Argentina

Uruguay & Paraguay

a Lonely Planet travel survival kit

Wayne Bernhardson

Argentina, Uruguay & Paraguay

2nd edition

Published by

Lonely Planet Publications
Head Office: PO Box 617, Hawthorn, Vic 3122, Australia
Branches: 150 Linden St, Oakland, CA 94607, USA
10a Spring Place, London NW5 3BH, UK
71 bis rue du Cardinal Lemoine, 75005 Paris, France

Printed by

SNP Printing Pte Ltd, Singapore

Photographs by
All photographs by Wayne Bernhardson or María Massolo except:
Robert Strauss (RS)
Deanna Swaney (DS)

Front cover: La Boca, Buenos Aires (Michael J Pettypool)
Title page: Theater, Isla Martín García, Buenos Aires Province, (Wayne Bernhardson)

First Published
August 1992

This Edition
April 1996

Although the author and publisher have tried to make the information as accurate as possible, they accept no responsibility for any loss, injury or inconvenience sustained by any person using this book.

National Library of Australia Cataloguing in Publication Data

Bernhardson, Wayne.
Argentina, Uruguay & Paraguay.

2nd ed.
Includes index.
ISBN 0 86442 336 5.

1. Argentina – Guidebooks. 2. Uruguay – Guidebooks.
3. Paraguay - Guidebooks. I. Massolo, María. II. Title.
(Series: Lonely Planet travel survival kit).

918.2

Wayne Bernhardson

Wayne Bernhardson was born in Fargo, North Dakota, grew up in Tacoma, Washington, and earned a PhD in geography at the University of California, Berkeley. He has traveled widely in Latin America, and lived for extended periods in Chile, Argentina and the Falkland (Malvinas) Islands. His other LP credits include *Chile & Easter Island*, *South America on a Shoestring*, *Baja California* and *Rocky Mountain States*. Wayne resides in Oakland, California.

María Massolo

María Massolo was born in Olavarría, Buenos Aires province, the 'cement capital' of Argentina, studied literature at Universidad de Buenos Aires, and holds an MA in folklore and a PhD in anthropology from the University of California at Berkeley. María lives in Oakland, California, with husband and co-author Wayne Bernhardson, their daughter Clío and their Alaskan Malamute Gardel. María divides her time among an academic career, traveling and translating.

From Wayne

Special mention to Fito and Mary Massolo of Olavarría, Buenos Aires province, and to Rodolfo Massolo (hijo).

Many Buenos Aires residents all contributed to pulling this together: Joaquín Allolio, Hebe Alicia Blanco, Adrián Harari and Cristina Messineo, and Federico Kirbus; Eduardo Tapia of the Centro Cultural Recoleta; Julio Sapollnik of the Palais de Glaçe; Carlos Reboratti and Perla Zusman at the Instituto de Geografía, Universidad de Buenos Aires; Nicholas Tozer, Michael Soltys and Andrew Graham-Yooll of the *Buenos Aires Herald*; Diego Curubeto of *Ambito Financiero*; Mario Banchik of Librerías Turísticas; Cristina Kobs of the Casa de Chubut; Mariano Besio of the Subsecretaría de Turismo de la Provincia de Santa Cruz; Teresa Cabrera of the Casa de Misiones; Gustavo Rocha of the Casa de Entre Ríos; Patricia Peluffo of the Casa de Jujuy; Monique Larraín of the *Guía Argentina de Tráfico Aéreo*; Alán Rodrigué of the *Guía Internacional de Tráfico*; Armando Schlecker of the *Guía Latinoamericana de Transportes*; Kevin Michael O'Reilly of the US embassy; and Laura Repetto of Badino Turismo. Georges Helft of San Telmo graciously permitted photography of his collection.

Thanks to Guillermo Botarques of the Dirección de Turismo in La Plata, Buenos Aires province; Mariano Adrián Gattari of Bahía Blanca; Victor Centurión of Paraná, Entre Ríos; Sixto Vásquez Zuleta (Toqo) of Humahuaca, Jujuy; María Marta and Raúl Balduzzi of Mendoza; Nora Kolton of the Dirección Municipal de Turismo in Santa Fe; Victoria Irene Holzkan of the Dirección de Turismo in Resistencia, Chaco; Oscar Aranda of the Dirección de Turismo in Corrientes; Gustavo Gil and Diana Seijo of Neuquén; Jane Williams of Estancia Huechahue, Neuquén; Orlando Cifuentes of the Secretaría Municipal de Turismo, Junín de los Andes, Neuquén; Carlos Massolo and Laura Alvarez of Villa Regina, Río Negro; María del Carmen Fernández of *Datos Andinos Patagónicos*, and Rosa Giménez and Natalia P de Chercover of the Secretaría Municipal de Turismo, Río Negro; Toncek Arko of Bariloche; Stella Maris Breit of Viedma, Río Negro; Marcela Gregorini and Simo Guañabenz of Puerto Madryn, Chubut; Gustavo Wofoy Diez and Laura Rodríguez of the Secretaría de Turismo y Medio Ambiente in Puerto Madryn; Emilio Antonio Balado and Estela Williams of the Municipalidad de Trelew, Chubut; Alejandro Tirachini of Puerto Deseado, Chubut;

Ricardo Berwyn of the Dirección Municipal de Turismo in Esquel, Chubut; María Sofía Lanza of the Dirección de Turismo in Comodoro Rivadavia, Chubut; and Julio César Lovece and Mario Oscar Pérez Ruiz Díaz of the Dirección de Turismo at the Municipalidad de Ushuaia.

In Uruguay, we appreciate the usual help from Michael Power of Maldonado, as well as Manuel Pérez Bravo of the Asociación de Hoteles y Restaurantes del Uruguay, and Juan Carlos Migues and Jorge Herrera of the Ministerio of Turismo in Montevideo. Gaye Maris of the US embassy in Montevideo also made a contribution.

In Asunción, Paraguay, I should mention Antonio van Humbeeck of the Instituto Moisés Bertoni, Charly Sandoval of InterTours, Juan Luis Ramírez of the Dirección de Parques Nacionales y Vida Silvestre, Sixto Medina Peña of Cruceros SRL, and Bob Neus of the US Peace Corps in Itauguá.

In Santiago, Chile, my longtime Chilean friend Martín Montalva Paredes and his family solved many problems. Víctor Maldonado and Marisa Blásquez rescued me from insupportable expense and inconvenience by offering me their garage for seven months. Claudia Blancaire Rosas and José Agustín Olavarría of Navimag in Santiago updated me on ferry services in Chilean Patagonia. María Isabel Bächler of United Airlines in Santiago helped avoid excess baggage charges on books and papers.

In Chilean Patagonia, contributors included Sr Florentino Yañez Yañez of Sernatur in Punta Arenas, Miguel Angel Muñoz R of Sernatur in Puerto Natales, and British Consul John C Rees of Punta Arenas.

In the Falkland Islands, Cherilyn King and Natalie Smith of the Falkland Islands Tourist Board were most directly helpful in this specific project. Gabriel and Claudette Ceballos, Ian and María Strange, Graham Bound, Janet Robertson and Steve Beldham also made their contributions.

In California, thanks to Peter Grace of Oakland, and Miguel Helft of Berkeley and Out There Trekking. Jack Deasy of the US State Department in Washington, DC, provided some last minute info.

Guy Mellet and Patricia Magnin of Geneva, Switzerland, were entertaining and informative companions in Punta Arenas, Ushuaia and Buenos Aires. Debbie Balanik and Donald Slaght of Edmonton, Alberta, shared conversation and insights in El Bolsón and Bariloche. Paul Arundale of Leeds, England, corrected some of my stereotyped notions on cycling in Argentina.

Thanks again to Tony and Maureen Wheeler for keeping me employed these several years, and a special thanks and acknowledgment to every one in Melbourne who treated me like royalty during the 21st anniversary travel summit there.

From the Publisher

Coordinating editor Kate Hoffman 'La Comandante' took charge of editing and proofing with the help of freelancers Sarah Lewis, Sandra Lopen Barker, and Jeff Campbell. The in-house cartographers – Alex Guilbert 'El Jefe', Cyndy Johnsen, Chris Salcedo, Hayden Foell, and Becca Lafore – created the majestic maps with help from freelancers Blake Summers and Scott Noren. Chris Salcedo 'El Dios', Hugh D'Andrade, and Mark Butler drew illustrations. Hayden Foell 'El Capitán' and Richard Wilson put all the pieces together in layout, and Carolyn Hubbard, Scott Summers, and Caroline Liou looked it all over and put it to rest.

This Book

The first edition of this book was researched and written by Wayne Bernhardson and María Massolo. Wayne Bernhardson researched and wrote this 2nd edition of *Argentina, Uruguay & Paraguay – a travel survival kit*. Thanks to Andrew Draffen for information on Brazil's Foz Do Iguaçu and to Deanna Swaney for information on Villazón and La Quiaca.

Warning & Request

Things change – prices go up, schedules change, good places go bad and bad places go bankrupt – nothing stays the same. So if you find things better or worse, recently opened or long since closed, please write and tell us and help make the next edition better!

Your letters will be used to help update future editions and, where possible, important changes will also be included as a Stop Press section in reprints.

All information is greatly appreciated and the best letters will receive a free copy of the next edition, or any other LP book of your choice.

Contents

URUGUAY

PARAGUAY

Map Legend

BOUNDARIES

—··—··—··— International Boundary

—···—···—··· Provincial/Department Boundary

AREA FEATURES

Park

NATIONAL PARK   National Park

HYDROGRAPHIC FEATURES

Water

Coastline

Creek

River, Waterfall

Swamp, Spring

ROUTES

Freeway

Major Road

Minor Road

Unpaved Road

Foot Trail

Ferry Route

Railway, Railway Station

Metro, Metro Station

ROUTE SHIELDS

RN 12 Ruta Nacional   RP 65 Ruta Provincial   Argentina

1 Ruta Nacional   11 Ruta Secundaria   Uruguay

2 Ruta   Paraguay

SYMBOLS

✪ **NATIONAL CAPITAL**
◉ **Provincial/ Department Capital**
● City
● Town

■ Hotel, B&B
▲ Campground
⌂ Hostel
⬥ RV Park
▼ Restaurant
♟ Bar (Place to Drink)
☕ Café

✚ Airfield
✈ Airport
∴ Archaeological Site, Ruins
⑤ Bank, ATM
⚾ Baseball Diamond
☻ Bus Depot, Bus Stop
🚏 Cathedral
⌒ Cave
✝ Church
⌐ Embassy
🐟 Fishing, Fish Hatchery
⋈ Foot Bridge
⁂ Garden
⛽ Gas Station

↑ Golf Course
☉ Hospital, Clinic
🛕 Lighthouse
🔺 Mission
🔱 Monument
▲ Mountain
🏛 Museum
♪ Music, Live
← One-Way Street
⌂ Observatory
🅿 Parking
🔺 Park
)(Pass
🍴 Picnic Area

★ Police Station
🏊 Pool
✉ Post Office
⛷ Skiing, Alpine
🎿 Skiing, Nordic
⛵ Shipwreck
❖ Shopping Mall
🏛 Stately Home
☎ Telephone
⬛ Tomb, Mausoleum
🚶 Trailhead
🍷 Winery
🐘 Zoo

Note: not all symbols displayed above appear in this book.

Introduction

Argentina, Uruguay, and Paraguay comprise the bulk of the region commonly known as South America's "Southern Cone", which stretches from the tropics to, by some accounts, the South Pole. Within this region visitors encounter a remarkable variety of both natural and cultural attractions. The magnificent desolation of Patagonia and the high Andes contrast dramatically with the urban frenzy of Buenos Aires, one of the world's largest and most cosmopolitan cities.

For many travelers, the region's natural wonders will be the primary attraction. In the early 20th century, Argentina was one of the first South American countries to designate national parks. Its southern Andean cordillera offers a string of alpine parks where awesome glaciers spill icebergs into blue-green lakes of incomparable beauty. The central cordillera features the highest peaks in the Western Hemisphere, while the northern deserts are, in their own way, no less impressive. These thinly populated areas also contain unusual wildlife. In vivid contrast are the massive concentrations of sub-Antarctic wildlife on the southern Patagonian coastline. Argentina also shares the awesome Iguazú Falls with Brazil and Paraguay.

Because of the cultural domination of overseas immigrants, ecological historian Alfred Crosby has called Buenos Aires and its immediate hinterlands a "neo-Europe," in which trans-Atlantic arrivals and their cultural baggage – domestic plants and animals, and weeds – transformed the natural environment and ensured the eventual demise of the way of life of the relatively few indigenous people who inhabited the area in the 16th century. According to Crosby, the most aggressive weeds were the Europeans themselves, whose overwhelming numbers created a society which never truly accepted its New World uniqueness nor its ultimately derivative nature. It

did, however, maintain important economic and cultural links with Europe, feeding its parent with grains and beef, contributing to world literature through Borges and others, and exporting the tango to European salons. For such reasons, Argentina is one Latin American country in which Europeans, North Americans, and Anglophones can feel at ease and travel relatively inconspicuously.

Uruguay, the economy and culture of which closely resemble those of the Argentine Pampas, is a political buffer between giant Brazil and Argentina, while isolated Paraguay is South America's "empty quarter," a hot, sparsely populated, subtropical lowland best known, until recently, for the unusually durable military dictatorship of General Alfredo Stroessner.

Historically, Uruguay is the most stable and democratic of the three countries, but the recent regional democratic revival has made all three countries more inviting destinations. There is still uncertainty whether democratic institutions will endure, but many signs are positive and, at present, one can travel through all three countries without fear of arbitrary arrest and detention.

This was not the case through the 1970s and early 1980s, when Argentina's military government fought its infamous Dirty War against "subversives" before losing both power and prestige during the military confrontation with Britain in the South Atlantic war of 1982, commonly referred to as the Falklands War. Uruguay suffered a similar, only slightly less brutal, experience at the hands of its military, while Paraguay endured institutionalized authoritarian rule for decades until 1989 when General Stroessner was ousted and replaced with a reform-minded (if not entirely untainted) colleague. In 1993 the country selected a civilian president.

Present-day Argentina also includes northwestern areas with significant indigenous populations once more closely integrated with the pre-Columbian civilizations of Peru and Bolivia. Throughout the colonial era, when Buenos Aires was a near-forgotten backwater, cities like Tucumán and Salta provided mules and essential provisions for the vital mining economy of the central Andes.

In addition, only late in the 19th century, after a brutal war of extermination against mounted Indians and with the assistance of a new wave of European immigration, did the Argentine state incorporate enormous, thinly populated Patagonia into its effective orbit. These persistent regional distinctions challenge the frequently expressed ideal of *argentinidad*, a uniform Argentine nationality.

Even today, despite economic disorder, Argentina's relative prosperity attracts immigrants from adjacent lands like Chile and Bolivia. It also presents the visitor with a greater geographical and cultural diversity than one might expect. With Uruguay and Paraguay, it offers complementary natural and cultural attractions for an extended stay.

The Falkland (Malvinas) Islands are a special case. Politically, they are one of the world's last colonial relics, yet there is no doubt that the people, by and large, are content with their political status. The islands are easily accessible by air from Punta Arenas, Chile.

While the Falkland Islands are steeped in history, visitors will be most impressed by the wild island landscapes and especially the tame, abundant, and accessible wildlife. Except for the nearly constant wind, the climate is surprisingly benign; yet short of Antarctica itself, there is no better place to see the birds and mammals characteristic of the world's most southerly regions.

Argentina

Facts about Argentina

HISTORY
Pre-Colonial Era

Conventional histories portray Argentina as a homogeneous society founded on European immigration, but the country's pre-Columbian and colonial past, and even the present, are more complex than this misleading stereotype. When Europeans first arrived in South America in the 16th century, they encountered peoples living in diverse economic and social systems. In the Andes the Europeans found dense populations, while in the tropical and temperate forests they met semisedentary agricultural peoples. In the Amazon and on the Patagonian steppes, they noted the nomadic hunters and gatherers.

On the eastern slopes of the central Andes, on the periphery of the civilizations of Peru and Bolivia, Diaguita Indians irrigated maize fields that supported permanent villages between present-day Salta and San Juan. Other groups, like the Comechingones near Córdoba, practiced a similar livelihood. To the east, in the forested Río Paraná delta across the Chaco scrubland, smaller Guaraní populations of shifting cultivators relied on maize, along with tuber crops like manioc (cassava) and sweet potatoes. Over most of the region, though, highly mobile peoples hunted the guanaco (a wild relative of the Andean llama) and the rhea (a flightless bird resembling the ostrich) with bow and arrow or *boleadoras* (heavily weighted thongs). In the far south, groups like the Yahgans gathered shellfish and bird eggs.

Invasion of the New World

Ironically, even after a papal treaty ratified the Spanish-Portuguese division of the Americas in 1494, the structure of Indian societies more strongly influenced the economic and political structure of colonial society than the edicts of peninsular authorities. The first Spaniards sought gold and silver above all, and ruthlessly appropriated precious metals through outright robbery when possible or by other more brutal means, such as forced slavery in mines. El Dorado, the legendary city of gold, eluded them, but they soon realized that the true wealth of the Indies consisted of the surprisingly large Indian populations they encountered in Mexico, Peru, and elsewhere.

The Spaniards exploited the indigenous populations of the New World through legal mechanisms like the *encomienda*, best translated as "entrustment," by which the Crown granted an individual Spaniard rights to Indian labor and tribute in a particular village or area. Institutions like the Catholic Church also held encomiendas. In theory, Spanish legislation required the holder of the encomienda to reciprocate at least with instruction in the Spanish language and the Catholic religion, but in practice imperial administration was inadequate to ensure compliance and avoid the worst abuses. Spanish overseers worked Indians mercilessly in the mines and extracted the maximum in agricultural produce.

In the most densely populated parts of the Americas, some *encomenderos* became extraordinarily wealthy, but the encomienda system failed when Indian populations died off rapidly. This was less because of overwork and physical punishment than because the Indians, isolated for at least 10,000 years from the diseases of the Old World, could not withstand the onslaught of smallpox, influenza, typhus, and other microbial killers. In some parts of the New World, introduced diseases reduced the native population by more than 95%.

In most of Argentina and the other modern River Plate countries (Uruguay and Paraguay), the encomienda was less significant than in the Andes. Ironically, the most

ARGENTINA

Diaguita

PACIFIC
OCEAN

Huarpe

Guaraní

Querandí

Charrúa

Araucanians

Puelche

ATLANTIC
OCEAN

Tehuelche

Chono

**Major
Indian Groups**

Alacaluf

Ona

Yahgan   Haush

Colonial Times

Indian resistance discouraged early settlement of the lower River Plate. Potential settlers preferred Asunción, founded in 1537 in the upper Paraná, but the region's most significant early economic links were not directly with Spain but with silver-rich Alto Perú (now Bolivia), where the bonanza mine at Potosí financed Spanish expansion, and with Lima, capital of the Viceroyalty of Peru. Although Spanish forces re-established Buenos Aires by 1580, it long remained a backwater in comparison to Andean settlements such as Tucumán (founded in 1571), Córdoba (1573), Salta (1582), La Rioja (1591), and Jujuy (1593). Spaniards from Chile settled the cities of Mendoza (1561), San Juan (1562), and San Luis (1596) in what became known as the Cuyo region. The Tucumán region provided mules, cloth, and foodstuffs for Alto Perú; Cuyo produced wine and grain, while Buenos Aires languished.

The colonial decline of the Indian population in northwestern Argentina and their relatively small numbers in the rest of the country produced a maldistribution of land that mirrored such shifts in other Latin American countries but which took on particularly Argentine characteristics. The appearance of *latifundios*, or large landholdings, came about after the virtual disappearance of the Indian population made the encomienda obsolete. Spanish immigrants and *criollos* (American-born Spaniards) responded by acquiring large tracts of the best land for agriculture and livestock; this new institution, the *hacienda*, bore some resemblance to its feudal Spanish namesake, though it differed considerably in detail. As Indian populations gradually recovered or merged with the Spanish to form a mixed-race *mestizo* population, they found that the best lands had been monopolized and that their only economic alternatives were cultivation of small plots *(minifundios)* on inferior lands or dependent labor on the large estates.

Although the hacienda was never as important in Argentina as it was in Peru or

highly organized Indian peoples were the easiest to subdue and control, since they were accustomed to similar forms of exploitation. In hierarchical states like the Inca Empire, the Spaniards rather easily occupied the apex of the pyramid.

The semisedentary and nomadic peoples of the riverine lowlands and the southern Pampas, though, put up determined resistance. In 1536, Querandí Indians routed Pedro de Mendoza's garrison at Buenos Aires within five years of its establishment, and even into the late 19th century, parts of the Pampas were not safe for White settlers. Abandoned Spanish livestock multiplied rapidly on the fine pastures of the Pampas, where horses greatly aided the Indians's mobility and ability to strike. Not until the so-called Conquista del Desierto, a de facto war of extermination against the Pampas Indians in the late 19th century, could the European usurpers relax their guard.

ARGENTINA

ARGENTINE NATIONAL & PROVINCIAL PARKS & RESERVES

1 Monumento Natural Laguna de los Pozuelos
2 PN Baritú
3 PN Calilegua
4 PN Los Cardones
5 PN Finca el Rey
6 Reserva Natural Formosa
7 PN Río Pilcomayo
8 PN Chaco
9 PN Mburucuyá
10 PN Iguazú
11 PP Talampaya
12 PP Ischigualasto
13 PP Aconcagua
14 PP Tupungato
15 PP Sierra de las Quijadas
16 PN Díamante
17 PN El Palmar
18 PN Lihué Calel
19 PN Laguna Blanca
20 PN Lanín
21 PN Nahuel Huapi
22 PN Los Arrayanes
23 PN Lago Puelo
24 PN Los Alerces
25 RP Península Valdés
26 RP Punta Tombo
27 PN Perito Francisco P Moreno
28 Monumento Natural Bosques Petrificados
29 PN Los Glaciares
30 PN Tierra del Fuego

Argentina

0   200   400 km

**Provinces of
Argentina**

War scene from *San Martín Libertador de América*

Mexico, the livestock *estancia* came to play a critical role in the development of Argentine society. When the Spaniards returned to the estuary of the River Plate in the late 16th century, they found that the cattle and horses abandoned decades earlier had proliferated almost beyond belief as the primary agents in what historian Alfred Crosby has called "ecological imperialism." With commerce severely restricted except under Spanish mercantile regulation, the inhabitants of colonial Buenos Aires looked to livestock for their livelihood. Without these livestock, the legendary gaucho of the Pampas could never have existed, but their growing commercial importance also brought about his extinction.

Growth & Independence

Though isolated and legally prohibited from direct European commerce for nearly two centuries, the people of Buenos Aires pursued a flourishing contraband trade with Portuguese Brazil and nonpeninsular Euro-pean powers. When Buenos Aires became capital of the new Viceroyalty of the River Plate in 1776, it was explicit acknowledgment that the region had outgrown Spain's political and economic domination. Previously Buenos Aires had been governed as the tail end of a long, indirect supply line, via the Caribbean, Panama, and Peru. This was frustrating for criollos, who wished to carry on direct trade between Buenos Aires and Spain.

Toward the end of the 18th century, criollos became increasingly dissatisfied and impatient with peninsular authority in all parts of the continent. The expulsion of British troops who briefly occupied Buenos Aires in 1806 and 1807 gave the people of the River Plate new confidence in their ability to stand alone, which they asserted in the revolution of May 25, 1810.

Independence movements throughout South America united to expel Spain from the continent by the 1820s. Under the leadership of General José de San Martín and others, the United Provinces of the River Plate, Argentina's direct forerunner, declared independence at Tucumán in 1816. Ironically, British financial and logistical support made it possible for Argentina and its allies to break the Spanish yoke. In the process, Bolivia and Paraguay became independent countries rather than remaining part of the former Viceroyalty of the River Plate.

After achieving independence, the provinces were united in name only. With no truly effective central authority, the regional disparities that Spanish rule had obscured became more obvious. This resulted in the rise of the *caudillos*, or local strongmen, who resented and resisted Buenos Aires as strongly as Buenos Aires had resisted Spain. Argentine educator and president Domingo F Sarmiento, himself a product of the provinces, indicted the excesses of demagogic caudillos in his classic *Life in the Argentine Republic in the Days of the Tyrants* (1845). At the same time the caudillos commanded great and often admirable personal loyalty. In 1833 Charles Darwin observed in his notes that

The Paths of the Liberators

The two major figures of South American independence, Simón Bolívar and José de San Martín, converged on the center from the periphery. Bolívar, born wealthy in Caracas, began in the north, while San Martín, of more humble origins on the former Jesuit mission of Yapeyú on the Río Uruguay, led the charge from the south.

In retrospect, it is no surprise that the leaders should come from the backwaters of the Spanish empire, since Spanish control was strongest in Peru, where it had been established on the foundation of the indigenous Inca state. In the far-flung viceroyalties of Nueva Granada and the Río de la Plata, Bolívar and San Martín developed a criollo sense of identity that a privileged education in Spain did nothing to eradicate.

Still, the two differed greatly in temperament. Bolívar, by all accounts, was a passionate man who, when his young Spanish wife died, sublimated his energy first in grandiose plans for

Simón Bolívar

Spanish American independence, which took many years to win. Despite early setbacks, his intensity and populist ability to inspire the masses – even when they failed to understand or did not agree with his ideas – proved a greater strength than his limited military skills. By sheer persistence and force of will, he turned former adversaries into supporters, and his movement gained strength.

San Martín, by contrast, was more methodical and conservative. Though he immediately left for London on hearing of the events of the Revolution of May 1810 and prepared to return to Buenos Aires, his actions were those of a professional soldier who had spent 20 years in the ranks. Rather than leap into battle, he first trained and organized his forces; especially in the logistically and strategically demanding liberation of Chile, which involved crossing the high Andes and surprising royalist forces at Chacabuco, his troops' discipline served them well.

After liberating Chile, San Martín, who disdained political ambition for himself, sailed north to drive the royalists out of Lima (though they remained strong elsewhere) and then north to a now famous meeting with Bolívar at Guayaquil, Ecuador. The apolitical Argentine found himself in conflict with Bolívar, whose political ambitions were boundless if largely praiseworthy; San Martín saw the essential expediency of installing a powerful leader, even a monarch, to avoid the disintegration of Peru, while Bolívar insisted on a constitutional republic. In a complicated exchange that aroused ill feeling among partisans of both leaders, the Venezuelan won the day and San Martín returned to the south.

In the long run, though, both were disappointed. The proliferation of *caudillos*, local warlords who acted from selfish motives, appalled both great soldier-statesmen and set an often deplorable pattern for most of the 19th century. San Martín returned to an Argentina racked by internal dissension and left for self-imposed exile in France almost as soon as he arrived, never to return. Bolívar's dream of the strong republic of Gran Colombia was shattered by difficulties which led to the secession of Ecuador and the separation of Colombia and Venezuela. Just before being exiled, he died of pulmonary tuberculosis in the Colombian town of Santa Marta. ■

José de San Martín

Juan Manuel de Rosas "by conforming to the dress and habits of the Gauchos . . . obtained an unbounded popularity in the country" and that he "never saw anything like the enthusiasm for Rosas . . . ."

In theory, the great controversy in Argentine politics was between the Federalists of the interior, who advocated provincial autonomy, and the Unitarists of Buenos Aires, who upheld central authority. The Federalists, associated with conservative provincial landowners but supported by much of the rural working class, resented Buenos Aires as much as Madrid. The Unitarists, led by intellectuals like Bernardino Rivadavia, were more cosmopolitan and looked to Europe for capital, immigrants, and ideas. For nearly two decades, bloody and vindictive conflicts between the two factions left the country nearly exhausted. A common salutation on documents of the period was "Death to the Unitarist savages!"

The Reign of Rosas

In practice, differences between Federalists and Unitarists sometimes owed as much to convenience as conviction. Juan Manuel de Rosas came to prominence as a caudillo in Buenos Aires province and undoubtedly represented the interests of rural elites whose power depended on their estancias and *saladeros* (tanneries and salting works). But he also helped centralize political power in Buenos Aires and set other ominous precedents in Argentine political life, creating the *mazorca*, his ruthless political police, and institutionalizing torture. According to Domingo F Sarmiento:

The central consolidated despotic government of the landed proprietor, Don Juan Manuel Rosas . . . applied the knife of the Gaucho to the culture of Buenos Ayres, and destroyed the work of centuries – of civilization, law and liberty.

Even allowing for Sarmiento's partisan rhetoric, Rosas's opportunism and continual military adventures required a large standing army, consuming an increasing percentage of public expenditures, and the

dictator required all overseas trade to be funneled through the port of Buenos Aires rather than be shipped directly to the provinces.

Despite the efforts of the Federalists, Buenos Aires continued to dominate the new country. After the Unitarists and even some of Rosas's former allies finally forced him from power in 1852, succeeding decades and economic developments confirmed the city's primacy. Rosas himself spent the last 25 years of his life in exile in Southampton, England.

The Roots of Modern Argentina

The expulsion of Rosas ushered in a new era in Argentine development. Sheep estancias, producing enormous quantities of wool in response to the nearly inexhaustible demand of English mills, supplanted the relatively stagnant cattle estancias. According to Argentine historian Hilda Sábato, the province of Buenos Aires was in the vanguard of this process, integrating Argentina into the global economy and, simultaneously, consolidating the country as a political entity. Steadily, European immigrants assumed important roles in crafts and commerce. In nearby areas of Buenos Aires province, small farms known as *chacras* supplied the city's food, but sheep displaced the semi-wild cattle of the surrounding estancias. In the periphery of the province, though, cattle estancias operated much as before.

Politically, the Constitution of 1853, still in force today despite its frequent suspension, signified the triumph of Unitarism, even allowing the president to dissolve provincial administrations despite lip service to federal principles. The economic expression of Unitarism was Liberalism, an openness to foreign capital which even now raises the hackles of many Argentine nationalists. As used in Argentina, the term Liberalism means something very different from what it does in Western Europe and North America.

According to historian David Rock, Liberalism had three main aspects: foreign investment, foreign trade, and immigration.

In the late 19th century, all three inundated the Humid Pampas, Mesopotamia, and Córdoba, if barely lapping at the edges of some interior provinces. Basque and Irish refugees became the first shepherds, as both sheep numbers and wool exports increased nearly tenfold between 1850 and 1880. Some of these herders were independent family farmers on relatively small units, but the majority were sharecroppers, and the land itself remained in the hands of traditional large landowners.

After 1880, Argentina became a major producer of cereal crops for export, and it still is today. The Humid Pampas were the focus of this development, the origins of which lay in midcentury colonization projects focused on attracting European settlers. Estancieros rarely objected to occupation of lands that were nominally theirs, because new settlers provided a buffer between themselves and the still troublesome Indians. Swiss, German, French, and Italian farmers proved successful in provinces like Santa Fe and Entre Ríos.

Such developments did not eliminate latifundios. The government sold public lands at bargain prices to pay its debts, which encouraged speculators and reduced independent farming opportunities for immigrants, whose only agricultural alternatives were sharecropping or seasonal labor. Many remained in Buenos Aires, steadily increasing the city's share of the country's population.

British capital, amounting to one-third of Britain's total Latin American investment by 1890, dominated the Argentine economy. Most went to infrastructural improvements such as railroads, which rapidly made the cart roads of the Pampas obsolete. By the turn of the century, Argentina had a highly developed rail network, fanning out from Buenos Aires in all directions, but the economy was ever more vulnerable to international fluctuations like the depression in 1870 that followed the Franco-Prussian War.

These conditions stimulated a debate over foreign investment that anticipated 20th-century controversies over "dependence" and economic autonomy through industrial diversification and protectionism. In fact, the only industries that benefited from protection were agricultural commodities such as wheat, wine, and sugar. These in turn benefited large landholders and encouraged further land speculation and concentration. Speculation led to a boom in land prices and paper money loans that depreciated in value, causing near collapse of the financial system toward the end of the 19th century.

By reducing opportunities for family farming, land speculation and commodity exports also encouraged urban growth. The port city of Buenos Aires, which rapidly modernized in the 1880s, nearly doubled its population through immigration during that decade alone. Urban services such as transportation, power, and water improved steadily. Because of the capital's increasing importance, it became an administratively distinct federal zone (the Capital Federal), effectively seceding from its namesake province. Outside the Pampas, uneven development exaggerated regional inequality.

From the mid-1890s until WWI, Argentina's economy recovered enough to take advantage of the enormous opportunities presented by beef, mutton, and wheat exports. Because of inequities in land distribution, however, this prosperity was less broad-based than it might have been. Industry could not absorb all the immigrants, and with the onset of the Great Depression, the military took power under conditions of indecisive and ineffectual civilian government, as well as considerable social unrest. An obscure colonel, Juan Domingo Perón, was the first Argentine leader to try to come to grips with the economic crisis in a comprehensive manner.

Juan Perón & His Legacy

Born in Buenos Aires province in 1895, Juan Perón emerged from obscurity in the 1940s to become Argentina's most revered, and most despised, political figure. During his youth and rather mediocre military career, he became familiar with virtually

The Peróns

Lieutenant-General Juan Perón (diehard supporters refuse to separate his name and rank) was an Argentine enigma, embodying the contradictions of the country itself. Perón and his second wife Eva continue to occupy an enduring place in the country's political mythology. Rising to power through the elitist institution of the military, he still enjoyed broad popularity among the public at large. Leader of a Roman Catholic country, he incited his followers to attack the Church. Attracting people of intense and passionate convictions, he could appeal ambiguously to followers from across the political spectrum – for an equivalent in the English-speaking world, one would have to imagine Margaret Thatcher with resolute partisans ranging from Militant Tendency to the National Front. Irreconcilable factions within Perón's Justicialist party warred with each other, sometimes with words and often with bullets and bombs, while each ardently professed its allegiance to the man and his ideals.

During the era of Argentina's greatest power and prestige, Perón insightfully assessed the country's shortcomings as well as its strengths. When the Perón family relocated to Patagonia for an unsuccessful attempt at sheep farming, he saw firsthand the most unsavory aspects of large, paternalistic sheep estancias, controlled almost exclusively by British interests. Recognizing that the sheepherders and other workers of the Pampas were not far removed from his own humble origins, he treated them on a basis of equality. As a young military officer, he witnessed the miserable physical and educational state of rural conscripts, casualties of an inequitable social order. Sent to restore order in several labor disputes, he proved an attentive listener to working-class concerns, mediating labor settlements on the railways and sugar *ingenios* (factories) of the subtropical north.

Perón first came to national prominence after a military coup deposed President Ramón Castillo in 1943. Sensing an opportunity to assist the country's forgotten working class, Perón settled for a relatively minor post as head of the National Department of Labor. In this post, his success at organizing relief efforts after a major earthquake in the Andean city and province of San Juan earned praise throughout the country. In the process he also met Eva Duarte, the actress who would become his second wife and make her own major contribution to Argentine history.

During sojourns as Argentine military attaché in Fascist Italy and Nazi Germany, Perón had grasped the importance of spectacle in public life, and he had the personal charisma to put it into

the entire country from its subtropical north to its sub-Antarctic south. As Perón grew to maturity, Argentina was one of the world's most prosperous countries, but its prosperity was narrowly based on commodity exports such as meat, grain, and wool.

The *oligarquía terrateniente*, or landed elite, benefited most from the export economy and resisted attempts to promote diversification through domestic industrialization. Correctly or not, many Argentines came to perceive the country's agricultural sector as beholden to foreign "liberal," especially British, interests.

This was not an unreasonable interpretation. British capital built most of the railways that radiated from Buenos Aires like spokes from the hub of a wheel, bringing agricultural commodities to the capital for shipment to Europe. In return, inexpensive British products flooded domestic markets and retarded local industry.

Perón associated a new economic order for Argentina with domestic industrialization and economic independence. In this sense, he appealed to conservative nationalists, who distrusted the cosmopolitan landowning elite, and to radical working-class elements, who objected to the role of foreign capital. Almost until his death, Perón avoided alienating either sector even as they conducted a virtual civil war with each other.

After being dislodged from his labor post and briefly incarcerated by jealous fellow officers, Perón ran for and won the presidency of Argentina in 1946 and again in 1952. Until Perón was ousted in 1955, his reforms and programs benefited working-class interests in matters of wages, pensions, job security, and working conditions. University education ceased to be the privilege of the elite, but instead became available to any capable individual. Many

practice. With the equally charismatic "Evita" at his side or on her own, he transformed the country's political culture and economy, addressing massive rallies from the balcony of the Casa Rosada. Giving voice to the disenfranchised masses, the Peróns enlisted them in his cause and alienated traditionally powerful sectors of Argentine society. He created a powerful institution, the General Confederation of Labor (CGT), which overwhelmed rival labor organizations.

The Peróns made little attempt to disguise their demagoguery and ambition. Evita once wrote that "there are two things of which I am proud: my love for the people and my hatred for the oligarchy." Despite huge congressional majorities, Perón's authoritarian tendencies led him to govern

A charismatic speaker, Eva Perón often rallied the working class in support of her husband.

by decree rather than by consultation and consensus. His excessively personalistic approach created a political party, known formally as "Justicialist" but popularly and universally as "Peronist," which has never been able to transcend a stagnant reliance on its founder's charisma. He did not hesitate to use or condone intimidation and torture for political ends, although such activities never reached the level they did during the state terrorism of the late 1970s. Argentine literary great Jorge Luis Borges was among those who suffered Perón's caprice.

Yet during the decade they lived together, the Peróns also broadened the range and popular appeal of Argentine politics in many positive ways. Besides legitimizing the trade-union movement and extending political rights and economic benefits to working-class people, they managed to secure voting rights for women by 1947. Unfortunately, they could not or would not overcome the atmosphere of tension and confrontation that colored Argentine politics for more than three decades after Evita's death in 1952. ■

Argentines gained employment in the expanding state bureaucracy.

Perón promoted industrialization and economic self-sufficiency. Coming to power at a time of global crisis, just after WWII, he may have had no alternative but to foster state involvement since Europe, Argentina's traditional source of capital, was in economic ruin. In any event, his policies had broad support from both traditional working-class supporters and a military that feared dependence on foreign sources for raw materials and munitions.

Economic shortcomings, including rising inflation, undermined the latter stages of Perón's presidency. He also failed to disavow a virulent and often violent anticlerical campaign that divided the country toward the end of his first presidency. In late 1955, he himself fell victim to the so-called Revolución Libertadora, a coup that sent him into exile and initiated nearly three decades of disastrous military government, with only brief interludes of civilian rule.

Perón's Exile & Return

After Perón left the country, Argentina's military government banned the Justicialist party, which split into several factions. Even to speak Perón's name in public was suspect; Anglo-Argentines would often refer to him as "Johnny Sunday," a gloss on Perón's Christian names "Juan Domingo." Perón himself wandered to Paraguay, Panama (where he met his third wife, dancer María Estela Martínez, known better by her stage name, Isabelita), Venezuela, the Dominican Republic, and eventually to Spain in 1961, where he remained for 12 years.

During exile, Perón and his associates constantly dreamed of their return to Argentina. Perón acquired a bizarre retinue of advisors, including his mysterious personal secretary, José López Rega, a spiritualist and extreme right-wing nationalist who was Perón's Svengali or Rasputin. At Perón's Puerta de Hierro mansion in Madrid, where Evita Perón's embalmed body lay in state after being rescued from an anonymous grave in Italy in 1971, López Rega reportedly conducted rituals over the casket to imbue Isabelita with Evita's charismatic qualities.

In the late 1960s, increasing economic problems and political instability, including strikes, political kidnappings, and guerrilla warfare, marked Argentine political life. In the midst of these events, the opportunity for Perón to return finally arrived in 1973, when the beleaguered military relaxed their objections to the Justicialist party and loyal Peronist Hector Cámpora was elected president. Cámpora himself was merely a stalking-horse for Perón and soon resigned, paving the way for new elections handily won by Perón.

After an 18-year exile, Perón once again symbolized Argentine unity, but there was no substance to his rule. His anticipated arrival at Buenos Aires airport, attended by hundreds of thousands of people on a dark winter's night, resulted in violent clashes between supporters across the broad spectrum of Argentine politics. Chronically ill, Perón died in mid-1974, leaving a fragmented country. His ill-qualified wife Isabelita, elected as his literal running mate but under the influence of López Rega, inherited the presidency.

In this chaotic political climate, armed conflict was the rule rather than the exception. The urban Montoneros, a left-wing, anti-imperialist faction of the Peronist movement, went underground, kidnapping and executing enemies, bombing foreign enterprises, and robbing banks to finance their armed struggle. The Ejército Revolucionario Popular (People's Revolutionary Army, known by its acronym ERP) undertook guerrilla warfare in the mountainous forests of Tucumán province. López Rega's Alianza Anticomunista Argentina (AAA, or Argentine Anti-Communist Alliance) took the law into its own hands, assassinating labor leaders, academics, and others it considered "subversive."

The Dirty War (1976 – 1983)

In March 1976, unable to maintain civil order or control inflation, which sometimes exceeded 50% per month, Isabel Perón's government fell in a bloodless and widely anticipated military coup. Placed under house arrest, she eventually went into exile in Spain, where her main interest appeared to be challenging Imelda Marcos and Nancy Reagan for the world's most extravagant wardrobe.

If the coup itself was bloodless, its aftermath was not. During the so-called Proceso de Reorganización Nacional, the military government of General Jorge Rafael Videla instituted a reign of terror unparalleled since the days of Rosas. Military officers occupied nearly every position of political importance in the entire country.

In theory and rhetoric, the Proceso was a comprehensive effort at reforming the bloated state sector and stabilizing the economy by eliminating corruption, thus creating the basis for economic growth and an enduring democracy; in practice, it

Forced to flee Argentina in 1955, Juan Perón plotted his return for 18 years from abroad.

was one more chapter in a history of large-scale government corruption in the name of development, accompanied by an orgy of state-sponsored or tolerated violence and anarchy.

The army's superior firepower quickly eliminated the naive, inept, and outmanned ERP in Tucumán. The more sophisticated and intricately organized Montoneros posed a greater challenge and were eventually eliminated only in the infamous Guerra Sucia (Dirty War), which claimed thousands of innocent victims. Operating with state complicity, paramilitary death squads like the AAA were responsible for countless other casualties.

The "Disappeared"

In eliminating ERP and the Montoneros, the dictatorship made little effort to distinguish among those who actively fought against it and aided the guerrillas, those who openly or privately sympathized with the guerrillas without assisting them, and those who expressed reservations about the indiscriminate brutality used to carry out the military's campaign. Only a few highly visible and courageous individuals and organizations publicly criticized the regime, and at great personal risk.

During these years, to "disappear" meant to be abducted, detained, tortured, and probably killed with no hope or pretense of legal process. The armed forces and police ran numerous illegal detention centers, the most notorious of which was the Escuela de Mecánica de la Armada (ESMA, or Navy Mechanics's School) in an exclusive northern suburb of Buenos Aires. For anyone crossing the street, even at midday, the presence of a black Ford Falcon, without number plates and occupied by four men in sunglasses, induced outright terror.

The dictatorship almost never acknowledged illegal detention of individuals, although it sometimes reported their deaths in battles or skirmishes with "security forces." Inexplicably, a few escaped or were released, but their stories gained more notoriety outside Argentina than within. A few courageous individuals, like Nobel

Peace Prize winner Adolfo Pérez Esquivel, and groups, such as the famous "Madres de la Plaza de Mayo," kept their stories in public view. Las Madres still parade in front of Buenos Aires' Casa Rosada presidential palace every Thursday.

No one knows exactly how many people died during the Dirty War. In 1986 *Nunca Más*, the official report commissioned by civilian president Raúl Alfonsín and presented by the prestigious novelist Ernesto Sábato listed 9000 cases, but some estimates are three times greater. Ironically, the Dirty War ended only when the Argentine military attempted a real military objective.

The Falklands War

In mid-1982, a cartoon in the Argentine magazine *Humor* depicted "La Libertad Argentina" (a female figure equivalent to the US Statue of Liberty or England's Britannia) in a public park with her four children and their toys: an army general with a tank, an admiral with a destroyer, an air force brigadier with a jet fighter, and a smartly dressed civilian with a bridge. When another woman remarks how expensive it is to raise children, La Libertad responds "You're telling me!"

Despite public homage to economic growth and stabilization, Argentina's economy continued to decline during military rule. On the one hand, the government enacted strict monetarist economic measures, including a fixed exchange rate to eliminate speculation on the dollar, but it failed to reduce annual inflation to less than three digits. It did, however, increase unemployment and undermine local industry through cheap imports. Lip service to austerity brought in billions of dollars in loans, which were invested in grandiose public works projects such as the nearly unused toll highway between downtown Buenos Aires and the airport at Ezeiza, while public officials pocketed much of the money and sent it overseas to Swiss bank accounts. Meanwhile, the military acquired the latest in European technology, including the deadly Exocet missile.

Under the weight of its import splurge

and the burden of debt, the economy collapsed in chaos. Almost overnight, devaluation reduced the peso to a fraction of its former value, and inflation again reached astronomical, rather than merely high levels. The Proceso was coming undone.

In an orderly transition in early 1981, General Roberto Viola replaced General Videla as de facto president, but Viola's ineffectuality led to his replacement by General Leopoldo Galtieri before the end of the year. Under Galtieri, rapid economic deterioration and popular discontent, manifested in the first mass demonstrations at the Casa Rosada since before the 1976 coup, led to desperate measures. To stay in power, Galtieri launched an April 1982 invasion to dislodge the British from the Falkland Islands, claimed by Argentina as the Malvinas for nearly a century and a half.

Overnight, the nearly unopposed occupation of the Malvinas unleashed a wave of nationalist euphoria that subsided almost as fast as it crested. Acting on faulty advice from his civilian foreign minister Nicanor Costa Méndez, Galtieri underestimated the determined response of British Prime Minister Margaret Thatcher, herself in political difficulties, and the ability of Britain's naval task force to absorb heavy losses to attain a remote goal. After only 74 days, Argentina's ill-trained, poorly motivated, and ineffective forces surrendered ignominiously, and the military meekly prepared to return government to civilian hands. In 1983, Argentines elected Raúl Alfonsín, of the Unión Cívica Radical (UCR, or Radical Civic Union), to the presidency.

For more detailed information on the war, see the section on the Falkland Islands.

Aftermath

In his successful presidential campaign, Alfonsín pledged to try those military officers responsible for human-rights violations during the Dirty War. Junta members, including Videla, Viola, and Admiral Emilio Massera, were tried and convicted of kidnapping, torture, and homicide. Evidence uncovered by the commission that produced *Nunca Más* was critical to their convictions. Videla and Massera received life sentences, though in virtual luxury accommodations in a military prison.

When the government attempted to extend trials to junior officers, many of whom protested that they had been merely "following orders," those officers responded with uprisings in several different parts of the country. These might have toppled the government, but conversely had they been more forcefully resisted, they might have effectively subjugated the military to civilian control. The timid administration succumbed to military demands and produced a *Ley de la Obediencia Debida* (Law of Due Obedience), allowing lower-ranking officers to use the defense that they were "following orders", as well as a *Punto Final* (Stopping Point), beyond which no criminal or civil prosecutions could take place. These measures eliminated prosecutions of notorious individuals like navy captain Alfredo Astiz (the "Angel of Death"), who was implicated in the disappearance of a Swedish-Argentine teenager and the highly publicized deaths of two French nuns thrown into the Río de la Plata from an airplane.

The Law of Due Obedience and the Stopping Point did not eliminate the divisive impact of the Dirty War on Argentine politics; after 1987, the military reasserted its role in politics despite internal factionalism. One especially disconcerting element has been the emergence of the overtly fascist *carapintada* movement of disaffected junior officers. In December 1990, prior to a visit by US President George Bush, the carapintadas (so-called after their custom of painting their faces with camouflage markings) occupied army headquarters across from the Casa Rosada and elsewhere in Buenos Aires in the hope of encouraging the military establishment to join them in overthrowing President Carlos Menem, himself a prisoner of the military during the Dirty War.

Ironically and astonishingly, Menem himself contributed to the controversy in an unexpected and unwarranted manner. Just after Christmas 1990, he pardoned Videla,

Massera, and their cohorts despite overwhelming evidence that the Argentine public opposed such measures. He also pardoned former Montonero guerrilla Mario Firmenich who, some speculated, still had access to substantial funds that might benefit Menem's Peronist party. US journalist Martin Anderson has argued that Firmenich was a double agent who collaborated with the military government's intelligence services while participating in armed resistance, but the evidence for this is scanty.

In 1991, Menem aroused further controversy when he ordered Argentine warships to the Persian Gulf in support of the allied effort to liberate Kuwait (the ships gave logistical support, but did not participate in combat). Both right- and left-wing nationalists resented the president's apparent obsequiousness toward the USA, but the definition of an overtly military mission for Argentine forces was something of a novelty; since then they have undertaken other international missions, such as serving as peacekeepers in the former Yugoslavia. Kept busy with such tasks, the military has been remarkably quiet over the past few years, and no one anticipates overt military domination of Argentina, but it would be premature to dismiss completely the specter of military intervention in civilian matters.

During the presidential campaign of 1995, the human rights issues of the Dirty War resurfaced spectacularly when journalist Horacio Verbitsky wrote *El Vuelo* (The Flight; Editorial Planeta, Buenos Aires), a book based on interviews with former navy captain Adolfo Scilingo. Troubled but unrepentant, Scilingo acknowledged that he himself participated in regular weekly flights in which the navy threw political prisoners, alive but drugged, into the Atlantic Ocean. While such reports had long circulated, this was the first time any participant had openly admitted responsibility, and it ignited a clamor of protest for a more complete accounting of the disappeared – even though Alfonsín's due obedience law and Menem's pardons had eliminated any possibility of further prosecutions. Another revelation was that military chaplains had counseled and comforted the perpetrators of the killings.

Taken by surprise, President Menem attacked Scilingo's credibility and encouraged the country not to reopen old wounds, though some suggested that the president was trying to cover a bleeding gash with a Band-Aid. Inconsistencies among the administration's spokespersons as to the possibility of lists of the disappeared undercut the president's statements, and, despite initial denials, more material soon became available. A complete accounting still seems a long range goal, since the military destroyed many records before surrendering power in 1983 and probably hid others overseas. Nevertheless, many people believe that, because so many of the participants are still alive, a more complete record is likely to come about – even though some groups, like the Madres de la Plaza de Mayo, have vowed to seek a list of the murderers, not the disappeared.

Scilingo's "confession" set off a chain of events that has yet to end. Despite Menem's continued pleas to put the matter aside, Army Chief of Staff General Martín Balza went on nationwide television to apologize to the country for the Army's conduct during the Dirty War, Air Force Chief of Staff General Juan Paulik did likewise for his branch, and Roman Catholic Bishop Jorge Novak regretfully admitted the Church's collaboration. Navy officials, however, remained conspicuously silent and even spoke of promoting the disreputable Astiz, precipitating a minor diplomatic confrontation with France.

GEOGRAPHY & CLIMATE

With a total land area of about 2.8 million sq km, excluding the South Atlantic islands and the Antarctic quadrant it claims as national territory, Argentina is the world's eighth-largest country, only slightly smaller than India. On the South American continent, only neighboring Brazil is larger. The distance from La Quiaca on the Bolivian border to Ushuaia in Tierra del Fuego is nearly 3500 km, about the same as from

ARGENTINA

PACIFIC OCEAN

Gran Chaco

Río Paraná

Río Uruguay

Cordillera de los Andes

Río de la Plata

Pampas

ATLANTIC OCEAN

Patagonia

Tierra del Fuego   **Physiographic Regions**

Havana to Hudson's Bay or from the Sahara to Scotland.

Argentine geographers acknowledge four major physiographic provinces: the Andes, the lowland North, the Pampas, and Patagonia. Each of these, however, has considerable variety in its own right, since altitude as well as latitude plays a major role in Argentine geography. Most of the country is a midlatitude lowland, but the Andean chain runs the length of the country's western border, diminishing in altitude in the south. The Andes separate Argentina from Chile, while rivers form its borders with Uruguay, Brazil, and Paraguay. Its relatively short Bolivian frontier has both mountainous and riverine areas. (For temperatures, see Climate Charts on page 755.)

The Andes

The Andean chain runs the length of Argentina from the Bolivian border in the north to the South Atlantic, where the chain disappears. Its greatest elevations presented a formidable western barrier to colonizers

entering from Peru after the Spanish invasion of the New World. In this northwestern region, a string of oasis settlements from Jujuy and Salta southward to Mendoza developed, with communications links to Lima rather than to Buenos Aires. This area's colonial architecture, primarily but not exclusively ecclesiastical, is the most significant in Argentina. Here the mestizo population most closely resembles that of Peru and Bolivia, where indigenous traits are dominant.

Rainfall can be erratic, although rain-fed agriculture is feasible from Tucumán northward. In most areas, perennial streams descending from the Andes provide irrigation water. In the extreme north lies the southern extension of the Bolivian *altiplano*, a thinly populated high plain between 3000 and 4000 meters altitude, punctuated by even higher volcanic peaks. The inhabitants reside in scattered mining settlements, and there are a few llama herders; the zone is too arid for the more valuable but delicate alpaca. Vegetation consists of sparse bunch grasses *(ichu)* and low, widely spaced shrubs, known collectively as *tola*. Although days can be surprisingly hot (sunburn is a very serious hazard in the high altitude tropics), frosts occur almost nightly. In the summer rainy season, travelers should be prepared for potential flash floods and even snow at higher elevations.

South of Tucumán, rainfall is inadequate for crops, but irrigation has brought prosperity to the wine-producing Cuyo region, which consists of the provinces of Mendoza, San Juan, and San Luis. La Rioja and Catamarca are much less well-to-do. Much of this area resembles the Great Basin of the western US, with north-south mountain ranges separated by salt flats or very shallow lakes.

On the region's far western edge is the massive Andean crest, featuring 6960-meter Aconcagua, South America's highest peak. The area can be hot in summer but pleasant the rest of the year despite cool nights in winter. On occasion the Zonda, a dry wind descending from the Andes, causes dramatic temperature increases and, consequently, serious physical discomfort.

The Chaco & Mesopotamia

East of the Andes and their foothills, northern Argentina consists of tropical and subtropical lowlands. In the arid western area, known as the Argentine Chaco and part of the much larger Gran Chaco region which extends into Bolivia, Paraguay, and Brazil, open savannas alternate with almost impenetrable thorn forests. In the provinces of Santiago del Estero, Chaco, Formosa, and northern Santa Fe and Córdoba, summers are brutally hot.

Between the Paraná and Uruguay rivers, where the provinces of Entre Ríos and Corrientes comprise most of the area known as Mesopotamia, rainfall is sufficient to support swampy lowland forests as well as upland savanna. The province of Misiones, a politically important salient surrounded on three sides by Brazil and Paraguay, is even more densely forested and contains part of the awesome Iguazú Falls, which descend from the Paraná Plateau of southern Brazil.

Rainfall decreases from east to west; for example, Corrientes's annual average rainfall of about 1200 mm contrasts with Santiago del Estero's 500 mm, which is insufficient for rain-fed agriculture because evaporation is so high. Shallow summer flooding is common throughout Mesopotamia and the eastern Chaco, while only the immediate river floodplains become inundated in the west. The Chaco has a well-defined winter dry season, which is even more pronounced the farther west one travels, while Mesopotamia's rainfall is more evenly distributed throughout the year.

The Pampas

Bordering the Atlantic Ocean and the Río de la Plata and stretching nearly to Córdoba and the central Andean foothills, the Pampas are the political and economic heartland of modern Argentina. Argentine industry and agriculture are concentrated here; outside the federal capital of Buenos Aires and its industrial suburbs, most settlements are cookie-cutter farm towns resembling, in some ways, their counterparts in the US Midwest.

The Pampas are more properly subdivided into the Humid Pampas, along the coastal littoral (coastal region), and the Arid Pampas of the western interior and the south. More than a third of the country's population lives in and around Buenos Aires, whose humid climate resembles New York City's in the spring, summer, and autumn. Annual rainfall exceeds 900 mm, but several hundred kilometers westward it is less than half that. Buenos Aires' winters are humid but relatively mild.

The Pampas are an almost completely level plain of wind-borne loess (fine-grained silt or clay ranging in color from beige to gray) and river-deposited sediments, once covered by lush native grasses and now occupied by grain farms and cattle and sheep estancias. The absence of relief makes the area vulnerable to flooding from the relatively few small rivers that cross it. Only the granitic Sierra de Tandil (484 meters) and the Sierra de la Ventana (1273 meters) in southwestern Buenos Aires province, and the Sierra de La Pampa disrupt the otherwise monotonous terrain. The seacoast of Buenos Aires province features attractive, sandy beaches at resorts like Mar del Plata and Necochea, which *porteños* (inhabitants of the capital) overrun in January and February.

Patagonia & the Lake District

Patagonia is that region south of the Río Colorado, consisting of the provinces of Neuquén, Río Negro, Chubut, and Santa Cruz. It is separated from Chilean Patagonia by the Andes, although their crest is much lower than in the north of the country; Cerro Tronador, at 3554 meters the highest peak in Parque Nacional Nahuel Huapi near Bariloche, dwarfs all surrounding summits by at least 1000 meters.

The cordillera is still high enough, though, that Pacific storms drop most of their rain and snow on the Chilean side. In the extreme southern reaches of Patagonia, this rain shadow effect does not prevent the

ARGENTINA

accumulation of sufficient snow and ice to form the largest Southern Hemisphere glaciers outside Antarctica. Hiking, trekking, skiing, and mountaineering are common recreational activities, depending on the season. Outdoors enthusiasts should be prepared for changeable and inclement weather.

East of the Andean foothills, the cool, arid Patagonian steppes support huge flocks of sheep, almost all the wool of which is exported to Europe. In organization and operation, Patagonian sheep estancias resemble their counterparts in New Zealand and Australia, although ecological conditions are very different. The Atlantic maritime influence generally keeps temperatures relatively mild even in winter, when more uniform atmospheric pressure moderates the strong gales that blow most of the year.

Except for urban clusters like Comodoro Rivadavia (the center of Argentina's petroleum industry) and Río Gallegos (wool and meat packing), Patagonia is thinly populated. Tidal ranges along the Atlantic coast are too great for major port facilities. In the valley of the Río Negro and at the outlet of the Río Chubut, there is farming and fruit orchards.

Tierra del Fuego

The southernmost permanently inhabited territory in the world, the "Land of Fire" consists of one large island (Isla Grande), unequally divided between Chile and Argentina, and many smaller ones, some of which have been objects of contention between the two Southern Cone powers. When Europeans first passed through the Strait of Magellan, which separates Isla Grande from the Patagonian mainland, the fires stemmed from the activities of the now almost extinct Yahgan Indians; nowadays, they result from the flaring of natural gas in the region's oilfields.

The northern half of Isla Grande, which resembles the Patagonian steppes, is devoted to sheep grazing for wool and mutton, while its southern half is mountainous and partly covered by forests and glaciers. Despite a reputation for inclemency, it would be more accurate to call the weather changeable. As in Patagonia, winter conditions are rarely extreme, although trekking and outdoor camping are not advisable except for experienced mountaineers. For most visitors, the brief daylight hours in winter may be a greater deterrent than the weather. Skiing is possible in Ushuaia, along with outstanding views of the famous Beagle Channel.

ECOLOGY & ENVIRONMENT

Argentina's diverse environments have spawned environmental challenges ranging from the heavy industrial pollution of the Riachuelo waterway in Buenos Aires to deforestation in subtropical Misiones Province to overgrazing on the Patagonian steppes. A joint Argentine-Paraguayan hydroelectric project in Itaipú proved an economic and ecological boondoggle. Among the current major issues is the proposed placement of a nuclear waste dump in the Patagonian province of Chubut, a development that has induced many towns to declare themselves "non-nuclear municipalities." And recently, government officials have proposed dredging the Río Paraná into Paraguay and southern Brazil to provide deep-water access for ocean-going vessels – a project that might desiccate the famous wetlands of the Pantanal.

FLORA & FAUNA

Because Argentina is so large and varied in its environments, it supports a wide range of flora and fauna. The country's subtropical rainforests, palm savannas, high-altitude deserts and high-latitude steppes, humid temperate grasslands, alpine and sub-Antarctic forests, and coastal areas all support distinctive biota that will be unfamiliar to most visitors, or at least to those from the Northern Hemisphere. To protect these environments, Argentina has created an extensive system of national parks, briefly described below. More detailed descriptions of both the parks and their characteristic species can be found in separate entries in geographical chapters and sidebars.

Endangered Species

The Convention on International Trade in Endangered Species of Wild Fauna and Flora (CITES) is a diplomatic agreement regulating trade in biotic resources, including plants and animals, which are either in immediate danger of extinction, or else threatened or declining so rapidly that they may soon be in danger of extinction. Regulations are complex, but in general such species are either protected from commercial or noncommercial exploitation or subject to severe restrictions. In many instances, all commerce of a given species is prohibited; in most others, the export of plants and animals in a given country is prohibited without express authorization from that country's government.

Under CITES, most species are assigned either to Appendix I (endangered, under immediate threat of extinction without remedial action) or Appendix II (threatened, perhaps regionally endangered); some recovering species have been reassigned from Appendix I to Appendix II. Appendix III listings cover species that require close monitoring to determine their degree of vulnerability to extinction.

Travelers should take special care not to hunt, purchase, or collect the following species of plants and animals found in Argentina, Uruguay, Paraguay, and the Falkland Islands, nor should they purchase products made from these plants and animals. Note that US customs no longer permits the importation of birds even with CITES permits from the appropriate country, and that the US Marine Mammal Protection Act prohibits the importation of any marine mammal products whatsoever.

Appendix I

Flora
Alerce (Chilean falsh larch)
(*Fitzroya cupressoides*)

Mammals
Andean cat (*Felis jacobita*)
Beaked whales (*Berardius* or *Mesoplodon* sp*)
Blue whale (*Balaenoptera musculus*)
Bottlenosed whales (*Hyperodon* spp)
Brazilian tapir (*Tapirus terrestris*)
Chacoan giant peccary (*Catagonus wagneri*)
Fin whale (*Balaenoptera physalus*)
Giant armadillo (*Priodontes maximus*)
Humpback whale (*Megaptera novaeangliae*)
Jaguarundi (*Felis yagouarundi*)
Long-tailed otter (*Lutra platensis*)
Maned wolf (*Chrysocyon brachyrus*)
Marine otter (*Lutra felina*)
Marsh deer (*Blastocerus dicotemus*)
Minke whale (*Balaenoptera acutorostrata*)
Pampas deer (*Ozotocerus bezoarticus*)
Pink fairy armadillo (*Clamyphorus truncatus*)
Pudú (*Pudu pudu*)

Pygmy right whale (*Caperea marginata*)
Sei whale (*Balaenoptera borealis*)
South Andean huemul (*Hippocamelus bisulcus*)
Southern right whale (*Eubalaena australis*)
Southern river otter (*Lutra provocax*)
Sperm whale (*Physeter catodon*)
Vicuña (*Vicugna vicugna*)

Birds
Andean condor (*Vultur gryphus*)
Black-fronted piping-guan (*Pipile jacutinga*)
Darwin's rhea (*Pterocnemia pennata*)
Eskimo curlew (*Numenius borealis*)
Glaucous macaw (*Anodorhynchous glaucus*)
Harpy eagle (*Harpia harpyja*)
Red-spectacled parrot (*Amazona pretrei pretrei*)
Solitary tinamou (*Tinamus solitarius*)

Reptiles
Argentine boa constrictor
(*Boa constrictor occidentalis*)
Broad-snouted caiman (*Caiman latirostris*)
Yacaré (caiman) (*Caiman crocodilus yacare*)

Appendix II

Mammals
Argentine gray fox (*Dusicyon griseus*)
Guanaco (*Lamo guanicoe*)
La Plata river dolphin
Pontoporia (*Stenodelphis blainvillei*)
Pampas fox (*Dusicyon gymnocercus*)
Southern elephant seal (*Mirounga leonina*)
Southern fur seal (*Arctocephalus australis*)

Birds
Caracaras *Falconidae* (all species in family except those on Appendix I)
Chilean flamingo (*Phoenicopterus ruber chilensis*)
Greater rhea (*Rhea americana albescens*)

*All cetaceans (whales and porpoises) not in Appendix I are in Appendix II, but not all are listed individually here. ■

NATIONAL & PROVINCIAL PARKS

Argentina's national parks lure visitors from around the world. One of Latin America's first national park systems dates from the turn of the century, when explorer and surveyor Francisco P Moreno donated 7500 hectares (29 sq miles) near Bariloche to the state in return for guarantees that the parcel would be preserved for the enjoyment of all Argentines. This area is now part of Parque Nacional Nahuel Huapi in the Andean lake district.

Since then, the country has established many other parks and reserves, mostly but not exclusively in the Andean region. There are also important provincial parks and reserves, such as Península Valdés, that do not fall within the national park system but deserve attention. In general, the national parks are more visitor oriented than the provincial parks, but there are exceptions to this; Parque Nacional Perito Moreno has almost no visitor services, while Reserva Provincial Penísula Valdés has good services.

Note that Argentine park personnel, including rangers, are generally very cautious and patronizing with respect to activities beyond the most conventional, and they will often exaggerate the difficulty of hikes and climbs.

Before seeing the national parks, visitors to Buenos Aires should stop at the capital's national parks office for maps and brochures, which are often in short supply in the parks themselves. There may be a charge for some of these. (See the Information section in the Buenos Aires chapter.)

Monumento Natural Laguna de los Pozuelos

A large, high-altitude lake in Jujuy province supports abundant bird life, including three species of flamingos, on its 16,000 hectares (61 sq miles).

Parque Nacional Baritú

On the Bolivian border in Salta province and accessible by road only through Bolivia, this park contains 72,000 hectares (274 sq miles) of nearly virgin subtropical montane forest.

Parque Nacional Calilegua

In Argentina's northerly province of Jujuy, this scenic unit of 76,000 hectares (289 sq miles) protects a variety of ecosystems, from *yungas* (transitional, subtropical lowland forest) to humid, subtropical montane forest to sub-alpine grassland.

Parque Nacional Los Cardones

Although its formal creation is pending, this scenic montane desert park west of Salta protects the striking cardón cactus, which in the past has been used for timber and other purposes.

Parque Nacional Finca El Rey

In the eastern part of Salta Province, this lush, mountainous park protects 44,000 hectares (162 sq miles) of subtropical and coniferous Andean forest.

Parque Nacional Río Pilcomayo

On the Paraguayan border in the province of Formosa, this reasonably accessible park protects 60,000 hectares (228 sq miles) of subtropical marshlands and palm savannas harboring birds, mammals, and reptiles like the caiman or *yacaré*.

Parque Nacional Chaco

In Chaco province, this very accessible but little-visited park offers 15,000 hectares (57 sq miles) of dense, subtropical thorn forests, marshes, and palm savannas, as well as colorful birds.

Parque Nacional Mburucuyá

On the north side of the famous Esteros de Iberá, this newly declared 15,060-hectare (57-sq-mile) marshland reserve is southeast of the city of Corrientes.

Parque Nacional Iguazú

In the northeastern province of Misiones, on the border with Brazil and Paraguay, this very popular park contains the awesome Iguazú Falls, featured in the popular film *The Mission*. It also preserves nearly

A   B

C   D

E   F

A: Parque Provincial Talampaya
B: Guanacos
C Flower, Parque Nacional Lanín

D: Parque Nacional Lanín
E: Children, Humahuaca
F: Gaucho

A	B
C	D
E	F

A: King penguins, Saunders Island
B: Lago Cisne, Parque Nacional
   Los Alerces
C Quechua market seller

D: Hikers, Tierra del Fuego
E: Colonial governor, Stanley
F: Southern elephant seal

55,500 hectares (211 sq miles) of subtropical rainforest, with abundant birds, mammals, and reptiles.

Parque Nacional El Palmar
Readily accessible from Buenos Aires, this 8500-hectare (32-sq-mile) park on the Río Uruguay in Entre Ríos province protects the last extensive stands of *yatay* palm savanna, elsewhere destroyed or threatened by grazing. It is also an excellent place to see birds.

Parque Provincial Talampaya
In western Rioja province, among desert landscapes reminiscent of the southwestern US, this 270,000-hectare (1026-sq-mile) park is a fauna and flora reserve with major paleontological and archaeological resources.

Parque Provincial Ischigualasto
In northern San Juan province, also popularly known as *Valle de la Luna* (Valley of the Moon), this park is a scenic paleontological preserve between sedimentary ranges of the Cerros Colorados and Cerro Los Rastros.

Parque Nacional Diamante
In the province of Entre Ríos, south of the city of Paraná, this 2458-hectare (9-sq-mile) unit protects the islands and gallery forests (forests that grow along streams in regions that otherwise cannot support them) of the northern delta region.

Parque Nacional Sierra de las Quijadas
Covering about 150,000 hectares (570 sq miles) in the northwest corner of San Luis province, this newly designated national park has desert canyons that resemble those of San Juan's Parque Provincial Ischigualasto (see above).

Parque Provincial Aconcagua
The province of Mendoza has set aside 71,000 hectares (270 sq miles) surrounding the Western Hemisphere's highest peak, 6960-meter Aconcagua, a major destination for mountaineers from around the world.

Parque Provincial Tupungato
The 6650-meter summit of Mendoza's second major provincial park is, according to most mountaineers, a more interesting and challenging destination than Aconcagua.

Parque Nacional Lihué Calel
Relieving the desert monotony, this picturesque 9900-hectare (38-sq-mile) park in La Pampa province has salmon-colored peaks and isolated valleys that support a surprising range of fauna and flora, including pumas, guanacos, foxes, rheas, vizcachas, and flowering cacti. There are also numerous Araucanian Indian petroglyphs and some historical buildings.

Parque Nacional Laguna Blanca
Surrounded by ancient volcanoes and lava flows near the city of Zapala in Neuquén province, this lake supports nesting colonies of black-necked swans, plus Andean flamingos and other distinctive birds. The lake and surrounding parklands cover more than 11,000 hectares (42 sq miles).

Parque Nacional Lanín
The snow-covered, symmetrical cone of the Lanín volcano is the centerpiece of this large (378,000 hectares, 1436 sq miles) northern Patagonian park, near the mountain resort of San Martín de los Andes. Fishing is a popular pastime. Equally worthwhile, if less imposing, are the extensive forests of "monkey puzzle trees" (*Araucaria* sp) and southern beech (*Nothofagus* sp).

Parque Nacional Nahuel Huapi
Lago Nahuel Huapi, an enormous trough carved by Pleistocene glaciers, filled by meltwater and surrounded by impressive peaks, is the focus of this scenic, 758,000-hectare (2880-sq-mile) park. The city of Bariloche is the best base for visiting the park, the most highly developed in the Argentine system.

Parque Nacional Los Arrayanes

Surrounded on all sides by the much larger Parque Nacional Nahuel Huapi, this park on a small peninsula near the resort of Villa La Angostura protects pure stands of the unique *arrayán* tree, a member of the myrtle family.

Parque Nacional Lago Puelo

Lago Puelo, an aquamarine, low-altitude lake in northwestern Chubut province, drains into the Pacific near the town of El Bolsón (Río Negro province) and is surrounded by high Andean peaks. Covering 23,700 hectares (90 sq miles) along the Chilean border, the park makes for an interesting if infrequently used border crossing.

Parque Nacional Los Alerces

Along the Andean crest in Chubut province, west of the city of Esquel, this very attractive park protects 263,000 hectares (1000 sq miles) of the unique Valdivian forest ecosystem, which includes impressive specimens of the *alerce* tree, resembling the California redwoods.

Reserve Provincial Península Valdés

Although not part of the national park system, the Chubut provincial reserve of Península Valdés is an important destination for wildlife enthusiasts. Marine mammals, including whales, sea lions, and elephant seals, are the main attraction, but there are also Magellanic penguins and other unusual seabirds. Along the Patagonian coast are many smaller reserves with breeding colonies of seabirds and marine mammals.

Reserva Provincial Punta Tombo

Also not part of the national park system, this scenic provincial reserve south of Trelew in Chubut has an enormous nesting colony of burrowing Magellanic penguins and other seabirds.

Parque Nacional Perito Francisco P Moreno

Named for the founder of the Argentine park system, this nearly inaccessible unit of 115,000 hectares (437 sq miles) in northwestern Santa Cruz province protects a series of awesome glacial lakes, surrounding Alpine peaks and Andean-Patagonian forest. Wildlife includes herds of guanaco, the lowland counterpart of the domesticated llama of the central Andes. For real solitude, this park and Monumento Natural Bosques Petrificados are the best bets.

Monumento Natural Bosques Petrificados

On the Patagonian steppe in northern Santa Cruz province, this isolated 10,000-hectare (38-sq-mile) park features immense specimens of petrified *Proaraucaria* trees from an era prior to the creation of the Andes when the region contained a dense, humid forest.

Parque Nacional Los Glaciares

One of Argentina's "must see" attractions is the famous Moreno Glacier, one of few in the world that is currently advancing, but the awesome peaks of the Fitzroy Range invite a much longer stay. Southern beech forests cover substantial zones of the 600,000-hectare (2280-sq-mile) park.

Parque Nacional Tierra del Fuego

Argentina's only shoreline national park, this unit on the Beagle Channel stretches inland to envelop alpine glaciers and peaks within its 63,000 hectares (240 sq miles). There are marine mammals, seabirds, shorebirds, and extensive forests of southern beech.

GOVERNMENT & POLITICS

After the end of military dictatorship in 1983, Argentina returned to the Constitution of 1853, which established a federal system similar to that of the US. There are separate executive and bicameral legislative branches, an ostensibly independent judiciary, and a theoretical balance of power among the three.

In 1994 a constitutional convention amended the document to permit re-election of the president while reducing the term to four years (from the previous six-year single term). It also eliminated the legal requirement that the president be a Roman Catholic, added an additional senator for each province and the city of Buenos Aires, and lengthened the legislative year.

The president and the Congreso Nacional (comprising a 254-member Cámara de Diputados and a 72-member Senado) are popularly elected, as are provincial governors and legislatures. In practice, the president is far more powerful than a North American counterpart and frequently governs by decree without consulting the Congreso; the president can also, and frequently does, intervene in provincial matters. When the constitutional convention established re-election of the president, it also created the office of Jefe de Gabinete, a sort of executive prime minister responsible to the Congreso.

Administratively, the country consists of a federal district (the city of Buenos Aires proper), plus 23 provinces, the territories of the South Atlantic islands (including the Falklands and South Georgia, under British administration), and the Argentine Antarctic (where territorial claims are on hold by international agreement).

Political Parties
Although personality is often more important than party, the spectrum of Argentine political parties is broad. At least 18 different parties are represented in Congress, but the most important are the Peronists (Justicialists) of the late Juan Perón and current President Carlos Menem, and the Unión Cívica Radical (misleadingly called the "Radicals") of former President Raúl Alfonsín, who generally represents middle-class interests. Though Argentines of all classes normally participate in political discussion, which does not always constitute dialogue, some observers have recently expressed concern over apathy among younger voters who have traditionally formed the activist sector of their parties.

Until the 1940s, when Perón revolutionized Argentine politics by overtly appealing to labor unions and other under-represented sectors of society, the Radicals vied against parties tied to traditional conservative landowning interests for electoral supremacy. Within the Peronist party, there are deeply divided factions which, in the mid-1970s, even conducted open warfare against each other.

Currently these divisions are less violent, but there is still considerable friction between the official "neoliberal" adherents of President Menem, who has attempted to reduce the role of the state in economic matters and limit the influence of militant labor, and leftist and nationalist elements that see Menem's policies as capitulation to foreign institutions like the World Bank and International Monetary Fund. Ultra-nationalist factions within the Justicialist party are not much happier despite their loathing of the left.

Menem has forged an open association with the conservative Unión del Centro Democrático (UCeDé, or Democratic Center Union) and its leader, Alvaro Alsogaray, whose counsel is a source of great irritation to leftists and nationalists. Other parties, much less numerous and influential, include the Partido Intransigente (PI, or Intransigent Party), the Democracia Cristiana (Christian Democrats), and the Movimiento para Integración y Desarollo (MID, or Movement for Integration and Development). The Movimiento Para la Dignidad e Independencia (MODIN, or Movement for Dignity and Independence) is a right-wing extremist party headed by former carapintada leader Aldo Rico, a retired colonel who attempted to overthrow the elected government of former Radical President Raúl Alfonsín.

In some provinces, local political parties are especially important. In Neuquén, for instance, the Sapag family's Partido Popular Neuquino has been responsible for some of the most progressive social policies in the entire country. In the province of Catamarca, the Saadi family is known for the most egregious corruption, even by Argentine standards.

Current Politics

Rising political figures in the country include current economy minister Domingo Cavallo, author of the government's controversial but, to this point, effective "convertibility" policy; Peronist ex-Governor Ramon "Palito" Ortega of Tucumán (a former crooner who once attempted to get the federal government to subsidize a financial disaster he suffered in bringing Frank Sinatra to Buenos Aires); ex-Santa Fe Governor Carlos Reutemann (who first came to public prominence as a Formula One racing driver); and former World Cup soccer coach Julio César Menotti (a possible successor to Reutemann, who is constitutionally ineligible for re-election in Santa Fe). Buenos Aires provincial Governor Eduardo Duhalde, Menem's former vice-president, lacks their celebrity but is a strong presidential candidate for the year 1999. Menem's vice-president, former Interior Minister Carlos Ruckauf, is another possibility despite dismissive comments from opponents within his own party that he was chosen because he was "shorter and uglier than the president."

The Radicals chose Río Negro Governor Horacio Massaccessi to run against Menem, but many Argentines think that the party lost its identity by acquiescing in the so-called "Pacto de Olivos," which permitted Menem to run for re-election despite a constitutional prohibition. The center-left coalition known as Frente del País Solidario (Frepaso, the national arm of Frente Grande, which has done well in Buenos Aires municipal elections) chose dissident Peronist José Octavio Bordón of Mendoza as its presidential candidate, with porteño Carlos "Chacho" Alvarez (nicknamed "Metrovías" because, like the subway, he never leaves Buenos Aires) as his running mate. The MID and the Unidad Socialista (Socialist Unity) are part of the Frepaso alliance, which has yet to prove that it is more than an ephemeral force in national politics.

In the 1995 presidential elections, which Menem won by a substantial plurality over Bordón, with Massaccessi a weak third, the

After President Menem discounted confessions of torture and executions at the Escuela de Mecánica de la Armada (SAMA or Naval Mechanics' School) under the military dictatorship of 1976 – 83, the *Buenos Aires Herald* published this cartoon by Rober Bobrow (courtesy of the *Buenos Aires Herald*).

Partido Justicialista won majorities in both houses of the Congreso Nacional. In the Cámara de Diputados, the Peronists have 131 seats, while the Radicals have 70, Frepaso 28, and minor and regional parties 29. In the Senate, the Peronists have 39 seats, the Radicals 21, and the other dozen belong to a variety of lesser regional parties. One of the most encouraging results was the extremely poor showing of Rico's MODIN.

In addition to the Menem-Cavallo economic policies, major issues in the recent past have been Menem's authoritarian tendencies and corruption in his administration (one influential banker referred to the country as a "kleptocracy"). Even before winning a second term, he spoke of running again in 2003 (which would require a further constitutional amendment), he has not refrained from ruling by decree, rather than consulting with Congress over legislation, and has even interfered in the federal courts.

At one point, the administration proposed a libel law including a "defamation of the dignity of the dead" clause that could theoretically result in imprisonment of, for example, a historian writing a critical biography of San Martín. According to *Buenos Aires Herald* editor Andrew Graham-Yooll,

"Argentina has made its national heroes into saints, probably in the assumption that if debate on the actions of politicians of old is prevented, then discussion of present-day officials can be discouraged." Another less comprehensive law would permit the Argentine Senate to jail journalists for up to three days for "lack of respect."

Certain issues have aroused suspicion of the administration, including a drug-money laundering case involving the president's in-laws, sluggish and unsuccessful police investigations of the bombings of the Israeli embassy and Asociación Mutua Israelita Argentina (AMIA) cultural center (see the section on Population & People), and revelations that the Argentine ambassador to Saudi Arabia had apparently accepted large bribes to grant citizenship to Middle Eastern terrorists.

Nevertheless, the divided opposition has been ineffective in pursuing such matters, and many Argentines seem uninterested. Probably the most effective criticism has come from the *vox populi*, where Menem is referred to as *El Mufa* – a slang term implying a "jinx." (Professional athletes have suffered misfortunes such as broken bones soon after meeting the president, who regularly scrimmages with the national soccer team, and one racing boat driver, shortly after shaking hands with him, lost the hand in an accident.) According to popular belief, it is bad luck to use Menem's name when talking about him, so many now obliquely refer to him as "Méndez."

The Military

Since 1930, when the military overthrew Radical President Hipólito Yrigoyen, it has played a crucial if not always public role in Argentine politics. Generals have often worn the presidential sash, most recently between 1976 and 1983. It is sometimes difficult to determine whether the frequent coups occur when the military feel themselves "obliged" to intervene because of civilian incompetence, corruption, and disorder, or whether military activities themselves create conditions that undermine the civil order.

The military coup that overthrew constitutional President María Estela Martínez de Perón ("Isabelita") was bloodless, not unexpected and, even among moderate sectors of the populace, not unwelcome. After Juan Perón's death, people honestly yearned for relief from economic chaos and the erosion of public order, in which violent strikes, bombings, and kidnappings were everyday occurrences.

In the aftermath of the coup, though, military rule was savage. The services operated dozens of clandestine detention centers, including that at the infamous Escuela de Mecánica de la Armada (ESMA, or Naval Mechanics's School) in Buenos Aires, where opponents and presumed opponents of the government were tortured and frequently murdered under the ideology of the "national security doctrine." (See the History section above.)

The military themselves are traditionally a privileged sector in Argentine society. More frequently used to control the civilian population than to fight foreign enemies, the military failed miserably in confronting Britain during the Falklands/Malvinas War of 1982 but soon recovered its technological capacity despite heavy material losses. The air force, which suffered the heaviest material losses despite a creditable performance under difficult conditions, quickly replaced its lost hardware despite a grave economic crisis that foolish military action had worsened.

President Carlos Menem has made some headway in redefining the military's mission by involving them, despite nationalist objections, in international operations like the Gulf War of 1991 and peacekeeping operations elsewhere around the world. At the same time, despite his own incarceration at the hands of the military during the Dirty War, he inexplicably pardoned the highest-ranking criminals and even, at the end of 1994, gratuitously praised them for their contribution to saving the country from "chaos." In response, human rights groups such as the Madres de La Plaza de Mayo have continued to publicize the whereabouts and activities of individuals

ARGENTINA

like the notorious Astiz, and, in an extraordinary episode, Army Chief of Staff Eduardo Bauza went on nationwide television to apologize to the public for his service's role in the repression. The navy, however, has remained unrepentant.

The recent abolition of compulsory military service, once universal for all males above the age of 18, is a hopeful sign of the diminished influence of the Argentine military; it has also reduced the size of the army. Even with improved wages and working conditions, however, the services have been unable to achieve recruitment quotas, and even officers have suffered salary cuts due to recent budget crises.

Many Argentines continue to view the military with a mixture of distaste and anxiety over its ambiguous role in society. The cover photograph of a recent magazine article on the "power of secretaries" in business depicted several young women in military dress uniform rather than the presidential sash, a symbol of civilian authority.

Geopolitics

Besides the national security doctrine, one of the mainstays of military ideology and influence is the idea of geopolitics, a 19th-century European doctrine interpreted in a peculiarly Argentine way. According to this world view, first elaborated by German geographer Friedrich Ratzel and later exaggerated in National Socialist (Nazi) ideology in the 1930s, the state is akin to a biological organism that must grow (expand) or die. This means effective occupation of the territories that the state claims as its own, through which the state comes into conflict with other states. Such thinking was clearly a major factor in General Galtieri's decision to invade the Falkland Islands in 1982.

Other South American countries, particularly Brazil and Chile, share this perspective. Chile's former dictator, General Augusto Pinochet, has even written a textbook entitled *Geopolítica*, while his Argentine and Brazilian counterparts discuss topics like the "Fifth Column" of Chilean immigrants (largely illiterate sheep shearers

from the economically depressed island of Chiloé) in Patagonia or the justification of territorial claims in the Antarctic in accordance with each country's longitudinal "frontage" on the icebound continent. In one instance, an Argentine military government transported a pregnant woman to Antarctica to give birth there and strengthen its case for "effective settlement."

The tenets of geopolitics are most popular among, but not restricted to, the military, who publish obsessively complex articles in journals like *Estrategia* (Strategy). Although some of these analyses are much more sophisticated than others, it would be a mistake to dismiss any of them too easily. Once during an interview, an Argentine naval officer observed that, "For us, the Malvinas are a pact sealed in blood." So long as such attitudes persist, the militarization of Argentine society remains a significant issue.

ECONOMY

Relating the tale of a relative who found an unusable "treasure" of 10 billion old pesos in the mountains of Córdoba, one of the characters in Osvaldo Soriano's recent novel *Una Sombra Ya Pronto Serás (Shadows)* remarks that "a country where finding a fortune is a waste of time isn't a serious country."

Indeed, Argentina's inability to achieve its potential, despite its abundant natural resources and its highly literate and sophisticated population, has mystified outside observers for decades. A country that, at the turn of the century, resembled now prosperous Australia and Canada has regressed instead of keeping pace with those countries. Burdened with a monstrous foreign debt unlikely ever to be repaid, its middle class is shrinking, while the working class and the poor have little hope of advancement. Despite the recent stability of the Menem administration, it is difficult to find any Argentine truly optimistic about the country's future.

Ever since the colonial era, the Argentine economy has relied on agricultural export commodities – hides, wool, beef, and grains – gleaned from the fertile Pampas. Self-sufficient in petroleum and other energy resources, the country has been unable to capitalize on these advantages despite a superficial prosperity. With a per capita GDP of nearly US$6800 (a figure exaggerated by an overvalued peso), Argentina is one of Latin America's wealthiest countries, but its economy is in a state of perpetual chaos. To repay the crippling international debts of US$62 billion (thousand million) would require all export earnings for 27 months; Mexico's foreign debt, by contrast, equals only 13 months of that country's exports.

Encouraged by international institutions, Argentina's borrowing binge of the 1970s and 1980s funded gigantic, capital-intensive projects offering no obvious economic advantages to the country but myriad opportunities for graft and corruption. These undertakings, like the Yacyretá dam on the upper Río Paraná, fostered economic speculation that contributed to the country's chronic inflation, which consistently exceeded 100% per annum and was often much higher.

One of Argentina's problems has been inequities in the rural sector, where problems resemble those of other Latin American countries. The richest agricultural lands of the Pampas remained under the control of relatively few individuals – unlike Canada or the US, where family farmers benefited from a more broadly based prosperity. With other rural people relegated to marginal lands or a role as dependent labor on large estates, Argentina reproduced the classic Latin American pattern of latifundio versus minifundio. Institutions like the powerful Sociedad Rural maintained the power of the landholding elite.

Perón's rise to power demonstrated that the structure of rural society was inadequate for broader prosperity, that Argentina needed to develop its industrial base, and that workers needed to share in the development of Argentine industry. At the time, there was probably no alternative to state involvement in industry, but its dominance over succeeding decades outlived its usefulness.

During the Menem administration, Economy Minister Domingo Cavallo has drastically slashed the state sector, once the economy's largest, by selling off corrupt or inefficient state enterprises such as ENTel (the state telephone company), Aerolíneas Argentinas, and Yacimientos Petrolíferos Fiscales (YPF, or the state oil monopoly). Indeed, the usefulness of many state employees can be questioned when the day after the announcement of the impending privatization of ENTel, so many people came to work that there were insufficient desks for all of them.

Argentines refer to individuals who hold multiple government jobs as *ñoquis*, after the traditional potato pasta served in Argentine households on the 29th of each month – the implication is that they appear on the job just before their monthly paychecks are due. Such practices have contributed to ruinous inflation rates, often exceeding 50% per month. While the prevalence of ñoquis has declined in the federal bureaucracy (between 1990 and 1995, state employment fell from one million to 370,000), reform has barely touched provincial governments.

For better or worse, the Menem administration has apparently broken the inflationary spiral by reducing the public sector deficit, selling off inefficient state enterprises, and restricting the activities of militant labor unions. Cavallo has managed to tame inflation, at least temporarily, by means of a "convertibility" law that pegged the peso at one to one with the dollar – in effect establishing a gold standard as the government would print no more pesos than its hard currency reserves. Inflation for 1994 was less than 4% – an astonishingly low figure by Argentine standards – but the figure for January 1995 was an unexpected and alarming 1.2%, which government economists prayed was only a blip on the screen rather than an omen of any return to the bad old days. So far this seems to be the case, and in March 1995 there was a virtually unprecedented *deflation* of -0.4%.

Selling off state assets like Aerolíneas Argentinas, YPF, and ENTel was a one-time bonanza that reduced or eliminated budget deficits in the short term and increased productivity, but a more efficient tax system will have to achieve such gains in the future. The legacy of state domination has fostered a large informal sector that operates parallel to the official economy in providing goods and services. One recent study claimed that only 40% of Argentina's workers functioned in the "official" economy – the remainder labored independently, were often paid in cash, and avoided taxes entirely.

The reduction of the state sector has also brought costs that often do not fit into conventional accounting systems. In April 1995, for instance, the privatized YPF dumped waste oil into the Río de la Plata near Buenos Aires's popular Reserva Ecológica, on the rationale that "we had to get rid of the waste somehow and this looked like the only solution." A state-controlled YPF might not have done things any differently, but this intentional discharge also came at a time when the company had contracted to clean up the area's waters.

Whether the "rationalization" of the Argentine economy envisaged by Menem and Cavallo will be successful is uncertain, but similar measures over the last 15 years have failed many times. The administration's pleas for austerity and its promises that things will get better ring false when the president himself accepts a US$50,000 sports car as a gift from potential foreign investors, and a prominent labor leader declares that "nobody in Argentina ever got rich by working." There have also been objections to Cavallo's methods; according to former President Alfonsín, Cavallo is "authoritarian, a madman and a basilisk. He is an authoritarian who has served in authoritarian governments and holds no democratic beliefs."

One of the side effects of privatization has been increasing unemployment, which the government sees as an essential structural adjustment but which ordinary people

worry may be a more enduring problem. In mid-1995, official unemployment figures stood at 12.2%, with a probable undercount in rural areas, and it then rose to nearly 20% as the economy contracted in the aftermath of President Menem's re-election. In part, provincial governments have taken up the slack by hiring more people for their own state-run enterprises, but their reliance on federal government revenue-sharing causes serious difficulties; for instance, Río Negro governor and Radical presidential candidate Horacio Massaccessi was in the position of having to ask his main political rival, President Menem, for funds to pay provincial employees. In May 1995, dissatisfied provincial employees forced the resignation of Radical governor Eduardo Angeloz and trashed the city of San Juan after provincial Governor Jorge Escobar reduced wages by 30% for any state employee earning more than US$400 per month (the legal monthly minimum wage is only US$200 in a country where living expenses are not much less than in Europe or North America).

Late in 1994, Cavallo's convertibility policy came under criticism as budget deficits rose and Argentina declined to accept an IMF loan because of international oversights, forcing a minor stock market crisis and a run on the dollar. The crash of the Mexican peso in January 1995 put considerable pressure on the Argentine economy, but to this point the convertibility policy has resisted devaluation pressures that would probably unleash a new round of serious inflation.

One should not disregard the psychological factor in Argentina's economic disorder. Argentines so routinely expect prices to rise that, before the administration raised the value added tax (VAT, or *impuesto de valor agregado*, IVA) in early 1995, businesses immediately talked of raising prices – some by considerably more than the 3% increase in the tax rate. Individuals are so accustomed to paying the asking price of an item before it goes up that they will rarely, if ever, shop around in search of a better price.

ARGENTINA

Mercosur

The recent customs union of Brazil, Argentina, Uruguay, and Paraguay, known as "Mercosur", is the first attempt by "developing" countries to establish a free trade area, and the union should in theory facilitate commerce among the four countries and reduce prices for imported goods. Nobody should get too excited too soon, however – at present the policy only requires the four countries to impose a common external tariff on most imported goods, but internal customs barriers remain in place to protect local and national industries.

There is no common labor market, such as in the European Union, so Brazilian, Paraguayan, and Uruguayan workers are officially unwelcome in Argentina – and vice versa. At present, undocumented foreign laborers are being persecuted in much the same manner as Mexican workers residing in the USA.

Tourism

Tourism makes a substantial contribution to the Argentine economy; in 1993, over 3.5 million foreigners visited the country, while the income from *turismo receptivo* exceeded US$3600 million (this figure does not take into account domestic tourism, which is also an important economic

Tourism and textiles continue to be important for the country's economy.

factor). Excluding citizens of the neighboring countries of Brazil, Chile, Uruguay, and Paraguay, the greatest number of foreign visitors to Argentina are the French, followed by Americans, Spaniards, and Italians. Tourism employs nearly half a million Argentines and accounts for about 20% of the country's export earnings.

POPULATION & PEOPLE

Argentina's population of 32.3 million is unevenly distributed. More than a third reside in Gran Buenos Aires (Greater Buenos Aires), which includes the Capital Federal and its suburbs in the Buenos Aires province. More than 86% live in urban areas; the other major population centers are Rosario (Santa Fe province), Córdoba, Tucumán, Mendoza, and Bahía Blanca (Buenos Aires province). South of Patagonia's Río Colorado the population is very small and dispersed.

From the early 19th century, the Unitarist faction in Argentine politics had followed the dictum of Juan Bautista Alberdi, a native of Tucumán, who argued that "to govern is to populate." Unitarists saw Europe as a model for independent Argentina's aspirations, and they did everything possible to promote European immigration. Alberdi's ideas retain great appeal, surviving especially among geopoliticians who dream of filling the country's vast empty spaces, Patagonia and even Antarctica, with more Argentines.

Unlike the central Andean countries, which had large, urbanized Indian populations when Europeans appeared on the scene, the Pampas core of present-day Argentina was sparsely populated by hunting and gathering peoples. Except in the northwest, where early colonization proceeded from Peru and Bolivia, European immigrants displaced relatively small numbers of indigenous peoples. From the mid-19th century on, the trickle of Europeans became a flood, as Italians, Basques, Welsh, English, Ukrainians, and immigrants of other nationalities inundated Buenos Aires as they did New York City. Italian surnames are even more common than Spanish ones, though Italo-Argentines do not constitute a cohesive, distinctive group in the way that Italian-Americans do in many cities in the US.

Some groups have retained a distinctive cultural identity, such as the Anglo-Argentines throughout the country and the Welsh in Chubut province (despite the eclipse of Welsh as a living language). In some areas there are agricultural settlements with a definable ethnic heritage, for instance, the Germans of Eldorado in Misiones province, the Bulgarians and Yugoslavs of Roque Sáenz Peña in the Chaco, and the Ukrainians of La Pampa.

Buenos Aires' Jewish community of about 400,000, the world's eighth largest, has drawn unfortunate attention due to the bombing of the Israeli embassy in 1992 and the particularly lethal terrorist destruction of the Asociación Mutua Israelita Argentina (AMIA) in July 1994, when a bomb killed at least 86 people as it leveled the Jewish cultural center. Progress in identifying the culprits has been agonizingly slow, but according to press reports, in late 1995, some 15 people were arrested and charged with planning or facilitating the attack. About 10 are noncommissioned officers in the army. The bombing has had a chilling effect on the Jewish community in Buenos Aires; most Jewish synogogues and centers have been heavily fortified, and security guards check everyone upon entry.

Middle Eastern immigrants, though not numerous, have attained great political influence. The most obvious case is current President Carlos Menem, of Syrian ancestry, who rose to prominence in the province of La Rioja. Although a vocal and perhaps opportunistic Catholic (Catholicism was a formal requirement for the presidency when he was first elected), his marriage to his now-estranged wife, Zulema Yoma, was arranged; both Zulema and their daughter, Zulemita, are active Moslems who planned a pilgrimage to Mecca after the death of Carlos Jr in a helicopter accident.

The Saadis in Catamarca and the Sapags in Neuquén province are other influential political families of Middle Eastern

origins, while Colonel Mohammed Alí Seineldín (a fanatical Catholic despite his name) is an imprisoned leader of the army's fascist carapintada movement. Argentines refer indiscriminately to anyone of Middle Eastern ancestry (except Jews or Israelis) as a *turco* (Turk), sometimes but not always with racist connotations.

The Buenos Aires suburb of Escobar has a conspicuous Japanese community, but non-European immigrants have generally not been welcome; despite the upheavals in Asia over the past decade-plus, only a relative handful of immigrants from that region have entered Argentina. Nevertheless, an abundance of Chinese restaurants have opened in the past decade, the common Korean surname Kim fills nearly a page in the Buenos Aires telephone directory, and Asian faces are a more common sight than in the past.

Many Chileans live in Argentine Patagonia, but their usual status as dependent laborers on sheep estancias marginalizes their position in Argentine society. Bolivian highlanders often serve as seasonal laborers *(peones golondrinas* or swallows) in the sugar harvests of northwestern Argentina; some have moved to Buenos Aires, where they mainly work in the construction industry. Numerous Paraguayans and Uruguayans also reside permanently in Argentina. As the Menem administration's increasingly rigid economic policies have swelled unemployment, some Argentines have begun to scapegoat undocumented foreign workers, even though those workers (like Mexicans in the USA) fill economic niches that few Argentines choose to fill themselves – willingly or otherwise.

Estimates of the country's indigenous population range from 60,000 to 150,000, but the Instituto Nacional de Estadística places the figure around 100,000. The largest groups are the Quechua of the northwest and the Mapuche of northern Patagonia, but there are important populations of Matacos, Tobas, and others in the Chaco and in northeastern cities such as Resistencia and Santa Fe. The Alfonsín administration was surprisingly sympathetic to Indian issues, but the Menem government appears indifferent.

EDUCATION

Argentina's 94% literacy rate is one of Latin America's highest. From the age of five to 12, education is free and compulsory, though attendance is low in some rural areas. The comprehensive secondary education system follows the French model, with no elective courses. Elite public secondary schools such as the Colegio Nacional Buenos Aires, where the teachers are also university instructors, are unequaled by other public or private institutions, although some bilingual schools are very prestigious.

Universities are traditionally free and open, but once students have chosen a specialization, their course of study is extremely rigid. Ready access to higher education has glutted Buenos Aires with large numbers of professionals, such as doctors and lawyers, who are not easily absorbed into the city's economy, but are reluctant to relocate to the provinces. Private universities exist, but public universities like Buenos Aires, Córdoba, and La Plata are more prominent.

In addition to university education, there is a tertiary system for the preparation of teachers, who do not need a university degree. Individuals who are not academically oriented can choose vocational training.

ARTS

Many Argentine intellectuals have been educated in European capitals, particularly Paris. In the 19th and early 20th centuries, Buenos Aires self-consciously emulated French trends in art, music, and architecture, but many Argentines have made their mark outside the country's borders.

Popular Music

Argentine rock musicians such as Charly García (formerly a member of the important group Sui Generis) and Fito Páez (dismissed by some as excessively commercial) have recorded overseas. García performed a version of the Argentine national anthem much along the lines of Jimi Hendrix's "Star-Spangled Banner"; after a judge dismissed a lawsuit which alleged that García lacked "respect for national symbols," the *Buenos Aires Herald* editorialized that García's defense was a victory over "extremist nationalist sectors" which had too long "imposed their warped and often authoritarian views on the rest of society."

Les Luthiers is a group in tie and tails who build many of their unusual instruments from scratch and satirize the middle class and the military. Many performers are more conventional and derivative, but before you report an Elvis sighting in Buenos Aires, make sure it isn't Sandro, a living Argentine clone of the King (the advent of Sandro impersonators in the boliches of the Boca district may be sending a message to the man known to his devotees as "El Maestro").

Increasingly popular Argentine groups, playing "rock nacional," include Soda Stereo, Los Divididos, and especially Los Ratones Paranóicos, who opened for the Rolling Stones on their spectacularly successful five-night stand in Buenos Aires in February 1995 (longtime Stones associate Andrew Loog Oldham has produced one of the Ratones's albums). Also on the bill with the Stones were Las Pelotas and local blues artist Pappo.

Porteño blues band Memphis La Blusera has worked with American legend Taj Mahal. Singer Patricia Sosa's closest counterparts in the English-speaking world would be Janis Joplin or, today, perhaps Melissa Ethridge. The appropriately named Dos Minutos group emulates the Ramones, who themselves have played Buenos Aires several times.

Tango & Folk Music

Probably the best known manifestation of Argentine popular culture is the tango, both as music and dance, with important figures such as the legendary Carlos Gardel, the late Julio Sosa and Astor Piazzola, and contemporaries like Susana Rinaldi, Eladia

Once associated with the working class and the brothels, the tango attained broad popularity in the early 20th century.

Blásquez, and Osvaldo Pugliese. The late Atahualpa Yupanqui was a giant of Argentine folk music, along with contemporaries Mercedes Sosa, Tarragó Ross, Leon Gieco (modern enough to adopt a rap style at times), and Conjunto Pro Música de Rosario.

Classical Music, Dance & Theater

The palatial Teatro Colón, home of the Buenos Aires opera, is one of the finest facilities of its kind in the world. Classical music and ballet, as well as modern dance, appear here and at similar venues. Buenos Aires has a vigorous theater community, equivalent in its own way to New York, London, or Paris, but even in the provinces, live theater is an important medium of expression.

Literature

Argentine writers of international stature include Jorge Luis Borges, Julio Cortázar, Ernesto Sábato, Manuel Puig, Osvaldo Soriano, and Adolfo Bioy Casares, much of whose work is readily available in English translation. Argentine women writers are best known for poetry and essays, but little of their work is available in translation. One exception is Victoria Ocampo, whose essays were included in a recent biography by Doris Meyer entitled *Against the Wind and Tide*. Borges is best known for his short stories but also for important poetry. His erudite language and references sometimes make him inaccessible to readers without a solid grounding in the classics, even though his material often deals with everyday porteño and rural life. Sábato's *On Heroes and Tombs* is a psychological novel that explores people and places in Buenos Aires. Originally published in 1961, it was a cult favorite among Argentine youth. Try also his novella *The Tunnel*, the engrossing story of a porteño painter so obsessed with his art that it distorts his relationship to everything and everyone else.

Cortázar, while a Parisian resident, nevertheless emphasized clearly Argentine characters in novels such as the experimentally structured *Hopscotch* and *62: A Model Kit*. The landmark 1960s film *Blow-Up* was based on one of his short stories. Manuel Puig's novels, including *Kiss of the Spider Woman* (which was made into a movie), *The Buenos Aires Affair*, and *Betrayed by Rita Hayworth*, focus on the ambiguous role of popular culture in Argentina.

Bioy Casares's hallucinatory novella *The Invention of Morel* also deals with the inability or unwillingness to distinguish between fantasy and reality; it was a partial inspiration for the highly praised film *Man Facing Southeast*. His *Diary of the War of the Pig* is also available in translation.

Osvaldo Soriano, perhaps Argentina's most popular contemporary novelist, wrote *A Funny Dirty Little War*, later adapted into a film, and *Winter Quarters*. In Soriano's *Shadows*, the English translation of *Una Sombra Ya Pronto Serás* (the title comes from the lyrics of a popular tango), the protagonist is lost in an Argentina where the names are the same, but all the familiar landmarks and points of reference have lost their meaning. A film version has recently been made.

Film

Despite the limited resources available to directors, Argentine cinema has achieved international stature, especially since its post-Dirty War renaissance. Argentina has left its mark on Hollywood and vice versa. Carlos Gardel flashed his smile in several Spanish-language films, including *El Día Que Me Quieras*, and Hollywood used Argentina as a location under forced circumstances – Juan Perón's economic policies prohibited studios from exporting profits made from their movies, so some studios used the profits to film in Argentina; the epic *Taras Bulba* (1962), for instance, was filmed partly around Salta. Fay Dunaway appeared much later in the truly atrocious *Eva Perón* (filmed in 1981 as an NBC-TV miniseries and now available on video), for which Dunaway's salary probably comprised 90% of the budget.

Readers who know Spanish may enjoy *Ambito Financiero* film critic Diego Curubeto's *Babilonia Gaucha*, an entertaining exploration of the relationship between Hollywood and Argentina.

Visual Arts

Given its French origins, official public art tends toward the pompously monumental, but there also exists a thriving alternative and unconventional art scene, grudgingly acknowledged by the arbiters of official taste. Buenos Aires is the focus of the country's arts community, but there are also unexpected outliers such as the city of Resistencia, capital of Chaco province. There are many important art museums and galleries in Buenos Aires and elsewhere.

Architecture

Argentina lacks the great pre-Columbian monuments of Peru and Bolivia, though a few significant archaeological sites dot the Andean Northwest. This latter region,

Opened in 1908 with the spectacular *Aida*, Teatro Colón remains one of the world's premier opera houses.

however, has notable if not abundant Spanish colonial architecture in cities such as Salta and Tucumán, and villages in isolated areas like the Quebrada de Humahuaca and surrounding areas. Other areas for colonial architecture, or at least atmosphere, include San Antonio de Areco and Carmen de Patagones in Buenos Aires province. The city of Buenos Aires itself has scattered colonial examples, but it is essentially a turn-of-the-century city whose architectural influences are predominantly French. Recent architecture tends to the pharaonic and impersonal, with a substantial number of modernistic buildings in the downtown area.

Architects in the Andean lake district of northern Patagonia have adapted Middle European styles into some of the region's most appealing urban landscapes, but recent tacky construction in cities like San Carlos de Bariloche has overwhelmed its appeal. Southern Patagonia, while not famous for its architecture, has an intriguing and unique "Magellanic" style of wooden houses with metal cladding, also present in southern Chile.

CULTURE & SOCIETY

English-speaking visitors will find Argentina more accessible than other Latin American countries because of its superficial resemblance to their own societies. In contrast to countries like Peru and Bolivia, with their large indigenous populations, foreign travelers are relatively inconspicuous and can more easily integrate themselves into everyday life. Argentines are gregarious and, once you make contact with them, much more likely to invite you to participate in their regular activities than would, say, Quechua llama herders in Bolivia.

One of these activities, which you should never refuse, is the opportunity to *tomar un mate* (drink *mate*). Drinking *mate* (pronounced "mah-tay"), or Paraguayan tea, is an important ritual throughout the River Plate countries and to a lesser degree in Chile, but especially so in Argentina. In the

south, it is drunk bitter, but in the north people take it with sugar and *yuyos* (herbs).

Sport is extremely important to Argentines. Most people know Argentine athletes through its World Cup champion soccer teams, featuring players such as Diego Maradona and Daniel Passarella (the latter now coach of the national team), and tennis stars Guillermo Vilas and Gabriela Sabatini, but rugby, polo, golf, skiing, and fishing also enjoy great popularity. Soccer, though, is the national obsession. The teams River Plate and Boca Juniors, the latter based in Buenos Aires' immigrant Italian neighborhood of La Boca, are both nationwide phenomena.

RELIGION

Roman Catholicism is the official state religion but, as in many other Latin American countries, evangelical Protestantism is making inroads among traditionally Catholic believers. Even within the Catholic religion, popular beliefs diverge from official doctrine – one of the best examples is the cult of the Difunta Correa, based in San Juan province, to which hundreds of thousands of professed Argentine Catholics make annual pilgrimages and offerings despite an aggressive campaign by the Church hierarchy against her veneration.

Spiritualism and veneration of the dead have remarkable importance for a country that prides itself on European sophistication. Novelist Tomás Eloy Martínez has observed that Argentines honor their national heroes, such as San Martín, not on the anniversary of their birth but of their death, a habit that indirectly parallels the celebrations of saint's days. Visitors to Recoleta and Chacarita cemeteries in Buenos Aires – essential sights for comprehending Argentine culture – will see steady processions of pilgrims communicating with icons like Juan and Evita Perón, psychic Madre María, and tango singer Carlos Gardel by laying hands on their tombs and leaving arcane offerings.

Official Catholicism has provided Argentina with some of its most impressive monuments, from the modest but picturesque churches of the Andean Northwest to the Jesuit missions of Mesopotamia, the colonial cathedral of Córdoba, and the neo-Gothic basilica of Luján in the province of Buenos Aires. A lack of attention to the role of religion will limit anyone's understanding of Argentine society.

Like other Argentine institutions, the Church has many factions. During the late 1970s and early 1980s, the official Church generally supported the de facto military government despite persecution, kidnapping, torture and murder of religious workers. These workers, adherents of the movement toward "Liberation Theology," often worked among the poor and dispossessed in both rural areas and the *villas miserias* (shantytowns) of Buenos Aires and other large cities. Such activism has resumed in today's more permissive political climate, but the Church hierarchy remains obstinate: The Archbishop of Buenos Aires, for example, has defended President Menem's pardon of the convicted murderers and torturers of the Proceso, and it appears that official chaplains acquiesced in the atrocities of the Dirty War by counseling the perpetrators.

LANGUAGE

Spanish is the official language, but some immigrant communities retain their language as a badge of identity. Italians are the single largest immigrant group, and the Italian language is widely understood, while the Anglo-Argentine community retains a precise, clipped English – short-wave listeners who stumble onto Radio Argentina Al Exterior may momentarily assume they've found the BBC. While many Argentines study English as a second language, outside Buenos Aires it is often only in tourist offices, major hotels, and travel agencies catering to foreigners that you will encounter individuals with a good working knowledge of the language. In Chubut province, despite the persistence of many Welsh cultural traditions, the Welsh language itself has nearly disappeared, though there are some indications of a revival.

No one should ignore the country's 17

El Voseo

Argentines, Uruguayans, and Paraguayans commonly use the *voseo*, a relict 16th-century form of *tuteo* or the second person singular. As a consequence, even if your Spanish is good, you'll hear verbs pronounced differently in the usual *tú* form. With voseo regular verbs change their stress and add an accent, while irregular verbs do not change internal conjugation but add a terminal accent. Imperative forms also differ, but negative imperatives are identical in both the tuteo and the voseo.

In the sample list below, the first verb of each ending is regular, while the second is irregular. The tú form is given to show the contrast – the pronoun is included for clarity, though most Spanish speakers normally omit it.

Verb	Tuteo/Imperative	Voseo/Imperative
hablar (to speak)	tú hablas/habla	vos hablás/hablá
soñar (to dream)	tú sueñas/sueña	vos soñás/soñá
comer (to eat)	tú comes/come	vos comés/comé
poner (to put)	tú pones/pon	vos ponés/poné
admitir (to admit)	tú admites/admite	vos admitís/admití
venir (to come)	tú vienes/ven	vos venís/vení

Some of the most common verbs, like *ir* (to go), *estar* (to be), and *ser* (to be) are identically irregular in both the tuteo and the voseo. Argentines continue to use the possessive pronoun *tu* (¿Vos tenés tu lápiz?) and the reflexive or conjunctive object pronoun *te* (¿Vos te das cuenta?). If you have trouble grasping all this, don't worry – people will understand if you use tuteo.

An Argentine inviting a foreigner to address him or her informally will say *Me podés tutear* (You can call me "tú") rather than *Me podés vosear* (You can call me "vos"), even though the expectation is that both will use "vos" forms in subsequent conversation. ∎

native languages, though some are spoken by very few individuals. In the Andean Noroeste, Quechua speakers are numerous, although most are bilingual in Spanish. In the southern Andes, there are at least 40,000 Mapuche-speaking Indians. In northeastern Argentina, there are about 15,000 Guaraní speakers, an equal number of Tobas, and about 10,000 Matacos.

Argentine Spanish

Spanish in Argentina, and the rest of the River Plate region has characteristics that readily distinguish it from the rest of Latin America. Probably the most prominent are the usage of the pronoun *vos* in place of *tu* for "you," and the trait of pronouncing the letters "ll" and "y" as "zh" (as in "azure") (these letters are pronounced like the "y" in "you" in the rest of Latin America). These differences will easily identify an Argentine elsewhere in Latin America or overseas. Note that in American Spanish, the plural of the familiar "tu" or "vos" is *ustedes* rather than *vosotros*, as in Spain. Argentines and other Latin Americans will understand continental Spanish, but may find it quaint or pretentious.

Every visitor to Argentina should make an effort to speak Spanish – the basic elements are easily acquired. If possible, take a brief night course at your local university or community college before departure. Even if you can't speak very well, Argentines are gracious hosts and will encourage your Spanish, so there is no need to feel self-conscious about vocabulary or pronunciation. There are many common cognates, so if you're stuck, try Hispanicizing an English word – it is unlikely you'll make a truly embarrassing error. Do not, however, admit to being "embarazada" unless you are in fact pregnant (see the sidebar on false cognates below for other usages to be avoided).

Vocabulary

There are many differences in vocabulary between European and American Spanish, and among Spanish-speaking countries in the Americas. There are also considerable

Lunfardo

Below are a few of the more common, and innucuous, lunfardo usages that you may hear on the streets of Buenos Aires and throughout the country.

guita	money
laburo	work
morfar	to eat
palo	ten pesos
pibe	guy, dude
piola	cool
pucho	cigarette
quilombo	a mess

regional differences within these countries not attributable to accent alone. The language of Mesopotamia, for example, includes many words from the aboriginal Guaraní, while the speech of Buenos Aires abounds with words and phrases from the colorful slang known as *lunfardo*. Although you shouldn't use lunfardo words unless you are supremely confident that you know their *every* implication (especially in formal situations), you should be aware of some of the more common everyday usages. Check the glossary for some of these.

Argentines and other South Americans normally refer to the Spanish language as *castellano* rather than *español*.

Phrasebooks & Dictionaries

Lonely Planet's *Latin American Spanish* phrasebook, by Anna Cody, is a worthwhile addition to your backpack. Another exceptionally useful resource is the *University of Chicago Spanish-English, English-Spanish Dictionary*; its small size, light weight, and thorough entries make it perfect for travel.

Pronunciation

Spanish pronunciation is, in general, consistently phonetic. Once you are aware of the basic rules, they should cause little difficulty. Speak slowly to avoid getting tongue-tied until you become confident of your ability.

Pronunciation of the letters *f, k, l, n, p, q,*

s, and *t* is virtually identical to English. Although *y* is identical in most Latin American countries when used as a consonant, most Argentines say "zh" for it and for *ll*, which is a separate letter. *Ch* and *ñ* are also separate letters, with separate dictionary entries.

Vowels Spanish vowels are very consistent and have easy English equivalents.

a is like "a" in "father."
e is like "ai" in "sail."
i is like "ee" in "feet."
o is like "o" in "for."
u is like "u" in "food." After consonants other than "q," it is more like English "w." When the vowel sound is modified by an umlaut, as in "Güemes," it is also pronounced "w."
y is a consonant except when it stands alone or appears at the end of a word, in which case its pronunciation is identical to Spanish "i."

Consonants Spanish consonants generally resemble their English equivalents, but there are some major exceptions.

b resembles its English equivalent but is undistinguished from "v." For clarification, refer to the former as "b larga," the latter as "b corta." The word for the letter itself is pronounced like English "bay."
c is like the "s" in "see" before e and i, otherwise like English "k."
d closely resembles "h" in "feather."
g is like a guttural English 'h' before Spanish "e" and "i," otherwise like "g" in "go."
h is invariably silent. If your name begins with this letter, listen carefully when immigration officials summon you to pick up your passport.
j most closely resembles English "h" but is slightly more guttural.
ñ is like "ni" in "onion."
r is nearly identical to English except at the beginning of a word, when it is often rolled.
rr is very strongly rolled.
v resembles English, but see "b," above.

x is like "x" in "taxi" except for very few words for which it follows Spanish or Mexican usage as "j."
z is like "s" in "sun."

Diphthongs Spanish is an easy language to pronounce as each vowel is pronounced separately except when they occasionaly create a diphthong – a combination of two vowels forming a single syllable. In Spanish, the formation of a diphthong depends on combinations of "weak" vowels ("i" and "u") or strong ones ("a," "e," and "o"). Two weak vowels or a strong and a weak vowel make a diphthong, but two strong ones are separate syllables.

A good example of two weak vowels forming a diphthong is the word *diurno* (during the day). The final syllable of *obligatorio* (obligatory) is a combination of weak and strong vowels.

Stress Stress, often indicated by visible accents, is very important, since it can change the meaning of words. In general, words ending in vowels or the letters "n" or "s" have stress on the next-to-last syllable, while those with other endings have stress on the last syllable. Thus *vaca* (cow) and *caballos* (horses) both have the stress on their next-to-last syllables.

Visible accents, which can occur anywhere in a word, dictate stress over these general rules. Thus *sótano* (basement), *América*, and *porción* (portion) all have stress on different syllables. When words appear in capitals, the written accent is generally omitted but is still pronounced.

Greetings & Civilities
In their public behavior, Argentines are very conscious of civilities, sometimes to the point of ceremoniousness. Never, for example, approach a stranger for information without extending a greeting like *buenos días* or *buenas tardes*.

yes	*sí*
no	*no*
thank you	*gracias*
you're welcome	*de nada*

hello	*hola*
good morning	*buenos días*
good afternoon	*buenas tardes*
good evening/night	*buenas noches*
goodbye	*adiós, chau*
I don't speak much Spanish.	
Hablo poco castellano.	
I understand.	
Entiendo.	
I don't understand.	
No entiendo.	

Useful Words & Phrases

and	*y*
to/at	*a*
for	*por, para*
of/from	*de, desde*
in	*en*
with	*con*
without	*sin*
before	*antes*
after	*después*
soon	*pronto*
already	*ya*
now	*ahora*
right away	*en seguida*
here	*aquí*
there	*allí*
Where?	*¿Dónde?*

Where is . . . ?	*¿Dónde está . . . ?*
Where are . . . ?	*¿Dónde están . . . ?*
Is there...? Are there...?	*¿Hay?*
How much does it cost?	*¿Cuanto cuesta?*
here	*aquí*
When?	*¿Cuando?*
How?	*¿Cómo?*
I would like . . .	*Me gustaría . . .*
coffee	*café*
tea	*té*
beer	*cerveza*
How much?	*¿Cuanto?*
How many?	*¿Cuantos?*

Countries

The list below contains only countries whose spelling differs in English and Spanish.

Denmark	*Dinamarca*
England	*Inglaterra*
France	*Francia*
Germany	*Alemania*
Great Britain	*Gran Bretaña*
Ireland	*Irlanda*
Italy	*Italia*
Japan	*Japón*
Netherlands	*Holanda*
New Zealand	*Nueva Zelandia*

¡POR FAVORO, NO PRESERVATIVO, PLEASE!

No Preservatives

False cognates are words that appear very similar but have different meanings in different languages; in some instances, the differences are so great that they can lead to serious misunderstandings. The following is a list of some of these words in English with their Spanish cousins and their meaning in Spanish. Note that this list deals primarily with the River Plate region, and usages may differ in other areas.

English	Spanish	Meaning in Spanish
actual	actual	current (at present)
carpet	carpeta	looseleaf notebook
embarrassed	embarazada	pregnant
introduce	introducir	introduce (as an innovation)
precise	preciso	necessary
present (verb)	presentar	introduce (a person)
preservative	preservativo	condom

Peru	*Perú*
Scotland	*Escocia*
Spain	*España*
Sweden	*Suecia*
Switzerland	*Suiza*
United States	*Estados Unidos*
Wales	*Gales*

Getting Around

airplane	*avión*
train	*tren*
bus	*colectivo, micro, omnibus*
ship	*barco, buque*
car	*auto*
taxi	*taxi*
truck	*camión*
pickup	*camioneta*
bicycle	*bicicleta*
motorcycle	*motocicleta*
hitchhike	*hacer dedo*

I would like a ticket to . . .
  Quiero un boleto/pasaje a . . .
What's the fare to . . . ?
  ¿Cuanto cuesta hasta . . . ?
When does the next plane/train/bus leave for...?
  ¿Cuando sale el próximo avión/tren/ómnibus para . . . ?
Is there a student/university discount?
  ¿Hay descuento estudiantil/universitario?
Do you accept credit cards?
  ¿Trabajan con tarjetas de crédito?
first/last/next
  primero/último/próximo
first/second class
  primera/segunda (or turista) clase
single/return (roundtrip)
  ida/ida y vuelta
sleeper
  camarote
left luggage
  guardería, equipaje

Accommodations

Below you will find English phrases with useful Spanish equivalents for Argentina, most of which will be understood in other Spanish-speaking countries.

hotel	*hotel, pensión, residencial*

Is/Are there . . . ?	*¿Hay . . . . ?*
single room	*habitación para una persona*
double room	*habitación doble*
What does it cost?	*¿Cuanto cuesta?*
per night	*por noche*
full board	*pensión completa*
shared bath	*baño compartido*
private bath	*baño privado*
too expensive	*demasiado caro*
discount	*descuento*
cheaper	*mas económico*
May I see it?	*¿Puedo verla?*
I don't like it.	*No me gusta.*
the bill	*la cuenta*

Around Town

tourist information	*oficina de turismo*
airport	*aeropuerto*
train station	*estación de ferrocarril*
bus terminal	*terminal de buses*
bathing resort	*balneario*
post office	*correo*
letter	*carta*
parcel	*paquete*
postcard	*postal*
airmail	*correo aéreo*
registered mail	*certificado*
express mail	*puerta a puerta*
stamps	*estampillas*
person to person	*persona a persona*
collect call	*cobro revertido*

Toilets

The most common word for 'toilet' is *baño*, but *servicios sanitarios* (services) is a frequent alternative. Men's toilets will usually bear a descriptive term like *hombres, caballeros*, or *varones*. Women's restrooms will say *señoras* or *damas*.

Geographical Expressions

The expressions below are among the most common you will encounter in this book and in Spanish language maps and guides.

bay	*bahía*
bridge	*puente*
cape	*cabo*
farm	*chacra*

ARGENTINA

ARGENTINA

glacier	glaciar, ventisquero
highway	carretera, ruta
hill	cerro
lake	lago
marsh	estero
mount	cerro
mountain range	cordillera
national park	parque nacional
pass	paso
ranch	estancia
river	río
waterfall	cascada, catarata, salto

Numbers

Should Argentina's hyperinflationary times return, you may have to learn to count in very large numbers.

1	uno	17	diecisiete
2	dos	18	dieciocho
3	tres	19	diecinueve
4	cuatro	20	veinte
5	cinco	21	veintiuno
6	seis	22	veintidós
7	siete	30	treinta
8	ocho	31	treinta y uno
9	nueve	40	cuarenta
10	diez	50	cincuenta
11	once	60	sesenta
12	doce	70	setenta
13	trece	80	ochenta
14	catorce	90	noventa
15	quince	100	cien
16	dieciseis	101	ciento uno

102	ciento dos	1200	mil doscientos
110	ciento diez	2000	dos mil
120	ciento veinte	5000	cinco mil
130	ciento treinta	10,000	diez mil
200	doscientos	50,000	cincuenta mil
300	trescientos	100,000	cien mil
400	cuatrocientos	1,000,000	un millón
500	quinientos		
600	seiscientos		
700	setecientos		
800	ochocientos		
900	novecientos		
1000	mil		
1100	mil cien		

Days of the Week

Monday	lunes
Tuesday	martes
Wednesday	miércoles
Thursday	jueves
Friday	viernes
Saturday	sábado
Sunday	domingo

Time

Telling time is fairly straightforward. Eight o'clock is *las ocho*, while 8:30 is *las ocho y treinta* (literally, eight and thirty) or *las ocho y media* (eight and a half). However, 7:45 is *las ocho menos quince* (literally, eight minus fifteen) or *las ocho menos cuarto* (eight minus one quarter). Times are modified by morning *(de la mañana)* or afternoon *(de la tarde)* instead of am or pm. It is also common to use the 24-hour clock, especially with transportation schedules.

Facts for the Visitor

PLANNING
When to Go
For residents of the Northern Hemisphere, Argentina offers the inviting possibility of enjoying two summers in the same year, but the country's great variety can make a visit in any season worthwhile. Buenos Aires' urban attractions transcend the seasons, but popular Patagonian destinations such as the Moreno Glacier in Santa Cruz province are best in summer. The Iguazú Falls in subtropical Misiones province are best in the southern winter or spring, when heat and humidity are less oppressive, at which time skiers could also visit Andean resorts like Bariloche or Las Leñas.

What to Bring
Argentina is a mostly temperate, midlatitude country, and seasonally appropriate clothing for North America or Europe will be equally suitable here. In the subtropical north, especially in summer, you will want lightweight cottons, but at higher elevations in the Andean Northwest and the high latitudes of Patagonia, warm clothing is desirable even in summer.

Backpackers are not prejudiced against in Argentina, and many young Argentines take to Patagonia and other remote parts of the country on a shoestring themselves. Cheaper Argentine outdoor equipment is generally inferior than that made in North America or Europe, so bring camping supplies from home. Higher quality products will be very expensive.

Maps
The Automóvil Club Argentino (ACA), at Av del Libertador 1850 in Buenos Aires, publishes maps, which are regularly updated, of the country and each province. You may also find them at specialty bookshops like Edward Stanford's in London or in the map rooms of major university libraries. At about US$10 each, an entire set of provincial maps costs upwards of US$200, but they are indispensable for motorists and an excellent investment for any other traveler in Argentina – members of foreign automobile clubs can purchase them at discount prices. In most major Argentine cities, ACA has a service center that sells these maps, although not every center stocks all of them.

Tourist offices in Buenos Aires and the provinces stock maps of considerable use to visitors – the province of Neuquén does an exemplary job. These vary in quality but are usually free. Members of American Automobile Association (AAA) and its affiliates can obtain that organization's South American road map, which is adequate for initial planning but not for on-the-road use. The late Australian cartographer Kevin Healy's vivid three-sheet *South America* is really reference material, packed with information but not suitable for taking along on a trip.

For topographic maps, the best source is Buenos Aires' Instituto Geográfico Militar, at Cabildo 381, reached by bus No 152 and open from 8 am to 1 pm. These maps are much more difficult to obtain outside the capital.

SUGGESTED ITINERARIES
Since Argentina is a very large country, itineraries will depend on time and mode of transport. Visiting the country's most popular attractions – the city of Buenos Aires, the Cataratas del Iguazú and the Moreno Glacier in Parque Nacional Los Glaciares – would require a minimum of about ten days by airplane, but this would be very rushed, and at least two weeks is desirable. Add in other key destinations like Península Valdés, the city of Ushuaia, the lake district around Bariloche, and Chile's Parque Nacional Torres del Paine

(a popular stop for visitors to Los Glaciares) and at least a month is on the docket.

Traveling overland on a budget, the same destinations would justify two months or upwards, with the possible addition of Cuyo and the Andean Northwest. If the money holds out, dedicated overland travelers could easily spend around six months in the country without much backtracking or repetition.

HIGHLIGHTS

For most visitors from overseas, Argentina's principal attractions are both cultural and natural, but as in all countries, some of the least frequented sights deserve more attention, while a few of the best known destinations hardly warrant a stop.

The following list, starting in the north and working south, includes some of the country's best known tourist attractions and some lesser but still deserving ones in its most remote corners.

Quebrada de Humahuaca The scenic desert canyons of the Andean Northwest, with their large Indian populations and colonial churches, are an outlier of the central Andean countries.

Cataratas del Iguazú Despite the increasing commercialization of the surrounding area, the thunderous falls at Iguazú are still one of the continent's most breathtaking sights.

Esteros del Iberá Some travelers find this marshland in Corrientes province even more appealing than Brazil's Pantanal, but it's much less visited.

Córdoba Argentina's second largest city is Buenos Aires' cultural rival, with monumental colonial and ecclesiastical architecture, not to mention the nearby Sierras.

Buenos Aires A self-consciously European sophistication, combined with the romantic image of the tango, is only the stereotypical trademark of a city that has much more to offer.

Delta del Paraná Less than an hour from Buenos Aires, the myriad channels of the Río de la Plata are a welcome escape from the noise, heat, and congestion of the capital.

The Pampas The gaucho, a cultural icon and modern anachronism, remains Argentina's enduring image in towns like San Antonio de Areco and surrounding estancias, many of which encourage paying guests. Religious pilgrimage centers like Luján, with its monumental cathedral, are worth a visit.

Cuyo Argentina's wine country also features recreational attractions like Mendoza's Parque Provincial Aconcagua and San Juan's offbeat Difunta Correa shrine.

Lake District Soaring volcanoes, shimmering lakes, sprawling forests, and trout-rich rivers make the eastern slopes of the Andes a recreational paradise. Its traditional focus is San Carlos de Bariloche, on Lago Nahuel Huapi, but many other places are more suitable for extended visits.

Península Valdés The unique, abundant wildlife and desert scenery of the Patagonian coast draw visitors to this popular wildlife reserve near Puerto Madryn, in Chubut province. Punta Tombo is a comparable attraction, but even the barren Patagonian steppe exercises a powerful hold on the imagination.

Moreno Glacier In Santa Cruz province, one of the world's few advancing glaciers is even more awesome when the lake behind it causes it to burst at regular intervals (about every four years).

Torres del Paine In Chilean Patagonia, South America's finest national park is a miniature Alaska.

Tierra del Fuego The town of Ushuaia is itself overrated, but the wild coastal and alpine scenery around it justify a trip to the terminus of Ruta Nacional (RN) 3.

TOURIST TRAPS

Argentina has its share of gaudy and costly tourist traps, or places that are simply distasteful or overrated. Like the previous list, this one starts in the north and works south.

Villa Carlos Paz On a large artificial reservoir outside the city of Córdoba, Villa Carlos Paz is an even more ghastly version of Mar del Plata in summer, without the appeal of surf or sea lions.

Mar del Plata Your best chance of being a traffic fatality is to attempt to drive down Ruta Provincial (RP) 2 from Buenos Aires to this summer madhouse, where porteños flock to socialize with the same people they see the rest of the year, elbowing them for space on the beach. The rest of the year, it's a relatively normal and even attractive place.

Bariloche The setting is incomparable, but the lake district's largest city has encroached on Parque Nacional Nahuel Huapi, and its high-rise timeshares have overwhelmed the architectural integrity of its landmark Centro Cívico.

El Calafate At the gateway to the Moreno glacier, Calafate's merchants are notorious for disregard of their captive clientele. Where else in the world would a restaurant owner blame a customer for a fly in the beer glass?

TOURIST OFFICES

Almost every city or town has a tourist office, usually on or near the main plaza or at the bus terminal. Each Argentine province also has its own representation in Buenos Aires; most, though not all, of these are well organized, often offering a computerized database of tourist information, and are well worth a visit before heading for the provinces. A few municipalities, mostly the Atlantic coastal resorts of Buenos Aires province, have separate offices in Buenos Aires.

The best organized provincial offices are those of Buenos Aires, Chubut, Entre Ríos, Jujuy, Misiones, Río Negro, and Tierra del Fuego.

Local Tourist Offices

The offices listed below are provincial tourist offices located in Buenos Aires unless indicated otherwise.

Buenos Aires
    Callao 235 (☎ 371-7045)
Catamarca
    Córdoba 2080 (☎ 374-6891)
Chaco
    Callao 322 (☎ 476-0961)
Chubut
    Sarmiento 1172 (☎ 382-8126)
Córdoba
    Callao 332 (☎ 372-6566)
Corrientes
    4th floor, San Martín 333 (☎ 394-7432)
Entre Ríos
    Suipacha 844 (☎ 328-9327)
Formosa
    Hipólito Yrigoyen 1429 (☎ 381-7048)
Jujuy
    Santa Fe 967 (☎ 393-6096)
La Pampa
    Suipacha 346 (☎ 326-0511)
La Rioja
    5th floor, Viamonte 749 (☎ 326-1140)
Mar del Plata (municipal)
    Santa Fe 1175 (☎ 811-4466)
Mendoza
    Callao 445 (☎ 371-0835)
Misiones
    Santa Fe 989 (☎ 322-0677)
Neuquén
    Perón (ex-Cangallo) 687 (☎ 326-6812)
Pinamar (municipal)
    5th floor, Florida 930 (☎ 315-2679)
Río Negro
    Tucumán 1916 (☎ 371-7066)
Salta
    5th floor, Roque Sáenz Peña 933 (☎ 326-1455)
San Clemente del Tuyú (Muncipalidad de la Costa)
    Bartolomé Mitre 1135 (☎ 381-0764)
San Juan
    Sarmiento 1251 (☎ 382-5291)
San Luis
    Azcuénaga 1087 (☎ 822-3641)
Santa Cruz
    25 de Mayo 277 (☎ 343-3653)
Santa Fe
    Montevideo 373 (☎ 375-4570)

Santiago del Estero
  Florida 274 (☎ 326-9418)
Tierra del Fuego (Instituto Fueguino de Turismo)
  Santa Fe 919 (☎ 322-8855)
Tucumán
  Bartolomé Mitre 836 (☎ 345-3656)
Villa Carlos Paz (municipal)
  Lavalle 623, 2nd floor (☎ 322-0053)
Villa Gesell (municipal)
  Bartolomé Mitre 1702 (☎ 374-5199)

Tourist Offices Abroad

The larger Argentine consulates, such as in New York and Los Angeles, usually have a tourist representative in their delegation. Local representatives of Aerolíneas Argentinas often have similar information at their disposal.

Australia
  1st floor, MLC Tower, Woden, ACT 2606
  (☎ 06-282-4555)
Canada
  Suite 620, 90 Sparks St, Ottawa, Ontario
  (☎ 236-2351)
  Suite 605, 1010 Saint Catherine St West,
  Montréal, Québec (☎ 866-3810)
UK
  53 Hans Place, London SW1 XOLA (☎ 0171-589 3104)
USA
  1600 New Hampshire Ave NW, Washington,
  DC 20009 (☎ 202-939-6411)
  12 West 56th St, New York, NY 10019
  (☎ 212-603-0400)
  Suite 1450, 5005 Wilshire Blvd, Los
  Angeles, CA (☎ 213-954-9155)
  800 Brickell Ave, Penthouse 1, Miami, FL
  33131 (☎ 305-373-1889)
  20 N Clark St, Suite 602 Chicago, IL 60602
  (☎ 312-263-7435)
  Suite 1810, 2000 S Post Oak Rd, Houston,
  TX 77056 (☎ 713-871-8935)

VISAS & DOCUMENTS
Passports

Passports are obligatory for all visitors except for citizens of bordering countries. Argentina presently enjoys a civilian government, and the police and military presence are relatively subdued, but the police can still demand identification at any moment. It is advisable to carry your passport at all times, especially if there is political unrest. In general, Argentines are very document oriented, and your passport is essential for cashing traveler's checks, checking into a hotel, and many other routine activities.

Visas

Argentina has eliminated visas for many but not all international tourists. In theory, upon arrival all non-visa visitors must obtain a free tourist card, good for 90 days and renewable for 90 more. In practice, immigration officials issue them only at major border crossings, such as at airports and on the ferries and hydrofoils between Buenos Aires and Uruguay. If you lose your card, it probably won't be a major catastrophe, but you shouldn't be careless with it. At most exit points, immigration officials will provide immediate replacement; that is, the bureaucracy may require you to fill one in even though you're leaving the country.

Nationals of the USA and most Western European countries do not need visas to enter Argentina; thanks to improved relations with Argentina, Britons are among this group. Australians and New Zealanders, who do need visas, must submit their passports with a payment of US$30 and may need a return or onward ticket. Ordinarily, the visa will be ready the following day. The Argentine consulate in Santiago, Chile, is particularly efficient.

Argentina has a wide network of embassies and consulates, both in neighboring countries and overseas. Some are very accommodating, while others (most notably those in Colonia, Uruguay, and La Paz, Bolivia) act as if your visit is a major nuisance. Renewing a nearly expired visa at a consulate other than the one that issued it can be nearly impossible; it is easier to get a new passport from your own consulate and then request a new Argentine visa.

Visa Extensions

As mentioned, Argentine tourist cards are valid for 90 days. For a 90-day extension, visit the office of Migraciones (☎ 312-7985) at Av Antártida Argentina 1365 in Buenos Aires or in provincial capitals, or go to provincial delegations of the federal police. There may be a nominal charge. In areas where the police are unaccustomed to dealing with immigration matters, the process can be tedious and time-consuming.

If you wish to stay longer than six months, it is much easier to cross the border into a neighboring country for a few days and then return. You can then stay an additional six months in Argentina. Although it is possible to obtain residence in Argentina, leaving the country then becomes problematic and you cannot take advantage of tourist regulations with respect to Argentine customs and duties.

Re-Entry Visas

Individuals born in Argentina, even of foreign parents, are considered Argentines and may encounter difficulties entering the country with non-Argentine documents. In one instance, officials harassed a retired US army colonel, who was born in Buenos Aires, for lacking proof of completing obligatory military service in Argentina. Argentine passports renewed overseas expire upon re-entry into Argentina, and renewing them with the federal police can be a tiresome experience on a short trip.

Very short visits to neighboring countries usually do not require visas. Most importantly, you need not waste time obtaining a Brazilian visa to cross from the Argentine town of Puerto Iguazú to Foz do Iguaçu if you return the same day, although you must show your passport. The same is true at the Bolivian border town of Villazón near La Quiaca, the Paraguayan crossing at Encarnación near Posadas.

Driver's License & Permits

Motorists need an International Driving Permit to complement their national or state licenses, but they should not be surprised if police at the numerous roadside checkpoints do not recognize it or, even worse, claim it is invalid and try to exact a bribe. Politely refer them to the Spanish translation on the card.

EMBASSIES
Argentine Embassies Abroad

Argentina has diplomatic representation throughout Latin America, North America, Western Europe, and many other regions, including Australia. The following are most likely to be useful to prospective visitors. For more detailed information on overseas delegations, see the Tourist Offices Abroad section above.

Australia
    1st floor, MLC Tower, Woden, ACT 2606 (☎ 06-282-4555)
Bolivia
    2nd floor, 16 de Julio 1486, La Paz (☎ 35-3089), corner of Bolívar & Ballivián, Tarija
Brazil
    2nd floor, Praia de Botafogo 228, Rio de Janeiro (☎ 551-5198)
    8th floor, Rua Araújo 216, São Paulo (☎ 256-8555)
Canada
    Suite 620, 90 Sparks St, Ottawa, Ontario K1P 514 (☎ 613-236-2351)
    2000 Peel St, Montréal, Québec H3A 2W5 (☎ 514-842-6582)
Chile
    Vicuña Mackenna 41, Santiago (☎ 222-8977)
    2nd floor, Cauquenes 94, Puerto Montt (☎ 25-3966)
    21 de Mayo 1878, Punta Arenas
Paraguay
    Banco Nación, España at Perú, Asunción (☎ 21-2320, 21-2321)
    Cabañas & Mallorquín, Encarnación
UK
    53 Hans Place, London SW1 XOLA (☎ 0171-584-6494; consulate ☎ 589-3104)
USA
    1600 New Hampshire Ave NW, Washington, DC 20009 (☎ 202-939-6411)
    12 W 56th St, New York, NY 10019 (☎ 212-603-0400)
    Suite 210, 5005 Wilshire Blvd, Los Angeles, CA 90036 (☎ 213-954-9155)
    800 Brickell Ave, Penthouse 1, Miami, FL 33131 (☎ 305-373-1889)
    205 N Michigan Ave, Suite 4209, Chicago, IL 60601 (☎ 312-819-2610)
    2000 Post Oak Blvd, Suite 1810, Houston, TX 77056 (☎ 713-871-8935)
    2 Canal St, Suite 915, New Orleans, LA 70130 (☎ 504-523-2823)
    229 Peach Tree St, Suite 1401, Atlanta, GA

30303 (☎ 404-880-0805)
Oficina 819, Edificio Mercantil, Av Ponce de Leon, Parada 27, Hato Rey, Puerto Rico 00918 (☎ 809-754-6500)
Uruguay
Franklin D Roosevelt 442, Carmelo (☎ 2266)
Av General Flores 230, Colonia (☎ 2093)
Sarandí 3193, Fray Bentos (☎ 2638)
Río Branco 1281, Montevideo (☎ 90-0897, 92-0667)
Leandro Gómez 1034, Paysandú (☎ 2253)
Edificio Santos Dumont, Punta del Este (☎ 41106)
General Artigas 1134, Salto (☎ 2931)

Foreign Embassies in Argentina

Every European and South American country and many others throughout the world have embassies and consulates in Buenos Aires. The following list contains those most likely to be of use to independent travelers.

Australia
Villanueva 1400 (☎ 777-6580)
Belgium
8th floor, Defensa 113 (☎ 331-0066)
Bolivia
Av Belgrano 1670 (☎ 381-0539)
Brazil
5th floor, Carlos Pellegrini 1363 (☎ 394-5227, 394-5260)
Canada
Tagle 2828 (☎ 805-3032)
Chile
9th floor, San Martín 439 (☎ 394-6582)
Denmark
9th floor, Leandro N Alem 1074 (☎ 312-6901)
France
3rd floor, Santa Fe 846 (☎ 312-2409)
Germany
Villanueva 1055 (☎ 778-2500)
Ireland
Suipacha 1380 (☎ 326-2612)
Israel
10th floor, Av de Mayo 701 (☎ 342-1465)
Italy
MT de Alvear 1149 (☎ 325-6135)
Japan
Paseo Colón 275 (☎ 343-2561)
Mexico
Larrea 1230 (☎ 821-7170)
Netherlands
Av de Mayo 701 (☎ 334-4000)

Norway
3rd floor, Esmeralda 909 (☎ 312-1904)
Paraguay
Viamonte 1851 (☎ 812-0075)
Peru
San Martín 969 (☎ 311-7582)
Spain
Guido 1760 (☎ 811-0078)
Sweden
3rd floor, Corrientes 330 (☎ 328-3088)
Switzerland
10th floor, Santa Fe 846 (☎ 311-6491)
UK
Doctor Luis Agote 2412 (☎ 803-7070)
Uruguay
Las Heras 1907 (☎ 807-3044)
USA
Colombia 4300 (☎ 774-4533)

CUSTOMS

Argentine customs officials generally pass along foreign visitors, but if you cross the border frequently and carry electronic equipment such as cameras or a laptop computer, it is helpful to have a typed list of your equipment, including serial numbers, to be stamped by authorities. At Buenos Aires' Aeropuerto Internacional Ezeiza, you will likely be asked whether you are carrying such goods, which are much more costly in Argentina than overseas. Entering Argentina from Paraguay or Chilean Patagonia, where cheap electronics are also available, you may experience very thorough baggage checks.

Depending on where you have been, customs authorities focus on different things. Travelers coming into Argentina from the central Andean countries may be searched for drugs, while those from central Chile or from Brazil should know that fruit and vegetables are likely to be confiscated. Even after passing customs, which may be some distance from the actual border, you are subject to inspection by police at checkpoints that are usually at provincial borders or important highway junctions. *Never* carry firearms.

MONEY

Traditionally, Argentine money presents real problems for visitors unaccustomed to

ARGENTINA

hyperinflation and without sufficient zeros on their pocket calculators – when Argentine economists spoke hopefully of single-digit inflation, they meant *per month*. Since the institution of Domingo Cavallo's convertibility policy in early 1991, however, inflation has fallen to record lows, and the peso has remained fixed against the dollar. Still, given Argentina's history of financial instability, travelers should keep a close watch on the exchange markets and current economic events; it is still not wise to keep large amounts of cash in local currency.

Costs

At times of economic instability, which is often enough, Argentines panic and buy US dollars, the exchange rate collapses, and the country can become absurdly cheap for the visitor with hard currency. Presently, though, the economy is relatively stable, but the country is nearly as expensive as Europe or North America. Inflation has remained relatively high in some sectors, so that prices for hotels, restaurants, and similar travelers' services have increased more rapidly than others in the economy at large. In 1994, when the aggregate inflation rate was only 4%, transportation costs nevertheless increased by nearly 19%. Some Argentines even prefer to take their holidays in less expensive countries like the USA and have acquired the ironic nickname "démedos" because, on their visits to Miami, they find consumer items so cheap that they tell the clerk to "give me two."

This does not mean that budget travel is impossible. Certain important costs, such as modest lodging, food, and some transportation, will be lower than in Europe or North America, even if higher than in surrounding countries. After overcoming the initial shock, travelers arriving from inexpensive countries such as Bolivia should be able to spend a rewarding time in Argentina by adapting to local conditions. By seeking out cheaper hospedajes and residenciales, carrying a tent to take advantage of campgrounds, and dining selectively, judicious travelers can control costs. In par-

ticular, those accustomed to eating every meal in a restaurant in neighboring countries will not be able to do so in Argentina; consider sandwich fixings from the market and splurge on an occasional treat elsewhere.

Still, you should probably allow a minimum of US$30 per day for food and lodging, and congratulate yourself if you can get by on less. Prices given in this book are subject to wild fluctuations.

ATMs

Cajeros automáticos (ATMs) are increasingly abundant in Argentina and can also be used for cash advances on major credit cards like MasterCard and Visa. Many but not all ATMs will dispense either dollars or Argentine pesos.

Credit Cards

The most widely accepted credit cards are Visa and MasterCard. MasterCard, affiliated with the local Argencard, is more widely accepted than Visa, and travelers with UK Access should insist on their affiliation to MasterCard. American Express, Diner's Club, and others are also valid in many places. Because lost or stolen credit cards are vulnerable to abuse, credit card holders should consider a protection plan to insure themselves against serious financial loss.

Credit card users should be aware of two complications. Some businesses add a *recargo* (surcharge) of 10% or more to credit card purchases because of high bank charges and the time between the purchase and their own receipt of payment. The flip side of this practice is that some merchants give a discount of 10% or more for cash purchases.

Second, the amount you pay depends upon the exchange rate at the time your purchase is posted to your overseas account, which can be weeks later. If the local currency is depreciating, your purchase price may be a fraction of the dollar cost you calculated at the time.

International Transfers

Travelers who have suffered lost or stolen cash and credit cards have found the American Express Money Gram a quick and efficient (if costly) means of transferring funds from their home country to Argentina. Amex has a major office in Buenos Aires as well as representatives throughout the country, which are indicated in the text.

Currency

The present unit of currency is the peso ($), which replaced the *austral* on January 1, 1992. The austral had replaced the *peso argentino* in 1985, which had replaced the *peso ley* in 1978, which had replaced the ordinary *peso* some years earlier. One new peso equals 10,000 australs, on a par with the US dollar.

Paper money comes in denominations of 1, 2, 5, 10, 20, 50, and 100 pesos. One new peso equals 100 *centavos*; coins come in denominations of 1, 5, 10, 25, and 50 centavos, though few merchants want anything to do with one centavo coins. Tattered Argentine banknotes seem to stay in circulation for decades, but few banks or businesses will accept torn, worn, or defaced banknotes.

At present, US dollars are legal tender almost everywhere, and, for the most part, it's unnecessary to change US cash into pesos. It's wise to carry some pesos, however, since institutions such as the post office and some bus companies, as well as a few nationalistic businesspeople, refuse to accept US currency.

Traditionally, the provinces of the Jujuy, Salta, and Tucumán sometimes issue their own paper money, known as *bonos* (bonds), for local use; these are only valid in the province of issue and have expiration dates beyond which they become worthless, so dispose of them locally and on time. As of early 1995, only Tucumán still had bonos in circulation.

Currency Exchange

US dollars are by far the preferred foreign currency, although Chilean and Uruguayan pesos can be readily exchanged at the borders. Even when the dollar is relatively weak, only Buenos Aires will have a ready market for European currencies.

Exchange rates can be volatile. As of September 1991, for example, the rate for the previous currency was just below 10,000 australs per US dollar, but earlier in mid-December 1990, the dollar had sunk below 5000 australs until a minor economic crisis and intensified domestic demand by Argentines planning overseas holidays drove the rate up dramatically. At present, there is no black market, and you can change money freely, but in times of crisis visitors should be aware of changes in the so-called "parallel rate." For the most up-to-date information, see *Ambito Financiero*, Argentina's equivalent of *The Wall Street Journal* or *Financial Times*, or the English-language daily *Buenos Aires Herald*.

Cash dollars can be exchanged at banks, *casas de cambio* (exchange houses), hotels, and some travel agencies, and often in shops or on the street. Cash dollars earn a much better rate of exchange and avoid commissions of up to 10% or more levied on traveler's checks, which are increasingly difficult to cash anywhere and specifically *not* recommended. If you are confident of your ability to carry cash safely, it is a much better alternative.

At press time, the exchange rates were as follows:

Australia	A$1	=	$0.74
Bolivia	Bol$1	=	$0.20
Brazil	BraR$1	=	$0.90
Chile	Chi$1000	=	$2.40
France	FFr1	=	$0.21
Germany	DM1	=	$0.72
Italy	It£1000	=	$0.63
Japan	Jpn¥100	=	$1.14
Paraguay	Par₲1000	=	$0.50
United Kingdom	UK£1	=	$1.60
United States	US$1	=	$1
Uruguay	Urg$100	=	$14

Tipping & Bargaining

In restaurants, it is customary to tip about 10% of the bill, but in times of economic distress Argentines themselves frequently overlook the custom. In general, waiters and waitresses are poorly paid, so if you can afford to eat out, you can afford to tip. Even a small *propina* will be appreciated.

Bargaining is not the way of life in Argentina as it is in Bolivia or Peru, but in the Andean Northwest and in artisan markets throughout the country it is customary. Even in Buenos Aires, downtown shops selling leather and other tourist items will listen to offers. Late in the evening, some hotels may give a break on room prices; if you plan to stay several days, they almost certainly will. Many better hotels will give discounts up to 30% for cash payment.

Note that Argentina's hefty 21% *impuesto de valor agregado* (IVA, or value added tax, VAT) is in some cases refundable for foreign tourists; see the entry on Things to Buy below.

POST & TELECOMMUNICATIONS

The post office and telephone services are among the most intractable problems in modern Argentina. Both are traditionally corrupt and inefficient. Telephone infrastructure is almost hopelessly antiquated, although recent developments offer slight encouragement.

Far more dependable than the post office are both Argentine domestic couriers, such as Andreani and OCA, and international couriers like DHL and Federal Express. The latter two have offices only in the largest cities, like Buenos Aires, while the former two usually serve as their connections to the interior of the country.

Postal Rates

Postal rates are among the highest in the world. Domestic letters weighing 150 grams or less cost US$0.75, while postcards cost US$0.50. International letters of 20 grams or less cost US$0.75 to bordering countries, US$1 elsewhere in the Americas, and US$1.25 outside the Americas. International express mail services, including overnight, are much more expensive but a better value because of their dependability.

Airmail packages are expensive, while surface mail is much cheaper but even less dependable.

Sending Mail

Encotesa or Correo Argentino is the recently privatized postal and telegraph service. It is frequently paralyzed by strikes and "work-to-rule" stoppages, resulting in enormous accumulations of mail that never reaches its final destination. Send essential overseas mail *certificado* (registered) or *puerta a puerta* (express, literally "door to door") to ensure its arrival. Mail containing money or anything else of value is likely to be opened, the valuable contents expropriated, and anything else tossed in the trash.

When addressing a letter to Argentina, note that the house number usually follows rather than precedes the street name, while the postal code precedes rather than follows the name of the town or city. Thus a typical postal address would be as follows:

Carlos Saúl Méndez
Avenida Corrientes 1724
1013 Buenos Aires
ARGENTINA

Receiving Mail

You can receive mail via Poste Restante or Lista de Correos, both equivalent to general delivery, at any Argentine post office. Instruct your correspondents to address letters clearly and to indicate a date until which the post office should hold them; otherwise, they will be returned or destroyed.

Post offices have imposed heavy charges, up to US$1.50 per letter, on Poste Restante services, so if you can arrange to have mail delivered to a private address such as a friend's residence or a hotel you will avoid this surprisingly costly and bureaucratic annoyance.

It is also worth remembering that Argentines often refer to Buenos Aires proper as the "Capital Federal," which works as a destination on mail.

ARGENTINA

Telephone

French and Spanish interests run the two new telephone companies, which are Telecom, north of Buenos Aires, and Telefónica, south of the capital (actually, the two have divided the capital in half, on either side of Av Córdoba). Under ENTel, the former government monopoly, service was so difficult to obtain that Buenos Aires apartments with telephones would sell for many thousands of dollars more than those without. The government claims that the present duopoly, with some of the highest telephone rates in the world, will improve the situation. Even so, decades are likely to pass before the superannuated phone system is even adequate. Many affluent porteños have resorted to cellular phones because of the expense and difficulty of getting a line; installation of a new line in the capital still costs nearly US$1000.

Telecom and Telefónica have assumed control of most of ENTel's long-distance offices, although some provinces and smaller towns operate their own telephone cooperatives, and there are now many privately run *locutorios* (long-distance offices). If possible, make overseas calls outside costly peak business hours; there is usually a 20% discount between 10 pm and 8 am weekdays, and all day on weekends. Even these rates are no bargain.

You can make collect calls to North America or Europe from most but not all offices – ask before you try, or you may have to pay the cost out of pocket. In major cities, you can make credit card calls to some countries, often on direct lines to overseas operators (see International Direct Dialing below). The system is hopelessly overloaded on and near major holidays like Christmas.

Most public telephones operate on tokens known as *fichas* or *cospeles*, which are basically of equal value but differ for local and long-distance service. For local calls, one cospel gives you about three minutes. Both fichas and cospeles are available from street-corner kiosks as well as phone company offices, but kiosks normally tack on 10% or more for their own

profit. Phone cards are now widely available and more convenient than a pocketful of tokens. Phone debit cards *(tarjetas)* are available in values of 25, 50, 100, and 150 fichas.

Most public phones are inexplicably located on noisy corners that make hearing very difficult. In most of Patagonia, however, enclosed phone booths shut out the noise. Note that some hotel telephones will register a call as completed within 20 or 30 seconds, whether or not anyone has answered, so hang up quickly if there's no response.

When calling or answering the telephone, the proper salutation is *"hola"* (hello). Exchange pleasantries before getting to the point of your conversation. When calling a central number or business switchboard, you may be asked for an *interno* (extension number).

Emergency & Information Convenient three-digit numbers are available for Asistencia Pública (Emergency, ☎ 107), Policía (Police, ☎ 101), Bomberos (Fire Department, ☎ 100), and Información (Directory Information, ☎ 110).

International Direct Dialing From those parts of Argentina that have Discado Directo Internacional (DDI, or International Direct Dialing), it is now possible to get direct access to home-country operators for collect and credit card calls from both private and public telephones; this is usually much cheaper than going through the Argentine carriers. Note that private locutorios will only rarely permit their facilities to be used for such calls, since they make no profit on them. The following countries provide such an alternative:

Brazil	☎ 0055-800-666-111	
Chile	☎ 0056-800-888-111	
France	☎ 0033-800-999-111	
Italy	☎ 0039-800-555-111	
Spain	☎ 0034-800-444-111	
USA	☎ 001-800-200-1111	ATT
	☎ 001-800-333-1111	MCI
	☎ 001-800-777-1111	Sprint

Germany is conspicuous by its absence, having no agreement with Argentina for collect or credit card calls.

Fax

Most locutorios offer fax services. In addition to fax services, Encotesa also provides telegraph and telex services.

Email

Online addicts will find Argentina a trying destination because the government strictly controls electronic data transmissions. Even university researchers rarely have direct desktop access; instead, they frequently have to go through a gatekeeper who spends only a few hours a day at the terminal. The best bet for sending or retrieving electronic communications is to rely on a friend with access.

BOOKS

Buenos Aires is a major publishing center and has many excellent bookshops on or near Av Corrientes, which is a delightful area to browse. For details, see the chapter on Buenos Aires. For information on Argentine literature see Arts in the Facts about Argentina chapter.

Guidebooks

Other guidebooks can supplement and complement this one, especially if you are visiting additional South American countries. One obvious endorsement is the 6th edition of Lonely Planet's *South America on a Shoestring*, a collaborative effort by several authors. LP also has guides for Ecuador & the Galápagos Islands, Peru, Colombia, Venezuela, Bolivia, Brazil, and Chile & Easter Island, as well as an updated *Latin American Spanish phrasebook*.

If you plan to do some trekking, or even some short walks, a good companion is Clem Lindenmayer's *Trekking in the Patagonian Andes* (Lonely Planet), a detailed guide to 24 walks in Chilean and Argentine Patagonia, which includes contour maps.

Now edited by Ben Box, the *South American Handbook* has been the standard guide to the continent since the 1920s, but its annual updating is a bit misleading because the area covered is so large that many sections are quickly outdated. Nevertheless, its encyclopedic comprehensiveness and observant humor make it great armchair reading for travelers of every kind. Since 1991, a separate volume covers Mexico and Central America.

The *APA Insight Guides* series has volumes on Buenos Aires and Argentina that are excellent in cultural and historical analyses, with outstanding photographs, but lacking on the nuts-and-bolts of everyday travel. Many typographical errors mar the Argentina volume.

Readers competent in Spanish will find *La Guía Pirelli: Buenos Aires, Sus Alrededores y Costas del Uruguay* full of illuminating historical and cultural material on the capital and nearby areas. However, the maps are very inadequate, and it seems to have been written on the assumption that every tourist has a new BMW and stays in five-star hotels; by their standards, Hotel Plaza Francia, luxurious and pricy by most estimates, ranks as a budget accommodation. Pirelli also publishes a guide to the entire country with the same strengths and shortcomings; both may be available in English, but the English language editions are less up-to-date than the Spanish versions.

Travel

Argentina has inspired some excellent travel writing, most notably Bruce Chatwin's indispensable *In Patagonia*, one of the most informed syntheses of life and landscape for any part of South America or the entire world. Avoid Paul Theroux's irritatingly patronizing *The Old Patagonian Express*; Theroux does everything possible to isolate himself from the people he travels among.

American scientist George Gaylord Simpson's *Attending Marvels: A Patagonian Journal* starts, surprisingly, with an account of the coup against President Hipólito Yrigoyen in 1930. The late British naturalist Gerald Durrell wrote several light but entertaining accounts of his travels in Argentina, from Jujuy to Patagonia, in *The Drunken Forest* and *The Whispering Land*, available in inexpensive paperback editions. Make a special effort to locate Lucas Bridges' *The Uttermost Part of the Earth*, in which he describes his life among the Indians of Tierra del Fuego. Bridges' father was one of the earliest missionary settlers from the Falkland Islands and compiled an important dictionary of the Yahgan language.

Don't overlook works of greater antiquity. Charles Darwin's *Voyage of the Beagle* is as fresh as yesterday, and his account of the gauchos on the Pampas and in Patagonia vividly evokes a way of life that no longer really exists, but to which Argentines still pay symbolic homage. William Henry Hudson's *Idle Days in Patagonia* is a romantic account of the 19th-century naturalist's adventures in search of migratory birds. Also try his *Far Away and Long Ago*.

One of the more unusual, unlikely pieces of travel literature in recent years is Ernesto Guevara's *The Motorcycle Diaries: A Journey Around South America*, an early 1950s account of two Argentine medical students who rode a dilapidated motorcycle across northern Patagonia and into Chile before abandoning it to continue their trip by stowing away on a coastal freighter. Guevara, who died in 1967 in Bolivia, is better known by the common Argentine nickname "Che."

History
General For an account of early European exploration of Argentina and elsewhere in South America, see JH Parry's *The Discovery of South America*. Although it does not focus specifically on Argentina, James Lockhart and Stuart Schwartz's *Early Latin America* makes an unusual but persuasive argument that the structures of native societies were more important than Spanish domination in the cultural transitions of the colonial period. Uruguayan writer Eduardo Galeano presents a bitter indictment of

European conquest and its consequences in *The Open Veins of Latin America: Five Centuries of the Pillage of a Continent*. Do not miss Alfred Crosby's fascinating account of the ecological transformation of the Pampas in comparison with other mid-latitude lands settled by Europeans in his *Ecological Imperialism: The Biological Expansion of Europe, 900 – 1900*.

For the South American wars of independence, including Argentina, a standard work is John Lynch's *The Spanish-American Revolutions 1808 – 1826*. One of the best known contemporary accounts of postindependent Argentina is Domingo Faustino Sarmiento's *Life in the Argentine Republic in the Days of the Tyrants*, an eloquent but often condescending critique of the Federalist caudillos and their followers from the Unitarist perspective of the country's second constitutional president. Also worthwhile is Lynch's *Argentine Dictator: Juan Manuel de Rosas, 1829 – 1852*. José Luis Romero analyzes the conflict between Unitarism and Federalism in *A History of Argentine Political Thought*.

James Scobie's *Argentina: A City and a Nation* has gone through many editions and is now a standard account of the country's development. The most up-to-date, comprehensive history of the country is David Rock's *Argentina 1516 – 1987: From Spanish Colonization to the Falklands War and Alfonsín*.

For an account of Britain's role in Argentina's 19th-century development, see HS Ferns's *Britain and Argentina in the Nineteenth Century*. More recent is Alistair Henessy and John King's edited collection of essays, *The Land That England Lost: Argentina and Britain, A Special Relationship*, which goes beyond the strictly political to deal with intriguing cultural topics like the English tango fad just prior to WWI.

Several historians have compared Argentina, Australia and Canada as exporters of primary products such as beef and wheat, and their subsequent economic development. These include Tim Duncan and John Fogarty's *Australia & Argentina – On Par-*

Top: Congreso Nacional, Buenos Aires
Left: Tango musicians, La Boca, Buenos Aires
Right: Tomb of President Nicolás Avellaneda, Recoleta Cemetery

Top Left: Billboard of Carlos Gardel, Buenos Aires
Top Right: Basilica of Luján, Buenos Aires Province
Bottom: Fountain, Plaza del Congreso, Buenos Aires

allel Paths, DC Platt and Guido di Tella's edited *Argentina, Australia and Canada – Studies in Comparative Development, 1970 – 1985*, and Carl Solberg's *The Prairies and the Pampas: Agrarian Policy in Canada and Argentina, 1880 – 1930*.

For an interpretation of the role of the gaucho in Argentine history, see Richard W Slatta's *Gauchos and the Vanishing Frontier*. More recently, Slatta has compared the gauchos with stockmen of other countries in the beautifully illustrated *Cowboys of the Americas*. A recent book, offering a kind of intellectual history of the country, is Nicholas Shumway's *The Invention of Argentina*.

Perón & His Legacy A standard biography is Robert Alexander's *Juan Domingo Perón*. Another important book is Frederick Turner and José Enrique Miguens's *Juan Perón and the Reshaping of Argentina*. Also look at Joseph Page's *Perón: A Biography*, and Robert Crassweller's *Perón and the Enigma of Argentina*. A fascinating, fictionalized version of Perón's life, culminating in his return to Buenos Aires in 1973, is Tomás Eloy Martínez's *The Perón Novel*.

Eva Perón speaks for herself, to some degree, in her ghost-written biography *La Razón de Mi Vida* (My Mission in Life). VS Naipaul suggests that political violence and torture have long permeated Argentine society in his grim but eloquent essay *The Return of Eva Perón*. Also try JM Taylor's *Eva Perón: The Myths of a Woman*.

The Military, Politics & Geopolitics One good general overview of the military in Latin America is John J Johnson's *The Military and Society in Latin America*. Robert Potash has published two books on military interference in Argentine politics: *The Army and Politics in Argentina, 1928 – 1945: Yrigoyen to Perón*, and *The Army and Politics in Argentina, 1945 – 1962: Perón to Frondizi*.

For analysis of the notion of geopolitics in Argentina, see Philip Kelly and Jack Child's edited volume, *Geopolitics of the Southern Cone & Antarctica*. A more general account, dealing with Chile, Brazil, and Paraguay as well, is César Caviedes' *The Southern Cone: Realities of the Authoritarian State*.

The Dirty War The classic first-person account of state terrorism in the late 1970s is Jacobo Timmerman's *Prisoner Without a Name, Cell Without a Number*. *Nunca Más*, the official report of the National Commission on the Disappeared, systematically details military abuses during the 1976 to 1983 period. John Simpson and Jana Bennett's *The Disappeared: Voices from a Secret War* is a good general account. A highly regarded first novel on the Dirty War is US writer Lawrence Thornton's *Imagining Argentina*.

Contemporary Argentine Politics

For an analysis of the contradictions in Argentine society, read Gary Wynia's *Argentina in the Post-War Era: Politics and Economic Policy-making in a Divided Society*. A recent collection on the democratic transition is Monica Peralta-Ramos and Carlos Waisman's *From Military Rule to Liberal Democracy in Argentina*. David Erro's *Resolving the Argentine Paradox: Politics and Development, 1966 – 1992* provides a good analysis of contemporary Argentine politics and policies through the early Menem years, though it may be overly optimistic about current trends.

Geography & Natural History

There are several readable texts that integrate Latin American history with geography. Try Arthur Morris's *South America*, Harold Blakemore and Clifford Smith's collection *Latin America*, which includes a detailed chapter on the River Plate countries, and *The Cambridge Encyclopedia of Latin America*, which is rather broader.

For Argentina's national parks, do not overlook William Leitch's beautifully written and comprehensive *South America's National Parks*, which is superb on environment and natural history but much weaker on practical aspects of South American travel. Birders might acquire the 4th edition of T Narosky and D Yzurieta's *Guía para la Identificación de las Aves de Argentina y Uruguay*, also available in English as *Birds of Argentina and Uruguay*.

Foreign Literature

Writers from other countries have dealt with Argentine themes. Banned by the military dictatorship of the Proceso, Peruvian novelist Mario Vargas Llosa's *Aunt Julia and the Scriptwriter* offers amusing but ironic and unflattering observations of what other Latin Americans think of Argentines. Graham Greene's *The Honorary Consul*, made into an atrocious film starring Richard Gere, is a semi-satirical account of the kidnapping of an insignificant British diplomat by a small but committed revolutionary group in the slums of Corrientes.

FILM

Many Argentine films, made both before and after the Dirty War, are available on video. María Luisa Bemberg, perhaps Argentina's best known contemporary director, died of cancer in mid-1995. Her historically based films often illuminate the Argentine experience, particularly the relationship between women and the church – *Camila* (nominated for an Oscar as best foreign film in 1984) recounts the tale of Catholic socialite Camila O'Gorman, who fell in love and ran away from Buenos Aires with a young Jesuit priest in 1847, before the repressive government of Rosas found and executed them both. Bemberg's English-language film *Miss Mary* (1986), starring Julie Christie, focuses on the experience of an English governess of upper-class Argentine children, while *I, the Worst of All* (1990) tells the life of the 17th-century Mexican nun Sor Juana Inés de la Cruz. Bemberg's last directorial effort, *I Don't Want to Talk About It* (1992), is an unusual love story starring Marcelo Mastroianni; filmed in the Uruguayan city of Colonia, across the river from Buenos Aires, it metaphorically explores issues of power and control in a provincial town.

Director Luis Puenzo's *The Official Story* deals with the delicate and controversial theme of adoption of children of missing people by those responsible for their disappearance during the Dirty War; it stars Norma Leandro, who has also worked in English-language films in the US. One truly creepy feature, which ironically depicts many amusing aspects of porteño life, is the English-language film *Apartment Zero*, in which an Anglo-Argentine film buff takes a morbidly curious interest in his mysterious North American housemate. Eliseo Subiel's *Man Facing Southeast* (1986) takes part of its inspiration from Adolfo Bioy Casares' unusual novella *The Invention of Morel*.

Héctor Babenco directed *Kiss of the Spider Woman*, set in Brazil but based on Manuel Puig's novel, an intricate portrayal of the way in which the police and the military abuse political prisoners and exploit informers. *Las Locas de la Plaza de Mayo* is a documentary tribute to the mothers and grandmothers who defied the Proceso by marching every Thursday in front of the Casa Rosada. *The Night of the Pencils* also deals with the Dirty War.

A recent release is director Adolfo Aristarain's *A Place in the World*, a story that has been compared to the classic Hollywood Western *Shane*. Based on Osvaldo Soriano's novel, *A Funny Dirty Little War* comically depicts the very serious matters of fractious politics and consequences of a possible military coup in a small provincial town. *Don Segundo Sombra*, based on Ricardo Güiraldes' gauchesco novel, is a coming-of-age-on-the-Pampas film set in the village of San Antonio de Areco. *La Patagonia Rebelde*, which often plays university campuses and repertory houses in the USA, is a historical account of the Anarchist rebellion in Santa Cruz province at the turn of the century. Federico Pinos Solano, also a leftist candidate for president in 1995, has directed films such as *El Viaje*, *El Exilio de Gardel,* and *Sur*. See

Arts in Facts about Argentina for more information on the film industry.

MEDIA

Argentina is the most literate country in South America, and it supports a wide spectrum of newspapers, magazines, and book publishers despite its unceasing economic crisis. In recent years, the end of government monopoly in the electronic media has opened up the airwaves to a greater variety of programming than in the past. Argentine cinema does a great deal with limited resources.

Freedom of the press is far greater than under the military dictatorship, but abuses still occur – provincial journalists have received physical and even death threats, and, in one case, Mendoza police may have illegally entered a hotel room and intimidated three visiting Chilean journalists. The present government has withheld official advertising from newspapers that have investigated official corruption too vigorously for its taste.

Newspapers & Magazines

Both in the federal capital and the provinces, there is a thriving daily press with unambiguous political tendencies. The most important porteño dailies are the venerable *La Prensa* and *La Nación* (the latter founded by President Bartolomé Mitre) and the middle-of-the-road tabloid *Clarín*, which has an excellent Sunday cultural section. *Página 12*, which does not publish Mondays, provides a refreshingly intelligent leftist perspective and often breaks important stories that mainstream newspapers are slow to cover. Although not doctrinaire, it often succumbs to irritating, self-indulgent cleverness: Continual ironic references to President Menem's one-time economy minister as "Sup-Erman González" quickly grows tiresome.

The English language daily *Buenos Aires Herald* covers Argentina and the world from an Anglo-Argentine perspective, with emphasis on business and commerce, but its perceptive weekend summaries of political and economic developments are a must

for visitors with limited Spanish; its Sunday edition now includes Britain's *Guardian Weekly* at no extra charge. The *Herald* has a well-deserved reputation for editorial boldness – during the Dirty War of the late 1970s and early 1980s, the paper was so outspoken in condemning military and police abuses that its editor had to go into exile because of threats against him and his family. *Argentinisches Tageblatt* is a German-language weekly that appears on Saturday.

Ambito Financiero is the daily voice of Argentina's business community, centered around Calle San Martín in Buenos Aires. *El Cronista Comercial* is its afternoon rival.

Magazines such as *El Porteño* offer a forum for Argentine intellectuals and contribute greatly to the cultural life of the capital and the country. The monthly *Humor* caricatured the Argentine military during the Dirty War and even during the early nationalist hysteria of the Falklands conflict; in safer times, it has lost much of its edge but is still worth reading. Avoid its soft-porn spinoff, *Humor Sexo*.

Radio & TV

The most popular station, the nationwide Radio Rivadavia, is a combination of top 40 and talk radio, but there are many others on the AM band. In Buenos Aires, at least a dozen FM stations specialize in styles from classical to pop to tango.

Legalization of nonstate television and the cable revolution have brought a wider variety of programming to the small screen. To be sure, there are countless game shows, dance parties, and soap-opera drivel *(novelas)*, but there is also serious public affairs programming on major stations at prime viewing times such as Sunday evening. Foreigners can tune in to CNN for news and ESPN for sports. Spanish and Chilean stations are also available

PHOTOGRAPHY & VIDEO

The latest in consumer electronics is available, but import duties make cameras and film very expensive, up to three times their cost in North America or Western Europe –

ARGENTINA

one shop in Río Gallegos wanted US$20 for a lens cap costing less than US$5 in the States. Developing is equally expensive. Bring as much film as you can; you can always sell anything you don't need to other travelers. Locally manufactured film is reasonably good, but no cheaper than imported.

Color slide film can be purchased cheaply in Asunción, Paraguay, or in the free zones at Iquique and Punta Arenas, Chile. These are also good places to replace lost or stolen camera equipment, as prices are only slightly higher than in North America, even if the selection is not so great.

TIME

For most of the year, Argentina is three hours behind Greenwich Mean Time (GMT), but this varies among provinces. The city and province of Buenos Aires observe daylight saving time (summer time), but most provinces do not. Exact dates for the changeover vary from year to year.

ELECTRICITY

Electric current operates on 220 V, 50 cycles. In downtown Buenos Aires, Calle Talcahuano has a large concentration of shops specializing in transformers and adapters for appliances.

WEIGHTS & MEASURES

The metric system is universal and obligatory, but country folk commonly use the Spanish *legua* (league, equaling about 5 km) to indicate distance. See the inside back cover for a conversion chart.

LAUNDRY

In recent years, self-service laundries have become more common in both Buenos Aires and provincial cities, but they tend to be more expensive than their equivalent in the USA or Europe. Laverap has branches in most major cities. Most inexpensive hotels will have a place where you can wash your own clothes and hang them to dry. In some places maid service will be

reasonable, but agree on charges in advance.

TOILETS

In terms of cleanliness and sanitation, Argentine toilets are probably better than in most of the rest of South America, but there is considerable regional variation – in subtropical rural areas like the Gran Chaco and parts of the Northwest Andean, standards can be lower. For the squeamish, the better restaurants and cafes are good alternatives. Always carry your own toilet paper.

HEALTH

Although emergency medical care in Argentina's public hospitals is good and usually free of charge, international travelers should take out comprehensive travel insurance before they leave home. If you're from a country with socialized medicine, you should find out what you'll need to do in order to be reimbursed for out-of-pocket money you may spend.

In general, Argentina presents few serious health hazards, although a few cases of cholera were reported after the major 1991 outbreak in Peru. Before traveling, US residents can contact the International Travel Hotline (☎ 404-332-4559), a voicemail service at the Centers for Disease Control and Prevention (CDC) in Atlanta. Even more useful is the CDC's automated Fax Information Service (☎ 404-332-4565), which provides printouts of the most current information on health conditions in specific regions by immediate return fax. Just call the number, indicate which country you want information on (Argentina, the Falklands, Paraguay, and Chile is 220180; Paraguay is 220170), and provide a fax number. For the latest details while in Argentina, contact your country's consulate in Buenos Aires.

If you do become ill in Argentina, don't hesitate to seek medical help at hospitals or clinics. While some of these will have more English-speaking staff (for instance, the British Hospital in Buenos Aires), most doctors have a working knowledge of English.

Travel Health Guides

A number of books provide good information on travel health:

Staying Healthy in Asia, Africa & Latin America, by Dick Schroeder, is probably the best all-round guide. It's compact but very detailed and well organized.

Travelers' Health, by Doctor Richard Dawood, is comprehensive, easy to read, authoritative, and highly recommended, but rather large to lug around.

Where There Is No Doctor, by David Werner, is a very detailed guide, more suited to those working in countries where health facilities are few than to travelers.

Backpacking in Chile and Argentina, by Hilary Bradt and John Pilkington, has a good section on the hazards of hiking and camping in the Southern Cone countries.

Travel with Children, by Maureen Wheeler, offers basic advice on travel health for younger children.

Predeparture Preparations

Health Insurance It's a good idea to get a travel insurance policy to cover theft, loss, and medical problems. There are a wide variety of policies, and your travel agent will have recommendations. International student travel policies handled by STA Travel or other student travel organizations are usually a good value. Some policies offer lower and higher medical expenses options, but the higher one is chiefly for countries like the USA with extremely high medical costs. Check the small print.

- Some policies specifically exclude "dangerous activities" such as scuba diving, motorcycling, and even trekking. If these activities are on your agenda, avoid this sort of policy.
- You may prefer a policy that pays doctors or hospitals directly, rather than one that requires you to pay first and claim later. If you have to claim later, keep all documentation. Some policies ask you to call back (reverse charges) to a center in your home country for an immediate assessment of your problem.
- Check whether the policy covers ambulance fees or an emergency flight home. If you have to stretch out, you will need two seats, and somebody has to pay for it!

Medical Kit All standard medications are available in well-stocked pharmacies, and many common prescription drugs can be purchased legally over-the-counter in Argentina. A possible kit list includes:

- Aspirin, acetominophen, or panadol, for pain or fever
- Antihistamine (such as Benadryl), which is useful as a decongestant for colds, and to ease the itch from allergies, insect bites, or stings or to help prevent motion sickness
- Antibiotics, which are useful for traveling off the beaten track, but they must be prescribed, and you should carry the prescription with you (see note below)
- Kaolin preparation (Pepto-Bismol), Immodium, or Lomotil, for stomach upsets
- Rehydration mixture, to treat severe diarrhea, which is particularly important if you're traveling with children
- Antiseptic, mercurochrome, and antibiotic powder or similar "dry" spray, for cuts and grazes
- Calamine lotion, to ease irritation from bites or stings
- Bandages, for minor injuries (minimize use in hot climates)
- Scissors, tweezers, and a thermometer (airlines prohibit mercury thermometers)
- Insect repellent, sunscreen lotion, lip balm, and water purification tablets

Antibiotics are specific to the infections that they treat. Ideally, they should be administered only under medical supervision and never taken indiscriminately. Take only the recommended dose at the prescribed intervals and continue using it for the prescribed period, even if symptoms disappear earlier. Stop immediately if there are any serious reactions, and don't use the antibiotic at all if you are unsure if you have the correct one.

Health Preparations Make sure you're healthy before you start traveling. If you are embarking on a long trip, make sure your teeth are in good shape. Argentine dentists are excellent, especially in Buenos Aires. If you do happen to require dental work and the US dollar is strong against the peso, the charge may be rather cheap. If you wear glasses, take a spare pair and your prescription. You can get new spectacles made quickly and competently, depending on the prescription and frame you choose; replacing contacts may prove a bit more time-consuming. If you require a particular medication, take an adequate supply and bring a prescription in case you lose your supply.

Immunizations Argentina requires no vaccinations for entry from any country, but if you are visiting neighboring tropical countries you should consider prophylaxes against typhoid, malaria, and other diseases. The farther off the beaten track you go, the more necessary it is to take precautions.

It is important to understand the distinction between vaccines recommended for travel in certain areas and those required by law. Essentially the number of vaccines subject to international health regulations has been dramatically reduced over the last 10 years. Currently, yellow fever is the only vaccine subject to international health regulations. Vaccination as an entry requirement is usually only enforced when coming from an infected area.

On the other hand, a number of vaccines are recommended for travel in certain areas. These may not be required by law but are suggested for your personal protection. All vaccinations should be recorded on an International Health Certificate, which is available from your physician or government health department.

Plan ahead for getting your vaccinations: Some of them require an initial shot followed by a booster, while some vaccinations should not be given together. It is recommended you seek medical advice at least six weeks prior to travel. Note that smallpox has now been wiped out around the world, so immunization is no longer necessary.

Most travelers from Western countries will have been immunized against various diseases during childhood, but your doctor may still recommend booster shots against measles or polio, diseases still prevalent in many developing countries. The period of protection offered by vaccinations differs widely, and some are contraindicated if you are pregnant.

In some countries immunizations are available from airport or government health centers. Travel agents or airline offices will tell you where. Vaccinations include:

Tetanus & Diphtheria Boosters are necessary every 10 years, and protection is highly recommended.

Hepatitis A The most common travel-acquired illness can be prevented by vaccination. Protection can be provided in two ways: with the antibody gamma globulin (see below) or with a new vaccine called Havrix, which provides long-term immunity (possibly more than 10 years) after an initial course of two injections and a booster at one year. It may be more expensive than gamma globulin but certainly has many advantages, including length of protection and ease of administration. It is important to know that as a vaccine it will take about three weeks to provide satisfactory protection – hence the need for careful planning prior to travel.

Gamma globulin is not a vaccination but a ready-made antibody which has proven very successful in reducing the chances of hepatitis infection. Because it may interfere with the development of immunity, it should not be given until at least 10 days after administration of the last vaccine needed; it should also be given as close as possible to departure because it is at its most effective in the first few weeks after administration, and the effectiveness tapers off gradually between three and six months.

Basic Rules & Precautions

Care in what you eat and drink is the most important health rule; stomach upsets are the most likely travel health problem (between 30% and 50% of travelers in a two-week stay experience this), but the majority of these upsets will be relatively minor. Don't become paranoid; after all, trying the local food is part of the experience of travel.

Water Although the aging water supply system of Buenos Aires has come under scrutiny for its chemical content, there is almost no danger of dysentery or similar ailments. In remote rural areas, where latrines may be close to wells, one should exercise caution. One geographical area of concern is the "Impenetrable" of the central Chaco, north of Roque Sáenz Peñal, which has been the only region in the country to experience recent outbreaks of cholera.

Bottled drinking water, both carbonated and noncarbonated, is widely available in Argentina. If you prefer to purify water yourself, the simplest way is to boil it thoroughly – vigorous boiling for 10 minutes should be satisfactory even at a high altitude (where water boils at a lower temperature, and germs are less likely to be killed).

Simple filtering will not remove all dangerous organisms, so if you cannot boil water it should be treated chemically. Chlorine tablets (Puritabs, Steritabs, or other brand names) will kill many but not all pathogens, including Giardia and amebic cysts. Iodine is very effective in purifying water and is available in tablet form (such as Potable Aqua), but follow the directions carefully – too much iodine can be harmful.

If you can't find tablets, tincture of iodine (2%) or iodine crystals can be used. Four drops of tincture of iodine per liter or quart of clear water is the recommended dosage; let the treated water stand for 20 to 30 minutes before drinking. Iodine crystals can also be used to purify water, but this is a more complicated process, as you must first prepare a saturated iodine solution (iodine loses its effectiveness if exposed to air or becomes damp, so keep it in a tightly sealed container). Flavored powder will help disguise the taste of treated water and is a good idea if you are traveling with children.

Food North Americans, Europeans, and Australasians who are not vegetarians will find Argentine food relatively bland and easy on the stomach. Salad greens and other fresh vegetables are safe to eat in virtually every part of the country.

Remember that if your food is poor or limited in availability, if you're traveling hard and fast and therefore missing meals, or if you simply lose your appetite, you can soon start to lose weight and compromise your immune system.

Everyday Health
Normal body temperature is 98.6°F or 37°C; more than 4°F or 2°C higher indicates a "high" fever. The normal adult pulse rate is 60 to 80 per minute (children 80 to 100, babies 100 to 140). It is important to know how to take a temperature and a pulse rate.

Respiration (breathing) rate is also an indicator of illness. Count the number of breaths per minute: Between 12 and 20 is normal for adults and older children (up to 30 for younger children, 40 for babies). People with a high fever or serious respiratory illness (like pneumonia) breathe more quickly than normal. More than 40 shallow breaths a minute is usually an indication of pneumonia.

Medical Problems & Treatment
Potential medical problems can be broken down into several categories. First, there are the problems caused by extremes of temperature, altitude, or motion. Then there are diseases and illnesses caused through poor environmental sanitation, animal or human contact, and insect bites or stings. Simple cuts, bites, and scratches can also cause problems.

Self-diagnosis and treatment can be risky, so wherever possible, seek qualified help. Although we do give drug dosages in this section, they are for emergency use only. Medical advice should be sought where possible before administering any drugs. An embassy or consulate can usually recommend a good place to go for such advice.

Climatic & Geographical Ailments
Sunburn & Heat Exhaustion Although Argentina is mostly a temperate country, its

northern provinces lie within the Tropic of Capricorn, and the heat of the sun's direct rays can be devastating, especially at high altitudes. In the western Chaco and other desert regions, where summer temperatures can exceed 40°C, dehydration is a very serious problem. In far southern Patagonia and Tierra del Fuego, where the protective ozone layer has dissipated because of aerosol fluorocarbons, sun protection is also a good idea despite the frequent overcast weather.

Use a sunscreen and take extra care to cover areas not normally exposed to sun. Quality sunglasses and a Panama hat or baseball cap are excellent ideas. You should also use zinc cream or some other barrier cream for your nose and lips. Calamine lotion is good for mild sunburn.

Dehydration or salt deficiency can cause heat exhaustion. Take time to acclimatize to high temperatures and make sure that you get enough liquids. Salt tablets may also help. Salt deficiency is characterized by fatigue, lethargy, headaches, giddiness, and muscle cramps. Vomiting or diarrhea can also deplete your liquid and salt levels. Anhydrotic heat exhaustion, caused by the inability to sweat, is quite rare. Unlike the other forms of heat exhaustion it is likely to strike people who have been in a hot climate for some time, rather than newcomers. Always carry – and use – a water bottle on long trips.

Heat Stroke Long, continuous periods of exposure to high temperatures can leave you vulnerable to this serious, sometimes fatal, condition, which occurs when the body's heat-regulating mechanism breaks down and body temperature rises to dangerous levels. Avoid excessive alcohol intake or strenuous activity when you first arrive in a hot climate.

Symptoms include feeling unwell, lack of perspiration, and a high body temperature of 102°F to 105°F (39°C to 41°C). It's wise if you're traveling with others to watch for these signs in your companions; heat stroke is often more obvious to others than to the victim. Immediately get out of

the sun, remove clothing, cover with a wet sheet or towel, and fan continually. Hospitalization is essential for extreme cases.

Hypothermia At high altitudes in the mountains or high latitudes in Patagonia, cold and wet conditions can kill. Changeable weather at high altitudes can leave you vulnerable to exposure: After dark, temperatures in the mountains or desert can drop from balmy to below freezing, while high winds and a sudden soaking can lower your body temperature too rapidly. If possible, avoid traveling alone; partners are more likely to avoid hypothermia successfully. If you must travel alone, especially when hiking, be sure someone knows your route and when you expect to return.

Seek shelter when bad weather is unavoidable. Woolen clothing and synthetics, which retain warmth even when wet, are superior to cottons. A quality sleeping bag is a worthwhile investment, although goose down loses much of its insulating qualities when wet. Carry high-energy, easily digestible snacks such as chocolate or dried fruit.

Get hypothermia victims out of the wind or rain, remove their clothing if it's wet, and replace it with dry, warm clothing. Give them hot liquids – not alcohol – and high-calorie, easily digestible food. In advanced stages it may be necessary to place victims in warm sleeping bags and get in with them. Do not rub victims, but place them near a fire or, if possible, in a warm (not hot) bath.

Fungal Infections Fungal infections, which occur with greater frequency in hot weather, are most likely to occur on the scalp, between the toes or fingers (athlete's foot), in the groin (jock itch or crotch rot), and on the body (ringworm). You get ringworm (which is a fungal infection, not a worm) from infected animals or by walking on damp areas, like shower floors.

To prevent fungal infections wear loose, comfortable clothes, avoid underwear made of artificial fibers, wash frequently, and dry carefully. If you do get an infection, wash the infected area daily with a disinfectant or medicated soap and water, and rinse and dry well. Apply an antifungal powder, try to expose the infected area to air or sunlight as much as possible, and wash all towels and underwear in hot water as well as changing them often.

Altitude Sickness From the passes between Mendoza and Chile northward to the Bolivian border, altitude sickness *(apunamiento* or *soroche)*, also known as acute mountain sickness (AMS), represents a potential health hazard. In the thinner atmosphere above 3000 meters or even lower in some cases, lack of oxygen causes many individuals to suffer headaches, nausea, shortness of breath, physical weakness, and other symptoms that can lead to very serious consequences, especially if combined with heat exhaustion, sunburn, or hypothermia.

There is no hard and fast rule as to how high is too high: AMS has been fatal at altitudes of 3000 meters, although it is much more common above 3450 meters. It is always wise to sleep at a lower altitude than the greatest height reached during the day. A number of other measures can prevent or minimize AMS.

For mild cases, everyday painkillers such as aspirin or *chachacoma*, an herbal tea made from a common Andean shrub, will relieve symptoms until your body adapts. In the Andean Northwest, coca leaves are a common remedy, but authorities frown upon their usage even by native peoples, who sell them surreptitiously in the markets of Jujuy, Salta, and other towns. If you experience AMS symptoms, avoid smoking, drinking alcohol, eating heavily, or exercising strenuously. Most people recover within a few hours or days as their body produces more red blood cells to absorb oxygen, but if symptoms persist, it is imperative to descend to lower elevations. Following some simple guidelines will help:

• Ascend slowly – take frequent rest days, spending two to three nights for each climb of 1000

meters (3000 feet). If you reach a high altitude by trekking, acclimatization takes place gradually, and you are less likely to be affected than if you fly direct.
• Drink extra fluids. The mountain air is dry and cold, and you lose moisture as you breathe.
• Eat light, high-carbohydrate meals for more energy. Snacks such as chocolate or dried fruit are easily available in Argentina.
• Avoid alcohol, which may increase the risk of dehydration.
• Avoid sedatives.

Motion Sickness Eating lightly before and during a trip will reduce the chances of motion sickness. If you are prone to motion sickness, try to sit in a place that minimizes disturbance, for example, near the wing on aircraft or near the center on buses. Fresh air usually helps, while reading or cigarette smoke doesn't. Commercial anti-motion sickness preparations, which can cause drowsiness, have to be taken before the trip commences; once you already feel sick, it's too late. Ginger, a natural preventative, is available in capsule form.

Jet Lag Jet lag usually occurs when a person travels by air across more than three time zones (each time zone usually represents a one-hour time difference); however, some people experience it crossing only two zones. Many of the functions of the human body (such as temperature, pulse rate, and emptying of the bladder and bowels) are regulated by internal 24-hour cycles called circadian rhythms. When we travel long distances rapidly, our bodies take time to adjust to the "new time" of our destination, and we may experience fatigue, disorientation, insomnia, anxiety, impaired concentration, and loss of appetite. These effects will usually be gone within three days of arrival, but there are ways of minimizing the impact of jet lag:

• Rest for a couple of days prior to departure; try to avoid late nights and last-minute dashes for traveler's checks, passports, and other important items.
• Try to select flight schedules that minimize sleep deprivation; arriving late in the day means

you can go to sleep soon after you arrive. For very long flights, try to organize a stopover.

- Avoid excessive eating (which bloats the stomach) and alcohol (which causes dehydration) during the flight. Instead, drink plenty of noncarbonated, nonalcoholic drinks such as fruit juice or water.
- Avoid smoking, as this reduces the amount of oxygen in the airplane cabin even further and causes greater fatigue.
- Make yourself comfortable by wearing loose-fitting clothes and perhaps bringing an eye mask and ear plugs to help you sleep.

Diseases of Poor Santitation
Diarrhea A change of water, food, or climate can all cause the runs; diarrhea brought on by contaminated food or water is more serious. Despite all your precautions you may still have a mild bout of travelers' diarrhea, but a few rushed toilet trips with no other symptoms is not indicative of a serious problem. Moderate diarrhea, involving half a dozen loose movements in a day, is more of a nuisance.

Dehydration is the main danger with any diarrhea, particularly for children who can dehydrate quite quickly. Weak herbal tea with a little sugar, soda water, or soft drinks allowed to go flat and diluted 50% with water are all good fluid replacements. With severe diarrhea a rehydrating solution is necessary to replace minerals and salts.

Commercially available oral rehydration salts (ORS) are very useful; add the contents of one packet to a liter of boiled or bottled water. In an emergency you can make up a solution of eight teaspoons of sugar to a liter of boiled water and provide salted crackers at the same time. You should stick to a bland diet as you recover.

Lomotil or Imodium can be used to bring relief from the symptoms, although they do not actually cure the problem. Only use these drugs if absolutely necessary – eg, if you *must* travel. For children Imodium is preferable. Do not use these drugs if the person has a high fever or is severely dehydrated. Antibiotics may be useful in treating diarrhea that is watery, with blood and mucous, and/or accompanied by a fever.

The recommended drugs (adults only) would be either norfloxacin, 400 mg twice daily for three days, or ciprofloxacin, 500 mg twice daily for three days.

The drug bismuth subsalicylate has also been used successfully. The dosage for adults is two tablets or 30 ml and for children it is one tablet or 10 ml. This dose can be repeated every 30 minutes to one hour, with no more than eight doses in a 24-hour period.

The drug of choice for children would be co-trimoxazole (Bactrim, Septrin, Resprim) with dosage dependent on weight.

Dysentery This serious illness, caused by contaminated food or water, is characterized by severe diarrhea, often with blood or mucus in the stool. There are two kinds of dysentery: bacillary and amebic. Bacillary dysentery is characterized by a high fever and rapid onset; headache, vomiting, and stomach pains are also symptoms. It generally does not last longer than a week, but it is highly contagious. Amebic dysentery is often more gradual in the onset of symptoms, with cramping abdominal pain and vomiting less likely; fever may not be present. It is not a self-limiting disease: It will persist until treated and can recur and cause long-term health problems.

A stool test is necessary to diagnose which kind of dysentery you have, so you should seek medical help urgently. In case of an emergency the drugs norfloxacin or ciprofloxacin can be used as presumptive treatment for bacillary dysentery, and metronidazole (Flagyl) for amebic dysentery.

For bacillary dysentery, norfloxacin 400 mg twice daily for seven days or ciprofloxacin 500 mg twice daily for seven days are the recommended dosages.

If you're unable to find either of these drugs, then a useful alternative is co-trimoxazole 160/800 mg (Bactrim, Septrin, Resprim) twice daily for seven days. This is a sulpha drug and must not be used by people with a known sulpha allergy.

In the case of children the drug co-trimoxazole is a reasonable first-line treatment. For amoebic dysentery, the recommended adult dosage of metronidazole (Flagyl) is one 750-mg to 800-mg capsule three times daily for five days. Children ages 8 to 12 years should have half the adult dose; the dosage for younger children is one-third the adult dose.

An alternative to Flagyl is Fasigyn, taken as a two gram daily dose for three days. Alcohol must be avoided during treatment and for 48 hours afterward.

Giardiasis Commonly known as Giardia, and sometimes "Beaver Fever," this intestinal parasite is present in contaminated water. Giardia has even contaminated apparently pristine rushing streams in the backcountry.

Symptoms are stomach cramps, nausea, a bloated stomach, watery, foul-smelling diarrhea, and frequent gas. Giardia can appear several weeks after exposure to the parasite; symptoms may disappear for a few days and then return, a pattern which may continue. Tinidazole, known as Fasigyn, or metronidazole (Flagyl) are the recommended drugs for treatment. Either can be used in a single treatment dose. Antibiotics are useless.

Hepatitis Hepatitis is a general term for inflammation of the liver. There are many causes of this condition: drugs, alcohol, and infections are but a few. The discovery of new strains has led to a virtual alphabet soup, with hepatitis A, B, C, D, E, and a rumored G. These letters identify specific agents that cause viral hepatitis. Viral hepatitis is an infection of the liver, which can lead to jaundice (yellow skin), fever, lethargy, and digestive problems. It can have no symptoms at all, with the infected person not aware that he or she has the disease. Travelers shouldn't be too paranoid about this apparent proliferation of hepatitis strains; hep C, D, E, and G are fairly rare (so far), and following the same precautions as for A and B should be all that's necessary to avoid them.

Viral hepatitis can be divided into two groups on the basis of how it is spread. The first route of transmission is via contaminated food and water, and the second route is via blood and bodily fluids.

Hepatitis A is a very common disease in most countries, especially those with poor standards of sanitation. Most people in developing countries are infected as children; they often don't develop symptoms, but do develop lifelong immunity. The disease poses a real threat to the traveler, as people are unlikely to have been exposed to hepatitis A in developed countries.

The symptoms are fever, chills, headache, fatigue, feelings of weakness, and aches and pains, followed by loss of appetite, nausea, vomiting, abdominal pain, dark urine, light-colored feces, and jaundiced skin; the whites of the eyes may also turn yellow. You should seek medical advice, but in general there is not much you can do apart from resting, drinking lots of fluids, eating lightly, and avoiding fatty foods. People who have had hepatitis must forgo alcohol for six months after the illness, as hepatitis attacks the liver, and it needs that amount of time to recover.

The routes of transmission are via contaminated water, shellfish contaminated by sewerage, or foodstuffs sold by food handlers with poor standards of hygiene. Taking care with what you eat and drink can go a long way toward preventing this disease. If there is any risk of exposure, additional cover is highly recommended. This cover comes in two forms: gamma globulin and Havrix. Gamma globulin is an injection in which you are given the antibodies for hepatitis A, which provide immunity for a limited time. Havrix is a vaccine that gives lasting immunity by encouraging your body to develop its own antibodies.

Hepatitis B, which used to be called serum hepatitis, is spread through contact with infected blood, blood products, or bodily fluids; for example, through sexual contact, unsterilized needles, and blood transfusions. Other risk situations include having a shave or getting a tattoo in a local shop, or having your ears pierced. The symptoms of type B are much the same as type A except that they are more severe and may lead to irreparable liver damage or even liver cancer. Although there is no treatment for hepatitis B, a cheap and effective vaccine is available; the only problem is that for long-lasting cover you need a six-month course. The immunization schedule requires two injections at least a month apart followed by a third dose five months after the second.

Hepatitis C is similar to B but seems to lead to liver disease more rapidly. Often referred to as the "Delta" virus, Hepatitis D only occurs in chronic carriers of hepatitis B. Hepatitis E is a very recently discovered virus, of which little is yet known. It appears to be rather common in developing countries, generally causing mild hepatitis, although it can be very serious in pregnant women. Care with water supplies is the only current prevention, as there are no specific vaccines for this type of hepatitis. At present it doesn't appear to be too great a risk for travelers.

**Diseases Spread by Animals & People
Rabies** Dogs are noted carriers of rabies. Any bite, scratch, or even lick from a warm-blooded, furry animal should be cleaned immediately and thoroughly. Scrub with soap and running water, and then clean with an alcohol solution. If there is any possibility that the animal is infected, medical help should be sought immediately. Even if the animal is not rabid, all bites should be treated seriously as they can become infected or can result in tetanus. A rabies vaccination is now available and should be considered if you are in a high-risk category – eg, if you intend to explore caves (bat bites can be dangerous) or work with animals.

Tetanus Tetanus is difficult to treat but is preventable with immunization. Tetanus occurs when a wound becomes infected by a germ which lives in the feces of animals or people, so thoroughly clean all cuts, punctures, or animal bites. Tetanus is also known as lockjaw, and the first symptom may be discomfort in swallowing, or stiffening of the jaw and neck; this is followed by painful convulsions of the jaw and the whole body.

Sexually Transmitted Diseases Sexual contact with an infected partner spreads these diseases. While abstinence is the only 100% effective preventative, using condoms also reduces your risk. Gonorrhea and syphilis are the most common of these diseases; sores, blisters, or rashes around the genitals, discharges, or pain when urinating are common symptoms. Symptoms may be less marked or not observed at all in women. Syphilis symptoms eventually disappear completely, but the disease continues and can cause severe problems in later years. The treatment of gonorrhea and syphilis is by antibiotics.

There are numerous other sexually transmitted diseases, and effective treatment is available for most. However, there is no cure for herpes, and there is also currently no cure for AIDS (see below).

HIV/AIDS "En Argentina no hay SIDA, porque hay 35 millones de forros." (In Argentina, there's no AIDS, because there are 35 million scumbags (condoms).) – slogan on a T-shirt in Santiago del Estero. Despite this self-deprecating but misleading comment on Argentine society, HIV/AIDS exists, though not on the scale that it does in Brazil or parts of the USA – there are roughly 5000 cases in the country, the second-highest number on the continent after Brazil's 55,000. AIDS also certainly exists in Uruguay and Paraguay, but it is not (yet) the widespread disaster that it is in Brazil; Paraguay may be more under threat in the long term due to its close Brazilian connections. For referrals to AIDS support groups, see the "Useful Organizations" entry.

HIV (the Human Immunodeficiency Virus) may develop into AIDS (Acquired Immune Deficiency Syndrome). HIV is a major problem in many countries. Any exposure to blood, blood products, or bodily fluids may put the individual at risk. Infection can come from practicing unprotected sex or sharing contaminated needles.

Apart from abstinence, the most effective preventative is always to practice safe sex using condoms. It is impossible to detect the HIV-positive status of an otherwise healthy-looking person without a blood test.

HIV/AIDS can also be spread through infected blood transfusions; many countries cannot afford to screen blood for transfusions. It can also be spread by dirty needles – vaccinations, acupuncture, tattooing, and ear or nose piercing can potentially be as dangerous as intravenous drug use if the equipment is not clean. If you do need an injection, ask to see the syringe unwrapped in front of you, or better still, take a needle and syringe pack with you overseas – it is a cheap insurance package against HIV infection.

Fear of HIV infection should never preclude treatment for serious medical conditions. Although there may be a risk of infection, it is very small indeed. A good resource for help and information is the US Centers for Disease Control AIDS hotline (☎ 800-343-2347).

Cholera The cholera epidemic that has swept Peru and some other South American countries has so far not spread among the general population of Argentina, Uruguay, and Paraguay, but it would be wise to take minimum precautions. Avoid raw seafood, and do not consume ice in drinks in areas where drinking water may be suspect. The "Impenetrable" of the mid-Chaco, an area little frequented by foreigners, has been the site of Argentina's only cholera outbreaks.

The disease is characterized by a sudden onset of acute diarrhea with "rice water" stools, vomiting, muscular cramps, and extreme weakness. Seek medical help fast and treat for dehydration, which can be extreme. If there is an appreciable delay in getting to the hospital, then begin taking tetracycline (one 250 mg capsule four times daily for adults, one-third to one-half of this dosage for children).

A cholera vaccine exists, but is not very effective, and is not required as a condition of entry to any country in the world.

Hydatidosis Spread by contact with dogs that have eaten the entrails of infected sheep, this highly contagious disease is prevalent in areas like Argentine and Chilean Patagonia, where sheep numbers are very high, and dogs may come into contact with them. Though not cause for panic, it is a potentially serious matter; do not eat homemade sausages in this region, and avoid contact with the sheep dogs in particular.

Shellfish Poisoning In Argentine and Chilean Patagonia, most notably in Tierra del Fuego, collection of shellfish is not advisable and, in many cases, not permitted because of toxic "red tide" conditions.

Insect-Borne Diseases

Chagas' Disease Darwin may have suffered from this parasitic disease, transmitted by a bug that lives in mud (adobe) huts and comes out to feed at night. The bite is often mistaken for that of a bed bug, but early symptoms of Chagas' disease include a hard, violet-colored swelling appearing in about a week at the site of the bite, followed by swelling of the lymph glands or by a fever. The long-term complications can be quite serious and can eventually lead to death years later. Most cases of Chagas' disease have appeared in Brazil, but travelers should avoid sleeping in or near mud huts. If you have no other choice, sleep under a mosquito net, use insecticides and insect repellents, and check for hidden insects.

Malaria There is a minor risk of malaria in rural areas of northern Argentina, bordering Bolivia in Salta and Jujuy provinces. Chloroquine is the recommended medication here.

Yellow Fever Yellow fever is a very low-risk matter in Argentina and Uruguay, which do not require vaccination certificates, and only slightly higher in Paraguay.

ARGENTINA

Nevertheless, a certificate is a good idea for anyone visiting neighboring tropical countries.

Cuts, Bites & Stings

Cuts & Scratches Skin punctures can easily become infected in hot climates and may be difficult to heal. Treat any cut with an antiseptic such as Betadine. When possible avoid bandages and Band-Aids, which can keep wounds wet.

Bites & Stings Bee and wasp stings are usually painful rather than dangerous. Calamine lotion will give relief, and ice packs will reduce the pain and swelling. Some spiders have dangerous bites, and scorpion stings are very painful, but neither is likely to be fatal. Bites are best avoided by not using bare hands to turn over rocks or large pieces of wood.

Bites from snakes do not cause instantaneous death, and antivenins are usually available. Seek medical help, if possible with the dead snake for identification. Don't attempt to catch the snake if there is even a remote possibility of being bitten again. In the case of a snake bite, avoid slashing and sucking the wound, avoid tight tourniquets (a lightly constricting band above the bite can help), avoid ice, keep the affected area below the level of the heart, and move it as little as possible. Do not ingest alcohol or any drugs. Stay calm and get to a medical facility as soon as possible.

In the case of spiders and scorpions, there are no special first-aid techniques. A black widow spider bite may be barely noticeable, but the venom can be dangerous, and if you're bitten you should seek medical attention immediately. Centipede, bee, wasp, and antbites may be relieved by application of ice.

If you are hiking a long way from the nearest phone or other help, and you are bitten or stung, you should hike out and get help, particularly in the case of snake and spider bites. Reactions are often delayed for up to 12 hours, and you can hike out before then. It is recommended to hike with a companion.

Ticks Ticks are a parasitic arachnid that may be present in brush, forest, and grasslands, where hikers often get them on their legs or in their boots. The adults suck blood from hosts by burying their head into skin, but are often found unattached and can simply be brushed off. However, if one has attached itself to you, pulling it off and leaving the head in the skin increases the likelihood of infection or disease.

To avoid ticks, use insect repellent. If one should embed itself in you, avoid yanking it out with a tweezers, as this usually breaks off the body from the head, which can cause infections. Instead, rub on Vaseline, alcohol, or oil to induce it to let go, or press it with a very hot object like a match (the lighted end of a cigarette works well, if you have one). The tick should back out and can then be disposed of. Always check your body for ticks after walking through a tick-infested area. If you get sick in the next couple of weeks, consult a doctor.

Bedbugs & Lice Bedbugs live in various places, but particularly in dirty mattresses and bedding. Spots of blood on bedclothes or on the wall around the bed can be read as a suggestion to find another hotel. Bedbugs leave itchy bites in neat rows. Calamine lotion may help.

All lice cause itching and discomfort. They make themselves at home in your hair (head lice), your clothing (body lice), or in your pubic hair (crabs). You catch lice through direct contact with infected people or by sharing combs, clothing, and the like. Powder or shampoo treatment will kill the lice, and infected clothing should then be washed in hot water.

Women's Health

Gynecological Problems Poor diet, lowered resistance due to the use of antibiotics for stomach upsets, and even contraceptive pills can lead to vaginal infections when traveling in hot climates. Wearing skirts or loose-fitting trousers and cotton underwear help prevent infections.

Yeast infections, characterized by a rash, itching, and discharge, can be treated with a vinegar or even lemon-juice douche or with yogurt. Nystatin suppositories are the usual medical prescription. Trichomonas is a more serious infection; symptoms are a discharge and a burning sensation when urinating. Male sexual partners must also be treated, and if a vinegar-water douche is not effective, seek medical attention. Flagyl is the prescribed drug.

Pregnancy Most miscarriages occur during the first three months of pregnancy, so this is the most risky time to travel. The last three months should also be spent within reasonable distance of good medical care, as quite serious problems can develop at this time. Pregnant women should avoid all unnecessary medication, but vaccinations and malarial prophylactics should still be taken where possible. Additional care should be taken to prevent illness, and particular attention should be paid to diet and nutrition. Abortion is illegal in Argentina.

WOMEN TRAVELERS
Attitudes toward Women
In Argentina, International Women's Day becomes yet another occasion to "send her flowers," but for women traveling alone, the country is probably safer than Europe, the USA, and most other Latin American countries – although you should not be complacent. Buenos Aires is more notorious than the provinces for annoyances like unwelcome physical contact, particularly on crowded buses or trains. If you're physically confident, a slap or a well-aimed elbow should discourage any further contact. If not, a scream is also very effective.

Other nuisances include crude language and *piropos*. Crude language, generally in the presence of other males, usually emphasizes feminine physical attributes. If you respond aggressively ("Are you talking to me?"), you will probably put your aggressor to shame. One clever New Yorker found that a bogus wedding ring

worked wonders in deterring unwanted admirers.

There is no good definition of the piropo, but most Argentine males would consider it the masculine art of approaching a woman in public and commenting on her femininity or attractiveness. This is an idealized definition because piropos are most often vulgar, even though some are creative and even eloquent (one cited in the *Buenos Aires Herald* was, "Oh God, the sky is parting and angels are falling"). While irritating, such verbal aggression rarely becomes physical. On occasions when persistent suitors trail you for blocks, the best means of discouraging their pursuit is to completely ignore them.

Precautions
Single women checking in at low-budget hotels, both in Buenos Aires and the provinces, may find themselves objects of suspicion, since prostitutes often frequent such places. In the provinces, women traveling alone are objects of curiosity, since Argentine women generally do not do so. You should interpret questions as to whether you are running away from parents or a husband as expressions of concern.

If you hitchhike, always exercise judgment and avoid getting into a vehicle with more than one man: Argentine males rarely find it necessary to demonstrate their machismo except in the company of women males.

GAY & LESBIAN TRAVELERS
While Argentina is a strongly Catholic country, and homosexuality is taboo to many (former military dictator Juan Carlos Onganía recently caused a furor by stating he would not have a homosexual friend), there are enclaves of tolerance in Buenos Aires (particularly Av Santa Fe and Recoleta), the Paraná Delta, and some other areas. Argentine males in general are much more physically demonstrative than their counterparts in North America and Europe, so certain behaviors like kissing (at least on the cheek, in greeting) or a vigorous embrace may seem innocuous even to some

who object to homosexuals. Lesbians walking hand-in-hand will attract relatively little attention, since Argentine women frequently do so, but this would be very conspicuous behavior for males. When in doubt, it's better to be discreet.

DISABLED TRAVELERS

Travelers with disabilities will find Argentina difficult at times; the wheelchair-bound in particular will find Buenos Aires' narrow sidewalks, which are frequently in disrepair, difficult to negotiate; crossing streets is also a problem, since Argentine drivers are a challenge to even the most agile and physically fit adults. Nevertheless, Argentines with disabilities get around – one of the most famous works of contemporary Argentine fiction is Ernesto Sábato's *On Heroes and Tombs*, which includes an extraordinary "Report on the Blind" that is based, in part, on the author's observations in Buenos Aires (Sábato, however, is not himself blind).

SENIOR TRAVELERS

Senior travelers should encounter no particular difficulties traveling in Argentina where older citizens traditionally enjoy a great deal of respect; on crowded buses, for instance, most Argentines will readily offer their seat to an older person. Senior discounts on transportation and most other services are, however, virtually a thing of the past.

TRAVELING WITH CHILDREN

Argentina is extremely child-friendly in terms of safety, health, people's attitudes, and family-oriented activities, although there are regional differences. When we did research for the first edition of this book, we took our 2½-year-old daughter Clío on the road with us part of the time; we also returned there for an entire year when she was four and bilingual.

We thought that since Clío was a good walker, we did not need a stroller; in retrospect that was a serious mistake. If we had had our folding stroller, she would have been able to rest or take naps in it instead of

in our arms or on our shoulders. Furthermore, in museums it would have been a good way of keeping track of her. Argentina is not a place where children risk getting kidnapped, but there is always the chance of them getting lost in crowds.

Even if a child does get lost, someone will usually try to help. One afternoon Clío left our apartment in downtown Buenos Aires, went down the stairs, and walked out the door into the street. The minute she stepped out, the heavy iron-and-glass door closed behind her. When I realized she was gone, I rushed downstairs and saw her crying outside, where a formally dressed young man was gently calming her down and asking her if she remembered her apartment number.

People are also very helpful on public transport; often someone will give up a seat for a parent and child, but if that does not occur, an older person may offer to put the child on his or her lap. Sometimes this happens so spontaneously that you find someone pulling a child out of your arms. Remember, this is a country where people frequently touch each other (to get someone's attention you may touch him or her on the arm and say "*Disculpe...*"), so your children will be patted on the head and caressed quite a bit.

In terms of food and health, there are no major concerns in most parts of Buenos Aires, but we usually drank bottled water. In general, this had to do more with the horrible taste of chemicals and chlorine in the tap water than with health risks. Most restaurants provide a wide selection of food suitable for children (vegetables, pasta, meat, chicken, fish); however, we rarely ordered a separate dish for Clío because Argentine portions are abundant, and we always shared. Waiters have no problem bringing an extra dish and cutlery, although in some places there may be an additional charge. The real treat for all of us, particularly in the warm months, was Argentina's superb ice cream, which comes in a tremendous variety of both fruit-juice-based and creamy flavors. Clío also loved to eat the local croissants for breakfast; they are small and come in sweet and unsweetened varieties.

Our main concern was bathrooms. In general, public toilets are often poorly kept, so we avoided them as much as possible. On the occasions when Clío could not wait, her mother held her so she would not touch the toilet. Always carry toilet paper with you, since it is nonexistent in public lavatories. Moreover, while a woman may take a young boy into the ladies' room, it would be socially unacceptable for a man to take a girl into a men's room.

Unless you are traveling by plane, remember that distances are long, and trips seem never-ending. We were lucky enough to have a truck with a camper shell open to the cab. At all times we had a bed and Clío's special blanket ready for her, so when she tired of playing games or singing with us, she rested or slept comfortably. Similarly, we would prepare a bed for her in buses and trains.

In Argentina breast-feeding in public is very much related to ethnicity; in the more indigenous areas, women breast-feed their babies in the markets, but I don't recall ever seeing a mother breast-feeding in public in Buenos Aires. However, there is always the possibility of going to a cafe and covering yourself with a baby blanket. The drawback in this case, of course, would be the inevitable cigarette smoke.

Clío loved Buenos Aires, the size and fast pace of which fascinated her; the Obelisco, a downtown landmark, gave her a reassuring sense of familiarity. We encouraged her to identify it from a bus or taxi, or in our walks, and make her guess if someone was looking from the tiny window at the top.

Buenos Aires offers a good selection of children's cultural activities, including theater, movies, and music events, which are listed in a special newspaper column. Most of these activities take place during the winter school recess (early to mid-July), but they are also very crowded. We tried to balance indoor activities and museum visits, which were tiring for all of us, by spending time at open spaces like the

Plaza Francia near Recoleta, where she could use the playground, or the Plaza de Mayo, where she could chase pigeons. Some campgrounds also have secure playgrounds where children can play and make instant friendships, transcending language or cultural barriers.

If in Buenos Aires children are liked, in the interior they are treated like royalty. One of the hardest rules for Clío was to be polite and accept candy from passersby with a *gracias* but not eat it. Elderly people, men in particular, often carry candy and give it to passing children; their intentions are good, but we always made her put it in the nearest garbage can. Visiting a family is even more problematic; in most cases children will be offered candy, sodas, or sweets. When we felt she had had too much, we solved the problem by telling white lies such as, "She has a problem with sugar so the doctor recommends keeping it to a minimum."

In parts of northern Argentina cholera is a problem, and although government rhetoric often tries to minimize it, we liked to play it safe by not eating uncooked vegetables or unpeeled fruits and using mineral water even to brush our teeth. Regional foods, such as *empanadas*, tend to be spicier than in the central or southern parts of the country, so in those places Clío ate much more pasta and grilled meats. Hotel employees never denied us boiling water, and budget hotels often allowed us to use their kitchen to make pasta or soups.

Unlike Buenos Aires, where life moves really fast, the provincial cities enjoy a calmer, healthier pace; the usually lively town centers are virtually abandoned during afternoon siesta. Even in later trips, when Clío was five-years-old, we found this rhythm more suited to her needs.

USEFUL ORGANIZATIONS

ASATEJ (☎ 311-6953, fax 311-6840), Argentina's nonprofit student travel agency and an affiliate of STA Travel, is on the 3rd floor, Florida 835, 1005 Buenos Aires. The agency is eager to encourage low-budget

ARGENTINA

travelers, and you need not be a student to take advantage of their services.

There is a small network of about 30 youth hostels throughout the country for which a youth hostel card is desirable, though not always imperative. It's better to obtain membership overseas since it's generally cheaper – the initial year's membership in Argentina costs anywhere from US$48 to US$60, depending on the age of the member, though renewal is half-price. Contact the Asociación Argentina de Albergues de la Juventud (☎/fax 476-1001), 2nd floor, Oficina 6, Talcahuano 214, 1013 Buenos Aires. This office also serves as a travel agency, issues international student cards, and has a message board for travelers (mostly young Argentines) seeking companions for extended trips.

The Administración de Parques Nacionales (☎ 311-0303, ext 165), at Santa Fe 690 in Buenos Aires, provides information on national parks, but it is ill-prepared to deal with queries on any but the most popular and accessible ones, like Iguazú and Nahuel Huapi. It stocks a small number of publications of interest to conservationists and wildlife enthusiasts. Visitors specifically interested in fly-fishing should contact the Asociación Argentina de Pesca de Mosca (☎ 773-0821) at Lerma 452, 1414 Buenos Aires.

Another address of interest to conservationists is the wildlife organization Fundación Vida Silvestre Argentina (☎ 331-4864), Defensa 245, Buenos Aires 1065 (in the San Telmo barrio). Membership starts at US$35 per year and includes the group's newsletter *Otioso*; memberships at US$60 per annum also includes its magazine *Revista Vida Silvestre*. Hours are 9:30 am to 6 pm weekdays.

Birding enthusiasts might contact the Asociación Ornitológica del Plata (☎ 312-8958) at 25 de Mayo 749, 2nd floor in Buenos Aires. The Argentine affiliate of Greenpeace (☎ 962-2291) is at Mansilla 3046 in Buenos Aires, a few blocks from the Agüero station on Línea D of the Subte (underground).

Buenos Aires has two AIDS-related support organizations. Cooperación, Información y Ayuda al Enfermo de SIDA (COINSIDA, ☎ 383-2788) is an information and assistance center for those with AIDS or HIV; it's at Talcahuano 309, 5th floor, Departamento 10. Línea SIDA (☎ 922-1617) is at Zuviría 64.

DANGERS & ANNOYANCES

Although street crime appears to be increasing in Argentina, personal security is a minor problem compared to most other South American countries or to cities like New York or Washington, DC. Violent crime is rare in Buenos Aires, and both men and women can travel in most parts of the city at any time of day or night without excessive apprehension. Take precautions against petty theft, such as purse snatching, especially on slow-moving trains, where thieves may grab your bag, run through the aisle, and jump off while the train is still in motion. Temperley Station, in the southern suburbs of Buenos Aires, has a particularly bad reputation.

US residents concerned with domestic travel conditions in Argentina or any other country can obtain recorded travel information from the US Department of State Bureau of Consular Affairs by calling ☎ 202-647-5225.

Police & Military

The police and military may be of more concern than common criminals. Both military and police officials have been found responsible for extrajudicial killings of prisoners and conscripts, for which some officials have gone to prison, but foreign visitors are more likely to experience petty harassment. For motorists, so-called safety campaigns often result in citations for very minor equipment violations, which carry very high fines – up to US$200 for an inadequate emergency brake. In most cases, corrupt officers will settle for less expensive *coimas* (bribes), but this requires considerable caution and tact on your part. A discreet hint that you intend to phone your consulate may limit or eliminate such

ARGENTINA

problems – often the police count on foreigners' ignorance of Argentine law. For further information, see the Getting Around chapter.

The military retains considerable influence even under civilian government. Avoid approaching military installations, which often display the warning, "No stopping or photographs – the sentry will shoot." In the event of a military coup or other emergency, state-of-siege regulations suspend all civil rights; carry identification at all times, and make sure someone knows your whereabouts. Contact your embassy or consulate for advice.

Fireworks
A recent cause for concern is the widespread availability of fireworks, which are high-powered, poorly regulated, and very dangerous. Especially around holidays like Christmas and New Year's, thoughtless fireworks enthusiasts set off firecrackers in the streets and even toss them from highrise apartments (when these go off between tall buildings, the echo chamber effect mimics the bombing of Hanoi). It may be better to refrain from walking the streets of Buenos Aires at these times.

Terrorism
The state terrorism of the 1970s and 1980s has subsided, but deadly attempts on Jewish/Israeli centers in Buenos Aires have raised questions as to the government's commitment to public safety. In the months prior to the bombings, anti-Semitic incidents were increasingly common.

Smoking
Many Argentines are heavy smokers – women as well as men – even though most will acknowledge the habit is unhealthy. If lung cancer is not the leading cause of death, it's only because so many Argentines perish in traffic accidents first. In what might be the ultimate example of "unclear on the concept," I once saw a porteño jogger with a lit *pucho* in his mouth.

Long distance and local buses, the Buenos Aires subway, and some other areas are legally smoke-free, even if enforcement is lax – moviegoers seem to think that the credits at the end of a film include orders to light up. Thanks to recent municipal legislation, many restaurants and confiterías in Buenos Aires have set aside smoke-free areas. Travelers bothered by second-hand smoke in an inappropriate setting, such as a taxi, will find it more productive to appeal to common courtesy by pleading *alergia* (allergy) than by becoming indignant.

BUSINESS HOURS & PUBLIC HOLIDAYS
Traditionally, business hours in Argentina commence by 8 am and break at midday for three or even four hours, during which people return home for lunch and a brief siesta. After the siesta, shops reopen until 8 or 9 pm. This schedule is still common in the provinces, but government offices and many businesses in Buenos Aires have adopted a more conventional 8 am to 5 pm schedule in the interests of "greater

efficiency" and, especially in the case of government, reduced corruption.

There are numerous national holidays on which government offices and businesses are closed. The following list does not include provincial holidays, which may vary considerably.

January 1
    Año Nuevo (New Year's Day)
March/April (dates vary)
    Viernes Santo/Pascua (Good Friday/Easter)
May 1
    Día del Trabajador (Labor Day)
May 25
    Revolución de Mayo (May Revolution of 1810)
June 10
    Día de las Malvinas (Malvinas Day, commemorating the establishment of the "Comandancia Política y Militar de las Malvinas" in 1829)
June 20
    Día de la Bandera (Flag Day)
July 9
    Día de la Independencia (Independence Day)
August 17
    Día de San Martín (Anniversary of San Martín's death)
October 12
    Día de la Raza (Columbus Day)
December 25
    Navidad (Christmas Day)

ACTIVITIES

Argentines are very fond of a variety of sports, both as participants and spectators, but soccer *(fútbol)* is the most widespread. In *villas miserias* (shantytowns), children will clear a vacant lot, mark the goal with stones, and make a ball of old rags and socks to pursue their pastime, but even in exclusive country clubs the sport is popular. Argentine professional soccer is world-class, although many of the best athletes play in Europe because salaries there are much higher. In 1978 and 1986, Argentina won the World Cup.

Other popular sports include tennis, basketball, auto racing, cycling, rugby, field hockey, and polo. Some of these, especially rugby and polo, are confined to elite sectors. Skiing, although expensive, is gaining

popularity, as are other outdoor recreational activities such as canoeing, climbing, kayaking, trekking, windsurfing, and hang gliding. Recently, paddle ball (a sort of hybrid between tennis and handball) has gained major popularity, with courts springing up around the country.

For the more sedate pastime of learning Spanish, there are many schools in Buenos Aires (see the Buenos Aires chapter for details).

Skiing

Although surprisingly little known to outsiders, some outstanding skiing is offered in Argentina. Most locations offer superb powder, good cover, and plenty of sunny days, but prices are not cheap. Many fields are near large towns, so you don't even need to stay on the mountain but can stay cheaply nearby. Many resorts have large ski schools with instructors from all over the world, so even language is not a problem. At some of the older resorts equipment can be a little antiquated, but in general the quality of skiing more than compensates.

There are three main areas in which skiers can indulge themselves: the southern Cuyo region, featuring Las Leñas and Los Molles near Malargüe; the lakes district, including the Cerro Catedral complex near Bariloche and Chapelco near San Martín de los Andes; La Hoya area near Esquel; and the world's most southerly commercial skiing near Ushuaia in Tierra del Fuego.

For more details, refer to the relevant geographical entries in this book. Ski tours can be booked through travel agents, especially adventure tour specialists; see the Getting There & Away chapter for details.

Trekking

Argentina's vast open spaces offer plenty of wilderness walks for foreigners and Argentines alike. The most popular areas are the southern Andean national parks along the Chilean border, from Lanín south to Los Glaciares, and Tierra del Fuego, though the high Andean reaches around Aconcagua, west of Mendoza, are increasingly popular. The northern Andes around the Valle de Humahuaca are also good, but plenty of Argentines enjoy the gentler Sierra de la Ventana in Buenos Aires province and Sierras de Córdoba.

See the LP guide *Trekking in the Patagonian Andes* by Clem Lindenmayer for more information on southern Andean walks.

Mountaineering

Aconcagua, west of Mendoza, is a magnet for climbers, but there are plenty of other high peaks in the Andes – many of them more interesting than South America's highest point, which is a relatively straightforward walkup for experienced mountaineers in good physical condition. The Fitzroy Range in Parque Nacional Los Glaciares, Santa Cruz province, is another popular area, as are the mountains of Parque Nacional Nahuel Huapi, around Bariloche. In the province of Buenos Aires, the Sierra de la Ventana is a good area for technical climbing, but provincial park rangers are astonishingly patronizing toward anyone who wants to do anything other than a simple hike.

White-Water Rafting

This increasingly popular activity takes place on the rivers that descend from the Andean divide, from Mendoza south into Chubut province. The main possibilities are the Río Mendoza and Río Diamante in the Cuyo region, the Río Hua Hum and Río Meliquina near San Martín de los Andes, and the Río Limay and Río Manso near Bariloche. Some of these, most notably the Limay, are relatively gentle Class II floats, but most of the rest are Class III-plus white-water.

Golf

Golf is an increasingly popular avocation with Argentina's leisured class; some clubs and courses are very elitist, but most are open to the public. For a complete list of courses in the country, contact the Asociación Argentina de Golf (☎ 325-7498), Av Corrientes 538, 1043 Buenos Aires.

Polo

The annual Campeonato Argentino Abierto Argentino de Polo (Argentine Open Polo Championship), held in the Buenos Aires barrio of Palermo, celebrated its centenary in 1993. Participation is not exactly for the masses, but most polo events are open to the public free of charge; for current information, contact the Asociación Argentina de Polo (☎ 331-4646), Hipólito Yrigoyen 636 in Buenos Aires, which keeps a list of activities scheduled throughout the country.

Shoppers interested in polo gear can visit La Martina (☎ 478-9366) at Paraguay 661, or La Polera (☎ 806-0586) at Uriburu 1710 in Buenos Aires. La Martina also organizes full-day polo lessons, with afternoon matches, on the outskirts of the capital.

WORK

It is not unusual for visiting travelers to work as English-language instructors in Buenos Aires, but wages are much lower than they would be in the US. Check the classified section of the *Buenos Aires Herald*. Residence and work permits are fairly easy to obtain, but the effort may not be worth it. Travelers can obtain work during the fruit harvests in areas like Río Negro Valley and El Bolsón in Patagonia, but don't expect to do much more than break even.

Ideally, in Argentina and the rest of Latin America, there should be work for someone who can mend the fractured English that so often appears in brochure translations.

ACCOMMODATIONS

The spectrum of accommodations in Argentina ranges from campgrounds to five-star luxury hotels. Where you stay will depend on your budget and standards, your location, and how thorough a search you care to make in an unfamiliar destination, but you should be able to find something reasonable by North American, European or Australian criteria. You may also find yourself invited into Argentine homes and should not hesitate to accept under most conditions. This section details the lodging alternatives.

Note that, in many circumstances, tourist offices are very reluctant to recommend budget accommodations or even to admit that they exist. This is partly because some of the cheapest accommodations can be pretty squalid, but mostly because the staff have the idea that foreigner visitors should stay in *hoteles de categoria*, the best available (and usually very expensive) lodging. Often, with gentle persistence, you can extract information on more economical alternatives.

Hotel checkout times can vary but are often as early as 10 am and rarely any later than noon. While most places are flexible within reason, some will add on an extra day; it's a good idea to verify each hotel's policy and to give advance notice if you need any extra time.

Many establishments offer half or full board for an additional charge above the room rate. Half board means breakfast and lunch or dinner, and full board includes all three meals.

Camping & Refugios

If traveling on a budget, especially coming overland from the central Andean countries, do not dismiss the idea of camping in Argentina – by doing so, you may be able to keep expenses for accommodations at roughly what you would pay for hotels in Bolivia or Peru. Nearly every Argentine city and many smaller towns have municipal (or recently privatized) campgrounds where you can pitch a tent for about US$5 per night – sometimes more, sometimes less, occasionally even free. Most Argentines arrive in their own automobiles, but backpackers are welcome.

These usually woodsy sites have excellent facilities – hot showers, toilets, laundry, a *fogón* (firepit) for cooking, restaurant or *confitería*, a grocery, sometimes even a swimming pool – and are often very central. Personal possessions are generally secure, since attendants keep a watchful eye on the grounds, but don't leave costly items such as cameras lying around unnecessarily.

There are drawbacks, though. Argentines are renowned *trasnochadores* (night people). During summer vacations, it is not unusual for them to celebrate their *asado* (barbecue) until almost daylight, so in extreme cases you may find sleep difficult unless you can isolate yourself on the margins of the campground – often the least desirable parts. On the other hand, you may be invited to join in one of these gregarious groups. Otherwise, avoid the most popular tourist areas in the prime vacation months of January and February.

For comfort, invest in a good, dome-style tent with rainfly before coming to South America, where camping equipment is costlier and often inferior. A three-season sleeping bag should be adequate for almost any weather conditions. A good petrol or kerosene-burning stove is also a good idea, since white gas *(bencina)* is expensive and available only at chemical supply shops or hardware stores. Firewood is a limited and often expensive resource which, in any event, smudges pots and pans. Bring or buy mosquito repellent, since many campsites are near rivers or lakes.

There are, of course, opportunities for more rugged camping in the national parks and their backcountry. Parks have both organized sites resembling those in the cities and towns and more isolated, rustic alternatives. Some parks have *refugios*, basic shelters for hikers in the high country. For details, see the entries under the respective national parks.

Hostels

There are several youth hostels in Buenos Aires and throughout the provinces. The following list outlines where they are; see the entries on the different cities for more information.

Buenos Aires – Mar del Plata, San Bernardo, San Fernando, and Pinamar

Córdoba – Villa General Belgrano, Villa María, Capilla de Monte, and Cura Brochero

Chubut – Puerto Madryn, Comodoro Rivadavia, and El Bolsón

Jujuy – Humahuaca
Mendoza – Guaymallén and Cañon del Atuel
Misiones – Puerto Iguazú, Posadas, and Monte-
carlo
Neuquén – San Martín de los Andes
Río Negro – Bariloche
Salta – Salta and Cafayate
Santa Cruz – Puerto Deseado and El Calafate
Tucumán – the city of Tucumán

Most do not insist on a youth hostel card, but they usually charge a bit more for non-members. Since hostels are generally open in summer only, especially in the provinces, it's a good idea to phone before heading over. Sponsored by UNESCO, the nonprofit Asociación Argentina de Albergues de la Juventud (☎ 476-1001) is on the 2nd floor at Talcahuano 214, Buenos Aires. It's open weekdays 11 am to 7 pm.

Hospedajes, Pensiones & Residenciales

These offer cheap accommodations but the differences between them are sometimes ambiguous; all may even be called hotels. Rooms and furnishings are modest, usually including beds with clean sheets and blankets. Never hesitate to ask to see a room. While some have private bathrooms, more often you will share toilet and shower facilities with other guests.

An *hospedaje* is usually a large family home with a few extra bedrooms (the bath is shared). Often they are not permanent businesses but temporary expedients in times of economic distress. Similarly, a *pensión* offers short-term accommodations in a family home but may also have permanent lodgers. Meals are sometimes available. *Residenciales*, which are permanent businesses, figure more commonly in tourist office lists. In general, they occupy buildings designed for short-stay accommodations, although some (known euphemistically as *albergues transitorios*) cater to clientele who intend only *very* short stays, perhaps two hours or so. Occasionally prostitutes frequent them, but so do young Argentine couples with no other indoor alternative for their passion. It may

not always be obvious whether a place is an albergue transitorio, though some are very candid about their business; except for a little noise, such activities should not deter you, even if you have children.

Hotels

Hotels proper vary from one-star basic accommodations to five-star luxury, but you should not assume a perfect correlation between these classifications and their standards – many one-star places are a better value than three- and four-star lodgings. In general, hotels provide a room with attached private bath, often a telephone, and sometimes *música funcional* (elevator Muzak) or television. Normally they will have a confitería or restaurant and may include breakfast in the price. In the top categories you will have room and laundry service, a swimming pool, a bar, shopping galleries, and other luxuries.

Rentals & Homestays

House and apartment rentals can save you money if you're staying in a place for an extended period. In resort locations, such as Mar del Plata, Bariloche, or Paso de la Patria, you can lodge several people for the price of one by seeking an apartment and cooking your own meals. Check the tourist office or newspapers for listings.

During the tourist season, mostly in the interior, families rent rooms to visitors. Often these are excellent bargains, permitting access to cooking and laundry facilities and hot showers, as well as encouraging contact with Argentines. Tourist offices in most smaller towns, but even in cities as large as Salta or Mendoza, maintain lists of such accommodations.

Estancias

An increasingly popular way of passing an Argentine vacation is to stay at an estancia, both in the area around Buenos Aires and as far as remote Patagonia. Many of the new estancias that are taking guests are barely prepared for an influx of tourists, and may even boot their own children out of bed to accommodate them.

FOOD
The Argentine Diet

Ever since Spanish livestock transformed the Pampas into enormous cattle ranches, the Argentine diet has relied on meat, but there is more ethnic and regional variety to Argentine cuisine than most people expect. Most people will quickly recognize the influence of Italian immigrants in such pasta dishes as spaghetti, lasagna, cannelloni, and ravioli, but should not overlook the tasty *ñoquis* (gnocchi in Italian), an inexpensive staple when the budget runs low at the end of the month. Traditionally, ñoquis are a restaurant special on the 29th of each month, but in times of economic crisis people may joke that "this month we'll have ñoquis on the 15th."

Beef, though, is the focus of the diet; no meal is truly complete without it. In fact, the Spanish word *carne* (meat) is synonymous with beef – lamb, venison, and poultry are all something else. The most popular form is the *parrillada*, a mixed grill of steak and other cuts that no visiting carnivore should miss. A traditional parrillada will include offal such as *chinchulines* (small intestines), *tripa gorda* (large intestine), *ubre* (udder), *riñones* (kidneys), and *morcilla* (blood sausage), but don't let that put you off unless you're a vegetarian.

Since the early 1980s, health food and vegetarian fare have won a niche in the diets of some Argentines, but outside Buenos Aires and a few other large cities vegetarian restaurants are less common. You will find Chinese food in the capital but not often elsewhere; the quality is not outstanding but some offer *tenedor libre* or *diente libre* (all you can eat) for those on a budget. High-cost and high-quality international cuisine is readily available if your budget is unlimited.

Some regions have very distinctive food. The Andean Northwest is notable for spicy dishes, more closely resembling the food of the central Andean highlands than the bland fare of the Pampas. From Mendoza north, it is common to find Middle Eastern food. Argentine seafood, while not so varied as Chilean, deserves attention, even though Argentines are not big fish eaters. In the Patagonian lake district, game dishes like trout, boar, and venison are regional specialties, while river fish in Mesopotamia and Misiones are outstanding. In the extreme south, where wool and mutton are important commodities, lamb often replaces beef in the typical asado.

Places to Eat

There are different kinds of eating places in Argentina. If you're on a very low budget in the northern provinces, you may want to frequent the markets, where meals are often very cheap, but otherwise try the *rotiserías* (delis), which sell dairy products, roast chicken, pies, turnovers, and *fiambres* (processed meats). Such places often have restaurant-quality food for a fraction of the price.

Avoid fast-food clones such as *Pumper Nic*, which are neither as cheap nor even as good as their North American cousins. For fast food, try the bus or train terminal cafeterias or the common *comedor*, which usually has a limited menu, often including simple but filling fixed-price meals. Comedores also often serve *minutas* (short

---

Meatless Meals in Cattle Country

Argentine cuisine is known for red meat, but vegetarians no longer have much trouble making do except, perhaps, in the most out of the way places. Since the 1980s, vegetarian restaurants have become commonplace in Buenos Aires and not unusual elsewhere, and nearly all of them have the additional appeal of being tobacco-free.

Even standard parrillas serve items acceptable to most vegetarians, such as green salads (often large enough for two people) and pasta dishes like raviolis, canelones and ñoquis – but before ordering pasta be certain it doesn't come with a meat sauce. To be served a meatless dish in out of the way places, try pleading allergies and remember that *carne* (meat) is beef – chicken, pork, and the like are something else, since sometimes referred to as *carne blanca* (white meat). Vegans will find far fewer menu options. ∎

orders) such as steak, eggs, *milanesa* (breaded steak), salad, and french fries.

Confiterías serve mostly sandwiches, including *lomito* (steak), *panchos* (hot dogs), and hamburgers. *Restaurantes* are distinguished by much larger menus – including pasta dishes, parrillada, and fish – professional waiters, and often more elaborate decor. There is, though, a great difference between the most humble and the most extravagant.

Meals in Argentine restaurants are generally relaxed affairs. Breakfasts are negligible, but other meals can last for hours. Lunch starts around midday, but dinner starts later, much later, than in English-speaking countries. Almost nobody eats before 9 pm, and it is not unusual to dine after midnight even on weeknights.

An important part of the meal, whether at home or in the restaurant, is the *sobremesa*, dallying at the table to discuss family matters or other events of the day. No matter how long the lines outside, no Argentine restaurateur would even dream of nudging along a party that has lingered over coffee long after the food itself is history.

Snacks

One of the world's finest snacks is the empanada, a tasty turnover filled with vegetables, hard-boiled egg, olive, beef, chicken, ham and cheese, or other fillings. These are cheap and available almost everywhere – buy them by the dozen in a rotisería before a long bus or train trip. Empanadas *al horno* (baked) are lighter than empanadas *fritas* (fried). Travelers coming from Chile will find Argentine empanadas very different.

Pizza, a common snack in markets and restaurants, is one of the cheapest things on the menu when purchased by the slice. In many pizzerías, it is cheaper to eat standing at the counter than to take a seat. Toppings are standardized – not customized as in North America – but there are more options when buying an entire pizza rather than slices. For slices, try *fugazza*, a delicious cheeseless variety with sweet onions which is very cheap, or *fugazzeta*, which adds

cheese. Mozzarella is the most popular cheese. Many Argentines eat their pizza with *fainá*, a dense chickpea (garbanzo) dough baked and sliced to match.

For Argentines at home or on the road, a common afternoon snack is *mate con facturas*, mate with sweet pastries. If you go to visit an Argentine family in the afternoon, stop by the bakery to bring some along.

Breakfast

Argentines eat little or no breakfast. The most common breakfast items are coffee, tea, or *yerba mate* with *tostadas* (toast), *manteca* (butter), and *mermelada* (jam). In cafes, *medialunas* (small croissants), either sweet or *saladas* (plain), accompany your *café con leche* (coffee with milk). A mid-morning breakfast may consist of coffee plus a *tostado*, a thin-crust toasted sandwich with ham and cheese, and a glass of fresh-squeezed orange juice.

Main Dishes

Argentines compensate for skimpy breakfasts with enormous lunches, usually begun about noon or 1 pm, and dinners, never earlier than 9 pm and often much later. Beef, in a variety of cuts and styles of preparation, is the most common main course.

An asado or parrillada is the standard, ideally prepared over charcoal or a wood fire and accompanied by *chimichurri*, a tasty marinade. French fries or salad will usually accompany it. Serious carnivores should not miss *bife de chorizo*, a thick, tender, juicy steak. *Bife de lomo* is short loin, *bife de costilla* or *chuleta* is T-bone steak, while *asado de tira* is a narrow strip of roast rib. *Vacío* is sirloin. *Matambre relleno* is stuffed and rolled flank steak, baked or eaten cold as an appetizer. Thinly sliced, it makes excellent sandwiches and is usually available at rotiserías.

Most Argentines prefer their beef *cocido* (well done), but on request restaurants will serve it *jugoso* (rare) or *a punto* (medium). *Bife a caballo* comes with two eggs and french fries.

Carbonada is a beef stew with rice, potatoes, sweet potatoes, maize, squash, chopped apples, and peaches. *Puchero* is a slow-cooking casserole with beef, chicken, bacon, sausage, blood sausage, maize, peppers, tomatoes, onions, cabbage, sweet potatoes, and squash; the cook may also add garbanzos or other beans. It is accompanied by rice cooked in the broth. *Milanesa*, a breaded steak usually fried but sometimes baked, is one of the cheapest and commonest short-order items on the menu. More elaborate versions are available – *milanesa napolitana* with tomato sauce and mozzarella, and *milanesa maryland*, made with chicken and accompanied by fried bananas and creamed corn.

Chicken dishes are good. *Pollo* sometimes accompanies the standard parrillada, but also comes separately with french fries or salad. The most common fish is *merluza* (hake), usually fried in batter and served with mashed potatoes. Spanish restaurants are good for well-prepared seafood.

Desserts

Fresh fruit is the most common *postre* in Argentine homes, where uncouth Americans and Australians will find that cultured Argentines peel oranges and all other fruit (except grapes) carefully with a knife. In restaurants, *ensalada de fruta* (fruit salad), *flan* (egg custard), or *queso y dulce* (cheese with preserved fruit, sometimes known as *postre vigilante)* are frequent choices. The "dulce" can consist of *batata* (sweet potato) or *membrillo* (quince). Flan will be topped with *crema* (whipped cream) or *dulce de leche*, a sweet caramelized milk which is an Argentine specialty. *Almendrado*, vanilla ice cream rolled in almonds, is also common.

Argentine *helado* (ice cream) deserves special mention. Coming from the Italian tradition, it is the continent's best and comparable to the best anywhere in the world. Chains like *Massera*, located throughout the country, are not bad, but you will find the best Argentine ice cream at smaller *heladerías* that make their own in small batches on the premises or nearby – look for the words *elaboración propia* or *elaboración artesanal*. Often such places have many dozens of flavors, from variations on

---

Mate

No other trait captures the essence of *argentinidad* (argentinity) as well as the preparation and consumption of *mate* (pronounced "mah-tay"), perhaps the only cultural practice that transcends barriers of ethnicity, class, and occupation. More than a simple drink like tea or coffee, *mate* is an elaborate ritual, shared among family, friends, and coworkers. In many ways, sharing is the point of *mate*.

Yerba mate is the dried, chopped leaf of *Ilex paraguayensis*, a relative of the common holly. Also known as "Paraguayan tea," it became commercially important in the colonial era on the plantations of the Jesuit missions of the upper Río Paraná. Europeans quickly took to the beverage, crediting it with many admirable qualities. The Austrian Jesuit Martin Dobrizhoffer wrote that *mate* "provokes a gentle perspiration, improves the appetite, speedily counteracts the languor arising from the burning climate, and assuages both hunger and thirst."

Unlike many American foods and beverages, though, mate failed to make the trip back to Europe. After the Jesuits' expulsion in 1767, production declined, but since the early 20th century it has increased dramatically.

Argentina is the world's largest producer and consumer of yerba mate. Argentines consume an average of five kg per person per year, more than four times their average intake of coffee, although Uruguayans consume twice as much per capita as Argentines. It is also popular in parts of Chile, in southern Brazil, and in Paraguay.

Preparing mate is a ritual in itself. In the past, upper-class families even maintained a slave or servant for the sole purpose of preparing and serving it. Nowadays, one person takes responsibility for filling the mate (gourd) almost to the top with yerba, heating but not boiling the water in a *pava* (kettle), and pouring it into the vessel. People sip the liquid from a *bombilla*, a silver straw with a bulbous filter at its lower end which prevents the leaves from entering the tube.

Gourds can range from simple calabashes to carved wooden vessels to the ornate silver

conventional vanilla and chocolate to common and exotic fruits and unexpected mixtures. During winter, when Argentines rarely eat ice cream, the best places offering these homemade specialties often close.

DRINKS

Everything from marriage proposals to business transactions to revolutions may start in cafes, where many Argentines spend hours on end over a single cup of coffee. Cafes also serve beer, wine, and hard liquor.

Bars are where people go to drink alcohol. In large cities, gentrified bars may be called pubs (pronounced as in English). In small towns, bars are a male domain, and the few women who frequent them are likely to be prostitutes.

The most famous and distinct Argentine drink is *mate*, a cultural bellwether. There are few drinking restrictions of any kind, although legally you must be 18 years old to drink alcohol in public.

Soda

Argentines drink prodigious amounts of soft drinks, from the ubiquitous Coca-Cola to 7UP to the local tonic water, Paso de los Toros, which is probably your best choice. Mineral water, both carbonated *(con gas)* and plain *(sin gas)*, is widely available, but tap water is potable almost everywhere. If there is no carbonated mineral water, ask for *soda*, which in small-town cafes and restaurants comes in large siphon bottles. Soda is usually the cheapest thirst quencher.

Juice

Jugos are not so varied as in tropical South America. For fresh-squeezed orange juice, ask for *jugo de naranja exprimido* – otherwise you may get tinned juice (oranges are very cheap in Argentina but, when turned into fresh juice, their value miraculously increases tenfold). *Pomelo* (grapefruit), *limón* (lemon), and *ananá* (pineapple) are also common. *Jugo de manzana* (apple juice) is a specialty of the Río Negro region of Patagonia, but it's available everywhere.

ARGENTINA

museum pieces of the 19th century. Bombillas also differ considerably, ranging in materials from inexpensive aluminum to silver and gold with intricate markings, and in design from long straight tubes to short, curved ones.

There is an informal etiquette for drinking *mate*. The *cebador* (server) pours water slowly near the straw to produce a froth as he or she fills the gourd. The gourd then passes clockwise and this order, once established, continues. A good cebador will keep the *mate* going without changing the yerba for some time. Each participant drinks the gourd dry each time. A simple *gracias* will tell the server to pass you by.

There are marked regional differences in drinking *mate*. From the Pampas southwards, Argentines take it *amargo* (without sugar), while to the north they drink it *dulce* (sweet) with sugar and *yuyos* (aromatic herbs). Purists, who argue that sugar ruins the gourd, will keep separate gourds rather than alternate the two usages. In the withering summer heat, Paraguayans drink *mate* ice-cold in the form of *tereré*.

An invitation to drink mate is a sign of acceptance and should not be refused, even though *mate* is an acquired taste and foreign novices may find it bitter and very hot at first. On the second or third round, both the heat and bitterness will diminish. It is poor etiquette to hold the mate too long before passing it on, but it probably will not affect either your health or finances despite Dobrizhoffer's warning:

" . . . by the immoderate and almost hourly use of this potation, the stomach is weakened, and continual flatulence, with other diseases, brought on. I have known many of the lower Spaniards who never spoke ten words without applying their lips to the gourd containing the ready-made tea. If many topers in Europe waste their substance by an immoderate use of wine and other intoxicating liquors, there are no fewer in America who drink away their fortunes in potations of the herb of Paraguay." ■

Licuados are milk-blended fruit drinks, but on request can be made with water. Common flavors are banana, *durazno* (peach), and *pera* (pear).

Coffee, Tea & Chocolate

Serious coffee drinkers will be delighted to find that even in the smallest town, your coffee will be an espresso (accompanied by enough packets of sugar to fuel a Brazilian Volkswagen). *Café chico* is a thick, dark coffee served in a very small cup. *Cortado* is a small coffee with a touch of milk, usually served in a glass – for a larger portion ask for *cortado doble*. *Café con leche* (a latte) is similar but contains more milk, and is served for breakfast – don't make the mistake of ordering it after lunch or dinner in a restaurant, when you should request a cortado.

Tea, produced domestically in the provinces of Corrientes and Misiones, is also a common drink. Usually it comes with lemon slices, but if you drink it with milk, do not order *té con leche*, a tea bag immersed in warm milk. Rather, ask the waiter for *un poquito de leche*.

Argentine hot chocolate can be delicious. For breakfast, try a *submarino*, a semisweet chocolate bar dissolved in a glass of steamed milk. Prices vary greatly. Even *chocolate*, which is made with powdered cocoa, can be surprisingly good, especially in Bariloche.

Alcoholic Drinks

Beer, wine, whiskey, and gin should satisfy most visitors' alcoholic thirst, but don't refrain from *ginebra bols* (which differs from gin) and *caña* (cane alcohol), which are national specialties.

Quilmes, brewed in the Buenos Aires suburb but available everywhere, is an excellent beer. Bieckert is another popular brand. In bars or cafes, ask for the excellent *chopp* (draft or lager).

Argentine wines get less publicity abroad than Chilean ones, but reds *(tintos)* and whites *(blancos)* are both excellent and inexpensive (when prices on almost everything else skyrocket, wines miraculously remain reasonable, and a bottle of good wine may be cheaper than a liter of Coca-Cola). Especially at home, where jug wines are present at almost all meals, Argentines often mix their wine with soda water.

Wineries in the major growing areas, near Mendoza, San Juan, La Rioja, and Salta, offer tours and tastings. Among the best known brands are Orfila, Suter, San Felipe, Santa Ana, and Etchart. Try to avoid cheap, boxed wines such as Termidor.

ENTERTAINMENT

Dance Clubs

Argentines are fond of music and dancing. Dance clubs both in Buenos Aires and the provinces open late and close even later – nobody would go before midnight and things don't really jump before 2 am. After sunrise, when the clubs close, partygoers head to a confitería or home for breakfast before collapsing in their beds. This is nearly as common on weekdays as on weekends. Recorded rather than live music is the norm.

Nightclubs

Except in Buenos Aires, where there are good tango, rock and jazz clubs, nightclubs tend to be disreputable places. Places listed in the *Buenos Aires Herald* as nightclubs are usually the more respectable ones; but in a Spanish context, the word 'nightclub' tends to imply a fairly seedy place with bar girls who are thinly disguised prostitutes.

Theaters

Both in Buenos Aires and the provinces, live theater is well attended and high quality, from the classics and serious drama to burlesque. Av Corrientes is Buenos Aires' Broadway or West End, but even in places like Villa Regina, a small town in Río Negro province, there are several active theater groups and venues for performances.

There are two main types of theater, one a well-supported official theater and the other a more underground type that improvises and operates on a shoestring budget, often performing in public places like parks and plazas, or even in rented houses. Despite their limited budgets, these can be surprisingly professional.

Cinemas

Traditionally, Argentines jam the cinemas, although outside Buenos Aires the video revolution has brought about the closure of many theaters that once counted on being the only show in town. Still, in the capital and larger cities, major theaters offer the latest films from Europe, the US, and Latin America. Repertory houses, cultural centers, and universities provide a chance to see classics or less commercial films you may have missed.

In Buenos Aires, the main cinema districts are along Lavalle, Av Corrientes, and Av Santa Fe, and the inner suburb of Belgrano. Prices have risen in recent years and now match those in North America or Europe, but most cinemas offer substantial discounts midweek. On weekends, there are *transnoches* (late-night showings) after midnight.

SPECTATOR SPORTS

By far the most popular spectator sport is *fútbol* (soccer); the British origins are apparent from the names of many of the best teams like Boca Juniors, River Plate, Newell's Old Boys, and others. Argentina has twice won the World Cup, at home in 1978 and again on the road in 1986.

Unfortunately, as in Britain, Argentine soccer has become prone to violence between partisans of opposing teams, even resulting in so-called accidental deaths. These *barras bravas* are a serious deterrent to many middle-class spectators who otherwise enjoy the sport.

For an account of the sport's development and history in the Southern Cone, see British sociologist Tony Mason's brief and rather misleadingly titled *Soccer in South America*, which deals almost exclusively with Argentina, Uruguay, and Brazil.

Ticket prices for first division teams start at around US$10 for *popular* (standing room), but *platea* (fixed seating) runs about US$20 to US$40 or more, depending on the location of the seat and the importance of the match. The regular season starts in August or September and ends with championships in July, though it breaks in January for the Copa de Verano, a friendly tournament. For more information, contact the Asociación del Fútbol Argentino (☎ 371-4276) at Viamonte 1366, Buenos Aires.

Other popular spectator sports include automobile racing, horse racing, polo, boxing, tennis, and, increasingly, basketball. Many North American athletes unable to play professional basketball in the US or Europe have come to Argentina, improving the quality of play. In 1995, the Argentine national team defeated the US team for the gold medal in the Pan American Games in Mar del Plata.

THINGS TO BUY

As Argentine food is famous for beef, so Argentine clothing is famous for leather. In Buenos Aires, many downtown shops cater to the tourist trade in leather jackets, handbags, and shoes. Quality and prices can vary greatly, so shop around before buying. Shopkeepers are aggressive but sometimes open to bargaining.

Argentines are very fashion-conscious, with the latest styles displayed along Florida and Santa Fe in Buenos Aires and on main shopping streets in cities throughout the country. Bariloche is especially well known for woolen goods. The best prices are available just before seasonal changes, as shops try to liquidate their inventory. Jewelry is another quality Argentine product, made frequently with 18-carat gold.

Mate paraphernalia make good souvenirs. Gourds and bombillas range from simple and inexpensive aluminum, often sold in street kiosks, to elaborate and expensive gold and silver from jewelry stores or specialty shops. In the province of Salta, the distinctive *ponchos de Güemes* are a memorable choice.

In artisans' *ferias*, found throughout the country, the variety of handicrafts is

The Menem Trucho

For two decades of economic chaos and inflation, Argentines have been coping with changing currencies, from the peso ley to the peso argentino to the austral to the current peso. At times, walletfuls of million-peso notes have barely bought a cup of coffee, while balancing bank accounts has consistently challenged the capacities of handheld calculators. Consumers would barely learn to deal with a deluge of zeros before they were slashed in the latest monetary reform.

No one, however, was quite prepared for the crisp new notes that appeared at the end of 1991 bearing a portrait of President Carlos Menem and the text "Un Valor Que Estabilizó El País" – "A Courage That Stabilized the Country." On the reverse side appeared an etching of the Casa Rosada, the presidential palace, and the imprint of the "Partido Justicialista Nacional," Menem's own Peronist party.

After the initial success of Economy Minister Domingo Cavallo's convertibility plan, the administration was justifiably proud of Argentina's almost unprecedented single-digit inflation. So proud was Menem's personal friend Armando Gostanian, a wealthy clothes manufacturer and director of the Casa de Moneda (National Mint), that he arranged the printing of thousands of these superficially credible bank notes on embossed official paper in honor of the president.

To the administration's opponents, however, these "Menem truchos" (bogus Menems) became yet another symbol of corruption, arrogance, and impunity. Although Gostanian's partisan indiscretion apparently cost the state no money, it fell into a gray area under a counterfeiting law that prohibits the production of anything resembling official currency. Four years later, Gostanian remains head of the Casa de Moneda and the "Menem trucho" has become a minor collector's item. ∎

extensive. There are good places in Buenos Aires (San Telmo's Plaza Dorrego, Recoleta's Plaza Francia, and Belgrano's Plaza General Belgrano), Mendoza, Bariloche, and El Bolsón. In the summer, the Atlantic coast has many others.

Argentines are well read and interested in both national and world literature, and Buenos Aires has a superb selection of general and special interest bookshops. Since the end of the military dictatorship, the capital has re-established itself as a publishing center; in April, the Fería Internacional del Libro (book fair) is South America's largest, with over 600 exhibitors and more than a million visitors.

Foreign and foreign-language books tend to be very expensive, but there's a good selection (including this and other Lonely Planet guides) at Buenos Aires' better bookstores and, occasionally, those in the interior.

Refunds of IVA (VAT)

Under limited circumstances, foreign visitors may obtain IVA refunds on purchases of Argentine products upon their departure from the country. A "Tax Free" (in English) window decal identifies participants in this program, but always verify their status before making your purchase.

To obtain a refund of this 21% tax, present your passport and tourist card to the merchant for purchases of US$200 or more; the merchant must enter the amount of the refund on the reverse of the invoice and paste an equivalent quantity of stamps on the form, the triplicate of which you will also receive. On leaving the country, you must have your purchase separate from the rest of your baggage for inspection; a customs official will check it and seal the invoice.

With this invoice, branches of Banco de la Nación at Buenos Aires' Aeropuerto Internacional Ezeiza, Aeroparque Jorge Newbery (for flights to some neighboring countries), and the capital's river ports at Dársena Norte and Dársena Sur will refund your money in pesos, then change it into US dollars. These branch banks are open 24 hours daily.

Getting There & Away

AIR

Buenos Aires' Aeropuerto Internacional Ministro Pistarini (more commonly known as Ezeiza) has excellent air connections from North America, Europe, the UK, and Australia/New Zealand, plus more costly routes from southern Africa across the Atlantic via Brazil. Alternately, travelers can fly to a neighboring country such as Chile or Brazil and continue overland to Argentina. Be aware that international flights within South America tend to be very costly unless purchased for intercontinental travel, though limited student and discount fares are available. One-way international tickets are usually very expensive.

Some travelers wishing to visit widely separated regions, for example, from Asia to South America, take advantage of Round-the-World (RTW) fares on the same trip. One possibility is the Qantas/Aerolíneas Argentinas ticket that lets you circle the globe with stops in New Zealand, Europe, and Southeast Asia, but similar fares are available on other airlines.

Major Airlines

Major international airlines to Argentina include: Aeroflot, Aeroperú, Air France, All Nippon Airways, American Airlines, Areolíneas, Argentinas, British Airways, Cubana, Japan Airlines, Korean Air, Ladeco, Lloyd Aéreo Boliviano, Malaysia Airlines, Pluna, Qantas Airways, South Africa Airways, Swissair, TAP (Air Portugal), United Airlines, Varig, and Vasp.

Baggage & Other Restrictions

On most domestic and international flights you are limited to two checked bags, or three if you don't have a carry-on. There could be a charge if you bring more or if the size of the bags exceeds the airline's limits. It's best to check with the individual airline if you are worried about this. On some international flights the luggage allowance is based on weight, not numbers; again, check with the airline.

If your luggage is delayed upon arrival (which is rare), some airlines will give a cash advance to purchase necessities. If sporting equipment is misplaced, the airline may pay for rentals. Should the luggage be lost, it is important to submit a claim. The airline doesn't have to pay the full amount of the claim; rather, they can estimate the value of your lost items. It may take them anywhere from six weeks to three months to process the claim and pay you.

Smoking Flights to and from Argentina, as well as those within the country, have non-smoking sections, but Argentine airports allow smoking throughout.

Illegal Items Items that are illegal to take on a plane, either in checked or carry-on baggage, include aerosols of polishes, waxes, and so on; tear gas and pepper spray; camp stoves with fuel; and divers' tanks that are full. Matches should not be checked.

Travelers with Special Needs

If you have special needs of any sort – a broken leg, dietary restrictions, dependence on a wheelchair, responsibility for a baby, fear of flying – you should let the airline know as soon as possible so that they can make arrangements accordingly. You should remind them when you reconfirm your booking (at least 72 hours before departure) and again when you check in at the airport. It may also be worth calling several airlines before you make your booking to find out how they would handle your particular needs.

Airports and airlines can be surprisingly helpful, but they do need advance warning. Most international airports can provide

Air Travel Glossary

Baggage Allowance This amount will be written on your ticket. Usually one 20-kg item, which goes in the hold, and one carry-on item are the maximum, but many airlines allow more for international flights.

Bucket Shop An unbonded travel agency specializing in discounted airline tickets.

Bumped Just because you have a confirmed seat doesn't mean you're going to get on the plane (see Overbooking).

Cancellation Penalties If you have to cancel or change an Apex ticket, there are often heavy penalties involved; insurance can sometimes be taken out against these penalties. Some airlines impose penalties on regular tickets as well, particularly against "no show" passengers.

Check In Airlines ask you to check in a certain amount of time prior to flight departure (usually two hours on international flights). If you fail to check in by 30 minutes before the flight and it is overbooked, the airline can cancel your booking and give your seat to somebody else.

Confirmation Having a ticket written out with the flight and date you want doesn't mean you have a seat until the agent has checked with the airline that your status is 'OK' or confirmed. Meanwhile, you might only have 'on request' status.

Lost Tickets If you lose your airline ticket, an airline will usually treat it like a traveler's check and, after inquiries, issue you another one. Legally, however, an airline is entitled to treat it like cash and if you lose it, then it's gone forever. Take good care of your tickets.

No Shows No shows are passengers who fail to show up for their flight, sometimes due to unexpected delays or disasters, sometimes due to simply forgetting, sometimes because they made more than one booking and didn't bother to cancel the one they didn't want. Full-fare passengers who fail to turn up are sometimes entitled to travel on a later flight. The rest of us are penalized (see Cancellation Penalties).

On Request An unconfirmed booking for a flight (see Confirmation).

Open Jaws A return ticket with which you fly out to one place but return from another. If available, this can save you backtracking to your arrival point.

Overbooking Airlines hate to fly planes with empty seats, and since every flight has some passengers who fail to show up (see No Shows), airlines often book more passengers than they

---

escorts from check-in desk to plane where needed, and there should be ramps, lifts, accessible toilets and reachable phones. Aircraft toilets, on the other hand, are likely to present a problem; travelers should discuss this with the airline at an early stage and, if necessary, with their doctor.

Guide dogs for the blind will often have to travel in a specially pressurized baggage compartment with other animals, away from their owner, though smaller guide dogs may be admitted to the cabin. Guide dogs are not subject to quarantine as long

as they have proof of being vaccinated against rabies.

Deaf travelers can ask that airport and inflight announcements be written down for them.

Children under two travel for 10% of the standard fare (or free, on some airlines), as long as they don't occupy a seat. (They don't get a baggage allowance either.) "Skycots" should be provided by the airline if requested in advance; these will take a child weighing up to about 10 kg. Children between two and 12 can usually occupy a seat for half to two-thirds of the full fare,

have seats. Usually the excess passengers balance those who fail to show up, but occasionally somebody gets bumped. If this happens, guess who it is most likely to be? The passengers who check in late.

Reconfirmation At least 72 hours prior to departure time of an onward or return flight, you must contact the airline and 'reconfirm' that you intend to be on the flight. If you don't do this, the airline can delete your name from the passenger list and you could lose your seat. You don't have to reconfirm the first flight on your itinerary or if your stopover is less than 72 hours. It doesn't hurt to reconfirm more than once.

Restrictions Discounted tickets often have various restrictions on them – advance purchase is the most usual one (see Apex). Others include restrictions on the minimum and maximum period you must be away, such as a minimum of 14 days or a maximum of one year (see Cancellation Penalties).

Tickets Out Many countries enforce an entry requirement that you have an onward or return ticket – in other words, a ticket out of the country. If you're not sure what you intend to do next, the easiest solution is to buy the cheapest onward ticket to a neighboring country or a ticket from a reliable airline that can later be refunded if you do not use it.

Transferred Tickets Airline tickets cannot be transferred from one person to another. Travelers sometimes try to sell the return half of their ticket, but officials can ask you to prove that you are the person named on the ticket. This is unlikely to happen on domestic flights, but on an international flight, tickets may be compared against passports.

Travel Agencies Travel agencies vary widely, and you should ensure that you use one that suits your needs. Some simply handle tours, while full-service agencies handle everything from tours and tickets to car rental and hotel bookings. A good one will do all these things and can save you a lot of money, but if all you want is a ticket at the lowest possible price, then you really need an agency specializing in discounted tickets. A discounted ticket agency, however, may not be useful for other things, such as hotel bookings.

Travel Periods Some officially discounted fares, Apex fares in particular, vary with the time of year. There is often a low (off-peak) season and a high (peak) season. Sometimes there's an intermediate, or shoulder, season as well. At peak times, when everyone wants to fly, not only will the officially discounted fares be higher but so will unofficially discounted fares. Or there may simply be no discounted tickets available. Usually the fare depends on your outward flight – if you depart in the high season and return in the low season, you pay the high-season fare. ■

and they do get a baggage allowance. Strollers can often be taken on as hand luggage.

Buying Tickets

From almost everywhere, South America is a relatively expensive destination, but discount fares can reduce the bite considerably. In addition to a straightforward round-trip ticket, a ticket to Argentina can also be part of a Round-the-World ticket. There are often significant seasonal discounts, so try to avoid peak travel times, which include the month of December, the summer months, and religious and patriotic holidays. It's best to consult with the airlines about these holidays, because dates for many can vary.

The plane ticket will probably be the single most expensive item in your budget, and buying it can be intimidating. It is always worth putting aside a few hours to research the current state of the market. Start shopping for a ticket early – some of the cheapest tickets must be purchased months in advance, and some popular flights sell out early. Talk to other recent travelers – they just might be able to stop you from making some of the same old mistakes. Look at the ads in newspapers and magazines, consult reference books, and watch for special offers.

Airlines can supply information on routes and timetables, but they do not supply the cheapest tickets except during fare wars and the competitive low season. Travel agents are usually a better source of bargains. Whether you go directly through an airline or use an agent, always ask the representative to clarify the fare, the route, the duration of the journey, and any restrictions on the ticket.

Most major airlines have ticket "consolidators" offering substantial discounts on fares to Latin America, but things change so frequently that even weekly newspaper listings are soon out of date. Among the best sources of information on cheap tickets are the Sunday travel pages of major US newspapers, such as the *New York Times*, *Los Angeles Times*, or *San Francisco Examiner*. If you're in a university town, check campus newspapers like Berkeley's *Daily Californian*. There will usually be a listing for the local affiliate of the Council on International Travel Exchange (CIEE, or Council Travel) or the Student Travel Network (STA); you don't have to be a student to take advantage of their services (see below for listings of the US offices).

Similar listings are available in the travel sections of magazines like *Time Out* and *TNT* in the UK, or the Saturday editions of newspapers like the *Sydney Morning Herald* and *The Age* in Australia. Ads in these publications offer cheap fares, but don't be surprised if they happen to be sold out when you contact the agents: They're usually low-season fares on obscure airlines with conditions attached.

Cheap tickets are available in two distinct categories: official and consolidator. Official ones have a variety of names including advance-purchase fares, budget fares, Apex, and super-Apex. Consolidator tickets are simply discounted tickets that the airlines release through selected travel agents (not through airline offices). The cheapest tickets are often nonrefundable and require an extra fee for changing your flight. Many insurance policies will cover this loss if you have to change your flight for emergency reasons. Return (roundtrip) tickets usually work out cheaper than two one-way fares – often *much* cheaper.

See the sidebar on the types of tickets you can purchase. Discounts on such fares are often available from travel agents, but usually not in Latin America, where discount ticketing is unusual. Standby can be a cheap way of getting from Europe to the US, but there are no such flights to Argentina or other parts of South America. Foreigners in Argentina may now pay for international air tickets in local currency, but since the new Argentine peso has stabilized at par with the dollar, there is presently no advantage to doing so.

One of the cheapest means of getting to South America is via courier flights, in which travelers trade all or part of their baggage allowance for a highly discounted fare and agree to accompany business equipment or documents. The major drawbacks to this, in addition to baggage being limited to carry-on items, are the relatively short travel period and the very limited number of gateway airports in Europe and North America.

You may decide to pay more than the rock-bottom fare by opting for the safety of a better-known travel agent. Established firms like STA Travel, which has offices worldwide, Council Travel in the USA, and Travel CUTS in Canada are valid alternatives, and they offer good prices to most destinations.

Once you have your ticket, write down its number, together with the flight number and other details, and keep the information somewhere separate. If the ticket is lost or stolen, this will help you get a replacement.

Remember to buy travel insurance as early as possible.

Note: Use the fares quoted in this book as a guide only. They are approximate and based on the rates advertised by travel agents and airlines at press time. Quoted airfares do not necessarily constitute a recommendation for the carrier.

Ticket Options

There are several types of discount tickets to South America. The following are the main ones:

Apex Advance purchase excursion (Apex) tickets must be bought well before departure, but they can be a good deal if you know exactly where you will be going and how long you will be staying. Usually only available on a return basis, with a 14- or 21-day advance purchase requirement, these have minimum- and maximum-stay requirements (usually 14 and 180 days respectively), allow no stopovers and stipulate cancellation charges.

Courier Flights This relatively new system, which businesses use to ensure the arrival of urgent freight without excessive customs hassles, can mean phenomenal bargains for travelers who can tolerate fairly strict requirements, such as short turnaround time – some tickets are valid for only a week or so, others for a month, but rarely any longer. In effect, the courier company ships business freight as your baggage, so that you can usually take only carry-on luggage, but you may pay as little as US$480 for a ticket from New York to Buenos Aires and back.

Discounted Tickets There are two types of discounted fares – officially discounted (see Promotional Fares) and unofficially discounted. The lowest prices often impose limitations such as flying with unpopular airlines, inconvenient schedules, or unpleasant routes and connections. A discounted ticket can save you other things than money – you may be able to pay Apex prices without the associated Apex advance booking and other requirements. Discounted tickets only exist where there is fierce competition.

Economy Class Valid for 12 months, economy-class (Y) tickets have the greatest flexibility within their time period. However, if you try to extend beyond a year, you'll have to pay the difference of any price increase in the interim period.

Excursion Fares Priced midway between Apex and full economy fare, these have no advance booking requirements but may require a minimum stay. Their advantage over advance purchase is that you can change bookings and/or stopovers without surcharge.

Full Fares Airlines traditionally offer first-class (coded F), business-class (coded J) and economy-class (coded Y) tickets. These days there are so many promotional and discounted fares available from the regular economy class that few passengers pay full economy fare.

MCO "Miscellaneous charges orders" (MCOs) are open vouchers for a fixed US dollar amount, which can be exchanged for a ticket on any IATA (International Air Transport Association) airline. In countries that require an onward ticket as a condition for entry, such as Panama or Colombia, this will usually satisfy immigration authorities. In a pinch, you can turn it into cash at the local offices of the airline from which you purchased it.

Point-to-Point This discount ticket is available on some routes in return for waiving stopover rights, but some airlines have entirely eliminated stopovers.

Promotional Fares Officially discounted fares like Apex fares that are available from travel agents or direct from the airline.

RTW Some excellent bargains are possible on "Round-the-World" tickets, sometimes for less than the cost of a return excursion fare. You must travel round the world in one direction and cannot backtrack; you are usually allowed five to seven stopovers.

Standby A discounted ticket with which you can fly only if there is a seat free at the last moment. Standby fares are usually only available on domestic routes. ■

Round-the-World Tickets Round-the-World (RTW) tickets have become very popular in the last few years. Airline RTW tickets are often real bargains and can work out to be no more expensive or even cheaper than an ordinary return ticket. Prices start at about UK£850, A$1800, or US$1300.

The official airline RTW tickets are usually put together by a combination of two airlines, and permit you to fly anywhere you want on their route systems as long as you do not backtrack. Other restrictions are that you must usually book the first sector in advance, and cancellation penalties apply. There may be restrictions on the number of stops permitted, and tickets are usually valid from 90 days up to a year. An alternative type of RTW ticket is one put together by a travel agent using a combination of discounted tickets.

Although most airlines restrict the number of sectors that can be flown within the USA and Canada to four, and some airlines black out a few heavily traveled routes (like Honolulu to Tokyo), stopovers are otherwise generally unlimited. In most cases a 14-day advance purchase is required. After the ticket is purchased, dates can be changed without penalty and tickets can be rewritten to add or delete stops for US$50 each.

The majority of RTW tickets restrict you to just two airlines. For instance, Qantas flies in conjunction with American Airlines, Delta Air Lines, Northwest Airlines, Canadian Airlines, Air France, and KLM. Qantas RTW tickets, with any of the aforementioned partner airlines, cost US$3247 or A$3099.

For travelers starting in Australia or Argentina, one possibility is the combined ticket offered by Qantas and Aerolíneas Argentinas. Beginning from Sydney or Buenos Aires, you can stop in New Zealand, London, Paris, Bahrain, Singapore, and other cities, although you must arrange the itinerary in advance. It does not, unfortunately, permit North American stopovers, but similar fares are available in the USA and Canada. The price for the Aerolíneas-Qantas ticket is A$3000 in Sydney or US$3124 in Buenos Aires (the latter figure represents about 15% more than the former, so it is cheaper to buy in Australia).

Aerolíneas has additional RTW agreements with Air New Zealand, British Airways, Cathay Pacific, KLM, Singapore Airlines, and Thai Airways International. The Aerolíneas-British Airways ticket (A$2250) allows one side trip in South America and another in Europe. British Airways and Qantas Airways offer a RTW ticket called the Global Explorer that allows you to combine routes on both airlines to a total of 28,000 miles for US$2999 or A$3099.

Canadian Airlines offers numerous RTW combinations, such as one with Philippine Airlines for C$2790 that could include Manila, Dubai, Pakistan, and Europe; another with KLM that could include Cairo, Bombay, Delhi, and Amsterdam for C$3149; and a third with South African Airways that could include Australia and Africa for C$3499.

To/From the USA

From the USA, the principal gateways to South America are Miami, New York, and Los Angeles. Recently privatized Aerolíneas Argentinas is the national carrier, but other airlines serving Buenos Aires include All Nippon Airways, American Airlines, British Airways, Japan Airlines, Korean Air, Ladeco, Lloyd Aéreo Boliviano, United Airlines, and Varig.

Líneas Aéreas Paraguayas (Lapsa or Air Paraguay) is traditionally a budget carrier via Miami, but its recent acquisition by the Ecuadorian airline Saeta may alter this focus; US domestic carriers usually make the connection with Miami. As of mid-1995, it was still offering a US$545 round-trip, valid for 45 days, between Miami and Buenos Aires. Lapsa (☎ 800-795-2772 toll-free in North America) also sells passes valid for travel to other South American countries in conjunction with international flights to its Asunción hub.

AeroPerú (☎ 800-777-7717) offers a Visit South America fare that includes a return flight from the US to Lima, and six coupons for flights within the continent to any of the following cities: Guayaquil, La Paz, Santiago, São Paulo, Rio de Janeiro, and Buenos Aires. Valid for 60 days and available only in the USA, low-season tickets cost US$1099 from Miami, US$1299 from Los Angeles. Additional international coupons cost US$100 apiece, while internal coupons for Peruvian flights cost US$40 apiece. High-season tickets, from July 1 to August 1 and December 15 to January 15, cost US$200 more.

Aerolíneas Argentinas and Austral offer a domestic air pass that is convenient for visiting widely separated parts of the country (for more details, see the Getting Around chapter), but note that such tickets must usually be bought outside the country, and sometimes can only be bought in conjunction with an international ticket.

Council Travel CIEE, or Council Travel, (☎ 800-226-8624) has agencies in the following cities:

Berkeley, CA
    2486 Channing Way (☎ 510-848-8604)
Boston, MA
    Suite 201, 729 Boylston St
    (☎ 617-266-1926)
La Jolla, CA
    UCSD Student Center, B-023
    (☎ 619-452-0630)
Los Angeles, CA
    10904 Lindbrook Drive (☎ 213-208-3551)
New York, NY
    16th floor, 205 E 42nd St (☎ 212-661-1450)
Pacific Beach (San Diego), CA
    943 Garnett Ave (☎ 619-270-6401)
San Francisco, CA
    530 Bush St (☎ 415-421-3473)
Seattle, WA
    1314 NE 43rd St, Suite 210
    (☎ 206-632-2448)

Student Travel Network STA (☎ 800-825-3001) has offices in the following cities:

Boston, MA
    297 Newbury St (☎ 617-266-6014)

Chicago, IL
    429 S Dearborn St (☎ 312-786-9050)
Los Angeles, CA
    7202 Melrose Ave (☎ 213-934-8722)
New York, NY
    10 Downing St (☎ 212-627-3111)
Philadelphia, PA
    3730 Walnut St (☎ 215-382-2928)
San Francisco, CA
    51 Grant Ave (☎ 415-391-8407)
Seattle, WA
    4341 University Way NE (☎ 206-633-5000)
Washington, DC
    2401 Pennsylvania Ave, Suite G
    (☎ 202-887-0912)

Courier Flights In the USA, New York and Miami are the only choices for courier flights to South America. For the widest selection of destinations, try the following companies: Now Voyager (☎ 212-431-1616, fax 334-5253), 74 Varick St, Suite 307, New York, NY 10013; Air Facility (☎ 718-712-0630) or Travel Courier (☎ 718-738-9000) in New York; Linehaul Services (☎ 305-477-0651) in Miami; or Discount Travel International (☎ 305-538-1616) in Miami or (☎ 212-362-3636, fax 362-3236), 169 W 81st St, New York, NY 10024.

For the latest information on courier and other budget fares, send US$5 for the latest newsletter or US$25 for a year's subscription to Travel Unlimited, PO Box 1058, Allston, MA 02134. Another source of information is the *Air Courier Bulletin* of the International Association of Air Travel Couriers (☎ 407-582-8320), 8 South J St, PO Box 1349, Lake Worth, FL 33460, whose US$35 annual membership includes the alternate monthly newsletter *Shoestring Traveler* (not related to Lonely Planet).

To/From Canada

There are direct services from Canada to South America as well as those via the US. Aerolíneas Argentinas, British Airways, and Ladeco serve Montreal, while Aerolíneas Argentinas and Canadian Airlines International fly from Toronto.

Travel Cuts, the Canadian national student travel agency, has offices across the country. You don't need to be a student to make use of their services. Contact them at 171 College St, Toronto, Ontario M5T 1P7 (☎ 416-977-3703, fax 977-4796).

To/From the UK & Europe

It is generally cheaper to fly from Europe via New York or Miami rather than directly to South America, but direct services to Buenos Aires are available with Aeroflot, Aerolíneas Argentinas, Air France, Alitalia, British Airways, Iberia, KLM, Lufthansa, Pluna, Swissair, and TAP (Air Portugal).

So-called "bucket shops" in London can provide the best deals; check out newspapers or magazines like the Saturday *Independent* or *Time Out* for suggestions. Currently the cheapest fares from London to Buenos Aires run about UK£369 one-way, UK£599 return.

If traveling from the UK, you will probably find that the cheapest flights are being advertised by obscure bucket shops whose names haven't yet reached the telephone directory. Many such firms are honest and solvent, but there are a few rogues who will take your money and disappear, to reopen elsewhere a month or two later under a new name. If you feel suspicious about a firm, don't give them all the money at once – leave a deposit of 20% or so and pay the balance on receiving the ticket. If they insist on cash in advance, go elsewhere. And once you have the ticket, call the airline to confirm that you are booked on the flight.

Since bucket shops come and go, it's worth inquiring about their affiliation with the Association of British Travel Agents (ABTA), which will guarantee a refund or alternative if the agent goes out of business. The following are reputable London bucket shops:

Campus Travel
    52 Grosvenor Gardens, London SW1
    (☎ 0171-730-3402)
Journey Latin America
    16 Devonshire Rd, Chiswick, London W4
    2HD (☎ 0181-747-3108)

Passage to South America
    (☎ 0171-602-9889)
STA Travel
    86 Old Brompton Rd, London SW7 (☎ 0171-937-9962)
    117 Euston Rd, London NW1
South American Experience
    47 Causton St, London SW1
    (☎ 0171-976-5511)
Trailfinders
    194 Kensington High St, London W8
    (☎ 0171-938-3939)
    42-50 Earls Court Rd, London W8
    (☎ 0171-938-3366)

In Berlin, check out the magazine *Zitty* for bargain fare advertisements. Throughout Western Europe and the UK you can find agencies that provide bargain fares. Here are some possibilities:

France
    Council Travel, 31 Rue Saint Augustine, Paris 2ème (☎ 1-42.66.20.87)
    Council Travel, Rue des Pyramides, Paris 1er (☎ 1-44.55.55.44)
Germany
    Alternativ Tours, Wilmersdorferstrasse 94, Berlin (☎ 030-881-2089)
    SRID Reisen, Bergerstrasse 1178, Frankfurt (☎ 069-43-01-91)
    SRS Studentenreise Service, Marienstrasse 23, Berlin (☎ 030-281-5033)
Ireland
    USIT Travel Office, 19 Aston Quay, Dublin (☎ 01-679-8833)
Italy
    CTS, Via Genova 16, Rome (☎ 06-46 791)
Netherlands
    NBBS, Rokin 38, Amsterdam
    (☎ 020-642-0989)
    Malibu Travel, Damrak 30, Amsterdam
    (☎ 020-623-6814)
Spain
    TIVE, Calle José Ortega y Gasset, Madrid (☎ 91-401-1300)
Switzerland
    SSR, Leonhardstrasse 5 & 10, Zürich
    (☎ 01-261-2956)

The only apparent courier flights from Europe are to Rio de Janeiro; Courier Travel Service (☎ 0171-351-0300), 346 Fulham Rd, London SW10 9UH, charges UK£425 for a 28-day return fare.

To/From Australia & New Zealand

The most direct is Aerolíneas Argentinas' weekly transpolar flight from Sydney via Auckland, which is an obvious connection for buyers of the Aerolíneas-Qantas RTW fare (see the Round-the-World Tickets section). From Argentina, the flight stops in Río Gallegos before crossing the pole. Otherwise, LanChile's trans-Pacific flights to Santiago have ready connections to Buenos Aires, but some travelers have found it cheaper to go via London or Los Angeles.

STA Travel is a good place to inquire for bargain airfares; you needn't be a student to use their services.

Adelaide
> Level 4, the Arcade, Union House, Adelaide University (☎ 08-223-6620, 08-223-6244, fax 08-224-0664)

Brisbane
> Shop 25 & 26, Brisbane Arcade, 111-117 Adelaide St, Brisbane 4000 (☎ 07-221-3722, fax 07-229-8435)

Canberra
> Arts Centre, GPO Box 4, ANU, Canberra 0200 (☎ 06-247-0800, fax 06-247-9786)

Hobart
> Ground Floor, Union Building, University of Tasmania, Hobart 7005 (☎ 002-243-496, fax 002-243-738)

Melbourne
> 220 Faraday St, Carlton 3053 (☎ 03-9347-6911)

Perth
> 1st Floor, New Guild Building, University of West Australia, Crawley 6009 (☎ 09-380-2302, fax 09-380-1010)

Sydney
> 1st Floor, 732 Harris St, Ultimo 2007 (☎ 02-212-1255, fax 02-281-4183)

To/From Asia & Africa

Carriers serving Buenos Aires directly from Asia, usually via North America, include All Nippon Airways (with Aerolíneas Argentinas), Japan Airlines, and Korean Air. Varig and Vasp also have good connections via Rio de Janeiro or São Paulo.

Malaysia Airlines flies twice weekly from Kuala Lumpur to Buenos Aires via Cape Town and Johannesburg. South Africa Airways flies weekly from Johannesburg to Buenos Aires via Rio de Janeiro or São Paulo.

To/From Mexico

Aerolíneas Argentinas and Ladeco serve Buenos Aires from Mexico City (Ladeco also from Cancún), while AeroPerú, American, Cubana, and Lloyd Aéreo Boliviano provide less direct services.

To/From Neighboring Countries

Bolivia La Paz is the principal destination, but some flights continue to Santa Cruz de la Sierra. Aerolíneas also flies to Santa Cruz via Córdoba and Salta. Lloyd Aéreo Boliviano flies to Santa Cruz and Cochabamba, and to Santa Cruz and La Paz.

Brazil From Ezeiza airport in Buenos Aires, Rio de Janeiro and São Paulo are the main destinations for many airlines, but Aerolíneas also offers flights from Ezeiza to Porto Alegre and Florianópolis. In addition, it flies from Aeroparque to Rio and São Paulo, both direct and via Córdoba; from Mar del Plata to Rio and São Paulo; and from Córdoba and Tucumán to Rio and São Paulo.

Chile Many airlines fly between Buenos Aires and Santiago, but Aerolíneas Argentinas also flies from Santiago to Mendoza, as does the Chilean airline Ladeco. Ladeco has additional flights from Santiago to Neuquén, Argentina, via Mendoza.

TAN, the regional airline of Neuquén province, connects Bariloche with Puerto Montt, Chile. Several minor airlines fly between Punta Arenas, Chile, and destinations in Santa Cruz province and Argentine Tierra del Fuego.

Paraguay Asunción is Paraguay's only air connection with Buenos Aires; flights leave from both Aeropuerto Jorge Newbery (Aeroparque) and Ezeiza in Buenos Aires. The only direct carriers are Aerolíneas Argentinas and Lapsa, though many other South American airlines also pass through Asunción.

ARGENTINA

Uruguay There are numerous flights from Aeroparque to Montevideo, while a few long-distance international flights continue from Ezeiza in Buenos Aires to Montevideo. From Aeroparque, the only other Uruguayan destinations are Punta del Este and Colonia del Sacramento.

LAND

There are multitudinous crossings from the neighboring countries of Chile, Bolivia, Paraguay, Brazil, and Uruguay. Some are very easy, some very difficult and time-consuming (the latter are usually far more interesting).

Andean Routes to/from Chile

Except in far southern Patagonia, every land-crossing border with Chile involves crossing the Andes. Some passes close in winter. The only rail crossing, from Antofagasta to Salta, is not a regular passenger service.

Chilean visas (probably best obtained in the traveler's home country or in Buenos Aires) are obligatory for citizens of the following countries: African countries, France, Guyana, Haiti, Kuwait, Mexico, New Zealand, Suriname, and Communist countries (the latter a shrinking category, presumably). The rest usually only need a Chilean tourist card, obtainable at the border point. For some reason, French nationals can only get single-entry visas.

Salta to Calama Buses from Salta to Calama, with connections to Antofagasta and Iquique, now cross the Andes via a combination of national and provincial highways to Jujuy, Susques, and the Paso de Jama, in the summer months only. The 4275-meter Huaytiquina pass to the south, reached from Salta via RN 51 and RP 37, is still open to automobiles and trucks, but traffic is almost nonexistent, so forget about hitching. There may be passenger rail service to the Chilean border at Socompa, but only freight service beyond, though the Chilean train will sometimes take passengers. See the chapter on Salta for details.

San Juan to La Serena Dynamited by the Argentine military during the Beagle Channel dispute of 1978-79, the 4779-meter Agua Negra Pass at the western end of RN 150 is now open to automobiles and trucks, but regular bus service is still on hold.

Mendoza to Santiago Many bus companies serve the Libertadores border crossing, the most popular between the two countries, via RN 7 from the city of Mendoza. *Taxi colectivos*, which carry up to five passengers, are faster, more comfortable, and only slightly more expensive. Winter snow sometimes closes the route, but never for long. See the Mendoza entry of the Cuyo chapter for details.

Lake District Routes

There are a number of scenic crossings between the Argentine and Chilean lake districts, some involving bus-boat shuttles. These are popular routes during summer, so make bookings in advance whenever possible.

Neuquén & Zapala to Temuco The most northerly lake district route, RN 22, reaches the border at 1884-meter Pino Hachado pass, directly east of Zapala and Neuquén, continuing to Temuco via Lonquimay and Curacautín, along the upper Río Biobío. Alternative RP 13, slightly to the south, uses the 1298-meter Icaima Pass. Both have occasional bus traffic in summer.

San Martín/Junín de los Andes to Temuco On the Argentine side, RP 60 skirts the northern slopes of Volcán Lanín to the Tromen pass (known to Chileans as Mamuil Malal), closed in winter. On the Chilean side, the road passes Currarehue, Pucón, and Villarica. There is summer bus service, often heavily booked, on this route.

San Martín de los Andes to Valdivia From San Martín a daily ferry sails up Lago Lacar to Argentine customs at Hua Hum, while buses use the shoreline RP 48 to arrive at the same spot, where a local bus continues to the Chilean settlement of Pirehueico, where a ferry crosses the lake of the same name to Puerto Fuy. From Puerto Fuy there is bus service via Choshuenco and Panguipulli to Valdivia.

Bariloche to Osorno via Puyehue On the north shore of Lago Nahuel Huapi, RN 231 is the quickest land crossing in the lake district; on the Chilean side, the highway traverses Parque Nacional Puyehue.

Bariloche to Puerto Montt, via Lago Todos los Santos Extraordinarily popular in summer, this bus-boat combination is feasible as a single through ticket or in stages via several scenic villages.

From Bariloche, there are frequent bus services to Llao Llao's Puerto Pañuelo, where a ferry sails west on Lago Nahuel Huapi to Puerto Blest. After a short bus ride, passengers cross Lago Frías by launch, go through Argentine immigration at Puerto Frías, and continue by bus over the Pérez Rosales pass to Peulla for the ferry to Petrohué, at the west end of Lago Todos los Santos.

Southern Patagonian Routes
Since the opening of Chile's Carretera Austral (Southern Hwy) beyond Puerto Aysén, it has become more common to cross between Chile and Argentina south of Puerto Montt. There are also several crossing points in extreme southern Patagonia and Tierra del Fuego.

Lago Puelo to Puelo South of El Bolsón, a footpath/stock trail leads across the Chilean border to the Seno de Reloncaví (Reloncaví Sound), with connections to the city of Puerto Montt. This is approximately a three-day journey.

Esquel to Puerto Ramírez There are two possible crossings in this area. From Esquel there are colectivos on RN 259 to Futaleufú, across the Chilean border, with connections to Chaitén; on the Chilean side, the highway continues southwest to Puerto Ramírez and then turns northwest to

Puerto Piedra and Chaitén. The alternative takes RP 17 and RP 44 to Corcovado (there is a bus service along this route) to Argentine customs at Carrenleufú. Soon after the border is the town of Palena, where the road jogs northwest to meet the highway from Futaleufú.

Comodoro Rivadavia to Coihaique There are two weekly buses, often heavily booked, from Comodoro Rivadavia to via Río Mayo via RP 26, RP 20, and RP 22. A more southerly route, with no public transport, goes over the Paso Huemules to Balmaceda and Coihaique via RP 55.

Los Antiguos to Chile Chico & Puerto Ibañez A bus from Los Antiguos (where there are connections to the Patagonian coastal town of Caleta Olivia) goes to Chile Chico three times daily. From Chile Chico there's a ferry to Puerto Ibañez on Lago General Carrera (which is called Lago Buenos Aires on the Argentine side). An alternative goes northwest from Perito Moreno via RP 45 and RP 72 to Puerto Ibañez, avoiding the ferry crossing, but there's no public transport.

Calafate & Río Turbio to Puerto Natales & Parque Nacional Torres del Paine There are frequent buses between Puerto Natales and the Argentine coal town of Río Turbio, where many Chileans work; from Río Turbio there are connections to Río Gallegos. Twice weekly or more in summer, there are direct buses from Torres del Paine and Puerto Natales to Calafate, the gateway to Argentina's Parque Nacional Los Glaciares.

Río Gallegos to Punta Arenas There are many buses daily between Punta Arenas and Río Gallegos; the trip takes six hours.

Tierra del Fuego to Punta Arenas From Río Grande there are two buses weekly to Porvenir, in Chilean Tierra del Fuego, where a three-hour ferry trip or a 10-minute flight takes you to Punta Arenas. There are also direct buses twice weekly from

Ushuaia to Punta Arenas via the Primera Angostura ferry crossing.

To/From Bolivia

The Bolivian border offers one major and two minor crossing points into Argentina. There are both rail and road connections at La Quiaca/Villazón in the province of Jujuy, while the Aguas Blancas and Yacuiba crossings are in the province of Salta.

La Quiaca to Villazón From Jujuy and Salta, there are many daily buses up the Quebrada de Humahuaca on RN 9 to La Quiaca, but there is no longer any passenger rail service on the Argentine side. At La Quiaca, you must walk or take a cab across the Bolivian border to catch a bus or train to La Paz.

Aguas Blancas to Bermejo From Orán, reached by bus from either Salta or Jujuy via RN 34 and RN 50, take a bus to Aguas Blancas and the Bolivian border town of Bermejo, where a bridge now crosses the river of the same name. From Bermejo, you can catch a bus to Tarija.

Pocitos to Yacuiba From Jujuy or Salta there are buses on RN 34 to Tartagal and on to the border at Pocitos/Yacuiba. From Yacuiba, there are trains to Santa Cruz de la Sierra.

To/From Paraguay

There are two direct border crossings between Argentina and Paraguay, plus one requiring a brief detour through Brazil. Another may open if the massive Yacyretá hydroelectric project on the Río Paraná is ever completed.

Clorinda to Asunción There are frequent bus services between Asunción and Clorinda (in Formosa province) via the Puente Internacional Ignacio de Loyola, which is renowned for ferocious customs checks.

Posadas to Encarnación Buses run frequently on the Puente Internacional Beato Roque González, the new international bridge across the Paraná River. However, it's still possible to take a launch between the river docks even though the rising waters behind Yacyretá Dam have submerged low-lying parts of both cities.

Puerto Iguazú to Ciudad del Este Frequent buses connect Puerto Iguazú in Misiones province to the Brazilian city of Foz do Iguaçu, with easy connections to Ciudad del Este (ex-Puerto Presidente Stroessner).

To/From Brazil

The most common overland crossing is between Puerto Iguazú in Misiones province and Foz do Iguaçu, but you can also go from Paso de los Libres, in Corrientes province, to Uruguaiana, Brazil, and on to Porto Alegre. The most obscure crossings are a launch/ferry across the Río Uruguay from Santo Tomé (north of Paso de los Libres) to the Brazilian village of São Borja, and another in the province of Misiones, from San Javier to Puerto Xavier.

Direct bus service connects Buenos Aires with Rio de Janeiro and São Paulo.

To/From Uruguay

Travelers worried about seasickness on the ferry or hydrofoil will find direct buses from Buenos Aires to Montevideo, but these are slower and less convenient than the land/river combinations across the Río de la Plata, which are detailed below. All other land connections are across the Río Uruguay in Entre Ríos province.

Gualeguaychú to Fray Bentos Three buses a day cross the Puente Internacional Libertador General San Martín, with good connections to Montevideo from Mercedes, the first town beyond Fray Bentos.

Colón to Paysandú The Puente Internacional General José Gervasio Artigas links these two cities, south of Parque Nacional El Palmar.

Concordia to Salto The bridge across the Salto Grande hydroelectric complex, north of Concordia, unites these two cities north of Parque Nacional El Palmar. There are also scheduled launches across the river.

RIVER & SEA
From Buenos Aires, there are several ways to Uruguay that involve ferry and hydrofoil, and often require combinations with buses. The only other maritime service is the erratic boat from Ushuaia, Tierra del Fuego, to Puerto Williams, on Chile's Isla Navarino. For details, see the appropriate geographical entries.

Buenos Aires to Colonia From Buenos Aires there are two ferries (three hours) and several hydrofoils (one hour) daily to Colonia, with direct bus connections to Montevideo (three hours more).

Buenos Aires to Montevideo The quickest and most convenient river services to Montevideo are the comfortable, high-speed ferries that carry passengers to the Uruguayan capital in only 2½ hours from downtown Buenos Aires.

Tigre to Carmelo & Nueva Palmira Passenger launches cross the estuary of the Río de la Plata from the Buenos Aires suburb of Tigre. You can reach the docks from Retiro Station or via the No 60 bus ("Tigre") from Av Callao. From Carmelo there are good connections to Montevideo.

Ushuaia to Puerto Williams Service on the erratic passenger ferry from Ushuaia to Puerto Williams on Isla Navarino (reached by plane or boat from Punta Arenas) suffers frequent interruptions.

DEPARTURE TAXES
International passengers leaving from Buenos Aires' Ezeiza airport pay a US$13 departure tax, also payable in local currency. On flights of less than 300 km to neighboring countries, such as Uruguay, the tax is only US$5.

There is no tax for land departures, but users of the new hydrofoil port at Dársena Norte pay US$6 to travel to Colonia, Uruguay, or US$10 to Montevideo.

TOURS
Myriad companies offer tours to Argentina, but most focus on the attractions of Buenos Aires, Iguazú, and the Moreno Glacier. A few also include trips to Ushuaia and Tierra del Fuego. Other parts of the country get short shrift, so if you're interested in those areas, you may have to make arrangements in Buenos Aires.

Increasingly, both Argentine and foreign companies have become involved in nature-oriented tourism (popularly, but not always accurately, known as *turismo ecológico* or *turismo aventura*). In Buenos Aires, Patagonia Wilderness operates climbing and hiking trips, some of them very challenging, such as ones to Cerro Torre and Aconcagua. They will design custom trips with knowledgeable local guides. Contact them at ☎ 334-5134, 8th floor, Av Julio A Roca 610, 1067 Buenos Aires. USA-based Out There Trekking (☎/fax 510-895-9956), PO Box 5431, Berkeley, CA 94705, is primarily a mountaineering company that arranges 20-day ascents to Aconcagua (a nontechnical climb with a gradual approach and extended acclimatization period).

Other well-established North American companies operating in Argentina include Wilderness Travel (☎ 510-548-0420, 800-247-6700), 801 Allston Way, Berkeley, CA 94710; and Mountain Travel Sobek (☎ 510-527-8100, 800-227-2384), 6420 Fairmount Ave, El Cerrito, CA 94530. Both have lavishly illustrated catalogs of their numerous excursions to Patagonia and the Andean Lake District, which range from easy day hikes with accommodations at hotels and campgrounds, to strenuous treks and climbs with nights spent bivouacking in the backcountry.

Patagonia Wildland Adventures (☎ 206-365-0686, 800-345-4453), 3516 NE 155th St, Seattle, WA 98155, arranges 10-day itineraries through local guides and outfitters for as few as two persons for

US$1295 per person (land cost). Another possibility is Lost World Adventures (☎ 404-971-8586, fax 977-3095, 800-999-0558). For visitors with limited time, such trips may be ideal, especially in areas like Patagonia where logistics can be difficult.

Similar companies exist in Europe and Australia. Journey Latin America (☎ 0181-747-8315), 16 Devonshire Rd., Chiswick, London W4 2HD, takes smallish groups to Latin America, specializing in tours for one or two people. Explore Worldwide (☎ 0252-34-4161), 1 Frederick St, Aldershot, Hants GU11 1LQ, and Melia Travel (☎ 0181-491-3881), 12 Dover St, London W1X 4NS, are also Latin American specialists.

In Australia, try World Expeditions, which has two offices: 441 Kent St, Sydney, NSW 2000 (☎ 02-264-3366) and 1/393 Little Bourke St, Melbourne, Victoria 3000 (☎ 03-9670-8400, 1-800-803-688). Although Peregrine Bird Tours (☎ 03-9727-3343), 2 Drysdale Place, Mooroolbark, Victoria 3138, often schedules trips to Argentina, they have none planned for 1996. However, they may organize some if they get enough requests. Peregrine Adventures (which is not affiliated with Peregrine Bird Tours), 258 Lonsdale St, Melbourne, Victoria 3000 (☎ 03-9663-8611), also sometimes runs tours.

In Germany, Argentoura Travel (☎/fax 089-673-3072), Gustav-Heinemann-Ring 42, 81739 München, operates very comfortable back-roads excursions through both northern and southern Argentina in their custom-designed Traction Mobil (available for charter trips as well). Their Patagonian trips take place in the summer months, while the northern trips, to Chile's Atacama Desert and the Argentine provinces of Mendoza, San Juan, Salta, and Tucumán, are in winter. Owners Frank and Heike Neumann speak excellent English.

Argentoura's Buenos Aires agent is Kraft Travel Service (☎ /fax 793-4062), E Lamarca 343, 1º Piso, No 17, 1640 Martínez, Provincia de Buenos Aires, while their Patagonian representative is Cumbres Patagónicos (☎ /fax 0944-23831), Villegas 222, San Carlos de Bariloche, Río Negro.

WARNING

The information in this chapter is particularly vulnerable to change: Prices for international travel are volatile, routes are introduced and cancelled, schedules change, special deals come and go, and rules and visa requirements are amended. Airlines and governments seem to take a perverse pleasure in making price structures and regulations as complicated as possible. You should check directly with the airline or a travel agent to make sure you understand how a fare (and ticket you may buy) works. In addition, the travel industry is highly competitive, and there are many lurks and perks.

The upshot of this is that you should get opinions, quotes, and advice from as many airlines and travel agents as possible before you part with your cash. The details given in the chapter should be regarded as pointers and are not a substitute for your own careful, up-to-date research.

Getting Around

AIR

Argentine air traffic, routes, and fares have undergone a major transformation since the privatization of Aerolíneas Argentinas, which handles domestic as well as international routes, and Austral, which handles domestic routes only. These two airlines, which charge identical fares, have the most extensive services, but some existing secondary airlines have expanded their routes, and others have come into existence. Both secondary and new airlines have undercut the very high existing fare structure of the established carriers. Apparently in response, Aerolíneas and Austral have introduced a supplementary fare system which, with some restrictions, offers cheaper alternatives.

Perhaps the single greatest shortcoming of the air transport system is that many major cities have connections only through Buenos Aires. For example, to fly from Salta to Mendoza, a distance of 950 km, one must actually travel a total of 2250 km by first flying to Buenos Aires (1270 km) and then making the 980-km connection to Mendoza.

Línea Aéreas Privadas Argentinas (LAPA) has begun to provide competition for Aerolíneas and Austral on many routes, though it has fewer planes and a much smaller total capacity. Dinar Líneas Aéreas, a recent startup, flies to the northwestern cities of Tucumán, Salta, and Jujuy, and to Puerto Iguazú.

Líneas Aéreas del Estado (LADE), the air force's passenger service, flies mostly to Patagonian destinations, but reduced state subsidies have resulted in greatly diminished services. Transportes Aéreos Neuquén (TAN), the provincial airline of Neuquén, has fairly extensive schedules from Mendoza in the north to El Calafate in the south, while Sapse goes from Buenos Aires all the way to Esquel. But other Patagonian carriers, including Kaikén

Líneas Aéreas and Líneas Aéreas Pingüino in Santa Cruz and Tierra del Fuego provinces, have smaller and slower planes. The only non-Patagonian carrier of this sort is Líneas Aéreas de Entre Ríos (LAER), which connects Paraná, Santa Fe, and other cities of the littoral with Buenos Aires and the Atlantic beach resorts of Buenos Aires province.

Note that in the summer and around holidays, all flights in Patagonia may be heavily booked, and it is advisable to make reservations as far in advance as possible. Flying with LADE or TAN is sometimes cheaper than covering the same distance by bus, but demand is heavy and flights are often booked (usually overbooked) well in advance. With polite insistence and a convincing story, you can often get a seat on a LADE flight in town, but in desperation do not hesitate to go to the airport, where you may well find a plane with tens of empty seats.

Fares

The cost of flying in Argentina has risen dramatically in recent years; consult the accompanying map for the most recent standard airfare structure, which indicates the range of fares from least to most expensive. One low-cost alternative on some airlines is *banda negativa*, in which limited seats on a selected list of flights every month are available for discounts of 40% or so. Often, but not always, these are night flights and require advance purchase, but they are excellent bargains.

Aerolíneas and Austral, apparently under pressure from their competitors, have introduced a series of modified fares including *Tiempo Libre*, with discounts up to 50% on selected flights based on advance purchase and confirmed departure and return dates, valid from one week to 60 days; the similar *Escapada*, with discounts up to 25%, valid

ARGENTINA

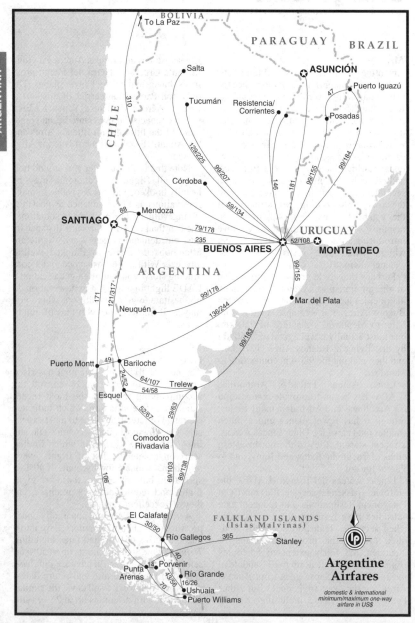

BOLIVIA
To La Paz

PARAGUAY

BRAZIL

ASUNCIÓN

Salta

Tucumán

Resistencia/
Corrientes

Puerto Iguazú

47

Posadas

310

129/225

99/207

Córdoba

59/134

146

181

99/155

99/184

CHILE

SANTIAGO

88

Mendoza

79/178

235

BUENOS AIRES

URUGUAY

52/108

MONTEVIDEO

ARGENTINA

99/155

121/317

171

99/178

Neuquén

136/244

Mar del Plata

99/183

Puerto Montt

49

Bariloche

24/52

64/107

Trelew

54/58

Esquel

52/67

29/63

Comodoro
Rivadavia

69/103

89/138

106

El Calafate

30/50

FALKLAND ISLANDS
(Islas Malvinas)

Río Gallegos

365

Stanley

40

14

Porvenir

Punta
Arenas

43/56

Río Grande

16/26

70

Ushuaia

Puerto Williams

**Argentine
Airfares**

*domestic & international
minimum/maximum one-way
airfare in US$*

four to ten days; *Conozca Patagonia* and *Conozca Cataratas* for visitors to Patagonia and to Iguazú; and inexpensive *Express Cabotaje* fares to Córdoba (US$49) and Mendoza (US$59). For more details, see the respective geographical entries or, in the country, representatives for Aerolíneas or Austral.

Air Passes

Aerolíneas Argentinas' "Visit Argentina" fare, also valid on Austral, lets you fly anywhere served by either airline so long as you make no more than one stop in any city except for an immediate connection, but it is more expensive and less flexible than in the past. Theoretically, the pass must be purchased outside Argentina or Uruguay, but some LP correspondents claim to have bought them in Buenos Aires.

Four flight coupons cost US$450 and are valid for 30 days; additional coupons, up to a maximum of eight, cost US$120 each. One coupon must be used for each numbered flight. A flight from Puerto Iguazú to Bariloche, for example, requires the use of two coupons rather than one as in the past, because there is a stopover to change planes in Buenos Aires. Conditions permit one change of itinerary without charge, but each additional change requires a payment of US$50.

An interesting new option is the mileage-based Mercosur Pass, which allows travelers to visit widespread areas in Brazil, Paraguay, Argentina, and Uruguay on virtually any major carrier in those countries but must include at least one international flight. Details are rather complex, but the fare structure is thus:

Distance (nautical miles)	Fare
1000 – 1900	US$225
1901 – 2500	US$285
2501 – 3200	US$345
3201 – 4200	US$420
4201 – 5200	US$530
5201 – 6200	US$645
6201 – 7200	US$755
7201 – plus	US$870

Properly organized, this can be cheaper than some domestic air passes, such as Aerolíneas' Visit Argentina Pass, but you need a patient travel agent to make the optimum itinerary.

Timetables

Aerolíneas, Austral, and the other airlines publish detailed timetables to which they adhere very closely. LADE will sometimes leave early if the flight is full or nearly full, so don't arrive late at the airport. There is a listing of the principal airline offices, both international and domestic, in the Buenos Aires chapter, and of regional offices in each city entry.

Departure Tax

Argentine domestic flights carry a departure tax of about US$3, not included in the price of the ticket. At the airports of Chapelco (San Martín de los Andes), Reconquista, and Goya, the tax is only US$1.50.

BUS

Argentine bus services cover a large portion of the country's extensive road network. Long-distance buses are generally large, comfortable, and sometimes faster than you might like. Most have toilets and serve coffee or snacks; a few provide on-board meals, but most stop at reasonably good, moderately priced restaurants.

Most cities and towns have central bus terminals at which each company has a separate office; some, like El Bolsón, have a cluster of offices in the same general area. Most companies post fares and schedules prominently, but only a few distribute printed schedules (Andesmar, which has extensive routes throughout the country, is the best in this regard).

Some long-distance companies offer reclining seats at premium prices, but ordinary bus seats on main routes are more than adequate even on very long trips. Local or provincial services (known as *común*) are usually more crowded, make very frequent stops, and take much longer than direct *(expreso)* services.

Federal regulations now prohibit smoking on buses throughout the country, but many Argentines (including drivers) appear not to be aware of the fact. Nevertheless, a polite reminder is usually sufficient to get the offender to stub it out.

Reservations

Reservations are generally unnecessary, but during holiday periods or on routes where seats are limited, it's a good idea to buy your ticket as far in advance as possible. Christmas, New Year's, and Easter are obvious times, but do not overlook the winter holidays around Independence Day (July 9), when public transportation can also be very crowded.

Usually a trip to the bus terminal the day before you travel will suffice. The major exceptions are the infrequent international services on relatively remote routes such as Salta to Antofagasta (Chile) or Comodoro Rivadavia (Chubut) to Chile Chico (Chile) via Caleta Olivia (Santa Cruz) and Los Antiguos. Purchase tickets for these and other infrequent routes as early as possible.

Costs

Bus fares are considerably costlier than in the Andean countries and somewhat more expensive than in Chile. The Dirección Nacional de Transportes has fixed a standard rate of about US$0.036 per km, but a good rule of thumb is US$3 per hour of journey. Bus services, however, are private rather than state-operated, and bus fares respond more quickly to market conditions and inflation than do train fares.

Sample bus fares from Buenos Aires are as follows:

Destination	Fare
Rosario	US$15
Mar del Plata	US$25
Paraná	US$26
Bahía Blanca	US$32
Córdoba	US$30
Mendoza	US$40
Puerto Iguazú	US$45
Puerto Madryn	US$64
Salta	US$64
Bariloche	US$80
Río Gallegos	US$107

Promotional fares are sometimes available, so inquire at several companies before buying your ticket.

Depending on the company, university students and teachers sometimes receive 20% discounts on intercity bus fares, though this practice is less common than in the past. It is helpful to have student or university identification, which need not be current, but often just asking for the discount will be sufficient. Credit cards are usually not accepted for discount fares.

TRAIN

Private operators have recently assumed control of the profitable freight service on the formerly state-owned railways, but they have shown no interest in providing passenger service except on commuter lines in and around Buenos Aires. The provinces of Buenos Aires, Río Negro, Chubut, Tucumán, and La Pampa continue to provide much-reduced passenger service.

Train trips are often but not always longer than bus trips, and are subject to frequent delays, breakdowns, and strikes. If the railroads do go on strike, you may find that your ticket is useless, although you should be able to get a refund.

Timetables

In Buenos Aires, the Mitre, Belgrano, and San Martín lines operate from Estación Retiro; the Roca line from Estación Constitución; the Urquiza line from Estación Federico Lacroze; and the Sarmiento line from Estación Once. From Retiro, Constitución, and Once, there are suburban commuter services as well as intercity services. All four stations are served by the underground (Subte).

Operated by the provinces of Buenos Aires and Río Negro, the Ferrocarril Roca serves the Atlantic beach resort of Mar del Plata, other destinations in Buenos Aires province, and northern Patagonia as far as Bariloche in Río Negro province. From

Ingeniero Jacobacci, on the line to Bariloche, a picturesque narrow-gauge spur goes to Esquel.

Operated by the province of Tucumán, the Ferrocarril Mitre goes to Rosario, Santiago del Estero, and Tucumán. The Ferrocarril Sarmiento, though primarily a commuter line, still links the capital to Santa Rosa in La Pampa province. The Belgrano, San Martín, and Urquiza lines are now primarily commuter railways for Gran Buenos Aires, but the Urquiza and Belgrano also have some tourist excursions in Buenos Aires province.

Classes

There are four classes of passenger service, not all of which are found on every train. *Coche cama* or *dormitorio*, a sleeper compartment, is the costliest but most comfortable on long journeys such as Constitución-Bariloche. *Pullman* is considerably cheaper, with air-conditioning and reclining seats somewhat larger than those in *primera* (1st class). Primera is very acceptable in almost all circumstances, especially since the price difference is minimal compared to that of *turista* (tourist or 2nd class), with its rigid bench seats.

For trips of more than a few hours, and especially on overnight trips, avoid turista class. There may be slight variations on all these categories.

Reservations

Because they are cheaper than buses, trains can be very crowded. During holiday periods such as Christmas and around Independence Day (July 9), it is very important to buy tickets as far in advance as possible. At most major stations, ticket purchases are now computerized and tickets will show date of travel *(fecha)*, departure time *(sale)*, carriage number *(coche)*, and seat *(asiento)*. When traveling with friends or family, Argentines often ignore seat assignments, but do not hesitate to insist on your proper seat or even call the conductor to straighten out any problems.

Costs

Argentine train fares are still lower than bus fares on comparable routes, but reduced state subsidies have meant increased prices. Presently the train fare for the 24-hour trip from Constitución to Bariloche, for example, is US$98 in a dormitorio, US$66 in Pullman, and US$53 in primera.

CAR & MOTORCYCLE

Because Argentina is so large, many parts are easily accessible only by motor vehicle despite the country's extensive public transport system. Especially in Patagonia, where distances are great and buses can be infrequent, you cannot easily stop for something interesting at the side of the road and then continue on your merry way by public transport.

Unfortunately, operating a car is expensive. Although Argentina is self-sufficient in oil, the price of *nafta* (petrol) has risen to world levels at about US$0.80 per liter, although *gas-oil* (diesel fuel) is only about one-third of that. Unleaded fuel is widely available in provincial capitals and along main paved routes in the central part of the country, but it can still be difficult to find off the beaten track. The situation is improving as more vehicles using unleaded come on the market.

Distances are comparable to those in North America or Australia, pushing costs

even higher unless shared by several people. In some areas, most notably Buenos Aires province, tolls on recently privatized highways are very high – as much as US$4 per 100 km.

Formally, you must have an International or Inter-American Driving Permit to supplement your national or state driver's license. In practice, police rarely examine these documents closely and generally ignore the latter. They do not ignore automobile registration, insurance, and tax documents, which must be up to date. Except in Buenos Aires, security problems are few, and you should not drive in Buenos Aires anyway.

Although motorbikes have become fashionable among some Argentines, they are very expensive, and I have never seen a rental company offering motorcycles in Argentina.

You may encounter certain words on the road that are worth heeding:

bache	pothole
cruce ferrocarril	railroad crossing
guardaganado	cattle guard
vado	dip

Rental

Major international rental agencies such as Hertz, Avis, and AI have offices in Buenos Aires and in major cities and other tourist areas throughout Argentina. To rent a car, you must have a valid driver's license and be at least 21 years of age; some agencies may not rent to anyone younger than 25. It may also be necessary to present a credit card such as MasterCard or Visa.

Even at minor agencies, rental charges are now very high. The cheapest and smallest vehicles go for about US$27 per day plus US$0.27 per km (you can sometimes negotiate a lower rate by paying in cash rather than by credit card); rates are even higher in Patagonia. When you factor in the cost of insurance and gasoline, operating a vehicle becomes very pricey indeed unless you have several people to share expenses. Although unlimited mileage deals do exist, they usually only apply to weekly or longer periods and are very expensive. One potentially worthwhile tactic is to make a reservation with one of the major international agencies in your home country, which can sometimes guarantee lower rates.

If you camp out – feasible in or near most cities as well as the countryside – rather than staying in hotels, the money you save may offset a good part of the rental cost.

Purchase

If you are spending several months in Argentina, purchasing a car is an alternative worth exploring, but it has both advantages and disadvantages. On the one hand, it is more flexible than public transport and is likely to be cheaper than rentals, which can easily reach US$100 per day. If you resell it at the end of your stay, it may turn out even more economical. On the other hand, any used car can be a risk, especially on the rugged back roads of Patagonia. When the gearbox gave out on our Peugeot pickup, we were fortunate enough to be in Bariloche, where it was easily but not cheaply repaired.

If you purchase a car, you must deal with the exasperating Argentine bureaucracy. You must have the title (*tarjeta verde* or green card), and license tax payments must be up-to-date. As a foreigner, you may find it very useful to get a notarized document authorizing your use of the car, since the bureaucracy does not move quickly enough to change the title easily. In any event, Argentines rarely do so because of the expense involved – even vehicles 30 years old or more often bear the original purchaser's name.

As a foreigner you may own a vehicle in Argentina, but, in theory at least, you may not take it out of the country even with a notarized authorization, although certain border crossings, such as Puerto Iguazú, appear to be more flexible. On the other hand, at Gualeguaychú in Entre Ríos province, Argentine customs were adamant in refusing permission for temporary export even with the legal owner's permission.

Contact your consulate for assistance and advice, but hardly anyone can prevail against a truly determined customs official.

Argentina's domestic automobile industry has left a reserve of serviceable used cars in the country. The most popular models are Peugeot 404s and Ford Falcons, for which parts are readily available, but do not expect to find a dependable used car for less than about US$3000. Prices will be higher for a *gasolero*, a vehicle that uses cheaper diesel fuel.

Insurance

Liability insurance is obligatory in Argentina, and police may ask to see proof of insurance at checkpoints. Fortunately, unlike many services in Argentina, it is reasonably priced; a four-month policy with US$1 million in coverage costs as little as US$90 (paid in cash), and it is also valid, with slightly reduced coverage, in the neighboring countries of Chile, Bolivia, Paraguay, Brazil, and Uruguay. Since Chilean companies, for example, cannot provide such extensive coverage outside their own borders, foreign motorists may find it worthwhile to cross from Santiago to Mendoza to arrange a policy.

Among reputable Argentine insurers are Seguros Belgrano, Seguros Rivadavia, and the Automóvil Club Argentino (ACA).

Road Rules & Hazards

Once, in the province of Buenos Aires, an Argentine driver passed us at very high speed *on the left side* of a traffic island separating one-way lanes at a major T-intersection. In another instance, in the province of Salta, an enormous truck blithely ignored a red light to pass us at an intersection where dozens of schoolgirls were crossing the highway on their way home for lunch. Yet another time, after dark in the province of Neuquén, a car traveling in excess of 150 km per hour *without headlights* passed and nearly collided with a large bus headed in the opposite direction. On furlough from prison in Santa Fe, where he was serving time for murdering his wife, former world middle-

weight boxing champion Carlos Monzón imposed his own death sentence in a high-speed highway accident in January 1995.

These incidents are not unusual – after 2000 traffic deaths in the first two months of 1995, the Argentine television network Telefé referred to the highway slaughter as the "Guerra del Tránsito" (the Traffic War). Anyone considering driving in Argentina should know that Argentine drivers are reckless, aggressive, and even willfully dangerous, ignoring speed limits, road signs, and even traffic signals. Traffic accidents are the main cause of death for Argentines between the ages of five and 35.

Theoretically, most Argentine highways have an 80 km/hour speed limit, though some have been raised to 100 km/hour, but hardly anybody pays attention to these or any other regulations. In the summer of 1991, Argentine President Carlos Menem drove his Ferrari Testarossa (a questionable gift from two Italian industrialists who later obtained rights to the prestigious Hotel Llao Llao near Bariloche) to the Atlantic coast resort of Pinamar, a distance of about 400 km, in a little over three hours. In 1994, Argentina's traffic fatality rate of 1200 per million vehicles was about five times that in Italy (241 per million) or the USA (229 per million).

Argentine police contribute almost nothing toward traffic safety. Shortly before Menem's excursion, the Buenos Aires provincial police had announced a major summer safety campaign, but they were directed *not* to interfere with a red Ferrari traveling at high speed to the Atlantic coast. In the summer of 1995, a check of violators approaching toll booths in excess of 150 km on RN 2 to Mar del Plata found that many of them were federal and provincial politicians, who were merely "advised" to "set an example" by obeying traffic laws.

Tailgating is another serious hazard – it is not unusual to see half a dozen cars a meter or less apart, waiting for their chance to overtake a truck which itself may be exceeding the speed limit. During the Pampas harvest season, pay particular attention to slow-moving farm machinery which, though not a hazard in its own right, brings out the worst in impatient Argentine motorists. Night driving is inadvisable; in some regions animals may roam on the road, but more often, many drivers seem to believe they can see in the dark and, consequently, do not bother to use headlights.

In fact, you will rarely see police patrolling the highways, where high-speed, head-on crashes are common, but you will meet them at major intersections and roadside checkpoints where they conduct meticulous document and equipment checks. A notoriously bad spot is the intersection of RN 9 and RN 14 at Zárate, in Buenos Aires province. Provincial borders also are frequently sites for these annoying inspections; especially irritating are the opposite ends of the tunnel beneath the Río Paraná, which connects the towns of Santa Fe (Santa Fe province) and Paraná (Entre Ríos province).

If one of these policemen asks to check your turn signals (which almost no Argentine bothers to use), brake lights, or hand brake, it may well be a warning of corruption in progress. Such equipment violations carry fines up to US$200, but equipment checks are most commonly pretexts for graft – the police may claim that you must pay the fine at a local bank which may not be open until the following day or, on a weekend, until Monday. If you are uncertain about your rights, state in a very matter-of-fact manner your intention to contact your embassy or consulate. Offer a *coima* only if you are confident that it is "appropriate" and unavoidable.

Astonishingly, in a country where nearly everyone drives dangerously fast even on very bad roads, a new traffic law that went into effect in 1995 *raises* speed limits to 120 km per hour on highways and 130 km per hour on motorways. Under the same law, drivers must carry their title document (*tarjeta verde* or green card; for foreign vehicles, customs permission is the acceptable substitute), emergency reflectors (*valizas*), and one-kilo fire extinguishers. Headrests are also required for the driver and each passenger, and motorcycle helmets are now obligatory.

Automóvil Club Argentino

If you drive in Argentina, especially with your own car, it may be worthwhile to become a member of the Automóvil Club Argentino (ACA), which has offices, service stations, and garages throughout the country, offering free road service and towing in and around major cities. However, ACA also recognizes members of its overseas affiliates, such as the American Automobile Association (AAA), as equivalent to its own members and grants them the same privileges, including discounts on maps, accommodations, camping, tours, and other services. Membership costs about US$30 per month, which is more expensive than most of its overseas counterparts.

ACA's head office (☎ 802-6061) is at Av del Libertador 1850, Palermo, in Buenos Aires. ACA has offices in every major city.

BICYCLE

Bicycling is an interesting, inexpensive alternative for traveling around Argentina – if you camp, it could make your trip nearly as cheap as in the Andean countries.

There are many good routes for bicycling, especially around the Patagonian lake district and in the Andean Northwest – the highway from Tucumán to Tafí del Valle, the direct road from Salta to Jujuy, and the Quebrada de Cafayate would be exceptionally beautiful rides on generally good surfaces.

While many Argentines use bikes for transportation, bicycling is an increasingly popular recreational activity. Many towns do have bike shops, but high-quality bikes are expensive and repair parts can be hard to come by. Bicycle rentals (primarily mountain bikes) are available in cities and towns such as Mendoza, Bariloche, and other towns in the Lake District, where recreation is an important industry. Racing bicycles are suitable for some paved roads, but these are often narrow; a *todo terreno* (mountain bike) would be safer and more convenient, allowing you to use the unpaved shoulder and the very extensive network of graveled roads throughout the country. Argentine bicycles are improving in quality but are still not equal to their counterparts in Europe or the US.

There are two major drawbacks to bicycling in Argentina. One is the wind, which in Patagonia can slow your progress to a crawl. Argentine motorists, with total disregard of anyone but themselves, are the other. On many of the country's straight, narrow, two-lane highways, they can be a real hazard to bicyclists, but LP reader Paul Arundale, who has cycled extensively through the Southern Cone, suggests less-traveled secondary roads as excellent alternatives:

Argentina is a wonderful country for cycling, as it is covered by a network of unsurfaced smooth earth or rough stone roads. This means that you can cycle anywhere in the country, even out of Buenos Aires and other large cities, without having to compete for road space with the speedy traffic on the main roads, as long as you are prepared with a good map and plenty of food and water.

On these unsurfaced roads traffic is maybe one or two pickup trucks per day and, without exception, overtaking vehicles move completely across to the left-hand side of the road, which is not the case on main roads. There are several unsurfaced routes crossing the Andes into Chile, such as the Caracoles to Cochrane road in the south and the Bardas Blancas to Talca and the Jáchal to Vicuña routes either side of Santiago, which offer ideal, traffic-free cycling for the well prepared. There are few fences near these roads, and a tent can be pitched anywhere.

Readers interested in more detailed information on cycling in South America can find more material in Bruce Junek's *Cycling in Latin America*.

HITCHHIKING

Along with Chile, Argentina is probably the best country for hitching in all of South America. The major drawback is that Argentine vehicles are often stuffed with families and children, but truckers will frequently pick up backpackers. At the *servi-centros* at the outskirts of large Argentine cities, where truckers gas up their vehicles, it is often worthwhile to solicit a ride.

Women can and do hitchhike alone, but they should exercise caution and especially avoid getting into a car with more than one man. In Patagonia, where distances are great and vehicles few, hitchers should expect long waits and carry warm, windproof clothing. A water bottle is also a good idea, especially in the desert north. Carry some snack food.

There are a few routes along which I would discourage hitching. RN 40, from Calafate to Perito Moreno and Río Mayo, carries very little traffic and is virtually hopeless, though I have met one person who did it successfully. The scenic route from Tucumán to Cafayate is very difficult past Tafí del Valle. The Andean crossing from Salta to Antofagasta, Chile, is utterly futile.

BOAT

There are limited opportunities for boat or river travel in Argentina, except for regular international services across the Río de la Plata to Uruguay, across the Andean lakes to Chile, and the very erratic services from Ushuaia, Tierra del Fuego, to Puerto Williams, Chile, on Isla Navarino.

There is a passenger ferry from Rosario, Santa Fe province, across the Río Paraná to Victoria, Entre Ríos. There are also numerous boat excursions around the River Plate Delta from Tigre, a suburb of Buenos Aires. Every winter, there is a river cruise up the Paraná to Asunción, Paraguay. Ask for details at travel agencies in the capital.

LOCAL TRANSPORT
To/From the Airport

In most Argentine cities, each airline has a minibus operating in tandem with the flight schedule; sometimes Aerolíneas Argentinas and Austral combine their operations. There is also usually a city bus which stops at the airport.

In Buenos Aires, there is a variety of ways to get to either the domestic airport

Aeroparque or the international airport at Ezeiza. See the chapter on Buenos Aires for details.

Bus

Even small Argentine cities have extensive public transportation networks, usually bus systems. Except when conducting "work-to-rule" stoppages, Buenos Aires' bus drivers go for speed before safety, and there have been serious accidents in which buses have run over pedestrians on the sidewalk as well as the street.

Buses are clearly numbered and usually carry a placard indicating their final destination. Since many identically numbered buses serve slightly different routes, pay attention to these placards. When you board a bus, tell the driver your final destination and he will indicate the fare; most buses now have automatic fare machines that issue the ticket and make change. Do not lose this ticket, which may be checked en route.

Train

Despite reductions in long-distance services, there remains an extensive system of commuter trains from Constitución, Retiro, Once, and Lacroze stations to the suburbs of Gran Buenos Aires. There are also trains between Rosario and its suburbs. During railroad strikes, trains may operate on severely reduced schedules.

Underground

Buenos Aires is the only Argentine city with a subway system. Although undergoing renovation, it is still an excellent way of getting around the city center. For details, see the Buenos Aires chapter.

Taxi & Remise

Like New Yorkers, the porteños of Buenos Aires make frequent use of taxis, which are digitally metered and reasonably priced. Outside Buenos Aires, meters are common but not universal, and it may be necessary to agree upon a fare in advance. Drivers are generally polite and honest, but there are exceptions; be sure the meter is set at zero. It is customary to round off the fare as a tip.

In areas such as Patagonia, where public transportation can be scarce, it is possible to hire a cab with a driver for the day to visit places off the beaten track. If you bargain, this can actually be cheaper than a rental car, but negotiate the fee in advance.

Remises are radio taxis without meters that generally offer fixed fares within a given zone. They are an increasingly popular form of transportation and are slightly cheaper than taxis. Unlike taxis, they may not cruise the city in search of fares.

Buenos Aires

When the recent Radical government of President Raúl Alfonsín proposed moving the seat of government to the small northern Patagonian city of Viedma, powerful opposition soon forced him to abandon the plan. His failure vividly illustrated the persistent dominance of Buenos Aires; the relatively small Capital Federal (federal district) and Gran Buenos Aires (Greater Buenos Aires), which includes nearby suburbs in Buenos Aires province, is home to nearly 40% of Argentina's 33 million citizens. Almost everyone admits that this concentration of political and economic power is undesirable, but the residents of large and important cities such as Córdoba and Rosario most vigorously criticize the capital's primacy.

HISTORY

Buenos Aires dates from 1536, when Spanish explorer Pedro de Mendoza camped on a bluff overlooking the Río de la Plata, possibly at the site of present-day Parque Lezama. Mendoza's oversized expedition, comprising 16 ships and nearly 1600 men, arrived too late in summer to plant crops, and the few Querandí Indians reacted with hostility when the Spaniards forced them to seek food. Scant provisions and incessant Indian resistance led some members of the expedition to sail up the Paraná, where they founded the city of Asunción among the more sedentary and obliging Guaraní peoples. Within five years, the Spaniards had completely abandoned Buenos Aires to the Querandí.

More than four decades passed before the Spaniards of Asunción, led by Juan de Garay, reestablished themselves on the west bank of the Río de la Plata. Even then, at the end of a tenuous supply line stretching from Madrid via Panama and Lima, Buenos Aires was clearly subordinate to

119

Asunción; the city managed to survive but did not flourish. Garay himself died at the hands of the Querandí only three years later.

Over the next two centuries, Buenos Aires grew slowly but steadily on the basis of enormous herds of feral cattle and horses that had proliferated on the Pampas. As local frustration with Spain's mercantile restrictions grew, merchants began to smuggle contraband transported on Portuguese and British vessels. In 1776 Buenos Aires' promotion to capital of the new Viceroyalty of the River Plate, which

included the famous silver district of Potosí, was palpable recognition that the adolescent city had outgrown Spain's parental authority.

In the late colonial history of Buenos Aires and the country, the British invasions of 1806 and 1807 were a major turning point; after first seeming to cooperate with British forces, criollo forces repelled them. Only three years later influential criollos, on the pretext that Spain's legitimate government had fallen, confronted and deposed Viceroy Cisneros. As described by American diplomat Caesar Rodney, the

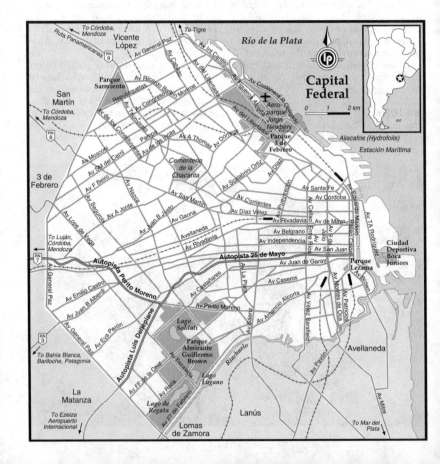

architects of the revolution and the people of the city showed remarkable restraint and maturity:

At some periods of the revolution, when the bands of authority were relaxed, the administration actually devolved into the hands of the inhabitants of the city. Hence, it might have been imagined, endless tumult and disorder would have sprung up, leading directly to pillage and bloodshed. Yet no such disturbances ever took place; all remained quiet . . . . The people have in no instance demanded victims to satisfy their vengeance; on the contrary, they have sometimes, by the influence of public opinion, moderated the rigor with which their rulers were disposed to punish the guilty.

Six years later, in Tucumán, the United Provinces of the River Plate declared independence but failed to resolve the conflict between two elite sectors: the landowners of the interior, concerned about preserving their economic privileges, and the residents of Buenos Aires (not yet the capital), who maintained an outward orientation toward overseas commerce and European ideas. After more than a decade of violence and uncertainty, Federalist caudillo Juan Manuel de Rosas asserted his authority over Buenos Aires.

When Charles Darwin visited Buenos Aires in 1833, shortly after the ruthless Rosas took power, he was impressed that the city of 60,000 was

large; and I should think one of the most regular in the world. Every street is at right angles to the one it crosses, and the parallel ones being equidistant, the houses are collected into solid squares of equal dimensions, which are called quadras. On the other hand the houses themselves are hollow squares; all the rooms opening into a neat little courtyard. They are generally only one story high, with flat roofs, which are fitted with seats, and are much frequented by the inhabitants in summer. In the center of the town is the plaza, where the public offices, fortress, cathedral . . . stand. Here also, the old viceroys, before the revolution had their palaces. The general assemblage of buildings possesses considerable architectural beauty, although none individually can boast of any.

Rosas' reign lasted nearly another three decades, during which time (ironically) Buenos Aires' influence grew despite his perhaps opportunistic Federalist convictions. His overthrow opened the city to European immigration, and the population grew from 90,000 in 1854, to 177,000 in 1869, to 670,000 by 1895. By the turn of the century, Latin America's largest city had more than a million inhabitants.

In the 1880s, when the city became the official federal capital, the indignant authorities of Buenos Aires province moved their government to a new provincial capital at La Plata. Still, as the agricultural exports boomed and imports flowed into the country, the port city became even more important. According to British diplomat James Bryce, none of the leaders of Glasgow, Manchester, or Chicago "shewed greater enterprise and bolder conceptions than did the men of Buenos Aires when on this exposed and shallow coast they made alongside their city a great ocean harbour."

Immigration and growth brought problems of course, as families crowded into substandard housing, merchants and manufacturers kept wages low, and labor became increasingly militant. In 1919, under pressure from landowners and other elite sectors, the Radical government of President Hipólito Yrigoyen ordered the Army to suppress a metalworkers' strike in what became known as La Semana Trágica (the Tragic Week), setting an unfortunate precedent for the coming decades.

In the 1930s, ambitious municipal governments undertook a massive downtown modernization program, as broad avenues like Santa Fe, Córdoba, and Corrientes obliterated narrow colonial streets. Since WWII, sprawling Gran Buenos Aires has absorbed many once-distant suburbs. Smaller in population than Mexico City or São Paulo, Buenos Aires remains Argentina's dominant economic, political, and cultural center. But a city that once prided itself on its European sophistication and livability now shares the same problems as other Latin American megacities – pollution, noise, decaying infrastructure, and declining public services, unemployment and underemployment, and spreading shantytowns.

Not all signs are negative. Since the restoration of democracy in 1984, Buenos Aires is once again a lively place, where political and public dialogue are freewheeling, the publishing industry has rebounded, and the arts and music flourish within the limits of economic reality. Fewer foolish public works projects, like the motorway to Ezeiza Airport, are being built. Buenos Aires may have seen its best days, but it should survive to offer the visitor a rich and unique urban experience.

ORIENTATION

At first glance, Buenos Aires may appear to be as massive and imposing as New York or London, but a brief orientation suffices for an exploration of the city's compact, regular center and the most accessible *barrios* (neighborhoods) on foot. On brutally hot and humid summer days, bus, underground, and taxi services are good alternatives.

The traditional focus of activity is the Plaza de Mayo, where hundreds of thousands have rallied to cheer Perón or jeer Galtieri. Both the cathedral and remaining portions of the original Cabildo are also here, at the east end of Av de Mayo. At the west end is the Plaza del Congreso, and the stately but now rather drab Congreso building, desperately in need of a facelift after years of disuse. Street names change on each side of Av de Mayo.

A pedestrian's nightmare, the broad Av 9 de Julio forms a second north-south axis, simultaneously encompassing Cerrito and Carlos Pellegrini north of Av de Mayo, and Lima and Bernardo de Irigoyen south of Av de Mayo. It runs from Plaza Constitución in the south to Av del Libertador, which leads to the city's exclusive northern suburbs and their spacious parks.

One of the most popular tourist zones is the *microcentro* north of Av de Mayo and east of 9 de Julio, an area that includes the Florida and Lavalle *peatonales* (pedestrian malls), Plaza San Martín, and the important

commercial and entertainment areas along Avs Corrientes, Córdoba, and Santa Fe. Florida is a peatonal for its entire length from Plaza San Martín to Diagonal Roque Sáenz Peña, while Lavalle is a peatonal only between Carlos Pellegrini and San Martín. Beyond Av Santa Fe are the chic neighborhoods of Recoleta and Palermo. South of the Plaza de Mayo are colorful, working-class San Telmo and La Boca.

North of downtown, the residential areas of Retiro and Recoleta are informally known as Barrio Norte. Along the river, the Av Costanera Rafael Obligado, more commonly known as "La Costanera," is a strip of restaurants and dance clubs, with occasional green spaces, that provides porteños' only real riverside access. Its major architectural landmark, the vaguely Tudor-style Club de Pescadores (Fishermen's Club), dates from 1937 and sits at the end of a 150-meter pier.

Street numbering is straightforward. Numbers on east-west streets start from zero near the waterfront, while those on north-south streets climb on each side of Av de Mayo. Only when you go outside the immediate center does numbering become more complicated.

Maps

Metrovías, the private operator of the Subte, publishes a very good pocket-sized map of its service area, which encompasses the great majority of the capital's tourist attractions; it's available free from most public information offices. Covering a smaller area on a larger scale, Guías Taylor's *Plano Turístico de la Ciudad de Buenos Aires* focuses on the microcentro and San Telmo, Recoleta, Boca, and Palermo barrios. Widely available from kiosks along Florida, it also contains a useful Subte diagram; oversized symbols for some landmarks detract from the map's readability.

For visitors spending some time in Buenos Aires, Lumi Transportes publishes *Capital Federal* and *Capital Federal y Gran Buenos Aires* in compact, ring-binder format, with all city streets and bus routes indexed. A similar worthwhile acquisition is the *Guía Peuser*.

INFORMATION
Tourist Offices
The Dirección Nacional de Turismo (☎ 312-2232), Av Santa Fe 883, is open weekdays 9 am to 5 pm; there's also a branch (☎ 480-0224) at Aeropuerto Internacional Ezeiza. Both have well-prepared English-speaking staff.

More convenient, for most purposes, are municipal tourist kiosks on Florida between Av Córdoba and Paraguay, at the intersection of Florida and Diagonal Roque Sáenz Peña, and at RM Ortiz and Av Quintana in Recoleta. These kiosks, which have excellent pocket-size maps in English and Spanish, as well as other brochures, are open weekdays 8:30 am to 8:30 pm, Saturdays 9 am to 7 pm, except for the one in Recoleta, which is open 10 am to 9 pm daily except Sunday, when it's open noon to 8 pm.

For more detailed information on the city, visit the municipal Dirección General de Turismo (☎ 476-3612, 371-1496) in the Centro Cultural San Martín, 5th floor, Sarmiento 1551. This office also organizes free guided walks of certain areas at 5 pm

Barrios of Buenos Aires

Saturdays and Sundays in summer, and at 3 pm the rest of the year, weather permitting.

For information and maps on the national parks, visit the Administración de Parques Nacionales (☎ 311-0303, ext 165), Santa Fe 690, which is at the north end of the Florida pedestrian mall.

The ACA central office (☎ 802-6061) in Palermo at Av del Libertador 1850 offers a wealth of member services and stocks a complete selection of provincial road maps.

Foreign Embassies

Buenos Aires has a large diplomatic corps from overseas and neighboring countries; for an extensive list, see the Facts for the Visitor chapter.

Immigration

The Dirección Nacional de Migraciones (☎ 312-3288) is located at Antártida Argentina 1335.

Money

While Domingo Cavallo's convertibility law has reduced the need to change money, dozens of exchange houses still line San Martín, Argentina's equivalent of Wall St or the City of London, south of Av Corrientes. There are many more to the north of Corrientes, along Corrientes itself, and on the Florida peatonal. The only real reason to use them is to cash traveler's checks, which are easier to change here than elsewhere in the country, or to exchange currencies other than US dollars, but an ATM card is a far better alternative. Cambio hours are generally 9 am to 6 pm weekdays, but a few open Saturday mornings. American Express, Arenales 707 near Plaza San Martín, will change its own traveler's checks without commission.

Downtown ATMs are now so common that it would be superfluous to mention any in particular. Holders of MasterCard and Visa can also get cash advances at most downtown banks between 10 am and 4 pm.

Lost or Stolen Credit Cards The following local representatives of major international banking institutions can aid travelers in replacing lost or stolen credit cards and/or traveler's checks:

American Express
    Arenales 707 (☎ 312-1661)
Diner's Club
    Carlos Pellegrini 1023 (☎ 815-4545)
MasterCard
    Hipólito Yrigoyen 878 (☎ 331-1021, 331-2559)
Visa
    Corrientes 1437, 3rd floor (☎ 954-2000)

Post

Public The architecturally distinctive Correo Central, Sarmiento 189, occupies an entire block along Av Leandro Alem between Av Corrientes and Sarmiento. Open weekdays 9 am to 7:30 pm, it's the only post office to deal with international express mail. It does not accept US dollars.

For international parcels weighing more than one kg, visit the Correo Internacional, on Antártida Argentina, near Retiro Station. Hours are weekdays 11 am to 5 pm.

When writing to addresses in Buenos Aires, bear in mind that Argentines often refer to the city as the "Capital Federal." Porteños often shorten this term further to "la capital."

Private Private-run international and national services are more dependable than Correo Argentino (ex-Encotel) but also more expensive. Federal Express (☎ 325-6551) is at Maipú 753, while DHL International (☎ 343-1687) is at Hipólito Yrigoyen 448. OCA (☎ 788-7777), which makes domestic connections for several international couriers, is at Echeverría 1238 in Belgrano. Private international mail services accept US dollars.

Telephones

Argentina's two phone companies, Telecom and Telefónica, have split the city down the middle at Av Córdoba; theoretically, everything north belongs to Telecom, while everything south is the responsibility of Telefónica, but occasionally there's a bit of overlap. Despite improvements in service and infrastructure since privatization, you will often find that, even if your call gets through, the person at the other end will be unable to hear you. Repairs can take weeks, and coordination between the two companies is very poor.

Most public telephones now work, though they are usually located on noisy corners. To make a local call, purchase *cospeles* (tokens) or more convenient phonecards from almost any kiosk or newsstand, or from street vendors. Should you get through, you will only be able to speak for about two minutes, so carry a pocketful of cospeles. There are two kinds of cospeles, one for local calls and one for long-distance.

Long-distance offices are usually very busy, especially during the evening (10 pm to 8 am) and weekend discount hours when overseas calls are most economical. Telefónica's most convenient and efficient office, open 24 hours, is at Corrientes 701, where direct links with operators in North America, Japan, Europe, and neighboring countries greatly simplify overseas collect or credit card calls (see Facts for the Visitor for a list of operator services). Otherwise, an attendant will give you a priority number and, when that number is called, a cashier will give you a ticket for a booth; once in the booth, you can either dial directly or request operator assistance. When you finish your call, pay the cashier.

Since the demise of ENTel, many locutorios have sprung up around central Buenos Aires, so it's usually not necessary to make a long detour simply to place a long distance or overseas call, or send or receive a fax. However, few locutorios care to handle collect or credit card calls, which must be placed at Telecom or Telefónica offices, or from a private telephone.

Buenos Aires' area code is 01.

Telegrams, Telex & Fax

International telegrams, telexes, and faxes can be sent from Encotel, which is still a state monopoly, at Corrientes 711 next door to the main Telefónica office.

Cultural Centers

One of Buenos Aires' best resources is the high-rise Centro Cultural San Martín (☎ 374-1251), which has free or inexpensive galleries, live theater, lectures, and films. Most visitors enter from Corrientes, between Paraná and Montevideo, but the official address is Sarmiento 1551, where a shaded alcove has changing exhibitions of outdoor sculptures and occasional free concerts on summer weekends.

At Junín 1930 in Recoleta, the Centro Cultural Ciudad de Buenos Aires (☎ 803-1041) also offers free or inexpensive events, such as art exhibitions and outdoor films on summer evenings.

The United States Information Agency's Lincoln Center (☎ 311-7148), Florida 935, has an excellent library that carries US newspapers and magazines. The center also has satellite TV transmissions from the US and often shows free, sometimes very unconventional, films. Hours are Monday, Tuesday, Thursday, and Friday 10:30 am to 6:15 pm, and Wednesday 5 to 9:30 pm. It's closed weekends and on US holidays.

Another source of information for North Americans is the Instituto Cultural Argentino-Norteamericano (☎ 322-3855, 322-4557), Maipú 672. The Instituto Goethe (☎ 315-3327), 1st floor, Av Corrientes 319 between 25 de Mayo and Reconquista, not far from Florida, offers German-language instruction, lectures and films. The Alianza Francesa (☎ 322-0068) is at Av Córdoba 936.

Travel Agencies

ASATEJ (☎ 311-6953, fax 311-6840), Argentina's nonprofit student travel agency and an affiliate of STA Travel, is on the 3rd floor, Oficina 319-B, at Florida 835. Open weekdays from 11 am to 7 pm, it has the cheapest airfares available (the US$159 roundtrip to Santiago, Chile, is only slightly more than the bus fare) and a brochure of discount offers at hotels, restaurants and other businesses for holders of international student cards. Some of its tours are remarkable bargains.

Another youth- and student-oriented

travel agency is the Asociación Argentina de Albergues de la Juventud (☎ /fax 476-1001), 2nd floor, Oficina 6, Talcahuano 214. It issues hostel memberships and international student cards, and has a message board for travelers (mostly young Argentines), seeking companions for extended trips.

American Express (☎ 312-0900, fax 315-1866), Arenales 707, will cash its own traveler's checks, but also offers many other travel services. Reader-recommended Swan Turismo (☎ 311-3537, fax 311-3537), Viamonte 464, will help renegotiate the Visit Argentina Pass and make connections with LADE or other airlines for which timetables are not easily available outside the country.

Bookstores

Buenos Aires' landmark bookshop El Ateneo (☎ 325-6801), Florida 340, has a large selection of travel books, including LP guides, but foreign language books are expensive. Librería ABC at Córdoba 685 and Hachette (☎ 322-6947) at Córdoba 936 have similar stock. Fondo de Cultura Económica (☎ 322-0825), Suipacha 615, is a major Spanish-language publisher that runs an expanding chain offering general interest material in addition to its own specialties in history, economics, sociology and the like.

For the most complete selection of guidebooks, including nearly every LP title in print, visit Librerías Turísticas (☎ 963-2866, ☎ /fax 962-5547) at Paraguay 2457 (Línea D, Subte Pueyrredón), near Barrio Norte. Its prices are also the most reasonable for foreign language guidebooks.

Visiting academics and curiosity seekers should explore the basement stacks at Platero (☎ 382-2215), Talcahuano 485, which stocks a remarkable selection of new and out-of-print books about Argentina and Latin America. The staff is knowledgeable in almost every field of interest, and trustworthy and efficient in packaging and sending books overseas. Another good shop with similar stock is Aquilanti (☎ 952-4546), Rincón 79 in the Congreso area.

French speakers can find a wide selection of reading material at Oficina del Libro Francés, with locations at Esmeralda 861 (☎ 311-0363) and Talcahuano 342, 2nd floor (☎ 46-4747).

Several street markets have good selections of used books, including those at Plaza Lavalle near Librería Platero; Av Santa Fe outside the Palermo Subte station; and outside the Primera Junta Subte station (end of the line for Línea A).

Film & Photography

Kinefot (☎ 374-7445), Talcahuano 248, has fast, high-quality developing of E-6 slide film, but it's not cheap. For prints, try Le Lab (☎ 322-2785) at Viamonte 624 or Laboclick at Esmeralda 444.

For minor camera repairs, visit Gerardo Föhse, in the basement at Florida 835, Local 37 (☎ 311-1139). For fast, dependable service on more complex problems, phone José Norres (☎ 326-0963), 4th floor, Oficina 403, Lavalle 1569, who accepts payment in US dollars only.

Medical Services

Buenos Aires' Hospital Municipal Juan Fernández (☎ 801-5555) is at Av Cerviño 3356 in Palermo, but there are many others, including the highly regarded British Hospital (☎ 304-1081) at Perdriel 74, a few blocks northwest of the Constitución train station.

Dangers & Annoyances

Personal security is a lesser concern in Buenos Aires than in most other Latin American cities, but travelers cannot afford to be complacent – pickpockets, purse-snatchers and the like certainly exist. Watch for common diversions such as the "inadvertent" collision that results in ice cream or some similar substance being spilled on an unsuspecting visitor, who loses precious personal possessions while distracted by the apologetic perpetrator working in concert with a thief (one LP reader has eloquently referred to them as "mustard artists").

Porteño drivers, like most Argentines,

jump the gun when the red light is about to turn green. Be especially wary of vehicles turning right; though pedestrians at corners and crosswalks have legal right-of-way, almost nobody behind the wheel concedes it. Other troublesome and potentially deadly hazards include potholes and loose tiles on city sidewalks, which can also be very slippery when wet – people have died after falling and striking their heads.

BARRIOS OF BUENOS AIRES

Most porteños "belong" to a *barrio* (neighborhood) where they have spent almost all their lives. Tourists rarely explore most of these, but five fairly central ones and one outlying barrio of Belgrano contain most of the capital's major attractions. The boundaries indicated below are more convenient than precise and sometimes even overlap, but they should orient you to the most important public buildings, parks and museums. Note that most museums charge about US$1 admission but are usually free of charge Wednesday or Thursday.

Plaza de Mayo & the Microcentro

Juan de Garay refounded Buenos Aires in 1580, just north of Pedro de Mendoza's encampment near Parque Lezama. In accordance with Spanish law, he laid out the large Plaza del Fuerte (Fortress Plaza), later called the Plaza del Mercado (Market Plaza). The Plaza de la Victoria was laid out after the victories over the British invaders in 1806 and 1807. It acquired its present name of **Plaza de Mayo** after the month in which the Revolution of 1810 occurred.

Major colonial buildings here included the **Cabildo** (see below), part of which still exists, and a church at a site now occupied by the **Catedral Metropolitana**. Inside the catedral is the tomb of the repatriated San Martín, who died in France. In the center of the plaza, the **Pirámide de Mayo** is a small obelisk over an earlier monument, around which the Madres de la Plaza de Mayo still march every Thursday afternoon in their

unrelenting campaign for a full accounting of Dirty War atrocities.

At the east end of the plaza, the **Casa Rosada** (presidential palace) begun during Sarmiento's presidency, occupies a site where colonial riverbank fortifications once stood – today it is more than a kilometer inland because of land filling. From its balcony, Juan Perón, General Leopoldo Galtieri, Raúl Alfonsín, and other Argentine politicians have convened throngs of impassioned Argentines when they deemed necessary a show of public support. In 1955, naval aircraft strafed the Casa Rosada and other downtown buildings in the so-called Revolución Libertadora, which toppled Perón.

Most other public buildings in the area were constructed in the 19th century, when Av de Mayo first connected the Casa Rosada to the **Plaza del Congreso** and the **Palacio del Congreso**, unfortunately obliterating part of the historic and dignified Cabildo in the process. British diplomat Bryce, though, found these developments symbols of progress:

One great thoroughfare, the Avenida de Mayo, traverses the center of the city from the large plaza in which the government buildings stand to the still larger and very handsome plaza which is adorned by the palace of the legislature. Fortunately it is wide, and being well planted with trees it is altogether a noble street, statelier than Piccadilly in London, or Unter den Linden in Berlin, or Pennsylvania Avenue in Washington . . .

The streets are well kept; everything is fresh and bright. The most striking new buildings besides those of the new Legislative Chambers, with their tall and handsome dome, are the Opera-house, the interior of which equals any in Europe, and the Jockey Club, whose scale and elaborate appointments surpass even the clubhouses of New York.

Modern Buenos Aires' faded elegance and failure to keep pace with European and North American capitals might surprise Bryce today, but visitors can still glimpse the city's "Belle Epoque", even though the focus of downtown activities has moved north along streets like Florida, Lavalle, and Avs Corrientes, Córdoba, and Santa Fe.

ARGENTINA

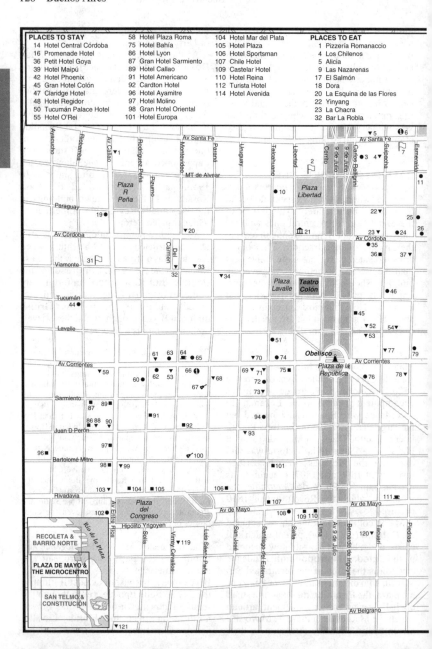

ARGENTINA

33	Coto	68	Pippo
34	La Casa China	69	Pizzería Güerrín,
37	Broccolino	70	Pizzería Los Inmortales
49	El Pulpo	71	Pizzería Serafín
52	La Estancia	73	Los Teatros
53	El Palacio de la Papa Frita	77	La Rural
54	La Casona del Nonno	78	Verde Esmeralda
56	Oriente	88	Cervantes II
59	El Toboso	90	Pizzería La Continental
61	Heladería Cadore	93	Vecchio Unione
64	Café La Paz	99	La Americana

103	Confitería del Molino
111	Café Tortoni
119	La Fonda de Montserrat
120	Swedish Club
121	La Cabaña

OTHER

2	Italian Consulate
3	LAER
6	Dirección Nacional de Turismo
7	French/Swiss Consulates
8	Manuel Tienda León
10	Caño 14
11	LAPA
12	Parques Nacionales
13	Lincoln Center
15	Peruvian Consulate
19	Clásica y Moderna
21	Teatro Cervantes/Museo Nacional del Teatro
24	Buquebus
25	Oficina del Libro Francés
26	Aliscafos
27	Ferrytur
28	Librería ABC
29	Municipal Tourist Kiosk
30	ASATEJ/Föhse Camera Repair
31	Paraguayan Consulate
35	Alianza Francesca, Hachette
38	Instituto Cultural Argentino-Norteamericano
40	Federal Express
41	Galerías Pacífico
43	Swan Turismo
44	Sapse Líneas Aéreas
46	Fondo de Cultura Económica
51	Librería Platero
57	Chilean Consulate
60	Teatro El Vitral
62	Teatro La Plaza, Paseo La Plaza, Cartelera Vca Mas
63	Teatro Presidente Alvear
65	Foro Gandhi
66	Centro Cultural San Martín, Teatro General San Martín
67	Oliverio
72	Oficina del Libro Francés
74	Teatro Blanca Podestá
76	Dinar Líneas Aéreas
79	Teatro Esmeralda
80	Telefónica/Encotel
81	Cotton Club de Buenos Aires
82	El Ateneo
83	Museo Mitre
84	Austral Líneas Aéreas
85	Instituto Goethe
94	Asociación Argentina de Albergues de la Juventud
95	Archivo y Museo Histórico del Banco de la Provincia de Buenos Aires Doctor Arturo Jauretche
100	El Subsuelo
102	Palacio del Congreso
108	Teatro Avenida
113	Municipal Tourist Kiosk
115	Aerolíneas Argentinas
116	Cabildo
117	DHL International
118	Casa Rosada

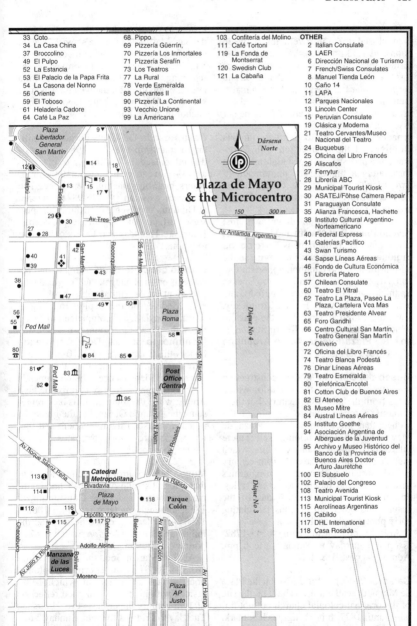

In the early part of the century Florida, then closed to motor vehicles between noon and 1:30 pm, was the capital's most fashionable shopping street – a status since lost to Av Santa Fe. Today both Florida and perpendicular Lavalle are pedestrian malls. Demolition of older buildings created the broad avenues of Corrientes (the theater district), Córdoba, and Santa Fe. The even broader Av 9 de Julio, with its famous **Obelisco** at the intersection with Corrientes, is a pedestrian's worst nightmare, but fortunately a tunnel runs underneath it. Two blocks north of the Obelisco, the **Teatro Colón** is Buenos Aires' major architectural and cultural landmark.

At the north end of downtown, just beyond **Plaza San Martín** and its magnificent *ombú* tree, is the famous **Torre de los Ingleses**, a Big Ben clone testifying to the partial truth of the common aphorism that "an Argentine is an Italian who speaks Spanish, wishes he were English, and behaves as if he were French." Ironically, since the 1982 Falklands War the plaza in which it stands, opposite Retiro Station, is now the **Plaza Fuerza Aérea Argentina** (Air Force Plaza).

Museo del Cabildo Modern construction has twice truncated the Cabildo, which dates from the mid-18th century, but there remains a representative sample of the arches that once crossed the Plaza de Mayo. The two-story building itself is more interesting than the scanty exhibits, which include mementos of the early 19th-century British invasions, some modern paintings in Colonial- and Independence-era styles, and religious art from missions of the Jesuits and other orders, plus fascinating early photographs of the plaza.

At Bolívar 65, the museum (☎ 343-1782) is open Thursday to Sunday 2 to 6 pm. Admission costs US$1.

Catedral Metropolitana Also on the Plaza de Mayo, the cathedral was built on the site of the original colonial church but not finished until 1827. It is a religious landmark, but it's an even more important national historical site, containing the tomb of José de San Martín, Argentina's most revered hero. In the chaos following independence, San Martín chose exile in France, never returning alive to the shores of Argentina even though, in 1829, the boat on which he was traveling to Montevideo dropped anchor in the harbor.

Casa Rosada Off-limits during the military dictatorship of 1976 – 1983, the presidential palace is no longer a place to avoid – you can even photograph the grenadiers guarding the main entrance. The basement museum (☎ 476-9841), entered at Hipólito Yrigoyen 219, exhibits the personal effects of Argentine presidents. Hours are Thursday and Friday only, noon to 6 pm.

Palacio del Congreso Costing more than twice its original budget, the Congreso set a precedent for Argentine public works projects. Modeled on the Capitol Building in Washington, DC, and completed in 1906, it faces the Plaza del Congreso, where the **Monumento a los Dos Congresos** honors the Congresses of 1810 in Buenos Aires and 1816 in Tucumán that led to Argentine independence. The monument's enormous granite steps symbolize the high Andes, while the fountain at its base represents the Atlantic Ocean, but the hordes of pigeons that stain the monument and foul its waters are poor surrogates for the Andean condor.

Museo Mitre Bartolomé Mitre was a soldier, journalist, and Argentina's first legitimate president under the Constitution of 1853, although his term ran from 1862 – 1868. After leaving office he founded the influential daily *La Nación,* which is still a porteño institution.

At San Martín 366, the Museo Mitre (☎ 394-7659) is an enormous colonial house (plus additions) in which Mitre resided with his family – a good reflection of 19th-century upper-class life. Hours are Tuesday to Friday 1 to 6 pm, Sunday 2 to 6 pm. Admission is US$1.

Teatro Colón For decades, visitors to Buenos Aires have marveled at the Teatro Colón (☎ 382-6632), a world-class facility for opera, ballet, and classical music, which opened in 1908 with a presentation of *Aida*. Occupying an entire block bounded by Libertad, Tucumán, Viamonte and Cerrito (Av 9 de Julio), the imposing seven-story building seats 2500 and has standing room for another 1000. Presidential command performances take place on the winter patriotic holidays of May 25 and July 9, but no events are scheduled in the summer months of January and February.

Guided tours, which cost US$5 and take place hourly between 9 am and 4 pm weekdays, and 9 am and noon Saturdays, are available in Spanish, English, German, French, Portuguese, and even Danish, but only Spanish and English are always available. On these very worthwhile tours, visitors see the theater all the way from the basement workshops (which employ over 400 skilled carpenters, sculptors, wigmakers, costume designers and other *técnicos*), as well as rehearsal rooms and the stage and seating areas.

Other Downtown Museums The well-organized **Archivo y Museo Histórico del Banco de la Provincia de Buenos Aires Doctor Arturo Jauretche** (☎ 331-1775), Sarmiento 362, is a superb introduction to Argentine economic and financial history from viceregal times to the present.

At the **Museo Nacional del Teatro** (☎ 815-8883, ext 195), in the Teatro Cervantes at Córdoba 1199 opposite Plaza Lavalle, prime exhibits include a gaucho suit worn by Gardel during his Hollywood film *El Día Que Me Quieras*. Also on display is the bandoneón belonging to Paquita Bernardo, the first Argentine musician to play the accordion-like instrument, who died of tuberculosis in 1925 at the age of 25. Admission is free.

A bit farther away, at Sarmiento 2573 between Larrea and Paso, the best exhibits at the **Museo del Cine Pablo D Hicken** (film museum, ☎ 952-4528) are models like that of the *Merrimac*, on which Sar-

miento sailed back to Argentina from the USA and learned that he had been elected president in absentia. Its Sala María Luisa Bemberg contains scenery from the director's well-known films *Camila*, *Yo, La Peor de Todas*, and *Miss Mary* (the latter in English, with Julie Christie). It's open weekdays 9 am to 4 pm.

San Telmo

South of the Plaza de Mayo, San Telmo is an artist's quarter where Bohemians find large spaces at low rents, but it's also the site of high-density slum housing in *conventillos* (tenements) once built as single-family housing for the capital's elite.

San Telmo is also famous for the rugged street fighting that took place when British troops invaded the city in 1806 and occupied it until the following year, when covert porteño resistance gave way to open counterattack. When British forces advanced up narrow Calle Defensa, an impromptu militia, supported by women and slaves pouring cauldrons of boiling oil and water from the rooftops and firing cannons from the balconies of the house at **Defensa 372**, routed the British back to their ships. Victory gave porteños confidence in their ability to stand apart from Spain, though independence had to wait another decade.

In this area, bounded by Alsina, Bolívar, Perú, and Moreno, the **Manzana de las Luces** (Block of Enlightenment) includes the Jesuit Iglesia San Ignacio, the city's oldest colonial church (see below). At Defensa and Humberto Primo, **Plaza Dorrego** is the site of the famous Sunday flea market, the Feria de San Telmo. A few blocks beyond, at Defensa and Brasil, **Parque Lezama** is the presumptive site of Pedro de Mendoza's original foundation of the city.

After yellow fever hit the once-fashionable area in the late 19th century, the porteño elite evacuated to higher ground west and north of the present-day microcentro. As immigrants poured into Argentina, many of the older houses became conventillos housing European families in cramped, divided quarters with inadequate sanitary facilities. These conditions still exist – look for crumbling older houses with laundry on the balconies; a good example is the sprawling edifice at the corner of Humberto Primo and Balcarce.

Manzana de las Luces In colonial times, this was Buenos Aires' center of learning and, to some degree, it still symbolizes high culture in the capital. The first to occupy the block were the Jesuits; on the north side of the Manzana, fronting on Alsina, two of the five original buildings remain of the Jesuit **Procuraduría**, currently undergoing restoration. After independence, the Universidad de Buenos Aires occupied this site, the entrance of which is at Perú 222.

Fronting on Bolívar, the **Iglesia San Ignacio**, with its rococo interior, dates from 1712; after the demolition of 1904, there remains only a single original cloister. It shares a wall with the **Colegio Nacional de Buenos Aires**, where generations of the Argentine elite have received secondary schooling and indoctrination.

Slow-paced tours conducted by the Instituto de Investigaciones Históricas de la Manzana de las Luces Doctor Jorge E Garrido (☎ 342-6973), Perú 272, provide the only regular public access to the block's interior. Tours (US$2) take place at 6 pm Friday, Saturday, and Sunday.

Museo Histórico Nacional Appropriately sited in Parque Lezama, this historical museum offers a panorama of the Argentine experience from its shaky beginnings to the present. The paintings in its Sala de la Conquista depicting the Spanish domination of wealthy, civilized Peru and Columbus' triumphant return to Spain contrast sharply with those of the Mendoza expedition's struggle on the shores of the Río de la Plata. There is also a map of Juan de Garay's second founding of the city four decades later.

In the Sala de la Independencia and other rooms are portraits of major figures like Simón Bolívar, his ally and rival San Martín both as a youth and disillusioned in

San Telmo & Constitución

0   150   300 m

PLACES TO STAY
1   Hotel Nogaró
10 Hotel Victoria
18 Hotel Bolívar
26 Hotel Carly
28 Hotel Zavalia
29 Albergue Juvenil

PLACES TO EAT
5   Laurak Bat
8   Taberna Baska
12 Nicole de Marseille
14 Último Tango
17 Hostal del Canigó
19 Jerónimo
21 La Casa de Esteban de Luca
22 Pizzería Las Marías II
23 La Tasca de San Fermín
24 Antigua Casca de Cuchilleros
30 La Carretería

OTHER
2   Museo de la Ciudad
3   Museo San Roque
4   Aerolíneas Argentinas
6   Casa de la Defensa/Museo
    Nacional del Grabado
7   Iglesia de Nuestra Señora
    del Rosario, Museo de la
    Basílica del Rosario
9   Museo del Traje
11 La Casa Blanca
13 A Media Luz
15 Hendrix
16 El Viejo Almacén
17 Teatro Margarita Xirgu
20 Los Dos Pianitos
25 Bar Sur
27 Museo de Arte Moderno,
    Instituto Nacional Belgrano
31 Museo Histórico Nacional

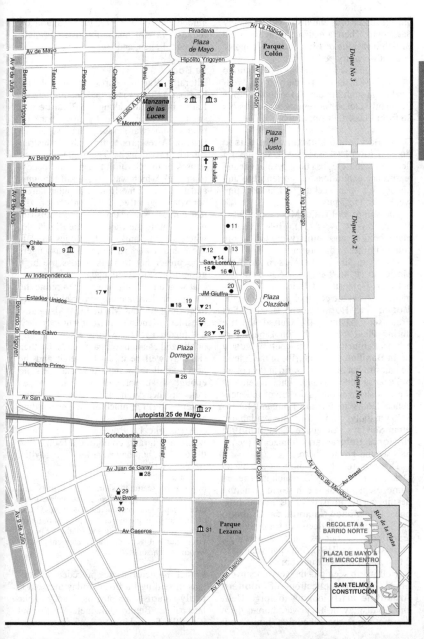

old age, and Rosas and his scowling enemy Sarmiento. There are also portrayals of the British invasions of 1806 and 1807, and of late 19th-century porteño life.

At Defensa 1600, the Museo Histórico (☎ 307-1182) is theoretically open Wednesday through Sunday, 2 to 6 pm, but it's frequently closed for repairs. Take bus No 86 from Plaza del Congreso.

Other San Telmo Museums The **Museo de la Ciudad** (☎ 331-9855), on the 1st floor at Alsina 412, has both permanent and temporary exhibitions on porteño life and history. It's open weekdays 11 am to 7 pm, weekends 3 to 7 pm.

The **Museo del Traje** (Museum of Dress & Uniforms, ☎ 343-8427), Chile 832, displays civilian and military clothing from colonial times to the present.

The main site of the **Museo de Arte Moderno** (☎ 46-9426) is at San Juan 350 between Defensa and Balcarce. For religious art from the colonial period, visit the **Museo San Roque** at the Basílica San Francisco, Alsina 340. Gutted by fire during the 1955 Revolución Libertadora against Perón, the late 18th-century **Museo de la Basílica del Rosario**, in the Iglesia de Nuestra Señora del Rosario at the corner of Defensa and Belgrano, contains relics of the British invasions and wars of independence. Hours are 9 am to 1 pm and 4:30 to 8:30 pm daily; guided tours are available at 3 pm Sundays. Alongside it, the **Instituto Nacional Belgraniano** lionizes Argentina's second-greatest hero.

The restored 19th-century Casa de la Defensa at Defensa 372, which may retain some elements of the historic structure despite an ill-advised 1970s remodeling, houses the **Museo Nacional del Grabado** (☎ 345-5300), a collection of mostly contemporary woodcuts and engravings. Admission costs US$2; it's open weekdays 2 to 6 pm, Sundays 1 to 6 pm.

Well worth seeing is the very unconventional private collection of **modern Argentine art** belonging to Jorge Helft and on display in his private home; there are no regularly scheduled hours, but

guided tours (☎ 307-9175) are available on request in Spanish, English, French, German, Italian, and Hungarian.

La Boca
Literally Buenos Aires' most colorful barrio, La Boca was settled and built up by Italian immigrants along the **Riachuelo**, a small waterway lined by meat packing plants and warehouses that separates Buenos Aires proper from the industrial suburb of Avellaneda. The brightly painted houses of the **Caminito**, a popular pedestrian walk which was once a rail terminus and takes its name from a popular tango, contributes greatly to La Boca's color. The rest comes from petroleum and industrial wastes tinting the waters of the Riachuelo, where rusting hulks and dredges lie offshore and rowers strain to take passengers who prefer not to walk across the high girder bridge to Avellaneda.

It would probably be easier to refine the oleaginous Riachuelo into diesel fuel than to clean it up, but María Julia Alsogaray, President Menem's environment secretary, has pledged to swim in it when a highly publicized cleanup campaign ends. By then she may well be in a wheelchair and the heavily polluted watercourse may be solid enough to support her; at present, when rains are heavy and tides are high, flood waters submerge much of the surrounding area.

Areas like La Boca were once places where immigrants could find a foothold in the country, but they were less than idyllic. Bryce described them as

a waste of scattered shanties . . . dirty and squalid, with corrugated iron roofs, their wooden boards gaping like rents in tattered clothes. These are inhabited by the newest and poorest of immigrants from southern Italy and southern Spain, a large and not very desirable element among whom anarchism is rife.

In fact, French Basques preceded the Italians in settling La Boca. Today the area is partly an artists' colony, the legacy of the late painter Benito Quinquela Martín, but it's still a flourishing working-class neighborhood. The symbol of community solidarity is the Boca Juniors soccer team, once the club of disgraced superstar Diego Maradona.

Tourists also come to La Boca to savor the atmosphere of **Calle Necochea**, which is lined with pizzerías and garish cantinas. When these places were still brothels, the tango was not the respectable, middle-class phenomenon it is today.

The No 86 bus from Congreso is the easiest route to La Boca, although Nos 20, 25, 29, 33, 46, 53, 64, and 97 also stop in the vicinity of the Caminito.

Museo de Bellas Artes de La Boca

Once the home and studio of Benito Quinquela Martín, La Boca's fine arts museum exhibits his work and that of other 20th-century Argentine artists. At Pedro de Mendoza 1835, the museum (☎ 301-1080) is open Tuesday to Saturday 8 am to 6 pm. Admission is free.

Recoleta

Northwest of downtown, the fashionable Recoleta takes its name from the Franciscan convent that dates from 1716, but it is best known for the **Cementerio de la Recoleta** (Recoleta Cemetery), an astonishing necropolis where, in death as in life, generations of the Argentine elite repose in ornate splendor. (For additional information, see the Life & Death aside below.)

Alongside the cemetery, the **Iglesia de Nuestra Señora de Pilar**, a colonial church consecrated in 1732, is a national historical monument; adjacent to it is the important **Centro Cultural Ciudad de Buenos Aires**. Within easy walking distance are the Museo Nacional de Bellas Artes (see below), and the **Centro Municipal de Exposiciones**, which hosts book fairs and other cultural events.

Recoleta was among the areas to which the upper-class porteños of San Telmo relocated after yellow fever outbreaks in the 1870s. It has many attractive public gardens and open spaces, including **Plaza Alvear**, **Plaza Francia** (where the capital's largest crafts fair takes place on Sun-

days), and several other parks stretching into the barrios of Palermo and Belgrano. One of the area's most characteristic and entertaining sights are its *pasaperros* (professional dog walkers) strolling with a dozen or more canines on leash.

Biblioteca Nacional After a decade of construction problems and delays, this ultra-modern Proceso-era project (☎ 806-4729) opened just a few years ago, but the plaster is already cracking on some of the landscaped outdoor terraces. Prominent Argentine and Latin American literary figures like Ernesto Sábato frequently offer lectures at the facility. Open weekdays from 10 am to 9 pm, it's at Agüero 2510.

Museo Nacional de Bellas Artes

Unquestionably the country's most important art museum, Bellas Artes (Fine Arts Museum, ☎ 803-0802) houses works by European masters like Renoir, Rodin, Monet, Toulouse-Lautrec and Van Gogh, as well as 19th- and 20th-century Argentine artists. At Av del Libertador 1473, it's open daily except Monday 12:30 to 7:30 pm; on Saturdays it opens at 9:30 am. Admission is free.

Museo Municipal de Arte Hispanoamericano Isaac Fernández Blanco

Containing an exceptional collection of colonial art, including silverwork, painting, costumes, and antiques, this museum (☎ 393-6318) occupies a colonial-style house with attractive gardens at Suipacha 1422. Hours are daily (except Mondays) 2 to 7 pm. Admission is US$2, but it's free Thursdays.

Museo de Motivos Argentinos José Hernández

Named for the author of the gaucho epic *Martín Fierro,* this museum (☎ 802-9967) really should be called Museo Carlos Daws after the Anglo-Argentine who donated most of the Argentine folk art on display here dating from prehistory through the colonial period to the present. It's open weekdays from 8 am to 7 pm and weekends 3 to 7 pm, at Av del

Libertador 2373. Admission costs US$1, but it's free Wednesdays.

Other Recoleta Museums The **Museo Eduardo Sívori**, a museum of Argentine art in the Centro Cultural Ciudad de Buenos Aires at Calle Junín 1930, is open Tuesday to Friday 3 to 8 pm, weekends 10 am to 8 pm. Sívori was an Italo-Argentine painter who studied in Europe but later returned to Argentine themes mainly inspired by rural life on the Pampas.

Only a few minutes' from the Museo Sívori, housed in the Palais de Glace at Posadas 1725, the **Salas Nacionales de Cultura** (☎ 804-4324) offers rotating cultural, artistic, and historical exhibitions. Once a skating rink, the unusual circular building is open weekdays 1 to 8 pm, weekends 3 to 8 pm.

The **Museo Nacional de Arte Decorativo** (National Museum of Decorative Arts, ☎ 802-6606) and the **Museo de Arte Oriental** (Museum of Oriental Art, ☎ 801-5988) share the same building at Av Libertador 1902. Both of them are open weekdays, 3 to 7 pm.

Palermo
Ironically, Juan Manuel de Rosas' most

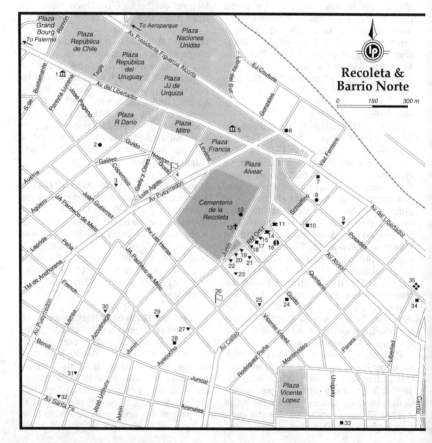

Recoleta & Barrio Norte

positive legacy is the wide open spaces of Palermo, beyond Recoleta on both sides of Av Libertador. Once the dictator's private retreat, the area became public parkland after his fall from power. One measure of the dictator's disgrace is that the man who overthrew him, Entre Ríos caudillo and former ally Justo José de Urquiza, sits here astride his mount in a mammoth equestrian monument on the corner of Sarmiento and Figueroa Alcorta; the surrounding Parque Tres de Febrero bears the date of Rosas' defeat at the battle of Caseros.

When British diplomat Bryce visited Buenos Aires after the turn of the 19th century, he marveled at the opulence of the porteño elite who frequented the area, and perhaps envisioned the capital's late 20th-century traffic congestion:

On fine afternoons, there is a wonderful turnout of carriages drawn by handsome horses, and still more of costly motor cars, in the principal avenues of the Park; they press so thick that vehicles are often jammed together for fifteen or twenty minutes, unable to move on. Nowhere in the world does one get a stronger impression of exuberant wealth and extravagance. The Park itself, called Palermo, lies on the edge of the city towards the river, and is approached by a well-designed and well-planted avenue.

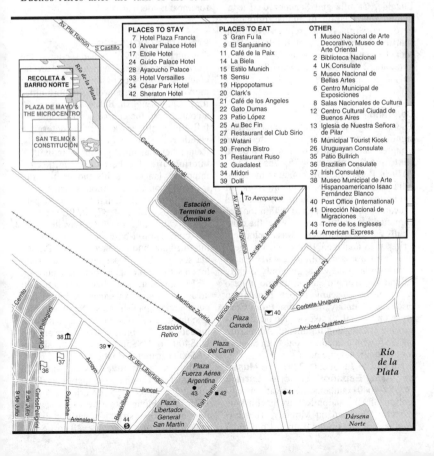

PLACES TO STAY
7 Hotel Plaza Francia
10 Alvear Palace Hotel
17 Etoile Hotel
24 Guido Palace Hotel
28 Ayacucho Palace
33 Hotel Versailles
34 César Park Hotel
42 Sheraton Hotel

PLACES TO EAT
3 Gran Fu la
9 El Sanjuanino
11 Café de la Paix
14 La Biela
15 Estilo Munich
18 Sensu
19 Hippopotamus
20 Clark's
21 Café de los Angeles
22 Gato Dumas
23 Patio López
25 Au Bec Fin
27 Restaurant del Club Sirio
29 Watani
30 French Bistro
31 Restaurant Ruso
32 Guadalest
34 Midori
39 Dolli

OTHER
1 Museo Nacional de Arte Decorativo, Museo de Arte Oriental
2 Biblioteca Nacional
4 UK Consulate
5 Museo Nacional de Bellas Artes
6 Centro Municipal de Exposiciones
8 Salas Nacionales de Cultura
12 Centro Cultural Ciudad de Buenos Aires
13 Iglesia de Nuestra Señora de Pilar
16 Municipal Tourist Kiosk
26 Uruguayan Consulate
35 Patio Bullrich
36 Brazilian Consulate
37 Irish Consulate
38 Museo Municipal de Arte Hispanoamericano Isaac Fernández Blanco
40 Post Office (International)
41 Dirección Nacional de Migraciones
43 Torre de los Ingleses
44 American Express

Now a major recreational resource for all porteños, Palermo contains the city's **Jardín Botánico Carlos Thays** (the botanical gardens, infested with feral cats), **Jardin Zoológico** (zoo), **Rosedal** (rose garden), **Campo de Polo** (polo grounds), **Hipódromo** (racetrack) and **Planetarium**.

As you might guess, some of these uses were not really for the masses, but elite sectors no longer have the park to themselves.

Museo del Instituto Nacional Sanmartiniano In Palermo Chico, occupying a small plaza at the junction of Aguado, Elizalde, Castilla and Sánchez de Bustamante, this bastion of undiscriminating hero worship is a replica of San Martín's home-in-exile at Boulogne-Sur-Mer, France. It's open weekdays 9 am to noon and 2 to 5 pm, weekends 2 to 5 pm only.

Belgrano

The outlying barrio of Belgrano has several significant museums. Once the site of the Congreso and executive offices, the **Museo Histórico Sarmiento** (☎ 783-7555), Cuba 2079 in Belgrano, now contains memorabilia of Domingo F Sarmiento, one of Argentina's most famous statesmen and educators. Always depicted with a look of perpetual indignation on his face, the classically educated Sarmiento was an eloquent writer who analyzed 19th-century Argentina from a cosmopolitan, clearly Eurocentric point of view. Lagging only slightly behind the Instituto Sanmartiniano in hero worship, the museum is open Tuesday to Friday and Sunday, 3 to 7 pm. From Congreso or Av Callao, take bus No 60, disembarking at Cuba and Juramento. Admission is US$1, with guided tours at 4 pm Sunday for no additional charge.

Nearby, at Juramento 2291, the **Museo de Arte Español Enrique Larreta** (☎ 784-4040) contains the private art collection of Hispanophile novelist Enrique Larreta. It's open on Monday, Tuesday, Wednesday, and Friday 9 am to 1 pm and 3

to 7:45 pm, weekends only 3 to 7:45 pm. Admission is US$2.

A few blocks away, at O'Higgins 2390, the **Museo Casa de Yrurtia** (☎ 781-0385) belonged to sculptor Rogelio Yrurtia (probably the country's greatest), who designed the building in Mudéjar style. Hours are Wednesday to Sunday, 3 to 7 pm. Admission costs US$1; there is no additional charge for informative guided tours, which take place at 4:30 pm on Saturday afternoons. The **Museo Líbero Badii** (☎ 784-8650), on the Barrancas de Belgrano at 11 de Setiembre 1990, contains the unconventional sculptures of one of Argentina's foremost modern artists.

LANGUAGE COURSES

Consult the Sunday classified section of the *Buenos Aires Herald,* which offers several columns' worth of possibilities, including individual tutoring, as well as opportunities for teaching English. Before signing up for a course, read the course description carefully, note all fees and try to determine whether it suits your particular needs. Remember that small groups or individual tutoring offer the best opportunities for improving language skills, though the latter is usually considerably more expensive.

The Instituto de Lengua Española para Extranjeros (ILEE, ☎ 375-0730, fax 864-4942), Oficina C, 7th floor, Lavalle 1619, has conversation-based courses at basic, intermediate, and advanced levels. Private classes cost US$17 per hour, while group lessons (no more than four students) are US$12 an hour; specialized instruction in areas like Latin American literature and commercial Spanish costs US$30 per hour. The institute can also help arrange accommodations in a private home for around US$400 to US$500 per month single, US$600 per month double.

Another alternative is the Instituto Nacional de Enseñanza Superior en Lenguas Vivas (☎ 393-7351), Carlos Pellegrini 1515. Monthlong intensive courses, with four hours of instruction daily at basic, intermediate or advanced level, cost $450.

Life & Death in Recoleta & Chacarita

Death is an equalizer, except in Buenos Aires. When the arteries harden after decades of dining at Au Bec Fin and finishing up with coffee and dessert at La Biela or Café de la Paix, the wealthy and powerful of Buenos Aires move ceremoniously across the street to Recoleta Cemetery, joining their forebears in a place they have visited religiously all their lives. Perhaps no other place says more about Argentina and Argentine society.

According to Argentine novelist Tomás Eloy Martínez, Argentines are "cadaver cultists" who honor their most revered national figures not on the date of their birth but of their death – Día de la Bandera (Flag Day) takes place on the date of designer Manuel Belgrano's death. Schoolchildren repeat the last words of San Martín, Belgrano and others like them. When the citizens of Ushuaia, Tierra del Fuego, decided to organize an annual cross-country ski event, they chose August 17, the date of San Martín's death.

Nowhere is this obsession with mortality and corruption more evident than at Recoleta, where generations of the elite repose in the grandeur of ostentatious mausoleums. It is a common saying and only a slight exaggeration that "it is cheaper to live extravagantly all your life than to be buried in Recoleta" – certainly some crypts cost considerably more than middle-class housing. Traditionally, money alone is not enough – you must have a surname like Anchorena, Alvear, Aramburu, Avellaneda, Mitre, Martínez de Hoz or Sarmiento. The remains of Evita Perón, secured in a subterranean vault, are an exception that irritates the presumptive aristocracy.

One reason for this is that the defunct often play a peculiar, and more than just symbolic, role in Argentine politics. Evita came to rest in Recoleta only after her embalmed body's odyssey from South America to an obscure cemetery in Milan to Perón's house in exile in Madrid and finally to Buenos Aires. (Embalming is an uncommon practice in South America.) The man responsible for her "kidnapping" was General Pedro Aramburu, a bitter political enemy of the Peróns who reportedly sought the Vatican's help in sequestering the cadaver after Perón's overthrow in 1955.

Aramburu himself was held for "ransom" by the left-wing Peronist Montoneros *after* his assassination in 1970. Only when the military government of General Alejandro Lanusse ensured Evita's return to Perón in Madrid did Aramburu's body reappear to be entombed in Recoleta, now only a few short "blocks" from Evita. Juan Perón himself lies across town, in the much less exclusive graveyard of Chacarita, which opened in the 1870s to accommodate the countless yellow fever victims of San Telmo and La Boca.

Although more democratic in conception, Chacarita has many tombs that match the finest in Recoleta. One of the most visited belongs to Carlos Gardel, the famous tango singer. Plaques from around the world cover the base of his life-size statue, many thanking him for favors granted – like Evita, Juan Perón, and others, Gardel is a near-saint to whom countless Argentines feel a quasi-religious devotion. The steady procession of pilgrims exposes the pervasiveness of spiritualism in a country that prides itself on European sophistication.

One of the best places to witness this phenomenon is the Chacarita tomb of Madre María Salomé, a disciple of the famous healer Pancho Sierra. Every day but especially on the second of each month (she died on October 2, 1928), adherents of her cult leave floral tributes – white carnations are the favorite – and lay their hands on her sepulcher in spellbound supplication. The anniversary of Gardel's death on June 26, 1935, is another major occasion, as pilgrims jam the streets between the tombs.

Organized tours regularly visit Recoleta Cemetery, open daily from 7 am to 6 pm on Calle Junín across from Plaza Alvear, but most visitors wander about on their own. For Evita's grave, ask directions to the relatively modest tomb of the "Familia Duarte" (her maiden name), but do not overlook the monuments to Mitre, Sarmiento, and other elite families. Outside the walls of the cemetery, the gourmet corridor of Calles Ortiz and Junín, along with the presence of a string of albergues transitorios on Calle Azcuénaga, raises interesting questions about the cultural connections between food, sex, and death in Argentina.

To visit Chacarita, which is not as major a tourist attraction as Recoleta, take Línea B of the Subte to the end of the line at Federico Lacroze, from which it is a short walk. Look for the tomb of "Tomás Perón", but do not miss those of Gardel, Madre María, poetess Alfonsina Storni, aviator Jorge Newbery, tango musician Aníbal "Pichuco" Troilo, and comedian Luis Sandrini. Hours are identical to those at Recoleta. ∎

Three-month courses, with four hours of instruction weekly, cost US$50 per month.

Tradfax (☎ 382-8741), Montevideo 205, 6th floor, offers three-hour daily classes in general Spanish for US$180 per week; commercial Spanish classes cost about US$30 more per week. Individual classes cost US$18 per hour. It also arranges lodging in nearby hotels from US$210 per week single, US$245 per week double.

The Universidad de Buenos Aires (UBA, ☎ 343-1196, fax 343-2733), 25 de Mayo 221, offers good instruction at its Laboratorio de Idiomas de la Facultad, but only for a few hours weekly; this is suitable if you're spending an extended period of time in the city, but not very efficient if your stay is brief.

ORGANIZED TOURS

Many agencies offer half-day and full-day city tours, but unless your time is very limited, try to get around on your own. The Dirección General de Turismo (☎ 371-1496, 476-3612), in the Centro Cultural San Martín at Sarmiento 1551, offers free guided tours of city barrios Saturdays and Sundays at 5 pm in summer, 3 pm the rest of the year. Phone or drop by to pick up a monthly list of their offerings.

Buenos Aires Tur (☎ 371-2304), Lavalle 1444, Oficina 16, offers city tours (US$14) by bus that visit locations in Palmero, Recoleta, the microcentro, San Telmo, and La Boca. These take place daily at 9:30 am and 2:30 pm, Sundays at 2 pm only. Other tours include afternoon visits to Tigre and the Delta (US$29; with lunch included US$60) and a gaucho fiesta in the province of Buenos Aires (US$60). Buenos Aires Visión (☎ 394-2986), Esmeralda 356, 8th floor, has similar itineraries and also arranges excursions to La Plata.

SPECIAL EVENTS

If you're in Buenos Aires for more than a very brief stay, see the municipal Dirección General de Turismo for its annual booklet listing special events in the city; one section of the booklet covers January through June, while the other covers July through December.

Restricted to a small area on Av de Mayo between Bolívar and Luis Sáenz Peña, Buenos Aires' annual Carnaval is a very modest celebration by Brazilian standards.

The annual book fair, the Feria del Libro, attracts more than a million customers the first three weeks of April; most exhibitors are from Latin America, but by no means all – in 1995, for example, there were displays from England, China, France, Ukraine, Norway, Armenia, and other countries. The event takes place at the sprawling Centro Municipal de Exposiciones (☎ 374-1251, ext 208) at Avs Figueroa Alcorta and Pueyrredón in Recoleta, and is important enough that the president of the country gives the opening address.

PLACES TO STAY

Buenos Aires has a wide variety of accommodations, from youth hostels and down-in-the-mouth hospedajes to simple family-oriented hotels to five-star luxury lodgings of jet-set stature. Given elevated service-sector prices, there are very few really good values, but affordable, acceptable accommodations are still available. Budget accommodations tend to be well past their prime but are not necessarily bad, and many midrange hotels are either showing their age or have been cheaply remodeled (this is even true of some top-end accommodations). There are, however, some good values in all categories, and a number of places still offer discounts up to 15% for cash.

In ascending order of desirability, the budget areas are Constitución near the southern train station (abundant), San Telmo (limited), the microcentro (limited), plus Av de Mayo and the Congreso area (abundant), but all these areas have both very good and very bad places. San Telmo is the most interesting zone, followed by Congreso for its access to the nightlife of Corrientes and Santa Fe. Both the microcentro and Congreso have decent midrange accommodations.

In areas such as Retiro, Recoleta, and Barrio Norte, top-end accommodations are the rule; budget travelers will find few alternatives, though some midrange places exist. The microcentro and Congreso also have additional top-end hotels.

Please note that the letter following the name of an establishment indicates which map it appears on: **M** for Plaza de Mayo & the Microcentro, **R** for Recoleta, and **S** for San Telmo. If there is no letter, that means the hotel is outside the extents of the map.

Places to Stay – bottom end

Hostels In a rambling but charming building at Brasil 675, near Constitución station, the official *Albergue Juvenil* (S, ☎ 394-9112) is easily reached by Subte. It has 90 beds, a TV lounge and a pleasant outdoor patio, but it can be noisy when groups from the provinces come to visit the capital. Prices run about US$9 per person with breakfast but without kitchen privileges. It sometimes closes between noon and 6 pm; IYH membership is obligatory.

Hostel membership is not obligatory at *Albergue Oroño* (☎ 581-6663, 581-9387), which charges US$7 per person, but it's far less central at Espinosa 1628 near Av San Martín, north of Parque Centenario. Take bus No 24 or No 166 from downtown.

In an older house near the Caballito branch of the Universidad de Buenos Aires, Juan Carlos Dima (☎ 432-4898) offers accommodations with private rooms, kitchen facilities, cable TV and phone for about US$10 per night.

Hotels Central, friendly, and attractive *Hotel Maipú* (M, ☎ 322-5142), Maipú 735, offers simple but pleasant rooms, some with balconies, for $19/24 with shared bath, $25 double with private bath. *Hotel O'Rei* (M, ☎ 393-7186), Lavalle 733 near Maipú, is the best located budget hotel, just a block from Florida, but rooms fronting directly onto Lavalle can be noisy. Several readers have griped about grumpy management, but others seem to find it just fine. Singles/doubles with shared bath cost US$19/25 double. Rates at *Hotel Bahía* (M, ☎ 382-1780), Av Corrientes 1212, are US$20; ask for student discounts. The owner's son speaks some English.

In San Telmo, probably the cheapest acceptable place is amiable, well-maintained *Hotel Zavalia* (S, ☎ 362-1990) at Juan de Garay 474 near Parque Lezama. Singles/doubles with shared bath cost only US$8/12, but the number of families with children means it can be noisy at times. Close to Plaza Dorrego is the rundown but passable *Hotel Carly* (S, ☎ 361-7710), Humberto Primo 464, for US$12/14 single/double with shared bath.

Also in San Telmo, *Hotel Victoria* (S, ☎ 361-2135), Chacabuco 726, has very good singles/doubles for US$15/25 with private bath; some rooms are a little musty, but it has a pleasant patio. *Hotel Bolívar* (S, ☎ 361-5105), Bolívar 886, is the barrio's budget favorite; several rooms have sunny balconies for US$17/22 a single/double with private bath.

Congreso is a good area for inexpensive lodging of decent quality. Despite indifferent staff, *Hotel Sportsman* (M, ☎ 381-8021) is a nice older building at Rivadavia 1425, with rooms for US$15/24 with shared bath, US$28/35 with private bath; the former is better value. Under the same management is the slightly better *Hotel Europa* (M, ☎ 381-9629), Mitre 1294, where rooms with private bath cost $35 double. At funky but passable *Hotel Plaza* (M, ☎ 371-9747), Rivadavia 1689, small singles with shared bath cost US$18, only slightly more with private bath (it's very unlikely to be confused with Retiro's exclusive Marriott Plaza Hotel).

Hotel Callao (M, ☎ 476-3534), in an interesting building at Av Callao 292, has singles with shared bath for around US$16, and rooms with private bath for US$27/38. Greatly improved *Gran Hotel Oriental* (M, ☎ 951-6427), Bartolomé Mitre 1840, has rooms with shared bath for US$16/18 and others with private bath for US$20/22. Still a decent value is friendly *Gran Hotel Sarmiento* (M, ☎ 476-2764), on a quiet block at Sarmiento 1892, where simple but

ARGENTINA

very clean rooms (some a bit cramped) with private bath cost US$25/35.

Places to Stay – middle

Near the Plaza del Congreso, shopworn *Hotel Mar del Plata* (M, ☎ 476-0466), Rivadavia 1777, charges about US$28/35 with shared bath, US$33/45 with private bath and breakfast. Friendly but funky *Hotel Versailles* (S, ☎ 811-5214), Arenales 1364, has spacious rooms and an excellent Barrio Norte location, but it's worn and past its peak for US$30/40.

In the microcentro, *Hotel Central Córdoba* (M, ☎ 311-1175), San Martín 1021, is modest but friendly, pleasant, quiet, very clean, and also very central; some rooms are small, but one might charitably call them cozy. Rates are US$32/42 with private bath. At *Hotel Plaza Roma* (M, ☎ 311-1679), Lavalle 110 near Leandro Alem, rooms with private bath and breakfast cost US$35/54. Once a leading budget hotel, *Petit Hotel Goya* (M, ☎ 322-9311) at Suipacha 748 is no longer cheap at US$40/50, but it's well maintained, friendly, spotless, central, quiet, and comfortable.

At the *Cardton Hotel* (M, ☎ 382-1697), an older mansion in good repair at Perón 1559 in Congreso, singles/doubles with cable TV start at US$30/40; under the same management is the thoroughly remodeled and recommended but slightly dearer *Hotel Americano* (M, ☎ 382-4223), nearby at Rodríguez Peña 265.

Hotel Molino (M, ☎ 374-8941), Callao 164, charges US$40/52 with air conditioning, private bath and telephone, but some rooms are small and front on this very noisy street. In a quiet building on a noisy street, the very clean and recommended *Hotel Ayamitre* (M, ☎ 953-1655), Ayacucho 106, has rooms with TV, phone, and air conditioning, but it's not quite the equal of the Americano, especially for US$55/70.

Many of the abundant midrange hotels around Av de Mayo are worn – though not dirty – or cheaply remodeled. Some travelers like the once-elegant *Hotel Reina* (M, ☎ 381-2496) at Av de Mayo 1120 near

Av 9 de Julio, where singles/doubles with shared bath cost US$20/30; those with private bath cost US$25/37. Some singles have been created by improvised partitions and are rather small.

Among the area's best values is the Art Nouveau *Chile Hotel* (M, ☎ 383-7877), Av de Mayo 1297, where rooms with private bath cost US$30/45. Although there's considerable street noise, its corner balconies have choice views of the Congreso Nacional and the Casa Rosada. Correspondents offer mixed reviews of *Hotel Avenida* (M, ☎ 331-4341), Av de Mayo 623, where singles/doubles cost US$35/45 with private bath; several consider its much improved bright, spacious and air-conditioned rooms a lesser value than other less expensive places – perhaps because the staff are less cheerful than the rooms.

For about US$40/55, the equally central *Turista Hotel* (M, ☎ 331-2281), Av de Mayo 686, has some adherents but has also drawn negative comment. For US$50/60 with breakfast, about half the price of other four-star accommodations, *Hotel Regidor* (M, ☎ 314-7917), Tucumán 451, is an excellent value but can be snooty toward casually dressed visitors. One correspondent praises centrally located *Promenade Hotel* (M, ☎ 312-5681), MT de Alvear 444, which charges about US$60/70 single/double, but another found its attractive lobby misleading given the "grubby, grimy and noisy" rooms above.

For US$47/60, the *Ayacucho Palace* (R, ☎ 806-0943), Ayacucho 1408, is close to Recoleta without Recoleta prices. In Recoleta proper, the otherwise dignified *Guido Palace Hotel* (R, ☎ 812-0341), Guido 1778, boasts an excellent location and an attractive 5th floor patio, but it also has scuffed walls and offers no real luxuries for US$60/70.

At the upper end of the category, rates start around US$60/70 at places like the *Tucumán Palace Hotel* (M, ☎ 311-2298), Tucumán 384, which has drawn some criticism for "deferred maintenance." Charming and friendly *Hotel Lyon* (M, ☎ 476-0100), Riobamba 251, has spacious, well-maintained suites with private bath, cable TV, telephone and other conveniences for US$64/72. Even larger ones cost only a few dollars more, making it a good value for a family.

Places to Stay – top end

Top-end hotels almost invariably quote prices in dollars but do accept Argentine currency; all of them take credit cards.

Owners of the convenient *Hotel Phoenix* (M, ☎ 312-4845), an architectural gem at San Martín 780, have made substantial investment in attempting to restore the place to its glorious heyday when it hosted the Prince of Wales; its 60 rooms now have modern conveniences as well as original antiques. Improvements have come at a price, though, and what was recently a midrange hotel now costs $79/90 single/double.

The four-star *Castelar Hotel* (M, ☎ 383-5000, fax 383-8388), in a magnificent building at Av de Mayo 1152, is one of the best top-end values for US$70/80 – only slightly more than some mediocre midrange places. *Hotel Nogaró* (M, ☎ 331-0091), on Diagonal Presidente Julio A Roca 562, is a bit tattered by four-star standards, but a 15% cash discount makes rooms that start at US$106/118 a little more palatable. Among its more appealing features is the good natural light in most rooms, not always common in the densely built microcentro.

Gran Hotel Colón (M, ☎ 325-1917), Carlos Pellegrini 507, charges US$144/158 for comfortable rooms, the verdant (thanks to large potted plants) balconies of which overlook the Obelisco at one of the capital's most famous (and noisiest!) intersections (9 de Julio and Corrientes). Few places can match the Old World charm of *Hotel Plaza Francia* (R, ☎ 804-9631), at Eduardo Schiaffino 2189 in Recoleta, where singles/doubles go for about US$135/180. If you plan to eat so much that walking back to the hotel would be an effort, the five-star *Etoile Hotel* (R, ☎ 804-8603), RM Ortiz 1835, is right on Recoleta's restaurant row. Standard suites start at

US$170 per night, plus the whopping 21% IVA, and reach US$350 per night plus IVA. The venerable, dignified *Claridge Hotel* (M, ☎ 322-7700), conveniently central at Tucumán 535, overcharges for very comfortable rooms with cable TV and other amenities, which cost US$254 a single/double.

The modern *Sheraton Hotel* (R, ☎ 311-6330) at San Martín 1225 is less central and convenient, with doubles well upwards of US$300; ditto for the *Caesar Park Hotel* (R, ☎ 814-5157), Posadas 1232 in Recoleta. If you're going to stay that far away and pay that much, you're better off at Recoleta's revered, elegant *Alvear Palace Hotel* (R, ☎ 804-4031), Av Alvear 1891, where doubles can reach $260 or more; pay another US$30 and take a suite (most of which have spas).

PLACES TO EAT

Food in Buenos Aires ranges from the cheap and simple to costly and sophisticated. Decent fixed-price meals are available for US$5 or less, but side orders like chips and soft drinks can drive a-la-carte prices up rapidly. Chinese tenedor libre restaurants provide the most food for the least money – as little as US$4 – but quality varies considerably.

In run-of-the-mill restaurants, standard fare is basic pasta like ravioli and gnocchi, short orders like milanesa, and the more economical cuts of beef, plus fried potatoes, green salads, and desserts; for just a little more, you can find the same sort of food but with better ingredients. More cosmopolitan meals are available at the capital's high-class restaurants, but these can be very costly. One place to catch up on the latest in *haute cuisine* is the "Good Living" section in the Sunday *Buenos Aires Herald,* where Dereck Foster also offers the latest on Argentine wines, but by his criteria "inexpensive" meals can easily cost US$15.

Porteños depend on cafés for hot and cold drinks, for meals, for socializing, and for entertainment, and some cafés meet all these needs while others fill only a few.

Let Them Eat Beef

When Charles Darwin rode across the province of Buenos Aires in the 1830s, he could not contain his astonishment at the gauchos' diet, which he himself followed out of necessity:

I had now been several days without tasting any thing besides meat: I did not at all dislike this new regimen; but I felt as if it would only have agreed with me with hard exercise. I have heard that patients in England, when desired to confine themselves exclusively to an animal diet, even with the hope of life before their eyes, have scarce been able to endure it. Yet the Gaucho in the Pampas, for months together, touches nothing but beef . . . . It is, perhaps, from their meat regimen that the Gauchos, like other carnivorous animals, can abstain long from food. I was told that at Tandeel, some troops voluntarily pursued a party of Indians for three days, without eating or drinking.

Many Argentines recognize that a diet so reliant on beef is unhealthy, but sedentary porteños continue to ingest it in large quantities. Visitors who don't make it a way of life can probably indulge themselves on the succulent grilled meat, often stretched on a vertical spit over red-hot coals in the picture windows of the city's most prestigious restaurants. ■

Some cafés are also bookstores. See Cafés in the Entertainment section for more about all of these.

Note that the name of each establishment is followed by a letter indicating which map it appears on: **R** for Recoleta, **M** for Plaza de Mayo & the Microcentro, and **S** for San Telmo. If there is no letter, the restaurant isn't on any map.

Parrillas

If you visit only one parrilla in Buenos Aires, ignore the rent-a-gauchos at *La Estancia* (M, ☎ 326-0330), Lavalle 941, and focus on excellent food at moderate prices. Other highly regarded but pricier microcentro parrillas include *La Cabaña* (☎ 381-2373) at Entre Ríos 436 (although recent reports suggest declining service), *La Chacra* (M, ☎ 322-1409) at Av Córdoba 941, *La Rural* (M, ☎ 322-2654) at Suipacha 453, and *Las Nazarenas* (M, ☎ 312-5559) at Reconquista 1132.

Dora (M, ☎ 311-2891), Av Alem 1016, is popular in part for its massive portions; menu prices look steep, but most dishes suffice for two people – the imposing half portion of bife de chorizo (US$9) weighs nearly half a kilo. LP correspondents have also praised its seafood and pasta, as well as "incredible" desserts (which *are* expensive). Nearby *El Salmón* (M, ☎ 313-1731), Reconquista 968, has a similar and slightly cheaper menu.

There are countless cheaper but ordinary downtown parrillas. Traditionally, one of the most popular and economical is *Pippo,* (M) at Paraná 356. The modest *Último Tango,* (S) Pasaje San Lorenzo 379 in San Telmo, attracts a crowd of mostly middle-aged men to its surprisingly good fixed-price lunches, enjoyed with background tango music, from US$5 to US$7 for three courses. A good, popular, and reasonable chain is *El Palacio de la Papa Frita* at Lavalle 735 (M, ☎ 393-5849), Lavalle 954 (☎ 322-1559), and Corrientes 1612 (☎ 326-8063).

Mobbed at lunch, *El Toboso* (M, ☎ 476-0519), Corrientes 1848, is a decent and moderately priced parrilla with other daily specials, but very expensive drinks (US$2.50 for mineral water) drive up the prices. The pâté with bread is a nice touch not found at other similar places.

Mandato (☎ 802-4258), Scalabrini Ortiz

3191 in Palermo, is a moderately priced parrilla and pasta place which may be the only place in Buenos Aires where you can go to talk baseball – owner Jorge Fuertes has coached the sport, is still an occasional softball player, and watches the game on cable; after midnight Fridays and Saturdays his place turns into a popular pub for neighborhood youth. On the Costanera, near Aeroparque, try *Los Años Locos* (☎ 783-5126), on Av Rafael Obligado at Pampa.

Italian

Italian establishments in Buenos Aires are either nicer restaurants or pizzerías, and although Argentina's abundance of Italian surnames might suggest otherwise, most so-called Italian food is actually hybrid Italo-Argentine. Exceptions to this rule tend to be pricey, but *La Casona del Nonno* (M, ☎ 322-9352), Lavalle 827, has good lunch specials for US$4 and a separate, well-ventilated nonsmoking section upstairs. Also very inexpensive is the *Vecchio Unione* (M, ☎ 372-7750), in the basement of the Sociedad Benevolenza di Italia at Perón 1372; its US$7 menú ejecutivo for lunch is a real bargain because they seem willing to substitute just about anything on the list. A bit dearer, but excellent and still reasonable by current standards, is *Broccolino* (M, ☎ 322-7652), Esmeralda 776.

Fiori y Canto (☎ 963-3250), on the edge of Palermo Viejo at Córdoba 3547, is an attractive combination of pizzería, parrilla, and pasta with particularly delicious homemade bread. *L'Altro Cesare* (☎ 781-7365), Monroe 2248 in Belgrano, is a very fine Italian restaurant with outstanding service and some innovative dishes – try the canelones con humita (corn) for US$8.

Buenos Aires has outstanding pizza. Unsung *Pizzería Güerrín,* (M) Corrientes 1372, sells very inexpensive slices of superb fugazza, fugazzeta and other specialities, plus excellent empanadas, cold lager beer to wash it all down, and many appealing desserts. It's cheaper to buy at the counter and eat standing up, but there is a much greater variety of toppings if you decide to be seated and served, or order an entire pizza to take out. Traditionally excellent *Pizzería Serafín,* (M) nearby at Av Corrientes 1328, is well worth a visit – their chicken empanadas are always good. At the corner of Callao and Mitre since 1936, *La Americana* (M) also has very fine pizza and exceptional empanadas, but the best chicken empanadas (usually breast meat) are at *La Continental,* (M) Callao 202 at Perón.

For a bit of nostalgia, visit the original branch of *Los Inmortales* (☎ 326-5303), at Corrientes 1369 beneath the conspicuous billboard of Carlos Gardel, to see the historic photographs of Gardel and his contemporaries; it also has branches at Lavalle 746 (☎ 322-5493), Av Callao 1165 (☎ 813-7551), and Av Alvear 1234 (☎ 393-6124). Part of a respectable chain, *Romanaccio* (M, ☎ 811-4071), Av Callao 1021, has a good nonsmoking section.

Another recommended pizzería is reader-endorsed *Las Marías II,* (S) at Bolivar 964-66 in San Telmo, with a friendly and efficient staff.

Spanish

Spanish restaurants are usually the best alternatives for seafood, which is generally not particularly prized by Argentines. In addition to a pleasant atmosphere, *Los Teatros* (M, ☎ 374-4946), Talcahuano 360 between Sarmiento and Corrientes, has outstanding seafood, chicken, and pasta dishes. Part of San Telmo's Casal de Catalunya cultural center at Chacabuco 863, *Hostal del Canigó* (S, ☎ 304-5250, 300-5252) serves Catalonian specialties like pollo a la punxa (chicken with calamari). Prices are not cheap (the fixed-price menú ejecutivo costs US$9), but portions are large. A nice touch is the glass of sherry before lunch.

Bar La Robla (M, ☎ 811-4484), Viamonte 1613, has both excellent seafood and standard Argentine dishes served in a pleasant environment at moderate prices. Although it's a chain, the food is far from monotonous, service is superb, and there's a small but clearly designated and effectively segregated tobacco-free area. Its

US$3.50 lunch specials, including an appetizer and a small glass of clericó, are an excellent value. Another branch is at Montevideo 194 (☎ 381-3435).

Cervantes II (M, ☎ 372-8869), Perón 1883, has enormous servings of standard Argentine fare, but is often so crowded that you may wish to take out your food; alternatively go late for lunch or early for dinner. They will enforce the nonsmoking section only if someone complains, however. Another possibility is *La Fonda de Montserrat* (M, ☎ 372-6282), Virrey Cevallos 178, which has barrio atmosphere and quick, friendly and excellent service. The food is fairly routine, but the lunch specials are a good value at around US$6.

San Telmo's *La Casa de Esteban de Luca* (S, ☎ 361-1582) serves very fine food at moderate prices in a restored colonial house at Defensa 1000. *El Pulpo* (M, ☎ 311-0330), Tucumán 400, is generally considered the city's best seafood restaurant. Try also *Antigua Casca de Cuchilleros* (S, ☎ 362-3811) at Carlos Calvo 319 in San Telmo. For Basque food, try *Laurak Bat* (S, ☎ 381-0642) at Belgrano 1174 or *Taberna Baska* (S) at Chile 980.

French

It's stretching it a bit to call *Nicole de Marseille* (S, ☎ 362-2340), Defensa 714, a French restaurant or even to call it Franco-Argentine, but its three-course weekday lunches for US$6 are a good value, with a wide choice of entrees and desserts. A new addition is the appealing *French Bistro* (R, ☎ 806-9331), at French 2301 and Azcuénaga in Barrio Norte.

Acknowledged as one of Buenos Aires' best restaurants, *Au Bec Fin* (R, ☎ 801-6894), Vicente López 1825 in Recoleta, has prices to match. *Hippopotamus* (R, ☎ 804-8310), Junín 1787, which includes a popular but very formal disco/nightclub, is in the same category with its reader-endorsed US$18 menú ejecutivo.

Asian

One of our most memorable bilingual menus came from a Chinese restaurant where an unusually creative mistranslation turned Spanish "camarones a la plancha" (grilled shrimp) into English "ironed shrimp." Despite this vivid image, most Asian food is Cantonese and unremarkable, but the tenedor libre restaurants, as cheap as US$4, are good options for budget travelers – if you choose wisely. Most also have salad bars with excellent ingredients, but also tack on a US$1 surcharge if you don't order anything to drink; prices for mineral water, soft drinks and beer are usually not outrageous, compared to upscale restaurants, but it's where these places make their profit.

There is little difference among these places, which also offer a variety of Argentine standards, but try *Macau* at Suipacha 477, *Doll* at Suipacha 544, *La Fronda* at Paraná 342, *Han Kung* at Rodríguez Peña 384, or *Yong Bin Kwan* at Rivadavia 2030.

A step up from most all-you-can-eats is *Gran Fu Ia* (R, ☎ 803-5522), Las Heras 2379 in Palermo Chico, a few blocks from Recoleta cemetery; the US$8 price tag for lunch or dinner reflects its higher quality, including items such as prawns not normally on the menu elsewhere, and spicy a-la-carte dishes that most Argentines shy away from. Other possibilities for better quality Chinese food include *La Cantina China* (M, ☎ 312-7391) at Maipú 976, *La Casa China* (☎ 371-1352) at Viamonte 1476, or *Oriente* (M) at Maipú 512.

Japanese food is becoming more common, with places like the expensive *Midori* (R, ☎ 814-5151) in the César Park Hotel at Posadas 1252 and *Sensu* (R, ☎ 804-1214) at Ortiz 1813. Figure about US$20 upwards for lunch or dinner.

Latin American & Regional

Buenos Aires Herald critic Dereck Foster notes that non-Argentine Latin American restaurants tend to start with good intentions and varied menus but often retreat to conventional local offerings. One place which may not do so is *La Casa de Orihuela* (☎ 951-6930), Alsina 2163 in the Congreso area, which serves exceptionally well-prepared Peruvian and regional dishes. Its US$6 fixed-price lunch is one of the city's best values, well worth a detour from other parts of town. The decor is pleasing, the service cheerful and efficient.

El Sanjuanino (R, ☎ 804-2909), Posadas 1515 in Recoleta, serves regional versions of Argentine dishes like empanadas, locro and sweets, and also delivers within the immediate area. Jujuy cuisine is the rule at friendly *La Carretería,* Brasil 656 (S, just beyond San Telmo). If you can't cross the Andes, there's passable Chilean seafood and other national dishes at *Los Chilenos,* (M) Suipacha 1042.

Middle Eastern

Renowned for being a good value, the *Restaurant del Club Sirio,* (R, ☎ 806-5764) Pacheco de Melo 1902 in Barrio Norte/Recoleta, has tenedor libre Monday to Saturday evenings for US$18. *Watani* (R, ☎ 806-0553), Junín 1460, is part of the Club Libanés, while reasonably priced *Al Shawarma de Aladino* (☎ 788-0328), Echeverría 2487 in Belgrano, is open for lunch and dinner Monday through Saturday. The latter has vegetarian specials, takeout service, and live music and dance Thursday, Friday, and Saturday nights.

International

Many new restaurants have opened in Plaza del Pilar, at Av Pueyrredón 2501 alongside the Centro Cultural Ciudad de Buenos Aires; more easily reached from the Calle Junín entrance to the Centro, they range from modest fast-food offerings to elaborate and sophisticated fare. One of the best values is *Munich del Pilar* (☎ 806-1111), whose US$9 weekday menú ejecutivo offers a choice of meat, chicken, or pasta entrées including drinks. *Molière* serves an excellent grilled salmon with appetizer and a large glass of house wine for US$15; service is well intentioned but erratic.

Several others in the complex are worth checking out, including *Café Champs Elysée* (more a confitería, with tantalizing desserts); *Caruso* (a pricey trattoría); *Campo del Pilar* (a parrilla); *Café Rex* (with cinematic décor); *La Doma* (expen-

sive fixed-price menu); *Mumy's* (pricey hamburgers, but some reasonable combinations); *Romanaccio* (pizza and pasta); *Fishy Bar* (fast food); and *Puerto Marisko* (pricey seafood).

If price is no object, check out Recoleta institutions like *Estilo Munich* (R, ☎ 804-4469) at RM Ortiz 1871, nearby *Gato Dumas* (R, ☎ 806-5802) at Junín 1747, or *Clark's* (R, ☎ 801-9502) at Junín 1777. Fixed-price lunches or dinners are in the US$20 to US$30 range, but a-la-carte meals can be much dearer. Attractive *Café de los Angeles* (R, ☎ 801-1844), Guido 1936, has a variety of relatively inexpensive lunch specials (beware the costly drinks and desserts). One of Recoleta's better values is *Patio López* (R, ☎ 807-0611), Vicente López 1955, where good lunches cost US$10, dinners US$12, with occasional specials.

Dolli (R, ☎ 327-2134), Av Libertador 312, has Mediterranean food in the US$30-plus range. *La Cátedra* (☎ 774-9859), Cerviño 4699 in Palermo (Subte Plaza Italia), serves an excellent three-course lunch, including a small bottle of wine and coffee, for US$12 weekdays; a-la-carte prices are significantly higher, but it has a US$7 salad bar.

An open secret is the popular smorgasbord at the *Swedish Club* (M, ☎ 334-1703), 5th floor, Tacuarí 143. Theoretically open to members only, it now takes place every Wednesday, but you can "request" an invitation by phone. They're particularly enthusiastic if you have a Swedish surname, but the US$26 price tag makes it a special event for most people.

A good, inexpensive choice in San Telmo is *Jerónimo* (S, ☎ 300-2624), Estados Unidos 407, where entrees cost between US$3 and US$5 and desserts are about US$1.50. Far more expensive is *La Tasca de San Fermín,* (S) on Carlos Calvo between Defensa and Balcarce.

Restaurant Ruso (M, ☎ 805-7079), Azcuénaga 1562 in Barrio Norte, is a new restaurant specializing in Russian food at reasonable prices (by Barrio Norte standards). Also in Barrio Norte, at Santa Fe

2321, is the attractive *Guadalest* (R, ☎ 825-6425), with fine pasta and imposing desserts – most of them large enough for two. It is one of the few places in town that takes the trouble to ask diners whether they prefer the nonsmoking section.

Vegetarian

Since the mid-1980s, the carnivorous capital has enjoyed a vegetarian boom, and nearly all of these restaurants have the additional appeal of being tobacco-free, including the self-service, tenedor-libre *Ratatouille,* Sarmiento 1810, for US$8. Reader endorsements include *Giardino,* with locations at Suipacha 429 and Lavalle 835, and *Verde Esmeralda* (M) at Esmeralda 370.

One of the most enduring vegetarian places, *La Esquina de las Flores* (M, ☎ 811-4729), at Av Córdoba 1599, also has a health-food store; its daily fixed-price meals cost US$10 (US$6 for children), but there are less expensive a-la-carte choices. The Esquina is also a cultural center, offering lectures and workshops on food, diet, health and similar topics, and has radio and TV programs.

It's not strictly vegetarian and prices are a bit upscale, but *Alicia* (M, ☎ 393-6981), Santa Fe 959, is a natural foods restaurant with an excellent takeout bakery – try the tasty barley biscuits. *Yinyang* is a macrobiotic restaurant with branches in the microcentro (M, ☎ 311-7798) at Paraguay 858 and in Belgrano (☎ 788-4368) at Echeverría 2444.

Fast Food

Argentine fast-food restaurants are generally inferior to standard inexpensive eateries, but there are exceptions. The Patio de Comidas on the lower level of the Galerías Pacífico on the Florida peatonal has a number of moderately priced fast-food versions of some very good restaurants for about US$5 to US$7 or so, including *Sensu* for Japanese, *Romanaccio* for pizza and pasta, and *Freddo* for ice cream. Since all have common seating, it's a good choice for groups unable to agree on where to eat.

The express cafeteria at supermarket *Coto,* Viamonte 1571, offers a variety of very inexpensive (US$3 or less) meals of good quality; there's zero atmosphere or maybe lots of it from another point of view – the entire main floor is blissfully tobacco-free.

The indigenous *Pumper Nic,* a McDonald's clone, has many locations throughout the city. In quality, however, it falls just short of *vomitivo.*

Ice Cream

For ice cream lovers, Buenos Aires is paradise. Our favorite, distinguished by the outline map of Italy above its otherwise unpretentious storefront, is *Heladería Cadore* (M) at Av Corrientes and Rodríguez Peña. Chocoholics should not miss their exquisite chocolate amargo (semisweet chocolate) or chocolate blanco (white chocolate), while the mousse de limón (lemon mousse) also merits special mention. Several locals recommend *Saverio,* which has branches on Corrientes and in Recoleta.

Also in Recoleta, try *Freddo* at Ayacucho and Quintana; Ortiz and Guido; and several other locations around the city. Despite its recent expansion (Aerolíneas Argentinas now serves Freddo's ice cream on international flights), quality does not seem to have suffered.

A recent discovery is *Recopa 2* (☎ 433-0104), Pedro Goyena 1401 in the Caballito neighborhood near the Facultad de Filosofía y Letras of the Universidad de Buenos Aires; its white chocolate with chocolate-covered almonds is unearthly.

ENTERTAINMENT

Carteleras along Av Corrientes sell heavily discounted tickets for entertainment events including movies, live theater, and tango shows; most tango shows aren't worth US$40, but they are for half that. Since the number of discount tickets may be limited, buy them as far in advance as possible. It's always worth trying, though, so if you want to see a movie on short notice just phone or drop by to see what's available – the most recently released hits are unlikely to be among the options.

Cartelera Vea Mas (☎ 372-7285, 372-7314, ext 219), Local 19 in the Paseo La Plaza complex at Corrientes 1660, is open daily 10 am to 11 pm. Cartelera Baires (☎ 372-5058), Local 25 in the Galería Teatro Lorange at Corrientes 1372, is open Monday through Thursday 10 am to 10:30 pm, Friday and Saturday 10 am to midnight, and Sunday 2 to 10:30 pm.

Please note that the letter following the name of an establishment indicates which map it appears on: **M** for Plaza de Mayo & the Microcentro, **R** for Recoleta, and **S** for San Telmo. If there is no letter, that means the hotel is outside the extents of the map.

Cafés

Café society is a major force in the life of Argentines in general and porteños in particular – they spend hours solving their own problems, the country's and the world's over a chessboard and a cheap cortado. Some cafés double as bookstores.

Founded in 1858, famous *Café Tortoni* (M, ☎ 342-4328), Av de Mayo 829, has occupied its present site only since 1893. Oozing 19th-century atmosphere out of the woodwork and onto the sidewalk, it showcases traditional jazz bands on weekends and has billiards in the back. The almost rococo interior at *Confitería del Molino,* (M) Av Callao 20, also merits a visit from anyone seeking turn-of-the-century ambience.

Av Corrientes is a favorite hangout for Argentine intellectuals. Famous for Bohemian atmosphere is the spartan *Cafe La Paz* (M, ☎ 46-5542), Av Corrientes 1599. *Café Pernambuco,* Av Corrientes 1680, also has good atmosphere for a cup of coffee or glass of wine. *Alimentari,* San Martín 899, has outstanding croissants.

Some of the porteño elite while away the hours on caffeine from *La Biela* (R, ☎ 804-0432), Quintana 598 across from the Cementerio de la Recoleta. The rest exercise their purebred dogs nearby, so watch your step in crossing the street to *Café de la Paix* (R, ☎ 804-6820), Quintana 595.

Another elegant place is the *Winter Garden* at the Alvear Palace Hotel (R).

In La Boca, *La Barbería* (☎ 21-8770) at Pedro de Mendoza 1959 has cold beer and cider on tap, good but pricey empanadas, sidewalk seating, and kitschy decor.

Several downtown bookstores are also cafés offering live music, poetry readings, occasional films and the like. The *Foro Gandhi* (M, ☎ 374-7501), Av Corrientes 1551, is an arts-oriented coffeehouse offering tango music and foreign film cycles at bargain prices. The very attractive *Clásica y Moderna* (M, ☎ 812-8707), Callao 892 near Córdoba, is a more upscale, haute-cuisine type of place; it also keeps the day's newspapers for patrons' convenience.

Dance Clubs

Dance clubs tend to the exclusive and expensive, such as *Hippopotamus* at Junín 1787, *Trump's* at Bulnes 2772 in Palermo, and *Africa* in the Alvear Palace Hotel (R). Cover charges are US$20 and upwards, and drinks are expensive.

Less expensive, with a young and lively crowd, is *Gallery,* Azcuénaga 1771 in Barrio Norte/Recoleta. The cover charge is US$6, while large drinks cost about US$5 each. *Hanoi* (☎ 806-5312), at Av Casares and Sarmiento in Palermo, has a high-priced restaurant and a US$15 cover charge; it's open to 6 am.

Theater

Live theater enjoys great popularity. *Corrientes,* between 9 de Julio and Callao, is the capital's Broadway or West End, but there are many other venues. One of the best places is the *Teatro General San Martín* (☎ 374-8611), Corrientes 1530, which has several auditoriums and frequent free events.

Other important venues include the *Teatro Presidente Alvear* (M, ☎ 374-6076) at Corrientes 1659; *Teatro Blanca Podestá* (M, ☎ 382-9140) at Corrientes 1283; *Teatro La Plaza* (M, ☎ 326-8781) at Corrientes 1660; *Teatro Avenida* (M, ☎ 381-3193) at Av de Mayo 1212; *Teatro El Vitral* (M, ☎ 371-0948) at Rodríguez Peña 344;

Gardel & the Tango

In June 1935, a Cuban woman committed suicide in Havana, while a woman in New York and another in Puerto Rico tried to poison themselves, all over the same man none of them had ever met. The man whose smiling photograph graced their rooms had himself just died in a plane crash in Medellín, Colombia. On his long odyssey to his final resting place in Argentina, Latin Americans thronged to pay him tribute in Colombia, New York, Rio de Janeiro, and Montevideo. Transported to Buenos Aires, his body lay in state at Luna Park stadium before a horse-drawn carriage took him to Chacarita Cemetery. The man was tango singer Carlos Gardel, *El Zorzal Criollo*, the songbird of Buenos Aires.

Born around 1880, only a decade before Gardel, the tango was the vulgar dance and music of the capital's *arrabales* or fringes, blending gaucho verse with Spanish and Italian music. Gardel created the *tango canción*, the tango-song, taking it out of the brothels and tenements and into the salons of Buenos Aires, but only after a roundabout odyssey to New York and Paris, where its acceptance legitimized it to the Argentine elite.

It was no accident that the tango grew to popularity when it did. In the late 19th century, the *Gran Aldea* (Great Village) of Buenos Aires was becoming an immigrant city, where frustrated and melancholic Europeans displaced gaucho rustics, who retreated gradually to the ever more distant countryside. The children of those immigrants would become the first generation of porteños, and the tango-song summarized the new urban experience.

Permeated with nostalgia over a disappearing way of life, the tango-song expressed the apprehensions and anxieties of individuals, ranging from mundane pastimes like horse racing and other popular diversions to more profound feelings towards the changing landscape of neighborhood and community, the figure of the mother, betrayal by women, and friendship or other important personal concerns. One tango compares the inevitable transformations of La Boca's "Caminito" with those in the singer's own life:

Caminito que entonces estabas	*Caminito of what you once were*
bordeado de trébol y juncos en flor . . .	*Bordered by clover and flowering rushes . . .*
una sombra ya pronto serás,	*A shadow you soon will be,*
una sombra, lo mismo que yo . . .	*A shadow just like me . . .*

Though born in France, Gardel came to epitomize the porteño. When he was three, his poor and single mother brought him to Buenos Aires, where he passed his formative years in a neighborhood near the Mercado de Abasto, a central produce market, near which many porteños en route to work now board the Subte at Estación Carlos Gardel. In his youth, he worked at a variety of menial jobs but also entertained neighbors with his singing. His performing career began after he became friends with Uruguayan-born José Razzano, forming the popular duo Gardel-Razzano, which lasted until Razzano lost his voice.

and *Teatro Esmeralda* (M, ☎ 322-3600) at Esmeralda 425. For complete listings, consult the *Buenos Aires Herald* or the entertainment section of *Clarín*.

Free theater presentations take place at several different sites, including the *Teatro Margarita Xirgu* alongside the Casal de Catalunya (☎ 300-5252) at Chacabuco 863/875 (performances are in Spanish rather than Catalan). Less conventional companies, most of which have no regular venue but appear sporadically around town, include *Casita de la Selva* (☎ 672-5700) at La Selva 4022 in the outlying barrio of Vélez Sarsfield, Catalinas Sur, La Runfla, La Diablo Mundo, and Las Calandracas.

Popular Music

Buenos Aires has a thriving rock and blues scene; for the latest information, consult Friday's "Suplemento Jóven" (which also lists free events) in *Clarín,* and the weekend editions of *Página 12*.

La Porteña jazz band plays Thursdays at *Bárbaro*, Tres Sargentos 415, which has pleasantly informal decor. *El Subsuelo* (M, ☎ 476-2479), in the basement at the Pasaje de la Piedad alleyway just off Mitre 1571, is an intimate (microscopically tiny) venue with good live music, including rock, blues and jazz. *Hendrix* (S), San Lorenzo 354, is worth a trip to San Telmo.

For live jazz, also try *Oliverio* (M,

From 1917, Gardel became a solo performer. His voice, his singing, and his personal charisma made him an immediate popular success in Argentina and other Latin American countries, although the Argentine elite still despised the music and what it stood for – the rise of a middle class that challenged its monopoly on power. Building on this popularity, Gardel appeared regularly on the radio and soon became a recording star. To broaden his appeal, he traveled to Spain and France, where widespread acceptance finally made him palatable even to the elite sectors of Argentine society, which once were scandalized by the tango's humble origins and open sensuality. Later he began a film career, which was cut short by his death.

In a sense, Gardel's early death rescued him from aging and placed him in an eternal present, where his figure is an icon that still dominates Argentine popular culture. One measure of this immortality is the common saying that "Gardel sings better every day." Photographs of Gardel, with his unmistakably charismatic smile, are everywhere – one laboratory in Buenos Aires sold more than 350,000 pictures in the first two decades after his death. The large, devoted community of his followers, known as Gardelianos, cannot pass a day without listening to his songs or watching his films.

Daily, there is a steady procession of pilgrims to his plaque-covered tomb in Chacarita Cemetery where, often, a lighted cigarette rests in the hand of his life-size statue. On December 11, 1990, the centenary of his birth, the tomb was smothered in floral tributes.

For an excellent account in English of Gardel's life, see Simon Collier's *The Life, Music, and Times of Carlos Gardel*, a serious biography that refrains from the most romantic exaggerations of the singer's fanatical devotees. ■

☎ 371-6877), downtown at Paraná 328, or the *Cotton Club de Buenos Aires* (M, ☎ 325-1708) at Corrientes 636. The very appealing *Merlyn Café* (☎ 786-3349), Cuba 2290 in Belgrano, showcases good live jazz and serves good and reasonably priced food.

Tango

Finding spontaneous tango is not easy, but plenty of places portray Argentina's most famous cultural export, for up to US$40 per show in San Telmo and La Boca. The best value is Plaza Dorrego's free city-sponsored *"Tango y Baile,"* on alternate Saturday nights in summer, which show-cases singers, musicians and dancers, and gives porteños of all ages and classes a chance to show their steps.

From its publicity, *La Casa Blanca* (S, ☎ 331-4621), Balcarce 668 in San Telmo, appears to take pride in hosting disgraced heads of state like Brazil's Fernando Collor de Mello and Mexico's Carlos Salinas de Gortari, and dropping the names of show-biz patrons like Omar Sharif, Oliver Stone, and Eric Clapton. Regular shows take place weekdays at 10 pm, Saturday at 9 and 11 pm.

Other San Telmo *tanguerías* include *El Viejo Almacén* (S, ☎ 362-3602) at Balcarce and Independencia, *Bar Sur* (S, ☎ 362-

6086) at Estados Unidos 299, the less formal *A Media Luz* (S, ☎ 331-6146) at Chile 316, and the very lively *Los Dos Pianitos* (S, ☎ 361-2188) at Pasaje Giuffra 305.

The flagrantly touristic but highly praised dinner show at *Tango Mío* (☎ 303-0568, 303-6970), Ituzaingó 1200 in La Boca, costs $55 and includes transport to and from the hotel, plus wine and champagne. *La Casa de Carlos Gardel* (in fact, once Gardel's home) is at Jean Jaurés 735, in the Abasto neighborhood (Subte Carlos Gardel or Pueyrredón). Downtown tango spots include *Caño 14* (M) at Talcahuano 975 and *Tanguería Corrientes Angosta* at Lavalle 750.

Several places provide **tango instruction**. The Universidad de Buenos Aires, 25 de Mayo 217, teaches beginners' from 6:30 to 8 pm Fridays, while more advanced students take the floor from 8 to 10 pm. Non-students pay $7. The Teatro Suizo, on Rodríguez Peña near Corrientes, also has inexpensive tango lessons.

Cinemas

Buenos Aires is famous for its cinemas, which play first-run films from around the world, but there is also an audience for unconventional and classic films. The main cinema districts are along the Lavalle peatonal, west of Florida, and on Corrientes and Santa Fe, all easy walking distance from downtown. The price of tickets has risen dramatically in recent years, but most cinemas offer half-price discounts

Wednesdays and sometimes for the first afternoon showing. Wednesday showings can be mobbed, so go early.

The *Sala Leopoldo Lugones* at the Teatro General San Martín, Av Corrientes 1530, offers thematic foreign film cycles as well as occasional reprises of outstanding commercial films.

Since Spanish translations of English-language film titles are often misleading, check the *Buenos Aires Herald* to be certain what's playing. Except for children's films and cartoon features, which are dubbed, foreign films almost always appear in the original language with Spanish subtitles.

SPECTATOR SPORTS

Buenos Aires has the highest density of first-division soccer teams in the world – eight of the country's 20 are based in the capital, while another five are in nearby suburbs. For information on tickets and schedules, contact the clubs listed below; where two addresses and telephone numbers appear, the first is club offices, while the second is the stadium, where tickets are normally purchased. *Entradas populares* (standing room) costs around US$10, while *plateas* (fixed seats) cost $20 and upward.

Argentinos Juniors
    Punta Arenas 1271 (☎ 551-6887)
    Boyacá 2152 (☎ 582-8949)
Boca Juniors
    Brandsen 805 (☎ 362-2260)
Ferrocarril Oeste
    Cucha Cucha 350 (☎ 431-9203)
    Martín de Gainza 244 (☎ 432-3989)
Huracán
    Av Caseros 3159 (☎ 91-6713)
    Av Almancio Alcorta 2570 (☎ 942-1965)
River Plate
    Av Presidente Figueroa Alcorte 7597
      (☎ 788-1200)
San Lorenzo y Almagro
    Av Fernández de la Cruz 2403 (☎ 923-9212)
    Av Perito Moreno between Av Fernández de
    la Cruz and Varela (☎ 924-3455)
Unión Española
    Fernández 2100 (☎ 613-0968)
    Santiago de Compostela 3801 (☎ 612-9648)
Vélez Sarsfield
    Av Juan B Justo 9200 (☎ 641-5663)

ARGENTINA

THINGS TO BUY
Compulsive shoppers will adore Buenos Aires. The main shopping zones are downtown, along the Florida peatonal and the more fashionable and more expensive Av Santa Fe, although Recoleta is another worthwhile area. Ritzy one-stop shopping centers, some of them recycled such as Florida's Galerías Pacífico (☎ 311-6323), Recoleta's Patio Bullrich (☎ 815-3501), and Palermo's Alto Palermo, have begun to take business away from the traditional commercial center.

Buenos Aires' best buys are jewels, leather goods, shoes, and typical souvenirs like *mate* paraphernalia. Among many leather shops, try Rossi y Carusso (☎ 811-5357) at Santa Fe 1601, Chiche Farrace (☎ 383-6233) at Av de Mayo 963, Carteras Italianas at Marcelo T de Alvear 720, Campanera Dalla Fontana at Reconquista 735, or Jota U Cuero at Tres Sargentos 439. Celina Leather (☎ 312-9207), Florida 971, gives 15% discounts to holders of student identification cards.

You can look just about anywhere along Av Corrientes or Florida for shoes, but try Andrea Carrera at Maipú 943 or Celine at Florida 793 for women's footwear. For men's shoes, try Guante at Florida 271 or Delgado at Florida 360.

For typical souvenirs, check out places like Artesanías Argentinas (☎ 812-2650) at Montevideo 1386, Friend's at Av Santa Fe and Esmeralda, Martín Fierro at Santa Fe 992, or Iguarán at Libertad 1260. Other places (offering student discounts) include Rancho Grande (☎ 311-7603) at Alem 564 and Patagonia at Córdoba 543. Several provincial tourist offices, especially those along Santa Fe and Callao, have small but worthwhile selections of regional crafts.

For an only-in-Buenos-Aires experience, visit the local outlet of Pierre Cardin (☎ 476-0560), which shares a building with the capital's chapter of the Communist party, at Callao 220.

Art Galleries
Most of Buenos Aires' dozens of art galleries offer fairly conventional works, either European or consciously derivative of European traditions. Nevertheless a few offer more locally based, innovative works, including Ruth Benzacar (☎ 313-8480) downstairs at Florida 1000; Federico Klem (☎ 311-2527) downstairs at Marcelo T de Alvear 636; Rubbers (☎ 393-6010) at Suipacha 1175; Vermeer (☎ 394-3462) across the street at Suipacha 1168; and Galería der Brücke (☎ 775-2175) at Av Libertador 3883 (under the railroad bridge in Palermo).

Markets
One of the capital's most interesting shopping districts is San Telmo, where a fascinating flea market, the Feria de San Telmo, takes place both Saturday and Sunday from 10 am to about 5 pm on Plaza Dorrego. Vendors prefer that customers not touch items on display. Prices have risen considerably at nearby antique shops, but there are good restaurants and often spontaneous live entertainment from buskers and mimes.

The Feria Artesanal Plaza General Manuel Belgrano, at Juramento and Cuba in Belgrano, takes place weekends and holidays 10 am to 8 pm, but it gets better as the day goes on – not until 4 or 5 pm do the real craftsworkers finally outnumber the kitsch merchants.

GETTING THERE & AWAY
Because of space limitations, very detailed air and bus schedules do not appear below, but most newspapers, including the *Buenos Aires Herald,* publish schedules of arriving and departing international flights; for domestic flight frequencies, consult the appropriate destination in other chapters. Bus services are very frequent to most major domestic destinations.

Air
International Many major international airlines have offices or representatives in Buenos Aires. Most of the following serve Ezeiza for long-distance international flights, but a few from neighboring countries use Aeroparque.

Aeroflot
    Av Santa Fe 816/822 (☎ 312-5573)
Aerolíneas Argentinas
    Paseo Colón 185 (M, ☎ 343-2071, 343-2089)
    Perú 2 (☎ 343-8551, 343-8559)
Aero Perú
    Av Santa Fe 840 (☎ 311-6431)
Air France
    Av Santa Fe 963 (☎ 327-0202)
Alitalia
    Suipacha 1111, 28th floor (☎ 321-8421)
American Airlines
    Av Santa Fe 881 (☎ 312-3640)
Avianca
    Carlos Pellegrini 1163, 4th floor
    (☎ 394-5990)
British Airways
    Av Córdoba 650 (☎ 325-1059)
Canadian Airlines International
    Av Córdoba 656 (☎ 322-3732)
Cubana de Aviación
    Sarmiento 552, 11th floor
Iberia
    Carlos Pellegrini 1163, 1st floor
    (☎ 327-2739, 327-2752)
Japan Airlines
    Av Córdoba 836, 11th floor (☎ 393-1896)
KLM
    Reconquista 559, 5th floor (☎ 480-9470)
Lacsa
    Viamonte 920, 1st floor (☎ 393-5546)
Ladeco
    Av Santa Fe 920 (☎ 326-9937)
LanChile
    Paraguay 609, 1st floor, (☎ 311-5334)
Lapsa (Air Paraguay)
    Cerrito 1026 (☎ 393-1527)
Lloyd Aéreo Boliviano (LAB)
    Carlos Pellegrini 141 (☎ 326-3595,
    326-6411)
Lufthansa
    Marcelo T de Alvear 636 (☎ 319-0600)
Pluna (Líneas Aéreas Uruguayas)
    Florida 1 (☎ 342-4420)
Saeta
    Cerrito 1026 (☎ 393-1527)
Swissair
    Av Santa Fe 846 (☎ 319-0000)
TAP (Air Portugal)
    Cerrito 1146 (☎ 811-0984)
Trans Brasil
    Florida 780 (☎ 394-8424
United Airlines
    Carlos Pellegrini 1165, 5th floor
    (☎ 326-9111)
Varig
    Florida 630 (☎ 329-9200, 329-9201)

Vasp
    Av Santa Fe 784 (☎ 311-2699)
Viasa
    Carlos Pellegrini 1163, 1st floor
    (☎ 326-5082)

Domestic & Regional Most domestic and some regional flights leave from Aeroparque Jorge Newbery, a short distance north of downtown, but a few use Ezeiza. To Uruguay, in particular, services from Aeroparque are cheaper and more efficient than the major international airlines at Ezeiza.

Aerolíneas Argentinas – This airline has extensive domestic and international routes. Paseo Colón 185 (M, ☎ 343-2071, 343-2089) or Perú 2 (☎ 343-8551, 343-8559)

Austral Líneas Aéreas – Close partners Austral and Aerolíneas share an identical fare structure. Both serve nearly every major Argentine city between Bolivia and the Beagle Channel. Corrientes 485 (M, ☎ 325-0777)

Dinar Líneas Aéreas – This new airline flies to the northwestern Argentine destinations of Tucumán, Salta, and Jujuy. Fares are lower than Aerolíneas' or Austral's, but capacity is limited. Diagonal Roque Sáenz Peña 933 (M, ☎ 326-0135)

Líneas Aéreas del Estado (LADE) – The Air Force's commercial service serves Patagonian destinations exclusively. Perú 710, (☎ 361-0583)

Líneas Aéreas de Entre Ríos (LAER) – This airline flies to Mesopotamia, Santa Fe, La Pampa, and coastal Buenos Aires province. 5th floor, Carlos Pellegrini 1055 (M, ☎ 328-3932)

Líneas Aéreas Privadas Argentinas (LAPA) – LAPA has acquired many new planes and expanded routes to compete with Aerolíneas and Austral. Its capacity is still much smaller than its competitors, and flights are often booked far in advance. Also provides regional services to Colonia and Montevideo, Uruguay. MT de Alvear 790 (M, ☎ 314-1005)

Sapse Líneas Aéreas – This airline flies smaller planes to coastal Buenos Aires province and Patagonia. Fares are slightly more than half those of the larger airlines, but the limited number of flights are usually heavily booked. Tucumán 1920 (M, ☎ 371-7066)

Transporte Aéreo Costa Atlántica (TACA) – TACA flies small planes to Atlantic coastal destinations in summer. Bernardo de Irigoyen 1370, 1st floor (☎ 307-1956)

Bus

Buenos Aires' massive Retiro bus terminal is at Antártida Argentina and Ramos Mejía, a short distance from the Retiro train station. Its Centro de Informes y Reclamos (☎ 313-9594), Oficina 29 on the 2nd floor, provides general bus information and also monitors taxis serving the terminal; direct any complaint about taxi drivers to them.

Each of Retiro's 100-plus bus companies has a desk resembling an airline ticket counter (some of them shared). Discounted tickets are less prevalent than in the past, but student and university identification can still sometimes yield a reduction of 20% except on special promotions.

Space prohibits more than the following representative sample of information; for more detailed information, phone or visit the terminal. To the most popular destinations, departures are frequent and reservations are rarely necessary except during peak summer and winter holiday seasons, but purchasing your ticket a day ahead of time is still a good idea.

While the listing below is regionally organized, services do not always fit into convenient categories. Many Patagonian carriers, for example, stop in the Pampas of Buenos Aires province, while some serving Cuyo also continue to Chile. Bus companies and their regional destinations are given first, followed by tables of destinations, price, and estimated length of the trip.

International Destinations Bus compa-
nies with routes to other countries include the following:

Chevallier (☎ 313-3288) – Santiago, Chile

Chevallier Paraguaya (☎ 313-2349) – similar routes as La Internacional

El Rápido Internacional (☎ 315-0804) – Lima, Peru

Expreso Ormeño (☎ 313-2259) – Lima, Peru

Fénix Pullman Norte (☎ 313-0134) – Santiago, Chile.

General Urquiza (☎ 313-2771) – nightly service to Montevideo

La Internacional (☎ 313-3167) – Asunción, Paraguay, via Formosa and Clorinda.

Nuestra Señora de la Asunción (☎ 313-2325) – similar routes as La Internacional

Pluma (☎ 313-3839) – Brazilian destinations, including Foz do Iguaçu, Porto Alegre, Florianópolis, Camboriú, Curitiba, São Paulo, and Rio de Janeiro

Rápido Yguazú (☎ 313-4139) – Brazilian routes

TAC (☎ 313-2627) – Santiago, Chile

Tepsa (☎ 27-6591) – Lima, Peru

Destination	Fare	Duration
Asuncion	US$56-95	21 hours
Camboriú	US$90	27 hours
Curitiba	US$95	35 hours
Florianópolis	US$85	26 hours
Foz do Iguacu	US$60	19 hours
Lima, Peru	US$160	80 hours
Montevideo	US$25	9 hours
Porto Alegre	US$71	21 hours
Rio de Janeiro	US$117	48 hours
Santiago, Chile	US$60	21 hours
São Paulo	US$101	42 hours

To Atlantic Coast & the Pampas The
following bus companies go to points along the coast and in the Pampas.

Chevallier (☎ 313-3288) – Rosario and points north

Costera Criolla (☎ 313-2449) – Buenos Aires province, Bahía Blanca, Mar del Plata, northwestern Argentina, Patagonia, and Paraná

El Cóndor (☎ 313-3695) – Buenos Aires province, Bahía Blanca, Mar del Plata, northwestern Argentina and Patagonia

Empresa Antón (☎ 313-3051) – Mar del Plata and other beach resorts

La Estrella (☎ 313-3051) – Buenos Aires province, Bahía Blanca, northwestern Argentina, and Patagonia

La Internacional (☎ 313-3167) – Rosario and points north

La Unión (☎ 313-3797) – Rosario and points north

Micro Mar (☎ 313-3128) – Mar del Plata and other beach resorts

Río de la Plata (☎ 313-3580) – Mar del Plata and other beach resorts

Destination	Fare	Duration
Bahía Blanca	US$30	10 hours
Mar del Plata	US$25	7 hours
Rosario	US$20	6 hours

ARGENTINA

To Mesopotamia, Misiones & the Gran Chaco Try the following bus companies:

Ciudad de Posadas (☎ 313-4139) – Posadas, Puerto Iguazú, and Corrientes
El Norte Bis (☎ 313-2435) – Resistencia
El Rápido (☎ 315-0804) – littoral cities of Santa Fe, Paraná, and Corrientes
Empresa Kurtz (☎ 313-0950) – Posadas and Puerto Iguazú
Empresa Tata (☎ 313-3836) – Mesopotamian cities of Gualeguaychú, Colón and northerly destinations, passing Parque Nacional El Palmar
Expreso Río Paraná (☎ 313-3143) – Resistencia
Expreso Singer (☎ 313-2355) – Posadas and Puerto Iguazú
Flecha Bus (☎ 315-2781) – Paraná
Horiansky (☎ 97-6084) – Posadas and Puerto Iguazú
La Encarnaceña (☎ 313-2393) – Resistencia

Destination	Fare	Duration
Corrientes	US$32	14 hours
Gualeguaychú	US$20	3 hours
Paraná	US$26	7 hours
Posadas	US$35	14 hours
Puerto Iguazú	US$48	21 hours
Resistencia	US$43	15 hours
Santa Fe	US$21	6 hours

To Córdoba & the Andean Northwest Companies with routes to Córdoba and the Andean Northwest include:

Ablo (☎ 313-2835) – Rosario, Córdoba and its Sierras, and La Rioja
Cacorba (☎ 313-2588) – Córdoba and Catamarca
Chevallier (☎ 313-3288) – Rosario, Córdoba, Santiago del Estero, Catamarca, and points north
Colta (☎ 313-0590) – Sierras de Córdoba
El Santiagueño (☎ 313-2085) – Santiago del Estero
El Trébol (☎ 315-0808) – Termas de Río Hondo, Santiago del Estero, and Tucumán
La Estrella (☎ 313-3167) – Termas de Río Hondo, Santiago del Estero, and Tucumán
La Internacional (☎ 313-3167) – Salta and Jujuy
La Veloz del Norte (☎ 313-4309) – Salta and to the Bolivian border at Pocitos

Destination	Fare	Duration
Catamarca	US$50	16 hours
Córdoba	US$30	10 hours
Jujuy	US$77	22 hours
La Rioja	US$53	17 hours
Pocitos (Bolivia)	US$83	26 hours
Río Hondo	US$43	15 hours
Salta	US$65	22 hours
Santiago del Estero	US$39	14 hours
Termas de Río Hondo	US$43	15 hours
Tucumán	US$46	16 hours

To Cuyo To get to Cuyo, try one of the following bus companies:

Autotransportes San Juan (☎ 313-9625) – San Luis and San Juan
Chevallier (☎ 313-3288) – San Luis and Mendoza
Expreso Jocolí (☎ 311-8283) – San Luis and Mendoza
TAC (☎ 313-3627) – San Luis and Mendoza

Destination	Fare	Duration
Mendoza	US$52	13 hours
San Juan	US$54	16 hours
San Luis	US$45	12 hours

To Patagonia Bus companies with routes to Patagonia are:

Chevallier (☎ 313-3288) – Neuquén and Bariloche
Costera Criolla/Don Otto (☎ 313-2503) – coastal Patagonia: Tandil, Bahía Blanca, Puerto Madryn, Comodoro Rivadavia, and Río Gallegos
El Cóndor (☎ 313-3687) – Neuquén and Bariloche
El Sureño (☎ 315-288) – to Bariloche
El Valle (☎ 313-2441) – Bariloche, San Martín de los Andes
Empresa Pehuenche (☎ 311-8283) – Santa Rosa in La Pampa province, and to Neuquén
Expreso Pingüino (☎ 311-5440) – Río Gallegos, with connections to Punta Arenas, Chile
La Estrella (☎ 313-3051) – Neuquén and Bariloche, same routes as Costera Criolla/Don Otto as far as Comodoro
La Puntual (☎ 313-3742) – runs as far as Comodoro
TAC (☎ 313-3627) – Bariloche
Vía Bariloche (☎ 315-3122) – Bariloche

Destination	Fare	Duration
Bahía Blanca	US$28	10 hours
Bariloche	US$76	23 hours
Comodoro Rivadavia	US$82	24 hours
Neuquén	US$45	15 hours

Puerto Madryn	US$57	21 hours
Río Gallegos	US$107	40 hours
San Martín de los Andes	US$70	23 hours
Santa Rosa	US$37	9 hours
Tandil	US$15	6 hours

Train

Privatization of Ferrocarriles Argentinos has greatly reduced long-distance rail services. The Línea Mitre (☎ 312-6596) to Tucumán from Estación Retiro and the Línea Roca (☎ 304-0035) from Estación Constitución to Buenos Aires province and Bariloche continue to offer regular, though less frequent, passenger service. Retiro is near the bus terminal in downtown Buenos Aires, while Constitución is south of downtown; Línea C of the Subte links them. The Línea Sarmiento (☎ 861-0041) goes to Santa Rosa, La Pampa, on Monday, Wednesday, and Friday at 8 pm from Estación Once (Subte Plaza Miserere).

To Mar del Plata In season, as many as nine trains daily go to Mar del Plata; the ticket office at Constitución is open 7 am to midnight. Fares are US$40 Especial, US$30 Expreso, US$25 Pullman, US$19 Primera and US$14 Turista.

To Patagonia Servicios Ferroviarios Patagónicos' (Sefepa) ticket office at Constitución is open weekdays 9 am to 7 pm and Saturdays 9 am to 1 pm, as well as 6:30 to 7:30 am Wednesdays and Sundays (train days). It does not accept dollars or credit cards.

Sefepa's *Tren Tradicional* goes Wednesday at 7:40 am to Bahía Blanca (12 hours), Carmen de Patagones/Viedma (19 hours), San Antonio Oeste/Las Grutas (23 hours), Ingeniero Jacobacci (29 hours, the connection for the narrow gauge railroad to Esquel) and Bariloche (34 hours). Its more comfortable Sunday *Tren Español* has a similar schedule. Prices for destinations based on Primera/Pullman/Literas/Dormitorio classes are as follows:

Bahía Blanca	US$18/23/22/34
Viedma	US$31/33/32/49
Ingeniero Jacobacci	US$46/56/52/83
Bariloche	US$53/66/61/98

To Tucumán *El Tucumano* goes to Tucumán Monday, Wednesday, and Friday at 4 pm, via Rosario and Santiago del Estero (La Banda). The ticket office at Retiro is open weekdays 10 am to 6 pm, Saturdays 9:30 am to 1 pm. Fares based on Turista/Primera/Pullman classes are:

Rosario	US$10/12/16
La Banda	US$30/34/43
Tucumán	US$35/40/50

Boat

Buenos Aires has ferry and hydrofoil *(aliscafo)* services to Colonia, Uruguay, with bus combinations to Montevideo, and directly to Montevideo. These sail regularly from Dársena Norte, near downtown at Madero and Viamonte, or from Dársena Sur, Av Pedro de Mendoza 20 in La Boca. There is now a US$10 departure tax from these terminals.

Ferrytur (☎ 315-6800 or 300-1366 at Dársena Sur), Córdoba 699, sails the ferry *Ciudad de Buenos Aires* twice daily weekdays, daily weekends, to Colonia (2½ hours) and back. Regular fares are US$15 one-way, US$8 for children ages three to nine. One-way fares for automobiles start at US$40.

Ferrytur's hydrofoil *Sea Cat* goes to Colonia (one hour) three times daily, Monday to Saturday, and twice Sunday for US$25 one-way, US$45 return; children ages three to nine pay US$15/25. Both the ferry and hydrofoil make bus connections to Montevideo and Punta del Este. Fares may be higher on selected peak days and in summer. Aliscafos (☎ 314-2473), Córdoba 787, also runs several hydrofoils daily to Colonia.

Buquebus (☎ 313-4444), Córdoba 867, has three ferry sailings daily to Colonia on the *Eladia Isabel* and *Silvia Ana*. Their "Aviones de Buquebus" are high-speed ferries that reach Montevideo in 2½ hours and cost US$37 in turista, US$49 in primera; children ages two to nine pay

US$19/32. There are four sailings daily. A Buquebus colectivo leaves the Av Córdoba offices for Dársena Sur 1½ hours prior to every departure.

Cacciola (☎ 749-0329), at Lavalle 520 in the riverside suburb of Tigre, goes daily to Carmelo, Uruguay, at 8 am and 3:30 pm (US$11, US$7.50 for children). Movilán/Deltanave (☎ 749-4119) also goes to Carmelo, at 8:30 am and 3:30 pm. Línea Nueva Palmira (☎ 749-0537) goes to Nueva Palmira, Uruguay, daily at 7 am except Mondays, when it leaves at 4:30 am.

GETTING AROUND
To/From the Airport
Nearly all domestic flights and some to neighboring countries leave from convenient Aeroparque Jorge Newbery (☎ 771-2071), on the Costanera Av Rafael Obligado, only a few kms north of the city center. Aeropuerto Internacional Ministro Pistarini (commonly known as "Ezeiza", ☎ 480-0235), the international airport, is about 35 km south of downtown.

To reach Aeroparque, take city bus No 37C ("Ciudad Universitaria") from Plaza Italia; No 45 northbound from Constitución, Plaza San Martín or Retiro, as well as intermediate points; or No 160B from Av Las Heras or Plaza Italia. The fare is only about US$0.50.

The cheapest way to get to Ezeiza is to catch the No 86 bus (be sure it says "Ezeiza", since not all No 86s go to the end of the line), which starts in La Boca and comes up Av de Mayo past the Plaza del Congreso. To be assured of a seat, take the more comfortable "Servicio Diferencial" (about US$5). Theoretically neither allows very bulky luggage, though normal backpacks and suitcases should be permitted, but for a judicious tip you should be able to take almost anything. Because of heavy traffic, figure at least 1½ hours to Ezeiza.

Manuel Tienda León (☎ 314-3636, 314-2577), Santa Fe 790, runs a comfortable and efficient minibus service to Ezeiza (US$14 one-way), and also offers hotel pickup. Regular services begin at 4 and 5 am, then continue on the half hour until

11 pm. The hours for return services from Ezeiza are 6:30 am to 9:30 pm. The trip takes about 45 minutes, depending on traffic.

Manuel Tienda León service to Aeroparque (US$5) starts at 7:10 am, then continues on the half hour to 10:10 pm. Return service from Aeroparque starts at 7:50 am and stops at 10:50 am.

Taxis are expensive for individuals, costing about US$30, plus a US$2 surcharge for using the freeway, but may be cheaper than Manuel Tienda León if you have a group of three or four – negotiate with the driver.

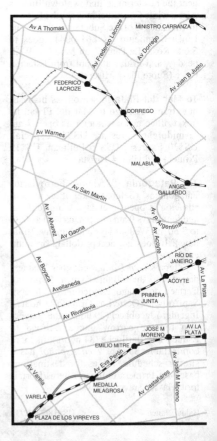

Bus

A large and complex bus system serves the entire Capital Federal and Gran Buenos Aires. For novices, the best guides are the *Guia Peuser,* sold at most kiosks and bookstores, which details almost 200 routes, accompanied by a foldout map; and *Capital Federal y Gran Buenos Aires* (commonly known as the "Guía Lumi"), which comes in a slightly larger but less unwieldy wire-binder format. However, not all No 60 buses, for example, go all the way to Tigre, nor do all No 86 buses go to Ezeiza – check the sign in the window to determine their ultimate destinations.

Many porteños have memorized the system and can instantly tell you which bus to take and where to get off for a particular destination. Unlike the Subte, fares depend on distance – on boarding, tell the driver where you're going and he will charge you accordingly. Most buses now have automatic ticket machines, which also make small change. Drivers are usually polite enough to give warning of your stop. If not, or if you find yourself at the back of a crowded bus, ask other passengers for advice and assistance. Anyone taller than Napoleon or Carlos Menem will have to bend over to see out the windows.

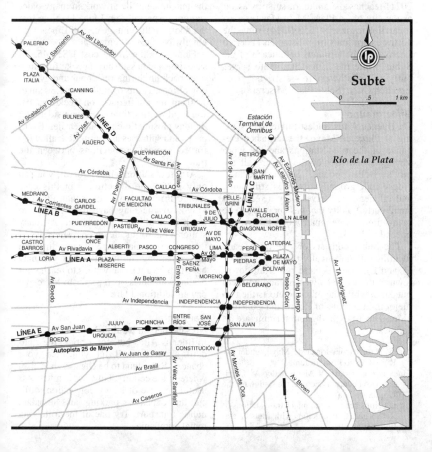

Like other motorists in the capital, bus drivers are fast and ruthless, and accidents involving buses are not that unusual. Hang on tight!

Train

Despite reductions in long-distance train service, local rail lines continue to serve most of Gran Buenos Aires. From Retiro, Ferrovías (the former Belgrano Norte line, ☎ 314-1444) goes to the city's northern suburbs, as does TMS Transporte Metropolitano General San Martín (☎ 772-5013).

From Constitución, Transportes Metropolitanos General Roca (TMR, ☎ 304-0021) reaches the southern suburbs as far as the city of La Plata. Metrovías (ex-Ferrocarril Urquiza, ☎ 553-9214) runs the northwestern lines from Estación Federico Lacroze, at the terminus of Línea B of the Subte, while the Línea Sarmiento serves outlying southwestern districts from Estación Once (Subte Plaza Miserere).

Underground

On Buenos Aires' oldest Subte line, starting at Plaza de Mayo, the tarnished elegance of the tiled stations and the worn vintage woodwork of the cars recall the city's "Belle Epoque." South America's oldest underground railway is still quick and efficient, but serves only a relatively small part of a city that has sprawled to be many times larger than when the system opened in 1913.

The Subte consists of five lines, each identified alphabetically (Líneas A, B, C, D, and E). Four of these run from downtown to the capital's western and northern outskirts, while the other connects the two major train stations of Retiro and Constitución. The lines and their termini are as follows:

Línea A runs from Plaza de Mayo, under Av Rivadavia, to Primera Junta.
Línea B runs from LN Alem, under Av Corrientes, to Federico Lacroze, the station for the Urquiza railway.
Línea C runs between the major train stations of Retiro and Constitución, with transfer stations for all other lines.
Línea D runs from Catedral, on the Plaza de Mayo, with a recent extension past Palermo to Ministro Carranza, at the junction of Av Cabildo and Av Dorrego.
Línea E runs from Bolívar, on the Av de Mayo, to Plaza de los Virreyes.

Privately operated Metrovías (☎ 553-9214 for complaints and comments between 10 am and 6 pm weekdays) has recently assumed control of operations and promises improvements in cleanliness, security, and emergency assistance. One of the first visible signs of progress is the introduction of comfortable new Japanese cars on Línea B, but the company also intends to restore the magnificent tile artwork in many older stations, especially on Línea D. Note that the doors on the vintage cars of Línea A do not always close automatically.

Fichas for the Subte cost US$0.45. To save time and hassle, buy a pocketful, since lines back up during rush hour and even at other times. Trains operate from 5:30 am to 1:30 am and are frequent on weekdays, but weekend waiting time can be considerable; Sunday closing time is much earlier. Backpacks and suitcases are permitted, allowing for convenient connections between the train stations.

At a few stations, like Alberdi, you can only go in one direction – in this case toward Primera Junta rather than Plaza de Mayo, so you may have to backtrack to reach your ultimate destination. At many stations, platforms are on opposite sides of the station, so make sure of your direction *before* passing the turnstiles, or you may have to backtrack many stops to reach your destination, unless you prefer to leave and pay an additional fare.

Car Rental

No sane person would recommend driving in Buenos Aires but, for a price, the standard agencies will let you take your chances. Rates tend to be cheaper than elsewhere in the country, but a car is much less useful because of heavy congestion, difficult and expensive parking, and abundant public transport. Try one of the following rental companies:

Top: Iguazú Falls, Misiones Province
Bottom: Parque Nacional El Palmar, Entre Ríos

Top Left: Cathedral, Paraná city
Top Right: Jesuit Church of La Campañía, Córdoba city
  Bottom: Sierras de Córdoba

AI
    Marcelo T de Alvear 678 (☎ 312-9475)
Alamo
    Florida 375, 2nd floor (☎ 325-7000)
Budget
    Santa Fe 869 (☎ 311-9870)
Dollar
    Viamonte 611, 11th floor (☎ 322-8409)
Hertz
    Ricardo Rojas 451 (☎ 312-1317)
Localiza
    Paraguay 1122 (☎ 375-1611)

Taxi
Buenos Aires' numerous, reasonably priced taxis are conspicuous by their black and yellow paint jobs. All are now digitally metered; it costs about US$1 to drop the flag and another US$0.10 per 100 meters. Drivers do not expect a big tip, but it's customary to let them keep small change; if you're carrying a large amount of luggage there may be a small additional charge. Remises (radio-taxis) tend to be marginally cheaper than the regular taxis that cruise the streets of the capital.

Almost all drivers are honest, but be certain the meter is set at zero; complaints are taken seriously. To make a complaint, you need the taxi and license numbers of the cab. Submit them to the service monitor at the bus terminal, who can provide a list of approximate standard fares.

When it rains, demand is high and taxis can be hard to find, so you may have to wait out the storm in a confitería.

Around Buenos Aires

Just outside the Capital Federal, in Buenos Aires province, are several more interesting and worthwhile attractions. Within commuting range of the capital (less than an hour by train, more than an hour by bus), the riverside suburb of Tigre is a popular weekend retreat and the best point of departure for exploring the Delta del Paraná and visiting historic Isla Martín García. It is also the departure point for passenger launches across the river to Carmelo and Nueva Palmira, Uruguay, but there is no ferry service for vehicles.

Isla Martín García was the site of an important naval battle during the wars of independence and later of a penal settlement still operating today. Several worthwhile tours offer an opportunity to explore the island.

TIGRE & THE DELTA
Tigre has older mansions, some of them dilapidated, that make walking around worthwhile, and the town is a popular weekend picnic destination. One of Tigre's best attractions is the **Puerto de Frutos** (fruit port), which holds a big weekend crafts fair and also offers good food at its restaurant.

Tigre is at the confluence of the Río Luján and the Río Tigre, beyond which is the 2000-km maze of waterways that constitutes the Delta. The main channel through the Delta is the Río Paraná de las Palmas.

Places to Stay & Eat
Hotels are relatively few in the Delta, but try *Hotel Laura* (☎ 749-3898) on Canal Honda off the Paraná de las Palmas for US$60 double with private bath weekdays, US$80 weekends. It also offers a US$15 excursion to the Delta. *Hotel I'Marangatú* (☎ 749-7350), on the Río San Antonio, charges US$80 during the week, US$100 weekends, while *La Manuelita* (☎ 749-0987), on the Río Carapachay, costs US$45 during the week, US$50 weekends. *Hotel Astor* is strictly an albergue transitorio.

On the Río Tres Bocas, about 20 minutes from Tigre by launch, *La Riviera* (☎ 749-6177, 749-5960) is a popular restaurant with good food, live music, and a frequently (but by no means exclusively) gay clientele. On weekends during Carnaval, the clientele are at their most outrageous.

Getting There & Away
Bus No 60 from Av Callao in Buenos Aires goes all the way to Tigre (1½ hours, US$1), but the Ferrocarril Mitre, leaving

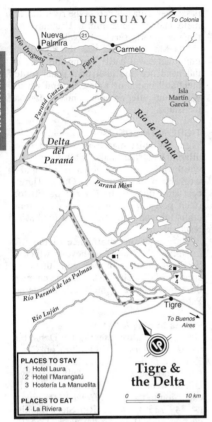

PLACES TO STAY
1 Hotel Laura
2 Hotel l'Marangatú
3 Hostería La Manuelita

PLACES TO EAT
4 La Riviera

Tigre & the Delta

0   5   10 km

ISLA MARTÍN GARCÍA

While navigating the densely forested channels of the Delta, en route to historic Martín García, visitors can easily imagine colonial smugglers hiding among the rushes. Just off the Uruguayan littoral, directly south of the city of Carmelo, the island is famous – or infamous – as a prison camp; four Argentine presidents have spent time in custody here, and the Servicio Penitenciario of Buenos Aires province still uses it as a halfway house for prisoners near the end of their terms. At present, though, it's more a combination of historical monument, nature reserve, and recreational retreat from the bustle of the capital.

History

In colonial times, Martín García was a bone of contention between Spain and Portugal. Unlike the sedimentary islands of the flood-prone Delta, the high ground of 180-hectare Martín García (27 meters above sea level) made it suitable for a fortress to guard the approach to the Uruguay and Paraná Rivers. Irish admiral Guillermo Brown gave the United Provinces of the River Plate their first major naval victory here in 1814, when a commando raid dislodged royalist troops who escaped to Montevideo. Both England and France took advantage of Argentine conflicts with Brazil to occupy the island at various times in the early 19th century.

For most of the 20th century, the Argentine navy has controlled the island. Nicaraguan poet Rubén Darío lived in what is now the natural history center while serving as Colombian consul in Buenos Aires at the turn of the century. During WWI, authorities briefly detained the crew of the German destroyer *Graf Spee,* sunk off Montevideo.

The Argentine military regularly confined political prisoners here, including Presidents Hipólito Yrigoyen (twice in the early 20th century), Marcelo T de Alvear (around the same time), Juan Domingo Perón (briefly in 1945), and Arturo Frondizi (1962 – 1963). Many speculate that the military dictatorship of 1976 – 1983 used

from Plataformas 1 or 2 at Retiro, is quicker when traffic is heavy. It's also cheaper (US$1.20 return).

Launches to Carmelo, Uruguay, leave daily at 8 am and 3 pm, charging $11 one-way plus $2 departure tax.

Getting Around

Interislena runs a series of lanchas colectivas from Tigre's Estación Fluvial to various destinations in the Delta for $3 to $5 per person, depending on the distance. They will drop or pick you up at any riverside dock – just flag them down as you would a bus.

the island as a Dirty War detention center and that sealed subterranean tunnels may contain evidence of such activity.

Things to See & Do

Martín García's main points of interest are its historic buildings. Four baterías, two on each side of the muelle (passenger pier), protect the perimeter of the town, and a faro (lighthouse) overlooks the cluster of buildings. The Oficina de Informes, uphill from the muelle, is also the headquarters of the Servicio Penitenciario, which manages halfway-house prisoners. Other buildings of interest to visitors include the ruins of the former Cuartel (naval barracks), the Panadería Rocio (a bakery dating from 1913), the extraordinarily decorative Cine-Teatro (theater), the Museo de la Isla, and the Casa de Ciencias Naturales, a house once occupied by Darío. At the northwestern end of the island, beyond a block of ruined and overgrown houses, vessels can no longer approach the Puerto Viejo (old

port) because sediments have clogged the anchorage. The cementerio (cemetery) contains the headstones of many conscripts who died in an epidemic in the early part of the 20th century.

The densely forested northern part of the island offers pleasant walks if you don't mind fending off the mosquitos. East of the airstrip, the Zona Intangible is closed to casual hikers because of its botanical value and the hazard of fire.

Comedor El Solís (see below) has a swimming pool open to the public.

Organized Tours

Without your own boat, the only practical way to get to the island is the guided tour from Cacciola's Terminal Internacional (☎ 749-0329) at Lavalle 520 in Tigre; tickets are also available at their office (☎ 322-0026) at Florida 520, 1st floor, Oficina 113 in Buenos Aires' microcentro. The enclosed catamaran leaves Tigre at 8 am, returning from Martín García at 5 pm

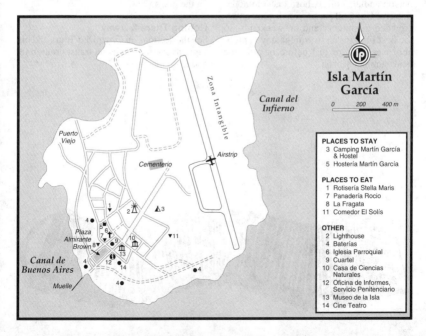

Isla Martín García

0   200   400 m

PLACES TO STAY
3 Camping Martín García & Hostel
5 Hostería Martín García

PLACES TO EAT
1 Rotisería Stella Maris
7 Panadería Rocio
8 La Fragata
11 Comedor El Solís

OTHER
2 Lighthouse
4 Baterías
6 Iglesia Parroquial
9 Cuartel
10 Casa de Ciencias Naturales
12 Oficina de Informes, Servicio Penitenciario
13 Museo de la Isla
14 Cine Teatro

ARGENTINA

(be dockside at 4 pm, however), and costs US$28 return. For US$42, the tour includes lunch at the Cacciola's La Fragata restaurant, but there are cheaper and better dining alternatives. Visitors camping on Martín García do not need to take the guided tour and pay only US$23 return.

On arrival at the island, Buenos Aires province collects a US$2 per person entrance fee to support the maintenance of its Reserva Natural y Cultural Isla Martín García. Passengers then split into two groups – those opting for the full excursion get a free aperitif, while the rest follows a very knowledgeable guide to the island's many well-preserved historic buildings. Very worthwhile if you understand Spanish, the 1½-hour tours leave plenty of time to explore the island on your own.

Places to Stay & Eat
Pleasant, shady *Camping Martín García* (☎ 413-2682 or 208-2883 for reservations, which are essential) costs US$3.50 per person and also offers hostel accommodations for US$6.50 per person. It can be very crowded in summer and on weekends, so the best time for an overnight stay is probably weekdays or just before or after the peak summer season.

Cacciola offers full-board overnight packages, including transportation, for US$105 per person at its *Hostería Martín García*; additional nights cost US$50 per person. Three-day, two-night packages with half-board cost US$109 and for US$35 with each additional day.

Comedor El Solís, with a US$8 tenedor libre including tasty boga and dessert, is a much better value than the expensive lunch at Cacciola's *La Fragata,* which is included in the full excursion. Drinks at Solís cost extra but are not outrageous. *Rotisería Stella Maris* also has decent simple meals and drinks, while the *Panadería Rocío* is renowned for its fruitcakes.

Things to Buy
Artisanal goods available on the island include mate gourds and wooden ships, along with the usual T-shirts and mugs manufactured elsewhere. Purchase these from small shops and individual artisans on the plaza.

Getting There & Away
See the sections on Organized Tours and on Tigre above for details on transportation to and from the island.

The Pampas

Argentina's celebrated Pampas are almost unrelentingly flat except for their extensive coastline, several small mountain ranges, and the delta of the Río de la Plata. These features give variety to the country's agricultural heartland, which comprises the provinces of Buenos Aires, La Pampa, and major parts of Santa Fe and Córdoba. Within this area are a surprising number of tourist attractions.

Buenos Aires province contains several important cities, particularly its capital of La Plata and the Atlantic port of Bahía Blanca. The colonial city of Luján is one of the most important religious centers in South America, while the interior town of San Antonio de Areco wears the emblem of Argentina's gaucho culture. Along the Atlantic coast lie many beach towns, the largest being Mar del Plata, to which porteños flock each summer. In the southern part of the province, there is scenic mountain country at Tandil and Sierra de la Ventana.

Rosario, a vital port for Argentina's agricultural commodities, is situated up the Río Paraná in Santa Fe province and vies with Córdoba for the status of "second city" in the republic. Rosario, however, is not even the capital of its own province – the colonial city of Santa Fe remains the seat of political power.

History

The aboriginal inhabitants of the Pampas were Querandí hunter-gatherers, less numerous and more dispersed than the sedentary, civilized peoples of the Andean Northwest or even the semisedentary Guaraní of the upper Paraná basin. Although they lacked both the plow and the domestic draft animals to cultivate the fertile Pampas, the Querandí had no real need for them – their subsistence came from hunting guanaco and rhea with boleadoras (also known as bolas) which, accurately thrown,

became entangled in the animal's legs and made it easy prey. Hunting was a communal rather than individual activity, and so long as game remained abundant on the Pampas' boundless pastures, the hard labor of cultivation was pointless.

The Querandí resisted the Spanish presence, besieging early settlements and preventing them from establishing any foothold in the area for more than half a century. Even after the definitive founding of the city of Buenos Aires in 1580, settlement of the Pampas proceeded slowly, only in part because Spain's mercantile policy favored already populous Peru and constrained potential rivals to Lima's political and economic primacy.

In many ways, feral animals accomplished what Madrid's early colonial policy actually discouraged – the spontaneous Europeanization of the Pampas. When the Spaniards abandoned their first settlement at Buenos Aires for the pleasures of Paraguay, they also left behind cattle and horses, which multiplied prodigiously in their absence.

During the centuries and even millennia before the arrival of the Spaniards, aboriginal peoples had transformed the Pampas environment through hunting and, especially, through fire. Frequent burning, a hunting technique to flush out game, prevented the re-establishment of *monte* (scrub forest) and directly benefited the grasses, which recuperated much more quickly. In turn, the new, succulent native grasses could support even more game.

Or more cattle. According to ecological historian Alfred Crosby, in 1619 (less than 40 years after the re-establishment of Buenos Aires), colonial officials informed Madrid that a harvest of 80,000 cattle per year for hides would not diminish the herds. One 18th-century visitor estimated the number of cattle south of modern Paraguay and north of the Río Negro at 48

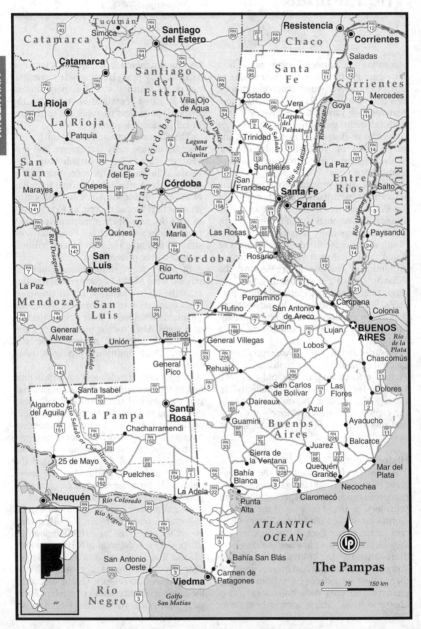

The Pampas

0   75   150 km

Over the undulating plains, where these great beds occur, nothing else can now live . . . I doubt whether any case is on record of an invasion on so grand a scale of one plant over the aborigines.

Unpremeditated introductions of European biota, then, were at least as important as European force in undermining indigenous resistance and opening the frontier to overseas immigrants.

Upon Argentine independence, the country's doors opened fitfully to foreign commerce. The Pampas' saladeros yielded only hides, tallow, and salt beef, products with limited overseas markets. This trade, in turn, benefited the relatively few estancieros with the luck to inherit or the foresight to grab large tracts of land. Some landowners did not survive the fall of Rosas, whose policies had encouraged the alienation of public lands for grazing establishments, but others prospered as Buenos Aires experienced a wool boom in the latter half of the 19th century.

From shortly after midcentury, the railroads, built largely with British capital, made it feasible to export wool and then beef, but the meat from rangy, unimproved criollo cattle did not appeal to British tastes. Improved breeds required more succulent feed, such as alfalfa, but the estancieros could not produce this on their enormous holdings with the skeletal labor force available to them. Consequently, their traditional opposition to immigration declined as they sought to attract tenant farmers to their holdings.

Although the estancieros had no intention of relinquishing their lands, the development of arable farming was an indirect benefit of the intensification of stock-raising. Cultivation of alfalfa required preparatory cultivation, so landowners rented their properties to *medieros* (sharecroppers), who raised wheat for four or five years before moving elsewhere, and thus landowners benefited both from their share of the wheat crop and from their new alfalfa fields. Still, shortly after the turn of the century, agricultural exports such as maize, wheat, and linseed exceeded the

million. Even granting the impossibility of a truly accurate estimate, the numbers were obviously very great.

Horses were also numerous. Like the Plains Indians of North America, Araucanians on both sides of the Andes quickly learned to tame and ride them, which bolstered their resistance to the invasion of their territories into the late 19th century. On horseback they were much more formidable opponents against imperial Spain and even independent Argentina, but as European immigration increased, the Indians' options were fewer, and the Pampas eventually fell to the cattle producers and farmers.

The wild cattle and horses left two enduring and related legacies: the culture of the gaucho, who persisted for many decades as a neohunter-gatherer and then as a symbol of argentinidad, an extreme but romantic Argentine nationalism; and environmental impoverishment, as grazing and opportunistic European weeds altered the native grasslands. Nineteenth-century observers such as Darwin and William Henry Hudson remarked on the rapid displacement of native plants by European artichokes and thistles in parts of the Pampas. Darwin wrote that in one area

very many (probably several hundred) square miles are covered by one mass of these prickly plants, and are impenetrable by man or beast.

value of livestock products such as hides, wool, and meat.

The Pampas are still famous for their beef, and estancias still dominate the economy, but smaller landholdings have increased in number and Argentina has remained a major grain exporter. The province of Santa Fe, where rain-fed maize is the principal crop, has a more democratic structure of land ownership, but almost everywhere agriculture is now highly mechanized and dependent on petroleum-based fertilizers and pesticides. In this sense, Argentina resembles other major grain-producing areas such as Australia, Canada, and the US. Near Buenos Aires and other large cities, though, there is intensive cultivation of fruits and vegetables, as well as dairy farming.

Northern Buenos Aires Province

Buenos Aires province is the largest, richest, most populous, and most important province in the country. Its area of 307,000 sq km makes it nearly twice the size of Uruguay, while its population, even excluding the federal district of the city of Buenos Aires, is more than triple Uruguay's three million. Its wealth lies in its soil; the yields of hides, beef, wool, and wheat for global markets placed an independent Argentina on the map in the 19th century.

From the mid-19th century, the province and city of Buenos Aires were the undisputed political and economic center of the country, but Buenos Aires' de facto secession as a federal zone subjugated the powerful province to national authority without completely eliminating its influence. By the 1880s, after a brief but contentious civil war, the province responded by creating its own model city of La Plata.

Outside the Capital Federal, a dense network of railroads and highways connects the agricultural towns of the Pampas, forming an astonishingly symmetrical pattern

on the provincial map, though the railroads carry far more freight than passengers. Most of these towns resemble each other as much as any part of the almost endlessly flat Pampas resembles another.

LA PLATA

After the city of Buenos Aires became Argentina's federal capital, Governor Dardo Rocha founded La Plata in 1882 to give the province its own new capital. After detailed study, Rocha selected Pedro Benoit's elaborate plan, greatly resembling that of Washington, DC, with major avenues and broad diagonals connecting its public buildings and numerous plazas. For two years, an army of laborers worked day and night to bring the plan to fruition.

La Plata's grandiose public buildings reflect Benoit's intention of building an important administrative, commercial, and cultural center, but the city does not overwhelm the human dimension. Buildings such as the well-kept Casa de Gobierno and Legislatura are better maintained than their federal counterparts, and make the city an attractive destination for either a day trip or an overnight excursion from the Capital Federal.

Rocha was the first rector of the Universidad Nacional de la Plata, founded by Joaquín V González and widely acknowledged as one of the best in the country; its original buildings have recently been restored to their former glory on Av 7, and the downtown sparkles with new restaurants. There are also several theaters and cultural centers and the campuses of the Universidad Tecnológica and the Universidad Católica.

Orientation

La Plata, 56 km southeast of Buenos Aires via RP 14, is a town of about 210,000, with a total population, including surrounding municipalities, of about 650,000. Its basic design is a conventional grid, but the superposition of numerous diagonals forms a distinctive diamond pattern, connecting the plazas and permitting traffic to flow smoothly between them. While most public

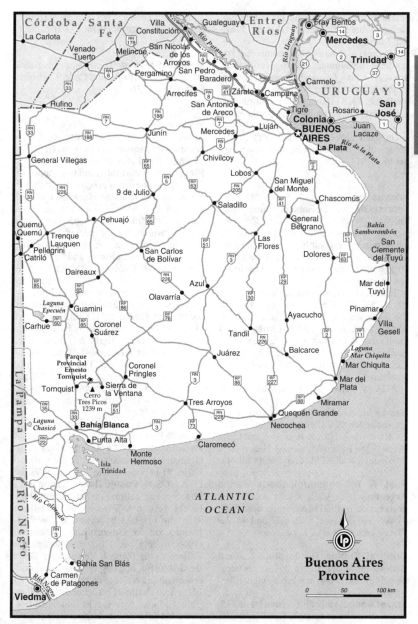

Buenos Aires Province

0   50   100 km

buildings are on or around Plaza Moreno, the commercial center is near Plaza San Martín.

All streets are named and numbered, but residents use numbers only to identify locations. Avenidas 1, 7, and 13 are main thoroughfares which run northwest-southeast, while Avs 44, 51, 53, and 60 run northeast-southwest. Diagonal 74 runs north-south, while Diagonal 73 runs east-west.

On each block, street numbers run in groups of 50 rather than the customary 100 per block.

Information

Tourist Offices The Entidad Municipal de Turismo (☎ 25-8334, 27-1535), Calle 47 No 740 between Calle 9 and Diagonal 74, has a friendly and helpful staff, but it keeps limited hours, from 8 am to 2 pm weekdays only. It distributes a sketchy city map and a few brochures.

The provincial Subsecretaría de Turismo (☎ 36357, 25-4576), on the 13th floor of the Torre Municipal at Calle 12 and Av 53, is very bureaucratic and has little printed matter, but if you can persuade them to let you up on the roof, there are magnificent views of the city. It's open 9 am to 3 pm weekdays.

ACA (☎ 30161) is at Calle 9 and Av 51.

Money Most banks and cambios are in the area bounded by Calles 6 and 8, and 46 and 50. Banco de la Nación is at Av 7 and Calle 49, as is the Banco Municipal. Banco de la Provincia has an ATM at Av 7 and Calle 47.

Post & Telecommunications Correo Argentino is at Calle 4 and Av 51; the postal code is 1900. Telefónica is at Calle 47 No 680 between Calles 47 and 48. La Plata's area code is 021.

Cultural Center The Instituto Cultural Británico, at Calle 12 No 869, hosts occasional cultural events and Friday night films.

Travel Agencies Titán Turismo (☎ 40495) is at Calles 43 and 6, while Los Diagonales

Tour (☎ 27-0657) is at Calle 11 No 1137. Confort Turismo (☎ 35140) is at Calle 6 No 668.

Medical Services The Hospital Español (☎ 21-0191) is located on Calle 9 between Calles 35 and 36.

Walking Tour

In the middle of **Plaza Moreno,** which occupies four square blocks between Calles 12 and 14 and Avs 50 and 54, La Plata's **Piedra Fundacional** (founding stone) of 1882 marks the city's precise geographical center. Across from the plaza, on Calle 14 between Avs 51 and 53, visit the neo-Gothic **Catedral** (begun 1885, completed 1903); inspired by its medieval counterparts in Cologne and Amiens, it has fine stained-glass windows and polished-granite floors. Dardo Rocha and his wife are buried here. The building's museum is open daily 8 am to noon and 2 to 7 pm.

On the opposite side of Plaza Moreno is the **Palacio Municipal** (1886), designed in German Renaissance style by Hannoverian architect Hubert Stiers; on either side, modern towers house most of the provincial government offices. Two blocks north, on Calle 10 between Avs 51 and 53, the unfinished **Teatro Argentino** replaces an earlier, much more distinguished building destroyed by fire.

Three blocks farther north, on Av 7 opposite Plaza San Martín, is the provincial **Palacio de la Legislatura,** also in German Renaissance style. To the west, on Calle 50 between Calle 6 and Av 7, the French classic **Pasaje Dardo Rocha** is La Plata's major cultural center. Detour three blocks west, to Av 7 between 47 and 48, to view the original buildings of the **Rectorado de la Universidad Nacional** (1905, once a bank) before returning via Calle 6 to the Flemish Renaissance **Casa de Gobierno,** housing the provincial governor and his retinue, on the north side of Plaza San Martín. If it's a hot day, stroll up Calles 54 and 5 to the landmark **Cervecería Modelo** for a cold lager beer.

ARGENTINA

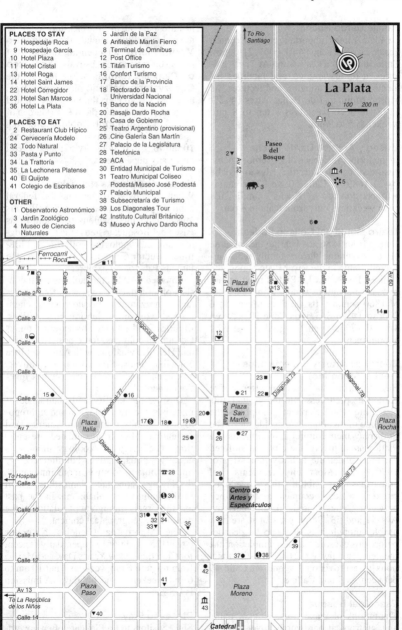

PLACES TO STAY
7   Hospedaje Roca
9   Hospedaje García
10 Hotel Plaza
11 Hotel Cristal
13 Hotel Roga
14 Hotel Saint James
22 Hotel Corregidor
23 Hotel San Marcos
36 Hotel La Plata

PLACES TO EAT
2   Restaurant Club Hípico
24 Cervecería Modelo
32 Todo Natural
34 Pasta y Punto
35 La Trattoría
35 La Lechonera Platense
40 El Quijote
41 Colegio de Escribanos

OTHER
1   Observatorio Astronómico
3   Jardín Zoológico
4   Museo de Ciencias
    Naturales

5   Jardín de la Paz
6   Anfiteatro Martín Fierro
8   Terminal de Omnibus
12 Post Office
15 Titán Turismo
16 Confort Turismo
17 Banco de la Provincia
18 Rectorado de la
    Universidad Nacional
19 Banco de la Nación
20 Pasaje Dardo Rocha
21 Casa de Gobierno
25 Teatro Argentino (provisional)
26 Cine Galería San Martín
27 Palacio de la Legislatura
28 Telefónica
29 ACA
30 Entidad Municipal de Turismo
31 Teatro Municipal Coliseo
    Podestá/Museo José Podestá
37 Palacio Municipal
38 Subsecretaría de Turismo
39 Los Diagonales Tour
42 Instituto Cultural Británico
43 Museo y Archivo Dardo Rocha

To Río
Santiago

La Plata

0   100   200 m

Paseo
del
Bosque

Pasaje Dardo Rocha

La Plata's most important cultural center, Pasaje Dardo Rocha (☎ 21-0061, 21-0066), Calle 50 between Calle 6 and Av 7, has galleries, a library/archive, and facilities for theater, concerts, movies, and lectures. Its Museo Municipal de Bellas Artes (☎ 27-1198) is open weekdays 8 am to 8 pm, weekends 5 to 9 pm.

Museo y Archivo Dardo Rocha

In the former residence of Governor Rocha, designed by Benoit, the Museo Rocha (☎ 21-1689) at Calle 50 No 933 contains artifacts donated by Rocha's family. It's open weekdays only from 8 am to 8 pm.

Teatro Municipal Coliseo Podestá

Dating from 1886 and bearing the surname of the Argentine theater family who pioneered drama in the River Plate region, the Coliseo Podestá is La Plata's most attractive and prestigious venue, with a capacity of 1360 persons. Its 1st-floor Museo José Podestá (☎ 24-8457), on Calle 10 between 46 and 47, is open for guided visits by appointment.

Centro de Artes y Espectáculos (Teatro Argentino)

Begun during the Proceso after a fire burned its predecessor to the ground, this pharaonic white elephant exemplifies the outcome of dictators who decide they need to display their cultural commitments (La Plata was, arguably, the city that suffered the most under the military repression of 1976-1983). Most city residents feel embarrassment about this oversized bunker, which occupies a full block between Calles 9 and 10, and between Avs 51 and 53. Some parts of it are now usable, though it is likely to be decades before this eyesore reaches completion; the theater company (☎ 21-4700) still functions in a provisional venue on Calle 49 between Av 7 and Calle 8.

Paseo del Bosque

Plantations of eucalyptus, gingko, palm, and subtropical hardwoods cover this 60-hectare park at the northeastern edge of town. Its facilities include the **Anfiteatro Martín Fierro,** an open-air facility that hosts summer drama festivals; the **Museo de Ciencias Naturales** (see below): the **Observatorio Astronómico** (open 7 am to 1 pm weekdays); the symbolic United Nations of the **Jardín de la Paz** (Garden of Peace); a small **Jardín Zoológico** (a zoo, open weekdays 9 am to 9 pm, weekends 10 am to 9 pm) along Av 52; and several university departments.

Museo de Ciencias Naturales

When Buenos Aires became the federal capital, provincial authorities built this museum, in the spacious park known as Paseo del Bosque, to house the archaeological and anthropological collections of lifetime director Francisco P Moreno, the famous Patagonian explorer.

Finished in 1889, the building itself consists of an attractive oval with four stories and a mezzanine with showrooms, classrooms, workshops, laboratories, offices, libraries, and storage. Its exterior mixes Corinthian columns, Ionic posterior walls, and Hellenic windows with Aztec and Inca embellishments. Since 1906, the university's school of natural sciences has functioned here.

Despite the quality and abundance of materials, the archaeological and anthropological exhibits from South America and Argentina suffer from outdated presentation. The extensive zoology display is equally unimaginative, but the recently opened botany room is more innovative, displaying "economic" plants (those useful to the indigenous inhabitants in the past and the largely immigrant population of the present) in geographical context.

The Museo de Ciencias Naturales (☎ 39125, 21-9066) is open daily (except for Christmas, New Year's Day, and May 1) from noon to 6 pm weekdays and 10 am to 6 pm weekends and holidays. Admission is US$2.

Places to Stay

Since visitors to La Plata are often government officials on per diem, hotels price their rooms accordingly. One of few budget hotels, the friendly but run-down *Hospedaje Roca* (☎ 21-4916), Calle 42 No 309, has singles/doubles for US$15/20 with shared bath, US$18/30 with private bath. Try also *Hospedaje García,* Calle 2 No 525.

Moderately priced *Hotel Saint James* (☎ 21-8089), Av 60 No 377, charges US$25/35 without breakfast. *Hotel Plaza* (☎ 21-0325), near the train station at Av 44 No 358, has rooms for US$30/40 without breakfast, but there is a budget double on the 3rd floor for US$30. Similar in price and standard is one-star *Hotel Roga* (☎ 21-9553) at Calle 54 No 334, where clean, comfortable rooms with private bath cost US$41/55.

At the top end are three-star lodgings such as *Hotel La Plata* (☎ 21-1365), Av 51 No 783 near Plaza Moreno, which has a nice restaurant; rooms go for US$45/60. *Hotel Cristal* (☎ 21-1393), Av 1 No 620, charges US$47/62, while rooms at *Hotel San Marcos* (☎ 42385), Calle 54 No 523, cost US$50/67.

Four-star *Hotel Corregidor* (☎ 25-6800), Calle 6 No 1026, offers rooms and many luxuries for US$82/95.

Places to Eat

Among the cheapest restaurants are traditional favorites such as *Everton,* Calle 14 between Calles 63 and 64, and *Club Matheu,* Calle 63 between Av 1 and Calle 2. Both offer limited but good menus at affordable prices. A bit more pricey but very pleasant is the *Restaurant Club Hípico* in the Paseo del Bosque.

For a good parrillada try *El Chaparral,* at Av 60 and Calle 117, which has excellent mollejas (sweetbreads). On Plaza Paso, *El Quijote* occupies a commonplace building at Avs 13 and 44, but it has delicious food, particularly the ensalada de frutos de mar (seafood salad). Local lawyers recommend the *Colegio de Escribanos,* Av 13 between Calles 47 and 48, especially their omelette surprise for dessert.

Pasta y Punto, Calle 47 No 787 between Calles 10 and 11, is a very fine, pleasantly decorated Italian restaurant which is a good value for the money, though it's not really cheap; next door is *Todo Natural,* a good natural foods market. Another popular Italian place is *La Trattoría* at Calle 47 and Diagonal 74. *La Lechonera Platense,* on Diagonal 74 between Calles 48 and 49, specializes in pork dishes.

The quintessential La Plata experience is the 85-year-old *Cervecería Modelo,* or simply *La Modelo,* at the corner of Calles 5 and 54. On a warm summer night, you can pass hours at their sidewalk tables, downing excellent *cerveza tirada* (lager beer) and complimentary peanuts – for something more substantial, try a lomito (beef sandwich) with chips. In winter there is plenty of space inside.

Entertainment

The *Cine Galería San Martín* (☎ 39-947) is on Av 7 between Calle 50 and Av 51.

Spectator Sports

Gimnasia y Esgrima La Plata (☎ 22-8620), the local soccer club, has offices at Calle 4 No 979, but the team plays at the *stadium* (☎ 21-4422) at the intersection of Calles 60 and 118. Buy tickets at the stadium, but always call first.

Getting There & Away

Bus The Terminal de Omnibus (☎ 21-0992) is at Calles 4 and 42. Río de la Plata (☎ 38537) has buses every half hour to Once, Constitución, and Retiro stations in Buenos Aires (US$2) and also offers a beach service to Pinamar and Villa Gesell.

Long-distance carriers include Costera Criolla (☎ 31185), which serves Mar del Plata, Miramar, Necochea, and Tandil, and El Cóndor/La Estrella (☎ 23-2745), which goes direct to Mar del Plata and to Bahía Blanca via Olavarría and Sierra de la Ventana. Liniers (☎ 39147) goes daily to Santa Rosa, La Pampa province, while Pampa (☎ 24-3064) has runs to Tandil and Necochea. Río Paraná (☎ 24-2036) goes to Bahía Blanca and Carmen de Patagones.

TAC (☎ 25-6943) goes daily to Mendoza via San Luis; at the same office, El Santiagueño goes to Santiago del Estero via Rosario, and Flecha Bus goes to Concordia. Empresa Tala (☎ 24-3064) has buses to Paso de los Libres and Corrientes. La Unión (☎ 24-0940) goes to Termas de Río Hondo.

General Urquiza (☎ 25-9292) and Expreso Córdoba Mar del Plata go to Córdoba and its Sierras, the latter with additional service to La Rioja. El Rápido Argentino (☎ 24-3062) goes to most provincial beach towns, from Mar de Ajó in the north to Necochea in the south.

Train The turn-of-the-century Estación Ferrocarril General Roca (☎ 21-9377, 21-2575), at Avs 1 and 44, features an interesting Art Nouveau dome and wrought-iron awning, but the lack of maintenance has left it less impressive than it once was. There are hourly train departures to Constitución (US$1, 1½ hours) via Quilmes or Temperley.

Getting Around
Buses to different places in the city stop by the train station.

AROUND LA PLATA
La República de los Niños
Evita Perón sponsored this scale version of a city for the education and enjoyment of children, completed shortly before her death in 1952. From the Plaza de la Amistad, a steam train circles this architectural hodgepodge of medieval European and Islamic styles, with motifs from Grimms' and Andersen's fairy tales. It includes a civic center with church, a (working) post office, courts and police station, shops, supermarket, restaurants, factories, a zoo and aquarium, and an educational farm, plus an artificial lake.

The **Museo Internacional del Muñeco**, a doll museum with domestic and imported dolls and puppets in the Moorish Casa de la Cultura, is open 10 am to 6 pm daily. Like most public works projects of its era, República de los Niños is

showing its age, but it's worth a visit if you have crabby kids to appease; otherwise, it's sort of a bargain-basement Disneyland.

República de los Niños (☎ 84-0194) is on Camino General Belgrano Km 7 and Calle 501, north of La Plata in the suburb of Manuel Gonnet. From Av 7 in La Plata, take bus No 518 or No 273; not all No 273 buses go all the way. Admission is US$3 per person, which includes aquarium and farm, but the train ride and doll museum require separate admission fees.

Río Santiago
Ghost factories like the Swift meat-packing plant, which employed 24,000 workers at its peak, haunt the port of Río Santiago, at the end of the Roca line past La Plata. Infrequent trains are usually packed with soldiers coming from and going to the military academy that functions there, so city bus No 214 (Berisso) is more frequent and dependable.

From the Río Santiago train station, it's also possible to take a boat to picturesque **Isla Paulino**, rarely visited by tourists, whose inhabitants cultivate grapes in the highly regarded *viñedos de la costa* (coastal vineyards).

LUJÁN
Buenos Aires' second founder, Don Juan de Garay, granted the lands around the Río Luján to Spanish pioneers, but incessant Querandí raids and the distance from Buenos Aires deterred settlement until the 17th century, when the settlement by the Río Luján became an important stop on the cart road west.

According to legend, in 1630 a wagon containing a painting of the Virgin en route from Brazil to a Portuguese farmer would not budge until the gauchos removed the painting. The image's devoted owner cleared the site and built a chapel where the Virgin had chosen to stay, about five km from present-day Luján. This image took the name of La Virgen de Luján and became Argentina's patron saint, but she now occupies the neo-Gothic basilica, one of the city's two main tourist attractions.

The other is a colonial historical museum complex.

Orientation
On the east bank of its namesake river, Luján is only 65 km from Buenos Aires via RN 7, so many people come from the federal capital for the day. Most places of interest, as well as hotels, are near the basilica, but Plaza Colón, five blocks southeast via Calle San Martín, is also a major center of activity.

Information
Tourist Offices There's an Oficina de Informes Turísticos (☎ 20032) at the bus terminal, but the staff at Dirección de Turismo (☎ 20453) in Edificio La Cúpula, at the west end of Lavalle, is more knowledgeable and better supplied with information and brochures.

Post & Telecommunications Correo Argentino is on Mitre between Colón and Mariano Moreno; Luján's postal code is 6700. The area code is 0323.

Basílica Nuestra Señora de Luján
Every year four million people from all over Argentina visit Luján to honor the Virgin for her intercession in affairs of peace, health, forgiveness, and consolation. The terminus of their pilgrimages is this huge neo-Gothic basilica, where the "Virgencita" (she is known by the affectionate diminutive) occupies a *camarín* (chamber) behind the main altar. Devotees have covered the stairs with plaques acknowledging her favors.

Every October since the Dirty War, a massive Peregrinación de la Juventud (Youth Pilgrimage) originates in Buenos Aires' Once Station, 62 km away. In the days of the military dictatorship, when any mass demonstration was forbidden, this walk had tremendous symbolic importance, but since the restoration of democracy it has become more exclusively devotional. The other large gathering of believers takes place May 8, the Virgin's day.

Near the basilica, the **Museo Devo-**cional houses *ex-votos* (gifts) to the Virgin, including objects of silver, wood, and wax, musical instruments, and icons from all over the world. It's open Tuesday to Friday from 1 to 6 pm, weekends from 10 am to 6 pm.

Complejo Museográfico Enrique Udaondo
Bounded by Calles Lezica y Torrezuri, Lavalle, San Martín, and Parque Ameghino, this museum complex occupies three full hectares. It includes the 30 rooms of the **Museo Colonial e Histórico**, housed in colonial buildings such as the **cabildo** and the so-called **Casa del Virrey** (no viceroy ever actually lived there). Exhibits cover the area's history from pre-Columbian times but stop abruptly in 1953. The **Museo de Transporte** has four showrooms, plus a patio with colonial wagons, a windmill, and a horse-powered mill.

Museum hours are Wednesday 12:30 to 4:30 pm, Thursday and Friday 11:30 am to 4:30 pm, and weekends 10:45 am to 6 pm. The combined library/archive is open weekdays 9:30 am to 6 pm but closes in January.

Places to Stay
Camping For about US$4 per person per day, *Camping 7* on RN 7 (Av Carlos Pellegrini) across the Río Luján is basic and less than perfectly maintained, but it's OK for a night. There is another more expensive *campground* along the river near the Dirección Municipal de Turismo at Edificio La Cúpula. Informally, pilgrims camp just about anywhere they feel like it.

Hospedajes & Hotels Several budget hotels cater to the pilgrims who come throughout the year. On the north side of the basilica is friendly *Hospedaje Carena* (☎ 21287), Calle Lavalle 114, with singles/doubles at US$12/15 with private bath. Similar in price and standards is *Hotel Santa Rita* (☎ 20981), Torrezuri 857 at Lezica, with small, musty, but clean rooms with private bath for US$15/20. Opposite the bus terminal, *Hospedaje Royal*

(☎ 21295), 9 de Julio 696, has small rooms at US$20/28.

Also nearby is the dark and worn but clean and friendly *Hotel Venecia,* Calle Brown 100, which has small rooms with private baths and fans for US$15/20. Rates are similar at *Hotel Victoria* (☎ 20582), Lavalle 136. South of the basilica is the once-elegant *Hotel de la Paz* (☎ 24034), 9 de Julio 1054, which is now worn around the edges. The owners are friendly and the rooms are acceptable at US$20/30.

The only two-star hotel, the *Real Hotel Luján* (☎ 20054), Av Nuestra Señora de Luján 816, is a good value at US$25/35, including private bath and telephone. For the most improbable hotel name in this major devotional center, we nominate *Hotel Eros* (☎ 21658), San Martín 129. Very clean, small rooms with no exterior windows cost US$25/35 with private bath.

Places to Eat
There is a slew of cheap, fixed-menu restaurants near the basilica along Av Nuestra Señora de Luján, where very aggressive waiters nearly yank tourists off the sidewalk. Off the central plaza, quiet *Restaurant Don Diego,* Colón 964, has excellent but pricey Argentine food. *Restaurante Match Point,* San Martín 199, is cheaper with smaller portions, and there are discounts for ACA members.

Highly regarded *L'eau Vive,* a convent-run restaurant at Constitución 2112 between Entre Ríos and Doctor Luppi, is at the south end of town.

Getting There & Away
Bus The Estación Terminal de Omnibus is at Av de Nuestra Señora del Rosario, four blocks north of the basilica. Transporte Luján (Línea 52) goes to Plaza Miserere (Estación Once) in Buenos Aires, while Transportes Atlántida (Línea 57) connects Luján with Palermo. Talsa goes frequently to Once for US$3.

There are also long-distance services. Empresa Argentina has three buses daily to

Mar del Plata (US$26), while Atlántida has similar but costlier services to Mardel (US$30), Pinamar, and Villa Gesell. La Estrella goes to San Juan (US$51) and to San Rafael, with connections to Mendoza, for US$48. General Urquiza serves Rosario (US$14) and Córdoba (US$36).

Train The Ferrocarril Sarmiento still runs daily trains to and from Estación Once (Plaza Miserere Subte) in Buenos Aires.

SAN ANTONIO DE ARECO
Dating from the early 18th-century construction of a chapel in honor of San Antonio de Padua (but named to reflect the river on which it's situated), this serene village is the symbolic center of Argentina's vestigial gaucho culture and host to the country's biggest gaucho celebration, Día de la Tradición, in November. Nestled in the verdant pampas of northern Buenos Aires province, it was the setting for Ricardo Güiraldes' famous novel *Don Segundo Sombra* (1927). Güiraldes' nephew Adolfo played the role of Don Segundo in the film version (1969), in which many locals served as extras.

Unlike most Argentine cities, San Antonio's street life centers not around the plaza but on the main commercial street of Alsina, where there's a wealth of quality artisanal goods – this is one of the best places in the country for typical souvenirs. It's an exceptionally popular weekend destination for porteños, but weekdays can be very quiet, and Monday is utterly dead except when roaring motor scooters decimate the town's normally bucolic ambience (San Antonio's narrow streets are notorious echo chambers). At least the cobbled streets around Plaza Ruiz de Avellano help slow the traffic.

Orientation
San Antonio is on the south bank of Río Areco, 113 km west of Buenos Aires via RN 8, which continues west to Pergamino, Río Cuarto, and Mercedes before meeting

ARGENTINA

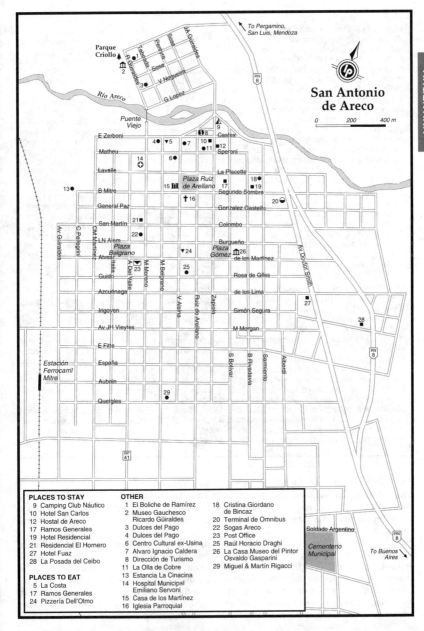

San Antonio de Areco

0   200   400 m

PLACES TO STAY
9   Camping Club Náutico
10 Hotel San Carlos
12 Hostal de Areco
17 Ramos Generales
19 Hotel Residencial
21 Residencial El Hornero
27 Hotel Fuaz
28 La Posada del Ceibo

PLACES TO EAT
5   La Costa
17 Ramos Generales
24 Pizzería Dell'Olmo

OTHER
1   El Boliche de Ramírez
2   Museo Gauchesco
    Ricardo Güiraldes
3   Dulces del Pago
4   Dulces del Pago
6   Centro Cultural ex-Usina
7   Alvaro Ignacio Caldera
8   Dirección de Turismo
11 La Olla de Cobre
13 Estancia La Cinacina
14 Hospital Municipal
    Emiliano Servoni
15 Casa de los Martínez
16 Iglesia Parroquial
18 Cristina Giordano
    de Bincaz
20 Terminal de Omnibus
22 Sogas Areco
23 Post Office
25 Raúl Horacio Draghi
26 La Casa Museo del Pintor
    Osvaldo Gasparini
29 Miguel & Martín Rigacci

The Rise & Romance of the Gaucho

No one could have predicted the respectability of that accidental icon, the Argentine gaucho, and even fewer completely understand him. The modern gaucho, dressed in baggy *bombacha*, a leather *rastra* round his waist, and a sharp *facón* in his belt, is the idealized version of a complex historical figure who remains in the Argentine conscience. Directly or indirectly, to Argentines and foreigners alike, he derives from the romantic portrayals of José Hernández's epic poem *Martín Fierro* and Ricardo Güiraldes' novel *Don Segundo Sombra*. Like his counterpart, the North American cowboy, the gaucho has received elaborate cinematic treatment. Ironically, only when he became a sanitized anachronism did he achieve celebrity.

Without the rich pastures of the Pampas and the cattle and horses that multiplied on them, the gaucho could never have flourished. In a sense, he replaced the Pampas Indian; usually a *mestizo*, he hunted burgeoning herds of cattle just as the Querandí Indians hunted the guanaco and rhea. So long as cattle were many, people few, and beef, hides, and tallow of limited commercial value, his subsistence and independence were assured. This achieved, he could amuse himself by gambling and drinking in the saloon or *pulpería*. Observers such as Domingo Sarmiento thought the gaucho indolent, but grudgingly acknowledged that he led a good life:

> Country life, then, has developed all the physical but none of the intellectual powers of the gaucho. His moral character is of the quality to be expected from his habit of triumphing over the forces of nature; it is strong, haughty, and energetic. Without instruction, and indeed without need of any, without means of support as without wants, he is happy in the midst of his poverty and privations, which are not such to one who never knew nor wished for greater pleasures than are his already. Thus if the disorganization of society among the gauchos deeply implants barbarism in their natures, through the impossibility and uselessness of moral and intellectual education, it has, too, its attractive side to him. The gaucho does not labor; he finds his food and raiment ready to his hand.

Even when Sarmiento wrote about the gaucho in the mid-19th century, their independent, self-sufficient way of life was already in decline. Just as the gauchos had replaced the Pampas Indians, the large landowners squeezed out the gauchos when the primitive livestock economy gave way to *saladeros,* which made use of a wider variety of products – processed hides, tallow, and salted beef.

For their saladeros, landowners needed labor; the gaucho, with his skills on horseback, was a desirable if unwilling source of manpower, but landowners were not reluctant to use their influence to coerce him. Classifying the gaucho as a "lawless" element, discriminatory laws soon required internal passports, and men without jobs could no longer travel freely over the Pampas. Punishment for "vagrancy" was often military conscription. As sheep replaced cattle on the Pampas, land was fenced and marked, forcing the gaucho to the fringes or onto the estancias.

Unlike the frontier, the estancia was not a democracy, and the gaucho was no longer his own master, even though his livestock skills were still in seasonal demand. He became instead a hired hand on an institution the physical aspects of which bespoke hierarchy: the *estanciero* (manager) resided in the *casco* (big house), while, if fortunate, the peons and their families lived in hovels or isolated *puestos* (outside houses) at the pleasure of the landowner – and the puestos themselves

RN 7 to San Luis and Mendoza. At the eastern approach to town, RP 41 heads toward RN 9, Rosario, and points north.

East of the river, San Antonio has a very regular grid, the formal focus of which is Plaza Ruiz de Arellano, bounded by Calles Lavalle, Arellano, Mitre, and Alsina (the main commercial drag). Street names change on each side of Arellano. Several points of interest are on or across the river, while San Antonio's numerous artisans are scattered around the downtown area.

Information

Tourist Office Friendly but sometimes patronizing to foreigners, San Antonio's Dirección de Turismo (☎ 3165) is on Castex between Arellano and Zapiola. It's open 7 am to 2 pm weekdays, 10 am to 5 pm weekends (when it serves up to 800 visitors daily). The office distributes a helpful pocket-sized guide, updated monthly, with a map and much other useful information. It also dispenses *Pregon Turismo,* a new tabloid-size publication

were a means of keeping an eye on remote properties. As European immigrants came to occupy many of these jobs, which often were detested by real gauchos, friction arose between gaucho "natives" and Italian "gringos"; however, despite resistance, the days of the free-roaming gaucho were over by the late 19th century.

Ironically, about this time Argentina discovered the gaucho's virtues in what has become known as *literatura gauchescha* (gauchesque literature, or literature *about* as opposed to *by* the usually illiterate gauchos). The poem *Martín Fierro* romanticized the life of the independent gaucho at the very time when, like the open-range cowboy of the American West, he was disappearing. Hernández deplored both opportunistic strongmen like Juan Manuel de Rosas, who claimed to speak for the gaucho, and "civilizers" like Sarmiento, who had no scruples about discarding the people of the countryside. The gaucho's fierce independence, so often depicted as lawlessness, became admirable, and Hernández almost single-handedly rehabilitated the image of the gaucho, as Argentines sought an identity in a country being transformed by immigration and economic modernization. Having fought alongside the gaucho, defending him in the public forums of his country and pleading for his integration into the country's future, Hernández was an eloquent spokesperson for the gaucho's positive values, which even Sarmiento admitted – courtesy, independence, and generosity. Urban Argentines soon elevated the gaucho to a mythical status, incorporating these values into their own system, but only after his fate was decided.

In 20th-century gauchesque literature, the most important work is *Don Segundo Sombra,* in which narrator Fabio Cáceres, an orphan, receives his "education" on the Pampas under the tutelage of a clearly idealized gaucho who symbolizes many of the same values as Martín Fierro. The novel's climax is the revelation that Fabio, who would have been helpless without his mentor, is in fact heir to a powerful landowning family – implying that Argentina's elite needed to remain in touch with their predecessors on the Pampas.

Readers interested in gauchesque literature can find *Martín Fierro,* one of the world's most translated books, in many editions. Less widely available but still translated into 16 languages since its original publication in 1927, *Don Segundo Sombra* appeared in English in 1935. The 1969 film version, available in some video stores specializing in foreign cinema, comes from Two World International Films (Beatles fans take note: John Lennon is credited as an extra in this film). ∎

that provides more detailed material on San Antonio's attractions.

Money San Antonio has no ATMs, but there are several banks. Visitors coming from Buenos Aires will find it easier to exchange money there first.

Post & Telecommunications Correo Argentino is at Alvear and Del Valle; the postal code is 2760.

There are several downtown locutorios on Alsina; San Antonio's area code is 0326.

Medical Services The Hospital Municipal Emiliano Servoni (☎ 2391) is at Lavalle and Moreno.

Walking Tour

San Antonio's compact center lends itself to walking. At the beginning of the 18th century, **Plaza Ruiz de Arellano** was the site of the corrals of the town's founding estanciero; in its center, the **Monumento a Vieytes** honors locally born Juan Hipólito Vieytes, a figure in the early independence movement. Around the plaza are several historic buildings, including the **Iglesia Parroquial** (parish church) and the **Casa de los Martínez** (site of the *casco* (main house) of the original Ruiz de Arellano estancia).

Conspicuously featured in the film version of *Don Segundo Sombra,* the **Puente Viejo** (1857) across the Río Areco follows the original cart road to northern Argentina; once a toll bridge, it's now a pedestrian crossing leading to the **Parque Criollo y Museo Gauchesco Ricardo Güiraldes,** San Antonio's major visitor attraction.

Ricardo Güiraldes and Segundo Ramírez, the real-life role model for Don Segundo Sombra, both lie in the **Cementerio Municipal** at the south end of town on Soldado Argentino.

Parque Criollo y Museo Gauchesco Ricardo Güiraldes

Inaugurated by the provincial government in 1938, a decade after Güiraldes' death, this elaborate museum is, on one level, a spurious Gaucholand of restored and/or fabricated buildings idealizing and fossilizing the history of the Pampas. On the other hand, its 90 hectares also provide an unalloyed introduction to the gaucho as a modern cultural phenomenon, allowing visitors to appreciate the degree to which this icon has infused contemporary Argentine society.

The centerpiece of the complex is the **Casa del Museo,** a 20th-century reproduction of an 18th-century casco, which includes a **Sala de los Escritores** on gaucho literature (including the desk and chair of Walter Owen, who translated *Martín Fierro* into English), a **Sala Pieza de Estanciero** with a wooden bed belonging to Juan Manuel de Rosas (perhaps the ultimate rural landowner), and a **Sala del Gaucho** with horsegear and various works of gauchesque art. Two rooms are dedicated to Güiraldes himself, another to his

wife Adelina del Carril de Güiraldes, and one to his painter cousin Alberto.

More authentic, or at least more venerable, than the Casa del Museo is the **Pulpería La Blanqueada,** a mid-19th century building displaying a credible recreation of a rural tavern. Alongside the pulpería are **La Tahona,** an 1848 flour mill brought here from the town of Mercedes, and the **Galpón y Cuarto de Sogas,** where the estancia might have stored its carriages. Nearby is **La Ermita de San Antonio,** a colonial-style chapel with some colonial artifacts.

North of the river on Camino Ricardo Güiraldes, reached via the Puente Viejo, the grounds and buildings of the Museo Gauchesco (☎ 2583) are open weekdays 10 am to 3 pm except Tuesday (when it is closed), weekends and holidays 10 am to 5 pm. Admission is US$2 for adults, US$1 for retired persons.

Centro Cultural ex-Usina

This interestingly retrofitted power plant comprises several galleries displaying local artists' and artisans' work, as well as historical materials on San Antonio and its residents. Among the interesting materials are original woodcuts by Adolfo Bellocq used to illustrate *Martín Fierro,* and copies of Florencio Molina Campos' amusing caricatures of gaucho life and culture, which appeared on millions of calendars distributed by the Alpargatas textile factory in the 1930s and 1940s.

The Centro Cultural is on Alsina between Matheu and Lavalle. Admission is free; hours are from 8 am to 1 pm weekdays, 10 am to 5 pm weekends.

La Casa Museo del Pintor Osvaldo Gasparini

Open daily 8 am to 8 pm, this museum (☎ 3930) features oils and watercolors with gaucho themes. It's at Av de los Martínez (ex-Alvear) 521, corner of Bolívar, opposite Plaza Gómez.

Estancia La Cinacina

For a day in the country, countless porteños

choose Estancia La Cinacina, where US$30 buys an all-you-can-eat asado, entertainment in the form of folkloric music and dance, a tour of the estancia's museum, and horseback riding. Estancia Cinacina (☎ 2045), at Mitre 9 only six blocks from Plaza Ruiz de Arellano, is less crowded and more comfortable on weekdays. Its Buenos Aires representative is Empresa Que La Opera (☎ 342-1986, 342-2841), Mitre 734, 10° B; tours including transportation from the capital cost US$60.

Special Events

Lasting a week in November, Fiesta de la Tradición (90 years old in 1996) celebrates San Antonio's gaucho past. By presidential decree, San Antonio is the "sede provincial de la tradición" (provincial site of tradition). The actual Día de la Tradición is November 10, but it's moved to the following Sunday for convenience. The festival includes lectures, artisanal exhibits, guided tours of historic sites, displays of gaucho horsemanship, folk dancing, and the like. If you're planning to visit San Antonio at this time, make reservations far in advance for the limited accommodations. June 13 is the Día del Santo Patrono (patron saint's day).

Places to Stay

San Antonio has decent but very limited accommodations; prices for lodging may rise on weekends, when reservations are advisable. Reservations are absolutely essential during the Fiesta de la Tradición in November.

The spacious, shady riverside *Camping Club Náutico,* just off Zapiola, has clean toilets and hot showers, but it is overpriced at US$10 per tent, plus US$5 per vehicle (first night only). The cheapest regular accommodations, by no means bad, are at the conveniently located *Hotel San Carlos* (☎ 3106) at Zapiola and Castex. *Hotel Residencial* (☎ 2166), Segundo Sombra and Rivadavia, is very comparable and slightly more expensive.

Residencial El Hornero (☎ 2733), at Moreno and San Martín, charges US$25 per person, while *Hotel Fuaz* (☎ 2487), at

Av Doctor Smith 488 near de los Lima, costs US$52 double with breakfast. San Antonio's most attractive accommodation is *Hostal de Areco* (☎ 4063), Zapiola 25, which charges US$30 per person with breakfast Sunday through Thursday, US$35 per person Friday and Saturday. Another good value, for US$20 per person Monday through Thursday or US$30 per person Friday through Sunday, is *La Posada del Ceibo* (☎ 4614) on Simón Segura/Irigoyen between RN 8 and Av Doctor Smith. *Ramos Generales,* Bolívar 66, offers excellent overnight accommodario for US$25/40 single/double, and the adjoining restaurant is good.

Places to Eat

Except for about half a dozen ice cream parlors on Alsina, San Antonio is surprisingly short of places to eat. The only halfway worthwhile place downtown is *Pizzería Dell'Olmo* (☎ 2506), Alsina 365, the appeal of which is greatly diminished by hordes of gum-chewing teenyboppers trying to display their sophistication by puffing on coffin nails. *La Costa* (☎ 2481), a parrilla at Belgrano and Zerboni, has a decent tenedor libre for about US$10.

Far better is *Ramos Generales,* Bolívar 66, a very new restaurant convincingly decorated as a turn-of-the-century general store. It suffers a bit from self-conscious cuteness, like the backward "S" on every signboard, but it has good homemade pasta and the like (hold the salt, though) at reasonable prices. They also offer excellent overnight accommodations.

Things to Buy

San Antonio's artisans are known throughout the country, with many of their apprentices practicing their trades in other cities and provinces. Mate paraphernalia, *rastras* (silver-studded belts), and *facones* (long-bladed knives), produced by skilled silversmiths, are among the most typical. Internationally known Raúl Horacio Draghi (☎ 4207), Guido 391, also works in leather; other top silversmiths include Miguel & Martín Rigacci, Av Quetgles

ARGENTINA

333, and Alvaro Ignacio Caldera (☎ 2599), Alsina 17.

For horse gear and gaucho clothing, check out Sogas Areco, Moreno 280. Cristina Giordano de Bincaz (☎ 2829), Sarmiento 112, sells weavings. El Boliche de Ramírez, on Güiraldes opposite the Museo Gauchesco, handles a bit of everything.

For artisanal chocolates, try La Olla de Cobre, Speroni 433. In addition to its restaurant, Ramos Generales, Bolívar 66, also produces homemade sweets, cheeses, and salami. Dulces del Pago (☎ 4751), Zerboni 136 or Nogueira 125, makes a variety of fruit preserves.

Getting There & Away
Bus The Terminal de Omnibus is at Av Doctor Smith and Gonzalez Gastellu. The main carriers are Chevallier, Empresa Argentina, and Rápido Argentino. Frequent buses to Buenos Aires take 1½ hours.

Train The Estación Ferrocarril Mitre is at Avs Güiraldes and Quetgles. On Sundays, *El Tren del Oeste* goes to San Antonio from Lacroze station in Buenos Aires.

AROUND SAN ANTONIO DE ARECO
Surrounding San Antonio de Areco are a number of estancias offering overnight accommodations in the range of US$125 per person, plus IVA, with full board; activities such as horseback riding, polo, and the like usually cost extra. Director María Luisa Bemberg shot part of her historical drama *Camila* at **Estancia La Bamba** (see the San Antonio tourist office for details on accommodations and tours).

Certainly the most historic of nearby estancias is the Güiraldes family's **Estancia La Porteña** (☎ 322-6023, 322-5694 in Buenos Aires), which dates from 1850 and has a garden designed by the renowned French architect Charles Thays, who was responsible for major public parks such as Buenos Aires' Jardín Botánico and Mendoza's Parque San Martín. **Estancia El Ombú** (☎ 92080; ☎ 793-2454 in Buenos Aires) belonged to General Pablo Ric-

chieri, who first inflicted universal military conscription on the country.

Atlantic Coast Beaches

For porteños and others from Buenos Aires province, summer means the beach, while the beach means the Atlantic coast in general and Mar del Plata in particular. Every summer millions of Argentines take a holiday from their friends, families, and coworkers, only to run into them on the beaches. Those who can't make it in person participate vicariously in the beach scene every afternoon on nationwide television.

Beach access is unrestricted, but *balnearios* (bathing resorts) are privately run, so access to toilets and showers is limited to those who rent tents. Legally, balnearios must have lifeguards, medical services, toilets, and showers. Most also have *confiterías,* paddleball courts (a current fad in Argentina), and even shops.

Even by Argentine standards, prices are hard to pin down, since they rise every two weeks from December 15 to February 15, and then decline slowly until the end of March, when most hotels and residenciales close. Those that stay open year round lower their prices considerably, though Semana Santa (Holy Week) is an excuse to raise them briefly.

North of Mar del Plata to Cabo San Antonio, gentle dunes rise behind the generally narrow beaches of the province. Southwest from Mardel to Miramar, steep bluffs highlight the changing coastline, although access is still good for bathing. Beyond Miramar, toward Monte Hermoso, the broad sand beaches delight bathers, fishing enthusiasts, and windsurfers.

MAR DEL PLATA
When Juan de Garay, founder of Buenos Aires, sailed along the Atlantic coast in 1581, he described the shoreline around present-day Mar del Plata as "*muy galana*"

(very beautiful), but Europeans were slow to occupy the area. Nearly two centuries later, in 1747, Jesuit missionaries tried to evangelize Indians from the southern Pampas, but the only reminder of their efforts is the body of water known as Laguna de los Padres.

More than a century later, Portuguese investors established a small town, El Puerto de Laguna de los Padres, with a pier and a saladero. Beset by economic problems in the 1860s, they sold the land to Patricio Peralta Ramos, who founded Mar del Plata proper in 1874. Peralta Ramos helped develop the area as an important commercial and industrial center and, later, as a beach resort. By the turn of the century, most upper-class porteño families owned a villa or summer residence in the city, some of which still grace the exclusive Barrio Los Troncos.

Since the 1960s, Mardel, as it is popularly known, has become the main holiday destination for middle-class porteños, who outnumber locals three to one during the summer. Multitudinous skyscrapers have risen because local authorities have failed to enforce building codes, leaving many of the finest beaches in the shade for much of the day.

As the "Pearl of the Atlantic" has lost its exclusivity, its architectural character, and its calm, the Argentine elite have sought refuge in more exclusive resorts such as Pinamar or Punta del Este, Uruguay. Mardel remains the most successful of Argentine beach towns; its large population and well-developed infrastructure are able to support events like 1995's Panamerican Games.

Mar del Plata still has many appealing qualities, but unless you can relax amid thousands of gregarious vacationers, you may prefer to visit in spring or fall, when prices are lower and the area's natural beauty is easier to enjoy.

Orientation

Mar del Plata, 400 km south of Buenos Aires, sprawls along eight km of beaches, but because of ceaseless construction, new neighborhoods are constantly being added.

The downtown area, containing most points of interest for visitors, is bound by Av JB Justo, running roughly west from the port, Av Independencia, which runs roughly northeast-southwest, and the Atlantic Ocean.

On street signs, the road running along the water is called Av Peralta Ramos, but most people refer to it as Blvd Marítimo. San Martín and Rivadavia are both pedestrian streets on summer evenings.

Information

Tourist Offices The Ente Municipal de Turismo (Emtur, ☎ 21777, 20853) has its main office at Blvd Marítimo 2267, opposite the casino; there's usually someone who speaks English on duty. Since Mar del Plata gets very crowded in summer, the staff copes with tourists in an almost assembly-line fashion, but the computerized information system is very efficient, providing good maps and descriptive brochures. It also distributes the new *Guía Turística Mar del Plata,* a slickly professional but very commercial booklet that lists only a portion of the services available in the city. Parts of it are in a reasonably readable English.

In summer only, there's a tourist office at the bus station, and there's also a provincial tourist office (☎ 25340) in the Rambla del Hotel Provincial, Blvd Marítimo 2500, Local 60.

ACA (☎ 20031) is at Av Colón 1450.

Money There are several cambios along San Martín and Rivadavia, including Jonestur at San Martín 2574 and Av Luro 3191; La Moneda at Rivadavia 2623; and Mar del Plata at Santiago del Estero 1732 and Luro 3071. There are many ATMs, mostly on Av Independencia. Banco de la Provincia is at San Martín 2563, and Banco de la Nación is at San Martín 2594.

Post & Telecommunications Correo Argentino has several branches: The main one is at Av Luro 2460, while others are at Av Luro 7099, 12 de Octubre 3346, and Sarmiento 2710. The postal code is 7600.

ARGENTINA

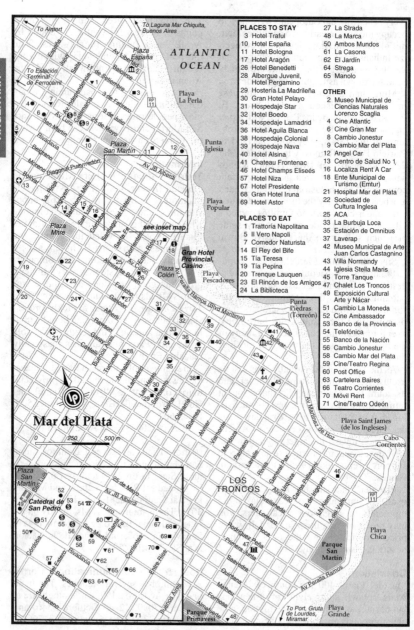

PLACES TO STAY
3 Hotel Traful
10 Hotel España
11 Hotel Bologna
17 Hotel Aragón
26 Hotel Benedetti
28 Albergue Juvenil,
   Hotel Pergamino
29 Hostería La Madrileña
30 Gran Hotel Pelayo
31 Hospedaje Star
32 Hotel Boedo
34 Hospedaje Lamadrid
36 Hotel Aguila Blanca
38 Hospedaje Colonial
39 Hospedaje Nava
40 Hotel Alsina
41 Chateau Frontenac
46 Hotel Champs Eliseés
57 Hotel Niza
67 Hotel Presidente
68 Gran Hotel Iruna
69 Hotel Astor

PLACES TO EAT
1 Trattoría Napolitana
5 Il Vero Napoli
7 Comedor Naturista
14 El Rey del Bife
15 Tía Teresa
19 Tía Pepina
20 Trenque Lauquen
23 El Rincón de los Amigos
24 La Biblioteca

27 La Strada
48 La Marca
50 Ambos Mundos
61 La Casona
62 El Jardín
64 Strega
65 Manolo

OTHER
2 Museo Municipal de
   Ciencias Naturales
   Lorenzo Scaglia
4 Cine Atlantic
6 Cine Gran Mar
8 Cambio Jonestur
9 Cambio Mar del Plata
12 Angel Car
13 Centro de Salud No 1,
16 Localiza Rent A Car
18 Ente Municipal de
   Turismo (Emtur)
21 Hospital Mar del Plata
22 Sociedad de
   Cultura Inglesa
25 ACA
33 La Burbuja Loca
35 Estación de Omnibus
37 Laverap
42 Museo Municipal de Arte
   Juan Carlos Castagnino
43 Villa Normandy
44 Iglesia Stella Maris
45 Torre Tanque
47 Chalet Los Troncos
49 Exposición Cultural
   Arte y Nácar
51 Cambio La Moneda
52 Cine Ambassador
53 Banco de la Provincia
54 Telefónica
55 Banco de la Nación
56 Cambio Jonestur
58 Cambio Mar del Plata
59 Cine/Teatro Regina
60 Post Office
63 Cartelera Baires
66 Teatro Corrientes
70 Móvil Rent
71 Cine/Teatro Odeón

Telefónica has its central office at Av Luro 2554, but there are locutorios at many places throughout town, including the train station, the bus terminal, and the airport. Mar del Plata's area code is 023.

Cultural Centers The Centro Cultural General Pueyrredón, at Catamarca and 25 de Mayo, offers a variety of activities ranging from film and theater to popular music, jazz, folklore, tango, and the like.

The Sociedad de Cultura Inglesa at San Luis 2498 has a library with newspapers, magazines, and books in English, as well as occasional films and lectures.

Travel Agencies There are several travel agencies at the bus terminal: Turismo Esplanada (☎ 51-2636), Local 27; Turismo La Plata (☎ 51-2153), Local 12; and Zenit Turismo (☎ 51-8733), Local 11.

Laundry There are many downtown laundries, including Laverap at Falucho 1572 and La Burbuja Loca at Las Heras 2471.

Medical Services Centro de Salud Municipal No 1 (☎ 20568) is at Av Colón 3294. Hospital Mar del Plata (☎ 22021) is at Castelli 2460. The Hospital Regional (☎ 77-0030) is at JB Justo 6700.

Walking Tour
A stroll past some of Mar del Plata's mansions offers vivid insights into the city's upper-class origins and its relatively recent past when it was still the exclusive playground of wealthy Argentines. Built in 1919, **Villa Normandy,** at Viamonte 2216, is one of few examples of the French style that survived the renovation craze of the 1950s; it is now the Italian consulate. On the hilltop, at Brown and Viamonte, is **Iglesia Stella Maris,** with its impressive marble altar. Its virgin is the patron saint of local fishermen. On the highest point of this hill, at Falucho and Mendoza, is the 88-meter **Torre Tanque**. The outstanding view from its *mirador* (overlook) justifies the climb, though it has recently been closed for reconstruction.

After descending Viamonte to Rodríguez Peña, walk toward the ocean to the corner of Urquiza. There stands the **Chalet Los Troncos,** from which this distinguished neighborhood took its name. The timber of the gate and fence are *quebracho* and *lapacho* hardwoods from the province of Salta. Lining Calles Urquiza, Quintana, Lavalle, Rodríguez Peña, Rivas, and Almafuerte are examples of more recent but equally elite design. To return to the center, try the longer route along Av Peralta Ramos, which offers beautiful views of the city from **Cabo Corrientes.**

Museo Municipal de Arte Juan Carlos Castagnino
Lovers of art and architecture should enjoy this museum (☎ 51-3232) at Av Colón 1189, in the Villa Ortiz Basualdo, once the summer residence of a prominent Argentine family. Built in 1902, its exterior resembles a Loire Valley castle, while the interior decor was imported from Belgium. The museum exhibits paintings, drawings, photographs, and sculptures by Argentine artists.

The museum is open every day but Wednesday from 10 am to 1 pm and 6 to 11 pm. Admission is US$2. Buses Nos 221, 581, 592, and 593 all go there.

Museo Archivo Histórico Municipal Villa Emilio Mitre
A superb collection of turn-of-the-century photographs, plus other exhibits, recalls Mardel's colorful past in this museum (☎ 21200) in Villa Mitre at Lamadrid 3870 between Matheu and Formosa, yet another former summer residence of the Argentine oligarchy. It also chronicles the demolitions that made room for the tacky high-rises that now blight the shoreline.

It's open every day except Monday from 4 to 8 pm; admission is US$1. Take bus No 523 to get there.

Museo Municipal de Ciencias Naturales Lorenzo Scaglia
Paleontological, archaeological, geological, and zoological exhibits are on display

in this museum (☎ 73-8791) at Libertad 2999, on Plaza España. The ground-floor aquarium features local fresh- and saltwater species. The museum's hours are normally 3 to 7 pm daily, but it was closed for repairs in 1995.

Banquina de Pescadores

Mar del Plata is one of the country's most important fishing ports and seafood processing centers. At the port's picturesque wharf, busy fishermen and stevedores on colorful wooden boats follow their daily routine, monitored by sea lions who have established a large – mostly male – colony on one side of the pier.

In the early morning, unfazed by the chilly sea breeze, the fishermen load their nets and crates before leaving to spend all day at sea. The lions follow suit. At about 5 pm, the pier gets noisy and hectic as the returning fishermen sort and box the fish, bargain for the best price, and tidy up their boats and tools. The sea lions return to seek or fight over a resting spot.

There are excellent opportunities for photography – separated by a fence, you can approach within a meter of the sea lions, then close the day in one of the port complex's great restaurants or, more cheaply, in one of the standing-room seafood cafeterias. Local buses Nos 221, 511, 522, 551, 561, 562, and 593 go to the wharf from the town center.

A related attraction is the tribute to Mar del Plata's fishing community in the **Museo del Hombre del Puerto Cleto Ciocchini** (☎ 80-1228), at Padre Dutto 383, about eight blocks north of the port. It's open daily from 6 to 10 pm; admission is US$2.

Gruta de Lourdes

Only 10 blocks from the port, at Magallanes 4100, lush vegetation covers this replica of the French grotto. It contains an image of Nuestra Señora de Lourdes, and a trail with the stations of the cross, which includes a kitschy model of Jerusalem with waterfalls, sound and light show, and mobile figures.

To reach the grotto from the port, walk along 12 de Octubre, the main commercial street in the area, to the 4100 block. Magallanes is the next block east. It's open daily 9 am to 7 pm, and admission is free. Bus No 522 goes there.

Exposición Cultural Arte y Nácar

Many travelers have remarked favorably on this museum at San Luis 1771 (☎ 91-5141), which hosues an impressive permanent collection of 52,000 shells representing 6000 species from around the world. The shells belong to collector Benjamín Sisterna. Hours are Monday to Saturday from 4 to 8 pm; admission is free.

Catedral de San Pedro

At San Martín and San Luis, this turn-of-the-century neo-Gothic building features gorgeous stained glass, an impressive central chandelier from France, English-tile floors, and a ceiling of tiles from other European countries.

Villa Victoria

The Argentine writer Victoria Ocampo, founder of the famous literary journal *Sur,* which was published between the World Wars, hosted literary salons of prominent intellectuals during the 1920s and 1930s at this museum and cultural center. At Matheu 1851 between Lamadrid and Arenales (☎ 92-0569), it's a prime example of prefabricated homes built in Norway and imported during Mar del Plata's "belle epoque." It's open daily from 10 am to 1 pm, and from 5 to 9:30 pm. Admission is US$2.

Mar del Plata Aquarium

This new facility (☎ 67-0700), at Av Martínez de Hoz 5600 in Punta Mogotes, is open daily from 10 am to midnight, but it's essentially an overpriced (US$15) trained-seals show. Buses Nos 221, 511, 581, and 717 go there.

Organized Tours

Emtur conducts free organized tours *(Paseos para Gente Inquieta)* of city sights such as the Banquina de Pescadores, the Centro Cultural Victoria Ocampo (in the Villa Victoria), and the like; register one day in advance at the Emtur office on Blvd Marítimo. Combi-Tur (☎ 30732) has more extensive, less specialized excursions leaving from Plaza Colón and Plaza San Martín.

For US$10, Anamora Yate Fiesta (☎ 89-0310) offers one hour harbor tours several times daily leaving from Dársena B at the port. Turimar (☎ 84-1450) has rather shorter weekend excursions, also departing from Dársena B.

Special Events
Mar del Plata's elaborate tourist infrastructure guarantees a wide variety of special events throughout the year, such as January's Fiesta Nacional del Mar (National Ocean Festival) and Fiesta Nacional de los Pescadores (National Fishermen's Festival). The city celebrates its founding on February 10, the date in 1874 when Buenos Aires provincial governor Mariano Acosta authorized the city's creation.

In the summer of 1995, Mar del Plata presented its first Festival Internacional de la Canción, with popular performers ranging from tacky salsa singer Ricky Maravilla to more respected figures like Charly García.

The Muestra de Cine Internacional (International Film Festival) takes place every odd-numbered year in March and November. In season there are many national golf, tennis, and polo tournaments and sailing regattas.

Places to Stay
It's worth reiterating that prices climb considerably from month to month during summer and fall in the off-season, when many hotels and residenciales close their doors. Prices indicated here are from early high season. The least expensive accommodations are near the bus terminal.

Places to Stay – bottom end
Camping South of town along RP 11 are several campgrounds, all very crowded in summer. Rates run around US$16 for up to four persons. Bus Rápido del Sud stops at each one.

Campamento Acuario, about 7½ km south of the lighthouse at Punta Mogotes, has complete facilities and offers ACA discounts. Farther along in tranquil La Serena is the shady, well-kept *Camping Suizo,* at Calles 11 and 20. Buses Nos 221 and 511 (Serena) go there from the town center.

At the northern entrance of town, in the beautiful multi-use Parque Camet is *Camping El Bosque de Camet,* at Williams and Villalobo. Bus Nos 221 and 541 go there.

Hostel A few blocks from the bus terminal, the *Albergue Juvenil* (☎ 27927) occupies a wing of Hotel Pergamino at Tucumán 2728. They have rooms with shared bath for about US$12 per person without breakfast, US$13 with breakfast.

Hospedajes & Hosterías At Sarmiento 2258 you'll find *Hospedaje Nava* (☎ 51-7611), a beautiful colonial-style house with a friendly owner. A room for four with a huge, clean, shared bath is about US$15 per person. Another excellent choice is *Hostería La Madrileña* (☎ 51-2072), Sarmiento 2955, which has clean, modest doubles with private bath at slightly higher prices.

Near the bus terminal at Lamadrid 2518, *Hospedaje Lamadrid* (☎ 25456) has decent singles/doubles for US$15/20 in the off-season, but it's pricier in summer. Also near the terminal are *Hospedaje Colonial* (☎ 51-1039) at Olavarría 2663 and *Hospedaje Star* (☎ 25044) at Falucho 1949. A recent reader's recommendation is *Hospedaje San Miguel,* on Tucumán. Centrally located *Hotel Niza,* run by three sisters at Santiago del Estero 1843, is an excellent value for US$18 per person with breakfast and private bath. *Gran Hotel Pelayo* (☎ 51-3579), Sarmiento 2899, is a good value at US$14 per person with breakfast.

Places to Stay – middle
At these one-star and two-star hotels, prices range from US$30 to US$40 per person. At

the lower end are *Hotel Alsina* (☎ 51-4465) at Alsina 2368, *Hotel Aragón* (☎ 23064) at Buenos Aires 1973, and *Hotel Boedo* (☎ 24695) at Brown 1771.

Costlier two-star hotels include *Hotel Bologna* (☎ 43369) at 9 de Julio 2542, *Hotel Champs Eliseés* (☎ 51-2692) at Rawson 233, *Hotel España* (☎ 20526) at Av Luro 2964, *Hotel Aguila Blanca* (☎ 86-2459) at Sarmiento 2455, and *Hotel Traful* (☎ 36650) at Yrigoyen 1190.

Places to Stay – top end

In the high season, rooms in this category start around US$75 and can range well upwards of US$100 per person. *Gran Hotel Iruna* (☎ 91-1060) is at Alberdi 2270. At the lower end of the price range, *Hotel Astor* (☎ 92-2916), Entre Ríos 1649, is also good. *Hotel Benedetti* (☎ 30031), is at Colón 2198, while *Hotel Presidente* (☎ 91-1183) is at Corrientes 1516.

Others include *Hotel Sasso* (☎ 84-0031), Av Martínez de Hoz 3545; *Chateau Frontenac* (☎ 20-1051), Alvear 2010, which has an excellent but expensive restaurant; and *Hotel Hermitage* (☎ 51-7235), Blvd Marítimo 2657, which is usually frequented by Argentine showbiz folks.

The most luxurious is the massive *Gran Hotel Provincial* (☎ 91-5949), Blvd Marítimo 2300, which was once a training school for hotel workers. It offers a famous casino, a restaurant, and a commercial gallery and comes recommended for its spacious rooms.

Places to Eat

Although Mar del Plata's numerous restaurants, pizzerías, and snack bars usually hire extra help between December and March, they have a hard time keeping up with impatient crowds of tourists. As a result, there are always long lines. The food is generally good, and at the restaurants in the Nuevo Complejo Comercial Puerto (the renovated old port) seafood is invariably excellent, though costly. Around the bus terminal you can find very cheap *minutas* or sandwiches.

For standard Argentine fare, try *Tía Pepina* (☎ 25309) at Yrigoyen 2699, *La Biblioteca* (☎ 46767) at Santa Fe 2633, or *Ambos Mundos* (☎ 20450) at Rivadavia 2644; the latter serves abundant minutas and good puchero de gallina (chicken stew) for moderate prices. *La Cantina de Armando,* at San Lorenzo and Catamarca, is also reasonable. *La Estancia de Don Pepito* (☎ 20471), at Blvd Marítimo 2235 across from the casino, is very reasonable and serves large portions of pasta, parrillada, and seafood; look for discount coupons on flyers at the tourist office and around town.

Of course there are many parrillas. Although a bit expensive, *Trenque Lauquen* (☎ 37149), Mitre 2807, is excellent. *La Marca* (☎ 51-8072), Almafuerte 253, is similar. *El Rey del Bife* (☎ 23957), Colón 2863, and *El Rincón de los Amigos* (☎ 25525), Córdoba 2588, are both more economical.

Italian cuisine is very popular among beachgoers. A small, moderate place with good dishes is *Tía Teresa* (☎ 29360), San Luis 2081. *Il Vero Napoli,* Belgrano 3408, has superb lasagna. *Trattoría Napolitana* (☎ 23850), 3 de Febrero 3158, has costly but excellent food, while *La Strada,* Entre Ríos 2642, is more moderate in price.

There are many pizzerías, which also sell good lager beer. *Joe,* at Lamadrid and Rawson, serves superb pizza and calzones. *Manolo,* Rivadavia 2371, has a variety of tasty pizzas. Also try *La Casona* at Santa Fe 1752 or *Strega* at Rivadavia 2320. The few vegetarian restaurants are all a good value – try *Comedor Naturista* at Salta 1571 or *El Jardín* (☎ 25539) at Rivadavia 2383, which offers all-you-can-eat meals for about US$8, including juices and dessert.

Alfajores (biscuit sandwiches filled with chocolate, dulce de leche, or fruit) are delicious for afternoon tea or *mate.* Havanna is a very popular brand, available at most grocery stores.

Entertainment

As in Buenos Aires, there are carteleras that offer half-price tickets to movies and live theater presentations. The Mar del

Plata branch of Cartelera Baires is at Santa Fe 1844, Local 33.

Cinema There are several first-run cinemas downtown, including the *Ambassador* (☎ 27271) at Córdoba 1673, the *América* (☎ 43240) and the *Atlas* (☎ 45001), both at Luro and Corrientes, the *Atlantic* (☎ 73-0206) at Av Luro 3426, the *Gran Mar* (☎ 73-8128) at Salta 1545, the *Odeón* (☎ 42753) at Entre Ríos 1828, the *Regina* (☎ 30699) at San Martín 2426, and the *Santa Fe* (☎ 91-9728) at Santa Fe 1854.

Theater When Buenos Aires shuts down in January, many shows come from the capital to Mar del Plata. Theaters mostly cater to vacationers by showing comedies that range from *café concert* (stand-up comedy) to vulgar but popular burlesque.

The *Teatro Auditorium* (☎ 36001), part of the casino complex at Blvd Marítimo 2280, offers musical theater with quality actors from the capital; other venues include the *Corrientes* (☎ 37918) at Corrientes 1766, the *Regina* (☎ 30699) at San Martín 2426, and the *Odeón* (☎ 42753) at Entre Ríos 1828.

Dance Clubs After leisurely days at the beach, Argentines like to stay up all night dancing and socializing. Mar del Plata has lots to offer partygoers along Av Constitución, appropriately nicknamed Av del Ruido (Avenue of Noise), where dance clubs and nightclubs line both sides of the street. Among the current favorites are *Sobremonte, Chocolate, Gol, La Base, Aquelarre,* and *Azúcar.* Bus No 551 runs throughout the night.

Casino Unlike its flashier counterparts in Las Vegas or Reno, the *casino* (☎ 24081) at Mar del Plata's Gran Hotel Provincial is an elegant, black-tie venue at night, but it's less formal during the daytime. It's busy all day, especially after midnight.

Things to Buy
Mar del Plata is famous for sweaters and jackets. Shops along Av JB Justo, nick-named "Avenida del Pullover," have competitive, near-wholesale prices. To go shopping there, take bus No 561 or 562.

A multitude of boutiques along San Martín and Rivadavia cater to the fashion-conscious.

Getting There & Away
Air Aeropuerto Félix U Camet is on RN 2, 10 km north of the city. Both Aerolíneas Argentinas (☎ 25014) and Austral (☎ 23085, 72-8293 at the airport), with offices at the Gran Hotel Provincial, Blvd Marítimo 2300, have several daily flights to Buenos Aires (US$80) and a Sunday direct flight to São Paulo and Rio de Janeiro.

LADE (☎ 38220), also in the casino at Local 5, has a Tuesday flight to the capital for US$46. LAPA (☎ 92-2112), San Martín 2648 Local 5, has five flights daily and charges US$49 to US$69, depending on the schedule.

Bus Mardel's busy Estación de Omnibus (☎ 51-5404) is very central at Alberti 1602. Costamar (☎ 51-2843), Costera Criolla (51-2963), Chevallier (☎ 51-8447), El Cóndor (51-2110), and El Rápido (☎ 51-0874) run several buses daily to Buenos Aires in the summer. El Rápido Argentino (☎ 51-0874) travels to La Plata twice daily. Expreso Córdoba-Mar del Plata (☎ 51-8733) serves Córdoba, while Empresa Pampa (☎ 51-8478) goes to Bahía Blanca, with connections to Patagonia. TAC (☎ 41142) and Tirsa (☎ 51-3507) travel to Mendoza and other northern destinations. Ciudad de Posadas (☎ 51-0014) serves the Mesopotamian provinces of Entre Ríos, Corrientes, and Misiones.

Typical fares are: Buenos Aires US$22 (seven hours), La Plata US$18 (five hours), Bahía Blanca US$27 (seven hours), and Bariloche US$83 (19 hours).

Train The Estación Terminal de Ferrocarril (☎ 72-9553) is at Av Luro 4599, about 20 blocks from the beach. Líneas Ferrocarriles (☎ 23059) at San Martín 2300 also has downtown offices open daily until 9 pm and at the bus terminal (☎ 51-2501).

During the summer the tourist train *El Marplatense* travels three times daily to Buenos Aires. Reservations should be made far in advance, since it's usually booked solid through the season. One-way fares are Turista US$14, Primera US$16, and Pullman US$21.

Getting Around

Mar del Plata is a sprawling city, but it has excellent public transportation. Buses are frequent and reach just about every place in town. For local destinations, the tourist office can help.

Car Rental Try Avis (☎ 37850), Blvd Marítimo 2451; Angel Car (☎ 22993) at 3 de Febrero 2358; Localiza (☎ 20181) at Córdoba 2071; or Móvil Rent (☎ 26489), Luro 2240.

AROUND MAR DEL PLATA
Mar Chiquita

Along RP 11, 34 km north of Mar del Plata, the peaceful resort of Mar Chiquita is a paradise for swimming, fishing, and windsurfing (there's a windsurf regatta in December). Fed by creeks from the Sierras de Tandil and sheltered by a chain of sand dunes, its namesake estuary, Laguna Mar Chiquita, alternately drains into the ocean or absorbs seawater, depending on the tides.

In the nearby community of Santa Clara del Mar, at Niza 1065, the **Museo Paleontológico Pachamama** features paleoecological, botanical, zoological, and archaeological exhibits. From Mar del Plata's casino, Bus Rápido del Sur goes eight times daily to Mar Chiquita, where there are several campgrounds and hotels.

VILLA GESELL

In the 1930s, merchant, inventor, and nature-lover Carlos Gesell created this resort of zigzag, unpaved streets lined with acacias, poplars, oaks, and pines to stabilize its shifting dunes. Much more sedate than Mar del Plata, the town has a very small, stable population, although it attracts many summer visitors. Middle- and working-class people perceive Villa Gesell as exclusive and stay away, but backpackers and campers can pursue both traditional beach-oriented activities and less conventional ones like horseback riding.

Orientation

Villa Gesell is 100 km northeast of Mar del Plata via RP 11, and about 450 km south of Buenos Aires via RP 11, the scenic but dangerous coastal highway. Avenida 3, the only paved road, parallels the beach and runs from Av Buenos Aires, at the edge of the Barrio Norte suburb, south to the bus terminal and most of the campgrounds.

With few exceptions, streets in Villa Gesell are numbered rather than named. Outside Barrio Norte, the town center consists of 10 Alamedas, running east-west, and 145 Paseos, running north-south. Barrio Norte lies between the beach in the east and Circunvalación in the west, and between Av Buenos Aires in the south and Calles 307 and 312 in the north.

Avenida 3, with its pedestrian mall, is Villa Gesell's shopping and entertainment center, with teahouses, specialized bakeries, and high-class restaurants, plus artisan shops, boutiques, and video arcades. Everything is within walking distance, and the concentration of hotels and restaurants would probably dismay its founder.

Information

Tourist Offices The Dirección de Turismo (☎ 68596), at Av Buenos Aires and Circunvalación near the golf course at the northern entrance to town, has friendly staff but very poor maps. There's another office in the Municipalidad (☎ 63055) at Av 3 No 820, plus several booths throughout the city with information on accommodations, places to eat, and bus schedules.

ACA (☎ 62272) is on Av 3, between Paseos 112 and 113.

Post & Telecommunications Correo Argentino is on Av 3 between Paseos 105 and 106. The postal code is 7165.

Villa Gesell's telephone code is 0255.

Medical Services The Hospital Municipal Arturo Illía (☎ 62618) is located at Calle 123 and Av 8.

Things to See & Do
The **Museo Histórico Municipal** (☎ 68624), at Alameda 202 and Calle 302, has guided tours daily between 9 am and 1 pm, and between 4 and 9 pm.

At the **Muelle de Pesca,** at Playa and Paseo 129, the 15-meter pier offers year-round fishing for mackerel, rays, shark, and other fish. You can rent bicycles at El Loco de los Bicis, Av 3 and Paseo 119.

Riding is a popular activity at places like the **Escuela de Equitación San Jorge,** at Circunvalación and Paseo 102, where you can rent horses independently or take guided excursions. Local golfers frequent the **Club de Golf** at the western entrance to town.

Organized Tours
El Trencito de Villa Gesell (☎ 68354), actually a bus, leaves from Plaza Carlos Gesell at 10 am, 5 and 7 pm for a two-hour excursion past the Casa de Don Carlos Gesell, the pine forest, the amphitheater, the pioneer houses, the pier, and the bus terminal. It costs US$5 per person, but children under five ride free.

Agencia Playa Médanos (☎ 63118), Av 3 and Paseo 111, runs trips to Faro Querandí, the local lighthouse. The trip takes up to 10 passengers in US Army 4WD jeeps on a 30-km trip over dunes, stopping along the way for photography, swimming, and exploring. The lighthouse itself, one of the highest and most inaccessible in the country, soars impressively above the surrounding dense forest. Four-hour trips, leaving daily at 9 am and 3:30 pm, cost US$22 per person.

Places to Stay
Accommodations in Villa Gesell are abundant, but there's really no such a thing as an inexpensive, basic hospedaje with shared bath – most places include private bathroom and even a telephone. Listings below

constitute only a fraction of the possibilities. For the most up-to-date price information, and to make reservations, contact Macroempresa Turismo (☎ 811-2376), Montevideo 708, 2° Piso, Oficina 5, Buenos Aires.

Places to Stay – bottom end
Camping Camping is the cheapest accommodation only if you are part of a group of four, since campgrounds have a minimum rate of about US$23 per group of four. Except for one exception, all close at the end of March.

On the north end of town, both *Camping Africa* (☎ 68507), Av Buenos Aires and Circunvalación, and *Camping Caravan* (☎ 68259), Paseo 101 and Circunvalación, have swimming pools. *Camping California* (☎ 68346) is on Av Buenos Aires and Circunvalación, while *Campamento del Sol* (☎ 68001), Blvd Silvio Gesell and Paseo 102, is open until April. Nearby *Camping El Faro* is on Blvd Silvio Gesell and Paseo 101. *Autocamping Europa* (☎ 68292) is at Alameda 214 and Calle 304, alongside Camping California. *La Arboleda Camping* (☎ 62634) is located at Paseo 107 between Avs 5 and 6.

The campgrounds on Av 3 at the south end of town include *Camping Casablanca* (☎ 60771) at Paseo 172, *Camping Mar Dorado,* and *Camping Monte Bubi* at Av 3 and Paseo 168.

The youth hostel/campground *El Coyote* (☎ 68448) is at Alameda 212 and Calle 304 bis.

Hospedajes & Hotels Figure on about US$30 to US$40 for doubles in places such as *Hospedaje Aguas Verdes* (☎ 62040), at Av 5 between Paseos 104 and 105, and *Hospedaje Sarimar,* Av 3 between Paseos 117 and 118. The enormous *Hospedaje Inti Huasi* (☎ 68365), Alameda 202 and Av Buenos Aires, has rooms with private bath and includes breakfast.

Hospedajes that open all year include *Hospedaje Villa Gesell* (☎ 62393) at Av 3 and Paseo 108 and *Hospedaje Bellavista* (☎ 62293) at Paseo 114 between Avs 1 and

3. The small *Hospedaje Viya* (☎ 62757), Av 5 between Paseos 105 and 106, includes breakfast. *Hospedaje Antonio* (☎ 62246), Av 4 between Paseos 104 and 106, has some rooms with shared bath and some with private bath.

Among the slightly more expensive one-star hotels are *Hotel Torremolinos* (☎ 62389) at Paseo 111 and Playa, and *Hotel Maracas* (☎ 68779) at Av 1 and Paseo 103. Both *Hotel Cantábrico* (☎ 62835), Av 2 and Paseo 102, and *Hotel Demi* (☎ 62658), Av 3 and Paseo 111, remain open all year. Prices run around US$40 to US$60 double.

Places to Stay – middle
There are several two-star hotels, with prices from about US$50 to US$70, but only three are open all year. *Hotel Romadrid* (☎ 68368) is at Paseo Costanero between Av Buenos Aires and Alameda 201, *Hotel El Loco Chávez* (☎ 62452) is at Av 3 and Paseo 125, and *Hotel Colón* (☎ 62310) is at Av 4 and Paseo 104.

Places to Stay – top end
The most expensive hotels in town start at about US$80 double and rise to around US$170. Try *Hotel Coliseo* (☎ 63420), Av 1 and Paseo 107, or *Hotel Terrazas Club* (☎ 63214), Av 2 between Paseos 104 and 105, both of which have swimming pools. *Hotel Gran Internacional* (☎ 68672) is on Paseo 103 between Av 1 and Paseo Costanero.

Places to Eat
There is a wide variety of restaurants in Villa Gesell, mostly along Av 3, catering to all tastes and budgets. *La Jirafa Azul* (☎ 62431), on Av 3 between Av Buenos Aires and Paseo 102, has long had a reputation for being cheap and good. It serves a standard menu. Owner-operated *Cantina Arturito* (☎ 63037), Av 3 No 186 between Paseos 126 and 127, serves large portions of exquisite homemade pasta, as well as shellfish and home-cured ham, at medium to expensive prices. Also costly but serving exotic game and international cuisine amid very pleasant decor is *Restaurant El Establo* at Av 3 and Av Buenos Aires.

For tasty seafood go to *Marisquería El Gallego,* Av 3 between Paseos 108 and 109, which has good but not cheap paella. *Los Sobrinos,* on Av 4 between Paseos 104 and 105, also specializes in seafood.

For good sandwiches and hamburgers and super-friendly attention from the owners, try *Sangucheto,* Paseo 104 between Avs 3 and 4. Also good and family-attended, with some health food and drinks, is *La Martona,* Paseo 107 between Avs 2 and 3. For moderately priced takeout try the rotisería *El Faro* at Av 3 and Paseo 119.

Entertainment
Music The European country-style Playa Hotel, Alameda 205 and Calle 304 in Barrio Norte, established Villa Gesell as a vacation resort; every summer, the *Sociedad Camping Musical* organizes chamber music concerts in its auditorium. Other musical events, such as the Encuentros Corales (a gathering of choirs from around the country) take place at the town's *Anfiteatro del Pinar* (amphitheater), Av 10 and Paseo 102.

Theater The *Casa de la Cultura,* Av 3 and Paseo 109, offers live theatrical productions in summer.

Cinemas Villa Gesell has three cinemas: the *Cine Atlantic* on Paseo 105 between Avs 2 and 3; the *Cine Teatro Atlas* on Paseo 108 between Avs 3 and 4; and the two-screen *Cine San Martín* on Paseo 105 between Avs 2 and 3.

Dance Clubs Dance clubs include *Chocolate* at Av 1 and Paseo 103 bis, *Dixit* on Paseo 106 between Avs 3 and 4, *Le Brique* on Av 3 between Av Buenos Aires and Av 1, and *Tango* on Av 2 between Paseos 102 and 104.

Things to Buy
The Feria Artesanal, Regional y Artística takes place daily on Av 3, between Paseos 112 and 113, from mid-December through

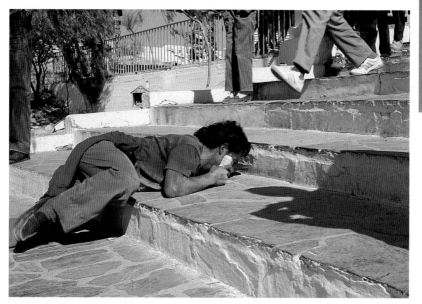

Top: Pilgrims bringing presents to Difunta Correa, San Juan Province
Left: Parque Provincial Talampaya, La Rioja Province
Right: Pucará fortifications, Tilcara, Jujuy Province

Cerro Torre, Parque Nacional Los Glaciares, Santa Cruz Province

mid-March and during Semana Santa and winter holidays.

Getting There & Away

Air Aerolíneas Argentinas (☎ 68228), at Av Buenos Aires and Av 10 in town, has flights to/from Villa Gesell daily in summer. Líneas Aéreas Entre Ríos (LAER, ☎ 68169), Av Buenos Aires between Paseos 205 and 206, flies to and from Buenos Aires three times weekly, while Transporte Aérea Costa Atlántica (TACA, ☎ 68585), Av Buenos Aires and Alameda 211, flies daily to the capital in summer.

Aerolíneas charges around US$80, while LAER and TACA are cheaper at US$60.

Bus The Terminal de Omnibus (☎ 66058) is at Av 3 and Paseo 140, on the south side of town. Some long-distance buses stop at the Mini Terminal (☎ 62340) at Av 4, between Paseos 104 and 105.

Empresa Río de la Plata (☎ 62224), a block from the Mini Terminal, has several direct buses daily to Buenos Aires (seven hours) in summer, as does Antón (☎ 63215), Paseo 108 between Avs 3 and 4. Fares are around US$20.

PINAMAR

Architect Jorge Bunge, of a well-known elite Argentine family, founded and designed the sophisticated resort of Pinamar in 1944 as a tranquil, elegant refuge for upper-class porteños. Its beautiful beaches, extensive forests, sandy streets, luxury homes and hotels, chic shops, and posh restaurants have made Pinamar the "in" place for Argentines who needn't work for a living.

Bathed by a tropical current from Brazil, its waters are pleasantly warm and its clean beaches slope gradually into a sea abundant with fish. Other adjacent resorts, such as Ostende and Valería del Mar, differ little but offer more moderate prices. Cariló, also nearby, has a very exclusive, country-club atmosphere but merits a visit for those wishing to glean insights into upper-class Argentine life. Do not let the security gates

deter you from entering, although you will probably be asked to leave your name.

Orientation

Pinamar, 120 km north of Mar del Plata via RP 11 and 320 km southeast of Buenos Aires via RN 2, was planned around an axis formed by Av Libertador, running parallel to the beach, and Av Bunge, running perpendicular to the beach. In the areas on either side of Bunge, the streets in the original city plan form two large fans, which make orientation a bit tricky at first, but the newer parts of town follow a conventional grid pattern.

Pinamar's commercial area is very compact, since residents are zealous about zoning codes. Most shops, restaurants, and hotels are on or within a few blocks of Av Bunge, the main thoroughfare.

Information

Tourist Offices The busy Secretaría de Turismo (☎ 82796), Av Bunge 456 at Libertador, has a good pocket map with useful descriptions of Pinamar, Valería, Ostende, and Cariló. ACA (☎ 82744) is at Del Cangrejo 1575.

Post & Telecommunications Correo Argentino is at Jasón 524. The telephone office is at Jasón and Shaw; Pinamar's area code is 0254.

Medical Services The Hospital Municipal (☎ 82390) is at Calle Shaw 250.

Things to See & Do

Pinamar is another outdoors center where, besides sunbathing and swimming, people enjoy a variety of water sports, including surfing, windsurfing, water-skiing, kayaking, and, of course, fishing. Also popular are golf (on the city's attractive course), horseback riding, tennis, paddleball, and hiking in the woods. Unfortunately, roaring dune buggies, both on the beach and even along nature trails, are also popular.

Places to Stay

Pinamar has no really cheap accommoda-

ARGENTINA

tions, though there's a youth hostel in nearby Ostende. There are only a few hospedajes, but plenty of hotels, motels, and hosterías that are invariably full during the season, so reservations are a must.

Other long-stay options include house rentals (information is available at the tourist office or at Casa de Pinamar in Buenos Aires) and apart-hotels. The following section emphasizes categories more than prices, which are comparable to those in Villa Gesell.

Places to Stay – bottom end

Camping Three campgrounds, charging around US$15 per site, serve the area between Ostende and Pinamar. *Autocamping Moby Dick* (☎ 86045), on Av Víctor Hugo and Tuyú in Ostende, has a dense tree canopy. *Camping Saint Tropez,* at Quintana and Nuestras Malvinas in Mar de Ostende, has a good beachfront location, but is small. *Camping Ostende* is on Cairo and Av La Plata in Ostende.

Hostel The youth hostel (☎ 82908), at Nuestras Malvinas and Sarmiento in Ostende, is a friendly place, offering dormitories and kitchen facilities in an interesting beachfront building. Rates are $12 per person.

Hospedajes & Hosterías Starting at around US$30 double, hospedajes in Pinamar include *Hospedaje Las Acacias* at Del Cangrejo 1358, *Hospedaje Rose Marie* (☎ 82522) at Las Medusas 1381, and *Hospedaje Valle Fértil* (☎ 84799) at Del Cangrejo 1110.

Among the one-star hotels, ranging in price from US$45 to US$65 double depending on whether it's low or high season, are *Hotel Berlín* (☎ 82320) at Rivadavia 326, *Hotel Sardegna* (☎ 82760) at Jasón 840, *Hotel Riviera* (☎ 82334) at Del Tuyú 51, and *Hotel Yacanto* (☎ 82367) at Rivadavia 509.

Places to Stay – middle

Mid-range accommodations start around US$60 in low season and rise to about US$80 in the summer peak. *Posada del Rey* (☎ 82267), at Del Tuyú 98, offers an optional continental breakfast in its pleasant surrounding garden; it's also taken over the former Hotel Zita, now *Posada del Centro* (☎ 82241), at Av Constitución 556. *Hotel San Marcos* (☎ 82424) is at Del Mejillón 1089.

Places to Stay – top end

Rates at *Hotel La Golondrina* (☎ 82240), Av Constitución 590 at Robinson Crusoe, start around US$80 double, rising to US$120 in the peak season. Similarly priced *Hotel El Bufón del Rey* (☎ 82323), Delfines 81 at Odiseo, has an intriguing French sculpture of a jester with twins in his arms, who supposedly helps those who desire children. The owners welcome visits from nonguests.

The most expensive in this group are the four-star, ultramodern *Hotel del Bosque* (☎ 82480), at Av Bunge 1550, and *Hotel Algeciras* (☎ 85550), Av Libertador 75 between Del Tuyú and Jonas. Doubles run some US$90 to US$115 in low season, US$150 to US$175 in high season.

Places to Eat

From the local rotiserías to the most exclusive restaurants, food in Pinamar is superb but costly. *Con Estilo Campo,* Av Bunge and Marco Polo, serves great pork and chivito a la parrilla (grilled kid goat). For good paellas, cazuelas (a substantial soup made with a large piece of chicken or beef, corn of the cob, and rice) and empanadas tucumanas (traditionally on the spicy side), try *El Negro B* at Rivadavia 350.

International cuisine is the highlight at *Matarazzo Party,* Av Bunge and Júpiter, serving unusual Italian food including varieties of cheeses and cantimpalo (a special salami), dips with smoked venison and toasted almonds for hors d'oeuvres, great salads, and the famous spaghetti Matarazzo, with nine different sauces. Since it is tenedor libre, you can take your choice. The dessert list includes vanilla ice cream with hot strawberry sauce. Since it is always crowded, you may need reservations. *Mamma Liberata,* Av Bunge and Simbad el Marino, and *Club Italiano,* Eneas and Cazón, also offer tasty pasta.

El Vivero, Avs Bunge and Libertador, is an enormous but high-quality vegetarian restaurant. Despite its name, *Paxapoga* (☎ 84985), Avs Bunge and Libertador, is a parrilla and pasta place open all year.

Pizzería La Reja, Jasón and Robinson Crusoe, offers 25 varieties of pizza and great empanadas including traditional ones with hand-chopped beef, either to eat there or to go.

German cooking, mostly breads and cakes, can be found at *Tante* (☎ 82735), De las Artes 35, and *Zur Tanne,* Rivadavia and De las Artes.

Getting There & Away
Air Aerolíneas Argentinas (☎ 83299), Av Bunge 799, flies to Villa Gesell and Pinamar in summer, as does LAPA (☎ 84300), Shaw 600.

Bus The Terminal de Omnibus is on Av Shaw between El Pejerrey and Lenguado. Empresas Antón (☎ 82378) and Río de la Plata (☎ 82247) service Buenos Aires, as do Expreso Paraná (☎ 85068) and Central Argentino (☎ 83397). Córdoba Mar del Plata (☎ 82885) goes to the interior, while Costamar (☎ 82885) connects the beaches.

SAN CLEMENTE DEL TUYÚ
Partido de la Costa, a county 320 km southeast of Buenos Aires, is the closest resort area to the capital. It consists of 11 localities, the northernmost of which, San Clemente del Tuyú, is a few kilometers from Punta Rasa, the southern tip of Bahía Samborombón.

These beaches are less attractive than those further south and much less exclusive. While they also receive large numbers of tourists in summer, visitors are mostly working-class people who arrive by public transportation and enjoy traditional beach activities such as sunbathing and fishing. Housing is modest and the towns, with a few exceptions, are undistinguished, but all

have very enthusiastic people working to promote tourism.

San Clemente stands out from the rest of the Partido de la Costa – not only is its large wooded park, El Vivero Cosme Argerich, very attractive, but its location near Cabo San Antonio puts it on the flyway for migratory birds from as far away as Alaska and Canada. Mundo Marino, a theme park with a serious commitment to marine conservation, attracts youngsters and adults alike.

Orientation
San Clemente's streets are mostly numbered, with east-west avenidas perpendicular to the beach and north-south calles parallel to it, but a series of fan-shaped barrios near the beach makes parts of the city plan confusing north of the ACA campground (roughly in the center of town). Some avenidas have Roman rather than Arabic numerals.

Information
Tourist Office The Oficina de Turismo (☎ 21478), at Calle 2 No 2090, is friendly but has few maps or brochures.

Post & Telecommunications Correo Argentino is at Calle 4 No 2037; San Clemente's postal code is 7105. Telefónica is at Calle 4 No 2152; the telephone code is 0252.

Medical Services The Hospital Municipal (☎ 21132) is at Av San Martín 500.

Mundo Marino
Argentina's third most popular tourist destination in terms of numbers of annual visitors, Mundo Marino reflects the commitment of the Méndez family to marine wildlife conservation. The facility rescues, treats, and, in some circumstances, keeps orcas (killer whales), sea lions, dolphins, sea otters, and seabirds. Their research-, education-, and conservation-oriented park is well designed and immaculately maintained, with spacious enclosures. The US$6 entry fee is reasonable for what you get.

ARGENTINA

Mundo Marino (☎ 21071) is on the north end of town, at Av Décima No 157. All shows take place in the open, so bring sunscreen. Local bus No 500 goes there from every town of Partido de la Costa.

Estación Biológica de la Fundación Vida Silvestre
At the south end of Bahía de Samborombón, this research station in Punta Rasa is both a good fishing area (for corvina negra) and an interesting place for bird watchers. Ask for information at the tourist office.

Places to Stay
San Clemente's high season, like the rest of the Atlantic coast, is January and February, while lower-priced accommodations are available in the medium season (October to December and the month of March); the price differential is around 20%. During the rest of the year, many places close.

Places to Stay – bottom end
Camping Several campgrounds at the entrance of San Clemente all charge about US$3 per person and US$3 per tent per day. These include *Camping Kumelcan 1* (☎ 22059), Calle 48 and Av 7; *Camping Kumelcan 2* (☎ 21752), Calle 50 and 33 bis; and *Autocamping El Tala* (☎ 21593), Calle 9 bis and 72. All are some distance from the beach.

Right downtown is the shady *Camping del ACA* (☎ 21124), Av II No 96, which is mostly for members but you can "join" on the spot. Rates are about US$15 for up to four people, tent, and car, including electricity. The bathroom and washing facilities are excellent.

Hospedajes & Hotels San Clemente has a number of reasonably priced, comfortable hotels with high-season prices around US$15 to US$22 per person. *Hotel Riviera* (☎ 21679), Calle 21 No 312, and *Hospedaje Quinta Av* (☎ 21035), Calle 5 No 1561, are both a good value in this category, while *Hospedaje Pereyra,* Calle 13 No 90, is slightly more expensive but includes breakfast. *Hotel Acuario* (☎ 21357), Av San Martín 444, is comparable.

Places to Stay – middle
Mid-range hotels run about US$22 to US$28 per person with breakfast at places such as two-star *Hotel Correa* (☎ 21212), Talas del Tuyú 2883. *Hotel Savoia* (☎ 21107), Av San Martín 267, charges US$25 with "normal" breakfast and US$30 with "abundant" breakfast.

At *Hotel Casino* (☎ 21315), Calle 16 No 71, rates are US$30 per person with breakfast but US$40 with half-pension. There is a 10% discount for cash.

Places to Stay – top end
Hotel Morales (☎ 21207), Calle 1 No 1856, charges US$70 double, but for twice that you can have all meals included. Four-star *Hotel Fontainbleu* (☎ 21187), Costanera and Calle 3 Sur, is the most expensive and luxurious hotel in the city at US$55 per person with breakfast, but nearby *Hotel Altair* (☎ 21429), Calle 3 No 2283, is equally comfortable and more reasonably priced.

Places to Eat
Restaurant Oraya, Calle 1 between Avs 13 and 14, has reasonable prices and a good pollo al ajillo (chicken with garlic). *Restaurant-Parrilla La Quebrada,* Calle 1 between Avs 13 and 22, is family-oriented, basic, and cheap. *Pizzería Gugupa,* Calle 1 No 2426, has tasty pizza. *El Rey del Calzón* specializes in Neapolitan calzone.

Getting There & Away
San Clemente's Parador de Omnibus (☎ 21340) is at Calle 10 and Av San Martín. Empresa Río de la Plata (☎ 31340), Calle 3 between Avs 1 and 15, has daily buses to Buenos Aires for about US$24. Empresa Costamar, at Av San Martín and Calle 3, goes to Buenos Aires, Pinamar, Villa Gesell, and Mar del Plata. El Rápido, Calle 21 No 132, also has a service from Buenos Aires to Mar del Plata that stops at every resort. Río Paraná, Chevallier, Plus-

mar, and Rutatlántica are some other bus companies.

Alvarez Hermanos, Calle 15 and Av 20, connects Gran Buenos Aires with the beaches to Villa Gesell, as does CAT, San Martín 157, which goes all the way to Miramar.

MIRAMAR

Dating from the turn of the century, this small, pleasant family resort, nicknamed La Ciudad de los Niños (City of Children), did not attract mass tourism until the 1950s. Lacking nightlife and entertainment despite the presence of a casino, Miramar's safety and friendliness attract families with young children. Bicycling is safe and pleasant, so that children and adults alike use bicycles both in town and in the Vivero Municipal Florentino Ameghino, a densely forested park covering 500 hectares. Vacationers spend most days relaxing on the clean, gently sloping beaches.

Orientation

From Cabo Corrientes in Mar del Plata, car-clogged RN 11 follows spectacular cliffs southwest past the summer presidential residence at Chapadmalal and holiday complexes belonging to different trade unions (a legacy of Peronism) before finally arriving at Miramar, 45 km southwest of Mar del Plata, 450 km from Buenos Aires, and 102 km northeast of Necochea.

Miramar's city plan mimics that of La Plata, with numbered streets and diagonals starting at the central plaza and ending at peripheral plazas, allowing for easy access to places and smoothly flowing traffic. Even-numbered streets run parallel to the sea in a roughly east-west direction, while odd-numbered streets run north-south.

Common practice has imposed the use of names for some arterial roads: Av B Mitre (Av 23), Calle 9 de Julio (Calle 21), Calle Legarra (Calle 19), Av H Yrigoyen (Av 9), Diagonal Fortunato de la Plaza to the north, Diagonal Illia to the east, Diagonal R Mitre to the south, and Diagonal J Dupuy to the west.

Information

Tourist Offices

Egatur, the Ente General Alvarado de Turismo (☎ 20190), Calle 28 at Calle 21, sells a very thorough city guide for about US$2. It also has free brochures and a useful map. ACA (☎ 61-0682) is at Diagonal Fortunato de la Plaza 1733.

Money

Cambio Ibertur is on Calle 21, between Calles 18 and 20. Banco de la Nación is at Av Mitre 1501; Banco Provincia is at Calle 21 No 1209.

Post & Telecommunications

Correo Argentino is on Calle 17 at Calle 32; the postal code is 7067. Telefónica is at Diagonal F de la Plaza 1451. Miramar's area code is 0291.

Travel Agencies

There are two travel agencies in Miramar: Anuschka Tours (☎ 21119) at Calle 21 No 787, and Droppy Tours (☎ 20735) at Calle 24 No 1130.

Medical Services

The Hospital Municipal (☎ 20837) is at Diagonal Dupuy 1550.

Places to Stay – bottom end

There is a variety of accommodations in Miramar, where rates are generally lower than at other resorts.

Camping

Camping El Durazno is on RP 11 toward Mar del Plata, two km from the center of town. It has clean plots, with electricity and sanitary facilities, for about US$4 per person per day. There are other campgrounds in nearby Mar del Sud – *Camping Mar del Sud* charges about US$3.50 per person.

Hospedajes & Hotels

Several modest hospedajes start at about US$12 per person. These include *Hospedaje Familia* (☎ 20788) at Calle 23 No 1701; nearby *Hospedaje Dorimar* (☎ 21109) at Calle 24 No 1839; and *Hospedaje España* at Calle 14 No 1046. *Hospedaje Laurana* (☎ 22462), Calle 11 No 1728, is clean and pleasant.

One-star hotels offer rooms with private bath for about US$15 to US$20 per person. Try *Hotel Santa Eulalia II* (☎ 20091), Calle 15 at Calle 20; *Hotel Miramar* (☎ 21617), Calle 21 No 974; *Hotel Ideal* (☎ 20259), Calle 21 No 632; *Hotel Cervantes* (☎ 20387), Calle 24 No 1110; and *Hotel Castilla* (☎ 20938), Calle 21 No 1032.

Places to Stay – middle
Two-star hotels in this category run to about US$25 to $30 per person. Possibilities are *Hotel Montecarlo* (☎ 20469) at Calle 16 No 1050, *Hotel Carolina* (☎ 20925) at Calle 11 No 1114, *Hotel Domani* (☎ 20978) at Av 9 No 1034, and *Hotel Continental* (☎ 20895) at Calle 19 No 1168.

Places to Stay – top end
There are several three-star hotels, including *Hotel América* (☎ 20847) at Diagonal Mitre 1114, and the *Grand Hotel* (☎ 20358) at Calle 29 No 586. Both charge around US$35 to US$40 per person. *Hotel Palace* (☎ 20258), at Calle 23 No 774, includes meals.

Places to Eat
Food in Miramar is considerably less expensive than in Mar del Plata or most other beach resorts. *Círculo Italiano,* Av 9 between Calles 28 and 30, serves abundant Italian dishes, as does *Río Nápole,* on Calle 21 at Calle 30. *Restaurant El Aguila,* Calle 19 No 1461, has a standard Argentine menu. *El Estribo,* Calle 30 between Calle 19 and 21, has good parrillada. For seafood, especially shellfish, try *El Muelle,* Costanera at 37, and *Mesón Español,* Av 26 No 1351.

Restaurante Punto y Banca, Fortunato de la Plaza 1426, offers good seafood and pasta. *Parrilla Rancho Grande,* Calle 23 No 1022, has a better-than-average tenedor libre. *La Posta de Facundo,* Av 9 No 1053, is good, but it closes in winter. Good rotiserías with food to go include *Katty,* Calle 21 No 780; *Popeye,* Av 26 between Avs 19 and 21; and *Valería,* Calle 25 No 620.

Entertainment
Miramar has several cinemas: *Cine Astral,* Calle 21 between Calles 30 and 32; the *Gran Rex* (☎ 20370) on Calle 21 between Calles 18 and 20, and *Cine Atlántico* (☎ 20167) on Calle 21 between Calles 30 and 32.

Several confiterías on the Costanera offer dancing at night, including *Aramaçao* and *Seeb,* both at the intersection of Calle 37.

Getting There & Away
Air Miramar has flights to Buenos Aires during summer only, from the Aeródromo five km north of town on RP 77. Aerolíneas Argentinas (☎ 21553) is at 9 de Julio 710. Austral (☎ 20735) is at Calle 24 No 1130.

Bus For a small town, Miramar has excellent bus connections despite the lack of a central terminal. Several companies have offices (☎ 23359) at Av Mitre 1701, and others are located at Calle 32, at the corner of Calle 19. Companies at Mitre include El Rápido del Sur, which has buses to Mar del Plata. CAT travels to different areas of Gran Buenos Aires, and Micromar goes to the Capital Federal also.

Costera Criolla (☎ 20747), Calle 32 at Calle 19, travels to Necochea, while El Pampa, at the same office, goes to Bahía Blanca. Fares to Buenos Aires (eight hours) cost about US$30.

Train The Ferrocarril Roca (☎ 20657), on Av 40 between Calles 15 and 17, has daily service to Buenos Aires and Bahía Blanca.

NECOCHEA
Famous for its wide, sandy beaches, dunes, and casino, Necochea is a popular, tranquil, family-oriented resort on the Río Quequén Grande, 500 km south of Buenos Aires and 125 km southwest of Mar del Plata via RP 88. The town counts many Danes among its permanent population.

Orientation
The south-flowing Quequén Grande divides the city in half. East of the river, all streets are numbered 500 and above, while

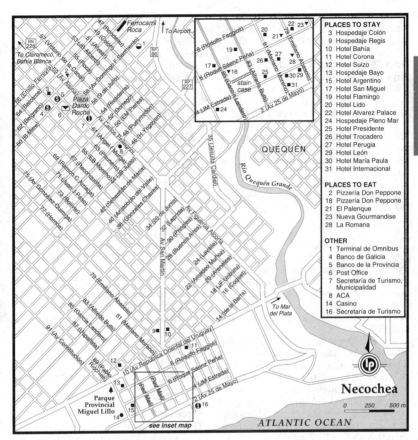

PLACES TO STAY
3 Hospedaje Colón
9 Hospedaje Regis
10 Hotel Bahía
11 Hotel Corona
12 Hotel Suizo
13 Hospedaje Bayo
15 Hotel Argentino
17 Hotel San Miguel
19 Hotel Flamingo
20 Hotel Lido
22 Hotel Alvarez Palace
24 Hospedaje Pleno Mar
25 Hotel Presidente
26 Hotel Trocadero
27 Hotel Perugia
29 Hotel León
30 Hotel María Paula
31 Hotel Internacional

PLACES TO EAT
2 Pizzería Don Peppone
18 Pizzería Don Peppone
21 El Palenque
23 Nueva Gourmandise
28 La Romana

OTHER
1 Terminal de Omnibus
4 Banco de Galicia
5 Banco de la Provincia
6 Post Office
7 Secretaría de Turismo, Municipalidad
8 ACA
14 Casino
16 Secretaría de Turismo

QUEQUÉN

Necochea

ATLANTIC OCEAN

0   250   500 m

west of the river street numbers run from 2 to the low 100s in the center. Even-numbered streets run parallel to the sea, while odd numbers run perpendicular. Bridges at Calle 46 (Yrigoyen) and Calle 10 (Av República Oriental del Uruguay) connect the two areas.

The focus of tourist activity is the regular grid between Av 10 (República Oriental del Uruguay) and the beach, a pedestrian-friendly area surrounded by Parque Provincial Miguel Lillo; Calle 83 (Alfredo Butti) is its main commercial street.

Avenida 59 (Alsina), also RN 228, changes names several times. North of Av 58 (Sarmiento) and Plaza Dardo Rocha, it is Alsina; south of Av 58 it is Av Carlos Pellegrini as far as the Diagonal San Martín, where it becomes Av Figueroa Alcorta.

Information
Tourist Offices The Secretaría de Turismo (☎ 22175, ext 238/240/241) is in the Municipalidad at Calle 56 No 2969, but the most convenient office (☎ 22182) is at Av 2 (25 de Mayo) and Calle 79 (Abasolo). ACA (☎ 22106) is located at Av 59 No 2073.

Money There are ATMs at Banco de Galicia, Calle 60 (Mitre) 3164, and Banco de la Provincia, Calle 60 (Mitre) 3000.

Post & Telecommunications Correo Argentino is at Av 58 (Sarmiento) and Calle 63 (Paunero). There are locutorios on Av 59 (Pellegrini) and Av 75 (González Quiroga); Necochea's area code is 0262.

Medical Services The Hospital Municipal (☎ 22405) is on Av 59 (Alsina) at the northern approach to town, between Calles 100 and 104.

Dangers & Annoyances Sunbathers on the beach have been run over by four-wheel motorcycles.

Things to See & Do
One of the city's more attractive features is **Parque Provincial Miguel Lillo,** a large green space along the beach; its dense pine woods are widely used for bicycling, horseback riding, and picnicking. Publicity brochures assert that its **casino** is "irresistible."

The Río Quequén Grande, rich in rainbow trout and mackerel, also allows for adventurous canoeing, particularly around the falls at Saltos del Quequén. At the village of **Quequén,** at the river's mouth, several stranded shipwrecks offer good opportunities for exploration and photography below sculpted cliffs. The **Faro** (lighthouse) is another local attraction.

Places to Stay – bottom end
Camping The *Camping Municipal* is in Parque Lillo, but there are also several private campgrounds along the beach.

Hospedajes & Hotels Most accommodations in Necochea are downtown, relatively close to the beach. The most reasonable are hospedajes such as *Hospedaje Regis* (☎ 25870) at Av San Martín 726 for US$15/20 single/double. Other comparable places are *Hospedaje Bayo* (☎ 23334) at Calle 87 No 338; *Hospedaje Colón* (☎ 24825) at Calle 62 No 3034; and *Hospedaje Pleno Mar* (☎ 22674) at Calle 87 No 230.

One-star hotels start around US$15 per person – try the simple but clean and quiet *Hotel Alvarez Palace* (☎ 23667), Av 79 No 304. Other possibilities include *Hotel Lido* (☎ 23918) at Calle 81 No 328; *Hotel Flamingo* (☎ 20049) at Calle 83 No 333; and *Hotel María Paula* (☎ 23903) at Calle 4 No 3927. *Hotel Suizo* (☎ 24008) is at Calle 22 No 4235.

Places to Stay – middle
There are numerous two-star hotels, such as *Hotel Argentino* (☎ 23661) at Calle 87 No 293; *Hotel Trocadero* (☎ 22589) at Calle 81 No 279; *Hotel Bahía* (☎ 23353) at Av San Martín 731; *Hotel Corona* (☎ 22646) at Av 75 No 371; and *Hotel Internacional* (☎ 24587) at Calle 81 No 232. Prices are about US$20 to US$30 per person.

Places to Stay – top end
Three-star hotels include *Hotel León* (☎ 24800) at Av 79 No 229; *Hotel Perugia* (☎ 22020) at Calle 81 No 288; and *Hotel San Miguel* (☎ 25155) at Calle 85 No 301. All charge about US$35 to US$40 per person. Four-star *Hotel Presidente* (☎ 23800), at Calle 4 No 4040, charges US$50 per person.

Places to Eat
La Romana, on Av 79 between Calles 4 and 6, is a great value with tenedor libre pasta for only US$4.50. *Nueva Gourmandise,* on Calle 77 at the corner of Calle 6, offers a US$6 daily special which is also an excellent value. *El Palenque,* Av 79 and Calle 6, has good parrillada and reasonable prices.

Pizzería Don Peppone (☎ 31364), on the Peatonal 85 at Av 4, offers good prices, fast service, and excellent quality; there's another branch (☎ 26390) at Av 59 No 2828.

Entertainment
Cine París (☎ 22273), Av 50 No 2874, shows first-run movies; another possibility is *Cine Océan* (☎ 23762), Calle 83 No 450.

There are several dance clubs on Calle 85 between Calles 2 and 6, including *Down Street, Mostaza,* and *Yamo.*

Getting There & Away
Air Aeropuerto Necochea (☎ 25826), 12 km north of town on RP 86, has summer flights with Sapse; the local representative is Diver Tour (☎ 28517), Calle 50 No 3128.

Bus The Terminal de Omnibus (☎ 22460) is on Av 58 (Sarmiento) between Calle 47 (Rondeau) and Av 35 (Jesuita Cardiel), near the river. Both El Cóndor (☎ 22120) and Costera Criolla (☎ 25553) have several buses daily to Buenos Aires ($25, seven hours). Empresa Córdoba Mar del Plata serves the interior, and there are often special services by other carriers in summer.

Train The Ferrocarril Roca (☎ 22182) has trains between Necochea and Constitución Station in Buenos Aires, via Tandil, three times weekly in each direction.

CLAROMECÓ
This tranquil village, with only 1000 permanent residents, has attractive beaches for sunbathing, swimming, surfing, and waterskiing, but it is most famous for its fishing. Nicknamed "Fisherman's Paradise," Claromecó holds a 24-hour fishing tournament every February, which attracts aficionados from all over the province. One year the winning entry was a 48-kg corvina negra.

Claromecó is off the main coastal routes at the mouth of the Arroyo Claromecó, 565 km from Buenos Aires at the end of RP 73, and 68 km south of Tres Arroyos on RN 3; it's 260 km east of Bahía Blanca. The Dirección de Turismo is at Calle 28 No 325.

Several campgrounds include the union-run *Luz y Fuerza,* which charges US$3 for adults, US$1.50 for children; privately run *Autocamping Las Dunas* is more expensive at US$12 for two persons, US$18 for four. Hotel accommodations are reasonably priced. Try *Residencial Suyal* for US$13 with breakfast, or *Residencial Céntrico* for

US$18 per person with breakfast. There are bus connections to Buenos Aires, Necochea, Bahía Blanca, and Mendoza from the Estación Terminal, Calle 28 No 327.

MONTE HERMOSO
With a current population of about 5000, Monte Hermoso has an interesting past tied to the 19th-century colonization of Buenos Aires province and the displacement of native peoples. In 1897 Don Esteban Dufaur, exiled by his father to develop the 4000-hectare El Recreo cattle estancia, blundered along with ex-convict labor for years before even finding a site where the shifting dunes would not cover the main house. Local Indians, not accepting his ownership, resisted establishment of the estancia, but by the turn of the century Dufaur had settled on a location, and the village of Monte Hermoso developed nearby. By 1917 Dufaur built his first hotel from a jettisoned cargo of lumber that washed up on the beach, and the village opened for tourism.

Orientation
The southernmost beach resort in Buenos Aires province, Monte Hermoso is 106 km east of Bahía Blanca and 633 km southwest of Buenos Aires, situated on RP 78 a short distance off RN 3. The main commercial street is Dufaur.

Information
Tourist Office The friendly Secretaría de Turismo (☎ 81123) is open all year in the bus terminal at Faro Recalada and Pedro de Mendoza. It offers an English version of its tourist guide to Monte Hermoso (for a charge), and adequate free maps and brochures.

Post & Telecommunications Encotesa is on Valle Encantado. The Cooperativa Telefónica is at Pedro de Mendoza 268; Monte Hermoso's telephone code is 0921.

Dangers & Annoyances Swimmers should note that occasional changes in water temperature can bring hordes of stinging jellyfish. Although these invasions do not last long, it happens every summer – to avoid discomfort, stay out of the ocean at these times.

Things to See & Do
Warm currents, broad, sandy beaches, and relative quiet attract vacationers to Monte Hermoso. It is also cheaper and less crowded than the more fashionable resorts to the north, with a good but not over-whelming tourist infrastructure, including several shady, spacious campgrounds and good, if standard, restaurants and pizzerías. Beaches, especially those toward the light-house on the east end of Av Costanera, are wide enough to accommodate large-court beach games like *paleta* (beach tennis).

Beaches closest to the **Faro Recolada** (lighthouse) are used almost exclusively for fishing, walking, and jogging. The light-house itself, 67 meters high, dates from 1906 and merits a visit for the panorama of the town, beaches, dunes, and the ocean. Emphasizing the area's natural history, Monte Hermoso's **Museo Municipal de Ciencias Naturales**, on the Av Costanera at Dufaur, contains exhibits on paleon-tology and archaeology, and a specialized collection of 120 different species of mollusks.

Places to Stay
Camping Monte Hermoso has several campgrounds, including two highly recom-mended ones. The village-like *Camping Americano* (☎ 81149), right on the beach west of town, has excellent facilities including a swimming pool, store, and recreation sites, but it is not cheap at US$5 per person, US$3 for the tent and US$2 for electrical hookup. Well-maintained and slightly cheaper *Autocamping Nuevo Mon-temar* (☎ 81183) is on Dufaur, about 1½ km away from the beach; its friendly owners give ACA discounts.

Hospedajes & Hosterías Hospedajes at Monte Hermoso, charging an average of about US$15 per person, include: *Hospe-daje Ambar,* Dufaur and Valle Encantado;

Hospedaje Rambla (☎ 81015), Dufaur 67; *Hospedaje Pec-Mar* (☎ 81195), Río Col-orado 445; *Hospedaje Mari-Car* (☎ 81223), Av Costa 58; and *Hospedaje Ripoll* (☎ 81237), Los Pinos and Traful.

More expensive is *Hostería La Goleta* (☎ 81142), Av Costanera at Calle 10, with singles/doubles at about US$40/50. *Nauta Motel* (☎ 81083), Dufaur 635, has similar prices and service.

Places to Eat
Monte Hermoso has reasonably priced restaurants such as *Parrilla La Rueda,* Los Pinos and Traful, which also prepares food to go. *Marisquería Rincón Basko,* Perón 50, has superb pollo al ajillo (garlic chicken) and shellfish dishes. The sidewalk *Pizzería Las Carabelas,* at Dufaur and Costanera, also serves good food.

Getting There & Away
The bus terminal is at Faro Recolada and Pedro de Mendoza. La Estrella/El Cóndor (☎ 81089) connects Monte Hermoso with Buenos Aires, and La Acción (☎ 81188) goes to Bahía Blanca several times daily. Andesmar has a wide network of services linking the interior provinces and Patago-nia with the coast.

Southern Buenos Aires Province

In only two parts of Buenos Aires province has does granitic bedrock tower above the deep sediments of the Pampas. Trending from northwest to southeast, the low moun-tain ranges of Tandilia and Ventania disrupt the monotony of the otherwise endlessly flat terrain. The easterly Sierras de Tandil are low, rounded hills whose peaks, not exceeding 500 meters, take the names of the counties they cross – Olavarría, Azul, Tandil, and Balcarce. The westerly Sierra de la Ventana, its jagged peaks reaching above 1300 meters in places, is more scenic and attracts hikers and climbers. Between the two ranges is a generally level area that slopes only gradually toward the bluffs and sandy beaches of the Atlantic coast, between Mar del Plata and Claromecó.

BAHÍA BLANCA

In an early effort to establish military control on the periphery of the Pampas, Colonel Ramón Estomba built the pompously named Fortaleza Protectora Argentina at the natural harbor of Bahía Blanca in 1828. In 1884 the railway connected the area with Buenos Aires, but another 11 years passed before Bahía Blanca officially became a city. Only in this century has it flourished in commerce and industry, primarily through agriculture and petrochemicals; it is also home to Puerto Belgrano, South America's largest naval base, and to the prestigious Universidad Nacional del Sur.

Bahía Blanca is more an important crossroads than a tourist city per se. Its location makes it the southern gateway to Buenos Aires province, the Atlantic outlet for produce from the Río Negro Valley, and the coastal approach to Patagonia.

Orientation

Bahía Blanca is 653 km southwest of Buenos Aires via RN 3, 530 km east of Neuquén via RN 22, and 278 km north of Viedma via RN 3. Plaza Rivadavia is the center of the town's grid. Street names change on either side of the plaza along Av Colón and Hipólito Yrigoyen.

Information

Tourist Offices Bahía Blanca's Oficina de Información Turística (☎ 55-1110), Alsina 45, is open weekdays 7:45 am to 1 pm. It's next door to the Municipalidad, which is at Alsina 65, across from Plaza Rivadavia; if you ring the bell at the Municipalidad on weekends, you may be able to get a map of the city.

ACA (☎ 55-0076) has offices at Chiclana 305, where members can park in a reasonably priced garage.

Foreign Consulate The Chilean Consulate (☎ 25808) is at Güemes 102.

Money Cambios keep short hours, usually closing by 4 pm. Try Cambio Pullman at San Martín 171, Cambio Iberotur at Soler 144, or Cambio Florida at Belgrano 187.

Bank hours are 8 am to 2 pm in summer, 10 am to 4 pm in winter. Banco del Sud, next to the Municipalidad on Plaza Rivadavia, has a cambio open 10 am to 3 pm weekdays. Banco de la Nación is at Estomba 52, and Banco de la Provincia is at Chiclana and Undiano. There are several ATMs in the vicinity of Plaza Rivadavia.

Post & Telecommunications Correo Argentino is at Moreno 34; the postal code is 8000.

Telefónica is at O'Higgins 249, but there are several locutorios in the vicinity of Plaza Rivadavia. Bahía Blanca's area code is 091. Note that Bahía Blanca's phone system is undergoing major renovation, and many current numbers may soon change.

Travel Agencies Travel agencies include Viajes Bahía Blanca (49767) at Drago 63, Viajes Toa (☎ 49150) at San Martín 108, and Turmundo (☎ 49150) at Soler 156.

Laundry Laverap is at Colón 197.

Medical Services The Hospital Italiano (☎ 51-0055) is at Necochea 675, while the Hospital Municipal (☎ 22222) is at Estomba 968.

Bookstores Librería Pampa Mar, Alsina 245, and Rayuela Libros (named for a famous novel by Julio Cortázar), at the corner of Alsina and San Martín, are both very fine downtown bookstores.

Things to See & Do

On Saturday mornings, the city closes Calle Alsina between Dorrego and San Martín, making it a pleasant site for an outing; otherwise the only pedestrian mall is on LM Drago, between O'Higgins and Donado.

Within the Municipalidad, on Plaza Rivadavia, is Bahía Blanca's **Museo de**

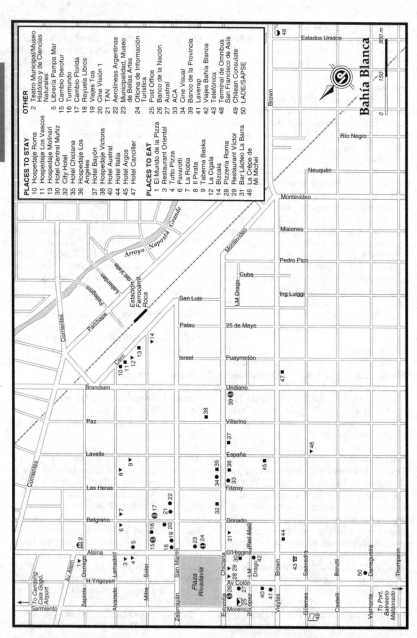

PLACES TO STAY
10 Hospedaje Roma
11 Hospedaje Los Vascos
13 Hospedaje Molinari
30 Hotel Central Muñiz
32 City Hotel
35 Hotel Chiclana
36 Hospedaje Los Angeles
37 Hotel Bayón
38 Hospedaje Victoria
40 Hotel Austral
44 Hotel Italia
45 Hotel Argos
47 Hotel Canciller

PLACES TO EAT
1 El Mundo de la Pizza
3 Restaurant Oriental
4 Tutto Pizza
6 Pavarotti
7 La Robla
8 Il Pirata
9 Taberna Baska
12 La Cigala
14 Bizcaia
28 Pizzería Roma
29 Restaurant Victor
31 Bar Lácteo La Barra
46 La Crêpe de Mi Michel

OTHER
2 Teatro Municipal/Museo Histórico y de Ciencias Naturales
5 Librería Pampa Mar
15 Cambio Iberotur
16 Turmundo
17 Cambio Florida
18 Rayuela Libros
19 Viajes Toa
20 Cine Visión 1
21 TAN
22 Aerolíneas Argentinas
23 Municipalidad, Museo de Bellas Artes
24 Oficina de Información Turística
25 Post Office
26 Banco de la Nación
27 Austral
33 ACA
34 Cine Visual
39 Banco de la Provincia
41 Laverap
42 Viajes Bahía Blanca
43 Telefónica
48 Terminal de Omnibus San Francisco de Asís
49 Chilean Consulate
50 LADE/SAPSE

Bellas Artes. The neoclassical **Teatro Municipal,** on Alsina just north of Dorrego, is the city's main performng arts center. In the same building is the **Museo Histórico y de Ciencias Naturales** (Historical and Natural Sciences Museum), open every day except Monday, 4 to 9 pm. The entrance is on Calle Soler.

Places to Stay – bottom end

Camping There is a basic municipal campground at *Balneario Maldonado* (☎ 29511), four km from the center at the southwestern end of town. Open all year, it has saltwater swimming pools, but hot water and electricity are available in summer only. Fees are US$4 per person. *Camping Cala Gogó,* on Sarmiento Km 4 in Aldea Romana east of Bahía Blanca, is open all year.

Hospedajes & Hotels Across from the train station on Av Cerri, several cheap but run-down hospedajes charge about US$10 single, US$20 double; surprisingly, there are none near the bus terminal. Try *Hospedaje Molinari* (☎ 22871) at Cerri 719, *Hospedaje Los Vascos* (☎ 29290) at Cerri 747, or recommended *Hospedaje Roma* (☎ 38500) at Cerri 759. Four blocks away is *Hospedaje Victoria* (☎ 20522) at General Paz 84.

On Chiclana, closer to Plaza Rivadavia, accommodations are better but slightly pricier. *Hotel Bayón* (☎ 22504), Chiclana 487, charges about US$12/22 single/double with shared bath, US$16/28 with private bath. Comparable *Hospedaje Los Angeles,* Chiclana 367, is very clean.

Places to Stay – middle

Hotel Chiclana (☎ 30436), Chiclana 370, and *Hotel Canciller* (☎ 38270), Brown 667, have singles/doubles at US$25/35 with private bath. Friendly *Hotel Central Muñiz* (☎ 20021), O'Higgins 23, has rooms with private bath starting at US$32/43. Pleasant *Hotel Italia* (☎ 20121), Brown 181, has nice rooms with bath for US$33/40; a good restaurant is on the premises. *City Hotel* (☎ 30176), Chiclana 228, charges US$35/50 for rooms with telephone, air-con, and private bath.

Places to Stay – top end

Prices and standards are very similar at Bahía Blanca's three-star, top-end hotels. *Hotel Austral* (☎ 56-1700), Av Colón 159, has comfortable rooms with TV and telephone for about US$79/89. *Hotel Argos* (☎ 40001) is at España 149.

Places to Eat

There are several acceptable restaurants in Bahía Blanca, though none is really memorable. Food is basic, abundant, and inexpensive at *El Cholo* at RN 3 Sur, Km 696, the province's most popular truck stop. Also cheap is *La Cigala,* across from the train station at Cerri 757. There are several parrillas and inexpensive pizzerías around Plaza Rivadavia, including *Tutto Pizza* at Alsina 248, *Pizzería Roma* at Chiclana 21, and *Restaurant Víctor* (☎ 23814) at Chiclana 83, which also has seafood. Other good pizzerías include *El Mundo de la Pizza* (☎ 45054) at Dorrego 55 and *Il Pirata* at Lamadrid 360.

For breakfast, try *Bar Lácteo La Barra,* Chiclana 155, which has good, fresh orange juice and tasty grilled sandwiches. *Taberna Baska* (☎ 21788), Lavalle 284, serves appetizing, reasonably priced Spanish food. *El Aljibe,* at Donado and Thompson, offers a conventional Argentine menu but is somewhat pricey. *Restaurant Oriental,* on Alsina between Lamadrid and Soler, is a Chinese tenedor libre charging US$10.

Local residents recommend *Gambrinus* (☎ 22380), a choppería (a beer joint with food) at Arribeños 164 near Hotel Italia; the Italian trattoría *Pavarotti* (☎ 51-4874) at Belgrano 272; *La Robla* (☎ 55-1307), across the street from Pavarotti; *Bizcaia* (☎ 20191) at Soler 769 near Av Cerri; and *La Barraca Sur* on Av Cerri. Cheap and excellent *La Crêpe de Mi Michel,* at España and Saavedra, is run by a Frenchman who went around the world on a bicycle and decided to stay in Bahía.

Entertainment

For first-run movies, try the *Cine Visual* (☎ 51-8503) at Chiclana 452 or the *Cine Visión 1* at Belgrano 137.

Things to Buy

On weekends there's a Feria de Artesanos (artisans' market) on Plaza Rivadavia, opposite the Municipalidad.

Getting There & Away

Air Austral (☎ 21383; 86-0299 at the airport), Colón 59, flies twice daily to Buenos Aires except Sunday, when there is only a single flight. Austral flies to Comodoro Rivadavia, Río Gallegos, and Río Grande daily except Sunday. Aerolíneas Argentinas (☎ 26934) maintains offices at San Martín 298, but no longer flies into or out of Bahía Blanca.

LADE (☎ 21063) and SAPSE (☎ 37697) share offices at Darregueira 21. LADE flies Mondays to Viedma (US$30), San Antonio Oeste (US$40), and Puerto Madryn (US$61), and on Tuesdays to Mar del Plata (US$49) and Aeroparque (US$68). SAPSE flies Monday and Thursday to Bariloche (US$95) and Esquel (US$130).

TAN (☎ 55-0963) is in the Galería Visión 2000, Oficina 80, at San Martín 216. It flies Sunday to Choele Choel (US$35) and Neuquén (US$91).

Bus The comfortable Terminal de Omnibus San Francisco de Asís (☎ 29616), Estados Unidos and Brown, is about two km east of Plaza Rivadavia. Bahía Blanca is a major transport node for southern Buenos Aires province and points south.

Costera Criolla (☎ 21075), La Estrella (☎ 34846) and El Cóndor (☎ 34846) serve Buenos Aires (US$30, ten hours) several times daily. Pampa (☎ 24121) goes to Mar del Plata (US$21) and Necochea, while El Valle (☎ 30134) travels to Neuquén (US$30) and Zapala, via the Río Negro Valley, four times daily. Don Otto (☎ 55-2585) has buses to coastal Patagonian destinations daily at 8 am, and to Río Gallegos (US$72) on Wednesdays. La Puntual (☎ 31146) goes as far as Comodoro Rivadavia (US$47, 15 hours), also stopping in Viedma, Puerto Madryn, and Trelew (US$42, 12 hours).

Ticsa (☎ 23481) serves San Luis and San Juan daily. La Acción (☎ 55-1974) goes to Monte Hermoso. TUP and TUS (☎ 49245) have buses to Córdoba. Andesmar (☎ 25462) runs very extensive routes toward the interior provinces and Patagonia.

Train The once-seigniorial Estación Ferrocarril Roca (☎ 21168), Av Cerri 750, is run-down and lacks any comfortable place to wait for connections. There are daily trains to and from Estación Constitución (in Buenos Aires). Fares are about 20% less than the comparable bus ride, but the train is slower and can be erratic.

Servicios Ferroviarios Patagónicos (Sefepa) runs southbound rail service to Carmen de Patagones/Viedma (seven hours), San Antonio Oeste/Las Grutas (11 hours), Ingeniero Jacobacci (22 hours), and Bariloche (27 hours). Its southbound *tren tradicional* from Consititución passes through Bahía Blanca Wednesday evenings at 7:18 pm, while its more comfortable *tren español* stops here Sunday evenings at the same hour. The tren español also has a separate service starting in Bahía Blanca at 1 pm Wednesday. Northbound services stop in Bahía Blanca at 3:18 am Saturday (tren español) and Tuesday (tren tradicional).

Getting Around

To/From the Airport Aeropuerto Comandante Espora (☎ 21665) is 15 km east of town on the naval base, RN 3 Norte, Km 674. City bus No 10 goes to the airport, but Austral provides its own transport (US$3) at 7 and 8 am, and 4:30 and 8:05 pm.

Bus Local buses Nos 505, 512, 514, 516, and 517 go to the bus terminal from downtown. Bus No 514 along Av Colón goes to Balneario Maldonado.

Car Rental Try AT (☎ 43944) at Colón 169; Alquilauto (☎ 24444) at Güemes 14; Localiza (☎ 51-4141) at Roca 381; or Dollar Rent a Car (☎ 56-2526) at Colón 194.

SIERRA DE LA VENTANA

Only a short distance north of Bahía Blanca but resembling the Sierras de Córdoba, this charming, slow-paced village is popular with Argentines but underappreciated by foreigners. Its more conventional facilities include a casino, golf links, and swimming pools, but it also offers opportunities for hiking, climbing, riding, bicycling, kayaking, and two rivers for fishing. There are comfortable, if limited, accommodations and good food.

Orientation

Sierra de la Ventana refers both to the mountain range and to this town, which is 125 km north of Bahía Blanca via RN 33 to Tornquist, and then RP 76. It is 602 km from Buenos Aires via RN 3 to Azul, RN 226 to Olavarría, and RP 76.

The Río Sauce Grande divides the village into two sectors: Sierra de la Ventana proper (Villa Tivoli), with government offices and businesses, and the residential barrio of Villa Arcadia. Avenida San Martín is the main street, with most services near the train station. Locals generally ignore street names.

Information

Tourist Office Alongside the train station, the Oficina de Turismo y Delegación Municipal (☎ 91-5032), Roca 15 at Av San Martín, has a useful packet of maps and flyers. It's open daily 7 am to 1 pm and 4 to 9 pm except Sunday, when it's open 7 am to 1 pm and 4:30 to 8 pm.

Money Banco de la Provincia is at San Martín 260, but it has no ATM.

Post & Telecommunications Correo Argentino and Telefónica are alongside each other on Av Roca near Alberdi. Sierra de la Ventana's postal code is 8168; the telephone code is 091.

Laundry Laverap is on Güemes near San Martín.

Places to Stay – bottom end

Camping There are several free *campsites* along the Río Sauce Grande, with access to toilets and showers at the nearby municipal swimming pool (US$2.50).

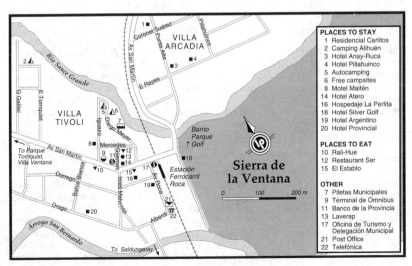

PLACES TO STAY
1 Residencial Carlitos
2 Camping Alihuén
3 Hotel Anay-Ruca
4 Hotel Pillahuinco
5 Autocamping
6 Free campsites
8 Motel Maitén
14 Hotel Atero
16 Hospedaje La Perlita
18 Hotel Silver Golf
19 Hotel Argentino
20 Hotel Provincial

PLACES TO EAT
10 Rali-Hue
12 Restaurant Ser
15 El Establo

OTHER
7 Piletas Municipales
9 Terminal de Omnibus
11 Banco de la Provincia
13 Laverap
17 Oficina de Turismo y
    Delegación Municipal
21 Post Office
22 Telefónica

If you prefer an organized campground, try *Autocamping* (☎ 91-5100), on Diego Meyer, which has good facilities at US$4 per adult, US$2 per child. *Camping Alihuén,* at the north end of Calle Tornquist, charges US$4 per person.

Hospadajes & Hotels Sierra de la Ventana's good, moderately priced accommodations include *Hotel Argentino,* Roca 122, and *Hospedaje La Perlita* (☎ 91-5020), Islas Malvinas and Pasaje 3, both of which charge US$15 per person. *Residencial Carlitos* (☎ 91-5011), at Coronel Suárez and Punta Alta in Villa Arcadia, offers doubles for US$21, but it is a bit standoffish. *Hotel Pillahuinco* (☎ 91-5024), on Rayes between Punta Alta and Pillahuinco in Villa Arcadia, has rooms for US$15 per person, US$18 with breakfast; other meals are also available.

Places to Stay – middle
ACA's *Motel Maitén* (☎ 91-5073), Iguazú 93 at Mercedes, is a good value at US$18 per person for members and US$23 for nonmembers; rates include breakfast. *Hotel Atero* (☎ 91-5002), Av San Martín and Güemes, has singles for US$20 with breakfast. *Hotel Anay-Ruca,* Rayes and Punta Alta in Villa Arcadia, has singles at US$27 with breakfast and US$40 with half-board.

Places to Stay – top end
Hotel Silver Golf (☎ 91-5079), at Barrio Parque Golf, has singles at US$50 with meals. The most expensive accommodations are at *Hotel Provincial* (☎ 91-5025), on Drago between Bahía Blanca and Islas Malvinas, which charges US$55 per person with half-pension, US$70 with all meals.

Places to Eat
Besides hotel restaurants, try *Restaurant Espadaña* on RP 76 (one km from the village) and the great and only parrilla *Rali-Hue,* on Av San Martín between Bahía Blanca and Islas Malvinas. *Restaurant Ser* (☎ 91-5055), on Güemes just off the main drag, has good pizza and pasta, with large portions, but drinks are expensive. *El*

Establo, on San Martín between Islas Malvinas and Av Roca, is a passable pizzería.

Getting There & Away
Sierra de la Ventana's modest Terminal de Omnibus is at San Martín and Iguazú. La Estrella has nightly buses to Buenos Aires (US$25, 7½ hours) at 11:40 pm, with an 8:05 am service to La Plata via Coronel Suárez. There are also buses to Bahía Blanca, via Tornquist, at 6:40 am and 7:45 pm daily.

Getting Around
Expreso de la Sierra runs three times daily weekdays and Sundays between Sierra de la Ventana and Tornquist, stopping at Saldungaray, Villa Ventana, and Abra de la Ventana. There is reduced service twice daily Saturdays and holidays.

AROUND SIERRA DE LA VENTANA
Villa Ventana
This friendly, small village, 17 km north of Sierra de la Ventana, has shady lanes, a riverside balneario with a municipal campground, and an excellent teahouse, *El Rincón de la Villa,* that alone justifies a stop if you're in the area.

Cerro Tres Picos
Although it is not part of Parque Provincial Ernesto Tornquist (see below), 1239-meter Cerro Tres Picos, seven km west of Sierra de la Ventana, is a fine choice for a backpack trip. The tourist office in Sierra de la Ventana can provide details on the hike, which requires crossing the property of Estancia Cerro Colorado.

Parque Provincial Ernesto Tornquist
The imposing wrought-iron gates at the entrance to this scenic 6700-hectare park belonged to the Tornquists, an elite Argentine family of financiers who donated the lands to the province. Although small, the park has an informative visitors center with a well-organized display on local ecology, enhanced by an audiovisual presentation. The **Corral de Recrías** contains local

fauna, mostly deer and guanaco, and there's also a forestry station.

Hiking is a popular activity, both independently and with rangers. In summer there are daily five-km guided walks to the corral at 11 am, and 4:30 and 7 pm; to other parts of the reserve on Fridays and Sundays at 6:30 pm; and four-hour trips to the gorge at **Garganta del Diablo** (Devil's Throat) Saturdays at 9 am and 1 pm, and by request on weekdays.

The best hike in the park is **Cerro de la Ventana**. From the trailhead, it takes about two hours to the 1136-meter summit, which gives dramatic views of surrounding hills and the distant Pampas. Rangers in the trailer at the trailhead collect a US$1 entry fee and routinely deny permission to climb after 1 pm for this occasionally steep but short, well-marked, and otherwise very easy hike. Insistent hikers can get permission by signing a waiver; in fact, a later start is better because you'll have the view to yourself instead of sharing it with dozens of porteño tobacco addicts who manage to huff and puff their way to the crest of what is probably the country's most-climbed peak. Some might find it easier if they left their spray paint cans behind.

Other worthwhile sights are the Indian caves at **Las Cuevas del Toro de Corpus Cristi** and the gorge at **Garganta Olvidada.** Hours for the visitors center are 9 am to 12:30 pm, and 4 to 8:30 pm daily. An audiovisual presentation is given daily at 10:30 am and at 4:30 and 6:30 pm.

At the trailhead, the friendly *Campamento Base* has good shade, clean baths, and excellent hot showers for US$4 per person. *Hotel El Mirador,* on RP 76 near Cerro de la Ventana, has singles/doubles at US$35/50 with breakfast.

TANDIL

On a plain surrounded by a horseshoe-shaped range of hills, Tandil developed from Fuerte Independencia, a military outpost established in 1823 by Martín Rodríguez. Today it serves as an important agricultural and livestock area and is a manufacturing center for cement, limestone, and dairy products. The local campus of the Universidad del Centro de la Provincia de Buenos Aires is well known for its agronomy and computer science departments.

Tandil (population 81,000) traditionally attracts masses of visitors during Easter Week, when they flock to Calvario, a hill ostensibly resembling the site of Christ's crucifixion at Golgotha, but the town does have other features worth seeing.

Orientation

Tandil is 384 km from Buenos Aires via RN 3 and RN 226, and 170 km from Mar del Plata via RN 226. The downtown area is bounded by Avs Rivadavia to the west, Avellaneda to the south, Buzón to the east, and del Valle to the north. Street names change at the intersections of Avellaneda/Estrada and Rivadavia/Dorrego. The main commercial streets are Rodríguez and 9 de Julio, while the principal center of social activity is Plaza Independencia, a two-block area bounded by Rodríguez, Belgrano, Chacabuco, and Pinto.

Information

Tourist Offices The Subsecretaría de Turismo (☎ 32073), 9 de Julio 555, distributes a none-too-good city map and some useful brochures, with directions on reaching points of interest by public transport.

ACA (☎ 25463) is at Rodríguez 399.

Post & Telecommunications Both Correo Argentino and Telefónica are at Rodríguez 630. Tandil's postal code is 7000; the area code is 0293.

Medical Services Hospital Municipal Ramón Santamarina (☎ 22011) is located at Paz 1406.

Things to See

Tandil has two worthwhile museums. The historic **Museo Tradicionalista Fuerte Independencia,** at 4 de Abril 845, is open daily except Monday from 4 to 8 pm. The **Museo de Bellas Artes,** at Chacabuco

367, is open daily except Sunday from 5 to 8 pm.

At the southwestern corner of town, **Parque Independencia** offers good views of the city, particularly at night. The **Dique del Fuerte,** two km from the city, is a huge reservoir where the Balneario Municipal operates three swimming pools.

For many years, a 300-ton boulder balanced precariously atop legendary **Cerro La Movediza** before falling, but the site still attracts visitors. In the early 1870s, one of the most notorious incidents in provincial history began here when a group of renegade gauchos, followers of an eccentric healer Gerónimo de Solané, popularly known as Tata Dios, gathered here to distribute weapons before going on a murderous rampage against European settlers and recent immigrants in central Tandil. A few years later, Francisco Fernández dramatized the incident in his play *Solané.*

Places to Stay
Camping On the road to Dique del Fuerte, clean and shady *Camping Municipal Pinar de la Sierra* charges US$8 per tent (up to four people) per day. It has a grocery and hot showers. Some but not all No 500 (yellow) buses go there – ask the driver.

Hospedajes & Hotels Friendly, modest, and tidy *Hotel Kaikú* (☎ 23114), Mitre 902, is a good value at US$10/14 single/double with breakfast. *Hotel Cristal* (☎ 25951), Rodríguez 871, is very basic but also cheap at US$10 per person. *Hospedaje Savoy* (☎ 25602), Alem and Mitre, is an old-fashioned family hotel, with a confitería for breakfast or snacks; the congenial owner charges US$12/20 for rooms with private bath.

At *Hotel Austral* (☎ 25606), 9 de Julio 725, rates are US$20/28 for rooms with private bath, but tourist discounts are available upon request. Across from Plaza Independencia is the very pleasant *Plaza Hotel* (☎ 27160), General Pinto 438, where rooms with private bath, telephone, and TV cost US$35/45 with breakfast; its confitería

serves the best coffee in town, and its restaurant is also highly regarded.

Places to Eat
Probably the cheapest place to eat is the *Comedor Universitario,* a stone house at the corner of Maipú and Fuerte Independencia, just south of Plaza Independencia. For great pollo a la piedra (grilled chicken) try *Restaurant El Nuevo Don José,* Av Monseñor De Andrea 269. *Restaurant El Estribo,* San Martín 759, has tasty pork. At *La Farola,* Pinto 681, the dish to order is pejerrey, a tasty mackerel. For parrillada, go to *Parada 4,* Rodríguez and Constitución. The restaurant at Plaza Hotel (see above) is also good.

Getting There & Away
Bus Tandil's Terminal de Omnibus (☎ 25585), Av Buzón and Portugal, may be the world's only bus station to have a casino on site. La Estrella (☎ 26018) and Río Paraná (☎ 24812) go to Buenos Aires three times daily; Río Paraná also goes to coastal destinations from Bahía Blanca to Pinamar and Villa Gesell. El Rápido (☎ 26171) travels to Mar del Plata every two hours, and also heads west to Santa Rosa, La Pampa. Costera Criolla (☎ 25970) goes to La Plata and Buenos Aires; Pampa (☎ 24249) goes to Necochea and La Plata.

TAC (☎ 25275) serves the west to Mendoza, while Transporte San Juan, in the same office, goes to the city of San Juan. Others in the same office include Tirsa to Rosario and Expreso Córdoba-Mar del Plata. Empresa Jocolí (☎ 24249) provides additional services between Mendoza and Mar del Plata.

Getting Around
Bus Tandil's excellent public transportation system reaches every important sight. Bus No 500 (yellow) goes to Dique del Fuerte and the municipal campground. No 501 (red) goes to the bus terminal, while No 503 (blue) goes to Cerro La Movediza, the university, and the bus terminal.

Car Rental Localiza (☎ 34002) is at Av España 555.

AROUND TANDIL
Estancia Acelain

On the wealthy estancias of Buenos Aires province there remain many opulent cascos. This one, 54 km northwest of Tandil, belonged to Hispanophile writer Enrique Larreta (1875–1961), whose erudite historical novels made him famous (Larreta's house in the Buenos Aires barrio of Belgrano is also a museum). Built in 1924 with local stone, it features furnishings and ornaments which, following Larreta's love for the Old Country, were brought from Spain. The chapel has beautiful stained-glass windows made in Germany.

Dense woods surround the buildings of the estancia, which also has a natural lagoon with good mackerel fishing.

Santa Fe Province

Along with Buenos Aires province to the south, Santa Fe is the heartland of the Humid Pampas, an agricultural area of phenomenal fertility even though its northernmost areas are part of the drier, less fertile Chaco. Many groups of Indians, including the Toba and Mocoví, resisted and disrupted early Spanish settlements here.

Marginal during colonial times, Santa Fe grew dramatically after independence, especially with the expansion of the railroads. Unlike the province of Entre Ríos, a virtual island on the opposite bank of the Río Paraná, Santa Fe benefited from better overland communications to Buenos Aires and the cities to the north and northwest.

Although caudillos such as Estanislao López and other large estancieros controlled the province, they put up minimal resistance to colonization by small farmers because Indians had deterred expansion of the estancias. Large landowners believed agricultural colonization would benefit them by reducing both the Indian threat and

their burden of taxes. In the second half of the 19th century, according to historian David Rock, land under cultivation increased from almost nil to 1.5 million hectares, mostly in family farms, a dramatic contrast to the latifundos of Buenos Aires province.

Agricultural expansion contributed to the growth of the port of Rosario, which soon surpassed the provincial capital of Santa Fe in size and importance. In southern Santa Fe, wheat cultivation helped double the province's population between 1895 and the outbreak of WWI. As the industrial and agricultural significance of Córdoba grew, so did that of Rosario, which was Córdoba's connection to the exterior.

About 4000 Mocoví Indians remain dispersed throughout the province of Santa Fe. The largest concentration is in Recreo, a small village of sharecroppers and artisans 17 km north of Santa Fe, but there are additional communities in Helvecia and San Javier, northeast of Santa Fe.

SANTA FE

In 1573 Juan de Garay, on an expedition from Asunción, founded Santa Fe de la Vera Cruz on the Río San Javier, a secondary tributary of the Paraná. In the mid-17th century, though, the Spaniards wearied of constant Indian raids, floods, and isolation, so the local *cabildo* (town council) moved the city, stock and block, southward to its present site near the confluence of the Río Salado and the main channel of the Paraná. Although the city was rebuilt on the exact urban plan of abandoned Santa Fe La Vieja, a neo-Parisian building boom in the 19th century and more recent construction have left only isolated colonial buildings. Those that remain, though, are well worth seeing.

Although still capital of its province, Santa Fe's population of about 350,000 leaves it second in economic power to burgeoning Rosario, a major road and rail junction. Still, the capital is an important agroindustrial center, transshipping and processing regional produce, and building and distributing farm machinery.

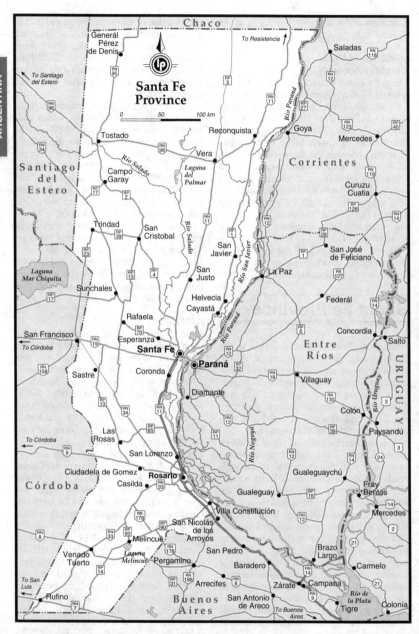

Santa Fe Province

0   50   100 km

The river and its fluctuations continue to be a powerful, inescapable force in local life; events upstream dramatically affect the city. In 1964 Laguna Setúbal desiccated because of drought in the upper Paraná basin; in 1983 the river rose to 9.2 meters, well above its stable level of 4.2 meters, destroying the bridge that connected the city with El Rincón and Paraná, across the river in Entre Ríos. A new bridge now links these areas, but the twisted Puente Colgante (Hanging Bridge) testifies to the river's power.

Beyond the city, the river has fostered a little-known but intriguing way of life among the people of "suburban" villages like Alto Verde. When the river rises, these fisherfolk evacuate their houses for temporary refuge in the city, but when the floods recede they rebuild their houses on the same spot. The *baqueanos* of the islands know the marshes and dense forests of the middle Paraná as well as porteños know the corner of Florida and Corrientes.

Orientation

Tributaries of the Paraná surround Santa Fe, but the main channel flows about 10 km east of the city. An access canal connects the port of Santa Fe with the Río Colastiné and the Paraná. The Río Salado meanders west of the city, while Laguna Setúbal, a wide, shallow section of the Río Saladillo, borders it on the east.

RN 11 links Santa Fe with Rosario (167 km) and Buenos Aires (475 km) to the south and with Resistencia (544 km) and Asunción, Paraguay, to the north. Between Rosario and Santa Fe, the faster *autopista* (motorway) A-008 parallels the ordinary route. To the east, RN 168 connects Santa Fe with its twin city of Paraná (25 km), Entre Ríos province, although the Uranga Sylvestre Begnis tunnel beneath the main channel of the Paraná is maintained by the province.

All of the city's remaining colonial buildings are within a short walk of Plaza 25 de Mayo, the functional center of the town. Avenida San Martín, north of the Plaza, is the major commercial street;

between Juan de Garay and Eva Perón (Catamarca), it is an attractive *peatonal* (pedestrian mall).

Information

Tourist Offices Santa Fe's helpful, motivated, and well-informed Dirección Municipal de Turismo has several branches, the most convenient of which (☎ 30982) is at the bus terminal, Belgrano 2910. It has maps, loads of brochures, and much other detailed information in loose-leaf binders, available for perusal. It's open daily from 7 am to 1 pm and 2 to 8 pm.

At the southern highway approach to town, the Boca del Tigre office (☎ 59-8774) is open weekdays from 7 am to 1 pm and 2 to 8 pm, Saturday from 7 am to 1 pm, and Sunday from 2 to 8 pm. The office at the Paseo del Restaurador (☎ 42274), north of downtown at Blvd Zavalla and JJ Paso, keeps the same hours.

ACA (☎ 43999) is at Av Rivadavia 3101, near Suipacha, with a second branch (☎ 31949) at Pellegrini and Av San Martín.

Money Tourfe, San Martín 2500, collects 3% commission on traveler's checks. One traveler reports that Banco Bica, which also has an ATM at San Martín 2453, refused to change less than US$500. Banco de la Nación and Banco de la Provincia are on opposite sides of Av San Martín at Tucumán.

Citibank has an ATM at San Martín and La Rioja, while Banco Río has one at San Martín and Tucumán.

Post & Telecommunications Correo Argentino is at Av 27 de Febrero 2331, near Mendoza; the postal code is 3000. Telecom long-distance telephone services are at the post office, upstairs at the bus terminal, in the Galería del Teatro at San Martín and Juan de Garay, and at Crespo 2336 across from Plaza España. Santa Fe's area code is 042.

Travel Agency Vacaciones Felices (☎ 31079), Mendoza 2615, is the Amex representative.

ARGENTINA

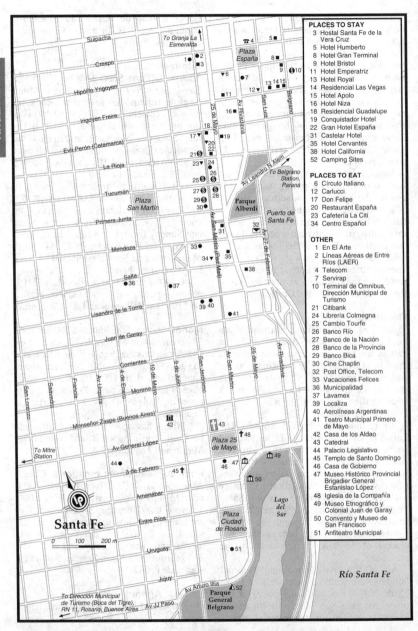

PLACES TO STAY
3   Hostal Santa Fe de la Vera Cruz
5   Hotel Humberto
8   Hotel Gran Terminal
9   Hotel Bristol
11 Hotel Emperatriz
13 Hotel Royal
14 Residencial Las Vegas
15 Hotel Apolo
16 Hotel Niza
18 Residencial Guadalupe
19 Conquistador Hotel
22 Gran Hotel España
31 Castelar Hotel
35 Hotel Cervantes
38 Hotel California
52 Camping Sites

PLACES TO EAT
6   Círculo Italiano
12 Carlucci
17 Don Felipe
20 Restaurant España
23 Cafetería La Citi
34 Centro Español

OTHER
1   En El Arte
2   Líneas Aéreas de Entre Ríos (LAER)
4   Telecom
7   Servirap
10 Terminal de Omnibus, Dirección Municipal de Turismo
21 Citibank
24 Librería Colmegna
25 Cambio Tourfe
26 Banco Río
27 Banco de la Nación
28 Banco de la Provincia
29 Banco Bica
30 Cine Chaplin
32 Post Office, Telecom
33 Vacaciones Felices
36 Municipalidad
37 Lavamex
39 Localiza
40 Aerolíneas Argentinas
41 Teatro Municipal Primero de Mayo
42 Casa de los Aldao
43 Catedral
44 Palacio Legislativo
45 Templo de Santo Domingo
46 Casa de Gobierno
47 Museo Histórico Provincial Brigadier General Estanislao López
48 Iglesia de la Compañía
49 Museo Etnográfico y Colonial Juan de Garay
50 Convento y Museo de San Francisco
51 Anfiteatro Municipal

Bookstore Librería Colmegna, San Martín 2546, has a good selection of Argentine history and literature.

Laundry Lavamex is on 9 de Julio between Salta and Lisandro de la Torre. Servirap is at Rivadavia 2834.

Medical Services The Hospital Provincial José María Cullen (☎ 21001) is at Lisandro de la Torre and Freire, west of downtown.

Historic Center
Santa Fe is one of Argentina's oldest cities, but the 20th century has changed its face considerably – in 1909, for example, the French Renaissance-styled **Casa de Gobierno** (Government House) replaced the demolished colonial cabildo on Plaza 25 de Mayo. The **Palacio Legislativo** is four blocks west on 3 de Febrero, between 4 de Enero and Urquiza.

Many of the remaining colonial buildings are museums, although several revered churches still serve their original functions. The exterior simplicity of the Jesuit **Iglesia de la Compañía**, on Plaza 25 de Mayo at Av San Martín and Av General López, masks a much more ornate interior. Dating from 1696, it's the best preserved colonial church in the province.

The **Templo de Santo Domingo**, at 3 de Febrero and 9 de Julio, dates from the mid-17th century but has undergone several modifications. Its interior is Ionian, while the exterior is a combination of Ionian and Roman styles; atop stands a pair of symmetrically placed bell towers and a dome.

The **Casa de los Aldao,** Monseñor Zaspe (Buenos Aires) 2861, is a restored two-story house from the early 18th century. Like others of the period, it has a tile roof, balconies, and meter-thick walls.

Santa Fe's museums are generally open 8:30 am to 12:30 pm and 3 to 7 pm on weekdays, and from 9:30 am to 12:30 pm and 4 to 7 pm on weekends and holidays.

Convento y Museo de San Francisco
Built in 1680, Santa Fe's single most outstanding historical landmark has walls more than a meter thick, supporting a roof whose Paraguayan cedar and hardwood beams are held together with fittings and wooden spikes rather than nails. Like many other colonial churches, its floor plan duplicates the Holy Cross. The doors are the original, handworked ones, while the baroque pulpit is laminated in gold. Besides these architectural features, the church contains many colonial works of art.

Note the tomb of Father Magallanes, killed by a·jaguar which, driven from the shores of the Paraná during the floods of 1825, took refuge in the church. The church also holds the coffins of the Santa Fe caudillo Estanislao López and his wife. Parts of the interior patio are open to the public, but do not go beyond into the cloisters.

Adjacent to the church is a **historical museum** (☎ 23303) covering both secular and religious topics from both colonial and republican eras. One interesting exhibit is the Sala de los Constituyentes, containing wax figures of the representatives to the assembly that wrote the Argentine Constitution of 1853.

The church and convent are at Amenábar 2257 near Av San Martín, just south of Plaza 25 de Mayo.

Museo Histórico Provincial Brigadier General Estanislao López
In a damp but well-preserved building from the late 17th century, this museum contains permanent exhibits on the 19th-century civil wars, provincial governors (and caudillos), period furnishings, and religious art, as well as a room with changing displays on more contemporary themes.

At San Martín 1490, the museum (☎ 22760) is closed Mondays, but may open on request – try knocking on the door or standing around looking lost.

Museo Etnográfico y Colonial Juan de Garay
The most interesting single display in this

ARGENTINA

museum (☎ 35857) is a scale model of the original settlement of Santa Fe La Vieja. Besides the excellent collection of Spanish colonial artifacts from excavations at the former site near present-day Cayastá, indigenous basketry, Spanish ceramics, and coins and money are on display. The staff is very patient and helpful in explaining details of the exhibits. It's at 25 de Mayo 1470 at Av Arturo Illia.

Granja La Esmeralda

On the northern outskirts of Santa Fe, this experimental farm also contains a worthwhile zoo that concentrates on fauna native to the province, mostly in spacious enclosures. The most impressive specimens are tropical birds such as toucans, big cats such as pumas and jaguars, and the giant anteater.

Admission is US$1; hours are from 7 am to 7 pm. Bus No 10 bis, which crosses the San Martín peatonal, goes to the Granja.

Places to Stay – bottom end

Camping There is no formal campground in Santa Fe proper, but the city tolerates free camping along the Lago del Sur in Parque General Belgrano, at the south end of Av San Martín; look for Argentine campers. The nearest formal campground is at San José del Rincón, 12 km east of Santa Fe across the bridge, accessed by Servitur bus.

Hotels Several inexpensive accommodations are exactly opposite the bus terminal or a short distance away. The absolute cheapest is *Residencial Las Vegas,* Irigoyen Freire 2246, where singles/doubles cost only US$10/16; *Residencial Guadalupe,* Eva Perón (Catamarca) 2575, is slightly more expensive at US$12/18. *Hotel Humberto* (☎ 55-0409), Crespo 2222, charges US$16/22.

At *Hotel Gran Terminal* (☎ 32395), Hipólito Yrigoyen 2222, rooms with shared bath cost US$15 per person, while those with private bath cost US$20/32; *Hotel Royal* (☎ 27359), Irigoyen Freire 2256, charges about the same. Comparably priced *Hotel Apolo* (☎ 27984), across from the bus terminal at Belgrano 2821, is clean but dark. *Hotel Bristol* (☎ 35044), Belgrano 2859, has air-con rooms with shared bath for US$17/28, with private bath US$27/35. *Hotel Alem* (☎ 55-6875), at Sarmiento 2799 on the corner of Av Alem, five blocks east of Belgrano, is a reasonable choice for US$20/30.

There are a few budget choices slightly closer to the center. Modern and undistinguished *Hotel California* (☎ 23988), 25 de Mayo 2190, is very friendly but has only a dozen rooms, all with private bath. Rates are US$17/30. *Hotel Cervantes* (☎ 40178), 25 de Mayo 2277, charges US$20/30.

Places to Stay – middle

A good choice is *Hotel Niza* (☎ 22047), Rivadavia 2755, where rooms with private bath, air-con, and telephone cost US$26/40. An even better choice, perhaps the best value in town, is *Hotel Emperatriz* (☎ 30061), at Irigoyen Freire 2440 between 25 de Mayo and Rivadavia, occupying a remodeled private house that once belonged to an elite santafesino family. It's quiet, friendly, and dignified for US$30/38 with private bath. The large, impersonal, and rather noisy *Castelar Hotel* (☎ 20141), 25 de Mayo 2349, charges US$32/48; some larger rooms are slightly more expensive.

Places to Stay – top end

At unpretentious *Gran Hotel España* (☎ 21016), 25 de Mayo 2647, rates start at US$44/60. If you have money to burn, the owners of the Gran Hotel España will happily accept it across the street at the *Conquistador Hotel* (☎ 55-1195), 25 de Mayo 2676, which is more modern but no better at US$72/92. Slightly cheaper, and probably superior, is *Hostal Santa Fe de la Vera Cruz* (☎ 55-1740), Av San Martín 2954, where rates are US$64/86.

Places to Eat

On Belgrano, across from the bus terminal, several very good, inexpensive places serve Argentine staples such as empanadas, pizza, and parrillada. At San Martín and La

Rioja, try *Cafetería La Citi* for coffee and sandwiches.

For a downtown splurge, try *Restaurant España* (☎ 55-6481) at Av San Martín 2642. North of downtown, at Blvd Galvez and San Luis 3499, *Las Leñas* (☎ 29946) is a good but pricey parrilla. *Carlucci* (☎ 35176), Irigoyen Freire 2300, has fine Italian food. The *Círculo Italiano* (☎ 20628), Hipólito Yrigoyen 2457 between 25 de Mayo and Rivadavia, prepares good and moderately priced lunch specials. The *Centro Español,* San Martín 2219, has a classy Spanish restaurant. *Don Felipe,* on San Martín between Eva Perón (Catamarca) and La Rioja, is worth a look.

Tourists flock to riverside *El Quincho de Chiquito* (☎ 62608), some distance north of downtown at Brown and Obispo Vieytes, but so do locals. Because of its enormous size, service is pretty impersonal, but it still serves outstanding grilled river fish such as boga and sábalo and exceptional hors d'ouevres like fish empanadas. In practice, if not in theory, it's all you can eat for about US$10 to US$15 plus drinks. Take bus No 16 on Av Gálvez, which parallels Suipacha four blocks to the north.

Entertainment
Cinema *Cine Chaplin* (☎ 26856), at the back of a gallery on San Martín between Tucumán and Primera Junta, shows recent films.

Theater Designed in the French Renaissance style so common in turn-of-the-century Argentina, the *Teatro Municipal Primero de Mayo* (☎ 21653, 37777), at Av San Martín 2020, offers drama and dance performances.

Things to Buy
En El Arte (☎ 20030), Local 11 in the Galería via Macarena at San Martín 2945, has a good selection of local and regional crafts. Owner Fabián Pinnola is also a good source of information on the goods he handles.

Getting There & Away
Air Aerolíneas Argentinas (☎ 20713) is at Lisandro de la Torre 2633. It has nonstop flights to Buenos Aires weekday mornings, Tuesday, Thursday, and Friday afternoons, and every evening. The one-hour trip costs US$73.

Líneas Aéreas de Entre Ríos (LAER, ☎ 40170), San Martín 2984, flies daily except Saturday to Buenos Aires (US$65).

Bus The Oficina de Informes (☎ 40698) at the Estación Terminal de Omnibus, Belgrano 2940, is open 6 am to midnight; it posts all fares for destinations throughout the country, so it is not necessary to run from window to window for comparison.

About every hour throughout the day and night, Etacer buses (☎ 20941) leave for Paraná for US$2.

El Rápido (☎ 41314) goes to Rosario (US$9, two hours) and Buenos Aires (US$19, six hours). La Internacional (☎ 43514) and Micro Ejecutivo (☎ 42618) also go to Rosario and Buenos Aires; at the same window as Micro Ejecutivo, Zenit goes to Mar del Plata (US$47, 13 hours).

El Norte Bis (☎ 29725) serves Corrientes (US$10 hours, US$32). Ciudad de Posadas (☎ 42172) also goes to Resistencia, Corrientes, and Posadas (US$38, 12 hours), as does Empresa Kurtz, which continues to Puerto Iguazú (US$50, 16 hours). Expreso Singer (☎ 30306) stops in Santa Fe en route between Córdoba and Posadas. Puerto Tirol (☎ 55-7013) also serves Buenos Aires, Corrientes, and Formosa.

El Turista (☎ 55-8696) has inexpensive services to Córdoba and its sierras, as does El Serrano (☎ 23943). TAC (☎ 30306) goes to Mendoza. Several carriers serve Patagonian destinations, including Alto Valle (☎ 30306) to Neuquén (US$80, 16 hours) and Tirsa (☎ 39690) to Bariloche. To Bahía Blanca, the coastal gateway to Patagonia, try TUS (☎ 29122), Central Argentino (☎ 30306), or Costera Criolla (☎ 42618).

La Pehna (☎ 39690) has international services to Porto Alegre and Florianópolis, Brazil; other Brazilian carriers include El Catarinense (☎ 55-8696), Norosur

(☎ 44362), and Pluma (☎ 30306). Godoy (☎ 43514) goes to Asunción, Paraguay (13 hours); Cora (☎ 29122) has runs to Montevideo, Uruguay (12 hours).

Getting Around

To/From the Airport City bus L goes to Aeropuerto Sauce Viejo (☎ 70642), seven km south of town on RN 11.

Car Rental Localiza (☎ 31465) is at Lisandro de la Torre 2665.

AROUND SANTA FE
Alto Verde

Shaded by enormous willows and other trees, Alto Verde is a picturesque fishing village on Isla Sirgadero, accessible only by canoe for most of the year. In really wet years, when the Paraná floods and destroys their houses, fishing families abandon the island for Santa Fe, returning and rebuilding when the flood waters recede. To reach the village, catch a launch from Puerto del Piojo, in the port complex at the east end of Calle Mendoza in Santa Fe.

San José del Rincón

The shady earthen roads of San José del Rincón still offer a few colonial buildings and an excellent **Museo de la Costa** (Museum of the Coast). Many santafesinos maintain weekend homes here, where camping and fishing are popular pastimes. Local gardeners cultivate ornamental flowers, such as gladiolus bulbs, for sale in the city.

Servitur buses from Santa Fe go directly to Rincón.

Cayastá

Cayastá, the site of Santa Fe La Vieja, is 78 km northeast of Santa Fe on RP 1. The Río San Javier has eroded away part of the original site, including half of the Plaza de Armas, but recent excavations have revealed the sites of the cabildo and the Santo Domingo, San Francisco, and Merced churches. Authorities have erected protective structures to guard the remains of these buildings. For educational purposes,

they have also reconstructed a typical period house with furnishings.

Excavations have also uncovered numerous colonial artifacts, some of them exhibited in the nearby **Museo de la Colonización y Población del Virreyanto de la Plata,** and others in the Museo Etnográfico in present-day Santa Fe. Hours are from 8 am to 7 pm on weekdays and 10 am to noon and 3 to 6 pm on weekends, but you can usually talk your way onto the grounds even when it's closed.

About two km north of the ruins on RP 1, *Comedor Cayastá* is an excellent value, offering full meals with salad and dessert for US$4 or less; service is friendly and attentive. There is regular bus service from the capital.

ROSARIO

Arguably the second city of the republic (a status disputed by Córdoba), Rosario sits on a bluff above the west bank of the main channel of the Río Paraná, 320 km upstream from Buenos Aires. The first European inhabitants settled informally around 1720 without sanction from the Spanish Crown. After independence Rosario quickly superseded Santa Fe as the province's economic powerhouse, but the more northerly capital held on to political primacy to the irritation of rosarinos.

The first trunk railway in the country connected Rosario with Córdoba and, later, with Mendoza and Tucumán. The Central Argentine Land Company, an adjunct of the railroad, was responsible for bringing in agricultural colonists from Europe for whom Rosario was a port of entry. Between 1869 and 1914 Rosario's population multiplied nearly tenfold to 223,000, easily overtaking the capital in numbers.

Rosario is a 19th-century city with no colonial pretensions, but its many French Renaissance buildings are typical of turn-of-the-century Argentine architecture. Some refer to it as the "Chicago of Argentina" because of its industrial importance and role in exporting the produce of a large agricultural heartland – despite its distance up the Paraná, the port can accommodate

ARGENTINA

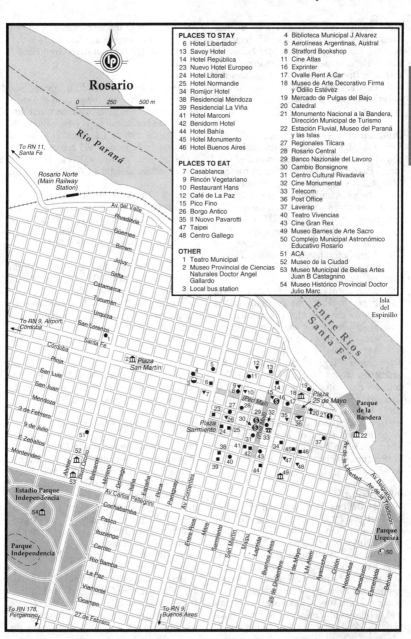

Rosario

0   250   500 m

Río Paraná

To RN 11,
Santa Fe

Rosario Norte
(Main Railway
Station)

PLACES TO STAY
6   Hotel Libertador
13   Savoy Hotel
14   Hotel República
23   Nuevo Hotel Europeo
24   Hotel Litoral
25   Hotel Normandie
34   Romijor Hotel
38   Residencial Mendoza
39   Residencial La Viña
41   Hotel Marconi
42   Benidorm Hotel
44   Hotel Bahía
45   Hotel Monumento
46   Hotel Buenos Aires

PLACES TO EAT
7   Casablanca
9   Rincón Vegetariano
10   Restaurant Hans
12   Café de La Paz
15   Pico Fino
26   Borgo Antico
35   Il Nuovo Pavarotti
47   Taipei
48   Centro Gallego

OTHER
1   Teatro Municipal
2   Museo Provincial de Ciencias
     Naturales Doctor Angel
     Gallardo
3   Local bus station

4   Biblioteca Municipal J Alvarez
5   Aerolíneas Argentinas, Austral
8   Stratford Bookshop
11   Cine Atlas
16   Exprinter
17   Ovalle Rent A Car
18   Museo de Arte Decorativo Firma
     y Odilio Estévez
19   Mercado de Pulgas del Bajo
20   Catedral
21   Monumento Nacional a la Bandera,
     Dirección Municipal de Turismo
22   Estación Fluvial, Museo del Paraná
     y las Islas
27   Regionales Tilcara
28   Rosario Central
29   Banco Nazionale del Lavoro
30   Cambio Bonsignore
31   Centro Cultural Rivadavia
32   Cine Monumental
33   Telecom
36   Post Office
37   Laverap
40   Teatro Vivencias
43   Cine Gran Rex
49   Museo Barnes de Arte Sacro
50   Complejo Municipal Astronómico
     Educativo Rosario
51   ACA
52   Museo de la Ciudad
53   Museo Municipal de Bellas Artes
     Juan B Castagnino
54   Museo Histórico Provincial Doctor
     Julio Marc

ocean-going vessels as easily as Buenos Aires. Its waterfront access, where many new restaurants grace the older buildings along the costanera, is a feature nearly absent in Buenos Aires. Many visitors are nationalistic Argentines who cherish Rosario as "Cuna de la Bandera" (Cradle of the Flag).

Orientation

Rosario's size and port status make it a node for several major highways and railroads. Passing through Rosario en route to Córdoba, RN 9 is also the major motorway connecting it with Buenos Aires. Heading north to Santa Fe are RN 11 and its parallel motorway, A-008, while RN 178 goes south to the prosperous farm zone around Pergamino, in Buenos Aires province, and RN 33 heads southwest to Venado Tuerto. Motorists can bypass the city on the Av Circunvulación.

Rosario displays a very regular grid pattern except where the curvature of the bluffs above the river channel dictates otherwise – much of this area is open space, with excellent views of and access to the river. Traditionally, the focus of urban activities is Plaza 25 de Mayo, but the pedestrian streets of San Martín and Córdoba are the centers of commerce. The center's shady plazas offer relief from the heat, while beyond the plaza the center streets are tree-shaded and the many new plantings of palms are signs of municipal vigor. There are some 70 sq blocks of open space in Parque Independencia, southwest of downtown.

Information

Tourist Offices The Dirección Municipal de Turismo (☎ 37-1295) is in the new Centro de Convenciones General Juan Domingo Perón at Cafferata 729, directly opposite the bus terminal. It's open weekdays only from 8 am to 3 pm and distributes maps and a monthly bulletin of what's happening in town. It maintains a secondary office (☎ 40-8583), open weekends and holidays only from 9 am to 7 pm, at the Galería de Honor de las Banderas de América, part of the Monumento Nacional a la Bandera complex at Santa Fe 581.

ACA (☎ 41278) is at Blvd Oroño and 3 de Febrero.

Money Numerous cambios along San Martín and Córdoba change cash and traveler's checks, the latter with the usual discount and commission. Try Bonsignore at San Martín 998 or Exprinter at Córdoba 960. Banco Nazionale del Lavoro has an ATM at San Martín 902, but there are several others along the Córdoba peatonal.

Post & Telecommunications Correo Argentino is at Córdoba 721, on Plaza 25 de Mayo; the postal code is 2000. Telecom is at San Luis 936 between Maipú and San Martín. Rosario's area code is 041.

Cultural Center The Centro Cultural Rivadavia (☎ 24-8382), Av San Martín 1080, is a good place to find out what's happening in Rosario. It shows free or inexpensive films, and hosts dance and theater events. Its galleries provide a showcase for the very active local art community.

Bookstore Stratford Bookshop, on Mitre between Santa Fe and Córdoba, sells English-language books.

Laundry Laverap is at Rioja 607.

Monumento Nacional a la Bandera

Topped by a 78-meter tower, the Monument to the Flag at Santa Fe 581 is architect Angel Guido's exercise in patriotic hubris. The colossal boat-shaped monstrosity has a bow that shelters the crypt of General Manuel Belgrano, designer of the Argentine flag. Every June, Rosario celebrates La Semana de la Bandera (Flag Week), climaxed by ceremonies on June 20, the anniversary of Belgrano's death.

Heroic sculptures by Alfredo Bigatti and José Fioravanti and bas-reliefs by Eduardo Barnes symbolically represent the regions of the country and various patriotic figures. Its museum (☎ 21-4972), containing the

limited hours, Wednesday 2:30 to 4 pm and Sunday 4 to 6:30 pm, the murals can be seen whenever the building is open.

Historical Museums

The **Museo Histórico Provincial Doctor Julio Marc** (☎ 21-9678) in Parque Independencia contains some pre-Colombian and colonial exhibits, but concentrates on post-independence materials. It's open Tuesday to Friday 9 am to 12:30 pm and 3 to 6:30 pm, weekends from 3 to 6:30 pm. Another historical museum is the municipal **Museo de la Ciudad** (☎ 82-4552), Blvd Oroño 2350, open Wednesday to Sunday 9 am to noon and 3 to 7 pm.

Art Museums

The fine-arts **Museo Municipal de Bellas Artes Juan B Castagnino** (☎ 21-7310), at Avs Pellegrini and Oroño, is open Tuesday to Friday 4 to 10 pm; it houses a permanent collection of European and Argentine art, with occasional contemporary exhibitions. The **Museo Barnes de Arte Sacro** (☎ 48-3784), Laprida 1235, exhibits sculptures from the man responsible for parts of the Monument to the Flag. It's open Thursday 4 to 6 pm.

There are wider-ranging art collections at the **Museo de Arte Decorativo Firma y Odilio Estévez** (☎ 48-2544), Santa Fe 748. Hours are Wednesday to Friday 4 to 8 pm, weekends 2 to 8 pm.

Science Museums

Those interested in the environment and wildlife may wish to visit the **Museo Provincial de Ciencias Naturales Doctor Angel Gallardo** (☎ 25-7969) at Moreno 758 near Plaza San Martín, open Tuesday to Friday 9 am to 12:30 pm and Tuesday, Friday, and Sunday 3 to 6 pm.

Those interested in more distant environments can visit the planetarium at the **Complejo Municipal Astronómico Educativo Rosario** (Municipal Observatory, ☎ 48-3084) in Parque Urquiza, which has shows Saturday and Sunday from 5 to 6 pm. Tuesday and Thursday, from 9 to 10 pm, visitors can view the austral skies

General Manuel Belgrano designed the Argentine flag.

original flag embroidered by Catalina de Vidal, is open daily from 9 am to 1 pm and 4 to 7 pm, except Mondays when hours are 4 to 7 pm only. Every Wednesday at 8:15 am, there's a flag ceremony with a military band.

One redeeming attribute of the monument is the good view of the Paraná waterfront from the foot of Av Córdoba.

Museo del Paraná y Las Islas

Life on the river – flora, fauna, and people – is the focus of this museum on the 1st floor of the waterfront Estación Fluvial, Av Belgrano and Rioja. It's a much more worthwhile sight than the pretentious Monumento a la Bandera because of the romantic but fascinating murals of local painter Raúl Domínguez: *Recorrido del Paraná* (Exploring the Paraná), *Cortador de Paja* (Thatch Cutter), *El Paraná y Sus Leyendas* (The Paraná and Its Legends), *El Nutriero* (The Otter Trapper), *Creciente* (In Flood), *Bajante* (In Drought), and others. While the museum proper (☎ 48-2136) has very

through its 2250-mm refractor telescope and 4500-mm reflecting telescope.

River Excursions

Weekends and holidays, the *Ciudad de Rosario I* (☎ 25-7895) cruises the Río Paraná at 4 and 6:30 pm from the Estación Fluvial. On the same days and from the same depot, the *Delta Queen* takes a whirl around the islands of the Paraná, stopping and picking up passengers out for the day. Trips depart every 1½ hours starting at 8 am till dark.

Special Events

Besides La Semana de la Bandera (see Monumento Nacional a la Bandera, above), Rosario holds its own Semana de Rosario in the first week of October and the national Encuentro de las Colectividades, a tribute to the country's immigrants, in November or December.

Places to Stay – bottom end

Camping *Camping 26 de Noviembre* is in the Ciudad Universitaria at the south end of Av Belgrano, near its intersection with Blvd 27 de Febrero. Anyone intending to camp here must ask permission in person from the Asociación del Personal de la Universidad Nacional de Rosario, Córdoba 1900.

Hotels Friendly, inexpensive *Hotel Normandie* (☎ 21-2694), Mitre 1030, has singles/doubles for US$14/23 with shared bath, US$20/27 with private bath. Comparably priced *Hotel Bahía* is at Maipú 1254. Centrally located *Residencial La Viña* (☎ 21-4549), 3 de Febrero 1244, is a good value for US$15/25.

Hotel Litoral (ex-Nuevo Hotel Linton, ☎ 21-1426), at Entre Ríos 1043 across from noisy Plaza Sarmiento, has attractive balconies opening out from many of its rooms, which cost US$20/30. For about the same price, *Residencial Mendoza* (☎ 24-6544), Mendoza 1246, includes breakfast. Fans are provided, but air conditioning is extra.

Near the bus terminal, *Hotel Residencial* (☎ 37-3413), Pasaje Quintanilla 628, has

good singles without TV for US$19; singles/doubles with TV go for US$21/30.

Places to Stay – middle

Friendly, recently upgraded *Hotel Buenos Aires* (☎ 24-2034), Buenos Aires 1063, offers singles/doubles for US$25/30, with the possibility of multi-day discounts. *Romijor Hotel* (☎ 21-7276), Laprida 1050, has quiet patio rooms for US$27/40. The *Savoy Hotel* (☎ 48-0071), San Lorenzo 1022, maintains a shabby dignity for about US$24/42.

At *Hotel Marconi* (☎ 49115), San Juan 1077, rates are US$30/35 with private bath. The nearby *Benidorm Hotel* (☎ 21-9368) at San Juan 1049 is comparably priced. The dark but friendly *Hotel Monumento* (☎ 40-6446), Buenos Aires 1020, is a bit costlier at US$33/41.

Near the bus terminal, at Pasaje Quintanilla 657, *Hotel Gran Confort* (☎ 38-0486) has rooms with private bath for US$24/38. Directly across from the terminal, at Santa Fe 3554, modern *Hotel Embajador* (☎ 38-6367) charges US$30/42.

Places to Stay – top end

Top of the line places, such as *Nuevo Hotel Europeo* (☎ 24-0382) at San Luis 1364, start at about US$51/62. *Hotel República* (☎ 24-8580), San Lorenzo 955, charges US$59/72. The best in town is *Hotel Libertador* (☎ 24-1005), at the corner of Córdoba and Corrientes, which charges US$69/84.

Places to Eat

Probably the best value in town is *Pico Fino,* San Martín 783, which offers a varied menu of Argentine and international food, outstanding service, and very reasonable prices. They'll even make half-pizzas (four portions) for solo diners, and the fresh-squeezed orange juice for less than US$2 is a good value.

Italian or Italian-derived food is big in Rosario. One of the best places is an outstanding rotisería alongside *Restaurant Rich,* San Juan 1031 near the Centro Cultural Rivadavia. Moderately priced *Casa-*

blanca, Córdoba 1471, serves typical Italo-Argentine food such as canneloni and ravioli, along with cold lager beer.

Despite its self-consciously Italian name, *Il Nuovo Pavarotti* at Laprida 988 is a medium-priced parrilla. *Rincón Vegetariano,* on Mitre between Santa Fe and Córdoba, is a meatless alternative. The *Centro Gallego,* Buenos Aires 1127, serves fixed-price all-you-can-eat meals, while *Restaurant Hans,* Mitre 775, is also economical. *Taipei,* Laprida 1121, is a Chinese tenedor libre.

Confitería *Café de La Paz,* Sarmiento and San Lorenzo, draws big crowds. For an upscale dinner, try *Borgo Antico* at Ricardone 131.

Entertainment
Cinema The *Cine Monumental* (☎ 21-6289) at San Martín 999, the *Cine Gran Rex* (☎ 21-3805) at San Martín 1139, and the *Cine Atlas* (☎ 26-0252) at Mitre 643 show first-run movies.

Theater *Teatro Vivencias* (☎ 21-7045), Mendoza 1171, is an alternative theater venue.

Spectator Sports
Rosario has two first-division soccer teams. Newell's Old Boys (☎ 21-1180), in danger of relegation after the 1994-1995 season, has its offices and plays at *Estadio Parque Independencia.* Rosario Central (☎ 21-0000) has offices at Mitre 857, but its stadium (☎ 38-9595) is at Blvd Avellaneda and Av Génova. Tickets are sold at the stadium, but always call the office to check on game times.

Things to Buy
For regional handicrafts, check out Regionales Tilcara at Ricardone 130, or the Paseo del Arte artisans' market, which takes place Friday, Saturday, and Sunday in Plaza Sarmiento; in summer it occasionally takes place during the week.

The Mercado de Pulgas del Bajo is a picturesque flea market that takes place weekend and holiday afternoons at Av Belgrano and Buenos Aires.

Getting There & Away
Air Aerolíneas Argentinas and Austral (☎ 48-0185) share offices at Santa Fe 1410. Aerolíneas has at least two flights daily to Buenos Aires (US$61), while Wednesday and Sunday flights from Aeroparque continue to São Paulo and Rio de Janeiro. Austral flies weekdays only to Córdoba (US$63).

Bus The Estación Mariano Moreno (☎ 372384, 372385, 372386) is at Cafferata 702, near Santa Fe. Bus No 101 from Calle San Juan goes there.

Chevallier (☎ 38-5551) has services southeast to Buenos Aires (US$15, four hours), west to Córdoba, southwest to Neuquén and Bariloche (US$76, 23 hours), north to Tucumán, and northeast to Corrientes. Ablo/Costera Criolla (☎ 39-7186) passes through Rosario en route from Buenos Aires to Córdoba (US$20, six hours) and on to La Rioja, and also goes to Mar del Plata, Bahía Blanca, and Comodoro Rivadavia. El Rápido/Tata (☎ 39-8493) connects Buenos Aires, Rosario, Santa Fe, Santiago del Estero, and Corrientes, while ESAP goes to Buenos Aires, La Plata, and Mar del Plata. La Unión/La Veloz del Norte (☎ 37-0466) serves Santiago del Estero, Tucumán, and Salta, while TAC (☎ 38-9706) has buses to Mendoza, Buenos Aires, and Córdoba. El Santiagueño stops in Rosario en route between La Plata and Santiago del Estero.

Ciudad de Posadas/Expreso Panamericano (☎ 38-4752) goes to Resistencia, Corrientes, and Posadas, as do Kurtz and El Norte Bis. Puerto Tirol (☎ 39-5894) stops in Rosario en route between Buenos Aires and Formosa. Empresa Argentina (☎ 39-4398) goes to La Plata (US$22, six hours) and Mar del Plata, while Tirsa (☎ 39-0842) goes to Mar del Plata and Bariloche. Casilda (☎ 37-0579) serves the Sierras de Córdoba. El Trebol/La Estrella goes to Tucumán.

Rosario has international services with

La Internacional (☎ 38-8748) to Asunción and Ciudad del Este (Paraguay), and Pluma to Porto Alegre and Rio de Janeiro (Brazil). Cora (☎ 38-0038), El Rápido Internacional and Monticas/Empresa General Artigas (☎ 30-4164) go to Montevideo (Uruguay). Encon goes to Montevideo, Piriápolis, and Punta del Este.

Train For intercity passenger service on the Ferrocarril Mitre, three times weekly between Retiro (Buenos Aires) and Tucumán, use Estación Rosario Norte (☎ 39-2429), Av del Valle 2700. Bus No 120 from Calle San Juan and Mitre goes there.

Getting Around
To/From the Airport Aerolíneas Argentinas runs direct buses to Aeropuerto Fisherton, eight km west of town.

Bus Rosario has a very extensive public bus system, mostly leaving from the local bus station around Plaza Sarmiento.

Train The Ferrocarril Mitre also runs local trains to suburbs such as Fisherton.

Car Rental Try Ovalle (☎ 21-6592) at Santa Fe 837.

La Pampa Province

For most Argentines, the province of La Pampa is like the Great Plains or the prairies for Americans and Canadians – a place you cross to get somewhere else. Primarily an agricultural zone, it was settled later than the province of Buenos Aires because Indian resistance deterred European incursions much longer, and because its erratic rainfall made agriculture more unpredictable than in the Humid Pampas toward the Atlantic. It borders six other provinces: Río Negro, Nequén, Mendoza, San Luis, Córdoba, and Buenos Aires.

No one would visit Argentina just to go to La Pampa, even though its capital city of

Santa Rosa is an attractive administrative and service center, but its little-known Parque Nacional Lihué Calel more than justifies a detour from the standard routes to and from Patagonia. Travelers returning from Neuquén to Buenos Aires will find its tranquil granitic peaks a very interesting alternative.

Despite the monotony implied by its name, La Pampa offers a variety of environments, including rolling hills with native *caldén* forests, desert zones with saline lakes which support flamingos and other birds, and extensive native grasslands.

SANTA ROSA
In the midst of the Pampas, 600 km from Buenos Aires, Santa Rosa de Toay was not legally founded until 1892. French, Spanish, and Italian immigrants arrived with the expansion of the railroads at the turn of the 19th century, but one measure of its continuing isolation and insignificance was that, until 1951, the surrounding area remained a territory rather than a province. Santa Rosa is now a clean, pleasant city with a population of about 80,000.

Orientation
Santa Rosa is only 80 km from the Buenos Aires provincial border on RN 5, which is paved all the way from the Federal Capital. RN 35 goes north to Córdoba and southeast to Bahía Blanca.

North of Av España, the city consists of a standard grid centered on Plaza San Martín and its surrounding streets, where most businesses are located. A more recent focus of activity is the modern Centro Cívico on Av Pedro Luro, seven blocks east. One km west, Laguna Don Tomás is a major recreational resource for city residents. In the quadrant southwest of the junction of Av España and Av Pedro Luro, streets trend northwest to southeast, rather than north to south.

Information
Tourist Offices The enthusiastic and helpful Dirección Provincial de Turismo

(☎ 24404) is at Av Pedro Luro and Av San Martín, directly across from the bus terminal. The English-speaking staff have maps and brochures, and there's an interesting selection of local handicrafts in the Mercado Artesanal (see below). Hours are weekdays 7 am to 8 pm, weekends 9 am to noon and 4 to 8 pm.

The Municipalidad maintains a Centro de Información Turística at the bus terminal, open 24 hours. ACA (☎ 22435) is at Av San Martín 102, at the corner of Coronel Gil.

Money Several banks will change money, though not traveler's checks. Banco de la Nación is at Av Roca 1, at the southeast corner of Plaza San Martín, but there are several others, including Banco Dorrego and Banco Hispano Corfin, along Av Pellegrini, one block west and one block north. Banco de la Pampa has an ATM on Av Luro, alongside the provincial tourist office, and another at Pellegrini 255.

Post & Telecommunications Correo Argentino is at Hilario Lagos 258 near Rivadavia; Telefónica is next door. Santa Rosa's postal code is 6300, while the area code is 0954.

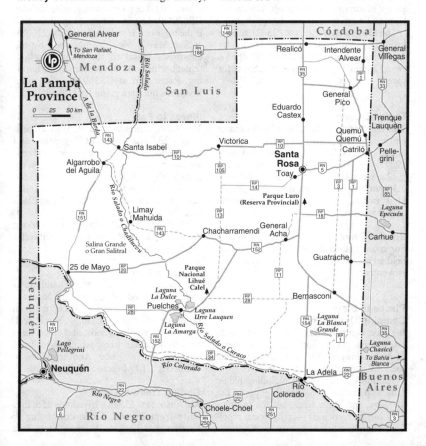

Travel Agencies Santa Rosa has a number of downtown travel agencies, including Swiss Travel (☎ 25952) at Pellegrini 219 and Vega Viajes (☎ 33415) at Garibaldi 426.

Medical Services The Hospital Lucio Molas (☎ 27033) is at Raúl P Diaz and Pilcomayo, two km north of downtown.

Museums

At Pellegrini 190, the **Museo de Ciencias Naturales y Antropológicas** (☎ 22693) contains natural science, archaeological, historical, artisanal, and fine-arts collections. Hours are 8 am to 5 pm weekdays except in summer, when it's open mornings only, and 6 pm to 1 am Sundays.

The **Museo de Artes** (☎ 27332), at 9 de Julio and Villegas, contains works by Argentine and provincial artists. It's open 8 am to 1 pm daily, with extended hours for special exhibits.

Teatro Español

This theater (☎ 24520), Santa Rosa's major performing arts venue, dates from the turn of the century but was not finished until 1927. At Hilario Lagos 54, it's open to the public weekdays 10 am to noon and 4 to 6:30 pm; weekend hours depend on scheduled events, which take priority over casual visits.

Special Event

For more than a decade, Santa Rosa has held a Festival de Jazz the first weekend of November.

Places to Stay

Camping One of Argentina's last remaining free *campgrounds* is the comfortable site at Laguna Don Tomás, at the west end of Av Uruguay. From the bus terminal, take the local Transporte El Indio bus.

Facilities are excellent, including picnic tables, parrillas, a swimming pool, hot showers, and shade trees, but the mosquitoes can be ferocious – bring some repellent. There is a fitness course for joggers.

Hospedajes, Hosterías & Hotels Except for camping, really cheap accommodations are hard to find. The most reasonable is *Hospedaje Mitre* (☎ 25432), a short distance from the bus terminal at Emilio Mitre 74. Singles/doubles with shared bath are US$15/27, while those with private bath are about US$21/34. Rates are virtually identical at *Hostería Santa Rosa* (☎ 23868), Hipólito Yrigoyen 696. At *Hostería Río Atuel* (☎ 22597), conveniently across from the bus terminal at Av Pedro Luro 356, rooms with private bath are slightly costlier at US$28/42.

The central *Hotel San Martín* (☎ 22549), Alsina 101, has rooms with private bath for US$29/49. The uncontested top of the line is the high-rise *Hotel Calfucurá* (☎ 23608), at San Martín 695, distinguished by the enormous mural of the Indian cacique (chief), which climbs the sides of the building. Rates start at US$69/88, with more luxurious quarters going for US$83/106.

Places to Eat

The *Club Español* (☎ 23935) at Hilario Lagos 237 has excellent Argentine and Spanish food, outstanding service, and reasonable prices. For regional specialties, try *Rancho de Pampa Cuatro* at Corrientes 69, opposite the bus terminal. At *Señor Quintana,* Urquiza 336, the US$11 parrillada includes a superb buffet.

There are several other parrillas along Av Pedro Luro and a number of confiterías around Plaza San Martín.

Things to Buy

For traditional gaucho-style handicrafts and similar goods, don't miss the Mercado Artesanal in the tourist office, with its excellent selection, including horse gear, silverwork, woolen goods, and wood carvings from caldén trees, which cover large areas of the province. Another place to check out is El Matrero at Pellegrini 86.

Getting There & Away

Air Austral (☎ 22388), Rivadavia 256, flies daily from Buenos Aires, continuing to Viedma and back to Buenos Aires in a

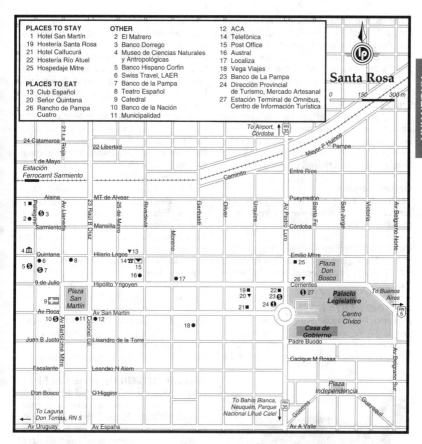

PLACES TO STAY	OTHER	12 ACA
1 Hotel San Martín	2 El Matrero	14 Telefónica
19 Hostería Santa Rosa	3 Banco Dorrego	15 Post Office
21 Hotel Calfucurá	4 Museo de Ciencias Naturales	16 Austral
22 Hostería Río Atuel	y Antropológicas	17 Localiza
25 Hospedaje Mitre	5 Banco Hispano Corfin	18 Vega Viajes
	6 Swiss Travel, LAER	23 Banco de La Pampa
PLACES TO EAT	7 Banco de la Pampa	24 Dirección Provincial
13 Club Español	8 Teatro Español	de Turismo, Mercado Artesanal
20 Señor Quintana	9 Catedral	27 Estación Terminal de Omnibus,
26 Rancho de Pampa	10 Banco de la Nación	Centro de Información Turística
Cuatro	11 Municipalidad	

Santa Rosa

counter-clockwise pattern. The fare to either Viedma or Buenos Aires is US$105.

LAER (☎ 25952), Pellegrini 219, flies Monday, Wednesday, and Friday from Buenos Aires to Santa Rosa (US$99) and General Pico (US$21), then back to Buenos Aires.

Bus The Estación Terminal de Omnibus (☎ 22952, 22249) is at the Centro Cívico, Av Pedro Luro 365. Chevallier (☎ 27056) has four buses daily to Buenos Aires (US$28, six hours), plus one bus daily to San Martín de los Andes and Bariloche (US$50, 21 hours). Chevallier has the only

regular service that passes Parque Nacional Lihué Calel (US$22) en route to Neuquén (US$28); it leaves Wednesday at midnight. El Valle and Alto Valle (☎ 22952 for both) go to Neuquén as well.

Empresa Pehuenche (☎ 22952) also goes to Neuquén and Buenos Aires. La Estrella (☎ 32841) has additional service to Buenos Aires, while Liniers (☎ 31113) goes to La Plata. El Rápido (☎ 31113) serves Mar del Plata.

TUS (☎ 32140) has services to the Mesopotamian littoral, while TUP (☎ 32140) goes to Comodoro Rivadavia and Caleta Olivia. Andesmar (☎ 32841) buses between Mendoza (12 hours) and Bahía Blanca (4½ hours), and between Mendoza and Caleta Olivia (19 hours), stop in Santa Rosa. Ticsa (☎ 22952) goes to San Juan, while Dumas and Jocolí, both at the same office as Ticsa, go to San Luis.

Train The Ferrocarril Sarmiento (☎ 33451) is at Alsina and Pellegrini, but services have declined and are much slower and less convenient than buses. There continue to be trains to Estación Once (in Buenos Aires) Sunday, Wednesday, and Friday at 10 pm.

Getting Around
To/From the Airport Taxis will carry passengers to the airport, three km from town, for about US$3.

Car Rental Driving is the best way to visit Parque Nacional Lihué Calel. Try Localiza (☎ 25773) at Moreno and Hipólito Yrigoyen.

AROUND SANTA ROSA
Reserva Provincial Parque Luro
Originally a private hunting reserve, this 7500-hectare park, 35 km south of Santa Rosa, now belongs to the province of La Pampa. Doctor Pedro Luro, an influential early resident, imported exotic game species such as Carpathian deer and European boar into its pastures and native caldén forests. He also built an enormous French-style mansion (now a museum), formerly known as the Castle, to accommodate foreign hunters.

With the decline of sport hunting by the European aristocracy during and after WWI, followed by the Great Depression, the reserve fell into disrepair, and animals escaped through holes in the fences. During and after WWII, another landowner exploited its forests for firewood and charcoal, grazed cattle and sheep, and bred polo ponies. Since its acquisition by the province in 1965, it has served as a recreational and historical resource for the people of La Pampa, offering a visitors center, bikepaths, and several short hiking trails.

Parque Luro is open daily except Monday, 9 am to 8 pm in summer and 9 am to 5 pm the rest of the year. Besides the museum, there are picnic areas, a small zoo, and a collection of turn-of-the-century carriages. Camping is possible in a new campground for about US$3 per person. There is also a modest admission charge.

PARQUE NACIONAL LIHUÉ CALEL
Like the Sierras de Tandil and the Sierra de la Ventana in Buenos Aires province, Parque Nacional Lihué Calel (a Pehuenche phrase meaning Sierra de la Vida or the Range of Life) is a series of small, isolated mountain ranges and valleys in an otherwise nearly featureless landscape, situated 226 km southwest of Santa Rosa. Its salmon-colored, exfoliating granites, resembling parts of the Joshua Tree National Monument in California's Mojave Desert, do not exceed 600 meters but still offer a variety of subtle environments, which change with the season and even with the day, providing a refuge from the monotony of the Pampas.

Though Lihué Calel is a desert, receiving only about 400 mm rainfall per annum, water is an important factor in the landscape. Sudden storms can bring flash floods

If you're lucky, you may catch a glimpse of a puma while at Parque Nacional Lihué Calel.

or create impressive ephemeral waterfalls over the nicks in the granite near the visitors center. Even when the sky is cloudless, the subterranean streams in the valleys nourish the monte, a scrub forest with a surprising variety of plant species. Within the park's 10,000 hectares exist 345 species of plants, nearly half the total found in the entire province.

In this thinly populated area survives wildlife now extinct in the Humid Pampas farther east – on my most recent visit, I saw a puma *(Felis concolor)* in the park campground, although the large cats are not common. Other cats are more likely to be seen, including Geoffroy's cat *(Felis geoffroyi)* and the yaguarundi *(Felis yagouaroundi)*. There also remain other large mammals like the guanaco *(Lama guanicoe)*, which is more common on the Patagonian steppe, and smaller species such as the *mara* or Patagonian hare *(Dolichotis patagonicum)* and *vizcacha (Lagostomus maximus)*, a wild relative of the domestic chinchilla.

The wide variety of birds includes the rhea or *ñandú (Rhea americana)* and many birds of prey including the *carancho* or crested caracara *(Polyborus plancus)*. Although you are not likely to encounter them, be aware of the highly poisonous pit vipers commonly known as *yarará (Bothrops spp.)*.

Until General Roca's so-called Conquista del Desierto (Conquest of the Desert), Araucanian Indians successfully defended the area against European invasion. Archaeological evidence, including numerous petroglyphs, is proof of their presence and of that of their ancestors. Lihué Calel was the last refuge of the Araucanian cacique (leader) Namuncurá, who hid for several years before surrendering to Argentine forces.

Things to See & Do
From the park campground, an excellent signed nature trail follows an intermittent stream through a dense thorn forest of caldén *(Prosopis caldenia),* a local species of a common worldwide genus, and other typical trees. This trail leads to a petroglyph site, unfortunately vandalized since 1927. The exceptionally friendly and knowledgeable rangers accompany visitors if their schedule permits.

During and after rainstorms, the granite boulders on the upper stream course briefly form spectacular waterfalls. There is a marked trail to the 589-meter peak which bears the unwieldy name of **Cerro de la Sociedad Científica Argentina,** but the climb is gradual enough in any direction that you can choose your route. Watch for flowering cacti such as *Trichocereus candicans* between the boulders, but be advised that the granite is very slippery when wet. From the summit, there are outstanding views of the entire Sierra and its surrounding marshes and salt lakes, such as Laguna Urre Lauquen to the southwest.

If you have time or a vehicle, hike or drive to the **Viejo Casco,** the big house of the former Estancia Santa María before the provincial government expropriated the land, which was later transferred to the national park system. It is possible to make a circuit via the **Valle de las Pinturas,** where there are more, undamaged petroglyphs. Ask the rangers for directions.

Places to Stay
Near the visitors center is a very comfortable *campground* with shade trees, picnic tables, firepits, clean toilets, cold showers (summer weather is hot enough for them to be acceptable), and electricity until 11 pm. Nearby you're likely to see foxes, vizcachas, and many, many birds. There is no charge, but bring food – the nearest available supplies are at the town of Puelches, 35 km south. On the highway, it is possible to stay at the *ACA Hostería,* which charges US$20/30 single/double and also has a restaurant.

Getting There & Away
Most buses between Santa Rosa and Neuquén now use RP 20; the only remaining regular bus service using RN 152 from Santa Rosa to Chelforó (on RN 22 in Río

ARGENTINA

Negro province) is Chevallier's weekly service to Neuquén at midnight Wednesday, which drops passengers at Lihué Calel in the predawn hours for US$22.

Recently, however, Rapibus (☎ 28903) at Av Luro 1340 in Santa Rosa has begun a minibus service to and from the town of Puelches (US$12) on Monday, Wednesday, and Friday at 6 am; it passes Lihué Calel en route. The only other alternative would be to take a bus to the RP 152 junction at El Carancho and hitch south from there.

Argentine Mesopotamia

Mesopotamia is that part of Argentina between the Paraná and Uruguay rivers, comprising the provinces of Entre Ríos, Corrientes, and Misiones. Historically, the rivers' winding channels and sandbars made navigation difficult above present-day Rosario (Santa Fe province), while their breadth made cross-river communications equally awkward. In effect, Mesopotamia was an island. The area between and along the rivers is commonly known as the littoral.

Subtropical Misiones, northeast of Corrientes, is Argentina's political geographic peninsula between the Paraná and Uruguay, nearly surrounded by the countries of Paraguay and Brazil. Its most spectacular attraction is the awesome series of waterfalls known collectively as the Cataratas del Iguazú, the location for the successful film *The Mission*. Corrientes borders both Brazil and Uruguay to the east, and the provinces of Chaco and Santa Fe to the west.

History

In history and geography, Mesopotamia differs greatly from the Argentine heartland. Nomadic hunter-gatherers populated the temperate Pampas when Europeans first arrived, but the Guaraní peoples, from northern Entre Ríos through Corrientes and into Paraguay and Brazil, were semisedentary agriculturalists, raising sweet potatoes, maize, manioc, and beans. Riverine fish also played an important role in their diet.

Rumors of wealthy Indian civilizations first drew Europeans to the region. Pedro de Mendoza led the earliest expedition to the Río de la Plata, the estuary formed by the two rivers, but his founding of Buenos Aires in 1536 proved ephemeral when Querandí Indians drove out his sick, starved, and ill-prepared men, delaying the city's re-establishment for nearly half a century. The following year, Mendoza's lieutenant Pedro de Ayolas established a beachhead in the upper Paraná at Asunción, where the Spanish could obtain food and supplies from the friendlier Guaraní. Settlement thus proceeded southward from Asunción rather than northward from Buenos Aires. Corrientes was founded in 1588, and Santa Fe about the same time. For further information on early Spanish settlement in the upper Paraná, see the Paraguay section of this book.

Jesuit missionaries helped colonize the upper Uruguay and Paraná rivers, concentrating the native Guaraní populations in settlements and at least approaching the Spanish ideal of reciprocal rights and responsibilities in dealing with native peoples. To be sure, the Jesuit fathers exploited native labor on their *yerba mate* (Paraguayan tea) plantations, but they also conscientiously taught the Spanish language, Catholic religion, and other European customs to their charges. Portuguese slavers' and secular Spaniards' jealousy of the missions' economic success and their monopolization of the Indian labor force led to expulsion of the Jesuits and the disintegration of mission communities, but their ruins, which today attract many visitors to Misiones province, are monuments to an extraordinary period of history. The presence of the Guaraní is reflected in many place names and linguistic survivals, such as the common usage of the words *gurí*, meaning "child," by the general populace. Perhaps 15,000 Guaraní remain in the region

Entre Ríos Province

This province's name literally describes its location between the region's two major waterways. Covered by rolling grasslands, with gallery forests lining its riverbanks, Entre Ríos has always supported livestock enterprises, but it is also an important

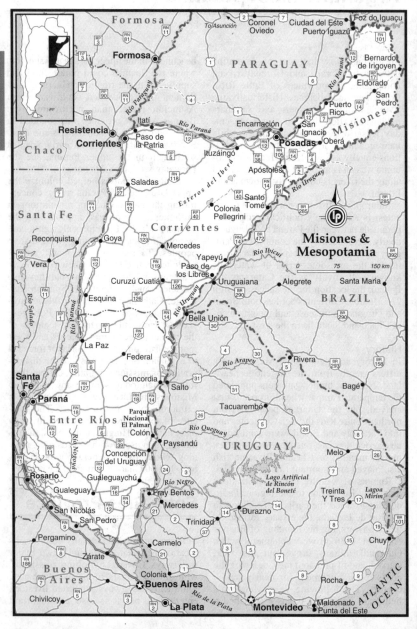

Misiones &
Mesopotamia

agricultural center. Fiercely independent from Buenos Aires, at one time even declaring itself an independent republic, it ironically became a Unitarist stronghold after dictator Juan Manuel de Rosas took power there. Local caudillo Justo José Urquiza, commanding an army of provincial loyalists, Unitarists, Brazilians, and Uruguayans, was in large part responsible for the demise of Rosas and the eventual adoption of Argentina's modern constitution.

The provincial economy formerly resembled that of Buenos Aires. Large landowners, including Urquiza himself, controlled extensive cattle estancias. Like their Buenos Aires counterparts, these estancias salted their beef and prepared hides for export at riverside locations. By the 1880s, colonization schemes managed to settle 15,000 European immigrant farmers in the province, including Russo-Germans south of Paraná and Russian Jews near Basavilbaso west of Concepción.

In the early years of the 20th century, improved cattle breeds began to displace Entre Ríos' native criollo types. Poor rail connections with Buenos Aires, not established until 1908 and even then via ferry rather than bridges, retarded economic modernization. Locally built meat freezer plants brought greater prosperity, but construction of the Zárate-Brazo Largo bridge across the Río de la Plata delta has enabled much of the livestock processing industry to move south to Buenos Aires province.

For visitors, Entre Ríos' principal attractions are the rivers and their recreational opportunities. These include camping and fishing in winter, spring, and autumn, when the weather is not oppressively hot. Parque Nacional El Palmar, established to protect the region's declining native palm forests, is only a few hours north of Buenos Aires on the Río Uruguay. There are several bridges across the river to the neighboring republic of Uruguay.

PARANÁ
One of Mesopotamia's oldest cities, Paraná is also the provincial capital. Although it has no official founding date, most residents associate it with the establishment of the Parroquia (parish) del Rosario de la Bajada in 1730. From 1853 to 1861, it was capital of the short-lived Argentine Confederation, but eventually lost its primacy to Buenos Aires. In April 1994 it hosted the Convención Constituyente, which rewrote the Argentine constitution to permit President Carlos Menem to run for re-election.

Paraná is a pleasant, modern city (population 250,000) whose major attraction is the river itself, accented by large public parks and campgrounds. The most important public buildings date from the 19th century. Paraná and neighboring Santa Fe, across the river, take pride in having built the subfluvial Uranga Silvestre Begnis (ex-Hernandárias) tunnel, which connects the two cities, despite apathy and, later, active opposition from the federal government. Paraná is an unusual hotbed of interest in North American softball, having hosted national and international tournaments, including the 1995 Panamerican Games.

Orientation
Paraná sits on a high bluff on the east bank of the Río Paraná, 500 km north of Buenos Aires via RN 9 to Rosario and RN 11 to Santa Fe; approaches through southern Entre Ríos are shorter but slower because of substandard roads. Its city plan is more irregular than most Argentine cities, with numerous diagonals, curving boulevards, and complex intersections. Plaza 1 de Mayo is the town center, through which Calle Jose de San Martín is a peatonal for six blocks. On Saturday mornings, virtually the entire town congregates for a *paseo* (outing) here.

Except for Calle San Martín, street names change on all sides of the plaza. At the west end of Calle San Martín, Parque Urquiza extends more than a kilometer along the riverfront and the bluffs above it. Many other attractive parks and plazas are scattered throughout the city.

Information
Tourist Offices The Secretaría de Turismo Municipal (☎ 22-1632) is at 25 de Mayo

ARGENTINA

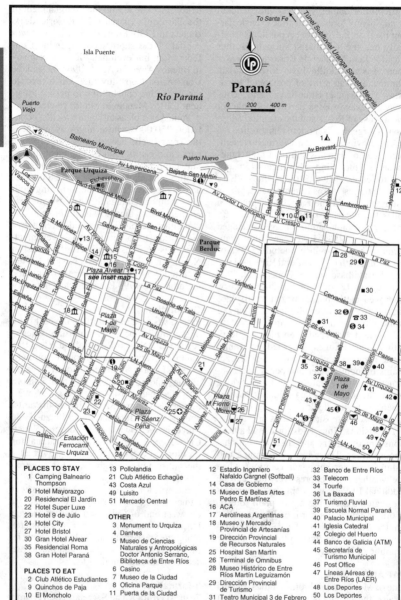

Paraná

Río Paraná

To Santa Fe

Túnel Subfluvial Uranga Silvestre Begnis

Isla Puente

Puerto Viejo

0   200   400 m

Balneario Municipal

Puerto Nuevo

Av Bravard

Parque Urquiza

Av Laurencena

Bajada San Martín

Av Doctor Laurencena

Av Crespo

Parque Berduc

Plaza Alvear

see inset map

Plaza 1 de Mayo

Av Urquiza

Plaza M Fierro Moreno

Plaza R Sáenz Peña

Estación Ferrocarril Urquiza

Plaza 1 de Mayo

Av Urquiza

La Paz

PLACES TO STAY
1 Camping Balneario Thompson
6 Hotel Mayorazgo
20 Residencial El Jardín
22 Hotel Super Luxe
23 Hotel 9 de Julio
24 Hotel City
27 Hotel Bristol
30 Gran Hotel Alvear
35 Residencial Roma
38 Gran Hotel Paraná

PLACES TO EAT
2 Club Atlético Estudiantes
9 Quinchos de Paja
10 El Moncholo

13 Pollolandia
21 Club Atlético Echagüe
43 Costa Azul
49 Luisito
51 Mercado Central

OTHER
3 Monument to Urquiza
4 Danhes
5 Museo de Ciencias Naturales y Antropológicas Doctor Antonio Serrano, Biblioteca de Entre Ríos
6 Casino
7 Museo de la Ciudad
8 Oficina Parque
11 Puerta de la Ciudad

12 Estadio Ingeniero Nafaldo Cargnel (Softball)
14 Casa de Gobierno
16 Museo de Bellas Artes Pedro E Martínez
17 ACA
17 Aerolíneas Argentinas
18 Museo y Mercado Provincial de Artesanías
19 Dirección Provincial de Recursos Naturales
25 Hospital San Martín
26 Terminal de Omnibus
28 Museo Histórico de Entre Ríos Martín Leguizamón
29 Dirección Provincial de Turismo
31 Teatro Municipal 3 de Febrero

32 Banco de Entre Ríos
33 Telecom
34 Tourfe
36 La Baxada
37 Turismo Fluvial
39 Escuela Normal Paraná
40 Palacio Municipal
41 Iglesia Catedral
42 Colegio del Huerto
44 Banco de Galicia (ATM)
45 Secretaría de Turismo Municipal
46 Post Office
47 Líneas Aéreas de Entre Ríos (LAER)
48 Los Deportes
50 Los Deportes

44, on the Plaza 1 de Mayo; daily hours are from 8 am to 8 pm. There are branches at the bus terminal, at the Oficina Parque (☎ 23-3677) on the riverfront at Bajada San Martín and Av Laurencena, and at the newly constructed Puerta de la Ciudad (Gates of the City) at Av Crespo and Calle Florida.

The Dirección Provincial de Turismo (☎ 21-3231) is at Laprida 5.

ACA (☎ 21-1522) is at Buenos Aires 333, near Laprida.

Money Tourfe, the local cambio, and Banco de Entre Ríos, both on the San Martín peatonal, are as good as any, but there are also ATMs nearby – Banco de Galicia has one at the corner of San Martín and Perú.

Post & Telecommunications Correo Argentino is at 25 de Mayo and Monte Caseros; the postal code is 3100.

Telecom is at San Martín 735, on the peatonal. Paraná's area code is 043.

Medical Services Hospital San Martín (☎ 23-4545) is at Presidente Perón 450, near Gualeguaychú.

Walking Tour

Walkers can see most of Paraná's key buildings in a short stroll starting at Plaza 1 de Mayo, where the post office occupies the erstwhile site of **General Urquiza's residence.** The **Iglesia Catedral** (Cathedral) has been on the plaza since 1730, though the current building dates only from 1885; its museum is open from 5 to 7 pm daily. When Paraná was capital of the Argentine Confederation, the Senate deliberated at the present **Colegio del Huerto,** behind the Catedral at 9 de Julio and 25 de Mayo.

A block west, at Corrientes and Av Urquiza, are the **Palacio Municipal** (1889) and the **Escuela Normal Paraná** (Paraná Normal School), founded by the famous educator and President DF Sarmiento. Across Calle San Martín, at 25 de Junio 60,

is the **Teatro Municipal 3 de Febrero** (1908). At the north end of the San Martín peatonal is **Plaza Alvear,** with a cluster of several important museums. A block west, bounded by Córdoba, Laprida, and Santa Fe, the **Centro Cívico** contains the provincial **Casa de Gobierno** and other government offices. Farther west, along the diagonal Av Rivadavia, is the **Biblioteca de Entre Ríos,** the provincial library.

You can continue to **Parque Urquiza,** walk the length of the park, and double back at the foot of San Martín to return to Plaza 1 de Mayo. The park has a number of significant monuments, including the **Monumento a Urquiza,** and also features the new **Museo de la Ciudad,** at the corner of Av Laurencena and San Martín.

Museo de la Ciudad

Only very recently inaugurated, the Museo de la Ciudad (☎ 23-4454) focuses on Paraná's urban past and surroundings. On the costanera Av Laurencena in Parque Urquiza, it's open Monday 3 to 7 pm, Tuesday to Saturday 9 am to noon and 3 to 6 pm, and Sunday 5 to 9 pm.

Museo Histórico de Entre Ríos Martín Leguizamón

This modern, well-arranged museum (☎ 21-2735) at Plaza Alvear, Laprida and Buenos Aires, flaunts the regional pride of entrerrianos. The knowledgeable but patronizing guides go to rhetorical extremes to emphasize the importance of provincial caudillos and their role in Argentine history. There are excellent collections of portraits and 19th-century artifacts of provincial life.

Admission charges are nominal. Hours are Tuesday to Friday 8:30 am to noon and 2 to 8 pm, Saturday 9 am to noon and 3 to 6 pm, and Sunday 9 am to noon.

Museo de Bellas Artes Pedro E Martínez

This subterranean museum (☎ 21-1527), just off Plaza Alvear at Buenos Aires 355, displays oil paintings, illustrations, and sculptures by provincial artists. Morning hours are Tuesday to Sunday, 9 am to noon all year. Winter afternoon hours are 3 to 6 pm Tuesday to Saturday; in summer, afternoon hours are 5 to 8 pm.

Museo y Mercado Provincial de Artesanías

At Av Urquiza 1239, this combined crafts center and museum (☎ 22-4540) displays and sells handicrafts from throughout the province. Materials include wood, ceramics, leather, metal, bone, iron, and others. Hours are 8:30 am to 12:30 pm daily except Sunday, and 4 to 8 pm weekdays only.

Museo de Ciencias Naturales y Antropológicas Doctor Antonio Serrano

This partially remodeled museum (☎ 21-2635) at Av Rivadavia 462, containing natural history and archaeological specimens, is open Tuesday to Friday 8:30 am to noon and 1:30 to 6 pm, Saturday from 9 am to noon and 3 to 6 pm.

Túnel Subfluvial Uranga Silvestre Begnis

Until this tunnel beneath the Río Paraná opened in 1969, the provincial capitals of Paraná and Santa Fe had to rely on ferryboats for interurban transport. The federal government, then building a bridge between Buenos Aires province and southern Entre Ríos, refused even to allow the two provinces to build a bridge, a right reserved to Buenos Aires. This forced the provinces into the more difficult and costly (US$60 million) alternative – the 2.4-km tunnel beneath the Paraná's main channel. On its 25th anniversary in 1994, the tunnel was renamed to honor former Entre Ríos governor Raúl Lucio Uranga and former Santa Fe governor Carlos Silvestre Begnis, who tenaciously promoted the project despite federal opposition.

Free of charge, hourly guided tours of the tunnel include a film and visit to the control center; any bus to Santa Fe will drop you at the tunnel entrance. Daily hours are 8 am to 6 pm all year.

Motorists should be aware of irritating document checks from the provincial police at each end of the tunnel. The toll for passenger vehicles is US$2.

Activities

Fishing River fishing is a popular local pastime, and tasty local game species like boga, sábalo, dorado, and surubí reach considerable size. Licenses are available through the Dirección Provincial de Recursos Naturales at Monte Caseros 195. For more detailed information, see the entry on Paso de la Patria, Corrientes province.

Water Sports Boating, water-skiing, windsurfing, and swimming are popular pastimes for much of the year. Sporting goods are available at Los Deportes (☎ 21-3991), at 9 de Julio 178 and Calle San Martín 732.

River Excursions Hour-long excursions on the motor vessel *Realidad II* leave from the Puerto Nuevo at Costanera and Vélez Sarsfield daily at 5:20 pm, costing US$7; make reservations at Turismo Fluvial (☎ 22-5104), San Martín 960. The *Realidad II* also runs passengers over to nearby Isla Puente for picnics and the like, for US$2.50 roundtrip; departures are more or less hourly between 10:30 am and 8 pm.

Special Events

Every January, Paraná hosts the Fiesta Provincial de Música y Artesanía Entrerriana, featuring regional folk music. In October, the Fiesta Provincial del Inmigrante acknowledges immigrants' contributions to provincial development.

Perhaps the most unusual event is February's recently revived Maratón Internacional Hernandárias-Paraná, an 88-km swim that attracts contestants from around the world. First held in 1965 – 1966, the race was not held again until 1993 (when the winner was Germany's Christof Wandratsch) and 1994 (when the winner was Canada's Gregory Streppel). It is part of Paraná's annual Fiesta del Río.

At Diamante, 44 km south of Paraná, the January Fiesta Nacional de Jineteada y

Folklore celebrates gaucho culture and music. Diamante also is the site of the Fiesta Provincial del Pescador (Provincial Fisherman's Festival) in February.

Places to Stay – bottom end

Camping There are numerous campgrounds in and around Paraná. Closest to downtown and to Parque Urquiza is shady *Camping Balneario Thompson* (☎ 22-1998), which can be noisy on weekends when locals gather for all-night asados. The cold showers are of no concern in the summer, but choose your time in more changeable spring and autumn weather. Sites cost US$8 for two persons, US$10 for four. Buses Nos 1 and 6, with the sign "Thompson," go between the campground and the center. Beware of *jejenes,* annoying biting insects, along the river in summer.

There are other good campgrounds at *Toma Vieja* (☎ 24-2622), the old waterworks, a few kiometers outside town but accessible by bus No 5, and at *Los Arenales* (☎ 24-3727), reached by bus No 1 (red). Prices are roughly comparable to Balneario Thompson.

Hotels Compared to Santa Fe, accommodations in Paraná are fairly limited in all categories and not particularly cheap. The best budget place is *Hotel City* (☎ 21-0086) at Blvd Racedo 231, directly opposite the train station, with a wonderful patio garden and cool rooms with high ceilings. Singles/ doubles are US$19/30 with private bath, slightly less with shared bath; unlike other lower priced places, it accepts credit cards.

Prices are similar at *Hotel 9 de Julio* (☎ 21-3047), 9 de Julio 674, half a block from the train station; at *Residencial El Jardín* (☎ 22-1685) at Belgrano 386; and at downtown *Residencial Roma* at Urquiza 1061. *Hotel Bristol* (☎ 21-3961), near the bus station at Alsina 221 between Ruiz Moreno and Av Echagüe, is more expensive at US$24/35, but clean and attractive.

Places to Stay – middle

The modern but drab *Hotel Super Luxe* (☎ 21-2787), Villaguay 162 between 9 de

Julio and Monte Caseros, has rooms with private bath at US$30/45. *Gran Hotel Alvear* (☎ 22-0000), San Martín 637, charges US$42/58.

Places to Stay – top end

Gran Hotel Paraná (☎ 22-3900), at Urquiza 976 on Plaza 1 de Mayo, has rooms with private bath and many other conveniences for about US$55/77, but the new kid on the block is the five-star *Hotel Mayorazgo* (☎ 23-0333), in Parque Urquiza at Etchevehere and Miranda, where singles/doubles with a full buffet breakfast cost US$115/145.

Places to Eat

River fish is the local specialty; for a bargain on tasty grilled boga, try the takeout *Pollolandia* (☎ 21-3671), Tucumán 418, which also grills chicken over coals. Traditionally one of Paraná's best restaurants is *Luisito* (☎ 21-6912), 9 de Julio 140.

Other recommended restaurants include *El Moncholo* at Av Crespo and Scalabrini, *Quinchos de Paja* (☎ 23-1845) at Av Laurencena and Bajada San Martín, the *Club Atlético Echagüe* (☎ 21-2099) at 25 de Mayo 555, and the *Club Atlético Estudiantes* (☎ 21-8440) at the west end of Av Laurencena. *Don Charras* (☎ 22-3186) is a highly regarded parrilla at Av Raúl Uranga 1127. You might also try *Los Quinchos,* which is at Bravard 280, near Balneario Thompson.

A good palce to stock up on food is the *Mercado Central.* For ice cream, go to *Costa Azul,* Calle San Martín 1059. Ice cream shops on the littoral invariably have water coolers, a welcome relief in the oppressive summer heat.

Entertainment

Theater The municipal *Teatro 3 de Febrero* at 25 de Junio 60 puts on exhibitions of local art, inexpensive films, and other activities.

Casino If you have money to spare, you can gamble at the casino at *Etchevehere* in Parque Urquiza, but remember that the

Spanish term for slot machine is *traga-monedas* (coin-swallower). Winter hours are from 9 pm to 3 am, summer hours from 9:30 pm to 3:30 am.

Dance Clubs *La Baxada* is an Art Deco-style club on Av Urquiza, next to the former Plaza Hotel. Other nightspots worth checking out are *Escándolo* on Av Estrada, west of the Puerto Viejo, and *Danhes,* near the Urquiza monument at the west end of Av Rivadavia.

Spectator Sports
In 1995 Paraná hosted the men's and women's Panamerican Games softball championships at its Estadio Ingeniero Nafaldo Cargnel, near the entrance to the tunnel to Santa Fe, but the sport has been popular since the 1960s. From the number of children and teenagers walking around town in softball uniforms, you might think you were in a small town in the American Midwest on a summer weekend; to talk baseball or buy a new glove or bat, visit Víctor Centurión's specialty shop Béisbol y Softbol, in the gallery at Gran Hotel Paraná, Urquiza 976.

Both youth and adult leagues play on the city's eight fields, three of which are lit at night. Both slow- and fast-pitch versions are popular; the level of play varies, but it can be excellent. Games take place almost every night at the *stadium,* with free admission except for special events like regional or national championships.

Getting There & Away
Air Aerolíneas Argentinas (☎ 21-0003) has offices at Corrientes 563, but flights leave from Santa Fe's airport at Sauce Viejo. See Getting There & Away for Santa Fe for details.

Líneas Aéreas de Entre Ríos (LAER, ☎ 21-6375, 23-0347), 25 de Mayo 119, flies from Paraná to Aeroparque (US$65) four times daily on weekdays, but only once daily on weekends. It has its own minibus service to Aeropuerto Ciudad de Paraná, just outside the city limits.

Bus The new Terminal de Omnibus (☎ 22-1282) is on Av Ramírez between Posadas and Moreno, opposite Plaza Martín Fierro. Paraná is a center for provincial bus services, but Santa Fe is more convenient for long-distance trips. About every hour throughout the day and night, Etacer buses (☎ 21-6809) leave for Santa Fe for US$2.

El Rápido (☎ 23-2080) has seven buses daily to Rosario (US$11, three hours) and five to Buenos Aires (US$26, eight hours), as does Flecha Bus. San José also goes to Rosario, while Empresa Tata goes to northern littoral destinations between Paraná and Corrientes, including La Paz, Esquina, and Goya. Basa/Costera Criolla (☎ 21-6872) has long-distance services to Córdoba, Buenos Aires, Mar del Plata, Neuquén, and Bariloche. Empresa Kurtz offers service to Puerto Yguazú, as does El Litoral. Ciudad de Paraná (☎ 24-2037) goes to Córdoba and TAC to Mendoza.

International carriers include Cora, which goes to Montevideo, Uruguay, and Singer, which travels to Porto Alegre, Brazil.

LA PAZ
On the east bank of the Paraná, about 160 km northwest of the provincial capital, La Paz is known for excellent fishing and good camping. In February it celebrates the Fiesta Nacional de Pesca Variada de Río (national river fishing festival). It also has a regional museum.

The tourist office (☎ 2-2389) is at Echagüe 787. La Paz's postal code is 3190, while the area code is 0437. For modest accommodations, try the basic and rather cramped *Residencial Las Dos M* (☎ 21303) at Urquiza 825, where singles/doubles cost US$12/20. For more comfort there's *Hotel Rivera* (☎ 21419) at San Martín 367 for US$17/27 or *Hotel Milton* (☎ 22232) at Italia 1029 for US$27/39.

GUALEGUAYCHÚ
Founded in 1783 by Tomás de Rocamora, Gualeguaychú (population 85,000) is the first substantial town encountered by travelers arriving in Entre Ríos from Buenos

Aires. While not a major destination for most foreigners, it has considerable historical interest, offers good river recreation, holds one of Argentina's best carnivals, and leads to the most southerly bridge crossing into Uruguay.

Orientation
Some 220 km north of Buenos Aires and 13 km east of RN 14, Gualeguaychú sits on the east bank of the Río Gualeguaychú, a tributary of the Uruguay. Plaza San Martín, occupying four square blocks, is the center of its very regular grid pattern. RN 136 bypasses the city center en route to the Puente Internacional General Libertador San Martín, a toll bridge leading to the Uruguayan city of Fray Bentos.

Information
Tourist Offices The Dirección Municipal de Turismo (☎ 23668) is on Av Costanera near the bridge across the Río Gualeguaychú. It's open 8 am to 10 pm in summer and 8 am to 8 pm in winter, and has good brochures and a list of accommodations, but poor-quality maps. ACA (☎ 26088) is at Urquiza and Chacabuco.

Foreign Consulate Uruguay has a consulate (☎ 26168) at Rivadavia 510.

Money Casa Goyo, on Ayacucho near Calle San Martín, changes cash dollars but not traveler's checks. It's open weekdays 8 am to noon and 4 to 7:30 pm, Saturdays 8 am to noon.

Banco de la Nación is at 25 de Mayo 920, and Banco de Entre Ríos is at 25 de Mayo and España. There's an ATM at 25 de Mayo 851. Banco de la Provincia is on 25 de Mayo between España and Chacabuco.

Post & Telecommunications Correo Argentino is at Urquiza and Angel Elías; the postal code is 2820.

There are long-distance cabinas at the bus terminal and elsewhere around town. Gualeguaychú's area code is 0446.

Medical Services The Hospital Centenario (☎ 27831) is at 25 de Mayo and Pasteur.

Things to See
A handful of colonial buildings remain in Gualeguaychú, in addition to more recent ones important in Argentine political and literary history. During the civil wars of the mid-19th century, Giuseppe Garibaldi once occupied the **Museo Haedo,** the oldest house in town and the municipal museum; at San José 105 just off Plaza San Martín, it's open daily 8 am to noon and 7 to 9 pm. The colonial **Casa de Andrade,** at Andrade and Borques, now contains the Centro Artesanal San José, with a good selection of handicrafts. In the mid-19th century it belonged to entrerriano poet, journalist, diplomat, and politician Olegario Andrade.

At Fray Mocho 135, **Casa de Fray Mocho** was the birthplace of José S Álvarez, founder of the famous and influential satirical magazine *Caras y Caretas* at the turn of the century; Fray Mocho was his pen name. The **Casa de la Cultura,** an unusual building at 25 de Mayo 734 dating from 1920, has occasional public exhibitions and contains the city's **Museo Arqueológico.** At Urquiza 705, the **Teatro Gualeguaychú,** inaugurated in 1914 with a performance of *Aida,* still hosts symphony, ballet, and theater.

The **Museo Ferroviario** is an open-air exhibit of steam locomotives, dining cars, and other hardware from provincial rail history. It's at the Estación Ferrocarril Urquiza, on Piccini at the end of Maipú.

Across the river, **Parque Unzué** is a spacious greenbelt for swimming, picnicking, camping, fishing, and relaxing.

River Tours
Expreso Ciudad de Gualeyguaychú offers two-hour guided river tours, leaving from the Puerto Municipal; for details, contact the Dirección Municipal de Turismo on the costanera.

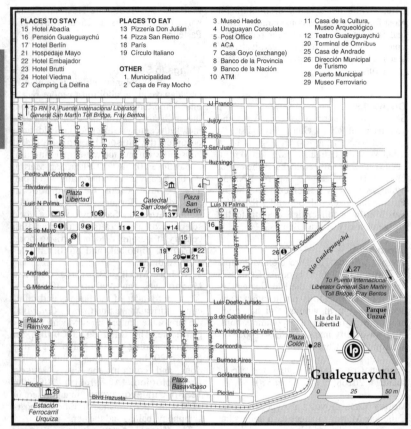

PLACES TO STAY
15 Hotel Abadía
16 Pensión Gualeguaychú
17 Hotel Berlín
21 Hospedaje Mayo
22 Hotel Embajador
23 Hotel Brutti
24 Hotel Viedma
27 Camping La Delfina

PLACES TO EAT
13 Pizzería Don Julián
14 Pizza San Remo
18 París
19 Círculo Italiano

OTHER
 1 Municipalidad
 2 Casa de Fray Mocho
 3 Museo Haedo
 4 Uruguayan Consulate
 5 Post Office
 6 ACA
 7 Casa Goyo (exchange)
 8 Banco de la Provincia
 9 Banco de la Nación
10 ATM
11 Casa de la Cultura,
     Museo Arqueológico
12 Teatro Gualeguaychú
20 Torminal de Omnibus
25 Casa de Andrade
26 Dirección Municipal
     de Turismo
28 Puerto Municipal
29 Museo Ferroviario

Gualeguaychú

Special Events

Gualeguaychú is a party town, with several important festivals. Its summer Carnaval has a national and even international reputation, so if you can't go to Rio or Bahía, make a stop here any weekend from mid-January to late February. Every October for the past 30 years, high school students have built and paraded floats through the city during the Fiesta Provincial de Carrozas Estudiantiles.

Other celebrations include the folkloric Abrazo Celeste y Blanco (after the colors of the Argentine flag) and numerous *jinete-adas* (rodeos) throughout the course of the year.

Places to Stay

Camping There are good facilities at *Camping La Delfina* (☎ 23984), in Parque Unzué on the far side of the river, but take plenty of mosquito repellent in summer. Fees are US$8 for two people, US$10 for four.

Hospedajes & Hotels Most reasonably priced hotels are near the bus station. The cheapest is the clean and friendly *Pensión*

Gualeguaychú, 25 de Mayo 456 near Nieves, where rooms with shared bath are US$10 per person. At *Hospedaje Mayo* (☎ 27661), on Bolívar 550 at 3 de Febrero, singles/doubles with private bath cost US$12/20. *Residencial Marina* (☎ 27159), 25 de Mayo 1031, has quiet, spacious rooms with good beds for US$15/25. *Hotel Brutti* (☎ 26048), Bolívar 571, charges around US$15 per person, while *Hotel Abadía* (☎ 27675), Calle San Martín 588, charges US$20/35 with breakfast.

At mid-range *Hotel Viedma* (☎ 24262), Bolívar 530, singles/doubles cost US$32/49 with breakfast. *Hotel Berlín* (☎ 26085), Bolívar 733, has rooms for about US$45/65, also with breakfast. Closest to luxury is three-star *Hotel Embajador* (☎ 24414), at Calle San Martín and 3 de Febrero, which also has a casino. Rates are only slightly higher than the Berlín, and breakfast is included.

Places to Eat

Most restaurants are along the costanera, but try also the *Círculo Italiano* (☎ 22155) at Calle San Martín 647, near Pellegrini, or *Paris* (☎ 23850) at Pellegrini 180. *Pizzería Don Julián* (☎ 25112) is at Urquiza 607, while *Pizza San Remo* (☎ 26891) is at 25 de Mayo 634.

Getting There & Away

The Terminal de Omnibus (☎ 27987) is very central at Bolívar and Monseñor Chalup (ex-Chile). Buenos Aires is three hours plus and US$20 away, with frequent services by San José, El Rápido, Flecha Bus (☎ 24070), and El Tata. Ciudad de Gualeguay has five buses daily to Paraná (US$20, six hours) via Larroque, Gualeguay, and Victoria. Three times weekly, El Serrano goes to Córdoba (US$38, 11 hours) via Santa Fe. Ciudad de Gualeguaychú has daily buses to Corrientes.

Daily except Sunday, ETA has three buses to Fray Bentos, Uruguay, two of which continue to Mercedes. Fares are US$4 to Fray Bentos and US$5 to Mercedes. For Montevideo, make connections in Fray Bentos.

CONCEPCIÓN

On the Río Uruguay east of the junction of RN 14 from Buenos Aires and RP 39 to Paraná and midway between Gualeguaychú and Parque Nacional El Palmar, Concepción de Uruguay is a crossroads town whose tourist services make it a worthwhile stopover for travelers on long trips north. The area's major tourist attraction is the **Palacio San José**, General Urquiza's palatial residence 35 km west of town, where Urquiza was assassinated by the forces of his rival, Ricardo López Jordán.

Concepción's Subsecretaria Municipal de Turismo (☎ 0442-25820), at 9 de Julio 844, provides information for visitors. Inexpensive but surprisingly convenient accommodations, less than two blocks south of the central Plaza General Francisco Ramírez, are available for about US$17/27 single/double at *Residencial Centro* (☎ 27429) at Manuel Moreno 130, or *Residencial La Posada* (☎ 25461) at Manuel Moreno 166. The *Grand Hotel* (☎ 25586), north of the Plaza at Eva Perón 114, charges US$42/60 for two-star facilities. There are also campgrounds at the Balneario Municipal Itapé at the south end of Av 3 de Febrero and at Banco Pelay north of town. Both charge around US$7 for two persons.

There are several restaurants just north of the Plaza, including *Flippini* (☎ 27963) and *La Delfina*(☎ 22851), both at Eva Perón and Rocamora, and *Isondú* (☎ 22636) at Eva Perón 90.

The Terminal de Omnibus is at General Galarza and Blvd Benigno T Martínez, ten blocks west of the Plaza.

COLÓN

One of three major border crossings in Entre Ríos, Colón sits on the west bank of the Río Uruguay, connected to the Uruguayan city of Paysandú by the Puente Internacional General Artigas. Founded in 1863, Colón has been an attractive tourist destination due to its beautiful riverine landscape and fine beaches, but flooding in recent years, due to upstream dam discharges, has wiped out several of them. In

ARGENTINA

mid-February, the city hosts the Fiesta Nacional de la Artesanía, a crafts fair that features live folkoric entertainment by national figures. Its tenth anniversary was celebrated in 1995.

Four km from Colón is the **Molino Forclaz,** the area's first flour mill. It's also worth visiting the nearby village of **San José,** eight km west, where in 1857 European pioneers established the country's second agricultural colony; an interesting regional museum displays period tools and memorabilia.

The Subsecretaría de Turismo (☎ 21233) is at Emilio Gouchon and the Av Costanera Gobernador Quirós. Correo Argentino is at Artigas and 12 de Abril; Colón's postal code is 3280. The telephone code is 0447.

Places to Stay & Eat
Two municipal *campgrounds* charge US$8 double per site. For other cheap accommodations, try the friendly, recommended *Residencial Chacabuco* (☎ 21734), a few blocks from the plaza at Chacabuco 185, which is a good place to meet other travelers and perhaps arrange a shared remise to Parque Nacional El Palmar. Rates are

US$15/20 single/double. *Residencial Verwei* (☎ 21972), 25 de Mayo 10, is slightly dearer at US$20/30. For eats, try the anonymous *tenedor libre* at Alem and Urquiza for about US$6.

Getting There & Away
Colón's Terminal de Omnibus is at Rocamora and 9 de Julio. From Colón you can catch a bus to the entrance of Parque Nacional El Palmar.

PARQUE NACIONAL EL PALMAR
In the 19th century, the native yatay palm covered large parts of Entre Ríos, Uruguay, and southern Brazil, but the intensification of agriculture, ranching, and forestry throughout the region destroyed much of the palm savannas and inhibited reproduction of the species. On the west bank of the Río Uruguay, midway between Colón and Concordia, 8500-hectare Parque Nacional El Palmar preserves the last extensive stands of *Syagrus yatay* on the Argentine littoral. The state acquired this former cattle estancia, one of the Argentine park system's most visited units, in 1966.

Most of the remaining palms in El

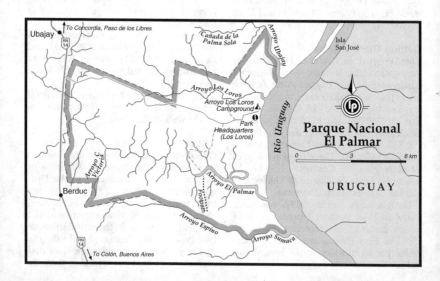

Palmar are relics, some more than two centuries old, but under protection from grazing and fire they have once again begun to reproduce. Reaching a maximum height of about 18 meters, with a trunk diameter of 40 cm, the larger specimens clustered throughout the park accentuate a striking and soothing subtropical landscape that lends itself to photography. The grasslands and the gallery forests along the river and creeks shelter much wildlife, including birds, mammals, and reptiles.

The park is remarkably tranquil and undeveloped, despite its proximity to population centers, so most activities are oriented toward the park's natural attractions. Park admission, collected at the entrance on RN 14, is US$2.50 per person.

Things to See & Do

Centro de Interpretación Across from the campground at Los Loros, the visitors center (☎ 90586) has displays on natural history, including a small herpetarium (reptile house), and offers slide shows in the evening. Unfortunately, many of the excellent color blowups of landscape, flora, and fauna have faded over the years and badly need replacement. There is a confitería next door at which you can get food and drink. The *intendencia* (park administration) was once the casco of the estancia.

Wildlife Viewing To view wildlife, go for walks along the watercourses or through the palm savannas, preferably in early morning or just before sunset. The most conspicuous bird is the *ñandú* or rhea *(Rhea americana)*, but there are also numerous parakeets, cormorants, egrets, herons, storks, caracaras, woodpeckers, and kingfishers. Among the mammals, the *carpincho* or capybara, a semiaquatic rodent weighing up to 60 kg, and the vizcacha, a relative of the chinchilla, are common sights, but there are also foxes, raccoons, and wild boars.

Vizcachas inhabit the campground at Arroyo Los Loros, where their nocturnal squeaks and reflective eyes sometimes disturb campers, but they are totally harmless. The same is not true of the yarará *(Bothrops alternata)*, a highly poisonous pit viper inhabiting the savannas. Bites are not common, but watch your step and wear high boots and long trousers when hiking. The enormous toads that invade the showers and toilets at night are harmless.

Río Uruguay There is excellent access to the river for swimming and boating from Arroyo Los Loros campground, as well as a series of short hiking trails comprising **El Paseo de la Glorieta**. You can rent canoes at the campground store.

Arroyo Los Loros A short distance by gravel road from the campground, this is a good place to observe wildlife.

Arroyo El Palmar Five km from Los Loros is Arroyo El Palmar, a pleasant stream with a beautiful swimming hole, accessible by a good gravel road. It is a fine place to see birds and, crossing the ruined bridge, visitors can walk for several kilometers along a palm-lined road now being reclaimed by savanna grasses.

Places to Stay

Fortunately, there are no hotels in the park and the only alternative is to camp at Los Loros (☎ 0447-93031), which has shady level sites, hot showers, a store, and a confitería. Campers pay a one-time fee of US$4 per tent as well as US$4 per person per day. The nearest hotels are in the cities of Concordia, about 50 km north of the park entrance on RN 14, and Colón, about the same distance south.

Getting There & Away

El Palmar is 360 km northwest of Buenos Aires on RN 14, a major national highway, so there are frequent north-south bus services. Any bus from Buenos Aires, Gualeguaychú, or Concepción del Uruguay will drop you at the park entrance, as will any bus making the run from Colón to Concordia. There is no public transport to the visitors center and camping area, but hitching should not be difficult.

CONCORDIA

Originally settled in 1769, this clean and attractive agricultural and livestock center on the Río Uruguay offers the most northerly border crossing in the province of Entre Ríos, via the Salto Grande hydroelectric project, to the Uruguayan city of Salto. Concordia's formal foundation dates from 1832 with the construction of its Catedral San Antonio de Padua. Visitors come for its riverside beaches and fishing.

Orientation

Concordia (population 140,000) is 431 km north of Buenos Aires and 65 km north of Parque Nacional El Palmar via RN 14. Its very regular grid centers on Plaza 25 de Mayo, where most of the main public buildings are; street names change on each side of Calle Urquiza, which runs north-south on the west side of the Plaza. One block west of the Plaza, Calle Entre Ríos is a popular peatonal between Bernardo de Irigoyen and Undinarraín (do not confuse east-west Bernardo de Irigoyen for the north-south thoroughfare Av Hipólito Yrigoyen, one block west of the Plaza, which leads to the bus station).

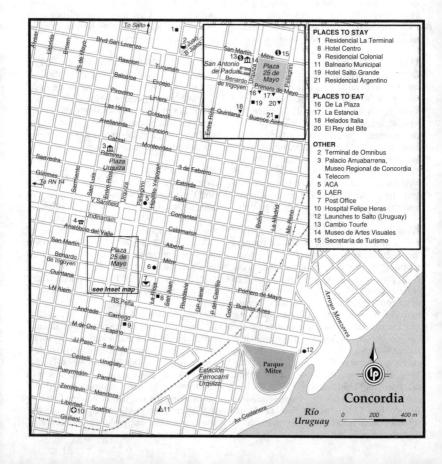

PLACES TO STAY
1   Residencial La Terminal
8   Hotel Centro
9   Residencial Colonial
11 Balneario Municipal
19 Hotel Salto Grande
21 Residencial Argentino

PLACES TO EAT
16 De La Plaza
17 La Estancia
18 Helados Italia
20 El Rey del Bife

OTHER
2   Terminal de Omnibus
3   Palacio Arruabarrena,
    Museo Regional de Concordia
4   Telecom
5   ACA
6   LAER
7   Post Office
10 Hospital Felipe Heras
12 Launches to Salto (Uruguay)
13 Cambio Tourfe
14 Museo de Artes Visuales
15 Secretaría de Turismo

Concordia

Río Uruguay

0   200   400 m

Information
Tourist Offices The municipal Secretaría de Turismo (☎ 21-2137, 21-3905), Mitre 64, is open daily 7 am to 9:30 pm.

ACA (☎ 21-3478) is at Pellegrini and Corrientes.

Money Tourfe, San Martín 43, will change money, but there are several ATMs in the vicinity of Plaza 25 de Mayo.

Post & Telecommunications Correo Argentino is on Hipólito Yrigoyen between 1 de Mayo and Buenos Aires; the postal code is 3200.

Telecom is on San Luis between Undinarraín and Aristóbulo del Valle. Concordia's telephone code is 045.

Medical Services Hospital Felipe Heras (☎ 21-2580) is at Entre Ríos 135.

Things to See
On the west side of Plaza 25 de Mayo, the 19th-century **Catedral San Antonio de Padua** is the city's signature landmark. Also near the Plaza, at Urquiza 636, is the **Museo de Artes Visuales,** which emphasizes local artists and also includes a sample of regional handicrafts.

At the corner of Entre Ríos and Ramírez facing Plaza Urquiza, the **Palacio Arruabarrena** (1919) is a French-style building that contains the **Museo Regional de Concordia.** In the riverside Parque Rivadavia, at the northeastern edge of town, is the ruins of **Castillo San Carlos** (1888), built by a French industrialist who mysteriously abandoned the property years later. French writer Antoine de Saint-Exúpery briefly lived in the building and wrote about his experiences in the area.

Eighteen km north of town, the 39-meter-high Represa Salto Grande and its 80,000-hectare reservoir is a joint Argentine-Uruguayan project that also supports a road and railway bridge linking the two countries. Its Oficina de Relaciones Públicas (☎ 21-2600) arranges tours of the project.

Special Events
Fishing enthusiasts crowd Concordia during January's Fiesta Nacional de la Boga, in search of the region's tastiest river fish. The city holds its Fiesta Nacional de Citricultura (National Citrus Festival) in December.

Places to Stay
Camping The most convenient camping place, also close to the port for crossings to Salto, is the *Balneario Municipal* at the foot of San Juan, beyond the railroad tracks.

Residenciales & Hotels For the cheapest lodging, try *Residencial La Terminal* (☎ 21-1758) at Hipólito Yrigoyen 1313, but there are better, more central, and only slightly dearer accommodations like *Residencial Argentino* (☎ 21-5767) at Buenos Aires and Pellegrini, or *Residencial Colonial* (☎ 22-1448) at Pellegrini 443; rates are around US$15/25 single/double. At the east end of Calle Coldaroli near the beach at Playa Nebel, *Residencial Betanía* (☎ 21-5456) charges US$15 per person.

Midrange accommodations are available at *Hotel Centro* (☎ 21-7746), at the corner of La Rioja and Buenos Aires, for US$38/47, while the most commodious, upscale lodging is four-star *Hotel Salto Grande* (☎ 21-3916) at Urquiza 575, where rooms start at US$68/80.

Places to Eat
Despite a name that brands it as a parrilla, *La Estancia* (☎ 21-1150), 1 de Mayo 93, serves excellent grilled fish like surubí, boga, and dorado, all at moderate prices.

El Rey del Bife (☎ 21-2644), Pellegrini 568, concentrates on parrilla but also serves pasta and seafood. *De La Plaza,* on 1 de Mayo between Urquiza and Pellegrini, is a more upscale alternative. For ice cream, try *Helados Italia* on Urquiza between Bernardo de Irigoyen and Quintana.

Getting There & Away
Air LAER (☎ 21-1551), La Rioja 622, flies daily to Buenos Aires (US$65), sometimes

in the morning but more often in the evening. The airport is north of town, on the road to Salto Grande.

Bus The Terminal de Omnibus (☎ 21-7235) occupies the triangle formed by Blvd San Lorenzo, Hipólito Yrigoyen, and the diagonal Juan B Justo. Chadre buses to Salto leave at noon and 6 pm, while Flecha Bus services leave at 11:30 am and 6:30 pm. Note that there are no Sunday buses to Salto.

Long-distance buses between Buenos Aires and the provinces of Corrientes and Misiones resemble those passing through Gualeguaychú, Concepción, and Colón. Flecha Bus has five buses daily to the capital (US$23, six hours), while Tata, Itapé, and Sudamericano provide additional services. Flecha Bus has additional direct service to La Plata.

Boat From the port at the east end of Roque Sáenz Peña, launches cross the river to Salto weekdays at 8 and 10 am, noon, and 3 and 6:30 pm; weekend and holiday crossings are at 9 am, noon, and 3 and 6:30 pm. The fare is US$3.

Corrientes Province

Like Entre Ríos, Corrientes traditionally has been an isolated province with a strong regional identity. Southern Corrientes' low, rolling terrain, with its productive agriculture, closely resembles Entre Ríos. The alluvial grasslands of the north, however, support mostly livestock except where interrupted by marshes like the Esteros del Iberá, a potential national park with wildlife comparable to Brazil's better known Pantanal. Gallery forests are common along the many watercourses, but plantations of exotic conifers also flourish in the warm, humid climate. Winter and early spring are the best times for a visit because summer can be oppressively hot.

During the colonial era, settlement in Corrientes advanced southward from Para-

guay. Indian resistance discouraged a permanent Spanish presence until 1588, with the founding of the city of Corrientes. Jesuit priests were the region's most effective colonizers until their expulsion from South America in 1767; their most southerly mission, at Yapeyú on the Río Uruguay, was also the birthplace of Argentina's greatest hero, General José de San Martín.

Since independence, Corrientes' economy has relied on livestock, first cattle and, more recently, sheep. The province's distance from markets discouraged attempts to improve its cattle breeds until well into the 20th century. In recent years, forestry and timber processing have become important industries. Efforts at encouraging provincial industry through large-scale energy developments like the trouble-plagued hydroelectric project at Yacyretá have been unsuccessful so far.

For visitors, the Río Paraná and its fishery may be the province's greatest attraction. Both the city and province of Corrientes also hold the country's most notable celebrations of Carnaval. The city has many historic buildings dating to colonial times.

CORRIENTES
Founded just below the confluence of the Río Paraná and the Río Paraguay by Spaniards moving south from Asunción in 1588, the provincial capital of Corrientes is one of Argentina's oldest and most historic cities. Originally called Vera de los Siete Corrientes, after its founder Juan Torres de Vera y Aragón and after the shifting currents of the Paraná, it suffered repeated Indian uprisings before establishing itself permanently. In the early 19th century, it was part of the short-lived "República de Entre Ríos." On the opposite bank of the Paraná is Resistencia, capital of Chaco province.

Orientation
Overland connections from Buenos Aires, 1025 km south via RN 12 and other roads, are good. Corrientes' extremely regular grid centers on Plaza 25 de Mayo, though

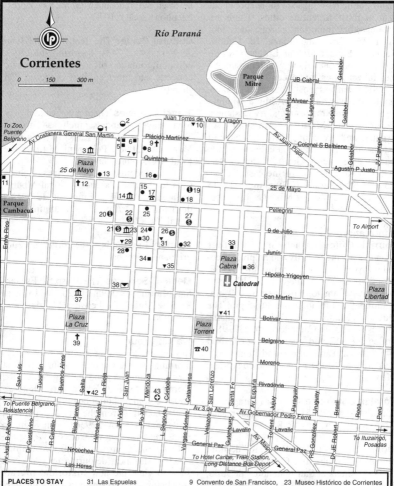

ARGENTINA

Corrientes

0   150   300 m

Río Paraná

Parque Mitre

To Zoo, Puente Belgrano

Av Costanera General San Martín

Juan Torres de Vera Y Aragón

Plácido Martínez

Quintana

Plaza 25 de Mayo

Parque Cambacuá

Entre Ríos

Av Juan Pujol

Colonel S Balbiene

Agustín P Justo

25 de Mayo

Pellegrini

9 de Julio

To Airport

Junín

Hipólito Yrigoyen

Plaza Cabral

Catedral

San Martín

Plaza Libertad

Plaza La Cruz

Bolívar

Belgrano

Moreno

Plaza Torrent

Rivadavia

Av 3 de Abril

Av Gobernador Pedro Ferré

San Juan

Tucumán

Buenos Aires

Salta

La Rioja

San Juan

Mendoza

Catamarca

San Lorenzo

Santa Fe

Av España

Jujuy

Paraguay

Uruguay

Brasil

Roca

Perú

To Puente Belgrano, Resistencia

Av Juan B Alberdi

Dr Gustavino

R Castillo

Blas Parera

Hroes Civiles

J F Vidal

Pío XII

L Segovia

Vargas Gómez

Velazco

Gutemberg

Lavalle

Av Maipú

Torrent

R S González

Dr J E Robert

To Ituzaingó, Posadas

Necochea

General Paz

General Paz

Las Heras

To Hotel Caribe, Train Station, Long Distance Bus Depot

PLACES TO STAY
4 Hospedaje Robert
5 Hotel Colón
6 Hotel Hostal del Pinar
11 Gran Hotel Turismo
30 Orly Hotel
33 Hotel Corrientes
34 Hotel Guaraní
36 Hotel San Martín

PLACES TO EAT
7 Heladería Trieste
10 Yapeyú
29 Mercado Central
31 Las Espuelas
35 La Cueva del Pescador
41 Pizzería Los Pinos
42 Gran Rancho

OTHER
1 Estación Terminal de Colectivos Urbanos
2 Resistencia-Corrientes Bus Depot
3 Museo de Artesanía Folklórica
8 Monumento a la Gloria, Historical Murals
9 Convento de San Francisco, Museo Franciscano
12 Iglesia de la Merced
13 Casa de Gobierno
14 Museo de Bellas Artes Dr Juan Ramón Vidal
15 Teatro Oficial Juan de Vera
16 ACA
17 Telecom
18 Laverap
19 Dirección Provincial de Turismo
20 Turismo Taragüí
21 Banco del Iberá (ATM)
22 Banco de la Provincia (ATM)
23 Museo Histórico de Corrientes
24 Cine Colón
25 Quo Vadis
26 Banco de Galicia (ATM)
27 Cambio El Dorado
28 4WD Empresa de Viajes de Turismo
32 Austral
37 Museo de Ciencias Naturales Amado Bonpland
38 Post Office
39 Iglesia de la Cruz/Santuario de la Cruz del Milagro
40 Telecom
43 Hospital Escuela San Martín

major public buildings are more spread out than in most Argentine cities. There are several other important plazas, including Plaza La Cruz and Plaza JB Cabral. Between Salta and San Lorenzo, Calle Junín is a peatonal along which most commercial activities are concentrated.

Calle Junín and most other areas of interest to the visitor are within a triangle formed by three main streets: Av Costanera General San Martín, north-south Av España, and Av 3 de Abril, a westward extension of Av Gobernador Ferré, which leads to the Puente General Manuel Belgrano to Resistencia. To the east, RN 12 parallels the Paraná to Ituzaingó and to Posadas, the capital of Misiones province.

Information

Tourist Offices
Much improved over recent years, the friendly and helpful Dirección Provincial de Turismo (☎ 27200, 24565) is at 25 de Mayo 1330. It's open weekdays 7 am to 1 pm and 3 to 9 pm, Saturday 9 am to noon and 5 to 8 pm. The Dirección Municipal de Turismo maintains offices in Parque Cambacuá (☎ 23779) at Pellegrini 542 and also at Plaza Cabral (☎ 28845) at San Lorenzo and Junín.

ACA (☎ 24545) is at 25 de Mayo and Mendoza.

Foreign Consulate
There is a Paraguayan consulate (☎ 27945) at Gobernador Ruiz 2746, reached by bus No 8.

Money
Cambio El Dorado is on 9 de Julio between Córdoba and Catamarca. Banco de la Provincia at San Juan and 9 de Julio, Banco de Galicia on Córdoba between 9 de Julio and Junín, and Banco del Iberá at 9 de Julio 1002 have ATMs.

Post & Telecommunications
Correo Argentino is at the corner of San Juan and Av San Martín; the postal code is 3400. Telecom has long-distance services at Pellegrini 1175, between Mendoza and San Juan, but it's only open from 7 am to 9 pm; there's a 24-hour office on Catamarca

between Belgrano and Moreno. Corrientes' telephone code is 0783.

Cultural Center
The Teatro Oficial Juan de Vera (☎ 27743), honoring the city's colonial founder, offers classical music concerts and other cultural events at San Juan 637.

Travel Agencies
There are several downtown travel agencies, such as Turismo Taragüi (☎ 22236) at La Rioja 730; Quo Vadis (☎ 23096), Pellegrini 1140, is the local Amex representative.

For less conventional services such as trips to the new Parque Nacional Mburucuyá, contact 4WD Empresa de Viajes de Turismo (☎/fax 33269), Junín 1062, Local 12.

Laundry
Laverap is at the corner of Pellegrini and Córdoba.

Medical Services
The Hospital Escuela San Martín (☎ 20895, 30026, 30113) is at Av 3 de Abril 1251, between Mendoza and Córdoba.

Walking Tour
In Corrientes' stifling summer heat, early-morning or late-afternoon hours are best for sightseeing. A good starting point is the **Convento de San Francisco,** Mendoza 450, a colonial church beautifully restored in 1939. Dating from the city's founding, it has a museum (☎ 22936) open 8 am to noon and 5 to 9 pm weekdays.

From the Convento, walk west along Plácido Martínez, detouring up Calle San Juan to view the new **historical murals** (see below) before strolling along the tree-lined Av Costanera, past the small but interesting **Jardín Zoológico.** Beyond the zoo are excellent views of the **Puente Belgrano,** the bridge which crosses the Paraná to Resistencia. Returning by Edison and Bolívar, stop at the **Santuario de la Cruz del Milagro** on the south side of Plaza La Cruz, containing a 16th-century cross that, according to legend, defied all efforts of rebellious Indians to burn it.

Continue along Bolívar and up San Lorenzo to the **Catedral** on Plaza Cabral, which contains the mausoleum and statue of local caudillo Colonel Genaro Berón de Astrada. From Plaza Cabral, return along the Junín peatonal to Salta and back toward the river, passing Plaza 25 de Mayo. An alternative route continues north on San Lorenzo to attractive **Parque Mitre.**

Monumento a la Gloria & Historical Murals

Recently the east side of Calle San Juan, between Plácido Martínez and Quintana, has been transformed into a shady, attractive park. A new monument honors the Italian community and a series of striking historical murals, extending over 100 meters around the corner onto Quintana, chronicles the city's history since colonial times. It's a very attractive addition to a block that already features the colonial Convento de San Francisco.

Museo Histórico de Corrientes

The city's historical museum, 9 de Julio 1044, has exhibits of weapons, antique furniture, and coins, as well as exhibits dealing with religious and civil history. It's open weekdays 8 am to noon and 4 to 8 pm, and also has a library.

Museo de Bellas Artes Doctor Juan Ramón Vidal

The fine-arts museum, at San Juan 634 opposite the Teatro Vera, emphasizes sculpture but has frequent special exhibitions. Opening hours are Tuesday to Saturday 9 am to noon and 6 to 9 pm.

Jardín Zoológico

On the Av Costanera at the foot of Calle Junín, Corrientes' zoo has a small selection of provincial wildlife, including caimans, capuchin monkeys, toucans, pumas, and Geoffrey's cat. The enclosures are small, but most of the animals appear healthy. Hours are 10 am to 6 pm daily.

Museo de Ciencias Naturales Amado Bonpland

Founded by and named for Alexander von Humboldt's naturalist companion, who spent much of his life in the province and is buried at Paso de Los Libres, this natural-history museum, at Av San Martín 850, has some good fossils but is otherwise unexceptional. Opening hours are weekdays 9 am to noon and 4 to 9 pm.

El Carnaval Correntino

Inspired by immigrants from the provincial town of Paso de Los Libres on the Brazilian border, Corrientes' traditionally riotous carnival nearly disappeared until a recent revival, and it's once again an event worth watching. Celebrated on weekends (Friday, Saturday, and Sunday) in the carnival season, it attracts comparsas from neighboring provinces and countries to the parade along Av Ferré; crowds have reached as many as 80,000.

Places to Stay – bottom end

Camping The nearest campground to Corrientes is *Punta Molina,* five km from downtown, reached by bus No 8 out Av Libertad (the eastward continuation of Pellegrini and Av Gobernador Ruiz); sites cost US$5 plus US$1 per vehicle. Slightly farther out is *Puente Pesoa,* beyond the provincial police checkpoint at the junction of RP 12 and RN 3, reached by bus No 6 (Riachuelo). Municipal sites in Paso de la Patria and Resistencia are other dependable alternatives.

Hotels Accommodations are relatively scarce and expensive in Corrientes, and generally inferior to those in nearby Resistencia. During Carnaval, however, the provincial tourist office maintains a list of *casas de familia* where lodging generally ranges from US$10 to US$20 per person.

Among the most reasonable regular accommodations are the basic *Hotel Colón* (☎ 24527), La Rioja 437, where singles/doubles with shared bath cost US$15/25 and rooms with private bath are US$23/33, but recent reports suggest falling standards.

It is near the city's many pleasant riverfront parks.

Other budget places include *Hospedaje Robert* (no phone) at La Rioja 415, *Hospedaje Belgrano* (☎ 61788) at Almirante Brown (the extension of Calle Belgrano) 2619, and *Residencial Necochea* (☎ 65476) at Héroes Civiles (the southward extension of La Rioja) 1898. Rates are around US$17/26 with shared bath.

Hotel Caribe (☎ 69065), close to the bus terminal at Maipú 2590, charges US$29/42 with private bath.

Places to Stay – middle
Gran Hotel Turismo (☎ 29112), in attractive, parklike grounds on the Av Costanera General San Martín at 25 de Mayo, has a swimming pool, a restaurant, and a bar, and is a good value at US$42/50. Slightly cheaper at US$35/48, and with similar facilities but less attractive surroundings, is *Hotel Corrientes* (☎ 65026), at Calle Junín 1549 on Plaza Cabral. The *Orly Hotel* (☎ 27248), San Juan 867, charges about US$41/50 for rooms that are small and frayed about the edges, but spotlessly clean. *Hotel San Martín* (☎ 60870) at Santa Fe 955 is comparably priced.

Places to Stay – top end
At the four-star, high-rise *Hotel Hostal del Pinar* (☎ 69060), on the riverfront at Plácido Martínez and San Juan, rooms with private bath are about US$46/67. *Hotel Guaraní* (☎ 27203), Mendoza 970, is more expensive (and overpriced) at US$55/73.

Places to Eat
The Junín peatonal has many cafes and confiterías, but shuts down during the midday heat. For cheap eats, look in and around the *Mercado Central* (central market) on Junín between La Rioja and San Juan. *Pizzería Los Pinos,* at Bolívar and San Lorenzo, is a good fast-food choice.

Las Espuelas, Mendoza 847, is an outstanding parrilla, but prices have risen enough that it's not quite the value it once was. At lunchtime, you may wish to take advantage of its air conditioning, but the outdoor patio can be pleasant for dinner. *Yapeyú,* on the costanera at Vera 1352, is also a worthwhile parrilla.

For surubí and other river fish, try *Gran Rancho* at 3 de Abril 935. *La Cueva del Pescador* (☎ 22511), Hipólito Yrigoyen 1255 between Mendoza and Córdoba, is another very fine fish restaurant with good atmosphere and high but not outrageous prices.

Heladería Trieste, at the corner of San Juan and Quintana, has very fine ice cream and a very welcome water cooler.

Entertainment
The *Cine Colón* is on 9 de Julio between San Juan and Mendoza.

Spectator Sports
Mandiyú (☎ 23651), Corrientes' first-division soccer team, plays at Av Armenia 4601, east of downtown. One of the league's traditional doormats, it nevertheless usually manages to avoid relegation.

Things to Buy
Local crafts are available at the Museo de Artesanía Folklórica, in a colonial house at Salta and Quintana. Hours are 7:30 am to 12:30 pm and 2 to 6 pm weekdays except Tuesdays (when it is closed), and Saturdays 9 am to noon and 3 to 6 pm.

Getting There & Away
Air Austral (☎ 23918), Calle Junín 1301 at Córdoba, flies daily to Buenos Aires (US$146), but there are also flights from nearby Resistencia, both with Austral and Aerolíneas Argentinas.

Bus Resistencia has better long-distance bus connections, especially to the west and northwest. Local buses to Resistencia (US$2) leave from the local bus terminal, on Av Costanera General San Martín at La Rioja, at frequent intervals throughout the day. El Rápido (☎ 63734) goes to provincial destinations like Goya and Esquina.

Empresa Ciudad de Posadas (☎ 64910) and Kurtz (☎ 63590) have regular runs to Posadas, the capital of Misiones province, where there are connections to the former Jesuit missions and to Puerto Iguazú. Chevallier has bus service to Paraná, Santa Fe, Rosario, and Buenos Aires (US$40,14 hours). Tata/Central El Rápido (☎ 63227) runs an identical route, and also goes to Córdoba. They also provide services to Paso de Los Libres, on the Brazilian border, via the interior city of Mercedes, which has good access to the Esteros del Iberá. Co-Bra (☎ 62243) offers direct service to Brazil.

Empresa Tala (☎ 63577) goes to a wide variety of destinations both domestic (Formosa, Concordia, Buenos Aires, La Plata) and foreign (Uruguaiana, Brazil, and Asunción, Paraguay). El Zonda (☎ 63842) connects Corrientes with Buenos Aires, Posadas, and Puerto Iguazú, and also crosses the Chaco to Tucumán. Itatí (☎ 60279) is another important Buenos Aires and regional carrier. Puerto Tirol (☎ 60279) serves the western bank of the Paraná, with routes running from Formosa south to Buenos Aires.

Getting Around
To/From the Airport Local bus No 8 goes to Corrientes' Aeropuerto Doctor Fernando Piragine Niveyro (☎ 25056, 24894), about 10 km east of town on RN 12. Austral runs a minibus to Resistencia in accordance with flight schedules.

Bus The long-distance bus terminal, the Estación Terminal de Transporte Gobernador Benjamín S González (☎ 62243, 60137) is on Av Maipú. From the local bus station on Av Costanera, take bus No 6.

Car Rental For visiting remote places like the Esteros de Iberá, arrange car rentals through Turismo Taragüi (☎ 22236), La Rioja 730.

PASO DE LA PATRIA
This small, placid resort, about 30 km northeast of Corrientes at the confluence of the Paraguay and Paraná, has a national and international reputation for sport fishing, making tourism the backbone of the local economy. High season is July to September; early October to early March is the closed season. Only the main street is paved, so it can be very muddy when it rains. Paso de la Patria can be very expensive, it but offers outstanding opportunities for dedicated fishing enthusiasts.

Information
The tourist office (☎ 94007) is at 25 de Mayo 518. Paso de la Patria's postal code is 3904, while the telephone code is 0783.

Fishing
Besides the famous dorado, local sport fish include the surubí (weighing up to 70 kg), the exceptionally tasty boga, sábalo, pejerrey, pacú, patí, manduví, manduve, mangrullo, chafalote, and armado. Methods include trolling, spinning, and fly casting. Night fishing is possible.

Prices for fishing holidays start at about US$90 per person per day, including boat, guide, and an evening parrilla to feast on the day's catch. For further information on fishing holidays, contact Luís Maríns (☎ 94218), 25 de Mayo 470, 3904 Paso de la Patria, Provincia de Corrientes.

Special Event
The annual Fiesta Internacional del Dorado lasts four days in mid-August. The highlight is a competition for the largest specimens of the carnivorous dorado *(Salminus maxiliosus)*, known as the "tiger of the Paraná" for its fighting nature. The dorado weighs up to 25 kg, and the minimum allowable catch size is 75 cm. Entry costs US$60 per person.

Places to Stay
There are few budget accommodations in Paso de la Patria, but several campgrounds charge about US$5 to US$6 per tent per day, plus US$3 per vehicle, with all facilities. Many correntinos have weekend houses here and often rent them to visitors. Prices for a two-bedroom house start around US$50 per day for up to six persons. For more information, contact the tourist office.

ARGENTINA

One alternative for local accommodations is *Le Apart Hotel* (☎ 94174), 25 de Mayo 1201, which charges US$120 per day with breakfast for up to four persons.

Getting There & Away
There is frequent bus service to and from Corrientes.

ESTEROS DEL IBERÁ
Esteros del Iberá, a nearly trackless wilderness occupying 13,000 sq km in the north-central part of the province, is a wildlife area comparable to Brazil's Pantanal do Mato Grosso. Although plans for a national park are on hold, the marshes are a cornucopia of plant and animal species deserving of a visit despite its difficult access.

Aquatic plants and grasses dominate the marsh vegetation, while trees are relatively few. The most notable wildlife species are reptiles like the cayman, mammals like the capybara, pampas, and swamp deer, and some 280 species of birds. At the settlement of Colonia Pellegrini, on Laguna Iberá, it's possible to organize canoe trips into the marshes. Much of the wildlife is nocturnal.

There are no hotels, but camping is possible on the site. The best place to purchase supplies is the town of Mercedes, 107 km southwest of Colonia Pellegrini.

Organized Tours
Since the logistics of visiting the Esteros are awkward, organized tours can be a good alternative. In the region, contact Turismo Operativo Misionero at either Urquiza and Zapiola, Posadas (☎ 0752-27591); at Mariano Moreno 58 in Puerto Iguazú (☎ 0757-21240); or at Av Corrientes 753, Buenos Aires (☎ 01-393-3476).

For four-day trips based at an estancia on the north side of the Esteros, near the village of Loreto, contact Aquatours (☎/fax 01-314-7798), Maipú 812, Piso 3°, Oficina G, Buenos Aires.

Getting There & Away
Colonia Pellegrini, 353 km southeast of Corrientes via RN 12 and RP 123, and 241 km northwest of Paso de Los Libres via RN 123, is the best center for visiting the Esteros. There is regular public transportation between Paso de Los Libres and Corrientes to Mercedes, where RP 40 leads northeast to Colonia Pellegrini.

There is occasional truck transport from Mercedes to Colonia Pellegrini, and hitching may be possible. Taxis with drivers can be hired, but Corrientes is the nearest place to hire a car without a driver.

PASO DE LOS LIBRES
Brazilian influence made Paso de Los Libres, a town of 25,000 on the Río Uruguay, the "Cradle of the Carnaval of Corrientes." About 700 km north of Buenos Aires and 370 km south of Posadas on RN 14, it has the only truly convenient international border crossing in the province, to the much larger Brazilian city of Uruguaiana on the opposite bank of the river. Brazilians come here to load up on consumer trinkets.

Orientation
On the west bank of the Uruguay, Paso del Los Libres has a standard rectangular grid, centered on Plaza Independencia. The principal commercial street is Av Colón, one block west. Most points of interest are nearby, but the international bridge to Uruguaiana is about ten blocks southwest.

Information
There is no tourist office in the town center; for information, try the facilities at the entrance to the international bridge to Uruguaiana, where ACA has an office.

Money Alhec Tours, Av Colón 901 at Juan Sitja Min, will change cash but not traveler's checks.

Post & Telecommunications Correo Argentino is at General Madariaga and Juan Sitja Min. The postal code is 3230. Telecom is at General Madariaga 854, half a block north of the Plaza; the telephone code is 0772.

Medical Services Hospital San José (☎ 21404) is on Calle T Alisio, on the east side of Plaza España.

Bonpland's Tomb

Paso de Los Libres is the final resting place of Amado (Aimé) Bonpland, the famous naturalist and travel companion of Alexander von Humboldt on the latter's epic South American journey in the early 19th century. Bonpland eventually settled in Corrientes, where he founded the province's first natural-history museum.

The frequently visited tomb is in the Cementerio de la Santa Cruz, just beyond the bus station, about 10 blocks from the center via Av San Martín. Ask the attendant for directions to "El sabio Bonpland."

Places to Stay & Eat

Paso de Los Libres' *Camping Municipal*, just north of the train station, charges US$10 per site. The cheapest regular lodging is *Residencial Colón Hotel,* Av Colón

1065, which charges US$15 per person for a room with private bath. Shabby but comfortable *Hotel Buen Confort* (☎ 21848), Coronel López 1091, has rooms with bath and very welcome air conditioning for US$20/30.

ACA has a restaurant near the border complex, but try also *La Victoria* (☎ 21577), Colón 585.

Getting There & Away

Air LAER (☎ 22395), Colón 1007, flies to Concordia and Buenos Aires (US$84) several times weekly. There is a larger airport on the Brazilian side of the border.

Bus The Terminal de Omnibus (☎ 21608) is at Av San Martín and Santiago del Estero. Expreso Singer and Crucero del Norte pass through Paso de Los Libres three times daily en route between Buenos Aires and Posadas (six hours). Empresa Tala goes daily to La Plata.

There are also daily buses to Paraná and

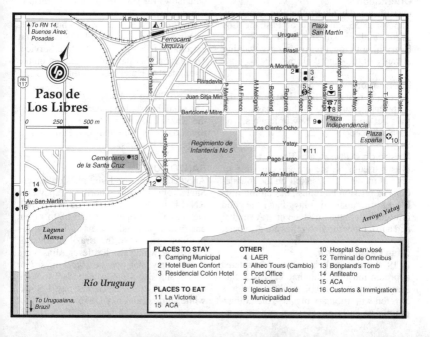

PLACES TO STAY	OTHER	10 Hospital San José
1 Camping Municipal	4 LAER	12 Terminal de Omnibus
2 Hotel Buen Confort	5 Alhec Tours (Cambio)	13 Bonpland's Tomb
3 Residencial Colón Hotel	6 Post Office	14 Anfiteatro
	7 Telecom	15 ACA
PLACES TO EAT	8 Iglesia San José	16 Customs & Immigration
11 La Victoria	9 Municipalidad	
15 ACA		

ARGENTINA

Santa Fe, and daily service to Rosario except for Thursdays. Daily, except Thursday, Paso de Los Libres is a stopover between Córdoba and Puerto Iguazú.

Provincial bus services run three times daily to Corrientes, to Goya, twice daily to Santo Tomé via Yapeyú, and daily to Sauce via Curuzú Cuatiá.

YAPEYÚ

Founded in 1626, this southernmost Jesuit mission once had a population of more than 8000 Guaraní Indians who tended as many as 80,000 cattle. After the order's expulsion in 1767, the Indians dispersed and the mission fell into ruins. In 1778, José de San Martín, Argentina's greatest national hero, was born in a modest house whose ruins still exist in a protected site. Many of the houses in this quiet, charming riverside village of 1500 people are built of red sandstone blocks salvaged from the mission buildings.

Orientation

On the west bank of the Río Uruguay, Yapeyú is 55 km north of Paso de Los Libres and six km southeast of RN 14. Everything in town is within easy walking distance of the central plaza.

Information

Yapeyú's tourist office, just inside the portal at the entrance to town, has helpful staff but no maps and few brochures. The telephone code is 0772.

Museo de Cultura Jesuítica

This museum on the plaza, consisting of several modern kiosks built on the foundations of mission buildings, has an interesting photographic display that is a good introduction to the mission zone. A sundial and a few other mission relics are also here.

Casa de San Martín

In 1938 the federal government completed a pretentious temple that encloses San Martín's modest birthplace. The interior is covered with tributary plaques, including a prominent one from General and de facto President Jorge Rafael Videla, a convicted (though pardoned) Dirty War lifer, attesting to his "most profound faith" in San Martín's ideals of liberty.

Museo Sanmartiniano

Next door to San Martín's birthplace, in a house dating from the Jesuit era, this museum contains a number of artifacts and documents from San Martín and his family. Opening hours are erratic.

Places to Stay & Eat

Yapeyú has limited accommodations. The most reasonable place is the *Camping Municipal* near the river, where sites cost US$5 with hot showers. Insects can be abundant, and the most low-lying sites can flood in heavy rain – select your tent site carefully.

Hotel San Martín, on the plaza at Sargento Cabral 712, is bright and cheerful for $15/20 single/double. *El Parador Yapeyú* (☎ 93056), at the entrance to town, has bungalows for US$30/40. *Hotel Paraíso* is comparable.

Restaurant Bicentenario has well-prepared food, reasonable prices, and extremely friendly and attentive service. There is another passable restaurant on the plaza, next to Hotel San Martín.

Getting There & Away

The small bus station is two blocks south of the plaza. Crucero del Norte stops several times daily en route between Paso de Los Libres and Posadas.

SANTO TOMÉ

Another stop on the Jesuit mission circuit, Santo Tomé is 140 km north of Yapeyú via RN 14. Its **Museo Histórico Regional**, Navajas 844, is open weekdays 8 to 11 am and 5 to 7 pm, and also has a library. It's possible to cross to the Brazilian town of São Borja, which also has Jesuit ruins, via a launch/ferry that operates weekdays 7 to 10 am and 1 to 4 pm, weekends 7 to 9 am and 1 to 4 pm. Passengers pay US50¢, while automobiles pay US$6.

There is an ACA hotel (☎ 0756-20162)

at Patricio Bertrán and Belgrano, plus several nearby campgrounds along Av San Martín. Crucero del Norte goes three times daily to Posadas.

Misiones Province

On the map of Argentina, Misiones is the political geographic peninsula surrounded by the ocean of Brazil and Paraguay. Its outstanding natural feature is the Cataratas del Iguazú (Iguazú Falls) on the upper Paraná, one of South America's major

natural attractions, but the cultural landscape of ruined Jesuit missions also draws large numbers of visitors.

Unlike the rest of Argentine Mesopotamia, Misiones is mountainous. The Sierra Central, separating the watersheds of the two major rivers, reaches elevations up to 800 meters, although it only rarely exceeds 500 meters. The natural vegetation is mostly subtropical forest, though some large stands of native Araucaria pines remain; however, the forest cover in the province declined from 2.5 million hectares to 1.1 million hectares between 1914 and 1983.

ARGENTINA

The Jesuit Missions

After the Spaniards realized that America was not a storehouse of precious metals, they sought their wealth through the encomienda, a grant of native labor that also assigned them the responsibility of catechizing "their" Indians and teaching them Spanish. Although Spaniards rarely lived up to their part of the bargain, the encomienda successfully overcame problems of economic organization in settled, densely populated areas like Mexico and Peru – at least until the Indians died out from smallpox and other introduced diseases. But the encomienda was ineffective in areas where the Indians were less sedentary and their political organization less centralized. This was the case on the upper Paraná of Paraguay and Argentina, where Spanish encomenderos controlled only very small amounts of Indian labor.

Enter the Jesuit order, whose history differed greatly from the mendicant orders of the Middle Ages. Unhindered by vows of poverty and with a genius for organization, the Jesuits brought about a major political, economic, and cultural transformation among the semisedentary Guaraní. Their remarkable success also aroused envy and intrigue against them.

The Jesuits began their activities in 1607 in eastern Paraguay, an area largely overlooked by secular Spaniards. Sixteen of the 30 missions that operated in the 18th century were in present-day Argentina, mostly in Misiones but a few in Corrientes, while the remainder were equally distributed between modern Paraguay and Brazil. Their organizational principle was *reducción* or *congregación*, the common Spanish practice of concentrating the Indians, breaking their nomadic habits and reorganizing their political structure. Because the area was so isolated, the Jesuits had little competition until the success of their enterprise became apparent.

The first challenge to the Jesuits came from the Portuguese slave raiders of São Paulo, known as *paulistas* or *bandeirantes*. Only two decades after their establishment, 11 of the first 13 missions were destroyed and their native inhabitants abducted. The Jesuits responded by moving operations westward and raising an army to repel any further incursions. The evacuation of the missions was an epic event – the Jesuits and Indians rafted down the Paraná to the precipitous Guairá Falls (now inundated by the Brazilian-Paraguayan Itaipú dam), descended to their base, and built new rafts to continue the journey. Thousands of Indians perished, but the Jesuits successfully re-established themselves at new sites.

Slavers were not the only menace. Some local *caciques* (chiefs) resented the Jesuit conversion of their peoples, while the physical concentration of the Indians accelerated the spread of European diseases to which they had little natural immunity. Between 1717 and 1719, for example, an epidemic killed off nearly a sixth of the mission population. Travel between missions spread the contagion. In succeeding decades, discontent among secular Spaniards *(comuneros)* in Corrientes led to invasions just as devastating as those of the bandeirantes. Eventually, these disturbances and exaggerated rumors of Jesuit intrigue resulted in the order's expulsion in 1767.

The physical organization of the Jesuit missions was nearly identical to that of Spanish secular municipalities. Spanish colonial ordinances had dictated the Roman grid system based upon a central square from which all streets extended at right angles. The Jesuits imitated this form but usually enclosed the plaza with buildings whose function was religious rather than secular – the church, priests' quarters, and classrooms. This pattern is obvious in the plan of San Ignacio Miní, the best restored of the Argentine missions. Often earthworks or a trench surrounded the settlement for purposes of defense.

The mission economy was largely agricultural and diversified. The Indians raised their own

Economically, Misiones is the country's largest producer of *yerba mate,* the staple drink of Argentines and of many Uruguayans, Paraguayans, and Brazilians. Most yerba plantations are just east of the provincial capital of Posadas, but the central uplands also support large monocultures of tea. In recent years forestry has become important, with large plantations of northern hemisphere pines replacing the native Araucarias.

History

Misiones province is best known for the Jesuit settlements *(reducciones* or *congregaciones)* for which the province is named. From 1607, after finding the nomadic Indians of the Chaco poor candidates for missionary instruction, the Jesuits established 30 missions among the semisedentary Guaraní in the upper Paraná, in present-day Argentina, Brazil, and Paraguay. Perhaps as many as 100,000 Indians

subsistence crops (maize, sweet potatoes, and cassava) but also labored on communal fields. *Yerba mate* was the most important plantation crop, but cotton, citrus, and tobacco were also significant. Within the settlement itself, intensive vegetable gardening yielded carrots, tomatoes, beans, peas, radishes, and beets. Outside the settlement, native herders tended the mission's numerous livestock. When the Jesuits were expelled, San Ignacio Miní had a population of 3200 but possessed ten times that many cattle and more than twice that many sheep and goats.

Life on the reducción was probably less idyllic than portrayed in the film *The Mission*, but the labor was certainly less odious than elsewhere. The Jesuits closely regulated many aspects of everyday life such as education and dress, but their exuberant approach to work made mission residence sufficiently attractive that many Indians willingly chose it over the grim certainties of the encomienda. With the aid of skilled German priests, the Guaraní learned crafts and trades like weaving, baking, carpentry, cabinetmaking, and even the design of musical instruments. Unfortunately, these skills were useless to them in the post-mission world. ∎

lived in these settlements, which resembled other Spanish municipalities but operated with a political and economic autonomy that made them the envy of other Iberian settlers, who resented the missions' wealth and their monopoly on the Indian labor that made that wealth possible. The missions competed with secular producers in the cultivation and sale of *yerba mate,* then the region's only important commodity.

The conflict between the Jesuits and

other Iberians, both Spanish and Portuguese, was the background for the popular English-language film *The Mission,* with Robert De Niro and Jeremy Irons. Non-Jesuit settlers in the region, where the encomienda was less important than elsewhere in Spanish America, realized that they could never compete with the Jesuits unless they could persuade the Spanish crown to grant them Indian labor. The Jesuits resisted these efforts politically and even militarily, but their success eventually undermined their own position; Spanish concerns that they were becoming an autonomous state-within-a-state resulted in their expulsion from the New World in 1767.

The Jesuits' high degree of organization is apparent in ruins like San Ignacio Miní, with its enormous plaza, imposing church, and extensive outbuildings. Unlike most secular Spaniards and many other monastic orders, they took seriously their obligation to instruct indigenous peoples in the Spanish language and Catholic religion, but they also taught music, literature, and the arts. Much of the elaborate sandstone statuary that embellishes the ruins is the work of Guaraní sculptors.

Long before expulsion, the missions had begun to suffer *malocas* (Portuguese slave raids) and other setbacks – despite their good intentions, the Jesuits' concentration of Indians in fixed settlements made them more vulnerable to epidemics like smallpox. In the political vacuum after 1767, mission communities disintegrated rapidly and much of the area lapsed into virtual wilderness. Densely forested areas became a refuge for Indians lacking the protection of the missions but unwilling to submit to the demands of secular Spaniards.

During the 19th century, Argentina, Brazil, and Paraguay contested the territory, but after the War of the Triple Alliance (1865 – 1870) between Paraguay, on the one hand, and Argentina, Uruguay, and Brazil, on the other, Argentina took definitive control. Precise boundaries were not yet finalized, but European colonization proceeding from Corrientes by the mid-19th century soon intensified. Exploitation of wild *yerba mate* spurred settlement but resulted in large concessions of land to a very few individuals and companies. The federal government confiscated many of these holdings when their owners failed to survey and carry out improvements and, soon after, actively encouraged small-scale agricultural settlement.

By the turn of the century, colonists represented many nationalities: Poles, Brazil-

ians, Argentines, Paraguayans, Italians, Russians, Germans, Spaniards, French, Swedish, unspecified Asians, Swiss, Arabs, Danes, British, Greeks, and North Americans. The most successful were the German colonists around Eldorado on the upper Paraná, but the entire province preserves a polyglot heritage acknowledged by all its residents.

Potentially the most ironic episode in provincial history never came to pass. During the depression of the 1930s, British officials in the Falkland Islands briefly considered relocating Islanders to a colonization project at Victoria, near Eldorado, but gave up the project on the rationale that Falklanders were not suited for the humid subtropics. In the 1950s, Japanese immigrants settled successfully in the province, but most recently there has been a further influx of Brazilians. Besides agriculture, forestry, and some mining, tourism is now a major factor in the provincial economy.

For a superb account of the environment and colonization in Misiones from colonial times to the present, see Robert Eidt's *Pioneer Settlement in Northeast Argentina.* For the history of the Jesuit mission era, see Nicholas P Cushner's *Jesuit Ranches and the Agrarian Development of Colonial Argentina, 1650 – 1767.*

Visitors who read Spanish well may wish to acquire the *Guía Turística de Misiones* (Posadas: Editora y Difusora de Guías SRL, 1994), which focuses on the province and has gone through 13 editions.

POSADAS

Named for Gervasio Antonio de Posadas, who decreed the creation of Entre Ríos and Corrientes while briefly holding the position of Director of the Provincias Unidas in 1814, the city of Posadas is Misiones' provincial capital and commercial center. As part of Corrientes province, Posadas first developed after the War of the Triple Alliance because of its strategic location. When the federal government made Misiones a separate territory in the 1880s, Corrientes reluctantly surrendered Posadas, which became the territorial capital and the gateway to the pioneer agricultural communities of interior Misiones. In 1912, the Urquiza railway connected the city with Buenos Aires.

Despite its recent pioneer past, Posadas is a modern city of 200,000, and it is losing some of its low-lying areas to flooding from the Yacyretá hydroelectric project. In summer, plentiful shade trees moderate the otherwise oppressive heat and humidity. For most travelers, it will be a brief stopover en route to Paraguay or Iguazú, but no one should miss the restored Jesuit missions at San Ignacio Miní, about 50 km

east, or at Trinidad on the Paraguayan side of the border. The Yacyretá hydroelectric project is a different sort of monument.

Orientation

Posadas is on the south bank of the upper Río Paraná, 1310 km north of Buenos Aires by RN 14, 310 km east of Corrientes via RN 12, and 300 km southwest of Puerto Iguazú, also via RN 12. Since April 1990, a handsome international bridge has linked Posadas with the Paraguayan city of Encarnación, across the river, but launches still operate between the port areas of the two

PLACES TO STAY
1 Albergue Juvenil
6 Hotel Canciller
7 Hotel de
   Turismo Posadas
11 City Hotel
16 Posadas Hotel
18 Hotel Continental
24 Residencial Misiones
27 Hotel Julio César
28 Residencial Colón
29 Hotel Libertador
32 Le Petit Hotel
35 Hotel Horianski
36 Gran Hotel Misiones
37 Residencial Nagel
38 Residencial Neumann

PLACES TO EAT
10 Los Pinos
19 La Querencia
20 La Ventana
26 Heladería
   Costa Blanca
30 El Estribo

OTHER
2 Launches to Paraguay
3 Paraguayan Consulate
4 Telecom
5 Teatro El Desván
8 Austral
9 Post Office
12 Casa de Gobierno
13 Banco Nazionale
   del Lavoro (ATM)
14 Museo de Ciencias
   Naturales e Históricas
15 Cine Sarmiento
17 ACA
21 Liverpool Libros
22 Avis
23 Secretaría de
   Estado de Turismo
25 French Consulate
31 Turismo Guatá
33 Tigre, Expreso Singer
34 Terminal de Omnibus

Posadas

0   200   400 m

Río Paraná

Parque
República
del Paraguay

ARGENTINA

cities. Customs and immigration formalities for both countries take place on the Argentine side of the river.

Plaza 9 de Julio is the center of Posadas' standard grid. The city center, 14 blocks square, is circumscribed by four major thoroughfares: Av Corrientes in the west, Av Guacurarí in the north, Av Roque Sáenz Peña on the east, and Av Mitre to the south. Avenida Mitre leads east to the new international bridge to Paraguay.

Theoretically, all streets in the city center have recently been renumbered, but new and old systems exist side-by-side, creating great confusion to nonresidents, since most locals strongly prefer the old system. Wherever possible, the information below refers to unambiguous locations rather than street numbers; if street numbers are given, the new number appears first with the old number in parentheses.

Information

Tourist Offices The exceptionally helpful, well-organized, and well-informed Secretaría de Estado de Turismo (☎ 33185) is at Colón 1985 (ex-393) between Córdoba and La Rioja. It has numerous maps and brochures, and is open weekdays 6:30 am to 12:30 pm, and 2 to 8 pm. Holiday and weekend hours are 8 am to noon and 4 to 8 pm.

ACA (☎ 36955) is at Córdoba and Colón.

Foreign Consulates Paraguay has a consulate (☎ 23850) on San Lorenzo between Santa Fe and Sarmiento, open weekdays from 8 am to noon. It's friendly and has a few brochures and basic maps.

Brazil's consulate (☎ 24830), at Mitre 1242 (631) near the entrance to the Encarnación bridge, offers same-day visa service and does not insist on a photograph. Hours are weekdays 9 am to 1 pm and 4 to 6:30 pm.

France has a consulate (☎ 23519) at La Rioja and General Paz.

Money Cambio Mazza, on Bolívar between San Lorenzo and Colón, will change traveler's checks. Banco Nazionale del Lavoro has a convenient ATM on Bolívar, at the southeastern corner of Plaza 9 de Julio, but there are several others downtown.

Post & Telecommunications Correo Argentino is at Bolívar and Ayacucho; the postal code is 3300. Telecom is at Colón and Santa Fe, but there are additional long-distance telephones on Junín between Bolívar and Córdoba, open 7 am to midnight. Posadas' area code is 0752.

Travel Agencies To arrange tours to nearby sights like Yacyretá or the Jesuit ruins at San Ignacio, Santa Ana, and Loreto for about US$30, try Turismo Guatá (☎ 28583), Salta 1853.

At Urquiza (the westward extension of Guacurarí) and Zapiola, Turismo Operativo Misionero (☎ 27951) runs trips to less accessible natural attractions like the Esteros del Iberá and parts of Parque Nacional Iguazú.

Bookstore Liverpool Libros, at the corner of Ayacucho and La Rioja, has English-language books.

Medical Services The Hospital General R Madariaga (☎ 23112) is about one km south of downtown, at Av López Torres 1177.

Museo de Ciencias Naturales e Históricas

The natural-history section of this very worthwhile museum, on San Luis between Córdoba and La Rioja, focuses on invertebrates, vertebrates, and the geology and mineralogy of the province; it also has an excellent serpentarium, an aviary, and an aquarium. Its historical section stresses prehistory, the Jesuit missions, and modern colonization.

Normal hours are Tuesday to Friday 8 am to noon and 3 to 7 pm, weekends 9 am to noon. During winter holidays, hours are 9 am to noon and 3 to 8 pm daily except Monday. Every July morning at 10 am there is a demonstration of how to extract snake venom.

Museo Regional de Posadas
At the north end of Alberdi near Parque República de Paraguay, this museum has an interesting collection of stuffed natural-history specimens, ethnographic artifacts, and historical relics.

Places to Stay – bottom end
Camping The campground at the Balneario Municipal on the river is cramped, noisy, and overpriced at US$3 per person, plus US$3 per vehicle; locals overrun the place on weekends in particular, so sleep is impossible. It's not recommended, but there's no nearby alternative.

Hostel For US$8 per night, there are hostel accommodations at *Albergue Juvenil* (☎ 23700) at the Anfiteatro MA Ramírez, on the riverfront at the north end of Alberdi.

Residenciales & Hotels Posadas offers a reasonable selection of relatively inexpensive accommodations, though you might also consider the better values over the border in Encarnación, Paraguay. One popular place is *Residencial Misiones* (☎ 30133), on Av Azara between La Rioja and Córdoba, where singles/doubles with private bath are US$15/25, but recent visitors have questioned its standards. A good, comparably priced choice is *Residencial Neumann* (☎ 24675), on Roque Sáenz Peña between Mitre and Santiago del Estero. *Residencial Nagel* (☎ 25656), at Pedro Méndez and Uruguay, charges US$16 per person.

Others in this range charge around US$20/31. These include *Hotel Horianski* (☎ 22673) at Av Mitre and Líbano, *City Hotel* (☎ 33901) on Colón opposite Plaza 9 de Julio, and *Gran Hotel Misiones* (☎ 22777) on Líbano at Barrufaldi near the bus terminal, which also has a restaurant. A reader recommendation, seconded by locals, is *Le Petit Hotel* (☎ 36031), on Santiago del Estero between Rivadavia and Buenos Aires, which has rooms with private bath for US$20/30 .

Places to Stay – middle
Midrange places start around US$22/32, like the visually appealing but distinctly unfriendly *Residencial Colón* (☎ 25085), on Colón between Entre Ríos and Catamarca. Despite its impersonal appearance, the high-rise *Hotel de Turismo Posadas* (☎ 37401), at Bolívar and Junín, is much friendlier and its balconies have excellent river views; rates are US$25/38. *Residencial Carioca* (☎ 24113), on Mitre near the Expreso Singer bus terminal, has rooms for US$25/30, while *Hotel Canciller* (☎ 31602), at Junín and San Martín, charges US$31/40 with private bath but without breakfast.

Places to Stay – top end
Hotel Continental (☎ 27045), on Bolívar opposite Plaza 9 de Julio, charges US$48/68 for rooms with private bath and breakfast. *Hotel Libertador* (☎ 36901), on San Lorenzo between Catamarca and Salta, offers similar services at slightly lower prices, around US$50/60.

At the top-of-the-line *Posadas Hotel* (☎ 30801), on Bolívar between Colón and San Lorenzo, rooms with bath and breakfast are US$60/65. The *Hotel Julio César* (☎ 27930), on Entre Ríos between San Lorenzo and Colón, is Posadas' only four-star hotel, for US$65/80 with breakfast.

Places to Eat
There are many interchangeable, inexpensive eating places along San Lorenzo west of the plaza, but parrillas are the standard, with several excellent ones. The spiffiest is *La Querencia* (☎ 37117) on Bolívar, across from Plaza 9 de Julio. *La Ventana* (☎ 37581), Bolívar 1725 (580) between Av Azara and Calle Buenos Aires, has a varied menu with large portions and reasonable prices – at least for some items.

El Estribo, at the corner of Tucumán and Ayacucho, has a US$4 lunch menu in addition to its roasted chicken specialty. *Los Pinos,* on San Lorenzo between Bolívar and San Martín, is one of Posadas' better pizzerías.

For ice cream, try *Costa Blanca* at the corner of Ayacucho and Entre Ríos.

Entertainment
Cine Sarmiento is on Córdoba between San Lorenzo and Ayacucho. *Teatro El Desván,* a provincial theater company on Sarmiento between Colón and San Lorenzo, offers works by major Spanish-language playwrights like Federico García Lorca. There is also a children's theater.

Things to Buy
Posadas has a good selection of artisanal products. Try La Barraca, next door to Teatro El Desván, or El Payé, around the corner on Colón, where there is a good selection of *mate* paraphernalia (gourds and bombillas), basketry, wood carvings, and ceramics.

Getting There & Away
Air Austral (☎ 32889, 35031), at the corner of Ayacucho and San Martín, flies twice daily between Posadas and Buenos Aires except Saturdays, when there's a morning flight only.

Bus The main Terminal de Omnibus (☎ 25800) is at Av Mitre and Uruguay, but Tigre and Expreso Singer (☎ 24771) have a separate terminal three blocks west. There are excellent regional and long-distance services.

Singer has daily service to Buenos Aires (US$30, 13½ hours; US$55 in *coche cama* sleepers) and intermediate points, and to Santa Fe (14 hours) and Córdoba (US$41, 19½ hours). Other carriers serving Buenos Aires include El Crucero (☎ 27653), Crucero del Norte (☎ 27897), Empresa Kurtz (☎ 22393), Metro Bus Klein (☎ 25800), Expreso Via Bariloche (☎ 35788), and Empresa Tigre Iguazú (☎ 26210). Ciudad de Posadas (☎ 24331), El Norte Bis (☎ 22393), Horianski (☎ 29334), and Kurtz all go to Rosario (16 hours).

Singer also has international services daily to Asunción (5½ hours) all year and

three times weekly to Porto Alegre, Brazil (12 hours) in summer. Nuestra Señora de la Asunción (☎ 24404) also docs the Asunción route.

To Puerto Iguazú, the Martignoni, Cotal, and Tigre busses take 5½ hours express but much longer on the local (stopping) bus. Fares are about US$20. Tigre's earliest bus to San Ignacio Miní that departs at a reasonable hour leaves at 6:10 am; departures are hourly thereafter.

Ciudad de Posadas, Martignoni, and Kurtz all run buses to Corrientes (US$18, five hours) and Resistencia, with connections across the Chaco to northwestern Argentina. Cotal has service to Mendoza (34½ hours) via Santiago del Estero (18½ hours), Catamarca, La Rioja, and San Juan.

Since the opening of the international bridge, there are buses from Posadas to Encarnación, Paraguay, leaving every 15 minutes from the corner of Mitre and Junín, opposite the bus terminal. With border formalities, the trip can take an hour, but is often quicker; fares are US$1 *común,* US$2 *servicio diferencial* (with air-con).

Boat Launches across the Paraná to Encarnación (US$1) continue to operate despite the new bridge, although they may cease because the reservoir behind Yacyretá dam floods the low-lying parts of the two cities. For the moment, they leave from the dock at the east end of Av Guacurarí.

Getting Around
To/From the Airport Austral has its own minibus to Aeropuerto Internacional Posadas, 12 km southwest of town via RN 12, but the No 8 bus also goes there from San Lorenzo between La Rioja and Entre Ríos.

Car Rental Try Avis (☎ 32745), across from ACA at Córdoba and Colón.

AROUND POSADAS
Yacyretá Dam
A vivid lesson in foreign debt, this gigantic hydroelectric project is actually in Corrientes province near the town of Ituzaingó,

but is more accessible from Posadas. At Ituzaingó, 1½ hours from Posadas by bus, the Argentine-Paraguayan Entidad Binacional Yacyretá has given up trying to put this boondoggle in the best possible light, instead delegating the responsibility to Ri-Mar-Os Tur (☎ 0786-20546), which now charges US$3.50 to visit the installations. Tours leave at 8, 9, 10, and 11 am, and 2, 3, 4, and 5 pm from the Centro Cultural (☎ 21278) on the main plaza. A museum displays artifacts unearthed in the process of construction and a scale model of the project, and you can also see the enormous city built to house the dam workers. Guides are well rehearsed, but the bus rarely slows and never stops for photographs. For a more complete analysis of the Yacyretá debacle, see Gustavo Lins Ribeiro's *Transnational Capitalism and Hydropolitics in Argentina: the Yacyretá High Dam.*

Visitors opting to stay overnight might try moderately priced *Hotel Géminis* (☎ (0783) 20324) at Corrientes 943 or the more elaborate *Hotel Yaciretá* (☎ 20577) at Buenos Aires and Loreto. Empresa Ciudad de Posadas (☎ 20111) links Ituzaingó with Corrientes and Posadas.

Santa Ana

Buses from Posadas will drop passengers at the clearly marked turnoff to the ruins at Santa Ana (founded 1633), at Km 43 along RN 12. Mostly covered by the luxuriant rain forest and strangler figs, the settlement's outlines are nevertheless clear. The walk from the junction is one km.

Loreto

Founded in 1632 by Padre Antonio Ruiz de Montoya, Loreto saw the first book published in what is now Argentina in the year 1700; *Martirologio Romano* (Roman Martirology) was later translated into Guaraní. Buses from Posadas will also stop here, at Km 48 along RN 12, but the distance from the highway to the ruins is greater than at Santa Ana.

SAN IGNACIO & SAN IGNACIO MINÍ

Visitors can see the ruins of San Ignacio Miní, the former reducción, on a day trip from Posadas, but lodging in the appealing village of San Ignacio gives more time to explore. Other sights, besides the ruins, include the house of Uruguayan writer Horacio Quiroga and the provincial museum. The town is very small, and everything is within easy walking distance.

San Ignacio is 56 km east of Posadas via RN 12. From the highway junction, the broad Av Sarmiento leads about one kilo-

---

Megawatts for Megabucks

Upon its projected completion in 1997, Yacyretá Dam will form a monstrous reservoir of 1800 sq km which will submerge the Paraná more than 200 km upstream, inundate low-lying areas of Posadas and Encarnación, require the relocation of nearly 40,000 people, and connect Ituzaingó with the Paraguayan city of Ayolas in a new border crossing. Presumably it will provide energy for industrial development in Argentina's northern provinces, increasing Argentine and Paraguayan electricity supplies by 50%. As of early 1995, its four functioning turbines were generating 2.8 million megawatts of power, and water was lapping at the sidewalks of the older parts of Encarnación. The remaining 16 turbines are due to come on line in 1998.

While the stated rationale for development of Yacyretá was energy demand, informed analysts believe that geopolitics played a more important role in Juan Perón's last government, which proposed the project in 1973. Current Argentine President Carlos Menem himself once called the project "a monument to corruption" which may cost eight times the original estimate of US$1.5 billion (thousand million); it presently stands at US$8.5 billion. Despite Menem's original, publicly stated intention of stopping the project, his government solicited further loans to continue construction and has resisted compensating Paraguay for the relocation of those displaced by the rising waters (it will flood five times as much Paraguayan as Argentine territory). There are attempts to privatize the project in order to get buyers to assume the debt, with the incentive of permitting sales to Brazil, but this would do away with a proposed 15% reduction in the domestic price of electricity in Argentina. ∎

meter to Calle Rivadavia, which leads four blocks east to the ruins. San Ignacio's area code is 0752.

San Ignacio Miní

San Ignacio Guazú, founded in 1609 but abandoned after repeated attacks by Brazilian slavers, was the forerunner of San Ignacio Miní, which was founded in 1632 on the Río Yabebiry and later shifted a short distance away. At its peak, in 1733, it had a Guaraní population of nearly 4000. Its ruins, rediscovered in 1897 and restored after 1943, are among the region's most impressive, though Trinidad and Jesús on the Paraguayan side of the river have more imposing hilltop sites. Admission to the ruins costs US$2.50.

San Ignacio's architecture belongs to a style known as "Guaraní baroque." Designed by Italian Jesuit architect Juan Brasanelli, the enormous red sandstone church, 74 meters long and 24 meters wide with walls two meters thick at their base, was the focal point of the settlement. Adjacent to the tile-roofed church, which was embellished with bas-relief sculptures by Guaraní artists, was the cemetery and the priests' cloisters. In the same complex were classrooms, a kitchen, a dining room, and workshops. On all sides of the Plaza de Armas were the Indians' living quarters.

Museo Provincial Miguel Nadasdy

On Av Sarmiento near the turnoff to the ruins, this museum displays the archaeological and ethnological collections of a dedicated Romanian immigrant. Focus on the exhibits, which include stone tools, a complete dugout canoe, and 19th-century weapons, and try to overlook the caretaker's bizarre theories of local prehistory. Opening hours are 7:30 am to noon and 3:30 to 7 pm daily.

Casa de Horacio Quiroga

Uruguayan-born of Argentine parents, Quiroga was a poet and novelist who also

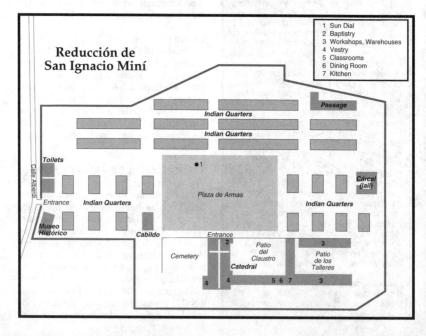

Reducción de San Ignacio Miní

1 Sun Dial
2 Baptistry
3 Workshops, Warehouses
4 Vestry
5 Classrooms
6 Dining Room
7 Kitchen

Passage

Indian Quarters

Indian Quarters

Toilets

Calle Alberdi

Cárcel (jail)

Entrance   Indian Quarters   Plaza de Armas   Indian Quarters

• 1

Museo Histórico

Entrance

Cabildo   Entrance

Cemetery   Patio del Claustro   Patio de los Talleres

2   3

Catedral

4   4   5 6 7   3

dabbled in other activities, taking some of the earliest photographs of the rediscovered ruins at San Ignacio and farming cotton (unsuccessfully) in the Chaco. He lived in San Ignacio from 1910 to 1917, when his first wife committed suicide (as did Quiroga himself, terminally ill, 20 years later).

Unlike Enrique Larreta's Hispanicist nostalgia and Ricardo Güiraldes' gauchesco romanticism, Quiroga's regionally based stories transcend both time and place without abandoning their setting. Some of his short fiction is available in English translation in *The Exiles and Other Stories,* while Pedro Orgambide has recently published *Horacio Quiroga: Una Biografía.* The house is open daily 8:30 am to 7:30 pm.

Places to Stay & Eat
Camping At the *free site* just beyond the entrance to the ruins, there are no sanitary facilities and the urchins who hang out there may disturb your sleep. Try instead Hospedaje Los Salpeterer (see below), where two can pitch a tent on the grounds for US$6.

Hospedajes, Hosterías & Hotels The cheapest accommodation is German-run *Hospedaje Los Salpeterer* at Sarmiento and Centenario, a short walk from the bus terminal. Rooms with shared bath cost US$7 per person with access to kitchen facilities, while those with private bath cost US$10. Another possibility is *Hospedaje El Descanso,* a bit farther from the ruins at Pellegrini 270. Highly recommended *Hotel San Ignacio* (☎ 70047), Sarmiento 823, has singles/doubles with bath for about US$20/30.

Hostería Tom (☎ 70003), Independencia 469, has rooms with bath and air-con for US$30/35, as well as a pool and a decent restaurant. There are several more places to eat across from the entrance to the ruins, where *El Jardín* has good, filling dinners starting at US$4.

Getting There & Away
The bus terminal is at the north end of Sarmiento. Empresa Tigre and other companies have 26 daily buses to Posadas (US$3.50), the last of which leaves at 10:40 pm. Tigre has buses to Puerto Iguazú (US$17 direct) at 6:10 am, 2:10 pm, and 8:10 pm. Other buses along RN 12 will stop readily en route in either direction.

PUERTO IGUAZÚ
At the confluence of the Río Paraná and the Río Iguazú, the village of Puerto Iguazú hosts most visitors to the Argentine side of Iguazú Falls, which are only 15 km away. Despite the area's popularity, prices for food and accommodations are surprisingly reasonable. Some visitors stay at Foz do Iguaçu, on the Brazilian side, but certain nationalities (including Americans and Australians) need a visa to do so.

Orientation
Some 300 km northwest of Posadas via paved RN 12, Puerto Iguazú has a very irregular city plan, but fortunately is small enough to find your way around easily. The main drag is the diagonal Av Victoria Aguirre, which enters town in the southeast, but most tourist services are just north of Av Victoria Aguirre in a rabbit warren of streets that cross each other at odd angles.

From the Hito Argentino, at the confluence of the rivers at the west end of Av Tres Fronteras, you can see both Brazil and Paraguay. (The Hito Argentino is a small obelisk marking Argentine territory; all three countries have a similar landmark on their side of the junction between the Paraná and Iguazú rivers.)

Information
Tourist Offices The Secretaría de Turismo (☎ 20800), Av Victoria Aguirre 311, is open weekdays from 8 am to 8 pm, weekends from 8 am to noon and 4:30 to 8 pm.

ACA (☎ 20165) is on the highway to the park, just beyond Camping El Pindó.

Foreign Consulate Brazil's impressively efficient consulate, on Av Victoria Aguirre

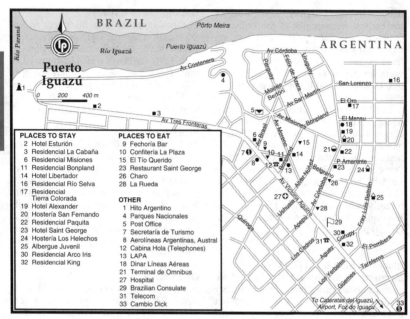

Puerto Iguazú

PLACES TO STAY
2 Hotel Esturión
3 Residencial La Cabaña
6 Residencial Misiones
11 Residencial Bonpland
14 Hotel Libertador
16 Residencial Río Selva
17 Residencial
   Tierra Colorada
19 Hotel Alexander
20 Hostería San Fernando
22 Residencial Paquita
23 Hotel Saint George
24 Hostería Los Helechos
25 Albergue Juvenil
30 Residencial Arco Iris
32 Residencial King

PLACES TO EAT
9 Fechoría Bar
10 Confitería La Plaza
15 El Tío Querido
23 Restaurant Saint George
26 Charo
28 La Rueda

OTHER
1 Hito Argentino
4 Parques Nacionales
5 Post Office
7 Secretaría de Turismo
8 Aerolíneas Argentinas, Austral
12 Cabina Hola (Telephones)
13 LAPA
18 Dinar Líneas Aéreas
21 Terminal de Omnibus
27 Hospital
29 Brazilian Consulate
31 Telecom
33 Cambio Dick

between Av Córdoba and Curupy, turns around visa applications in as little as half an hour. Public hours are weekdays from 8 am to noon.

Money Change cash or traveler's checks at Cambio Dick (☎ 20545), Av Aguirre 471, where there is also a market for Brazilian reals and Paraguayan guaraníes, but note some reports of very high commissions on checks. Before buying Brazilian currency, ask other travelers about black market trends in Foz do Iguaçu.

Post & Telecommunications Correo Argentino is at Av San Martín 780; the postal code is 3730.

Telecom is at Av Victoria Aguirre 146 Sur, between Los Cedros and Aguay, but Cabina Hola is a convenient locutorio on Aguirre near Bonpland. Puerto Iguazú's area code is 0757.

Travel Agency Turismo Operativo Misionero (☎ 21240), Mariano Moreno 58, arranges trips to less frequented sections of Parque Nacional Iguazú and to less frequented destinations such as the Esteros del Iberá.

Medical Services The hospital is at Av Victoria Aguirre and Ushuaia.

Time Note that Argentina is an hour behind Brazil, which means that 7 am in Brazil is 6 am in Argentina.

Organized Tours
Many of Puerto Iguazu's operators offer day tours to the Brazilian side of the falls. These include a meal and a trip to Itaipú dam and Ciudad del Este in Paraguay, and cost about US$25. One traveler recommendation is Turismo Cuenca del Plata (☎ 20338), on Paulino Amarante near Hostería Los Helechos.

Places to Stay
Both Puerto Iguazú and Foz do Iguaçu have many suitable places to stay in all price

ranges. Foz usually tends to be a bit cheaper and Brazilian food may be a welcome change for anyone tired of beef, but the grossly overvalued Brazilian real has recently upset this traditional balance and the Argentine side may be slightly cheaper; even though the Argentine peso is itself overvalued, the accommodations here are of better value than in other parts of Argentina. The near absence of street crime in Puerto Iguazú may tip the balance for some travelers.

Note that higher prices often prevail during Semana Santa and during Argentine winter holidays in July, and occasionally in January if demand is heavy.

Places to Stay – bottom end
Camping *Camping El Pindó*, at Km 3½ of RN 12 on the edge of town, charges US$3 per person and US$3 per vehicle. *Camping Americano* (☎ 20820), at Km 5, charges US$3 per person and US$3 per tent; some recent visitors have complained of dirtiness at the site.

Hostels Puerto Iguazú's *Albergue Juvenil* (☎ 20529), at Fray Luis Beltrán 116, charges US$6 with breakfast included. *Hostería Los Helechos* (☎ 20338), at Paulina Amarante 76 near Beltrán, is a superb value for US$15/25, though a bit dearer in high season. *Hostería San Fernando* (☎ 21429), at Av Córdoba 693 opposite the bus terminal, has shown recent improvement.

Residenciales & Hotels *Residencial Arco Iris* (☎ 20636), Curupy 152, is very popular with travelers for US$15/20 single/double with private bath. Shady At Victoria Aguirre 915, *Residencial King* (☎ 20360) has attractive grounds and a swimming pool for about the same price. Other desirable places in this category include *Residencial Paquita* (☎ 20434) at Av Córdoba 158 for US$15/22 and *Residencial Bonpland* (☎ 20965) at Bonpland 33. *Residencial La Cabaña* (☎ 20564) is farther out, on Av Tres Fronteras 530 at Urquiza, and

more expensive at US$15/20 in low season, US$20/30 in peak season.

For US$12/20 single/double or even cheaper in the off season, Tidy *Residencial Río Selva* (☎ 21555), San Lorenzo 140, is slightly dearer at US$15/22, and also has a pool. Another inexpensive choice is *Residencial Misiones* (☎ 20991), at Av Victoria Aguirre 389 near Calle Brasil, for about US$15/25. *Residencial Tierra Colorada* (☎ 20649), at El Oro 265, charges US$12/15 for rooms with private bath in low season, US$20/25 in peak season.

Places to Stay – middle
Somewhat costlier are *Hotel Alexander* (☎ 20249) at Av Córdoba 222 for US$25/35 in low season, US$35/45 in high season, and the perennial favorite *Hotel Saint George* (☎ 20633), at Córdoba 148, for US$30/35 in low season, US$40/50 in high season; it also has a swimming pool. The declining *Hotel Libertador* (☎ 20570) at Bonpland 475 has lost some of its former prestige. Rates are US$30/40 in low season, US$36/48 in high season.

Places to Stay – top end
Quite near the national park, *Hotel Esturión* (☎ 20020, fax 20414), at Av Tres Fronteras 650, offers singles/doubles for US$80/90 with breakfast. For just a little more, about US$112/135, indulge yourself at the hideously ill-situated *Hotel Internacional Iguazú* (☎ 20296, fax 20311), near the visitors center at Parque Nacional Iguazú, but rooms with a view of the falls cost US$147/177. If you have a package tour with meals included, obtain meal coupons before dining or you may end up paying extra.

Places to Eat
There are many places to eat in town, but there's also rapid turnover. For the cheapest eats, stroll around the triangle formed by Av Brasil, Perito Moreno, and Ingeniero Eppens. One reader recommends the Saturday fruit market at Córdoba and Félix de Azara.

The *Fechoría Bar* (☎ 20182), at Eppens 30 near Brazil, is a good breakfast choice. *La Plaza* is a lively confitería on Aguirre near Brazil. Recommended parrillas include *Tomás* (☎ 20850) at the bus terminal (the former owner is an accomplished harpist), *Charo* (☎ 21529) at Córdoba 106, and *La Rueda* on Córdoba near Victoria Aguirre. After hearing wildly contradictory readers' opinions of *Restaurant St George* in the Hotel St George (☎ 20633), Córdoba 148, I returned recently and found both food and service superb, but increasingly pricey. Another popular choice is *El Tío Querido* (☎ 20750), on Bonpland alongside Hotel Libertador.

Getting There & Away

Air Aerolíneas Argentinas (☎ 20168) is at Aguirre 295, offering services to Buenos Aires' Aeroparque ($184), as well as Tuesday and Saturday international service to and from São Paulo and Rio de Janeiro. Austral shares these offices, but currently has no flights to or from Yguazú. Aerolíneas "Conozca Cataratas" fare offers a 35% discount on roundtrips from Buenos Aires, valid three to five days only.

Dinar Líneas Aéreas (☎ 20566), a new airline at Córdoba 236, flies to Aeroparque (US$130) Thursday and Sunday afternoons. LAPA (☎ 20214), Bonpland 110 Local 7, has a similar schedule, but charges only US$99.

There are international services across the border, as well as Brazilian domestic services.

Bus The Terminal de Omnibus is at Avs Córdoba and Misiones. Companies with services to and from Posadas are Cotal, Horianski, Kurtz, Kruse, Martignoni, Aristóbulo del Valle, Empresa Iguazú, and Expreso Tigre Yguazú (☎ 20854). Expreso Singer (☎ 21581) has direct service to Córdoba and to Buenos Aires (US$45, 22 hours). It also has provincial services to the sierra immigrant town of Oberá. Other companies, some with slightly cheaper service to the capital, include Crucero del Norte (☎ 20291), Klein, Kurtz, Tony Tur (continuing to Mar del Plata), and Vía Bariloche, which continues to Bariloche (with a nearly ten-hour layover). Ciudad de Posadas (☎ 20854) goes to Corrientes. Cotal has direct service to Mendoza, a 40-hour marathon via Santiago del Estero and San Juan.

Getting Around

To/From the Airport Expreso Aristóbulo del Valle (☎ 20348, 20490), Entre Ríos 239, charges US$3 to the airport and will pick up passengers at their hotels; phone for reservations. A taxi will run around US$18.

Bus Buses to Parque Nacional Iguazú (US$2) leave hourly from 6:40 am to 8:15 pm from the bus terminal – catch an early one to avoid the heat and the hordes of tour buses that swarm around the falls about 11 am, when noisy Brazilian helicopters also begin their flights. The entrance fee for the park can be paid in Argentine pesos or US dollars.

Frequent buses cross to Foz do Iguaçu (US$2) and to Ciudad del Este, Paraguay from the bus terminal.

Car Rental Try Avis (☎ 20020) at the Hotel Esturión, Av Tres Fronteras 650, Localiza (☎ 20975) at Victoria Aguirre 279, or AI (☎ 20748) at Hotel Internacional Iguazú.

Taxi For a group of three persons or more hoping to see both sides of the falls as well as Ciudad del Este and the Itaipú hydroelectric project, a shared cab or remise can be a good idea; figure about US$60 to US$70 for a full day's sightseeing. Contact the Asociación de Trabajadores de Taxis (☎ 20282) at Aguirre and Brasil, or simply approach a driver.

PARQUE NACIONAL IGUAZÚ

Near the visitors center at Parque Nacional Iguazú, a plaque credits Alvar Nuñez Cabeza de Vaca with the discovery of the awesome Iguazú Falls in 1541, but he was at best the first European to view them. For

Around
Cataratas del Iguazú

the Guaraní Indians of the region and their predecessors, these impressive falls had been the source of legend for millennia.

According to Guaraní legend, the falls originated when an Indian warrior named Caroba incurred the wrath of a forest god by escaping down the river in a canoe with a young girl named Naipur, with whom the god had become infatuated. Enraged, the god caused the riverbed to collapse in front of the lovers, producing a line of precipitous falls over which Naipur fell and, at their base, turned into a rock. Caroba survived as a tree overlooking his fallen lover.

The geological origins of the falls are simpler and more prosaic. In southern Brazil, the Río Iguazú passes over a basaltic plateau that ends abruptly just east of the confluence with the Río Paraná. Where the lava flow stopped, at least 5000 cubic meters of water per second plunges more than 70 meters into the sedimentary terrain below – during floods, the volume can be many times greater. Prior to reaching the falls, the river divides into many channels with hidden reefs, rocks, and islands separating the many visually distinctive falls that together form the famous *cataratas*. In total, the falls are more than two km across.

You can see many of the falls up close via a system of *pasarelas* (catwalks), which offer unmatchable views. The most awesome is the semicircular Garganta del Diablo (Devil's Throat), a deafening and dampening but indispensable part of the experience.

Parque Nacional Iguazú occupies a total area of about 55,000 hectares, 6000 hectares of which constitute a Reserva Nacional, allowing for commercial development in the immediate area of the falls. Above the falls, the river itself is suitable for canoeing, kayaking, and other water sports.

Other attractions are well worth seeing, including substantial areas of subtropical rain forest, with unique flora and fauna – there are thousands of species of insects, hundreds of species of birds, and many mammals and reptiles.

Dangers & Annoyances

As Cabeza de Vaca wrote, the currents of the Río Yguazú are indeed strong and swift; in January 1995, an American tourist who attempted to swim from the mainland to Isla San Martín, below the falls, was swept downriver and drowned. It should go without saying that no one should get too close to the falls themselves. No one has ever gone over the cataratas, in a barrel or otherwise, and lived to tell about it.

Cataratas del Iguazú

Before seeing the falls themselves, have a quick look around the visitors center, which has a small museum and, depending on the budget, informational brochures. The tower near the visitors center offers a good overall view, but walking around is the best way to see the falls. Plan your hikes before or after the midmorning influx of tour buses. At midday, you can take a break from the heat at the restaurant and confitería here.

Formerly, an interconnected series of catwalks led to all the falls from the visitors center, but floods in 1983 destroyed a section and isolated those that go to Garganta del Diablo, the single most impressive cascade. You can still reach Garganta del Diablo by a good dirt road that goes to Puerto Canoas (hourly buses cost $1 for the four-km ride), whereas a $5 launch takes you to the remains of the pasarela to the overlook. At Ñandú, there is a confitería and, a bit farther on, a free rudimentary campground. Beyond the confitería, the road may not be passable to ordinary cars after heavy rain.

You can see most of the falls by roaming at will on the trails and catwalks around the visitors center; descending to the river, you can take a launch across to **Isla Grande San Martín,** the cost of which is now included in the park entry fee. Although the trip takes only a few minutes, the island offers views not available elsewhere and insulates you from the masses on the mainland. Swimming and picnicking are popular activities. After returning to the mainland, you can catch a bus or taxi to Ñandú, where another catwalk leads across the river to the Garganta del Diablo.

Of all the sights on earth, the **Garganta del Diablo** must come closest to the experience of sailing off the edge of a flat earth imagined by early European sailors. On three sides, the deafening cascade plunges to a murky destination; the vapors soaking the viewer blur the base of the falls. It is difficult to abandon a site of such menacing attraction, where you can still sense the awe that the native peoples of the region must have felt. Faced with this spectacle, though, early Spaniards showed only a practical indifference; Cabeza de Vaca reported that

the current of the Yguazú was so strong that the canoes were carried furiously down the river, for near this spot there is a considerable fall, and the noise made by the water leaping down some high rocks into a chasm may be heard a great distance off, and the spray rises two spears high and more over the fall. It was necessary, therefore, to take the canoes out of the water and carry them by hand past the cataract for half a league with great labor.

Similar attitudes in the present may have resulted in the use of the word "Iguazú" in a common line of Argentine toilet bowls, but at least since 1943, when the federal government incorporated the area into its national park system, hundreds of thousands of visitors have felt much greater emotion than the Spanish explorers. Still, relatively few venture beyond the immediate area of the falls to appreciate the park's other scenery and wildlife.

Flora & Fauna

Despite pressures for development and deforestation, Parque Nacional Iguazú presents a nearly pristine area of subtropical rain forest, with more than 2000 identified plant species, countless insects, 400 species of birds, and many mammals and reptiles. High temperatures, rainfall, and humidity encourage a diverse habitat.

Resembling the tropical Amazonian rain forest to the north, the forests of Misiones consist of multiple levels, the highest of

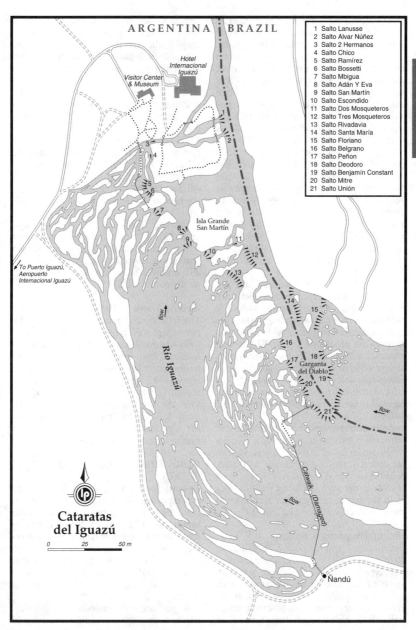

ARGENTINA

ARGENTINA   BRAZIL

Hotel
Internacional
Iguazú

Visitor Center
& Museum

1   Salto Lanusse
2   Salto Alvar Núñez
3   Salto 2 Hermanos
4   Salto Chico
5   Salto Ramírez
6   Salto Bossetti
7   Salto Mbigua
8   Salto Adán Y Eva
9   Salto San Martín
10 Salto Escondido
11 Salto Dos Mosqueteros
12 Salto Tres Mosqueteros
13 Salto Rivadavia
14 Salto Santa María
15 Salto Floriano
16 Salto Belgrano
17 Salto Peñon
18 Salto Deodoro
19 Salto Benjamín Constant
20 Salto Mitre
21 Salto Unión

Isla Grande
San Martín

To Puerto Iguazú,
Aeropuerto
Internacional Iguazú

Río Iguazú

flow

flow

Garganta
del Diablo

flow

Catwalk (Damaged)

flow

Cataratas
del Iguazú

0   25   50 m

Ñandú

them a closed canopy of trees more than 30 meters high. Descending, there are several additional levels of trees, plus a dense growth of shrubs and herbaceous plants on the ground. One of the most interesting species is the *guapoy* or strangler fig *(Ficus monckii),* an epiphyte which uses a large tree for support until it finally asphyxiates its host. This species covers the ruins of many abandoned Jesuit mission buildings found elsewhere in the province.

Other epiphytes take advantage of their hosts without harming them. Orchids use the limbs of large trees like the lapacho *(Tabebuia ipe)* or *palo rosa (Aspidosperma polyneuron)* for support only, absorbing essential nutrients from rainfall or the atmosphere. At lower levels in the forest, you will find wild specimens of yerba mate *(Ilex paraguariensis),* which Argentines and other residents of the River Plate region use for tea.

Mammals and other wildlife are not easily seen in the park, because many are either nocturnal or avoid humans – which is not difficult in the dense undergrowth. This is the case, for instance, with large cats such as the puma and jaguar. The largest mammal is the tapir *(Tapirus terrestris),* a distant relative of the horse, but the most commonly seen is the coatimundi *(Nasua nasua),* related to the raccoon. It is not unusual to see iguanas and do watch out for snakes.

Birds deserve special mention. Many of the species most of us normally see in pet shops can be found in the wild here, including toucans, parrots, parakeets, and other colorful species. The best time to see them is early in the morning along watercourses or in the forest, although the trees around the visitors center do not lack flocks.

Hiking, Bicycling & Rafting
Because the forest is so dense, there are relatively few trails, but walks along the road past Ñandú will usually reward you with views of wildlife. About 400 meters from the visitors center, along the road, is the entrance to the **Sendero Macuco** nature trail, which leads through dense forest to an almost hidden waterfall. The main trail is almost completely level, but a steep lateral drops to the base of the falls; the trail here is muddy and slippery – watch your step and figure about an hour each way. Early morning would be the best time for the trip, with better opportunities to see wildlife. Another trail goes to the *bañado,* a marsh that abounds in bird life. Take mosquito repellent.

To get elsewhere in the forest, hitch or hire a car to go out RN 101 toward the village of Bernardo de Irigoyen. Few visitors explore this part of the park, but it is still nearly pristine forest. Macuco Tours, at the visitors center, can arrange trips to this area.

Floating Iguazú, at the visitors center, arranges 4WD trips to the Yacaratia forest trail, organizes rafting excursions, and also rents mountain bikes. La Gran Aventura also arranges recommended raft/boat trips on the river for US$25.

Getting There & Away
The falls are 20 km from Puerto Iguazú by paved highway. Buses leave from Av Victoria Aguirre to the visitors center at hourly intervals between 7 am and 7 pm. The return schedule is similar. Entry to the park costs US$3 per person and includes the launch to Isla Grande San Martín. If you miss the last regular bus, inquire at the front desk of the Hotel Internacional for the employees' bus, which returns to Puerto Iguazú around 8 pm.

PARQUE NACIONAL FOZ DO IGUAÇU (BRAZIL)
To reach the Brazilian side of the falls, take the Argentine Tres Fronteras or the Brazilian Pluna or Itaipú bus over the Puente Internacional Tancredo Neves, which commemorates the popular Brazilian President-elect who died before he could take office in 1985. The trip takes about half an hour and costs US$2; buses run about every 15 minutes Monday to Saturday, hourly on Sunday.

If you are only crossing for the day, border formalities are minimal; you should not need a Brazilian visa, but you do need your passport, though neither Argentine nor Brazilian authorities should stamp it unless you are remaining in Brazil (in which case you may need a visa, depending on your nationality). At various times, readers have reported that Australian, New Zealand, French, British, and US citizens need a visa to cross to Foz do Iguaçu, so check in advance; one report suggests that a photo and a form at the border will suffice. Because of recent abuses of Brazilian tourists by US immigration, Brazilian authorities have begun to enforce such matters more tightly. If possible, get a visa before leaving your home country; otherwise, try to get it in a major capital like Buenos Aires.

The bus will drop you at the bus terminal at the city of Foz do Iguaçu, from which you can catch the Transbalan bus marked "Cataratas" to the falls. There is an admission charge of US$3 to the park, payable in Brazilian currency only. The bus drops you at the park's complex of hotels and parking lots, where a hillside catwalk leads to the falls themselves. There is an excellent overview of the falls, but you cannot approach them as closely as on the Argentine side.

The Brazilian side of the falls is more commercial than the Argentine side, but the hotels fit better into the landscape than the Argentine constructions. Argentine officials have complained that low-flying Brazilian helicopters, which offer aerial views of the falls for US$50, have disturbed wildlife, including nesting birds.

FOZ DO IGUAÇU (BRAZIL)
Having grown from a small town of 35,000 to a city of 190,000 as a result of the Itaipú hydroelectric scheme, the Brazilian border town of Foz do Iguaçu is a frenzied place with considerable street crime, particularly at night.

Orientation
Foz do Iguaçu is at the confluence of Rios Iguaçu and Paraná, 630 km south of Curitiba by BR-277. The Ponte Presidente Tancredo Neves links the city to Puerto Iguazú, Argentina, across the Río Iguazú, while the Ponte da Amizade connects it to Ciudad del Este, Paraguay, across the Río Paraná; 15 km upstream is Itaipú, the world's largest hydroelectric project.

Foz do Iguaçu has a compact center with a fairly regular grid, presenting no great difficulties of orientation. Av das Cataratas, at the southwest edge of town, leads 20 km to the world-famous falls via BR-469 and toward the Argentine border. Westbound BR-277 leads to Ciudad del Este.

Information
Tourist Offices Foztur maintains six information booths, all with maps, lists of hotels (one-star and above only), and tourist newspapers with descriptions of the attractions in English. All the staff are helpful, most speak English, and some also speak Italian, Spanish, or German. Teletur (☎ 1516) maintains a 24-hour information service with English-speaking operators.

There are information booths in the city at Rua Rio Branco (open 6:30 am to 10 pm), at the rodoviária (6 am to 6 pm), at the airport (9 am until the last plane), at Ponte Tancredo Neves on the Argentine border (8 am to 6 pm), just before the Ponte da Amizade on the Paraguayan border (8 am to 8 pm), and at the northern entrance to the city on BR-277 (7 am to 6 pm).

Money Recently, cambios have been giving more favorable rates in Foz do Iguaçu than elsewhere in Brazil. Try Cambio Dick in Foz, near the old bus station at Av Brasil 40, or Frontur at Av Brasil 75. There are plenty of others, but these two change both cash and traveler's checks.

Post & Telecommunications The post office is on Praça Getúlio Vargas. International phone calls can be made from Rua Rui Barbosa 475, or Rua Marechal Floriano Peixoto 1222. Foz do Iguaçu's area code is 045.

Visas Visitors spending the day outside Brazil will not require visas, but those intending to stay longer must go through

ARGENTINA

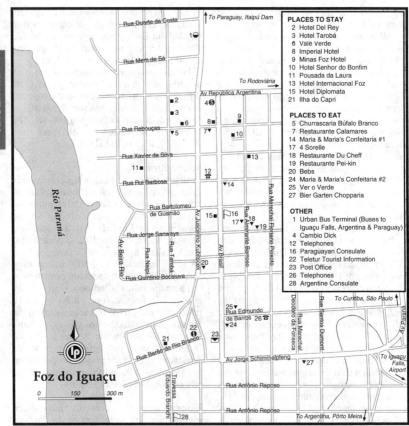

Foz do Iguaçu

0   150   300 m

PLACES TO STAY
2 Hotel Del Rey
3 Hotel Tarobá
6 Vale Verde
8 Imperial Hotel
9 Minas Foz Hotel
10 Hotel Senhor do Bonfim
11 Pousada da Laura
13 Hotel Internacional Foz
15 Hotel Diplomata
21 Ilha do Capri

PLACES TO EAT
5 Churrascaria Búfalo Branco
7 Restaurante Calamares
14 Maria & Maria's Confeitaria #1
17 4 Sorelle
18 Restaurante Du Cheff
19 Restaurante Pei-kin
20 Bebs
24 Maria & Maria's Confeitaria #2
25 Ver o Verde
27 Bier Garten Choppraria

OTHER
1 Urban Bus Terminal (Buses to
  Iguaçu Falls, Argentina & Paraguay)
4 Cambio Dick
12 Telephones
16 Paraguayan Consulate
22 Teletur Tourist Information
23 Post Office
26 Telephones
28 Argentine Consulate

the formalities. The Argentine consulate (☎ 574-2969), at Travessa Eduardo Branchi 26, is open weekdays 9 am to 2 pm. The Paraguayan consulate (☎ 523-2898), Rua Bartolomeu de Gusmão 738, is open weekdays 8:30 am to 1 pm and 3 to 6 pm.

Itaipú
Free guided tours of the Itaipú dam, 19 km from Foz, take place six times daily: at 8, 9, and 10 am, and 2, 3, and 4 pm; for more details on the project, see the Ciudad del Este entry in the Eastern Paraguay chapter. From Foz's downtown local bus terminal, take the "Conjunto C" bus (US50¢), which

runs north along Av Juscelino Kubitschek every 20 minutes from 5:30 am until 11 pm. Their last stop is at the Ecomuseu (worth a look), about 400 meters from the Itaipú visitors center.

Special Event
Foz's Pesca ao Dourado (Dorado Fishing Contest) takes place the last week of October.

Places to Stay
Foztur keeps a complete list of rated (one-star and up) hotels, but they don't have information about the real cheapies. Some

visitors have warned against official-looking locals with badges who direct backpackers to inferior accommodations.

Places to Stay – bottom end

Camping Just before the entrance to the park, *Camping Club do Brasil* (☎ 574-1310) is 600 meters up a dirt track to the left. It costs US$9 per person, and has a restaurant and swimming pool. Closer to the city of Foz, woodsy *Internacional* (☎ 574-2184) costs US$4 per person and also rents cabins for US$25 that can hold up to six people. It's a couple of kilometers out of Foz on the road to the falls' right-hand side and is well posted.

Hotels Around the old bus station are lots of cheap hotels, but the area is pretty seedy in the evenings. Popular with travelers is *Hotel Senhor do Bonfim* (☎ 572-1849), in a small, dead-end street just off Rua Almirante Barroso. They charge US$7 per person for dormitory accommodations with breakfast, and have fans in every room. The nearby *Minas Foz Hotel* (☎ 574-5208) at Rua Rebouças 641, has *apartamentos* (rooms with private bath) for US$8 per person without breakfast.

At Rua Rebouças 335 is *Vale Verde* (☎ 574-2925), the former youth hostel, which has received a few complaints from readers about the paper-thin walls and lack of privacy, but the lady who runs the place is helpful. She charges US$6 per person without breakfast, but for an extra US$1 you can eat it in the cafe out front.

The best place for budget travelers is inconspicuous *Pousada da Laura* (☎ 574-3628) at Rua Naipi 629 – look carefully for the sign. Laura speaks English, French, and Spanish, and her pousada is clean, safe, and friendly. You can even watch TV (from the USA via satellite) with the family in the living room. On a quieter, tree-lined street close to the local bus station, it costs US$7 per person with breakfast.

Places to Stay – middle

At *Ilha do Capri* (☎ 523-2300), Rua Barão do Rio Branco 409, singles/doubles go for US$20/30. It's handy for buses, close to a few eateries, and has a pool and a good breakfast. A bit cheaper is the *Consul* (☎ 574-5712) at Rua Rui Barbosa 1343. They rent small, air-con apartamentos for US$10/15 single/double, without breakfast.

The *Imperial Hotel* (☎ 523-1299) at Av Brasil 168 is a reasonable choice, with apartamentos for US$14/19 single/double, but the front rooms tend to get a bit noisy. *Hotel Diplomata* (☎ 523-1615), Av Brasil 678, also has a pool and charges US$30/40 single/double.

The *Hotel Del Rey* (☎ 523-2027) and the *Hotel Tarobá* (☎ 574-3890) are next door to each other on Rua Tarobá near the junction with República Argentina. Both charge US$30 for a double. The Del Rey has a pool and larger rooms, but both are well located for catching buses.

Places to Stay – top end

At the top end, the classiest place to stay is the *Hotel das Cataratas* (☎ 74-2666), right at the falls. Singles/doubles cost US$90/100, but Brazil airpass holders can get a 15% discount. Back in town, the five-star *Hotel Internacional Foz* (☎ 74-4855), at Rua Almirante Barroso 345, charges US$100 for a single and US$120 for a double.

Places to Eat

The best buffet deal in town is *Restaurante Calamares* at Rua Rebouças 476. At US$4 for all you can eat, it's the place to go for an energy boost after a hard day at the falls. Along Rua Almirante Barroso between Rua Jorge Sanways and Rua Xavier da Silva are lots of good places. For Italian food, *4 Sorelle* is at No 650. For seafood, *Restaurante Du Cheff* is at No 683. It's expensive, but excellent.

Readers have recommended *Maria's and Maria Confeitaria* for their baked goods, sandwiches, and hot chocolate. They have two locations, both on Av Brasil, at Nos 495 and 1285. *Pastel Mel*, in the third lane of Av Juscelino Kubitschek at No 26, has 30 different types of pancakes (US$3 each) and 20 types of pastels (US$1 each).

A good churrascaria is *Búfalo Branco* at Rua Rebouças 530. *Restaurante Pei-kin,* Rua Jorge Sanways 765, serves fair Chinese food. Vegetarians can lunch at *Ver o Verde* at Rua Barros 111 from 11 am to 3 pm. It has a cheap, self-serve buffet for US$4. *Bebs* at Av Juscelino Kubitschek 198 is a popular student hangout that gets pretty lively. The *Bier Garten Chopparia,* on the corner of Av Jorge Schimmelpfeng and Rua Marechal Deodoro da Fonseca, serves a good variety of pizza, steaks, and chops. It's in a pleasant setting, and gets crowded at night.

Getting There & Away
Air There are frequent flights from Foz do Iguaçu to Asunción, Buenos Aires, Rio, and São Paulo. VASP (☎ 523-2212) is at Av Brasil 845; Transbrasil (☎ 574-1734) is at Av Brasil 1225; and Varig/Cruzeiro (☎ 523-2111) is at Av Brasil 821.

Bus From Foz do Iguaçu to Curitiba (US$16, 12 hours), there are seven daily buses on BR-277. To São Paulo, eight buses make the 15-hour trip (US$26). To Rio there are six buses per day (US$36, 22 hours).

Getting Around
To/From the Airport For US50¢, catch a "P Nacional" bus, which runs every 20 minutes from 5:30 am until 7 pm, then hourly until 12:40 am; the trip takes 30 minutes. A taxi costs US$20.

To/From the Bus Terminal All long-distance buses arrive and depart from the new Rodoviária, six km from the center of town on Av Costa e Silva. To get to the center, walk down the hill to the local bus stop and catch an "Anel Viaria" bus – it says "Centro" in nice, big letters. They start at 5:30 am and run every 15 minutes until 1:15 am.

Bus All local buses leave from the urban bus terminal on Av Juscelino Kubitschek. On weekdays the first "Cataratas" bus to the Brazilian side of the falls (US80¢) leaves the terminal at 8 am and runs every two hours until 6 pm; the last one leaves the falls at 7 pm, after which cabs charge extortionist rates to return to Foz. At the park entrance, the bus waits while you pay the US$3 entry fee (in Brazilian currency only). On weekends and public holidays, the first bus leaves the terminal at 8 am, the second at 10 am; thereafter buses leave every 40 minutes until 6 pm.

Buses to Puerto Iguazú (US$1.20) start at 7 am and run every 15 minutes (every 50 minutes on Sunday) until 8:50 pm. Buses for Ciudad del Este begin running at 7 am and leave every ten minutes.

The Gran Chaco

The Gran Chaco is a lowland of savannas and thorn forests extending from about 30° south latitude into Paraguay, eastern Bolivia, and western Brazil. Together, Chaco and Formosa provinces comprise the bulk of the Argentine Chaco, though parts of the region also fall within the boundaries of the western provinces of Salta and Santiago del Estero, as well as the northern edges of Santa Fe and Córdoba. Summer is brutally hot; in winter there are occasional frosts. Rainfall is high in the east on the border with Corrientes, but low toward the west, where irrigation is essential for agriculture.

Traditionally, the region's economy depends on agriculture and forestry, particularly exploitation of *Quebrachia lorentzii*; this tree's common name, *quebracho* (axebreaker), derives from its rock-hard wood. The quebracho was once an unsurpassed source of natural tannin for leather processing, while the related *quebracho colorado* served for timber, firewood, and charcoal. Presently, the region is experiencing accelerating forest clearance for rain-fed agriculture as cotton and oil crops, especially sunflowers, become more important. Petroleum exploration is proceeding in the area north of Castelli, along the border between the two provinces.

The mostly roadless western half of Chaco province is popularly known as El Impenetrable. Except between the main cities of the eastern Chaco, such as Resistencia and Formosa, roads can be very bad and communications difficult. Crossing the northern Chaco, in Formosa province, can be particularly challenging; LP reader Christián Gaebler had the following experience in 1993:

Trying to get from Bolivia to Paraguay through northern Argentina, we had an incredible two-day trip, starting by bus in the morning from Pocitos to Embarcación and going on to Los Blancos. There, at 10 pm, the bus driver told all passengers that he would go back to Embarcación because the road was closed for buses. Los Blancos may have 200 inhabitants. Some of the Argentinian passengers hired a pickup to go on and we went three hours through heavy rain over an incredibly muddy road. Two times the pickup threatened to get stuck in the meter-deep mud. After midnight, we arrived in by this time Venice-like Ingeniero Juárez and spent the entire night in the only dry place – the bus station. Bus service had been suspended, so we went to the railway station in the morning.

Unfortunately, at the beginning of the year, all passenger service had ceased, so only freight trains were going. Because the railway was the only passable way to Formosa, many people gathered at the station. The railway employees decided to let the people go by train and added an old caboose to a long freight train, which took them half the day to arrange. The train left at 3 pm, and went with a speed of 25 km/h. So we reached the village at the beginning of the paved road, Estanislao del Campo, at 3 am the next morning. A bus to Formosa left at 5 am, reaching Formosa at 7:30 am. So we had a journey of about 48 hours for a distance of 800 km in a flat area.

While paved RN 81 continues to advance westward, reaching the town of Las Lomitas 60 km west of Estanislao del Campo, the rainy winter can still present problems, and travelers should anticipate delays.

Guía de la Provincia de Formosa, published by the provincial Dirección de Turismo in 1986, is hard to find but worth acquiring for those who read Spanish well.

History

In colonial times, Europeans avoided the hot, desolate Chaco, where the few hunter-gatherer peoples were resistant to colonization and not sufficiently numerous to justify their pacification for encomiendas. Today, about 20,000 Guaycurú (Toba, Mocoví) and Mataco peoples remain in both the region's interior and urban areas.

The earliest Spanish settlement was probably Concepción del Bermejo, founded in 1585 but abandoned in 1632 due to Indian resistance and rediscovered only recently, 75 km north of present-day Roque Sáenz Peña. After the mid-18th century, Jesuit missionaries had some success among the Abipone people, but their expulsion from the Americas in 1767 again delayed European settlement.

Permanent settlement of the Argentine Chaco came much later. Oppressive summer heat, Indian resistance, and poisonous snakes discouraged exploration of its dense thorn forests until the mid-19th century, when woodcutters from Corrientes entered the region's forests to exploit the valuable quebracho. This eventually opened the region to agricultural expansion, which has primarily taken the form of cotton and cattle production.

Colonization proceeded from the province and city of Corrientes but was not really permanent until 1872. Resistencia, founded in 1750 as the Jesuit reducción of San Fernando del Río Negro, was the jumping-off point for woodcutters. The two railroads built across the Chaco have made it easier to get logs to Resistencia and Formosa, where there is sufficient water to process the tannin.

Most of the region's agricultural devel-

opment took place after 1930, when cotton production increased rapidly. New settlers of mostly central European origin – Austrians, Bulgarians, Czechs, Russians, Yugoslavs, and some Spaniards – came via the Humid Pampa. The agricultural frontier continues to expand westward, as the quebracho forests are cleared for wood and charcoal, although the erratic rainfall in the western Chaco makes rain-fed agriculture risky.

RESISTENCIA

First settled in 1750, the capital of Chaco province grew rapidly with the growth of the tannin industry and subsequent agricultural progress. Surprisingly, for a town that developed on the frontier, it is proudest of its fine-arts tradition and prefers to be known as the "city of sculptures" or "the open-air museum" for the many statues, often very unconventional, in virtually every public space. Probably the frontier tradition of wood carving helped establish this unique cultural oasis; there is also an important university, as well as several cultural centers and many museums.

Orientation

Linked to Corrientes by the Belgrano

Due to Indian resistance, the first Spanish settlement in the Chaco was abandoned in 1632.

bridge across the Paraná, Resistencia (population 300,000) is not directly situated on the river; an eastbound road connects it to the small port of Barranqueras. It is 1019 km north of Buenos Aires on RN 11 via Rosario and Santa Fe.

Plaza 25 de Mayo, occupying four square blocks, is the focus of the city center. Street names change on each side of the plaza. Av Sarmiento is the main access route from RN 16, which leads east to the Belgrano bridge and west to Roque Sáenz Peña, continuing across the Chaco to Salta and Santiago del Estero. Av 25 de Mayo leads northwest from the plaza to RN 11, which also goes north to Formosa and the Paraguayan border at Clorinda.

Information

Tourist Offices The Dirección Provincial de Turismo (☎ 23547), so poorly marked it's easy to miss, is upstairs at JB Justo 135. The staff is friendly and well informed, and there's occasionally an English speaker among them. It's open weekdays 7:30 am to 1 pm and 3 to 7:30 pm. A tourist kiosk on the plaza keeps less dependable hours.

ACA (☎ 70507) is at Av 9 de Julio and Av Italia, three blocks from Plaza 25 de Mayo.

Money Cambio El Dorado, at the corner of Yrigoyen and Pellegrini, changes traveler's checks at reasonable rates, while Banco del Chaco, at Güemes and Yrigoyen, is open between 10 am and 1 pm and charges a uniform commission of US$8 on traveler's checks regardless of the amount. Banco de la Nación is directly on the plaza at Av 9 de Julio.

There are ATMs at Banco de Boston at JB Justo 171; Banco Roberts at JB Justo 151; and Banco Río at Rawson 124.

Post & Telecommunications Correo Argentino faces Plaza 25 de Mayo at Sarmiento and Yrigoyen; the postal code is 3500.

Telecom is at the corner of JM Paz and JB Justo, a block from Plaza 25 de Mayo. Resistencia's area code is 0722.

ARGENTINA

ARGENTINA

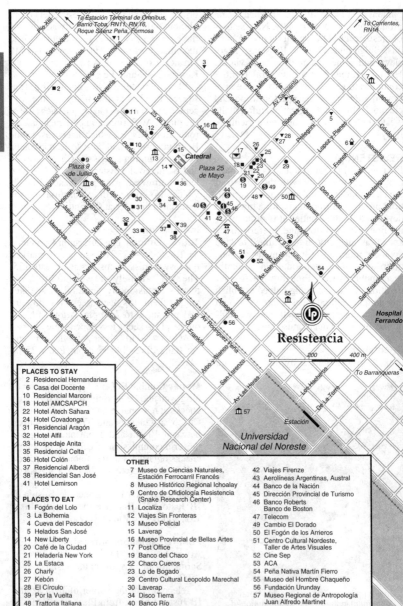

PLACES TO STAY
2 Residencial Hernandarias
6 Casa del Docente
10 Residencial Marconi
18 Hotel AMCSAPCH
22 Hotel Atech Sahara
24 Hotel Covadonga
31 Residencial Aragón
32 Hotel Alfil
33 Hospedaje Anita
35 Residencial Celta
36 Hotel Colón
37 Residencial Alberdi
38 Residencial San José
41 Hotel Lemirson

PLACES TO EAT
1 Fogón del Lolo
3 La Bohemia
4 Cueva del Pescador
5 Helados San José
14 New Liberty
20 Café de la Ciudad
21 Heladería New York
25 La Estaca
26 Charly
27 Kebón
28 El Círculo
39 Por la Vuelta
48 Trattoria Italiana

OTHER
7 Museo de Ciencias Naturales,
   Estación Ferrocarril Francés
8 Museo Histórico Regional Ichoalay
9 Centro de Ofidiología Resistencia
   (Snake Research Center)
11 Localiza
12 Viajes Sin Fronteras
13 Museo Policial
15 Laverap
16 Museo Provincial de Bellas Artes
17 Post Office
19 Banco del Chaco
22 Chaco Cueros
23 Lo de Bogado
29 Centro Cultural Leopoldo Marechal
30 Laverap
34 Disco Tierra
40 Banco Río

42 Viajes Firenze
43 Aerolíneas Argentinas, Austral
44 Banco de la Nación
45 Dirección Provincial de Turismo
46 Banco Roberts
   Banco de Boston
47 Telecom
49 Cambio El Dorado
50 El Fogón de los Arrieros
51 Centro Cultural Nordeste,
   Taller de Artes Visuales
52 Cine Sep
53 ACA
54 Peña Nativa Martín Fierro
55 Museo del Hombre Chaqueño
56 Fundación Urunday
57 Museo Regional de Antropología
   Juan Alfredo Martinet

Cultural Centers The Centro Cultural Leopoldo Marechal, Pellegrini 272, has regular art exhibitions and performances; it's open weekdays 9 am to noon and 7 to 9 pm. The Centro Cultural Nordeste (☎ 22649), Arturo Illía 353, has similar facilities.

Travel Agencies Among the best established travel agencies are Viajes Firenze (☎ 33333) at JB Justo 148 and Sin Fronteras (☎ 31055) at Necochea 70.

Laundry Laverap has two sites, one at Vedia 23 and the other at Vedia 319.

Medical Services Hospital Ferrando (☎ 25050) is at Av 9 de Julio 1101, near Mena.

Sculptures

There is insufficient space to detail the astonishing number of sculptures in the city; in any case, the number is constantly growing. The tourist office distributes a map with addresses of 75 of them. A walk around early in the morning before the suffocating summer heat makes a good introduction to the city. The **Museo Provincial de Bellas Artes,** which concentrates on sculpture, is at Mitre 150; it's open Tuesday to Friday 8 am to noon and 6 to 8:30 pm. Another center for Resistencia's arts community is the **Taller de Artes Visuales,** Arturo Illía 353, open weekdays 9 to 11:30 am and 4 to 7 pm.

One small monument deserves special explanation. The shattered piece in **Plaza 25 de Mayo**, near the corner of Alvear and Av Sarmiento, was a memorial to a guerrilla group massacred by the army in 1976 after surrendering and laying down their weapons in the village of Margarita Belén, 17 km north of Resistencia. Erected in 1986 with the concurrence of all major political parties, it was vandalized within a few days of its placement; the building opposite the memorial was used for torture during the Dirty War. Provincial governor Luis Palacios, founder of the party known

as Acción Chaqueña, was a military official during the Proceso.

El Fogón de los Arrieros

This privately owned museum (☎ 26418), famous for an eclectic collection of art objects from around the Chaco, Argentina, and the world, was the driving force behind Resistencia's progressive displays of public art; it also features the wood carvings of local artist Juan de Diós Mena. At Brown 350, it's open 8 to 11:30 am Monday to Saturday; the museum's bar, renowned for its ambience, is open 9 to 11 pm Wednesday through Friday. There is an admission charge of US$2 for the morning session; call before visiting.

Museo Policial

Before dismissing the idea of visiting the police museum, be assured you can ignore the grisly photos of auto accidents, sensationalistic accounts of crimes of passion, and the predictable drug-war rhetoric and focus on the fascinating exhibits on *cuatrerismo* (cattle rustling, still widespread in the province today) and social banditry – one elaborate display is a surprisingly sympathetic description of the careers of two late 1960s outlaws who, after killing a policeman, lived for five years on the run, helped by the *humildes* (poor rural people) of the province.

The museum is at Roca 233, between Necochea and Vedia. Hours are 9 am to noon and 6 to 8 pm Tuesday to Friday, and 6 to 9 pm Sunday and holidays. Police officers accompany visitors on guided tours.

Museo Regional de Antropología Juan Alfredo Martinet

Archaeology, rather than the much broader field of anthropology, is the focus of this museum at the Universidad Nacional del Noreste; its major display details the failed Spanish settlement at Concepción del Bermejo. There are ethnographic exhibits as well, but uncritical acceptance of Argentine scholar Angel Rosenblat's very low and largely superseded estimates for the aboriginal population of the Americas at

European contact illustrates the difficulties provincial universities face in keeping up with more recent research. At Av Las Heras 727, the museum is open weekdays 8 am to noon and 4 to 9 pm; admission is free.

Museo Histórico Regional Ichoalay

Named for a cacique who negotiated a peace settlement with the Spanish governor of Corrientes in 1750, the poorly organized provincial history museum features ethnographic materials relating to Chaco Indians and exhibits on European colonization. Within a school at Donovan 425, opposite Plaza 9 de Julio, it's supposedly open weekdays 8 am to noon and 2 to 5:30 pm, but visitors may have to track down the staff for access.

Museo de Ciencias Naturales

Recently relocated to the former Estación Ferrocarril Francés (French Railroad Station) on Laprida near Pellegrini, this museum has a good collection of stuffed birds of the region but is otherwise unexceptional, although it has a friendly and dedicated staff. It's open weekdays 8 am to noon.

Other Museums

A new **Museo de la Escultura en Madera** (Museum of Wood Sculptures) is due to open near the Domo del Centenario, a performing arts amphitheater in Parque 2 de Febrero, north of downtown. The recently established **Museo del Hombre Chaqueño** (Museum of the Chaco Man, ☎ 26112), Arturo Illía 655, focuses on the colonization of the Chaco.

Centro de Ofidiología Resistencia

Reptile-lovers will be unable to resist a visit to the Snakle Research Center (☎ 42-2867), specializing in the study of the region's snakes. The center has audiovisual programs. At Santiago del Estero 488, it's open daily after 6:30 pm, but phone ahead.

Barrio Toba

About 1500 Toba Indians inhabit this modern government reducción, which appears to be cohesive and well-maintained, if impersonal in appearance. At its **Cooperativa de Artesanos** some of the ceramics are very cheap and gaudy, but the *yiscas* (string bags) and other goods show traditional skills. To reach the barrio, take bus No 7 from Plaza 25 de Mayo.

Special Events

The second week of July, Resistencia hosts the Concurso Nacional e Internacional de Escultura y Madera, a competition in which the participants have seven days to carve a trunk of urunday (a native tree) into a work of art. For more information, contact the Fundación Urunday (☎ 36694), Av San Martín 465.

In August, the Exposición de Ganadería shows the region's best livestock.

Places to Stay – bottom end

Camping *Camping Parque 2 de Febrero,* 15 blocks from the center at Av Avalos 1100, has outstanding facilities but may be a bit crowded and noisy in high season – not least because of the dance clubs across Av Avalos. Fees are reasonable at US$4 per person, and the staff are very friendly and helpful.

Hostel The *Casa del Docente* (☎ 24564), French 555, offers beds for US$7 per night.

Residenciales, Hospedajes & Hotels

Resistencia has a wider selection of modest accommodations than nearby Corrientes, but it's not top quality. The cheapest in town is the rather depressing *Hospedaje Anita,* Santiago del Estero 45, where triples with shared bath costs US$20. *Residencial Aragón,* Santiago del Estero 154, is only slightly more expensive at US$15/20 single/double, but it is also pretty dreary.

Despite a run-down exterior, *Residencial Alberdi,* Av Alberdi 317 between Ameghino and Obligado, has decent rooms with shared bath for US$18 per person, but it is often full. Nearby at Rawson 304, comparably priced *Residencial San José* (☎ 26062) is ramshackle but clean, and one of the rooms is truly enormous.

Three other places charge about US$20/25 with private bath: *Residencial Marconi* (☎ 21978) at Perón 332, *Residencial Hernandarias* (☎ 27088) at Av Hernandarias 215, and *Hotel Colón* (☎ 22861) at Santa María de Oro 149. *Residencial Celta* (☎ 22986) at Alberdi 210 is a bit more expensive.

Places to Stay – middle

Hotel Atech Sahara (☎ 22970), at Güemes 160, charges US$20 per person. Other midrange hotels start about US$20/26, like *Hotel AMCSAPCH* (formerly ESMIRNA, ☎ 22898; its unwieldy name consists of the initials of the union that recently acquired it) at Yrigoyen 83 on Plaza 25 de Mayo. So-so *Hotel Alfil* (☎ 20822), on Santa María de Oro between Av Moreno and Santiago del Estero, costs US$35 for a double but charges extra for a room with air-conditioner.

Places to Stay – top end

Hotel Lemirson (☎ 22277), Rawson 167, charges US$43/65. Resistencia has no real luxury lodging, but try *Hotel Covadonga* (☎ 22875), at Güemes 200, which charges US$58/78.

Places to Eat

North and northwest of Plaza 25 de Mayo, along Güemes and Pellegrini, several new and attractive confiterías and ice cream shops have opened, rejuvenating this part of town. One of the new places is the very attractive *Café de la Ciudad,* formerly a sleazy bar, at the corner of Yrigoyen and Pellegrini; alongside it on Yrigoyen, equally new *Heladería New York* has outstanding ice cream. *Helados San José,* at Pellegrini and Saavedra, also has a wide selection of ice cream.

An old mainstay is *El Círculo* at Güemes 350, with decent fixed-price meals and huge portions. Most restaurants are parrillas, like recommended *La Estaca* at Güemes 202, but for variety try *Por la Vuelta* at Obligado 33 for international food or *Trattoria Italiana* at Yrigoyen 236. Pricey *La Bohemia* (☎ 42251), in an old

house at Corrientes 366, has tango shows Friday nights; reservations are advisable. Recent readers' recommendations include *Gran Munich* at the corner of Güemes and Brown, and inexpensive *New Liberty,* a snack bar at Roca 155 near the cathedral.

Cueva del Pescador, Av Paraguay 24, is a very fine fish and seafood restaurant that also has a branch across the river in Corrientes. Other places worth checking out include *Charly* (☎ 29491) at Güemes 215 for international cuisine and local river fish, *Kebón* at Güemes and Don Bosco for international cuisine, and *Fogón del Lolo* at Alvear 750 for parrillada.

Entertainment

Music For live music, try the *Peña Nativa Martín Fierro,* Av 9 de Julio 699 at José Hernández, Friday and Saturday nights in winter.

Cinema *Cine Sep,* Colón 164, shows recent films.

Dance Clubs Try *Tierra,* at Santa María de Oro 251, or *Desequilibrio,* at Av Moreno 850.

Things to Buy

Besides the artisans' cooperative at Barrio Toba (see above), check out Lo de Bogado, at Güemes 174, for a good selection of Indian and non-Indian handicrafts, including hammocks, yiscas, and the like. For leather goods, go to Chaco Cueros at Güemes 160.

Getting There & Away

Air Aerolíneas Argentinas (☎ 22854) and Austral (☎ 27389) are both at Rawson 99 across from the plaza. Aerolíneas flies to Buenos Aires Wednesday, Friday, and Sunday nights, while Austral flies there Monday, Tuesday, Thursday, and Saturday afternoons. Both Aerolíneas Argentinas and Austral also fly from nearby Corrientes.

Bus Resistencia is an important hub of bus travel for destinations in all directions; its

new Estación Terminal de Omnibus
(☎ 46986, 46987), at Av MacLean and Islas
Malvinas, replaces the dilapidated downtown terminal. Godoy Resistencia buses
make the rounds between Corrientes and
Resistencia at frequent intervals throughout
the day.

La Internacional (☎ 26924) goes south to
Reconquista, Santa Fe, Rosario, and
Buenos Aires (US$43, 15 hours); west to
Roque Sáenz Peña; and north to Formosa
and Asunción (Paraguay). El Norte Bis
(☎ 24522) serves the same routes to the
south and also east to Posadas. Puerto Tirol
(☎ 35170) sends daily buses to Buenos
Aires and half a dozen buses daily to
Formosa.

La Estrella (☎ 25221) connects with
Roque Sáenz Peña and also goes to the
village of Capitán Solari, near Parque
Nacional Chaco, four times daily. La
Estrella and Cacorba (☎ 21521) alternate
daily service to Córdoba.

Central Sáenz Peña (☎ 21521) has four
daily buses to Roque Sáenz Peña and alter-
nates with La Velóz del Norte in crossing
the Chaco to Salta (US$40, 16 hours) daily,
while El Rayo (☎ 21123) takes a more
southerly route to Santiago del Estero and
Tucumán. Cotal (☎ 21521) serves Mendoza and San Juan on Tuesday, Thursday,
and Saturday via Catamarca and La Rioja.
Ciudad de Posadas (☎ 34907) goes to
Posadas (three buses daily), to Puerto
Iguazú (daily), and to Mar del Plata (twice
weekly). Kurtz (☎ 38804) also goes to
Puerto Iguazú.

Godoy SRL (☎ 20730, 23824) heads
north to Formosa, the border town of Clorinda, and Asunción, and it also goes to
Naick-Neck and Laguna Blanca, near
Parque Nacional Pilcomayo. Other international carriers to Asunción include El Tala
(20959) and Brújula.

Getting Around

To/From the Airport Aeropuerto San
Martín is six km south of town on RN 11;
take bus No 3 (black letters) from the post
office on Plaza 25 de Mayo.

To/From the Bus Station Take bus No 3
or No 10 from the Casa de Gobierno (near
the post office) on Plaza 25 de Mayo.

Car Rental Localiza (☎ 39255) is at Roca
460.

PARQUE NACIONAL CHACO

Preserving a variety of diverse ecosystems
adapted to subtle differences in relief, soils,
and rainfall, this very accessible but little-
known park preserves 15,000 hectares of
the humid eastern Chaco. It is 115 km
northwest of Resistencia via RN 16 and
RP 9.

Ecologically, Parque Nacional Chaco
falls within the "estuarine and gallery
forest" subregion of the Gran Chaco, but
the park encompasses a variety of marshes,
open grasslands, palm savannas, scrub

Ñandú, also known as a rhea, resembles a
small ostrich.

forest, and denser gallery forests. The most widespread system is the *monte fuerte,* where mature specimens of quebracho, algarrobo, and lapacho reach above 20 meters, while lower stories of immature trees and shrubs provide a diversity of habitats at various elevations.

Scrub forests form a transitional environment to seasonally inundated savanna grasslands, punctuated by *caranday* and *pindó* palms. More open grasslands have traditionally been maintained by human activities, including grazing and associated fires, but these are disappearing. Marshes and gallery forests cover the smallest areas, but they are biologically the most productive. The meandering Río Negro has left several shallow oxbow lakes in which dense aquatic vegetation flourishes.

Mammals are few and rarely seen, but birds are abundant, including the rhea, jabirú stork, roseate spoonbill, cormorants, common caracaras, and other less conspicuous species. The most abundant and widely distributed insect species is the mosquito, so plan your trip during the relatively dry, cool winter and bring insect repellent.

Activities
Hiking and bird watching are the principal activities, best done in early morning or around sunset. Park service personnel are extremely hospitable and will accompany visitors if their duties permit. Some inundated areas are accessible only while **horseback riding;** inquire for horses and guides in Capitán Solari, six km east of the park.

Places to Stay & Eat
At Capitán Solari, you may find basic accommodations, but *camping* is the only alternative at the park itself. Fortunately, there are numerous shaded sites with clean showers (cold water only) and toilets, despite many ants and other harmless *bichos* (creatures). A tent or other shelter is essential. There are fire pits, picnic tables, plenty of wood lying around for fuel, and no fees, but beware of Panchi, the rangers'

pet monkey, who will steal anything not tied down.

Weekends can be crowded with people from Resistencia, but at other times you may have the park to yourself. Sometimes on weekends a concessionaire from Resistencia sells meals, but it's better to bring everything you need from Resistencia or Capitán Solari.

Getting There & Away
Capitán Solari is 2½ hours from Resistencia by bus; La Estrella has four buses daily, at 6:30 am and 12:30, 5:30, and 8 pm; return buses from Capitán Solari to Resistencia leave at 5:30 and 11:30 am and 5 pm.

From Capitán Solari, you will have to walk or catch a lift to the park entrance; the road may be impassable for motor vehicles in wet weather. If possible, avoid walking in the midday heat.

ROQUE SÁENZ PEÑA
Properly speaking, this city of 75,000 people, 168 km west of Resistencia, goes by the rather cumbersome name of Presidencia Roque Sáenz Peña, after the term of the Argentine leader responsible for the adoption of electoral reform and universal male suffrage in 1912.

Primarily a service center for cotton and sunflower growers, Roque Sáenz Peña's main visitor attraction, especially in winter, is its thermal baths, which were fortuitously discovered by drillers seeking potable water in 1937. The city is very hot in summer and, except around the plazas, almost treeless. Several immigrant communities have their own clubs, including Italians, Yugoslavs, and Bulgarians. The city, which also has one of the country's better zoos, is the gateway to the "Impenetrable" of the central Chaco.

Orientation
Roque Sáenz Peña straddles RN 16, which connects Resistencia with Salta. Its regular grid plan centers on willow-shaded Plaza San Martín; Av San Martín is the principal commercial street.

Information

Tourist Offices The Oficina Municipal de Turismo (☎ 22135) is at Av San Martín and 9 de Julio. ACA (☎ 20471) is at Rivadavia and 25 de Mayo.

Money Try Banco Nordecoop, 25 de Mayo 464, or Banco de la Nación, Av San Martín 301.

Post & Telecommunications Correo Argentino is at Belgrano 602, on the corner of Mitre; the postal code is 3700.

Telecom is at Rivadavia 435 between 9 de Julio and 25 de Mayo, but there's also a locutorio at Av San Martín 919. Roque Sáenz Peña's area code is 0714.

Travel Agency Tobas Tour (☎ 21723) is at 9 de Julio 479.

Medical Services Hospital 4 de Junio (☎ 21404) is at Las Malvinas 1350.

Termas de Sáenz Peña

Consciously developed for tourism, this complex of saunas, mineral baths, and Turkish baths also offers massage, a spa, physical therapy, and other services. In summer, you may notice little difference

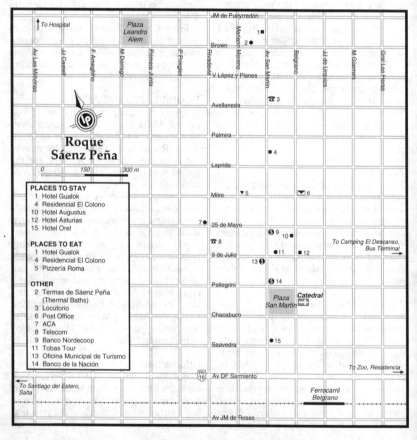

Roque Sáenz Peña

0   150   300 m

PLACES TO STAY
1 Hotel Gualok
4 Residencial El Colono
10 Hotel Augustus
12 Hotel Asturias
15 Hotel Orel

PLACES TO EAT
1 Hotel Gualok
4 Residencial El Colono
5 Pizzería Roma

OTHER
2 Termas de Sáenz Peña
   (Thermal Baths)
3 Locutorio
6 Post Office
7 ACA
8 Telecom
9 Banco Nordecoop
11 Tobas Tour
13 Oficina Municipal de Turismo
14 Banco de la Nación

between air and water temperature, which is about 45°C. Situated at Brown 541 between Av San Martín and Mariano Moreno, it's open weekdays from 7 am to noon and 3:30 to 10 pm, Saturdays from 2:30 to 9 pm. Thermal baths cost US$5, Turkish baths US$7, and saunas US$10 per person.

Parque Zoológico y Complejo Ecológico
At the junction of RN 16 and Ruta 95, three km east of downtown, this spacious and nationally renowned zoo and botanical garden emphasizes regionally important birds and mammals rather than ecological exotics. Featured species are tapir and jaguar.

The zoo (☎ 22145) has two large artificial lakes frequented by migratory waterfowl. Bus No 2 goes from the center to the zoo, which is within reasonable walking distance if it's not too hot. Admission is US50¢ per adult, plus US$1 per vehicle. Hours are 7 am to 7 pm daily.

Fiesta Nacional del Algodón
In May, Roque Sáenz Peña hosts the national cotton festival. Chaco province grows nearly two-thirds of the country's total cotton crop.

Places to Stay
Camping *Camping El Descanso,* the former municipal site along the eastern approach to town just north of RN 16, now charges US$6 per site. It has good, shady facilities, but it can be very noisy on weekends. You can reach it by bus No 1 from the center.

Residenciales & Hotels The best bargain is *Residencial El Colono* (☎ 22338), at Av San Martín 755, between Laprida and Palmira, where singles with shared bath are US$11. It also has a good restaurant with sidewalk seating. *Hotel Asturias* (☎ 20210), Belgrano 402, charges about US$13 per person for rooms without air conditioning, US$25/35 for singles/doubles with air-con.

At *Hotel Orel* (☎ 20101), Av San Martín 131, and *Hotel Augustus* (☎ 22068), Belgrano 483, rates are around US$15/23 with shared bath, US$21/33 with private bath; the Augustus tacks on 50% for air-con. Four-star *Hotel Gualok* (☎ 20521), Av San Martín 1198, part of the thermal baths complex, charges US$41/57; it also has a restaurant.

Places to Eat
Besides Residencial El Colono, which has a good restaurant, and the restaurant at Hotel Gualok, there are numerous restaurants and confiterías along Av San Martín. Also try *Pizzería Roma,* an appealing place at Av Mitre and Mariano Moreno.

Getting There & Away
The Terminal de Omnibus (☎ 20280) is east of downtown, on Petris between Avellaneda and López y Planes. It can be reached by bus No 1 from Av Mitre.

La Internacional (☎ 25340) and El Tata (☎ 25321) both go to Buenos Aires (US$61, 17 hours). El Rayo (☎ 20280) crosses the Chaco to Santiago del Estero, while Central Sáenz Peña (☎ 20222) and La Estrella (☎ 21553) both go to Resistencia. Central Sáenz Peña serves many other provincial destinations.

FORMOSA
Much like North American teenagers in their automobiles, the teenagers of Formosa, capital of its namesake province, race up and down the main drag (Av Doctor Luis Gutniski) in platoons of underpowered motor scooters. Like Resistencia, Formosa's numerous sculptures – not just monuments – show a surprising cultural element. This steamily hot city of 150,000 people may also have the highest density of ice creameries in the country.

Orientation
Formosa is 169 km north of Resistencia and 113 km south of Clorinda, on the border with Paraguay, via RN 11. It is also possible, though still not easy, to cross the northern Chaco via RN 81 and continue to

ARGENTINA

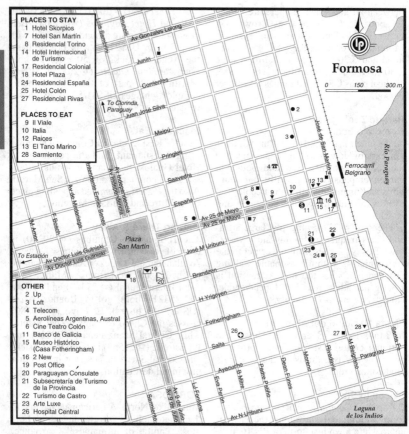

PLACES TO STAY
1   Hotel Skorpios
7   Hotel San Martín
8   Residencial Torino
14 Hotel Internacional
    de Turismo
17 Residencial Colonial
18 Hotel Plaza
24 Residencial España
25 Hotel Colón
27 Residencial Rivas

PLACES TO EAT
9   Il Viale
10 Italia
12 Raices
13 El Tano Marino
28 Sarmiento

OTHER
2   Up
3   Loft
4   Telecom
5   Aerolíneas Argentinas, Austral
6   Cine Teatro Colón
11 Banco de Galicia
15 Museo Histórico
    (Casa Fotheringham)
16 2 New
19 Post Office
20 Paraguayan Consulate
21 Subsecretaría de Turismo
    de la Provincia
22 Turismo de Castro
23 Arte Luxe
26 Hospital Central

Formosa

Bolivia. The Ferrocarril Belgrano no longer
carries passengers across the Chaco to
Embarcación.

Av Doctor Luis Gutniski, as RN 11 is
known through town, heads eastward to
Plaza San Martín, a four-block public park
beyond which Av 25 de Mayo, the heart of
the city, continues to the shores of the Río
Paraguay. From the north side of Plaza San
Martín, Av Independencia is RN 11,
heading north to Clorinda and Paraguay,
although the Av Circunvalación does allow
motorists to avoid the downtown area.

Unlike many Argentine towns, street
names do not change on either side of the
plaza but rather along either side of Av
Gonzales Lelong, seven blocks north of the
plaza.

Information
Tourist Office The Subsecretaría de
Turismo de la Provincia (☎ 26502) is at
Brandzen 117. It's open 7 am to 1 pm
weekdays.

Foreign Consulate Paraguay has a consulate on Fontana between Brandzen and
Uriburu.

ARGENTINA

Money Banco de Galicia operates an ATM at Av 25 de Mayo 160.

Post & Telecommunications Correo Argentino is on Plaza San Martín at Av 9 de Julio 930; Formosa's postal code is 3600.

Telecom is on Rivadavia between España and Saavedra; the area code is 0717.

Cultural Center The Cine Teatro Colón, on Av 25 de Mayo between Dean Funes and Moreno, is no longer a cinema but instead hosts occasional live theater performances and exhibitions.

Travel Agency Try Turismo de Castro (☎ 27483) at Brandzen 75.

Medical Services The Hospital Central (☎ 26194) is at Salta 545.

Museo Histórico
In the Casa Fotheringham, a pioneer residence that was the province's first Casa de Gobierno, the municipal historical museum focuses on the foundation and development of Formosa (originally part of the Paraguayan Chaco until the War of the Triple Alliance). It's at the corner of Belgrano and Av 25 de Mayo.

Special Events
Formosa's annual Fiesta del Río, lasting a week in mid-November, features an impressive nocturnal religious procession in which 150 boats from Corrientes sail up the Río Paraguay. There are also sports competitions, including swimming, kayaking, windsurfing, and sailing.

In February, Formosa celebrates Carnaval on weekends, while Día de la Fundación de Formosa celebrates the city's founding on April 8. The Fiesta de la Virgen de la Catedral honors the Virgen del Carmen, Formosa's patron saint, on July 16.

Places to Stay – bottom end
Camping *Camping El Bosquecillo,* about 15 km south of town, is serviced by city bus

No 1 (Empresa San Martín). The campground is free but has almost no facilities.

In town, ACA at Av Gutnisky 3025 will sometimes permit people to park or pitch a tent overnight on its spacious grounds.

Residenciales Formosa has no real bargain accommodations, but *Residencial Rivas* (☎ 20499), at Belgrano 1399 near the old bus terminal, offers clean, comfortable singles/doubles for about US$20/25. *Residencial España* (☎ 29348), Belgrano 1032, costs about the same, as do *Residencial Torino* at Moreno 709, *Residencial Colonial* (☎ 26345) at San Martín 897, and *Residencial Real* (☎ 27851) at Belgrano and Av González Lelong.

Places to Stay – middle
Mid-range accommodations all cost around US$30/40. They include *Hotel Colón* (☎ 20719) at Belgrano 1068, *Hotel San Martín* (☎ 26769) at Av 25 de Mayo 380, *Hotel Plaza* (☎ 26767) at Uriburu 920, and *Hotel Skorpios* (☎ 20894) at Mitre 98.

Places to Stay – top end
Both the *Hotel Colón* and *Hotel Plaza* have somewhat costlier, more comfortable rooms in the US$40/55 range, but the modernistic *Hotel Internacional de Turismo* (☎ 30935) at San Martín 759 is the most impressive in town. "Executive" singles/doubles cost US$65/78, though there are also some rooms in the US$45/65 range.

Places to Eat
Raices (☎ 27058), Av 25 de Mayo 65, and *El Tano Marino* (☎ 20628), next door at Av 25 de Mayo 55, both offer good, reasonably priced meals in pleasant surroundings. *Italia,* Rivadavia 792, serves pizza and pasta, and *Il Viale,* Av 25 de Mayo 275, is a confitería. *Sarmiento,* San Martín 1338, serves beef and seafood.

Entertainment
Formosa's several popular dance clubs all have English names: *2 New* (at Av 25 de Mayo 18), *Loft* (at Belgrano 545), and *Up* (at Belgrano 636).

Things to Buy
Arte Luxe, at Brandzen 104 opposite the tourist office, has the best selection of crafts in town.

Getting There & Away
Air Aerolíneas Argentinas (☎ 29314) and Austral (☎ 29392) occupy the same building at Av 25 de Mayo and Mitre, but only Austral has flights to Buenos Aires (US$163) leaving daily except Tuesday and Saturday.

Bus Formosa's sparkling new Estación Terminal de Omnibus is on Av Gutniski and Antártida Argentina, 15 blocks west of Plaza San Martín. Godoy SRL (☎ 30816, 33330) goes to Clorinda (on the Paraguayan border), Resistencia, and Buenos Aires (US$50, 18 hours). Puerto Tirol (☎ 33320) has frequent service to Resistencia and Corrientes, with daily service to Buenos Aires. El Norte Bis (☎ 33500) passes through Formosa daily en route from Clorinda to Buenos Aires. El Tala (☎ 33353) goes daily to La Plata via Resistencia, Corrientes, and Buenos Aires.

Cacorba (☎ 33488) serves Córdoba five times weekly. Empresa Atahualpa (☎ 20030), Padre Patiño 969, crosses the Chaco to Salta Thursday and Saturday. Empresa Giroldi (☎ 31700) crosses the northern Chaco as far as Embarcación, in the province of Salta, where connections to Bolivia are possible.

Navarro (☎ 23598), at the corner of Alberdi and Corrientes, runs buses to Clorinda and Laguna Naick-Neck (Parque Nacional Río Pilcomayo) daily at 5:30 am and 2 and 8 pm.

Getting Around
Aeropuerto El Pucú is only four km south of town along RN 11, so cabs are an inexpensive alternative.

CLORINDA
Renowned for ferocious customs checks, Clorinda is the border crossing to Asunción, Paraguay, via the Puente Internacional San Ignacio de Loyola; some officials at Puerto Falcón on the Paraguayan side are conspicuously corrupt. Empresa Godoy (☎ 21110) crosses the border at regular intervals from Clorinda's station at San Martín and Paraguay, where Navarro buses to Parque Nacional Río Pilcomayo also depart.

Formosa is a more pleasant place to stay, but if you're stuck, there's inexpensive lodging at *Residencial Ortega* (☎ 21593), Libertad 1213, for US$15/20 single/double. *Residencial San Martín* (☎ 21211), 12 de Octubre 1150, is comparably priced. Clorinda's area code is 0718.

PARQUE NACIONAL RÍO PILCOMAYO
West of Clorinda, the wildlife-rich marshlands of 60,000-hectare Parque Nacional Río Pilcomayo, resembling Parque Nacional Chaco in its ecology and environments, hug the Paraguayan border. Its outstanding feature is shimmering **Laguna Blanca** where, at sunset, yacarés lurk on the lake surface. Other wildlife, except for birds, is likelier to be heard than seen among the dense aquatic vegetation.

From the park's campground, a wooden *pasarela* (walkway) leads to the lakeshore, where there is a platform overlook about five meters high, plus three lake-level platforms for swimming and sunbathing (the water is barely a meter deep). It's especially tranquil and appealing late in the day, after picnickers and daytrippers have returned to Clorinda and Formosa, but carry plenty of mosquito repellent.

Places to Stay & Eat
Parque Nacional Río Pilcomayo's free camping facilities are seldom used except on weekends; automobiles cannot enter the *campground* proper but must park nearby. There are showers in the bathrooms, but the water is saline and most people prefer the lake, which offers relief from the heat. Just outside the park entrance, a small shop sells basic food and cold drinks, including beer.

At the town of Laguna Blanca, 11 km beyond the turnoff, accommodations are available at *Hotel Guaraní,* at San Martín and Sargento Cabral.

Getting There & Away

Navarro runs buses from Formosa and Clorinda along RN 86 to Laguna Naick-Neck, where there is a well-marked turnoff to the ranger station at Laguna Blanca. From the turnoff, you'll have to hike or hitch the last five km to Laguna Blanca.

Córdoba

Córdoba, a transitional province between the Andes and the Pampas, is a very popular destination for Argentine tourists but much less frequented by foreigners. Excluding Patagonia, it lies in the virtual center of the country, bounded by the Andean provinces to the northwest, Cuyo to the southwest, the Chaco to the northeast, and the Pampas to the southeast. Most of the province is agricultural, but its major attractions are the city of Córdoba and its scenic mountain hinterland, the Sierras de Córdoba. Many of the province's features appeal to conventional tastes, but newly paved roads have improved accessibility to opportunities off the beaten track. Historical attractions are especially abundant, diverse, and appealing.

The city of Córdoba, capital of the province, holds a special place in colonial and modern Argentine history. It is Argentina's second city and a longtime rival with Buenos Aires for political, economic, and cultural supremacy. From the early 17th century, its churches and universities were among Latin America's best, while Buenos Aires languished at the end of Spain's circuitous mercantile supply route. Today, it remains one of Argentina's most important industrial centers, especially important as the heart of the Argentine automotive industry.

The geologically complex Sierras, consisting of three longitudinal ranges reaching as high as 2800 meters, stretch 500 km from north to south, separating the Pampas from the Andes. Giving birth to several east-flowing rivers, prosaically named Primero (First), Segundo (Second), Tercero (Third), and Cuarto (Fourth), the Sierras offer literally hundreds of small towns and even tinier villages. In the northeast of the province, the Río Primero drains into the Laguna Mar Chiquita, a shallow, inland sea.

The Sierras's attractions range from reservoirs, artificial sandy beaches, noisy dance clubs, and gaudy casinos of tacky resorts like Villa Carlos Paz to more sedate places like Cosquín or Candonga. Outside the peak summer season, prices for accommodations can be much lower and bargaining is possible, but many places close by the end of March. The Sierras's dense network of roads, many well paved but others graveled, make them good candidates for bicycle touring – Argentine drivers here seem a bit less ruthless than elsewhere in the country. A mountain bike is still the best choice, but a racing bike would suffice if you plan your itinerary well.

History

Before the arrival of the Spaniards, the sedentary Comechingones Indians occupied the area around Córdoba. Like their counterparts farther north, they were maize cultivators, but they also herded llamas and collected the fruit of the algarroba tree. Proficient warriors, they effectively resisted the Spanish for a brief period – by one account, they shot a Spaniard so full of arrows that he "looked like San Sebastián," a famous Christian martyr.

The Spaniards also found that the local Indians lacked the hierarchical political structure that had facilitated efforts to bring other tribes under the encomienda system:

It is notorious that no village which has a cacique is the subject of another cacique or pueblo. These people are in such anarchy that in all the encomiendas which exist or are being established each pueblo and cacique is mentioned by itself even if there are only two Indians.

Jerónimo Luis de Cabrera founded the city of Córdoba in 1573. It quickly became the center for Spanish activities in the region, with a strong missionary presence facilitated by its agricultural potential and the readily accessible construction materials,

ARGENTINA

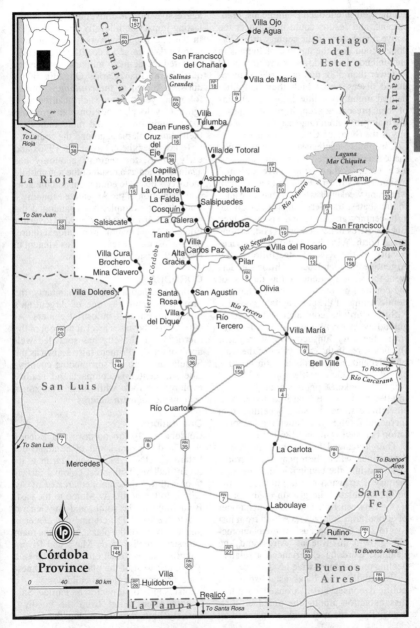

Córdoba
Province

0   40   80 km

but the well-intentioned Dominicans, Franciscans, and Jesuits could not protect the native population. In the century after Córdoba's founding, the number of Indians in encomienda declined from more than 6000 to fewer than 500, due primarily to introduced diseases to which they had little natural immunity. Little evidence remains of their presence except in place names – the major mountain range southwest of the city is the Sierra de Comechingones.

Córdoba's ecclesiastical importance made it a center for education, fine arts, and architecture. Many impressive colonial monuments still grace the center of town where, on weekends when the bustling auto traffic abates, travelers can still absorb the 17th-century ambience and visualize how Buenos Aires depended on its connections to the north. With the creation of the Viceroyalty of the River Plate, followed by Argentine independence, Córdoba underwent the same reorientation as the rest of the country, becoming subject to the economic whims of the port capital.

Still, Córdoba continued to assert its autonomy in many ways. Royalist forces from the city unsuccessfully resisted Buenos Aires in the early years of the wars of independence; Córdoba's conservative clergy, under the cry "Religion or Death," were outspoken opponents of Unitarist intellectuals like Bernardino Rivadavia. Nevertheless, the city soon benefited from increased foreign trade, doubling its population between 1840 and 1860.

Things changed, as they did in the rest of Argentina, when European immigrants swarmed into the country in the late 19th century. Expansion of the railways in the 1870s stimulated the growth of the province – between 1882 and 1896, the number of agricultural colonies increased from just five to 176. Still, because of the phenomenal growth in Buenos Aires and the Pampas, Córdoba experienced a relative decline on a country-wide level.

Eventually, the local establishment's political conservatism aroused so much dissatisfaction among the populace that, especially in the university, it spawned an aggressive reform movement that had a lasting impact both locally and nationally. In the late 1960s, university students and auto workers forged a coalition that nearly unseated the de facto military government of General Juan Carlos Onganía in an uprising known as the *cordobazo*. In the following years, many such insurrections, ignited by local conditions but growing increasingly broader and more radical in their aims, took place around the country.

Today, after the chaos of the 1970s and early 1980s, the region's economy has again declined as a result of the automobile industry's obsolete equipment and the general stagnation of the Argentine economy – Renault, for example, has abandoned the city of Córdoba. Provincial Governor Eduardo Angeloz remains a national figure, having lost a close race to Carlos Menem in the 1989 presidential elections.

CÓRDOBA

With more than a million inhabitants, the provincial capital is one of Argentina's major cultural and industrial centers. At 400 meters above sea level at the foot of the Sierra Chica, the city has sprawled well north of the Río Primero (also known as the Suquía) and into the surrounding countryside. Its center is compact and readily explored on foot, while industrial zones occupy the southern suburbs.

Orientation

Córdoba is 710 km northwest of Buenos Aires and 330 km south of Santiago del Estero via RN 9. Plaza San Martín is its urban nucleus, with most colonial attractions within a quadrant demarcated by Av Olmos to the north, Av Maipú to the east, Blvd Junín to the south, and Av General Paz to the west. The commercial center is just northwest of the plaza, where the main pedestrian malls, 25 de Mayo and Rivera Indarte, intersect each other. Calle Obispo Trejo, just west of the plaza, has the finest concentration of colonial buildings.

Just south of downtown, Parque Sarmiento offers relief from the bustling, densely built downtown, but the largest

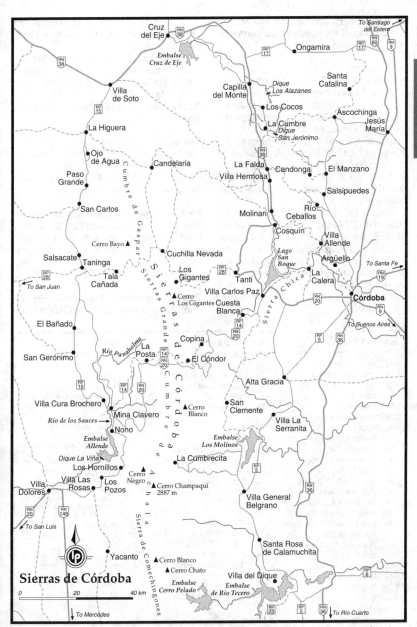

Sierras de Córdoba

0   20   40 km

open space is Parque General San Martín, on the banks of the Suquía on the northwest outskirts of town.

Information

Tourist Offices The provincial Subsecretaría de Turismo (☎ 23-3248), inside a gallery at Tucumán 25, is open weekdays 7 am to 2 pm, but is less helpful than the municipal Dirección de Turismo (☎ 22-5761) at Casa del Obispo Mercadillo, downstairs at Calle Rosario de Santa Fe 39 on Plaza San Martín. It also has a branch (☎ 24-5758) at the nearby cabildo, open weekdays 8 am to 9 pm, weekends 9 am to noon and 5 to 8 pm.

There is another branch of the provincial office (☎ 23-4169) at the bus terminal, Blvd Perón (ex-Reconquista) 380, open weekdays 7:30 am to 8:30 pm, weekends 8 am to 8 pm; if arriving by bus or at the nearby train station, look here first for the latest information on hotels. An additional office (☎ 81-1241) is at the Aeropuerto Internacional.

ACA (☎ 21-4636) is at Av General Paz and Humberto Primo, eight blocks north of Plaza San Martín.

Córdoba has no youth hostel, but the local affiliate of Hostelling International f(☎ 23-3954), Caseros 862, can issue hostel cards and provide information on hostels in the province. It's open 8 am to 1 pm weekdays.

Money For changing cash or traveler's checks (the latter with a hefty commission), try Exprinter at Rivadavia 39 or Barujel at San Martín 37. There are ATMs downtown and at the bus station.

Post & Telecommunications Correo Argentino is at Av General Paz 201; central Córdoba's postal code is 5000. Telecom is at Av General Paz 36, but there are several locutorios downtown and at the bus station. Córdoba's area code is 051.

Travel Agencies For tours around Córdoba, try Oceania (☎ 23-6082) at Calle

PLACES TO STAY		PLACES TO EAT		OTHER	
9	Hotel Garden	2	Mercado Norte	20	Cabildo
12	Hotel Claridge	38	Pizzería Italiana	21	Cambio Barujel
14	Hospedaje Vásquez	44	La Cabaña de Rubén	22	Cambio Exprinter
23	Hotel Crillon	49	Pizzería San Merino	24	Viajes Oceania
26	Hotel Sussex	50	Café Pause	25	Austral
28	Hotel Felipe II	51	Café Jameo	27	Museo Histórico Provincial Marqués de Sobremonte
29	Hospedaje Dory's			40	LAPA
30	Hotel Florida	**OTHER**		41	Colegio Nacional de Monserrat
31	Residencial Thanoa	1	ACA	42	Seminario Convictorio de San Javier, Universidad Nacional de Córdoba
32	Corona Hotel	3	Hospital de Urgencias		
33	Residencial El Crishsol	4	Córdoba Open Plaza		
34	Hotel Riviera	5	Aerolíneas Argentinas	43	Iglesia de la Compañía
35	Residencial Mallorca	6	Córdoba Rent a Car (Hotel Astoria)	45	Iglesia de Santa Teresa y Convento de Carmelitas, Descalzas de San José, Museo de Arte Religioso Juan de Tejeda
36	Hotel Viña de Italia	7	Post Office		
37	Residencial Central	10	TAN		
39	Hotel Termini Roma	11	Mundo Aborígen		
48	Residencial San Francisco	13	Viajes Aeroturis	46	Museo de la Ciudad
53	Hospedaje Suzy	15	Simonelli Viajes (Amex)	47	Al Rent A Car (Hotel Dorá)
54	Residencial El Cielo	16	Subsecretaría de Turismo	52	Avis
55	Bristol Hotel	17	Museo Doctor Genaro Pérez	56	Nueva Estación Terminal de Omnibus de Córdoba (NETOC)
58	Hotel de la Cañada				
59	Hotel Gran Rex	18	Telecom	57	Swept
		19	Dirección de Turismo-Obispo Mercadillo	60	Club Andino de Córdoba

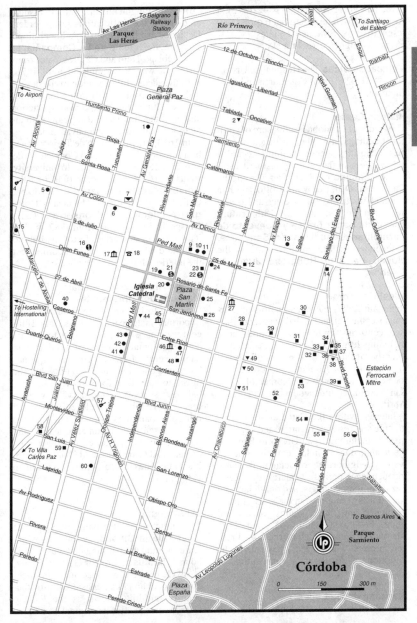

ARGENTINA

Córdoba

0   150   300 m

Rivadavia 96 or Aeroturis (☎ 42-1872) at Av Olmos 351. The American Express representative is Simonelli Viajes (☎ 21-6575), Av Figueroa Alcorta 50.

Medical Services The Hospital de Urgencias (☎ 21-0243) is at Catamarca and Blvd Guzmán.

Historic Center

The center of Córdoba is a treasure of colonial buildings and other historical monuments. Besides specific buildings detailed below, see also the recently restored 18th-century **cabildo** on Plaza San Martín; the **Casa del Obispo Mercadillo,** with a colonial wrought-iron balcony at Rosario de Santa Fe 39; and the 18th-century **Iglesia de Santa Teresa y Convento de Carmelitas Descalzas de San José,** Independencia 122, which contains the **Museo de Arte Religioso Juan de Tejeda.**

Iglesia Catedral

Begun in 1577, the construction of Córdoba's cathedral proceeded over more than two centuries under several architects, including Jesuits and Franciscans. Consequently, it shows a variety of styles, crowned by its Romanesque dome. It's located on the southwest corner of Plaza San Martín, at Independencia and 27 de Abril.

Interred within the Catedral are several notable figures in Argentine and regional history, including Deán Gregorio Funes (a cleric and educator in late colonial times as well as an important politician in the early independence period); General José María Paz (a military strategist and politician who fought as a young man in the wars of independence and, later, against Rosas and other Federalist caudillos); and Fray Mamerto Esquiú (a Catamarca-born Franciscan priest who played a key role in the adoption of Argentina's constitution of 1853).

Manzana de las Luces

Like Buenos Aires, Córdoba has its own "Block of Enlightenment," initially associated with the influential Jesuit order. Designed by the Flemish Padre Philippe Lemaire, the **Iglesia de La Compañía,** at Calle Obispo Trejo and Caseros, dates from 1645 but was not completed until 1671, with the successful execution of the design of Lemaire's timber roof in the form of an inverted ship's hull. It has a modest exterior and an ornate but tasteful interior, with an altarpiece carved of Paraguayan cedar.

In 1613, Fray Fernando de Trejo y Sanabria founded the Seminario Convictorio de San Javier, which, elevated to university status in 1622, was the forerunner of the **Universidad Nacional de Córdoba,** Calle Obispo Trejo 242. The nearby **Colegio Nacional de Monserrat,** Calle Obispo Trejo 294, dates from 1782, but has its origins in an earlier Jesuit institution. The building is considerably modified, but the interior cloisters are original.

Museo Histórico Provincial Marqués de Sobremonte

Claiming to be one of the country's most important historical museums, this 18th-century house once belonged to Rafael Nuñez, colonial governor of Córdoba and later Viceroy of the Río de la Plata; it has 26 rooms and five interior patios, but the most notable feature is a wrought-iron balcony supported by carved wooden brackets. Exhibits include collections of religious paintings, Indian and gaucho weapons, musical instruments, leather and wooden trunks, furniture, and other miscellanea. At Calle Rosario de Santa Fé 218, it's open Tuesday to Friday 8:30 am to 1:30 pm.

Art Museums

Not quite what its name implies, the **Museo de la Ciudad,** at Entre Ríos 40, features modern paintings; it has erratic hours. The **Museo Doctor Genaro Pérez,** at Av General Paz 33, specializes in three-dimensional arts in an unusual turn-of-the-century building known as the Palacio Garzón, named after its original owner.

Climbing

For information on climbing or exploring the Sierras de Córdoba, contact the Club Andino de Córdoba at Duarte Quiros 1591 or Calle Obispo Trejo 658. It's open Wednesdays 8:30 to 11 pm and Saturdays 11 am to 1 pm.

Special Events

During the first three weeks of April, the city puts on a large crafts market (locally called "FICA") at the city fairgrounds, which is on the north side of town near the Chateau Carrera stadium. Córdoba celebrates the founding of the city on July 6. Mid-September's Feria del Libro is a regional book fair, smaller than Buenos Aires' but still significant enough to draw literary figures of the stature of Eduardo Galeano and Osvaldo Soriano. Córdoba is a notable regional publishing center.

Places to Stay – bottom end

Camping The nearest site is in Parque General San Martín, 13 km from downtown. City bus No 31 from Plaza San Martín leaves you at the Complejo Ferial, an exhibition and entertainment complex about one km from the campground, so you'll have to walk or hitch the last stretch.

The campground itself is spacious, but the newly planted trees provide only limited shade. Showers and toilets could be cleaner and the water supply is undependable, but it's a passable place to stay. Charges are around US$4 per site.

Hospedajes, Residenciales & Hotels

As usual, most economy lodging is near the bus terminal and the train station. Without a doubt, the cheapest in town is *Residencial Thanoa* at Calle San Jerónimo 479, near Calle Paraná. Quiet, friendly, and very basic but not too bad, it costs just US$10 per person with shared bath. Spotlessly clean *Hospedaje Suzy,* Entre Ríos 528, has singles for just US$8 with shared bath (no doubles). Indifferent *Residencial El Crishsol* (not to be confused with Hotel Gran Crisol), Calle San Jerónimo 581, is bottom-of-the-barrel accommodations at about the same price. Try instead the basic *Residencial El Cielo,* Balcarce 324, for US$12 single.

Hospedaje Dory's, San Jerónimo 327, is dark and dingy, but quiet, with rooms at US$12/18 single/double with private bath. Slightly more expensive than Dory's, *Residencial Central* (☎ 21-6667), Blvd Perón 150 near the train station, is also dingy but rooms are very clean. *Hospedaje Vásquez* (☎ 23-8268), Santiago del Estero 188, has 15 plain rooms with private bath and ceiling fans for US$10 per person.

Not quite equal to its Buenos Aires namesake is *Hotel Claridge* (☎ 21-5741), 25 de Mayo 218, which has rooms with balcony and balky air conditioning on a quiet pedestrian street for US$18/34 single/double. Other modest alternatives for about US$20/30 include *Residencial Mallorca* (☎ 23-9234) at Av Balcarce 73 and *Residencial San Francisco* at Buenos Aires 272. At comparably priced, two-star *Bristol Hotel* (☎ 23-2216), Pasaje Corrientes 64 (also called Pasaje Tomás Oliver), the aircon appears not to work.

Places to Stay – middle

The modern *Welcome Hotel* (☎ 71-4228), JL de Cabrera 189, is close to the Belgrano train station, with doubles for US$25. *Valle Hotel* (☎ 71-4228), under the same management at Cabrera 197, is a small one-star hotel for US$25/35 single/double. Near the Mitre train station at Entre Ríos 687, the modern *Hotel Termini Roma* has rooms with private bath for US$30/45 single/double.

The attractive, well-maintained *Hotel Garden* (☎ 21-4729), 25 de Mayo 35, is a good value for about US$26/46 single/double. Downtown *Hotel Florida* (☎ 22-8373), Rosario de Santa Fé 459, offers rooms for US$32/45 single/double with private bath. The modern *Hotel Gran Rex* (☎ 23-8659), Vélez Sarsfield 600, charges US$28/42 single/double, while the *Corona Hotel* (☎ 22-8789), San Jerónimo 574, charges US$35/50 single/double. Reader-recommended *Hotel Felipe II* (☎ 21-4752),

San Jerónimo 279, has quiet singles/doubles for US$30/50.

Places to Stay – top end

Hotel Viña de Italia (☎ 22-0972), San Jerónimo 611, is modern but inviting at US$45/59. Close to the train and bus terminals, *Hotel Riviera* (☎ 23-5303), Calle Balcarce 74, charges about US$66 double. At *Hotel Córdoba* (☎ 24-3825), on the east side of Parque Sarmiento at Av Sabattini 459, rooms cost US$68/85 single/double.

Hotel Sussex (☎ 22-9071), a beautiful building at San Jerónimo 125, costs US$60/90 single/double. *Hotel Crillon* (☎ 21-6093), at Calle Rivadavia 85, is comparable. A bit outside the center is the wood, brick, and concrete *Hotel de la Cañada* (☎ 21-4649) at Av Alvear 580 near San Luis.

Places to Eat

The municipal *Mercado Norte* at Calle Rivadavia and Oncativo has excellent inexpensive eats – pizza, empanadas, and lager beer. Many other inexpensive places line Blvd Perón, near the train and bus terminals, and side streets like San Jerónimo, where numerous video bars serve meals – the evening's shows are posted outside, taking precedence over the food. *Pizzería Italiana,* at Calle San Jerónimo 610, is a decent choice despite its unimpressive appearance. *Pizzería San Merino,* at the corner of Chacabuco and Entre Ríos, is also worth a try.

For lunch, *La Cabaña de Rubén* at Calle Obispo Trejo 169 has a good selection of reasonable, fixed-price meals as well as other more elegant dishes. *Estancia La María,* 9 de Julio 364, is a parrilla with its menu in French, German, English, and Italian. Recommended cafes include *Café Jameo* at Chacabuco 294, corner of Corrientes, and *Café Pause* at Chacabuco 216, corner of Entre Ríos.

Entertainment

Córdoba Open Plaza, Av Colón 600, has live music until 4 am. *Swept,* at Hipólito Yrigoyen 419, is also very popular.

Spectator Sports

Córdoba has two first division soccer teams, Belgrano and Talleres de Córdoba. The *Belgrano Stadium* (☎ 80-0852) and offices are at Arturo Orgaz 510, while the *Talleres de Córdoba stadium* is at at General Ricchieri 1595 and its offices (☎ 23-3576) at Rosario de Santa Fe 11.

Things to Buy

For indigenous crafts of the Wichí, Toba, Pilagá, Colla, and Calchaquí peoples of the northern provinces, check out Mundo Aborígen, 25 de Mayo 73, which is also a research and information center. Regionales La Fama, 9 de Julio 336, has good alpaca woolens.

Getting There & Away

Air Córdoba has better air services, including international flights, than any other city in Argentina except Buenos Aires. Aerolíneas Argentinas (☎ 21-5003) is at Av Colón 520. Its Monday 12:15 pm flight from Aeroparque (US$134) continues to Salta and to Santa Cruz, Bolivia, while its midday flight Monday, Thursday, and Friday goes to São Paulo and Rio de Janeiro. There's also a Sunday-morning flight to Tucumán and Río.

Aerolíneas has at least two flights daily to Buenos Aires, while Austral (☎ 34883), Buenos Aires 59, has nearly as many to Buenos Aires as well as 17 flights weekly to Mendoza, a Monday flight to Tucumán and Jujuy, and a Wednesday flight to Tucumán, Salta, and Jujuy. Aerolíneas has recently undercut discount carrier LAPA's US$59 fare to the capital, offering a US$49 fare with 24-hour advance purchase.

LAPA (☎ 22-0188), Caseros 355, flies two or three times daily to Buenos Aires, and Tuesday, Thursday, and Saturday to Tucumán and Salta. TAN (☎ 22-4634), 25 de Mayo 49, flies Tuesday, Thursday, and Sunday to Neuquén (US$129).

Bus Rarely is a bus terminal an attraction in its own right, but the Nueva Estación Terminal de Omnibus de Córdoba (NETOC, ☎ 23-4199, 23-0532) at Blvd

Perón 300 deserves a visit even if you're not taking a trip. Facilities include two banks, an ATM, a pharmacy, a travel agency, public telephones, a post office, a day-care center, first aid, a photo lab, more than 40 shops, restaurants, and other utterly unexpected services – including hot showers.

Almost as an afterthought, it has dozens of different bus companies serving local, provincial, national, and international destinations. Carriers to Buenos Aires (US$30, 10 hours) include Costera Criolla (☎ 22-6160), Ablo (☎ 23-4095), General Urquiza (☎ 21-0711), and Cacorba (☎ 23-7666), which also serves Resistencia and Formosa five times weekly. General Urquiza continues to La Plata. In addition to Buenos Aires and Rosario, Chevallier (☎ 22-5898) has buses to Catamarca (US$20).

TUS/TUP (☎ 21-5240) serve Bahía Blanca, Tandil, Santa Rosa (La Pampa), and Bariloche (five times weekly, 22 hours; US$105, but ask about student and retiree discounts). Empresa Córdoba Mar del Plata (☎ 22-6969) goes to Atlantic coastal resorts, as do Empresa Miramar (☎ 23-0588) and Mar Chiquita (☎ 21-4611).

Socasa (☎ 23-5469) goes to San Juan twice weekly, with a 20% discount on roundtrip fares. Expreso Uspallata (☎ 25-3066) and TAC (☎ 23-7666) go to Mendoza (US$35, eight hours), with connections to Santiago, Chile. Tas Choapa (tel 25-6054) also has Chilean connections via Mendoza.

Veloz del Norte (☎ 23-9011) goes to Salta (US$54, 12 hours) and Orán, on the Bolivian border, while Panamericano (☎ 55-0501) goes to Tucumán and continues to Bolivian border crossings at La Quiaca and Pocitos. El Tucumano (☎ 23-2179) has similar regional services; Balut (☎ 21-2062) serves Salta and Jujuy.

La Estrella (☎ 25-6054) crosses the Chaco to Roque Sáenz Peña, Reconquista, and Resistencia three times a week, and goes to the northwestern cities of Catamarca, Tucumán, Salta, and Jujuy and also to Patagonian destinations like Neuquén. El Serrano (☎ 22-9751) has buses to Santa Fe, Gualeguaychú, and Corrientes, while Ciudad de Paraná (☎ 21-6213) goes to Paraná and other Mesopotamian destinations. Expreso Singer (☎ 21-2073) offers through buses to Posadas (US$41, 19½ hours) and Puerto Iguazú. Cora (☎ 25-4765) serves Montevideo (US$47) four times weekly, with connections to Brazil. Expreso Encon (☎ 22-4222) goes to Paso de los Libres on the Brazilian border via Colón and Concordia.

Many companies serve Córdoba's Sierra hinterlands, including Sierras de Calamuchita (☎ 22-6080), La Capillense (☎ 23-9671), Colta (☎ 22-1951), and Transportes La Cumbre (☎ 21-2472).

Train The Estación Ferrocarril Mitre (☎ 22-4168) is at Blvd Perón 101, at the east end of San Jerónimo just north of the bus terminal. Note that services to and from Buenos Aires are presently suspended and unlikely to resume.

The tourist-oriented Tren de las Sierras (☎ 82-2252) goes Thursday through Sunday to Cosquín (US$5, three hours), La Falda, La Cumbre, Huerta Grande (US$8), Capilla del Monte (US$10), and Cruz del Eje. It doesn't leave from the main station but from the station at Rodríguez del Busto and Manuel Cardeñoza in the suburb of Barrio Alto Verde. City buses Nos 50, 51, 54, and 56 go there from downtown.

Getting Around

To & From the Airport Aeropuerto Pajas Blancas (☎ 81-0696) is 15 km north of town. From the bus terminal, take the Empresa Ciudad de Córdoba (☎ 24-0048) bus marked "Salsipuedes," which enters the airport. Airport Kombis (☎ 92-2361) leaves from Hotel Sussex, San Jerónimo 125.

Bus City buses require cospeles, which are available for US65¢ from kiosks.

Car Rental For the circuits in the Sierras de Córdoba, a car would be extremely useful, though a bicycle would be an excellent alternative. Try Avis (☎ 22-2483 at Corrientes 452; ☎ 81-6473 at the airport);

AI (☎ 21-2031 at Hotel Dorá, Entre Ríos 78; ☎ 81-7157 at the airport); Localiza (☎ 72-9343) at Castro Barros 1155; or Córdoba Rent a Car (☎ 21-5091) at Hotel Astoria, Av Colón 164.

LA CALERA

Just 18 km northwest of downtown Córdoba, it's an easy day trip to La Calera's simple 17th-century **Jesuit chapel** (which has been restored and modernized). There are many parrillas, a municipal campground, and dozens of roadside stands selling regional specialties like salami and fresh bread for your picnic. Stop at places whose handmade signs advertise salami casero and pan casero.

VILLA CARLOS PAZ

Only 36 km from Córdoba on the shores of so-called Lago San Roque (in reality, a large reservoir), Villa Carlos Paz is merely a minor-league, freshwater Mar del Plata, but remains enormously popular with Argentines. The Secretaría de Turismo (☎ 25059) is at San Martín and Yrigoyen, with a branch office (☎ 21624) at the Estación Terminal de Omnibus, San Martín 400. The postal code is 5152, the telephone code 0541.

ACA's Centro Turístico (☎ 22132), which includes a *campground,* is directly on the reservoir at Av San Martín and Nahuel Huapi. The private *Bahía del Gitano* (☎ 22947), at Azopardo and Artigas, charges US$5 per person for campers. There are many expensive hotels like *Hotel Portal del Lago* (☎ 24931), as well as cheaper but still comfortable accommodations like *Hostería Alpenrose* (☎ 25595), and an abundance of residenciales and hospedajes.

Cotap has frequent buses to Córdoba from the Estación Terminal de Omnibus, San Martín 400; some long-distance companies start and end their Córdoba routes here.

COSQUÍN

Known for its Festival Nacional del Folklore (national folklore festival), held every January for more than 30 years, Cosquín has recently added classical music and ballet performances to the mix. The festival has declined by most accounts, but the surrounding countryside still makes the town one of the more appealing destinations near the provincial capital, which is 63 km away on RN 38. Cosquín's postal code is 5166; the area code is 0541.

East of town, **Cerro Pan de Azúcar** offers good views of the Sierras and, on a clear day, the city of Córdoba. Hitch or walk (buses are few) five km to a saddle where there is an *aerosilla* (chairlift) to the top; a steep 25-minute walk to the 1260-meter summit will save you US$5. Also at the saddle is a confitería whose owner, a devotee of Carlos Gardel, has decorated his business with Gardel memorabilia and built a mammoth statue of the great man.

Places to Stay

There is a good *campground* at Santa María de la Punilla, just south of Cosquín. In town, owner-operated *Rincón Serrano* (☎ 51311), A Sabattini 739, is very friendly and quiet, with an attractive patio with a parrilla for asados. In season, prices are about US$27/37 single/double, but off-season rates may be half that.

Other reasonably priced accommodations include *Residencial Alí* (☎ 52424), Tucumán 809, which charges US$15 per person plus US$3 for breakfast; lunch and dinner cost US$8 each. *Residencial Esteleta* (☎ 51473), Catamarca 138, charges US$15/24 single/double, but is only open in summer. *Hotel del Valle* (☎ 52802), San Martín 330, costs US$25/35, while the *Gran Sierras Hotel* (☎ 52120) charges US$63/83.

Getting There & Away

La Calera and El Serranito run buses from Cosquín to Córdoba.

LA FALDA

This woodsy village, 78 km from Córdoba at the base of the precipitous Sierra Chica, may be the most pleasant resort in the immediate area of the capital. The narrow, zigzag road across the Sierra Chica to Salsipuedes, Río Ceballos, and back to Córdoba climbs to 1500 meters at Cerro El Cuadrado, but the best views are back to the west. There are no buses over this route, but enough auto traffic that hitching should be possible in the high season. Dedicated joggers can get an excellent workout.

La Falda has two noteworthy museums. The **Museo de Trenes en Miniatura** (Miniature Train Museum), open 9 am to 9 pm daily, costs US$2. The **Museo Arqueológico Ambato** (archaeological museum) is open 9 am to noon and 3 to 8 pm; admission is US$1.

ACA has a service station (☎ 22674) at Avs España and Edén. Wella Viajes, Av Edén 412, No 12, arranges hiking and trekking in the Sierras.

La Falda's postal code is 5172; the area code is 0548.

Places to Stay & Eat

Nearby Villa Hermosa's *Camping Municipal* charges US$3 per person; while you're there, check out the historical museum in the old train station.

La Falda's lowest-priced lodging is *Hospedaje San Remo* (☎ 22409), Av Argentina 105, where simple rooms go for US$10 per person. *Hotel Majestic* (☎ 22117), Capital Federal 140, is also reasonably priced at US$15 per person, about the same price as recommended *Hostería Marín* (☎ 22640), Güemes 134.

Quiet, clean, and friendly *Hotel El Piccolo* (☎ 23343), Uruguay 51 near Av Edén, charges US$14 per person with private bath; it does a great deal of repeat business. *Old Garden Residencial* (☎ 22842), Capital Federal 28, has a pool and beautiful gardens but is notably more expensive at US$44 double. Try also *Hotel de la Ciudad* (☎ 51376), only half a block from the bus station at Salta 726.

There are a number of decent restaurants along Av Edén, such as *Confitería Kattak* at Edén 444.

Things to Buy

Avs Eden and España are the main shopping districts; try the woolens at Martex, Av España 446. At the former train station is the Feria Artesanal del Andén, open 6 pm to 1 am in summer.

Getting There & Away

La Calera and El Serranito have buses to and from Córdoba (US$3.50).

CANDONGA

Candonga's 18th-century Jesuit chapel is a minor masterpiece in a very picturesque, isolated canyon. At one time it was part of the Jesuit Estancia Santa Gertrudis, whose overgrown ruins, including buildings, a large stone wall, and an aqueduct, can still be seen. While there is no public transportation directly to the site, there is enough traffic that you should be able to hitch from El Manzano, 40 km north of Córdoba (try Empresa Ciudad de Córdoba or Sierras de Córdoba).

A day trip is worthwhile, but there are good accommodations at *Hostería Candonga* (☎ 71-0683 in Córdoba for reservations). For US$35 per person you get a room plus all meals, including well-prepared Argentine and regional specialties like *asado con cuero,* locro, empanadas, and homemade desserts.

JESÚS MARÍA

After losing their operating funds to pirates off the coast of Brazil, the Jesuits produced and sold wine from Jesús María to support their university in colonial Córdoba. One of the finest Jesuit estancias, Jesús María featured a diverse economy based on irrigated vineyards, orchards and croplands, livestock, and ancillary industries. Presently, the town of Jesús María, 51 km north of Córdoba via RN 9, is home to the annual Fiesta Nacional de Doma y Folklore, a celebration of gaucho horsemanship and customs.

Set among very attractive grounds, the church and convent now constitute the **Museo Jesuítico Nacional de Jesús María**, open weekdays 8 am to noon and 2 to 7 pm (3 to 7 pm in summer), weekends 2 to 6 pm (3 to 7 pm in summer) only;

admission is US$1. The museum has good archaeological pieces from the region's Comechingones Indians, including maps of the missionary trajectory, plus well-restored (though dubiously authentic) rooms including the kitchen and toilets, and displays of artwork, coins, and 19th-century dishware.

Five km away is the colonial post house of **Sinsacate**, site of a wake for the murdered La Rioja caudillo Facundo Quiroga in 1835. It's open 3 to 7 pm daily from mid-November to mid-March, 2 to 6 pm daily the rest of the year, but the caretaker is rarely punctual. Admission costs US$1.

Ciudad de Córdoba and Cadol run buses to and from the town of Jesús María.

SANTA CATALINA
Only about 12 km north of Ascochinga, but more easily reached from Jesús María, this Jesuit estancia was perhaps the richest and most elaborate in the region. It is now in private hands, but open to visits.

ALTA GRACIA
Only 35 km southwest of Córdoba, Alta Gracia's most notable attraction is its former **Jesuit church** and estancia, which supplied food and other provisions for the Jesuits in the city until their expulsion in 1767. One of its owners was Santiago Liniers, one of the last officials to occupy the post of Viceroy of the River Plate. Although he was a hero for resisting the British invasion of Buenos Aires in 1806, Liniers was executed for his loyalty to Spain and opposition to independence for Argentina. He is now buried in his native France; the house is a museum.

There is also a museum in the house occupied by the late Spanish composer Manuel de Falla.

Colta (☎ 21920) has direct bus service to Buenos Aires (US$47, 13 hours).

VILLA GENERAL BELGRANO
About 90 km southwest of Córdoba via RP 5, Villa General Belgrano flaunts its Teutonic origins as a settlement of unrepatriated survivors from the sunken German battleship *Graf Spee* near Montevideo during WWII. Its Oktoberfest is the *Fiesta Nacional de la Cerveza*. The postal code is 5194; the area code is 0546.

Places to Stay
Camping San José (☎ 62496) charges US$4 per person and US$3 per site. There are two youth hostels: *El Rincón* (☎ 61323), 600 meters from the bus terminal, charges only $7 per person with kitchen privileges, while *Estancia Alta Vista* (☎ 62238), 17 km from town, charges $25 with half-pension (no kitchen privileges).

Typical lodging includes *Hotel Bavaria* (☎ 61476), El Quebrada 21, for US$40/58 single/double, and *Hotel Prater* (☎ 61167), El Quebrada 4, for US$29 per person. For more upscale lodging, try *Hotel Edelweiss* (☎ 61284) and *Hotel Bremen* (☎ 61133), both charging around US$77/96 single/double. In the more remote, scenic village of La Cumbrecita, try *Hotel Las Verbenas* (☎ 98405).

Getting There & Away
Valle de Calamuchita buses serve Villa General Belgrano from Córdoba.

CANDELARIA
Only the church and casco remain of this late 17th-century estancia east of La Higuera. In this remote part of the Sierras, the thick walls and buttresses, iron-clad algarroba doors, and hideaways give evidence of defensive functions in an area where Indian resistence was intense. The estancia is about 220 km northwest of Córdoba via RP 28, the most direct road, but it's also accessible from RP 15, the Altas Cumbres route.

MINA CLAVERO
Mina Clavero's therapeutic mineral waters began to attract vacationers from Córdoba before the turn of the century, when Doña Anastasia Fabre de Merlo opened the first guesthouse on the advice of the famous "gaucho priest" José Gabriel Brochero, who had gotten to know the area in the

course of his evangelical activities. A century later, Mina Clavero is an important resort with hotels, campgrounds, restaurants, and vacation homes along the Río de los Sauces. Its limpid streams, rocky waterfalls, and verdant, idyllic mountain landscapes provide a relaxing environment for visitors to leave behind the faster-paced life of Córdoba and Buenos Aires.

Orientation

Mina Clavero is 170 km southwest of Córdoba via RN 20, near its junction with RN 15, the splendid Nuevo Camino de las Altas Cumbres (Highway of the High Peaks). It sits at the confluence of Río de Los Sauces and Río Panaholma, in the Valle de Traslasierra between the eastern Sierras Grandes and Cumbre de Achala and the western Sierra de Pocho. Below the confluence, both streams become the Río Mina Clavero, which divides the town.

Avenida San Martín is the principal street of a relatively irregular town plain, but Mina Clavero's small size and compactness make finding your way around fairly easy. Walking is the main means of transportation.

Information

Tourist Offices The Dirección de Turismo (☎ 70171) is at Av San Martín 1464, near the bridge. ACA (☎ 70197) is at Córdoba and Ramón Carcano.

Money Banco de la Nación, Av San Martín 898, and Banco de la Provincia, Av San Martín 1982, will change cash US dollars.

Post & Telecommunications Correo Argentino is at Av San Martín and Pampa de Achala; the postal code is 5889. Telecom is at Av San Martín and Intendente Vila. Mina Clavero's area code is 0544.

Medical Services The Hospital Vecinal (☎ 70285) is at Fleming 1332.

Places to Stay

For a complete list of Mina Clavero's numerous hospedajes and residenciales, check the tourist office, but note that there are few accommodations after the end of March, when the town almost rolls up the sidewalks. Most one-star hotels include breakfast, private bath, and similar services. Unless otherwise indicated, rates are for late-season doubles; midseason prices may be higher.

Camping *Autocamping El Faro,* three km south of Mina Clavero toward Nono, is the only campground open all year. It has very pleasant, shady grounds along the river, with impeccable bathrooms, hot showers, and good laundry facilities. Daily charges are US$5 per person, including vehicle and electricity.

Hospedajes & Residenciales Bottom-end accommodations, which are very decent, start at around US$12 per person at *Residencial Aire y Sol* (☎ 70226) at Rivadavia 551; slightly dearer for US$26 double is *Hospedaje Italia* (☎ 70232) at Av San Martín 1176. *Hospedaje Franchino* (☎ 70395), Mitre 1544 charges US$18/30 single/double, while *Hospedaje Las Moras* (☎ 70704) at Urquiza 1353 and *Residencial El Parral* (☎ 70005) at Intendente Vila 1430 both cost around US$30 double.

Hosterías, Hotels & Motels *Hostería Champaquí* (☎ 70343), San Lorenzo 1430, is an excellent value with singles at US$15 with half pension. *Hotel Milac Navira* (☎ 70278), Oviedo 1407, charges US$18, while the reasonable *Hotel Agüero* (☎ 70439) at 12 de Octubre 1139 and *Hotel España* (☎ 70123) at Av San Martín 1687 cost US$20.

A bit more upscale are *Hotel Aguirre* (☎ 70239) at Av San Martín 1168 for US$44 double, *Hotel La Morenita* (☎ 70347) at Urquiza 1138 for US$42 double, and *Hotel Marengo* (☎ 70224) at Av San Martín 598 for US$44/54. *Hotel Molino Blanco* (☎ 70124), Urquiza 1266, has rooms at US$50 double.

Hotel Rossetti (☎ 70012), Mitre 1434, charges US$56/110, while fancy *Motel du Soleil* (☎ 70066), at Mitre and Libertad at the entrance to town, has doubles at US$80 with breakfast.

Places to Eat

Parrilla La Costanera, on Av Costanera by the river, has a good *diente libre* (all-you-can-eat) deal. *Restaurant Lo de Jorge,* on Poeta Lugones, serves good, abundant parrillada at reasonable prices. *La Nona,* Mitre 1600, has tasty pasta.

Other good choices include *Di Solito* at San Martín 1234 and *Del Carmen* at San Martín and Lugones for pizza, and *Trattoria El Gringo,* San Martín 1022, for Italian food. Other alternatives include *Montecarlo* on Av Mitre, *Stop* on Av San Martín, and *El Pial* at Mitre and Milac Navira.

Getting There & Away

The Terminal de Omnibus is at Mitre 1191. Empresas El Petizo (☎ 70425) and Pampa de Achala have several daily buses to Córdoba and Villa Dolores; El Petizo also goes to Merlo, in San Luis province. TAC (☎ 70420) has daily service to Merlo, San Luis, and Buenos Aires, while Colta (☎ 70433) stops here en route between Córdoba and Mendoza. Chevallier (☎ 70433) goes daily to Buenos Aires (US$45, 17 hours).

AROUND MINA CLAVERO
Museo Rocsen

Operated by JJ Bouchon, an anthropologist, curator, and collector who first came to Argentina in 1950 as cultural attaché in the French Embassy, this eclectic museum displays more than 11,000 pieces ranging from European furniture and Pacific seashells to Peruvian mummies and musical instruments. While these materials might sound incompatible, the collection is so well presented that individual exhibits truly re-create the ambience of a rural rancho or German bedchamber. Particularly well done are the entrance's Rincón del Oligarca de Campo (Rural Landowner's Corner) and Rincón del Oligarca de Ciudad (Urban Elite Corner).

The museum is in the pastoral village of Nono, a one-time Indian settlement nine km south of Mina Clavero. Hours are from 10 am to 6 pm daily. The museum shop sells well-made ceramic reproductions of artifacts at very reasonable prices.

VILLA LAS ROSAS

Charming Villa Las Rosas, 31 km south of Mina Clavero, stands out among several small villages along the Altas Cumbres route, since it provides the most direct route to the summit of 2790-meter **Cerro Champaquí,** the province's highest peak. In the Municipalidad, the tourist office (☎ 94407) can provide a map with a list of local guides.

For accommodations, try the municipal campground or *Hostería Las Rejas, Hotel Sierras Grandes, Hotel Vila,* or *Hotel Micheletti. Restaurant Los Horcones* serves typical regional food.

YACANTO

About 15 km south of Villa Las Rosas is the village of Yacanto, site of the *Golf Club and Hotel Yacanto* (☎ 0544-82075), whose turn-of-the-century building and surrounding manicured parkland once belonged to the British railways. Hiking, tennis, and horseback riding are popular activities here, where business people from Córdoba and Buenos Aires take a break from stressful city life. It's worth a visit even if you can't afford the US$65/90 single/double for full lodging.

In nearby San Javier, cheaper lodging is available at *Hostería San Javier,* for US$52 single with all meals.

Cuyo

Settled from and part of colonial Chile, the Andean provinces of Mendoza, San Juan, and adjacent San Luis still retain a strong regional identity, and their substantial mestizo population distinguishes them from Buenos Aires and the Pampas. The formidable barrier of the Andes is the backdrop for one of Argentina's most significant agricultural regions, which produces grapes for wine, mostly for the internal market, rather than beef and grain for export; the term "Cuyo" derives from the Huarpe Indian term *cuyum,* meaning "sandy earth."

Cuyo lies in the rain shadow of the massive Andean crest, where 6960-meter Cerro Aconcagua is the highest peak in the Americas, but enough snowfall accumulates on the eastern slopes to sustain the rivers that irrigate the extensive vineyards of the lowlands, despite the dry climate. Because of these advantages, *mendocinos,* inhabitants of the province of Mendoza, call their home La Tierra de Sol y Buen Vino (Land of Sun and Good Wine).

With its varied terrain and gentle climate, Cuyo also offers outdoor recreation year round. Possible summer activities include climbing, trekking, riding, white-water rafting, canoeing, fishing, water-skiing, hang-gliding, windsurfing, and sailing. Downhill skiing is a popular if costly winter pastime. Many travelers visit Mendoza en route between Santiago (Chile) and Buenos Aires, but one should not overlook the other provinces, particularly San Juan, for off-the-beaten-track possibilities.

Mendoza Province

For most of its history Mendoza has been isolated from both the other Andean provinces and the distant Pampas. This largely resulted from an accident of history – the settlement of Cuyo from Chile.

Like their counterparts farther north in Tucumán, Cuyo's Huarpe Indians practiced irrigated agriculture. Their population was large enough to encourage Spaniards to cross the 3850-meter Uspallata pass from Santiago to establish encomiendas, but the impossibility of traversing the mountains in winter stimulated economic independence and invited political initiative. Still, trans-Andean communications were the rule, with links to Lima via Santiago rather than northward to Tucumán and Bolivia. For nearly two centuries, Buenos Aires remained a remote backwater.

Irrigated vineyards first became important during colonial times, along with fattened cattle for the Santiago market, but isolation limited the region's prosperity – 17th-century Carmelite priest Antonio Vásquez de Espinosa observed that "There are very good vineyards from which they make quantities of wine which they export in carts via Córdoba to Buenos Aires," yet "the people are very poor, with few possibilities and no help from headquarters, being so distant and remote."

Local vintners developed commerce across the Andes to Santiago and sold 7300 barrels a year to interior markets by the late 18th century, when Cuyo became part of the Intendencia de Córdoba within the Viceroyalty of the River Plate, but Argentine independence closed these outlets for their produce, and the economy declined rapidly. Darwin, in 1835, remarked that "nothing could appear more flourishing than the vineyards and the orchards of figs, peaches and olives," yet he also noted that "the prosperity of the place has much declined of late years."

Only after the arrival of the railroad in 1884 did prosperity return, permitting expansion of grape and olive cultivation, plus alfalfa for livestock. As provincial

307

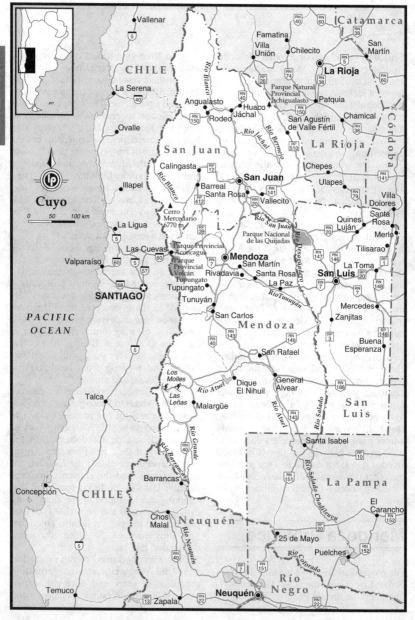

ARGENTINA

authorities like Governor Emilio Civit promoted modernization of the irrigation system, an influx of Italian immigrants transformed the countryside, and federal economic policies protected the growing domestic industry. The area under vineyard cultivation grew from 6400 hectares in 1890 to 45,000 hectares by 1910; 100,000 hectares by 1934; 175,000 hectares by 1960; and reached 240,000 hectares before leveling off in the 1970s. Despite the centralization of water management, the vineyards remain relatively small, owner-operated enterprises, most not exceeding 50 hectares. Since 1913, the annual Fiesta de la Vendimia has celebrated the famous provincial wines.

While minerals are relatively insignificant within the province, it has major oil and gas fields that provide 25% of Argentina's petroleum; coupled with hydroelectric development in the nearby Andes, this has fostered industrial development. The province's location on a major international transit route has greatly aided the tourist economy. Besides the towering Andean landscape and its poplar-lined vineyards and orchards, the province offers several provincial nature parks and reserves and important thermal baths. It's a popular destination for both summer and winter holidays.

MENDOZA

Founded in 1561 and named for Chilean Governor García Hurtado de Mendoza, the provincial capital sits 761 meters above sea level at the foot of the Andes in the valley of its namesake river. With a population of 700,000, it is the most important administrative and commercial center in the region, with an important state university and a growing industrial base supported by nearby oil fields. Earthquakes have often shaken the city, most recently in 1985.

Except during its long siesta hours, Mendoza is a lively city. Its bustling and attractive downtown, where locals congregate to read the latest headlines on the chalkboards in front of the daily newspaper *Los Andes,* is surrounded by tranquil neighborhoods

where, every morning, meticulous shopkeepers and housekeepers swab the sidewalks with kerosene to keep them shining. The *acequias* (irrigation canals) along its tree-lined streets are visible evidence of the city's indigenous and colonial past, even where modern quake-proof construction has replaced fallen historic buildings.

History

When Vásquez de Espinosa visited Mendoza in the early 17th century, he found it a modest place with only "40 Spanish residents and over 1500 Indians to convert and civilize," under the supervision of Franciscan, Mercederian, and Jesuit convents. The Governor of Chile appointed a Mendoza-based *corregidor* (magistrate) as his representative in Cuyo, but creation of the Viceroyalty of the River Plate in 1777, which eventually subjected the province to the Intendencia of Córdoba, was the beginning of a reorientation toward Bueno Aires.

In 1814, Mendoza played a major role in the Spanish American wars of independence, as General José de San Martín chose the city to train his Ejército de los Andes prior to crossing the Andes to liberate Chile. Only a few years later, though, Darwin found post-independence Mendoza depressing:

To my mind the town had a stupid, forlorn aspect. Neither the boasted alameda, nor the scenery, is at all comparable with that of Santiago; but to those who, coming from Buenos Aires, have just crossed the unvaried Pampas, the gardens and orchards must appear delightful.

The arrival of the railroad, along with the modernization of provincial irrigation works, returned Mendoza to prosperity. Today 80% of the country's wine comes from bodegas in and around the city, but construction of oil-fired and hydroelectric power plants has encouraged the development of petrochemicals and light industry, diversifying the city's economic base and related services, and thus promoting population growth. This has not been without cost: The expansion of the Universidad

ARGENTINA

ARGENTINA

PLACES TO STAY
1 Hotel Margal
3 Hotel Laerte
4 Hotel Vigo
5 Hotel Alcázar
6 Hotel Petit
13 Hotel Rincón Vasco
19 Hotel Necochea
20 Hotel Balbi
23 Hotel Montecarlo
29 Hotel El Torreón
30 Hotel Royal
31 Hotel Vecchia Roma
32 Hotel City
33 Imperial Hotel
37 Hotel Escorial
39 Hotel Provincial
41 Hotel Nuevo Horizonte
42 Hotel Castelar
44 Hotel Argentino
45 Hotel San Martín
47 Hotel Castillo
61 Plaza Hotel
79 Gran Hotel Huentala
84 Hotel Aconcagua
85 Hotel Lucense
96 Hotel Galicia
97 Hotel Center
99 Residencial Central
104 Hotel Terminal
105 Residencial Evelyn
106 Residenciales 402, San
     Fernando, Betty

PLACES TO EAT
2 Centro Andaluz
12 Café Mediterráneo
16 Rincón de La Boca
17 La Estancia
21 Café La Avenida

22 Montecatini
24 La Marchigiana
25 Mercado Central
31 Vecchia Roma
34 Trevi
40 Sociedad Libanesa
50 Dalí
54 El Vergel
59 La Casa de Tristán Barraza
60 Trattoria Aveni
69 Il Tucco
71 La Selecta
81 Línea Verde
89 Club Español
91 Vieja Recova
94 Asia
102 Trattoria La Veneciana

OTHER
7 Centro de Información y
   Asistencia al Turismo
8 Canadian Bicicletas
9 Museo Popular Callejero
10 Empresa Jocolí
11 Esquí Mendoza
   Competición
14 Turismo Mendoza
15 Telefónica
18 Operadores Mendoza
26 Iglesia, Convento y
   Basílica de San Francisco
27 Migraciones
28 Banco de la Nación
35 Cine Mendoza
36 Avis
38 Italian Consulate
43 Localiza Rent A Car
46 Turismo Mamb
48 Banco de Galicia (ATM)
49 Hunuc Huar Expeditions/
   Vida y Aventuras

51 Banco de Mendoza
52 Y Libros
53 Cine Lavalle
55 Cine Emperador
56 Cine Opera
57 Cine Gran Rex
58 Instituto Dante Alighieri
62 Cámara de Diputados
63 LAPA/TAN
64 Ladeco
65 LanChile
66 Cambio Exprinter
67 Fonobar
68 Aerolíneas Argentinas
70 Citibank (ATM)
72 Centro de Información y
   Asistencia al Turismo
73 Mercado Artesanal
74 Subsecretaría de Turismo
75 Aymará Turismo
76 Cambio Santiago
77 Rubén Simoncini Libros
78 Turismo Sepean
80 Al Rent A Car
82 Instituto Cultural Argentino
   Norteamericano
83 Museo del Pasado Cuyano
86 Laverap
87 La Lavandería
88 Club Andino Italiano/Centro
   Italiano
90 German Consulate
92 ACA
93 Austral
95 Dollar Rent A Car
98 Hospital Central
100 Terraza Mirador/Dirección
    Municipal de Turismo
101 Post Office
103 Terminal de Omnibus

Nacional de Cuyo, for example, displaced squatters from the western outskirts of the city, north of Parque San Martín.

Orientation

Mendoza is 1040 km west of Buenos Aires via RN 7 and 340 km northwest of Santiago de Chile via the Los Libertadores border complex, whose trans-Andean tunnel has supplanted the higher Uspallata route. Strictly speaking, the provincial capital proper is a relatively small area with a population of only about 130,000, but the inclusion of adjacent suburbs of Gran Mendoza (Greater Mendoza) in the departments of Las Heras (to the north), Guaymallén (to the east), Godoy Cruz (to the south), plus nearby Maipú and Luján de Cuyo, swells the population to more than 700,000.

Undergoing a major renovation at the time of writing, Plaza Independencia occupies four sq blocks in the city center; on its east side, the Cámara de Diputados (provincial legislature) is painted celeste (sky blue) and white, the Argentine national colors. On weekends open-air concerts and an artisans' market often take place on the Plaza.

Two blocks from each of the corners of Plaza Independencia, four smaller plazas are arranged in a virtual orbit. Beautifully tiled, recently restored Plaza España deserves particular attention.

Often on weekdays but zealously on Saturdays, mendocinos socialize at the numerous sycamore-shaded coffee houses on Av San Martín, which crosses the city from north to south. The poplar-lined Alameda, beginning at the 1700 block of San Martín, was a traditional site for promenades in the 19th century. Avenida Las Heras, also shaded by sycamores, is the principal commercial street.

A good place to orient yourself is the **Terraza Mirador,** the rooftop terrace of the Municipalidad, 9 de Julio 500, which offers panoramic views of the city and surroundings. It's open to the public Monday and Friday 8 am to noon, and Tuesday, Thursday, and Saturday 4 to 7 pm.

Information

Tourist Offices For most purposes, the municipal Centro de Información y Asistencia al Turismo (☎ 24-5333) on the Garibaldi peatonal, near Av San Martín, is the best and most convenient source of information; it's open 9 am to 9 pm, has good maps and very detailed informational handouts, and there's usually an English speaker on hand. The best available map, sold here for US$6, is Guía Roja's *Todo Mendoza – Planos Gran Mendoza y Provincia,* which includes the capital and all its surrounding suburbs, with a good index of street names. Another Centro de Información (☎ 25-1925) is at Las Heras 670.

At Av San Martín 1143, the provincial Subsecretaría de Turismo (☎ 20-2800) is open weekdays 7 am to 9 pm. The friendly staff operate an excellent computerized information system, but most of them seem to be on automatic pilot, and dealing with them is like an encounter with voice mail – you have to listen to all the options before

speaking to a human being. They have good maps, but no other brochures. The Dirección Municipal de Turismo (☎ 24-6500) in the Municipalidad, at 9 de Julio 500, is more bureaucratic.

There's also an Oficina de Informes (☎ 31-3001), open 7 am to 11 pm, in the bus terminal.

ACA (☎ 31-3510) is at Av San Martín and Amigorena.

Foreign Consulates Several Latin American and European countries maintain consulates in Mendoza; the most important appear below.

Bolivia
　　Eusebio Blanco & 25 de Mayo (☎ 29-2458)
Chile
　　Olascoaga 1071 (☎ 25-5024)
France
　　Chile 1754 (☎ 29-4715)
Germany
　　Montevideo 127, 1st floor, No 6 (☎ 29-6539)
Israel
　　Olascoaga 838 (☎ 38-0642)
Italy
　　Necochea 712 (☎ 23-1640)
Spain
　　Agustín Alvarez 455 (☎ 25-3947)

Immigration Migraciones (☎ 38-0569) is at Av España 1425.

Money Cambio Santiago, Av San Martín 1199, is one of the few places open Saturdays (until 8 pm); it takes a 2% commission on traveler's checks. Exprinter, another large but efficient cambio, is at Av San Martín 1198.

The massive Banco de Mendoza, a historic building at the corner of Gutiérrez and 9 de Julio, also has a branch at the bus terminal. Banco de la Nación, another architectural landmark, is at Necochea and 9 de Julio. Citibank, Av San Martín 1099, changes currency between 7:30 and 10:30 am only, but also has an ATM just outside the door. Banco de Galicia has an ATM at Necochea 202, but there are many others in the downtown area.

Post & Telecommunications Correo Argentino is at Avs San Martín and Colón; central Mendoza's postal code is 5500. Telefónica is at Chile 1574, but there are many other locutorios, such as Fonobar, Sarmiento 23 (where you can order a drink while you make your call). The telephone code is 061.

Cultural Centers The Instituto Cultural Argentino Norteamericano (☎ 24-1719) is at Chile 985. There are also branches of the Alianza Francesa (☎ 23-4614), at Chile 1754, and the Instituto Dante Alighieri (☎ 25-7613), at Espejo 638. The Instituto Goethe (☎ 24-9407), Morón 275, often shows German films.

Travel Agencies Many commercial travel agencies organize trips in the city, the surrounding provincial countryside, and neighboring San Juan and San Luis. These include Turismo Mendoza (☎ 25-7743) at Las Heras 559, Turismo Sepean (☎ 24-0162) at San Juan 1070, and Empresa Jocolí (☎ 23-0466) at Las Heras 601. For details of services, see the Organized Tours entry below.

Bookstores Y Libros (☎ 25-2822), Av San Martín 1252, has a large book selection that includes Spanish-language versions of many LP guides, and may have English-language versions. Rubén Simoncini Libros (☎ 20-2988), San Juan 1108, has a large, up-to-date selection of magazines in English, but prices are sky-high.

Laundry Laverap is at Colón 497, and La Lavandería at San Lorenzo 352.

Medical Services Mendoza's Hospital Central (☎ 24-8657) is at José F Moreno and Alem.

Ruinas de San Francisco
Located in the Ciudad Vieja (Old Town) at the corner of Ituzaingó and Fray Luis Beltrán, these misnamed ruins, which occupy the entire block, belong to a Jesuit-built church/school dating from 1638. After the Jesuits' expulsion in 1767, the Franciscans, whose own church was demolished in the 1782 earthquake, took over.

Museo Fundacional
One could call Mendoza's sparkling new Museo Fundacional empty, but it would be more accurate to call it spacious, as the high-ceilinged structure on Plaza Pedro del Castillo protects excavations of the colonial Cabildo, destroyed by an earthquake in 1861, and of the slaughterhouse then built on the Cabildo's foundations. At that time, the city's geographical focus shifted west and south to its present location.

The museum starts at the beginning – the Big Bang – and works through all of human evolution as if the city of Mendoza were the culmination of the process. Nevertheless, for all the subtle pretensions, it's one of the few Argentine museums that acknowledges either the indigenous Huarpes' role in the region's development or its mestizo culture. There are several good dioramas of the city at various stages of its development, a decent selection of historical photographs (most of them lamentably small), and ancient and modern artifacts.

Open Monday to Saturday 8 am to 8 pm, Sunday 3 to 10 pm, the air-conditioned facility (☎ 25-6927) at Alberdi and Videla Castillo has a small confitería and a shop selling credible reproductions of archaeological pieces. Admission is US$1.50 for adults, US$1 for students.

Museo Popular Callejero
This unusual outdoor museum along Av Las Heras, between 25 de Mayo and Perú, consists of a series of encased dioramas depicting the changes in one of Mendoza's major avenues since its creation in 1830 as Callejón de las Maruleilas, in a dry watercourse. The dioramas depict typical scenes as it became Calle de la Circunvalación (1863), Calle de las Carretas (an informal, common name dating from 1880), Calle Las Heras (1882, after San Martín's contemporary and colleague, Gregorio de Las Heras), Calle del Ferrocarril (1885, for obvious reasons), Boulevard de las

Palmeras (1908, for the palm trees planted along it), and Calle de los Inmigrantes (1912). Because it's on the street, it's open to viewing 24 hours a day.

Iglesia, Convento & Basílica de San Francisco

Many cuyanos consider this church's image of the Virgin of Cuyo, patron of San Martín's Ejército de los Andes (Army of the Andes), miraculous because it survived Mendoza's devastating 1968 earthquake. In the Virgin's semicircular *camarín* (chamber), visitors leave tributes to her and to San Martín; a mausoleum within the building holds the remains of San Martín's daughter, son-in-law, and granddaughter, all repatriated from France in 1951. At Necochea 201, the church's public hours are Monday to Saturday, 10 am to noon.

Museo Histórico General San Martín

José de San Martín's name graces parks, squares, and streets everywhere in Argentina, but the Libertador is especially dear to Mendoza, where he resided with his family and recruited and trained his army to cross into Chile. At Remedios Escalada de San Martín 1843, the museum (☎ 25-7947) is open weekdays only, 9 am to noon.

Museo de Bellas Artes Emiliano Guiñazú (Casa de Fader)

Paintings and sculptures by Argentine artists, particularly mendocinos, add flavor to this art museum (☎ 96-0224) in a distinguished historical residence in the suburb of Luján de Cuyo. From downtown, take bus No 200 to San Martín 3651.

Other Museums

At Montevideo 544, the historical **Museo del Pasado Cuyano** (☎ 24-1092) has collections of documents and period furniture. It opens weekday mornings 9 am to noon, and Tuesday and Friday afternoons, with guided tours at 11 am.

The **Museo Municipal de Arte Moderno** (☎ 25-7279), underground at Plaza Independencia, features contemporary sculpture.

Acuario Municipal

Mendoza's municipal aquarium (☎ 25-3824) contains both local and exotic fish, the most interesting of which are species from the Río Paraná. At Ituzaingó and Buenos Aires, it's open daily 10 am to noon and 3 to 9 pm; take the "Dorrego" trolley.

Parque San Martín

Originally forged for the Turkish Sultan Hamid II, the impressive gates to this 420-hectare park west of downtown came from England. Designed by architect Carlos Thays in 1897 and donated to the provincial government by two-time Governor and later Senator Emilio Civit, the park itself has 50,000 trees of about 700 different species, and is popular for weekend family outings and other activities. The famous **Cerro de la Gloria** features a monument to San Martín's Ejército de los Andes for their liberation of Argentina, Chile, and Peru from the Spanish. On clear days, views of the valley make the climb especially rewarding.

Within the park, several **museums** focus on archaeology, mineralogy, and natural history, including the Museo de Ciencias Naturales y Antropológicas Juan Cornelio Moyano (☎ 24-7666), the Museo Domingo Faustino Sarmiento (☎ 23-0971), and the Museo Mineralógico Manuel Telechea (☎ 24-1794). The Museo Arqueológico de la Universidad Nacional de Cuyo (☎ 23-3461), part of the Facultad de Filosofía y Letras, stresses American archaeology.

Bus No 110 ("Favorita") from around Plaza Independencia or Plaza España goes to the park, continuing to the **Jardín Zoológico** (☎ 25-0130), in an impressive hillside setting. The zoo is open Tuesday to Sunday 9 am to 7 pm.

Activities

Mendoza and its Andean hinterland constitute one of Argentina's major outdoor recreation areas, with several agencies organizing expeditions for climbers, trekkers, and hikers, rafting trips on the Río

Mendoza and other rivers, mule trips, and the like. Among these agencies are the following and their specialties:

Andesport (climbing, trekking, mule trips)
Rufino Ortega 390 (☎ 24-1003)
Arroyo Hondo (mule trips)
Sáenz Peña 173, Luján de Cuyo (☎ 98-0459)
Aymará Turismo (mule trips, trekking, rafting)
Avenida San Martín 1173 (☎ 24-3607)
Betancourt Rafting (rafting, mountain biking)
Ruta Panamericana 2149, Godoy Cruz (☎ 39-1949)
Hunuc Huar Expeditions (climbing, hiking, trekking)
España 1340, 8th floor, Oficina 16
Piuquén Viajes (mule trips, trekking across the Andes)
Alvarez 332 (☎ 25-3984)
Rumbo al Horizonte (climbing, skiing, expeditions, adventure courses)
Caseros 1053, Godoy Cruz (☎ 22-6826)
Turismo Mamb (rafting, trekking, mule trips)
Espejo 391 (☎ 23-0646)
Vida y Aventuras (rafting, riding, trekking)
España 1340, 11th floor, Oficina 16 (☎ 38-1287)

Climbing & Mountaineering For the latest information, contact the Club Andinista Mendoza (☎ 24-1840), Pasaje Lemos s/n, the Club Andino Italiano (☎ 29-3973) in the Centro Italiano at Patricias Mendocinas 843, Fernando Grajales (☎/fax 29-3830) at José Francisco Mendoza 898, 5500 Mendoza, or Rudy Parra at Aconcagua Trek (☎/fax 24-2003), Güiraldes 246, Dorrego.

Cycling & Mountain Biking Both road cycling and, increasingly, mountain biking are popular activities in and around Mendoza. For bicycle-oriented events, see the Special Events section below.

Navegante EV&T (☎ 31-0145) runs 5½-hour, 25-km mountain-bike tours every morning and afternoon in the precordillera of Mendoza for US$30, and also rents mountain bikes. To rent mountain bikes for a very reasonable US$15 per day, visit Canadian Bicicletas (☎ 29-8868), in the Galería Argentina, Local 23, at Av Las Heras 682.

Skiing For purchase and rental of ski equipment, try Esquí Mendoza Competición (☎ 25-2801) at Las Heras 583 or Rezagos de Ejército (☎ 23-3791) at Mitre 2002.

White-water Rafting The major rivers are the Mendoza and the Diamante, near San Rafael, with trips ranging from half-day excursions (US$30) to overnights (US$190) and three-day expeditions (US$350). In addition to the agencies mentioned above, readers have also recommended Ríos Andinos (☎ 96-0955).

Organized Tours

The city of Mendoza and the popular tourist areas to the west toward the Chilean border are suitable for day trips or for a circuit through areas of scenic river valleys, foothills, soaring mountains, and medicinal thermal springs.

Several travel agencies (see the separate listing above for addresses and telephone numbers) organize trips to these areas. Turismo Mendoza offers tours of the city (US$12), the wineries and Dique Cipoletti (US$13), to Villavicencio (US$17), and to the high cordillera around Potrerillos, Vallecitos and Uspallata (US$28). More distant excursions like Cañon del Atuel (US$39), San Juan (US$29), and San Luis are also possible, as are ski trips. Others offering similar excursions include Turismo Cóndor and Turismo Sepean.

Special Events

Mendoza's biggest annual event, the Fiesta Nacional de la Vendimia (wine harvest festival), lasts about a week from late February to early March. It features a parade on Av San Martín with floats from each department of the province, as well as numerous concerts and folkloric events, terminating with the coronation of the festival's queen in the amphitheater of Parque San Martín.

In February, bicyclists may wish to participate in the provincial equivalent of the Tour de France, the Vuelta Ciclística de

Mendoza. In July and August, the Festival de la Nieve features ski competitions.

Places to Stay

Mendoza has abundant accommodations in all categories. The tourist booth at the bus terminal may help find good rooms at bargain prices, while the downtown office also keeps a list of casas de familia, offering accommodations from about US$10 to US$15 single.

Places to Stay – bottom end

Camping Recently renovated, convenient *Churrasqueras del Parque* (☎ 29-6656), in Parque General San Martín, has good facilities, but its popular parrilla means it can be noisy late at night, especially on weekends. It's open January to March only; fees are US$2.50 per person, per tent, and per vehicle. Take bus Nos 50, 100, or 110 from downtown.

Bus No 110 continues to *El Challao,* six km north of downtown, which charges US$7 for two persons and US$1 for each additional person. Woodsy *Parque Suizo* (☎ 30-2575, 25-2995), nine km from downtown in Las Heras, charges US$5 per person and US$2.50 for children, plus US$3 per tent. Each has clean, hot showers, laundry facilities, electricity, and a grocery store.

Hostel Mendoza's *Albergue Juvenil* (☎ 26-3300), Tirasso 2170 in Guaymallén, offers beds for US$8 per night, without kitchen privileges.

Hotels & Residenciales Mendoza's cheapest accommodations are just north of the bus terminal, on Güemes and nearby streets. For US$9/13 single/double, friendly *Residencial San Fernando,* Güemes 448, has small rooms with sagging beds, but compensates partly with a pleasant patio. Comparable nearby places include *Residencial Betty* at Güemes 456; funky and barely passable *Residencial 402* at (surprisingly) Güemes 402; and *Residencial Evelyn* at Güemes 294. *Hospedaje Eben-Ezer* (☎ 31-2635), Alberdi 580, is

another cheapie near the bus terminal, and so is the recommended *Hospedaje Carmen,* Güemes 519.

Downtown *Hotel Montecarlo* (☎ 25-9285), General Paz 360, is very reasonably priced at US$10 per person. Recommended *Hotel Galicia* (☎ 20-2619), San Juan 881, is central, clean, and friendly for US$15/20 single/double with shared bath, US$30 private bath. Equally central *Hotel Vigo* (☎ 25-0208), Necochea 749, is perhaps one of the best inexpensive hotels in town, a bit rundown but with a nice garden; rates are US$15/26 for singles/doubles. Modest, friendly *Hotel Lucense* (☎ 24-5937), Chile 759, has rooms with shared bath for about US$15/24 single/double. Look for the sidewalk greenery at appropriately named *Residencial El Jardín,* which is an excellent value for US$25 double, at Güemes and Yapeyú near the bus terminal.

Reports are unenthusiastic about *Residencial Central* (☎ 29-1361), 9 de Julio 658, which has singles/doubles for US$15/25.

Places to Stay – middle

Midrange hotels start around US$20/30 single/double, including clean and pleasant *Hotel Escorial* (☎ 25-4777), San Luis 263, and *Hotel San Remo* (☎ 23-4068), north of downtown at Av Godoy Cruz 477. *Hotel Center* (☎ 24-1184), at Alem 547 near the bus terminal, is basic but no longer really cheap, with singles/doubles at US$23/36. Nearby, similarly priced *Hotel Terminal* (☎ 31-3893), Alberdi 261, is very tidy and comfortable but rooms are rather small.

For about US$25/35 single/double, enthusiastically recommended *Hotel Laerte* (☎ 25-5041) is a modern but homey place on Leonidas Aguirre 19. Comparable *Hotel Petit* (☎ 23-2099), Perú 1459, is clean, with a friendly staff, as is the recommended *Imperial Hotel* (☎ 23-4671), downtown at Las Heras 84. Other lower midrange places include *Hotel Alcázar* (☎ 23-4808) at Perú 1460, *Hotel Nuevo Horizonte* (☎ 25-3998) at Gutiérrez 565, which has good heat and air conditioning, and *Hotel Margal* (☎ 25-2013) at Av JB Justo 75.

Due to its good value and excellent location, *Hotel Rincón Vasco* (☎ 23-3033), Las Heras 590, is becoming a travelers' favorite; rates are US$30/40 single/double, but try negotiating cheaper rates. *Hotel City* (☎ 25-1343), General Paz 95, charges US$30/39 single/double. Slightly dearer midrange places, all with similar standards and prices around US$35/50 single/double, include comfortable and very central *Hotel Necochea* (☎ 25-3501), Necochea 541; *Hotel Castillo* (☎ 25-7370), Gutiérrez 572; *Hotel Castelar* (☎ 23-4245), Gutiérrez 598; *Hotel Vecchia Roma* (☎ 23-1515), España 1615; *Hotel Provincial* (☎ 25-8284), Belgrano 1259; *Hotel San Martín* (☎ 38-0677), Espejo 435; *Hotel Argentino* (☎ 25-4000), Espejo 455; and *Hotel América* (☎ 25-6514), JB Justo 812.

Places to Stay – top end

Hotels in this category start at about US$45/65 single/double, with continental breakfast, at *Hotel El Torreón* (ex-Nevada, ☎ 23-3900) at España 1433-39. In the Ciudad Vieja, *Hotel Royal* (☎ 38-0675), Av Las Heras 145, is a good value for US$48/52 single/double. *Hotel Balbi* (☎ 23-3500), Las Heras 340, has singles/doubles for US$68/80, while *Gran Hotel Huentala* (☎ 20-0766), Primitivo de la Reta 1007, charges US$63/82 single/double.

In a beautiful neocolonial building at Chile 1124, the stylish and highly recommended *Plaza Hotel* (☎ 25-6300) dates from 1925; it's a good value at US$68/85 single/double. *Hotel Aconcagua* (☎ 24-2321), San Lorenzo 545, charges US$73/110 single/double, but has been criticized for noise, "deferred maintenance," and glacially sluggish checkouts.

Places to Eat

Many of Mendoza's varied restaurants, pizzerías, cafes, and snack bars are downtown, but diners should not hesitate to look elsewhere. Probably the best value in town is the *Mercado Central*, at Av Las Heras

and Patricias Mendocinas, where a variety of stalls offer inexpensive pizza, empanadas, sandwiches, and groceries in general; its exceptional value and great atmosphere make it one of Mendoza's culinary highlights.

Parrillas are of course ubiquitous. Despite their Italian monikers, *Boccadoro* (☎ 25-5056), Mitre 1976, and *Trattoria Aveni,* 25 de Mayo 1163, are parrillas, the latter with some interesting fish dishes. *La Casa de Tristán Barraza* (☎ 23-3242), Av Sarmiento 658, and the inexpensive *La Estancia,* Las Heras 435, are other possibilities.

Several places specialize in pasta, however, including recommended *Montecatini* (☎ 25-2111), at General Paz 370, and *Trevi* (☎ 23-3195) at Las Heras 70 (outstanding lasagna). There are two locations for *Il Tucco,* at Emilio Civit 556 near the entrance to Parque San Martín and at Sarmiento 42 (☎ 29-2265), both with excellent food and moderate prices. *Vecchia Roma* (☎ 25-1491), alongside its namesake hotel at Av España 1619, has superb Italian cuisine, good service, and medium-to-high prices. *La Marchigiana* (☎ 23-0751), Patricias Mendocinas 1550, serves Italo-Argentine food. For pizza, try *Rincón de La Boca,* with good fugazzeta (hard to find in Mendoza) and chopp (draft or lager), plus friendly service and sidewalk seating at Las Heras 485.

Vieja Recova, Av San Martín 924, emphasizes seafood, while the *Centro Andaluz* (☎ 30-6637) at Leonidas Aguirre 35 has tasty paella. *Club Español* (☎ 24-3825) at Montevideo 244 has typical Spanish food, with moderate fixed-price meals. *Café Mediterráneo,* Las Heras 596, has interesting and moderately priced lunch specials, as does *Dalí* at Espejo 121.

Middle-Eastern immigrants have left a notable imprint on provincial cuisine – try the *Sociedad Libanesa* (☎ 23-0093) at Necochea 538 or *Café La Avenida* at Las Heras 341. The popular *Asia,* San Martín 821, is one of few tenedor libre Chinese restaurants in town, while *Línea Verde* at Montecaseros 1177 is a good, wholesome, and reasonable vegetarian restaurant.

Another good vegetarian choice is *El Vergel* (☎ 25-0053), Catamarca 76.

Longtime Mendoza residents recommend *La Selecta,* near the corner of Primitivo de la Reta and Garibaldi; *Trattoria La Veneciana* (☎ 24-4666) at Av San Martín 739 near Zapata for pasta; and *El Retortuño* (☎ 31-6300), on Calle Dorrego near Adolfo Calles in Guaymallén, for regional specialties. The latter has live music on weekend evenings; take the "Dorrego" trolley from downtown.

Entertainment
Dance Clubs Downtown discotheques include *Die for You* at Aristides Villanueva 256, *Frisco* at San Martín 300, and *Saudades* at San Martín and Barraquero. There are many others in the suburb of Chacras de Coria, on the southern outskirts of Mendoza.

Cinemas The *Microcine Municipal Davíd Eisenchlas* (☎ 29-6500), in the basement of the Municipalidad at 9 de Julio 500, shows occasional art films; the Universidad Nacional del Cuyo also runs the *Cine Mendoza* (☎ 25-2015) at San Juan 1427.

Commercial cinemas include *Cine Emperador* (☎ 38-0190) at Lavalle 71, the *Gran Rex* (☎ 23-3958) at Buenos Aires 63, the *Lavalle* (also ☎ 23-3958) at Lavalle 55, and the *Opera* (☎ 38-0456) at Lavalle 54. Mendoza also has a drive-in, the *Autocine El Cerro* (☎ 25-2015) on Av Champagnat, just north of the Ciudad Universitaria – Joe Bob says check it out.

Things to Buy
Weekends, an outdoor Mercado Artesanal takes place on Plaza Independencia.

Visit the Mercado Artesanal (☎ 24-8645), downstairs at Av San Martín 1133, for provincial handicrafts, including a superb display of vertical loom weavings (Huarpe-style), from the northwest of the province, and horizontal looms (Araucanian-style) from the south, baskets woven in Lagunas del Rosario, and braided, untanned-leather horse gear. Prices are reasonable, and the staff is very knowledge-

able and eager to talk about crafts and the artisans, who receive the proceeds directly. A must-see, the market is open weekdays 8 am to 1 pm.

Getting There & Away
Air Aerolíneas Argentinas (☎ 20-4185), Sarmiento 82, flies daily to Santiago, Chile, and several times daily to Buenos Aires (US$178). Ladeco (☎ 29-9336), Sarmiento 144, has 14 flights weekly to Santiago, Mendoza's only other international services. Aerolíneas has recently undercut discount carrier LAPA's US$79 fare to the capital, offering a US$59 fare with 24-hour advance purchase.

Austral (☎ 20-2200), Av San Martín 921, has three flights every weekday to Buenos Aires, but fewer on weekends; schedules to Córdoba (US$77) are similar.

LAPA (☎ 29-1061), España 1012, which flies weekday mornings and every afternoon except Sunday to Buenos Aires, has the cheapest regular fares, but flights are very crowded and you usually need to reserve at least a week ahead of time. TAN (☎ 34-0240), also at España 1012, has nine flights weekly to Neuquén (US$121), some of which stop at Chos Malal or Rincón de los Sauces.

Bus Mendoza's sprawling Terminal de Omnibus (☎ 26-0980, 25-6870) is at Av Gobernador Videla and Av Acceso Este, in Guaymallén (really just across the street from downtown). Hot showers are available here for US$2.

TAC has several buses daily to Buenos Aires (US$54, 14 hours) and others to Rosario, Mar del Plata, Bariloche, Córdoba (US$35, eight hours), La Rioja, and points farther north, and to Santiago (US$25, seven hours), Valparaíso, and Viña del Mar in Chile. It also goes daily except Sunday and Monday to Malargüe/Las Leñas. There are frequent services to San Rafael, and one bus daily to Merlo.

La Estrella and Libertador (☎ 31-0361) have daily buses to San Juan, La Rioja, Catamarca, and Tucumán (US$46, 14 hours). Empresa del Sur y Media Agua

(☎ 31-2570) has six buses daily to San Juan (US$11, two hours), while La Veloz del Norte has a daily bus to Salta (US$61, 19 hours) via San Juan.

Empresa Jocolí (☎ 31-4409) has a daily bus to Buenos Aires via San Luis and service to the Sierras de Córdoba as far as La Falda (US$38, 12 hours) via San Luis; it also goes to Santa Rosa de La Pampa and Mar del Plata, and has three buses daily to Merlo. Empresa Cotal (☎ 31-6933) has buses to Posadas and Puerto Iguazú (US$98, 36 hours) three times weekly, with stops at destinations like Santiago del Estero, Roque Sáenz Peña, Resistencia, and Corrientes.

Colta (☎ 31-2840) has daily service to Cordoba via the scenic Altas Cumbres route, as does La Cumbre. Expreso Uspallata (☎ 31-3309) takes the same route to Córdoba, crosses the pampas to Buenos Aires, and goes frequently to Uspallata, Cacheuta, and Potrerillos; it leaves twice daily to Las Cuevas, weekends and holidays at 6:10 am to Puente del Inca, and every morning and afternoon to Malargüe and San Rafael. El Rápido (☎ 31-6267) also goes to Neuquén and Salta. Empresa Alto Valle has daily buses to Neuquén.

Andesmar (☎ 31-3953, 31-2057) has the most extensive southbound services, including a connection to Comodoro Rivadavia (29 hours) and Caleta Olivia (32 hours) via Neuquén (US$46, 13 hours) and Puerto Madryn (24 hours), continuing Tuesday, Thursday, and Saturday to Río Gallegos (41 hours); there is also daily direct service to Bariloche (20 hours) and Esquel (25 hours), and service three times weekly to Zapala (15½ hours).

In summer Andesmar buses reach destinations on the southern coast of Buenos Aires province: Bahía Blanca (19 hours), Monte Hermoso (20½ hours), Necochea, Miramar, and Mar del Plata, all via Santa Rosa, La Pampa (12 hours). They also travel north to Tucumán (15½ hours), Salta (19 hours), and Jujuy (20 hours); one of these continues to the Bolivian border at Pocitos. El Rápido has direct international services to Lima and Montevideo.

Central Argentino stops at all northern beach resorts in Buenos Aires province en route to Villa Gesell, three times weekly in summer, and goes daily to Rosario.

Getting Around

Mendoza is more spread out than most Argentine cities, so you will need to walk or learn about the bus system to get around. Local buses and trolleys cost around US50¢, more for longer distances like the trip to the airport.

To/From the Airport Aeropuerto Internacional Plumerillo (☎ 30-7837, 30-6484) is six km from downtown on RN 40. Bus No 60 ("Aeropuerto") from Calle Salta goes straight to the terminal.

Bus The modern and very busy Terminal de Omnibus (☎ 26-0980, 25-6870) is at Avs Gobernador Videla and Acceso Oeste in Guaymallén, just beyond Mendoza city limits. To get there, take the "Villa Nueva" trolley from Lavalle, between Av San Martín and Calle San Juan.

Rental cars can be hard to get at the airport, so it may be easier in town. Try Avis (☎ 25-7802), on La Rioja between Buenos Aires and Entre Ríos; Dollar (☎ 20-1231) at Primitivo de la Reta 931; Localiza (☎ 25-4200) at Gutiérrez 453, or AI (☎ 20-2666) at San Juan 1012. Rates are high – AI charges US$75 per day for a Fiat 147, US$90 for a Renault 12 with 100 km free per day. Additional km cost US20¢ each.

AROUND MENDOZA

There are varied sights and recreational opportunities in and near Mendoza. Almost all of them are possible day trips, but some more distant ones would be more suitable for at least an overnight stay.

Wineries

Most wineries near Mendoza offer tours and tasting. The most convenient is **Bodega Toso** (☎ 38-0244), Alberdi 808 in Guaymallén; highly recommended as friendly and informative, it's open 7:30 am to 6 pm weekdays, 8:30 to 11:30 am Saturdays. Bus No 2 and trolley "Dorrego" go there from Av España, but it's also an easy walk from downtown Mendoza – from the corner of San Martín and Lavalle, go seven blocks east to Alberdi, then turn right one block south to the winery.

Southeast of downtown at Ozamis 1040 in Maipú, **Bodega La Colina de Oro** (ex-Giol, ☎ 97-2090) is open weekdays 9 am to 12:30 pm and 3 to 6:30 pm, Saturdays 9 am to 12:30 pm; winter afternoon hours are 2:30 to 6 pm. Take bus No 150 or 151 from downtown.

On Mitre in Coquimbito, Maipú, **Bodega Peñaflor** (☎ 97-2388) is open weekdays 8 am to 4 pm. Bus Nos 170, 172, and 173 go there. Also in Coquimbito is **Bodega La Rural** (☎ 97-2013), on Montecaseros, whose Museo Francisco Rutini displays winemaking tools used by 19th-century pioneers, as well as colonial religious sculptures from the Cuyo region. It opens weekdays 9 to 11 am and 3 to 6:30 pm, Saturdays 9 am to 11 am only. It produces the highly regarded San Felipe wines.

At Roca and Urquiza, Villa Nueva, Guaymallén, **Bodega Santa Ana** (☎ 26-3222) opens weekdays 8:30 am to 5 pm. Bus No 200 ("Buena Nueva via Godoy Cruz") goes there. **Bodega Escorihuela** (☎ 22-0215), Belgrano 1188 in Godoy Cruz, is open weekdays 9:30 am to 4:30 pm. Take bus No "T."

One of the author's favorite wineries is **Bodega Orfila** (☎ 0623-20637) in the eastern suburb of Rivadavia.

Calvario de la Carrodilla

A national monument since 1975, this church in Carrodilla, Godoy Cruz, houses an image of the Virgin of Carrodilla, the patron of vineyards, brought from Spain in 1778. A center of pilgrimage for mendocinos and other Argentines, it also has a sampling of indigenous colonial sculpture. Reached by bus Nos 10 and 200, it's open weekdays from 10 am to noon and 5 to 8 pm.

Cacheuta

In the department of Luján de Cuyo, 36 km from Mendoza, Cacheuta (altitude 1237 meters) is famous for its medicinal thermal waters and pleasant microclimate. Since 1986, the facilities at *Hotel Termas de Cacheuta* (☎ 061-38-0022, fax 25-9000) have undergone modernization and singles/doubles now cost US$96/160 with all meals, hot tubs, massage, mountain bikes, and recreation programs; slightly cheaper apartments are available for around US$60 per person for a minimum of four persons. The local mailing address is Buenos Aires 536, Mendoza; in Buenos Aires (☎ 322-8430, fax 322-5672), the mailing address is Tucumán 676.

There is also a restaurant, *Mi Montaña,* and a *campground* at Km 39 of RN 7.

Potrerillos

The road to the Andean resort of Potrerillos (altitude 1351 meters), 45 km from Mendoza, passes through a typical precordillera landscape along the Río Blanco, the main source of drinking water for the capital. Bird-watching is excellent in summer.

There are two hotels, the luxurious *Gran Hotel Potrerillos* (☎ 23-3000) and the more modest *Hotel de Turismo.* There is also an ACA campground, on RN 7 at Km 50, which costs US$8 per site for members, and US$10 for nonmembers. The town also contains the restaurant *Armando* and a gas station.

Villavicencio

Early travelers were unimpressed with Villavicencio. In the 1820s, Francis Bond Head wrote that "the post of Villavicencio, which in all the maps of South American looks so respectable, now consists of a solitary hut without a window, with a bullock's hide for a door, and with very little roof," while Darwin found it a "solitary hovel" when he spent a few years there. Neither could ever have anticipated the *Gran Hotel de Villavicencio,* with thermal baths in a spectacular mountainous setting. The hotel itself has been closed for nearly a decade because of legal entanglements, but was due to reopen at the end of 1995. Mineral water from the region is sold throughout the country.

Panoramic views make the *caracoles* (winding roads) to and beyond Villavicencio (altitude 1800 meters), 51 km from Mendoza, an attraction in itself. There is free camping alongside *Hostería Villavicencio,* which serves simple meals. Expreso Jocolí (☎ 061-23-0466, 25-1750), Las Heras 601 in Mendoza, runs buses to Villavicencio Wednesday, Saturday, and Sunday.

Ski Resorts

While wine ages in the barrels, the soil lies barren, and the poplars stand leafless, the snow attracts visitors to the province of Mendoza. Four ski resorts, particularly the fashionable Las Leñas, bring skiers from Argentina and overseas. Two of them, the nearest to Mendoza, are covered here; for Las Leñas and Los Molles, see the relevant information under Malargüe below.

Vallecitos Ranging between 2900 and 3200 meters in the Cordón del Plata, only 80 km northeast of Mendoza, Vallecitos is the area's smallest (only 88 hectares with six downhill runs) and least expensive ski resort. It's open from early July to early October; for more information, contact Valles del Plata (☎ 31-1957), Av Acceso Este 650, San José, Guaymallén.

Since the resort is so close to Mendoza, most skiers stay there, but *Hostería La Canaleta* (☎ 31-2779) has four-bunk rooms with private bath, a restaurant, and a snack bar. The cheapest accommodations are *Refugio San Antonio,* which has rooms with shared bath and a restaurant.

Los Penitentes Both scenery and snow cover are excellent at Los Penitentes, 165 km from Mendoza, which offers downhill and cross-country skiing at an altitude of 2580 meters. Lifts and accommodations are very modern; the maximum vertical drop on its 21 runs is more than 700 meters. For detailed information, contact the Los Penitentes office (☎ 29-4868, 29-5500) at San Lorenzo 433, Mendoza.

Hostería Los Penitentes (☎ 23-1200) has double and quadruple rooms with private bath, plus a restaurant and bar. Another resort hotel is three-star *Hostería Ayelén,* and five apartment buildings in Los Penitentes offer maid service, bar, and reception. For relatively inexpensive accommodations at nearby Puente del Inca, contact Gregorio Yapurai (☎ 30-5118 in Mendoza), who has cabañas with hot water, kitchen, and fridge for US$18 per person.

Confitería La Herradura is a skiers' hangout. A small market also keeps long hours.

Dique El Carrizal

Dique El Carrizal, 54 km southwest of Mendoza, gathers the waters of the Río Tunuyán mainly for irrigation, but also for swimming, windsurfing, and the like; its proximity to the city has made it a popular recreation and camping area.

Parque Provincial Volcán Tupungato

You can cross the high Andes route taken by part of San Martín's Andean army on an eight-day pack trip with guides from Turismo Masnú Barros (☎ 0622-22444), at Sarmiento and Echeverría in Tunuyán, 82 km south of Mendoza via RN 40.

USPALLATA

In an exceptionally beautiful valley surrounded by polychrome mountains, 105 km west of Mendoza at an altitude of 1751 meters, this crossroads village along RN 7 is a good base for exploring the surrounding area. There's a good rock-climbing area known as Cerro Montura on the route up to Paso de los Libertadores and Parque Provincial Aconcagua, but farther up the valley the rock is too friable for safe climbing. Uspallata may become a zona franca (duty-free zone) because of its proximity to Valparaíso, Chile.

Orientation & Information

Uspallata's tourist office, open daily 8 am to 8 pm except Monday, is a kiosk along-

side the YPF gas station. There is a post office (postal code 5545) and a branch of Banco de Mendoza. Uspallata's area code is 0624.

Things to See
One km north of the highway junction, a signed lateral leads to ruins and a museum at the **Bóvedas Históricas Uspallata,** a metallurgical site since pre-Columbian times. There are dioramas of battles on General Gregorio de Las Heras' campaign across the Andes in support of San Martín. About four km north of Uspallata on the road to Villavicencio, in a volcanic outcrop near a small monument to San Ceferino Namuncurá, is a faded but still visible set of **petroglyphs,** also worth seeing.

Motorists en route to Mendoza should consider taking the **Caracoles de Villavicencio,** a good gravel road even more scenic than paved RN 7. Ignore the sign at Uspallata that restricts the descent *(bajada)* to 2 to 8 pm and the ascent *(subida)* to 7 to 11 am; it's now open to two-way traffic at all hours. About three km past the entrance to the Caracoles is a memorial to Darwin, who discovered fossil *Araucaria* trees here. The high point, at 3800 meters and 26 km from Uspallata, is the **Cruz del Paramillo,** a way station for the Virgin of Fátima, with great views of the Andean peaks to the west.

Places to Stay & Eat
Uspallata's poplar-shaded *Camping Municipal* (☎ 20009), 500 meters north of the junction on the road to Villavincencio, charges only US$3 per site. The north end

of the facilities, near the wood-stoked hot showers, is much quieter and the best place to pitch a tent.

Built by the Confederación de Empleados de Comercio in the late 1940s, *Hotel Uspallata* (☎ 20003) is a bit shopworn since its Peronist glory days but still offers expansive grounds, tennis courts, a huge swimming pool, a bar, a bowling alley, pool tables, and a restaurant. For just US$20/37 single/double, it's the best value in town, and one of the best in the country.

Simple but very friendly *Hostería Los Cóndores* (☎ 20002), half a block west of the highway junction, costs US$30/35 single/double, but is a lesser value than the Uspallata; the bathrooms are huge, however. Outside town on RN 7, the highly recommended but still not outrageously expensive *Hotel Valle Andino* (☎ 20033), has an indoor pool. Rates are US$34/58 single/double for lodging alone, US$38/66 with breakfast, US$49/88 with half-pension, and US$60/110 with all meals. Facilities include an indoor pool, tennis courts, game room, reading room, and TV lounge.

Behind the YPF station, *Dónde Pato* and *Parrilla San Cayetano* (☎ 20049) are both convenient stops offering decent food for travelers en route to and from Chile.

Getting There & Away
Expreso Uspallata provides regular bus service between Mendoza and Uspallata, as far as Puente del Inca. Buses between Mendoza and Santiago will carry passengers to and across the border, but are often very full. Wednesdays at 8 am, a bus leaves Hotel Uspallata to Termas de Villavicencio (US$15), a scenic trip well worth doing.

PARQUE PROVINCIAL ACONCAGUA
North of RN 7, nearly hugging the Chilean border, Parque Provincial Aconcagua protects 71,000 hectares of the wild high country surrounding South America's highest summit, 6962-meter Cerro Aconcagua. Passing motorists can stop to enjoy the view of the peak from **Laguna Horcones,** a two-km walk from the parking lot just

north of the highway, where there's a ranger available 8 am to 9 pm weekdays, 8 am to 8 pm Saturdays. There's also a ranger at Las Leñas, on the Polish route up the Río de las Vacas to the east.

Aconcagua

Often called the "roof of the Americas," the volcanic andesite summit of Aconcagua covers a base of uplifted marine sediments. The origin of the name is uncertain; one possibility is the Quechua term *Ackon-Cahuac,* meaning "stone sentinel," while another is the Mapuche phrase *Acon-Hue,* signifying "that which comes from the

other side." Italian-Swiss climber Mathias Zurbriggen made the first recorded ascent in 1897; since then, the peak has become a favorite destination for climbers from around the world, even though it is technically less challenging than other nearby peaks, most notably Tupungato to the south. In 1985, the Club Andinista Mendoza's discovery of an Inca mummy at 5300 meters, on the mountain's southwest face, proved that the high peaks were a sacred funerary site in pre-Columbian times.

Reaching the summit of Aconcagua requires a commitment of at least 13 to 15

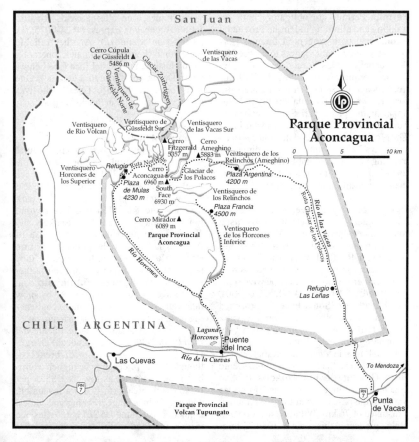

days, including time to get acclimatized; some climbers prefer the longer but more scenic, less crowded, but also more technical Polish route. Potential climbers should acquire RJ Secor's new climbing guide *Aconcagua;* there's less detailed information in the 3rd edition of *Backpacking in Chile & Argentina.*

Nonclimbers can trek to base camps and refugios beneath the permanent snow line; note that tour operators and climbing guides set up seasonal tents at the best campsites en route to and at the base camps, so independent climbers and trekkers usually get the leftover spots.

Permits Permits are obligatory both for trekking and climbing in Parque Provincial Aconcagua; park rangers at Laguna Horcones will not permit visitors to proceed up the Quebrada de los Horcones without one. These permits, which cost US$40 for trekkers and US$80 for climbers, are valid for three weeks and available only in Mendoza, at the provincial Subsecretaría de Turismo (☎ 20-2800), Av San Martín 1143. The process is routine, and the office is open weekdays 7 am to 9 pm. A shorter, three-day trekking permit is available for US$15, but its lack of flexibility makes it a poorer deal than the permit for the longer period.

Routes There are three main routes up Aconcagua. The most commonly used route, approached by a 40-km trail from Los Horcones, is the **Ruta Noroeste** (Northwest Route) from Plaza de Mulas, 4230 meters above sea level, where there is now a rather luxurious and expensive refugio (☎ radio-telephone 24-0075, 24-3350). The **Pared Sur** (South Face), approached from the base camp at Plaza Francia via a 36-km trail from Los Horcones, is a very demanding technical climb.

From Punta de Vacas, 15 km southeast of Puente del Inca, the longer but more scenic **Ruta Glaciar de los Polacos** (Polish Glacier route) first ascends the Río de las Vacas to the base camp at Plaza Argentina, a distance of 76 km. Wiktor Ostrowski and others pioneered this route in 1934. Climb-

ers on this route must carry ropes, screws, and ice axes, in addition to the usual tent, warm sleeping bag and clothing, and plastic boots. This route is more expensive because it requires the use of mules for a longer period.

Mules The cost of renting cargo mules, which can carry about 60 kg each, has gone through the roof of the Americas – the standard fee among outfitters is US$120 for the first mule from Puente del Inca to Plaza de Mulas, though two mules cost only US$160. One party of three paid US$300 to get their gear to the Polish route base camp and back.

For mules, one alternative is Ricardo Jatib's Aconcagua Express (☎ 24-0075, fax 38-0654 in Mendoza). Another reliable muleteer is Fernando Grajales, operating from Hostería Puente del Inca (see below) from December through February. One party recommends Carlos Cuesta, who lives next to the cemetery at Puente del Inca.

Puente del Inca

One of Argentina's most striking natural wonders, this natural stone bridge over the Río Mendoza is 2720 meters above sea level and 177 km from Mendoza. (The Río de las Cuevas just south of the park becomes the Río Mendoza just beyond Punta de Vacas.) From here trekkers and climbers can head north to the base of Aconcagua, south to the pinnacles of **Los Penitentes** (so-named because they resemble a line of monks), or even farther south to 6650-meter **Tupungato,** an impressive volcano partly covered by snow fields and glaciers that is a more challenging technical climb than Aconcagua.

The very pleasant *Hostería Puente del Inca* (☎ 061-29-4124 in Mendoza) charges US$40/50 single/double with breakfast, though posted prices may be higher. Multibed rooms may be as low as US$25 per person with breakfast. It has a restaurant, and may help arrange trekking and mules. Dinner costs around US$15 but, writes one visitor, the food there "tastes better *after* the climb." Climbers and trekkers can also pitch tents by the church here.

Cristo Redentor

Pounded by chilly but exhilarating winds, nearly 4000 meters above sea level on the rugged Argentine-Chilean border, the high Andes make an fitting backdrop for this famous monument, erected after settlement of a territorial dispute between the two countries in 1902. The view is a must-see either with a tour or by private car (since the road is no longer a border crossing into Chile), but the first autumn snowfall closes the hairpin road to the top. At Las Cuevas, 10 km before the border, travelers can stay at *Hostería Las Cuevas.*

Organized Tours

Many of the adventure-travel agencies in and around Mendoza arrange excursions into the high mountains; for their names and addresses see the Activities entry under Mendoza. A reliable North American operator organizing Aconcagua climbs is OTT Expeditions (☎ 510-865-9956), PO Box 5431, Berkeley, California 94705.

Aconcagua The most established operators are Fernando Grajales (☎ /fax 29-3830), José Francisco Mendoza 898, 5500 Mendoza, and Rudy Parra's Aconcagua Trek (☎ /fax 24-2003), Güiraldes 246, 5519 Dorrego, Mendoza.

Sol Andino (☎ 29-1544), Martínez de Rosas 489 in Mendoza, also offers treks to the mountain, starting from Hostería Ayelén in the village of Los Penitentes, and rafting on the Río Mendoza. Several guides from the Asociación de Guías de Montaña lead two-week trips to Aconcagua, among them Alejandro Randis, Soler 721, Mendoza; and Daniel Rodríguez, Cervantes 1697, Godoy Cruz. The trips leave from Mendoza by bus to Puente del Inca, then follow the Ruta Noroeste, partly on mule. Another independent mountain guide is Juan Carlos Pedernera, who lives opposite the cemetery at Km 1143 in Uspallata.

Pared Sur Operadores Mendoza (☎ 25-3334, 23-1883) at Las Heras 420, Mendoza, has trips of three and six days from Puente del Inca, partly by horse or mule, usually contracted with Fernando Grajales (see above). Trips follow the route that climbers attempting the difficult south face of Aconcagua must traverse.

SAN RAFAEL

Founded as a military outpost, San Rafael (population 80,000) is now a modern commercial and industrial center whose winemakers, particularly Suter, Bianchi, and Lávaque, have earned a national and international reputation; about 60,000 hectares of the surrounding area are vineyards. Like Mendoza, its acequias remind the visitor that the area is a desert, irrigated by the Río Atuel and the Río Diamante, and it's surrounded by scenic mountains much less frequented than those farther north. Its clean sidewalks, tree-lined streets, and parks are a local pride. The city has recently made a special effort to attract tourists.

Orientation

San Rafael is 230 km southeast of the city of Mendoza via RN 40 and RN 143 and 189 km northeast of Malargüe via RN 40. The main thoroughfare is RN 143, known as Av Hipólito Yrigoyen west of Av El Libertador/Av San Martín, the city's main north-south axis. East of Libertador/San Martín, RN 143 is known as Av Bartolomé Mitre. Most areas of interest to visitors are northwest of the Yrigoyen-San Martín intersection.

Information

Tourist Offices The Dirección Municipal de Turismo (☎ 24217), at the corner of Av Hipólito Yrigoyen 745 and Av Balloffet, has helpful staff and great brochures and maps. It's open 7 am to 8:30 pm daily, to 11 pm in summer.

Money Banco de la Nación is at Yrigoyen and Avellaneda, while Banco de Mendoza is at Libertador and Mitre.

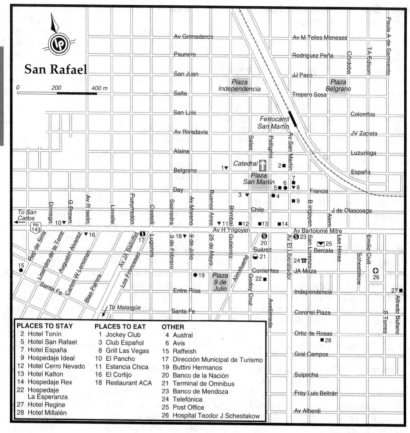

ARGENTINA

San Rafael

0   200   400 m

PLACES TO STAY
2 Hotel Tonín
5 Hotel San Rafael
7 Hotel España
9 Hospedaje Ideal
12 Hotel Cerro Nevado
13 Hotel Kalton
14 Hospedaje Rex
22 Hospedaje
   La Esperanza
27 Hotel Regine
28 Hotel Millalén

PLACES TO EAT
1 Jockey Club
3 Club Español
8 Grill Las Vegas
10 El Pancho
11 Estancia Chica
16 El Cortijo
18 Restaurant ACA

OTHER
4 Austral
6 Avis
15 Raffeish
17 Dirección Municipal de Turismo
19 Buttini Hermanos
20 Banco de la Nación
21 Terminal de Omnibus
23 Banco de Mendoza
24 Telefónica
25 Post Office
26 Hospital Teodor J Schestakow

Post & Telecommunications Correo
Argentino is at San Lorenzo and Barcala,
while Telefónica is at San Lorenzo 131.
San Rafael's postal code is 5600; the area
code is 0627.

Travel Agencies Agencies arranging local
excursions include Buttini Hermanos
(☎ 21423) at Corrientes 495 and Raffeish
(☎ 24456), República de Siria 296, which
organizes white-water rafting and trekking
trips in southern Mendoza province.

Medical Services San Rafael's Hospital

Teodor J Schestakow (☎ 24290) is at Emilio
Civit 151, at the corner of Corrientes.

Things to See
Worthwhile city sights are **Parque Hipólito Yrigoyen** at the west end of town, the
Catedral at Belgrano and Pellegrini on the
north side of Plaza San Martín, and the
Museo de Historia Natural, six km from
downtown on Isla Río Diamante, an island
in the middle of the river.

Places to Stay – bottom end
Camping On Isla Río Diamante, six km

east of downtown, *Camping El Parador* (☎ 27983) charges US$5 per tent site.

Hospedajes & Hotels *Hospedaje Ideal* (☎ 22301), Av San Martín 184, is the cheapest in town at US$14/23 for singles/doubles. Other inexpensive places are *Hospedaje La Esperanza* (☎ 22382) at Avellaneda 263 for US$15/26 single/double with shared bath, US$19/32 with private bath; and *Hospedaje Rex* (☎ 22177) at H Yrigoyen 56 for US$17/29 single/double. *Hotel Cerro Nevado* (☎ 28209), H Yrigoyen 376, charges US$21/32 single/double.

Places to Stay – middle
Hotel España (☎ 24055), Av San Martín 270, has rooms with private bath for US$24/40 single/double in its "sector colonial" (cheap wing), while rates for its cushier "sector celeste" is US$29/49 single/double, with a 10% discount if you pay cash. A block away at Av San Martín 327, *Hotel Tonín* (☎ 22499) has rooms for US$28/44 single/double. *Hotel Turis* (☎ 28090), Alvarez Condarco 340 between 25 de Mayo and Gutiérrez, is clean but basic and less central, with rooms for US$28/41 single/double. *Hotel Regine* (☎ 21470), Independencia 623, costs US$30/48 single/double with breakfast.

Places to Stay – top end
Hotel Kalton (☎ 30047), H Yrigoyen 120, is reasonable for US$36/64 single/double with breakfast. For US$40/70 single/double with breakfast, *Hotel Millalén* (☎ 22776), Ortíz de Rosas 198, is not the value it once was. Three-star *Hotel San Rafael* (☎ 30127), at Day 30, is top-of-the-line for US$48/78 single/double with breakfast.

Places to Eat
Try *Restaurant ACA* (☎ 22444) at H Yrigoyen 522, the elaborate *Club Español* (☎ 22907) at Salas and Day, *Jockey Club* (☎ 22336) at Belgrano 338, or *El Encuentro* at Coronel Plaza (the eastward extension of Santa Fe) and Patricias Mendocinas. The local parrillas are on Av H

Yrigoyen: *El Cortijo* at No 999, *El Pancho* at No 1110, and *Estancia Chica* at No 366. *Grill Las Vegas* (☎ 21390), San Martín 226, is a decent but unexceptional parrilla.

Getting There & Away
Air Austral (☎ 30036), Day 95 at Pellegrini, flies to Buenos Aires (US$172) Monday, Wednesday, and Friday.

Bus San Rafael is served by most of the same bus lines as Mendoza; the Terminal de Omnibus is on Coronel Suárez between Avellaneda and Almafuerte.

Alto Valle (☎ 23731) has nightly buses to Neuquén. Andesmar (☎ 27720) goes twice daily to Río Gallegos via Puerto Madryn and Comodoro Rivadavia, twice daily to Neuquén, daily to Bariloche, twice daily to Santa Rosa, and daily to Bahía Blanca. It has also northbound service twice daily to San Juan, La Rioja, Catamarca, Tucumán, Salta, and Jujuy, and goes Monday, Wednesday, and Friday mornings to Santiago, Chile.

TAC (☎ 22209) has at least 10 buses daily to Mendoza, seven to Malargüe, one to Córdoba, one to San Luis, one to Neuquén, one to Mar del Plata, five weekly to Bariloche, and three weekly to Las Leñas. Empresa Del Sur y Media Agua goes daily to San Juan. Expreso Uspallata (☎ 25153) goes several times daily to Mendoza, daily to Córdoba, and to Las Leñas weekends and holidays.

La Estrella (☎ 22079), Uspallata, and TAC go nightly to Buenos Aires (US$46, 13 hours).

Getting Around
Rental cars are available at Avis (☎ 22515) at Day 28, and at Sánchez Ariel (☎ 21189), Av Bartolomé Mitre 1178.

AROUND SAN RAFAEL
Cañón del Atuel
South along the Río Atuel, toward El Nihuil, a winding road passes through a spectacular, multicolored ravine that locals compare to the Grand Canyon of the Colorado, but much of Cañón del Atuel has

been submerged by three hydroelectric dams. The road crosses the Sierra Pintada, where there are interesting petroglyphs on the **Cuesta de los Terneros,** 32 km from San Rafael.

There's a *youth hostel* (☎ 26394) that charges US$50 for six-person bungalows.

Dique El Nihuil

El Nihuil, 79 km from San Rafael, is one of the main water-sports centers in the province. Its 9600-hectare reservoir, Dique El Nihuil, has a constant breeze that makes it particularly good for windsurfing and sailing; other activities include swimming, canoeing, and fishing. The *Camping Club de Pescadores* (☎ 26087) charges US$10 for tent sites, and has some bungalows that rent for US$60 for up to four persons; it also has a restaurant and store. In El Nihuil there are more restaurants and a gas station. TAC has buses from San Rafael at 6 am, 11 am, and 6:30 pm.

GENERAL ALVEAR

An agricultural town of 41,000 on the banks of the Río Atuel, General Alvear is the southeastern gateway to Mendoza province. In the late 19th century, General Diego de Alvear acquired the rich valley lands that originally belonged to the Indian cacique Goico and populated them with immigrants to form an agricultural colony. Among the main products are wine, fruits, vegetables, fodder, timber, and olives. You can visit the wineries along the poplar-lined roads around town.

Orientation & Information

General Alvear is 90 km east of San Rafael via RN 143. The main thoroughfares, Av Libertador and Av Alvear, divide the town into quadrants, with street names modified by directional indicators.

The Municipalidad, Av Alvear Oeste 550, provides tourist information. The area code for General Alvear is 0625.

Places to Stay & Eat

There are a few cheap hotels, in addition to several confiterías and pizzerías, along Av Alvear. Friendly *Hotel Avenida,* Av Alvear Este 254, has triples for US$12 per person, with a bath shared between every two rooms. Bathrooms are a bit rundown but have hot water. Downstairs is a comedor where large portions of basic food cost very little.

Other inexpensive places are *Hotel Grosso* (☎ 20392) at Ingeniero Lange 31 for US$20/35 single/double, and *Hotel Salamanca* (☎ 22700) on Av Alvear Este near República del Líbano for US$18/30 single/double. *Hotel Buenos Aires* (☎ 20393), Lange 54, charges US$25/44 single/double.

Things to Buy

Wine is the thing to buy, from wine shops or supermarkets. Wine shops include Vinería Blanco at Av San Martín 463, Vinería El Turista at Mitre 2576, and Vinería Favimar at Av San Martín 235.

MALARGÜE

Pehuenche Indians hunted and gathered in the valley of Malargüe, a term that derives from a Mapuche word meaning either "Place of Rocky Mesas" or "Place of Corrals." Spanish conquistador Francisco de Villagra reached the area in 1551. As in most regions of the country, the 19th-century advance of European agricultural colonists displaced and dispossessed the original inhabitants. Today petroleum is the principal industry, followed by uranium-processing for the Comisión Nacional de Energía Atómica, but Malargüe is also a center for outdoor activities.

Malargüe has a wealth of archaeological and paleontologic sites, but nearby cave paintings and petroglyphs are closed for study. Two fauna reserves, Payén and Laguna Llancanelo, are also close by, and caving is possible at Caveran de las Brujas and Pozo de las Animas. Las Leñas offers excellent skiing in winter and pleasant hiking in summer.

Orientation & Information

Malargüe is 189 km southwest of San Rafael via paved RN 40. The Dirección de

Turismo (☎ 71060) is in the Municipalidad at Fray Inalicán and N Uriburu.

The area code for Malargüe is 0627.

Places to Stay & Eat

Malargüe has abundant, reasonably priced accommodations, though prices can rise during the ski season. Both the *Camping Municipal Malargüe* (☎ 71059) and the *Camping Polideportivo* are on Alfonso Capdeville, at the north end of town.

The cheapest regular accommodations are *Hospedaje Sheril* (☎ 71337), which charges US$10 per person, and *Hospedaje Eben-Ezer* (☎ 71224), where singles/doubles with shared bath cost only US$11/20. In the US$15/25 single/double range are *Hotel Theis* (☎ 71429) at Av San Martín 938 and *Hotel Rioma* (☎ 71065) at Fray Inalicán 68. *Hotel Bambi* (☎ 71237), Av San Martín 410, charges US$20/35 single/double with private bath. *Hotel Turismo* (☎ 71042), Av San Martín 224, costs US$30/48 single/double.

Getting There & Away

Between them, TAC and Expreso Uspallata run at least five buses daily to San Rafael.

Getting Around

Transportes Diego Berbel, at Emilio Civit and Salas, has buses to Las Leñas and other nearby destinations. Chaltén Aventura, Av San Martín 113, has smaller vehicles for guided tours or excursions.

AROUND MALARGÜE
Caverna de Las Brujas

The Cave of the Witches is a limestone cave on Cerro Moncol, eight km from Bardas Blancas along RN 40 and 72 km south of Malargüe; JA Barros, Av San Martín 997 in Malargüe, has tours to Caverna de Las Brujas, and guides for hire. The nearby Bosques Petrificados de Llano Blanco, containing petrified Araucaria trees over 120 million years old, is six km from the village of Llano Blanco.

Los Molles

Los Molles is a small, quiet resort along RP 222 in the transverse valley of the Río Salado, 55 km northwest of Malargüe. Single 1100-meter lifts carry skiers up to the relatively gentle slopes, covering 90 hectares, while the thermal baths provide a local attraction. On the road to more exclusive Las Leñas, Los Molles' only hotel is the 155-room *Hotel Los Molles,* but there are also a couple of small guesthouses. It is much cheaper to stay here and ski at Las Leñas, but Los Molles lacks the larger resort's nightlife.

LAS LEÑAS

Designed primarily to attract wealthy foreigners, Las Leñas is Argentina's most self-consciously prestigious ski resort, but despite the glitter it's not totally out of the question for budget travelers. Since opening in 1983, it has attracted an international clientele who spend their days on the slopes and nights partying until the sun comes up.

Open mid-June to early October, with international competitions every year, Las Leñas is 445 km south of Mendoza, 200 km southwest of San Rafael, and only 70 km from Malargüe, all via RN 40 and RP 222. Its 33 runs cover 3300 hectares; the area has a base altitude of 2200 meters, but the slopes reach 3430 meters for a maximum drop of 1230 meters. One of the runs has lights and music twice a week, and there is a ski school with classes at several levels, taught in Spanish, English, French, German, Italian, and Portuguese.

Outside its ski season, Las Leñas is also attempting to attract summer visitors who enjoy weeklong packages stressing activities like windsurfing, mountain biking, horseback riding, and hiking. Rates start around US$490/$700 single/double with half-board; arrange both winter and summer holidays through Badino Turismo (☎ 326-1351, fax 393-2568), Perón 725, 6th floor, in Buenos Aires.

Lift Tickets

Prices for lift tickets vary considerably throughout the ski season, which runs from mid-June to late September. Children's tickets are discounted about 30%. In 1995, adult three-day passes ranged from US$75 to US$115, four-day passes from US$100 to US$155, seven-day passes from US$150 to US$250, and 14-day passes from US$270 to US$450.

Ski Packages

Two hotels on or near the slopes offer ski packages that include seven nights' accommodations with unlimited skiing and varying meal plans. Children ages four to 11 get a 20% discount, while children under four are free.

Hotel Piscis' adult rates for ski packages range from US$1177 to US$2744 for single accommodations near the slopes and from US$1258 to US$2942 for singles right on the slopes. Rates for doubles go from US$978 to US$2128 near the slopes and from US$1044 to US$2277 on the slopes. Each additional adult costs from US$531 to US$866. Singles at Hotel Escorpio range from US$918 to US$2128 and doubles from US$769 to US$1661. Each extra adult costs US$432 to US$712.

In addition, "apart-hotels" (dormitory-style lodgings) offer similar packages but without meals. Parties of two to three pay from US$416 to US$873 per person, and parties of four to seven pay US$368 to US$781 per person. For more hotel information, see the entry for Places to Stay & Eat, below.

Places to Stay & Eat

Las Leñas has a small village with four luxury hotels (☎ 0627-71100 for all), the most extravagant of which is 99-room *Hotel Piscis,* with wood-burning stoves, a gymnasium, sauna facilities, a swimming pool, the restaurant *Las Cuatro Estaciones,* a bar, a casino, and shops. The others are 47-room *Hotel El Escorpio,* 34-room *Hotel Géminis,* and 40-room *Hotel Acuario.* There are also has self-catering "apart-hotels," moderately priced dormitories with five to eight beds and shared bathrooms, the restaurant *El Brasero,* and a supermarket, but budget travelers can stay much more cheaply at Los Molles, 20 km down the road, or at Malargüe, 70 km away.

Getting There & Away

In season, there are charter flights from Buenos Aires to Malargüe for US$320 roundtrip, including transfers to and from Las Leñas. Airport transfers alone cost US$25 roundtrip to Malargüe, US$90 to San Rafael.

There is scheduled bus service in season from both Malargüe and San Rafael with Expreso Uspallata.

San Juan Province

If you can disregard the desiccated carcasses of cattle and horses struck by trucks and buses along RN 40 between Mendoza and San Juan, consider stopping to purchase melons and brightly painted gourds arranged in eye-catching geometric patterns at the colorful roadside fruit stands that line the way. While not a major destination for most foreign travelers, the province offers some truly appealing cultural attractions and nearly unexplored backcountry.

The province of San Juan is promoting the improvement of RN 150 over the Andes to La Serena and Coquimbo, Chile, in order to achieve a closer economic integration with its western neighbor that might benefit both. Although the 4750-meter Agua Negra pass is considerably higher than the heavily used Uspallata alternative near Mendoza, the drier climate means lower snowfall and theoretically better accessibility, though the Uspallata route is rarely closed for long.

SAN JUAN

Despite its provincial capital status, modern construction, and wide, tree-lined avenues, San Juan retains the rhythm and cordiality of a small town. With an annual average of nine hours of sun daily, its nickname is Residencia del Sol (Residence of the Sun). El Zonda, the dry north wind, often brings extreme heat and very high pressure, slowing the pace of local activities. As in

Mendoza, the streets are empty during siesta hours, between noon and 4 pm.

Founded as San Juan de la Frontera in 1562 by Juan Jufré de Loaysa y Montesso, the desert city struggled in its early years – in the early 17th century, Vásquez de Espinosa remarked that its 24 Spanish residents were "poverty stricken" and "powerless" to convert the area's 800 Huarpe Indians. Throughout the colonial period and to the present, San Juan has lagged behind larger and more influential Mendoza; though surrounding vineyards and orchards have grown and improved, it has not been able to attract supporting industries and lies off the region's principal transit routes.

A massive 1944 earthquake, after which Juan Perón's relief efforts first made him a major public figure, destroyed the city center; completely rebuilt since then, the downtown sparkles from the efforts of full-time custodians who sweep the sidewalks and water and patrol the parks and plazas, shooing people off the manicured lawns. As in Mendoza, people swab the sidewalks with kerosene to keep them shining.

Orientation

San Juan is 170 km north of Mendoza via RN 40, which passes through San Juan from north to south, and 1140 km from Buenos Aires. Like most Argentine cities, San Juan's grid pattern makes orientation very easy; the addition of cardinal points to street addresses helps even more. East-west Av San Martín and north-south Calle Mendoza divide the city into quadrants. The functional center of town is south of Av San Martín.

Information

Tourist Offices The Subsecretaría de Turismo (☎ 22-7219), Sarmiento 24 Sur near Av San Martín, has a good map of the city and its surroundings, plus useful information and brochures on the rest of the province, particularly Parque Provincial Ischigualasto (Valle de la Luna or "Valley of the Moon"). Opening hours are 8 am to noon and 4 to 8 pm daily.

For visitors interested in tours, the friendly and knowledgeable staff will provide a list of guides throughout the province. At the entrance, artisanal pottery, crafts, wines, and dried fruits are for sale. ACA (☎ 22-6625) is at 9 de Julio 802.

Money Cambio Cash at Tucumán 210 Sur and Cambio Santiago at General Acha 52 Sur are the main moneychangers, but many travel agencies also exchange cash. Banco de San Juan has an ATM at Rivadavia 44 Este, and Banco Multicrédito is at Laprida and Mendoza.

Post & Telecommunications Correo Argentino is at Av Ignacio de la Roza 259 Este; the postal code is 5400. Telefónica is at Laprida 180 Oeste, but there are many convenient locutorios. San Juan's area code is 064.

Travel Agencies Several travel agencies organize trips to the interior or to other provinces. Try Yafar Turismo (☎ 21-4476) at Caseros 90 Sur, Yanzón Viajes y Turismo (☎ 22-2420) at Calle Mendoza 322 Sur, Mario Agüero Turismo (☎ 22-3652) at General Acha 17 Norte, or Turismo Sol Sanjuanino (☎ 22-6018) at Av España 33 Norte.

Medical Services The Hospital Rawson (☎ 22-2272) is at General Paz and Estados Unidos.

Casa de Sarmiento

Domingo Faustino Sarmiento's prolific writing as politician, diplomat, educator, and journalist made him a major public figure both within and beyond Argentina. Exiled in Chile during the government of Rosas, he wrote the famous polemic *Life in the Argentine Republic in the Days of the Tyrants,* readily available in English translation and still used in many South American history courses; from 1868 to 1874, he was the first Argentine president of the interior province.

A fierce critic of caudillos like Buenos Aires' Rosas and his gaucho followers, Sarmiento argued that Unitarism embodied

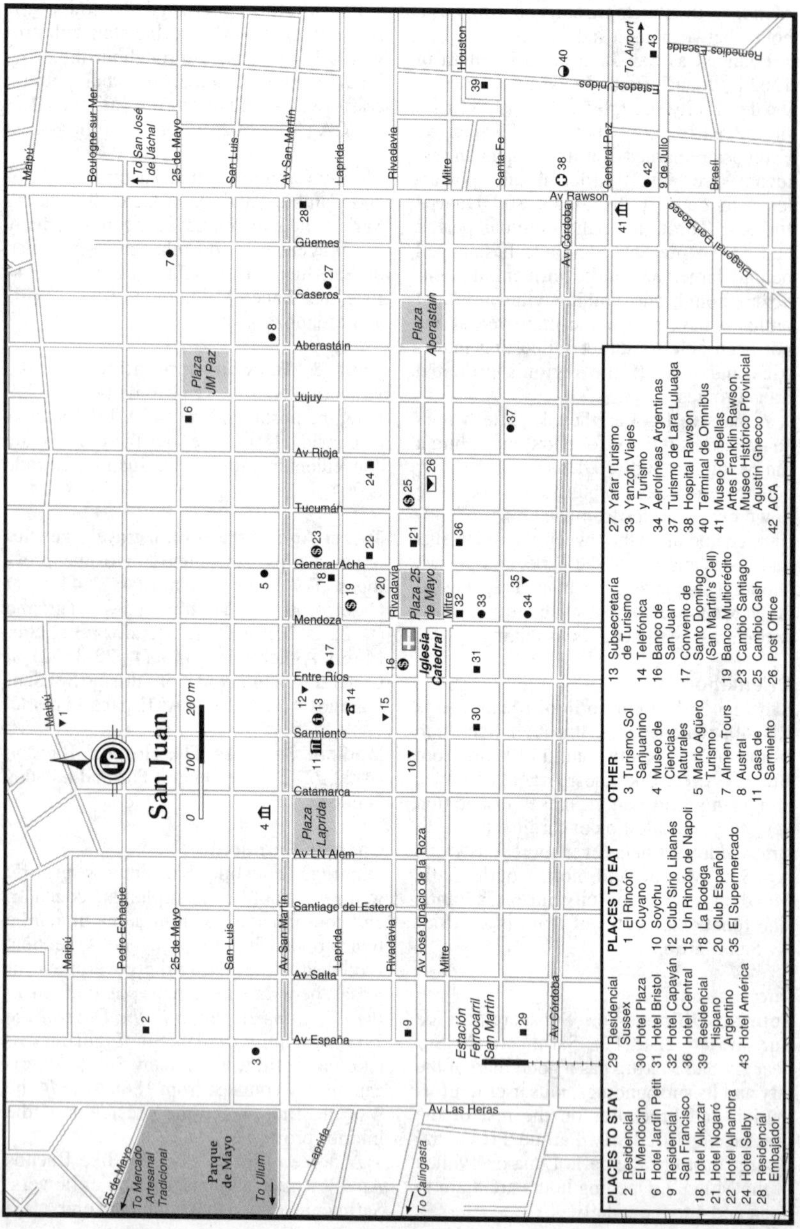

San Juan
0 100 200 m
To San José de Jáchal
To Mercado Artesanal Tradicional
To Ullum
To Calingasta
To Airport
Parque de Mayo
Plaza Laprida
Plaza JM Paz
Plaza 25 de Mayo
Plaza Aberastain
Iglesia Catedral
Estación Ferrocarril San Martín
Maipú
Pedro Echagüe
Boulogne sur Mer
25 de Mayo
San Luis
Av San Martín
Laprida
Rivadavia
Av José Ignacio de la Roza
Mitre
Santa Fe
Av Córdoba
General Paz
9 de Julio
Brasil
Av Rawson
Estados Unidos
Remedios Escalada
Diagonal Don Bosco
Houston
Av España
Av Salta
Santiago del Estero
Av LN Alem
Catamarca
Sarmiento
Entre Ríos
Mendoza
General Acha
Tucumán
Av Rioja
Jujuy
Aberastain
Caseros
Güemes
Av Las Heras
PLACES TO STAY
2 Residencial El Mendocino
6 Hotel Jardín Petit
9 Residencial San Francisco
18 Hotel Alkazar
21 Hotel Nogaró
22 Hotel Alhambra
24 Hotel Selby
28 Residencial Embajador
29 Residencial Sussex
30 Hotel Plaza
31 Hotel Bristol
32 Hotel Capayán
36 Hotel Central
39 Residencial Hispano Argentino
43 Hotel América
PLACES TO EAT
1 El Rincón Cuyano
10 Soychu
12 Club Sirio Libanés
15 Un Rincón de Napoli
18 La Bodega
20 Club Español
35 El Supermercado
OTHER
3 Turismo Sol Sanjuanino
4 Museo de Ciencias Naturales
5 Mario Agüero Turismo
7 Almen Tours
8 Austral
11 Casa de Sarmiento
13 Subsecretaría de Turismo
14 Telefónica
16 Banco de San Juan
17 Convento de Santo Domingo (San Martín's Cell)
19 Banco Multicrédito
23 Cambio Santiago
25 Cambio Cash
26 Post Office
27 Yafar Turismo
33 Yanzón Viajes y Turismo
34 Aerolíneas Argentinas
37 Turismo de Lara Luluaga
38 Hospital Rawson
40 Terminal de Omnibus
41 Museo de Bellas Artes Franklin Rawson, Museo Histórico Provincial Agustín Gnecco
42 ACA

"civilization" on the European model, while Federalism represented unprincipled "barbarism," resulting in

the final formation of the central consolidated despotic government of the landed proprietor Don Juan Manuel Rosas, who applied the knife of the gaucho to the culture of Buenos Ayres, and destroyed the work of centuries – of civilisation, law and liberty.

Ironically, most of Sarmiento's knowledge of the Pampas and their gauchos was secondhand, as he never crossed the country overland until after the fall of Rosas. His *Recuerdos de Provincia* recounted his childhood in this house and his memories of his mother, Doña Paula Albarracín, who paid for part of the house's construction by weaving cloth in a loom under the fig tree that still stands in the front patio. The museum (☎ 22-4603), at Sarmiento 21 Sur, is open daily except Monday.

Museo de Bellas Artes Franklin Rawson
Named after the local 19th-century painter, this museum (☎ 22-8104), at General Paz 737 Este, offers a good overview of Argentine art. Its valuable collection includes paintings, sculptures, drawings, and engravings by well-known artists such as Rawson himself, Prilidiano Pueyrredón, Raymond Monvoisin (a Frenchman who lived in Argentina), Ernesto de la Cárcova, Antonio Berni, Raúl Soldi, Lino Spilimbergo, Emilio Petorutti, Raquel Forner, and others.

Museo Histórico Provincial Agustín Gnecco
In the same building as the Museo de Bellas Artes, this museum has a notable collection of historical material related to San Juan's colonial life and political development. It also has some archaeological artifacts and a great coin collection assembled by the historian for whom it is named.

Convento de Santo Domingo
At Av San Martín and Entre Ríos, the present Dominican convent, constructed after the earthquake, lacks the grandeur of the 17th-century original, the order's richest in the territory.

The only part of the old building to survive the quake was the cell occupied by San Martín during his visits to San Juan in 1815, which has a small museum at Laprida 96 Oeste. San Martín held meetings here, soliciting political and financial support for his Ejército de los Andes, one local division of which liberated Coquimbo and La Serena, Chile. The original furnishings and some other materials are on display. It's open Tuesday to Sunday.

Iglesia Catedral
Inaugurated in 1979, the modern and rather ugly cathedral is at Calle Mendoza and Rivadavia, across from Plaza 25 de Mayo. Italian artists designed and sculpted the bronze doors and the main ornaments inside.

Museo de Ciencias Naturales
At Av San Martín and Catamarca, this museum has an interesting collection of plants, animals, minerals, and rocks from the province. The museum has conducted studies of important paleontologic sites at Ischigualasto and Ullum, with a comprehensive collection of fossils.

Mercado Artesanal Tradicional
Inaugurated in 1985 to promote local handicrafts, the market is in the Parque de Mayo, at 25 de Mayo and Urquiza, beneath the Auditorio Juan Victoria. Particularly attractive are the brightly colored *mantas* (shawls) of Jáchal, and the warm ponchos. Besides textiles, there are pottery, riding gear, and basketry, as well as traditional silver knife handles, *mate* gourds, and key chains. The market is open weekdays.

Wineries
For a sample of the region's famous *blanco sanjuanino* (white wine), visit the **Bodega Bragagnolo** (☎ 21-1305), on RN 40 and Av Benavídez in the suburb of Chimbas. Besides table and reserve wines, the winery produces excellent dessert wines, such as *mistela* and *moscato dulce* (muscatel), and

additional products such as juices, raisins, and the regional specialty *arrope de uva,* a kind of grape jam.

In the suburb of San Martín, **Bodega Peñaflor** manufactures the popular but mass-produced Termidor wines and will also give tours. Catch bus No 13 ("San Martín") on Av Córdoba.

Organized Tours

San Juan travel agencies, in addition to those above, run trips to some of the province's better but less easily accessible visitor attractions. Almen Tours (☎ 21-3848), 25 de Mayo 698 Oeste, goes to Parque Provincial Ischigualasto (US$52, without food), Calingasta/Barreal (US$35), Dique Ullum (US$16), and Jáchal/Pismanta (US$42). Turismo de Lara Luluaga (☎ 21-4703), Santa Fe 353 Oeste, does both overland (US$70) and aerial (US$110) tours of Ischigualasto.

Raphael Joliat, a Swiss citizen living in San Juan, conducts backcountry vehicle tours of San Juan province for between US$70 and US$120 per person per day; contact him through Covalle Bus (☎ /fax 23-0058) at the bus terminal.

Places to Stay – bottom end

Camping *Camping El Pinar,* the municipal site, is on Av Benavídez Oeste, six km from downtown; reached by Empresa de la Marina buses, it has a small artificial lake, a swimming pool, and a forest plantation. Charges are US$3 per person and US$2 per tent. There are other sites west of the city, where Av San Martín becomes RP 14 to Dique Ullum and Parque Rivadavia. Take bus No 23 or No 29.

Residenciales & Pensions There are several conveniently located, inexpensive places to stay in San Juan, most of which rent rooms by the hour. Near the train station at Av España 248 Sur, *Residencial San Francisco* (☎ 22-3760) has modest but clean singles/doubles for US$15/20. Similar in standard are *Residencial El Mendocino* (☎ 22-5930) at España 234 Norte for US$25 double, and *Residencial Sussex* at

España 402 Sur.

Near the bus terminal, the small rooms at friendly *Residencial Hispano Argentino,* Estados Unidos 381 Sur, cost US$12 per person with shared bath. *Residencial Embajador* (☎ 22-5520), Av Rawson 25 Sur, has nice, clean rooms at US$18/30 single/double.

Tidy *Hotel Central* (☎ 22-3174), Mitre 131 Este, offers the best inexpensive accommodations in town; it's central but quiet, has firm beds, and costs US$18 per person with private bath.

Places to Stay – middle

There is more variation in price than in standard and services of hotels in this category. All offer telephones, heating, air conditioning, and parking garages. Some have a restaurant or confitería.

The best values in this category are *Hotel América* (☎ 21-4514), 9 de Julio 1052 Este, which charges US$25/36 single/double with private bath, and *Hotel Plaza* (☎ 22-5179), Sarmiento 344 Sur, where rates are US$29/38.

Hotel Alhambra (☎ 22-8280), General Acha 180 Sur, has rooms for US$34/46 single/double. In the same range are *Hotel Selby* (☎ 22-4777) at Av Rioja 183 Sur, *Hotel Bristol* (☎ 22-2629) at Entre Ríos 368 Sur, and *Hotel Jardín Petit* (☎ 21-1825) at 25 de Mayo 345 Este.

Places to Stay – top end

The costliest hotels in San Juan are comfortable but less luxurious than those in Mendoza. *Hotel Capayán* (☎ 22-5122), Mitre 31 Este, has rooms for US$38/51 single/double, while *Hotel Nogaró* (☎ 22-7501), Ignacio de la Roza 132 Este, has rooms for US$45/61. Five-star *Hotel Alkazar* (☎ 21-4965), Laprida 82 Este, charges US$55/65 single/double with breakfast.

Places to Eat

Like Mendoza, San Juan has a varied international cuisine at private clubs operated by different cultural associations. *Club*

Sirio Libanés (☎ 22-9884), Entre Ríos 33 Sur, serves moderately priced Middle-Eastern food in a very pleasant environment of beautifully conserved tiles and woodwork. The more somber *Club Español* (☎ 22-3389), Rivadavia 32 Este, has ordinary food and erratic service. *La Bodega* (☎ 21-4965), in the Hotel Alkazar at Laprida 82 Este, is a sumptuous, expensive French restaurant.

La Nona María, west of downtown at Av San Martín and Perito Moreno, has excellent pasta. *El Rincón Cuyano,* Sarmiento 394 Norte, has a standard Argentine menu, but the food is good, service friendly, and prices reasonable. Near the outskirts of town, on Av Circunvalación near Av San Martín, *Wiesbaden* has good German food. The vegetarian restaurant *Soychu,* Ignacio de la Roza 223 Oeste, serves a highly recommended tenedor libre lunch. *El Supermercado,* on General Acha between Santa Fe and Córdoba, is a traditional market with good paella.

There are several parrillas on Av Circunvalación, including recommended *La Bodega del 800* at the corner of Tucumán and *Nahuel* at the corner of Salta. *Bonnanit* and *Mikonos* are on Av San Martín, as is *Las Leñas* (☎ 23-2100) at Av San Martín 1670 Oeste (corner of Zavalla), *El Gordo* (corner of Alvear), and *Las Cubas* (corner of Perito Moreno). *Bigotes,* Las Heras between 9 de Julio and General Paz, has tenedor libre beef, chicken, and salads for a reasonable price.

For a good inexpensive lunch, try *Restaurant Avenida* at 9 de Julio Este and General Acha, half a block from the ACA. Pizzería *Un Rincón de Napoli,* Rivadavia 175 Oeste, has a wide selection of toppings and good beer; it's a bit dingy, but also prepares food to go. *Pirandello,* on San Martín west of downtown, is an outstanding sandwich place.

Getting There & Away
Air Aeropuerto Las Chacritas (☎ 25-0486) is 13 km southeast of town on RN 20. Aerolíneas Argentinas (☎ 22-0205), Mendoza 468 Sur, flies nightly to Buenos Aires (US$178). Austral (☎ 21-4038) is at Aberastaín 2 Norte; its daily (except Sunday) flight from Córdoba to Mendoza stops briefly in San Juan before returning to Córdoba (US$71).

Bus The Terminal de Omnibus (☎ 22-1604) is at Estados Unidos 492 Sur. Empresa Del Sur y Media Agua has frequent buses to Mendoza (two hours) and daily service to Rosario and Neuquén (US$54). Autotransportes San Juan has three afternoon buses to Buenos Aires (US$40, 16 hours), and also goes to Mar del Plata (US$56) daily at noon.

Empresa Socasa has two buses daily to Córdoba (US$25), one direct and the other via La Rioja. Buses 20 de Junio also goes to Córdoba, but takes the scenic Altas Cumbres route. La Estrella (☎ 22-1365) has direct buses to Mendoza, La Rioja (six hours), Catamarca (eight hours), and Tucumán (13 hours). Libertador (☎ 22-1232) also stops here en route between Mendoza, La Rioja, Catamarca, and Tucumán.

Ticsa buses travel daily to Bahía Blanca and three times weekly to Neuquén and Zapala. On Wednesday a bus also goes to San Martín de los Andes, and on Friday and Sunday to Bariloche. Wednesday and Friday mornings it has buses to Viedma, and Tuesdays and Fridays to Santiago de Chile (US$30, nine hours).

TAC has daily service to Chile (Santiago, Valparaíso, and Viña del Mar), plus five buses to Mendoza. It also serves northern San Juan, (Jáchal and Pismanta), Bariloche (US$72) to the south, and the eastern destinations of San Luis, Merlo, and Paraná.

Empresa Iglesia travels to provincial destinations only. Empresa Vallecito has a daily bus to Caucete, the Difunta Correa shrine (US$3), and San Agustín del Valle Fértil.

AROUND SAN JUAN
Dique Ullum
Only a short distance west of San Juan, this reservoir is a center for nautical sports – swimming, fishing, kayaking, water-skiing, and windsurfing.

Museo Arqueológico La Laja

Focusing on the prehistory of San Juan, this museum (part of the provincial university) has seven display rooms, organized chronologically from the Fortuna culture of 6500 BC to the Incas and their trans-Andean contemporaries, with mummies, basketry, tools of many different materials, sculptures, petroglyphs, and the remains of cultivated plants.

The Moorish style building was once a hotel that featured thermal baths, which are still in use – after your visit, have a hot soak. Outdoors are reproductions of natural environments, farming systems, petroglyphs, and house types, all built to scale.

To reach the museum, 25 km north of San Juan in the village of La Laja, take bus No 20 ("Albardón") from Av Córdoba in San Juan. Only three buses a day, at 8 am and 1 and 4 pm, go all the way; if you miss any of them, take any bus No 20 to Las Piedritas and hitch a ride the last five km with trucks or other vehicles going to the quarry across from the museum.

Reserva Nacional El Leoncito

West of San Juan, RP 12 climbs the valley

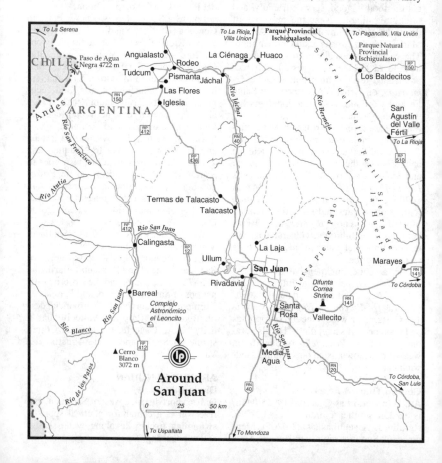

of the Río San Juan, between the Sierras del Tigre to the north and the Sierra del Tontal to the south, before arriving at the village of Calingasta and intersecting southbound RP 412, to Barreal and Uspallata in Mendoza province. South of Barreal, 76,000-hectare Reserva Nacional El Leoncito occupies a former estancia typical of the Andean precordillera and is the site of two observatories, the **Complejo Astronómico El Leoncito** and the **Observatorio Astronómico Doctor Carlos U Cesco.**

Calingasta has two modest hotels, *Hotel Calingasta* and *Hotel La Capilla,* and a municipal *campground.* Barreal has a wider range of accommodations, including *Posada San Eduardo* (☎ 0648-41046) for US$20 with breakfast, the *Hotel de Turismo* (☎ 0648-41000), four small pensions and two *campgrounds.* There are also several restaurants, including recommended *Isidoro.* The bus from San Juan costs US$11, and another bus runs between Calingasta and Uspallata Tuesdays and Fridays.

DIFUNTA CORREA SHRINE
At Vallecito, about 60 km east of San Juan, the shrine of the popular saint Difunta Correa is one of the most fascinating, offbeat cultural attractions in all of Argentina. While patronizing and pejorative, Sarmiento's commentary on Argentine rural religion in the 19th century provides some idea of what to expect:

To this, that is, to natural religion, is all religion reduced in the pastoral districts. Christianity exists, like the Spanish idioms, as a tradition which is perpetuated, but corrupted; coloured by gross superstitions and unaided by instruction, rites, or convictions.

Places to Stay & Eat
Reasonably comfortable accommodations are available at *Hotel Difunta Correa* for about US$18 per person, and there's one inexpensive *hostería,* but accommodations are more abundant and much better in San Juan. Pilgrims camp almost anywhere they feel like it.

There is good street food and a decent restaurant in the village; for dining, there are two quinchos with minutas and *Comedor Don Roque,* which has terrific soup and empanadas on Sundays; it's on RN 20 at the entrance to the village.

Getting There & Away
Empresa Vallecito goes daily from San Juan to the shrine (US$3), but any other eastbound bus, toward La Rioja or Córdoba, will drop off passengers at the site. Another alternative is to take a bus to Caucete, midway between San Juan and Vallecito, and go to the offices of Fundación Cementerio Vallecito, where you can catch a lift with the water trucks that serve the shrine.

JÁCHAL
Founded in 1751 and known as the Cuna de la Tradición (Cradle of Tradition), Jáchal, surrounded by vineyards and olive groves, is a charming village with a mix of older adobes and more contemporary brick buildings where weavers still make the famous Jachallero ponchos and blankets on 19th-century looms. Jachalleros, the local residents, are renowned for their crafts and fidelity to indigenous and gaucho traditions; in November, the Fiesta de la Tradición pays homage to and reinforces this way of life.

Across from the main plaza, the **Iglesia San José,** a national monument, houses the *Cristo Negro* (Black Christ) or *Señor de la Agonía* (Lord of Agony), a grisly leather image with articulated head and limbs, brought from Potosí in colonial times.

Places to Stay & Eat
There are several campgrounds in the vicinity of Jáchal. *Hotel San Martín* (☎ 0647-20431), at Etchegaray and Florida, has clean singles/doubles for US$15/23 with shared bath, US$20/30 with private bath. Accommodations at *Hotel Plaza* (☎ 0647-20431), San Juan 545, are comparable but slightly more expensive. *El Chatito Flores,* half a block off the plaza, has good but moderately priced meals.

The Difunta Correa & Her Legend

Legend has it that during the civil wars of the 1840s, Deolinda Correa followed the movements of her sickly conscript husband's battalion on foot through the deserts of San Juan, carrying food, water, and their baby son in her arms. When her meager supplies ran out, thirst, hunger, and exhaustion killed her, but when passing muleteers found them, the infant was still nursing at the dead woman's breast. There are many versions of this story, but the main points are the same, despite uncertainty that she ever even existed. Commemorating this apparent miracle, her shrine at Vallecito is widely believed to be the site of her death.

Difunta literally means "defunct"; Correa is her surname. Technically she is not a saint but rather a "soul," a dead person who performs miracles and intercedes for people – the child's survival was the first of a series of miracles attributed to her. Since the 1940s, her shrine, originally a simple hilltop cross, has grown into a small village with its own gas station, school, post office, police station, and church. At 17 chapels or exhibit rooms, devotees leave *ex-votos* (gifts) in exchange for supernatural favors. In addition, there are two hotels, several restaurants, a commercial gallery with souvenir shops, and offices for the nonprofit organization that administers the site.

A visit to the shrine is an unusual and worthwhile experience even for nonbelievers. The religious imagery and material manifestations resemble no other Christian shrine in Latin America – some people build and leave elaborate models of homes and cars obtained through her intercession. Pilgrims, locals, and even merchants are all eager to talk about the Difunta. It is perhaps the strongest popular belief system in a country that harbors a variety of unusual religious practices independent of Roman Catholicism, the official state religion, even if clearly related to it. They tell of miraculous cures, assistance at difficult childbirth, economic windfalls, and protection of travelers.

In fact, truckers are especially devoted. From La Quiaca, on the Bolivian border, to Ushuaia in Tierra del Fuego, you will see roadside shrines with images of the Difunta Correa, wax candles, small bank notes, and the unmistakable bottles of water left to quench her thirst. At some sites, there appears to be enough parts to build a car from scratch – do not mistake wheels, brake shoes and crankshafts for piles of trash – but refrain from taking anything away unless you really need it, since it is said that she also has a vengeful streak.

Despite lack of government support and the open antagonism of the Catholic Church, the shrine has grown as belief in the Difunta Correa has become more widespread. People visit the shrine all year round, but at Easter, May 1, and Christmas, up to 200,000 pilgrims descend on Vallecito. There is more activity on weekends than during the week. ■

Getting There & Away

TAC has several buses daily between Jáchal and San Juan, with connections to Mendoza.

AROUND JÁCHAL

A day trip on RN 40, north of San Juan, passes through a beautiful landscape of rich folkloric traditions, rarely seen by foreigners. East of Jáchal, the road climbs the precipitous **Cuesta de Huaco**, with a view of Los Cauquenes dam, before arriving at the village of **Huaco**, whose 200-year-old **Viejo Molino** (flour mill) justifies the trip. It is the birthplace of poet Don Buenaventura Luna, who put the Jachallero culture in the map.

Backtracking to RN 150, you cross the **Cuesta del Viento** and pass through the tunnels of Rodeo west of Jáchal to the department of Iglesia, home of the precordillera thermal baths of **Pismanta**. Its

42° waters are recommended for rheumatic ailments, circulation, and general cleansing and relaxation. For US$45/721 single/double, *Hotel Termas de Pismanta* has rooms with private bath, all meals at its restaurant/confitería, and a swimming pool.

RN 150 continues westwards to La Serena and Coquimbo, both in Chile, via the recently reopened **Paso de Agua Negra** (altitude 4722 meters). Inquire in San Juan about bus services on this route.

South of Pismanta, RP 436 returns to RN 40 and San Juan. Another worthwhile stop is **Iglesia**, a small Andean town where people cultivate fruit (mostly apples), make goat and cow cheeses, and weave guanaco blankets, ponchos, and saddlebags.

SAN AGUSTÍN DE VALLE FÉRTIL

Founded in 1788, San Agustín de Valle Fértil (population 6000) is a cheerful village where people sit on the sidewalks on summer evenings greeting passersby, and there are as many bicycles as automobiles; even the usually aggressive Argentine motorist appears to appreciate the relaxed pace. It lies among the Sierras Pampeanas, gentle sedimentary mountains cut by impressive canyons, 247 km northeast of San Juan via RN 141 and RP 510, which continues to Ischigualasto and La Rioja.

Thanks to San Agustín's temperate climate and high rainfall, the colorful hills, rivers, exuberant flora, and varied fauna contrast dramatically with the desert landscapes of the rest of the province. Visitors to Parque Provincial Ischigualasto frequently stay at the town, which celebrates the anniversary of its founding on April 4.

The main economic activities are farming and animal husbandry, and mining of quartz, mica, and marble, plus smaller quantities of granite, gold, and iron. Américo Cortés and Griselda Elizondo of the Dirección de Turismo (on General Acha· directly across from the plaza) are exceptionally helpful, providing general information, chatting about the town's traditional artisans, and recommending walks

along the Río Seco del Valle. They can also help arrange excursions into the backcountry sierras and canyons by car or mule. The office is open weekdays 7 am to 1 pm and 5 to 10 pm, Saturdays 8 am to 1 pm only. The Banco de San Juan is open Mondays only.

San Agustín is small enough that locals pay little attention to street addresses, so ask directions or use the LP map. At press time, this town had not yet been integrated into the national and international direct dial telephone system.

Things to See & Do

Spending a day by the Río Seco is pleasant and relaxing, whether fishing, sunbathing, or walking. About 300 meters across the river are the petroglyphs of **Piedra Pintada**; about 500 meters farther north are the **Morteros Indígenas** (Indian mortars). At the north end of town, near the Escuela Agrotécnica, is the Diaguita archaeological site known as the **Meseta Ritual.**

The village of **La Majadita,** seven km from San Agustín by mule or cart, is only reachable during the winter dry season, since the road crosses the river several times. You can find lodging at a local rancho, where you can eat kid goat and goat cheese, and have fresh milk in the morning.

Places to Stay & Eat

No longer the bargain it once was, the *Camping Municipal* now charges US$8 per site. Shady *Camping Valle Fértil,* the former ACA site, has better facilities for US$10, but try bargaining if it's not crowded. Given its popularity among sanjuaninos, it gets very crowded during long weekends and holidays.

The cheapest and most pleasant places are private homes. Four families all charge about US$9/12 for singles/doubles with shared bath: *Pensión Patrocinio Romero, Pensión Doña Zoila, Pensión Nicolás Mercado,* and *Pensión Villalón.*

There are also several hospedajes: *Hospedaje San Agustín* has rooms at US$8/13 with private bath and hot water, plus a restaurant/confitería. Similar in price, but with shared baths, is *Hospedaje Los Olivos.* At *Hospedaje Santa Fe* rooms with shared bath cost US$10 to US$12 per person. *Hospedaje Ischigualasto* charges US$12 per person.

Until it closed recently, the costliest place was the spectacularly sited *Hostería del ACA,* which had great views of the valley and the reservoir and a good restaurant/confitería. It may reopen.

Besides the hotel restaurants, try *Restaurant Keoma,* a pleasant family-run parrilla, *Pizzería La Plaza,* and *Rancho Criollo,* also a parrilla.

Getting There & Away

From San Juan (US$12, three hours), take Empresa Vallecito buses or hitch a ride with the mining trucks. There are buses to La Rioja Mondays and Fridays (US$7), which can drop off passengers at the turnoff to Ischigualasto.

Ask at the tourist office to arrange a private car to Parque Provincial Ischigualasto for about US$80; otherwise, remises cost about US$200.

San Agustín de Valle Fértil

0   250   500 m

PLACES TO STAY	PLACES TO EAT	OTHER
5 Camping Municipal	10 Restaurant Keoma	1 Morteros Indígenas
6 Hostería del ACA	15 Pizzería La Plaza	2 Piedra Pintada
7 Camping Valle Fértil	18 Rancho Criollo	3 Meseta Ritual
8 Pensión Nicolás Mercado		4 Escuela Agrotécnica
9 Hospedaje San Agustín		12 Telefónica
11 Pensión Doña Zoila		13 Post Office
17 Pensión Patrocinio Romero		14 Iglesia Nuestra Señora
19 Hospedaje Santa Fe		del Rosario
20 Hospedaje Los Olivos		16 Dirección de Turismo
22 Pensión Villalón		21 ACA Service Station

PARQUE PROVINCIAL ISCHIGUALASTO

Over time the persistent action of water has exposed a wealth of fossils, some 180 million years old from the Triassic period, in Parque Provincial Ischigualasto, named for an early Paleo-Indian culture and comparable to North American national parks like Bryce Canyon or Zion. Its museum displays some of these fossils, including the carnivorous dinosaur *Herrerasaurus* (not unlike *Tyrannosaurus rex*) and a good diorama of the park's paleo-environments.

Known colloquially as one of South America's many *Valles de la Luna* (Valleys of the Moon), Ischigualasto is a desert valley between two sedimentary mountain ranges, the Cerros Colorados in the east and Cerro Los Rastros in the west. Over millennia, at every meander in the canyon, the waters of the nearly dry Río Ischigualasto have carved distinctive shapes in the monochrome clay, red sandstone, and volcanic ash. Predictably, some of the these forms have acquired popular names: Cancha de Bochas (The Ball Court), El Submarino (the Submarine), and El Gusano (The Worm). The desert flora of algarrobo trees, shrubs, and cacti complement the eerie landforms.

From the visitors center, isolated 1748-meter **Cerro Morado** is a three- to four-hour walk gaining nearly 800 meters in elevation and yielding outstanding views of the surrounding area. Take plenty of drinking water and high energy snacks.

Places to Stay & Eat

Camping is permitted at the visitors center, which also has a confitería with simple meals and cold drinks; dried fruits and bottled olives from the province are also available. There are toilets and showers, but because water must be trucked in, don't count on them.

Getting There & Away

Ischigualasto is about 80 km north of San Agustín via RP 510 and a paved lateral to the northwest. Given its size and isolation, the only practical way to visit the park is by vehicle. After you arrive at the visitors center and pay the US$3 entrance fee, one of the rangers will accompany your vehicle on a two-hour, 45-km circuit through the park. Some roads within the park are unpaved and can be impassable after rain, necessitating a shorter trip.

If you have no vehicle, ask the tourist office in San Agustín about hiring a car and driver there. Alternatively, contact the park in advance so that the park ranger off duty during your visit can be hired as a guide, using his vehicle. The ranger will pick you up at the police checkpoint at Los Baldecitos on RP 510, reached by the Empresa Vallecito bus to La Rioja. Write to Dante Herrera at Parque Provincial Ischigualasto, (5449) San Agustín del Valle Fértil, Provincia de San Juan.

San Luis Province

Popularly known as *La Puerta de Cuyo* (the door to Cuyo), the province of San Luis draws many Argentine visitors, but very few foreigners visit the province's delightful hill country, resembling the Sierras de Córdoba. Its major attraction is the picturesque town of Merlo, but newly designated Parque Nacional Las Quijadas, in the northern part of the province, is a nature reserve comparable to San Juan's Parque Provincial Ischigualasto.

Within Cuyo's strong regional identity, residents of the province resolutely assert their own singularity as *puntanos*. The provincial government publishes a tourist guide, in both Spanish and readable English, with a small but good atlas of the province; it's available at the Casa de San Luis in Buenos Aires or at the Dirección de Turismo in the city of San Luis.

SAN LUIS

Founded in 1594 and capital of its namesake province, San Luis is the eastern gateway to Cuyo. During the 1970s and 1980s, this small but lively city of 110,000 people grew and attracted industry through a program of industrial promotion and tax incentives.

Orientation

On the north bank of the Río Chorrillos, San Luis is 260 km from Mendoza via RN 7, 456 km from Córdoba via RN 148, and about 850 km from Buenos Aires via either RN 7 or RN 8. The commercial center is along the parallel streets of San Martín and Rivadavia between Plaza Pringles in the north and Plaza Independencia in the south.

Information

Tourist Offices The Dirección Provincial de Turismo (☎ 23957), open weekdays 8 am to 1 pm and 4 to 8 pm, is at the triangular intersection formed by Junín, San Martín, and Av Illia. Its flashy brochures are short on information, but the staff can provide more thorough material, including a fairly complete list of hotels with budget alternatives. There's also an Oficina de Información Turística at the Terminal de Omnibus.

ACA (☎ 23188) is at Av Illia 401, corner of Constitución.

Money Alituris, Colón 733, changes dollars and Chilean pesos weekdays 8 am to noon, Saturdays 8:30 am to 12:30 pm. The banks are mostly around Plaza Pringles, including Banco de la Nación at San Martín and Pringles and Banco de San Luis at Rivadavia and Pringles. Banco de Galicia has an ATM at Belgrano 901, at the corner of Rivadavia.

Post & Telecommunications Correo Argentino is at Arturo Illia and San Martín; the postal code is 5700. Telefónica is at Colón and Lavalle. San Luis's area code is 0652.

Travel Agencies Besides Alituris, try Dasso Viajes (☎ 26616) at Rivadavia 615 or Turismo La Cumbre (☎ 28041) at Colón 978.

Medical Services The Hospital Regional (☎ 22627) is at Av República Oriental del

Uruguay 150 (the eastward extension of Bolívar).

Iglesia Catedral

Local materials, including provincial woods like algarrobo for windows and frames and white marble for steps and columns, complement the French tiles of the 19th-century cathedral, on Rivadavia across from Plaza Pringles.

Iglesia de Santo Domingo

Across from Plaza Independencia, the present church and convent dates from the 1930s, but reproduces the Moorish style of the 17th-century building it replaced. Part of the old church is visible next door inside the **Archivo Histórico Provincial** (historical archives), with striking algarrobo doors, on 25 de Mayo.

Mercado Artesanal

Dominican friars at this market, next to Iglesia de Santo Domingo on 25 de Mayo, sell gorgeous handmade wool rugs as well as ceramics, onyx crafts, and weavings from other parts of the province. It's open weekdays 7 am to 1 pm.

Places to Stay – bottom end

Residencial San Antonio (☎ 22717), at the corner of Av Lafinur and Av España, is the cheapest in town at US$12/20 with breakfast, while *Hotel César* (☎ 20483), Falucho 163, costs US$14 per person. *Residencial Buenos Aires* (☎ 24062), Buenos Aires 834, has modest but adequate rooms for US$14/25 single/double. *Residencial María Eugenia* (☎ 30361), 25 de Mayo 741, has large, very clean rooms with shared bath for US$15/25 single/double; since all rooms front onto an enclosed hall, it can be noisy during the day, but it's quiet at night. Similar in price and standards are *Residencial Casablanca* (☎ 23206), Belgrano 1046; *Residencial 17* (☎ 23387), at Estado de Israel 1475; and *Residencial Rivadavia* (☎ 22437), across the street at Estado de Israel 1470. The latter two are both near the bus terminal. *Residencial Los Andes* (☎ 22033), Ejército de los Andes 1180, has

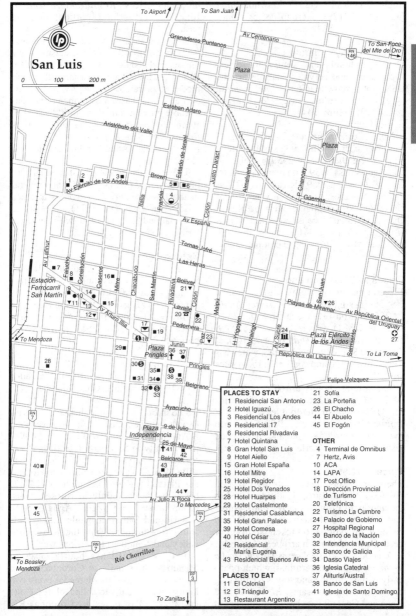

ARGENTINA

PLACES TO STAY
1 Residencial San Antonio
2 Hotel Iguazú
3 Residencial Los Andes
5 Residencial 17
6 Residencial Rivadavia
7 Hotel Quintana
8 Gran Hotel San Luis
9 Hotel Aiello
15 Gran Hotel España
16 Hotel Mitre
19 Hotel Regidor
25 Hotel Dos Venados
28 Hotel Huarpes
29 Hotel Castelmonte
31 Residencial Casablanca
35 Hotel Gran Palace
39 Hotel Comesa
40 Hotel César
42 Residencial
   María Eugenia
43 Residencial Buenos Aires

PLACES TO EAT
11 El Colonial
12 El Triángulo
13 Restaurant Argentino

21 Sofía
23 La Porteña
26 El Chacho
44 El Abuelo
45 El Fogón

OTHER
4 Terminal de Omnibus
7 Hertz, Avis
10 ACA
14 LAPA
17 Post Office
18 Dirección Provincial
   de Turismo
20 Telefónica
22 Turismo La Cumbre
24 Palacio de Gobierno
27 Hospital Regional
30 Banco de la Nación
32 Intendencia Municipal
33 Banco de Galicia
34 Dasso Viajes
36 Iglesia Catedral
37 Alituris/Austral
38 Banco de San Luis
41 Iglesia de Santo Domingo

singles/doubles for US$17/23, while *Hotel Iguazú* (☎ 22129), Ejército de los Andes 1582, charges US$18/30.

Places to Stay – middle

Midrange hotels are similar in price, appearance, and services, starting around US$20/30 single/double at *Hotel Comesa* (☎ 22996), Colón 667; *Hotel Mitre* (☎ 24599), Mitre 1045, costs US$20/32 single/double.

Hotel Castelmonte (☎ 24963), Chacabuco 769, charges US$25/35 single/double, while *Hotel Huarpes* (☎ 25597), Belgrano 1568, costs US$24/39 with breakfast. *Hotel Gran Palace* (☎ 22059), Rivadavia 657, has a pleasant atmosphere and nice rooms for US$24/43 single/double with breakfast. One good-value place is the pleasant *Gran Hotel España* (☎ 25051), Arturo Illia 300, with rooms at US$28/39 including breakfast.

Places to Stay – top end

Top-end accommodations start at around US$36/48 single/double at *Hotel Aiello* (☎ 25609), Illia 431, and at *Gran Hotel San Luis* (☎ 22881), Illia 470, for US$39/49. Try also *Hotel Dos Venados* (☎ 22312), at Perón and República del Líbano, which has a good restaurant and confitería; room rates are US$39/49.

The priciest hotels are *Hotel Regidor* (☎ 24756) at San Martín 804, with rooms for US$40/60 single/double, and *Hotel Quintana* (☎ 29548), at Illia 546, with rooms for US$48/58. The latter has a good restaurant and confitería.

Places to Eat

There are many restaurants doing good business in San Luis. Traditional dishes include locro (a thick maize soup), empanadas de horno (baked empanadas), and cazuela de gallina (chicken soup). For desert, try quesillo con arrope or figs.

A good breakfast place is *Confitería La Terminal* at the bus terminal, which opens early in the morning and serves terrific café con leche with croissants. *El Abuelo,* at J Roca and General Paz, has good lunches at

moderate prices. *Restaurant Argentino,* Illia 352, serves large portions of good pasta.

Sofía (ex-Taberna Vasca), at Colón and Bolívar, has mostly Spanish cuisine – try the seafood dishes. *El Colonial* (☎ 20828), Pedernera 1460, has a pleasant setting and moderate prices. *El Triángulo,* at Caseros 866 and Illia, has a varied menu and reasonable prices. *La Porteña* (☎ 23807), Junín 696, is another good choice, as is *Restaurant San Antonio* (☎ 22717) at Ejército de los Andes 1600, next door to Hotel Iguazú.

There are also a few parrillas on RN 20, most notably *Piros* (☎ 25506), and several in the town center: *El Fogón* is at Roca 1515, *El Chacho* (☎ 23271) at Playas de Miramar and San Juan, and *Patio Quieto* at Uriburu and Rivadavia.

Getting There & Away

Air Austral (☎ 23407), Colón 733, flies Monday, Wednesday, and Friday afternoons to San Rafael (US$56) and Buenos Aires (US$172); Tuesday, Thursday, and Saturday afternoon flights go to Buenos Aires via Río Cuarto (US$37), in Córdoba province.

LAPA (☎ 22499), Illia 331, flies weekday mornings, as well as Tuesday, and Thursday evenings, to Villa Mercedes (US$19) and Buenos Aires (US$69).

Bus San Luis's Terminal de Omnibus is on España between San Martín and Rivadavia.

Autotransportes San Juan (☎ 24998) travels daily to San Juan, four times daily to Buenos Aires (US$45, 12 hours) via Villa Mercedes and Río Cuarto, and to Mar del Plata (US$50). Chevallier (☎ 24937) has three buses nightly to Buenos Aires. Empresa del Sur y Media Agua goes to Rosario and San Juan, while Ticsa heads south to Bariloche (via the Río Negro valley and Neuquén) four times weekly.

TAC (☎ 23110) has hourly buses to Mendoza, three daily to Córdoba, one to Rosario, buses to Villa Mercedes every two hours, and two daily to Villa Dolores. Colta (☎ 25248) has buses to Córdoba, Río

Cuarto, Villa Mercedes, La Falda, Cosquín, Carlos Paz, and Mendoza. They also have a direct bus to Santiago de Chile. Empresa Dasso (☎ 25386) travels to small provincial towns.

Jocolí (☎ 20716) goes to Mendoza, Buenos Aires, Mar del Plata, and Santa Rosa. It also covers provincial destinations: Villa Mercedes, Merlo, San Martín, Unión, Trapiche, Florida, and Pozo de los Funes.

Getting Around
Hertz and Avis both have offices at Hotel Quintana, Illia 546. Dasso Viajes (☎ 26616), Rivadavia 615, also has rental vehicles.

AROUND SAN LUIS
Parque Nacional
Sierra de las Quijadas
Resembling San Juan's Parque Provincial Ischilgualasto, this newly designated national park sets aside 150,000 hectares of sedimentary desert canyons among the Sierra de las Quijadas, whose peaks reach a maximum elevation of 1200 meters at Cerro Portillo.

Buses from San Luis to San Juan will drop visitors at the village of Hualtarán, about 110 km northwest of San Luis via RN 147 (the highway to San Juan), which is the main entry point to the park. From Hualtarán a six-km lateral leads west to a viewpoint overlooking the **Potrero de la Aguada**, a scenic depression beneath the peaks of the Sierras, which collects the runoff from much of the park and is a prime wildlife area. Services are yet very limited in the area and travelers should bring all supplies with them, including water.

MERLO
Founded in 1797, the hill resort of Merlo struggles to retain the colonial atmosphere imparted by its church, plaza, and other buildings against a wave of modern construction. In the northeastern corner of the province, 900 meters above sea level on the western slope of the Sierras de Comenchingones, Merlo's mountainous locale and gentle climate make it a popular resort, but

one that is much less frequented than the better known Sierras de Córdoba. The permanent population is about 8000.

Orientation & Information
Merlo is 180 km from San Luis via RP 20 to La Toma and RN 148 to Santa Rosa del Conlara. The Oficina de Informes (☎ 75155), Coronel Mercau 605, has complete information on hotels and campgrounds, but little on outdoor activities.

Correo Argentino is at Coronel Mercau 579; the postal code is 5881. Telefónica is at Juan de Videla 112; the area code is 0544.

Places to Stay
Despite its size, Merlo has abundant accommodations that tend to be crowded in summer, around Semana Santa, and during the winter holidays in July. At these peak times, rates indicated below can rise by a third or more.

Places to Stay – bottom end
Camping Empresa Virgen del Valle buses go to El Rincón, about two km from the town center, where the shady and tidy *Camping Municipal* has superb views of the Sierra. It charges US$5 per site.

Residenciales, Hotels, & Motels
Merlo's cheapest lodging is *Residencial Oviedo,* (☎ 75193) Coronel Mercau 799, where singles/doubles with bath cost US$12/20; slightly more expensive is *Residencial El Castaño* (☎ 75327), on the elegant Av del Sol.

Several places charge about US$15/25 single/double: *Hotel La Llegada* at Sarmiento 405, *Hotel El Molino* at Rincón del Este s/n, and *Residencial Chiquita* (☎ 75218) at Coronel Mercau 479. SMATA, the Argentine automobile workers' union, runs *Motel 27 de Abril* (☎ 75219), at Av Dos Venados 1277, which has an incredible setting and is open to the public if space is available.

Places to Stay – middle
Midrange accommodations start around US$30 double with breakfast at places like

the very intimate *Posada Ignali* (☎ 75274), at Av San Martín 684. *Residencial Planetario* (☎ 75412), at Av del Sol and Marte, is comparably small, and has rooms with bath for US$20/32 single/double.

Others in this category include *Hotel Contilo* (☎ 75293) at Los Tilos and P Conti, *Residencial Amancay* (☎ 75311) at Av del Sol 500, *Hotel Mirasierras* (☎ 75045) at Av del Sol and Pedernera, *Residencial Sierras Verdes* (☎ 75340) at Av del Sol 458, *Residencial Piscu Yaco* (☎ 75419), with attractive gardens, at Av del Sol 231, and *Motel Algarrobo* (☎ 75208) at Av del Sol 1120.

Places to Stay – top end
Three-star *Hotel Casablanca* (☎ 75084), Av del Sol 50, charges US$35/65 single/double with breakfast.

The most expensive hotels in town are *Hotel Parque* (☎ 75110), Av del Sol 821, with singles at US$55 per person with all meals; and *Hotel Clima Tres* (☎ 75297), at Av del Sol 416, which charges US$50 double or US$50 per person with all meals included.

Places to Eat
The very good, inexpensive *Restaurant Plaza* is at Perón (ex-España) 58, near the Casa del Poeta and the ACA station. *Mangrullo,* Colón 684, is an attractive parrilla; similar to it is *La Estanzuela* at Av del Sol 2. Most hotels, especially top-end ones, have restaurants that are open to the general public as well as to guests.

Getting There & Away
The Terminal de Omnibus (☎ 75157) is at Coronel Pringles 535. Empresa Jocolí (☎ 75328), TAC, and El Serrano connect Merlo to Buenos Aires (US$45, 12 hours), while Chevallier, Jocolí, and TAC also link Merlo with San Luis and Mendoza. Sierras Córdobesas heads north into Córdoba province, as do Casilda and El Petizo.

The Andean Northwest

Argentina's most "traditional" region, the Andean Northwest *(Noroeste Andino)* consists of the provinces of Jujuy, Salta, Tucumán, La Rioja, Catamarca, and Santiago del Estero, all of which had thriving cities when Buenos Aires was still an insignificant backwater. The region's tangible pre-Hispanic and colonial past make the trip south from Peru and Bolivia to the Argentine heartland a journey through time as well as space. Even today, the northern provinces resemble the Andean countries as much or more than they do the cultural core of the Argentine Pampas, and substantial Quechua Indian communities exist as far south as Santiago del Estero.

In pre-Columbian times, the Noroeste was the most densely populated part of what is now Argentina, containing perhaps two-thirds of the population. Several indigenous groups, the largest of which was the Diaguita, practiced irrigated maize agriculture in the valleys of the eastern Andean foothills; they also cultivated complementary crops like potatoes, beans, squash, and *quinoa* (a native Andean grain) at different altitudes. While their numbers were smaller and their political organization less complex than the native civilizations of Peru and Bolivia, they could mobilize enough labor to build agricultural terraces and military fortifications. Other groups included the Lules, southwest of present-day Salta, the Tonocote, around Santiago del Estero, and the Omaguaca of Jujuy.

Decades before the European invasion, the Incas began to expand their influence among the Diaguita and other southern Andean peoples; Vásquez de Espinosa wrote that "they came to render obedience" to the Inca Viracocha, who sent "delegates down there to take possession and to see that they were instructed and disciplined in his false religion." The area remained peripheral to but oriented toward the agri-cultural Andean civilizations rather than toward the foragers of the Pampas; when Spaniards replaced the Inca at the apex of political authority, they benefited from this orientation and reinforced it, founding cities as they advanced south.

The first Spaniard to visit the region was Diego de Almagro, whose expedition from Cuzco to Santiago, Chile, traced the eastern side of the Andes before crossing the heights of the Puna de Atacama. En route, Almagro and his men passed through present-day Jujuy and Salta, but it was decades before the Spaniards established permanent settlements in the region, known in colonial times as "Tucumán." The Spaniards hoped that Indian populations would be sufficiently large for substantial enco-miendas, but the area never provided the wealth of labor and tribute that Peru did.

The earliest Spanish city, founded in 1553, was Santiago del Estero, but Indians destroyed several others before the successful founding of San Miguel de Tucumán (1565), Córdoba (1573), Salta (1582), La Rioja (1591), and San Salvador de Jujuy (1592). The Cuyo region, including the cities of Mendoza and San Juan, was settled from Santiago, Chile, across the Andes about the same time as Tucumán, while Catamarca was founded more than a century later.

These settlements were not impressive in their infancy – according to historian David Rock, the number of Spaniards in the Tucumán region did not exceed 700 at the end of the 16th century. Still, they established the basic institutions and visible features of Spanish colonial rule that still survive in many modern Argentine cities: the *cabildo* (town council), the church, and the rectangular plaza surrounded by a cluster of public buildings. Spanish citizens received rights to the labor of local Indians from the governor or the members of the cabildo, but as the Indians

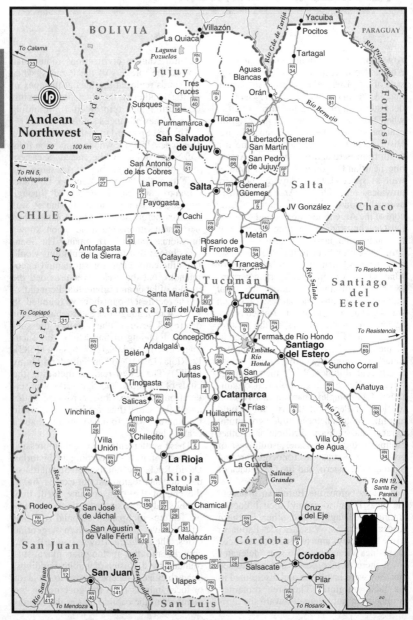

fell to European diseases and Spanish exploitation over the next century, encomiendas lost most of their economic value. In Santiago del Estero, for example, 12,000 Indians labored on 48 encomiendas in 1582, while in 1673 the remaining 34 encomiendas had only 3358 Indians.

During the colonial period, Tucumán was in the economic orbit of the bonanza silver mine at Potosí, in modern Bolivia. Spanish activities started with the provision of mules and the cultivation of cotton and production of textiles, but as the region recovered from 17th-century depression (due largely to labor shortages), sugar cane eventually dominated the economy. In part, the Spaniards had no alternative to this northward orientation, since the crown's mercantile policy decreed that commerce between Spain and the colonies had to be routed through Lima, by sea to Panamá, across the isthmus to the Caribbean, and then across the Atlantic.

Only after the creation of the Viceroyalty of the River Plate in 1776 did this orientation change, as Buenos Aires began to emerge from the shadow of Lima. The opening of the Atlantic to legal shipping toward the end of the colonial period, followed by political independence, relegated Jujuy and Salta provinces to economic marginality, but the adoption of a sugar monoculture reversed Tucumán's economic orientation and increased its importance in the new country. Completion of a railroad from Córdoba in 1874 spurred a dramatic threefold production in sugar by the end of the decade. By 1914, 100,000 hectares of sugar cane, mostly in Tucumán, were yielding 250,000 tons per annum, enough to satisfy Argentina's domestic demand.

Sugar continues to dominate the provincial economy, occupying more than 60% of the total agricultural land and causing social, economic, and ecological problems. Large farms and factories characterize the industry, whose seasonal labor requirements during the winter *zafra* (harvest) contribute to high unemployment the rest of the year. Tobacco is a distant second, and

citrus is locally significant, but attempts to further diversify the agricultural economy have had limited success despite some progress with soybeans.

Travelers should be aware that in this part of the country, not every establishment or organization has a phone. This is especially true in smaller towns and villages.

Jujuy Province

Bounded by Bolivia to the north, Chile to the west, and Salta province to the south and east, Jujuy is a southern extension of the high Andean steppe *(altiplano)*, where soaring volcanic peaks tower over saline lakes *(salares)* above 4000 meters in the thinly populated west. To the east, a lower range of foothills gives way to deeply dissected river valleys like the Quebrada de Humahuaca, whose Río Grande has exposed spectacular desert land forms, before opening onto subtropical lowlands toward the Gran Chaco. Jujuy has several wildlife and fauna reserves, though access to them is generally not easy.

One of Argentina's smallest and poorest provinces, Jujuy has suffered a 30% reduction in real GDP since President Menem took office in 1990. Nevertheless, it is rich in archaeological and cultural resources. The province's very name may be evidence of Inca influence – according to Incan nobleman Guamán Poma de Ayala, the region's Inca-designated governors went by the Quechua title of *Xuxuyoc*, a word early European residents Hispanicized as "Jujuy" (another explanation is that the Spanish corrupted the name of the Río Xibi Xibi). In colonial times it gained a certain prosperity through the cultivation of sugar cane under Jesuit missionaries and, well after independence, British investors. Tobacco is the second most important crop.

Like several other provinces, Jujuy has suffered considerably in the economic transition of the Menem administration. In March 1995, disgruntled state workers protesting unpaid salaries attempted to burn the provincial Casa de Gobierno to the ground.

Although a handful of colonial remains are still around Plaza Belgrano in San Salvador de Jujuy, most sites of interest are in the provincial countryside, especially the villages of the Quebrada de Humahuaca.

Budget travelers approaching Jujuy from Bolivia via the border complex of Villazón/La Quiaca are likely to find Argentine prices an unpleasant shock. Before panicking and dashing back across the border, look at alternatives for cheaper lodging, food, and transportation suggested in this chapter and elsewhere in the book. A handful of travelers arrive via the trans-Chaco highways from Resistencia or Formosa; for approaches from the south, see the entry for Salta below.

SAN SALVADOR DE JUJUY

At the southern end of the Quebrada de Humahuaca, where the valley broadens and the climate is perpetually springlike at 1200 meters, the Spaniards founded San Salvador de Jujuy (commonly known as "Jujuy") in 1592 as the most northerly of their colonial cities in present-day Argentina. The town's proper name of San Salvador de Jujuy distinguished it as a Spanish settlement and also avoided confusion with nearby San Pedro de Jujuy.

In the early 17th century, according to Vásquez de Espinosa, Jujuy had about "100 Spanish residents, mostly muleteers, who freight flour, corn, cheese, and other foodstuffs to the Chichas and Lipes mines; they have mule and cattle ranches, and drive their stock to Potosí." During the wars of independence, at the command of General Manuel Belgrano, residents evacuated the city to avoid falling into royalist hands; August's week-long celebration of the *éxodo jujeño* (Jujuy exodus) is the city's (and the province's) biggest annual event.

Orientation

At the mouth of the Quebrada de Humahuaca, Jujuy (population 200,000) sits above the flood plain of the Río Grande at its confluence with the smaller Río Xibi

Xibi, 1650 km from Buenos Aires. National Ruta 9 leads north up the Quebrada Humahuaca, while RN 66 leads southeast to a junction with RN 34, the main highway to Salta (though not the most direct). For motorists, southbound RN 9 is a much shorter, though winding and narrow, alternative route to Salta.

Jujuy consists of two main parts: the old city, with a fairly standard grid pattern between the Río Grande and the Río Xibi Xibi, and a newer area south of the Xibi Xibi that sprawls up the nearby hills. Shanty towns crowd the flood plain of the Río Grande beneath the San Martín bridge,

BOLIVIA

To Calama

Lago Colorado

Cordillera de Lipez

San Pedro de Atacama

Andes

Lago de Vilama

Paso de Jama

RP 70

Jujuy & Salta Provinces

0   50   100 km

Paso Huaytiquina

RP 37

RP 51

To RN 5, Antofagasta

RP 27

RP 27

RP 17

CHILE

RP 43

Catamarca

Cordillera

Cerro Galán 6600 m

Antofagasta de la Sierra

which leads to San Pedro de Jujuy by an attractive but little-used route.

Plaza Belgrano, the city center, is surrounded by the main public buildings. Belgrano, the main commercial street, becomes a pedestrian mall at its 700 block between Necochea and Lavalle.

Information
Tourist Offices The Dirección Provincial de Turismo (☎ 28153) is at Belgrano 690. The staff can be surprisingly indifferent to visitors but have an abundance of maps, brochures, and other materials. Hours are 7 am to 1 pm and 3 to 8 pm daily. A satellite office at the bus terminal is open 8 am to noon and 3 to 8 pm.

In summer and during July winter holidays, the Municipalidad maintains an office on Almirante Brown at the approach to town.

ACA (☎ 22568) is at Senador Pérez and Alvear.

Foreign Consulates The Bolivian consulate (☎ 22010), Arenales 641, is open weekdays 8 am to 1 pm. Others consulates include Spain (☎ 28193), at Ramírez de Velasco 362, and Italy (☎ 23199), at Av Fascio 660.

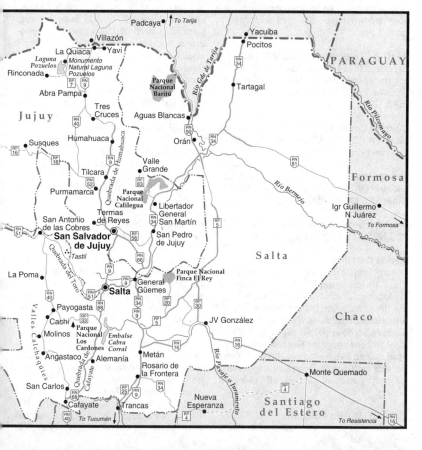

Money Cambio Dinar, at Belgrano 731, or Noroeste Cambio, almost next door at Belgrano 711, are efficient and will cash traveler's checks, but commissions are substantial. Local banks include Banco de la Provincia at Alvear and Lamadrid, and Banco Río at Alvear 802.

National Parks & Reserves For information on national parks and other reserves, visit the provincial Dirección General de Fauna y Parques, upstairs at Alvear 412, opposite the train station. It has good information on the condition of roads to parks such as Calilegua and El Rey (in Salta province), plus free informational publications and brochures. It's open weekdays 7 am to 1 pm.

Post & Telecommunications Correo Argentino is at Lamadrid and Independencia; the postal code is 4600. Telecom is at Senador Pérez 141. Jujuy's area code is 0882.

Cultural Centers Built in 1901, the Teatro Mitre (☎ 22782), Alvear 1009, sponsors plays and similar cultural events.

Travel Agencies For excursions, try Tea Turismo (☎ 22357) at 19 de Abril 485, or Dinar SRL (☎ 25353) at Belgrano 731.

Medical Services Hospital Pablo Soria (☎ 22025) is at Güemes and General Paz.

Iglesia Catedral

Dating from 1763, Jujuy's Cathedral on Plaza Belgrano replaced a 17th-century predecessor destroyed by Calchaquí Indians. Its outstanding feature, salvaged from the original church, is the gold-laminated Spanish Baroque pulpit, probably built by local artisans under the direction of a European master. In the shaded colonnade along the side entrance on Belgrano, a lively and interesting artisans' market sells excellent pottery.

Cabildo (Museo Policial)

Also on the plaza, this colonial building with its attractive colonade deserves more attention than its museum, which uncritically pays homage to authority with grisly photographs of crimes and accidents. The museum is open weekdays 10 am to 1 pm and 3 to 9 pm, Saturdays 10:30 am to 12:30 pm and 6:30 to 9 pm, and Sundays 6:30 to 9 pm.

Museo Histórico Provincial

Seven large rooms of this colonial house are devoted to distinct topics in provincial history, including the house's original owners, religious and colonial art, the independence period, the evacuation of Jujuy, provincial governors, 19th-century fashion, and the death of General Juan Lavalle. Lavalle, a hero of the wars of independence, became a victim of the civil wars after being reportedly struck by a bullet through the house's impressive wooden door.

At Lavalle 256, between Belgrano and San Martín, the museum is open daily 8:30 am to 12:30 pm and 3 to 7 pm. There is a nominal admission charge.

Iglesia Santa Bárbara

Several paintings from the well-known Cuzco school decorate the walls of this colonial church at Lamadrid and San Martín.

Mercado del Sur

Jujuy's lively southern market, opposite the bus terminal, is a real Indian market where foodstuffs and other necessities are for sale. Quechua men and women swig *mazamorra* (a pasty maize soup, served cold) and surreptitiously peddle coca leaves (officials usually tolerate coca use and sale by native peoples).

Special Events

In August Jujuy's biggest event, the week-long Semana de Jujuy, celebrates Belgrano's evacuation of the city during the wars of independence. The next largest, October 7, is the pilgrimage to the Virgin of Río Blanco & Paypaya. The March harvest festival is called Festival de la Humita y El

Folclor, while in May the town honors the mining industry through the Fiesta de la Minería. In September, the Fiesta Nacional y Latinoamericana de los Estudiantes is a student celebration.

Places to Stay – bottom end

Camping Jujuy's *Camping Municipal* is on Av Bolivia, three km north of Parque San Martín; take bus No 4 from the center. It's friendly, facilities are clean, and there is occasional hot water and increasing shade as the newly planted trees take over. Sites cost US$5 for vehicle, tent, and up to four persons.

Residenciales Jujuy's ample budget accommodations are mostly near the train station and bus terminal. Among the cheapest in town, the friendly *Residencial Río de Janeiro* (☎ 23700), west of the bus terminal at José de la Iglesia 1356, offers rooms for US$13 double with shared bath, US$14 with private bath; both have good hot showers. Declining *Residencial Los Andes* (☎ 24315), a few blocks east of the terminal at República de Siria 456, is OK in a pinch for US$11/16 single/double with shared bath, US$13/19 with private bath.

One recommended cheapie is *Residencial Norte* (☎ 22721), opposite the train

ARGENTINA

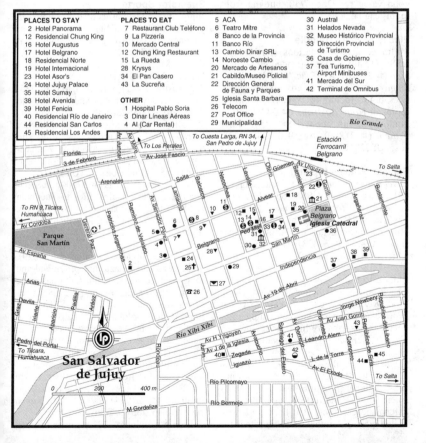

PLACES TO STAY	PLACES TO EAT		
2 Hotel Panorama	7 Restaurant Club Teléfono	5 ACA	30 Austral
12 Residencial Chung King	9 La Pizzería	6 Teatro Mitre	31 Helados Nevada
16 Hotel Augustus	10 Mercado Central	8 Banco de la Provincia	32 Museo Histórico Provincial
17 Hotel Belgrano	12 Chung King Restaurant	11 Banco Río	33 Dirección Provincial
18 Residencial Norte	15 La Rueda	13 Cambio Dinar SRL	de Turismo
19 Hotel Internacional	28 Krysys	14 Noroeste Cambio	36 Casa de Gobierno
23 Hotel Asor's	34 El Pan Casero	20 Mercado de Artesanos	37 Tea Turismo,
24 Hotel Jujuy Palace	43 La Sucreña	21 Cabildo/Museo Policial	Airport Minibuses
35 Hotel Sumay		22 Dirección General	41 Mercado del Sur
38 Hotel Avenida	**OTHER**	de Fauna y Parques	42 Terminal de Omnibus
39 Hotel Fenicia	1 Hospital Pablo Soria	25 Iglesia Santa Barbara	
40 Residencial Río de Janeiro	3 Dinar Líneas Aéreas	26 Telecom	
44 Residencial San Carlos	4 AI (Car Rental)	27 Post Office	
45 Residencial Los Andes		29 Municipalidad	

station at Alvear 444, with shared-bath doubles for US$12, private-bath doubles for US$14, and a decent restaurant. Friendly and central *Hotel Belgrano* (☎ 30393), at Belgrano 627 across from the tourist office, charges US$12/15 single/double with shared bath, US$15/18 with private bath. Other reasonable alternatives include *Residencial Chungking* (☎ 28142) at Alvear 627, for US$12/14 with shared bath, US$15/20 with private bath, and *Residencial San Carlos* (☎ 22286) at Republica de Siria 459, for US$14/21 with shared bath, US$15/18 with private bath. Two-star *Hotel Asor's* (☎ 23688), Urquiza 462, is a good value for US$17/30, but the front rooms can be noisy.

Places to Stay – middle

Midrange accommodations start around US$27/42 at the recommended *Hotel Avenida* (☎ 22678), Av 19 de Abril 469. *Hotel Sumay* (☎ 35065), Otero 232, charges US$36/48 including breakfast, while rooms at *Hotel Augustus* (☎ 34750), Belgrano 715, run about US$36/54. *Hotel Fenicia* (☎ 31800), Av 19 de Abril 427, costs US$39/59.

Places to Stay – top end

Hotel Internacional (☎ 31599), at Belgrano 501, charges about US$50/65, while rates at four-star *Hotel Panorama,* Belgrano 1295, are US$65/84 with breakfast. Jujuy's other four-star accommodation is *Hotel Jujuy Palace* (☎ 30433), Belgrano 1060, which charges US$65/80.

Places to Eat

Check bottom-end hotels for good, cheap food. *Restaurant Club Teléfono,* Alvear 1050, also has basic but nourishing four-course meals for very little money. *El Pan Casero,* Belgrano 619, is a natural-foods bakery.

Upstairs at the *Mercado Central,* at Alvear and Balcarce, several restaurants serve regional specialties that are generally spicier than in the rest of Argentina – try chicharrón con mote (stir-fried pork with boiled maize). Another local favorite is the modest-looking but interesting *La Sucreña,* on Leandro Alem east of the bus terminal, which serves a spicy sopa de maní. *La Pizzería,* Alvear 921, is a good choice for pizza.

Look for standard Argentine fare at parrillas like *La Rueda,* Av Lavalle 329, and moderately priced *Krysys* (☎ 26288), Balcarce 272. Misleadingly named, *Chung King* (☎ 28142), Alvear 627, has an extensive Argentine menu and fine service. On and near the Belgrano peatonal you'll find numerous confiterías and excellent ice creameries, most notably *Helados Nevada.*

Spectator Sports

Jujuy's first division soccer team, Gimnasia y Esgrima (☎ 28011), has offices at Güemes 1031 but plays at the stadium at Av El Exodo 78.

Getting There & Away

Air Austral (☎ 27198), San Martín 735, flies weekday mornings and evenings to Aeroparque (US$230), the morning flights stopping at Santiago del Estero (US$83); there's also a Saturday morning and Sunday evening flight. Monday, Wednesday, and Saturday flights leave for Tucumán (US$55) and Córdoba (US$133).

Dinar Líneas Aéreas (☎ 37100), at Senador Pérez 308, Local 3, flies to Tucumán (US$45) and Aeroparque (US$184) every weekday afternoon; on Friday there are two flights.

Bus The Terminal de Omnibus (☎ 26229), at Dorrego and Iguazú, has provincial and long-distance services, but Salta has more alternatives. Panamericano (☎ 27281) goes south daily to Tucumán (US$15, five hours) and Córdoba, and heads north to destinations in the Quebrada de Humahuaca as far as the Bolivian border at La Quiaca (US$20, seven hours), plus isolated *puna* settlements like El Moreno, Susques, and Olaroz Chico. Cooperativa Norte (☎ 26911) also goes to Humahuaca. Atahualpa's (☎ 23914) Salta – La Quiaca service also stops in Jujuy.

Empresa Balut (☎ 22134) goes to Orán

and the other Bolivian border crossing at Pocitos, while Empresa Itatí crosses the Chaco weekly to Corrientes and Iguazú. Balut, Panamericano, and La Internacional (☎ 22134) all go to Buenos Aires (US$64, 22 hours).

Andesmar (☎ 33293) runs southbound buses to Salta, Tucumán, Catamarca (9½ hours), La Rioja (12 hours), San Juan (18 hours), and Mendoza (20 hours).

Chile-bound buses from Salta stop in Jujuy before crossing the Paso de Jama to Calama and Iquique (US$60); make reservations as far in advance as possible.

Getting Around
To/From the Airport Tea Turismo, 19 de Abril 485, runs minibuses to Aeropuerto El Cadillal, 27 km southeast of town, for US$5.

Car Rental AI (☎ 29697) is at Senador Pérez 398, Localiza (☎ 23346) at Almirante Brown 695. Avis is at Abonado 211 (☎ 26030) and at Aeropuerto El Cadillal (☎ 91501).

AROUND JUJUY
Termas de Reyes
Don't leave Jujuy without visiting these thermal baths, northwest of town on the slopes of the scenic canyon of the Río Reyes, reached easily and cheaply from the bus terminal. Rustic facilities are free, but for US$6 you can wallow in the enormous, comfortable tubs at *Hotel Termas de Reyes* (☎ 35500). Although the hotel's public baths were not constructed for the view, it's still a worthwhile experience; its outdoor swimming pool also charges US$6 for day use for non-guests.

The hotel serves only a costly fixed-price lunch, so take along some food. For those who prefer to overnight, room rates of US$38/53 single/double include breakfast and in-room facilities; for US$47/72 you get dinner as well.

For exceptional views, one reader recommends hiking up the steep hill crowned by a crucifix behind the hotel. The route, which takes 1½ to two hours, follows a

green pipe from a point just beyond the small bridge before the kiosk.

QUEBRADA DE HUMAHUACA
The long, narrow Quebrada de Humahuaca, north of Jujuy, is an artist's palette of color splashed on barren hillsides dwarfing the hamlets where Quechua peasants scratch a living from irrigated agriculture and scrawny livestock. Though less fertile than in past centuries, the valley still supports a way of life not so different from that described by Vásquez de Espinosa in the 17th century:

> Omaguaca is an Indian village; the valley is fertile and abounds in wheat, corn, potatoes, and other native and Spanish root crops and fruit; it is all covered with small Indian villages and Spanish ranches . . . . There are some large rivers which flow with great turbulence.

Because the Spaniards colonized this area from Peru in the late 16th century, it has many cultural features that recall the Andean countries, particularly the numerous historic adobe churches. Earthquakes leveled many of the originals, which were often rebuilt in the 17th and 18th centuries with thick walls, simple bell towers, and striking doors and paneling constructed from the wood of the unusual *cardón* cactus. Whether you come south from La Quiaca or head north from Jujuy, there's something interesting every few kilometers on this colonial post route between Potosí and Buenos Aires.

The valley's main settlement is the village of Humahuaca, 130 km from Jujuy, but there are so many worthwhile sights that the convenience of an automobile would be a big plus if you have a group to share expenses. Otherwise, buses are frequent enough that you should be able to do the canyon on a "whistle-stop" basis, flagging down a bus when you need one. Excellent accommodations are available in Tilcara, only 88 km from Jujuy, if things go more slowly than expected.

It is best to visit the Quebrada in the morning, when there's little wind and before the afternoon heat. Travelers recommend the right side of the bus for better views.

Purmamarca
In this tiny village a few kilometers west of RN 9 via RP 52, the polychrome Cerro del los Siete Colores (Hill of Seven Colors) forms the backdrop for a noteworthy 17th-century **colonial church.** The village has a Mercado Artesanal on the main plaza, and two small casas de familia offer accommodations for about US$10 per day; there are several restaurants, including *Comedor Ruta 52.*

La Posta de Hornillos
Part of a chain that ran from Lima to Buenos Aires during viceregal times, this beautifully restored way station, 11 km north of the Purmamarca turnoff, was the scene of several important battles during the wars of independence. The informal but informative guided tours make this an obligatory stop on the way up the Quebrada.

Maimará
From an overlook on RN 9, only a few kilometers south of Tilcara, the astounding hillside cemetery of this picturesque valley settlement beneath the hill known as La Paleta del Pintor (the Painter's Palette) is a can't-miss photo opportunity. The town also has a worthwhile anthropological and historical museum.

Uquía
The 17th-century **Iglesia de San Francisco de Paula** in this roadside village displays a restored collection of paintings from the Cuzco school, featuring the famous *Angeles arcabuceros,* angels armed with Spanish colonial weapons. It is normally closed except during mass; intending visitors should ask at the house of Adriana Valdivieso, two blocks south of the plaza – she keeps the 17th-century key and will accompany visitors to the church.

TILCARA
At an elevation of 2461 meters, Tilcara features a classic Andean *pucará,* a fortification commanding unobstructed views of the Quebrada de Humahuaca in several directions. Its many museums and other interesting features, including its reputation as an artists' colony, make for a highly desirable stopover. Many jujeños have weekend houses here, where hiking in the surrounding hills is a popular diversion.

Travelers should note the large monolith marking where RN 9 to Humahuaca crosses the Tropic of Capricorn.

Orientation
Tilcara, on the east bank of the Río Grande, is connected by a bridge to RN 9, which leads south to Jujuy and north to Humahuaca and La Quiaca. Its central grid is irregular beyond the village nucleus, focused on Plaza Prado. As in many small Argentine villages, people pay little attention to street names and numbers.

Information
Little formal information is available, but El Antigal, a hotel and restaurant, distributes a small, useful brochure about the town. The Cooperativa Telefónica is on the ground floor of the Hotel de Turismo, Belgrano 590. Tilcara's area code is 0882, the same as Jujuy's.

El Pucará
Rising above the sediments of the Río Grande valley, an isolated hill provided the site for this reconstructed pre-Columbian fortification, one km from the village center. Admission is US$2. There are even better views from the hill on the road leading to the fort; from the south end of the bridge across the Río Huasamayo, it's an easy 15-minute climb to the top.

Museo Arqueológico Doctor Eduardo Casanova
The Universidad de Buenos Aires runs this outstanding, well-displayed collection of regional artifacts. Located in a beautiful colonial house on the Plaza Prado, it's open

daily 9 am to 6 pm; admission is US$1.50, but is free on Tuesdays.

Museo Ernesto Soto Avendaño

Ernesto Soto Avendaño, a sculptor from Olavarría in the province of Buenos Aires, spent most of his life in Tilcara and designed the appalling monument to the heroes of Argentine independence in Humahuaca. This collection of his better work is open Tuesday to Saturday, 9 am to noon and 3 to 6 pm. The museum's on the plaza.

Museo José Antonio Terry

Also located in a colonial building on the plaza, this museum features the work of a Buenos Aires-born painter whose themes were largely rural and indigenous – his oils depict native weavers, market and street scenes, and portraits. Hours are Tuesday to Sunday, 9 am to 5 pm. Admission is US$2, but Thursdays are free.

Special Events

Tilcara celebrates several festivals throughout the year, the most notable of which is January's Enero Tilcareño, with sports, music, and cultural activities. February's Carnaval is equally important in other Quebrada villages, as is April's Semana Santa (Holy Week). August's indigenous Pachamama (Mother Earth) festival is also worthwhile.

Places to Stay & Eat

Autocamping El Jardín, on Belgrano near the river, is a very congenial place with hot showers and attractive vegetable and flower gardens, all for US$4 per person. There is an adequate free site, with picnic tables, near the YPF petrol station along the highway, but it has no potable water or sanitary facilities.

Residencial El Edén, on Rivadavia 1½ blocks from the central Plaza Prado, charges US$7/10 single/double for rooms with sagging beds and shared bath (cold showers only), but it's clean and friendly. Juan Brambati and family offer lodging for up to four people at US$10 per person, with breakfast and dinner extra; in addition, Juan can arrange trekking and vehicle tours. Write Juan Brambati, 4624 Tilcara, Provincia de Jujuy, for more information or booking.

Residencial El Antigal (☎ 95020), also on Rivadavia, half a block from the plaza, is probably the best choice in town at US$20/30 with private bath, hot water, and an outstanding restaurant – try the *locro,* a spicy stew of maize, beans, beef, pork, and sausage. *Restaurant Pucará,* on the plaza, is also popular.

Utilitarian, two-star *Hotel de Turismo* (☎ 95002), Belgrano 590, is slightly cheaper than El Antigal, with private bath; its swimming pool only rarely functions.

Getting There & Away

The main bus station is on Plaza Prado. There are nine buses daily to Jujuy, four of which continue to Salta. Northbound services to Humahuaca and La Quiaca also stop in Tilcara.

HUMAHUACA

Picturesque Humahuaca, the largest settlement between Jujuy and the Bolivian border, is a village of narrow, cobbled streets and adobe houses, with a large Quechua Indian population. Nearly 3000 meters above sea level, it is the most popular destination for budget travelers exploring the Quebrada. Locals occasionally target tourists aggressively, offering unsolicited guide services.

Orientation

Humahuaca, straddling the Río Grande east of RN 9, is very compact, and everything is within easy walking distance. The town center is between the highway and the river, but there are important archaeological sites across the bridge.

Information

Tourist Office The tourist office, in the cabildo at Tucumán and Jujuy, is open weekdays only.

Post & Telecommunications Correo Argentino is on Buenos Aires, across from the plaza; the postal code is 4630. The Cooperativa Telefónica, on the main floor of the Hotel de Turismo on Buenos Aires, is open 7 am to 8 pm daily, but there's also a locutorio at the corner of Tucumán and Jujuy. Humahuaca's area code is 0887.

Medical Services The Hospital Belgrano (☎ 09) is at Santa Fe 34. It's open 8 am to 1 pm and 2 to 6 pm, but there is always someone on duty for emergencies.

Cabildo
Municipal offices occupy the cabildo, famous for its clock tower, from which a life-size figure of San Francisco Solano emerges daily at noon to deliver a benediction. Both tourists and locals gather in the plaza to watch the spectacle, but arrive early – the clock is erratic and the figure appears only very briefly.

Iglesia de la Candelaria
Built in 1641, Humahuaca's church contains an image of the town's patron saint as well as 18th-century oils by Marcos Sapaca, a painter of the Cuzco school. It's on the plaza.

Monumento a la Independencia
This monstrosity dominates the hill overlooking Humahuaca, but is not the best work of Tilcara sculptor Ernesto Soto Avendaño. The Indian statue is a textbook example of *indigenismo,* a distorted nationalist tendency in Latin American art and literature to romantically extol the virtues of native cultures that were overwhelmed by European expansion.

Museo Folklórico Regional
Local writer and Quechua activist Sixto Vázquez Zuleta, who prefers his Quechua name of Toqo, runs the museum and the youth hostel in which it's located. He is a gold mine of information on local history and culture. At Buenos Aires 435/447, the museum is open 8 am to 8 pm daily, but for guided tours only for groups larger than

three or four. Price for admission and tour is US$2 per person. Toqo speaks little English but passable German.

Special Events
Besides the Carnaval Norteño, celebrated throughout the Quebrada in February, Humahuaca observes February 2 as the day of its patron saint, the Virgen de Candelaria.

Places to Stay
Camping The municipal site across the bridge remains closed. It's possible to park or pitch a tent there for free, but there are no faciltities.

Hostels, Hospedajes, Residenciales & Hotels The most popular budget accommodation is the *Albergue Juvenil* at Buenos Aires 435, which does not require an international youth-hostel card. For US$5 per person, it offers hot showers, kitchen facilities, and the opportunity to encounter both ·Argentine and international travelers. Unlike most Argentine hostels, it's open all year.

There are two simple, inexpensive hotels. *Residencial Humahuaca,* at Córdoba 401 near Corrientes, half a block from the bus terminal, charges US$10/15 single/double for rooms with shared bath, US$13/18 with private bath. *Residencial Colonial* (☎ 21007), Entre Ríos 110, costs US$10/15 with shared bath, US$15/20 with private bath. Also check out *Pensión La Coyita,* just north of the bus terminal.

Two-star *Hotel de Turismo,* Buenos Aires 650, is the town's top-end lodging at US$16/24 with private bath, although the interior is very run-down.

Places to Eat
Regional dishes, such as goat, are sometimes on the menu. Near the bus terminal, *Restaurant El Rancho* doesn't look like much, but has outstanding spicy empanadas and *humitas* (corn tamales). There is an acceptable confitería at the bus terminal, and recent readers' recommendations include *Restaurant Cacharpaya* on Jujuy

between Santiago del Estero and Tucumán (for tamales, empanadas, and chicken), upscale *Restaurant Humahuaca* at Tucumán 22, *Restaurant El Fortín* on Buenos Aires just north of Salta, *Cafetería Belgrano* (good pizza) near the railway line, and *Peña de Fortunato,* at the corner of San Luis and Jujuy (for regional cuisine and live folk music).

Things to Buy
Visit the handicrafts market, near the train station, for woolen goods, souvenirs, and the atmosphere. The quality is excellent, but travelers heading north will probably find similar items at lower prices in Bolivia.

Getting There & Away
The Terminal de Omnibus is very central at Belgrano and Entre Ríos. Panamericano has four buses daily to Jujuy, five to Tres Cruces and La Quiaca. Atahualpa has six daily to Jujuy, three to Salta, and five to La Quiaca, plus weekend service to the mining settlement of Mina El Aguilar. Balut has another five to La Quiaca (US$25, 2½ hours) and offers 20% student discounts. Cooperativa Norte sends seven buses daily to Jujuy.

Transportes Mendoza offers a Saturday service to the scenic Andean village of Iruya; ask at the Almacén Mendoza convenience store where the buses depart (which they may not do at all in summer when it rains). There are also twice-weekly buses to the remote altiplano settlement of Susques, which has a hotel, an interesting Andean church. Nearby is the Monumento Natural Laguna de los Pozuelos, an important wildlife reserve.

AROUND HUMAHUACA
Coctaca
Ten km from Humahuaca by a dirt road leading north from the east side of the bridge across the Río Grande, Coctaca is northwestern Argentina's most extensive pre-Columbian ruins, covering about 40 hectares. Although they have not yet been excavated, many of the ruins appear to have

been broad agricultural terraces on an alluvial fan, but there are also obvious outlines of clusters of buildings. The nearby school is training guides to the site.

In the rainy season the road may be impassable. It is possible to walk to the ruins, but leave before the heat of the day and take water. After crossing the bridge across the Río Grande in Humahuaca, follow the road north and bear left until you see the village of Coctaca.

LA QUIACA
Near Abra Pampa, 90 km north of Humahuaca, paved RN 9 becomes a graveled road that climbs steeply to the high steppe *(altiplano)* typical of western Bolivia. Except during the summer rainy season, nightly frosts make agriculture a precarious activity; people concentrate subsistence efforts on livestock that can survive on the sparse *ichu* grass – llamas, sheep, goats, and a few cattle. Off the main highway, look for occasional flocks of the endangered vicuña, a wild relative of the llama and alpaca. At the end of the highway is the border crossing of La Quiaca and its Bolivian twin, Villazón.

Orientation
A bridge across the Río Villazón links La Quiaca with Villazón. To get to Argentine and Bolivian customs you have to walk or get a ride from taxi colectivos to the bridge, then cross it on foot. Hours are limited at Argentine customs, from 7:30 am to noon and 3 to 6 pm weekdays, 9 am to 11 am weekends and holidays.

Information
For maps or motorist services, visit the ACA station on RN 9 at Bustamente just north of Belgrano. Banco de la Nación will not cash traveler's checks, so you may have to cross to Villazón to change at Universo Tours.

Correo Argentino is at Sarmiento and San Juan, and Telecom is at San Martín and Av España. La Quiaca's postal code is 4650; the area code is 0885.

The Bolivian Consulate at the corner of

San Juan and Arabe Siria, one block south of Hotel Turismo, charges a hefty US$15 for a visa. You may be able to get one more cheaply and expeditiously in a larger city like Salta or Jujuy.

Manca Fiesta (Fiesta de las Ollas)
Artisans from throughout the altiplano bring their wares to La Quiaca for this popular event, which takes place the third and fourth Sundays of October.

Places to Stay
Accommodations are cheaper on the Bolivian side, but try very basic *Alojamiento Pequeño* at Bolívar and Balcarce, or *Hotel Frontera* on 25 de Mayo, for about US$7 per person. Recommended by several LP correspondents, *Hotel Cristal* (☎ 2255), Sarmiento 543, charges about US$17/28 for singles/doubles. The best value is the *Hotel de Turismo* (☎ 2243), at San Martín and Arabe Siria, where rates are US$17/27 with private bath.

Getting There & Away
Panamericano and Atahualpa have frequent bus connections to Jujuy and Salta. The bus stops at 25 de Mayo and Av España. There is no longer any southbound rail service.

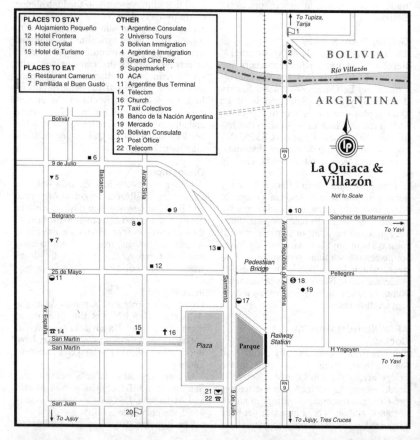

PLACES TO STAY
6 Alojamiento Pequeño
12 Hotel Frontera
13 Hotel Crystal
15 Hotel de Turismo

PLACES TO EAT
5 Restaurant Camerun
7 Parrillada el Buen Gusto

OTHER
1 Argentine Consulate
2 Universo Tours
3 Bolivian Immigration
4 Argentine Immigration
8 Grand Cine Rex
9 Supermarket
10 ACA
11 Argentine Bus Terminal
14 Telecom
16 Church
17 Taxi Colectivos
18 Banco de la Nación Argentina
19 Mercado
20 Bolivian Consulate
21 Post Office
22 Telecom

To Tupiza, Tarija

BOLIVIA

Río Villazón

ARGENTINA

La Quiaca & Villazón

Not to Scale

Bolívar
9 de Julio
Balcarce
Arabe Siria
Belgrano
25 de Mayo
Av España
San Martín
San Juan
To Jujuy

Sanchez de Bustamente
To Yavi
Avenida República de Argentina
Pellegrini
Pedestrian Bridge
Sarmiento
Railway Station
Plaza
Parque
H Yrigoyen
To Yavi
9 de Julio
To Jujuy, Tres Cruces

AROUND LA QUIACA

In the Indian village of Yavi, 16 km east from La Quiaca via paved RP 5, the 17th-century **Iglesia de San Francisco** is renowned for its altar, paintings, and wood carvings of San Francisco, San Juan Bautista, San José, Santa Ana, and San Joaquín. Hours are Tuesday to Friday 9 am to noon and 3 to 6 pm, Saturday 9 am to noon, but you may still have to track down the caretaker to get in.

Nearby is an interesting **colonial house** that belonged to the Marqués Campero, whose marriage to the holder of the original encomienda in this reducción created a family that dominated the regional economy in the 18th century.

Flota La Quinqueña provides regular public transport from La Quiaca to Yavi, but shared cabs are another alternative. Near Yavi there are several short hikes in the **Cerros Colorados,** including one to rock paintings and petroglyphs at **Las Cuevas** and another to springs at **Agua de Castilla.**

MONUMENTO NATURAL LAGUNA DE LOS POZUELOS

At an altitude of nearly 4000 meters, this lake covers more than 16,000 hectares. Three species of flamingos and many other birds breed along its shores, where you may also see the endangered vicuña. There are archaeological sites as well.

Because the park is so large and isolated, a car is the best transportation alternative, but carry extra fuel; there is no petrol available beyond Abra Pampa, midway between Humahuaca and La Quiaca. Occasional heavy summer rains can make the unpaved routes off the main highway impassable.

From Abra Pampa, Panamericano and Vilte have mid-morning buses to Rinconada, west of the lake, where there are simple accommodations. On request, the bus will drop you off at the Río Cincel ranger station, where camping is possible; with luck, you can accompany the rangers on their rounds. For more information, ask at the tourist office in Jujuy or at the Centro Cultural in Abra Pampa.

PARQUE NACIONAL CALILEGUA

On the eastern borders of Jujuy province, the high and arid altiplano gives way to the dense, subtropical cloud forest of the Serranía de Calilegua, whose preservation is the goal of this accessible, 75,000-hectare park. At the park's highest elevations, about 3600 meters, verdant Cerro Hermoso reaches above the forest and offers boundless views of the Gran Chaco to the east. Bird life is abundant and colorful, but the tracks of rare mammals, such as the puma and jaguar, are easier to see than the animals themselves.

Information

Park headquarters (☎ 0886-22046) is in the village of Calilegua just off RN 34, just north of Libertador General San Martín. Donated by the Ledesma sugar mill, the building includes a visitors' center with exhibits on the region's national parks, including Calilegua, Baritú, El Rey, and Laguna Pozuelos. The staff can also give you the latest information on road conditions, since many areas are inaccessible during the summer rainy season. Buses Veloz del Norte, between Salta and Orán, stop at the excellent and reasonable restaurant belonging to the Club Social San Lorenzo, next door to park headquarters.

Flora & Fauna

Receiving 2000 mm of precipitation a year, but with a defined winter dry season, Calilegua comprises a variety of ecosystems correlated with altitude. The "transitional *selva*," at elevations between 350 and 500 meters, consists of tree species common in the Gran Chaco, such as lapacho and *palo amarillo,* which drop their leaves in the winter. Between 550 and 1600 meters, the "cloud forest" forms a dark, dense canopy of trees more than 30-meters tall, punctuated by ferns, epiphytes, and lianas, covered by a thick fog in summer and autumn. Above 1200 meters, the "montane forest" is composed of "pines" (a general term for almost any conifer, such as cedar), *aliso,* and *queñoa.* Above 2600 meters this grades into moist puna grasslands, which become drier as one goes west toward the Quebrada de Humahuaca.

The 230 species of birds include the condor, brown eagle, torrent duck, and the colorful toucan. Important mammals, rarely seen in the dense forest, include tapir, puma, jaguar, collared peccary, and otter.

Things to Do

Nature-oriented activities will be the focus of any visit to Calilegua. The best places to view birds and mammals are near the stream courses in the early morning or very late afternoon, just before dark. From the ranger station at Mesada de las Colmenas, follow the steep, rugged, and badly overgrown trail down to a beautiful creek usually marked with numerous animal tracks, including those of large cats. The descent takes perhaps an hour, the ascent twice that.

There are excellent views from 3600-meter Cerro Hermoso, although there are no detailed maps; ask rangers for directions. Ordinary vehicles cannot go far past the Mesada de las Colmenas, but the road itself offers outstanding views of Cerro Hermoso and the nearly impenetrable forests of its steep ravines.

From Valle Grande, beyond the park boundaries to the west, it's possible to hike to Humahuaca along the Sierra de Zenta or to Tilcara, but the treks take at least a week. For details, see the 3rd edition of Bradt Publications' *Backpacking in Chile and Argentina* (1994).

Places to Stay

Camping is the only way to stay in the park itself. The developed free site at Aguas Negras, on a short lateral road near the ranger station at the entrance, may not have bathrooms and running water available. Beware of mosquitos, which are a lesser problem at higher elevations.

Although there are no other developed campsites, you can camp on a level area at the ranger station at Mesada de las Colmenas, which has great open views to the east.

There are several residenciales in nearby Libertador General San Martín, such as

Residencial Gloria, Urquiza 270, for US$10 per person with shared bath.

Getting There & Away

Infrequent public transportation is available to Valle Grande for about US$15 one-way; inquire at the park visitors' center for the most current information. Otherwise, it should be possible to hitch to the park and Valle Grande with the logging trucks that frequently pass through the park. Start from the bridge at the north end of the town of Libertador General San Martín, where there is a good dirt road through mostly shady terrain to Aguas Negras, eight km away.

Salta Province

In the northwest, Salta offers travelers a wide variety of terrains and a surprising number of historical sites. Salta, the best-preserved colonial city in Argentina, is the center for excursions to the montane subtropical forests of Parque Nacional Finca El Rey, the polychrome desert canyons of El Toro and Cafayate, along with their vineyards, and the sterile but scenic salt lakes and volcanoes of the high puna. Hundreds of archaeological sites and colonial buildings testify to Salta's importance in pre-Hispanic and colonial times, even though it declined with Argentine independence.

In colonial times, Salta's marshy but fertile Lerma Valley pastured thousands of mules that were bred on the Pampas of Buenos Aires and sold at an annual fair – in the 17th and 18th centuries, as many as 70,000 animals per year found their way to Bolivia and Peru, where they performed a wide variety of tasks in the mining industry. Independence and political fragmentation reduced this trade, a blow from which Salta has never completely recovered. In the early 20th century, it briefly reoriented itself toward supplying beef to the nitrate mines of Chile's Atacama Desert, across the Andes, but this trade declined as petroleum-based fertilizers replaced mineral nitrates in the world economy. Today, Salta is primarily an agricultural province, dependent on sugar cane, tobacco, and bananas, plus an increasing tourist trade, with minor contributions from mining and petroleum.

SALTA

Founded in 1582 by Hernando de Lerma, Salta lies at 1200 meters in a basin surrounded by verdant peaks. This valley's perpetual spring attracted the Spaniards, who could pasture animals in the surrounding countryside and produce crops that could not grow in the frigid Bolivian highlands, where the mining industry created enormous demand for hides, mules, and food. When extension of the Belgrano railroad made it feasible to market sugar to the immigrant cities of the Pampas, the city recovered to some degree from its 19th-century economic decline.

Orientation

At the town of General Güemes, RN 9 veers sharply west, climbing gradually through endless cane fields before dropping steeply into the Lerma Valley and the city of Salta. From the central Plaza 9 de Julio, Salta's conventional grid pattern extends in all directions until it ascends the eastern overlooks of Cerro 20 de Febrero and Cerro San Bernardo, where the streets hug their contours.

Although Salta has sprawled considerably over the past several years, most points of interest are within a few blocks of Plaza 9 de Julio. The commercial center is southwest of the plaza, where both Alberdi and Florida become pedestrian malls between Caseros and Av San Martín. North-south streets change their names on either side of the plaza, but the names of east-west streets are continuous.

Information

Tourist Office The Empresa Salteña de Turismo (Emsatur, ☎ 21-5927), at Buenos Aires 93 near Alvarado, has some brochures and maps, but is most helpful in locating accommodations in private houses. Hours are 8 am to 9 pm daily. The smaller office at the bus terminal closes for siesta between 1 to 4 pm.

ACA (☎ 21-0002) is at Rivadavia and Mitre.

Foreign Consulates The Bolivian consulate (☎ 21-1927) is at Santiago del Estero 179. France has a consulate (☎ 21-2226) at Santa Fe 20, while Germany's (☎ 22-0916) is at Güemes 1156.

Money Cambio Dinar, Mitre 101 on Plaza 9 de Julio, will change cash and traveler's checks, the latter at a very unfavorable rate with high commission. Try also Banco de la Nación at Mitre and Av Belgrano.

Post & Telecommunications Correo Argentino is at Dean Funes 140, between España and Av Belgrano; the postal code is 4400. For long-distance telephone service, go to Telecom at Vicente López 146 (open around 8 am to 7 pm) or at Belgrano 824 near 20 de Febrero (open 24 hours). Salta's area code is 087.

Immigration Migraciones (☎ 21-4857) is at Maipú 35, 11 blocks west of Plaza 9 de Julio.

Travel Agencies It is difficult to recommend one of Salta's dozens of travel agencies over the others. Try Saltur (☎ 21-2012) at Caseros 525 or, for student bargains, check out ATESA (Asociación Turismo Estudiantil Argentino) at Zuviría 522.

Bookstore The English-language bookstore Iei-Inglés, at Zuviría 518, has a modest selection of reading material.

Walking Tour

A number of colonial buildings in Salta's historic center have been turned into important museums, but even visitors arriving on Monday, when most are closed, can absorb the colonial atmosphere by a walk around the area. To see most of the buildings, walk north from the corner of Florida

ARGENTINA

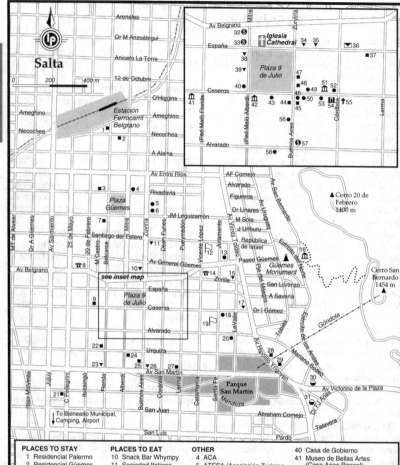

Salta

0   200   400 m

PLACES TO STAY
1   Residencial Palermo
2   Residencial Güemes
3   Residencial Astur
7   Residencial Balcarce
9   Hotel Provincial
20   Residencial Royal
21   Casa de Familia Toffoli
22   Residencial Florida
24   Hotel Italia
25   Residencial Elena
27   Hotel Las Tinajas
28   Hotel Petit
29   Hotel Continental
37   Residencial España
44   Hotel Regidor
45   Hotel Salta
47   Victoria Plaza Hotel
48   Hotel Colonial

PLACES TO EAT
10   Snack Bar Whympy
11   Sociedad Italiana
15   Trattoría Mamma Mia
17   Viejo Jack
23   Mercado Central
26   Restaurant Alvarez
34   Heladería Gianni
35   La Posta
38   Café del Consejo
39   Cafe Río

OTHER
4   ACA
5   ATESA (Asociación Turismo
     Estudiantil Argentino)
6   Iei-Inglés
8   Telecom
12   Bolivian Consulate
13   López Fleming Rent A Car
14   Telecom
16   Museo Antropológico
     Juan M Leguizamón
18   Convento de San Bernardo
19   French Consulate
30   Empresa Géminis
     (buses to Chile)
31   Terminal de Omnibus
32   Banco de la Nación
33   Cambio Dinar
36   Post Office
40   Casa de Gobierno
41   Museo de Bellas Artes
     (Casa Arias Rengel)
42   Cabildo/Museo Histórico
     del Norte
43   Saltur
45   Ruiz Moreno
46   AI (car rental)
49   LAPA
50   Aerolíneas Argentinas/Austral
51   Museo de Arte Popular
52   Tiwanaku
53   Turismo Tren a las Nubes
     (Movitren)
54   Casa Uriburu
55   Iglesia San Francisco
56   Dinar Líneas Aéreas
57   Empresa Salteña
     de Turismo (Emsatur)
58   Avis

and Alvarado, turning east on Caseros past the plaza to Av Hipólito Yrigoyen. Head north to Belgrano and go right until you reach the Güemes monument, backtracking down Belgrano to Buenos Aires and back to Alvarado. Ask at the tourist office for its brochure on the *Circuito Peatonal*.

Museo Histórico del Norte

The 18th-century cabildo housing this museum, on Plaza 9 de Julio, is worthwhile in its own right, but it also holds collections of religious and modern art, period furniture, and historic coins and paper money, plus horse-drawn and ox-drawn vehicles, including an old postal wagon and a hearse. At Caseros 549, its hours are Tuesday to Saturday 10 am to 2 pm and 3:30 to 7:30 pm, Sunday 10 am to 2 pm. Admission is US$1.

Iglesia Catedral

This 19th-century church contains the ashes of General Martín Miguel de Güemes, a native Salteño and hero of the wars of independence, as well as those of other important historical figures; even today, the gauchos of Salta province proudly flaunt their red-striped *ponchos de Güemes*. The church is at España 596, on the corner of Mitre.

Museo de Bellas Artes

Lodged in the two-story colonial mansion of the Arias Rengel family, the fine-arts museum displays both modern painting and sculpture. Its adobe walls are two meters thick; the interior patio features a wooden staircase that leads to a hanging balcony. At Florida 18, the building and museum are open daily except Monday, 9 am to 1 pm and 3 to 9 pm. Admission is US$1.

Casa Uriburu

The family of José Evaristo Uriburu, who was twice President of the Republic (both times briefly), lived in this 18th-century house at Caseros 417. It has a well-preserved collection of period furniture, and is open Tuesday to Saturday 10 am to 2 pm and 3:30 to 7:30 pm.

Iglesia San Francisco

Ornate almost to the point of gaudiness, with a highly conspicuous bell tower, this brightly painted church at Caseros and Córdoba is an unmistakable Salta landmark. It's open daily 7 am to noon and 5:30 to 9 pm.

Convento de San Bernardo

Only Carmelite nuns can enter this 16th-century convent, but visitors can approach the blindingly whitewashed adobe building (you might want sunglasses) to admire the algarrobo door, which was carved in the 18th century. At Caseros and Santa Fe, it was originally a hermitage, later a hospital, and later still a convent proper.

Museo de Arte Popular

This private institution at Caseros 476 exhibits representative crafts from throughout the Americas, focusing on Mexico, Peru, Argentina, Chile, Brazil, and Paraguay. Some items are for sale in a shop on the main floor. Admission is US$1; opening hours are Monday to Saturday from 9:30 am to 12:30 pm and 5:30 to 9:30 pm, except for Wednesday mornings.

Cerro San Bernardo

For outstanding views of Salta and its surroundings, take the *teleférico* (gondola) from Parque San Martín to the top and back (US$6 roundtrip). A trail up the hill begins at the Güemes monument at the top of Av General Güemes.

Museo Antropológico Juan M Leguizamón

On the lower slopes of Cerro San Bernardo, at Ejército del Norte and Polo Sur, this modern museum has good exhibits of local ceramics, especially from the Tastil site in the Quebrada del Toro, but also contains some outdated and even bizarre material on the peopling of the Americas – including one panel suggesting that humans might have reached the Americas originally via Antarctica.

It is open Tuesday to Friday 8:30 am to 12:30 pm and 2:30 to 6:30 pm, Saturday

3 to 6:30 pm, Sunday 4 to 6:30 pm; admission is US$1.

Places to Stay – bottom end

Camping *Camping Municipal Carlos Xamena* (☎ 23-1341), one of Argentina's best campgrounds, has the capacity for 500 tents and also features one of the west's largest swimming pools (it takes a week to fill in the spring). Fees are US$2 per car, US$3 per tent, US$2 per adult, and US$1 per child. Its major drawback is that in summer, when salteños flock here to catch some rays, they play unpleasantly loud music for the swimmers and sunbathers. Mercifully, they switch off the sound system by early evening. You can purchase food and drinks at the nearby supermarket.

From downtown, take bus No 13 ("Balneario"), which also connects with the train station.

Hostels Salta's official *Albergue Juvenil* (☎ 31-2891), Buenos Aires 930, is proving such a popular budget alternative, priced at $8 per person with kitchen facilities, that reservations are desirable. To get there, take bus No 12 from the terminal. *Residencial San Jorge* (☎ 21-0443), at Esteco 244 (two blocks south and six blocks west of Plaza 9 de Julio), also offers hostel accommodations for US$8 per person with shared bath, US$12 per person with private bath. Take local bus No 3 or No 10 from the Terminal de Omnibus.

Casas de Familia, Residenciales & Hotels

Emsatur maintains a list of private houses that are an excellent alternative to bottom-end hotels. One of the most popular and central is at Mendoza 915, run by María de Toffoli, one of three sisters (the other two occupy and let rooms in their own houses at Mendoza 917 and Mendoza 919). All have pleasant patios, kitchen facilities, and spotless bathrooms, for about US$10 per person.

Between the bus terminal and downtown is *Residencial Royal*, Alvarado 107, which is reasonably quiet and has singles/doubles with shared bath for US$10/14. *Residen-*

cial Elena (☎ 21-1529), Buenos Aires 256, in a neocolonial building with an attractive interior patio, offers rooms for US$15/22 single/double but seems reluctant to accept single travelers. Another possibility is *Residencial España* (☎ 21-7898), España 319, for US$16/22.

Italian-run *Hotel Italia* (☎ 21-4050), very central at Alberdi 231 near Urquiza, charges about US$17/22 for plain but spacious and sunny rooms. Comparably priced and equally central is the architecturally undistinguished *Residencial Florida* (☎ 21-2133), Urquiza 722 near Florida.

Most inexpensive accommodations are near the train station rather than the bus terminal, even though rail service has virtually disappeared. Directly across from the station on Ameghino, all comparable in price to Residencial Royal, are *Residencial Colón, Residencial Splendid, Residencial Tito,* and *Residencial Roma*. On Necochea between Balcarce and Mitre, *Residencial Güemes* is similar. *Residencial Balcarce* (☎ 21-8023), Balcarce 460, is also near the train station and offers rates of about US$15/22, as does *Residencial Astur* (☎ 21-2107), a few blocks away at Rivadavia 752. A recent discovery is *Residencial Palermo* (☎ 22-0426), Balcarce 980, which has good facilities for US$12 single.

Places to Stay – middle

Several reasonably priced mid-range hotels are near the bus terminal, starting around US$22/32 at *Hotel Las Tinajas* (☎ 23-3796), Lerma 288. *Hotel Petit* (☎ 21-3012), at Hipólito Yrigoyen 225, charges US$25/36, while *Hotel Continental* (☎ 31-0575), at Hipólito Yrigoyen 295, costs US$28/40. Downtown near Plaza 9 de Julio, try *Hotel Regidor* (☎ 31-1305) at Buenos Aires 8 for US$23/39, or *Hotel Colonial* (☎ 31-0760) at Zuviría 6 for US$27/39.

Places to Stay – top end

Another step up is the *Victoria Plaza Hotel* (☎ 31-0334), at Zuviría 16, which charges about US$36/48 for standard rooms but US$48/60 for VIP quarters. At attractive, centrally located *Hotel Salta* (☎ 21-1413), Buenos Aires 1 at Caseros, rates start at US$55/74 and rise as high as US$73/90, but several readers have found it a less than outstanding value. Try also *Hotel Provincial* (☎ 21-8993) at Caseros 786, ranging from US$51/75 up to US$75/110.

Places to Eat

One of the best and cheapest places to eat is Salta's large and lively *Mercado Central,* Florida and San Martín, where you can supplement inexpensive pizza, empanadas, and humitas with fresh fruit and vegetables. Even if you're not a budget traveler, you should pay the market a visit.

There are many cheap restaurants, pizzerías, and confiterías around Belgrano and Zuviría. Despite its unappealing moniker, *Snack Bar Whympy* at Zuviría 223 is good, inexpensive, and filling. *Restaurant Alvarez* (☎ 21-4523), Av San Martín and Buenos Aires, also has large portions of good, cheap food. The *Sociedad Italiana,* Zuviría and Santiago del Estero, has quality four-course meals for about US$6. *Café del Consejo,* a confitería on Mitre opposite the Plaza, serves the cheapest lager beer in town. Reader-recommended *Cafe Río* (☎ 21-1296) is at Mitre 41.

La Posta (☎ 21-7091), España 476, is a highly recommended but pricey parrilla. *Viejo Jack*, at Av Virrey Toledo 145, and *Viejo Jack II* (☎ 22-1206), Av Reyes Católicos 1465, are separate branches of a popular parilla that has drawn enthusiastic reviews from readers. For Italian food, check out *Trattoría Mamma Mia,* Virrey Toledo 200.

Despite its very modest decor, *Heladería Gianni,* España 486, is one of Argentina's best ice cream shops.

Things to Buy

For useful souvenirs, the most noteworthy place is the provincially sponsored Mercado Artesanal at the west end of Av San Martín, accessed by bus Nos 2, 3, or 7 from Av San Martín. Articles for sale include native handicrafts like hammocks, string

bags, ceramics, basketry, leather work, and the region's distinctive ponchos.

Tiwanaku, Caseros 424, also has good-quality pottery, ceramics, copperware, and woolens. There is another interesting shop at Catamarca 82.

In the cabildo, Horacio Bertero is a protegé of silversmith Raúl Horacio Draghi, the best known artisan in San Antonio de Areco.

Getting There & Away

Air Aerolíneas Argentinas (☎ 31-5738) and Austral (☎ 31-0258) share offices at Caseros 475. Salta is a brief stopover on Monday's Aerolíneas roundtrip flights between Aeroparque and Santa Cruz de la Sierra, Bolivia (US$127), which also stop in Córdoba (US$128). There's at least one Austral flight daily to Buenos Aires (US$225), while Austral's Monday and Wednesday flights from Córdoba and Tucumán to Jujuy (US$12) also stop here.

Dinar Líneas Aéreas (☎ 31-0606), Buenos Aires 46, Local 2, flies Monday, Tuesday, Thursday, Friday, and Saturday to Tucumán (US$30) and Buenos Aires (US$180).

LAPA (☎ 21-0386), Caseros 492, flies Tuesday, Thursday, and Saturday afternoons to Aeroparque (US$129) via Tucumán (US$29).

Bus Salta's Terminal de Omnibus (☎ 21-4716), on Av Hipólito Yrigoyen southwest of downtown, has frequent services to all parts of the country. Most companies are located in the terminal, but a few have offices nearby or elsewhere in town.

La Veloz del Norte (☎ 21-2465) serves Mar del Plata (US$85, 29 hours), Buenos Aires (US$64, 22 hours), Santa Fe (US$50, 15 hours), Mendoza (US$61, 19 hours), San Juan (US$50, 17 hours), Córdoba (US$45, 16 hours), Resistencia (US$40, 16 hours), La Rioja (US$35), Catamarca (US$26), and Santiago del Estero (US$20). Panamericano (☎ 21-2460) has frequent service to Tucumán (US$17), Santiago del Estero, and Córdoba, plus Mar del Plata. Andesmar (☎ 31-0263) goes to Mendoza and other destinations in Cuyo, and even farther south to Patagonia.

Atahualpa (☎ 21-4795) runs several buses daily to Jujuy and up the Quebrada de Humahuaca to La Quiaca (nine hours), as well as across the northern Argentine Chaco to Formosa Tuesdays and Thursdays, and to Antofagasta, Chile (Wednesdays, summer only). Empresa Géminis (☎ 21-2758) also has summer crossings on Saturdays to Antofagasta (US$40), and serves Calama, Iquique (US$50), and Arica (US$55). Buses to Chile are few and always very full, so buy your ticket well in advance if possible at the office at Dionísio Puch 117, opposite the terminal.

El Indio (☎ 21-9519) leaves three times daily for Cafayate (US$15, four hours), and sends daily buses up the Quebrada del Toro to San Antonio de los Cobres (US$14). Empresa Marco Ruedas (☎ 21-4447), Islas Malvinas 393, serves the altiplano village of Cachi.

Train The Ferrocarril Belgrano (☎ 21-3161) is at Ameghino 690, but no longer offers regular passenger services. One of Salta's popular attractions, however, is the scenic ride to and beyond the mining town of San Antonio de los Cobres on the famous Tren a las Nubes (Train to the Clouds) – contact Turismo Tren a las Nubes (☎ 21-6394, fax 31-1264), Caseros 443, or see the entry on San Antonio de los Cobres for details.

The local freight, leaving Wednesdays at about 7 am, is a cheaper alternative to get to San Antonio de los Cobres, or do the 29-hour marathon ride to the Chilean border at Socompa (US$30 roundtrip). From San Antonio de los Cobres you can catch a return bus to Salta, but see also the separate entry on Tren a las Nubes.

Getting Around

To/From the Airport Aeropuerto Internacional El Aybal (☎ 23-1648) is southwest of town on RP 51; buses to and from the airport cost US$3.

To/From the Bus & Train Station Local bus No 5 connects the train station and downtown with the bus terminal on Av Hipólito Yrigoyen, which is southeast of downtown. Bus No 13 connects the station with the municipal campground.

Car Rental Renting a car is a good way to see Salta and its countryside, but it's far from cheap – one reader spent US$1150 to rent a Volkswagen Golf from Avis (☎ 21-7575), Alvarado 537, for nine days. Other agencies include López Fleming (☎ 21-5797) at General Güemes 92 and at the airport; AI (☎ 31-0875) at Caseros 489; Localiza (☎ 31-1021) and Ruiz Moreno (☎ 21-2069) at Buenos Aires 1 in Hotel Salta.

NATIONAL PARKS OF SALTA PROVINCE

Salta has three important national parks, but only one, Los Cardones, is easily accessible. Baritú must be approached through Bolivia, while Finca El Rey is inaccessible only during the rainy summer.

Parque Nacional Los Cardones

There is some confusion whether Parque Nacional Los Cardones yet constitutes a park or ever will, but whether official or not, it occupies some 70,000 hectares on both sides of the winding highway from Salta to Cachi across the Cuesta del Obispo. Only 100 km from Salta, the park takes its name from the candelabra cactus known as the cardón (*Trichocereus pasacana*), the park's most striking plant species.

In the absence of forest in the Andean foothills and the puna, the cardón has long been an important source of timber for rafters, doors, window frames, and similar uses. As such, it is commonly found in native construction and in the region's colonial churches. According to Argentine writer Federico Kirbus, clusters of cardones is a good indicator of an archaeological site: The Indians of the puna ate its sweet black seed which, after passing through the intestinal tract, readily sprouted around their latrines.

Pending finalization of park status, Los Cardones has no visitor services, but this should not deter prospective visitors. Buses between Salta and Cachi will drop you off or pick you up. If visiting Buenos Aires before going to Salta, drop by the Parques Nacionales office to check the latest information; otherwise, try the Emsatur office in Salta.

Parque Nacional Baritú

Hugging the Bolivian border in Salta province, Baritú is the most northerly of the three Argentine parks conserving subtropical montane forest. Like Calilegua (see the entry under Jujuy province) and Finca El Rey (see below), it protects diverse flora and harbors a large number of endangered or threatened mammals, including black howler and capuchin monkeys, the southern river otter, Geoffroy's cat, the jaguar, and the Brazilian tapir. The park's emblem is the *ardilla roja* (yungas forest squirrel), which inhabits the moist montane forest above 1300 meters.

At present, the only access to Baritú is through Bolivia, where southbound travelers from Tarija may want to inquire about entry via a lateral off the highway, which goes to the border station at Bermejo/Aguas Blancas. For information in Argentina, contact the visitors' center at Parque Nacional Calilegua (☎ 0886-22046) in the village of Calilegua, Jujuy province.

Parque Nacional Finca El Rey

Confined to a narrow strip no wider than about 50 km, Argentina's subtropical humid forests extend from the Bolivian frontier south of Tarija almost to the border between Tucumán and Catamarca provinces. Parque Nacional Finca El Rey, comprising 44,000 hectares almost directly east of Salta, is the most southerly of Argentine parks protecting this unusual habitat, the most biologically diverse in the country. It takes its name from the estancia that formerly occupied the area, the expropriation of which led to the park's creation.

The park's emblem is the giant toucan, appropriate because of the abundant bird life, but the mosquito might be just as appropriate. Most of the same mammals found in Baritú and Calilegua are also present here. The staff maintain a vehicular nature trail along the Río Popayán and plan to make a foot trail. For up-to-date information and reservations at the park's comfortable hostería, contact the visitors' center at Calilegua (☎ 0886-22046).

As the crow flies, Parque Nacional Finca El Rey is only about 100 km from Salta, but via RN 9, RP 5, and RP 20 it is more than 200 km from the provincial capital. There is public transport as far as the junction of RN 9 and RP 5, but even if you can hitch to the second junction, there's almost no traffic for the last 46 km to park headquarters. In the summer rainy season, only 4WD vehicles will be able to pass.

QUEBRADA DE CAFAYATE

Salta's Lerma Valley receives abundant rainfall from summer storms which drop their load on the slopes surrounding the city, but higher ranges of peaks to the south and west inhibit the penetration of subtropical storms. In several areas, the rivers that descend from the Andes have carved deep *quebradas* (canyons) through these arid zones, exposing the multicolored sedimentary strata, which underlay the surface soils.

Many of these layers have eroded to strange, sometimes unearthly formations, which southbound travelers from Salta can appreciate from paved RN 68, but which are even more intriguing when explored up close. For its extraordinary scenery, the canyon deserves national or provincial park status. Properly speaking, the Quebrada de Cafayate is the Quebrada del Río de las Conchas, after the river that eroded the canyon.

Beyond the tiny village of Alemanía, about 100 km south of Salta, the scenery changes suddenly and dramatically from verdant hillsides to barren, reddish sandstones. To the east, the Sierra de Carahuasi is the backdrop for distinctive land forms

ARGENTINA

bearing evocative names like Garganta del Diablo (Devil's Throat), El Anfiteatro (The Amphitheatre), El Sapo (The Toad), El Fraile (The Friar; a nearby farm sells empanadas and cold drinks), El Obelisco (The Obelisk), and Los Castillos (The Castles). Just north of Cafayate, Los Médanos is an extensive field of sand dunes.

Getting There & Away

Other than renting a car (possible in Salta but not in Cafayate) or the ideal alternative, riding a bicycle, the only ways to see the Quebrada are to take the bus, hitch, or walk. Tours from Salta are brief and regimented. You can disembark from any of El Indio's buses anywhere in the canyon and a succeeding bus will pick you up, but be aware of the schedules between Salta and Cafayate, since you probably don't want to get stuck in the canyon after dark (although there are worse places to camp if you have your tent along). The same holds if you hitch between the most interesting sites – you may want to catch one of the buses if it gets late.

Walking will allow you to see the canyon at your own pace, but carry food and plenty of water in this hot, dry environment. A good place to start is the impressive box canyon of Garganta del Diablo. Remember that the most interesting portion is much too far to walk in a single day, so see as much as you can before continuing to Cafayate – you can always double back the next day.

CAFAYATE

Several major Argentine vintners, including highly regarded Etchart and Michel Torino, have vineyards near Cafayate, whose warm, dry, and sunny climate makes it ideal for the cultivation of wine grapes. The most important town in extreme southwestern Salta province, it's a popular tourist destination, but is not overrun with visitors.

Orientation

Cafayate sits at 1660 meters at the foot of the Calchaquí Valley, near the junction between RN 40, which goes northwest to Molinos and Cachi, and RN 68, which goes to Salta through the Quebrada de Cafayate. Through town, RN 40 is Av Güemes. As in many small provincial towns, few people bother with street names.

Information

The tourist information kiosk on Güemes, opposite the plaza, keeps erratic opening hours. It's better to change money in Salta, but try Banco de la Nación on the plaza, or the larger shops or hotels.

Correo Argentino is on Güemes, toward the north end of town; the postal code is

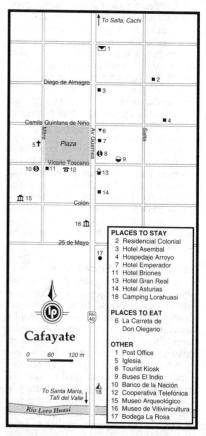

PLACES TO STAY
2 Residencial Colonial
3 Hotel Asembal
4 Hospedaje Arroyo
7 Hotel Emperador
11 Hotel Briones
13 Hotel Gran Real
14 Hotel Asturias
18 Camping Lorahuasi

PLACES TO EAT
6 La Carreta de Don Olegario

OTHER
1 Post Office
5 Iglesia
8 Tourist Kiosk
9 Buses El Indio
10 Banco de la Nación
12 Cooperativa Telefónica
15 Museo Arqueológico
16 Museo de Vitivinicultura
17 Bodega La Rosa

Cafayate

0   60   120 m

To Salta, Cachi

Diego de Almagro

Camila Quintana de Niño

Mitre

Plaza

Av Güemes

Salta

Vicario Toscano

Colón

25 de Mayo

To Santa María, Tafí del Valle

Río Loro Huasi

4427. Long-distance phone calls can be an agonizingly time-consuming experience at the Cooperativa Telefónica on the south side of the plaza. Cafayate's area code is 0868.

Museo Arqueológico
Señor Rodolfo Bravo, a dedicated aficionado and expert on the region, gives guided tours of his astounding personal collection of Calchaquí (Diaguita) ceramics, in his house on Calle Colón, for US$1 per person. There are also colonial and more recent artifacts, such as elaborate horse gear and wine casks. Drop in at any reasonable hour.

Museo de Vitivinicultura
On Güemes near Colón, this museum details the history of local wine production. Ask at Bodega La Rosa and other bodegas about tours and tasting; the Etchart tour has been recommended. A local specialty is the sweet white *torrontés.*

Special Events
Cafayate's annual Fiesta del Virgen, in early October, is worth a visit if you're in the area.

Places to Stay
Camping Although it can be dusty when the wind blows, the municipal *Camping Lorahuasi* at the south end of town charges US$2 per car, per person, and per tent, for excellent facilities, including hot showers and a swimming pool. There is a small grocery, but you can also buy food in town, which is just a ten-minute walk.

Hostel *Hotel Gran Real* (☎ 21231), Güemes 128, has limited hostel accommodations with kitchen facilities for $12.

Residenciales & Hotels Cafayate has a fine selection of hotels in all categories except luxury. The best budget choice is probably *Residencial Colonial* (☎ 21223), Diego de Almagro 134, which charges US$12 per person with shared bath, but may lack hot water at times. *Hospedaje Arroyo,* Quintana de Niño s/n (*sin numero,*

without a street address), may be even a bit cheaper. For US$25/32 single/double, *Hotel Briones* (☎ 21270), on the plaza at Vicario Toscano 80, is a lesser value than it once was, but still has a decent confitería.

At US$25/35 per single/double, ACA's *Hostería de Cafayate* (☎ 21296) on RN 40 is a bargain for members but costs US$40/50 for non-members. Slightly costlier are the *Hotel Emperador* (☎ 21268) at Güemes 42, and the *Hotel Gran Real* (☎ 21231) at Güemes 128. The latter has a dingy downstairs confitería and may be closed except in summer.

Several others are higher priced at about US$35/50, including *Hotel Asembal* (☎ 21065), at Güemes and Almagro, and *Hotel Asturias* (☎ 21040) at Güemes 154.

Places to Eat
Local cuisine focuses on parrillada, and sometimes puts decor before food, as at *La López Pereyra.* You can also try *La Carreta de Don Olegario,* on Güemes at the plaza, but there are several cheaper places, such as *El Gordo.*

Things to Buy
Cafayate has many young artists and craftspeople; check the Mercado Artesanal, on the plaza near the tourist office, for local handicrafts.

Getting There & Away
El Indio, on Toscano between Güemes and Salta, has three buses daily to Salta (US$15, four hours), except Thursday when there are four. There are also four daily to San Carlos, up the Valle Calchaquí, and one to Angastaco (US$7).

Use the daily buses to Santa María to visit the important ruins at Quilmes (see below), in Tucumán province. Several buses weekly connect Cafayate with the city of Tucumán via a very scenic and worthwhile route through Tafí del Valle.

VALLES CALCHAQUÍES
In this valley, north and south of Cafayate and one of the main routes across the Andes to Chile and Peru, Calchaquí Indians put up

Argentina's best restored archaeological site is in Quilmes.   WAYNE BERNHARDSON

some of the stiffest resistance to Spanish colonial rule. In the 17th century, plagued with labor shortages, the Spaniards twice tried to impose forced labor obligations on the Calchaquíes, but found themselves having to maintain armed forces to prevent the Indians from sowing crops and attacking pack trains.

Military domination did not solve Spanish labor problems, since their only solution was to relocate the Indians as far away as Buenos Aires, whose suburb of Quilmes bears the name of one group of these displaced people. The last of the descendants of the 270 families transported to the viceregal capital had died or dispersed by the time of Argentine independence.

When their resistance failed, the Calchaquíes lost the productive land that had sustained them for centuries and would have done so much longer. According to American geographer Isaiah Bowman, who visited the area in the 1920s, "So fertile is the soil of the Calchaquí valley . . . that alfalfa lasts for twenty five years without resowing . . . ." Those riches found their way into the hands of Spaniards who formed large rural estates, the haciendas of the Andes.

Quilmes

Although it is in the province of Tucumán, the pre-Hispanic fortress of Quilmes is only 50 km south of Cafayate and many travelers will approach it from this direc-

tion. Probably the best restored archaeological site in all of Argentina, this pucará deserves a visit despite its location five km off the main highway. See the Tucumán chapter for details.

Angastaco

Angastaco resembles other oasis settlements placed at regular intervals in the Valles Calchaquíes, with vineyards, fields of peppers, and ruins of an ancient pucará. There is also an archaeological museum.

Hostería Angastaco (☎ 087-25-0830 in Salta) has rooms for US$20 per person with breakfast and a swimming pool; dinners costs about US$7, and the manager's daughter also organizes horseback rides for about US$7 per hour. In addition to the hostería, there is also a cheaper residencial. Friday at 11 am, Expreso Marcos Rueda has a bus to Molinos, Cachi, and Salta, returning to Angastaco Sunday afternoons. There is a daily bus to Cafayate.

Molinos

Like Angastaco, Molinos was a way station on the trans-Andean route to Chile and Peru. Well into this century, pack trains passed here with skins, wool, blankets, and wood for sale in Salta and subsequent shipment to Buenos Aires. Molinos takes its name from the still-operative grain mill on the Río Calchaquí, and features an important 18th-century church. In the surrounding villages you can find the traditional "ponchos de Güemes" for sale. The 18th-century *Hostal Provincial de Molinos* (☎ 087-21-4871 in Salta) provides lodging for US$45/60 with breakfast.

Cachi

With its scenic surroundings, 18th-century church, and archaeological museum, Cachi is probably the most worthwhile stopover among the valley's more accessible settlements. There are several possibilities for lodging: the municipal campground and hostel, the modest *Hotel Nevado de Cachi* for US$10 per person, and the *Hostería ACA* (☎ 087-31-1157 in Salta), which has singles/doubles for US$18/30 for members, US$25/43 for non-members. The breakfast gets no raves, but there are several other restaurants.

You can reach Cachi either from Cafayate or, more easily and frequently, by the Marcos Rueda bus from Salta. This route passes across the scenic Cuesta de Obispo past the Parque Nacional Los Cardones (see above).

From Cachi, buses continue to La Poma, an old hacienda town which, for all practical purposes, is the end of the line. The road beyond, to San Antonio de los Cobres, is impassable except for vehicles with 4WD; it's much easier to approach San Antonio from Salta via the Quebrada del Toro.

San Antonio de los Cobres

In colonial times, transportation from northwestern Argentina depended on pack trains, most of which passed through the Quebrada de Humahuaca on the way to Potosí, but an alternative route crossed the rugged elevations of the Puna de Atacama to the Pacific and then continued to Lima. A member of Diego de Almagro's party, the first Spaniards to cross the puna, left an indelible account of the dismal 800-km crossing, which took twenty days in the best of times:

Many men and many horses froze to death, for neither their clothes nor their armor could protect them from the freezing wind . . . . Many of those who had died remained, frozen solid, still on foot and propped against the rocks, and the horses they had been leading also frozen, not decomposed, but as fresh as if they had just died; and later expeditions . . . short of food, came upon these horses and were glad to eat them.

For travelers across the Andes, the area around the bleak mining town of San Antonio de los Cobres (altitude 3700 meters) must have seemed an oasis, though even as late as 1914 it had a population below 1000. Until well into this century, it continued to be an important way station for drovers moving their stock across the mountains to arid Chile, whose narrow alluvial valleys could not produce the food needed for the nitrate miners of the Atacama Desert. Later, railroads and rugged highways supplanted mules for shipping food and supplies to Argentine mining settlements and across the Andes.

San Antonio de los Cobres is a largely Indian town, but the posters and political graffiti scribbled on its adobe walls serve as reminders that it's still part of Argentina. For truly intrepid travelers, it still offers one of the most interesting border crossings in all of Argentina, paralleling the routes of the mule drivers across the Puna de Atacama to the Pacific coast of Chile via the famous Train to the Clouds.

Places to Stay & Eat Until recently, San Antonio had only the most basic accommodations and food – and still, for the most part, what you see is what you get. What you get is basic lodging at *Hospedaje Belgrano* or *Hospedaje Los Andes,* for about US$8 per night per person, with plenty of blankets (nights are always cold at this elevation) and shared bath. Hospedaje Los Andes has a restaurant, but limited food and drink are also available in the few shops.

Recently the *Hostería de las Nubes* (☎ 90-9056) has attempted to fill the accommodations gap with 12 rooms with private baths, double-glazed windows, and a total of 30 beds. It also has a restaurant, central heating, and TV lounge; rates are

ARGENTINA

US$40/50 single/double, including breakfast, but can rise by 20% in the July-August peak season. Make reservations at Tren a las Nubes Turismo (☎ 087- 31-4984, fax 31-1264), Caseros 443 in Salta.

Getting There & Away There are five weekly buses from Salta to San Antonio de los Cobres (US$15, four hours) with El Quebradeño. See below for details on the picturesque El Tren a las Nubes trip from Salta to San Antonio de los Cobres and beyond.

Do not waste time trying to hitch across the Andes because there are almost no vehicles; even the summer buses operated by Géminis and Atahualpa from Salta now go via Jujuy and the Paso de Jama.

EL TREN A LAS NUBES & THE CHILEAN CROSSING

From Salta, the Tren a las Nubes (Train to the Clouds) leaves the Lerma Valley to ascend the multicolored Quebrada del Toro, continuing past the important ruins of Tastil as it parallels RN 51, which goes to the Huaytiquina pass and across the Andes to the Chilean oasis of San Pedro de Atacama. To reach the heights of the puna on the Chilean border, 571 km west, the track makes countless switchbacks and even spirals, passes through 21 tunnels more than 3000 meters in total length, and crosses 31 iron bridges and 13 viaducts. The trip's highlight, a stunning viaduct 64-meters high, 224-meters long, weighing 1600 tons, and spanning an enormous desert canyon at La Polvorilla, is a magnificent engineering achievement unjustified on any reasonable economic grounds. At Abra Chorillos, an altitude of 4575 meters makes this the fourth-highest operating line in the world.

From April to October, Tren a las Nubes Turismo (☎ 087-31-4984, fax 31-1264), Caseros 443 in Salta, operates the Tren a las Nubes service only as far as La Polvorilla; most trips take place weekends only, but can be more frequent during the July holidays. The train leaves at 7:05 am and returns to Salta at 10:15 pm. The fare is US$95 for the 438-km roundtrip, which reaches a maximum altitude of 4200 meters. Meals are additional, ranging from a US$11 fixed-price lunch in the dining car to sandwiches and hamburgers for US$3.50 to US$4.50. Some travelers have gotten slightly less comfortable "discount carriage" tickets for US$50.

Freight trains from Salta, which you may be able to catch in Rosario de Lerma or San Antonio de los Cobres, are a cheaper alternative to the Tren a las Nubes; for more details, see the Getting There & Away entry for the city of Salta. Freights are the only possibility from October to April, passing the gigantic salt lakes of the puna to the Chilean border station at Socompa, where it is feasible to catch the Chilean

---

Who's on the Train?

British capital and engineers built most of Argentina's railways, but the line from Salta to the Chilean border, used by the Tren a las Nubes, is one of few exceptions. First proposed in 1905, construction on the project was undertaken in 1921 and not finished until 1948.

New York-born Richard Maury, who also worked in Cuba and came to Argentina in 1906 at the age of 24, modified an earlier design for the awesome La Polvorilla viaduct and, with a crew of 1300 laborers, built a two-section steel bridge over the Río Toro. Buried in the village of Campo Quijano, the North American engineer is memorialized at a station known as Ingeniero Maury, 2358 meters above sea level.

Workers on the Huaytiquina line came from around the world. Legend has it that one of the immigrant applicants was a taciturn Yugoslav exile, who started at Campo Quijano and worked his way up the Quebrada de Toro before returning to Buenos Aires and, later, to Europe. In WWII, Josep Broz led a guerrilla struggle against the Nazis and, after the war, became president of his country. Most know him as Marshall Tito.

Readers interested in more detail should consult Federico Kirbus's *El Fascinante Tren a las Nubes* (Buenos Aires: Editorial El Ateneo, 1993), on sale in both Buenos Aires and Salta. ∎

Hopping the Scenic Night Train

Roland Nilsson of Sålen, Sweden, gives the following account of his experience on the cargo train from Salta to San Antonio de los Cobres:

"I was there in March, which meant that it was only the cargo train running. It was supposed to leave Salta Wednesday morning at 7:30 am, but the guy from the hostel told me that if I took the bus from Salta to Campo Quijano at 8:30 am, I would easily reach the train . . . .

"I took the bus together with two girls, and on the bus we met five other tourists who wanted to do the same thing. At the station in Campo Quijano we met two Germans who had arrived earlier. They said that the train officer refused to sell tickets to tourists. We tried anyway, but he refused. Half an hour later three more tourists arrived. They tried also, but the officer explained that the train was only for the locals, and he was not allowed to sell tickets to tourists. He said that we would have to take the other train (US$95). We said that at that time there was no other train and we also asked who would notice if he sold tickets to us?

" 'There's police aboard,' he said, 'and if they found out that I sold the tickets, they would fire me.' After two hours of arguing, he suddenly decided to sell 13 tickets.

"Now the clock was half past 11. The train was supposed to be there at 10:30 am. It arrived at 12:15 pm. We left the station (in the train) at 1 pm. Hurray! It was a pleasant, spectacular, comfortable journey for about three hours. At the General Manuel Solá station we stopped. The stop became very long and we asked, "What is the problem?"

"'No fuel,'" said the man from the train. 'We have to wait for another locomotive from Salta,' he continued.

"At 9:30 pm we left the station. Of course it was dark, so the beautiful scenery was impossible to see. As we were about 3000 meters above sea level, it became very cold during the night – no heating in the train.

"At 4 am we reached San Antonio de los Cobres. We had become a group of 14 tourists walking around looking for a place to stay. A guy from Salta knew a hotel which we went to. We rang the bell, knocked on the door, but nobody opened it. One of us found a window that was open, so he entered through that and tried to find somebody responsible inside. There was nobody there.

"It was very cold and we were all tired. The door was unable to open from inside, but it was warm there, so all 14 of us went through the window. Inside we looked for somebody working there but didn't find anyone.

"It was a new hotel with a fashionable lobby – we found it strange. In the reception we found the register and the keys, so we wrote notes about what we had done, who we were, which rooms we occupied and went to bed.

"The morning after, we expected to maybe find the police waiting for us or at least an angry hotel manager. But no problem. The staff were happy to have guests! They explained that the night porter had left during the night for some accident in the family. Normally the hotel is open 24 hours.

"Well, we all had thoughts of taking the bus back to Salta that day. But since we didn't see that much when we came, we decided to take the train back as well.

"'Friday morning at 9:30 am the train will leave,' they said. We were quite sure the train wouldn't leave at that time, so we sent a person there at 8:30 to check. At 2 pm, he said when he came back. At 6:30 pm we left the station on the train again. Of course, it was dark after half an hour. So once again on the scenic 'Tren a las Nubes' in the darkness!

"Anyway, the staff on the train were very friendly and helpful. It was a nice bar and a good kitchen, so we had a nice journey anyway. Arrived in Salta at 4 am.

"Conclusion: Be prepared to get frustrated. Don't expect that they take tourists on the cargo train. The next week, 12 persons came back to the hostel after being refused tickets!" ∎

freight to the Atacama Desert station of Baquedano on the Carretera Panamericana, about 100 km from the port of Antofagasta. On the Chilean side, this is a rugged, uncomfortable trip, not for the squeamish – the Chilean crew is disagreeable, and the train truly filthy.

At Socompa, 3900 meters above sea level, passengers must clear Argentine and Chilean immigration and customs before seeking permission to ride the infrequent westbound freights – it is not unusual to wait several days for a train. The Chilean station agent will radio for permission to carry passengers in the train's caboose; while permission is fairly routine, it is not guaranteed. Purchase a quantity of Chilean pesos before leaving Salta, since the agent may offer *very* unfavorable rates for US dollars.

From Socompa, the train descends with impressive views of 6051-meter Volcán Socompa to the east and 6739-meter Llullaillaco to the south, through vast monochrome deserts that few visitors to the continent ever see. At the abandoned mining station of Augusta Victoria, the crew may ask you to disembark while the train backtracks to another isolated mining outpost, but it will return. You may, however, wish to try hitching to Antofagasta – in this isolated area, mining trucks serve as informal public transport and almost certainly will stop. Otherwise, sleep in the abandoned station, which is far more comfortable than the caboose, until the train returns.

Tucumán Province

Tucumán is Argentina's smallest province, but its size belies its importance. From colonial times, when it was an important way station en route to Potosí, through the early independence period, and into the present, Tucumán has played a critical role in the country's political and economic history.

In contemporary Argentina, Tucumán means sugar. Unlike areas to the north, Tucumán benefits from both its proximity to the high Sierra de Aconquija to the west and the absence of a front range to the east. This permits warm, easterly winds to drop their moisture on the Sierra, bringing moderate winter temperatures – the area within 60 km of its slopes is frost-free. These humid slopes and dense, subtropical forests give birth to permanent streams for irrigation. While sugar monoculture has enabled the province to develop secondary industry, it has also created tremendous inequities in

wealth and land distribution, as well as ecological problems such as depletion of the soil. Yields per hectare have fallen in Tucumán in comparison with Salta and Jujuy.

The extreme west of the province is a high, arid extension of the Valles Calchaquíes, but the scenic area around Tafí del Valle is a climatic anomaly, a cool, damp valley between subtropical mountains and arid puna, where potatoes are the most important crop. The precipitous mountain road (RN 38 to RP 307) from Tucumán to Tafí de Valle is a spectacular trip no visitor to the area should miss.

TUCUMÁN

Although Tucumán (formally San Miguel de Tucumán) is the commercial and administrative center for the sugar industry, visitors find Tucumán's main appeal in its colonial and 19th-century historical sites and its access to the scenic Sierra de Aconquija. Founded in 1565 at the convergence of roads from Rosario, Córdoba, and Santa Fe, San Miguel de Tucumán and its hinterland were oriented toward Salta and Bolivia during most of the colonial period. Vásquez de Espinosa's early 17th-century description paints Tucumán as the most prosperous of the early Spanish cities:

It has as many as 250 Spanish residents; its climate is very hot and damp. It has in its neighborhood some Indian parishes in which are produced quantities of cotton cloth, canopies, bedspreads and other elaborate products. There are mule and cattle ranches in this district and it contains very fragrant and valuable timber, and on its plains countless numbers of wild cattle . . . It has an irrigation canal with which its vineyards, gardens and fields are watered.

Only during and after Argentine independence did Tucumán distinguish itself from the rest of the region. In the culmination of the ferment of the early 19th century, Tucumán hosted the congress that declared Argentine independence in 1816. Dominated by Unitarist merchants, lawyers, soldiers, and clergy, the Congress accomplished little else; despite a virtual boycott by Federalist factions, it failed to agree on

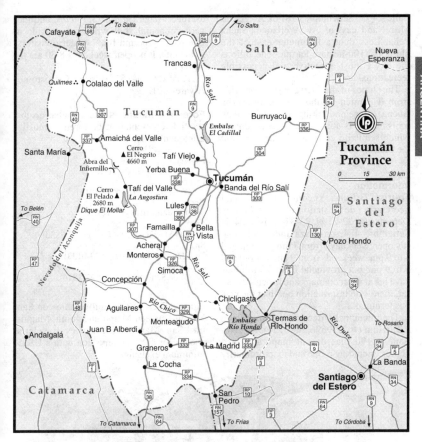

a constitution that would have institutionalized a constitutional monarchy in hopes of attracting European assistance.

Unlike other colonial cities of the Noroeste, Tucumán successfully reoriented its economy in the postindependence period. Modern Tucumán dates from the late 19th century and owes its importance to location – at the southern end of the frost-free zone of sugar cane production, it was just close enough to Buenos Aires to take advantage of access to the growing market of the federal capital. By 1874, a railroad connected Tucumán with Córdoba, permitting easy transport of this commodity, and

local and British capital contributed to the industry's growth.

Orientation

On the west bank of the Río Salí, only a few kilometers east of the precipitous Sierra de Aconquija, RN 9 passes Tucumán's eastern outskirts en route from Santiago del Estero to Salta. The Ferrocarril Mitre still provides rail connections with Buenos Aires, 1200 km southeast.

Tucumán's geographical focus is the rectangular Plaza Independencia, site of major public buildings like the Casa de Gobierno; street names change north and south of

Calle 24 de Setiembre, west of Av Alem/ Mitre, and east of Av Avellaneda/Sáenz Peña. Less than a kilometer east of the plaza, the 100-hectare Parque 9 de Julio is the city's most attractive and accessible recreational area.

The slopes of the Sierra, a short bus ride from Tucumán to the suburb of Yerba Buena, offer good hiking on gaucho stock trails. There is still a yearly rodeo during which semiwild cattle are herded in from the Sierra.

Information

Tourist Offices Tucumán's provincial Secretaría de Estado de Turismo y Deportes (☎ 22-2199, 23-3742) is at 24 de Setiembre 484, on Plaza Independencia. It's open weekdays from 7 am to 1 pm and 4 to 9 pm, weekends from 9 am to 1 pm and 5 to 9 pm, but provincial financial troubles have left it short on maps and brochures. So far, there's no information booth at the new bus terminal.

The municipal Dirección de Producción y Turismo (☎ 22-9696, 30-0756), Av Avellaneda 190, has decent maps and brochures, including a free and extraordinarily useful 35-page *Guía de Servicios,* and the very congenial staff will even provide a free parking permit for short-term visitors to the city. It is open weekdays 8:30 am to 4:30 pm.

ACA (☎ 31-1522) is at Crisóstomo Alvarez 901.

Foreign Consulates Tucumán has a substantial representation of foreign (mostly European) consulates.

Bolivia
    Mendoza 1095 (☎ 21-1852)
France
    25 de Mayo 518 (☎ 31-1913)
Germany
    9 de Julio 1015 (☎ 21-9102)
Italy
    San Martín 623, 1st floor (☎ 22-3830)
Spain
    Mate de Luna 4107 (☎ 33-0133)
Switzerland
    24 de Setiembre 524 (☎ 22-1816)

Money There are several cambios on San Martín between Maipú and Junín. Maguitur, San Martín 765, cashes traveler's checks for a 2% commission with a US$5 minimum exchange.

WAYNE BERNHARDSON
Goods from the countryside are hauled to town in brightly painted
horse carts for the Mercado de Abasto in Tucumán.

Downtown banks with ATMs include Banco de Boston at San Martín 736, Banco Quilmes at Maipú 762, Banco Francés at Santa Fe 596, Banca Nazionale del Lavoro at San Martín 879, and Banco Liniers Sudamericano at San Martín 764.

Post & Telecommunications Correo Argentino is at 25 de Mayo and Córdoba; the postal code is 4000. Telecom, at Maipú 480, does not permit collect or credit-card calls from its office, but there are many other locutorios. Tucumán's area code is 081.

Cultural Centers For information on what's happening in town, visit the Universidad Nacional de Tucumán's Centro Cultural Eugenio Flavio Virela (☎ 22-1692), 25 de Mayo 265, which has art exhibitions, an auditorium, and a small café, which is a quiet respite from the noisy downtown area. There are also crafts for sale.

The Centro Cultural Doctor Alberto Rougés, Laprida 31, has rotating exhibits of provincial painters.

Travel Agencies El Delfín Turismo (☎ 30-0608) is at 24 de Setiembre 368, but many other agencies offer travel services, as do most cambios.

Laundry Lavandería Marva is at Santiago del Estero 694, at the corner of Maipú.

Medical Services Hospital Angel C Padilla (☎ 21-9139) is at Alberdi 550.

Public Buildings & Museums
Tucumán is a historic city with a wealth of museums and other public buildings. The most imposing downtown landmark is the turn-of-the-century **Casa de Gobierno,** which replaced the colonial cabildo on Plaza Independencia. The **Basílica Santo Domingo** (1860), on 9 de Julio between Crisóstomo Alvarez and San Lorenzo, and the **Iglesia Catedral** (1845) at the corner of 24 de Setiembre and Congreso, are major ecclesiastical holdings. The **Museo de Arte Sacro,** a religious collection at the Catedral, was closed for repairs as of this writing.

The **Museo Iramain** has collections of sculpture and art on Argentine themes; at Entre Ríos 27, it's open weekdays 8 am to noon and 2 to 7 pm, Saturdays 8 am to noon only. Dating from 1905, the **Museo de Bellas Artes Timoteo Navarro** (☎ 31-0539), 9 de Julio 44, has changing exhibits, including some very imaginative sculptures; it's open weekdays 9:30 am to 12:30 pm and 5 to 8:30 pm, weekends 5:30 to 8:30 pm only.

Other noteworthy museums include the **Museo Histórico de la Provincia** (☎ 21-8250) at Congreso 56, the birthplace of President Nicolás Avellaneda, open 9 am to 12:30 pm weekdays and 5 to 8 pm daily; the **Museo Arqueológico** (☎ 22-1692), at 25 de Mayo 265, displays collections on northwestern Argentine prehistory weekdays 8 am to noon and 5 to 9 pm; and the **Museo Policial,** at Salta and Santa Fe, open weekdays 7:30 am to 1 pm.

Casa Padilla
This partly restored mid-19th-century house, alongside the Casa de Gobierno, first belonged to provincial Governor José Frías (1792-1874), then to his mayor son-in-law Angel Padilla and his son. At 25 de Mayo 36, the musuem (☎ 21-1610) displays a collection of European art and period furniture weekdays 9:30 am to 12:30 pm and 5 to 8 pm, Saturdays and holidays 9 am to 12:30 pm, and Sundays 5 to 8:30 pm.

Casa de la Independencia
Unitarist lawyers and clerics (Federalists boycotted the meeting) declared Argentina's independence from Spain on July 9, 1816, in this dazzlingly whitewashed late-colonial house. Portraits of the signatories line the walls of the room in which the declaration was signed.

The interior patio is a pleasant refuge from Tucumán's commercial bustle. At Congreso 151, 1½ blocks from Plaza Independencia, building hours (☎ 31-0826) are Tuesday to Friday 8:30 am to 1 pm and 3 to

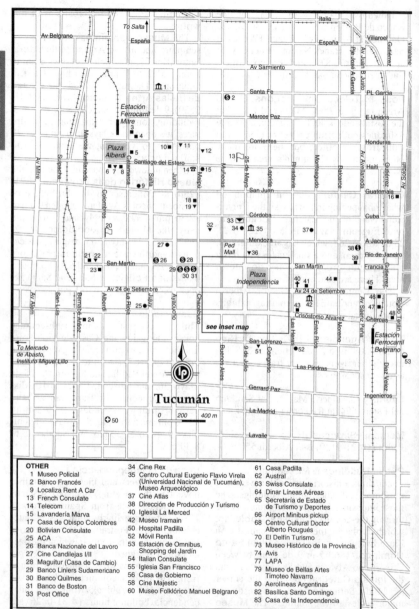

Tucumán

0   200   400 m

OTHER

1 Museo Policial	34 Cine Rex	61 Casa Padilla
2 Banco Francés	35 Centro Cultural Eugenio Flavio Virela	62 Austral
9 Localiza Rent A Car	(Universidad Nacional de Tucumán),	63 Swiss Consulate
13 French Consulate	Museo Arqueológico	64 Dinar Líneas Aéreas
14 Telecom	37 Cine Atlas	65 Secretaría de Estado
15 Lavandería Marva	38 Dirección de Producción y Turismo	de Turismo y Deportes
17 Casa de Obispo Colombres	40 Iglesia La Merced	66 Airport Minibus pickup
20 Bolivian Consulate	42 Museo Iramain	68 Centro Cultural Doctor
25 ACA	50 Hospital Padilla	Alberto Rougués
26 Banca Nazionale del Lavoro	52 Móvil Renta	70 El Delfín Turismo
27 Cine Candilejas I/II	53 Estación de Omnibus,	73 Museo Histórico de la Provincia
28 Maguitur (Casa de Cambio)	Shopping del Jardín	74 Avis
29 Banco Liniers Sudamericano	54 Italian Consulate	77 LAPA
30 Banco Quilmes	55 Iglesia San Francisco	79 Museo de Bellas Artes
31 Banco de Boston	56 Casa de Gobierno	Timoteo Navarro
33 Post Office	58 Cine Majestic	80 Aerolíneas Argentinas
	60 Museo Folklórico Manuel Belgrano	82 Basílica Santo Domingo
		83 Casa de la Independencia

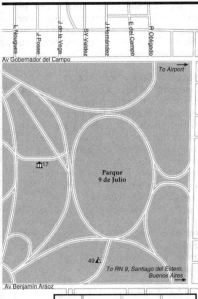

PLACES TO STAY

3 Hotel Norte
4 Hotel California
5 Hotel Tucumán
6 Hotel América
8 Residencial Viena
10 Hotel Miami/Albergue Juvenil
16 Gran Hotel de Tucumán
18 Hotel Maypol
21 Residencial Roni
23 Residencial Royal
24 Hospedaje La Estrella
39 Hotel Colonial
41 24 Palace Hotel
43 Hotel Impala
44 Residencial Independencia
45 Hotel Metropol
46 Hospedaje Autopista
47 Residencial El Parque
48 Hospedaje Charcas
62 Camping Las Lomitas

59 Residencial Florida
67 Hotel del Sol
71 Hotel Mediterráneo
75 Hotel Astoria
76 Hotel Petit
78 Hotel Premier
81 Hotel Francia

PLACES TO EAT

7 Plaza Alberdi
11 El Vesuvio
12 Restaurant Sirio Libanés
19 Restaurant de Tino
22 Paquito
32 Mercado del Norte
36 Café de la Fuente
51 El Duque
57 La Mesa
69 Feria de Artesanos Tucumanos
72 Adela

7:30 pm, weekends 9 am to 1 pm. Admission is US$1.

Museo Folklórico Manuel Belgrano

Occupying a colonial house that once belonged to the family of bishop José Eusebio Colombres, a major figure in the independence movement who also fostered local sugar cultivation, this pleasant and interesting museum features a good collection of River Plate horse gear, indigenous musical instruments and weavings, Toba wood carvings, Quilmes pottery, and samples of *randa* (an intricate lace resembling Paraguayan *ñandutí*) from the village of Monteros, 53 km south of Tucumán. Some items are for sale in the museum shop (☎ 21-8250). At 24 de Setiembre 565, it's open weekdays 7 am to 1 pm and 3 to 9 pm, weekends 9 am to 1 pm and 4 to 9 pm. Admission is free.

Casa del Obispo Colombres

In the center of Parque 9 de Julio, once bishop Colombres's El Bajo plantation, this 18th-century house contains the first ox-powered *trapiche* (sugar mill) of Tucumán's postindependence industry. Guided tours, in Spanish, explain the operation of the mill, some of the equipment of which is still in working order. Hours are weekdays 8 am to noon and 2 to 6 pm, weekends 9 am to 7 pm. Admission is US$1.

Instituto Miguel Lillo

The garden of this natural history museum has life-size replicas of dinosaurs and other fossils from Parque Provincial Ischigualasto in San Juan province. At Miguel Lillo 205, near the Mercado de Abasto, it's open weekdays 9 am to noon and 5:30 to 9 pm.

Mercado de Abasto

Photographers especially should not miss this colorful wholesale/retail market, one of South America's finest, where brightly painted horse carts from the countryside haul their goods to town. Unlike most markets, it is liveliest in mid- to late-afternoon, when the city's restaurateurs go to purchase their produce. At San Lorenzo and Miguel Lillo, it's ten blocks west and three blocks south of Plaza Independencia; the market cafés are very cheap places to eat.

Special Events
Celebrations of Día de la Independencia (Argentina's Independence Day) on July 9 are especially vigorous in Tucumán, the cradle of the country's independence. Tucumanos also celebrate the Batalla de Tucumán (Battle of Tucumán) September 24.

Activities
The staff at Tucumán's provincial Secretaría de Turismo y Deportes has information on a variety of outdoor activities, though its English-language brochure on the possibilities may be more amusing than illuminating:

Tucumán has many scenaries along its geography, apts to practice different sports: sailing, kayaks, hikking, trekking, polo, hanglidding, parashooting, fishing on the mountain rivers, canoing and all the already popular sports.

Tucumán proposes to you to penetrate its forests, valleys, and streams, traveling through its main adventure tourism's circuits.

Trekking and hiking are popular activities in the Sierra de Aconquija; one popular excursion is the four-day hike to Tafí del Valle. Lonely Planet correspondents have enthusiastically recommended Héctor Heredia ("El Oso" or "the Bear," ☎ 22-6205 or fax 30-2222) as a mountain guide for the Sierra, Tafí del Valle, and surrounding areas. Héctor can arrange extended treks in the provinces of Tucumán and Catamarca, and gives a good explanation of what to expect in advance. His address is Balcarce 1067, 4000 San Miguel de Tucumán, República Argentina.

Places to Stay
Tucumán's hotels are generally modern and lack character. The cheapest ones, near the old bus terminal, are generally shabby, but the area around Plaza Alberdi and the Ferrocarril Mitre is experiencing something of a revival, with upgraded but still reasonably priced accommodations and several new restaurants.

Places to Stay – bottom end
Camping Unfortunately, Tucumán's mayor closed the two convenient campgrounds in Parque 9 de Julio in late 1994, but information is included here on the chance that they may reopen. To reach *Las Lomitas,* the nearer and better of the two, either walk down Av Benjamín Aráoz past the university – it's about 20 minutes from the new bus terminal – or take bus No 1 from Crisóstomo Alvarez.

Fees are traditionally very low. The unfenced site is less secure than most Argentine campgrounds – although theft is unlikely, inform the attendant of any occurrences when you leave. If tent camping, choose your site carefully; lower-lying parts flood when it rains very heavily.

If Las Lomitas is not open, the nearest site is at Dique El Cadillal, a reservoir 20 km north of town via RN 9.

Hostel Tucumán's *Albergue Juvenil* (☎ 31-0265), Junín 580, charges US$15 with breakfast included. It occupies part of the mid-range Hotel Miami.

Hospedajes, Residenciales & Hotels
Near the Mitre station, try *Hotel Tucumán* (☎ 22-1809) at Catamarca 563, which is undergoing renovation; singles/doubles with shared bath cost US$10/14, with private bath US$14/21. Rundown *Hotel Norte,* Catamarca 639, is cheaper but seamier for US$10 per person, but the hot showers are good.

About five blocks south, *Residencial Royal* (☎ 21-8697), San Martín 1196 near Colombres, charges US$12/25. The comparably priced *Hotel Maypol* (☎ 21-8311), Maipú 342 between Córdoba and San Juan, is closer to downtown and has a good restaurant downstairs.

Rock-bottom at US$10/15 are *Hospedaje Charcas,* on Crisóstomo Alvarez near

Av Soldati, and *Hospedaje Autopista,* at the corner of Av Benjamín Aráoz and Sargento Gómez. Near the old bus terminal, friendly *Hospedaje La Estrella,* Av Benjamín Aráoz 36, has doubles for only US$20, but gets plenty of short-stay trade. Nearby and only slightly cheaper, dingy and noisy *Residencial El Parque,* Sargento Gómez 22, has an indifferent staff. *Residencial Independencia,* 1½ blocks away at Balcarce 50, charges US$15/25 with private bath. Friendly and central *24 Palace Hotel* (☎ 22-3855), 24 de Setiembre 233, is perhaps the best downtown value, with singles/doubles for US$18/28.

Places to Stay – middle

Residencial Florida (☎ 22-1785), just off the plaza at 24 de Setiembre 610, is friendly, quiet, and central, but very small; upstairs rooms have more and better light. Rooms with fans and shared bath are US$20/32, slightly more with private bath. At modern, boxy *Hotel Astoria* (☎ 21-7876), just off Plaza Independencia at Congreso 92, rates are US$25/33 with private bath; the street itself is very noisy.

Downtown, *Hotel Impala* (☎ 31-0371), at Cristóstomo Alvarez 274, is clean and modern for US$25/35 with private bath. *Hotel Petit* (☎ 21-3902), Cristóstomo Alvarez 675, is comparable but has slightly cheaper rooms with shared bath for US$20/30. Nearby *Hotel Francia* (☎ 22-9780), Cristóstomo Alvarez 467, costs US$33/45. *Hotel Colonial* (☎ 31-1523), San Martín 35 between Av Avellaneda and Balcarce, comes very highly recommended for US$30/40 – even though there's nothing remotely colonial about this very modern building.

Residencial Viena (☎ 31-0004), Santiago del Estero 1054 opposite the Mitre station, has rooms for US$20/30. *Residencial Roni* (☎ 21-1434), San Martín 1177, wins an award for one of the weirdest entrances to any Argentine hotel – a bridge across the hallway leads into the lobby – but rates are reasonable at US$22/25. An equally good value is spiffy *Hotel América* (☎ 22-4853), Santiago del Estero 1064, where basic rates

are US$28/40 but more comfortable VIP rooms go for US$33/45. Also near the Mitre station, *Hotel California* (☎ 22-9259) at Corrientes 985 charges US$29/42, while *Hotel Miami* at Junín 580 costs US$32/48.

Places to Stay – top end

At 24 de Setiembre 364, opposite Plaza Independencia, the modern but attractive *Hotel Mediterráneo* (☎ 31-0025) charges US$50/65 for rooms with cable TV and room service; English and French are spoken. *Hotel Premier* (☎ 31-0381), Cristóstomo Alvarez 502, charges US$55/65. More expensive but perhaps a lesser value are the central high-rises like *Hotel del Sol* (☎ 31-0393), Laprida 35, where rates are about US$66/86, and *Hotel Metropol* (☎ 31-1180), 24 de Setiembre 524, for US$70/90.

Near Parque 9 de Julio, a bit away from downtown at Av Los Próceres 380, five-star *Gran Hotel de Tucumán* (☎ 24-5000) is the city's best and most expensive for US$95/110.

Places to Eat

One of the best places to explore for inexpensive food is the colorful Mercado de Abasto (see separate entry above), but the more central *Mercado del Norte,* at Mendoza and Maipú, is another possibility.

Closer to downtown, try the outstanding *Feria de Artesanos Tucumanos,* on 24 de Setiembre half a block from Plaza Independencia. Behind its crafts shops, a variety of small stands prepare tasty regional specialties; the first one on your left as you enter has exceptional humitas and chicken empanadas. Other regional foods are available at *Restaurant de Tino,* Maipú 344 next to Hotel Maypol, and at *Paquito* (☎ 22-9021), San Martín 1165.

For breakfast, try *Café de la Fuente* (☎ 22-2074) at 25 de Mayo 183, where coffee or chocolate, two medialunas, a small glass of fresh squeezed orange juice, and a glass of soda water costs less than US$2; it's also air-conditioned.

Middle Eastern food is the specialty at

ARGENTINA

Adela (☎ 22-6533), 24 de Setiembre 358, and at *Restaurant Sirio Libanés* on Maipú between Corrientes and Santiago del Estero. *La Mesa,* San Martín 437, is a very good and reasonably priced parrilla by current Argentine standards, as is *Plaza Alberdi* on Santiago del Estero, across from Plaza Alberdi. *El Vesuvio,* at the corner of Junín and Corrientes, is an attractively remodeled parrilla. One LP reader has highly recommended *El Duque,* San Lorenzo 440.

Entertainment

Tucumán is large enough to have several cinemas showing recent international films, including *Candilejas I/II* (☎ 30-1901) at Mendoza 826, the *Cine Atlas* (☎ 22-0825) at Monteagudo 250, the *Rex* (☎ 21-7688) at 25 de Mayo 267, and the *Majestic* (☎ 21-7515) at 24 de Setiembre 666.

Getting There & Away

Air Aerolíneas Argentinas (☎ 31-1030), 9 de Julio 112, flies at least twice daily to Aeroparque (US$207); its Sunday evening flight stops in Córdoba (US$82). The only international flight is Sunday to Rio de Janeiro.

Austral (☎ 31-0427, 31-0889), at 24 de Setiembre 546 next to Hotel Metropol, has daily flights to and from Córdoba; northbound flights continue to Salta and/or Jujuy (US$55).

LAPA (☎ 30-2630), at Crisóstomo Alvarez 620, 1st floor, Oficina 3, flies Tuesday, Thursday, and Saturday to and from Buenos Aires (US$99); northbound flights continue to Salta (US$29).

Dinar Líneas Aéreas (☎ 22-2974), at 9 de Julio and 24 de Noviembre, has five flights weekly to Aeroparque (US$166), five to Salta (US$30), and six to Jujuy (US$45).

Bus At Brígido Terán 350, Tucumán's sparkling new Estación de Omnibus opened in December 1994. This major public works project has 60 platforms, a post office, telephone services, a supermarket, bars, and restaurants; in the complex, Shopping del Jardín's information booth

(☎ 30-6400, 30-2060), open daily 6:30 am to 11:30 pm, provides information on the Estación and the shopping center only. The entire scheme was the brainchild of the province's ambitious former governor, Ramón (Palito) Ortega, a onetime crooner with presidential hopes, who was constitutionally ineligible to succeed himself in office.

Aconquija (☎ 22-7620) goes to Tafí del Valle (US$9, three hours) at 10 am and 12:30 and 4 pm, and to Cafayate (US$20, seven hours) at 6 am and 2 pm daily. El Tucumano (☎ 22-6442) goes to Córdoba (8½ hours), Rosario, Buenos Aires, Termas de Río Hondo, Santiago del Estero, Salta (4½ hours), and Jujuy (5½ hours); Veloz del Norte (☎ 21-7860) has similar routes and also crosses the Chaco to Resistencia. Benjamín Aráoz (☎ 30-0934) has recliner *leito* service to Buenos Aires for US$80.

Panamericano (☎ 31-0544) heads north to Salta and Jujuy, and south to Córdoba. Bosio (☎ 22-8940) has similar routes and also goes to Mendoza. La Estrella (☎ 21-2098) goes daily to Mendoza via Catamarca and La Rioja, and also to Santa Fe, Rosario, Buenos Aires, Mar del Plata, Salta, Jujuy, Santa Rosa, and Neuquén. TAC (☎ 30-6663) goes to Catamarca, La Rioja, San Juan, Mendoza (US$48, 15 hours), Trelew, Puerto Madryn, Comodoro Rivadavia, Río Gallegos (US$151, 44 hours), Buenos Aires (US$57, 16 hours), Bariloche, Neuquén, and San Martín de los Andes. It also has international services to Santiago de Chile. Andesmar (☎ 22-5702) passes through Tucumán on its routes between Mendoza and Jujuy.

El Rayo (☎ 21-5850) crosses the Chaco to Roque Sáenz Peña, Resistencia, and Corrientes (US$34, 13 hours). Empresa Itatí goes to Posadas, Puerto Iguazú, and Buenos Aires (US$60, 20 hours). Atahualpa goes to Pocitos, on the Bolivian border, for US$30, and to Jujuy, Córdoba, Rosario, and Buenos Aires. Chevallier serves Rosario, Córdoba, and Buenos Aires more cheaply than Itatí. Cacorba (☎ 22-6111), El Galgo (☎ 26-6905), and La Unión (☎ 31-0653) all go to Termas de Río

Hondo (US$4, 1½ hours) and Santiago del Estero (US$5, two hours); Cacorba also goes to Córdoba and Buenos Aires. El Ranchilleño (☎ 22-2220) also has several buses daily to Termas de Río Hondo and Santiago del Estero.

Train From the Ferrocarril Mitre station (☎ 31-0725) at Catamarca and Corrientes, opposite Plaza Alberdi, *El Tucumano* goes to Buenos Aires via Santiago del Estero (La Banda) and Rosario Tuesday, Thursday, and Saturday. For fare information, see the Buenos Aires chapter.

Getting Around
To/From the Airport Aeropuerto Internacional Benjamín Matienzo (☎ 26-0121) is eight km east of downtown via Av Gobernador del Campo, the northern boundary of Parque 9 de Julio. Empresa Sáenz Alderete runs minibuses to the airport (US$2.50) that leave 1¼ hours before flight time from opposite the entrance to Gran Hotel Corona on Calle 9 de Julio, half a block from Plaza Independencia.

Bus City buses do not accept cash, so you must buy cospeles (US50¢ each) at downtown kiosks; they are less readily available outside the center.

Car Rental Try Móvil Renta (☎ 21-8635) at San Lorenzo 370, Avis (☎ 21-3373) at Congreso 60, Localiza (☎ 31-1352) at San Juan 959, or RentaCar (☎ 21-1372) at Av Soldati 380.

AROUND TUCUMÁN
Ruins of San José de Lules
Until 1767, this mission 20 km south of Tucumán was a Jesuit reducción among the region's Lule Indians. After the Jesuits' expulsion, the Dominicans assumed control of the complex, whose present ruins date from the 1880s and once served as a school. The small museum has replicas of colonial documents and a plethora of busts of various heroes of Argentine independence. There are numerous ghost stories

about the place, and legends of buried Jesuit treasure.

To get to Lules, a pleasant site for an afternoon outing, take the Trebol, Provincial, or El Centauro bus from downtown Tucumán.

TAFÍ DEL VALLE
From Tucumán, RN 38 heads southwest through sprawling cane fields, punctuated by the ingenios (industrial mills) of large sugar companies, before intersecting RP 307 at Acheral. From Acheral, the road snakes up the narrow gorge of the Río de los Sosas where, in places, the rising river has so eroded the highway that even a single vehicle can barely pass. On all sides dense, verdant subtropical forest covers the hills – this is the refuge where, in the late 1970s, the Argentine army wiped out the Ejército Revolucionario (ERP), ending their dreams of emulating Fidel Castro's success in the Sierra Maestra of Cuba, another sugar-producing zone.

About 100 km from Tucumán, the gorge opens onto a misty valley beneath the snowy peaks of the Nevado del Aconquija. When summer heat drives tucumanos out of the sweltering provincial capital, they seek refuge in the cool heights around the hill station of Tafí del Valle, whose permanent population of 6000 can briefly swell to 15,000 or more. Beyond Tafí, the newly paved road zigzags over the 3050-meter

---

Duendes & the Yastay

Tafí del Valle is known for its folklore, particularly stories of the mythical figures that live in the surrounding mountains. Among them is the yastay, known as the *dueño de los cerros* (owner of the mountains). When villagers go hunting or are searching for lost livestock, they need to bring an offering of yerba mate, gin, alcohol, or tobacco for the yastay; they sometimes sacrifice terneras to him. The hills are also home to duendes, the spirits of children who died unbaptized and are condemned to roam the hills for ten years, at which time their spirits go to heaven and their bodies to earth. ∎

ARGENTINA

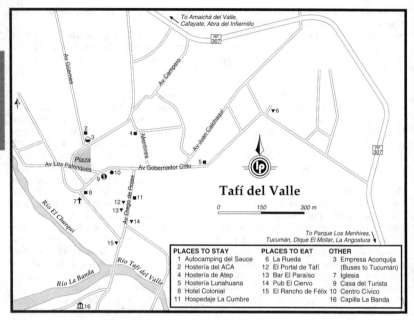

To Amaichá del Valle, Cafayate, Abra del Infiernillo

RP 307

Av Güemes

Av Campero

Av Juan Calchaquí

Menhires

RP 307

Plaza

Av Los Palenques

Av Gobernador Critto

Av Diego de Rojas

Río El Churquí

Río Tafí del Valle

Río La Banda

Tafí del Valle

0   150   300 m

To Parque Los Menhires,
Tucumán, Dique El Mollar, La Angostura

PLACES TO STAY	PLACES TO EAT	OTHER
1 Autocamping del Sauce	6 La Rueda	3 Empresa Aconquija
2 Hostería del ACA	12 El Portal de Tafí	(Buses to Tucumán)
4 Hostería de Atep	13 Bar El Paraíso	7 Iglesia
5 Hostería Lunahuana	14 Pub El Ciervo	9 Casa del Turista
8 Hotel Colonial	15 El Rancho de Félix	10 Centro Cívico
11 Hospedaje La Cumbre		16 Capilla La Banda

pass known as Abra del Infiernillo (Little Hell), an alternative route to Cafayate and Salta. It is possible to visit the impressive Diaguita Indians ruins at Quilmes.

Prior to the arrival of the Spaniards, Calchaquí Indians inhabited the Tafí valley, raising potatoes and herding llamas in dispersed settlements. After the Spanish conquest and decline of the encomienda, the Jesuits acquired the valley, which enjoyed a new prosperity until their expulsion in 1767. With Argentine independence, the isolated valley declined economically for more than a century until a new highway made it possible to get crops to market and tourists to the valley.

A temperate island in a subtropical sea, Tafí del Valle produces seed potatoes and fruits (apples, pears, and peaches) for Tucumán. It also pastures cattle, sheep, and, at higher altitudes, llamas; overgrazing and other unfortunate agricultural practices have turned some of the surrounding area into something resembling arid badlands,

surprising considering the humid, mid-latitude, high-altitude environment.

Typical products include sweets and dairy products – in early February, the town celebrates the **Fiesta Nacional del Queso** (National Cheese Festival). There is good fishing for trout and pejerrey in La Angostura, the reservoir formed by Dique El Mollar.

Orientation
At the north end of the reservoir formed by Dique El Mollar, Tafí del Valle sits 2000 meters above sea level. It is 70 km from Quilmes and 113 km from Cafayate via RP 307. Most public services are on or very near the Centro Cívico, which features an unusual semicircular plaza.

Information
Tafí's helpful Casa del Turista (☎ 21020) is open weekdays 7:30 am to 7:30 pm, weekends 10 am to 4 pm. There is an excellent small café in the Centro Cívico, but the

nearby peatonal is marred by a deafening video arcade.

Banco de la Provincia, in the Centro Cívico, will change US cash. Long distance telephones are also here; Tafí's area code is 0867.

Capilla La Banda

This 18th-century Jesuit chapel, acquired by the Frías Silva family of Tucumán on the Jesuits' expulsion and then expanded in the 1830s, was restored to its original configuration in the 1970s. Note the escape tunnel in the chapel. The small archaeological collection consists mostly of funerary urns, but also religious art of the Cuzco school, ecclesiastical vestments, and period furniture that once belonged to the Frías Silvas. Guided tours are available, and admission costs US$1.

The chapel is a short distance south of downtown, across the bridge over the Río Tafí del Valle and up the dirt road to the west.

Parque Los Menhires

More than eighty aboriginal granite monuments, resembling the standing stones of the Scottish Hebrides, cover the hillside at the southern end of La Angostura reservoir. Collected from various sites throughout the valley, these sculptures of human and animal forms had a ritual significance that archaeologists have not yet completely deciphered.

Hiking

Several nearby peaks and destinations make hiking in the mountains around Tafí del Valle an attractive prospect; try climbing 3000-meter **Cerro El Matadero,** a four- to five-hour climb; 3800-meter **Cerro Pabellón** (six hours); and 4600-meter **Cerro Negrito,** reached from the statue of Cristo Redentor on RN 307 to Acheral. The village of La Ciénaga is about seven hours away. The trails are badly marked, and no trail maps are available. Ask for more information at the tourist office.

Places to Stay

Tafí's recently reopened *Autocamping del Sauce* (☎ 21084) is acceptable for US$2.50 per person, but toilets and showers are very run-down; although the grounds are well kept, shade is limited (a lesser problem in overcast Tafí than elsewhere in the country). Bunks in small cabañas are available for US$5 per person, but these would be very cramped at their maximum capacity of four persons.

Hospedaje La Cumbre, Diego de Rojas 311, charges US$10 per person for rooms with shared bath, meals included, for US$4; *Hospedaje La Tinaja* and *Hospedaje Celia Correa* are comparable. The union-run *Hostería de Atep* (☎ 21061; ☎ 22-1602 in Tucumán) costs just US$12 for accommodations only, US$25 with all meals, while *Hotel Colonial* (☎ 21-4040 in Tucumán) charges US$25 per person with half-board. The well-kept *Hostería del ACA* (☎ 21027; ☎ 31-0603 in Tucumán) theoretically accepts members only, for US$27/40 single/double, but in practice they're much less discriminating.

Newer and much more upscale accommodations cost US$49/59 at *Hotel Tafí* (☎ 21007), Belgrano s/n, and for US$70/90 at *Hostería Lunahuana* (☎ 21330) at Av Gobernador Critto 540.

Places to Eat

Pub El Ciervo, on Diego de Rojas next to the YPF station, has moderately priced minutas, including humitas. Nearby locals congregate at *Bar El Paraíso* to eat an inexpensive dinner and watch Steven Seagal videos. *El Rancho de Félix* serves regional food and is probably the best choice in town, but *La Rueda* is also worth a look. *El Portal de Tafí* has repulsively kitsch decor, especially the animal skins stretched across the walls, but there's a good and varied menu of sandwiches, meat, and pasta.

Things to Buy

The crafts shop at the west end of the peatonal near the Centro Cívico has good pottery, jewelry, and blankets, but also a fair amount of dreck.

Getting There & Away
Tafí's bus station is on the north side of the plaza. Empresa Aconquija has buses to Tucumán at 4 and 6 am, and 1:30, 4:30, 6, and 10 pm.

Getting Around
Hourly in summer, every three hours in winter, local Aconquija buses do most of the circuit around Cerro El Pelado, in the middle of the valley. One goes on the north side, another on the south side, so it's possible to make a circuit of the valley by walking the link between them.

QUILMES
Dating from about 1000 AD, Quilmes was a complex urban settlement that occupied about 30 hectares and housed as many as 5000 people. The Quilmes Indians survived contact with the Incas from about 1480 AD, but could not outlast the siege of the Spaniards who, in 1667, deported the last 2000 Quilmes to Buenos Aires.

Quilmes' thick walls underscore its defensive functions, but clearly this was more than just a pucará. Dense construction sprawls both north and south from the central nucleus, where the outlines of buildings, in a variety of shapes, are obvious even to the casual observer. For revealing views of the form, density, and extent of the ruins, climb the trails up either flank of the nucleus, which offer vistas of the valley once only glimpsed by the defenders of the city. Give yourself at least half a day, preferably more, to explore the nucleus and the surrounding area.

There is a small museum at the entrance, whose US$2 admission charge also entitles you to explore the ruins. It is possible to camp on the site. Buses from Cafayate to Santa María or Tafí del Valle will drop passengers at the junction, but from there you'll have to walk or hitch (there is little traffic) five km to the ruins. It will probably be easier to get a lift back to the highway, since you can approach any vehicle visiting the ruins.

Santiago del Estero Province

The hot, subtropical lowland province of Santiago del Estero is a transitional area between the Gran Chaco and the Andes; cotton is the dominant crop. Its namesake capital is Argentina's oldest city, from which the region's other cities were founded. Termas de Río Hondo, the province's second city, is a popular winter resort known for its mild climate and thermal mineral waters.

SANTIAGO DEL ESTERO
Founded in 1553 by Francisco de Aguirre, the "Madre de Ciudades" (Mother of Cities) was Spain's first urban settlement in what is now Argentina; for centuries it was an important stopover between the Pampas and the mines of Bolivia. The city and province rely on agriculture, cotton being the most important crop, and irrigation supplements the sometimes undependable rainfall. Often, crops are grown on seasonally inundated *bañados* as flood waters recede; these areas shift with the annual movements of the Río Dulce.

In December 1993, provincial employees, disgruntled at not having been paid for four months, set fires that destroyed the interiors of two historical buildings. Tourist office brochures describe the event as "an energetic social protest," but the conflict was serious enough to bring federal intervention to the province. The fires proved to be only the first incidents of ongoing unrest.

Orientation
Santiago del Estero, with a population of about 200,000, sits on the west bank of the Río Dulce, 1045 km northwest of Buenos Aires. It is about 440 km north of Córdoba by RN 9, and 170 km southeast of Tucumán by the same highway.

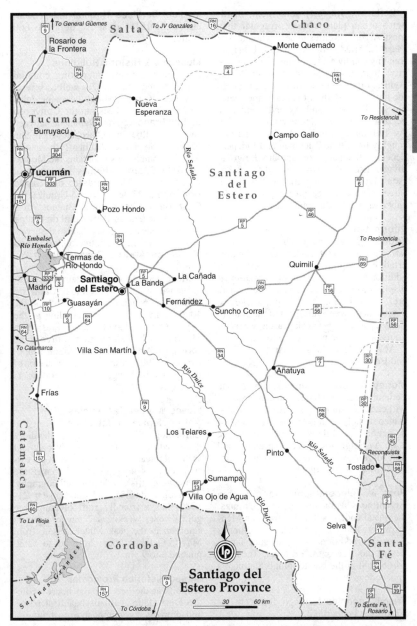

Santiago del
Estero Province

0   30   60 km

Reflecting its early settlement, Santiago's urban plan is more irregular than most Argentine cities. The town center is Plaza Libertad, from which Av Libertad, trending southwest to northeast, bisects the city; at its northern end, woodsy Parque Aguirre offers relief from summer heat. To the north and south of the plaza, the peatonal Av Tucumán and Av Independencia become important commercial areas, but Av Belgrano, crossing Av Libertad and roughly parallel to Tucumán and Independencia, is the main thoroughfare. Belgrano divides itself into Norte (north) and Sur (south) on each side of Av Rivadavia. Street names change on each side of Av Libertad and Av Belgrano.

Information

Tourist Offices The provincial Subsecretaría de Turismo (☎ 21-3253) is at Av Libertad 417, opposite Plaza Libertad. In addition to providing visitor information, it displays work by local artists. Hours hours are 7 am to 1 pm and 3 to 9 pm weekdays, 9 am to noon weekends most of the year; in the May to October peak season, weekend hours are 9 am to noon and 3 to 6 pm.

ACA (☎ 21-2270) is at Av Sáenz Peña and Belgrano.

Money Noroeste Cambios, on 24 de Setiembre between 9 de Julio and Urquiza, will change cash but not traveler's checks. Banco de la Nación is at 9 de Julio and 24 de Setiembre, while Banco de la Provincia is on Av Belgrano between Sarmiento and San Martín. Banco Crédito Argentino has an ATM at 24 de Setiembre 256.

Post & Telecommunications Correo Argentino is at Buenos Aires and Urquiza; the postal code is 4200. Telecom, on Mendoza between Independencia and Buenos Aires, has additional long-distance facilities at the Telecentro Peatonal, Tucumán 64/66, and at the bus terminal. Santiago's area code is 085.

Travel Agencies Santiago Tours (☎ 22-4726) is at Pellegrini 33.

Medical Services Hospital Independencia (☎ 21-1515) is at Av Belgrano 660 Norte.

Museums & Historic Buildings

Santiago has many interesting colonial buildings and museums, as well as several more recent ones. Besides the major sights described below, check out the **Convento de San Francisco** on Avellaneda between Av General Roca and Olaechea, where San Francisco Solano resided in a 16th-century cell; the complex also contains the **Museo de Arte Sacro** (religious art museum, ☎ 21-1548). The **Iglesia de Santo Domingo** at 25 de Mayo and Urquiza, the **Casa de los Taboada** at Buenos Aires 136, and the **Museo Provincial de Bellas Artes** at Independencia 222 also deserve a visit. At Mitre 127, visit the folkloric **Casa Museo de Andrés Chazarreta** (☎ 21-1905).

Monuments of more contemporary significance are the neocolonial **Casa de Gobierno** (which opened in 1953, on the 400th anniversary of the founding of the city), west of downtown on Plaza San Martín; and the **Palacio Legislativo** at the corner of Avellaneda and 25 de Mayo. Arson in 1993 destroyed the interiors of these two buildings, but restoration is underway.

Museo Wagner de Ciencias Antropológicas y Naturales

Chronologically arranged and splendidly displayed, this superb natural history and archaeological collection focuses on fossils, funerary urns (owls and snakes are recurring motifs), and Chaco ethnography. At Avellaneda 355, the museum (☎ 21-1380) has a friendly staff offering free guided tours weekdays 7 am to 1 pm in summer; in the peak winter season, from May to October, hours are 8 am to 12:30 pm and 3 to 9 pm.

Museo Histórico Provincial

Exhibits at the late-colonial house of Pedro Díaz Gallo, with its beautiful patios and colonnades, emphasize postcolonial

PLACES TO STAY
7   Residencial Santa Rita
8   Hotel Rodas
9   Residencial Emaus,
    Hotel Bristol
10 Residencial Iovino
20 Hotel Centro
25 Campamento Las Casuarinas
28 Hotel Libertador
32 Hotel Savoy
33 Residencial Petit Colonial
36 Hotel Palace
37 Hotel Florida
41 Gran Hotel

PLACES TO EAT
3   Taffik
4   Parrilla El Vasco
22 El Faro

23 La Casa del Folclorista
30 Mercado Armonía
34 Mía Mamma
38 Comedor Centro de Viajantes
40 Tequila Station
43 Comedor Universitario

OTHER
1   Hospital Independencia
2   Casa de Gobierno
5   ACA
6   Estación Terminal de Omnibus
11 Banco de la Provincia
12 Banco de la Nación
13 Iglesia de la Merced
14 Noroeste Cambios
15 Banco Crédito Argentino
16 Post Office
17 Museo Provincial de Bellas Artes

18 Museo Histórico Provincial
19 Iglesia de Santo Domingo
21 Convento de San Francisco,
    Museo de Arte Sacro
24 Zoo
26 Telecom
27 Casa Museo de Andrés Chazarreta
29 Santiago Tours
31 Telecom
35 Subsecretaría de Turismo
39 Austral
42 Casa de los Taboada
44 Museo Wagner de Ciencias
    Antropológicas y Naturales
45 Palacio Legislativo,
    Teatro 25 de Mayo

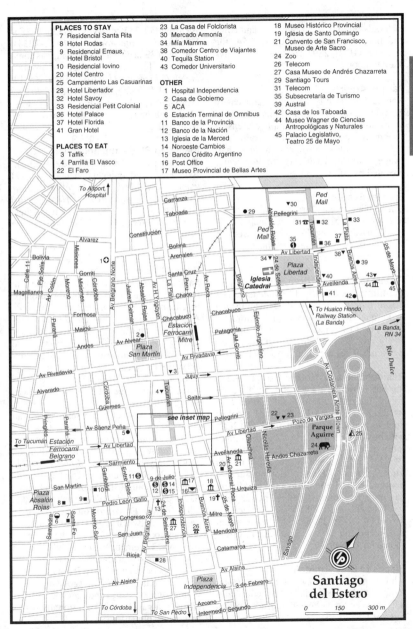

Santiago
del Estero

history, displaying religious and civil art, materials on elite local families, and coins and paper money. At Urquiza 354, the museum (☎ 21-2893) is open weekdays 8 am to noon.

Parque Aguirre

Named for the city's founder and easily accessible from downtown, this enormous park has a small zoo, camping areas, a swimming pool (when the erratic Río Dulce provides sufficient water), and (watch your step!) a drivers' training center operated by ACA.

Special Events

Santiago's chaotic Carnaval, in February, resembles celebrations in the Quebrada de Humahuaca. During the entire last week of July, santiagueños celebrate the founding of the city.

Places to Stay – bottom end

Camping The municipal *Campamento Las Casuarinas* is a pleasant, shady, secure area in Parque Aguirre, less than a kilometer from Plaza Libertad, but it can be oppressively crowded and deafeningly noisy on weekends. Fees are about US$5 per site.

Residenciales & Hotels Except around the bus terminal, there's not much really cheap lodging. *Residencial Santa Rita* (☎ 22-0625), Santa Fe 273, has singles/doubles with shared bath for US$12/20, with private bath for US$14/25; the comparably priced *Residencial Petit Colonial* (☎ 21-1261) is downtown at La Plata 65. Tiny *Residencial Emaus,* Moreno Sur 673 between Pedro León Gallo and San Martín, has only five rooms, but is friendly and spotlessly clean for US$13/22. *Residencial Iovino* (☎ 21-3311), near the bus terminal at Moreno Sur 602 at San Martín, offers rooms for US$19/30.

Places to Stay – middle

Almost next door to the terminal, *Hotel Rodas* (☎ 21-8484), at Pedro León Gallo 430 between Santa Fe and Saavedra, offers rates of US$26/38.

Downtown *Hotel Florida* (☎ 21-8664), Av Libertad 355, charges US$25/35. For US$28/35, *Hotel Savoy* (☎ 21-1234), Tucumán 39 near Plaza Libertad, has some character but very cramped bathrooms. *Hotel Palace* (☎ 21-2701), Tucumán 19, charges US$38/52. Rates at *Hotel Bristol* (☎ 21-8387), Moreno Sur 677 next to Residencial Emaus, are identical to those of Hotel Palace.

Places to Stay – top end

The four-star *Gran Hotel* (☎ 22-4383), at Avellaneda and Independencia, is a good value at US$48/65, as is *Hotel Libertador* (☎ 22-4383), Catamarca 47. *Hotel Centro* (☎ 21-4622), 9 de Julio 131, is the costliest in town at about US$60/70 with private bath.

Places to Eat

Santiago's *Mercado Armonía,* on Pellegrini between the Tucumán and Rojas peatonals, is cheap but less appealing than some Argentine markets. The *Comedor Universitario,* Avellaneda 364, has cheap if uninspiring food, but offers opportunities to meet local students. Better but still reasonably priced meals are available at the *Comedor Centro de Viajantes,* Buenos Aires 37; other inexpensive eating places are near the bus terminal.

There are several better restaurants and popular confiterías around Plaza Libertad, such as *Tequila Station* on Independencia between Av Libertad and Avellaneda. Moderately priced *Mía Mamma* (☎ 21-2242), 24 de Setiembre 15, has a very extensive menu of Italian dishes and parrillada, plus a good and inexpensive salad bar. *Parrilla El Vasco,* on the Tucumán peatonal between Jujuy and Salta, is another good choice. *Taffik,* at the corner of Jujuy and Tucumán, serves Middle Eastern food and also offers takeout service.

Alongside each other in Parque Aguirre on Av Libertad are *El Faro* (good draft beer with outdoor seating) and *La Casa del Folclorista,* a parrilla that occasionally offers live entertainment.

ARGENTINA

Entertainment
Within the same building as the Palacio Legislativo is the *Teatro 25 de Mayo* (☎ 21-4141), Santiago's prime theater venue.

Things to Buy
The Tucumán peatonal has an evening crafts market, featuring jewelry and leather goods.

Getting There & Away
Air Austral (☎ 22-4335), Buenos Aires 60, has flights weekdays only to Aeroparque (US$176) and to Jujuy (US$83).

Bus Santiago's aging Estación Terminal de Omnibus (☎ 21-3746) is at Pedro León Gallo and Saavedra, eight blocks south of Plaza Libertad. Santiago del Estero is a junction for important highways leading in several directions.

La Unión (☎ 21-3173) has 14 buses daily to Termas de Río Hondo (US$3), an hour to the northwest, continuing to Tucumán (US$7), and also goes to Rosario and Buenos Aires. Panamericano (☎ 21-5329) goes north to Salta (US$25, six hours) and Jujuy (US$28, seven hours), and leaves eight times daily for Córdoba; the express services are faster and more comfortable, but only slightly costlier, than the local buses. La Veloz del Norte goes to Buenos Aires, Rosario, Córdoba, Jujuy, Salta, Tucumán, and Pocitos, on the Bolivian border. Central Argentino goes to Tucumán, Buenos Aires (US$45, 13 hours), and La Plata.

Cotal goes to Mendoza, San Juan, Catamarca, Corrientes, and Posadas. TAC and Gutiérrez both go to Buenos Aires, while TAC has additional services to the Cuyo region. Libertador goes three times weekly to La Rioja (US$16), San Juan (US$32), and Mendoza (US$36). Bosio has daily buses to Catamarca (US$14), San Juan, La Rioja, and Mendoza.

El Santiagueño (☎ 22-0636) goes to Córdoba (US$19, six hours), as does Cacorba (☎ 21-3454), which sends five buses daily (US$18), as well as one daily to Buenos Aires (US$45, 16 hours). Chevallier (☎ 21-

5880), slightly cheaper to the federal capital, also has two daily buses to Rosario (US$25), plus service to Tucumán and Córdoba. La Estrella (☎ 21-3484) serves Santa Fe (US$30), Paraná (US$32), and Mar del Plata (US$52), while Empresa Tata (☎ 21-8251) goes to Rosario and Buenos Aires.

El Rayo crosses the Chaco to Roque Sáenz Peña (US$20), Resistencia (US$25), and Corrientes (US$27, nine hours), with connections to Puerto Iguazú, and also goes to Rosario and Buenos Aires; Empresa Martín goes to Resistencia, Corrientes, and Posadas as well. Patagonian carrier Ute Comahue goes to Neuquén, with connections to Bahía Blanca, Viedma, Bariloche, and Río Gallegos. Tus and Tup go to Santa Rosa de La Pampa and Patagonian destinations.

Train The Ferrocarril Mitre's station is in the suburb of La Banda. *El Tucumano,* which links Buenos Aires and Tucumán, stops here Mondays, Wednesdays, and Fridays northbound, and Tuesdays, Thursdays, and Sundays southbound.

Getting Around
Central Santiago del Estero is compact and walking suffices for almost everything except connections to the train station and the airport.

To/From the Airport Bus No 19 goes to Aeropuerto Mal Paso (☎ 22-2386), six km southwest of downtown on Av Madre de Ciudades.

Train From Moreno and Libertad in downtown Santiago, buses Nos 10, 14, 18, and 21 all go to the Ferrocarril Mitre station in La Banda.

TERMAS DE RÍO HONDO
With 12,000 beds in 190 hotels, plus rental apartments, houses, chalets, and three campgrounds in a town with just 25,000 permanent residents, Termas de Río Hondo lives and dies by tourism. Competition keeps prices reasonable, but outside the

peak winter season, May to October, most accommodations and many businesses shut down.

The primary attraction of Termas de Río Hondo is its thermal springs – even the most basic accommodations have hot mineral baths. Outside town, the 30,000-hectare Dique Frontal is a reservoir used for water sports like swimming, boating, fishing, and windsurfing.

The town proper has two unusual features – its triangular Plaza San Martín, and one of few monuments in the country with busts of both Juan and Evita Perón.

Orientation

Midway between Santiago del Estero and Tucumán, Termas de Río Hondo has a very irregular city plan, but the main thoroughfare is Av Alberdi (RN 9). Perpendicular Av Perón leads south to the Dique Frontal.

Information

Tourist Office The helpful Dirección Municipal de Turismo (☎ 21721), Caseros 132 between Rivadavia and Sarmiento, remains open 7 am to 9 pm daily, but closes for lunch from 1 to 3 pm in summer, 1 to 2 pm in winter. *El Frontal de Río Hondo,* the town's weekly newspaper, publishes a 24-page tourist supplement (US$2) of more than you ever wanted to know about thermal baths.

Money Only Banco de la Nación, on Caseros, does foreign exchange, but don't expect to change traveler's checks.

Post & Telecommunications Correo Argentino is on Av Alberdi between 9 de Julio and Maipú; the postal code is 4220. Telecom is at the corner of Sarmiento and Caseros; Termas de Río Hondo's area code is 0858.

Laundry Laverap is at Av San Martín 465, between Fleming and Yrigoyen.

Medical Services The Hospital Rural (☎ 21578) is at Antonino Taboada and Buenos Aires, west of downtown.

Places to Stay

Camping Along the river, several camp-grounds near downtown charge around US$3 per person: *Camping Mirador* (☎ 21392), *Camping del Río* (☎ 21985), and *Camping La Olla* (☎ 21857). Several km outside town, on the road to the Dique Frontal, *Camping del ACA* (☎ 21648) is friendly, shady, and spotless, but the noise from the *cucuyos* (insects in the trees) can be deafening in summer.

Hotels Most of Río Hondo's hotels close in summer, but a few remain open. Prices nearly double during the winter high season; those below are low season unless otherwise indicated. Among the best bargains are *Residencial El Parque* (☎ 21673) at Belgrano and Libertad for US$8 per person, *Residencial Mon Petit* (☎ 21822) at Alberdi 602, and *Hotel Las Vegas* (☎ 21010) at Absalón Rojas 17, both in the US$10 range.

Hotel Termal Los Felipe (☎ 21484), San Francisco Solano 230, costs US$12.50 per person in summer, US$20 per person in winter. *Hotel Los Olivos* (☎ 21313), Mar del Plata 455, charges US$15 per person.

The *Casino Center Hotel* (☎ 21346), Caseros 126, costs US$25 per person with breakfast in summer, US$35 in winter. Rates at four-star *Hotel Los Pinos* (☎ 21043), Maipú 20, are US$50 per person.

Places to Eat

For US$5, the dorado a la portuguesa at *La Cabaña de los Changos,* at Av Alberdi and Libertad, is an exceptional value, with more than enough for two persons; other fish dishes are also available. For other regional specialties at moderate prices, try *La Casa de Rubén,* a parrilla at Sarmiento and Caseros, and *Sabot,* on Caseros opposite Plaza San Martín, serving parrillada and international dishes. *Chorizo Loco,* at the corner of Alberdi and Sarmiento, specializes in grilled meats.

Heladería Trieste, at the corner Sarmiento and Caseros, serves Río Hondo's best ice cream.

ARGENTINA

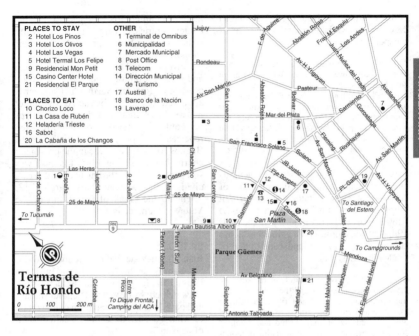

PLACES TO STAY
2 Hotel Los Pinos
3 Hotel Los Olivos
4 Hotel Las Vegas
5 Hotel Termal Los Felipe
9 Residencial Mon Petit
15 Casino Center Hotel
21 Residencial El Parque

PLACES TO EAT
10 Chorizo Loco
11 La Casa de Rubén
12 Heladería Trieste
16 Sabot
20 La Cabaña de los Changos

OTHER
1 Terminal de Omnibus
6 Municipalidad
7 Mercado Municipal
8 Post Office
13 Telecom
14 Dirección Municipal
   de Turismo
17 Austral
18 Banco de la Nación
19 Laverap

Getting There & Away

Air Austral (☎ 21631) is at Rivadavia 358. Flights from Buenos Aires to Santiago have a direct bus connection to Río Hondo.

Bus The Terminal de Omnibus (☎ 21513) is on Las Heras between España and 12 de Octubre, half a dozen blocks west of the plaza and two blocks north of Av Alberdi. La Unión (☎ 21722) sends 14 daily buses between Santiago del Estero and Tucumán that stop at Termas de Río Hondo, and also has buses to Buenos Aires (US$42, 15 hours) and La Plata. Chevallier (☎ 21085) has service to Tucumán, Buenos Aires, and La Plata, while Expreso Panamericano (☎ 21127) goes to Córdoba. La Estrella (☎ 21769) has buses to Buenos Aires and Mar del Plata, and San Cristóbal (also ☎ 21769) to Paraná, Entre Ríos, and Santa Fe. Libertador (☎ 21127) goes to Mendoza (19 hours) via Santiago del Estero, La Rioja, and San Juan.

Getting Around

Empresa 4 de Junio (☎ 21826) goes to the Dique Frontal for US50¢. Catch it downtown along RN 9 or Av Perón.

La Rioja & Catamarca Provinces

Among the modern provinces of Argentina, isolated La Rioja and Catamarca are poor relations, but they are rich in scenery, folklore, and tradition. Both were home to several important pre-Columbian cultures of mainly maize cultivators, who developed unique pottery techniques and styles – the region has many important archaeological sites. Inca influence did not touch the Diaguitas until the late 15th century, just before the arrival of the Spaniards.

Given the area's current economic distress, it seems remarkable that, in the early

16th century, Vásquez de Espinosa described La Rioja as, literally, an oasis of prosperity:

As one comes into the city, since the orange trees . . . are always covered and loaded down with blossoms, this entrance to the city for that distance of two leagues is a lovely cheering site, with the trees loaded with fruit the whole year round, and the great freshness and verdure; but what aids to make that spot seem the terrestrial Paradise or a bit of Heaven is the fragrance, sweetness, and perfume of the orange blossoms.

Irrigation brought water to the vineyards and fields, allowing for the planting of corn, wheat, sweet potatoes, and other root crops. Winemaking has proven to be La Rioja's most enduring industry. In the mid-19th century, Domingo Faustino Sarmiento compared the Riojano landscape to that of the Middle East:

In the reddish or ochreous tints of the soil, the dryness of some regions and their cisterns; also the orange-trees, vines and fig-trees bearing exquisite and enormous fruits, which are raised along the course of some turbid and confined Jordan. There is a strange combination of mountain and plain, fruitfulness and aridity, parched and bristling heights, and hills covered with dark green forests as lofty as the cedars of Lebanon.

This region has produced some of Argentina's most memorable historical figures, such as caudillos Facundo Quiroga, Chacho Peñaloza, and Felipe Varela – objects of Sarmiento's scorn in his famous diatribe against the rise of provincial strongmen. To balance the books, La Rioja also gave the country intellectuals like Joaquín V González, a writer, politician, and founder of La Plata university, and Arturo Marasso, writer and educator.

Presently, both provinces are economic backwaters with a low standard of living, especially in Catamarca, and people are leaving the countryside for the cities. The area is politically influential, though – President Carlos Menem and his mercurial family are riojanos, while the prominent Saadis have run Catamarca almost like a family fiefdom. Both, to some degree, are

modern counterparts of Facundo and his contemporaries, relying on personal loyalty rather than political principle for their support.

Corruption and nepotism are widespread and often get out of hand – in 1990, when Governor Ramón Saadi of Catamarca appeared to have obstructed the rape/ murder investigation of the son of one of his political protegés, a Catholic nun led repeated local protests that finally forced Buenos Aires to intervene in the provincial courts, but as of mid-1995, the case was still unresolved. According to a local priest, cited in the porteño daily *Página 12,* "Beneath the cloak of the Virgin of the Valley, Catamarca is a sewer."

LA RIOJA

Juan Ramírez de Velasco founded Todos los Santos de la Nueva Rioja in 1591. Dominican, Jesuit, and Franciscan missionaries helped "pacify" the Diaguita Indians and paved the way for Spanish colonization of what Vásquez de Espinosa called "a bit of heaven."

The city's appearance reflects the interaction between colonizer and colonized, the architecture combining European designs with native techniques and local materials. Many early buildings were destroyed in the 1894 earthquake, but the city has been entirely rebuilt. The recently restored commercial center, near Plaza 25 de Mayo, is a good replica of colonial architecture, as are several churches and private homes. The population is approximately 107,000.

Orientation

At the base of the picturesque Sierra de Velasco, La Rioja is 154 km southwest of Catamarca and 460 km northwest of Córdoba via RN 38, 515 km northeast of San Juan via a combination of national and provincial routes, and 1167 km north and west of Buenos Aires. It is relatively small, with all points of interest and most hotels within easy walking distance of each other.

Most of the major public buildings,

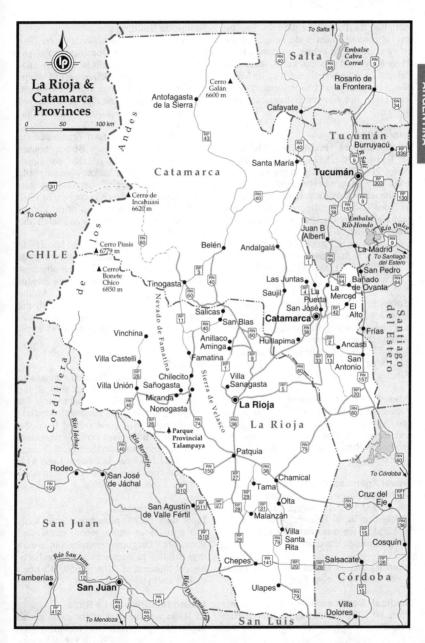

ARGENTINA

including the Palacio Legislativo, line the streets around Plaza 9 de Julio, but the city's commercial center surrounds Plaza 25 de Mayo and continues along east-west Pelagio Luna and north-south 25 de Mayo. North-south streets change their names at Rivadavia, but east-west streets are continuous.

Information

Tourist Offices The Dirección Municipal de Turismo (☎ 28834, 28839) is at Av Perón 715. The friendly, eager staff has a good city map and brochures of other provincial destinations. Hotel information includes only officially registered hotels, excluding many cheaper possibilities, but there is a list of casas de familia. Hours hours are 8 am to 1 pm and 4 to 9 pm weekdays, 8 am to noon Saturdays.

ACA (☎ 25381) is at Vélez Sarsfield and Copiapó.

Money La Rioja has no cambios, and bank hours are limited, but some travel agencies will change money. Banco de la Nación is at Belgrano and Pelagio Luna, while Banco de La Rioja is at Rivadavia and San Martín. Banco de Galicia has an ATM at San Nicolás de Bari and Buenos Aires.

Post & Telecommunications Correo Argentino is at Av Perón 764; the postal code is 5300. Telecom is at Pelagio Luna and Joaquín V González, with additional cabinas at Rivadavia 749. La Rioja's area code is 0822.

Travel Agencies Velasco Tur (☎ 26052) is at Buenos Aires 253, and Yafar Turismo (☎ 23053) is at Lamadrid 170. Trips to Parque Provincial Talampaya cost as much as US$150 for transportation alone, contracted through a taxi driver.

Laundry Mamá Espuma is at Av Perón 1066. Laverap is at Av Perón 946.

Medical Services Hospital Presidente Plaza (☎ 27814) is at San Nicolás de Bari Este 97.

Religious Buildings

La Rioja is a major devotional center. The **Convento de Santo Domingo** at Pelagio Luna and Lamadrid, built in 1623 by Diaguita Indians under the direction of Dominican friars, is Argentina's oldest convent. The date appears in the elaborately carved algarrobo door frame, also the work of Diaguita artists.

The **Convento de San Francisco,** at 25 de Mayo and Bazán y Bustos, houses the image of the Niño Alcalde, an important religious icon acknowledging the Christ Child as the city's mayor. This convent also contains the cell occupied in 1592 by San Francisco Solano, a priest known for educating native peoples and defending their rights.

The **Iglesia Catedral,** at San Nicolás de Bari and 25 de Mayo, contains the image of patron saint Nicolás de Bari, an object of devotion for both riojanos and the inhabitants of neighboring provinces. At the corner of Rivadavia and 9 de Julio, the **Iglesia de la Merced** replaced a Mercedarian church destroyed by the 1894 earthquake.

Museo Folklórico

This very interesting museum re-creates an authentic 19th-century house, with all the furnishings and objects necessary for everyday life; its shady patio with comfortable benches is a good refuge from the heat. One hall displays ceramic reproductions representing mythological beings from local folklore. At Pelagio Luna 811, it's open Tuesday to Sunday 8 am to noon and 4 to 8 pm.

Museo Inca Huasi

More than 12,000 pieces, including tools and artifacts of stone, wood, metal, and bone, plus Diaguita ceramics and weavings, fill this paleontological and archaeological museum at Alberdi 650. It's open daily 8 am to noon.

Museo Histórico de La Rioja

La Rioja was the land of the caudillos so deplored by Sarmiento, including the

ARGENTINA

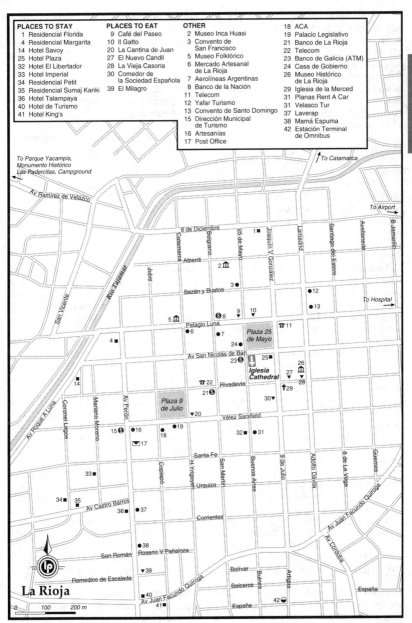

PLACES TO STAY
1 Residencial Florida
4 Residencial Margarita
14 Hotel Savoy
25 Hotel Plaza
32 Hotel El Libertador
33 Hotel Imperial
34 Residencial Petit
35 Residencial Sumaj Kanki
36 Hotel Talampaya
40 Hotel de Turismo
41 Hotel King's

PLACES TO EAT
9 Café del Paseo
10 Il Gatto
20 La Cantina de Juan
27 El Nuevo Candil
28 La Vieja Casona
30 Comedor de
   la Sociedad Española
39 El Milagro

OTHER
2 Museo Inca Huasi
3 Convento de
   San Francisco
5 Museo Folklórico
6 Mercado Artesanal
   de La Rioja
7 Aerolíneas Argentinas
8 Banco de la Nación
11 Telecom
12 Yafar Turismo
13 Convento de Santo Domingo
15 Dirección Municipal
   de Turismo
16 Artesanías
17 Post Office

18 ACA
19 Palacio Legislativo
21 Banco de La Rioja
22 Telecom
23 Banco de Galicia (ATM)
24 Casa de Gobierno
26 Museo Histórico
   de La Rioja
29 Iglesia de la Merced
31 Planas Rent A Car
31 Velasco Tur
37 Laverap
38 Mamá Espuma
42 Estación Terminal
   de Omnibus

To Parque Yacampis,
Monumento Histórico
Las Padercitas, Campground

To Catamarca

To Airport

Av Ramírez de Velazco

Río Tajamar

San Vicente

Catamarca

Jujuy

8 de Diciembre

Belgrano

25 de Mayo

Joaquín V González

Lamadrid

Santiago del Estero

Avellaneda

B Jaramillo

Alberdi

Bazán y Bustos

To Hospital

Pelagio Luna

Plaza 25
de Mayo

Av San Nicolás de Bari

Iglesia
Cathedral

Rivadavia

Mariano Moreno

Av Perón

Coronel Lagos

Av Roque A Luna

Plaza 9
de Julio

Vélez Sarsfield

Santa Fe

Copiapó

H Yrigoyen

San Martín

Buenos Aires

9 de Julio

Adolfo Dávila

8 de La Vega

Güemes

Urquiza

Corrientes

Av Castro Barros

San Román

Rosario V Peñaloza

Remedios de Escalada

Bolívar

Balcarce

Butnes

Artigas

España

España

Av Juan Facundo Quiroga

Av Córdoba

La Rioja

0   100   200 m

famous Facundo Quiroga, Felipe Varela, and Angel (Chacho) Peñaloza; many Argentines say that President Carlos Menem modeled himself on Facundo, even down to the muttonchops he used to wear. Offering some insight on the province's political development, this museum at Adolfo Dávila 79 contains Quiroga's stage-coach, military paraphernalia, and the die of the first coin used by his army.

Parque Yacampis

On the western outskirts of town at the foot of the Sierra de Velasco, this formerly well-landscaped park has become increasingly run-down, but still has panoramic views, a small zoo where some local fauna such as rheas run free, and a popular swimming pool.

Special Events

El Tinkunako This religious ritual, which takes place at midday December 31, re-enacts the original ceremony of San Francisco Solano's 1593 mediation between the Diaguitas and the Spanish conquerors. For accepting peace, the Diaguitas imposed two conditions: resignation of the Spanish *alcalde* (mayor), and his replacement by the Christ Child. Some riojanos wear indigenous clothing and sing traditional songs in a procession carrying the image of their patron saint, San Nicolás de Bari, to meet the Niño Alcalde in front of the Casa de Gobierno. In deference to the mayor, the saint bows three times.

La Chaya This folkloric festival, the local variant of Carnaval, attracts people from throughout the country. Its name, derived from a Quechua word meaning "to get someone wet," should give you an idea of what to expect. The festival takes place around the figure of Pujllay, the indigenous deity responsible for the happiness of the poor, who is born at Carnaval, lives for three days, and dies on Sunday.

Festival del Viñador This festival, honoring local vintners, takes place at the beginning of the March grape harvest in Villa

Unión. During the festival there is music, dancing, and tasting of the famous regional wines, particularly the artisanal *vino patero,* made by traditional foot stomping of the grapes.

Places to Stay – bottom end

Camping Parque Yacampis, at Av Ramírez de Velasco Km 3, has a free and shady but deteriorating campground whose swimming pool (not free) is its only redeeming feature. Several campgrounds occupy sites along RP 1 west of town, including *Country Las Vegas* at Km 7, *Sociedad Siriolibanesa* at Km 10, and *Balneario Los Sauces* at Km 12. Rates are around US$5 per tent and US$4 per person; to get there, catch city bus No 1 southbound on Perón, which goes nearly to the Las Vegas before turning around.

Residenciales La Rioja lacks a large tourist infrastructure, especially in budget hotels, but the tourist office maintains a list of casas de familia offering accommodations for about US$12 per person.

Residencial Sumaj Kanki, at Av Castro Barros and Coronel Lagos, provides modest but clean accommodations for about US$10 per person with shared bath, but can get a bit noisy. Around the corner, *Residencial Petit,* Lagos 427, offers singles with shared bath for US$13 and singles/doubles with private bath for US$20/35. Once a grand place, the building still conserves some of its past splendor, and the friendly, flexible owner allows some cooking and clothes washing.

Residencial Margarita, at Av Perón 407 behind a kiosk, has small, dark, but clean rooms at US$12 per person with bath. Another fairly central place is *Residencial Florida,* 8 de Diciembre 524, with small but comfortable rooms for US$12 with shared bath, US$15 with private bath. Since the elderly owner lives way out back, just walk in if nobody answers the bell.

Places to Stay – middle

Mid-range accommodations are relatively limited. *Hotel Savoy* (☎ 26894), Av Roque

A Luna 14, has comfortable rooms with bath, air-conditioning, and telephone for US$25/30, and has a bar and confitería for breakfast. Less central at Av Perón 951, *Hotel Talampaya* (☎ 24010) offers similar accommodations for US$23/35. Nearby *Hotel Imperial* (☎ 22478), at Mariano Moreno 345, charges US$25/35.

ACA's *Motel Yacampis* (☎ 25216), located in the run-down Parque Yacampis northwest of downtown, has singles/doubles at US$20/32 for members and US$30/48 for nonmembers; it also has a good restaurant and confitería.

Places to Stay – top end

Hotel El Libertador (☎ 26052), Buenos Aires 253, has rooms for US$40/60, with a 10% cash discount for ACA members. *Hotel Plaza* (☎ 25215), 9 de Julio and San Nicolás de Bari, offers rates of US$80/108, as well as room service, a swimming pool, and a bar.

Other top-end hotels are outside the center. At the southern entrance to town, *Hotel de Turismo* (☎ 25240), Av Perón and Av Quiroga, is a bit more luxurious than the others, with a swimming pool and solarium, and rooms for US$52/71. Nearby *Hotel King's* (☎ 25272) at Av Quiroga and Copiapó also has a swimming pool, but is cheaper at US$45/64.

Places to Eat

Regional cuisine, readily available at festivals and special events, can also be found at local restaurants. Some dishes to look for include: *locro* (stew), juicy and spicy empanadas differing from the drier ones of the Pampas, *chivito asado* (barbecued goat), *humita* (stuffed corn dough, resembling Mexican tamales), *quesillo* (a cheese specialty), and olives. Don't miss the local bread, baked in *hornos de barro* (adobe ovens). There is also a good selection of dried fruits, preserves, and jams from apples, figs, peaches, and pears. Don't hesitate to order house wines, which are invariably excellent.

Places serving regional specialties include *La Cantina de Juan,* Hipólito Yrigoyen 190; *La Vieja Casona,* Rivadavia 427; *El Milagro,* Av Perón and Remedios de Escalada; and *La Lala,* Av Quiroga and Güemes. All serve standard Argentine dishes like parrillada as well.

For Middle Eastern food, also a regional specialty, try *El Nuevo Candil,* part of the Sociedad Sirio Libanesa at Rivadavia 461. A good-value place is the *Comedor de la Sociedad Española,* 9 de Julio 237, with tasty Spanish food. *Il Gatto* (☎ 21899), Pelagio Luna 555, is part of a chain but still has very decent pizza and pasta at moderate prices. *Café del Paseo,* at the corner of Pelagio Luna and 25 de Mayo, is an appealing Spanish mission-style confitería.

Entertainment

Performers of the stature of Leon Gieco perform at *La Rioja's Coliseo La Quebrada,* 5½ km west of downtown on Av San Francisco, where there are also theatrical performances.

Things to Buy

La Rioja has unique weavings that combine indigenous techniques and skill with Spanish designs and color combinations. The typical mantas (bedspreads) feature floral patterns over a solid background. Spanish influence is also visible in silver work, including tableware, ornaments, religious objects, and horse gear. La Rioja's famous pottery is entirely indigenous – artists utilize local clay to make distinctive pots, plates, and flower pots. Vino riojano has a national reputation; Saúl Menem, father of the president, founded one of the major bodegas.

The Mercado Artesanal de La Rioja, Pelagio Luna 792, exhibits and sells these items and other popular artworks at prices lower than most souvenir shops. Artesanías, at the corner of Av Perón and Dalmacio Vélez, has outstanding pottery and weavings at good prices; it's open weekdays 9 am to 1 pm and 5 to 10 pm, Saturdays 9 am to 1 pm.

Getting There & Away

Air Aerolíneas Argentinas (☎ 27355,

26307), Belgrano 63, flies every morning except Sunday to Catamarca and Buenos Aires, with additional flights Wednesday and Friday afternoons.

Bus La Rioja's Estación Terminal de Omnibus (☎ 25453) is at Artigas and España.

Empresa El Cóndor (☎ 27572) travels daily to provincial destinations (Sanagasta, Castro Barros, Arauco, San Blas de los Sauces, and Chilecito), and daily except Saturday to Córdoba, Catamarca, and San Luis. Cacorba (☎ 33967) also goes to Córdoba. Transporte Chilecito (☎ 21273, 27733), Av San Francisco 326, has many daily buses to Chilecito.

Riojacor (☎ 26312) and El Rápido serve Córdoba three times daily, with student discounts, and also has buses to provincial destinations including Chilecito (three daily for US$8), Chepes (Fridays), and Villa Unión (daily). Cotal goes to Mendoza, Catamarca, Santiago del Estero, Reconquista, Resistencia, Corrientes, and Puerto Iguazú.

Expreso Nacate serves San Juan three times weekly. Transportes Libertador (☎ 27209) has daily buses to Mendoza (US$29, 9½ hours), San Juan (US$22, 7½ hours), Catamarca (US$11, two hours), and Tucumán (US$26, 4½ hours), and sends buses to Santiago del Estero (eight hours) three times weekly. Autotransporte Mendoza (☎ 27395) goes three times weekly to Mendoza (eight hours) and to Pocitos (ten hours), on the Bolivian border. Bosio (☎ 21011) also goes to Mendoza, San Juan, and Pocitos (US$50 roundtrip). Expreso El Riojano goes to Tucumán, Salta (US$35, 11 hours), Jujuy (US$36), and Pocitos.

Empresa Ablo (☎ 26444) has buses to Córdoba (US$12), Santa Fe, San Luis, Buenos Aires (US$45, 17 hours), and Mar del Plata. La Estrella (☎ 26306) goes to San Juan, Mendoza, Catamarca, Tucumán, and Jujuy. Empresa General Urquiza (☎ 26444) serves Santa Fe and Buenos Aires. Andesmar (☎ 22430) goes to Catamarca, Tucumán, Salta, Pocitos, and Mendoza, where it

has connections to Patagonian destinations like Bariloche, Esquel, and Río Gallegos.

Getting Around
To/From the Airport Aeropuerto Vicente Almonacid (☎ 25483) is east of town on RP 5, Km 7. Local bus No 3 goes there from Plaza 9 de Julio, while No 6 goes there from Perón and San Nicolás de Bari. An airport cab costs around US$6.

Car Rental There are two car rental agencies, Auto Tur (☎ 21687) at Santiago del Estero 32, and Planas (☎ 24065) at Buenos Aires 244.

AROUND LA RIOJA
Monumento Histórico Las Padercitas
According to legend, San Francisco Solano converted many Diaguita Indians at the site of this Franciscan-built colonial adobe chapel, now sheltered by a later stone structure, seven km west of town on RP 1. On the second Sunday of August, pilgrims convene to pay homage to the saint.

Dique Los Sauces
Beyond Las Padercitas, RP 1 climbs and winds past attractive summer homes, bright red sandstone cliffs, lush vegetation, and dark purple peaks whose cacti remind you that the area is semidesert. Balneario Los Sauces, 15 km from La Rioja at the dam, is a pleasant place for a leisurely picnic or outing.

From Balneario Los Sauces it is possible to hike or drive up the dirt road to Cerro de la Cruz (1680 meters), which affords panoramic views of the Yacampis Valley and the village of Sanagasta. The top also has a ramp for hang-gliding, a popular local activity.

VILLA SANAGASTA
At the end of paved RP 1 through the captivating valley of the Río Huaco, poplars line the narrow streets of summer homes and vineyards in the village of Sanagasta, 30 km from La Rioja. The town has a small, well-restored chapel, and an intriguing museum. *Hostería Achay Sacat*

(☎ 0822-92036) is very attractive and reasonably priced at US$25/35 single/double.

CHILECITO

Originally called Santa Rita, Chilecito acquired its current name from the presence of Chileans who worked the gold mines of Famatina in the 19th century; at one time, the provincial government briefly relocated here to escape the intimidation of Facundo Quiroga. Because of the importance of the mines, in 1892 Chilecito became the site of the second branch of the Banco de la Nación in the country. In 1903, Chilecito built one of the world's largest aerial engineering projects, the 34-km cable car to La Mejicana mine, which reaches an altitude of 4500 meters.

Although in the early 1900s there where 10 foundries in the area, agriculture has replaced mining as the main economic activity. The province's second-largest city

(population 32,000), Chilecito is famous for its wines, olives, and walnuts.

Orientation & Information

In a scenic valley at the foot of the massive Nevado de Famatina and Cerro Velazco, directly west of La Rioja, Chilecito is a roundabout 192 km from the provincial capital via RN 38 and RN 74. Its compactness rewards walkers.

Tourist Office The municipal Dirección de Turismo (☎ 2688), at Libertad and Profesor Cavero, has enthusiastic staff and good material. Director Alberto Decaro has written an excellent work on Parque Provincial Talampaya.

Money Banco de la Nación and Banco Provincia are on opposite corners of Plaza Sarmiento.

Post & Telecommunications Correo Argentino is at Joaquín V González and

ARGENTINA

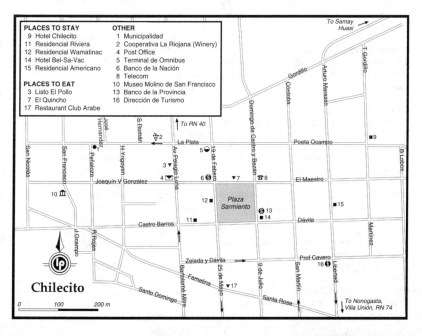

PLACES TO STAY
9   Hotel Chilecito
11 Residencial Riviera
12 Residencial Wamatinac
14 Hotel Bel-Sa-Vac
15 Residencial Americano

PLACES TO EAT
3   Listo El Pollo
7   El Quincho
17 Restaurant Club Arabe

OTHER
1   Municipalidad
2   Cooperativa La Riojana (Winery)
4   Post Office
5   Terminal de Omnibus
6   Banco de la Nación
8   Telecom
10 Museo Molino de San Francisco
13 Banco de la Provincia
16 Dirección de Turismo

Chilecito

0   100   200 m

B Mitre; the postal code is 5360. Telecom is at Castro y Bazán 27. Chilecito's area code is 0825.

Museo Molino de San Francisco

Chilecito founder Don Domingo de Castro y Bazán owned this colonial flour mill, whose museum houses an eclectic assemblage of archaeological tools, antique arms, early colonial documents, minerals, traditional wood and leather crafts, plus weavings and paintings. At J Ocampo 63, the building itself merits a visit, but the artifacts are a big plus. Hours hours are Tuesday to Sunday, 8 am to noon and 3 to 7 pm.

Samay Huasi

Doctor Joaquín V González, founder of the prestigious Universidad Nacional de La Plata, used this building, three km from Chilecito past La Puntilla, as his country retreat. Now belonging to the university, the building houses a natural sciences, archaeology, and mineralogy museum, and a valuable collection of paintings by Argentine artists. It's open Tuesday to Sunday, 8 am to noon and 3 to 7 pm.

Cooperativa La Riojana (Winery)

The province's largest winery, at La Plata 246, is open to visitors weekdays for tours and tasting.

Organized Tours

For information about guided tours of the Estación No 1 del Cable Carril, a historical monument displaying some of the machinery used for gold extraction, ask at the tourist office, which also has descriptions of nearby villages to visit and places to hike, as well as information on organized treks to Los Nevados del Famatina.

Places to Stay

The tourist office keeps a list of casas de familia, the cheapest accommodations in town, charging about US$8 per person. *Residencial Americano* (☎ 8104), Libertad 68, has singles/doubles for US$12/15, with shared bath. The very central *Residencial Wamatinac,* 25 de Mayo 19, costs

US$18/30. Rates at *Residencial Riviera,* Castro Barros 133, are US$24/35, and US$24/36 at *Hotel Bel-Sa-Vac* (☎ 2877), 9 de Julio and Dávila.

The best accommodations are at ACA's *Hotel Chilecito* (☎ 2801), at Poeta Ocampo and T Gordillo, which also has a good restaurant. Rooms with private bath are US$20/32 for members, US$30/48 for nonmembers.

Places to Eat

The hospitable owners of *Restaurant Club Arabe,* 25 de Mayo and Santa Rosa, offer great food despite a limited menu; in summer, ask for grapes fresh off the vine. *Listo El Pollo,* at Pelagio Luna 30, and *El Quincho,* Joaquín V González 50, serve parrillada. *El Gallo,* at Libertad and Illia, and *Toscanini,* at San Martín and Santa Rosa, offer standard Argentine menus.

Getting There & Away

The Estación Terminal de Omnibus is at La Plata and 19 de Febrero. Riojacor (☎ 2726) has daily buses to Villa Unión and La Rioja; Transporte Chilecito (☎ 2781), 19 de Febrero 194, goes to La Rioja many times daily. Ablo (☎ 2224) travels to Villa María (Córdoba province), Rosario, and Buenos Aires.

Expreso Santa Rita (☎ 2522) serves nearby locations, including Miranda, Famatina, and Tinogasta.

NONOGASTA

Only the roaring water of the acequias disrupts the peaceful, unpaved streets of this small town, birthplace of educator Joaquín V González. In a prosperous agricultural valley 16 km south of Chilecito, Nonogasta features charming adobe architecture (including Gonzalez's house and a 17th-century church), polite and friendly people, and good wines from Bodegas Nicarí.

CUESTA DE MIRANDA

With 800 turns, this mountain road through the Sierra de Sañogasta, about 56 km west of Chilecito, is one of the most spectacular in the northern Andes and one of the province's major scenic attractions. Although not paved, the surface is very smooth and wide enough for vehicle safety; still, sounding the horn before the innumerable blind turns is a good idea. At the highest point, 2020 meters above sea level, there is a vista from which the Río Miranda looks like a frozen silver ribbon below.

VILLA UNIÓN

In the valley of the Río Bermejo, at the intersection of RN 40 and RP 26, the inviting village of Villa Unión sits 1140 meters above sea level between the Nevados de Famatina and the precordillera. The austere modern church has very striking carvings made from cardón cactus.

On the outskirts of town, a mirador provides a panoramic view of valley, village, and surrounding mountains – don't let the 130 steps up the hill discourage you.

Villa Unión's area code is 0825.

Places to Stay & Eat

The highly recommended *Hostería Villa Unión* (☎ 7271), on the main street, is the de facto tourist office. It provides good accommodations, excellent information, and even changes money. Rooms cost US$7/13 single/double with shared bath, US$9/15 with private bath (no breakfast included). Group rates include room with private bath, breakfast, and dinner for about US$30 per person. The friendly and helpful owner has maps of the area drawn in the 1970s and 1980s by her now frail and elderly father, Ingeniero Bernard Lorenz. There are also detailed descriptions of the area.

Basic, friendly *Hospedaje Paola* charges US$8 for rooms with shared bath. Family-run *Comedor Hospedaje El Changuito* has a few beds, as well as good, cheap food (mostly minutas) and excellent regional wine.

Getting There & Away

Riojacor has a daily bus to Chilecito and La Rioja, via the Cuesta de Miranda. TAC has two weekly buses from San Juan.

PARQUE PROVINCIAL TALAMPAYA

Locals like to compare Talampaya, a 270,000-hectare fauna and flora reserve with major paleontological and archaeological resources, to Arizona's Grand Canyon. About 55 km south of Villa Unión, Talampaya means "Dry River of the Tala" in the Quechua language – a fitting description for this desert of hot days, chilly nights, infrequent but torrential summer rains, and gusty spring winds.

Only professional guides with 4WD vehicles offer tours through the colorful canyon to show its aboriginal petroglyphs and nesting condors, who scatter from their cliffside nests as vehicles invade their otherwise undisturbed habitat. On the usual two-hour tour from the visitors' center, the vehicle passes the vast dunes of **El Playón**, leading to the **Puerta de Talampaya** (Gate of Talampaya), entrance to the canyon. During a brief stop, passengers walk along a sandy trail to the petroglyphs and mortars.

Back on the road, the truck enters the breathtaking canyon, whose eastern wall reveals an enormous geological fault. The next major stops are at **El Balcón**, an extraordinary echo chamber where your voice seems to come back louder than your original call, and a nature trail to the **Bosquecillo** (Little Forest), a representative sample of native vegetation. On the return the major point is **El Cañón de los Farallones** (Canyon of Cliffs) where, besides condors and turkey vultures, you may see eagles and other birds of prey.

By making prior arrangements at the tourist office in Chilecito, it is possible to take a longer excursion traversing the entire canyon, and also to trek and hike. In addition to the US$3 park admission, the two-hour excursion costs US$35 per person for up to eight persons; proceeds go directly to the guide. If you can, sit in front with the guide one way, and in the back of the truck the other way.

Longer four-hour excursions to **Los Pizarrones** cost US$70 for up to eight persons, while a six-hour trip to **Los Cajones** costs US$110. An eight- to nine-hour trip

ARGENTINA

to the **Ciudad Perdida** or a ten-hour excursion to **Los Chañares** costs US$130.

Getting There & Away

Travelers without their own cars, on a limited budget, can take the El Cóndor bus from La Rioja to Pagancillo, 10 km from Talampaya, where most of the park personnel reside; from there they will help you get to the park, where it is necessary to pay for the excursions.

CATAMARCA

Spaniards founded Londres, the first city in present-day Catamarca province, as early as 1559, but hostile Indians delayed the permanent establishment of any city until 1683, when Don Fernando Mendoza de Mate de Luna founded San Fernando del Valle de Catamarca, or Catamarca for short. Economically, it has remained a provincial backwater, although major devotional holidays attract large numbers of visitors.

Except for its magnificent cathedral (a landmark that looks better by night), Catamarca's urban landscape is worn around more than just the edges. Reflecting the province's economic distress, its drab peatonal Rivadavia, which becomes a neon-lit consumerist enclave by night, has few places to sit and relax, while its well-designed Plaza 25 de Mayo shows seriously deferred maintenance. Images and murals of the Virgen del Valle are everywhere in the run-down town, leading many to wonder if all that Catamarca has left is its faith.

Orientation

Dense clouds often disrupt the view in the valley of the Río del Valle, flanked by the Sierra del Colorado in the west and the Sierra Graciana in the east, where Catamarca sits 156 km northeast of La Rioja and 238 km from Tucumán via RN 38, and 218 km from Santiago del Estero via RN 64.

Nearly everything is within walking distance in the city center, an area 12 blocks square enclosed by four wide avenues: Av Belgrano to the north, Av Alem to the east, Güemes to the south, and Virgen del Valle to the west. The focus of downtown is the beautifully designed Plaza 25 de Mayo (the work of Carlos Thays, who also designed Parque San Martín in Mendoza and Parque 9 de Julio in Tucumán), a shady refuge from the summer heat. South of the plaza, Rivadavia is a permanent peatonal between San Martín and Mota Botello, while beyond Mota Botello to Av Güemes it's closed to auto traffic from 8 am to 1 pm and 3 to 11 pm. North of Av Belgrano along Tucumán is Parque Adán Quiroga, another green space in this relatively treeless city.

Streets in Catamarca often change names; the most recent is Av Urquiza, recently renamed Av Virgen del Valle, while Calle Vicente Saadi has reverted to its original name of República.

Information

Tourist Offices The inconveniently located Dirección Municipal de Turismo (☎ 32647), at Virgen de Valle (ex-Urquiza) 951, is in the Manzana del Turismo (Tourism Block), a bit remote from both the bus terminal and downtown. It has only a basic city map, but the friendly and competent staff help make up for lack of brochures. It opens weekdays 7 am to 1 pm and 2 to 8 pm, weekends 8 am to noon and 3 to 8 pm. Around the corner on General Roca is the Dirección Provincial de Turismo.

ACA (☎ 24513) is at República 102.

Money Catamarca has no cambios, but you can exchange cash only at Banco de la Nación, San Martín 626, and Banco de la Provincia, República 480. Banco de Galicia has an ATM on Rivadavia between República and Esquiú.

Post & Telecommunications Correo Argentino is at San Martín 753; the postal code is 4700. Telecom, at Rivadavia 758, is painfully slow at arranging international calls. Catamarca's area code is 0833.

Travel Agencies Catamarca has an abundance of travel agencies, including Turi-Cat

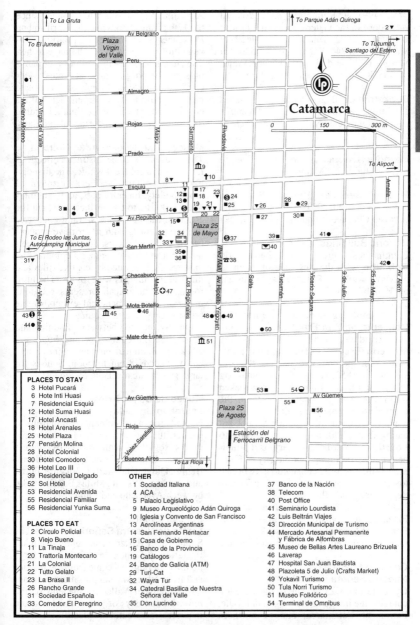

ARGENTINA

Catamarca

PLACES TO STAY
3 Hotel Pucará
6 Hote Inti Huasi
7 Residencial Esquiú
12 Hotel Suma Huasi
17 Hotel Ancasti
18 Hotel Arenales
25 Hotel Plaza
27 Pensión Molina
28 Hotel Colonial
30 Hotel Comodoro
36 Hotel Leo III
39 Residencial Delgado
52 Sol Hotel
53 Residencial Avenida
55 Residencial Familiar
56 Residencial Yunka Suma

PLACES TO EAT
2 Círculo Policial
8 Viejo Bueno
11 La Tinaja
20 Trattoría Montecarlo
21 La Colonial
22 Tutto Gelato
23 La Brasa II
26 Rancho Grande
31 Sociedad Española
33 Comedor El Peregrino

OTHER
1 Sociadad Italiana
4 ACA
5 Palacio Legislativo
9 Museo Arqueológico Adán Quiroga
10 Iglesia y Convento de San Francisco
13 Aerolíneas Argentinas
14 San Fernando Rentacar
15 Casa de Gobierno
16 Banco de la Provincia
19 Catálogos
24 Banco de Galicia (ATM)
29 Turi-Cat
32 Wayra Tur
34 Catedral Basilica de Nuestra
     Señora del Valle
35 Don Lucindo

37 Banco de la Nación
38 Telecom
40 Post Office
41 Seminario Lourdista
42 Luis Beltrán Viajes
43 Dirección Municipal de Turismo
44 Mercado Artesanal Permanente
     y Fábrica de Alfombras
45 Museo de Bellas Artes Laureano Brizuela
46 Laverap
47 Hospital San Juan Bautista
48 Plazoleta 5 de Julio (Crafts Market)
49 Yokavil Turismo
50 Tula Norri Turismo
51 Museo Folklórico
54 Terminal de Omnibus

(☎ 25499) at República 832, Yokavil (☎ 30066) in the Galería Paseo del Centro at Rivadavia 922, Tula Norri (☎ 29422) at Mate de Luna 744, Wayra Tur (☎ 25205) at Maipú 672, and Luis Beltrán Viajes (☎ 26538, 29422) at Chacabuco 1166.

Bookstore Catálogos, Sarmiento 518, has a quality selection of books on Argentine and regional history, as well as archaeology.

Laundry Laverap is on Mota Botello between Junín and Maipú.

Medical Services Hospital San Juan Bautista (☎ 24202, 22100) is on Ayacucho between Chacabuco and Mota Botello.

Historic Buildings
Catamarca's provincial **Casa de Gobierno** is on the west side of Plaza 25 de Mayo, while the **Palacio Legislativo** is on República between Caseros and Ayacucho.

The imposing neocolonial **Iglesia y Convento de San Francisco**, at Esquiú and Rivadavia, holds the cell of Fray Mamerto Esquiú, a 19th-century priest famous for speeches in defense of the constitution of 1853. A crystal box containing the priest's heart is now kept in a locked room after being stolen and left on the church's roof some years ago.

Now occupied by a private school but dating from 1890, the former **Seminario Lourdista** (Lourdist seminary) is a prominent landmark throughout the city of Catamarca, thanks to its conspicuous twin bell towers. It's on San Martín between Vicario Segura and 9 de Julio.

At the south end of Rivadavia, opposite Plaza 25 de Agosto, the **Estación del Ferrocarril Belgrano** is a striking landmark even though the trains no longer run.

Catedral Basilica de Nuestra Señora del Valle
Opposite Plaza 25 de Mayo, the Catedral contains the image of the Virgen del Valle, Patron of Catamarca, one of northern Argentina's most venerated images since the 17th century. Both in early April and on December 8, multitudes of pilgrims convene on Catamarca to pay homage to her. The church also has an exhibition of paintings of the virgin, an elaborate wood-carved altar to Saint Joseph, and an ornate baroque pulpit. The Virgen del Valle's crown, studded with more than a hundred diamonds, can be seen during the holidays.

Museo Arqueológico Adán Quiroga
This museum's three distinct collections fail to form a coherent whole. The first display hall contains a fine assortment of tools, pottery, funerary pots, and mummies from 3000 BC to the 18th century, but the arrangement, in a tedious, traditional style of glass cabinets with descriptive sequences of tools or objects, detracts from their quality. The second room, on colonial history, mixes disparate objects like rifles and musical instruments with fossils. The third room, also historical, presents religious material and the personal effects of the priest Fray Mamerto Esquiú.

On Sarmiento between Esquiú and Prado, the museum's opening hours are weekdays 8 am to 1 pm and 2:30 to 8 pm, and weekends 8 am to noon. Guides for large groups are available on request.

Museo de Bellas Artes Laureano Brizuela
Named for a prominent catamarqueño painter, the fine arts museum exhibits his works together with those by Varela Lezama, Roberto Gray, Antonio Berni, Benito Quinquela Martín, Vicente Forte, and others. It's at Mota Botello 239, between Ayacucho and Junín.

Special Events
Fiesta de Nuestra Señora del Valle The Sunday after Easter, in an impressive manifestation of popular religion, large numbers of pilgrims come from the interior and from other Andean provinces to honor the Virgen del Valle. At the end of the *novena* (nine days of prayer), she is taken in procession around the plaza.

Fiesta Nacional del Poncho In July, a crafts and industrial fair accompanies this festival of folkloric music and dance celebrating the importance of the poncho in the province. The shows, which attract well-known musicians, and exhibitions take place in the Manzana del Turismo on Av Virgen del Valle. Don't miss the scattered *peñas,* informal gatherings with music, dance, and typical food – ask the tourist office for suggestions.

Places to Stay – bottom end
Camping Catamarca's *Autocamping Municipal,* on RP 4 toward El Rodeo Las Juntas, is a pleasant spot about four km from downtown by the Río El Tala, in the foothills of the Sierra de Ambato. As a balneario, it presents two inconveniences: the major recreation site for people from the city, it gets loud and heavy use on weekends and holidays, and it also has ferocious mosquitos.

Bathrooms and showers are clean, and there is electricity. In summer, two swimming pools, one for adults and another for children, are also open. The confitería has a very friendly staff and basic food, but it's cheaper to buy your own in town.

Charges are US$6 per tent per day. Take bus No 10 from Convento de San Francisco, on Esquiú, or from the bus terminal on Vicario Segura. Climb to the top of the hill for a great view.

Casas de Familia, Residenciales & Hotels The tourist office keeps a list of casas de familia offering inexpensive lodging. Drab *Residencial Yunka Suma,* Vicario Segura 1255, is suitable for one night only at US$7 per person with shared bath. Still modest but notably better are *Pensión Molina* (☎ 22706) at República 721 and *Hotel Plaza* (☎ 26558) at Rivadavia 578, both for US$10 per person.

There are a number of basic hotels near the bus terminal. *Residencial Avenida* (☎ 22139), Av Güemes 754, is friendly, acceptable, and a bit tattered; it's not a great value at US$15/23 with shared bath,

US$19/27 with private bath. A block away at Av Güemes 841, *Residencial Familiar* (☎ 22142) has rooms with bath at US$15/24.

The equally friendly *Residencial Delgado* (☎ 26109), very central at San Martín 788/90, 1½ blocks from Plaza 25 de Mayo, charges US$15/25 with private bath. *Residencial Esquiú* (☎ 22284) Esquiú 365, charges US$18/27.

Places to Stay – middle
Prices vary greatly among mid-range places. The architecturally drab but otherwise congenial *Sol Hotel* (☎ 30803), Salta 1142, is a good value at US$20/28 with shared bath and kitchenette, US$27/37 with private bath; there are good views of town from the roof. For a pleasant place with friendly staff, try *Hotel Colonial* (☎ 23502), República 802, for US$27/37.

Similar in price, the improved *Hotel Comodoro* (☎ 23490), on República 855, is priced at US$30/40 with air-conditioning and private bath, but rooms with shared bath are an excellent value at US$15/25. The very central *Hotel Suma Huasi* (☎ 25199), Sarmiento 541, with rates of US$32/42, offers discounts to ACA members. *Hotel Pucará* (☎ 30698/688), Caseros 501, has pleasant rooms with television for US$35/45.

Places to Stay – top end
The modern *Hotel Inti Huasi* (☎ 25005), República 297, gives discounts to ACA members on its normal rates of US$40/52; prices are similar at central *Hotel Ancasti* (☎ 25974), Sarmiento 520. *Hotel Arenales* (☎ 30307), at Sarmiento 544, charges US$46/55, while *Hotel Leo III* (☎ 32080), Sarmiento 727, charges US$46/58. *Hotel Sussex* (☎ 24976, 30105), on the airport road, has rooms for US$48/59 and also has a swimming pool.

Places to Eat
The least expensive eateries cater to pilgrims. In the gallery behind the Catedral is *Comedor El Peregrino,* offering two courses (empanadas and pasta) for about

US$4, or a larger option including meat for US$6.

Other parrillas include *Rancho Grande,* at República 750, where a plentiful parrillada for two with salad and wine costs US$15; at night it has folk music. *La Tinaja* (☎ 29353) at Sarmiento 533 also has music and low prices, while *La Brasa II,* on Rivadavia just north of República, has takeout grilled chicken and empanadas. *Viejo Bueno,* on Esquiú between Maipú and Sarmiento, is another central parrilla. Much less central, at Av Castillo and Av Belgrano, *La Churrasquita* serves large portions of good beef.

La Colonial, República 574, is a good, moderately priced pizza and pasta place. Logically enough, the *Sociedad Italiana* at Moreno 152 also specializes in pasta, as does *Trattoría Montecarlo,* on República opposite Plaza 25 de Mayo.

The *Sociedad Española,* close to the tourist office at Virgen del Valle 725, has good seafood and traditional Spanish dishes. The *Círculo Policial,* open to the general public at Av Belgrano 1172, has very reasonable prices. For a more elegant place with a varied menu, try *Restaurant Maxims* at the Hotel Sussex, on RP 33.

Tutto Gelato, at the corner of República and Rivadavia, serves very fine ice cream.

Things to Buy

For Catamarca's well-known hand-tied rugs, visit the Mercado Artesanal Permanente y Fábrica de Alfombras at Virgen del Valle 945, next to the tourist office; the rugmakers work weekday mornings, 7 am to noon. Besides rugs, the market sells traditional ponchos, blankets, jewelry, red onyx sculptures, musical instruments, hand-spun sheep and llama wool, and basketry.

There's a small, informal crafts market evenings on the Plazoleta 5 de Julio, on the Rivadavia peatonal. Regional specialty shops are concentrated on Sarmiento, between Plaza 25 de Mayo and the Convento de San Francisco. Don Lucindo, on Sarmiento just south of San Martín, has a mixed selection – good stuff and kitsch – of pottery, basketry, wines, and fruits. Catamarca is the place to buy inexpensive, delicious walnuts, including *nueces confitadas* (sugared walnuts), which are very rich but tasty. Other local delicacies are olives, raisins, and wines.

Getting There & Away

Air Aerolíneas Argentinas (☎ 24460, 31000), at Sarmiento 589, has morning flights to Aeroparque daily, except Sundays, with afternoon flights Wednesdays and Fridays only.

Bus Catamarca's once depressing Terminal de Omnibus (☎ 23415), at Av Güemes 856, has been recently privatized and is undergoing a slow but much-needed facelift. Chevallier (☎ 30921) has two buses each evening to Buenos Aires (US$45, 16 hours; US$54 in coche cama), via Córdoba (US$16) and Rosario. Cacorba (☎ 23239) serves the same route.

La Estrella (☎ 23455) goes to Tucumán (4½ hours), Jujuy (9½ hours), Mendoza, and San Juan, while TAC goes to Córdoba, Tucumán, and Buenos Aires. Libertador (☎ 25745) stops at Catamarca en route to Mendoza (nine hours), San Juan (seven hours), La Rioja (US$6.50, 2½ hours), and Tucumán. Empresa Gutiérrez also goes to Tucumán. Andesmar (☎ 23777) has very extensive routes from the Bolivian border to Patagonia via Mendoza.

Cotil (☎ 23777) has buses to the Sierras de Córdoba via La Rioja (US$6.50), Chilecito, and Villa Unión. Bosio (☎ 23455) services Tucumán (US$10, six daily), Salta, La Rioja, San Juan, Mendoza, and Santiago del Estero. Cotal goes to Santiago del Estero (US$12, five hours), Reconquista (US$35, 16 hours), Corrientes (US$45, 17 hours), Posadas (US$58, 22 hours), San Juan (US$18, nine hours), and Mendoza (US$22, 11 hours). Robledo (☎ 30785) goes Tuesdays and Fridays to Patagonian destinations like Trelew (US$80) and Comodoro Rivadavia (US$122).

Getting Around

To/From the Airport For US$4 a downtown minibus will take you to Aeropuerto

Felipe Varela (☎ 24816), on RP 33, 22 km east of town.

Car Rental San Fernando Rentacar (☎ /fax 20830), República 476, 3rd floor, Oficina D, has vehicles for hire.

AROUND CATAMARCA
Parque Zoológico y Botánico de San Antonio

Although locals will recommend this park (☎ 23415), 13 km from Catamarca on RP 41, visitors should be aware of the crowded conditions under which its 350 animals (mostly Argentine species) suffer. To get there, take Bus No 203.

Gruta de la Virgen del Valle

According to local legend, in 1619 or 1620 the image of the Virgen del Valle appeared in this grotto seven km north of downtown on RP 32. The present image is a replica of that in Catamarca's Catedral, and the Gruta itself is now protected by a structure. Empresa Cotca's bus No 104 goes to the Gruta every 40 minutes.

Cuesta de El Portezuelo

In 20 km this hairpin road climbs more than 1000 meters to the top of the Sierras de Ancasti, affording ever more distant views of the city of Catamarca. There are several turnouts for panoramic vistas and photography, but since passenger buses no longer take this route, a private car or an organized tour are the only alternatives. Yokavil Turismo's daily tour, stopping short of the summit, costs US$10.

Villa Las Pirquitas

The Sierra de Famatina, the province's highest mountain range, is visible from the road to this picturesque village near the dam of the same name, 29 km north of Catamarca via RP 1. The foothills en route shelter small villages with hospitable people and interesting vernacular architecture. At the entrance to Villa Las Pirquitas, the house with the modest sign "Hay Pan" sells Catamarca's best home-baked bread.

Camping is possible in the basic balneario, where the shallows are too muddy for swimming. The very attractive *Hostería Municipal* (☎ 92030) offers great value at US$20/35 single/double with meals.

Empresa Cotca's bus No 101 leaves hourly for the village from Catamarca's bus terminal.

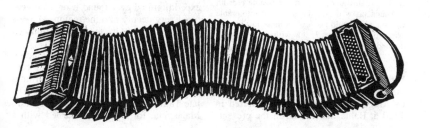

Patagonia

Argentina's most popular destination for adventurous and independent travelers is Patagonia, that enormous region south of the Río Colorado, just beyond the province of Buenos Aires, all the way to the Strait of Magellan. Beyond the straits is the archipelago of Tierra del Fuego, shared by Argentina and Chile.

History

Despite its seemingly monotonous landscape, the geography of Patagonia has long inspired the European imagination. Charles Darwin saw many exotic lands in his five years on the *Beagle,* but Patagonia remained longest and most vividly in his memory:

In calling up images of the past, I find that the plains of Patagonia frequently cross before my eyes; yet these plains are pronounced by all wretched and useless. They can be described only by negative characters; without habitations, without water, without trees, without mountains, they support merely a few dwarf plants. Why then, and the case is not peculiar to myself, have these arid wastes taken so firm a hold on my memory? Why have not the still more level, the greener and more fertile Pampas, which are serviceable to mankind, produced an equal impression? I can scarcely analyze these feelings: but it must be partly owing to the free scope given to the imagination. The plains of Patagonia are boundless, for they are scarcely passable, and hence unknown; they bear the stamp of having lasted, as they are now, for ages, and there appears to be no limit to their duration during future time. If, as the ancients supposed, the flat earth was surrounded by an impassable breadth of water, or by deserts heated to an intolerable excess, who would not look at these last boundaries to man's knowledge with deep but ill-defined sensations?

The origin of Patagonia's name is obscure, but one theory asserts that it derives from the region's native inhabitants, encountered by Magellan's crew as they wintered in 1520 at Bahía San Julián, in the present-day province of Santa Cruz. According to this explanation, the Tehuelche Indians, tall of stature and wearing moccasins that made their feet appear exceptionally large, may have led Magellan to adopt the name after the Spanish word *pata,* meaning paw or foot. On first encountering the Tehuelches, Antonio Pigafetta, an Italian nobleman on Magellan's crew, remarked with great exaggeration that one of them

was so tall we reached only to his waist, and he was well proportioned .... He was dressed in the skins of animals skillfully sewn together .... His feet were shod with the same kind of skins, which covered his feet in the manner of shoes .... The captain-general (Magellan) called these people Patagoni.

Bruce Chatwin, however, speculates that Magellan may have adopted the term "Patagon," describing a fictional monster from a Spanish romance of the period, and applied it to the aboriginal inhabitants of the area. In another parallel to the romance, Magellan abducted and attempted to take back to Spain two of these natives, but one escaped and the other died en route. This story found its way into English literature in Shakespeare's *The Tempest,* in which Caliban is abducted for the pleasure of a European monarch.

This was not the only fanciful account of the region. Since the early 16th century, the gold-hungry Spanish had spread tales of Trapalanda, an austral El Dorado somewhere in the southern Andes, but no early expedition had ever found it or even ventured very deeply into the region. Marvels like the Moreno Glacier remained unseen by Europeans until the 19th century.

It would be unfair to ignore less fanciful but more meaningful efforts, for Spain contributed scientists as well as fortune-seekers and plunderers to the region. The late 18th-century expedition of Alejandro Malaspina, for example, returned with a

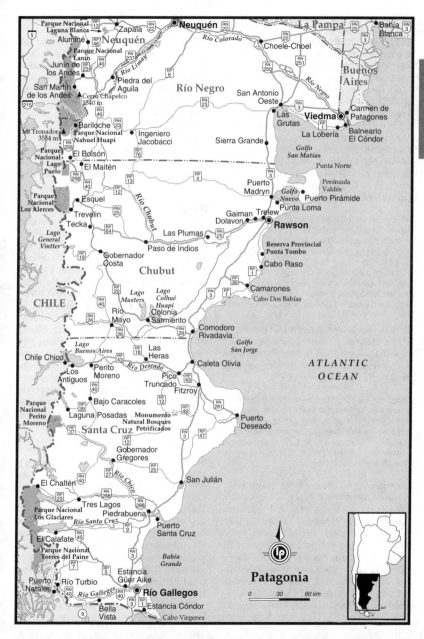

ARGENTINA

wealth of systematic information about Spain's American possessions, but Malaspina's unfortunate fall from political favor at court meant that he and his crew never received the recognition due them and their research. Iris Engstrad's *Spanish Scientists in the New World* contains a good account of Malaspina's and other Spaniards' scientific endeavors in the Americas.

Even after independence opened South America to visitors from countries other than Spain, Patagonia was among the last thoroughly explored areas. Undoubtedly, the most memorable early visit was Darwin's, as he dispelled some of the mystery and romance surrounding the Tehuelches:

We had an interview at Cape Gregory with the famous so-called gigantic Patagonians, who gave us cordial reception. Their height appears greater than it really is, from their large guanaco mantles, their long flowing hair, and general figure; on an average their height is about six feet, with some men taller and only a few shorter; and the women are also tall; altogether they are certainly the tallest race which we anywhere saw.

Darwin recognized, though, that the arrival of the white man meant the disappearance or subjugation of the Indian. Recording a massacre of Indians by Argentine soldiers, he ruefully observed:

Every one here is fully convinced that this is the justest war, because it is against barbarians. Who would believe that in this age in a Christian civilised country that such atrocities were committed? . . . Great as it is, in another half century I think there will not be a wild Indian in the Pampas north of Río Negro.

Darwin's predictions were remarkably precise. Although Patagonia remained a frontier for some decades, the inevitable occupation was bloody and brutal. In 1865 Welsh nationalists settled peaceably in eastern Chubut province and eventually spread westward, but from 1879 General Julio Argentino Roca carried out a ruthless war of extermination, known euphemistically as the Conquista del Desierto (Conquest of the Desert), against the region's first inhabitants. This war effectively

doubled the area under state control and opened up Patagonia to settlement.

Within a few years after the end of Roca's campaign, more than half a million cattle and sheep grazed former Indian lands in northern Patagonia. Eager to occupy the area before the Chileans could, the Argentine government made enormous land grants that became the large sheep estancias that still occupy most of the area today. In a few favored zones, such as the valley of the Río Negro near Neuquén, irrigated agriculture and the arrival of the railway encouraged colonization and brought eventual prosperity.

Geography & Climate

All of Argentine Patagonia lies in the rain shadow of the Chilean Andes, which block most Pacific storms. Consequently, except in a few locations along the Andean divide, the region is semi-arid to arid; Chilean Patagonia, more vulnerable to these westerly storms, supports a denser forest cover.

Although they drop their moisture in Chile, powerful westerlies blow almost incessantly across the Patagonian plains. Because of oceanic influence where the South American continent tapers toward the south, the region's climate is generally temperate, but winter temperatures can drop well below freezing. The Campo de Hielo Sur (southern continental ice field) extends from Chile into parts of Argentina.

Economy

The most obvious aspect of the economy is the sprawling sheep estancias that occupy almost every part of the region south of the Río Negro all the way to Tierra del Fuego. Cattle are fewer and much less important. The irrigated Río Negro valley, east of the city of Neuquén, has an ideal climate for fresh temperate fruits such as apples, which are sold throughout Argentina and also processed into products such as cider. Since extensive land uses like ranching employ relatively few people, the area south of the Río Negro is only thinly populated.

More important than sheep ranching is Patagonia's contribution to Argentina's energy supply. Major oil fields near Comodoro Rivadavia in Chubut province, Plaza Huincúl in Neuquén, and San Sebastián in Tierra del Fuego help make Argentina self-sufficient in petroleum, and the country even exports small amounts to neighboring countries. The coal reserves at Río Turbio, Santa Cruz province, are among the very few on the South American continent.

Tourism is a significant and growing part of the Patagonian economy. The region contains most of the country's national park lands, including three heavily visited units in the Andean lake district, where many Argentines spend their summer holidays: Nahuel Huapi and Los Arrayanes, near Bariloche; Lanín, near San Martín de los Andes; and Los Alerces, near Esquel.

These areas are also popular winter sports centers.

Farther south, Los Glaciares, near El Calafate, is also a major attraction. Access to several lesser known parks, like Perito Moreno and Bosques Petrificados, is difficult, but anyone who makes the effort to reach them will be well rewarded.

Río Negro & Neuquén Provinces

Río Negro and Neuquén together stretch from the Atlantic to the Andes. Most places of interest are near or along the Andes, but

ARGENTINA

The Patagonian Landscape

Visually, Patagonia has little in common with urbane Buenos Aires and the verdant Pampas provinces that surround the capital. On the sparsely vegetated plains of eastern Patagonia, visitors see a couple of straggling sheep and the occasional guanaco or rhea, but the few cities and towns are often hundreds of kilometers apart. Only a few sheltered and well-watered river valleys support any cultivation.

Traditionally, the Patagonian sheep estancia is the most important economic institution. Like the cattle estancia of the Pampas, it represents the concentration of large amounts of land in the hands of relatively few people, who employ a dependent, resident labor force. Like the cattle estancia, the sheep estancia served to also concentrate political power in the hands of a regional elite which, when threatened, has not been reluctant to use force to suppress discontent, although pay and working conditions have improved in recent decades.

Estancia names can be quietly eloquent. Many are optimistic, contrasting with the bleak steppes that surround them: *La Esperanza* (Hope), *Bella Vista* (Beautiful View), *La Armonía* (Harmony), *La Confianza* (Trust). Frequently they bear women's names: *La Julia, La Margarita, La Sarita*. A few commemorate an important date: *Primero de Abril, Tres de Enero*. Others bear indirect tribute to the aboriginal Tehuelches or Mapuches they dispossessed: *Pali Aike* (Place of Hunger), *Ototel Aike* (Place of Springs), *Choike Aike* (Place of the Rhea).

The central nucleus of an estancia usually consists of a settlement cluster, including the owner's or manager's casco, family housing for foremen and other married employees, and a bunkhouse for single men. There are also garages, workshops, a *pulpería* or company store, corrals, and a wool shed for shearing the sheep and storing the clip. Outside the settlement, sheep graze in the *campos*, fenced paddocks often thousands of hectares in size. In the more remote parts of the estancia, there will be an isolated puesto, where a resident shepherd will tend the sheep. Only during the spring shearing season will the sheep be gathered and brought into the settlement.

Most of the few cities in Patagonia, like Comodoro Rivadavia and Río Gallegos, are service centers for the estancias and the oil industry. Others, such as Bariloche, are tourist destinations in their own right. Wages are often much higher in Patagonia than elsewhere in the country, but few Argentines willingly relocate to what most perceive as an Argentine Siberia. When the recent Radical government of President Raúl Alfonsín proposed moving the seat of federal government from Buenos Aires to the northern Patagonian city of Viedma, shocked legislators and civil servants, accustomed to the amenities of the capital, forced him to reconsider and abandon the project. Much of Patagonia is still gaucho country, although the modern gaucho is now a dependent laborer whose past is idealized by Argentines in urban folklore festivals. ■

southbound visitors along the coast should at least stop over at Carmen de Patagones, a colonial relic.

Northern Patagonia's interior is mountainous, with alpine glaciers at the highest elevations. Near the Andean divide, diverse Valdivian forests cover the slopes, comprising extensive stands of southern beech, gigantic alerce, and the distinctive pehuén, known to English speakers as the monkey puzzle tree.

The native peoples of Río Negro and Neuquén were Puelches and Pehuenches (so-called for their dependence on the pehuén, the pine nuts of which formed the basis of their diet). Spaniards explored from the west in the late 16th century, but Mapuches who crossed the low Andean passes from Chile established their dominance in the region soon thereafter. Like the Plains Indians of North America, the Indians of Patagonia quickly learned to tame and ride the feral horses, which had multiplied on the Pampas, and used their new mobility to make life hard on anyone who invaded their territory. Like the Plains Indians, they suffered when the state decided their presence was intolerable.

During colonial times, Spanish expeditions sought but never found the "City of the Caesars," a southern El Dorado, but they did reach Lago Nahuel Huapi, still the centerpiece of the country's best known national park. Jesuit and Franciscan missionaries penetrated the region as early as the 17th century, but few survived the organized resistance of native peoples.

Only in the late 19th century did Argentina establish a permanent presence. The government placed such a high priority on settling the region that the Roca railway actually reached Neuquén before the turn of the century, but it did not connect the area to the port of Bahía Blanca in southern Buenos Aires province until the 1930s. The valley of the Río Negro soon became, according to one account, "a garden strip in a vast grazing region," as the government granted 100-hectare plots on the condition that each settler build a house, fence the land, and plant the poplar windbreaks that

remain a conspicuous element of the agricultural landscape. The Plaza Huincul oil fields between Neuquén and Zapala have contributed significantly to Argentina's energy self-sufficiency.

Travelers use Bariloche in Río Negro province as a base for exploring Parque Nacional Nahuel Huapi and other parks within a few hours north or south. Both winter and summer sports are popular. The city itself has rapidly overdeveloped, losing much of its former charm, but the surrounding countryside is still tranquil and pleasant.

CARMEN DE PATAGONES

The southernmost city in Buenos Aires province, this small town along RN 3 is the gateway to Patagonia. Founded in 1779, it conserves much of its late colonial heritage; its name derives from its patron Virgen del Carmen and from the region's first inhabitants. The town itself is often referred to simply as Patagones, but the townspeople are called *maragatos,* reflecting the origins of many colonists who came from the Spanish county of Maragatería in León. In 1827, during the war with Brazil, they repelled invaders superior in numbers and weapons.

Orientation

On the north bank of the Río Negro, 950 km south of Buenos Aires via RN 3, Carmen de Patagones (population 25,000) depends economically on the larger south bank city of Viedma, capital of Río Negro province. Launches loaded with maragatos regularly cross the river for work, school, shopping, and entertainment; the civic center and most historical landmarks are within a few blocks of the passenger pier. Two bridges connect Carmen de Patagones with Viedma. Both sides of the river have recreational balnearios, widely used for picnics and swimming in summer.

Information

Tourist Office The municipal Oficina de Turismo, at Comodoro Rivadavia 193 across from Plaza 7 de Marzo, provides a very helpful town map and an excellent walking tour guide.

Money To change money, try Banco de la Nación, Bynon 142; Banco de la Provincia de Buenos Aires, Comodoro Rivadavia and Alsina; and Banco del Sud at Avellaneda 16. All keep morning hours only.

Post & Telecommunications Correo Argentino is at Paraguay and Villegas; Carmen's postal code is 8504. There's a locutorio on Comodoro Rivadavia just south of Plaza Villarino; the area code is 0920.

Travel Agency Sudel Turismo (☎ 61594) is at Perito Moreno 6.

Walking Tour
The tourist office distributes a brochure (in Spanish only) describing the historic sites around Carmen de Patagones. Begin at **Plaza 7 de Marzo**; its original name, Plaza del Carmen, was changed after the 1827 victory over the Brazilians. Salesians built the **Iglesia Parroquial Nuestra Señora del Carmen** in 1883; its image of the Virgin, dating from 1780, is the oldest in southern Argentina. Visitors can see two of the original seven Brazilian flags captured in 1827 on the altar. Just west of the church, the **Torre del Fuerte** is the last vestige of the fort built in 1780, which once occupied the entire block. One block north, on 7 de Marzo, the elaborate **Teatro Español** dates from 1875.

Descending from the Torre del Fuerte, the **Escalinata** (steps), built in the 1960s, displays two cannons from forts that guarded the Patagonian frontier. At the bottom of the steps, **Rancho de Rial** (1820) is an adobe that belonged to Juan J Rial, the town's first elected mayor and later justice of the peace. At Mitre 27, the early-19th-century **Casa de la Cultura**, restored in 1981, was the site of a *tahona* (flour mill). Across the street, at the corner of Bynon and Mitre, **La Carlota** is now a museum, formerly a private residence, that is decorated with typical 19th-century furnishings. It's open weekdays from 10:30 to

11:30 am and from 7:30 to 8:30 pm, Sundays 7:30 to 8:30 pm only.

Mazzini & Giraudini was the home of prosperous merchants who owned the shop across the street from the pier. Its facade was restored in 1985. The house is part of the **Zona del Puerto** (port), which connected the town with the rest of the viceroyalty. At the **Solar Natal de Piedra Buena** is a bust of naval officer and Patagonian hero Luis Piedra Buena; the site at the foot of Bynon once included the general store, bar, and naval supply stores of his father.

One block west, what is now the **Casa Histórica del Banco de la Provincia de Buenos Aires** originally housed naval stores, but became in succession a girls' school, a branch of Banco de la Provincia, and then one of Banco de la Nación. Destroyed by a flood that ravaged Carmen de Patagone's riverside neighborhood and Viedma in 1899, it was rebuilt and occupied by several shops until its restoration by Banco de la Provincia in 1984. Since 1988, it has become a museum (☎ 62729), open weekdays 9 am to noon, daily 7 am to 9 pm. Nearby is **El Puerto**, a former waterfront bar.

Things to See
La Maragata, the first locomotive to arrive at Carmen de Patagones in 1921, is across from the train station at Juan de la Piedra at the north end of Italia. On Rivadavia five blocks west of Plaza 7 de Marzo, the **Cuevas Maragatas** (Maragatas Caves), excavated in the river bank, sheltered the first Spanish families who arrived in the 18th century. **Cerro de la Caballada**, where the battle with the Brazilians took place, offers a panoramic view.

Places to Stay
Viedma offers a wider choice of accommodations, but Carmen de Patagones does have three hotels. Probably the best value in town is *Residencial Reggiani* (☎ 61389), at Bynon 420 opposite Plaza Villarino, which has singles/doubles with shared bath for US$14/24 and with private bath for

ARGENTINA

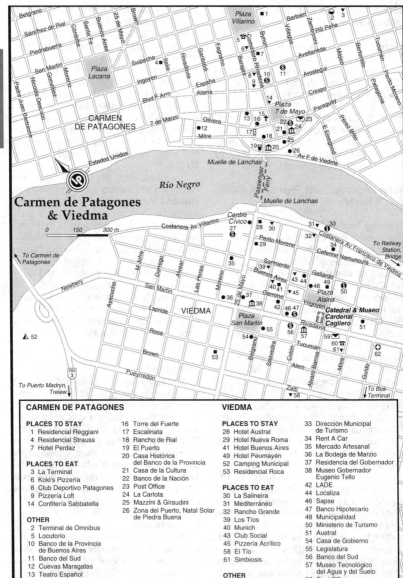

Río Negro

Carmen de Patagones
& Viedma

0   150   300 m

To Carmen de
Patagones

To Puerto Madryn,
Trelew

Plaza
Villarino

Plaza
Lacarra

CARMEN
DE PATAGONES

Plaza
7 de Mayo

Muelle de Lanchas

Muelle de Lanchas

Centro
Cívico

Costanera Av Villarino

Perito Moreno

Sarmiento

Buenos Aires

Garrone

VIEDMA

Plaza
San Martín

Plaza
Alsina

Catedral & Museo
Cardenal
Cagliero

Costanera Av Francisco de Viedma

To Railway
Station,
Bridge

To Bus
Terminal

CARMEN DE PATAGONES

PLACES TO STAY
1   Residencial Reggiani
4   Residencial Strauss
7   Hotel Perdaz

PLACES TO EAT
3   La Terminal
6   Koki's Pizzería
8   Club Deportivo Patagones
9   Pizzería Loft
14 Confitería Sabbatella

OTHER
2   Terminal de Omnibus
5   Locutorio
10 Banco de la Provincia
    de Buenos Aires
11 Banco del Sud
12 Cuevas Maragatas
13 Teatro Español
15 Municipalidad, Oficina de
    Turismo & Iglesia Parroquial
    Nuestra Señora del Carmen

16 Torre del Fuerte
17 Escalinata
18 Rancho de Rial
19 El Puerto
20 Casa Histórica
    del Banco de la Provincia
21 Casa de la Cultura
22 Banco de la Nación
23 Post Office
24 La Carlota
25 Mazzini & Giraudini
26 Zona del Puerto, Natal Solar
    de Piedra Buena

VIEDMA

PLACES TO STAY
28 Hotel Austral
29 Hotel Nueva Roma
41 Hotel Buenos Aires
49 Hotel Peumayén
52 Camping Municipal
53 Residencial Roca

PLACES TO EAT
30 La Salineira
31 Mediterráneo
32 Rancho Grande
39 Los Tíos
40 Munich
43 Club Social
45 Pizzería Acrílico
58 El Tío
61 Simbiosis

OTHER
27 Banco Provincia
    de Río Negro

33 Dirección Municipal
    de Turismo
34 Rent A Car
35 Mercado Artesanal
36 La Bodega de Marzio
37 Residencia del Gobernador
38 Museo Gobernador
    Eugenio Tello
42 LADE
44 Localiza
46 Sapse
47 Banco Hipotecario
48 Municipalidad
50 Ministerio de Turismo
51 Austral
54 Casa de Gobierno
55 Legislatura
56 Banco del Sud
57 Museo Tecnológico
    del Agua y del Suelo
59 Post Office
60 Telefónica
62 Hospital Artémides Zatti

US$18/28. Tiny but acceptable *Residencial Strauss* (☎ 62461) at Italia 393 has doubles for US$22. *Hotel Perdaz* (☎ 61495), at Comodoro Rivadavia and Irigoyen, has doubles for US$35, as well as multi-bed rooms at a slightly lower price per person, and also offers a reasonable breakfast.

Places to Eat
Restaurants include *La Terminal* at Barbieri and Bertorello, *Club Deportivo Patagones* at España and Rivadavia, and *Koki's Pizzería* at Comodoro Rivadavia 367. *Confitería Sabbatella* at Comodoro Rivadavia 218 is a pleasant café, while *Pizzería Loft* at Alsina 70 is also worth a try.

Getting There & Away
Connections with the rest of the country by bus, train, or plane are more frequent in Viedma. Patagones' Terminal de Omnibus (☎ 62666) is at Barbieri and Méjico, while the Ferrocarril Roca station is on Juan de la Piedra, at the north end of Italia. It's about 15 minutes between this station and the one in Viedma by train. The *balsa* (passenger launch) crosses the river on demand.

VIEDMA
In 1779, with his men dying of fever and lack of water at Península Valdés, Francisco de Viedma put ashore to found the city that would later take his name, on the bank of the Río Curru Leuvu (now the Río Negro). In 1879 it became the residence of the governor of Patagonia and the political and administrative center of the country's enormous southern territory. After territorial division, Viedma became the provincial capital and remained an important administrative site. A mostly modern city, it's less picturesque than Carmen de Patagones, but much livelier.

During the 1980s, Viedma enjoyed 15 minutes of fame when the Alfonsín administration proposed moving the federal capital here from Buenos Aires. Although these plans never materialized, some migrants who had anticipated the move have remained. In addition to numerous secondary schools, Viedma (population 45,000) houses a campus of the Universidad del Comahue, and a physical education center.

Orientation
On the south bank of the Río Negro, along RN 3 and only about 30 km from the Atlantic Ocean, Viedma is 960 km south of Buenos Aires, 275 km south of Bahía Blanca, and 180 km east of San Antonio Oeste. It's a compact town, suitable for walking, and the river itself is the focus of the city. Viedma's showpiece is the attractive Centro Cívico at 25 de Mayo and the Costanera Av Villarino.

Key provincial public buildings cluster around Plaza San Martín, including the Casa de Gobierno, the Residencia del Gobernador, and the Legislatura. Street names change on either side of Colón, except for Buenos Aires, which is continuous between 24 de Mayo and Yrigoyen.

Information
Tourist Offices In summer the Dirección Municipal de Turismo (☎ 27171), overlooking the river on the Costanera between Colón and Alvaro Barros, is open 8 am to 10 pm. The staff is attentive, competent, and highly motivated; local crafts and regional products are also for sale here, along with the tourist-oriented magazine *La Comarca que Viene.*

The provincial Ministerio de Turismo (☎ 24615), Gallardo 121, has brochures and information for the whole province. Expoventa Patagónica (☎ 31395), a private information office at RN 3 Km 696 that also sells regional products, is open 8 am to 2 pm and 5 to 11 pm.

ACA (☎ 22441) is at RN 3 Km 692.

Money Viedma has no cambios, but banks are open 8 am to 12:30 pm. Banco Hipotecario is at Colón and Rivadavia, and Banco Provincia de Río Negro is at the Centro Cívico. Banco del Sud has an ATM at San Martín and Colón.

Post & Telecommunications Correo Argentino is at Rivadavia 151, between

ARGENTINA

Alvaro Barros and Mitre; the postal code is 8500. Telefónica is at Mitre 531. Viedma's area code is 0920, the same as Carmen de Patagones.

Medical Services Hospital Artémides Zatti (☎ 22333) is at Av Rivadavia 351.

Museums

An impressive collection of tools, artifacts, and human remains of northern Patagonia's Tehuelche culture, as well as exhibits on European settlement, are on display at the **Museo Gobernador Eugenio Tello**, which also functions as a provincial research center in architecture, archaeology, physical and cultural anthropology, and geography. At San Martín 263, it's open weekdays 8:30 to 11:30 and daily from 7 to 9 pm.

The historical and ecclesiastical **Museo Cardenal Cagliero**, at Rivadavia 34, tells the story of the important Salesian Order, which catechized and educated Patagonian Indians. Near the cornor of Colón and Rivadavia, the **Museo Tecnológico del Agua y del Suelo**, an earth sciences oriented collection, is open weekdays 9 am to noon.

Organized Tours

Visitors should contact the municipal tourist office for walking tours on the **Circuito Histórico Cultural Viedma-Carmen de Patagones**, which covers the major historical landmarks and public buildings of both cities.

To get acquainted with the river, try the 1½-hour excursions on the catamaran *Curru Leuvu II*, which leaves from the Muelle de Lanchas (pier) Tuesdays to Sundays at 5 pm. The excursion fare is US$5 per adult and US$3 for children up to 12 years old.

Special Events

The Regata del Río Negro, in the second half of January, includes a weeklong kayak race that begins in Neuquén and ends in Viedma, a distance of about 500 km; in 1995, its 49 participants included several foreigners.

Places to Stay – bottom end

Camping The friendly riverside *Camping Municipal* west of RN 3, easily reached by bus from downtown, charges US$4 per person and an additional US$2 per tent. The partially shaded grounds are very tidy, although the plots are not clearly marked. Beware of the mosquitos in summer.

For noncampers, showers cost US$1; note that hot showers are available 7 pm to 7 am only – if you need an early shower, make it *very* early.

Hotels Except for camping, truly inexpensive accommodations are scarce in town. Clean, friendly *Hotel Nuevo Roma* (☎ 24510), 25 de Mayo 174, has singles/doubles with shared bath for US$12/15, with private bath for US$17/24; it also provides good, inexpensive food. *Hotel Buenos Aires* (☎ 24351), Buenos Aires 153, is basic for US$20 double.

Places to Stay – middle

The most economical mid-range choice is *Residencial Roca* (☎ 31241), Roca 347, where rooms cost US$25/38 with shared bath, US$30/45 with private bath. Overlooking Plaza Alsina, at Buenos Aires 334, *Hotel Peumayén* (☎ 25234) charges US$29/48. *Hotel Viedma* (☎ 23871) at Urquiza and Zatti is a good value for US$32/44.

Places to Stay – top end

Four-star *Hotel Austral* (☎ 22615), at Costanera Av Villarino 292, features nice river views for US$57/69.

Places to Eat

Locals mob popular *Pizzería Acrílico,* Saavedra 326, in the evening; it has flashy decor, good pizza, and mid-range prices except for the pasta, which is equally good but expensive by Argentine standards. Another worthwhile pizzería is *Los Tíos,* Belgrano 265.

Local parrillas worth trying include *El Tío* at Av Zatti and Colón and *Rancho Grande* at Av Villarino and Colón. For inexpensive meals, try the *Club Social* at Saavedra 246, 1st floor.

Simbiosis at Mitre 573 and *Munich* at Buenos Aires 169 have more varied menus. On the Costanera, *La Salineira* and *Mediterráneo* are both worth a look.

Things to Buy

Viedma's Mercado Artesanal (☎ 23207), Sarmiento 347, stocks varied regional crafts including wood carvings, silver work, ceramics, basketry, weavings, leather goods, and the like. Expoventa Patagónica (☎ 31395) at RN 3 Km 696, a private information office that also sells regional products, is open 8 am to 2 pm and 5 to 11 pm.

Mapuche Indian weavings are available at the municipal tourist office on the Costanera. The best place for wines is La Bodega de Marzio (☎ 22087), San Martín 319, which offers *vinos de la zona fría* (wines from cool climate grapes). Also try the pottery shop next to the post office.

Getting There & Away

Air Austral (☎ 22018), Yrigoyen 211, flies daily except Saturday to Buenos Aires (US$151) at 7 pm.

LADE (☎ 24420), Saavedra 403, has flights Mondays to San Antonio Oeste (US$21) and Puerto Madryn (US$34), and to Trelew (US$39) and Comodoro Rivadavia (US$79). Flights on Tuesdays go to Bahía Blanca (US$30), Mar del Plata (US$68), and Buenos Aires (US$97), and on Fridays to Neuquén (US$58) and Bariloche (US$101).

Sapse (☎ 21330) is at San Martín 57. It flies southbound Sundays to San Antonio Oeste (US$27), Bariloche (US$110), and El Bolsón (US$123); Mondays to San Antonio, General Roca (US$68), and Bariloche; Wednesdays to General Roca and Bariloche; Fridays to General Roca, Bariloche, El Bolsón, San Antonio Oeste, and Bariloche. Northbound flights to Buenos Aires (US$108) leave Sundays, Mondays,

Wednesdays, Thursdays, Fridays (twice), and Saturdays.

Bus Viedma's new Terminal de Omnibus is well south of downtown, at Guido 1580 and Av General Perón. La Puntual/El Cóndor (☎ 22748) has daily service north to Buenos Aires (US$62, 14 hours) and south along RN 3, and on Tuesdays and Fridays also goes to Bariloche (US$52, 19 hours). Fredes Turismo (☎ 30578), 7 de Marzo 726, also goes to the federal capital, while Codao has Wednesday and Saturday service to Bariloche (US$60, 14 hours).

Transportes Don Otto (☎ 25952) reaches Patagonian destinations along RN 3 as far south as Río Gallegos; at the same office, Transportadora Patagónica serves coastal destinations in Buenos Aires province, from Necochea to Mar del Plata. Transporte Mansilla (☎ 21385) goes to La Plata.

Central Argentino stops in Viedma en route between Rosario and Comodoro Rivadavia, while TUS/TUP (☎ 22748) links Viedma with Bahía Blanca, Santa Fe, and Córdoba. El Valle (☎ 22748) ascends the Río Negro valley to Neuquén and Bariloche, while Ticsa (☎ 21385) goes to Santa Rosa (La Pampa), San Luis, and San Juan.

Train Sefepa still runs northbound passenger trains on the Ferrocarril Roca (☎ 22130) at 10:56 pm Tuesday (to Bahía Blanca only, eight hours) and to Buenos Aires (20 hours) at 7:41 pm Fridays and 7:35 pm Mondays. Southbound trains to Bariloche (10 hours) leave at 7:18 pm Sundays, 8:53 pm Wednesdays, 3:11 pm Thursdays, and 6 pm Saturdays.

Getting Around

To/From the Airport Aeropuerto Gobernador Castello (☎ 22001) is on RP 51 southwest of town. There's no airport bus service, but it's close enough that cabs are reasonable.

Boat From the Muelle de Lanchas at the foot of 25 de Mayo, the launch *Ceferino Namuncurá* connects Viedma to Carmen de Patagones (US$0.40) on demand 6:30

am to 10 pm weekdays, 7 am to 9 pm Saturdays, and 9 am to 9 pm Sundays.

Car Rental Localiza (☎ 24307) is at Sarmiento 37. Rent A Car (☎ 30129) is at Namuncurá 78.

COASTAL RÍO NEGRO
Río Negro's 400 km of coastline attracts tourists with its many beaches, wildlife reserves, and summer resorts. The newly improved coastal highway RP 1 has opened up much of the area to recreation, but public transportation is limited and serves only a relatively small part of it.

Readers specifically interested in the San Antonio Oeste/Las Grutas area might acquire *La Costa Rionegrina* (Guías Regionales Argentinas/Ediciones Caleuche, Bariloche, 1993), a detailed guide that costs about US$3.

Balneario El Cóndor
This small resort, 32 km from Viedma, features a century-old lighthouse, the oldest in all of Patagonia. It has limited accommodations and a few restaurants, but there is a free campsite, plus excellent fishing for the tasty corvina. After the departure of the last tourists in late March, it shuts down for the winter.

Casino El Faro (☎ 25033) offers doubles with ocean views for US$60; other rooms are about US$10 cheaper. Empresa Ceferino (☎ 24542) buses to the balneario depart from Scheroni 383 in Viedma and cost US$2, continuing to La Lobería (US$4).

Centro de Interpretación Faunística Punta Bermeja (La Lobería)
This permanent colony of about 2000 southern sea lions (*Otaria flavescens*) is some 60 km south of Viedma via RP 1, on the north coast of the Golfo San Matías. At one time, commercial slaughter threatened the colony's survival, but the reserve has encouraged conservation, education, and research. The reserve's striking scenery features high bluffs with distinct strata and

The Patagonian hare *(mara)* inhabits scrub deserts and grasslands.

sandy beaches with occasional rock outcrops and tidal pools.

Activity at the colony is highly seasonal. The largest numbers occur during the spring mating season, when fights between males are common as they come ashore to establish harems of up to ten females each. From December onward, females give birth. The balcony from which visitors can watch, directly above the mating beaches, is safe and unobtrusive.

Numerous coastal birds frequent the area, both seasonally and permanently. The most common migrants are snowy sheathbills, gulls, cormorants, sandpipers, and oystercatchers. Black eagles, peregrine falcons, turkey vultures, and chimangos prey on the parakeets and swallows that nest in the cliffs, while the dunes provide a habitat for guanacos, rheas, maras (Patagonian hares), wildcats, vizcachas, skunks, foxes, armadillos, small reptiles, and rodents. The visitor center has a small interpretive exhibit on sea lions, a handful of stuffed pinnipeds and birds, and a confitería. It's possible to camp at barren *Camping La Lobería,* which has adequate sanitary facilities and a store, for US$2 per person and per tent.

West of La Lobería, RP 1 runs along

dunes covered by low grasses and native shrubs, then continues as a very dusty dirt road via Bahía Creek (excellent camping among immense dunes) to Punta Mejillón (site of another lobería with more difficult access). At Punta Mejillón the highway turns inland briefly before continuing west to intersect with paved RN 251, which returns to RN 3, near San Antonio Oeste.

Las Grutas

Rionegrinos congregate at Las Grutas (The Grottos), 179 km south of Viedma along RN 3, where, because of an extraordinary tidal range, the beaches can expand for hundreds of meters or shrink to just a few. Five formal *bajadas* (paths) provide access from town to the beaches. The town owes its name to the caves that the sea has eroded in the cliffs.

The Fiesta Nacional del Golfo Azul takes place in Balneario Las Grutas/San Antonio Oeste, during the first week of February. Outside peak season, Las Grutas's dunes, white sand beaches, and cliffs create a pleasant environment for walking, jogging, or simply relaxing; water sports like swimming, surfing, windsurfing, and diving are very popular. The abundant and rather costly hotels, 25 campgrounds, and (since 1988) a casino will discourage those in search of quiet and solitude – Las Grutas definitely gets crowded! Campgrounds charge from US$2 to US$6 per person, while rental houses are available for around US$35 per night for four persons. There are also timeshares.

The tourist office at Galería Antares, Primera Bajada, has good information about accommodations, as well as restaurant menus with prices. Tritón Turismo at Galería Casablanca, Local 15, Tercera Bajada, organizes ecologically oriented tours. There are hourly buses to San Antonio Oeste, 15 km away.

Sierra Grande

The southernmost town in eastern Río Negro province is the northernmost spot on RN 3 to purchase gasoline at "precios patagónicos" – less than half the price in Las Grutas/San Antonio Oeste. If at all possible, southbound motorists should avoid filling their tanks until they get here, and northbound motorists should not forget to do so.

BARILOCHE

Bariloche (formally San Carlos de Bariloche) is the urban center of the Argentine lake district and the base for exploring Parque Nacional Nahuel Huapi. In many ways, not all of them positive, it resembles European alpine resorts – the surrounding scenery is always pleasant and often spectacular, but crowds and traffic can be intolerable in the peak winter ski season and in summer. Uncontrolled growth has cost the city much of its former character as quaint neighborhoods have lost their views to multistory apartment buildings, and recent commercial development has impacted the lakefront.

Prior to the European invasion, native peoples freely crossed the Andean divide between Chile and Argentina via the Paso de los Vuriloches, south of the landmark Monte Tronador. Until the late 19th century, the Mapuche nation successfully resisted Argentine occupation, but General Roca's Conquista del Desierto made the area safe for immigrant settlers, many of them Germans who have left a visible imprint on the city's cultural landscape. Officially founded in 1902, the city really began to attract visitors after the southern branch of the Ferrocarril Roca arrived in 1934 and architect Ezequiel Bustillo adapted Central European styles into an attractive, tasteful urban plan.

Between 1980 and 1991, the population grew from 60,000 to more than 80,000, but even that impressive figure misleadingly understates the burgeoning numbers of hotels, time-shares, campgrounds and the like. The last decade's deplorable orgy of construction has overwhelmed Bustillo's efforts and, as a consequence, Bariloche has lost much of its perceived exclusivity; the silver lining is that prices have remained reasonable, and some even have fallen in recent years. The influx of visitors

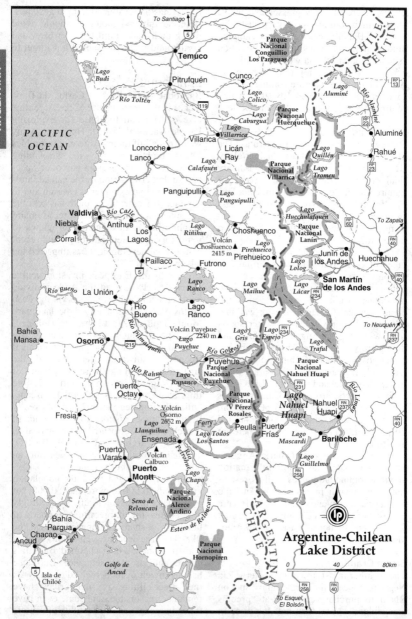

Argentine-Chilean Lake District

ARGENTINA

from South America's largest country has led to the ironic nickname "Brasiloche."

Bariloche has acquired some notoriety in recent years because former SS officer Erich Priebke, who fled here after allegedly overseeing a massacre of 335 Italian civilians near Rome at the end of WWII, has remained under house arrest while appealing extradition to Italy. The Menem administration, eager to mitigate Argentina's reputation as a haven for war criminals, has cooperated with the Italian request and has even created a Bariloche-based Instituto Contra la Discriminación, Xenofobia y Racismo (Institute Against Discrimination, Xenophobia, and Racism) to investigate such matters. In August 1995, however, an appeals court in General Roca rejected the Italian request, which proceeded to the Supreme Court in Buenos Aires, on the basis of an expired statute of limitations. In November 1995, the Supreme Court overturned the lower court's ruling, and Priebke was extradited to Italy for trial.

Orientation
On the south shore of Lago Nahuel Huapi's eastern end, 770 meters above sea level, Bariloche is 460 km southwest of Neuquén via RN 237. Entering the town from the east, RN 237 becomes the Costanera Av 12 de Octubre, continuing westward to the lakeside resort of Llao Llao. Southbound Calle Onelli becomes RN 258 to El Bolsón, on the border of Chubut province.

The city has a fairly regular grid pattern west of the Río Nireco and east of Bustillo's famous Centro Cívico, but north-south streets rise steeply from the lakeshore – some so steeply that they become staircases. The principal commercial area is along Av Bartolomé Mitre, but the new waterfront Puerto San Carlos, an overbuilt shopping center and marina, is taking some of the business a short distance north. Do not confuse similarly named Eduardo O'Connor and John O'Connor, which cross each other near the lakefront, or Perito Moreno and Ruiz Moreno, which intersect near Diagonal Capraro, at the east end of the downtown area.

Information
Tourist Offices The Secretaría Municipal de Turismo (☎ 23022) is at the Centro Cívico, at the east end of Av Bartolomé Mitre, across from the equestrian statue of General Roca. It is open from 8:30 am to 9 pm daily. It has many giveaways, including the blatantly commercial but still useful *Guía Busch,* which is loaded with basic tourist information about Bariloche and its surroundings, and is updated annually. The Ente Provincial del Turismo (☎ 23188), Palacios 217 1st floor, also operates a kiosk (☎ 22775, ext 23) at the Paseo de los Artesanos, Perito Moreno and Villegas. It's open daily from 9:30 am to 1 pm and from 5 to 8:30 pm.

Datos Andinos Patagónicos maintains a Centro de Información Turística (☎ 28999, 24531) at 20 de Febrero 24, next to the Club Andino Bariloche; it also publishes the homonymous *Datos Andinos Patagónicos,* a 224-page commercial guidebook that, among its many advertisements, has a great deal of useful information, excellent topographic maps, and suggestions for excursions in the immediate Bariloche area as well as to the rest of the lake district, from El Bolsón in the south to Aluminé in the north, and even across the border into Chile. If you read Spanish well and are spending more than a few days in the region, it can be a good investment for US$15.

ACA (☎ 23001) is at 12 de Octubre 785.

Foreign Consulates Of Bariloche's several consulates, all but Chile's are honorary.

Austria
  24 de Septiembre 230 (☎ 24873)
Chile
  Juan Manuel de Rosas 187 (☎ 23050)
Germany
  Ruiz Moreno 65 (☎ 25696)
Italy
  Villegas 135 (☎ 22020)
Spain
  Rolando 268 (☎ 22975)

Immigration Migraciones (☎ 23043) is at Libertad 191.

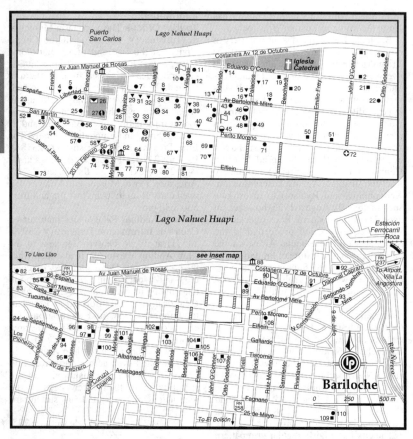

Money Change foreign cash and traveler's checks at Cambio Olano, Quaglia 238, which charges an extortionate 15% commission on traveler's checks. Bariloche is one of few Argentine cities outside Buenos Aires where currencies other than the US dollar will find a market.

Banks with ATMs include Banco de la Nación at Mitre 158, Banco de Crédito at Av San Martín 250, Banco del Sud at Mitre 424, Banco de Galicia at the corner of Moreno and Quaglia, and Banco de Quilmes at Mitre 433.

Post & Telecommunications Correo Argentino is next door to the municipal tourist office, at the Centro Cívico; the postal code is 8400. Just outside the tourist office are direct lines to the USA (ATT, MCI, Sprint), Japan, Spain, France, Italy, Chile, and Brazil for collect and credit card calls. There are several locutorios, the largest of which is at Bariloche Center at San Martín and Pagano. Bariloche's area code is 0944.

National Parks The Intendencia de Parques Nacionales (☎ 23111) is at San Martín 24. Another good source for parks information is the Club Andino Bariloche

ARGENTINA

(☎ 22266) at 20 de Febrero 30, which issues obligatory permits for trekking in Parque Nacional Nahuel Huapi. For further information, see the separate entry on Parque Nacional Nahuel Huapi below.

Cultural Centers There are occasional exhibitions at the Salón Cultural de Usos Múltiples (☎ 22775, ext 23), Perito Moreno and Villegas, which is also known by the unfortunate (at least in English) acronym SCUM.

Travel Agencies Bariloche may sink beneath lake level under the weight of its abundant travel agencies, most of which are along Av Bartolomé Mitre and its immediate cross streets. The Amex representative is Hiver Turismo (☎ 23792), Mitre 387.

Laundry Bariloche's laundries include Lavadero Huemul (☎ 20522) at Juramento 37, and Laverap on Rolando between Mitre and Perito Moreno.

Medical Services The Hospital Zonal (☎ 26100) is at Perito Moreno 601.

Storage Mochilas Guarderías, San Martín 82, stores backpacks and provides information as well.

Centro Cívico

The last decade's orgy of construction has eliminated most of Bariloche's European charm, but Bustillo's log and stone buildings housing the post office, tourist office, and museum still deserve a visit – if you can fend off the plaza photographers soliciting your portrait with their St Bernards or Siberian huskies. Come in the morning or at midday, before the shadows of the tawdry high-rise casino block out the sun.

Just north of the Centro Cívico, on the shores of Nahuel Huapi, builders have recently completed the massive new Puerto de San Carlos de Bariloche, a "recreational and shopping center" that includes an upscale marina for yachts and cruise ships. This monstrous eyesore has fortunately not blocked the view from the Centro Cívico, but it does little for the city's aesthetics.

Museo de la Patagonia

Lifelike stuffed animals, well-prepared archaeological and ethnographic materials, and critically enlightening historical evaluations on topics such as Mapuche resistance to the Conquista del Desierto and Bariloche's urban development make this diverse and recently remodeled museum on the Centro Cívico one of the best in the country. It has a specialized library, and there is a bookstore in the lobby.

Admission to the Museo de la Patagonia (☎ 22309) is US$2.50. Hours are Monday from 10 am to 1 pm, Tuesday from 10 am to Friday from 10 am to 12:30 pm and 2 to 7 pm, and Saturday from 10 am to 1 pm.

Other Museums

Bariloche's new **Museo Arquitectónico** (Architectural Museum, ☎ 25160), in the historic Oficina de Tierras at Elflein 6, is open weekdays 9 am to noon and 3 to 8 pm. Admission is free.

Bariloche's Club de Caza y Pesca, at 12 de Octubre and Onelli, operates the **Museo Ictícola** (☎ 22043), which addresses fish biology, the stocking of game fish, and fishing. It's open daily 2 to 8 pm; admission is free.

Hiking & Trekking

Countless hikes and treks are possible in Parque Nacional Nahuel Huapi; the Parques Nacionales office in Bariloche distributes a brochure with a simple map that rates hikes as easy, medium, or difficult and suggests possible loops; it is adequate for initial planning. Many of the hikes are detailed in LP's *Trekking in the Patagonian Andes*.

The Club Andino Bariloche (☎ 22266), 20 de Febrero 30, provides information and issues obligatory permits for trekking in Parque Nacional Nahuel Huapi; for US$3, their *Mapa General de la Guía de Sendas y Picadas* is cartographically mediocre, but has good trail descriptions of many popular hikes. Another good source of information and advice, especially for assistance in climbing the park's more difficult peaks, is the Asociación Argentina de Guías de Montaña (☎ 22567), Neumeyer 60.

Fishing

Fishing in Argentina's more accessible Andean-Patagonian parks, from Lago Puelo and Los Alerces in the south to Lanín in the north, draws visitors from around the world for both native and exotic species. The most popular introduced species are European brown trout, rainbow trout, brook trout, and landlocked Atlantic salmon, which reach impressive sizes. Native species, which should be thrown back, are generally smaller; these include *perca* (perch), *puyen*, Patagonian pejerrey, and the rare *peladilla*.

On larger lakes like Nahuel Huapi,

trolling is the preferred method, while fly-fishing is the rule on most rivers. Night fishing is prohibited. The season runs from mid-November to mid-April. For more information, contact the Club de Caza y Pesca (☎ 22403) at Costanera 12 de Octubre and Onelli.

Seasonal licenses, available from the Intendencia de Parques Nacionales at the Centro Cívico or the provincial department of Recursos Naturales at Morales and Elflein, cost US$100, while monthly licenses cost US$60 and weekly licenses US$30. Rental equipment is easily available in town.

Cycling & Mountain Biking

Bicycles are ideal for the Circuito Chico and other trips near Bariloche, where most roads are paved. Even the gravel roads are good, and Argentine drivers are less ruthless, slowing and even stopping for the scenery. Mountain bike rental, usually including gloves and helmet, costs about US$20 per day at a number of places.

For rentals, try Baratta e Hijos (☎ 22930) at Belgrano 50, Pochi (☎ 26693) at Perito Moreno 1035, Ramírez (☎ 25229) at 9 de Julio 961, Bikeway (☎ 24202) at Eduardo O'Connor 867, Bariloche Mountain Bike at Gallardo 375, Solo Bici (☎ 23574) at Neumeyer 40, and Honda Diéguez (☎ 28614) at Otto Goedecke 169, one block south of ACA.

Horseback Riding

Horseback excursions start at around US$60 per half day and US$120 per full day. Among them are Cabalgatas con Valery (☎ 60060) at Villa Catedral, the Club Hípico Bariloche (☎ 48193) at Av Bustillo Km 15.5, and Estancia Nahuel Huapi (☎ 23835).

Skiing

In winter, most people come to Bariloche for skiing; the runs around Bariloche were once South America's trendiest and best known, but other areas in Argentina (especially Las Leñas, near Mendoza) and Chile (Portillo and Valle Nevado) have pretty much superseded the Nahuel Huapi area, which is more popular with Argentines than foreigners. Gran Catedral, the largest and most popular area, amalgamates two formerly separate areas, Cerro Catedral and Lado Bueno, so skiers can buy one ticket valid for lifts in both areas. There is also the smaller Piedras Blancas area on Cerro Otto; for details, see the separate entry on Parque Nacional Nahuel Huapi below.

In addition to the ski schools at Gran Catedral, you might also contact Catedral (☎ 26402) at Juramento 190, 2nd floor, or the Club Andino Bariloche (☎ 24579) at 20 de Febrero 30. For rental equipment, try Baruzzi (☎ 24922) at Urquiza 250 or Martín Pescador (☎ 22275) at Rolando 257. Equipment is also available on site at Piedras Blancas and Gran Catedral.

White-Water Rafting

River rafting on the Río Limay (an easy Class 2 float) and the Río Manso (a Class 3 white-water descent with enough rapids to be interesting) have become increasingly popular in recent years. Among the companies offering these activities are Expediciones Náuticas (☎ 27502) at Rolando 268, Local 4; Safaris Acuáticos (☎ 32799) at Morales 564; and Rafting Adventure (☎ 32928), Av San Martín 82, 2nd floor. These are generally 20-km day trips that usually cost around US$65 and include a hearty lunch and Neoprene wet suits, helmets, and other equipment.

Other Water Sports

Sailing, windsurfing, canoeing, and kayaking have all become popular on Lago Nahuel Huapi and other nearby lakes and streams. For equipment rentals, try Baruzzi (☎ 24922) at Urquiza 250 or Martín Pescador (☎ 22275) at Rolando 257 opposite Cumbres Patagonia.

Organized Tours

Bariloche proper offers little beyond the opportunity to eat and drink well, and to see and be seen, but Parque Nacional Nahuel Huapi has many more possibilities. This section suggests some organized excursions, but consult the separate entry on Parque Nacional Nahuel Huapi for more detailed information.

City Tour Pochi's gaudy motorized *trencito* (little train) conducts regular city tours, starting at the Centro Cívico, but is hardly worthwhile unless you're too tired to walk. Trips to Isla Huemul, in Lago Nahuel Huapi, leave from Puerto San Carlos.

Half-day trips from Bariloche include Cerro Otto, Cerro Catedral (US$13 without chair lift access), the Circuito Chico west of town (US$13), Cascada de los Césares, and Isla Victoria and Parque Nacional Los Arrayanes (for more detailed information on the latter, see Villa La Angostura, Neuquén province). The latter can also be done as a full-day trip.

Other full-day trips include Puerto Blest and Laguna Frías (US$22), Cerro Tronador and Cascada Los Alerces via Lago Mascardi (US$29), the Circuito Grande to San Martín de los Andes via Siete Lagos (US$34), and the delightful town of El Bolsón (US$29). Beyond Villa Mascardi, 30 km south of Bariloche, scenic RN 258 to El Bolsón is no longer the stone-covered washboard surface it once was, but continuing road construction still makes day trips dusty, tiring, and inadvisable.

Catedral Turismo (☎ 25443) at Av Bartolomé Mitre 399 covers all these destinations, but so do many other travel agencies. Catedral Turismo also arranges the bus-boat combination over the Andes to Puerto Montt for US$90, which leaves weekdays at 9 am.

If you belong to ACA (☎ 23001) or any of their overseas affiliates, their office at Costanera 12 de Octubre 785 can arrange these excursions at discounts of at least 10%.

One more expensive but unique tour alternative is German-run Argentoura Travel. Their custom-designed vehicle does a half-day excursion on the Circuito Chico (US$39 including picnic) and a full-day circuit of the nearby Patagonian steppe (US$115), including a lunch stop at an estancia and mountain biking or horseback riding. English and several other languages are spoken. Their Bariloche representative is Cumbres Patagonia (☎ 23831), Villegas 222.

Special Events
In January and February, the Festival de Música de Verano puts on several different events, including the classical Festival de Música de Cámara (Chamber Music Festival), the Festival de Bronces (Brass Festival), and the Festival de Música Antigua (Ancient Music Festival).

In March, the Muestra Floral de Otoño allows the city's horticulturalists to show off their green thumbs, while the Salón Cultural de Usos Múltiples (SCUM) has displays of three-dimensional arts in April. May 3 is the Fiesta Nacional de la Rosa Mosqueta, after the fruit of the wild shrub used in many regional delicacies.

During the ski season, Bariloche holds its Fiesta Nacional de la Nieve (National Snow Festival), while in October horticulturalists show their early season colors at the Fiesta del Tulipán (Tulip Festival) and the Muestra Floral de Primavera (Spring Flower Show).

A December event is the Navidad Coral (Christmas Chorus).

Places to Stay
Bariloche's abundance of quality accommodations, ranging from camping and private houses to five-star hotels, makes it possible to find good values even in high season, but it's sometimes necessary to be patient. Some visitors may wish to look outside of town, where the ambience is more pleasant.

The municipal tourist office maintains a computer database with current prices, and the list below is only a cross-section of the possibilities.

Places to Stay – bottom end
Camping The nearest organized camping area to Bariloche is *La Selva Negra* (☎ 41013), three km west of town on the road to Llao Llao. Despite a few reports of unfriendly staff and less than perfect main-

tenance, it does have good facilities, and you can step outside your tent to pick apples in the fall. Fees are US$8 per site. Other sites between Bariloche and Llao Llao include *Camping Yeti* (☎ 42073) at Km 6.5, where sites cost US$7, and *Camping Petunia* (☎ 48152) at Km 13.5, which costs US$6.

Hostels Bariloche has two hostels, generally open only during summer and winter holidays. One is the popular *Albergue Alaska* (☎ 61564), 7½ km outside of town on the road to Llao Llao, which charges US$10 per person with kitchen privileges; it also has cooking and laundry facilities, rents mountain bikes, and arranges cheap tours and ski transfers. Bus Nos 10, 20, and 21 drop off passengers near the hostel. For reservations, contact the Asociación Albergues de la Juventud or the Asatej student travel agency in Buenos Aires (see the Buenos Aires chapter).

The other hostel is the more central *Albergue Los Andes* (☎ 22222), Perito Moreno 594, which charges US$13 but lacks a kitchen. Hostels will only be open during summer and winter holidays.

Casas de Familia Bariloche's best values are casas de familia, starting around US$10 per person at places like that of the Vallejos at Emilio Frey 635, between Tiscornia and Albarracín, which has hot showers and cooking facilities. The Ferreyra family (☎ 22556), Elflein 163, offers a more central possibility, while friendly Señora Heydée (☎ 25072) at Martín Fierro 1525 (firm beds, but the rooms are a little cramped) is near the bus/train station.

In the convenient, woodsy Barrio Belgrano, overlooking the Centro Cívico, you'll find several slightly dearer but agreeable and comparable choices. These include Señora Marianne Pirker (☎ 24873) at 24 de Septiembre 230, who also has an attractive one-bedroom apartment for US$20; Señora Rosa Arko (☎ 23109) at Güemes 691; Señora Carlotta Baumann (☎ 29689) at Av Los Pioneros 860; and Eloisa Lamuniere (☎ 22514) at 24 de Sep-

tiembre 71. The houses in this area all help each other out, so if one is full they'll refer you to their friends.

Residenciales, Hosterías & Hotels
Hospedaje El Mirador (☎ 22221), a converted private house at Perito Moreno 658, charges US$7 per person with shared bath and US$10 with private bath. At *Hospedaje Monte Grande* (☎ 22159), 25 de Mayo 1544, rates are US$12 per person.

Recommended *Hostería del Inca* (☎ 22644), Gallardo 252, has singles/doubles for US$10/20. For around US$12 per person, among the better values in regular accommodations are *Residencial Lo de Gianni* (☎ 33059) at Elflein 49 and *Residencial San Fernando* (☎ 25150) at 20 de Febrero 664. Convenient *Hostería Posada del Sol* (☎ 23011), Villegas 148, costs US$14 with breakfast. *Residencial Tito* (☎ 24039), at Eduardo O'Connor 745, is in an unimpressive building, but it's a friendly place and often full. It charges about US$15 per person.

Others in this category include quiet, comfortable *Residencial Nogaré* (☎ 22438) at Elflein 56 for US$10; *Residencial Martín* (☎ 22055) at 20 de Febrero 555 for US$12 per person, US$15 with breakfast; and *Residencial Torres* (☎ 23355) at Tiscornia 747 for US$15. The slightly more expensive *Casa Nogueira* (☎ 23648), Elflein 205, is fussy about backpackers. *Hotel Campana* (☎ 22162), Belgrano 165, is comparably priced but friendlier.

Places to Stay – middle
Many of Bariloche's mid-range accommodations are, for some inexplicable reason, overpriced compared to some of the better low-end places. For US$38 double, for example, the appealing *Residencial Wickter* (☎ 23248), Güemes 566, is a lesser value than other places in Barrio Belgrano. One of the better values is lakefront *Hotel Pilmayquén* (☎ 26175), Costanera 12 de Octubre 705 at John O'Connor, which offers rooms for US$20 per person. Two attractive hillside hotels are lesser values than they once were: *Hostería Ivalú*

(☎ 23237) at Frey 535 for US$40 double and *El Viejo Aljibe* (☎ 23316) at Frey 571 for US$25/40 single/double, both including breakfast.

Very centrally located *Hotel Internacional* (☎ 25938), Mitre 171, charges US$30/40 single/double. *Residencial Sur* (☎ 22677), Beschtedt 101 at Eduardo O'Connor, has very large beds in some very small rooms, with private bath, for US$30/45 single/double. This includes a generous breakfast, but even with a 10% discount for ACA members it's still a bit overpriced. Across the street, at Beschtedt 136, the unfortunately named *Hostería Piuké* (☎ 23044) charges US$45 double. At Eduardo O'Connor 702, just one block from the cathedral, inviting *Hostería El Ñire* (☎ 23041) charges US$30/40. Clean and quiet *Hostería La Sureña* (☎ 22013), San Martín 432, is comparably priced, as is recommended *Hotel Las Piedras II* (☎ 25594) at Palacios 235.

Places to Stay – top end

Upscale accommodations start at around US$60/80 single/double at *Hotel Aconcagua* (☎ 24718), San Martín 289, and *Hotel Carlos V* (☎ 25474), Morales 420. *Hotel Bella Vista* (☎ 22435), Rolando 351, charges US$68/90.

Five-star *Hotel Edelweiss* (☎ 26165), San Martín 202, charges US$108/135, while the budget-busters at *Hotel Lagos de la Patagonia* (ex-Panamericano, ☎ 25846), San Martín 536, extort US$188 double.

Places to Eat

For all its shortcomings, Bariloche has some of Argentina's best food. It's unlikely you'll have time or money enough to sample all the worthwhile restaurants, but a broad sample appears below.

Regional specialties deserve mention, include *jabalí* (wild boar), *ciervo* (venison), and *trucha* (trout); some places, like *Familia Weiss* (☎ 24829) at Palacios 167, specialize in smoked game and fish. At the vegetarian end of the spectrum, *La Esquina de las Flores,* the landmark Buenos Aires restaurant and natural foods market, has

recently opened a local branch at 20 de Febrero and Juramento.

French-Italian *Rigoletto* (☎ 26672) at Villegas 363 emphasizes pasta, lomo, and trout; alongside it is a parrilla, *El Boliche de Alberto 2 Restaurant Lennon* (☎ 23182), Perito Moreno 48 between Urquiza and Quaglia, is good, inexpensive, and decorated in a Beatles theme. The *Bagdad Café,* Eduardo O'Connor 1348, is a pub with a midday plato del día, usually something like ñoquis, for just US$3.

La Vizcacha (☎ 22109), at Rolando 279, is one of the country's best and cheapest parrillas, offering a pleasant atmosphere and outstanding service. Its standard parrillada for two includes not only the usual beef but also chicken breast, garnished with red peppers and parsley. In addition to butter, you get deer pâté and Roquefort cheese spreads. With a liter of house wine, the total bill comes to about US$20.

Another parrilla is *1810* (☎ 23922) at Elflein 167, although some LP correspondents have complained of high prices, indifferent service, and the staff's unwillingness to allow diners to share a portion. *La Andina* (☎ 23017), Elflein 95 at Quaglia, has been recommended for good food, large portions, and moderate prices – and no objections to portion-sharing.

Recommended *El Rincón,* Villegas 216, features parrillada, trout, and wild game, but it's not cheap. *Restaurant Jauja* (☎ 22952), Perito Moreno 220, has a good European-style menu but erratic service, relatively small portions, and upscale prices.

There are many pizzerías. *Cocodrilos* (☎ 26640), at Mitre 5, serves a very fine fugazzeta at a very reasonable price. Also try *La Andinita* (☎ 22257) at Mitre 56 for excellent fugazzeta, *El Mundo de la Pizza* (☎ 25910) at Mitre 370, or *Pizzaiola* (☎ 26181) at Pagano 275 just north of the Bariloche Center. *Pin 9,* Rolando 118, has good pizza and beer, but portions are small. A recent readers' recommendation is *Pizzería Vogue,* on Palacios opposite Familia Weiss.

La Alpina (☎ 25693), at Perito Moreno

98 at Quaglia, is a good and popular confitería, but there are innumerable others. *Copos*, open 24 hours at Mitre 392, serves good coffee and hot chocolate, and fresh croissants at reasonable prices. Befitting its name, *El Viejo Munich* (☎ 22336), Mitre 102, has excellent draft beer served with complimentary peanuts. Try also *Dino's* (☎ 25903) at Mitre 298.

Outstanding ice cream is available at *Helados Bari* (☎ 22305), España 7, a block from the Centro Cívico, *Melgari* at Mitre and Quaglia, and *Abuela Goye* (☎ 22276) at Quaglia 221.

The new Patio de Comidas in the waterfront Puerto San Carlos (☎ 27850) has several restaurants, including *Nino's Sandwichería* and the parrilla *Lanca-Hue*.

Entertainment
Cinema Cine Arrayanes (☎ 22860), Perito Moreno 39, is Bariloche's only remaining cinema.

Dance Clubs Several dance clubs along Av Juan Manuel de Rosas appeal to a youngish crowd but tend to be expensive – usually charging around US$30 for cover, which at least includes one drink. Among them are Cerebro (☎ 24948) at Rosas 405, Rockett (☎ 23257) at Rosas 424, and Grisú (☎ 22269) at Rosas 574.

Pub Moritz, Mitre 1530, attracts a slightly older crowd, about 25 to 30 years old. The Quincho del Hotel Bella Vista (☎ 22435), Rolando 351, features salsa and other Latin American music. Cauquén, at Km 13.8 on the Llao Llao road, is a parrilla that also features music for dancing. Tanguería and Gallery, San Martín 164, are also worth a look, as is La Farola at RN 258, Km 12.5.

Things to Buy
Bariloche is renowned for its sweets and confections. Del Turista and Fenoglio, across the street from each other on Mitre, are virtual supermarkets of chocolate and also good places for a cheap standup cup of coffee or hot chocolate, as well as dessert. Benroth, at Mitre and Quaglia, and Abuela Goye, at Villegas 232, are also good outlets for chocoholics.

Local craftsworkers display their wares in wool, wood, leather, and other media at the Paseo de los Artesanos, Villegas and Perito Moreno, between 10 am and 9 pm daily. The Mercado Artesanal, San Martín 459, also has local, regional, and Chilean handicrafts.

Getting There & Away
Air Aerolíneas Argentinas (☎ 23091, 22425) and LADE (☎ 23562) are both at Mitre 199. Aerolíneas has ten flights weekly to Buenos Aires (US$244), while LADE flies Mondays to Neuquén (US$43), Viedma (US$58), Trelew (US$64), and Comodoro Rivadavia (US$92); Fridays to Esquel (US$24), Puerto Madryn (US$64), Trelew, and Comodoro Rivadavia. Discount carrier LAPA (☎ 23714), Villegas 137, flies daily except Thursdays and Saturdays to Buenos Aires (US$149).

TAN (☎ 27889), Neuquén's provincial carrier, has offices at Villegas 144. It has flights to Esquel (US$34) and Calafate (US$140) Thursdays and Sundays; to Chapelco/San Martín de los Andes (US$25) and Neuquén (US$62) Mondays, Tuesdays, Wednesdays, and Fridays; to Neuquén only Thursdays and Sundays; to Puerto Montt, Chile (US$49), Wednesdays and Fridays; and to Comodoro Rivadavia (US$103) Wednesdays and Fridays. It offers senior citizen discounts, but only with payment in cash.

Sapse (☎ 28257), Palacios 266, flies to El Bolsón (US$23) Sundays and Fridays; to Esquel (US$30) Sundays, Mondays, and Thursdays; to San Antonio Oeste (US$72), Viedma (US$110), and Buenos Aires (US$136) Sundays and Fridays; to General Roca (near Neuquén, US$41), San Antonio Oeste, Viedma, and Buenos Aires Mondays; to Bahía Blanca (US$95) and Buenos Aires Sundays and Mondays; and to General Roca, Viedma, and Buenos Aires Wednesdays and Fridays.

Bus Bariloche currently uses the old train station as its Terminal Ferroviario

(☎ 26999), but most companies continue to have downtown offices, some of them shared, and drop off passengers there, creating gridlock in the narrow streets. Unless mentioned otherwise, the offices below are at the terminal. Shop around for the best deals, since there are frequent promotional fares.

Chevallier (☎ 23090), Perito Moreno 107, has daily departures at 2 pm for Buenos Aires (US$72, 22 hours) via Santa Rosa, La Pampa province; it also offers Tuesday and Sunday service to Rosario (US$76) via Santa Rosa (US$58). La Estrella (☎ 22140), Palacios 246, leaves daily for Buenos Aires at 3:20 pm via Bahía Blanca, and is slightly cheaper (US$60) to the capital. With El Valle (☎ 28589), Moreno 365, the trip to Buenos Aires costs US$70 via Neuquén (US$35) and Bahía Blanca (US$60). Coche cama service to Buenos Aires costs only US$5 more.

El Canario (☎ 26181, ext 258), Oficina 28 in the Bariloche Center at San Martín 127, has the cheapest fares (about US$55) to Buenos Aires; Vía Bariloche, in the same office, is slightly dearer. El Sureño (☎ 30122) goes nightly to Bahía Blanca (US$55) and Buenos Aires (US$60).

Tirsa (☎ 26999), Quaglia 197, goes Tuesdays and Sundays to Rosario (US$83, 24 hours). TUS (☎ 24565), Elflein and Rolando, serves Córdoba five times weekly (US$105, 22 hours).

Don Otto (☎ 26999) goes daily to El Bolsón (US$10), Esquel (US$21), and Comodoro Rivadavia (US$68, 14 hours), with connections to Río Gallegos (US$108; one correspondent calls the 28-hour plus voyage "agonizing"). Don Otto also has service to Trelew (US$51) and Puerto Madryn (US$55).

Charter (☎ 21689), Perito Moreno 138, runs two buses daily to El Bolsón (three hours, US$8). It also offers a faster (two hours) minibus service for US$11. Codao (☎ 26228) at John O'Connor 180, Mercedes (☎ 26999), and Vía Bariloche have similar bus service. Mercedes' two buses to El Bolsón continue to Esquel (five hours,

US$21); it also runs daily to Neuquén (US$30, seven hours) and, along with El Rápido, to Necochea (US$73), Miramar (US$80), and Mar del Plata (US$83). Vía Bariloche has additional daily long-distance service to Buenos Aires (US$95), connecting to Posadas (US$135) and Puerto Iguazú (US$150).

Andesmar (☎ 30211) also has a daily service to El Bolsón, continuing to Esquel (US$28); in addition, it has connections in Neuquén (US$30) for southbound Patagonian destinations. Andesmar's daily northbound services beyond Neuquén include stops in San Rafael (US$50) and Mendoza (US$61), with connections to San Juan (US$69), La Rioja (US$80), Catamarca (US$86), Tucumán (US$96), Salta (US$109), Jujuy (US$110), and Pocitos (US$124), on the Bolivian border.

TAC (☎ 26599), Mitre 86, runs three buses weekly to Mendoza (US$68, 22 hours) via Zapala (US$25) and San Rafael (US$56), with connections to Córdoba (US$88), and a daily service to Buenos Aires (US$69) and La Plata (US$73).

Turismo Algarrobal (☎ 23081) serves Villa La Angostura, on the north side of Lago Nahuel Huapi (US$6.50, two hours). La Puntual (☎ 26999) connects Bariloche with the provincial capital of Viedma (US$52, 16 hours), stopping en route at Ingeniero Jacobacci (US$14) for connections with the narrow gauge railway to Esquel. Codao also goes to Jacobacci, San Antonio Oeste, and Viedma, and to Villa Traful Friday mornings and afternoons.

Ko-Ko (☎ 23090), Perito Moreno 107, has buses to Junín de los Andes (US$19) and San Martín de los Andes (US$22), some via the longer paved La Rinconada (RN 40) route rather than the more scenic Siete Lagos route, on which paving is proceeding slowly.

Several companies cover the route between Bariloche and Chile. Mercedes (☎ 26999), Bus Norte (☎ 26228) at Juan O'Connor 180, TAS Choapa (☎ 26663), at Perito Moreno 138, and Cruz del Sur (☎ 24163) at San Martín 453, all go to Osorno and Puerto Montt, with connections to northern destinations. Fares vary between US$18 and US$25.

Train Sefepa (Servicio Ferrocarril Patagónico, ☎ 23172) leaves from the Estación Ferrocarril Roca across the Río Ñireco along RN 237. Mondays at 4:40 pm, the *tren tradicional* (no sleepers) does the 36-hour trip to Constitución station in Buenos Aires; Fridays at 8:48 pm it goes only as far as Viedma. The more comfortable *tren español* leaves at 5 pm Fridays for Constitución, while its Tuesday 8:18 pm service goes only to Bahía Blanca.

Fares vary depending on type or coach: primera, literas, pullman, or dormitorio. To Ingeniero Jacobacci, they range in price from US$7 to US$10 (no dormitorio); to San Antonio from US$18 to US$39; to Viedma from US$22 to US$49; to Bahía Blanca from US$34 to US$64; and to Constitución from US$53 to US$98.

Getting Around

To/From the Airport Aeropuerto Teniente Candelaria (☎ 22767) is 15 km east of town via RN 237 and RP 80. Sapse and TAN run their own minibuses to the airport, while LADE, LAPA, and Aerolíneas use Transporte Alí, which leaves Aerolíneas downtown offices 1½ hours before each flights. The price is US$3.

Bus From the corner of Moreno and Rolando, Codao (☎ 26228) and Micro Omnibus 3 de Mayo (☎ 26173) run hourly buses to Cerro Catedral for US$2.40 one-way. Codao uses Av de los Pioneros, while 3 de Mayo takes Av Bustillo. In summer 3 de Mayo goes four times daily to Lago Mascardi.

From 6 am to midnight, bus No 20 leaves every 20 minutes to the attractive lakeside towns of Llao Llao and Puerto Pañuelo.The No 10 bus also goes to Llao Llao via Colonia Suiza, seven times daily, allowing you to do the Circuito Chico (see the section on Parque Nacional Nahuel Huapi below) on inexpensive public transport. You can walk any section and flag down the buses en route.

Omnibus 3 de Mayo's No 50 bus goes to Lago Gutiérrez every 30 minutes, while in summer the company's Línea Mascardi goes to Villa Mascardi and Los Rápidos/ Lago Los Mosocos four times daily. Their Línea El Manso goes twice daily to Río Villegas and El Manso, on the southwestern border of the Parque Nacional Nahuel Huapi.

Car Rental Bariloche is loaded with all the standard car rental agencies and a few local ones to boot: AI (☎ 26420) at San Martín 235, Avis (☎ 25371) at Libertad 124, Budget (☎ 22482) at Perito Moreno 461, Dollar (☎ 22283) at Moreno 187, 1st floor, and Carro's (☎ 24869) at Mitre 26.

PARQUE NACIONAL NAHUEL HUAPI

In bequeathing the lands that comprise Parque Nacional Nahuel Huapi to the Argentine state in 1904, Francisco Pascasio Moreno stipulated that they "be conserved as a natural public park" and emphasized his desire that "the current features of their perimeter not be altered, and that there be no additional constructions other than those that facilitate the comforts of the cultured visitor." At present, however, as the oldest and one of the most heavily visited units in the Argentine system, Nahuel Huapi plays the same role as Yosemite in the United States, attracting so many people that the very values it presumes to uphold are at

The pudú is an endangered mammal.

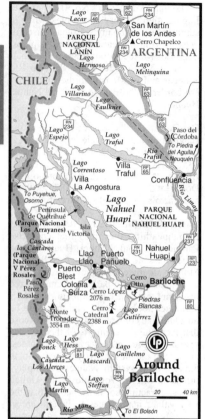

Around Bariloche

and covering more than 500 sq km that is the source of the Río Limay, a major tributary of the Río Negro. To the west a ridge of high peaks separates Argentina from Chile; the tallest is 3554-meter Tronador, an extinct volcano that still lives up to its name of "Thunderer" when blocks of ice tumble from its glaciers. During the summer months, wildflowers blanket alpine meadows.

Besides its scenery, Nahuel Huapi was created to preserve local flora and fauna, including its Andean-Patagonian forests and rare animals. Tree species are much the same as those found in Parque Nacional Los Alerces (see separate entry below), while the important animal species include the *huemul* or Andean deer *(Hippocamelus bisulcus)* and the miniature deer known as *pudú (Pudu pudu)*. Most visitors are not likely to see either of these, but several species of introduced deer are common, along with native birds. Both native and introduced fish species offer excellent sport.

The USA-based National Outdoor Leadership School (NOLS, ☎ 307-332-6973), 288 W Main St, Lander WY 82520, runs a "Semester in Patagonia" program, lasting 75 days (university credit possible), which takes place partly in Parque Nacional Nahuel Huapi. Most of the program takes place in Chile, however, where NOLS's local base is the town of Coyhaique.

Books

For trekking maps and information about hiking in the region, see Clem Lindenmayer's LP guide *Trekking in the Patagonian Andes* or, if you read Spanish, the locally published *Las Montañas de Bariloche* (Guías Regionales Argentinas, 1993) by Toncek Arko and Raúl Izaguirre. *Datos Andinos Patagónicos* (see the Information entry for Bariloche, above) contains useful contour maps and information on refugios in the park.

Claudio Chehébar and Eduardo Ramilo's *Fauna del Parque Nacional Nahuel Huapi* (Administración de Parques Nacionales & Asociación Amigos del Museo de la Pata-

risk. Some of Nahuel Huapi's problems stem from the fact that nearly half the park is a "national reserve," in which certain commercial activities are permitted or even encouraged, as opposed to having a strictly protected status. Another problem is nearby Bariloche's phenomenal growth from a modest village to an urban enclave that threatens its surrounding environment with noise, pollution, and sprawl.

Parque Nacional Nahuel Huapi occupies 750,000 hectares in mountainous southwestern Neuquén and western Río Negro provinces. Its centerpiece is Lago Nahuel Huapi, a glacial remnant over 100 km long

gonia Francisco P Moreno) is a guide to the park's animal life.

Circuito Chico

One of the most popular trips in the area, with excellent views, this excursion begins on Av Bustillo, on the outskirts of Bariloche, and continues to the tranquil resort of Llao Llao, named for the so-called "Indian bread" fungus. At Cerro Campanario, Av Bustillo Km 17, the Aerosilla Campanario (☎ 27274) carries passengers to a panoramic view of Lago Nahuel Huapi for US$7.

Llao Llao's Puerto Pañuelo is the point of departure for the boat-bus excursion across the Andes to Chile. Have a look at the grounds of the state-owned *Hotel Llao Llao* (☎ 48525, 48544), a national treasure that became a topic of political controversy when, in the summer of 1990-1991, two Italian businessmen who had given Argentine President Carlos Menem an expensive sportscar a few months earlier sought government permission to take over the hotel. They got it, and for a paltry US$290 per night, you, too,can enjoy what may be the country's single most prestigious lodging. In fact, that's the price for a "senior" room, but bargain "refugios" are available for US$135 double, suites for US$210, and "estudios" for US$270.

From Llao Llao you can double back to **Colonia Suiza**, named for its early colonists and the site of the annual Fiesta Nacional del Curanto (celebrating a typical dish of white and red meat, or vegetarian; it is very different from its Chilean namesake, a seafood stew). A modest confitería has excellent pastries, and camping is possible. The road passes the trailhead to 2075-meter **Cerro López**, a three-hour climb, before returning to Bariloche. At the top, it's possible to spend the night at the Club Andino Bariloche's *Refugio López* (☎ 26042 in Bariloche for reservations), where meals are also available.

Although travel agencies operate this as a tour, it's easily done on public transportation. For details, see the Getting Around entry for Bariloche.

Isla Victoria

In Lago Nahuel Huapi, Isla Victoria is a large island on which the Argentine park service trains park rangers, attracting students from throughout Latin America. Boats to Isla Victoria and to Parque Nacional Los Arrayanes on the Quetrihué peninsula leave from Puerto Pañuelo at Llao Llao, but you can visit Los Arrayanes more easily and cheaply from Villa La Angostura (see the separate entry under Neuquén province below). From Bariloche's Puerto San Carlos, the trip costs US$33; from Puerto Pañuelo, it costs US$25.

Cerro Otto

Cerro Otto (altitude 1405 meters) is an eight-km hike on a gravel road west from Bariloche. The Teleférico Cerro Otto (☎ 41035), at Km 5 on Av de Los Pioneros, carries adult passengers to the summit for US$15, children for US$5; a free bus leaves from the corner of Mitre and Villegas or Perito Moreno and Independencia to the base of the mountain. Bring food and drink – prices at the summit confitería are truly extortionate.

Piedras Blancas (☎ 25720, ext 1708) is the nearest ski area to Bariloche, at Km 6 on the road to Cerro Otto. There's a trail from Piedras Blancas to the Club Andino's *Refugio Berghof,* at an elevation of 1240 meters; make reservations, since there are only 20 beds.

Cerro Catedral

This 2400-meter peak, 20 km southwest of Bariloche, contains the area's most important ski center, the **Centro de Deportes Invernales Antonio M Lynch**. Several chair lifts and the Aerosilla Cerro Bellavista (US$8), which also operates during the summer, carry passengers up to 2000 meters, where there is a restaurant/confitería offering excellent panoramas. Several trekking trails also begin here; one relatively easy four-hour walk goes to Club Andino's *Refugio Emilio Frey,* where 40 beds and simple meals are available. This refugio itself is exposed, but there are sheltered tent sites in what is also Argentina's prime rock-climbing area.

There is a good mix of easy, intermediate, and advanced skiing runs, with some very steep advanced runs at the top and some tree runs near the base. The resort is popular, and crowds can sometimes be frustrating. Lift lines can develop, but lift capacity is substantial enough that waits are not excessive. One LP reader has complained that much of the lift equipment is outmoded, but improvements appear to be underway.

Lift passes at Gran Catedral start at US$32 per day for adults, US$26 for children; two-day and three-day passes get only small discounts, but one-week passes entail more substantial savings at US$192 for adults, US$156 for children. Rental equipment costs as little as US$9 per day, but quality equipment is considerably more expensive, ranging up to US$44 per day for competition equipment. Gran Catedral also has several ski schools at Villa Catedral, at the base of the lifts, including Robles Catedral (☎ 60050), Ski Club (☎ 60012), and Ski Total (☎ 60094).

Hostería del Cerro (☎ 60026), at the base of the lifts, charges US$123/176 single/double in the high season, but public transport from Bariloche is excellent, consisting of hourly buses from downtown with Micro Omnibus 3 de Mayo. There is also a good road to the large parking lot at the base of the ski area.

Monte Tronador

From Lago Mascardi, this full-day trip up a one-way dirt road goes to Pampa Linda, where camping is possible, and visits the Ventisquero Negro (Black Glacier) and the base of Tronador; traffic goes up in the morning (until 2 pm) and down in the afternoon (after 4 pm). For US$12 per person, the Club Andino Bariloche organizes transport to Pampa Linda daily at 9 am, returning at 5 pm, with Transporte RM (☎ 23918); some have found the trip itself dusty and unpleasant.

From Pampa Linda, hikers can approach the Club Andino's snowline *Refugio*

Meiling on foot and continue to Laguna Frías via the Paso de las Nubes; it's a five-to seven-hour walk to an elevation of 2000 meters. It's also possible to complete the trip in the opposite direction via the bus-boat-bus combination from Llao Llao/ Puerto Pañuelo to Puerto Blest, then hike up the Río Frías to Paso de las Nubes before descending to Pampa Linda via the Río Alerce.

Climbers intending to scale Tronador should anticipate a three- to four-day technical climb requiring experience on both ice and rock.

Places to Stay

There are numerous campgrounds in the Bariloche area. Besides those in the immediate Bariloche area, there are sites at Lago Mascardi, Lago Los Moscos, Lago Roca, Lago Guillelmo, and Pampa Linda. With permission from park rangers, campers can stay for free in certain areas. Refugios charge US$7 per night, US$2 for day use, and US$2 extra for kitchen privileges.

Within the park are a number of hotels tending to the luxurious. One of the best is *Hotel Tronador* (radiotelephone 26759) at the west end of Lago Mascardi on the road to Pampa Linda, where doubles cost US$125 with half-pension.

EL BOLSÓN

According to its reputation throughout Argentina and South America, El Bolsón is a tolerant mecca for ponytailed hippies who live on woodsy communes, drive VW Kombis, eat macrobiotic food, and make a living peddling handmade jewelry and pottery on the streets. In part, this image is accurate, making this sixties' anachronism and its surroundings a welcome relief from Bariloche's vulgar commercialism. Traditionally the utterly dismal highway between Bariloche and El Bolsón holds back the deluge of bourgeois porteños who overrun the Nahuel Huapi area throughout the year. Instead, El Bolsón invites backpackers.

El Bolsón's 3500 townspeople and their government were the first in Argentina to declare their hometown a "nonnuclear zone" and an "ecological municipality." This broadly supported policy was in part a response to the Menem administration's attempt (now abandoned) to locate a nuclear dump in nearby Chubut province. Communications are in fact better with northern Chubut than with Río Negro.

The local economy relies on tourism, agriculture, and forestry. Rows of poplar trees give a Mediterranean appearance to the chacras, most of which are devoted to hops (nearly three-quarters of the country's production), soft fruits such as raspberries and strawberries, and orchard crops such as cherries and apples. Beer and sweets made from the local harvest are excellent. Motorists should note that El Bolsón is the northernmost spot to purchase gasoline at Patagonian discount prices.

Orientation

Near the southwestern border of Río Negro province, El Bolsón lies in a basin surrounded by high mountains, dominated by the longitudinal ridges of Cerro Piltriquitrón to the east and the Cordón Nevado along the Chilean border to the west. At an

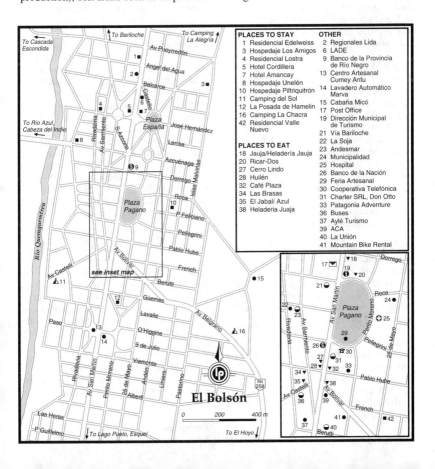

PLACES TO STAY
1 Residencial Edelweiss
3 Hospedaje Los Amigos
4 Residencial Lostra
5 Hotel Cordillera
7 Hotel Amancay
8 Hospedaje Unelén
10 Hospedaje Piltriquitrón
11 Camping del Sol
12 La Posada de Hamelin
16 Camping La Chacra
42 Residencial Valle Nuevo

PLACES TO EAT
18 Jauja/Heladería Jauja
20 Ricar-Dos
27 Cerro Lindo
28 Huilén
32 Café Plaza
34 Las Brasas
35 El Jabalí Azul
38 Heladería Juaja

OTHER
2 Regionales Lida
6 LADE
9 Banco de la Provincia de Río Negro
13 Centro Artesanal Cumey Antu
14 Lavadero Automático Marva
15 Cabaña Micó
17 Post Office
19 Dirección Municipal de Turismo
21 Vía Bariloche
22 La Soja
23 Andesmar
24 Municipalidad
25 Hospital
26 Banco de la Nación
29 Feria Artesanal
30 Cooperativa Telefónica
31 Charter SRL, Don Otto
33 Patagonia Adventure
36 Buses
37 Aylé Turismo
39 ACA
40 La Unión
41 Mountain Bike Rental

El Bolsón

elevation of 300 meters on the east bank of the Río Quemquemtreu, it is about 130 km from both Bariloche and Esquel on RN 258. South of Bolsón, in Chubut, the road is either paved or being paved, while the stretch of road 90 km north of Bolsón toward Bariloche is also undergoing improvement on what has been one of the worst road surfaces in all of Argentina.

From the south, RN 258 enters town as the diagonal Av Belgrano, but it briefly becomes Av Bolívar and north-south Av San Martín through the town. The principal landmark in the center of town is the semi-oval Plaza Pagano, which has a small artificial, and often dry, lake. Most services are nearby, but the majority of the area's natural attractions are outside town.

Information

Tourist Offices The Dirección Municipal de Turismo (☎ /fax 92604) is at Av San Martín and Roca, at the north end of Plaza Pagano. Though less attentive than it might be, it provides a good town map and brochures, along with complete, well-organized information on accommodations, food, tours, and services, but maps of the surrounding area are very poor. It's open 9 am to 9:30 am daily in summer, 9 am to 6 pm the rest of the year.

For motorists, ACA (☎ 92260) is at Avs Bolívar and San Martín.

Money El Bolsón has no ATMs or cambios. Banco de la Nación is at Av San Martín and Pellegrini, across from the south end of the Plaza Pagano, while Banco de la Provincia del Río Negro is just north of the tourist office, at the corner of San Martín and Dorrego.

Post & Telecommunications Correo Argentino is at Av San Martín 2608, near Dorrego; the postal code is 8430. The Cooperativa Telefónica is at Juez Fernández 429, at the south end of Plaza Pagano. El Bolsón's area code is 0944, the same as Bariloche's.

Travel Agencies Travel agencies include

Patagonia Adventure (☎ 92713) at Pablo Hube 418 and Aylé Turismo (☎ 92329) in the Galería del Cerro at San Martín and Castelli.

Laundry Lavadero Automático Marva is at the corner of San Martín and Paso.

Medical Services The Hospital de Area (☎ 92240) is on Perito Moreno, behind Plaza Pagano.

Radio La Señal, FM 89.1 Mhz, is El Bolsón's community-based, free-form radio station, offering an outstanding mix of folk, blues, jazz, and similar programs.

Dangers & Annoyances In early 1995, El Bolsón was the site of a mysterious viral outbreak which, by June, had claimed four lives. Initial speculation was that the virus, which killed its victims within 24 hours of infection, was similar to the rodent-born hantavirus of the southwestern USA, so travelers in the area should make special efforts to avoid places such as sheds and ruined houses, which may be frequented by rats and mice. Note that these rodents are only carriers of the virus, which seems to be transmitted via droppings. When the droppings are disturbed, the virus becomes airborne and is inhaled by victims.

Feria Artesanal

On Thursdays and Saturdays in summer, and Saturdays only the rest of the year, local craftspeople sell their wares at the south end of the Plaza Pagano from 10 am to 2 pm. It's also one of the best places in town to eat delicacies such as homemade empanadas and sausages, Belgian waffles with fresh raspberries, and locally brewed beer.

Festival Nacional del Lúpulo

Local beer gets headlines during the national hops festival, over four days in mid-February.

Activities

Rent mountain bikes at Perito Moreno

2355, behind the ACA gas station, by the hour, half-day, or full day.

Places to Stay – bottom end
Budget travelers are more than welcome in El Bolsón, where reasonable prices are the rule rather than the exception. The tourist office maintains a long list of private houses that offer lodging.

Camping Of El Bolsón's many campgrounds, the most central is dusty but shady municipal *Camping del Sol,* at the west end of Av Castelli, which has hot showers, a small confitería, and swimming in the river. Rates are US$4 per person per day. For US$5, *Camping La Chacra* (☎ 92111), off Av Belgrano one km from downtown, has more grass, less dust, and less shade. *Camping La Alegría* (☎ 92204), on Camino de los Nogales north of town, costs US$5 per person the first night, US$4 each succeeding night.

Hostel Hourly local buses go to *Albergue El Pueblito,* in Barrio Luján, about four km north of town. A good place to meet Argentine backpackers, this fine and friendly facility has room for 40 people and places to camp. Rates are US$8 with hostel card, US$9 without.

Hospedajes Although not quite up to the standards of the local tourist office, informal *Hospedaje Los Amigos,* on Islas Malvinas at the west end of Balcarce, is acceptable and charges about US$6 per person; with a tent you can camp in the garden for a bit less. For US$10 per person with shared bath, try *Hospedaje Piltriquitrón* at Saavedra 2729 or *Hospedaje Unelén* (☎ 92729) at Azcuénaga 350.

Residenciales & Hosterías A recent reader's recommendation is *Residencial Salinas,* Roca 641, which has rooms for US$10 that include a private log fire. Slightly more expensive is *Hostería Steiner* (☎ 92224), Av San Martín 600, which charges US$12/26 single/double. At *Residencial Edelweiss* (☎ 92594), Angel del Agua 360 near Av San Martín, rates are US$25 double with shared bath. *Residencial Lostra* (☎ 92252), Av Sarmiento 3212 at José Hernández, charges US$15 per person with private bath.

Places to Stay – middle
Mid-range accommodations start at around US$24/35 at *La Posada de Hamelin* (☎ 92030), at Granollers 2179, while *Residencial Valle Nuevo* (☎ 92087), at 25 de Mayo 2329, charges US$26/36. Clean, comfy *Hotel Amancay* (☎ 92222), Av San Martín 3217, has rooms with private bath for US$28/43.

Places to Stay – top end
At least until the autobahn from Bariloche brings the crowds, the three-star *Hotel Cordillera* (☎ 92235), Av San Martín 3210, is top of the line at US$51/64.

Places to Eat
Restaurants in El Bolsón mostly lack the variety of Bariloche, but the food is consistently a good value and often outstanding, thanks in large part to fresh, local ingredients and careful preparation. Probably the best and most economical place to eat is the *Feria Artesanal* (see separate entry above), where the goodies range from fresh fruit to Belgian waffles (with raspberries and cream), very cheap empanadas and sandwiches, frittatas, milanesa de soja (vegetarian milanesa), regional desserts, and many other goodies. You'll be tempted to sample everything.

Huilén (☎ 92480), at San Martín 2524, has superb breakfasts for as little as US$2.50. *Café Plaza,* at Av San Martín 2557, is a first-class confitería, while *Ricar-Dos,* behind the tourist office at Roca and Moreno, has above-average offerings. *Cerro Lindo,* Av San Martín 2526, has large, tasty pizzas, good music, and excellent, friendly service.

For a splurge, *Jauja* (☎ 92448), Av San Martín 2867, is one of Argentina's best values – though not cheap, ingredients are first-rate, the preparation is excellent, the decor (which includes imaginative flower arrangements) appealing, the music good but not noisy, and the service agreeable. Its very extensive menu includes pasta with tasty sauces, milanesa de soja, pizza, fish, vegetarian soup, homemade bread, and locally brewed beer. Save room to gorge yourself on the astoundingly good home-made, fruit-flavored ice cream next door at *Heladería Jauja,* one of Argentina's very best. The ice creamery has a smaller outlet, with fewer flavors, on Av San Martín near Bolívar.

El Jabalí Azul, at Sarmiento and Castelli, is an inexpensive but indifferent parrilla at Sarmiento 2530, but *Las Brasas* at Sarmiento and Hube is a superb choice for beef, and the service is excellent.

Things to Buy
There are plenty of goodies in El Bolsón. For fresh fruit and homemade jams and preserves, visit the berry plantations at Cabaña Micó, just a few blocks beyond the east end of Roca. The owners have a modern, water-saving drip and micro-spray irrigation system for their raspberries and strawberries. Other good places for regional sweets are Dulces del Doctor Miklos, on Balcarce near Av Sarmiento, and La Soja, the health-food store at Sarmiento and Ameghino. Heladería Jauja (see Places to Eat, above) and Regionales Lida, Av San Martín 3440, sell outstanding chocolate products.

Besides the twice-weekly Feria Arte-sanal (see above), there are several other outlets for local arts and crafts. Centro Artesanal Cumey Antu, Av San Martín 2020, sells Mapuche clothing and weav-ings; hours are 9 am to 1 pm. Taller Arte-sanal Sukal, two km outside town on the road to Cerro Piltriquitrón, sells dried flower arrangements and painted wood products, such as jewelry boxes.

Getting There & Away
Air LADE (☎ 92206), Castello 3253, flies to Bariloche (US$13), Chapelco (US$25), and Zapala (US$42) Wednesdays; to El Maitén (US$10), Esquel (US$16), and Comodoro Rivadavia (US$64) Thursdays.

The Sapse agent is at Turismo Ayle (☎ 92329), in the Galería del Cerro oppo-site the ACA station on San Martín. It flies Sundays to Bariloche (US$23), San Anto-nio Oeste (US$93), Viedma (US$123), and Buenos Aires (US$150); Fridays to Bari-loche, Viedma, and Buenos Aires.

Bus El Bolsón has no central bus terminal, but most companies are close to each other on or near Av San Martín. Several compa-nies go to Bariloche (US$10, three hours): Andesmar (☎ 92178) at Sarmiento 2678; Vía Bariloche (☎ 92161) at Roca 357 and San Martín; La Unión (☎ 92358) at San Martín and Berutti; Don Otto and Charter SRL (☎ 92333) at San Martín 2536 near Pablo Hube; and Mercedes (☎ 92727) on Castelli near San Martín.

Andesmar, Mercedes, and Don Otto go to Esquel (US$16, three hours), with Don Otto continuing to Comodoro Rivadavia. Mercedes also serves El Maitén, Neuquén, Mar del Plata, and Buenos Aires, but Andesmar has the most extensive north-bound connections. El Sureño (☎ 92178), Sarmiento 2678, also goes to Buenos Aires nightly (US$75, 26 hours).

Zabala Daniel (☎ 92145), Perito Moreno 2377 just north of the bike rental shop, has the only service to Esquel via Parque Nacional Los Alerces, at 11 am and 5 pm daily in summer, but there have been com-plaints about the availability of seats for those with open tickets to continue to Esquel.

Getting Around
Bus La Golondrina (☎ 92557) goes to Mallín Ahogado, leaving from the corner of Café Plaza, while buses to Río Azul leave from Bolsón Tour (☎ 92161), at the corner of Roca and San Martín.

Quimey Quipán (☎ 92483), Perito Moreno 2960, has buses to Lago Puelo (½ hour, US$3) and back at 7 and 9:30 am, and at 12:15, 3:30, 6, and 9 pm. Buses leave from the post office and the ACA station.

Taxi Some of Bolsón's taxi drivers have a

reputation for avarice, but try Radio Taxi Glaciar (☎ 92892); their driver Diógenes has been recommended for his local knowledge and reasonable prices.

AROUND EL BOLSÓN
Cabeza del Indio

On a ridge top eight km west of town, this metamorphic rock formation truly resembles a stereotypical profile of the "noble savage." Part of the trail traverses a narrow ledge that offers the best views of the formation itself, but by climbing from an earlier junction you can obtain better views of the Río Azul and, in the distance to the south, Parque Nacional Lago Puelo.

Cascada Mallín Ahogado

This waterfall on the Arroyo del Medio, a tributary of the Río Quemquemtreu, is ten km north of town, west of RN 258. Beyond the falls, a gravel road to the Club Andino Piltriquitrón's *Refugio Perito Moreno* (☎ 93912) offers lodging for US$6 per night, with a capacity of 80 persons. Meals are an additional US$8.

From the refugio, it's 2½ hours to the 2206-meter summit of **Cerro Perito Moreno**. In winter months, there's skiing at the Centro de Deportes Invernales Perito Moreno, where the base elevation is 1000 meters. The T-bar lifts reach 1450 meters.

Cascada Escondida

Downstream from Cascada Mallín Ahogado, this waterfall is eight km from El Bolsón. There is a footpath beyond the bridge across the river at the west end of Av Pueyrredón.

Cerro Piltriquitrón

Dominating the landscape east of Bolsón, the 2260-meter summit of this granitic ridge yields panoramic views across the valley of the Río Azul to the Andean crest along the Chilean border to the west. After driving or walking to the 1000-meter level (the 11-km road costs about US$15 by taxi), another hour's steep and dusty walk takes you to the Club Andino's *Refugio Piltriquitrón* (☎ 92024), where beds cost

US$7 per person – an outstanding value. Moderately priced meals are available, but bring your own sleeping bag.

Water is abundant along most of the route to the summit, but hikers should carry a canteen and bring lunch to enjoy at the top. From the refugio a steep footpath climbs along the rusted tow bar (only cross-country skiing is possible now), then levels off and circles east around the peak before climbing again precipitously up loose scree to the summit, marked by a brightly painted cement block. On a clear day, the tiring two-hour climb (conspicuously marked by paint blazes) rewards the hiker with views south beyond Lago Puelo, northwest to landmark Cerro Tronador, and beyond the border, the snow-topped cone of Volcán Osorno in Chile's Parque Nacional Vicene Pérez Rosales.

Cerro Lindo

Southwest of Bolsón, a trail from Camping Río Azul goes to *Refugio Cerro Lindo* (☎ 92763), where you can get a bed for US$6; meals are extra. It's about four hours to the refugio, where the trail continues to the 2150-meter summit.

El Hoyo

Just across the provincial border in Chubut, this town's microclimate makes it the local "fresh fruit capital." Nearby Lago Epuyén has good camping and hiking.

Parque Nacional Lago Puelo

In Chubut province, but only 15 km south of El Bolsón, this windy, azure natural lake is suitable for swimming, fishing, boating, hiking, and camping. There are regular buses from El Bolsón, but reduced service on Sunday, when you may have to hitch. Both free and fee campsites are at the park entrance; *Camping Lago Puelo* charges US$5 per person, including tent and vehicle.

With all the hubris of military bureaucracy, the Argentine navy maintains a mobile prefecture in a caravan near the dock, where the launches *Emanuel, Popeye 2000,* and *Elita* take passengers across the lake to Argentina's Pacific Ocean outlet at the Chilean border (US$20 per person), where's it's possible to continue by foot or horseback to the Chilean town of Puelo on the Seno de Reloncaví, with connections to Puerto Montt. This is roughly a three-day walk. For US$30, the launches also take passengers to El Turbio, at the south end of the lake, where there's a campground.

NEUQUÉN

Established as the capital of its namesake province because of its strategic location along the railroad at the junction of two major rivers, Neuquén is also an important service center for the agricultural towns of the Río Negro valley. As the road and rail gateway to the Andean lake district, it has good connections to Bariloche and Chile. A clean, modern city, it's not a major attraction, but it's well worth a day's stopover for its good restaurants and attractive parks.

Orientation

At the confluence of the Río Limay and the Río Neuquén, 265 meters above sea level, Neuquén (population 300,000) is the province's easternmost city. Paved highways go east to the Río Negro valley, west toward Zapala, and southwest toward Bariloche and the lake district.

Also known as Félix San Martín, east-west RN 22 is the main thoroughfare, a few blocks south of downtown (do not confuse Av San Martín, the obligatory homage to Argentina's national hero, with Félix San Martín). The principal north-south route is Av Argentina (Av Olascoaga south of the train station). Street names change on each side of Av Argentina and the train station. Several diagonals bisect the conventional grid.

Information

Tourist Offices The provincial Subsecretaría de Turismo (☎ 24089) is at Félix San Martín 182, corner of Río Negro, three blocks south of the train station. It is open weekdays 7 am to 9 pm, weekends 8 am to 9 pm. For tourist information, the province

of Neuquén is one of the best organized in the entire country, with free, up-to-date maps and brochures that contain truly useful material rather than glossy photos.

ACA (☎ 22325) is on the diagonal 25 de Mayo between Santa Fe and Buenos Aires.

Foreign Consulates Chile has a consulate (☎ 22727) at La Rioja 241; Spain has one (☎ 22466) at Alberdi 72.

Immigration Migraciones (☎ 22061) is at Santiago del Estero 466.

Money Neuquén has two cambios: Olano at the corner of J B Justo and Yrigoyen, and Pullman at Ministro Alcorta 144, between San Luis and La Pampa. Several banks have ATMs, including Banco Provincia and Banco Dorrego, alongside each other on Av Argentina between Rivadavia and Av Independencia, and Banca Nazionale del Lavoro, at the corner of Av Argentina and Rivadavia, which also issues US dollars.

Post & Telecommunications Correo Argentino is at Rivadavia and Santa Fe, at the intersection with the 25 de Mayo diagonal; the postal code is 8300. Telefónica is nearby on Alberdi, between Santa Fe and Córdoba. Neuquén's area code is 099.

Travel Agencies Neuquén has dozens of travel agencies, almost all of which are near downtown.

Medical Services Neuquén is known throughout Argentina for the quality of its medical services which, in some circumstances, are free. You should not hesitate to consult the Hospital Regional (☎ 43-1474) at Buenos Aires 421.

Art Museums

The **Sala de Arte Emilio Saraco**, in the old cargo terminal at the railroad station, has current art exhibits and is well worth a look if you're killing time waiting for a bus connection. It's free, and open weekdays 9 am to 8 pm, weekends 2 to 9 pm.

Also worth checking out is **Juntarte en**

ARGENTINA

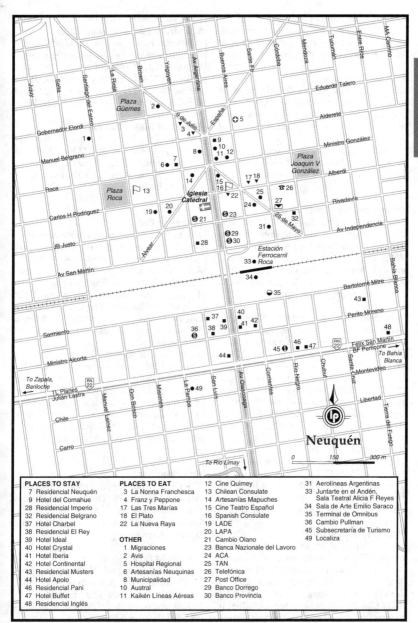

PLACES TO STAY
7 Residencial Neuquén
9 Hotel del Comahue
28 Residencial Imperio
32 Residencial Belgrano
37 Hotel Charbel
38 Residencial El Rey
39 Hotel Ideal
40 Hotel Crystal
41 Hotel Iberia
42 Hotel Continental
43 Residencial Musters
44 Hotel Apolo
46 Residencial Pani
47 Hotel Buffet
48 Residencial Inglés

PLACES TO EAT
3 La Nonna Franchesca
4 Franz y Peppone
17 Las Tres Marías
18 El Plato
22 La Nueva Raya

OTHER
1 Migraciones
2 Avis
5 Hospital Regional
6 Artesanías Neuquinas
8 Municipalidad
10 Austral
11 Kaikén Líneas Aéreas

12 Cine Quimey
13 Chilean Consulate
14 Artesanías Mapuches
15 Cine Teatro Español
16 Spanish Consulate
19 LADE
20 LAPA
21 Cambio Olano
23 Banca Nazionale del Lavoro
24 ACA
25 TAN
26 Telefónica
27 Post Office
29 Banco Dorrego
30 Banco Provincia

31 Aerolíneas Argentinas
33 Juntarte en el Andén,
    Sala Teatral Alicia F Reyes
34 Sala de Arte Emilio Saraco
35 Terminal de Omnibus
36 Cambio Pullman
45 Subsecretaría de Turismo
49 Localiza

el Andén, an outdoor art space across the tracks at the former passenger terminal, which is also the site of the **Sala Teatral Alicia F Reyes**, a performing arts venue.

Special Events

January's annual Regata del Río Negro is an internationally recognized kayak race that starts in Neuquén and ends a week later in Viedma, at the Atlantic mouth of the Río Negro.

The annual Expocultural Neuquén takes place in early February, offering good live music and other cultural events.

Places to Stay – bottom end

Camping *Camping Butaco* (☎ 48-5228) is at the Balneario Municipal along the Río Limay, at the west end of town; take bus No 103 from downtown to Obreros Argentinos and Copahue. Rates are US$2 per vehicle, US$2 per tent, and US$1 per person. It closes for camping after April 1.

Residenciales & Hotels Neuquén's hotels are numerous but not really a good value at the lower end of the spectrum. Dingy *Residencial Imperio* (☎ 22488), Yrigoyen 65, charges US$12/18 single/ double, while basic *Hotel Continental* (☎ 23757), Perito Moreno 90 at Corrientes, has rooms with private bath for US$15/20. *Residencial Inglés* (☎ 22252), Félix San Martín 534, costs US$15/25, which is slightly cheaper than *Residencial Belgrano* (☎ 42-4311), Rivadavia 283. *Hotel Buffet,* on Félix San Martín near the tourist office, charges US$15/22 for rooms with shared bath, slightly more with private bath, but the numerous single men loitering in the lobby may discourage single women.

Places to Stay – middle

Accommodations in the midrange start at around US$22/32 at *Residencial Neuquén* (☎ 22403), Roca 109; *Residencial Musters* (☎ 30237), at Tierra del Fuego 255, is slightly more expensive at US$22/29. *Hotel Charbel* (☎ 24143), San Luis 268, is comparably priced at US$25/35; it's simi-

lar to *Residencial Pani* (☎ 42287) at Félix San Martín 236, near Hotel Buffet.

Several hotels in the US$33/50 range are clustered around Av Olascoaga: *Hotel Crystal* (☎ 22414) at Olascoaga 268, *Hotel Ideal* (☎ 22431) at Olascoaga 243, *Hotel Iberia* (☎ 22372) at Olascoaga 294, and *Hotel Apolo* (☎ 22334) at Olascoaga 361.

Places to Stay – top end

The top of the line in Neuquén is five-star *Hotel del Comahue* (☎ 22439, 22440), at Av Argentina 387. Standard rates are US$98/109, but there is a 10% discount for payment in cash.

Places to Eat

The many confiterías along Av Argentina are all pleasant spots for breakast and morning coffee. *El Plato* (☎ 48-0359), Alberdi 158, has a good reputation for its US$5 lunch specials. *Franz y Peppone,* at 9 de Julio and Belgrano, is a good but unusual combination of Italian and German cuisine. *La Nueva Raya* (☎ 35435), Alberdi 59, has a varied, reasonable meat and seafood menu.

Las Tres Marías (☎ 24297), a parrilla at Alberdi 126, deserves special mention for its exceptionally diverse menu at moderate prices, in addition to cheap daily specials, in a pleasant environment with attentive service. *La Nonna Franchesca* (☎ 25291), 9 de Julio 56, has attractive decor in addition to outstanding pasta and French cuisine.

Entertainment

The Cine Teatro Español (☎ 42-2048), Av Argentina 271, shows current films, as does Cine Quimey, a two-screener on Ministro González between Av Argentina and Buenos Aires.

Things to Buy

Neuquén offers a good selection of regional handicrafts – try Artesanías Neuquinas (☎ 23806) at Roca 155. For Mapuche Indian crafts, visit Artesanías Mapuches (☎ 32155), Roca 62.

ARGENTINA

Getting There & Away

Air Aeropuerto Internacional Neuquén (☎ 31444), west of town on RN 22, has extensive domestic services and international services to Chile only.

Aerolíneas Argentinas (☎ 25087), Santa Fe 50, has no flights of its own to or from Neuquén. Austral (☎ 22409), Av Argentina 363, flies to Buenos Aires (US$178) three times daily except Saturdays, when it goes twice.

LADE (☎ 22453), at Brown 163, flies Friday afternoons to Bariloche (US$43), and Monday afternoons to Viedma (US$58), Trelew (US$64), and Comodoro Rivadavia (US$92).

LAPA (☎ 24540), Diagonal Alvear 135, flies weekday afternoons to Aeroparque (US$99).

Neuquén-based TAN (☎ 23076), 25 de Mayo 180, has the most extensive routes, serving northbound destinations as far as Córdoba (US$129, three times weekly), Bahía Blanca (US$91, twice), Santa Rosa (US$76, twice), Malargüe (US$66, three), and Mendoza (US$121, eight). Southbound Patagonian destinations include Chapelco/San Martín de los Andes (US$51, seven flights weekly), Bariloche (US$62, ten weekly), Esquel (US$71, five weekly), and El Calafate (US$170, on Thursdays and Sundays only).

Patagonian carrier Kaikén Líneas Aéreas (☎ 47-1333), Av Argentina 327, has flights Tuesdays and Thursdays to Mendoza (US$94); Mondays, Thursdays, and Saturdays to Trelew (US$74); and Wednesdays and Fridays to Trelew, Comodoro Rivadavia (US$110), Río Gallegos (US$176), Río Grande (US$187), and Ushuaia (US$198).

Chilean carrier Ladeco (☎ 73954), Miguel Muñoz 344, 1st floor, flies Mondays and Fridays to Temuco and Santiago.

Bus Neuquén's Terminal de Omnibus (☎ 24903) at Bartolomé Mitre 147 is a major hub for provincial, national, and international bus services. El Petróleo (☎ 48-4601) is the major provincial carrier,

with regular services to Zapala (US$9, three hours), Junín de los Andes (US$28, six hours), and San Martín de los Andes (US$30, seven hours).

El Valle (☎ 25168) runs the same routes, as well as some to Bariloche (US$30, seven hours), Bahía Blanca (US$30, eight hours), Mar del Plata, and Buenos Aires. Mercedes (☎ 23661) and Vía Bariloche also serve Bariloche. La Puntual (☎ 27054) goes to Viedma and Bahía Blanca, while Tirsa (☎ 23661) goes to Rosario (US$75, 14 hours).

Empresa Pehuenche (☎ 21951) goes to Buenos Aires (US$45, 15 hours) via Santa Rosa, La Pampa (US$25). La Estrella (☎ 23616) and Chevallier (☎ 23791) also serve the federal capital (US$75, with occasional promotional fares); both also go to Córdoba. TUS/TUP (☎ 20270) go daily to Córdoba (US$72, 17 hours) and also to San Martín de los Andes and Bariloche.

Alto Valle (☎ 43-4510) has service to Mendoza (US$45, 12 hours) as does TAC (☎ 25203) ; Alto Valle also goes to Esquel (US$51, 12 hours), Córdoba, and Paraná. Empresa del Sur y Media Agua (☎ 48-8778) goes to San Rafael, Mendoza, and San Juan.

Andesmar (☎ 33291) has the most extensive nationwide routes. Northbound, via Mendoza, it connects Neuquén with La Rioja (US$63), Catamarca (US$69), Tucumán (US$80), Salta (US$95), and Jujuy (US$96). Southbound, it goes to Bariloche, El Bolsón (US$42, ten hours), and Esquel (US$56), and to the Patagonian coastal destinations of Puerto Madryn (US$39, ten hours), Trelew (US$42, 11 hours), Comodoro Rivadavia (US$65, 15 hours), and Río Gallegos (US$111, 28 hours). Don Otto (☎ 2-3661) also goes to the far south.

Andesmar also crosses the Andes to the Chilean cities of Osorno (US$45), Valdivia (US$46), Temuco (US$49), Los Angeles (US$51), and Santiago (US$58). La Unión del Sud (☎ 484052) and Empresa San Martín (☎ 27054) use the scenic Tromen pass route to Villarica and Temuco. Igi Llaima (☎ 23661) also has routes to Chilean destinations.

Getting Around

There are several car rental agencies, including AI (☎ 30362) at Av San Martín 1269; Avis (☎ 30216) at Diagonal 9 de Julio 140; and Localiza (☎ 20875) at La Pampa 462. Neuquén is a good province to explore by automobile, but foreigners should know that RN 22, both east along the valley of the Río Negro and west toward Zapala, has some of Argentina's most dangerous drivers.

PIEDRA DEL AGUILA

Piedra del Aguila, 225 km southwest of Neuquén on RN 237, is a possible stopover en route to Bariloche, with its several residenciales and a municipal campground. The Delegación de Turismo is at the corner of General Winter and Conrado Villegas, directly on the highway. Piedra's area code is 0942.

Just outside Piedra del Aguila, Estancia Santa Teresa's *Ranch Hotel* (☎ 93125) offers lodging with full board, plus horseback riding, swimming, and tennis, for US$85 per person plus IVA per day. At Baja Colorada, 47 km farther south, the **Auca Cuyin** zoo of the Fundación Dehais displays fauna typical of the region.

ZAPALA

Windy, dusty, and economically depressed Zapala, the end of the line for the presently suspended northern branch of the Ferrocarril Roca, is a fairly ordinary desert mining town, but there are several worthwhile destinations nearby. Locals dream that the projected extension of the railroad to Las Lajas and to Lonquimay, across the Andes in Chile, will return prosperity to the area.

Orientation

Zapala is a junction for several important highways, including RN 22 east to Neuquén and north to Las Lajas, RN 40 southwest to Junín de los Andes and San Martín de los Andes and north to Chos Malal, and RP 13 west to Primeros Pinos. The main street is Av San Martín, an exit off the roundabout junction of RN 22 and RN 40.

Information

Tourist Office The Dirección Municipal de Turismo, a kiosk on the grassy median of Av San Martín at Almirante Brown, is open 7 am to 8 pm in summer, 8 am to 8 pm the rest of the year.

Money Banco de la Provincia del Neuquén, Cháneton 460, is open 7 am to 1:30 pm, and also has an ATM. Banco de la Nación is at Av San Martín and Etcheluz.

Post & Telecommunications Correo Argentino is at Av San Martín and Cháneton; the postal code is 8340. Telefónica is at Italia 248. Zapala's area code is 0942.

Medical Services The Hospital Regional (☎ 21256) is at Luis Monti 155.

Museo Olsacher

This small but significant private mineralogical museum contains more than 3500 exhibits, including numerous fossils, from 80 different countries. The owner, Señor Garatte, lives on site at Olascoaga 421, south of the train station. It is open from 4 pm onwards weekdays.

Places to Stay & Eat

Zapala's limited but decent accommodations are fairly costly except for the free *Camping Municipal,* on Calle Godoy, which has hot showers.

Residencial Coliqueo (☎ 21308), at Etcheluz 165, costs US$24 per person; *Residencial Huincúl* (☎ 21300), at Av Roca 311, charges around US$23/37 single/double, while *Nuevo Pehuén Hotel* (☎ 21360), a block from the bus station at Etcheluz and Vidal, is slightly more expensive but highly recommended at US$25/37. The best in town is three-star *Hotel Hue Melén* (☎ 22391), Almirante Brown 929, where rooms are US$40/74.

The best best for food are the restaurants at *Residencial Huincul, Residencial Odetto,* and *Hotel Hue Melén.* Try *El Chancho Rengo,* a confitería at Av San Martín and Etcheluz, for a light lunch.

Things to Buy

The Escuela de Cerámica (ceramics school) at Luis Monti 240 sells pottery made by students from local materials. Artesanías Neuquinas, at Av San Martín and Cháneton, sells regional crafts.

Getting There & Away

Air LADE (☎ 30134), Uriburu 397 at Etcheluz, flies Thursdays to Chapelco/San Martín de los Andes US$18), Bariloche (US$31), El Bolsón (US$42), El Maitén (US$42), Esquel (US$54), and Comodoro Rivadavia (US$92). Cabs to Aeropuerto Zapala (☎ 21879), south of town at the junction of RN 40 and RP 46, cost about US$5.

Bus The Terminal de Omnibus (☎ 21370) is at Etcheluz and Uriburu.

El Petróleo goes direct to Buenos Aires Sunday (US$65); otherwise, it's necessary to change at Neuquén. It also has two buses daily to San Martín de los Andes and daily service to the resort of Copahue, on the Chilean border. El Valle has runs to Buenos Aires, while Centenario goes to Buenos Aires and to ski areas at Copahue.

Ticsa serves San Juan and San Luis three times weekly, while TAC connects Mendoza (US$45) and Bariloche (US$20) via Zapala, also three times weekly in each direction. Chevallier goes daily to Buenos Aires in the late afternoon.

Four times weekly Igi Llaima and Ruta Sur cross the Andes to Temuco, Chile (US$40).

AROUND ZAPALA

Parque Nacional Laguna Blanca

Surrounded by striking volcanic deserts only 30 km from Zapala, Laguna Blanca is a shallow, interior drainage lake that formed when lava flows dammed two small streams. Too alkaline for fish, it nevertheless hosts many species of birds, including coots, grebes, upland geese, gulls, and even a few flamingos, but the 11,250-hectare park was created primarily to protect the black-necked swan *Cygnus melancoryphus,* which spends the entire year here. Its

The cisne de cuello negro (black-necked swan) stays year-round at Laguna Blanca.

breeding colonies, on a peninsula in the lake, have been fenced off to prevent their disturbance by livestock.

Ten km south of Zapala, the paved and well-marked RP 46 leads directly through the park toward the Andean town of Aluminé. Mondays, Wednesdays, and Fridays at 8 am, a bus leaves Zapala for Aluminé via Las Lajas and drops passengers at the ranger station, where there is a very basic and unsheltered campground, but this is very roundabout and it's better for returning from the park. If this schedule does not serve you, there is sufficient traffic on the route to make hitching feasible. A cab or remise is a reasonable alternative.

Ask the ranger, who also maintains a small exhibit of artifacts and natural history, for information on hiking. Bring all your own food – only 25th-century archaeologists will find any interest in the ruins of the intended visitor center and confitería, a white elephant that never found a concessionaire. It stands as a monument to unrealistic commercial expectations, but the unspoiled park itself should satisfy most visitors.

Primeros Pinos

This ski resort near Las Lajas, 55 km northwest of Zapala, has a 700-meter vertical drop.

ALUMINÉ

Aluminé, 103 km north of Junín de los Andes on RP 23, offers access to the northern sector of Parque Nacional Lanín; the Río Aluminé, paralleling the highway for most of its length, is one of the most highly regarded trout streams in the country.

For information, consult the Oficina de Informes Turísticos at the Plazoleta at the entrance to town. In early April, Aluminé celebrates the Fiesta del Pehuén in honor of the unique trees that cover the slopes of the Andes. Several nearby Mapuche Indian reservations sell traditional weavings. Aluminé's area code is 0942.

JUNÍN DE LOS ANDES

Founded in 1883 as a military outpost during the Conquista del Desierto, this modest livestock center on the Río Chimehuín calls itself the "trout capital" of Neuquén province. Less attractive but much less expensive than fashionable San Martín de los Andes, Junín (population 7400) can be a better base for exploring Parque Nacional Lanín, and also has a handful of interesting festivals and celebrations.

Orientation

Junín de los Andes is just south of the confluence of the Río Curruhue and the larger Río Chimehuín, which forms the city's eastern limit. Paved RN 234 (in town known as Blvd Juan Manuel de Rosas) is the main thoroughfare, leading 41 km south to San Martín de los Andes and 116 km northwest to Zapala via RN 40. North of town, graveled RP 23 heads to the fishing resort of Aluminé, while several secondary roads branch westward to Parque Nacional Lanín.

The city center is between the highway and the river. Do not confuse Av San Martín, which runs on the west side of Plaza San Martín, with Félix San Martín, two blocks farther west.

Information

Tourist Office The Secretaría Municipal

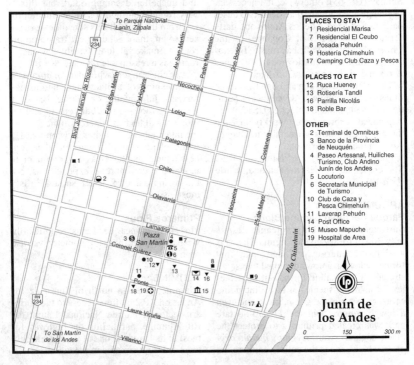

PLACES TO STAY
1 Residencial Marisa
7 Residencial El Ceubo
8 Posada Pehuén
9 Hostería Chimehuín
17 Camping Club Caza y Pesca

PLACES TO EAT
12 Ruca Hueney
13 Rotisería Tandil
16 Parrilla Nicolás
18 Roble Bar

OTHER
2 Terminal de Omnibus
3 Banco de la Provincia
   de Neuquén
4 Paseo Artesanal, Huilches
   Turismo, Club Andino
   Junín de los Andes
5 Locutorio
6 Secretaría Municipal
   de Turismo
10 Club de Caza y
    Pesca Chimehuín
11 Laverap Pehuén
14 Post Office
15 Museo Mapuche
19 Hospital de Area

Junín de
los Andes

0   150   300 m

de Turismo (☎ 91160), with its enthusiastically helpful staff, is at Padre Milanesio 596, corner of Coronel Suárez, on the main plaza. Hours are 7 am to 9:40 pm daily. Fishing permits are also available here.

Money Banco de la Provincia de Neuquén is on Av San Martín, opposite the plaza, between Suárez and Lamadrid.

Post & Telecommunications Correo Argentino is at Suárez and Don Bosco; the postal code is 8371. It's easiest to make local or long-distance calls from the locutorio on Padre Milanesio, opposite the plaza. Junín's area code is 0944.

Travel Agencies Huiliches Turismo (☎ 91670), Padre Milanesio 570, Local B, offers a variety of excursions, including trips to Lago Huechulafquen/Paimún (US$50 with lunch, hiking, and horseback riding); Termas de Lahuén Co (US$45 with lunch and thermal baths); and Lago Tromen (US$45 with lunch and hiking around Volcán Lanín). Cheaper half-day excursions, without lunch, are also available. Additional possibilities include a half-day rafting trip on the Río Hua Hum (US$45), a full-day cruise on Lago Lácar (US$28), visits to Estancia Huechahue (see separate entry below), and more adventurous possibilities such as climbing Lanín.

Laundry Laverap Pehuén is at Ponte 340.

Medical Services The Hospital de Area (☎ 91162) is at Ponte and Padre Milanesio.

Things to See & Do

Junín's surroundings are more appealing than the town itself, but the Salesian-organized **Museo Mapuche** at Ponte 540 is worth a look. In addition to ethnographic and historical materials, it also displays a selection of fossils and other natural history items.

Nearby Parque Nacional Lanín (see separate entry below) merits an extended visit for campers, hikers, climbers, and fishing enthusiasts. The Club Andino Junín de los Andes (☎ 91206), in the Paseo Artesanal at Padre Milanesio 568, can provide information on climbing Volcán Tromen and other excursions in the park.

Many North Americans and Europeans spend fishing holidays here; the Río Aluminé, north of Junín, is an especially choice area, but fishing is possible even within the city limits. Catch-and-release is obligatory in many local streams. For detailed information, contact the Club de Caza y Pesca Chimehuín (☎ 91186), Coronel Suárez 357; for equipment, visit the Fly Shop (☎ 91004) at San Martín 537 near the plaza. Neuquén fishing licenses cost US$100 for the season, US$60 monthly, or US$30 weekly; trolling licenses cost another US$60 for the season.

Special Events

Every year, Junín celebrates its own lively Carnaval del Pehuén with parades, costumes, live music, and the usual water balloons. No one will mistake it for Río de Janeiro or Bahía, but if you're in the area it can be entertaining.

In January, the Feria y Exposición Ganadera displays the best of local livestock – cattle, horses, and sheep, along with poultry and rabbits. There are also exhibitions of horsemanship, and local crafts exhibits, but this is the estanciero's show. Avergae folk get their chance at mid-February's Festival del Puestero.

Places to Stay

Camping The municipal Camping Club Caza y Pesca (☎ 91296), just three blocks east of the plaza on the banks of the Chimehuín, has the standard facilities. Fees are US$5 per person per day, plus an additional one-time charge of US$5 per tent. Showers, available 8 to 10 am and 8 to 10 pm, cost US$1.

Residenciales, Hosterías & Hotels

Junín's regular accommodations are modest in quality and not really any bargain. *Residencial Marisa* (☎ 91175), Blvd Rosas 360, charges US$20/25 single/double with private bath (breakfast extra).

ARGENTINA

Residencial El Ceubo (☎ 91182), near the plaza at Lamadrid 409, costs US$30 double, while *Posada Pehuén* (☎ 91569), Coronel Suárez 560, costs US$20 per person (breakfast not included).

Hostería Chimehuín (☎ 91132), overlooking the river at Coronel Suárez and 25 de Mayo, is an excellent value at US$25 per person with breakfast, US$45 with half-pension. At *Hotel Alejandro Primo* (☎ 91184), on busy Blvd Rosas at the northern outskirts of town, prices are US$30/50.

Places to Eat

Junín has fairly standard restaurants, although some local specialties like trout, wild boar, or venison may be available. *Ruca Hueney* (☎ 91113), Padre Milanesio 641, has the most extensive menu, with entreés in the US$6 to US$12 range. *Parrilla Nicolás,* Coronel Suárez 559, is also worth a look.

Roble Bar (☎ 91124), Ponte 331 near San Martín, is Junín's main pizzería, offering baked empanadas and sandwiches as well. At Coronel Suárez 431, just east of the plaza, *Rotisería Tandil* has excellent takeout empanadas.

Things to Buy

A wide selection of artisanal goods in various media, including wood, leather, wool, stone, and ceramics, is available at the Paseo Artesanal on Padre Milanesio, just north of the tourist office.

Getting There & Away

Air Aeropuerto Chapelco lies midway between Junín and San Martín de los Andes. For further information, see the Getting There & Away entry under San Martín de los Andes below.

Bus The Terminal de Omnibus (☎ 91110) is at Olavarría and Félix San Martín. La Unión del Sud (☎ 91030) has runs to Neuquén via Villa La Angostura, while Centenario (☎ 91458) uses the Zapala route to the provincial capital. El Petróleo also uses the Zapala route, but it continues

onward to Bahía Blanca, while La Puntual's (☎ 91030) Bahía Blanca service takes the route via La Rinconada and Piedra del Aguila. Ko-Ko (☎ 91458) has service to Bariloche via both the paved Rinconada route and the dusty but more scenic Siete Lagos alternative.

TAC (☎ 91458) heads north to Mendoza, as does Andesmar. TUS (☎ 91030) goes to Córdoba via Santa Rosa (La Pampa), while Chevallier (☎ 91458) provides services to Buenos Aires (US$60, 22 hours).

Empresa San Martín (☎ 91458) links Junín with neighboring San Martín de los Andes and crosses the Andes to Temuco, Chile, via the Tromen pass. Other carriers serving Chile include Igi-Llaima and Buses JAC, at the same number.

AROUND JUNÍN DE LOS ANDES
Estancia Huechahue

This Anglo-Argentine estancia, in a sheltered valley on the Ríos Aluminé and Collón Curá, about 30 km east of Junín on the road to Zapala, offers all-inclusive fishing (catch-and-release only), riding, and trekking holidays in pleasant surroundings both there and in Parque Nacional Lanín. Accommodations are very comfortable, amid owner Jane Williams's apple orchards and tranquil forest plantations.

The basic price of $150 per day includes transportation between the estancia and Bariloche or San Martín de los Andes, plus all meals and beverages (with minor exceptions). The estancia usually requires at least a couple days' advance notice prior to arrival; for further information, contact Jane Williams, Estancia Huechahue (☎ 0972-28276, 0944-91303; fax 0972-27111), 8371 Junín de los Andes, Provincia Neuquén.

SAN MARTÍN DE LOS ANDES

Thanks in part to a height limit on new construction, San Martín de los Andes still retains some of the charm and architectural unity that once attracted people to Bariloche, but the burgeoning hotels and restaurants and the ominous, insidious time-shares are rapidly transforming it into

ARGENTINA

PLACES TO STAY
1 Alberque Juvenil
2 Hotel Crismalú
4 Residencial Laura
8 Hostería Nevada
9 Hotel Colonos del Sur
10 Hostería La Cheminee
17 Residencial Italia
18 Residencial Villalago
20 Hostería La Masia
21 Hostería La Posta
   del Cazador
23 Hostal del Esquiador
24 Hostería de Chapelco
25 Residencial Los Pinos
26 Residencial Casa Alta
27 Hotel Aspen
28 Hostería Las Lengas
29 Hostería La Raclette

31 Hostería Las Lucarnas
50 Hostería Tisú
51 Hostería Anay
52 Hotel Nevegal
53 Hostería Peumayén
58 Hotel Chapelco Ski
65 Hostería Cumelén

PLACES TO EAT
13 Rotisería Viviana
14 Sayhueque
16 Piscis
40 La Crêperie
49 Café de la Plaza
60 Rotisería Alemana

OTHER
3 Centro Cultural Amankay,
   Cine Amankay

5 Grupo 3 de Turismo (Amex)
6 Trabunco
7 Grego Tour (Airport Buses)
11 La Pista
12 Hospital Rural Ramón Castillo
15 Bumps
18 Fiocca
19 HG Rodados (Mountain Bikes)
22 Terminal de Omnibus
   Navegación Lago Lácar
30 Casino
32 Post Office
33 Intendencia Parque
   Nacional Lanín
34 Al Filo
35 Museo Primeros Pobladores
36 Artesanías Mapuches
37 Secretaría Municipal de
   Turismo, Artesanías Neuquinas
38 Cooperativa Telefónica

39 Ensatur, La Pista
41 Fenoglio
42 Austral
43 Avis
44 TAN
45 Astete Viajes
46 Tiempo Patagónico,
   Mont Blanc, Cerro Torre
47 Al (By Mich)
48 Banco de la Nación
54 Kosem Artesanías
55 Wedlen
56 Cambio Andina
   Internacional
57 Laverap
59 LADE
61 Laverap
62 La Oveja Negra
63 Localiza
64 Claro Turismo, Localiza

San Martín de los Andes

a costly tourist trap. Founded as an army post in 1898, San Martín (population 17,000) has grown so rapidly in recent years that an inadequate sewage system has contaminated Lago Lácar's attractive beaches.

Orientation

Nestled amid attractive mountain scenery at the eastern end of Lago Lácar, 642 meters above sea level, San Martín straddles RN 234, which passes through town southbound to Villa La Angostura, on the north shore of Lago Nahuel Huapi. Northbound RN 234 heads to Zapala via Junín de los Andes.

Almost everything in San Martín de los Andes is walking distance from the Centro Cívico, while the shady lakefront park and pier are a delightful place to spend the afternoon. Bounding the Centro Cívico plaza along with Av Roca, Mariano Moreno, and Capitán Drury, Av San Martín is the main commercial street, running from the lakefront north toward the highway to Junín.

Information

Tourist Offices In an airy, modern building at the Centro Cívico (Avs San Martín and Rosas), the well-organized Secretaría Municipal de Turismo (☎ 27347) provides surprisingly candid information, such as warning visitors not to swim in polluted Lago Lácar. Open daily 7 am to 10 pm, it has details about hotels and restaurants, plus excellent brochures and maps, and also sells fishing licenses.

Ensatur (☎ 28654), a private business-oriented information service, is at Av San Martín 800.

Money Weekdays try Banco de la Nación at Av San Martín 687. The only official cambio is Andina Internacional at Capitán Drury 876.

Post & Telecommunications Correo Argentino is at the Centro Cívico, Roca and Coronel Pérez; the postal code is 8370. The Cooperativa Telefónica is at Capitán Drury

761, between Av San Martín and Roca. San Martín's area code is 0972.

National Parks Open weekdays only, the Intendencia of Parque Nacional Lanín (☎ 27233) is at Emilio Frey 749, in the Centro Cívico. Limited maps and brochures are available here.

Cultural Centers The Centro Cultural Amankay (☎ 28399) is at Roca 1154; within it is the Cine Amankay (☎ 27274).

Travel Agencies San Martín has many travel agencies, almost all near the Centro Cívico, along Av San Martín, Belgrano and Elordi. Grupo 3 de Turismo (☎ 28453), San Martín 1141, Local 1, is the local Amex representative.

Laundry Laverap (☎ 28820) is at Capitán Drury 880 and Villegas 972. Lavandería Marva is at Drury and Villegas.

Medical Services Hospital Rural Ramón Castillo (☎ 27211) is at Coronel Rohde and Av San Martín.

Museo Primeros Pobladores

Regional archaeological and ethnographic items such as arrowheads, spear points, pottery, and musical instruments are the focus of this museum, next door to the tourist office. There are also mineral and fossil exhibits. It's open weekdays 8 am to 2 pm and 4 to 8 pm.

Activities

The area in and around San Martín is well suited to mountain biking; for bike rentals, try H G Rodados (☎ 27345), Drury 988, or the lot alongside the Crêperie restaurant on Av San Martín. Rates run about US$15 per day.

For rafting on the Río Hua Hum or Meliquina, contact Tiempo Patagónico (☎ 27113) at San Martín 950 (US$45 with transfers), Ici Viajes (☎ 27800) at Villegas and Coronel Díaz, or El Claro Turismo (☎ 28876) at Villegas 977.

Trekking and climbing are also important activities in Parque Nacional Lanín. Horacio Peloso, known by his nickname "El Oso," is a highly regarded mountain guide who arranges trips and rents equipment for climbing Lanín. He's at Cerro Torre, San Martín 950 near Tiempo Patagónico.

Skiing at nearby Cerro Chapelco draws enthusiastic crowds in winter (see Cerro Chapelco section below). In town, ski rental equipment is available at Chapelco Sport, Av San Martín and Mascardi; Bumps at Villegas 566; Al Filo (☎ 27366) at San Martín 576; La Colina (☎ 27414) at San Martín 532; Mont Blanc at San Martín 950; La Pista at San Martín 800; Wedlen at Capitán Drury 864; and Fiocca at Villegas 717.

Special Events
February 4 is Día de la Fundación, the anniversary of the founding of San Martín de los Andes, which is celebrated with speeches, parades, and other festivities; the city will celebrate its centenary in 1998. The parade itself is an entertainingly incongruous mix of military, firefighters, gauchos, polo players, and fox hunters.

In December, the Christmas Fiesta Nacional de la Navidad Cordillerana lasts nearly two weeks but is most notable between Christmas Eve and New Year's Day.

Organized Tours
San Martín's several travel agencies offer tours to a number of outlying sights, among them Termas de Lahuén Co (US$30, full day); Siete Lagos and Villa La Angostura (US$30, full day); Lago Huechulafquen, Paimún, and Lanín (US$30, full day); and Cerro Chapelco (US$14, half-day).

Places to Stay
As a tourist center, San Martín is loaded with accommodations, but they are relatively costly in all categories except camping. The quality, however, is generally high.

Places to Stay – bottom end
Camping On the eastern outskirts of town at Av Koessler 2176, *Camping ACA* (☎ 27332) is a spacious, attractive campground charging US$5 per person; even if it's very crowded, it's easy to find a quiet (though perhaps less aesthetically pleasing) site. Similar facilities, at comparable prices, are available at *Catritre*, four km south of San Martín in Parque Nacional Lanín, and *El Molino* (☎ 26350), five km north of town.

Hostel San Martín's *Albergue Juvenil*, at 3 de Caballería 1164, charges $10 per person but lacks kitchen facilities. A recent reader suggestion is the informal church school on Capitán Drury between San Martín and Roca, which has rooms in summer for US$5 with shared bath, US$10 with private bath, but you may have to wait a while for the priest to show up.

Residenciales & Hotels Bottom-end accommodations start around US$20/30 single/double with private bath at *Residencial Los Pinos* (☎ 27207), nicely located at Almirante Brown 420, just outside the busy center. Since its remodelling, *Residencial Villalago* (☎ 27454), Villegas 717, has risen to US$35 double without breakfast. Others in this category include *Residencial Italia* (☎ 27590) at Coronel Pérez 977, *Residencial Laura* (☎ 27271) at Mascardi 632 for US$20 per person, and *Residencial Casa Alta* (☎ 27456) at Obeid 659 for US$40 double.

Places to Stay – middle
Midrange accommodations are abundant and generally a reasonable value. Typical are *Hotel Colonos del Sur* (☎ 27224) at Rivadavia 686 for US$30/45; *Hostería Tisú* (☎ 27231) at Av San Martín 771 for US$30/50; *Hostería Anay* (☎ 27514) at Capitán Drury 841 for US$34/50. Others include *Hostería Nevada* (☎ 27301) at Mariano Moreno 590, *Hotel Aspen* (☎ 27217) at Coronel Pérez 1127, and *Hostería Cumelén* (☎ 27304) at Elordi 931, all of which charge US$35/45.

A step up are *Hotel Crismalú* (☎ 27283), Rudecindo Roca 975, for US$38/52; *Hostería Las Lucarnas* (☎ 27085) at Coronel Pérez 632 for US$40/58; *Hostería La Raclette* (☎ 27664), Coronel Pérez 1170, for US$40/66; *Hotel Nevegal* (☎ 27484) at Av San Martín 817 for US$45/52; *Hostería Peumayén* (☎ 27232) at Av San Martín 851 for US$46/55; and *Hostal del Esquiador* (☎ 27674) at Coronel Rohde 975 for US$60 double. *Hotel Chapelco Ski* (☎ 27480), Belgrano 869, has rooms for US$45/60 single/double.

Places to Stay – top end
Top-end hotels start at US$39/75 at *Hostería La Posta del Cazador* (☎ 27501), Av San Martín 175, rising quickly to US$52/76 at *Hostería Las Lengas* (☎ 27659), Coronel Pérez 1175, and US$57/76 at *Hostería La Masia* (☎ 27688), Obeid 811.

San Martín's most luxurious accommodations are upscale places like five-star *Hotel Sol de Los Andes,* on a hill overlooking the southern approach to town, at US$68/90 single/double. *Hostería del Chapelco,* Brown 297, charges US$55 per person, while doubles cost US$120 at tasteful *Hostería La Cheminee,* downtown at Av Roca and Mariano Moreno.

Places to Eat
San Martín has a wide selection of excellent restaurants and confiterías. Though far from cheap, the pleasant sidewalk *Café de la Plaza* (☎ 28488), at Av San Martín and Coronel Pérez, is a decent breakfast choice. Stick with the basics like ham and cheese at the friendly, informal *La Crêperie* (☎ 28861), San Martín 820, whose dessert crêpes are made with sugary preserves rather than fresh fruit.

Rotisería Alemana (☎ 28186), San Martín 985, has a good US$4 lunch menu and other goodies as well. *Rotisería Viviana,* San Martín 489, has very cheap but excellent baked empanadas. Both are excellent choices for takeout food.

Piscis (☎ 27601), an outstanding mid-price parrilla at Villegas and Mariano Moreno, is mobbed in the evenings. *Sayhueque* (☎ 27006), a parrilla at Rivadavia 825, also draws big crowds.

Things to Buy
Many local shops sell regional products and handicrafts. Artesanías Mapuches, Rosas 770, offers local Indian weavings. La Oveja Negra (☎ 27248), at Av San Martín 1045, and Kosem, at Capitán Drury 846, also sell artisanal textiles. Chocolates are available at Fenoglio (☎ 27515), Av San Martín 836.

Getting There & Away
Air Austral (☎ 27003), Av San Martín 890, flies Mondays, Wednesdays, Fridays, and Sundays to Esquel (US$71) and Buenos Aires (US$236).

LADE (☎ 27672), Av San Martín 915, flies Wednesday afternoons to Zapala (US$18), and Thursday mornings to Bariloche (US$16), El Bolsón (US$25), El Maitén (US$26), Esquel (US$38), and Comodoro Rivadavia (US$84).

TAN (☎ 27872), Belgrano 760, flies Mondays, Tuesdays, Thursdays, Saturdays, and Sundays to Bariloche (US$25); Wednesdays and Fridays to Bariloche and Esquel (US$48); and eight times weekly to Neuquén (US$51).

Bus The Terminal de Omnibus (☎ 27044) is at Villegas and Juez del Valle. Regional carrier El Petróleo (☎ 27750) serves northern destinations (Aluminé, Junín de los Andes, Zapala), the Río Negro valley to the east, and the Chilean border at Pirehueico (US$5.50). Transportes Ko Ko (☎ 27422) goes to Villa la Angostura (US$13, three hours) and to Bariloche (5½ hours, US$22) by the scenic Siete Lagos route as well as by the longer but smoother Rinconada route. Centenario (☎ 28799) also goes to Villa la Angostura.

El Valle (☎ 28874) has four weekly buses to Buenos Aires (US$70, 23 hours), as do La Estrella (☎ 27750) and Chevallier

(☎ 27422). TAC (☎ 28874) goes to Mendoza Sundays and to Buenos Aires daily.

TUS (☎ 27750) goes to Córdoba Monday and Thursday mornings (US$94); on other days make connections in Bariloche. Buses JAC (☎ 28581) has four weekly departures for the Chilean destinations of Pucón, Villarica, Temuco, and Santiago. Igi-Llaima (☎ 27750) goes Tuesdays, Thursdays, and Saturdays at 6 am to Temuco (US$25), while Empresa San Martín (☎ 28508) goes Mondays, Wednesdays, and Fridays at the same hour. To Neuquén (US$22) there is frequent service with El Petróleo, Centenario, and La Unión del Sud (☎ 28581).

Boat Navegación Lago Lácar (☎ 27750), with offices in the Terminal de Omnibus, sails from the Muelle de Pasajeros (passenger pier) on the Av Costanera to Paso Hua Hum on the Chilean border, daily except Sundays at 9 am. The fare is US$20, plus a US$3.50 national park fee.

Getting Around

To/From the Airport Aeropuerto Chapelco (☎ 28398) is midway between San Martín and Junín, on RN 234. Transporte Caleuche (☎ 27115), Belgrano and San Martín, goes to Chapelco (US$6) Mondays, Tuesdays, Fridays, and Saturdays at 10 am, Sundays at 10:30 am. Grego Tour (☎ 28968), at Curruhuinca and Los Cipreses, also has airport buses.

To/From Parque Nacional Lanín Empresa San Martín goes daily to Huechulafquen (US$9) at 8 am, to Junín de los Andes (US$3) weekdays at 7 am and 1 and 7 pm, weekends at 9 am and 8 pm; to Lolog (US$2) several times daily; and to Catritre (US$1) frequently throughout the day.

Transportes Ko Ko runs four buses daily (US$2) to Lago Lolog.

Car Rental Car rental agencies include AI (By Mich) (☎ 27997) at Av San Martín 960, Avis (☎ 27704) at Av San Martín 998, Localiza (☎ 28876) at Villegas 977, and Trabunco (☎ 28931) at San Martín 1373.

AROUND SAN MARTÍN DE LOS ANDES

Cerro Chapelco

Cerro Chapelco's Centro de Deportes Invernales (☎ 0972-27460), 20 km southeast of San Martín, is one of Argentina's principal winter sports centers, with runs for beginners and experts, at a maximum elevation of 1920 meters. Rental equipment is available on site as well as in town.

Depending on snow conditions, provincial skiing championships are held every August. Also taking place in the first half of August is the Fiesta Nacional del Montañes, the annual ski festival.

Lift Tickets Lift tickets vary considerably from early to mid and late season, but the following prices should provide some idea what to expect. Full-season passes cost US$790 for adults, US$550 for children. The season runs from mid-June to mid-October. The prices vary depending on when you go – peak, mid-season, or low season. Half-day passes run from US$26 to US$13 for adults, US$21 to US$10 for children. Full-day passes range from US$32 to US$16 for adults and US$21 to US$10 for children. A single lift ticket for adults/children is US$13/8. Two-day passes for adults range from US$64 to US$32, for children US$51 to US$26. Three-day passes for adults are US$95 to US$48 and US$76 to US$38 for kids. Four-day passes are US$126 to US$63 for adults and US$101 to US$50 for kids. A weeklong ski pass for adults ranges from US$190 to US$95 and from US$152 to US$76 for children. For a 15-day pass expect to pay US$360 to US$180 for adults and US$288 to US$144 for children. Monthlong passes are also available for US$640 to US$420 for adults and US$450 to US$336 for children.

PARQUE NACIONAL LANÍN

Dominating the view in all directions from its position along the Chilean border, the 3776-meter snowcapped cone of Volcán Lanín is the centerpiece of Parque Nacional Lanín, which extends 150 km from Parque

Nacional Nahuel Huapi in the south to Lago Ñorquinco in the north. Created in 1937 to protect 379,000 hectares of native Patagonian forest, tranquil Lanín has so far avoided the commercial development blemishing Nahuel Huapi and Bariloche.

Parque Lanín has many of the same species that characterize more southerly Patagonian forests, such as the southern beeches *lenga, ñire,* and *coihue.* More botanically unique to the area, though, are extensive stands of the broadleaf deciduous southern beech *raulí (Nothofagus nervosa)* and the curious pehuén or monkey puzzle tree *(Araucaria araucana),* a member of

the pine family the nuts of which have long been a dietary staple for the Pehuenches and Mapuches. Note that only Indians may gather piñon nuts from the pehuenes.

Besides the views of Volcán Lanín and these unusual forests, the park has recreational attractions in the numerous finger-shaped lakes left behind by Pleistocene glaciers. Excellent campsites are abundant, though some of the less developed but more accessible ones are unfortunately dirty and polluted.

Information

The Intendencia de Parques Nacionales in San Martín de los Andes produces brochures on camping, hiking, and climbing in various parts of the park that are widely distributed in the area's tourist offices. Scattered throughout the park proper are several ranger stations that are good sources of information, but they usually lack printed matter.

Things to See & Do

From south to north, the towns of San Martín de los Andes, Junín de los Andes, and Aluminé are the best starting points for exploring Lanín, its lakes, and the back-country. This section begins at San Martín and works northward.

Lago Lácar From San Martín, at the east end of the lake, there is a bus service on RP 48, which parallels the shoreline to the Chilean border at Paso Hua Hum. A boat excursion also goes from San Martín to Hua Hum, where there is both organized and free camping, as well as numerous hiking trails.

Lago Lolog Fifteen km north of San Martín de los Andes, this largely undeveloped area has good camping, free of charge, and fishing. Transportes Ko Ko (☎ 27422) runs four buses daily (US$2) to Lago Lolog from San Martín.

Lago Huechulafquen The park's largest lake is also one of its most central and accessible areas, easily reached from Junín de los Andes despite limited public transport. From a junction just north of Junín, RP 61 climbs west to Huechulafquen and the smaller Lago Paimún, along the way offering outstanding views of Volcán Lanín and access to trailheads of several excellent hikes. Source of the Río Chimehuín, Huechulafquen offers outstanding fishing at its outlet.

From the ranger station at Puerto Canoa, a good trail climbs to a viewpoint on the shoulder of the volcano, where it is possible to hike across to the Tromen Pass or continue climbing to either of two refugios. One belongs to the army's Regimiento de Infantería de Montaña (RIM) and the other to the Club Andino Junín de los Andes (CAJA), but either can be a staging point for attempting the volcano's summit. See the Lago Tromen entry below for more detail on reaching the summit, including obtaining permits and equipment. The initial segment is an abandoned road, but after about 40 minutes it becomes a pleasant woodsy trail along the **Arroyo Rucu Leufu**, an attractive mountain stream; yellow paint blazes indicate the route where it is not obvious. Be on the lookout for hares, lizards, and tarantulas. Halfway to the refugio is an extensive pehuén forest, the southernmost in the park, which makes the walk worthwhile if you lack time for the entire route. The route to RIM's refugio, about 2450 meters above sea level, takes about seven hours one way, while the trail to CAJA's refugio takes a bit longer.

Another good backcountry hike circles **Lago Paimún**. This requires about two days from Puerto Canoa; you return to the north side of the lake by crossing a cable platform strung across the narrows between Huechulafquen and Paimún. An alternative hike that is much shorter goes from the very attractive campground at Piedra Mala to **Cascada El Saltillo**, a nearby forest waterfall. If your car lacks 4WD, leave it at the logjam "bridge" that crosses the creek and walk to Piedra Mala – the road, passable by any ordinary vehicle to this point, quickly worsens. Rental horses are available at Piedra Mala.

Along the highway are many campsites, some free and others inexpensive. Travelers camping in the free sites in the narrow area between the lakes and the highway must dig a latrine and remove their own trash. If you camp at the organized sites which, while not luxurious, are at least maintained, you'll support Mapuche concessionaires who at least derive some income from lands that were theirs alone before the state usurped them a century ago.

Fees at the *Raquithue* and *Piedra Mala* campgrounds are about US$3 per person; *Bahía Cañicul* is dearer at US$7 but grants ACA discounts. Limited supplies are available, but it is better and cheaper to bring them from Junín de los Andes.

Non-campers with money can stay at *Hostería Refugio Pescador* (☎ 91132) at Puerto Canoa or the three-star *Hostería Paimún* (☎ 91211), which both charge US$90 per person with all meals.

Lago Tromen This northern approach to Volcán Lanín, which straddles the Argentine-Chilean border, is also the shortest, and should open earlier in the season for hikers and climbers. En route from Junín, note the unique volcanic landforms, including the isolated El Mollar. Before climbing Volcán Lanín, ask permission at the Intendencia de Parques Nacionales in San Martín or, if necessary, of the Gendarmería (border guards) in Junín. It is obligatory to show equipment, including plastic tools, crampons, ice axe, and clothing – including sunglasses, sunscreen, gloves, hats, and padded jackets.

From the trailhead at the Argentine border station, it's five to seven hours to the CAJA refugio (☎ 91207, capacity 14 persons) at 2600 meters on the Camino de Mulas route; above that point, snow climbing equipment is necessary. There's a shorter but steeper route along the ridge known as the Espina del Pescado, where it's possible to stay at the RIM refugio (capacity 20 persons) at 2450 meters. Trekkers can cross the Sierra Mamuil Malal to Lago Huechulafquen via Arroyo Rucu Leufu (see above).

ARGENTINA

Hostería Lago Tromen (☎ 91238), on the north side of RP 60, offers accommodations with full board for US$135/180 single/double.

Lago Quillén Situated in the park's densest pehuén forests, this isolated lake is accessible by dirt road from Rahué, 17 km south of Aluminé, and has many good campsites. Other nearby lakes include Lago Rucachoroi, directly west of Aluminé, and Lago Norquinco on the park's northern border. There are Mapuche Indian reservations at Rucachoroi and Quillén.

Getting There & Away
Although the park is close to San Martín and Junín, public transport is minimal; see the sections on those towns for details. With some patience hitching is feasible in high season. Buses over the Hua Hum and Tromen passes from San Martín and Junín to Chile will carry passengers to intermediate destinations.

Pickup trucks from Junín will carry six or seven backpackers to Puerto Canoas for about US$5 per person.

VILLA LA ANGOSTURA
On the north shore of Lago Nacional Nahuel Huapi, placid Villa La Angostura is a scenic lakeside resort from which the most accessible natural asset is Parque Nacional Los Arrayanes. Nearby Cerro Bayo is a small but popular winter sports center.

Orientation
On the north shore of Lago Nahuel Huapi, about 100 km south of San Martín de los Andes, Villa La Angostura (at an altitude of 850 meters) is near the junction of RN 231 from Bariloche, which crosses the Andes to Puyehue and Osorno, Chile, and RN 234, which leads northward to San Martín de los Andes and Parque Nacional Lanín. Through town, RN 231 is known as Av Los Arrayanes and Av Los Lagos.

Villa La Angostura takes its name from the 91-meter isthmus that connects it with the Quetrihué Peninsula, which protrudes southward into the lake. In fact, the village consists of two distinct areas: El Cruce is the commercial center along the highway, while La Villa, three km south, is more residential but still has hotels, shops, services, and lake access. Unlike Bariloche, densely forested Villa La Angostura does not dominate its surroundings, so that, except along the highway, visitors are hardly aware of being in a town. The permanent population is about 2000.

Information
Tourist Office The helpful Dirección Municipal de Turismo (☎ 94124), with offices at the junction of Av Los Arrayanes and Av Los Lagos, has a good selection of maps and brochures.

Money Banco de la Provincia is on Av Los Arrayanes between Las Mutisias and Los Notros.

Post & Telecommunications Correo Argentino is in La Villa, on Nahuel Huapi; the postal code is 8403. There's a locutorio in the Galería Inacayal on Av Los Arrayanes, at El Cruce; the area code is 0944.

National Parks The local Intendencia (☎ 94152) is on Nahuel Huapi, in La Villa.

Travel Agencies Angostura Turismo (☎ 94405), on Av Arrayanes, organizes excursions and activities in the area.

Things to See & Do
Both town and the surrounding area are best seen on foot. From the local terminal on Av Los Lagos, just north of Los Arrayanes, Obalque (☎ 94124) buses can get you to most of the trailheads. Cabs and remises are also readily available.

Parque Nacional Los Arrayanes This inconspicuous and overlooked park, occupying the entire Quetrihué peninsula, protects remaining stands of the cinnamon-barked arrayán *(Myrceugenella apiculata)*, a member of the myrtle family. The peninsula's Mapuche name means "Place of the Arrayanes."

Park headquarters, near the largest concentration of arrayanes, is 12 km away at the southern end of the peninsula, but it's an easy three-hour walk on an excellent interpretive nature trail (brochures are available in the tourist office at El Cruce). Since regulations require hikers to leave the park by 4 pm, start early in the morning. Another alternative is to rent mountain bikes at El Cruce for US$5 per hour, but charges are lower for a full day. There are two small lakes along the trail; a recent report suggests that only guided excursions are now permitted.

From the park's northern entrance at La Villa, a very steep, 20-minute hike leads to two panoramic overlooks of Lago Nahuel Huapi.

Isla Victoria From the pier at La Villa's sheltered Bahía Mansa, it's possible to catch the boat to Isla Victoria and also to Bariloche.

Cerro Belvedere This four-km walk to an overlook offers good views of Lago Correntoso, Nahuel Huapi, and the surrounding mountains, then continues another three km to the 1992-meter summit. After visiting the overlook, retrace your steps to a nearby junction that leads to Cascada Inayacal, a 50-meter waterfall.

Centro de Ski Cerro Bayo From June to September, lifts carry skiers from the 1050-meter base up to 1700 meters at this relatively inexpensive winter resort (☎ 94189), nine km from El Cruce via RP 66. All facilities, including rental equipment, are available on site. Rates during the season depend on when you come – during the peak time, mid-season or low season. Children ages six to 12 qualify for discounts, while children five or younger and adults 65 and older ski for free. A half-day pass for adults ranges from US$16 to US$10 and for children from US$11 to US$7. A full-day pass for adults is US$26 to US$16, for children US$18 to US$11. Weekend lift

tickets are valid Fridays, Saturdays, and Sundays and cost US$70 to US$43 for adults, US$49 to US$30 for children. Weekly rates can include any six consecutive days and range from US$130 to US$80 for adults and US$91 to US$56 for children.

Siete Lagos From Villa La Angostura, RP 234 follows an especially scenic route past numerous alpine lakes to San Martín de los Andes. Tours from Bariloche and San Martín de los Andes regularly do this route, but there's also regularly scheduled public transportation; for details, see the Getting There & Away entry below.

Special Events

For four days during Holy Week, the Campeonato de Pesca Semana Santa attracts fishing enthusiasts to the area. The Fiestas Mayas in the second half of May celebrate local and national patriotic holidays.

Places to Stay

Camping *Camping El Cruce* (☎ 94145), on Av Los Lagos 500 meters beyond the tourist office, charges US$5 per person, US$4 each succeeding day. Their hot showers are dependable, but the toilets are sometimes dirty. Prices are roughly comparable at *Camping Correntoso* (☎ 94261), on Lago Correntoso north of town. There are also free sites along Lago Nahuel Huapi.

Residenciales, Hosterías & Hotels

Except for camping, accommodations tend to be pricey. *Residencial La Granja* (☎ 94193), on Nahuel Huapi in La Villa, is the most reasonable at US$20/35 for singles/doubles. *Residencial Don Pedro* (☎ 94269), on Belvedere in El Cruce, charges US$24/34. In La Villa, rates are around US$28/38 at *Hotel Río Bonito* (☎ 94110), on Topa Topa, and US$50/75 at lakeside *Hotel Angostura* (☎ 94424), on Nahuel Huapi, which also serves excellent food.

Hotel Correntoso (☎ 94424), north of El Cruce on RN 231, charges US$45/60 single/double. Three-star *Hostería Las Balsas* (☎ 94308), a few km south of El Cruce, charges US$75 per person with breakfast.

Places to Eat

There are several restaurants and confiterías along Los Arrayanes and its cross streets in El Cruce. *Parrilla Las Varas* (☎ 94405) alongside Turismo Angostura is a favorite, but Cantina Los Amigos (☎ 94322) on Los Taiques is also well established. For regional specialities in La Villa, try highly regarded but relatively expensive *Cuernavaca* (☎ 94234), on Nahuel Huapi.

Things to Buy

On weekends, artisans sell their own handicrafts from kiosks on the newly landscaped plaza, located at Blvd Nahuel Huapi between Las Frambuesas and Los Maquis, a block from El Cruce.

Getting There & Away

Villa La Angostura has no formal bus terminal, but all buses stop near the tourist office in El Cruce. Transporte Algarrobal (☎ 94426) on Los Arrayanes has two buses daily in each direction between Villa La Angostura and Bariloche (US$6.50). Transporte Unión del Sud (☎ 94322) connects Villa La Angostura with Neuquén (US$30) via San Martín de los Andes (US$10) and Junín de los Andes (US$12) three times weekly in each direction. For information and tickets, go to Cantina Los Amigos (☎ 94322) on Los Taiques. Andesmar (☎ 94124), on Av Los Lagos, also goes to San Martín del los Andes and Neuquén.

International services between Bariloche and Osorno and Puerto Montt (Chile) pass through Villa La Angostura, but they are often full. For Transporte Mercedes, Rápido, Argentino, Lanín, TAS Choapa, and Bus Norte, inquire at Cantina Los Amigos (☎ 94322).

VILLA TRAFUL

On the south shore of Lago Traful, about 80 km north of Bariloche on RP 65 in Parque Nacional Nahuel Huapi, Villa Traful offers excellent opportunities for camping, hiking, and fishing in a relatively undeveloped area. Codao has bus services to Bariloche Fridays at 9 am and 8:30 pm, while Colectivo Villa Traful has Tuesday and Friday services, leaving Villa Traful at 8 am and returning at 7 pm.

Other than camping, the cheapest lodging is *Hostería Villa Traful* (☎ 22181) at a modest US$18 per person with breakfast. The most extravagant is the *Rincón del Pescador* (☎/fax 0944-26215). Its glossy brochure offers "wall to wall wrags" and "scrumbled eggs for your breakfast" for US$80 per person. Accommodations are overpriced, but their trout dinner is worth a try.

Chubut Province

Argentina's third-largest province after Buenos Aires and Santa Cruz, Chubut takes its name from the Mapuche expression *Chupat,* meaning meandering river; stretching from the Atlantic to the Andes and producing up to 22 million kilos of wool yearly, the numerous sheep estancias of its eastern steppe surround the prosperous, irrigated Río Chubut valley. Road and air communications with Buenos Aires are exceptional, while an excellent paved highway links the coast with Chubut's portion of the scenic Argentine lake district, which is also accessible from the popular resort of Bariloche, in Río Negro province to the north.

History

Magellan's celebrated 16th-century expedition entered the Golfo Nuevo, site of present-day Puerto Madryn, but Europeans generally shunned Chubut until the mid-19th century. At that time Welsh nationalists, frustrated with English domination, sought a land where they could exercise sufficient political autonomy to retain their language, religion, and cultural identity. Deciding on desolate Patagonia, they appealed to the government of Argentina which, after initial misgivings due in part to the British presence in the Falkland Islands, offered them a land grant in the lower Río Chubut valley in 1863.

Disillusion and misfortune plagued the 153 first arrivals from the brig *Mimosa* in the winter of 1865. The Patagonian desert bore no resemblance to their verdant homeland, and several children died in a storm that turned a two-day coastal voyage into a 17-day ordeal. Only a handful of the immigrants were farmers in well-watered Wales, yet their livelihood was to be agriculture in arid Chubut. After near starvation in the early years, the colonists engineered suitable irrigation systems and increased their harvests, permitting the gradual absorption of more immigrants from Wales.

Eventually, the Welsh occupied the entire lower Chubut valley and founded the towns of Rawson (named for the Argentine minister who arranged their land grant), Trelew (after Lewis Jones, a founding member of the colony), Puerto Madryn (after colonist Love Parry, Baron of Madryn), and Gaiman (a Tehuelche word meaning Stony Point). Even so, by 1895 the territory's European population was fewer than 4000. Only after the turn of the century did immigration from Europe – Italian, Scottish, English, and other – and central Argentina completely transform the area.

All this immigration had been made possible by General Roca's ruthless Conquista del Desierto. To their credit, the Welsh did not participate in this slaughter of the Indians, but their settlement in the region constituted a foothold for the Argentine state in an area previously outside its authority.

With the outbreak of WWI, Welsh immigration ceased and there began a gradual process of assimilation into Argentine society. The province's cultural landscape still reflects the Welsh presence, though, with its stone buildings and monuments in typical villages like Dolavon, near Gaiman, and Trevelin, near Esquel. Cultural traditions such as tea houses and the *Eisteddfod*

(folk festival) in Gaiman endure. Younger people speak Spanish by preference (there are relatively few Welsh speakers under the age of 40), but a recent influx of tutors from Wales has led to a minor linguistic revival.

The most accessible book on the area is Anglo-Argentine writer Andrew Graham-Yooll's *The Forgotten Colony,* a comprehensive account of British immigration into Argentina that contains a chapter on the Welsh settlements. More specialized and thorough is Glyn Williams' historical geography *The Desert and the Dream: A History of the Welsh Colonisation of Patagonia, 1865 – 1915.* More recently he has produced *The Welsh in Patagonia: The State and the Ethnic Community.*

PUERTO MADRYN

Founded by Welsh settlers in 1886, this sheltered desert port has taken off as a tourist destination because its proximity to the provincial wildlife sanctuary of Península Valdés attracts foreigners, and the good beaches appeal to domestic tourist traffic. Only the street names disclose Puerto Madryn's Welsh origins – it took its name from Love Parry, Baron of Madryn – but despite modernization, the city has not succumbed to the gaudiness of lake district destinations like Bariloche. Puerto Madryn prides itself on environmental consciousness – like the rest of Chubut, it has declared itself a non-nuclear municipality. The local campus of the Universidad de la Patagonia is known for its departments of marine biology, computer science, and engineering.

Recent arrivals greatly outnumber self-identified "NICs" *(nacido y criado,* or "born and raised"). Between 1974, which saw the construction of the Muelle Storni (Storni pier) and Argentina's first aluminum plant (ALUAR), and 1988, the town's population multiplied nearly tenfold to 50,000; inadequate planning encouraged spontaneous housing and caused serious water and sewage problems. With the closure of fish processing plants and the reduction of ALUAR's activities, Madryn's

ARGENTINA

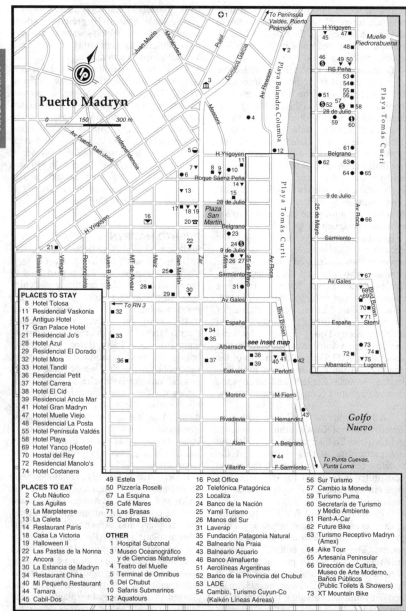

Puerto Madryn

0   150   300 m

To Península
Valdés, Puerto
Pirámide

Muelle
Piedrarabuena

Playa Balandra Columba

Playa Tomás Curti

Plaza
San Martín

Playa Tomás Curti

To RN 3

see inset map

To Punta Cuevas,
Punta Loma

Golfo
Nuevo

PLACES TO STAY
8   Hotel Tolosa
11   Residencial Vaskonia
15   Antiguo Hotel
17   Gran Palace Hotel
21   Residencial Jo's
28   Hotel Azul
29   Residencial El Dorado
32   Hotel Mora
33   Hotel Tandil
36   Residencial Petit
37   Hotel Carrera
38   Hotel El Cid
39   Residencial Ancla Mar
41   Hotel Gran Madryn
47   Hotel Muelle Viejo
48   Residencial La Posta
55   Hotel Península Valdés
58   Hotel Playa
69   Hotel Yanco (Hostel)
70   Hostal del Rey
72   Residencial Manolo's
74   Hotel Costanera

PLACES TO EAT
2   Club Náutico
5   Las Aguilas
9   La Marplatense
13   La Caleta
14   Restaurant París
18   Casa La Victoria
19   Halloween II
22   Las Pastas de la Nonna
29   Ancora
30   La Estancia de Madryn
40   Restaurant China
40   Mi Pequeño Restaurant
44   Tamara
45   Cabil-Dos

49   Estela
50   Pizzería Roselli
67   La Esquina
68   Café Mares
71   Las Brasas
75   Cantina El Náutico

OTHER
1   Hospital Subzonal
3   Museo Oceanográfico
     y de Ciencias Naturales
4   Teatro del Muelle
5   Terminal de Omnibus
6   Del Chubut
10   Safaris Submarinos
12   Aquatours

16   Post Office
20   Telefónica Patagónica
23   Localiza
25   Banco de la Nación
25   Yamil Turismo
26   Manos del Sur
31   Laverap
35   Fundación Patagonia Natural
42   Balneario Na Praia
43   Balneario Acuario
46   Balneario Almafuerte
51   Aerolíneas Argentinas
53   Banco de la Provincia del Chubut
53   LADE
54   Cambio, Turismo Cuyun-Co
     (Kaikén Líneas Aéreas)

56   Sur Turismo
57   Cambio la Moneda
59   Turismo Puma
60   Secretaría de Turismo
     y Medio Ambiente
61   Rent-A-Car
62   Future Bike
63   Turismo Receptivo Madryn
     (Amex)
64   Aike Tour
65   Artesanía Peninsular
66   Dirección de Cultura,
     Museo de Arte Moderno,
     Baños Públicos
     (Public Toilets & Showers)
73   XT Mountain Bike

population has declined to about 45,000, and the city is staking its future on its natural appeal.

Orientation

Puerto Madryn occupies a protected site on the Golfo Nuevo, just east of RN 3, 1371 km south of Buenos Aires, 439 km north of Comodoro Rivadavia, and only 65 km north of Trelew. Unlike most Argentine cities, but like many other towns in Patagonia, its activities do not cluster around the central Plaza San Martín, which features only a handful of businesses despite a popular nightly crafts market. Madryn's broad sandy beaches and the costanera Av Roca/Brown are the principal areas of interest to visitors.

Information

Tourist Office The Secretaría de Turismo y Medio Ambiente (☎ 70100) has a spacious new visitor center at Av Roca 223, near the corner of 28 de Julio. It's open daily 7 am to 1 am from mid-December to mid-March, but the rest of the year hours are 8 am to 2 pm and 3 to 9 pm. The staff has a reputation for helpfulness and efficiency, but sometimes falter at answering questions beyond the routine.

During summer, the center offers a series of videos and lectures at 9 pm daily – ask for the weekly program. For more in-depth history and natural history, or for a guided tour, contact Peter Seibt (German speaker) or Chris Fillmore (English) at 25 de Mayo 1016.

Money Local cambios include La Moneda at 28 de Julio 21, Local 4; Cuyun-Co (☎ 71772) at Av Roca 161; and Turismo Puma (☎ 73063) at 28 de Julio 48. Banco de la Nación, 9 de Julio 117, changes American Express traveler's checks, but also try Banco del Sud at Roque Sáenz Peña and 25 de Mayo, or Banco de la Provincia del Chubut at 25 de Mayo 154, which has an ATM. Banco Almafuerte, at the corner of Roque Sáenz Peña and 25 de Mayo, also cashes traveler's checks and has an ATM.

Post & Telecommunications Correo Argentino is at the corner of Belgrano and Gobernador Maíz; the postal code is 9120. Telefónica Patagónica, Marcos A Zar 289 on Plaza San Martín, permits overseas collect and credit card calls. Puerto Madryn's area code is 0965.

Cultural Centers The municipal Dirección de Cultura (☎ 72060), Av Roca 444, displays works by local artists and traveling exhibitions in its Salón Luis James, and also distributes a list of current cultural events in town.

Travel Agencies Turismo Receptivo Madryn (☎ 71048), Av Roca 303, is the local Amex representative.

Laundry Laverap is on 25 de Mayo between Sarmiento and Av Gales.

Medical Services Puerto Madryn's Hospital Subzonal (☎ 51240) is at Pujol 247.

Environment The Fundación Patagonia Natural (☎ 74363), Marcos A Zar 760, is a watchdog organization that monitors environmental issues in Chubut and elsewhere in Patagonia.

Showers Showers are available for US$1 in the Baños Públicos (public baths), which are downstairs at the Dirección de Cultura, Av Roca 444.

Museums & Monuments

In the historic Chalet Pujol, at the intersection of Domecq García and Menéndez, the **Museo Oceanográfico y de Ciencias Naturales** (☎ 51139) has commendable displays of Patagonian flora and fauna, both marine and terrestrial, and a library. There are panoramic views from the loft, which often has lectures and shows. It's open weekdays 9 to 11:30 am and 6 to 9 pm. Admission is US$2.

Puerto Madryn's **Museo de Arte Moderno** is at Av Roca 444. You can visit the **Alpesca** seafood processing plant by arrangement with their office; ask the

Secretaría de Turismo for details. In summer, **ALUAR** gives 1½ hour-tours of the aluminum plant daily at 9 am; make reservations at ALUAR headquarters the day before.

On the Costanera, toward the south end of town, the **Monumento a La Mujer Galesa** acknowledges the contribution of Welsh women to regional history. Six km south of downtown, along the waterfront road to Punta Cuevas, Luis Perlotti sculpted the **Monumento al Indio Tehuelche**, unveiled in 1965 on the centenary of the arrival of the Welsh colonists to acknowledge their debt to the province's native peoples.

Sunbathing & Water Sports

Puerto Madryn has a variety of beaches stretching from Aluar's Muelle Storni in the north to Punta Cuevas in the south and beyond; the most central of them have crowded balnearios. Because of industrial development near the pier, the northern **Playa Piedras** is less frequented but less attractive than more southerly beaches. Between Piedras and the Muelle Piedrabuena (the old pier), **Playa Balandra Columba** is an area popular for sailing lessons.

South of the Muelle Piedrabuena, **Playa Tomás Curti** is a popular windsurfing area that also attracts swimmers and sunbathers; Balneario Na Praia, on Blvd Brown between Lugones and Perlotti, rents windsurfing equipment and in-line skates. Balneario Acuario is the most central, developed, and crowded part of this area, but it's a lively place for cold beer, snacks, and the chance to mix with locals. To the south, **Playa Mimosa** and **Playa del Indio** are less protected from the constant wind, and even less protected from roaring jet skis. Diving is best south of **Punta Cuevas**.

For sailing excursions and lessons on the yacht *Gandul,* contact the Escuela Patagónica de Vela (☎ 71942), C Vigil 15. Three-hour cruises cost US$30 per person, but are half price for children ages 12 or less, free for those ages 5 and under. Three-

day training cruises around the Golfo Nuevo cost US$250 including accommodations and all meals, while charter cruises cost US$110 per day per person, with a minimum of four persons.

Several places arrange diving classes and excursions, including Safaris Submarinos (☎ 73800), Mitre 80, which has daily videos on diving and whales; Aquatours (☎ 95015) at the foot of the Muelle Piedrabuena, Roca and Yrigoyen; Expediciones de Buceo (☎ 71649) at Yrigoyen and Mitre; Patagonia Buceo, at Blvd Brown and Primera Rotonda; and Mundo Marino at Blvd Brown and Segunda Rotonda.

Mountain Biking

XT Mountain Bike, Av Roca 742, conducts guided tours and also rents mountain bikes by the hour, half day, or full day. Future Bike (☎ 72093), 25 de Mayo 302, charges US$25 per day.

Organized Tours

Tours of nearby attractions should be booked at least a day in advance. Yamil Turismo (☎ 73093), Sarmiento 427, offers trips to Península Valdés or Punta Tombo for as little as US$20, but fares tend to be competitive; Aike Tour (☎ 50720), Av Roca 353, is another good choice, offering trips in relatively small groups. Nearly all the guides speak English at Sur Turismo (☎ 73585), Av Roca 175, which organizes tours of the Madryn area and Península Valdés to match visitors' interests, including overland and submarine photographic safaris, educational tours, and whale watching. For small groups, Turismo Puma (☎ 71482), 28 de Julio 48, organizes nature walks, lasting about four hours, along the coast as well as in the countryside.

Places to Stay

In addition to the regular accommodations detailed below, the Secretaría de Turismo maintains a list of apartments for rent on a daily, weekly, or monthly basis. Prices usually range from US$10 to US$15 per day per person.

Places to Stay – bottom end

Camping Toward Punta Cuevas and the Monumento al Indio Tehuelche, the 800-site *Camping ACA* (☎ 81222) charges US$14 per day for up to four people with car, trailer, and tent, but US$18 for nonmembers. Of this area's several campgrounds, this is the only one with large trees offering some protection from the wind. Reservations are advisable for the busy summer months through Camping ACA, Punta Cuevas, Casilla de Correo 68, 9120 Puerto Madryn, Chubut.

Well designed but less sheltered, nearby *Camping Municipal Sud* (☎ 71924) has several categories of accommodations among its 1360 sites. Their "A" and "B" areas cost US$14 daily for four people, tent, car, and trailer, but their perfectly acceptable "C" and "D" areas are much cheaper at U$2.50 a day per person and US$2.50 per tent. They offer a 20% discount to ACA members and to those with student identification; children under six years old stay without charge. The entire complex closes from April to December.

The newest campground is the Club Náutico Atlántico Sud's *El Golfito* (☎ 71602). Its 300 sites are partly forested and have direct beach access. Nonmember prices are US$10 for four people, tent, and car, plus US$3 per additional person. There's also a small hostel for US$5 per person.

From town, city bus No 2 serves the southern campgrounds.

Hostel *Hotel Yanco* (☎ 71581), Av Roca 626, has hostel accommodations for $12 per person with breakfast, but no kitchen privileges.

Residenciales & Hotels *Antiguo Hotel* (☎ 73742) at 28 de Julio 149 is very friendly and pleasant despite its dark, narrow entrance and reports of "considerable night activity." Rooms cost US$10 per person with bath. *Hotel Tandil* (☎ 71017), J B Justo 770, also charges only US$10 per person.

The singles/doubles at *Residencial Jo's* (☎ 71433), Bolívar 75, are a good value for US$15/25, while *Residencial Petit* (☎ 71460) at M T de Alvear 845 has rooms with private bath at US$15 per person. Comparably priced are *Residencial El Dorado* (☎ 71026) at San Martín 545 and basic *Residencial Vaskonia* (☎ 72581) at 25 de Mayo 43 (probably the best budget hotel).

Another reasonable summer alternative is the Universidad de la Patagonia's *Residencial Ancla Mar* (☎ 51509), 25 de Mayo 874, which costs US$20/30.

Places to Stay – middle

Hotels & Residenciales *Hotel Azul* (☎ 50064), Gobernador Maíz 545, charges US$23/35. Slightly less central *Hotel Mora* (☎ 71424), Juan B Justo 654, is more expensive but mediocre. *Residencial La Posta* (☎ 72422), Av Roca 33, charges US$28/36 for small but clean rooms with bunk beds. *Hotel Yanco* (☎ 71581), Av Roca 626, has good views and a pleasant atmosphere, but the downstairs dance club makes sleep difficult some nights. Rates are US$25/39.

Gran Palace Hotel (☎ 71009), at 28 de Julio 390, has good upstairs rooms for US$30/40, but the downstairs rooms aren't as appealing. Singles/doubles at *Hotel Muelle Viejo* (☎ 71284), Yrigoyen 38, cost US$32/42, but beachfront *Hostal del Rey* (☎ 71156) at Blvd Brown 681 may be the best value in midrange accommodations at US$38/56.

With similar standards, the new, attractive, and central *Residencial Manolo's* (☎ 72390) at Av Roca 763 and *Hotel El Cid* (☎ 71416) at 25 de Mayo 850 are a bit more expensive at US$40/50. *Hotel Carrera* (☎ 50759) at Marcos A Zar 852 charges US$45/55, while *Hotel Gran Madryn* (☎ 72205) at Lugones 40 is very pleasant and well located for US$40/60. Less central but with very spacious rooms, the *Posada de Madryn* (☎ 74087) at Abraham Mathews 2951 charges US$42/60. Their restaurant offers a wide range of international dishes, and the hotel provides patrons with transportation to town and the airport.

Bungalows A self-catering alternative to hotels, *Ruca Hue Bungalows* (☎ 71791, 51267), Humphreys 209, charges US$60 for an apartment with six beds, private bath, an kitchen, and dining room.

Places to Stay – top end
Top-end hotels are primarily those with beach access. The major exception is the new and fairly impersonal *Hotel Tolosa* (☎ 71850), Roque Sáenz Peña 253, which charges US$50/60. Others in this category include *Hotel Costanera* (☎ 71038), at Blvd Brown 759, with rooms at US$55/62; and the *Hotel Playa* (☎ 51446), Av Roca 181, where rates are US$58/65. The priciest accommdations in town are at *Hotel Península Valdés* (☎ 71292) at Av Roca 163, which costs US$80/95.

Places to Eat
Puerto Madryn has a wide variety of good food at reasonable prices. Although beef is more expensive here than in the Pampas, there are several good parrillas, including the highly recommended *Estela* (☎ 51573) at Roque Sáenz Peña 28, *Las Brasas* (☎ 72152) at Av Roca 672, and *La Marplatense* at Roque Sáenz Peña 214. *La Estancia de Madryn,* in an old warehouse on Av Gales between Marcos A Zar and San Martín, has excellent food, reasonable prices, and great atmosphere – though some of that atmosphere comes from the heavy wood smoke used for grilling meat. The place is so spacious that it's difficult and expensive to heat, so it may be open in summer only.

La Esquina (☎ 72182), at Avs Roca and Gales, specializes in seafood and pasta, while *Mi Pequeño Restaurant* (☎ 51164), Av Roca 822, has seafood, pasta, and parrillada. *La Caleta* (☎ 73804), San Martín 156, is an expensive seafood venue, charging around US$20 per person, including a cold buffet. Along Ribera Norte, toward the Muelle Storni, the *Club Náutico* is good but a bit pricey; cheaper and very popular *Can-*

tina El Náutico (☎ 71404) is at Av Roca and Lugones.

There are a number of good pizzerías, including *Halloween II* (☎ 50909), with an extensive menu at 28 de Julio 338; a variety of empanadas are also available. *Pizzería Roselli* (☎ 72541), at Av Roca and Roque Sáenz Peña, is also extremely popular, but perhaps the best pizzas are the large ones at *Cabil-Dos* (☎ 71284), H Yrigoyen and Av Roca, which also serves great baked empanadas. Takeout service is available.

Ancora, at the corner of 25 de Mayo and 9 de Julio, is an outstanding pizza and pasta restaurant with pleasant, unpretentious decor, but note that the very low pasta prices are a bit misleading because the choice of sauce is additional. *Las Pastas de la Nonna* (☎ 50108), 9 de Julio 345, is a bit more expensive.

Cheaper alternatives include *Las Aguilas* (☎ 71980) at M A Zar 75 and *Restaurant París* (☎ 51701), Roque Sáenz Peña 112. Puerto Madryn has two Asian restaurants: *Restaurant China* at Marcos A Zar 752 and *Casa La Victoria* (☎ 73909), on 28 de Julio between Marcos Zar and San Martín, which advertises a US$10 Chinese tenedor libre.

Ice cream at *Café Mares,* at the intersection of Avs Gales and Roca, rates with Buenos Aires' best – try the chocolate and lemon mousses, and the white and bittersweet chocolates. For Welsh tea, Puerto Madryn's only alternative is *Tamara,* Av Roca 1250.

Entertainment
Teatro del Muelle, on Av Rawson (the northern extension of Av Roca) just beyond the Muelle Piedrabuena, has live performances Saturday nights at 11 pm. For current offerings, contact the Dirección de Cultura (☎ 72060), Av Roca 444.

Things to Buy
For homemade chocolate delicacies, try Artesanía Peninsular at Roca 320. Del Chubut (☎ 51311), at Roque Sáenz Peña 399, produces alfajores (cookie sandwiches filled with chocolate, dulce de leche, or

fruit) and tasty torta galesa (Welsh black cake).

Manos del Sur (☎ 72539), 9 de Julio 146, has an outstanding selection of souvenirs, natural foods, and artisanal products in ceramics, wood, wool, leather, and the like.

Getting There & Away

Air Although Puerto Madryn has had its own convenient Aeródromo El Tehuelche since 1989, nearly all commercial flights still arrive at Trelew, 65 km south (see the Getting There & Away entry for Trelew). The local airport tax is US$2.

LADE (☎ 51256), Av Roca 119, flies from Puerto Madryn to Buenos Aires (US$128) Tuesdays via San Antonio Oeste (US$25), Viedma (US$34), Bahía Blanca (US$61), and Mar del Plata (US$97). It also flies Mondays to Esquel (US$61), Bariloche (US$64), and Neuquén (US$64); and Fridays to Comodoro Rivadavia (US$48) via Trelew.

Cuyun-Co (☎ 50720), Av Roca 171, is the local agent for Kaikén Líneas Aéreas, which has flights Mondays and Saturdays to El Calafate (US$132), Río Gallegos (US$143), Río Grande (US$145), and Ushuaia (US$155). The airport tax is US$2.

Aerolíneas Argentinas (☎ 50110) has offices at 25 de Mayo 146.

Bus Puerto Madryn's Terminal de Omnibus is on H Yrigoyen between M A Zar and San Martín. Línea 28 de Julio (☎ 72056) runs frequent buses to Trelew (US$3) and back.

Empresa Andesmar (☎ 73764) has daily buses to Mendoza (23 hours) and Caleta Olivia (eight hours); three times weekly, this latter service continues to Río Gallegos (18 hours). Central Argentino (☎ 73764) goes to Comodoro Rivadavia (US$29, six hours), Bahía Blanca, and Rosario. TAC (☎ 50390), opposite the terminal, goes north to Buenos Aires, Córdoba (US$72, 18 hours), Tucumán, and Jujuy, west to Mendoza and south to Río Gallegos (US$73, 20 hours). Que Bus (☎ 73585), Av Roca 187, goes to La Plata and Buenos

Aires for US$100 return with meals included.

Empresa Don Otto (☎ 71575) has one daily direct bus to Buenos Aires, one to Comodoro Rivadavia, and one to Río Gallegos and intermediate stops. It also goes to Neuquén (US$39, 12 hours) five times weekly, and to Esquel (US$39, eight hours) four times weekly. El Condor/La Puntual (☎ 71125) also has daily bus service to Buenos Aires (US$57, 18 hours), four weekly to Bahía Blanca via Viedma and Carmen de Patagones, and four to Comodoro Rivadavia.

TUP (☎ 73764) travels three times weekly to Córdoba, and to Camarones and Comodoro Rivadavia. Mar y Valle (☎ 72056) has three buses weekly to Esquel.

Getting Around

To/From the Airport Aeródromo El Tehuelche (☎ 51287) is five km west of town, at the junction with RN 3; cabs are not expensive.

Southbound Línea 28 de Julio buses from Puerto Madryn to Trelew, which run every half hour, will stop at Trelew's Aeropuerto Internacional Almirante Zar on request. Aerolíneas Argentinas also runs a bus from Almirante Zar to Puerto Madryn (US$10), leaving 30 minutes after the flight arrival.

Car Rental Renting a car is the best way to see Puerto Madryn and its surroundings, especially Península Valdés. Rent-A-Car (☎ 71797), Av Roca 277, is open seven days a week. Localiza (☎ 71660) is at Belgrano 196, and Cuyun-Co (☎ 51845) at Av Roca 171.

AROUND PUERTO MADRYN
Reserva Faunística Punta Loma

This sea lion rookery, 17 km southwest of Puerto Madryn via a good but winding gravel road, has a visitor center and an overlook about 15 meters from the animals. Some travel agencies organize tours; otherwise, you can hire a car or taxi. Admission costs US$3 for adults, but retired people and students pay only US$1.

RESERVA FAUNÍSTICA PENÍNSULA VALDÉS

Sea lions, elephant seals, guanacos, rheas, Magellanic penguins, and many other seabirds are present in large numbers on the beaches and headlands of one of South America's finest wildlife reserves, but the big attraction is the southern right whale *Eubalaena australis,* known in Spanish as the *ballena franca.* Sheep estancias occupy most of the peninsula's interior, which includes one of the lowest continental depressions in the world, the salt flats of Salina Grande and Salina Chica, 42 meters below sea level.

Puerto Pirámide, the peninsula's only village, was the port of exit for salt from Salina Grande at the turn of the century, but it now depends exclusively on tourism; it's an excellent base for exploring the peninsula. Visited by right whales between mid-June and mid-December, its sandy white beaches and the warm clear waters of the Golfo Nuevo attract fishing and water sports enthusiasts. For visitors without cars, there is a sea lion colony only four km from town, with good views (and sunsets) across the Golfo Nuevo toward Puerto Madryn. During the season, launches can approach right whales in the harbor.

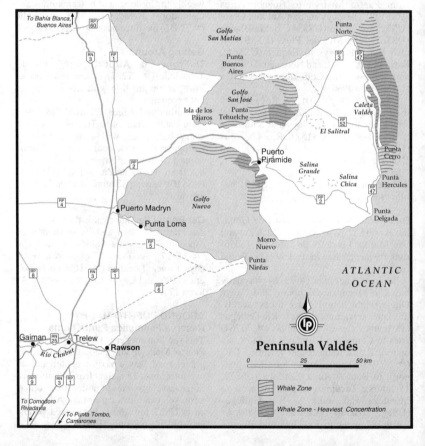

Península Valdés

0   25   50 km

Whale Zone

Whale Zone - Heaviest Concentration

Isla de los Pájaros

While most visitors to Península Valdés focus on whales, elephant seals, sea lions, penguins, and other marquee species, the area has a wide variety of birdlife, most of which will be new to visitors from the Northern Hemisphere. Most of these birds are also common in the rest of Patagonia and in Chile; only a handful, most notably the rock cormorant, night heron, crested duck, and steamer duck, breed here. Note that Spanish common names can vary between Argentina and Chile – sometimes for nationalistic reasons.

Linnaean Name	Spanish Common name	English Common name
Spheniscus magellanicus	Pingüino de Magallanes	Magellanic/Jackass penguin
Phoenicopterus chilensis	Flamenco austral	Chilean flamingo
Nycticorax nycticorax	Garza bruja	Black-crowned night heron
Haematopus ater	Ostrero negro	Black oystercatcher
H ostralegus	Ostrero común	Common oystercatcher
Phalacrocorax magallanicus	Cormorán de cuello negro	Rock cormorant
P olivaceus	Biguá	Olive cormorant
Charadrius falklandicus	Chorlo doble collar	Two-banded plover
Calidris fuscicollis	Chorlito rebadilla blanca	White-rumped sandpiper
Egretta alba	Garza blanca	Great egret
Larus dominicanus	Gaviota cocinera	Dominican/Kelp gull
L maculipennus	Gaviota capucho café	Brown-hooded gull
Lophonetta specularioides	Pato crestón	Patagonian crested duck
Tachyeres leucocephalus	Pato vapor cabeza blanca	White-headed steamer duck
Sterna hirundinacea	Gaviotín sudamericano	South American tern
S maxima	Gaviotín real	Royal tern
Calorsterna eurygnatha	Gaviotín pico amarillo	Yellow-beaked tern ■

About 18 km north of Puerto Madryn, paved RP 2 branches off RN 3 across the Istmo Carlos Ameghino to the entrance of the Península Valdés reserve; Chubut provincial officials collect a visitor fee of US$5 per adult, US$3 per child. The **Centro de Interpretación** here has a small exhibit of local fauna and flora, plus an observation tower with views across the desert to Golfo San José to the north and Golfo Nuevo in the south. In the Golfo San José, 800 meters north of the isthmus, **Isla de los Pájaros** is a bird sanctuary off-limits to humans but visible through a powerful telescope; it also contains a replica of a chapel built at Fuerte San José, the area's first Spanish settlement.

To visit remaining wildlife sites beyond Puerto Pirámide, it's essential to have a car or take an organized tour; the roads are gravelled, with occasional soft sand, but present no obstacle to prudent drivers. Just north of **Punta Delgada**, in the southeast corner of the peninsula, a large colony of sea lions and elephant seals is visible from the cliffs, but the better sites are farther north.

Caleta Valdés, on the eastern shore, is a sheltered bay with a long gravel spit onto which elephant seals haul themselves in the spring. They are easily photographed, but should not be approached too closely. Guanaco sometimes stroll across the beach. Between Caleta Valdés and Punta Norte is a substantial colony of burrowing Magellanic penguins. At **Punta Norte** itself is an enormous mixed colony of sea lions and elephant seals, with clearly marked trails and fences to discourage too close an encounter.

Dangers & Annoyances

At most wildlife sites, it is foolish to attempt to descend the precipitous, unconsolidated cliffs to get close to the animals. Even if you do make it down safely, male sea lions are quick, aggressive, and dangerous. Note that some areas are closed to all visitors, and you may have to be content to view them from a distance; ask park rangers for details.

Visitors contracting tours to Península Valdés should know that frustrated travelers have found that some trips spend too

Fauna of Península Valdés & Patagonia

The animal life of Península Valdés is generally typical of the entire Patagonian coast as far as Tierra del Fuego. This is especially true with respect to shorebirds, including penguins, and marine mammals, including whales and seals.

The following periods are the best for viewing marine and coastal wildlife at Península Valdés and most of the rest of Patagonia.

Species	Period
Birds (general)	All year
Penguins	October to March
Whales	June to mid-December
Sea lions	All year
Elephant seals	All year; summer months best

Penguins Until the era of European exploration in the 16th century, penguins were unknown outside the Southern Hemisphere, and these large flightless birds are still a novelty outside their range. The most northerly penguins are found in Ecuador's Galápagos Islands, but they are most numerous in the higher latitudes of Patagonia and Antarctica. The only species that regularly visits Península Valdés is the Magellanic or jackass penguin *(Spheniscus magellanicus).*

The first Europeans to see penguins were the Portuguese navigators who rounded the Cape of Good Hope in the late 15th century, but the first European to publicize them was Italian noble-man Antonio Pigafetta, the diarist on Magellan's expedition which circumnavigated the globe in the early 16th century. The late naturalist George Gaylord Simpson believes that Magellan's crew saw them at Punta Tombo, today a large reserve south of Puerto Madryn.

There are four species of the genus *Spheniscus.* In the South Atlantic, *S magellanicus* has a breeding range from Península Valdés, at about 42° S latitude, around the tip of South America to near Valparaíso, Chile, about 33° S in the colder Pacific. It spends winter at sea but comes ashore to breed in late September and hatch its eggs in shoreline burrows. Unable to feed them-selves until they can swim, chicks depend on their parents to feed them with regurgitated squid and other food ingested on daily trips to the ocean.

Penguins are awkward on land, tobogganing on their wings for speed when threatened. In the water they are swift and graceful, their webbed feet serving as rudders. In fact, it is not quite correct to call them flightless when, according to Simpson, "they fly in the water . . . . They are pro-pelled in the water by their wings, which move in unison as in usual flight and are as heavily muscled as those of aerial fliers."

Despite their enormous numbers, penguins have many predators. In the water, southern sea lions, leopard seals, and killer whales take adult birds. On land, eggs and chicks are vulnerable to gulls, skuas, and other large birds. Both aboriginal peoples, such as the Maori of New Zealand, and Europeans have consumed them for food; French naturalist Antoine Pernety, visiting the Falklands in the late 18th century, wrote that French colonists there ate penguins 'several times in ragouts, which we found to be as good as those made of hares'. Even today, Falkland Islanders collect penguin eggs in the spring, but no longer are penguins killed and boiled down for their oil, which was used to top off casks of whale and seal oil.

Magellanic penguins sometimes frequent the beach at Puerto Pirámides on Península Valdés. Otherwise you can see them along Caleta Valdés, although there are much larger numbers farther south at Punta Tombo and Cabo Dos Bahías. For information on other penguin species, see the chapter on the Falkland Islands, below. A readable account of the natural history of pen-guins, as well as a history of human encounters with them, is Simpson's *Penguins: Past and Present, Here and There.*

Whales The world's largest living animals comprise two orders: the toothed whales (including dol-phins, porpoises, and the killer whale *Orcinus orca)* feed mainly on fish and squid, while the baleen whales (including the southern right whale *Eubalaena australis)* trap plankton and krill (small crustaceans) as seawater filters through plates in their jaws. A layer of blubber beneath their skin insulates them from the cold ocean waters.

Their bodies black with white underbellies, killer whales frequent the waters around Península Valdés in pods. Males can reach more than nine meters in length and weigh as much as 950 kg, although most specimens of both males and females are considerably smaller. Their ominous dorsal fin is up to two meters high. Near the top of the food chain, they prey on fish, penguins, dolphins, seals, and, on rare occasion, larger whales.

Exploited for meat and oil, the slow moving right whale was a favorite target of whalers because, unlike other species, it remained floating on the surface after being killed; after more than half a century of legal protection, right whale populations are slowly recovering in the South Atlantic.

Averaging nearly 12 meters in length and weighing more than 30 tons, right whales enter the shallow waters of the Golfo Nuevo and the Golfo San José in spring to breed and bear their young. Whale-watching is possible from June to mid-December, but September and October are the best months. At Puerto Pirámide, launches take visitors out into the harbor for closer views.

Elephant Seals & Sea Lions The southern elephant seal *(Mirounga leonina)* and the southern sea lion *(Otaria flavescens)* belong to the order of pinnipeds or eared seals, which are widely distributed throughout Patagonia and other southern midlatitude and sub-Antarctic areas and islands.

Elephant seals take their common name from the male's enormous proboscis, which does indeed resemble an elephant's trunk. These ponderous animals reach nearly seven meters in length and weigh up to 4500 kg, but the females are so much smaller that it would be possible to mistake them for a different species. They spend most of the year at sea, diving several hundred meters for up to half an hour in search of squid and other fish.

Península Valdés has the only breeding colony of southern elephant seals on the South American continent. The bull elephant seal comes ashore in late winter or early spring, breeding shortly after the already pregnant females arrive and give birth. Dominant males known as "beachmasters" control harems of up to 100 females but must constantly fight off challenges from bachelor males. Fights are frequent and spectacular, leaving many adult males disfigured.

In the course of these fights, bulls accidentally crush many seal pups. Those that survive gain weight rapidly for about three weeks before being abandoned by their mothers, and they head to sea by the end of the year. There are substantial numbers of elephant seals at the Punta Norte reserve, but access to them is better on the gravel spit at Caleta Valdés.

Aggressive southern sea lions will occasionally drag away a helpless elephant seal pup, but they, too, feed largely on squid and the occasional penguin. The male is an imposing specimen, whose mane truly resembles that of an African lion. Like the African lion, it is surprisingly quick and aggressive on land. Do not approach them too closely for photographs. ■

much time at confiterías and too little time at wildlife sites; drivers apparently get kickbacks based on the amount of money spent at these stops. Before agreeing to any of these trips, try to speak to other travelers to learn about their experiences, discuss the tour with the operator to be sure that their expectations are the same as yours, and do not hesitate to relay complaints to the Secretaría de Turismo y Medio Ambiente in Puerto Madryn.

Whale Watching

From June to mid-December, several operators in Puerto Madryn and Puerto Pirámide offer whale-watching excursions on the waters of the Golfo Nuevo for about US$20. These companies include Hydrosport (☎ 95006), Pinino (☎ 95015), Sur Turismo (☎ 73585), Tito Botazzi (☎ 95050), and Peke Sosa (☎ 71291).

Although most such operators are scrupulous, provincial authorities have requested visitors to report to rangers or to the Seceretería de Turismo in Puerto Madryn) any instance of boats attempting to pursue, disperse, or round up whales; getting within 100 meters of any whale without cutting the motor; intercepting their course or navigating parallel with them; touching an animal with the boat; separating a mother from her young; and nearing an animal that is already under close observation by another boat.

Places to Stay & Eat

Accommodations in Puerto Pirámide are at least adequate and sometimes better, but are very limited. Since Av Roca, the only street, parallels the beach, all hotels have good beach access; note that the beach almost disappears during high tide. Change money in Puerto Madryn or Trelew.

Sites at Puerto Pirámide's *Camping Municipal*, though not well marked, are sheltered from the wind by dunes and trees. It has clean toilets, hot showers, and a store with groceries and cold beer, mineral water, and soft drinks. Prices are US$4 per person; because of extreme water shortages, showers (US$1) are carefully timed.

In summer, the place gets very crowded and somewhat noisy, but a persistent search should reward you with a quiet site.

There is basic but acceptable lodging at *Hospedaje El Español* (☎ 95031) for US$10 per person, with simple but clean rooms and toilets, plus hot showers. *El Libanés* (☎ 95007) has modest rooms in summer for US$20 per person with bath, slightly cheaper the rest of the year, and a small confitería that serves a reasonable breakfast. The most expensive accommodations are the *Hostería ACA* (☎ 95004), with singles/doubles for US$39/52 and a costly restaurant.

Pub Paradise (☎ 95030), a very casual, friendly place where the owner speaks fluent English, serves sandwiches and a broad selection of pizzas. Bed and breakfast are also available for US$20 per person.

Camping and fires are prohibited outside Puerto Pirámide, but highly recommended *Faro Punta Delgada* (☎ 0965-71910, fax 51218), Av Julio Roca 141 in Puerto Madryn, has 30 double rooms with private bath on the site of the old lighthouse. This is a good base for exploring the peninsula; rates are US$40 double, US$100 with full board.

Getting There & Away

On Tuesdays, Thursdays, Saturdays, and Sundays at 8:55 am, the Mar y Valle bus goes from Puerto Madryn to Puerto Pirámide (US$6.50), returning at 7 pm. The bus tours from Puerto Madryn, may allow passengers to get off at Puerto Pirámide and reboard another day for no additional charge, but verify that this is acceptable before doing so.

Getting Around

Hitchhiking in Península Valdés is nearly impossible, so to visit sites any distance from Puerto Pirámide, the alternatives are renting a car or taking an organized tour. Most travel agencies in Puerto Madryn organize day trips for about US$30, but competition is stiff. There are occasional bargains. Admission to the reserve is not included.

TRELEW

Actively courting tourists, Trelew is a convenient staging point for visits to the nearby Welsh villages of Gaiman and Dolavon, as well as the massive Punta Tombo penguin reserve. Founded in 1886 as a railway junction to unite the Chubut valley with the beaches of the Golfo Nuevo, it takes its Welsh name from Lewis Jones, who promoted expansion of the railway – *tre* means town, while "Lew" is short for Lewis. The town's first Eisteddfod (a poetry and music event still held in early September) took place in 1890, when the population did not exceed 80.

During the following 25 years, important developments took place: The railway reached Gaiman, the Welsh built their Salón San Davíd, and Italian immigrants constructed the Teatro Verdi. By 1915 the population had reached 4400, but it stabilized at this level until 1956, when federal government customs preferences promoted industrial development in Patagonia. Trelew became very attractive to immigrants from all over the country and, by

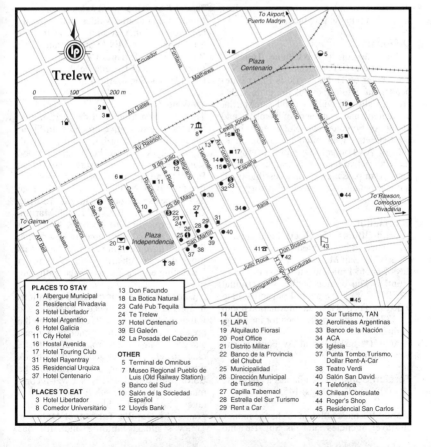

PLACES TO STAY
1 Albergue Municipal
2 Residencial Rivadavia
3 Hotel Libertador
4 Hotel Argentino
6 Hotel Galicia
11 City Hotel
16 Hostal Avenida
17 Hotel Touring Club
31 Hotel Rayentray
35 Residencial Urquiza
37 Hotel Centenario

PLACES TO EAT
3 Hotel Libertador
8 Comedor Universitario
13 Don Facundo
18 La Botica Natural
23 Café Pub Tequila
24 Te Trelew
37 Hotel Centenario
39 El Galeón
42 La Posada del Cabezón

OTHER
5 Terminal de Omnibus
7 Museo Regional Pueblo de Luis (Old Railway Station)
9 Banco del Sud
10 Salón de la Sociedad Español
12 Lloyds Bank
14 LADE
15 LAPA
19 Alquilauto Fiorasi
20 Post Office
21 Distrito Militar
22 Banco de la Provincia del Chubut
25 Municipalidad
26 Dirección Municipal de Turismo
27 Capilla Tabernacl
28 Estrella del Sur Turismo
29 Rent a Car
30 Sur Turismo, TAN
32 Aerolíneas Argentinas
33 Banco de la Nación
34 ACA
36 Iglesia
37 Punta Tombo Turismo, Dollar Rent-A-Car
38 Teatro Verdi
40 Salón San Davíd
41 Telefónica
43 Chilean Consulate
44 Roger's Shop
45 Residencial San Carlos

1970, its population had risen to 24,000. Around that time, Trelew became notorious for the massacre of political prisoners who escaped from the local prison and took over the airport for some hours.

The 1980s witnessed another wave of immigration for which city planners were unprepared – toward the end of the decade, the population had reached 90,000, but after 1989 the abandonment of industrial promotion policies led many to leave the area; the present population is around 85,000. Like El Bolsón, Trelew has declared itself a "non-nuclear municipality" because of objections to the federal government's plans to locate a nuclear waste dump in the province.

Orientation
In the valley of the Río Chubut, Trelew is 65 km south of Puerto Madryn along RN 3. The center of Trelew's grid is Plaza Independencia, while most of the main sights are on Calles 25 de Mayo and San Martín, at the north and south ends of the plaza, and along Av Fontana, two blocks east. East-west streets change their names on either side of Av Fontana. One of downtown's more attractive features is a series of semi-pedestrian passageways inaccessible to all but very small cars, traveling at very slow speeds.

Information
Tourist Offices The cheerful and competent Dirección Municipal de Turismo (☎ 20139), San Martín 171, is open weekdays 7 am to 1 pm and 5 to 8 pm in summer months. The branch at the bus terminal (☎ 20121) is open 8 am to 1 pm and 4:30 to 9:30 pm. There's also an information booth (☎ 33746) at the airport, open for incoming flights.

ACA (☎ 35197) is at Av Fontana and San Martín.

Foreign Consulate Chile has a consulate (☎ 20920) at Don Bosco 145.

Money It's most efficient to change money at travel agencies such as Sur Turismo

(☎ 34550), at Belgrano 326, which also changes traveler's checks. Banks, open 8 am to 1 pm, include Banco de la Nación at Av Fontana and Calle 25 de Mayo; Banco de la Provincia del Chubut at Rivadavia and 25 de Mayo; and Banco del Sud at 9 de Julio 320. The latter two have ATMs, as does Lloyds Bank at 9 de Julio 102.

Post & Telecommunications Correo Argentino is at Calle 25 de Mayo and Mitre; the postal code is 9100. Telefónica is at the corner of Julio Roca and Av Fontana; Trelew's area code is 0965.

Travel Agencies Local agencies organize tours to Península Valdés and penguin reserves at Punta Tombo. These include Sur Turismo (☎ 34081) at Belgrano 326; Punta Tombo Turismo (☎ 30658) at San Martín 150; and Estrella del Sur Turismo (☎ 31282) at San Martín 129.

Walking Tour
The Dirección Municipal de Turismo distributes an informative brochure, in Spanish and English, describing most but not all of the city's historic buildings. A good starting point is the **Museo Regional Pueblo de Luis** at the former railway station (1889), at the north end of Av Fontana; half a block south, on Fontana, the **Touring Club** began in 1906 as Hotel Martino before expanding to become, briefly at least, Patagonia's best hotel (a description that may have been faint praise). While its glory days are clearly gone, it's still an interesting edifice and a popular gathering place.

Banco de la Nación started operations in 1899 after being relocated from Rawson following floods on the Río Chubut, but the present building at the corner of Fontana and 25 de Mayo dates from 1922; note the clock tower. One block south and one block west, at San Martín and Belgrano, the **Salón San David** (1913) is a Welsh community center where the Eisteddfod often takes place. Half a block north on Belgrano, the **Capilla Tabernacl** (1889) is Trelew's oldest building and still has

Welsh-language services on alternate Sundays. Italian immigrants inaugurated the **Teatro Verdi**, on San Martín between Belgrano and Rivadavia, as a skating rink in 1914.

At the southeast corner of Plaza Independencia, the **Municipalidad** (1931) houses city offices; the plaza's most interesting feature is its Victorian gingerbread **Kiosco**, dating from 1910. On the west side of the plaza, on Calle Mitre, the **Distrito Militar** (1903) housed Trelew's first school; on the north side, at 25 de Mayo 237, Spanish immigrants built the **Salón de la Sociedad Española** (1920), which hosted local theater productions.

Museo Regional Pueblo de Luis

In the former railway station at Av Fontana and 9 de Julio, this museum focuses on historical photographs, clothing, and period furnishings but fails to explain the Welsh departure from the United Kingdom and the relation of the Welsh to the Argentine state. The train itself stopped running in 1961, but the antique steam engine and other machinery outside are worth a look.

The museum is open daily 7 am to 1 pm and 3 to 8 pm weekdays; admission costs US$2 for adults, US$1 for children.

Museo Paleontológico Egidio Feruglio

Saber-tooth tigers, dinosaur eggs the size of bowling balls, and a fossil spider (so large that arachnophobes may exit screaming) are among the outstanding specimens in this small but well-organized display, which also includes local dinosaurs, such as *Piatnitzkysaurus,* which are comparable to more famous Northern Hemisphere species like *Tyranosaurus rex* and *Apatosaurus* (brontosaurus).

At 9 de Julio 631, west of downtown, the museum (☎ 35464, 20012) is open weekdays 8:30 am to 12:30 pm, and 1:30 to 8 pm, Saturdays 9 am to noon and 2 to 9 pm, and Sundays and holidays 2 to 9 pm. Admission is US$4 for adults, and US$2 for university students, retirees, and children under 12 years old.

Special Events

Trelew's major cultural event is the Eisteddfod de Chubut, celebrating Welsh traditions, in early September. October 20's Aniversario de la Ciudad commemorates the city's founding in 1886.

The most conspicuously commercial event is early December's Fiesta Provincial del Pingüino. In late January, Trelew's Exposición Ganadera, Comercial y Agroindustrial showcases local livestock.

Organized Tours

Local travel agencies run excursions to most of the major sights in and around Trelew, including the city itself (US$20), Punta Tombo (US$30 plus the US$5 provincial admission charge), and the lower Río Chubut valley (US$15; US$27 with Welsh tea in Gaiman). Day trips to Península Valdés (US$40 plus the provincial admission charge) are more expensive here than those that depart from Puerto Madryn because it's an extra hour on the highway in each direction.

Places to Stay – bottom end

Camping Open October to March, *Camping Club Huracán* (☎ 34380), on RN 25 between the bridge and the traffic circle toward Comodoro Rivadavia, has only basic facilities.

Hostel Trelew's *Albergue Municipal* (☎ 20160), Mitre 37, has 40 dormitory-style beds available for US$5 per person. Hot showers and kitchen privileges are available.

Residenciales & Hotels Trelew's cheapest regular accommodations are basic *Residencial Urquiza* (☎ 31549), Urquiza 341, for US$10/18 single/double. *Hotel Argentino* (☎ 36134), Mathews 186, is clean and comfy but slightly dearer at US$12 per person.

Hostal Avenida (☎ 34172), near the bus terminal at Lewis Jones 49, is friendly, quiet, and clean for US$15/20 with shared bath and an inexpensive breakfast, but some of the beds sag. *Residencial San*

Carlos (☎ 31538), Sarmiento 758, has small but clean rooms at US$15/23 with bath. Popular with travelers, the modest rooms at *Residencial Rivadavia* (☎ 34472), Rivadavia 55, are a good value for US$15 per person with private bath. *Hotel Provincia* (☎ 31544) at H Yrigoyen 625, which also has a small restaurant, charges US$18/35.

Places to Stay – middle

The best mid-range value, if only for its silent film era atmosphere, is *Hotel Touring Club* (☎ 33998) at Av Fontana 240, which charges US$25/40; its confitería is a must for coffee or mid-morning aperitif. Prices are very reasonable by current Argentine standards, though service is a bit lethargic.

Hotel Amancay (☎ 31662), some distance from the center at Paraguay 953, charges US$20/30. *Hotel Galicia* (☎ 33803), at 9 de Julio 214, has nice rooms for US$25/40 with shared bath, while less convenient *Hotel Cheltum* (☎ 31384) at H Yrigoyen 1485 charges US$28/42 for small, dark rooms with private bath. *City Hotel* (☎ 35050), Rivadavia 254, costs US$30/40.

Places to Stay – top end

Downtown *Hotel Centenario* (☎ 36241), San Martín 150, costs US$48/70 and also has a restaurant, but the rooms are not really up to top-end standards. An alternative is *Hotel Libertador* (☎ 35132), at Rivadavia 73, which has a restaurant and a bar/confitería for US$53/70. The most expensive and luxurious in town is *Hotel Rayentray* (☎ 34702), Calle San Martín and Belgrano, which has a decent restaurant, swimming pools, a gym, and a sauna. Rates are US$90/110.

Places to Eat

The *Comedor Universitario,* at Fontana and 9 de Julio, offers wholesome meals at very low prices. Reader-recommended *Don Facundo* is at Av Fontana 213, corner of 9 de Julio.

Delikatesse (☎ 30716), west of downtown at AP Bell 434, offers wild game and other unusual foods as well as Italian cui-sine and pizza. *La Cantina,* at 25 de Mayo and AP Bell, specializes in pasta and sea-food, as do *La Posada del Cabezón* (☎ 20524), Don Bosco 23, and the recom-mended *El Galeón* (☎ 20011), at San Mar-tín 118.

Most people prefer an outing to Gaiman to sample its casas de té (Welsh tea houses), but *Te Trelew* at Pasaje La Rioja 361 may be worth a try for those who lack time for a side trip; the cost is US$12. Alongside it is *Café Pub Tequila.*

La Botica Natural is a natural foods grocery located on Av Fontana, alongside the Hotel Touring Club, which has an excellent confitería.

Things to Buy

The area's most famous product is the Welsh fruitcake. Some of the stores that sell them are Roger's Shop at Moreno 463, Torta Típica Galesa at AP Bell 315, La Galesa at Escalada 3531, and La Tienda del Sol on Pasaje La Rioja.

More conventional sweets are available at Chocolates Patagónicos, Soberanía Nacional 460, and Casa del Chocolate Huenüi, Belgrano 636. For beautiful leather goods, horse gear, and woolens, try Jagüel at 25 de Mayo 579.

Getting There & Away

Air At 25 de Mayo 33, Aerolíneas Argenti-nas (☎ 35297, 30016 at the airport) flies twice daily to Aeroparque (US$183), and daily to Río Gallegos (US$138) and Ushu-aia (US$157). Trelew is one of the cities on the itinerary for Aerolíneas "Conozca Pata-gonia" discount fare.

LADE (☎ 35740), Av Fontana 227, flies on Mondays to Puerto Madryn (US$13), Esquel (US$57), and Bariloche (US$64); Fridays to Neuquén (US$64) and Bari-loche; and Mondays and Fridays to Como-doro Rivadavia (US$40).

LAPA (☎ 23440), Av Fontana 285, has flights on Mondays, Wednesdays, and Sat-urdays to Aeroparque (US$99); Wednes-days to Comodoro Rivadavia (US$29); and Mondays and Fridays to Comodoro Riva-davia and Río Gallegos (US$89).

TAN (☎ 34550), Belgrano 326, flies on Tuesdays and Thursdays to Esquel (US$54) and Comodoro Rivadavia (US$30); on Mondays to Esquel only; on Wednesdays and Fridays to Comodoro Rivadavia and El Calafate (US$126); and on Wednesdays and Fridays (twice) to Neuquén (US$77).

Bus Trelew's Terminal de Omnibus (☎ 20121) is at Urquiza and Lewis Jones, six blocks northeast of downtown. Empresa 28 de Julio (☎ 32429) has frequent buses to Puerto Madryn (US$4), Gaiman (US$1.40), and Dolavon (US$2.60).

Empresa Mar y Valle (☎ 32429) has bus service to Puerto Pirámide Tuesdays, Thursdays, Saturdays, and Sundays, leaving Trelew at 7:45 am and returning from Puerto Pirámide at 6:30 pm. Empresas Rawson and 28 de Julio have buses to Rawson (US$1) every 15 minutes, starting at 5:30 am.

La Puntual (☎ 33748) has daily buses to Buenos Aires (US$76, 22 hours). Empresa Don Otto (☎ 32434) has two buses daily to Buenos Aires, two to Bahía Blanca, two to Comodoro Rivadavia (US$22, five hours), one to Puerto Deseado, one to Rio Gallegos (US$71, 18 hours), and one to Neuquén; it goes less frequently to Camarones (Mondays and Fridays) and Esquel (Tuesdays, Fridays, and Sundays). Que Bus (☎ 22760), Chile 185, offers roundtrips to La Plata and Buenos Aires for US$100.

Empresa Andesmar (☎ 33535) goes daily to Neuquén (US$38, ten hours) and Mendoza (US$76, 24 hours), to Caleta Olivia (US$25, ten hours), and three times weekly to Río Gallegos (US$68, 17 hours). Central Argentino, in the same office, goes to Viedma/Carmen de Patagones (US$28, seven hours), Bahía Blanca (US$45, 12 hours), and Rosario (US$100).

TAC (☎ 31452) has extensive coastal routes, including Comodoro Rivadavia, Caleta Olivia, and Río Gallegos southbound, and Bahía Blanca, La Plata, and Buenos Aires northbound, plus interior routes to the Cuyo region and the Andean Northwest.

Empresa TUP (☎ 21343) travels to Santa Rosa (US$46) and Córdoba (US$78) three afternoons weekly, and to Camarones and Comodoro Rivadavia three mornings a week.

Transportadora Patagónica (☎ 32428) goes to Bariloche (US$66) and has two buses weekly to Mar del Plata (US$72). Empresa Chubut (☎ 32806) goes daily to Esquel (US$35).

Getting Around
To/From the Airport Trelew's modern Aeropuerto Internacional Almirante Zar (☎ 33746) is on RN 3, five km north of town; despite its recent designation, there are no international flights yet. Buses from Trelew to Puerto Madryn will enter the airport to drop off passengers, while cabs cost about US$8.

Car Rental Several agencies rent cars in Trelew, the cheapest of which is Dollar (☎ 21438) at San Martín 148. Alternatives include Alquilauto Fiorasi (☎ 35344) at España 344; Rent a Car (☎ 20898) at San Martín 125; and Avis (☎ 34834) at Paraguay 105.

GAIMAN
One of the few demonstrably Welsh towns remaining in Patagonia, Gaiman (population 5000) owes its name (Stony Point) to the Tehuelche Indians who used to winter in the area, but modern visitors come to stuff themselves at the numerous and excellent Welsh tea houses.

The Welsh presence here dates from 1874, but later immigrants, including Creoles, Germans, and Anglos, also cultivated fruit, vegetables, and fodder in the lower Río Chubut valley. Industry followed later, including Argentina's only seaweed-processing plant, a nylon stockings factory, and a polyethylene packaging factory. It's the oldest municipality of Chubut province, 17 km west of Trelew via RN 25.

There's a Fonofax office on Av Tello between 25 de Mayo and 9 de Julio.

Things to See & Do
Welsh culture is still evident in the cut

ARGENTINA

stone construction along Av Eugenio Tello, as well as in local customs. Numerous tea houses offering a variety of homemade cakes and sweets, and the **Eisteddfod**, with choir singing and poetry competitions, still takes place regularly.

Architecturally distinctive churches and chapels of several denominations are scattered around town. The secondary school **Camwy** dates from 1899, while the **cemetery**, at the entrance to town, has many gravestones with inscriptions in Welsh. Nearby is the **Túnel del Ferrocarril** (railway tunnel), through which the first trains passed; its top offers a good view of the valley and town.

The old railway station, at the corner of Sarmiento and 28 de Julio, houses the **Museo Histórico Regional de Gaiman**, an excellent small museum attended by Welsh- and English-speaking volunteers, which has an intriguing collection of pioneer photographs and household items. Admission costs US$1.

One of the most interesting sights in Patagonia, or anywhere in conformist Argentina, is **Parque El Desafío**. Admission is US$5 for adults (US$4 per person for groups larger than three), US$2 for children, to what LP reader Paul Bruthiaux describes as

Gaiman's answer to Disneyland. It's a wonderful, wild, wacky miniature theme park built by local political protestor and conservationist Joaquín Alonso, exclusively from bits of string, bottles, cans, and other junk long before the rest of the world knew the meaning of recycling.

Places to Stay

Because Gaiman is primarily a day-trip destination from Trelew, its only accommodations are the fire station's *Camping Bomberos Voluntarios,* the small riverside municipal campground on Hipólito Yrigoyen between Libertad and Independencia. It can be inaccessible when it rains, and the floodplain soil can be soggy, but it has good picnic tables, clean toilets, and excellent showers, lacking only mirrors and hooks to hang your clothing. Sites cost a very reasonable US$2 per person.

Places to Eat

One cannot leave Gaiman without visiting one of the local Welsh tea houses, with their abundant home-baked sweets. While tea costs around US$10 or more, portions are large and they're a good value. Note that almost all tea houses get uncomfortably crowded when tour buses arrive, so try to avoid places with buses outside – or do something else until the buses leave. The tea houses are really the only place to eat in town, besides a couple of rotiserías.

Most tea houses open by 3 pm, so don't eat more than a light lunch. The oldest is *Plas y Coed,* at Miguel D Jones 123, run by Marta Rees, the original owner's daughter-in-law and a charming and wonderful cook, who speaks English. She personally makes sure that every client is satisfied, even offering a doggy bag to those who can't finish the spread.

Other possibilities include *Ty Gwyn* at 9 de Julio 147, *Casa de Té Gaiman,* on H Yrigoyen between Sarmiento and San Martín, *Elma* at Av Tello 571, *Te Newydd* at the corner of Av Tello and 9 de Julio, and *Ty Nain,* a beautiful house at H Yrigoyen 283.

The newest entry is *Te Ty Caerdydd* (☎ 91287), set among its own irrigated fields in a tasteful building with attractive gardens; they use their own fresh produce, include raspberries and apples, prepare a particularly good and light egg custard, and sell cakes to take away. Recorded Welsh choral music adds to the atmosphere of Patagonia's largest tea house, which is doing excellent business despite its relatively inconvenient location (at least for pedestrians) across the river; follow the signs along the bridge.

Things to Buy

Look for local crafts at the new Paseo Artesanal, at the corner of Av Tello and Miguel Jones, opposite the central Plaza Roca.

Getting There & Away

Stopping directly in front of Plaza Roca, Empresa 28 de Julio has several buses a day from Trelew via Gaiman to Dolavon. The return fare to Gaiman is US$2.80.

AROUND GAIMAN
Parque Paleontológico Bryn Gwyn
In the badlands along the Río Chubut, south of Gaiman via RP 5, Parque Paleontológico Bryn Gwyn is a Tertiary fossil site open to visitors for guided tours only. While the oldest sediments here date only about 40 million years, too recent for dinosaurs, there are interesting remains of terrestrial mammals in the volcanic Sarmiento formation, prior to the building of the Andes, and later marine mammals and fish of the Puerto Madryn and Gaiman formations, when the low-lying area was covered by subtropical seas.

The Museo Feruglio (☎ 35464), 9 de Julio 655 in Trelew, organizes three-hour excursions to the park, the costs (minivan rental for US$70 and a guide for US$30) are divided among a maximum of ten visitors. Trips normally leave at 8:30 am and 5 pm; make arrangements at least one day in advance. Admission costs an additional US$4 for adults, US$2 for children, and US$3 for retired people.

DOLAVON
Paved RN 25 leads another 18 km west from Gaiman to this historic Welsh agricultural town, the name of which means "River Meadow." The 1920s flour mill, today a museum, still has a functioning water wheel. It has a good campsite. There is one hotel, the *Hotel Pierse* (☎ 0965-92013), at 28 de Julio 45, and a tea house. Empresa 28 de Julio runs ten buses daily to Dolavon, via Gaiman, from the Trelew bus terminal.

RAWSON
Named for the Argentine minister who granted the Welsh refuge, Rawson (population 30,000) has always been a politically important town. The territorial capital since 1884, it became the provincial capital three years after Chubut attained provincial status in 1955. The modern Centro Cívico contains all government offices.

Since 1923 the long, attractive sandy beach has made the nearby suburb of Playa Unión a favorite holiday destination, but many visitors stay in Trelew, 20 km west via paved RN 25, which is far more important commercially and much more interesting historically and culturally.

Fishing boats return every afternoon to Puerto Rawson, at the mouth of the Río Chubut, where you can taste the catch at the cantinas near the pier. Playa Unión has a couple hotels, but can also be crowded with day trippers from Trelew and local tourists (mostly from the valleys) who keep summer houses at the beach.

Information
Tourist Office The Delegación Municipal de Turismo (☎ 96588) has a helpful office on the waterfront in Playa Unión, alongside Hotel Provincial. It's open 8 am to 7 pm daily from mid-December to mid-March.

Money Banco de la Nación is at the corner of Av San Martín and 25 de Mayo; Banco de la Provincia del Chubut is at Rivadavia 615. Travel agencies Turismo Rawson, Moreno 810, and Gallatts Turismo, Moreno 719, also change money.

Post & Telecommunications Correo Argentino is on the central Plaza Rawson, at the corner of Mariano Moreno and Vacchina; the postal code is 9103. Rawson's area code is 0965, the same as Trelew's.

Things to See
The **Capilla Maria Auxiliadora**, a chapel with interesting architecture and fine murals, keeps very limited hours. So does the **Museo Regional Salesiano** (☎ 82623), in the Colegio Don Bosco at Don Bosco 248, which has a significant collection of weapons used in the Conquista del Desierto, as well as fossils, minerals, and artifacts from the province. It is open Tuesdays and Fridays 10 am to noon, and Mondays, Wednesdays, and Thursdays 5 to 8 pm.

Also worth a look is the new **Museo de Rescate Histórico**, open 9 am to noon and 3 to 6 pm weekdays on Plaza Rawson.

Places to Stay & Eat

In Rawson proper, *Hospedaje San Pedro* (☎ 81721) at Belgrano 744 has singles/doubles for US$10/20 with shared bath. *Residencial Papaiani,* Alejandro Maíz 377, charges US$30/40, while the upgraded *Hotel Provincial* (☎ 81300) at Mitre 551 is frequented by visiting politicians. It has rooms for US$40/50 with bath, and also some triples. Its restaurant and confitería are also very good.

At Playa Unión, beachfront *Camping Siglo XXI* (☎ 81244), at the south end of Av Centenario, charges US$5 per person, with children ages eight and under free. Modest *Hostería Le Bon* (☎ 96638) at Rifleros 68 charges US$15 per person, US$20 with breakfast, while *Hotel Atlanser* on the Costanera Av Rawson is more expensive at US$30/35 single/double.

The local cantinas *El Marinero* and *Pleamar* offer a variety of fish and shellfish dishes.

Getting There & Away

Rawson has a new bus terminal on the road to Playa Unión. Empresas Rawson and 28 de Julio run buses from Trelew every 15 minutes weekdays, every half-hour Saturdays, and hourly Sundays and holidays. Buses run from 6 am to 1 am. Empresa Bahía connects downtown Rawson, Puerto Rawson, and Playa Unión.

La Puntual (☎ 82543) goes to Comodoro Rivadavia (five hours), Bahía Blanca (11 hours), and Buenos Aires (22 hours), but there are more connections in Trelew.

RESERVA PROVINCIAL PUNTA TOMBO

Half a million Magellanic penguins breed at Punta Tombo, the largest penguin nesting ground in continental South America, 110 km south of Trelew. There are many other species of seabirds and shorebirds, most notably king and rock cormorants,

giant petrels, kelp gulls, flightless steamer ducks, and black oystercatchers.

Early-morning visitors will beat the numerous tourist buses from Trelew. Most of the nesting area is fenced off; this does not prevent photographers from approaching the birds, since they pay no attention to the fences, but remember that penguins can inflict a bite serious enough to require stitches. They remain on land from September to April. Provincial officials charge a US$5 entry fee per person. Camping is forbidden.

There are three ways of getting there: by arranging a tour with a travel agency in Trelew (about US$30), hiring a taxi (about US$110), or renting a car, which permits you to remain as long as you wish. Graveled RP 1 from Trelew to the reserve, via Rawson, is in very good condition; alternative routes are poorly marked and hard on vehicles. Motorists can proceed south to Camarones (see below) via scenic but desolate Cabo Raso.

Note that tours may be canceled if bad weather makes the dirt roads impassable.

CAMARONES

Juan Perón's father operated a sheep estancia in the area around Camarones, and the town figures, perhaps apocryphally, in Tomás Eloy Martínez's *The Perón Novel.* From RN 3, about 180 km south of Trelew, newly paved RP 30 leads 72 km to this small, dilapidated but somehow charming fishing port where any weekend is certain to be a quiet one. Motorists should know that the town's only petrol station rarely has fuel. There is a Fiesta Nacional del Salmón (National Salmon Festival) every year.

Places to Stay & Eat

Open all year, the *Camping Municipal* near the Prefectura Naval on the waterfront charges nominal fees. *Residencial Bahía del Ensueño* and *Residencial Mar Azul* both have doubles for US$24. *Hotel Kau-i-keukenk,* at Sarmiento and Roca, is slightly more expensive at US$6 per person, but its restaurant deserves special mention – the friendly owner serves outstanding grilled salmon, cooked to order, exquisite escabeche de mariscos (marinated shellfish), and homemade flan at reasonable prices.

Getting There & Away
Mondays and Fridays, Empresa Don Otto leaves Trelew for Camarones (US$15, 3½ hours) at 8 am, returning the same day at 4 pm. The trip lasts 3½ hours and costs US$9 single. At 10 pm, a southbound Don Otto bus stops at the Astra service station on the junction with RN 3.

AROUND CAMARONES
Cabo Dos Bahías
This scenic nature reserve, 30 km southeast of Camarones, offers a wide selection of Patagonian marine and terrestrial wildlife, including penguins, other seabirds, sea lions, fur seals, guanacos, rheas, and foxes. Camping is possible at beaches en route and at the reserve itself. If you have no car, try hiring a taxi in Camarones.

Cabo Raso
Just a few families eke out a bleak existence at this virtual ghost town, about 85 km north of Camarones, on RP 1 to Punta Tombo. Camping is possible in the ruins near the shingle beach, where elephant seals sometimes haul themselves ashore.

COMODORO RIVADAVIA
While not a major destination in its own right, Comodoro Rivadavia is a frequent and worthwhile stopover for southbound travelers. Yacimientos Petrolíferos Fiscales (YPF), the former state oil company, spared no expense on the new petroleum museum in the suburb of General Mosconi; now operated by the Universidad de la Patagonia, it is one of the best of its kind in the world, and no visitor should miss it.

Fuel storage tanks and pipelines clutter the landscape nearly everywhere among the starkly scenic Atlantic beaches at the foot of steeply rising headlands such as 212-meter Cerro Chenque – Chubut's southernmost city (population 121,000) is the

powerhouse of the Argentine oil industry, providing about one-third of the country's production. Seismic survey lines crisscrossing the desert indicate subterranean blasting that may well have contributed to a massive landslide on Cerro Chenque, an area of poorly consolidated marine sediments, that destroyed sections of RN 3 in early 1995, isolating the northern suburbs and disrupting long-distance commerce.

Comodoro's other questionable distinction is the prevalence of what may be the largest soft-drink murals anywhere in the country and perhaps in the world – one covers the entire west-facing wall of the ten-story Hotel Comodoro. At least they're not neon.

History
Founded in 1901, Comodoro (as it is commonly known) boomed a few years later when workers drilling for water made the first major petroleum strike in the country. Foreign companies played a significant role in early oil development, but the state soon dominated the sector through YPF, "the first vertically integrated state petroleum industry outside the Soviet Union," according to historian David Rock (a money-loser as a state enterprise, YPF has since been privatized under the Menem administration). Argentina remains self-sufficient in petroleum and even exports small amounts to neighboring countries.

Orientation
Most of central Comodoro sits on a narrow wave-cut platform, behind which the hills rise steeply. RN 3 connects the city with Buenos Aires to the north and Río Gallegos to the south. Cerro Chenque, just north of the city center, is a stiff climb rewarded with outstanding views (since the Cerro Chenque slide occurred, however, climbing here may no longer be advisable or even feasible).

Unlike most Argentine cities, Comodoro has no central plaza around which major public buildings cluster. The principal commercial street is Av San Martín, which trends east-west below Cerro Chenque.

ARGENTINA

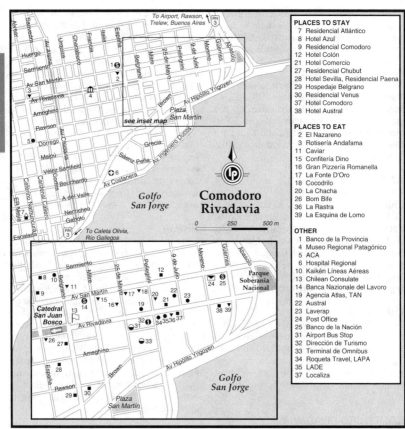

PLACES TO STAY
7 Residencial Atlántico
8 Hotel Azul
9 Residencial Comodoro
12 Hotel Colón
21 Hotel Comercio
27 Residencial Chubut
28 Hotel Sevilla, Residencial Paena
29 Hospedaje Belgrano
30 Residencial Venus
37 Hotel Comodoro
38 Hotel Austral

PLACES TO EAT
2 El Nazareno
3 Rotisería Andafama
11 Caviar
15 Confitería Dino
16 Gran Pizzería Romanella
17 La Fonte D'Oro
18 Cocodrilo
20 La Chacha
26 Bom Bife
36 La Rastra
39 La Esquina de Lomo

OTHER
1 Banco de la Provincia
4 Museo Regional Patagónico
5 ACA
6 Hospital Regional
10 Kaikén Líneas Aéreas
13 Chilean Consulate
14 Banca Nazionale del Lavoro
19 Agencia Atlas, TAN
22 Austral
23 Laverap
24 Post Office
25 Banco de la Nación
31 Airport Bus Stop
32 Dirección de Turismo
33 Terminal de Omnibus
34 Roqueta Travel, LAPA
35 LADE
37 Localiza

With the north-south Av Alsina (which becomes Av Chiclana) and the Atlantic shoreline, San Martín forms a triangle that defines the city center.

Information
Tourist Offices Comodoro's very helpful Dirección de Turismo (☎ 22376), at Pellegrini and Rivadavia, is open 7 am to 8 pm weekdays, 1 to 8 pm weekends in summer; it also has space at the bus terminal but depends on volunteer help there. ACA (☎ 24036) has excellent maps and information at its office, on Dorrego at Alvear.

Foreign Consulate The Chilean consulate (☎ 22414), at Rivadavia 671 between Mitre and Belgrano, is open weekdays 8 am to 1 pm.

Money Most of Comodoro's numerous banks and ATMs are along Av San Martín, including Banco de la Nación at San Martín 102, Banca Nazionale del Lavoro at San Martín 636, and Banco de la Provincia del Chubut at San Martín 833. Travel agencies along Av San Martín may also change cash, but not traveler's checks.

Post & Telecommunications Correo

Argentino is at Av San Martín and Moreno; the postal code is 9000. There are numerous downtown locutorios, including one at the bus terminal. Comodoro's area code is 0967.

Travel Agencies For visits to local attractions, try Roqueta Travel (☎ 26081), Rivadavia 396. There are many others on or near Av San Martín.

Laundry Laverap is at Rivadavia 287.

Medical Services The Hospital Regional (☎ 22542) is at Hipólito Yrigoyen 950.

Museo Regional Patagónico
Conspicuously rotting natural history specimens nearly overshadow this museum's interesting archaeological and historical items, including some good pottery and spear points, materials on early South African Boer immigrants, and a possible local encounter with members of Butch Cassidy's Wild Bunch. Still, compared with the state-of-the-art Museo de Petroleo, it's pretty insignificant. On the Av Rivadavia median, between Francia and Chacabuco, the museo (☎ 31707) is open 9 am to 7 pm weekdays, and is free of charge.

Places to Stay – bottom end
Camping There is no campground in Comodoro Rivadavia proper, but ACA has taken over the municipal site at Rada Tilly, a windy beach resort 15 km south on RN 3. Members pay US$3 per site, nonmembers US$4. Frequent local buses link Comodoro's Terminal del Omnibus with Rada Tilly.

Hostel Comodoro has official hostel accommodations at the *Residencial Atlántico* (☎ 23145) at Alem 30 (near Ceferino Namuncura); rates are US$12 with breakfast, but there are no kitchen facilities.

Residenciales & Hotels Deservedly, the most popular budget hotel by far is *Hotel Comercio* (☎ 32341), at Av Rivadavia 341, where the vintage bar and restaurant alone

justify a visit. Singles/doubles with shared bath cost US$10/12, but rooms with private bath are significantly higher at US$30 double.

Other hotels in this category include *Residencial Chubut* (☎ 28777), Belgrano 738 between Rivadavia and Ameghino, for US$22/29; *Hotel Sevilla* and *Residencial Paena,* both around the corner on Ameghino; *Residencial Venus,* on Rawson near Belgrano; and the quiet *Hospedaje Belgrano* (☎ 24313), at Belgrano 546. For US$30 double, *Hotel Colón* (☎ 22283), Av San Martín 341, has drawn some reader criticism for lack of cleanliness.

Places to Stay – middle
Not to be confused with high-rise Hotel Comodoro, *Residencial Comodoro* (☎ 22582) at España 919 costs US$25/39, as does comparable *Residencial Atlántico* (☎ 23145), Alem 30. *Hotel Azul* (☎ 34628), Sarmiento 724, charges US$30/49.

Places to Stay – top end
Hotel Austral (☎ 32200), Av Rivadavia 190, charges US$47/67 but offers a few bargain singles in the US$30 range, normally reserved for traveling salespeople. It also has a confitería.

Remodeled *Hotel Comodoro* (☎ 32300), 9 de Julio 770 at Av Rivadavia, has top-of-the-line singles/doubles at US$62/80.

Places to Eat
Confitería Dino, upstairs at the corner of San Martín and Mitre, is a cheap confitería that is good for breakfast, while *La Fonte D'Oro,* San Martín at 25 de Mayo, is its more expensive counterpart. At the corner of Rivadavia and Alvear, *Rotisería Andafama* (☎ 23882) prepares a wide variety of exquisite empanadas for takeout; the more central *La Chacha,* Pellegrini 827, has less diverse offerings.

Jammed with locals at lunchtime, *La Esquina de Lomo,* Rivadavia at Güemes, serves superb bife de chorizo and lasagna. Other parrillas include *La Rastra* at Rivadavia 348, the very popular *El Nazareno* (☎ 23725) at San Martín and España, and

Bom Bife at the corner of Rivadavia and España.

Caviar (☎ 33999), Belgrano 935, has a US$8 tenedor libre with pasta, US$16 with meats. *Cocodrilo,* San Martín 464, has good and inexpensive pasta, while *Gran Pizzería Romanella* (☎ 20823), 25 de Mayo 866, serves standard fare.

Entertainment
Rada Tilly's La Esquina Pub has a reputation for good live bands.

Getting There & Away
Comodoro Rivadavia has extensive air and road connections to coastal and interior destinations in Patagonia. RN 3 is entirely paved to Río Gallegos, while RN 26, RP 20, and RN 40 are paved to Esquel, the Andean foothill gateway to Parque Nacional Los Alerces.

Air Austral (☎ 22191), 9 de Julio 870, flies daily except Sundays to Bahía Blanca (US$135) and Buenos Aires (US$199) and twice daily nonstop to Buenos Aires except Sundays, when it goes only once. Southbound flights are daily except Sundays to Río Gallegos (US$103) and Río Grande (US$126). Comodoro is also one possible stop on Aerolíneas "Conozca Patagonia" discount fare.

Roqueta Travel (☎ 32400), Rivadavia 396, is the representative of LAPA, which flies Mondays and Fridays to Río Gallegos (US$69), and Mondays, Wednesdays, and Saturdays to Trelew (US$29) and Buenos Aires (US$99).

Flights on LADE (☎ 36181), Rivadavia 360 between Pellegrini and 9 de Julio, are frequently overbooked, but travelers stand a good chance of getting on at the airport itself. It flies Mondays to Trelew (US$40), Puerto Madryn (US$48), Esquel (US$52) and Bariloche (US$71); Fridays to Trelew, Viedma (US$79), Neuquén (US$92), and Bariloche (US$92); Wednesdays to Perito Moreno (US$34), Gobernador Gregores (US$47), El Calafate (US$74), Río Gallegos (US$79), Río Grande (US$107), and Ushuaia (US$121); Mondays to Puerto

Deseado (US$30), San Julián (US$47), Gobernador Gregores, El Calafate, Río Turbio (US$79), and Río Gallegos; Wednesdays to Esquel, El Maitén (US$61), El Bolsón (US$64), Bariloche, Chapelco/San Martín de los Andes (US$84), and Zapala (US$92); and Fridays to Río Mayo (US$26).

Agencia Atlas (☎ 35228), Rivadavia 439, is the representative of TAN, which flies Tuesdays and Thursdays to Esquel (US$67) and Trelew (US$60); Tuesdays and Thursdays to Puerto Deseado (US$39); Wednesdays and Fridays to Bariloche (US$103) and Puerto Montt (US$86; yes, that's right – the longer international flight costs less than the shorter domestic flight); Mondays and Thursdays to Río Gallegos (US$94) and Río Grande (US$121); Wednesdaysand Fridays to El Calafate (US$121); Wednesdays and Fridays to Trelew and Neuquén (US$138); and daily except Sundays to Neuquén only.

Kaikén Líneas Aéreas (☎ 21405), Sarmiento 733, flies Mondays, Wednesdays, and Fridays to Trelew and Córdoba; Tuesdays and Thursdays to Trelew, Neuquén, and Mendoza; daily except Sundays and Mondays to Río Gallegos, Río Grande, and Ushuaia; Mondays, twice Wednesdays, Fridays, and Sundays to Trelew; and daily except Sundays to Esquel and Bariloche.

Bus Comodoro's Terminal de Omnibus (☎ 27305) is at Ameghino and 25 de Mayo. La Puntual/El Cóndor (☎ 29176) has daily buses to Buenos Aires (US$82, 24 hours) via Viedma (US$40, ten hours) and Bahía Blanca (US$47).

Empresa Don Otto (☎ 24118) has almost identical service to Buenos Aires, but also goes daily to Río Gallegos (US$49, 11 hours), and daily to Esquel (US$33, eight hours), El Bolsón and Bariloche (US$47, 14 hours), to Neuquén, and to Viedma and Bahía Blanca.

Transportadora Patagónica (☎ 24118) goes to Río Gallegos southbound and to Trelew and Mar del Plata northbound. El Pingüino goes northbound to Buenos Aires and intermediates, and southbound to Río

Gallegos and points beyond, including El Calafate, Río Turbio, and the Chilean towns of Punta Arenas and Puerto Natales.

TAC has extensive routes southbound to Río Gallegos and northbound to Bahía Blanca and Buenos Aires, but also serves northwestern Argentine destinations via Santa Rosa, Córdoba, Santiago del Estero, Tucumán, and Jujuy.

Andesmar (☎ 28894) goes south to Caleta Olivia (one hour), and north to Trelew (US$32, six hours), Puerto Madryn, Santa Rosa, San Luis, Mendoza (31 hours), and San Juan, with connections to northwestern Argentina as well as to Chile. Transportes Robledo (☎ 28187) has service to Catamarca, while Transportes Ortiz (☎ 25723) stops in Comodoro en route between Río Gallegos and Tinogasta, in the province of Catamarca.

Central Argentino (☎ 28894) goes south to Caleta Olivia and north to Trelew, Puerto Madryn, Bahía Blanca, and Rosario. TUP (☎ 28493) goes southbound to Caleta Olivia and northbound to San Antonio Oeste, Santa Rosa, and Córdoba.

La Unión (☎ 22822) goes hourly to Caleta Olivia, with connections to Puerto Deseado (US$17, four hours), and twice daily to Perito Moreno and Los Antiguos (US$20, six hours). It also goes to Esquel, El Bolsón, and Bariloche.

Angel Giobbi (☎ 34841) departs at 1 am Mondays and Thursdays for Coyhaique, Chile (US$40) via Río Mayo, but these buses are often very full. Turistas provides additional services to Coyhaique. Etap (☎ 34841) also goes to Río Mayo.

Getting Around

To/From the Airport Aeropuerto General Mosconi (☎ 33355, ext 163) is north of the city, but the No 8 Patagonia Argentina (Directo Palazzo) bus goes there directly from the downtown bus terminal. As of the time of this writing, the slide at Cerro Chenque had disrupted connections.

To/From Rada Tilly Expreso Rada Tilly (☎ 51363) links Comodoro to the nearby beach resort about every half hour week-

days, less frequently weekends. The last bus leaves Comodoro's Terminal at 11:30 pm weekdays, 12.30 am Saturday nights/Sunday mornings, and 11:20 pm Sunday evenings.

Car Rental Rental cars are available at Localiza (☎ 32300), 9 de Julio 770.

AROUND COMODORO RIVADAVIA
Museo del Petróleo

Exceptionally vivid exhibits on the region's natural and cultural history, early and modern oil technology, and social and historical aspects of petroleum development are the strengths of what may be Argentina's best museum, and is certainly one of the best of its kind in the world. Historical photographs are especially outstanding, but there are also fascinating, detailed models of tankers, refineries, and the entire zone of exploitation. The grounds include the site of Comodoro's original gusher and an excellent display of restored antique drilling equipment and vehicles.

The video salon offers an impressive slide show, marred only slightly by its bombastic taped narration. The Universidad Nacional de Patagonia has recently taken over the facilities, originally organized by the former state oil agency YPF. Actually located in the suburb of General Mosconi (named for YPF's first administrator), a few kilometers north of Comodoro, the Museo (☎ 33300, Interno 5199) is on Lavalle between Viedma and Carlos Calvo. From downtown Comodoro, take either the No 7 Laprida or 8 Palazzo bus.

Admission is free. It's open weekdays 10 am to 8 pm, weekends 2:30 to 8:30 pm.

Astra Museum

About 15 km north of Comodoro on RN 3, this open-air display of early oil-drilling equipment also holds a small but impressive semisubterranean exhibit on Patagonian paleontology and minerals. Admission is free, but the mineral exhibit has very limited hours: Tuesdays 11 am to 1 pm, Wednesdays 2 to 4 pm, and Sundays 3 to 6 pm (with guided visits).

Petrified Forests

South of Colonia Sarmiento, an agricultural town 148 km west of Comodoro via paved RN 26 and RP 20, are two petrified forests more accessible than Monumento Natural Bosques Petrificados (see Santa Cruz province below). From Sarmiento, which is easily reached by Etap bus (US$10 one-way), it is possible to arrange a car and driver (about US$40) to the Ormachea (30 km) and Szlapelis (20 km farther) reserves; there is an additional admission charge of US$5. Travel agencies in Comodoro may offer occasional tours or suggestions.

RÍO MAYO

At the entrance to the army base of this dusty western crossroads, an enormous signboard declares the Argentine military's determination to retake the Falkland/ Malvinas Islands by force. Only gauchos and conscripts are likely to spend more than a night here, 274 km from Comodoro Rivadavia via paved RN 26 and RP 20. Graveled RN 26 continues west to Coyhaique, Chile, while rugged RN 40 heads south to Perito Moreno and Los Antiguos, and paved RP 22 and then RP 20 head north to Esquel, El Bolsón. and Bariloche.

If necessary, you should be able to change cash dollars at Banco de la Provincia del Chubut. Río Mayo's area code is 0903.

Things to See & Do

The small **Museo Regional**, Yrigoyen 552 at Belgrano, has exhibits on local ethnology and history. It's open Tuesdays to Saturdays, 10 am to noon and 3 to 7 pm. In the spring, the Festival Nacional de la Esquila features sheep-shearing competitions.

Places to Stay & Eat

Río Mayo has plenty of reasonable accommodations, the cheapest of which is the marginal *Hospedaje El Cóndor* for US$6 per person with shared bath. *Hotel San Martín,* Perito Moreno 693 at San Martín, charges US$8 per person with shared bath, and also has a restaurant/bar with takeout

food. Nicely remodeled *Hotel El Pingüino,* San Martín 640, charges US$12/25 for singles/doubles with private bath. Comparably priced and poorly remodeled *Hotel Covadonga,* San Martín 573, lost its classic Old West bar in the process, but still has a decent restaurant.

Getting There & Away

From the Terminal de Omnibus at Fontana and Irigoyen, Angel Giobbi has daily buses to Comodoro Rivadavia at 6:15 am, and goes to Coyhaique, Chile (US$23), Mondays and Thursdays at 6 am; the latter services, which start in Comodoro Rivadavia, are often very full.

Mondays and Thursdays at 1 am, Etap covers the 350 km to Esquel (US$33, seven hours) via Río Senguer, San Martín, Gobernador Costa and Tecka. There is no public transportation on RN 40 southward toward Perito Moreno and Los Antiguos, but patience may yield a lift.

GOBERNADOR COSTA

Midway between Río Mayo and Esquel, and also on the route between Esquel and Comodoro Rivadavia, this cattle town has good traveler's services, including its free *Camping Municipal.* Both *Residencial Jair* and *Hotel Vegas* have singles for US$10 with bath, as well as restaurants. Banco de la Provincia del Chubut will change cash dollars. On February 28, the town celebrates its annual festival, the Día del Pueblo.

Twenty km west of town, RP 19 leads to Lago General Vintter, in a less frequented part of the Argentine lake district, and several smaller lakes near the Chilean border. There is good trout and salmon fishing.

Getting There & Away

Provincial bus services are frequent. Empresa Don Otto has five weekly in each direction between Trelew and Esquel, and two in each direction between Comodoro Rivadavia and Bariloche. Angel Giobbi serves Río Mayo (see above) via Alto Río Senguer.

ESQUEL
In the foothils of western Chubut, sunny Esquel is the gateway to Parque Nacional Los Alerces and other Andean recreation areas, and the terminus for the picturesque narrow-gauge railway from Ingeniero Jacobacci in Río Negro province. Founded at the turn of the century, the town (population 23,000) is also the area's main commercial and livestock center. It takes its name from a Mapuche term meaning either "place of the thistles" or "bog."

Orientation
On the north shore of Arroyo Esquel, the town has a fairly standard grid pattern. RN 259 zigzags through town to a junction with RN 40, which heads north to El Bolsón and Bariloche, and southeast toward Comodoro Rivadavia. South of town, RN 259 leads to the Welsh settlement of Trevelin, with junctions to Parque Nacional Los Alerces and other Andean attractions.

Information
Tourist Offices Esquel's well-organized Dirección Municipal de Turismo (☎ 2369), at the corner of Sarmiento and Alvear, maintains a complete list of local hotels (with current prices), campgrounds, private houses, camping and lodging in Parque Nacional Los Alerces, travel agencies and tours, transportation, and recreation.

ACA (☎ 2383) is at 25 de Mayo and Ameghino.

Foreign Consulate There's an honorary Chilean consulate (☎ 2195, 2482) at Molinari 754.

Money Banks are open from 8 am to 1 pm. Banco de la Nación, Alvear and Roca, changes Amex traveler's checks only. Banco de la Provincia del Chubut has an ATM at Alvear 1131.

Post & Telecommunications Correo Argentino is at Alvear 1192, across from the bus station; the postal code is 9200. Esquel has several convenient locutorios,

including Su Central at 25 de Mayo 415, Unitel at 25 de Mayo 526, and Telefónica at San Martín 863. Esquel's area code is 0945.

Cultural Centers The Dirección Municipal de Cultura (☎ 2633), Belgrano 330, sponsors theater and music events.

Travel Agencies Esquel's many travel agencies include Esquel Tours (☎ 2704), Av Fontana 754, and Carlos Paz (☎ 3804) at the bus terminal. Patagonia Verde (☎ 2251), 9 de Julio 926, arranges less conventional activities like hiking, climbing, horseback riding, and the like.

Laundry Laverap is at Mitre 543.

Medical Services The Hospital Zonal (☎ 2131, 2226) is at 25 de Mayo 150.

Things to See & Do
Most of the area's attractions, most notably Parque Nacional Los Alerces, are around rather than in Esquel. The **Museo Indigenista**, part of the Dirección Municipal de Cultura, is at Belgrano 330 between Ameghino and Chacabuco. The **Estación Ferrocarril Roca**, at the corner of Brown and Roggero, is now also a museum, but travelers arriving by air or bus should still not miss the arrival of **La Trochita**, the narrow-gauge steam train (serious railroad fanatics will find the town of El Maitén, on the border of Río Negro province, even more interesting because of the extraordinary collection of antique rail equipment in its workshops).

Organized Tours
Travel agencies in Esquel sell tickets for the Circuito Lacustre boat excursion in Parque Nacional Los Alerces; obtaining a ticket here assures a place on this often crowded trip. Full-day excursions including the lake cruise, described in detail in the separate entry on the park, cost US$57 when sailing from Puerto Chucao, US$68 from Puerto Limonao. This includes transportation to and from the park, but you can

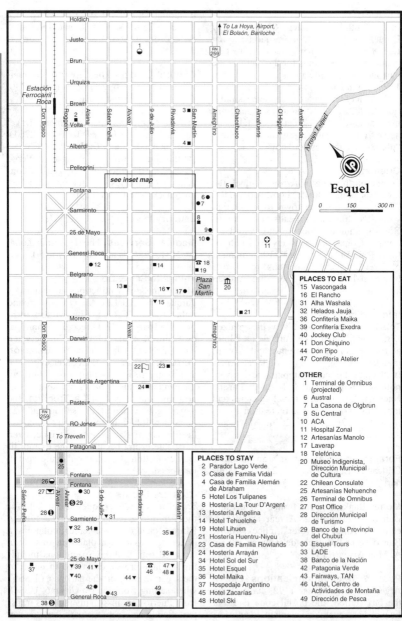

Esquel

0   150   300 m

PLACES TO EAT
15 Vascongada
16 El Rancho
31 Alha Washala
32 Helados Jauja
36 Confitería Maika
39 Confitería Exedra
40 Jockey Club
41 Don Chiquino
44 Don Pipo
47 Confitería Atelier

OTHER
1   Terminal de Omnibus
    (projected)
6   Austral
7   La Casona de Olgbrun
9   Su Central
10 ACA
11 Hospital Zonal
12 Artesanías Manolo
17 Laverap
18 Telefónica
20 Museo Indigenista,
    Dirección Municipal
    de Cultura
22 Chilean Consulate
25 Artesanías Nehuenche
26 Terminal de Omnibus
27 Post Office
28 Dirección Municipal
    de Turismo
29 Banco de la Provincia
    del Chubut
30 Esquel Tours
33 LADE
38 Banco de la Nación
42 Patagonia Verde
43 Fairways, TAN
46 Unitel, Centro de
    Actividades de Montaña
49 Dirección de Pesca

PLACES TO STAY
2   Parador Lago Verde
3   Casa de Familia Vidal
4   Casa de Familia Alemán
    de Abraham
5   Hotel Los Tulipanes
8   Hostería La Tour D'Argent
13 Hostería Angelina
14 Hotel Tehuelche
19 Hotel Lihuen
21 Hostería Huentru-Niyeu
23 Casa de Familia Rowlands
24 Hostería Arrayán
34 Hotel Sol del Sur
35 Hotel Esquel
36 Hotel Maika
37 Hospedaje Argentino
45 Hotel Zacarías
48 Hotel Ski

also buy the boat excursion separately if you have your own transportation.

There are also full-day trips to Futaleufú in Chile, Cholila/Lago Rivadavia (US$35), El Bolsón/Lago Puelo (US$48), and Corcovado/Carrenleufú. Half-day trips include the La Hoya winter sports complex (now under a private concessionaire), the nearby Welsh settlement of Trevelin and the Futaleufú hydroelectric complex (US$22), and the narrow-gauge railway to Nahuelpan (US$22).

Activities
Fishing The fishing season in local lakes and rivers runs from early November to mid-April. Seasonal licenses, which are valid throughout the Patagonian provinces of Chubut, Santa Cruz, Río Negro, and Neuquén, and in national parks, cost US$100. Weekly (US$30) and monthly (US$55) licenses are cheaper. The Dirección de Pesca (☎ 2503) is at Roca 571.

Mountain Biking Rental bikes are available (☎ 3924) in Esquel for US$5 per hour, with lower rates for full days.

Special Events
February's Semana de Esquel celebrates the founding of the city in 1906. The Fiesta Nacional de Esqui (national ski festival) takes place in September.

Places to Stay – bottom end
Camping Camping is popular and inexpensive in this part of the country. *Camping Millalén* (☎ 6164), Ameghino 2063 at Vuelta de Obligado, charges US$4 per adult, US$3 per child ages 10 or below. *Autocamping La Colina* (☎ 4962), Humphreys 554 near Darwin, costs US$3.50 per person and also has hostel accommodations for US$8/15 single/double.

Shady *Autocamping La Rural,* just south of town on the highway to Trevelin, charges US$5 per person, plus a one-time charge of US$5 per car, tent, and family group.

Casas de Familia The most reasonable places to stay are the casas de familia (family homes), for about US$10 to US$12 per person, some of which have private baths. Check the tourist office for the latest listings, but try Raquel Alemán de Abraham (☎ 2696) at Alberdi 529 for US$10 single with shared bath; Marta Vidal at San Martín 1590 for US$12 single with private bath; or Familia Rowlands (☎ 2578) at Rivadavia 330. Isabel Barutta (who speaks some English) runs the highly recommended *Parador Lago Verde* (☎ 2251), at Volta 1081 near the train station, for US$13/24 single/double with private bath.

Hospedajes, Hosterías & Hotels
Hospedaje Argentino (☎ 2237), at 25 de Mayo 862, is the cheapest of the formal accommodations at US$18/28 single/double. *Hospedaje Zacarías* (☎ 2270), General Roca 634, is slightly more expensive at US$20/30 with private bath.

Highly regarded *Hotel Ski* (☎ 2254), San Martín 961, charges US$20/35. Comparable places include *Hotel Lihuen* (☎ 2589), San Martín 822, for US$20/30; *Hostería Huentru-Niyeu* (☎ 2576), Chacabuco 606, for US$20/33; *Hostería Arrayán* (☎ 2082), Antártida Argentina 767, for US$20/35.

Places to Stay – middle
The recommended *Hotel Los Tulipanes* (☎ 2748), Fontana 365, is a good value at US$25 single; *Hostería La Tour D'Argent* (☎ 2530), at San Martín 1063, charges US$29/48 single/double. Similar prices and quality are available at *Hotel Maika* (☎ 2457), 25 de Mayo and San Martín.

Friendly but undistinguished *Hotel Esquel* (☎ 2534), San Martín 1044, charges US$30/40 with private bath. Comparably priced *Hostería Angelina* (☎ 2763), Alvear 758, has drawn praise for comfort, hospitality, and very substantial breakfasts, though some rooms are a bit small.

Places to Stay – top end
At three-star *Hotel Sol del Sur* (☎ 2189, 2427), 9 de Julio 1086, rooms cost around US$60/70 with breakfast. At *Hotel*

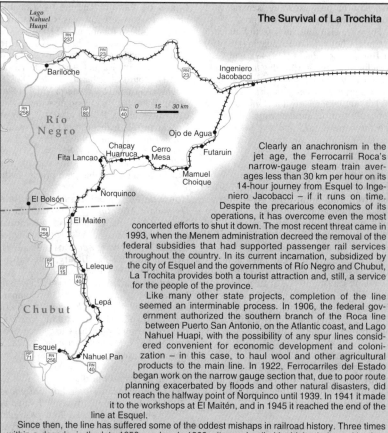

The Survival of La Trochita

Clearly an anachronism in the jet age, the Ferrocarril Roca's narrow-gauge steam train averages less than 30 km per hour on its 14-hour journey from Esquel to Ingeniero Jacobacci – if it runs on time. Despite the precarious economics of its operations, it has overcome even the most concerted efforts to shut it down. The most recent threat came in 1993, when the Menem administration decreed the removal of the federal subsidies that had supported passenger rail services throughout the country. In its current incarnation, subsidized by the city of Esquel and the governments of Río Negro and Chubut, La Trochita provides both a tourist attraction and, still, a service for the people of the province.

Like many other state projects, completion of the line seemed an interminable process. In 1906, the federal government authorized the southern branch of the Roca line between Puerto San Antonio, on the Atlantic coast, and Lago Nahuel Huapi, with the possibility of any spur lines considered convenient for economic development and colonization – in this case, to haul wool and other agricultural products to the main line. In 1922, Ferrocarriles del Estado began work on the narrow gauge section that, due to poor route planning exacerbated by floods and other natural disasters, did not reach the halfway point of Ñorquinco until 1939. In 1941 it made it to the workshops at El Maitén, and in 1945 it reached the end of the line at Esquel.

Since then, the line has suffered some of the oddest mishaps in railroad history. Three times within a decade, in the late 1950s and early 1960s, it was derailed by high winds, and ice has caused other derailments. In 1979, when a collision with a cow derailed the train at Km 243 south of El Maitén, the engine driver was the appropriately named Señor Bovino.

Probably the world's longest remaining functioning steam-train line, La Trochita stops at half a dozen stations, with another nine *apeaderos* (whistle stops) along its 402-km route; the Belgian Baidwin and German Henschel engines refill their 4000-liter water tanks at strategically placed pumps every 40 to 45 km. Most of the passenger cars, heated by wood stoves, date from 1922, as do the freight cars.

From Esquel's train station, which is now a museum, the **Tren Turístico** goes to Nahuel Pan, the first station down the line, 20 km east. The three-hour trip departs Wednesdays and Saturdays at 10 am and costs US$15; for a small additional fee, you can return with travel agencies by minibus. Pandering to readers of Paul Theroux's best-selling but whiningly dyspeptic and condescending account of his train travel through the Americas, the **Viejo Expreso Patagónico** (Old Patagonian Express) makes a special trip to El Maitén Thursdays at 11 am, returning at 4:30 pm; it's possible to return more quickly by bus. The best place to see and enjoy the variety of equipment available is the workshop at El Maitén. For details of the regular passenger service to Ingeniero Jacobacci, see the Getting There & Away entry for Esquel. ■

Tehuelche (☎ 2420/1), 9 de Julio 825, rates start around US$75/90, but fall to barely half that in the off-season. Ask for a room facing away from the noisy street.

Places to Eat

Food in Esquel is good but not exceptional. *Confitería Atelier* (☎ 3547), 25 de Mayo and San Martín, has excellent coffee and chocolate, and is open 24 hours. *Confitería Exedra* (☎ 2533) at 25 de Mayo and Alvear is also worth a visit, as is lively *Confitería Maika* (☎ 2457) at 25 de Mayo and San Martín.

Friendly, pleasant *Parrilla El Rancho,* Rivadavia 726, is a reasonable parrilla with a salad bar. *Restaurant Jockey Club,* Alvear 949, is comparable. *Vascongada* (☎ 4609), 9 de Julio and Mitre, has good food in generous portions, with friendly and attentive service. *Alha Washala,* at 9 de Julio and Sarmiento, is also highly regarded, along with *Don Chiquino,* 9 de Julio 964, which specializes in pasta. *Don Pipo* (☎ 3458), Rivadavia 920, has decent pizza. *Helados Jauja,* at Sarmiento and Alvear, has outstanding ice cream.

Things to Buy

La Casona de Olgbrun, San Martín 1137, has attractive but expensive copperwork and other artisanal crafts. Artesanías Manolo, Alsina 483, specializes in woodcraft. Artesanías Nehuenche, on Alvear between Fontana and Pellegrini, has Mapuche Indian crafts.

Getting There & Away

Air Austral (☎ 3413, 3614), Fontana 406, flies Mondays, Wednesdays, Fridays, and Sundays to Aeroparque (US$256).

LADE (☎ 2124), Alvear 1085, flies Mondays to Bariloche (US424), Fridays to Puerto Madryn (US$57), Thursdays to Comodoro Rivadavia (US$52), and Wednesdays to El Maitén (US$13), El Bolsón (US$16), Bariloche (US$24), Chapelco/San Martín de los Andes (US$38), and Zapala (US$54).

Fairways (☎ 3380), Roca 689, is the local representative of TAN (☎ 2427), which has flights Tuesdays and Thursdays to Trelew (US$54), and the same days to Comodoro Rivadavia (US$67). Fairways is also the agent for Sapse, which flies Sundays, Mondays, and Thursdays to Bariloche (US$30), Bahía Blanca (US$130), and Buenos Aires (US$150).

Kaikén Líneas Aéreas flies daily except Sundays to Bariloche (US$30), and Mondays, Wednesdays, and Fridays to Comodoro Rivadavia (US$55) and Trelew (US$58).

Bus Esquel's congested Terminal de Omnibus is at the corner of Avs Fontana and Alvear, but local authorities have projected a new terminal for the northern part of town, in the block bounded by Av Justo, 9 de Julio, Av Brun, and Av Alvear.

Transportes Automotores Mercedes (☎ 3012) runs twice daily to Bariloche (US$21, six hours); Empresa Don Otto's service to El Bolsón (US$12, 2½ hours) and Bariloche (six hours) via Epuyén is slightly cheaper. Don Otto (☎ 3012) also goes daily to Comodoro Rivadavia (US$38, eight hours), with connections to Río Gallegos (US$81), and four times weekly to Buenos Aires (US$95, 28 hours) via Trelew and Bahía Blanca. La Unión (☎ 3622) goes to Comodoro Rivadavia and Caleta Olivia. El Sureño (☎ 4748) goes to Buenos Aires via Bariloche.

Empresa Chubut (☎ 3012) has daily express service via Tecka to Trelew (nine hours) and Puerto Madryn (10 hours, US$39). Empresa Mar y Valle (☎ 3712) has six buses weekly via Paso de Indios, with slightly higher fares. Andesmar (☎ 3622) goes daily to Bariloche (US$23) and Mendoza (US$85), with connections to Salta, Jujuy, and other northwestern Argentine destinations. Angel Giobbi (☎ 4155) goes southbound to Comodoro Rivadavia via Río Mayo and Sarmiento, and northbound to El Bolsón.

For travelers unable to get a train ticket, Transportes Jacobsen (☎ 3528) connects Esquel with El Maitén and Ingeniero Jacobacci (US$10, five hours) Fridays at 8 am.

Codao (☎ 2924) serves nearby provincial destinations such as Trevelin, La Balsa, Corcovado, and Carrenleufú. Transportes Esquel (☎ 3529) goes to Parque Nacional Los Alerces daily at 8 am, and 2 and 7 pm; the first service combines with lake excursions. Fares are US$4.50 to the Intendencia, US$5 to Puerto Limonao, US$8.50 to Lago Verde, and US$9.50 to Lago Verde. Winter schedules may differ.

Zabala Daniel (☎ 2112) has the only service to El Bolsón (US$18) via Parque Nacional Los Alerces, at noon and 6 pm, but there have been complaints about the availability of seats for those with open tickets to continue to El Bolsón.

Train The Ferrocarril General Roca (☎ 2734) is at the corner of Brown and Roggero. Its narrow-gauge steam train *El Trencito* or *La Trochita* connects Esquel with the station at Ingeniero Jacobacci (☎ 0971-2089, 0971-2138), on the main line between Bariloche and Constitución (Buenos Aires). It leaves Jacobacci Tuesdays at 6 pm, arriving in Esquel at 7 pm; return service from Esquel leaves Wednesdays at 10 am, arriving at Ingeniero Jacobacci at midnight.

Primera fares are US$32.50 between Jacobacci and Esquel, while turista class is only slightly cheaper at $26.50 – and much less comfortable for long trips. Between Jacobacci and Constitución or Bariloche, there are reclining Pullman seats and sleepers; see entries for those cities for details and schedules.

Getting Around
Esquel Tours runs an minibus according to flight schedules at Aeropuerto Esquel, 20 km east of town on RN 40.

AROUND ESQUEL
La Hoya
Just 15 km north from Esquel, at an altitude of 1350 meters, this winter sports area is cheaper and less crowded than Bariloche, but skilled and experienced skiers consider it pretty tame. The season runs June to

October; equipment can be rented on site or in Esquel. There is a regular bus service from town, and several different lifts and runs on the slopes. For local information, contact the Centro de Actividades de Montaña (☎ 6166), Roca 687, in Esquel.

Lift Tickets Lift prices vary somewhat from early to mid- and late season. The season runs from mid-June to mid-October. Full-season passes cost US$260 for adults, US$170 for children; six-day passes cost US$70 for adults, US$50 for children; and 10-day passes are US$85 for adults, US$60 for children. A full-day pass ranges from US$18 to US$10 for adults and US$14 to US$10 for children. Half-day passes run from US$14 to US$7 for adults and US$11 to US$7 for children.

Cholila
Bruce Chatwin's literary travel classic *In Patagonia* recounts Butch Cassidy and the Sundance Kid's ranching efforts near this small town at the northeast entrance to Parque Nacional Los Alerces; US author Anne Meadows recently located their house, just off RP 71 at Km 21 near the conspicuously marked turnoff to the Casa de Piedra tea house, a short distance north of Cholila.

Zabala Daniel buses from Esquel to Parque Nacional Los Alerces and El Bolsón pass close enough for a fleeting glimpse of the house on the west side of the highway, but visitors with their own vehicle or time to spare can stop for a look at the overlapping log construction, typical of North America but unusual in this region. The current occupant of the rapidly deteriorating house, which is reached by the first gate to the right, is Aladín Sepúlveda. Ask permission before looking around or taking photographs.

Follow the signs to the Calderón family's *Casa de Piedra* (☎ 0945-98056), which offers tea, sweets, and preserves, as well as information; the Calderóns, of Spanish-Welsh-English-French Basque-Mapuche descent, also provide accommodations for US$25 per person, with breakfast, from

December to the end of March, and also during Semana Santa.

TREVELIN

Historic Trevelin, the only community in interior Chubut that retains any of its Welsh character, derives its name from the Welsh words for town *(tre)* and mill *(velin)*, after its first grain mill, now a museum. This pleasant town (population 5500) is suitable for either an overnight stay or a day trip from Esquel.

Orientation

Just 24 km south of Esquel via paved RN 259, Trevelin's urban plan is very unusual for an Argentine city – at the north end of town, eight streets radiate like the spokes of a wheel from Plaza Coronel Fontana. The principal of these, Av San Martín, is the southward extension of RN 259, toward Corcovado and the Chilean border at Futaleufú.

Information

Tourist Office From December to March, the exceptionally helpful Dirección de Turismo, Deportes y Actividades Recreativas (☎ 80120), directly on Plaza Coronel Fontana, is open daily from 8 am to 10:30 pm. Winter hours are 8 am to noon and 2 to 8 pm. It has some English-speaking staff, can help arrange guides, and also rents mountain bikes (inexpensively) and horses. Videos are available of activities like treks in Parque Nacional Los Alerces, organized by the Taller de Turismo Municipal.

Mapuche Indian weavings are on sale here, as are local ceramics.

Money Change money at Banco de la Provincia, corner of Av San Martín and Brown, but do so before noon.

Post & Telecommunications Correo Argentino is on Av San Martín, just off Plaza Coronel Fontana; the postal code is 9203. There's a locutorio at the corner of San Martín and Holdich; Trevelin's area code is 0945.

Medical Services Trevelin's hospital (☎ 80132) is at the corner of San Martín and John Evans.

Things to See & Do

Dating from 1918, the **Museo Molino Viejo** (☎ 80189) occupies the restored remains of the old grain mill (which was destroyed by fire). At the east end of 25 de Mayo, it's open 9 am to 9 pm in summer; the rest of the year hours are Wednesday 10 am to 4 pm, and Thursday to Sunday 2 to 8 pm. Admission costs US$2.

The Welsh chapel of **Capilla Bethel** (1910) is at the south end of town near

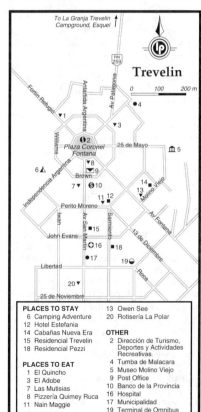

PLACES TO STAY
6 Camping Adventure
12 Hotel Estefania
14 Cabañas Nueva Era
15 Residencial Trevelin
18 Residencial Pezzi

PLACES TO EAT
1 El Quincho
3 El Adobe
7 Las Mutisias
8 Pizzería Quimey Ruca
11 Nain Maggie

13 Owen See
20 Rotisería La Polar

OTHER
2 Dirección de Turismo, Deportes y Actividades Recreativas
4 Tumba de Malacara
5 Museo Molino Viejo
9 Post Office
10 Banco de la Provincia
16 Teléfono
17 Municipalidad
19 Terminal de Omnibus

Ap-Iwan and Laprida. Two blocks northeast of Plaza Coronel Fontana, the monument **Tumba de Malacara** (☎ 80108) holds the remains of a horse whose bravery enabled its Welsh rider, John Evans, to escape a retaliatory raid by Araucanians who had been attacked by the Argentine army during the Conquista del Desierto. Admission to the site costs US$2.50.

Every Sunday in summer and on alternate Sundays the rest of the year, there is an artisans' market in Plaza Coronel Fontana.

Places to Stay

Camping The most central campground is *Camping Adventure,* the former municipal site, only a block southwest of Plaza Coronel Fontana. It's less attractive than some Argentine campgrounds, but recent improvements include hot showers, running water at every site, and spotless toilet facilities. Fees are US$4 per person, plus a one-time charge of US$2 per tent.

Three km north, on RN 259 to Esquel, *La Granja Trevelin* has slightly higher camping prices, but also has cabañas for US$10 per person. There are also activities such as horseback riding and yoga.

Residenciales & Hotels Trevelin has limited, modest, but pleasant accommodations. *Residencial Trevelin* (☎ 80102), Av San Martín 327, has singles/doubles with shared bath for US$17/28, slightly higher for rooms with private bath. *Hotel Estefania* (☎ 80148), at Perito Moreno and 13 de Diciembre, has similar prices and a good restaurant.

Often heavily booked in summer, *Residencial Pezzi* (☎ 80146) at Sarmiento 353 is a pleasant, family-run hotel with a large garden, charging US$16 per person, with dinner additional. For reservations, contact Señora Pezzi at the above address or in Buenos Aires (☎ 432-5542).

For decent family accommodations, try *Cabañas Nueva Era* (☎ 80295), on Molino Viejo just east of Av Fontana, or *Cabañas Chimpay* (☎ 80172), San Martín and Mimosa. Both charge around US$70 for four persons.

Places to Eat

Just as visitors to Trelew flock to Gaiman, so visitors to Esquel head to Trevelin for Welsh tea. The oldest tea house is *Nain Maggie* (☎ 80232), occupying a new building at Perito Moreno 179 but maintaining its traditional high standards. Along with a bottomless pot of tea, it offers sweets made from dulce de leche, chocolate, cream, rhubarb, cheese, traditional Welsh black cake, and scones hot from the oven. Service is attentive but unobtrusive. After a late afternoon here, you will probably skip dinner. Current prices are around US$10.

Other tea houses include *El Adobe* (☎ 80137) at 9 de Julio and Brown, *Las Mutisias* (☎ 80165) at Av San Martín 170, or *Owen See* (☎ 80295) on Molino Viejo near Av Fontana. If you're hungry for more than tea, sweets, or cheese, try *El Quincho* (☎ 80257), the local parrilla, on Fortín Refugio one block north of Plaza Coronel Fontana, or *Pizzería Quimey Ruca,* on 28 de Julio between San Martín and Av Fontana.

Cheese lovers will want to seek out homemade queso de Chubut. *Rotisería La Polar,* on San Martín between Libertad and 25 de Noviembre, has good takeout food.

Getting There & Away

The Terminal de Omnibus is at the corner of Libertad and Roca. There are eight Codao (☎ 2924) buses each weekday between Esquel and Trevelin, four on weekends, for US$1.50. There are three weekly to Río Grande/Futaleufú, on the Chilean border, Mondays, Wednesdays, and Fridays at 8 am, and five weekly to Carrenleufú, another Chilean border crossing. To travel north, you must first go to Esquel.

AROUND TREVELIN

Camping is possible on the road to the **Central Hidroeléctrico Futaleufú,** a dam project that submerged a chain of lakes in the southern part of Parque Nacional Los Alerces, 18 km west of Trevelin, in order to provide electricity for the aluminum plant at distant Puerto Madryn, 550 km to the east. *Autocamping Aikén Leufú* (☎ 2766), on the park boundary, charges US$5 for adults, US$3 for children, and also has cabañas for US$25 double.

On RN 259, 17 km south of Trevelin, a seven-km trail leads to a series of cascades known by its Welsh name, **Nant-y-Fall**. The Dirección de Turismo in Trevelin arranges excursions that allow hikers to start the hike at the north end and get picked up at the southern end, on RP 17. At Arroyo Baguilt, on RN 259 near the Chilean border, is the provincial **Estación de Salmonicultura** (salmon hatchery), open for visits weekdays, 7 am to 1 pm. *Camping Río Grande* (☎ 4403), 32 km west of Trevelin on RN 259, charges US$6 per person (children free of charge), while *Camping Puerto Ciprés* (☎ 3071), five km east of the border, charges US$5, with a one-time charge of US$5 per vehicle.

Near **Lago Rosario**, 24 km southwest of Trevelin via a lateral off RP 17, is a Mapuche Indian reservation. Just to its north, the **Sierra Colorada** offers good hiking.

PARQUE NACIONAL LOS ALERCES
Resembling the giant sequoia of California's Sierra Nevada, the *alerce* or Patagonian cypress *(Fitzroya cupressoides)* flourishes in the humid temperate forests of southern Argentina and Chile. Individual specimens of this strikingly beautiful and long-lived tree (one specimen may be more than 4000 years old) can measure more than four meters in diameter and exceed 60 meters in height. Like the giant sequoia, it has suffered from overexploitation because of its valuable timber. West of Esquel, this 263,000-hectare unit protects some of the largest remaining alerce forests.

Geography & Climate
Hugging the eastern slope of the Andes along the Chilean border, the peaks of Parque Nacional Los Alerces do not exceed 2300 meters, and their receding alpine glaciers are smaller and less impressive than the continental ice fields of Parque Nacional Los Glaciares to the south. They

have left, however, a series of nearly pristine lakes and streams that offer attractive vistas, excellent fishing, and other outdoor recreation. These include Lago Menéndez, Lago Cisne, and Lago Rivadavia. Many local place names derive from the Mapuche language, such as Lago Futalaufquen (Big Lake) and Futaleufú (Big River).

Because the Andes are relatively low here, westerly storms drop nearly three meters of rain annually to support the humid Valdivian forest. The eastern part of the park, though, is much drier. Winter temperatures average 2°C, but can be much colder. The summer mean high reaches 24°C, but evenings are usually cool.

Flora
While its wild backcountry supports some wildlife, Los Alerces exists primarily because of its botanical significance. Besides the alerce, other important coniferous evergreens and deciduous broadleaf trees characterize the dense, humid Valdivian forest, with its almost impenetrable undergrowth of *chusquea,* a solid rather than hollow bamboo. Conifers include another species of cypress *(Pilgerodendron uviferum)* and the aromatic Chilean incense cedar*(Austrocedrus chilensis)*.

The genus *Nothofagus* ("false beech," but commonly known as "southern beech"), to which most of the larger broadleaf tree species belong, exists only in the southern hemisphere. Local species include ñire *(Nothofagus antarctica)*, coihue *(Nothofagus dombeyi)*, and lenga *(Nothofagus pumilio)*. Another interesting species is the arrayán, the foliage and peeling, cinnamon-colored bark of which bears resemblance to the madrone of California. More extensive stands can be found at Parque Nacional Los Arrayanes, near Villa La Angostura in Neuquén province.

Information
The Intendencia is at Villa Futalaufquen, at the south end of the lake of the same name; for a good introduction to the park's natural history, stop at the **Museo y Centro del Interpretación** here. It also includes an

aquarium, and historical displays and documentation about the park's creation in 1937. Rangers provide information from 8 am to 9 pm daily in summer.

Circuito Lacustre

Traditionally, Los Alerces' most popular excursion sails from Puerto Limonao up Lago Futalaufquen through the narrow channel of the Río Arrayanes to Lago Verde, but recent dry years and low water levels have eliminated part of this segment, making it necessary to hike the short distance between Puerto Mermoud, at the north end of Lago Futalaufquen, and Puerto Chucao on Lago Menéndez.

Launches from Puerto Chucao handle the second segment of the trip to the nature trail to **El Alerzal**, the most accessible stand of alerces. The voyage from Puerto Chucao to El Alerzal lasts about 1½ hours each way and costs US$33; purchase tickets in Esquel to assure yourself a place on this popular trip. From Puerto Limonao, the excursion costs US$53. Scheduled departures are at 10 am from Limonao and 12:30 pm from Chucao, returning to Chucao at 4 pm and to Limonao at 7 pm.

The launch remains docked more than an

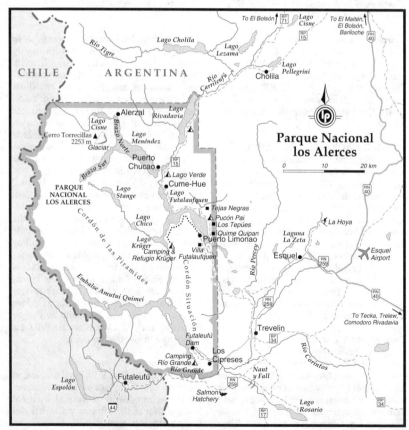

hour, sufficient for a deliberate hike around the loop trail that also passes Lago Cisne and an attractive waterfall to end up at **El Abuelo** (The Grandfather), the finest alerce specimen in the immediate area. Local guides are knowledgeable on forest ecology and conservation, but you may find the group uncomfortably large. If so, you may go ahead or lag behind the group, so long as you get back to the dock in time for the return trip.

Unfortunately, because of the fire hazard, backcountry camping is not permitted at El Alerzal or in other parts of the park's "zona intangible," which is open only to scientific researchers. There are several more interpretive trails near Lago Futalaufquen for day hikes, but the only alternative for trekkers is the trail from Puerto Limonao along the south shore of Futalaufquen to Lago Krüger (see below).

Things to See & Do

There are rock art sites on the **Río Desaguadero** near the Los Maitenes campground. Park rangers lead guided hikes to **Cerro Alto El Dedal** (US$7, six hours) from the trailhead near the Prefectura Naval at Puerto Bustillo, on the eastern shore of Lago Futalaufquen a few km north of the Intendencia; another nearby alternative, from the same trailhead, is **Cinco Saltos** (2½ hours). Carry water and food.

Since so much of the park is designated as inaccessible zona intangible, the longest possible hike is the 25-km trail along the south shore of Lago Futalaufquen to Refugio Krüger, a seven-hour trip that can be broken up by camping at Playa Blanca (park rangers claim the trip takes 12 hours, but are known to exaggerate). Boat excursions from Puerto Limonao to Puerto Lago Krüger cost US$20 per person.

Places to Stay

Camping Los Alerces has five organized campgrounds accessible by road, all of which have hot showers, picnic tables, groceries, and restaurants on site or nearby, and another accessible by foot or boat only. There are free campsites near some of these fee sites. Since park regulations do not control livestock, campers may be awakened by moos and cow bells rather than bird calls.

At *Camping Los Maitenes* (☎ 3622), 200 meters from the Intendencia on the road to Puerto Limonao, sites cost US$5 per person plus a one-time charge of US$3 per tent and/or vehicle. *Camping Pucón Pai* (☎ 3799), nine km from the Villa on the eastern shore of Lago Futalaufquen, charges US$5 per person and offers all meals for US$25 per day.

Camping Bahía Rosales (☎ 3622), at the north end of Futalaufquen 12 km from the Intendencia, also charges US$5 per day, while *Camping Lago Verde* on the eastern shore of its namesake lake 30 km from the Villa, charges US$5 per person with a one-time charge of US$3 for tent and/or vehicle, but also offers a 30% discount for backpackers not resident in Chubut. *Camping Lago Rivadavia* (☎ 4381), 42 km north of the Villa at the south end of the lake, charges US$5 per person plus a one-time charge of US$3 per tent/vehicle.

Camping & Refugio Lago Krüger, on its namesake lake, is accessible only by the 25-km foot trail that leaves from Hotel Futalaufquen, or by launch from Puerto Limonao. Camping costs US$6 per person plus a one-time charge of US$4, while the refugio, which has hot showers and other amenities, charges US$12 per person.

Cabañas & Hosterías Small- to medium-sized groups can rent cabins. *Cabañas Los Tepues,* eight km north of the Villa on the eastern shore of Lago Futalaufquen, rents cabins for US$100 per day for up to eight persons. Nearby *Cabañas Tejas Negras,* ten km north of the Villa, has five-person cabins for US$150, six-person cabins for US$180.

Also on Lago Futalaufquen, *Motel Pucón Pai* (☎ 2828) has singles/doubles with private bath for US$90 including breakfast, US$104/118 with half-pension. *Hostería Quime Quipan* (☎ 4134) at the south end of the lake charges US$50 per person for half-pension, with private bath, and also has cabins suitable for six or seven persons for US$120. *Hostería Cume Hue* (☎ 3639), 25 km north of the Villa, offers full pension for US$60 with shared bath, US$70 with private bath. The very dignified, tasteful *Hostería Futalaufquen* (☎ 4350), four km north of the Villa on the quieter western shore, is the park's most appealing accommodation, but it comes for a steep price – US$120 double with breakfast, plus the 18% IVA.

Getting There & Away

For details of getting to and from the park, see the entry on Esquel above.

EL MAITÉN

In open range country on the upper reaches of the Río Chubut, about 70 km southeast of El Bolsón, this small, dusty town deserves a visit primarily because of the workshops for La Trochita, the narrow-gauge railway between Ingeniero Jacobacci and Esquel. A graveyard for antique steam locomotives and other railroad hardware, it's an aficionado's dream and an exceptional subject for photography.

Every February, the Fiesta Provincial del Trencito commemorates the railroad that put El Maitén on the map and still keeps it there; it now doubles as the Fiesta Nacional del Tren a Vapor (National Steam Train Festival). Drawing people from all over the province and the country, it features riding and horse-taming competitions, live music (earplugs should be mandatory during performances by the provincial police band of Rawson), and superb produce and pastries, including homemade jams and jellies.

The *Camping Municipal,* directly on the river, charges US$2 per person but can get crowded and noisy during the festival. *Hostería La Vasconia,* on the plaza across from the train station, has rooms for US$15 per person, but vacancies are hard to come by during the festival.

Empresa Jacobsen stops at El Maitén en route from esquel to Ingeniero Jacobacci on Fridays. Mercedes buses from El Bolsón also stop here, and there's a minivan from El Bolsón Mondays, Wednesdays, Fridays, and Saturdays at 9 am.

For train services, see the Train entry for Esquel, above.

Santa Cruz Province

Santa Cruz province consists of three ecologically distinct zones: the Atlantic coast, the Patagonian *meseta* (steppe) extending several hundred km inland, and the Andean lake district, famous for its rugged glacial terrain. The Río Santa Cruz, born in the Fitzroy Range and the glacial troughs of lakes Viedma and Argentina, cuts through the steppe to form a deep, broad, and scenic canyon, eventually reaching the sea at Puerto Santa Cruz. Several lesser rivers also originate in the glaciers and lakes of the Andes.

Santa Cruz's aboriginal inhabitants were nomadic Tehuelche Indians, hunters of guanaco, rhea, and lesser wildlife. The first Europeans to set foot in the province came from Magellan's 1520 expedition, which wintered at San Julián and eventually circumnavigated the globe. The arid, windy meseta failed to attract Europeans until the 18th century, when Spain established a series of outposts including a whaling station at Puerto Deseado, and missionaries began to penetrate the region.

Even after Argentine independence, settlement lagged until opportunities in wool attracted British pioneers. Many settlers came from the Falkland Islands, where large grazing units had already occupied all available pastoral land. Many surnames are still common in both the Falklands and Santa Cruz.

Although vast Santa Cruz offered almost unlimited grazing over nearly 250,000 sq km, the human population grew very slowly. In 1895, it barely surpassed a thousand and in 1914 was still less than 10,000. The earliest towns were small ports such as San Julián, Santa Cruz, and Río Gallegos, which transferred the wool clip to ocean-going vessels.

Nowadays, the seven million-plus sheep in Santa Cruz are still the most conspicuous sector of the economy, but the province has also diversified with coal, oil, and tourism. RN 3, the principal north-south highway in Argentina, connects the fast-growing provincial capital of Río Gallegos with Buenos Aires and intermediate destinations. RN 3 south of Río Gallegos, to the Chilean border and Tierra del Fuego, is being paved.

For both Argentines and foreigners, Santa Cruz is a popular summertime destination because of Parque Nacional los Glaciares, which features both the famous Moreno Glacier, one of few in the world that is actually advancing, and the spectacular granite pinnacles of the Fitzroy Range. The coast and steppe, though much less popular, have their own charm; it is possible to see both maritime and terrestrial wildlife, and to visit the sheep estancias that made European settlement possible.

RÍO GALLEGOS

Founded in 1885 on the south bank of its namesake river, near the southern tip of Argentina, the provincial capital and port of 65,000 is the country's largest city south of Comodoro Rivadavia. It continues its tradition of service to the wool industry, but has also become an important center for energy development. The narrow-gauge railway from the coal deposits at Río Turbio, 230 km west near the Chilean border, discharges its cargo to ocean-going vessels here, while the Argentine state oil company operates a refinery with the crude oil from its nearby oilfields. For most travelers, Río Gallegos will only be a stopover en route to El Calafate and the Moreno Glacier, Punta Arenas or Tierra del Fuego, but a day spent here need not be a wasted one.

History

Bruce Chatwin's literary travelogue *In Patagonia* vividly retells the story of the Anarchist rebellion of 1921 and the Argentine army's subsequent massacre of laborers at Estancia La Anita. *La Patagonia*

Rebelde, a fictionalized film version based on Argentine historian Osvaldo Bayer's polemical history of the period, depicts the powerful Menéndez family of southern Patagonia and the Anglo-Argentine woolgrowers of Río Gallegos in a very unfavorable light. It sometimes shows at universities in Europe and the United States, and may be available on video.

Orientation

Central Río Gallegos has a standard Argentine grid pattern, centered on two major avenues, Av Julio Roca and Av San Martín, which run at right angles to each other; street names change on both sides of these avenues. Most areas frequented by visitors are in and around the southwest quadrant formed by Roca and San Martín, although the attractive, newly developed riverfront park at the north end of San Martín also deserves a visit. The most central open space, Plaza San Martín, is one block south of the junction of the two main avenues.

Information

Tourist Offices The energetic Subsecretaría de Turismo de la Provincia (☎ 22702), Av Roca 1551, is open weekdays 9 am to 8 pm. It has maps and a helpful list of accommodations (omitting the very cheapest and most unsavory alternatives), transport, and excursions.

The Dirección Municipal de Turismo (☎ 25951), at Los Inmigrantes and Río Negro, is primarily a business office, but it maintains a Centro de Informes (☎ 24999) at the bus terminal and another at Av San Martín and Av Roca.

ACA (☎ 20477) is at Orkeke 10, near the river.

Foreign Consulate The Chilean consulate (☎ 22364), M Moreno 148 between Fagnano and Rivadavia, is open weekdays 9 am to 2 pm.

Immigration Migraciones (☎ 20205) is at Urquiza 144.

ARGENTINA

PLACES TO STAY
4 Hotel Alonso
5 Hotel Ampuero
7 Hotel Punta Arenas
11 Hotel Nevada
13 Hotel Comercio
14 Hotel Covadonga
16 Hotel Viejo La Fuente
22 Hotel Liporace
23 Hotel Oviedo
25 Hotel Croacia
26 Hotel Cabo Vírgenes
39 Hotel Santa Cruz
40 Hotel París
45 Hotel Costa Río

PLACES TO EAT
6 Heladería Tito
8 Snack Bar Jardín
12 Le Croissant
17 Pietro
18 Restaurant Díaz
47 El Horreo, Pizzería Bertolo

OTHER
1 Museo Provincial Padre
   Jesús Molina
2 Subsecretaría de Turismo
   de la Provincia
3 Museo de los Pioneros
9 Locutorio

10 Cambio El Pingüino
15 LAPA
19 Localiza
20 ACA
21 Artesanías Keokén
24 Aike Lavar
27 Migraciones
28 Chilean Consulate
29 Telefónica
30 Rent A Car
31 Hospital Distrital
32 Dirección Municipal de
   Turismo, Museo de la
   Ciudad al Aire Libre

33 Aerolíneas Argentinas,
   Austral
34 Cambio Sur
35 El Pingüino
36 Banco del Sud
37 Post Office
38 Banco de la Nación
41 LADE
42 Interlagos Turismo
43 Tur Aike,
   Kaikén Líneas Aéreas
44 Banco de Crédito
46 Centro de Informes
48 Banco de la Provincia

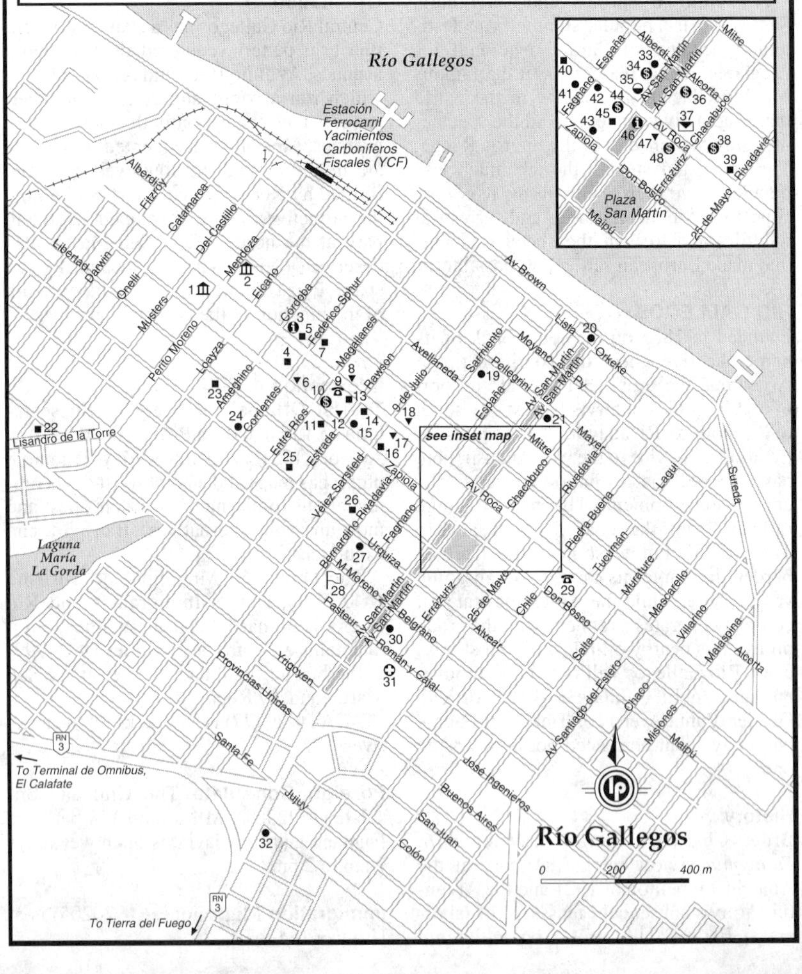

Río Gallegos

Money Cambio El Pingüino, Zapiola 469, will change cash dollars, traveler's checks (for a modest commission), and Chilean pesos. Cambio Sur, at Av San Martín 565 near Aerolíneas Argentinas, may have significantly better rates, especially when Argentine currency is unstable.

Most banks are on or near Av Roca, including Banco de la Nación at Roca 799, Banco de la Provincia at Roca 802, and Banco de Crédito at Roca 936. Banco del Sud has an ATM at Alcorta 32, just east of San Martín.

Post & Telecommunications Correo Argentino occupies an interesting building at the corner of Avs Julio Roca and San Martín; the postal code is 9400. Telefónica is at Av Roca and Chile, but there are numerous locutorios, the most central of which is at Av Roca 1328. Río Gallegos's area code is 0966.

Travel Agencies Among Gallegos' many travel agencies are Interlagos (☎ 22466) at Roca 998, El Pingüino (☎ 25332) at Zapiola 469, and Tur Aike (☎ 24503) at Zapiola 63. It's possible to buy a through ticket to the Moreno Glacier for US$60, a substantial savings over separate purchases. Most of these agencies also have branches in El Calafate.

Laundry Aike Lavar is at Corrientes 277.

Medical Services The Hospital Distrital is at Errázuriz and Ramon y Cajal.

Museums
At Perito Moreno 45 near Av Roca, the **Museo Provincial Padre Jesús Molina** has good exhibits on geology, Tehuelche ethnology (with excellent photographs), and local history. One of the grislier exhibits is the skull of a striker shot at Estancia San José, near the Fitzroy section of Parque Nacional Los Glaciares, in 1921. It's open daily 10 am to 5 pm, weekends 3 to 8 pm. The crafts shop next door has Tehuelche materials.

In a metal-clad house typical of southern Patagonia, the **Museo de los Pioneros** at Sebastián Elcano and Alberdi has displays of early immigrant life. It's open daily 3 to 8 pm. The **Museo de la Ciudad al Aire Libre**, on Av Los Inmigrantes near the rotonda at the south end of Av San Martín, is mostly an open-air display of antique farming equipment.

Places to Stay – bottom end
Camping Río Gallegos has no formal campground, but YPF's Estación de Servicio San Cristóbal, on RN 3 west of the bus terminal, has a large *playa* (parking lot) for passing truckers, where self-contained campers can park for free; it costs US$1 to use the separate toilets (which are free at the station proper) and US$2.20 for hot showers. Argentine backpackers generally crash where space is available, but there are even a few sites where people have pitched tents in a pinch.

Hotels Really inexpensive accommodations exist in Río Gallegos, but most of them are hard to recommend. The best alternative may be the dormitories in the *Gimnasio Juan B Rocha,* on Av Eva Perón just north of the bus terminal, for around US$5 per person; ask the staff at the tourist information booth there if it's open.

Several truly seedy places in and around the 600 block of Zapiola, between Ameghino and Corrientes, have singles for US$10 or less. *Pensión Esmeralda, Hotel Amanecer Argentino, Hotel Libertad,* and *Hotel Bar El Gaucho* have more than average numbers of serious drunks; women especially should avoid them.

Basic *Hotel Viejo La Fuente* (☎ 20304), Vélez Sarsfield 64, was once the best of the cheapest, with warm, clean, and spacious but basic singles, but at its current $15 per person it's a much poorer value than other nearby and only slightly dearer places. Boxy *Hotel Ampuero* (☎ 22189), Federico Sphur 38, charges US$17/30. *Hotel Cabo Virgenes* (☎ 22141), Rivadavia 259, costs US$20/30, as does *Hotel Oviedo* (☎ 20118) at Libertad 746.

Places to Stay – middle

In this category the best value is the simple but spotless, quiet, comfortable, and central *Hotel Covadonga* (☎ 20190), Av Roca 1244. Rooms with private bath are US$22/35, but rooms with washbasin and mirror (shared bath) cost only US$17/22. *Hotel Nevada* (☎ 22155), Zapiola 486, is also a good value for US$22/38. Other mid-range choices include *Hotel Liporace* (☎ 21937), Lisandro de la Torre 255, for US$22/30; *Hotel Punta Arenas* (☎ 22743), Federico Sphur 55, for US$25/36; and *Hotel París* (☎ 20111), Av Roca 1040, for US$29/42.

Places to Stay – top end

Top-end accommodations start at around US$39/53 at *Hotel Santa Cruz* (☎ 20601), Av Roca and Rivadavia. *Hotel Alonso* (☎ 22414), which is less central at Corrientes 33, charges US$39/56, as does *Hotel Croacia* (☎ 22997) at Urquiza 431. Modern, central *Hotel Comercio* (☎ 22172), Av Roca 1302, costs US$43/63, but rooms fronting on the street can be very noisy.

Hotel Costa Río (☎ 23412), Av San Martín 673, is the newest and costliest in town at US$75/100, offering discounts for cash and to ACA members.

Places to Eat

For a town of its size, Río Gallegos has few especially noteworthy eating places. Improving *Restaurant Díaz* (☎ 20203), Av Roca 1143, has reasonable minutas, as does *Snack Bar Jardín,* Av Roca 1311.

In the remodeled Sociedad Española, a historic building at Av Roca 862, is the attractive and highly regarded *El Horreo* (☎ 20060). Directly alongside it is equally appealing *Pizzería Bertolo,* but the latter has very indifferent service. *Pietro,* Av Roca 1148, is another good choice for pizza.

Le Croissant, at Zapiola and Estrada, has a wide variety of attractive baked goods, prepared on the premises. Nearby *Heladería Tito,* Zapiola and Corrientes, has very good and imaginative ice cream flavors, even by Argentine standards, but prices have risen unconscionably in the last few years. Try orange in white chocolate.

Entertainment

The new Cine Carrera, on Av Roca between San Martín and Fagnano, shows recent films.

Things to Buy

Local woolen goods, leather work, fruit preserves, sweets, and other items are available at Artesanías Keokén (☎ 20335), Av San Martín 336 between Mitre and Mayer.

Getting There & Away

From Río Gallegos, there are several Patagonian options: west to Chile's Puerto Natales and Parque Nacional Torres del Paine via Calafate and Parque Nacional Los Glaciares, or via the Argentine coal mining town of Río Turbio; or south to Punta Arenas and across the Strait of Magellan to Tierra del Fuego.

Air Aerolíneas Argentinas (☎ 22495), Av San Martín 545, has flights twice daily to Buenos Aires (US$236), and twice daily to Ushuaia (US$56) except Mondays and Thursdays, when it goes only once. It also has daily flights to Río Grande (US$48) except Mondays and Thursdays, and its twice-weekly transpolar flights from Buenos Aires to Auckland and Sydney stop here for refueling.

Austral, which shares offices with Aerolíneas, flies daily except Sunday to Comodoro Rivadavia (US$103), Bahía Blanca (US$175), Buenos Aires, and Río Grande. Río Gallegos is also one possible stop on Aerolíneas "Conozca Patagonia" discount fare.

LAPA (☎ 28382), Estrada 71, flies Mondays and Fridays to Comodoro Rivadavia (US$69), Trelew (US$89), and Buenos Aires (US$149), at the ungodly hour of 1:30 am.

LADE (☎ 22316), Fagnano 53, flies Mondays to Puerto Santa Cruz (US$22), Wednesdays to Río Grande (US$31) and Ushuaia (US$43), and Thursdays to El

Calafate (US$30), Gobernador Gregores (US$39), Perito Moreno (US$69), and Comodoro Rivadavia (US$79).

TAN (☎ 25259) has offices at the airport only. It flies Mondays and Thursdays to Río Grande (US$39), and Tuesdays and Fridays to Comodoro Rivadavia (US$94) and Neuquén (US$214).

Tur Aike (☎ 24503), at Zapiola 63, is the agent for Kaikén Líneas Aéreas, which has frequent flights to Ushuaia (US$51), usually with a stopover in Río Grande; Mondays, Wednesdays, and Fridays to Comodoro Rivadavia (US$94), Trelew (US$127), and Córdoba (US$231); Tuesdays and Thursdays to Comodoro Rivadavia, Trelew, Neuquén (US$176), and Mendoza (US$209); Mondays and Saturdays to El Calafate (US$50) and Puerto Madryn (US$143); Sundays to El Calafate, Comodoro Rivadavia, and Trelew; and Wednesdays to San Julián (US$55), Puerto Deseado (US$83), Comodoro Rivadavia, and Trelew.

El Pingüino (☎ 27326), at the corner of Roca and San Martín, is an established bus company that has recently moved into air transportation, so schedules and services may be irregular. It flies Mondays and Thursdays to Gobernador Gregores, Perito Moreno, Caleta Olivia, Comodoro Rivadavia, Río Mayo, and Trelew, and to El Calafate and back; Tuesdays and Fridays to El Calafate (US$40), Río Turbio, and back; Wednesdays and Sundays to El Calafate, Gobernador Gregores, Perito Moreno, and back, and to El Calafate, Río Turbio, and back; and Saturdays to Puerto Santa Cruz and Puerto Deseado.

Check out travel agencies for the Chilean airline Aerovías DAP, which flies Tuesdays, Thursdays, and Saturdays to Punta Arenas, Chile (US$49).

Bus Río Gallegos's Terminal de Omnibus is at the corner of RN 3 and Av Eva Perón. Río Gallegos is a major hub for provincial, long-distance, and international bus travel. Some but not all companies have convenient downtown offices.

El Pingüino, at Zapiola 445 (☎ 23338)

and downtown at Roca and San Martín (☎ 27326), goes twice daily to Río Turbio (US$15), Tuesdays and Saturdays to Puerto Natales, Chile (US$18, six hours), and daily to Punta Arenas (US$20, six hours) and to El Calafate (US$24). Buenos Aires, a nightly 40-hour marathon starting at 10 pm, costs US$107. There are also daily services north to the oil town of Caleta Olivia (US$30, eight hours) and intermediate points, and a Saturday service to the delightful Andean oasis of Los Antiguos (US$55, 17 hours). Transporte Mansilla (☎ 22701), San Martín 565, Transporte Vera, and Buses Ghisoni also do the six-hour trip to Punta Arenas.

Transportes Patagónicos (☎ 21215) also goes to Buenos Aires via Bahía Blanca (US$85), with connections via Comodoro Rivadavia (US$39) to Bariloche (US$104). Andesmar (☎ 25879) links Gallegos with coastal destinations as well as interior Patagonia, Cuyo, and the Andean Northwest. TAC goes to northern Patagonian destinations, including Neuquén, Zapala, and San Martín de los Andes, as well as Buenos Aires. Don Otto/Costera Criolla goes daily to Buenos Aires (US$121, 40 hours).

Empresa Ortiz has service to Córdoba (US$120), La Rioja (US$170), and Catamarca Thursdays at 7 am. Quebeck Tours (☎ 23130), 25 de Mayo 166, also serves Córdoba.

Interlagos Turismo (☎ 22466) at Roca 998 goes to El Calafate (US$25) and the Moreno Glacier. Midway on the five-hour journey to Calafate, most buses stop at the roadside confitería at La Esperanza, where the shockingly extortionate prices make bringing a snack advisable. Pingüino and Interlagos buses to Calafate leave from the airport 30 minutes after flight arrivals, but seats may be few.

Transporte San Lorenzo leaves Río Gallegos Thursdays for Piedrabuena and Gobernador Gregores (6½ hours, US$25). Transporte Greco goes to Gregores Tuesdays and Fridays at 2 pm (eight hours).

Train The world's most southerly functioning railway is the narrow-gauge coal train from Río Gallegos to Río Turbio. Yacimientos Carboníferos Fiscales (YCF), the state coal mining agency with offices at Gobernador Lista and Magallanes, operates the train and has limited passenger facilities, but it takes real persistence to get a seat. The YCF train leaves Friday for Río Turbio and returns Saturday.

Getting Around

To/From the Airport There is no regular public transport to or from Aeropuerto Internacional Río Gallegos except for cabs, which cost about US$6 to the city center. To save money, share a cab with other arrivals.

To/From the Bus Terminal Most long-distance companies have offices near downtown, but the Terminal de Omnibus is on the southern outskirts, at Av Eva Perón and RN 3, reached by bus Nos 1 or 12 (the placard must say "terminal") from Av Roca. Local buses in Río Gallegos are the country's most expensive at about US$1.20 per trip.

Car Rental Rent A Car (☎ 21321), Av San Martín 1054, rents cars for excursions to outlying places like Cabo Virgenes, as does Localiza (☎ 24417) at Sarmiento 237.

AROUND RÍO GALLEGOS
Estancia Güer Aike
At the junction of northbound RN 3 and westbound RP 5, about 30 km west of Río Gallegos, this estancia has 12 km of river frontage, offering trout fishing holidays for $275 per day with full pension. It's open November to April; for reservations, contact Truchaike (☎ /fax 394-3486), Esmeralda 719, 2º Piso B, 1007 Buenos Aires.

Cabo Virgenes
Some 30,000 Magellanic penguins nest at this colony at the end of RP 1, about 120 km southeast of Río Gallegos. There is no regular public transportation, but it may be possible to catch a lift with sheep farmers or oil workers at the clearly marked junction off RN 3 about 15 km south of town.

Camping is possible near the attractive but very exposed beach, but there are no facilities or even running water, though the small, isolated naval detachment may help. Provincial authorities have recently established a small information center staffed by a warden.

Estancias along RP 1 may provide a bed for the night, but try to arrange this in advance in Río Gallegos. Estancia Cóndor, a beautiful settlement midway to Cabo Virgenes, has a store that may sell supplies to passersby; in season, you can also watch sheep shearing here. If you wish to stay at this estancia, contact Artesanías Keokén in Río Gallegos. Estancia Monte Dinero (☎/fax 26900 in Río Gallegos), the closest estancia to the pingüinera, offers guided tours, meals, and lodging from October to April. By mail, contact Señor Ricardo Fenton, Casilla de Correo 86, 9400 Río Gallegos, Provincia de Santa Cruz, República Argentina. El Pingüino bus company in Río Gallegos may also organize visits.

RÍO TURBIO
Coal deposits, rare in South America, are the sole reason for this desolate border town, 270 km west of Río Gallegos via RN 40. Many, if not most, YCF employees are Chileans who commute from Puerto Natales, 30 km south. Paralleling the highway, a narrow-gauge railway hauls the coal to the port of Río Gallegos, but passenger services are sporadic and difficult to arrange.

Motorists will find RN 40 north of Río Turbio, from Estancia Tapi Aike to the junction with paved RP 5 at El Cerrito, much improved, permitting any vehicle to take this shortcut to El Calafate and avoid the much longer detour via La Esperanza. Buses between Puerto Natales and El Calafate also take this route now.

Río Turbio's Centro de Información Turística (☎ 21160) is on the Plazoleta Agustín del Castillo, in the center of town. The area code is 0902.

With permission, it is possible to visit the

mines; ask at the tourist office for details. In winter a small ski area operates outside town.

Places to Stay

Río Turbio's cheapest accommodation, usually occupied by miners, is the *Albergue Municipal* (☎ 21160) at Paraje Mina 1, where four-to-a-room dormitory beds cost US$10. Alternatives include the recommended *Hotel Gato Negro* (☎ 21226) on Roque Sáenz Peña, with singles/doubles at US$23/32 with private bath, and the slightly cheaper *Hotel Atlas* (☎ 21285) on Agustín del Castillo.

Getting There & Away

Air The airport is close enough to town for taking a cab to be a reasonable alternative. LADE (☎ 21224), Av Mineros 375, flies Monday afternoons to Río Gallegos (US$24) and Tuesday mornings to El Calafate (US$17), Gobernador Gregores (US$39), San Julián (US$33), Puerto Deseado (US$59), and Comodoro Rivadavia (US$79).

El Pingüino, Jorge Newbery 14 near Mineros, has flights on Sunday, Wednesday, and Saturday afternoons to El Calafate (US$30), and Sunday, Tuesday, and Friday evenings to Río Gallegos.

Bus Cootra runs a dozen buses every weekday to Puerto Natales (1½ hours) from Mineros and Agustín del Castillo, but weekend and holiday service is reduced. At the border, you change to a Chilean bus for the remainder of the trip.

TAC (☎ 21058), on Av Jorge Newbery near the YPF station, crosses the Patagonian steppe to Río Gallegos (US$20, six hours) daily at 4 am and 2 pm. Quebeck Tours (☎ 21422), at the corner of Hipólito Yrigoyen and Agustín del Castillo, about a block from the tourist kiosk, goes daily to Gallegos at 1 am.

El Pingüino, Jorge Newbery 14 near Mineros, goes to Río Gallegos (US$23) Tuesdays and Fridays at 7:20 pm, and to El Calafate (US$38) Wednesdays and Saturdays at 6:10 pm, Sundays at 8:10 pm.

EL CALAFATE

Neither attractive, interesting, picturesque, nor welcoming, El Calafate is nevertheless an almost inescapable stopover en route to some of Argentina's most impressive sights. In reality, it's an oversized encampment of rapacious merchants fixated on making a year's income in a few short months by maintaining high prices rather than increasing sales. Lest this sound like the complaint of a dyspeptic writer, many local residents concur and, to quote one LP correspondent, "there is no better description . . . even worse, unfriendly, expensive."

Formally founded in 1927, this onetime stage stop takes its name from the wild barberry *(Berberis buxifolia)*, which grows abundantly in the area. In summer, El Calafate swarms with porteño tourists, most of whom parade up and down the sidewalks of Av del Libertador San Martín, to the accompaniment of roaring motorcycles, before and after spending a few hours at the Moreno Glacier. January and February are the most popular months so, if possible, plan your visit just before or just after peak season. From May to September, visitors are fewer and prices may drop, but days are shorter and the main attractions less accessible (though not necessarily inaccessible).

Orientation

El Calafate is 320 km northwest of Río Gallegos via paved RP 5 and RP 11, and 32 km west of RP 5's junction with northbound RN 40, which heads toward the El Chaltén section of Parque Nacional Los Glaciares. Westbound RP 11 goes to the southern section of Parque Nacional Los Glaciares and the Moreno Glacier. RN 40 south to Río Turbio is greatly improved, permitting any vehicle to cut 100 km off the trip to Torres del Paine by avoiding the lengthy La Esperanza route.

El Calafate's main thoroughfare is Av del Libertador General San Martín, more conveniently known as "Av Libertador" or "San Martín." Because El Calafate is small, most everything is within easy walking distance of San Martín.

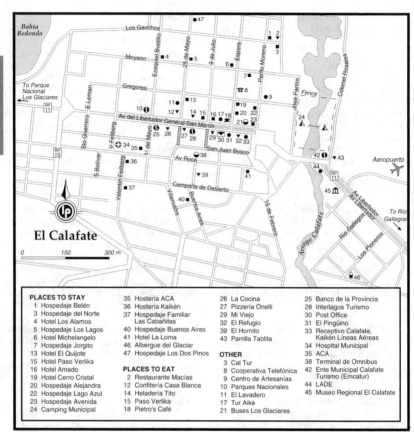

El Calafate

0   150   300 m

PLACES TO STAY
1   Hospedaje Belén
3   Hospedaje del Norte
4   Hotel Los Alamos
5   Hospedaje Los Lagos
6   Hotel Michelangelo
7   Hospedaje Jorgito
13 Hotel El Quijote
15 Hotel Paso Verlika
16 Hotel Amado
19 Hotel Cerro Cristal
20 Hospedaje Alejandra
22 Hospedaje Lago Azul
23 Hospedaje Avenida
24 Camping Municipal

35 Hostería ACA
36 Hostería Kaikén
37 Hospedaje Familiar
    Las Cabañitas
40 Hospedaje Buenos Aires
41 Hotel La Loma
46 Albergue del Glaciar
47 Hospedaje Los Dos Pinos

PLACES TO EAT
2   Restaurante Macías
12 Confitería Casa Blanca
14 Heladería Tito
15 Paso Verlika
18 Pietro's Café

26 La Cocina
27 Pizzería Onelli
29 Mi Viejo
32 El Refugio
39 El Hornito
43 Parrilla Tablita

OTHER
3   Cal Tur
8   Cooperativa Telefónica
9   Centro de Artesanías
10 Parques Nacionales
11 El Lavadero
17 Tur Aike
21 Buses Los Glaciares

25 Banco de la Provincia
28 Interlagos Turismo
30 Post Office
31 El Pingüino
33 Receptivo Calafate,
    Kaikén Líneas Aéreas
34 Hospital Municipal
35 ACA
38 Terminal de Omnibus
42 Ente Municipal Calafate
    Turismo (Emcatur)
44 LADE
45 Museo Regional El Calafate

Information

Tourist Offices Calafate's much improved Ente Municipal Calafate Turismo (Emcatur, ☎ 91090), a pseudo-chalet just before the bridge across the Arroyo Calafate at the eastern approach to town, is open 8 am to 10 pm daily. It keeps a list of hotels and prices, has maps, brochures, and a message board, and there's usually an English speaker on hand.

ACA (☎ 91004) is at Primero de Mayo and Av Roca.

Money Though (or because) Calafate is a tourist destination, changing money has traditionally been problematic, but the federal government's rigid convertibility policy has at least curtailed foreign exchange profiteering by local merchants.

Banco de la Provincia de Santa Cruz, Av Libertador 1285, will change cash dollars and traveler's checks (the latter with substantial commission), but it's open 10 am to 3 pm weekdays only. El Pingüino, Av Libertador 1025, also changes money, but it also imposes a substantial penalty in commission on traveler's checks.

Post & Telecommunications Correo Argentino is at Av Libertador 1133, between 9 de Julio and Espora; the postal code is 9405. Calafate's Cooperativa Telefónica is at Espora 194, between Moyano and Gregores; collect calls are not possible, and discounts are available only after 10 pm. The area code is 0902.

National Parks The Parques Nacionales office (☎ 91005), at Av Libertador 1302 at Ezequiel Bustillo, is open weekdays 7 am to 2 pm, and has brochures including a decent map (though not adequate for trekking) of Parque Nacional Los Glaciares. It is also in charge of remote Parque Nacional Perito Moreno, and can contact the ranger in charge there about visits.

Travel Agencies All of Calafate's numerous travel agencies can arrange excursions to the Moreno Glacier and other attractions in the area. Among them are Tur Aike (☎ 91389) at Av Libertador 1080, Receptivo Calafate (☎ 91116) at Av Libertador 945, Interlagos Turismo (☎ 91018) at Av Libertador 1175, and Cal Tur (☎ 91117) at Los Gauchos 813.

Laundry El Lavadero, 25 de Mayo 43, charges US$8 per load and is open every day, including Sunday afternoons.

Medical Services Calafate's Hospital Municipal (☎ 91001) is at Av Roca 1487.

Things to See
West and north of Calafate, **Parque Nacional los Glaciares** offers several of the most spectacular natural attractions in South America: the **Moreno Glacier**, the **Upsala Glacier**, and the **Fitzroy Range** of the southern Andes. For details, see the separate entry for the park below.

The **Museo Regional El Calafate**, Av Libertador 557, has been closed for remodeling – a seemingly permanent state of affairs. There is aboriginal rock art at **Punta Walichu** (☎ 91059), seven km east of town near the shores of Lago Argentino, but bogus reproductions of similar sites like Cueva de las Manos in northern Santa Cruz have corrupted whatever limited

integrity this recently privatized, grossly commercialized site might have had. Its absurd US$9 admission charge makes it one of the most flagrant tourist rip-offs in the entire country.

Places to Stay
Prices for accommodations can vary seasonally; the peak is usually January and February, but can extend from early November to late March at some places.

Places to Stay – bottom end
Camping Now fenced, the woodsy *Camping Municipal,* straddling the creek behind the tourist office, has separate sections for auto and tent campers, good toilets, hot showers, fire pits, and potable water; the entrance is on José Pantín, north of the bridge. Easy walking distance from anyplace in town, it costs US$8 per site.

Camping Los Dos Pinos (☎ 91271), at the north end of town at 9 de Julio 218, charges US$4 per person.

Hostel El Calafate's official youth hostel is *Albergue del Glaciar* (☎ 91243), on Calle Los Pioneros, east of the arroyo. Beds cost US$13 for members and nonmembers alike, including kitchen privileges, laundry facilities, and access to a spacious, comfortable common room. Director Mario Feldman speaks English, provides visitor information, and also organizes minibus excursions to local attractions. You can also make reservations in Buenos Aires (☎ 71-9344, 312-8486).

Hotel La Loma (☎ 91016), Av Roca 849, also offers hostel accommodations, in addition to mid-price rooms.

Hospedajes Prices can vary considerably with the season, but the cheapest places are family inns like the highly regarded *Hospedaje Alejandra* (☎ 91328), Espora 60, where rooms with shared bath cost US$10 per person. Comparably priced are *Hospedaje Los Dos Pinos* (☎ 91271) at 9 de Julio 358, the recommended *Hospedaje Buenos Aires* (☎ 91147) at Ciudad de Buenos Aires 296, *Hospedaje Lago Azul* (☎ 91419) at

Perito Moreno 83, *Hospedaje Belén* (☎ 91028) at Perito Moreno and Los Gauchos, *Hospedaje Avenida* (☎ 91159) at Av Libertador 902, and *Hospedaje Jorgito* (☎ 91323) at Moyano 943.

Places to Stay – middle

In low season, *Hospedaje del Norte* (☎ 91117), Los Gauchos 813 at José Pantín, charges US$15/24 for rooms with shared bath, while high season prices rise to US$20/30. Rooms with private bath cost US$20/30 in low season, US$25/36 in high season.

Several readers have praised *Cabañas del Sol* (☎ 91439), Av Libertador 1956, which charges US$20/26 in low season, US$31/40 in peak season. *Hospedaje Familiar Las Cabañitas* (☎ 91118), Valentín Feilberg 218, costs US$20/32 in low season, US$25/38 in peak season, while recommended *Hospedaje Los Lagos* (☎ 91170), 25 de Mayo 220 at Moyano, charges US$22/30 all year.

At *Hotel Paso Verlika* (☎ 91009), Av Libertador 1108, rates are US$30/40. Attractive *Hotel Cerro Cristal* (☎ 91088), at Gregores 989, costs US$22/30 in the off-season, US$25/38 peak season, while *Hotel Amado* (☎ 91023), at Av Libertador 1072, charges US$38/56. Members pay US$36/42 at the *Hostería ACA* (☎ 91004), Primero de Mayo 50, while nonmembers are welcome for US$48/55.

Places to Stay – top end

Several hotels charge upward of US$50 per night, including the stiflingly hot but otherwise pleasant *Hostería Kalkén* (☎ 91073) at Valentín Feilberg 119, which serves an excellent breakfast. Rates are US$50/65 in peak season, but barely half that in the off-season. *Hotel La Loma* (☎ 91016), Av Roca 849, costs US$51/64 in the November to March high season, but US$39/52 the rest of the year.

Hotel Michelangelo (☎ 91045), Moyano 1020, charges US$66/80 with breakfast, but is slightly cheaper in October. *Hotel El Quijote* (☎ 91017), Gregores 1191, charges US$80/95. In a class by itself is four-star

Hotel Los Alamos (☎ 91144), Moyano 1355, where rates are US$130/160 in peak season, US$96/120 the rest of the year.

Places to Eat

In general, Calafate restaurants are a poor value for the money. The most dependable is *Confitería Casa Blanca* (☎ 91402) at Av Libertador 1202, which has good pizza and reasonable beer, but beware the US$3.50 submarino; *Pizzería Onelli* (☎ 91184), across the street at Libertador 1197, also has its adherents. *Paso Verlika* (☎ 91009), Av Libertador 1108, is popular and reasonably priced, especially the pizza. *Pietro's Café*, at Av Libertador and Espora, also serves pizza, as does *El Hornito* (☎ 91443) at Buenos Aires 155, half a block south of the bus terminal.

Many hotels have restaurants, but avoid the rather tough chicken at *Hotel Amado*, Av Libertador 1072. The kitchen at *Hotel Michelangelo* (☎ 91045), Moyano 1020, offers decent food but (unusually for Argentina) in microscopic portions, and it's not cheap. More reasonable are *Parrilla La Tablita* (☎ 91065), at Coronel Rosales 24 across from the tourist office, and *Restaurante Macías*, on Los Gauchos opposite Hospedaje del Norte. The best ice cream is at *Heladería Tito*, now on Av Libertador between 25 de Mayo and 9 de Julio, but prices have risen sky-high – US$3 for a single-flavor cone.

Otherwise appealing *La Cocina* (☎ 91286), a new restaurant on Av Libertador with an innovative Italian menu, stubbornly charged the author for two beers even though the second was a replacement for the first, which had a fly in it. *Mi Viejo* (☎ 91691), Av Libertador 1111, is a good and popular but pricey parrilla. *El Refugio* (☎ 91318), Av Libertador 963, has an expensive international menu, but it's a good choice for a splurge.

Things to Buy

El Calafate's Centro de Artesanías is at Gregores and Perito Moreno.

El Puesto, at Gregores and Espora, has woolen clothing and other artisanal goods.

In the past few years there's been a proliferation of shops offering good but expensive homemade chocolates.

Getting There & Away

Air LADE (☎ 91262), Av Libertador 699, flies Mondays to Río Turbio (US$17) and Río Gallegos (US$30); Tuesdays to Gobernador Gregores (US$27), San Julián (US$33), Puerto Deseado (US$40) and Comodoro Rivadavia (US$74); Wednesdays to Río Gallegos, Río Grande (US$59), and Ushuaia (US$68); and Thursdays to Gobernador Gregores, Perito Moreno (US$31), and Comodoro Rivadavia.

El Pingüino (☎ 91273) is at Av Libertador 1025. It flies Wednesdays and Sundays to Gobernador Gregores, Perito Moreno, and Río Gallegos (US$40); Sundays, Tuesdays, and Fridays to Río Turbio (US$30) and Río Gallegos; and Mondays, Tuesdays, Thursdays, and Saturdays to Río Gallegos.

Receptivo Calafate (☎ 91116), Av Libertador 945, is the agent for Líneas Aéreas Kaikén, which flies Mondays and Saturdays to Puerto Madryn (US$132); Tuesdays, Wednesdays, Thursdays, and Fridays to Río Gallegos (US$50) and Ushuaia (US$83); and Saturdays, Sundays, and Mondays to Río Gallegos, Río Grande (US$69), and Ushuaia.

Bus El Calafate's new Terminal de Omnibus is on Av Roca, easily reached by a staircase from the corner of Av Libertador and 9 de Julio.

Buses Pingüino (☎ 91273) at Av Libertador 1025 and Interlagos (☎ 91018) at Av Libertador 1175 both cover the 320 km of RP 5 and RP 11, which is now completely paved between Calafate and Río Gallegos (US$25, six hours). On request, they will drop you at the Río Gallegos airport, saving you a cab fare.

During summer there is sometimes direct service to Parque Nacional Torres del Paine National Park on Tuesdays, Thursdays, and Saturdays at 8 am (US$45, ten hours). Buses Zaahj connects Calafate with Puerto Natales, Chile (US$28); it's cheaper to buy a return fare (US$44) in Puerto Natales.

Daily at 6 am during summer, Buses Los Glaciares (☎ 91158), Av Libertador 924, leaves Calafate for El Chaltén (US$25 one-way, US$50 with open return) and the Fitzroy Range. The return service leaves El Chaltén at 4 pm; winter schedules may differ. Cal Tur (☎ 91117) at Los Gauchos 813 also occasionally goes to Chaltén. Auto traffic between El Calafate and El Chaltén is almost non-existent, so hitching is very difficult.

PARQUE NACIONAL LOS GLACIARES

Nourished by several awesome glaciers that descend from the Andean divide, Lago Argentino and Lago Viedma in turn feed southern Patagonia's largest river, the Río Santa Cruz. Along with the Iguazú Falls, this conjunction of ice, rock, and water is one of the greatest attractions in Argentina and all of South America.

Its centerpiece is the breathtaking **Moreno Glacier** which, due to unusually favorable local conditions, is one of the planet's few advancing glaciers. A low gap in the Andes allows moisture-laden Pacific storms to drop their loads east of the divide, where they accumulate as snow. Over millennia, under tremendous weight, this snow has recrystallized into ice and flowed slowly eastward. The 1600 sq km trough of Lago Argentino, the country's largest single body of water, is unmistakable evidence that glaciers were once far more extensive than today.

As the 60-meter-high glacier advances, it periodically dams the **Brazo Rico** (Rico Arm) of Lago Argentino, causing the water to rise. Eventually, the melting ice below can no longer support the weight of the water behind it and the dam collapses in an explosion of ice and water. To be present when this spectacular cataclysm occurs is unforgettable; though it ruptures every four years on average, it has not done so since 1988.

Even in ordinary years, the Moreno Glacier merits a visit. It is no less an auditory than visual experience, as huge icebergs on the glacier's face calve and collapse into the **Canal de los Témpanos**

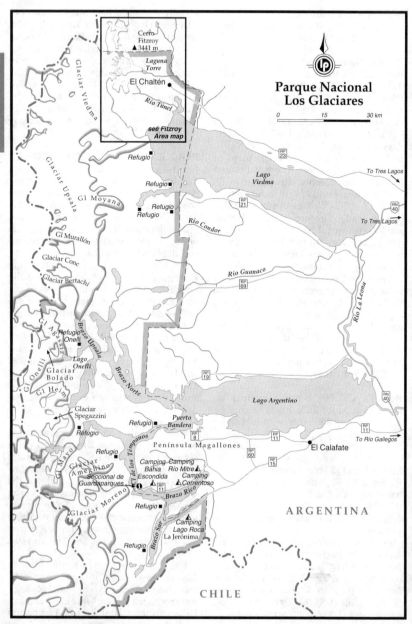

Parque Nacional
Los Glaciares

0   15   30 km

Top: Moreno Glacier, Parque Nacional Los Glaciares, Santa Cruz Province
Left: Cuernos del Paine, Parque Nacional Torres del Paine, Chile
Right: Parque Nacional Tierra del Fuego

Top: Canyon of Río Santa Cruz, Santa Cruz Province
Bottom: El Maitén, Chubut Province

(Channel of Icebergs). From a series of cat-walks and vantage points on the Península de Magallanes, visitors can see, hear, and photograph the glacier safely as these enor-mous chunks crash into the water. Because of the danger of falling icebergs and their backwash, it is no longer possible to descend to the shores of the canal.

Plans for a five-star hotel at the glacier overlook, which is private property, are on hold but nevertheless constitute a threat to the park; the understanding is that the same Italian group that obtained Hotel Llao Llao near Bariloche is behind the project, which would drastically alter the natural land-scape. At the same time, the current park-ing lot, which lacks any sanitary facilities whatsoever, is a different sort of problem and a real eyesore.

The Moreno Glacier is 80 km west of El Calafate via RP 11. The massive but less spectacular **Upsala Glacier**, on the Brazo Norte (North Arm) of Lago Argentino, is accessible by launch from Puerto Bandera, which is 45 km west of Calafate by RP 11 and RP 8. Many visitors recommend the trip for the hike to iceberg-choked **Lago Onelli**, where it is possible to camp at a refugio and return to Puerto Bandera another day.

In the most southerly section of the park at La Jerónima, **Cerro Cristal** is a rugged but rewarding hike beginning at the concrete bunker near the campground entrance. Hikers reaching the summit earn a view encompassing Torres del Paine in the south to Cerro Fitzroy in the north.

Places to Stay & Eat

On Península Magallanes, en route to the glacier, are two organized campsites with facilities including hot showers, fire pits, and the like: *Camping Río Mitre* is 53 km west of El Calafate, while *Camping Bahía Escondida* is 72 km from El Calafate and only eight km from the Moreno Glacier. Rates are US$5 per person. About midway between the two, *Camping Correntoso* is free but dirty; backpackers can also camp two nights near the Seccional de Guarda-parques, the ranger station at the glacier.

Also at the glacier is a confitería that has sandwiches and fixed-price lunches and dinner ranging from US$10 to US$14.

Hostería Los Notros (☎ 91437, fax 91816 in El Calafate) has a dozen rooms with glacier views starting at US$132/174 single/double in the off-season and rising to US$152/160 in peak season.

At *Camping Lago Roca* at La Jerónima on Brazo Sur, fishing (rental equipment is available) and horseback riding (US$10 per hour) are also possible. Camping prices are about US$5 per person; there is a confitería with meals for US$12, and hot showers from 7 to 11 pm.

Getting There & Away

The Moreno Glacier is about 80 km from Calafate via RP 11, a rough gravel road. Bus tours are frequent and numerous in summer, but off-season transportation can still be arranged. Calafate's numerous tour operators offer trips to all major tourist sites, but concentrate on the Moreno and Upsala glaciers; for specific operators see the entry for El Calafate or just stroll down Av Libertador. Some, like Interlagos, have English-speaking guides. The return fare to Moreno Glacier is about US$25 for the 1¼ hour (one-way) trip, while admission to the park costs an additional US$3.50.

EL Calafate's Albergue del Glaciar runs its own minivan excursions, leaving about 8:30 am and returning about 5 pm; Hotel La Loma has similar trips. Many visitors feel that day trips allow insufficient time to appreciate the glacier, especially if the inclement weather limits visibility. The changeable weather is almost sure to provide a window on the glacier at some time during your trip, but it is also worth exploring possibilities for camping nearby.

Several travel agencies offer brief hikes across the glacier itself. After crossing Brazo Rico in a rubber raft, you then hike with guides through the southern beech forest and onto the glacier. This all-day "minitrekking" excursion from El Calafate costs US$75. Full-day bus/motor launch excursions to the Upsala Glacier cost about

ARGENTINA

$55. Meals are extra and usually expensive; bring your own food.

Visitors for whom limited time is a problem, given the uncertainties of independent Patagonian travel, may wish to consider organized but not regimented tours. For details and addresses, see the Getting There & Away chapter.

FITZROY RANGE (CERRO FITZROY)

Sedentary tourists can enjoy the Moreno Glacier, but the Fitzroy Range is the area's mecca for hikers, climbers, and campers. The staging point for everything is the tiny, end-of-the-road settlement of **El Chaltén**, a monument to Argentina's prodigious capacity for bureaucracy. In this town where Chile and Argentina have recently settled one of the last of their seemingly interminable border disputes, virtually every inhabitant is a government employee.

Foolishly sited on the exposed floodplain of the Río de las Vueltas by a planner who never visited the area, the village of El Chaltén is a desolate collection of pseudo-chalets pummeled by almost incessant wind, but the magnificent surroundings more than compensate for any squalor. Ironically, the word itself, signifying "azure" in the Tehuelche language, was the name applied to Cerro Fitzroy. For all its faults, though, El Chaltén is a more agreeable place than El Calafate.

One of many fine hikes in the area goes to **Laguna Torre**, and continues to the base camp for climbers of the famous spire of **Cerro Torre**. There is a signed trailhead between the chalets and the rustic Madsen campground along the road to the north. After a gentle initial climb, it's a fairly level walk through pleasant beech forests and along the Río Fitzroy until a final steeper climb up the lateral moraine left by the receding Glaciar del Torre. From Laguna Torre, there are stunning views of the principal southern peaks of the Fitzroy Range. Allow at least three hours one-way.

While clouds usually enshroud the summit of 3128-meter Cerro Torre, look for the "mushroom" of snow and ice that caps the peak. This precarious formation is the final obstacle for serious climbers, who sometimes spend weeks or months waiting for weather good enough to permit their ascent. Protected campsites are available in the beech forest above Laguna Torre, but the small climber's refugio recently burned to the ground.

Another exceptional but more strenuous hike climbs steeply from the pack station at the Madsen campground; after about an hour plus, there is a signed lateral to excellent backcountry campsites at **Laguna Capri**. The main trail continues gently to **Río Blanco**, a base camp for climbers of Cerro Fitzroy, and then climbs very steeply to **Laguna de los Tres**, a high alpine tarn named in honor of the three Frenchmen who were first to scale Fitzroy. Condors glide overhead and nest in an area where, in clear weather, the views are truly extraordinary. Allow about four hours one-way, and leave time for contemplation and physical recovery after the last segment, on which high winds can be a real hazard.

More ambitious hikers can make a circuit through the Fitzroy Range that is shorter than the one in Torres del Paine, but still worthwhile; another possibility is Laguna del Desierto, north of Chaltén. Recent reports suggest some restriction on hiking this loop; ask for details at the ranger station in Chaltén. *Los Troncos,* a good private campground, lies along the circuit.

Places to Stay & Eat

There is free camping at Parques Nacionales' *Camping Madsen* in Chaltén, with running water and abundant firewood, but no toilets – you must dig a latrine. If you don't mind walking about ten minutes, shower at friendly *Confitería La Senyera* for about US$1; if you want a snack afterwards, try their enormous portions of chocolate cake. Other snacks and light meals are available, with prices, quality, and ambience superior to Calafate. *Camping Ruca Mahuida* charges US$6 per person, has meals and hot showers, and arranges local excursions. Other campsites, like *Posada Lago del Desierto,* charge about US$8 per

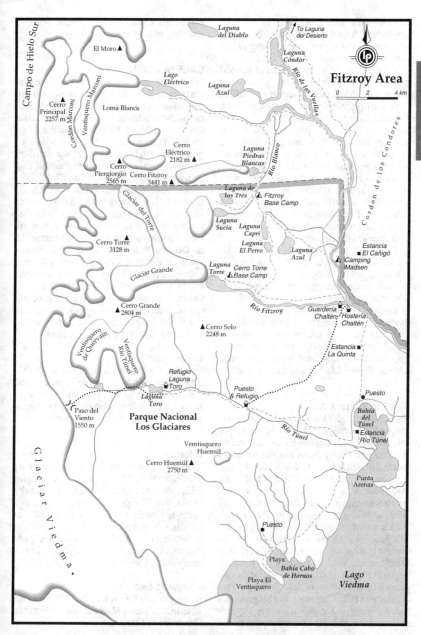

ARGENTINA

Campo de Hielo Sur

El Moro ▲

Laguna del Diablo

To Laguna del Desierto

Laguna Cóndor

Río de los Vueltas

Fitzroy Area

0   2   4 km

Cerro Principal 2257 m ▲

Cordón Marconi

Ventisquero Marconi

Lago Eléctrico

Laguna Azul

Loma Blanca

Cerro Eléctrico 2182 m ▲

Cerro Piergiorgio 2565 m ▲

Cerro Fitzroy 3441 m ▲

Laguna Piedras Blancas

Río Blanco

Glaciar del Torre

Laguna de los Tres

△ Fitzroy Base Camp

Cordón de los Condores

Laguna Sucia

Laguna Capri

Cerro Torre 3128 m ▲

Laguna El Perro

Laguna Azul

Estancia ■ El Cañigó
▲ Camping Madsen

Glaciar Grande

Laguna Torre

Cerro Torre ▲ Base Camp

Cerro Grande 2804 m ▲

Río Fitzroy

Guardería Chaltén
▲ ■ Hostería Chaltén

Ventisquero de Quervain

Ventisquero Río Túnel

▲ Cerro Solo 2248 m

Estancia ■ La Quinta

Refugio Laguna Toro ▲ ■

Laguna Toro

Puesto & Refugio ■

● Puesto

Bahía del Túnel
■ Estancia Río Túnel

Paso del Viento 1550 m

Parque Nacional Los Glaciares

Río Túnel

Vemtisquero Huemúl

Cerro Huemúl ▲ 2750 m

Punta Arenas

Glaciar Viedma ▪

● Puesto

Playa

Bahía Cabo de Hornos

Playa El Ventisquero

Lago Viedma

person. *Albergue Los Ñires* is a small (eight-bed) hostel that charges US$10 per person or US$4 per person for camping; its pub-restaurant is called *The Wall.*

Posada Lago del Desierto has four-bed cabins, with outside toilets but no hot water, for US$10 per person. It also offers very comfortable six-bed apartments, with kitchen facilities, private bath, and hot water, for US$17 per person; its hotel has doubles for US$80. Meals are expensive. *Cabañas Cerro Torre* has four-bed cabins with private bath for US$25 per person.

At the *Fitzroy Inn,* accommodations with half-board cost US$53 per person, but you might want to opt for a package for US$83 that includes return transportation from Calafate, one night's lodging, dinner, and breakfast; two-night packages cost US$110, while three nights cost US$134. *Estancia La Quinta,* on the outskirts of Chaltén, offers lodging for US$25 per person; make arrangements at agencies in Calafate.

For cheap eats, try the kitchen in Juan Borrego's converted bus, which is also a climbers' hangout. *Chocolatería Josh Aike* has been recommended for meals, while supplies (including fresh bread) are available at *Kiosko Charito* and *El Chaltén.*

Getting There & Away
El Chaltén is 220 km from El Calafate via paved RP 11, rugged RN 40, and even more rugged RP 23. See the entry on El Calafate for details on daily buses to Chaltén; buses normally return from El Chaltén at 4 pm.

Motorists should know that petrol is not available at El Chaltén except in very serious emergencies; carry a spare fuel can. The nearest gas station is at Tres Lagos, 123 km east of El Chaltén. Beyond the RP 23 junction, RN 40 is very bad, has no public transportation, and carries very little traffic of any kind, so returning to Río Gallegos is almost unavoidable for northbound travelers without vehicles. Between Tres Lagos and Bajo Caracoles, the highway has been greatly improved, permitting speeds between 65 and 80 kmh en route to the

small agricultural town of Perito Moreno and the junction to Los Antiguos.

CALETA OLIVIA
Less publicized than the Andean lake district, eastern Santa Cruz province, along the Atlantic coast and longitudinal RN 3, is not without interest. The oil port of Caleta Olivia, founded in 1901 to discharge cargo for the Buenos Aires-Cabo Vírgenes telegraph line, offers access to several petrified forests as well as the Andean oasis of Los Antiguos, a crossing point into Chile.

For southbound travelers on RN 3, Caleta Olivia (population 35,000) is the first stop in Santa Cruz province. Dominating the traffic circle in the town center, its most visible landmark is the **Monumento al Obrero Petrolero**, a 10-meter monument of the muscular oil worker known colloquially as "El Gorosito," in a style that might well be called "Peronist realism." Other industries include seafood processing and wool. If heading south towards Tierra del Fuego or east toward the Andes, you might opt to spend a night here.

Orientation
Entering Caleta Olivia from the north, RN 3 becomes part of Av Jorge Newbery and then Av San Martín (the main thoroughfare), before taking a dogleg at the monument, where it becomes Av Güemes.

Information
The friendly and enthusiastic Dirección de Turismo (☎ 62735) is at Av San Martín 272, also near the monument. Nearby banks will change cash but not traveler's checks. Correo Argentio is on Lavalle at Hipólito Yrogoyen. The most convenient locutorio is Telefonía Caleta, Av Independencia 1147 near Fagnano. Caleta Olivia's area code is 0967.

Things to See
In the Casa de Cultura, on Lavalle near San Martín, is the **Museo del Hombre** (Museum of Man).

Places to Stay

Camping at the *Balneario Municipal* (☎ 61082, ext 4) is the most economical alternative, at US$6 per person. There is 24-hour hot water and other services.

Otherwise, the most reasonable accommodations in town are comfortable *Residencial Las Vegas* (☎ 61177) at Hipólito Yrigoyen 2094, one block from El Gorosito, where rates are US$15 per person with private bath. *Hotel Capri* (☎ 61132), José Hernández 1145, costs US$20/30, while *Hotel Grand* (☎ 61393), at Mosconi and Chubut, is slightly more expensive at US$22/36. *Hotel Robert* (☎ 61452), Av San Martín 2151, costs US$38/41.

Places to Eat

Italo-Argentine food is available at *Gran Pizzería Romanella,* Güemes 2070. *El Hueso Perdido,* a parrilla, is downstairs at Hotel Grand. *El Puerto* and *El Abuelo,* the best and priciest in town, are both on Av Independencia, near El Gorosito.

Getting There & Away

Air El Pingüino (☎ 61929), with offices at the bus terminal, flies Mondays and Thursdays to Comodoro Rivadavia, Río Mayo, and Trelew; and Tuesdays and Fridays to Perito Moreno, Gobernador Gregores, and Río Gallegos.

Bus Caleta Olivia is a hub for bus travel in northern Santa Cruz province, as excellent paved roads lead north to Comodoro Rivadavia, south to Río Gallegos, and west to Los Antiguos. The Terminal de Omnibus is at Avs San Martín and Independencia, across from the monument.

La Unión (☎ 61134) departs hourly for Comodoro Rivadavia (US$4, one hour) between 7 am and 10 pm. Twice daily, morning and evening, it goes to isolated but picturesque Puerto Deseado (US$17, four hours), and to the town of Perito Moreno (not to be confused with the Moreno Glacier or with Parque Nacional

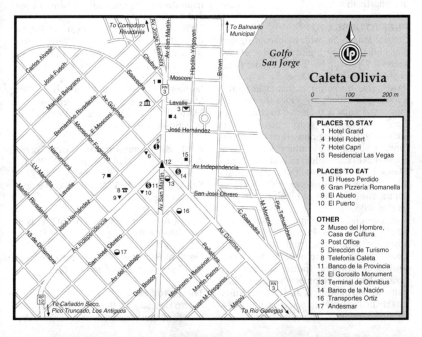

Caleta Olivia

0   100   200 m

PLACES TO STAY
1 Hotel Grand
4 Hotel Robert
7 Hotel Capri
15 Residencial Las Vegas

PLACES TO EAT
1 El Hueso Perdido
6 Gran Pizzería Romanella
9 El Abuelo
10 El Puerto

OTHER
2 Museo del Hombre,
   Casa de Cultura
3 Post Office
5 Dirección de Turismo
8 Telefonía Caleta
11 Banco de la Provincia
12 El Gorosito Monument
13 Terminal de Omnibus
14 Banco de la Nación
16 Transportes Ortiz
17 Andesmar

Perito Moreno) and Los Antiguos (US$30), on Lago Buenos Aires.

El Pingüino (☎ 61929) covers the 722 km to Río Gallegos (US$25, eight hours), with connections to Punta Arenas and Puerto Natales in Chile. There is a direct service to Buenos Aires (US$73, 32 hours) three times weekly with Empresa Don Otto (☎ 61237), but through buses from Río Gallegos will also take on northbound passengers. Don Otto also goes to Bariloche (US$65) four times weekly. El Pingüino also has daily runs to Perito Moreno and Los Antiguos. La Unión (☎ 2133), Belgrano 1565, has two buses per day.

Andesmar (☎ 61053), Lucio V Mansilla 1871, serves Cuyo and northwestern Argentina; schedules are similar to those from Comodoro Rivadavia. Transportes Ortiz, Peñaloza 1781, goes to Río Gallegos and Catamarca, while Transportadora Patagónica serves coastal destinations between Río Gallegos and Mar del Plata. TUP (☎ 61237) goes to Córdoba and intermediate destinations.

PUERTO DESEADO

Coastal Patagonia, with its barren steppes and bullet-riddled highway signs, almost seems a Wyoming-by-the-Sea, and off-the-beaten-track Puerto Deseado is one of those agreeable surprises that makes travel a rewarding experience. Once the port terminus of a railway projected to continue to Bariloche, in Río Negro province, this architecturally intriguing town of 8000 features a turn-of-the-century station that could have been plucked off the Great Plains, but is within sight of the Ría Deseado, a submerged estuary that provides habitat for thousands of seabirds and other marine wildlife.

In colonial times, Spain established a whaling station at Puerto Deseado, but when the *Beagle* anchored here in 1833, Darwin found only "ruins of an old Spanish settlement" where Indian attacks had "compelled the colonists to desert their half-finished buildings." In 1881 Argentina established a naval prefecture and, in 1884, the first permanent colonists arrived.

Orientation

When the federal government shortened southbound RN 3, which once ran through Puerto Deseado, by relocating the route to the interior of the province, it compensated Puerto Deseado in part by paving the 125 km of RN 281 from the Fitzroy junction to the city limits, where it becomes Av España. The main center of activity, though, is the axis formed by Avs San Martín and Almirante Brown, where there's a cluster of interesting historic buildings. The main open space is the Plaza Centenario 9 de Julio, bounded by San Martín, Rivadavia, Ameghino, and Sarmiento.

Information

Tourist Offices Deseado's Dirección Municipal de Turismo (☎ 70220), at Colón and Belgrano, is open weekdays 8 am to 8 pm, but the most convenient information post is in the Vagón Histórico, a historic rail car parked at San Martín and Almirante Brown. It's open daily 10 am to 1 pm and 4 to 7 pm.

On RN 281, 13 km west of Puerto Deseado in the village of Tellier, Bar Restaurant Apolo has maps and brochures of the town and the surrounding area.

Money Banco de la Nación is at San Martín 1001, Banco Almafuerte at San Martín 1082, and Banco de la Provincia at Don Bosco 1014.

Post & Telecommunication Correo Argentino is at San Martín 1075; Puerto Deseado's postal code is 9050. Telefonía San Martín is at San Martín 1320; the telephone code is 0967.

Travel Agencies Hito 45 (☎ 70231) is at Don Bosco 970.

Medical Services The Hospital Distrital (☎ 70200) is at Brown and Colón.

Things to See

Puerto Deseado has three superbly restored historical monuments, within a short dis-

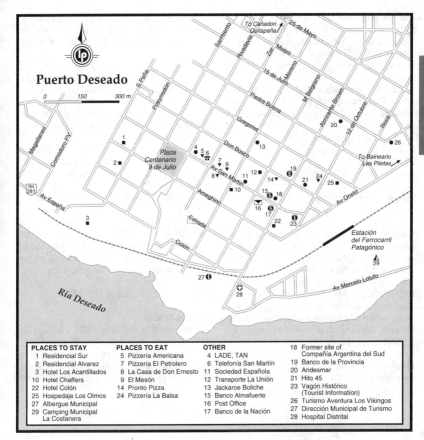

Puerto Deseado

0   150   300 m

Plaza Centenario 9 de Julio

Ría Deseado

To Cañadón Quitapeña

25 de Mayo

To Balneario Las Piletas

To Cañadón Quitapeña

Estación del Ferrocarril Patagónico

Av Marcelo Lotufo

PLACES TO STAY	PLACES TO EAT	OTHER	18 Former site of
1 Residencial Sur	5 Pizzería Americana	4 LADE, TAN	Compañía Argentina del Sud
2 Residencial Alvarez	7 Pizzería El Petrolero	6 Telefonía San Martín	19 Banco de la Provincia
3 Hotel Los Acantilados	8 La Casa de Don Ernesto	11 Sociedad Española	20 Andesmar
10 Hotel Chaffers	9 El Mesón	12 Transporte La Unión	21 Hito 45
22 Hotel Colón	14 Pronto Pizza	13 Jackaroe Boliche	23 Vagón Histórico
25 Hospedaje Los Olmos	24 Pizzería La Balsa	15 Banco Almafuerte	(Tourist Information)
27 Albergue Municipal		16 Post Office	26 Turismo Aventura Los Vikingos
29 Camping Municipal		17 Banco de la Nación	27 Dirección Municipal de Turismo
La Costanera			28 Hospital Distrital

tance of each other at Av San Martín and Almirante Brown. The most notable is the **Vagón Histórico** (1898) of the Ferrocarril Patagónico, a mixed cargo and passenger route than once hauled wool and lead from Chilean mines from Pico Truncado and Las Heras, 280 km northwest, and might have reached Bariloche had not the project been aborted. Colonel Héctor Benigno Varela used the car as his headquarters during the Anarchist rebellion of 1921; Varela, who personally executed gaucho rebel Facón Grande (Big Knife) at Jaramillo two days after reporting him killed in action, was himself assassinated by an anarchist in

Buenos Aires. In the latter days of the Proceso in 1980, the townspeople of Deseado demonstrated and blocked the roads out of town to keep the car here – an extraordinary event given the its symbolism in militant labor history.

A supermarket now occupies the former site of the **Compañía Argentina del Sud** (1919), while the vintage **Banco de la Nación** across the street consists of imposing lava blocks quarried nearby. One block west, at San Martín 1176, the **Sociedad Española** dates from 1915.

To the east, on Oneto, the imposing **Estación del Ferrocarril Patagónico** was the terminus for a line once projected to link up with the southern branch of the Ferrocarril Roca in Bariloche. The railroad closed in 1977, but the station is now undergoing restoration as municipal offices.

Another worthwhile sight is the **Museo de la Corbeta** *Swift*, open 8 am to 3 pm Wednesdays and Fridays, displaying relics of a ship sunk off the coast of Deseado in 1776 and discovered in 1984.

Places to Stay
Puerto Deseado has plenty of decent accommodations at moderate prices, ranging from camping to residenciales and hotels.

Camping Open all year, the *Camping Municipal La Costanera* on the waterfront Av Marcelo Lotufo charges only US$3.50 per tent, US$4 for car and tent, or US$4.50 for self-contained campers. It has good toilets and shower facilities, but the incessant winds can be a noisy nuisance and some of the tent sites are a bit stoney. Inexpensive trailers/cabañas are available for US$6 per person.

Hostel At Colón and Belgrano, the *Albergue Municipal* (☎ 70260) serves mostly

groups, but has rooms with private bath for US$12, US$8 without sheets; rooms with shared bath cost US$8, US$5 without sheets.

Hotels & Residenciales *Hotel Oneto* (☎ 70455), at Doctor Fernández and Oneto, has rooms with shared bath for US$13/22, while those with private bath go for US$18/30. Places with comparable prices include *Hospedaje Los Olmos* (☎ 70077) at Gregores 849, *Residencial Alvarez* (☎ 70053) at Pueyrredón 367, and *Residencial Sur* (☎ 70522) at Ameghino 1640. Rates at *Hotel Colón* (☎ 70304), Almirante Brown 438, range from US$22/30 to US$29/35.

Starting at US$23/38, hilltop *Hotel Los Acantillados* (☎ 70167), at Pueyrredón and España, has the best views in town but is well worn around the edges. Deseado's best accommodations are the sparkling new *Hotel Chaffers* (☎ 71246), at San Martín and Moreno, starting at US$35/49.

Places to Eat
Almost worth a detour in itself, *La Casa de Don Ernesto* (☎ 70150), San Martín 1245, has superior seafood and pasta dishes, plus what may be Patagonia's largest wine cellar; don't miss the "ensalada Punta

Cascajo" of chicken, lettuce, tomato, and potato. There's usually a nightly special for about US$7, and a half bottle of house wine costs only US$2. The Roquefort-butter spread is also very tasty, as are the creatively mistranslated "twisted shrimp" *(langostinos enrolladitos)*.

Pizzería El Petrolero, San Martín 1294, has very basic fixed price meals for US$8 – no bargain compared with Don Ernesto's superb food, and the service is not particularly good either. *Pizzería La Balsa* at 12 de Octubre 641, *Pizzería Americana* at San Martín 1362, and *Pronto Pizza,* Don Bosco 1055, are decent alternatives. *El Mesón,* on San Martín between Zar and Mariano Moreno, is another possibility.

Entertainment
The modernistic Jackaroe Boliche, a dance club at Moreno 633, looks as out of place in sleepy Puerto Deseado as its Australian-derived name might suggest.

Getting There & Away
Air The airport is about 6 km outside of town. The only transportation to and from it is taxis.

LADE and TAN share offices (☎ 70132) at San Martín 1380. LADE flies Mondays to San Julián (US$26), Gobernador Gregores (US$40), El Calafate (US$40), Río Turbio (US$59), and Río Gallegos (US$59), and Tuesdays to Comodoro Rivadavia (US$30). TAN flies Tuesdays and Wednesdays to Comodoro Rivadavia (US$39).

El Pingüino has recently established Saturday service to Puerto Santa Cruz and Río Gallegos.

Bus Transporte La Unión, on Belgrano between San Martín and Don Bosco, goes to Caleta Olivia (US$17, four hours) daily at 7 am and 3 pm. Andesmar has ticket offices on 15 de Julio between Almirante Brown and 12 de Octubre, but no services from Puerto Deseado itself.

AROUND PUERTO DESEADO
Reserva Natural Ría Deseado
The intrusion of the South Atlantic into the former river bed created several islands and other sites with nesting habitat for seabirds. These spots include Isla Chaffers (2000 pairs of Magellanic penguins), Banca Cormoranes (good photo access to the rock cormorant and the strikingly beautiful grey cormorant), and Isla de los Pájaros (nesting terns). The most interesting site, Isla de los Pingüinos, is 30 km offshore and has nesting rockhopper penguins and breeding elephant seals, but getting there costs a hefty US$500 for a maximum of five persons.

Gipsy Tours (☎ 72155, 71260), at the western approach to town, runs reasonably priced regular Sunday excursions along the ría, but is also available for charter at other times. Turismo Aventura Los Vikingos (☎ 70681), 15 de Julio 765, also operates excursions of varying itineraries and prices.

Balneario Las Piletas
When the tide is low enough to leave enormous tidal pools a few kilometers northeast of town isolated from the cold South Atlantic, residents of Puerto Deseado take advantage of the warming water to swim on summer days. Penguins sometimes come ashore where rugged lava flows, unusual in this part of Patagonia, have created some picturesque shoreline caves.

Gruta de Lourdes
Pilgrims flock to and camp at the entrance to this sacred site in an interesting volcanic canyon, about ten km west of Puerto Deseado via RN 281 and a short lateral, where there are plenty of devotional plaques and a pool at the base of a usually dry waterfall. Less devout visitors have decorated the otherwise scenic spot with spray paint. It's still worth a brief detour for visitors with their own vehicle.

Cañadon Quitapeña
Five km north of town via Zar, this scenic sheltered canyon has good camping but no services; consequently, it's most suitable

for those with their own vehicles, but it's worth a hike and a look.

MONUMENTO NATURAL BOSQUES PETRIFICADOS

In the Argentine national park system, natural monuments are the only units invulnerable to commercial exploitation, so the 15,000-hectare Monumento Natural Bosques Petrificados (Petrified Forest Natural Monument) contains no hotels, restaurants, confiterías, and other concessions as in Nahuel Huapi, Los Glaciares, and other overdeveloped parks. Bosques Petrificados has only its volcanic, polychrome desert landscape, fossilized forests, wildlife, and solitude to recommend it. Just off RN 3, 157 km south of Caleta Olivia, an excellent gravel road (along which guanacos are a common sight) leads 50 km west to the park.

During Jurassic times, 150 million years ago, this area enjoyed a humid, temperate climate, but intense volcanic activity leveled the forests that flourished here and buried them in volcanic ash. Erosion later exposed the mineralized *Proaraucaria* trees (ancestors of the modern *Araucaria,* a member of the pine family unique to the Southern Hemisphere), up to three meters in diameter and 35 meters in length. A short interpretive trail leads from park headquarters to the largest concentration of petrified trees. Until its legal protection in 1954, the area was consistently plundered for some of its finest specimens; do not perpetuate this unfortunate tradition by taking even the tiniest souvenir.

Other parts of the scenic desert park also merit exploration, but consult with park rangers before continuing far on the road toward the peak of Madre e Hijo (Mother and Son). You can pitch a tent for free near the dry creek, within sight of headquarters, which has a small display of local artifacts and fauna. Since there is no water at the site, bring your own if you have a vehicle. Otherwise, you *may* be able to obtain some from headquarters. Like the rest of Patagonia, it is extremely windy, but the clear

southern sky offers a spectacular display of stars at night.

There is no public transportation directly to the park, although you can rent a car in Comodoro Rivadavia or try hitching. Buses from Caleta Olivia will drop you at the junction, but you may wait several hours for a lift. Do not attempt hitching in winter, when the area is bitterly cold.

SAN JULIÁN

In the winter of 1520, Magellan's crew wintered in the sheltered harbor of San Julián, and in 1780 Antonio de Viedma established a colony that lasted only a few years. Only the wool boom of the late 19th century brought permanent settlement, thanks to pioneering Scots with surnames like Munro, McRae, and MacCaskill; from the turn of the century, the British-owned San Julián Sheep Farming Company was one of the region's most powerful economic forces. Seafood processing has become a secondary industry. If driving or hitching, you can break the long trip between Caleta Olivia and Río Gallegos here.

Orientation

San Julián (population 4500), 341 km south of Caleta Olivia and a few km east of RN 3, fills a small peninsula jutting into its protected namesake bay. Av San Martín, the main drag, is an eastward extension of the junction at RN 3.

Information

From mid-December to the end of February, the Municipalidad maintains an information office in a trailer at the highway junction; it's open 8:30 am to midnight weekdays, 10 am to midnight weekends. The small tourist kiosk downtown on San Martín is rarely open.

Almost all public services are near the east end of Av San Martín, close to the tip of the peninsula. Correo Argentino is at Av San Martín and Belgrano, while there are locutorios at San Martín and Pellegrini and at San Martín and Saavedra. Banco de la Nación occupies an attractive Victorian building at Mitre and Belgrano. San Julián's area code is 0962.

Things to See & Do

The **Museo Regional y de Arte Marino**, on Ameghino between Mitre and San Martín, features archaeological artifacts and historical exhibits on local estancias, as well as painting and sculpture. It's open weekdays 10 am to noon and 2 to 7 pm.

Ten km west of town, on RP 25 toward Gobernador Gregores, are the ruins of **Floridablanca**, Viedma's short-lived colony of 1780; ask at the tourist trailer for keys to the locked site. The Swift **Frigorífico** (mutton freezer), which operated between 1912 and 1967, is north of town.

Hired launches are available for visiting harbor rookeries of penguins, cormorants, and other seabirds at Banco Cormorán and Banco Justicia. Some of these sites are accessible by foot at low tide, but otherwise contact Carlos Cendrón (☎ 2856) at Brown 739, who charges about US$12 per hour.

Places to Stay & Eat

San Julián's *Autocamping Municipal* (☎ 2160), on the waterfront at the north end of Vélez Sarsfield, has first-rate facilities, including hot showers, a laundry, and a playground, for less than US$2 per person, plus US$4 per tent or car. There are other beachfront sites at Cabo Curioso (20 km north of town) and Playa La Mina, farther north, which has a sea lion rookery.

Hotel Colón, Av San Martín 301, is the cheapest accommodations in town. *Hotel Sada* (☎ 2013), Av San Martín 1112, has singles/doubles with bath for US$28/43, as does the *Hotel Municipal de Turismo* (☎ 2300), 25 de Mayo 917. *Hotel Alamo*, on RN 3, charges US$24/28.

Restaurant Sportsman, Mitre 301 at 25 de Mayo, has excellent parrillada and pasta (especially ñoquis) at reasonable prices. There are several other restaurants, including *Dos Anclas,* Berutti 1080, for seafood.

Getting There & Away

Air The airport is at the highway junction. LADE (☎ 2137), Berutti 985, flies Monday to Gobernador Gregores (US$22), El Calafate (US$33), Río Turbio (US$33), and Río Gallegos (US$33), and Tuesdays to Puerto Deseado (US$26) and Comodoro Rivadavia (US$47).

Kaikén Líneas Aéreas flies Wednesdays to Puerto Deseado, Comodoro Rivadavia (US$55) and Trelew, and to Río Gallegos (US$55) and Río Grande (US$80). (Kaikén only recently appeared in town; ask at the tourist office for directions.)

Bus The Terminal de Omnibus is on Vieytes between Rivadavia and Ameghino. Transportadora Patagónica's Río Gallegos-Buenos Aires services pick up passengers here, but any bus on RN 3 will take on passengers from the junction. Andesmar, Quebek Tours, and El Pingüino also operate from San Julián.

Transporte San Lorenzo has weekly services to Laguna Posadas, near the Chilean border, via Gobernador Gregores and Bajo Caracoles. This is the only feasible public transport to the junction to otherwise inaccessible Parque Nacional Perito Moreno (see the section on the park below).

GOBERNADOR GREGORES

Gobernador Gregores is the nearest town to Parque Nacional Perito Moreno. Although it is still more than 200 km east of the park, it's easier and cheaper to arrange a car and driver here rather than at the town of Perito Moreno, and it's a good place to stock up on supplies.

The free *Camping Municipal,* at Roca and Cañadón León, has hot showers. *Hotel San Francisco* (☎ 0962-91039), at San Martín and Sánchez, has singles/doubles for US$20/30.

LADE (☎ 91008), Colón 544, flies Mondays to El Calafate (US$27), Río Turbio (US$39) and Río Gallegos (US$39), and to San Julián (US$22), Puerto Deseado (US$40), and Comodoro Rivadavia (US$47). El Pingüino flies Mondays and Thursdays to Perito Moreno, Caleta Olivia, Comodoro Rivadavia, Río Mayo, and Trelew, and Wednesdays and Sundays to

Perito Moreno, El Calafate, and Río Gallegos.

Transporte San Lorenzo buses leave Gregores for Río Gallegos (6½ hours) via Piedrabuena Tuesdays at 1:30 pm. Transporte Greco goes to Gallegos Wednesdays and Sundays at 2 pm, taking eight hours.

PIEDRABUENA
On the north bank of the Río Santa Cruz, Piedrabuena is just east of RN 3, 127 km south of San Julián, and 235 km north of Río Gallegos. Although it has no major attractions, it is a common stopover. Hitchhikers, who must often wait in line at the junction near the ACA service station, confitería, and motel, can at least get food and drink here. North of town is a large army camp.

Orientation & Information
From RN 3, Av Belgrano goes directly into town, where it intersects the riverfront Av Gregorio Ibáñez, which becomes Av San Martín to the south. Tourist information is available at the municipal offices at Ibáñez and Gobernador Lista, while Banco de la Provincia de Santa Cruz is on Av San Martín. The area code is 0962.

Things to See & Do
At **Isla Pavón**, in the Río Santa Cruz about three km south of the highway junction, a museum honors Piedra Buena, who first raised the Argentine flag here in 1859. Fishing, water-skiing, and other aquatic sports are popular.

Places to Stay & Eat
Piedrabuena's *Camping Municipal Isla Pavón,* on the island itself, charges US$7 per site, and has 24-hour electricity and hot water. Showers cost US$2 per person.

Hotel Internacional (☎ 7197), Av Gregorio Ibáñez 99 across from the bus station, charges US$15 per person with shared bath. *Hostería El Alamo* (☎ 7249), Lavalle 8 at España, charges US$25/35 with private bath; some rooms have TV.

The *ACA Motel* (☎ 7245) is a good value at US$22/28 for members, but nonmem-

bers pay half that again; because it's small and good, it usually fills early. Its restaurant is dependable and reasonable. *Hotel Huayén* (☎ 7265), Belgrano 321, is comparable in price at US$30/38.

Getting There & Away
Piedrabuena's Terminal de Omnibus is at Ibáñez and Menéndez, but passing buses will also pick up passengers on RN 3. Forty-five km south of Piedrabuena, it may be possible to hitch to Calafate along RP 9, a decent gravel road that passes numerous estancias, with panoramic views of the canyon of the Río Santa Cruz, but hitching is generally difficult here because of heavy competition.

PERITO MORENO
Not to be confused with the Moreno Glacier in Parque Nacional Los Glaciares, nor with Parque Nacional Perito Moreno, the modest agricultural settlement of Perito Moreno is a brief stopover en route to the Andean oasis of Los Antiguos. Its main appeal is its relatively good access to the pre-Columbian rock art site of Cueva de las Manos, and to Parque Nacional Perito Moreno.

In mid-February, Perito Moreno celebrates its Festival Folklórico Cueva de las Manos, an annual musical event for the last 12 years.

Orientation
Perito Moreno's main thoroughfare, Av San Martín, leads north to RP 43, an excellent paved road that forks west to Los Antiguos and east toward Caleta Olivia. At the south end of town it becomes RN 40, a *very* rough highway to the bleak oasis of Bajo Caracoles and a junction to Parque Nacional Perito Moreno.

Information
The obliging Oficina Municipal de Turismo, San Martín 1222 between Mitre and Moreno, is open daily from 7 am to 9 pm except on weekends, when it closes between noon and 2 pm. Correo Argentino is on Av JD Perón, near Belgrano. Banco

de la Provincia de Santa Cruz, Banco de la Nación, and Hotel Belgrano will change cash dollars. Telefónica is at 9 de Julio 1514; Perito Moreno's area code is 0963.

Perito Moreno's Hospital Distrital (☎ 2040) is at Colón 1237.

Places to Stay & Eat

Camping Municipal, near the south end of town at Laguna de los Cisnes, is the cheapest place to stay. Sites cost US$1.50 per person, plus US$1 per car or tent, or rent one of their few cabañas for US$5 per person.

Hotel Argentino, at JD Perón and Belgrano, charges US$10 per person with no frills; *Hotel Santa Cruz,* around the corner on Belgrano, is similar. There are three other better and roughly comparable hotels: *Hotel Americano* (☎ 2074), San Martín 1327, for US$20/30 single/double; *Hotel Belgrano* (☎ 2019) at Av San Martín 1001 for US$22/30; and *Hotel Austral* (☎ 2042), San Martín 1381, for US$25/32. All the latter have restaurants, with meals ranging from US$7 to US$17 for lunch or dinner.

Getting There & Away

Air The airport is at the north end of town near the highway junction. Taxis are the only transportation between it and town.

LADE (☎ 2053) is at San Martín 1207, at the corner of Mariano Moreno. It flies on Wednesdays to Gobernador Gregores (US$31), El Calafate (US$52), Río Gallegos (US$69), Río Grande (US$100), and Ushuaia (US$113), and Thursdays to Comodoro Rivadavia (US$34).

Sr Carlos Matús, on San Martín just north of Saavedra, is the agent for Línea Aérea Pingüino, which flies Mondays and Thursdays to Caleta Olivia, Comodoro Rivadavia, Río Mayo, and Trelew, and Wednesdays and Sundays to Gobernador Gregores, El Calafate, and Río Gallegos.

Bus From Perito Moreno, you can proceed west to Los Antiguos, on Lago Buenos Aires, and cross into Chile, or else head east to Caleta Olivia and then north to Comodoro Rivadavia or south to Río Gallegos. El Pingüino (☎ 2019), at Hotel Belgrano at San Martín 1001, goes daily between Los Antiguos and Caleta Olivia, stopping at Perito Moreno, and also has weekly service to Río Gallegos (16 hours). La Unión (☎ 2133), Belgrano 1565, has two buses per day.

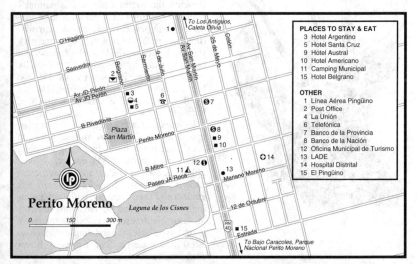

PLACES TO STAY & EAT
3 Hotel Argentino
5 Hotel Santa Cruz
9 Hotel Austral
10 Hotel Americano
11 Camping Municipal
15 Hotel Belgrano

OTHER
1 Línea Aérea Pingüino
2 Post Office
4 La Unión
6 Telefónica
7 Banco de la Provincia
8 Banco de la Nación
12 Oficina Municipal de Turismo
13 LADE
14 Hospital Distrital
15 El Pingüino

Perito Moreno

Laguna de los Cisnes

0   150   300 m

To Los Antiguos, Caleta Olivia

To Bajo Caracoles, Parque Nacional Perito Moreno

AROUND PERITO MORENO

About 25 km south of Perito Moreno on RN 40, Dutch-run **Estancia Telken** (☎ 0963-2079) offers accommodations for US$24 per person, with meals additional and rather expensive; camping costs US$15 for two persons with tent and vehicle. English is spoken here. Hiking and inexpensive horseback riding, as well as excursions to Cueva de las Manos, are possible.

RN 40 is very rough but scenic along the Río Pinturas, where the rock art of **Cueva de las Manos** (Cave of Hands) graces the most notable of several archaeological sites; it has a small information center. The Municipalidad of Perito Moreno has recently acquired a bus which, Sundays from mid-December to the end of February, carries passengers to Cueva de las Manos; prices are US$10 for adults and US$5 for children ages 6 and above. The bus leaves at 8 am from the tourist office on San Martín, and returns at 7 pm.

There is no public transportation southward toward **Parque Nacional Perito Moreno** (see separate entry below), and very little traffic of any sort, but a group may find a taxi and driver to go there.

BAJO CARACOLES

For motorists on RN 40, this tiny oasis has the only gasoline between Tres Lagos and Perito Moreno, a distance of nearly 500 km; south of Bajo Caracoles the highway is greatly improved, though infrequent heavy rain can still disrupt communications. The arrival of any vehicle is such an event that if you wait at the pump, the attendant will promptly come to you. Because gas deliveries can be infrequent, they may give northbound motorists only enough gas to get to Perito Moreno.

Surprisingly, in this bleak and remote place, *Hotel Bajo Caracoles* has basic but good accommodations for US$12 per person and very good (though not cheap) food.

PARQUE NACIONAL
PERITO FRANCISCO P MORENO

Beneath the Sierra Colorada, a painter's pallette of sedimentary peaks, herds of guanacos graze peacefully alongside aquamarine lakes in this gem of the Argentine park system. Honoring the system's founder but seldom visited by anyone but the friendly estancieros who live nearby, its 115,000 hectares abut the Chilean border, 310 km by RN 40 and RP 37 from the town of Perito Moreno.

Besides guanacos, there are also pumas, foxes, wildcats, perhaps *huemul* (Chilean deer), and many birds, including condors, rheas, flamingos, black-necked swans, upland geese *(cauquén)*, and crested caracaras (caranchos). Tehuelche Indians left evidence of their presence with rock paintings of guanaco and human hands in caves at Lago Burmeister. Outside the park boundary, glacier-topped summits such as 3700-meter Cerro San Lorenzo hover above the landscape.

Huemul

As precipitation increases toward the west, the Patagonian steppe grasslands of the park's eastern border become sub-Antarctic forests of southern beech, lenga, and coihue. Because the altitude exceeds 900 meters, considerably higher than more accessible southerly parks like Los Glaciares, weather can be severe. Summer visits are usually comfortable, but warm clothing and equipment are imperative at any season. Perito Moreno's quiet and solitude are a blessing, but visitors should be especially careful with fire in the frequent high winds. Bring all food and supplies, though water is pure and plentiful, and dead wood may be collected for fuel.

From its formal creation in 1936 until only a few years ago, Perito Moreno lacked visitors services, but it is now permanently staffed. Argentine ranger Adrián Falcone and his American wife, Tammy Olsen, welcome visitors and can be contacted through the Parques Nacionales office in El Calafate, which is in radio contact with the park, or by mail at Casilla 103, 9311 Gobernador Gregores, Provincia de Santa Cruz.

Places to Stay

Camping is an attractive possibility, but no longer the only one. One good site is just beyond the isthmus that separates the two arms of Lago Belgrano, about ten km west of Estancia Belgrano. In the interior of this peninsula, several smallish lakes harbor abundant waterfowl and offer sheltered backcountry campsites. Ask at Estancia Belgrano for directions to the pictographs at Lago Burmeister.

Estancia La Oriental, at the foot of Cerro León on the north shore of Lago Belgrano, welcomes campers, offers meals and accommodations, and also arranges transportation; for reservations, contact Manuel Lada (☎ 0962-2196), Rivadavia 936 in San Julián. It's open November to March.

LOS ANTIGUOS

Picturesque rows of Lombardy poplars are windbreaks for the irrigated chacras of Los Antiguos, a pleasant retreat on the southern shore of Lago Buenos Aires near the Chilean border, with good fishing and hiking in the surrounding countryside. Tourist facilities are good, but the area has not yet been overrun by outsiders; the abundant fresh fruit harvest, for lack of large nearby markets, is absurdly cheap.

Before the arrival of Europeans, Tehuelche Indians and their forerunners frequented this "banana belt" in their old age – the town's name is a near-literal translation of a Tehuelche usage meaning Place of the Elders. In August 1991, the eruption of Volcán Hudson on the Chilean side of the border covered both Los Antiguos and Chile Chico in volcanic ash and briefly forced their evacuation, causing the loss of as many as three harvests and the death of many livestock for lack of forage.

Orientation & Information

Los Antiguos occupies the delta formed by the Río Jeinemeni, which constitutes the border with Chile, and the Río Los Antiguos. As in many smaller Argentine towns, there are few street signs and even fewer street numbers, but east-west Av 11 de Julio runs the length of town. To the west, the avenue reaches and crosses the border to Chile Chico.

At the eastern portal to town, the Municipalidad maintains a tourist information office, open 7 am to 7 pm daily from September through March. In town, the Dirección de Cultura (☎ 9100) on Av 11 de Julio is open 7 am to 2 pm and 4 to 7 pm. Banco de la Provincia changes money.

Things to See & Do

In summer, **Lago Buenos Aires** is warm enough for swimming from the beaches at the municipal campground at the east end of Av 11 de Julio. Juan Carlos Pellón, owner of Hotel Argentino, will guide fishermen to pejerrey and rainbow trout on the lake. **Monte Zeballos**, 50 km south, offers good hiking in southern beech forests; the road to Monte Zeballos may be extended southward to Paso Roballos, permitting a scenic circuit around the volcanic

ARGENTINA

Meseta del Lago Buenos Aires via Lago Posadas, Bajo Caracoles, and Perito Moreno.

Since 1989, Los Antiguos has held an annual Fiesta de la Cereza (cherry festival), lasting three days in the second week of January. Other local fruits, including raspberries, strawberries, apples, apricots, pears, peaches, plums, and prunes, are equally delectable. You can stop to purchase these, and homemade fruit preserves, directly from the farms. Señora Regina de Jomñuk's Chacra El Porvenir is easy walking distance from the main avenue, but there are many others, including Belgian-run Chacra El Paraíso on the lakeshore.

Other local celebrations are Día del Lago Buenos Aires on October 29 and Día de los Antiguos on February 5.

Places to Stay & Eat
Los Antiguos's *Camping Municipal,* on the lakeshore at the east end of Av 11 de Julio, is one of the best and cheapest in Argentina. Forest plantings shelter the sites, each of which has tables and firepits, from the wind. Hot showers are available from 5:30 to 10 pm. Fees have recently risen but are still reasonable at US$2.25 per person, plus US$1.30 per tent and per vehicle. There are also a limited number of cabins, which can hold up to six persons, for US$8.50 per cabin.

Hotel Argentino, which charges US$18/32 single/double with private bath, also has excellent fixed-price dinners, with desserts of local produce and an outstanding breakfast for US$4, but prices have risen to US$14 for lunch or dinner. *Restaurant El Disco,* a parrilla, is a bit cheaper.

Getting There & Away
LADE and Pingüino serve the nearest airport, at Perito Moreno 64 km east. Buses El Pingüino and La Unión run between Caleta Olivia and Los Antiguos (US$20, six hours). Transportes VH crosses the border to Chile Chico (US$3 return) three times daily Monday to Thursday, once on Friday and Saturday, but never on Sunday.

Tierra del Fuego & Chilean Patagonia

Since the 16th-century voyages of Magellan to the 19th-century explorations of Fitzroy and Darwin on the *Beagle* and even to the present, this "uttermost part of the earth" has held an ambivalent fascination for travelers of many nationalities. For more than three centuries, its climate and terrain discouraged European settlement, yet indigenous people considered it a "land of plenty". Its scenery, with glaciers descending nearly to the ocean in many places, is truly enthralling.

The Yahgan Indians, now few in number, built the fires that inspired Europeans to give this region its name, famous throughout the world. The region consists of one large island, Isla Grande de Tierra del Fuego, and many smaller ones, only a few of which are inhabited. The Strait of Magellan separates the archipelago from the South American mainland.

History

In 1520 when Magellan passed through the strait that now bears his name, neither he nor any other European explorer had any immediate interest in the land and its people. In search of a passage to the spice islands of Asia, early navigators feared and detested the stiff westerlies, hazardous currents, and violent seas that impeded their progress. Consequently, the Ona, Haush, Yahgan and Alacaluf peoples who populated the area faced no immediate competition for their lands and resources.

All these groups were mobile hunters and gatherers. The Onas, also known as Selknam, and the Haushes subsisted primarily on terrestrial resources, hunting the guanaco and dressing in its skins, while the Yahgans and Alacalufes, known collectively as "Canoe Indians", lived primarily on fish, shellfish, and marine mammals. The Yahgans, also known as the Yamana, consumed the "Indian bread" fungus *(Cytarria darwinii)* that parasitizes the

ñire, a species of southern beech. Despite frequently inclement weather, they used little or no clothing, but constant fires (even in their bark canoes) kept them warm.

As Spain's control of its American empire dwindled, the area slowly opened to settlement by other Europeans, which led to the rapid demise of the indigenous Fuegians, whom Europeans struggled to understand. Darwin, visiting the area in 1834, wrote that the difference between the Fuegians, "among the most abject and miserable creatures I ever saw", and Europeans was greater than that between wild and domestic animals. On an earlier voyage, however, Captain Robert Fitzroy of the *Beagle* had abducted several Yahgans whom he returned after several years of missionary education in England.

From the 1850s, Europeans attempted to catechize the Fuegians. The earliest such instance ended with the death by starvation of British missionary Allen Gardiner. Gardiner's successors, working from a base at Keppel Island in the Falklands, were more successful despite the massacre of one party by Fuegians at Isla Navarino. Thomas Bridges, a young man at Keppel, learned to speak the Yahgan language and became one of the first settlers at Ushuaia, in what is now Argentine Tierra del Fuego. His son, Lucas Bridges, born at Ushuaia in 1874, left a fascinating memoir of his experiences among the Yahgans and Onas entitled *The Uttermost Part of the Earth* (1950).

Although the Bridges family and many of those who followed had the best motives, the increasing European presence exposed the Fuegians to diseases such as typhoid and measles, to which they had little resistance. One measles epidemic wiped out half the native population in the district, and recurrent contagion nearly extinguished them over the next half-century. Some early sheep ranchers made things worse with their violent persecution of the Indians, who had resorted to preying on domestic flocks as guanaco populations declined.

Since no other European power had had any interest in settling the region until Britain occupied the Falklands in the 1770s, Spain too paid little attention to Tierra del Fuego, but the successor governments of Argentina and Chile felt differently. The Chilean presence on the Strait of Magellan beginning in 1843 and increasing British mission activity spurred Argentina to formalize its authority at Ushuaia in 1884 and install a territorial governor the following year. In 1978 Argentina and Chile nearly went to war over claims to three small disputed islands in the Beagle Channel. International border issues in the area were only finally resolved in 1984, when an Argentine plebiscite ratified a diplomatic settlement.

Despite minor gold and lumbering booms, Ushuaia was for many years primarily a penal settlement for both political prisoners and common criminals. Sheep farming brought great wealth to some individuals and families, and it is still the island's economic backbone, although the northern area near San Sebastián has substantial petroleum and natural gas reserves. Since the 1960s, the tourist industry has become so important that flights and hotels are often heavily booked in summer. The spectacular mountain and coastal scenery in the immediate countryside of Ushuaia, including Parque Nacional Tierra del Fuego, attracts both Argentines and visitors from abroad.

Geography & Climate

Surrounded by the South Atlantic Ocean, the Strait of Magellan and the easternmost part of the Pacific Ocean, the archipelago of Tierra del Fuego has a land area of roughly 76,000 sq km, about the size of Ireland or South Carolina. The Chilean-Argentine border runs directly south from Cape Espíritu Santo, at the eastern entrance of the Strait of Magellan, to the Beagle Channel (Canal de Beagle), where it trends eastward to the channel's mouth at Isla

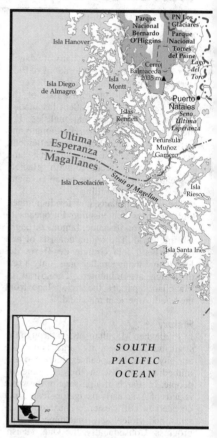

Nueva. Most of Isla Grande belongs to Chile, but the Argentine side is more densely populated, particularly around the substantial towns of Ushuaia and Río Grande. Porvenir (see the section on Chilean Patagonia) is the only significant town on the Chilean side.

The plains of northern Isla Grande are a landscape of almost unrelenting wind, enormous flocks of Corriedales (sheep), and oil derricks, while the island's mountainous southern part offers scenic glaciers, lakes, rivers and seacoasts. The mostly maritime climate is surprisingly mild, even in winter, but its changeability makes

Tierra del Fuego & Chilean Patagonia

warm, dry clothing important, especially on hikes and at higher elevations. The mountains of the Cordillera Darwin and the Sierra de Beauvoir, reaching as high as 2500 meters in the west, intercept Antarctic storms, leaving the plains around Río Grande much drier than areas nearer the Beagle Channel.

The higher southern rainfall supports dense forests of southern beech (*Nothofagus*), both deciduous and evergreen, while the drier north consists of extensive native grasses and low-growing shrubs. Storms batter the bogs and truncated beeches of the remote southern and western zones of the archipelago. Guanaco, rhea and condor can still be seen in the north, but marine mammals and shorebirds are the most common wildlife around tourist destinations along the Beagle Channel.

Books

Though its practical information is badly out of date, the 3rd edition of Rae Natalie Prosser Goodall's detailed, bilingual guidebook *Tierra del Fuego* is the most informed single source on the island's history and natural history. Rumors of a new edition persist, but the old one continues to be sold in local bookshops in Ushuaia.

Dangers & Annoyances

Collection of shellfish is not permitted because of toxic red tide conditions. Hunting is likewise illegal throughout the Argentine part of Tierra del Fuego.

Getting There & Around

Overland, the simplest route to Argentine Tierra del Fuego is via Porvenir, across the Strait of Magellan from Punta Arenas; for details, see the section on Chilean Patagonia. Transbordadora Austral Broom (☎ 21-8100), Anexo 21 in Punta Arenas, operates the roll-on, roll-off ferry *Baheia Azul*, which runs from Punta Delgada across the narrows at Primera Angostura to Chilean Tierra del Fuego. There's no public transportation to it. The ferry operates daily from 8 am to 11 pm; the half-hour crossing costs US$2 for passengers and US$13 for automobiles or pickup trucks. There are occasional breaks in service because of weather and tidal conditions.

The principal border crossing is San Sebastián, a truly desolate place about midway between Porvenir and Río Grande. Roads have improved considerably in recent years; they are unpaved on the Chilean side, but RN 3 is smoothly paved from San Sebastián past Río Grande as far as Tolhuín on Lago Kami, and paving was due to begin on the Tolhuín-Ushuaia portion over Paso Garibaldi in 1995.

Unlike the rest of Argentina, Tierra del Fuego has no provincial highways (*rutas provinciales*) as such, but has secondary roads that residents refer to as *rutas complementarias*. They're designated with a lowercase letter; references to such roads in this chapter will be 'RC-a', for example.

Tierra del Fuego

RÍO GRANDE

Founded in 1894 on the estuary of its namesake river, the bleak, windswept wool and petroleum service center of Río Grande is making a genuine effort to beautify and improve itself, but it still has a long way to go. A recent economic boom, sparked by duty-free status, has subsided and the local economy has stagnated. Most visitors will pass through quickly en route to Ushuaia, but the surrounding countryside is not completely without interest.

Orientation

Río Grande faces the open South Atlantic on RN 3, which leads 190 km south to Ushuaia and 79 km north to the Chilean border at San Sebastián. The main street is Av San Martín, which runs northwest-southeast. It crosses Av Islas Malvinas/-Santa Fe, as RN 3 is known through town. Most visitor services are along Av San Martín and along Av Manuel Belgrano between San Martín and the waterfront. Do not confuse the similarly named parallel streets 9 de Julio and 11 de Julio, which are two blocks (as well as two days) apart.

Information

Tourist Office The Instituto Fueguino de Turismo (Infuetur, ☎ 21373), in the lobby of the Hotel Los Yaganes at Belgrano 319, is open 10 am to 5 pm weekdays.

Foreign Consulate Chile has a consulate (☎ 22323) at Beauvoir 351, the southern extension of Av San Martín.

Money For money exchange, try Banco de la Nación, San Martín at 9 de Julio.

Post & Telecommunications Correo Argentino is at Ameghino 712, between Piedrabuena and Estrada; the postal code is 9420. Locutorio Cabo Domingo is at Av San Martín 458; the area code is 0964.

Laundry El Lavadero is located at Perito Moreno 221.

Medical Services Río Grande's Hospital Regional (☎ 22088) is at Av Belgrano 350.

Things to See

The most interesting historic site is the **Museo Salesiano**, 10 km north of town on RN 3, which was established by the missionary order that converted the Indians in this part of the island. Its several distinctive buildings contain excellent geological, natural history and ethnographic artifacts, but unfortunately the order does almost nothing interpretive with them.

Estancia María Behety, 20 km west of town, features the world's largest shearing shed. The Río Grande **Frigorífico** (mutton freezer) can process up to 2400 sheep per day.

Places to Stay

Because of its large number of single laborers, Río Grande is notorious for lack of quality budget accommodations. Patience and perseverance are necessary to find acceptable space, which may be a dormitory bed. Single women will probably prefer midrange hotels.

Places to Stay – bottom end

Hospedaje Irmary (☎ 23608), Estrada 743 between San Martín and Perito Moreno,

has beds for US$8 per person with shared bath, while *Hospedaje Noal* (☎ 22857), Rafael Obligado 557, charges US$13 per person with shared bath, US$15/35 single/ double with private bath and breakfast. At *Hostería Antares* (☎ 21853), Echeverría 49, rates are US$15 per person.

One of Río Grande's better choices, *Hospedaje Miramar* (☎ 22462) at Mackinlay 595, has clean, well-heated singles/ doubles at US$16 per person with shared bath, US$18 with private bath. Comparable in price and amenities, *Hospedaje Villa* (☎ 22312), San Martín 277, charges US$17 single, while *Hotel Rawson* (☎ 21352), Estrada 750, is slightly more expensive at US$18/28.

Places to Stay – middle to top end

ACA's *Hotel Los Yaganes* (☎ 30822), Belgrano 319, costs US$30/40 for members, US$42/53 for nonmembers. Rates at *Hotel Isla del Mar* (☎ 22883), Güemes 963, start at US$45/54.

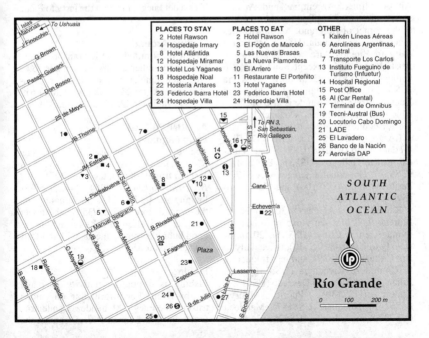

PLACES TO STAY	PLACES TO EAT	OTHER
2 Hotel Rawson	2 Hotel Rawson	1 Kaikén Líneas Aéreas
4 Hospedaje Irmary	3 El Fogón de Marcelo	6 Aerolíneas Argentinas,
8 Hotel Atlántida	5 Las Nuevas Brasas	Austral
12 Hospedaje Miramar	10 La Nueva Piamontesa	7 Transporte Los Carlos
13 Hotel Los Yaganes	11 El Arriero	13 Instituto Fueguino de
18 Hospedaje Noal	11 Restaurante El Porteñito	Turismo (Infuetur)
22 Hostería Antares	13 Hotel Yaganes	14 Hospital Regional
23 Federico Ibarra Hotel	23 Federico Ibarra Hotel	15 Post Office
24 Hospedaje Villa	24 Hospedaje Villa	16 AI (Car Rental)
		17 Terminal de Omnibus
		19 Tecni-Austral (Bus)
		20 Locutorio Cabo Domingo
		21 LADE
		25 El Lavadero
		26 Banco de la Nación
		27 Aerovías DAP

SOUTH
ATLANTIC
OCEAN

Río Grande

0   100   200 m

Enthusiastically recommended, *Posada de los Sauces* (☎ 32895), Elcano 839, charges US$55/70. *Federico Ibarra Hotel* (☎ 30071), Rosales 357, costs US$55/65, while rates at *Hotel Atlántida* (☎ 22592), Av Belgrano 582, are US$60/75.

Places to Eat
Hospedaje Villa, Hotel Federico Ibarra and Hotel Los Yaganes all have restaurants. You can also try *El Porteñito*, Lasserre 566 near Belgrano. For short orders and sandwiches, there are many confiterías in and around the center, including one at Hotel Rawson. *La Nueva Piamontesa* (☎ 21977), Av Belgrano 464, is an outstanding rotisería with reasonable takeout meals.

El Arriero, Av Belgrano 443 between Lasserre and Mackinlay, is a parrilla, as are *Las Nuevas Brasas* (☎ 22575) at Perito Moreno 635 and *El Fogón de Marcelo* (☎ 22585) at Estrada 817.

Getting There & Away
Air Aerolíneas Argentinas and Austral share offices (☎ 22748) at San Martín 607, at the corner of Belgrano. Aerolíneas flies twice daily to Ushuaia (US$26) and once daily to Buenos Aires (US$236), while Austral goes daily except Sunday to Río Gallegos (US$48), Comodoro Rivadavia (US$126), Bahía Blanca (US$204) and Buenos Aires. Río Grande is also one possible stop on Aerolíneas 'Conozca Patagonia" discount fare.

LADE (☎ 21651), Lasserre 447, flies Wednesday to Ushuaia (US$16) and Thursday to Río Gallegos (US$31), El Calafate (US$59), Gobernador Gregores (US$70), Perito Moreno (US$100) and Comodoro Rivadavia (US$107).

Kaikén Líneas Aéreas (☎ 30665), Perito Moreno 937, flies daily except Sunday to Punta Arenas, Chile (US$61), 20 times weekly to Ushuaia (US$30), twice daily to Río Gallegos (US$39), and less frequently to Comodoro Rivadavia (US$110), San Julián (US$80), Puerto Deseado (US$135), Trelew (US$130), Puerto Madryn (US$145), Neuquén (US$187), Mendoza (US$220) and Córdoba (US$253).

Aerovías DAP (☎ 30249), 9 de Julio 597, flies daily except Sunday to Punta Arenas, Chile (US$50).

Bus Río Grande's Terminal de Omnibus is at the foot of Av Belgrano on the waterfront, but most companies have offices elsewhere in town as well. Transportes Los Carlos (☎ 33871), Estrada 568, has daily buses to Ushuaia (US$20, four hours) in summer and less frequently in winter, when snow infrequently closes Paso Garibaldi. They also have service to Punta Arenas (US$30,10 hours) Monday and Friday at 7 am, and Tuesday, Thursday and Saturday at 7:30 am. Tecni-Austral (☎ 22620), Rivadavia 996, goes to Ushuaia daily at 7:30 am.

Transporte Pacheco (☎ 23382) goes to Punta Arenas Tuesday, Thursday and Saturday at 7:30 am. Transporte Senkovic (☎ 21339) goes Wednesday and Saturday at 6:30 am to Porvenir (US$20 one-way, US$36 return, seven hours) in Chilean Tierra del Fuego, meeting the ferry to Punta Arenas.

Getting Around
Given the limited public transportation, fishing and other excursions outside town are much simpler with a rental car, available from AI (☎ 22657) at Ameghino 612 or Avis/Tagle (☎ 22571) at Elcano 799.

AROUND RÍO GRANDE
Lago Fagnano
The huge glacial trough on RN 3 between Río Grande and Ushuaia merits a visit. A 100 km from Ushuaia, the beautifully sited *Hostería Kaikén* (☎ 0964- 24427) offers lodging for US$10/25 a single/double on the ground floor, US$15/35 on the upper floor, but it's often full. Its restaurant has good but rather costly meals, with indifferent service (at best).

Fishing
Fishing is a popular activity in many nearby rivers. For information on guided trips on the Fuego, Menéndez, Candelaria, Ewan and MacLennan Rivers, contact the

Club de Pesca John Goodall (☎ 0964-24324), Ricardo Rojas 606 in Río Grande. One highly recommended place is the *Hostería San Pablo* (☎ 0964-24638), 120 km southeast of Río Grande via RN 3 and RC-a, where there is good fly-fishing for trout and salmon on the Río Irigoyen. Rooms cost US$30/35 a single/double with breakfast included, while lunch or dinner costs an additional US$13.

USHUAIA

Over the past two decades, fast-growing Ushuaia has evolved from a village into a city of 42,000, sprawling and spreading from its original site, but the setting is still one of the most dramatic in the world, with jagged glacial peaks rising from sea level to nearly 1500 meters. The surrounding countryside is Ushuaia's greatest attraction, offering activities such as trekking, fishing, and skiing, as well as the opportunity to go as far south as roads go – RN 3 ends at Bahía Lapataia, in Parque Nacional Tierra del Fuego, 3242 km from Buenos Aires.

In 1870, the British-based South American Missionary Society made Ushuaia its first permanent outpost in the Fuegian region, but only artifacts, shellmounds, memories and Thomas Bridges' famous dictionary remain of the Yahgan Indians who once flourished in the area. Nearby Estancia Harberton, now open to visitors, still belongs to descendents of the Bridges family.

Between 1884 and 1947, Argentina incarcerated many of its most notorious criminals and political prisoners here and on remote Isla de los Estados (Staten Island). Since 1950, the town has been an important naval base that Argentina has used to support its claims to Antarctica, and in recent years it has become an important tourist destination.

Today Argentines and Chileans dispute which is the world's southernmost city, but fast-growing Ushuaia clearly overshadows modest Puerto Williams, across the Beagle Channel on Isla Navarino. Wages are higher than in central Argentina, thanks to industraial successes in electronics assembly, fishing and food processing, but so are living expenses. The boom is subsiding, though, and in early 1995 growing unemployment and the provincial government's inability to meet its payroll led to civil disturbances, during which police killed one demonstrator and injured several others.

Ushuaia is supposedly a free port, but foreign visitors will find few real bargains compared to Punta Arenas. In any event, the city is due to lose much of the preferential treatment it now enjoys with the imposition of IVA in 2003.

Orientation

Running along the north shore of the Beagle Channel, the recently beautified Av Maipú becomes Av Malvinas Argentinas west of the cemetery and, as RN 3, continues west to Parque Nacional Tierra del Fuego. The waterfront, its harbor protected by the nearby peninsula (site of the convenient airport), is a good place to observe shorebirds.

Unlike most Argentine cities, Ushuaia has no central plaza. Most hotels and visitor services are on or within a few blocks of Av San Martín, the principal commercial street, one block north of Av Maipú. North

ARGENTINA

Radical Radowitzky

One of Ushuaia's most famous inmates was Russian anarchist Simon Radowitzky, who assassinated Buenos Aires police chief Ramón Falcón with a bomb after a police massacre on May Day in 1909. Too young for the death penalty, Radowitzky received a life sentence at Ushuaia and briefly escaped to Chile with the help of Argentine anarchists to whom he was a hero. In 1930 Radical President Hipólito Yrigoyen ordered him released. The military dictatorship that overthrew Yrigoyen shortly thereafter confined several Radical political figures to Ushuaia, including writer Ricardo Rojas, and diplomat and former presidential candidate Honorio Pueyrredón (along with his vice-presidential candidate Mario Guido). ∎

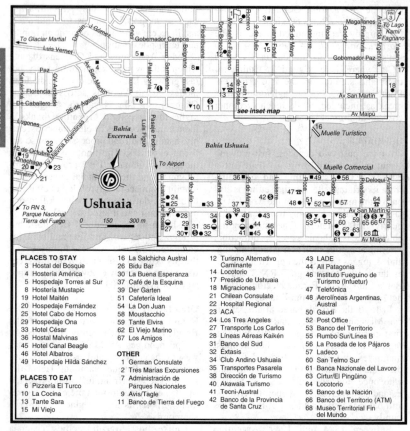

PLACES TO STAY
3 Hostal del Bosque
4 Hostería América
5 Hospedaje Torres al Sur
8 Hostería Mustapic
19 Hotel Maitén
20 Hospedaje Fernández
25 Hotel Cabo de Hornos
29 Hospedaje Ona
33 Hotel César
36 Hostal Malvinas
45 Hotel Canal Beagle
46 Hotel Albatros
49 Hospedaje Hilda Sánchez

PLACES TO EAT
6 Pizzería El Turco
10 La Cocina
13 Tante Sara
15 Mi Viejo

16 La Salchicha Austral
26 Bidu Bar
30 La Buena Esperanza
37 Café de la Esquina
39 Der Garten
51 Cafetería Ideal
54 La Don Juan
58 Moustacchio
59 Tante Elvira
62 El Viejo Marino
67 Los Amigos

OTHER
1 German Consulate
2 Tres Marías Excursiones
7 Administración de
   Parques Nacionales
9 Avis/Tagle
11 Banco de Tierra del Fuego

12 Turismo Alternativo
   Caminante
14 Locotorio
17 Presidio de Ushuaia
18 Migraciones
21 Chilean Consulate
22 Hospital Regional
23 ACA
24 Los Tres Angeles
27 Transporte Los Carlos
28 Líneas Aéreas Kaikén
31 Banco del Sud
32 Éxtasis
34 Club Andino Ushuaia
35 Transportes Pasarela
38 Dirección de Turismo
40 Akawaia Turismo
41 Tecni-Austral
42 Banco de la Provincia
   de Santa Cruz

43 LADE
44 All Patagonia
46 Instituto Fueguino de
   Turismo (Infuetur)
47 Telefónica
48 Aerolíneas Argentinas,
   Austral
50 Gaudí
52 Post Office
53 Banco del Territorio
55 Rumbo Sur/Línea B
56 La Posada de los Pájaros
57 Ladeco
60 San Telmo Sur
61 Banca Nazionale del Lavoro
63 Cirtur/El Pingüino
64 Locotorio
65 Banco de la Nación
66 Banco del Territorio (ATM)
68 Museo Territorial Fin
   del Mundo

of Av San Martín, streets rise very steeply, giving good views of the Beagle Channel.

Information

Tourist Offices The municipal Dirección de Turismo (☎ 32000) has moved to Av San Martín 660, between 25 de Mayo and Juana Fadul, with a branch at the airport for arriving planes and another at the port for arriving ships. They maintain a complete list of hotel accommodations and current prices and will assist in finding a room with private families; after closing time they post a list of available accommodations. They also have a message board, and the friendly, patient and helpful staff usually includes an English speaker and less frequently a German, French or Italian speaker. Hours are weekdays 8:30 am to 8:30 pm, Sundays and holidays 9 am to 8 pm.

The Instituto Fueguino de Turismo (Infuetur, ☎ 23340) is on the ground floor of Hotel Albatros at Maipú and Lasserre. ACA (☎ 21121) is at Malvinas Argentinas and Onachaga.

Foreign Consulates & Immigration

Chile has a consulate (☎ 22177) at Malvinas Argentinas 236, at the corner of Jainén.

ARGENTINA

It's open 9 am to 1 pm weekdays. Germany maintains a consulate (☎ 22778) at Rosas 516. Migraciones is at Yaganes 120.

Money Banco de la Nación is at Av San Martín 190 near Rivadavia, while Banco del Sud is at Av Maipú 781. Banco del Territorio, at San Martín 396 at Roca, cashes traveler's checks for a 3% commission; it also has an ATM at San Martín 152. Banco de la Provincia de Santa Cruz, Lasserre 140, charges a fixed US$7 fee, no matter what the value of the check.

Banca Nazionale del Lavoro, Maipú 297 (corner of Godoy), has an ATM connected to the Cirrus system. Banco de Tierra del Fuego has one at San Martín 1052.

Post & Telecommunications Correo Argentino is on Av San Martín, at the corner of Godoy. The local postal code is 9410.

There are convenient locutorios at Av San Martín 133 and Av San Martín 957. Telefónica is on Roca between Deloquí and Av San Martín. The Dirección de Turismo has a very convenient line for collect and credit card calls to Brazil, Chile, France, Italy, Japan, Spain, Uruguay and the USA (ATT, MCI, Sprint).

Ushuaia's area code is 0901.

National Parks The Administración de Parques Nacionales (☎ 21315), San Martín 1395, is open 9 am to noon weekdays.

Travel Agencies Ushuaia has nearly a score of travel agencies, among them Rumbo Sur/Línea B (☎ 22441) at Av San Martín 342; Akawaia Turismo (☎ 31371) at 25 de Mayo 64; All Patagonia (☎ 21117) at 25 de Mayo 31; and Turismo Alternativo Caminante (☎ 32723) at Don Bosco 319, which specializes in trekking.

Laundry Los Tres Angeles (☎ 22687) is at Rosas 139.

Medical Services Ushuaia's Hospital Regional (☎ 22950, emergencies ☎ 107) is at Maipú and 12 de Octubre.

Museo Territorial Fin del Mundo

The city of Ushuaia is restoring the original facade of this unusual block construction, dating from 1903 and atypical of Magellanic architecture, that once belonged to the family of early territorial governor Manuel Fernández Valdés. An informed, enthusiastic staff oversees exhibits on Fuegian natural history, aboriginal life, the early penal colonies (complete with a photographic rogues gallery), and replicas of an early general store and bank. There is also a bookstore and a good specialized library.

On the waterfront at Av Maipú and Rivadavia, the museum (☎ 21863) is well worth the US$2 admission charge (ask about student discounts). It's open Monday to Saturday from 4 to 8 pm.

Murals

On Av Maipú, along the waterfront, appears the striking mural of the Selknam/Ona "Hain" initiation ceremony described by Lucas Bridges in his classic account, *The Uttermost Part of the Earth*. Also along Av Maipú, between Don Bosco and Rosas, are some overtly political anti-nuclear, pro-environment murals.

Presidio de Ushuaia

As early as 1884, Argentina's federal government established a military prison on Isla de los Estados (Staten Island), at the east end of Tierra del Fuego, in part to support its territorial claims in a region inhabited only by hunters and gatherers with no state allegiance whatsoever. In 1902, it shifted the prison to Ushuaia and, in 1911, it merged with Ushuaia's Carcel de Reincidentes, which had encarcerated civilian recidivists since 1896.

The building (at its present size) held as many as 600 inmates in 380 cells designed for one prisoner each. It was closed as a penal institution in 1947 and incorporated into the naval base at the east end of Av San Martín. The Presidio is open to the public daily from 5:30 to 9 pm. Admission costs US$2; use the entrance at Yaganes and Gobernador Paz rather than the entrance to the base proper at Yaganes and San Martín.

Ferrocarril Austral Fueguino
Originally constructed to assist the logging industry during presidio days, Ushuaia's short-line, narrow-gauge railroad recently reopened as a tourist train under a 30-year concession, but it lacks permission to enter Parque Nacional Tierra del Fuego because the concessionaire jumped the gun on an environmental impact statement. At present its only stop is at Cascada La Macarena, where there's a tourist-trap reconstruction of a Selknam/Ona camp. The 3½-hour excursion would be a poor value at even a small fraction of the US$30 cost.

The Frozen South
One of the unanticipated, ironic dividends of the end of the Cold War has been the increasing accessibility of Antarctica at relatively reasonable prices. About 60% of Antarctic tourists leave from Ushuaia, where it's possible to arrange visits to the frozen continent with Russian research vessels that once benefitted from Soviet subsidies but must now pay their own way. To do so, they have begun to take paying passengers on 10- to 17-day Antarctic cruises on well-equipped, remodeled vessels.

Most of these cruises tend to the expensive, but if space is available it's sometimes possible to get on these vessels for as little as US$1200 for a week's voyage, everything included. Several Ushuaia travel agencies, most notably All Patagonia, arrange Antarctic excursions, but it's also worth going to the port and asking around.

Overseas operators arranging Antarctic tours include Mountain Travel Sobek (☎ 510-527-8100 or 800-227-2384), 6420 Fairmount Ave, El Cerrito, CA 94530; Marin Expeditions (☎ 416-964-9069, fax 416-964-2366, 800-263-9147), 13 Hazelton Ave, Toronto, ON M5R 2E1; Nature Expeditions International (☎ 800-869-0639), PO Box 11496, 474 Willamette, Eugene, OR 97440; and Natural Habitat Adventures (☎ 800-543-8917), 2945 Center Green Court South, Suite H, Boulder, CO 80301-9539.

One of the guidebooks presently available to Antarctica is Diana Galimberti's *Antarctica: An Introductory Guide* (Zagier & Urruty Publications, 1991). ∎

From Ushuaia's Plaza Cívica, on the waterfront at the Muelle Turístico, a bus leaves for the starting point at the municipal campground, eight km west of town.

Glaciar Martial
Just within the borders of Parque Nacional Tierra del Fuego lies Glaciar Martial, which hikers can reach via a magnificent walk that begins from the west end of Av San Martín. It passes the Parques Nacionales office and climbs the zigzag road (there are many hiker shortcuts) to the ski run seven km northwest of town. Transportes Pasarela (☎ 21735), Fadul 40, also runs five buses daily (US$5 return) to the Aerosilla del Glaciar, a chairlift that is open 10 am to 4:30 pm daily except Monday.

From the base of the Aerosilla (which costs US$5 and saves an hour's walk), the glacier is about a two-hour walk, offering awesome views of Ushuaia and the Beagle Channel. The weather is very changeable, so take warm, dry clothing and sturdy footwear.

Activities
All the travel agencies in Ushuaia arrange activities such as trekking, horseback riding, canoeing, mountain biking and fishing in and around Parque Nacional Tierra del Fuego and elsewhere on the island. See the Dirección de Turismo for a listing that rates these activities from *sin dificultad* (easy) to *pesado* (very difficult).

Fishing Fishing is a popular pastime for both Argentines and foreigners; the required license is available in Ushuaia from the Asociación Caza y Pesca at Maipú and 9 de Julio; the Administración de Parques Nacionales at San Martín 1395; or Transportes Pasarela at Juana Fadul 40. Fishing licenses cost US$40 monthly, US$30 for 15 days, US$20 weekly and US$10 daily.

Spinning and fly casting are the most common means of hooking brown trout, rainbow trout, Atlantic salmon, and other species. The nearest site is Río Pipo, five km west of town on RN 3. It is possible to visit the Estación de Piscicultura (trout hatchery) at Río Olivia, two km east of town.

Mountain Biking From October to April, local operators arrange mountain bike excursions ranging from a full day in Parque Nacional Tierra del Fuego to weeklong tours over Paso Garibaldi to Lago Kami, Lago Yehuin and Río Grande. Distances range from 50 to 95 km per day and, fortunately, the wind is usually at your back.

Skiing From June to mid-September, the mountains near Ushuaia have many suitable sites for both downhill and cross-country skiing, although only the period around Argentine winter holidays in early July is really busy. The main downhill area is Centro de Deportes Invernales Luis Martial (☎ 21423, 23340), seven km northwest of town, which has one 1300-meter run on a 23° slope, with a double-seat chairlift (maximum capacity 244 skiers per hour). The Club Andino Ushuaia (☎ 22335), Fadul 50, has a smaller area only three km from downtown on the same road.

East of Ushuaia, along RN 3 toward Paso Garibaldi, you'll find cross-country ski areas at the Club Andino's Pista Francisco Jermán five km from town; at Valle de los Huskies, 17 km from town; at Tierra Mayor, 21 km from town; at Las Cotorras, 26 km from town; and at Haruwen (☎ /fax 24058 in Ushuaia), 37 km from town. Rental equipment is available at each site for around US$30 per day. Each center provides its own transportation from the center of town.

Ushuaia's biggest ski event is the annual Marcha Blanca, a symbolic recreation of San Martín's historic crossing of the Andes, taking place on August 17, the date of the great man's death. Attracting up to 450 skiers, it starts from Las Cotorras and climbs to Paso Garibaldi.

Organized Tours
Overland Trips Local operators offer tours to the principal attractions in and around Ushuaia, including Parque Nacional Tierra del Fuego. Trips to historic Estancia Harberton (US$30), east of Ushuaia, can be arranged with sufficient notice, but no one should arrive unannounced; admission to the estancia costs an additional US$6 and includes a visit to the Bridges family cemetery. There are also half-day tours of the city (US$15 including the museum), tours to Lapataia/Parque Nacional Tierra del Fuego (US$15), and excursions over Paso Garibaldi to Lago Kami/Fagnano (US$30 full-day) and Río Grande.

Boat Trips Popular boat trips, with destinations such as the sea lion colony at Isla de los Lobos, leave from the Muelle Turístico (tourist jetty) on Maipú between Lasserre and Roca. Trips cost about US$30 for a 2½-hour excursion; with an extension to Bahía Lapataia, they cost US$45. The most commonly seen species is the southern sea lion *Otaria flavescens*, whose thick mane will make you wonder why Spanish speakers call it *lobo marino* (sea wolf). Fur seals, nearly extinct because of commercial overexploitation during the past century, survive in much smaller numbers. Isla de Pájaros, also in the Beagle Channel, has many species of birds, including extensive cormorant colonies. Trips to Estancia Harberton and its pingüinera (penguin colony) cost US$55.

Rumbo Sur/Línea B (see Travel Agencies, above) runs the luxury catamarans *Ana B* and *Ezequiel B*. A reader recommendation is Tres Marías Excursiones (☎ 21897, ask for Héctor), Romero 514; trips cost $10 per hour.

For weeklong sailboat excursions around Cape Horn or the Cordillera Darwin (for about US$1200 per person), contact travel agencies like All Patagonia, Caminante or Rumbo Sur.

Places to Stay
In the summer high season, especially January and February, demand for accommodations in Ushuaia is very high and no one should arrive without reservations; if you must arrive without reservations, try to do

so early in the day before everything fills up. Should you arrive without reservations and nothing is available, the 24-hour confitería at the Hotel del Glaciar (at Km 3.5 on the road to Glaciar Martial) is a good place to stay up drinking coffee. The tourist office does post a list of available accommodations outside the office after closing time.

Places to Stay – bottom end

Camping Ushuaia's free *Camping Municipal*, eight km west of town on RN 3 to Parque Nacional Tierra del Fuego, has minimal facilities. The *Camping del Rugby Club Ushuaia*, four km west of town, charges an extortionate US$15 per tent, but at least it offers reasonable facilities.

Other campsites, both free and for a fee, are at Parque Nacional Tierra del Fuego, but there are also others out RN 3 toward Río Grande and Valle de los Huskies. *Camping Río Tristen*, at the Haruwen winter sports center, has a dozen sites, with shared bathrooms and showers, for US$5 per tent (two people).

Casas de Familia The tourist office regularly arranges rooms in private homes, which tend to be cheaper than hotels; because these are usually available only seasonally and change greatly from year to year, you should arrange to stay in one only through the tourist office. Prices are usually in the US$20 per person range, occasionally slightly cheaper.

Hospedajes The cheapest permanent alternative is dilapidated *Hospedaje Ona*, 9 de Julio 27 at Av Maipú, where dormitory-style beds cost US$15 and weekly rates are slightly lower, but it's not really a good value. A better choice is *Hospedaje Torres al Sur*, Gobernador Paz 1437 between Onas and Patagonia, which charges $15 a single. The Dirección de Turismo discourages visitors from *Hospedaje Hilda Sánchez* (☎ 23622), Deloquí 391, but many travelers have found her place congenial, if crowded and a bit noisy at times. Rates are US$15 per person, and it's open all year.

Hostería Mustapic (☎ 21718), Piedrabuena 230, charges US$25/35 with shared bath, US$30/40 with private bath.

Places to Stay – middle

Midrange accommodations start around US$45/50 at *Hotel Maitén* (☎ 22745), 12 de Octubre 140, and *Hostería América* (☎ 23358), Gobernador Paz 1659. Enthusiastically recommended *Hospedaje Fernández* (☎ 21192), Onachaga 68 at Fitzroy, has doubles at US$49.

Other possibilities in this price range include *Hotel César* (☎ 21460) at Av San Martín 753, which offers singles/doubles for US$50/60, and *Hostal Malvinas* (☎ 22626) at Deloquí 609, with rooms for US$60/70.

Places to Stay – top end

Waterfront hotels have the best views and highest prices, but the most exclusive of them are not particularly good values; the most reasonable choice is ACA's *Hotel Canal Beagle* (☎ 21117), Av Maipú 599 at 25 de Mayo, which charges US$70/80. *Hotel Cabo de Hornos* (☎ 22187), Av San Martín at Rosas, costs US$69/79.

On the hillside at Magallanes and Fadul, *Hostal del Bosque* (☎ 21723) charges US$80/100. At *Hotel Ushuaia* (☎ 30671), Lasserre 933, rates are US$80/110, while at *Hotel Tolkeyén* (☎ 30532), on Estancia Río Pipo five km west of town on RN 3, rooms rent for US$90/100.

Badly overpriced *Hotel Albatros* (☎ 33446), Av Maipú 505 at Lasserre, charges US$120 with breakfast. For the same price, *Hotel del Glaciar* (☎ 30636), at Km 3.5 on the road to Glaciar Martial, is probably a better choice, but it's still hard to call it a good value at this price.

Five-star *Las Hayas Resort Hotel* (☎ 30710), at Km 3 on the road to Glaciar Martial, charges US$175/185 for singles/doubles that are "surrounded by natural beauty, invaiding the hotel through its wide windows". The hotel sometimes lacks staff to provide all the services of a hotel in its category.

Places to Eat

Meals both cheap and good are scarce in Ushuaia. On the waterfront near the Muelle Turístico, *La Salchicha Austral* (☎ 24596) is among the most reasonable, but *La Cocina*, on Av Maipú between Belgrano and Piedrabuena, is a phenomenal value by current Ushuaia standards, with excellent three-course meals like lomo a la champiñon (steak with mushrooms and French fries) for US$6.50. *Der Garten*, in the gallery alongside the tourist office on San Martín, has similarly priced weekday specials, as does *Los Amigos* (☎ 22473) at San Martín 150, which has a varied and interesting menu. *Pizzería El Turco* (☎ 23593), San Martín 1460, is also good and relatively inexpensive.

Café de la Esquina, at the corner of San Martín and 25 de Mayo, is Ushuaia's most popular confitería. At San Martín and Rosas, the long hours at the popular *Bidu Bar* (☎ 24605) make it a popular place to wait for the 3 am Punta Arenas bus; it has decent but not cheap meals. *Tante Sara*, at the corner of San Martín and Don Bosco, has outstanding ice cream and other desserts.

The US$12 tenedor libre at lively *Cafetería Ideal*, Av San Martín 393 at Roca, isn't really a bargain, but some travelers making it their only meal of the day find it a good choice. *Mi Viejo* (☎ 23565), Gobernador Campos 758, also has a tenedor libre special. *La Buena Esperanza*, at Maipú and 9 de Julio, has a handful of Chinese dishes.

At the pricier restaurants, reservations are essential for groups of any size. *Moustacchio* (☎ 23308), Av San Martín 298, has excellent food and service. *Tante Elvira* (☎ 21982, 21249), Av San Martín 234, also has a good reputation. *El Viejo Marino* (☎ 21911), Maipú 297, is a fairly expensive restaurant offering decent seafood. *La Don Juan* (☎ 22519), San Martín 345, is Ushuaia's only parrilla.

Entertainment

Éxtasis, at Maipú and 9 de Julio, is a popular pub/dance club. *La Posada de los Pájaros* (☎ 30610), at the corner of Deloqui and Godoy, is a popular cafe featuring live music on weekends. *San Telmo Sur*, Godoy 53, showcases Argentine rock and pop, while *Gaudí*, at Godoy 136, offers musical and comedy performances.

Things to Buy

Ushuaia is ostensibly a duty-free zone, but overseas visitors will find few bargains compared to Punta Arenas. Locally made chocolates are worth a taste.

Getting There & Away

Air Ushuaia has frequent air connections to Buenos Aires and to other parts of Patagonia, though its short runway, steep approach and frequent high winds have traditionally made landing here an adventure that timid flyers have preferred to avoid. A new 2700-meter runway will permit planes larger than 737s to land safely and Aerolíneas Argentinas' loss of a landing monopoly may soon permit long-distance competition from foreign airlines such as Ladeco, Varig, and Vasp. At press time, LAPA was due to begin flights into Ushuaia.

Aerolíneas Argentinas and Austral share offices (☎ 21091) at Roca 126. Aerolíneas flies daily to Río Gallegos (US$56), Trelew (US$157), and Buenos Aires (US$252); daily except Monday and Thursday to Río Gallegos, Río Grande (US$26), Buenos Aires; and Monday and Thursday to Río Grande and then Buenos Aires. Ushuaia is also a possible stop on Aerolíneas "Conozca Patagonia" discount fare.

LADE (☎ 21123), in the Galería Albatros at Av San Martín 564, has flights Thursday to Río Grande (US$16), Río Gallegos (US$43), El Calafate (US$68), Gobernador Gregores (US$82), Perito Moreno (US$113), and Comodoro Rivadavia (US$121).

Líneas Aéreas Kaikén (☎ 23663), San Martín 857, flies daily except Sunday to Punta Arenas, Chile (US$70); frequently to Río Grande (US$30), Río Gallegos (US$51), and El Calafate (US$83); five times weekly to Comodoro Rivadavia

(US$130) and Trelew (US$145); three times weekly to Córdoba (US$275); and less frequently to San Julián (US$120), Puerto Deseado (US$100), Puerto Madryn (US$155), Neuquén (US$198), and Mendoza (US$220).

Cirtur (☎ 21004), Maipú 237, is the agent for El Pingüino, which flies two or three times weekly to Río Gallegos (US$46), El Calafate (US$80), and Punta Arenas, in summer only.

Ladeco (☎ 31110), Godoy 115, flies Tuesday and Saturday to Punta Arenas (US$110), Puerto Montt, and Santiago. See travel agencies for Aerovías DAP, which flies Tuesday, Thursday, and Saturday to Punta Arenas (US$60), and Monday, Wednesday, and Friday to Puerto Williams, on Isla Navarino (US$37).

Bus There's no central bus teminal; all buses depart from company offices. Transporte Los Carlos (☎ 22337), Rosas 85, crosses Paso Garibaldi via Lago Fagnano to Río Grande; the bus departs daily at 7 pm (US$20, four hours); Friday to Monday there's an additional 7 am service, while Monday and Friday at 3 am it goes directly to Punta Arenas, Chile (US$48). Tecni-Austral (☎ 23396), in the Galería del Jardín at 25 de Mayo 50, also goes to Río Grande, daily at 6 pm.

For transportation to Parque Nacional Tierra del Fuego, see the Getting There & Away entry for the park.

Boat At 8 am on Saturday, in theory, the *Luciano Beta* crosses from Ushuaia to Puerto Williams, Chile (US$50, 1½ hours). This is very undependable and no one should count on it. Inquire at the tourist office.

From Puerto Williams, there are weekly sea and air connections to Punta Arenas. The *MV Tierra Australis* runs expensive cruises to Punta Arenas (3½ days, US$700) with accommodations and all meals included. See travel agents for details.

Getting Around

To/From the Airport Linked to town by a causeway, Aeropuerto Internacional Ushuaia is on the peninsula across from the waterfront. It's walking distance for backpackers, but cabs are moderately priced and there's also bus service along Av Maipú.

Car Rental Although rural public transport is better than at Río Grande, it is still limited. Rental rates for a Fiat Spazio start around US$30 per day plus US$0.30 per km, plus at least US$15 insurance daily; rental companies include Avis/Tagle (☎ 22744), San Martín and Belgrano, and Localiza (☎ 30663) at Hotel Albatros. Rates go up to US$120 per day plus mileage for a Toyota 4WD.

PARQUE NACIONAL TIERRA DEL FUEGO

Forests, bays, lakes, rivers, peaks, and glaciers attract many visitors and hikers to Argentina's only coastal national park, a 63,000-hectare unit extending from the Beagle Channel in the south along the Chilean border to beyond Lago Kami/Fagnano in the north. Just 18 km west of Ushuaia via RN 3, the park lacks the integrated network of hiking trails of Chile's Torres del Paine. There are several short hiking trails, but the one major trek is now off-limits because of misguided and inexplicable policies that have declared large but lightly impacted portions of the park a *reserva estricta*, closed to all access except for scientific research, while permitting the more accessible, so-called *zona de recreación* to be trashed almost beyond belief.

Information

Parques Nacionales maintains a Centro de Información at Bahía Lapataia, at the end of RN 3. There are also rangers at the park entrance and at Lago Roca. Park admission, payable at the ranger station on RN 3, is US$3.50 per person.

Books

South America's National Parks by William Leitch has a useful chapter on Parque

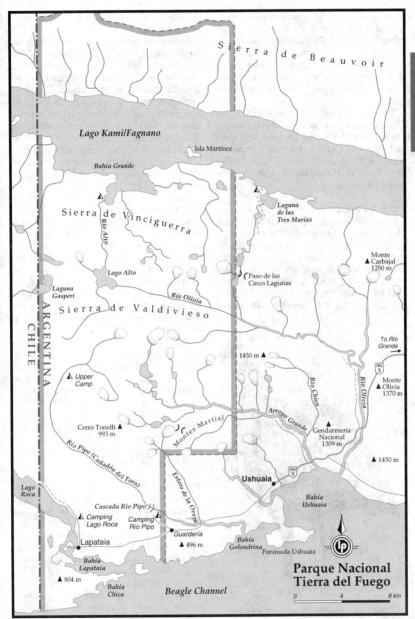

Sierra de Beauvoir

Lago Kami/Fagnano

Isla Martínez

Bahía Grande

Sierra de Vinciguerra

Laguna de las Tres Marías

Río Alto

Lago Alto

Monte Carbajal 1250 m

Paso de las Cinco Lagunas

Laguna Gasperi

Río Olivia

ARGENTINA
CHILE

Sierra de Valdivieso

1450 m ▲

To Río Grande

RN 3

Monte Olivia 1370 m

Upper Camp

Río Chico

Cerro Tonelli 993 m

Montes Martial

Arroyo Grande

Gendarmería Nacional 1309 m

Río Olivia

▲ 1450 m

Río Pipo (Cañadón del Toro)

Ushuaia

RN 3

Lago Roca

Estero de la Oveja

Bahía Ushuaia

Cascada Río Pipo

Camping Lago Roca

Camping Río Pipo

Guardería

▲ 496 m

Bahía Golondrina

Peninsula Ushuaia

Lapataia

Bahía Lapataia

▲ 804 m

Bahía Chica

Beagle Channel

Parque Nacional Tierra del Fuego

0   4   8 km

Nacional Tierra del Fuego, emphasizing its natural history. Several authors have contributed to Bradt Publications' *Backpacking in Chile & Argentina*, which describes treks in the area around Ushuaia but is skimpy on maps. Clem Lindemayer's *Trekking in the Patagonian Andes* is much more detailed.

Two useful guides for bird-watchers are Claudio Venegas Canelo's *Aves de Patagonia y Tierra del Fuego Chileno-Argentina* and Ricardo Clark's *Aves de Tierra del Fuego y Cabo de Hornos*. Claudio Villegas's *Aves de Magallanes* is also a worthwhile purchase.

Flora & Fauna

Three species of the southern beech *(Nothofagus)*, known by their common names coihue, lenga, and ñire, dominate the dense native forests. The evergreen coihue and deciduous lenga thrive on heavy coastal rainfall at lower elevations, but the deciduous ñire tints the Fuegian hillsides red during the fall months. Other tree

species are much less significant and not as conspicuous.

Sphagnum peat bogs in low-lying areas support ferns, colorful wildflowers, and the insectivorous plant *Drosera uniflora*; these may be seen on the self-guided nature trail **Sendero Laguna Negra**. To avoid damage to the bog and danger to yourself, stay on the trail, part of which consists of a catwalk for easier passage across the swampy terrain.

Land mammals are scarce, although guanacos and foxes exist; marine mammals are most common on offshore islands. Visitors are most likely to see two unfortunate introductions, the European rabbit and the North American beaver, both of which have caused ecological havoc and proved impossible to eradicate. The former numbers up to 70 per hectare in some areas, while the latter's handiwork is visible in the ponds and by the dead beeches along the **Sendero de los Castores** (Trail of the Beavers) to Bahía Lapataia. Originally introduced at Lago Kami/Fagnano in the 1940s, beavers quickly spread throughout the island.

Bird life is much more abundant, especially along the coastal zone, including Lapataia and Bahía Ensenada. The ranges of the Andean condor and the maritime black-browed albatross overlap ranges here, although neither is common. Shorebirds such as cormorants, gulls, terns, oystercatchers, grebes, steamer ducks, and kelp geese are common. The large, striking upland goose *(cauquén)* is widely distributed farther inland.

Trekking

Most park trails are very short, and the only remaining trek permitted in the park is a mere six km along the north shore of Lago Roca to the Chilean border. The extended trek from the Río Pipo campsite, across the Montes Martial and Sierra de Valdivieso to Lago Kami/Fagnano – a rugged 30-km trip – should be simple for experienced, independent hikers, but the reclassification of the area by Parques Nacionales has reduced or eliminated access. Turismo

The cauquén is also known as the upland goose

Top: Ross Road, Stanley
Left: Shearing at Port Louis, East Falkland
Right: King Penguins, Volunteer Point, East Falkland

Top: Loading wool on jetty, Weddell Island, West Falkland
Bottom: Sunset, Arch Islands, West Falkland

Alternativo Caminante in Ushuaia may still be able to undertake this trek. Take warm, dry clothing, good footwear, a sleeping bag, a tent, and plenty of food.

Because of Argentina's perpetual fiscal crisis and the military's proprietary attitude toward border zones, there are no official, detailed, easily available maps, but the route is fairly straightforward. Probably the best detailed walking map is the one contained in LP's *Trekking in the Patagonian Andes*.

Places to Stay

Since the Hostería Alakush at Lago Roca burned to the ground several years ago, camping is the only alternative for visitors wishing to stay in the park. The only organized campsite, *Camping Lago Roca*, charges US $4 per person and has a confitería and hot showers. Bring supplies from Ushuaia.

Camping Ensenada, Camping Las Bandurrias, Camping Laguna Verde, Camping Los Cauquenes, and *Camping Río Pipo* are free sites which, unfortunately, are disgracefully filthy. Since they lack even pit toilets and few people bother to dig latrines, toilet paper (and worse) is scattered everywhere.

Getting There & Away

During summer, Transporte Pasarela (☎ 21735), Fadul 40 in Ushuaia, goes to the park at 9:30 and 10 am, and 1, 5, and 7:30 pm, returning at 11 am, and 2, 6, and 8:30 pm. The roundtrip fare is US$10, and you need not return the same day.

Hitching to the park is feasible, but most Argentine families have little extra room in their vehicles.

Chilean Patagonia

Many people who visit Argentine Patagonia's popular natural attractions also visit Chilean Patagonia. Basic information on Chilean travel is provided here, but those

spending an extended period in other parts of Chile should obtain Lonely Planet's *Chile & Easter Island* guidebook.

Chilean Patagonia, a rugged, mountainous area battered by westerly winds and storms that drop enormous amounts of snow and rain on the seaward slopes of the Andes, consists of the regions of Aysén and Magallanes. The southern continental icefield separates the two; the Twelfth Region Magallanes and its capital of Punta Arenas are more easily accessible from Argentine Patagonia and Tierra del Fuego than from the Eleventh Region of Aysén or the Chilean mainland. The principal transportation from the mainland is by air, sea, or overland through Argentina.

Ona, Yahgan, Alacaluf and Tehuelche Indians, subsisting through fishing, hunting and gathering, were the area's original inhabitants. There remain very few individuals of identifiable Ona or Yahgan descent, while the Alacalufes and Tehuelches survive in much reduced numbers. In 1520, Magellan was the first European to visit the area, but early Spanish colonization attempts failed; tiny Puerto Hambre (Port Famine), on the strait south of Punta Arenas, is a reminder of these efforts. Nearby, the restored wooden bulwarks of Fuerte (Fort) Bulnes recall Chile's initial colonization in 1843, when President Manuel Bulnes ordered the army south to an area then only sparsely populated by indigenous peoples.

Punta Arenas itself owes its origins to the California Gold Rush, but its enduring prosperity derived from the wool and mutton industry that transformed both Argentine and Chilean Patagonia in the late 19th century. This prosperity was bolstered by maritime traffic originating in Europe, California, or Australia that passed through the strait. The opening of the Panama Canal in 1914 marked the beginning of a decline in traffic around Cape Horn, which in turn diminished the significance of the port in international trade.

Besides wool, the region's modern economy depends on commerce, provincial petroleum development, fisheries, and tourism. The province is the most prosperous in Chile, with the country's highest levels of employment, housing quality, school attendance, and public services. The region's impressive natural assets, particularly Parque Nacional Torres del Paine, have made it an increasingly popular destination for travelers.

Visas

Nationals of countries with which Chile has diplomatic relations, including the USA, Canada, Western Europe, Japan, Australia, and many others, need passports but not visas to enter the country. All visitors do need a tourist card, which is issued at the port of entry. Like the Argentine tourist card, it is valid for 90 days and renewable for another 90. Unlike the Argentine card, authorities take it very seriously, so guard it closely to avoid the hassle of replacing it. Chilean border officials are generally reasonable and friendly, however.

Customs

Chilean customs permits the importation of personal belongings, 500 cigarettes, 100 cigars, and two liters of alcoholic beverages, plus gifts and souvenirs. Normally customs officials are not difficult to deal with, although returning to Puerto Montt or Santiago from Punta Arenas (a free zone where electronic items are very cheap), you may encounter a thorough internal customs check. Unless you are carrying, say, half a dozen cameras of the same brand and model, you are not likely to be seriously inconvenienced.

Money & Costs

The recently revalued peso (Ch$) has appreciated from approximately 430 to 400 pesos per US dollar, making Chile increasingly expensive. Banknote denominations are Ch$500, Ch$1000, Ch$5000, and Ch$10,000 pesos, although breaking a Ch$10,000 note can be a great nuisance for small purchases. There are also coins of Ch$5, Ch$10, Ch$50 and Ch$100, but few items cost less than Ch$50.

For basic costs such as accommodations, food, and transport, foreign visitors will find Chile more expensive than the central Andean countries but still cheaper than Argentina. Chilean Patagonia, however, generally has a higher cost of living than the rest of the country because of its remoteness and relative isolation.

Health

Conditions are much the same as in Argentina; see the section on health in the Facts for the Visitor chapter. Chile does not demand any unusual health precautions, and no vaccinations are required as a condition of entry.

Getting There & Away

Visitors to Chilean Patagonia must arrive by air, by sea from mainland Chile, or overland through Argentina. Chile's two major airlines, LanChile and Ladeco, are both comfortable and efficient, as is National, which has fewer flights and is only slightly cheaper. Regular ferry services link Puerto Montt, on the Chilean mainland, and Puerto Natales, in Magallanes.

Within Chilean Patagonia, Aerovías DAP serves both Chilean and Argentine Tierra del Fuego, Río Gallegos, the Falkland (Malvinas) Islands, and Antarctica. There are ferries between Punta Arenas and Porvenir, in Chilean Tierra del Fuego.

Good, comfortable buses connect Punta Arenas, Puerto Natales, and Parque Nacional Torres del Paine, the main destinations for visitors in Chilean Patagonia.

PUNTA ARENAS

At the foot of the Andes on the western side of the Strait of Magellan, Patagonia's most interesting and liveliest city features many mansions and other impressive buildings dating from the wool boom of the late 19th and early 20th centuries. As the best and largest port for thousands of kilometers, Punta Arenas (population 110,000) attracts ships from the burgeoning South Atlantic fishery as well as Antarctic research and tourist vessels. Free port facilities have promoted local commerce and encouraged immigration from central

ARGENTINA

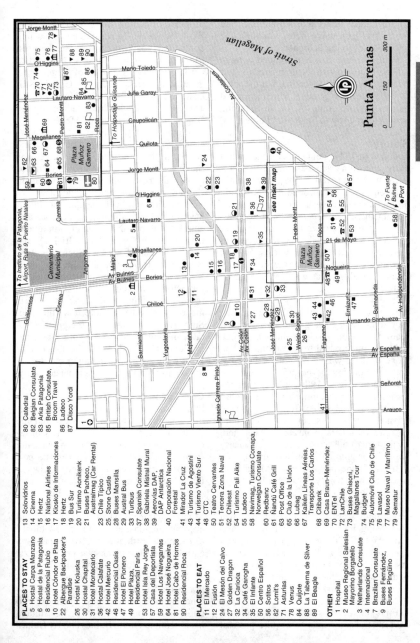

PLACES TO STAY
5   Hostal Carpa Manzano
6   Hostal de la Patagonia
8   Residencial Rubio
10 Hotel Cóndor de Plata
22 Albergue Backpacker's Paradise
26 Hostal Koluska
30 Hostal Chaptal
31 Hotel Montecarlo
36 Hostal Calafate
42 Hotel Mercurio
46 Residencial Oasis
47 Hotel El Pionero
49 Hotel Plaza, Residencial París
53 Hotel Isla Rey Jorge
57 Casa del Deportista
59 Hotel Los Navegantes
64 Hotel José Nogueira
81 Hotel Cabo de Hornos
90 Residencial Roca

PLACES TO EAT
11 El Mercado
12 Fusión
24 El Mesón del Calvo
27 Golden Dragon
32 La Carioca
34 Café Garogha
35 El Infante
50 Centro Español
56 Sottos
62 Lomit's
71 Asturias
78 Venus
84 Quijote
88 La Taberna de Silver
89 El Beagle

OTHER
1   Hospital
2   Museo Regional Salesian Mayorino Borgatello
3   Netherlands Consulate
4   Internacional
7   Brazilian Consulate
9   Buses Fernández, Buses Pingüino

13 Solovidrios
14 Cinema
15 Hertz
16 National Airlines
17 Kiosko de Informaciones
18 Hertz
19 Bus Sur
20 Turismo Aonikenk
21 Buses Pacheco, Australmag (Car Rental)
23 Chile Típico
25 Stone Castle
28 Buses Mansilla
29 Austral Bus
33 Turibus
37 Spanish Consulate
38 Gabriela Mistral Mural
39 Aerovías DAP, DAP Antartica
40 Corporación Nacional Forestal
41 Mirador La Cruz
43 Turismo de Agostini
44 Turismo Viento Sur
48 CTC
50 Teatro Cervantes
51 Tercera Zona Naval
52 Chilesat
54 Turismo Pali Aike
55 Ladeco
58 Navimag, Turismo Comapa, Norweigan Consulate
60 Redbanc
61 Ñandú Café Grill
63 Post Office
65 Club de la Unión
66 Lubag
67 Kalkén Líneas Aéreas, Transporte Los Carlos
68 Citibank
69 Casa Braun-Menéndez
70 ENTel
72 LanChile
73 Buses Ghisoni, Magallanes Tour
74 Budget
75 Automóvil Club de Chile
76 Lavasol
77 Museo Naval y Marítimo
79 Sematur
80 Catedral
82 Belgian Consulate
83 Arka Patagonia
85 British Consulate, Broom Travel
86 Ladeco
87 Disco Yordi

Chile; luxury items like automobiles are much less expensive here, although the basic cost of living is higher.

Punta Arenas has experienced a large influx of foreign visitors, compared to their relative paucity in Argentina, but the town is utterly dead on Sunday, which is a good day to explore some of the surrounding area or start a trip to Torres del Paine.

History

Founded in 1848, Punta Arenas was originally a military garrison and penal settlement that proved to be conveniently situated for ships headed to California during the Gold Rush. Compared to the initial Chilean settlement at Fuerte Bulnes, 60 km south, the town had a better, more protected harbor, and superior access to wood and water. For many years, English maritime charts had called the site "Sandy Point', and this became its rough Spanish equivalent.

In Punta Arenas' early years, its economy depended on wild animal products, including sealskins, guanaco hides and feathers; mineral products, including coal, gold and guano; and firewood and timber. None of these was a truly major industry, and the economy did not take off until the last quarter of the 19th century, after the territorial governor authorized the purchase of 300 purebred sheep from the Falkland Islands. The success of this experiment encouraged others to invest in sheep and, by the turn of the century, there were nearly two million animals in the territory.

In 1875, the population of Magallanes province was barely 1000, but European immigration accelerated as the wool market boomed. Among the most notable immigrants were Portuguese businessman José Nogueira; Irish doctor Thomas Fenton, who founded one of the island's largest sheep stations; and José Menéndez, an Asturian entrepreneur who would become one of the wealthiest and most influential individuals not just in Patagonia, but in all of South America.

First engaged solely in commerce, Menéndez soon began to acquire pastoral property, founding the famous Sociedad Explotadora de Tierra del Fuego, which controlled nearly a million hectares in Magallanes alone and other properties across the border – one of Argentina's greatest estancias, near Río Grande, still bears the name of his wife María Behety. Together with another important family, the Brauns, the descendents of Menéndez figured among the wealthiest and most powerful regional elites in all of Latin America. Although few remain in Punta Arenas (having relocated to Santiago and Buenos Aires), their downtown mansions remain symbols of Punta Arenas' golden age.

Menéndez and his colleagues could not have built their commercial and pastoral empires without the labor of immigrants from many lands: English, Irish, Scots, Croats, French, Germans, Spaniards, Italians and others. On all sides of José Menéndez' opulent mausoleum, modest tombstones in the municipal cemetery reveal the origins of those whose efforts made his and other wool fortunes possible. Since the expropriation of the great estancias, including those of the Sociedad Explotadora, in the 1960s, the structure of land tenure is more equitable, but energy has eclipsed wool in the regional economy.

Orientation

Punta Arenas sits on a narrow shelf between the Andes to the west and the Strait of Magellan to the east. Consequently, the city has spread north and south from its original center between the port and the Plaza de Armas, properly known as Plaza Muñoz Gamero. Street names change on either side of the plaza, but street addresses on the plaza itself bear the name Muñoz Gamero. Most landmarks, and accommodations, are within a few blocks of the plaza. Mirador La Cruz, at Fagnano and Señoret, four blocks west of the plaza, provides a good view of town and the strait.

Most city streets are one-way, though grassy medians divide Av Bulnes and a few other major thoroughfares. There are two main routes out of town: Av Costanera leads south to Fuerte Bulnes and Av Bulnes heads north past the airport to become Ruta 9 to Puerto Natales, which branches off to Ruta 255 to Río Gallegos, Argentina. Travelers coming from Argentina will find Chilean traffic much less hazardous.

Information

Tourist Offices Sernatur (☎ 22-5385), the Chilean state tourist agency, is at Waldo Seguel 689, just off Plaza Muñoz Gamero. It's open weekdays 8:15 am to 5:45 pm, and has a friendly, helpful, and well-informed staff. It publishes an annually updated list of accommodations and transport, and provides a message board for foreign visitors.

The municipal Kiosko de Informaciones (☎ 22-3798) in the 700 block of Av Colón, between Bories and Magallanes, is open weekdays 9 am to 7 pm all year, and Saturdays 9 am to 7 pm in summer.

The Automóvil Club de Chile (ACCHI, ☎ 24-3675), O'Higgins 931, is the equivalent of Argentina's ACA and honors auto club memberships of other countries.

Foreign Consulates The Argentine Consulate (☎ 26-1912), 21 de Mayo 1878, is open weekdays 10 am to 2 pm. There are also several European and other South American consulates:

Belgium
    Roca 817, Oficina 61 (☎ 24-1472)
Brazil
    Arauco 769 (☎ 24-1093)
Germany
    Av El Bosque 0398 (☎ 21-2866)
Italy
    21 de Mayo 1569 (☎ 24-2497)
Netherlands
    Sarmiento 780 (☎ 24-8100)
Norway
    Av Independencia 830, 2nd floor (☎ 24-1437)
Spain
    José Menéndez 910 (☎ 24-3566)
UK
    Roca 924 (☎ 24-7020)

Money Money changing is easiest at cambios and travel agencies along Lautaro Navarro, which are open weekdays and Saturday mornings, but not Sundays. Traveler's checks are much easier to negotiate than in Argentina, but many hotels and restaurants also accept US dollars at a fair rate of exchange. Bus Sur, at Magallanes and Colón, will cash traveler's checks for Saturday afternoon arrivals

Redbanc has an ATM at Bories 970, half a block north of the plaza, but there are several others in the area.

Hotel staff will change US dollars at fair rates, but Argentine currency is better changed before leaving Río Gallegos.

Post & Telecommunications Correos de Chile, the central post office, is at Bories 911 near José Menéndez, a block north of the plaza.

Long-distance telephone service is much better and much cheaper in Chile than in Argentina. Chile's country code is 56, and Punta Arenas' area code is 61. CTC has a long-distance office at Nogueira 1116, which is on the southwest corner of the plaza, while Chilesat has one at Errázuriz 856. ENTel also has an office at Lautaro Navarro 931.

National Parks The Corporación Nacional Forestal (CONAF, ☎ 22-3841) is at José Menéndez 1147.

Travel Agencies In addition to the agencies listed under Organized Tours below, also try Broom Travel (☎ 22-8312) at Roca 924 (in the same building as the British Consulate), Turismo Comapa (☎ 24-1437) at Av Independencia 840, and Turismo de Agostini (☎ 22-1676) at Fagnano 518.

Film & Photography A good, conscientious place for film developing, including slides, is Todocolor, Chiloé 1422 between Av Indepencia and Boliviana.

Laundry Lavasol (☎ 24-3607), O'Higgins 969, isn't as cheap as it used to be, but the service is still fast and efficient.

Medical Services The hospital is at Arauco and Angamos.

Walking Tour

The city is compact and the main sights can be seen quickly on foot. The logical starting place is the lovingly maintained **Plaza Muñoz Gamero**, landscaped with a variety of exotic conifers and an interesting Victorian kiosk (1910) that sometimes contains handicraft displays. In the plaza's center, donated by wool baron José Menéndez in 1920, is a monument to the 400th anniversary of Magellan's voyage; Magellan stands on a pedestal, flanked on a lower level by a Selknam Indian symbolizing Tierra del Fuego and a Tehuelche symbolizing Patagonia. Behind the famous Portuguese navigator are a globe and a copy of his log; beneath him is a mermaid with Chilean and regional coats of arms.

Around the plaza are the **Club de la Unión** (once the Sara Braun mansion, built by a French architect and recently restored as a hotel/restaurant), the **catedral**, and other monuments to the city's turn-of-the-century splendor. At the northeast corner of the plaza, the present Citibank was the headquarters of the famous and powerful Sociedad Menéndez Behety.

Half a block north, at Magallanes 949, is the spectacular **Casa Braun-Menéndez**, the famous family's mansion which is now a cultural center and regional history museum. Three blocks west of the plaza, the outlandish **stone castle** at Av España 959 belonged to Charly Milward, whose equally eccentric exploits inspired his distant relation Bruce Chatwin to write the extraordinary travelogue *In Patagonia*.

Four blocks south of the plaza, at the foot of Av Independencia, is the entrance to the **puerto** (port), which is open to the public. At the end of the pier, you may see ships and sailors from Spain, Poland, Japan, France, the USA and many other countries, as well as local fishing boats, the Chilean navy, and countless seabirds. At the corner of Colón and O'Higgins, four blocks northeast of the plaza, is a very fine **mural** of Nobel Prize-winning poet Gabriela Mistral.

Six blocks north of the plaza, at Bories and Sarmiento, is the **Museo Salesiano** (Salesian Museum). Another four blocks north is the entrance to the **Cementerio Municipal** (Municipal Cemetery), an open-air historical museum in its own right.

Things to See

Most of the reminders of Punta Arenas' golden age are open to the public; those that are not museums rarely object to interested visitors taking a look around.

Casa Braun-Menéndez Also known as the Palacio Mauricio Braun, this opulent mansion testifies to the wealth and power of pioneer sheep farmers in the late 19th century. The last remaining daughter of the marriage between Mauricio Braun (brother of Sara Braun) and Josefina Menéndez Behety (daughter of José Menéndez and María Behety) is in her nineties and living in Buenos Aires, but the family has donated the house to the state. Much of it, including original furnishings, remains as it did when still occupied by the family. At present, only the main floor is open to the public, but restoration may permit access to the upper floors.

The museum also has excellent historical photographs and artifacts of early European settlement. The admission fee is modest (US$1.20), but there's an extra charge for photographing the interior. Hours are Tuesday to Sunday from 11 am to 4 pm. Access to the grounds is easiest from Magallanes, but the museum entrance is at the back of the house.

Museo Regional Salesiano Mayorino Borgatello The Salesian College Museum, at Av Bulnes 374 near Sarmiento, features anthropological, historical and natural history exhibits from materials collected by a missionary order that was especially influential in European settlement of the region. In summer, it is open Tuesday to Sunday from 10 am to noon and from 3 to 6 pm; in winter, weekday hours are from 3 to 6 pm only, while weekend hours are identical to summer. Admission costs US$1.35.

Museo Naval y Marítimo Punta Arenas' new naval and maritime museum occupies the 2nd and 3rd floors at O'Higgins 989, at the corner of Pedro Montt. It's open weekdays from 9:30 am to 12:30 pm, Saturdays from 10 am to 1 pm, and daily except Sunday from 3 to 6 pm.

Cementerio Municipal The walled municipal cemetery, at Av Bulnes 949, tells a great deal about the history and social structure of the region. The first families of Punta Arenas flaunted their wealth in death as in life – wool baron José Menéndez's extravagant tomb is, according to Bruce Chatwin, a scale replica of Rome's Vittorio Emmanuel monument. But the headstones among the topiary cypresses also tell the stories of Anglo, German, Scandinavian and Yugoslav immigrants who supported the wealthy families with their labor. There is also a monument to the now nearly extinct Onas. Open daily, the cemetery is about a 15-minute walk from the plaza, but you can also take any taxi colectivo from the entrance of the Casa Braun-Menéndez on Magallanes.

Instituto de la Patagonia Part of the Universidad de Magallanes, the Patagonian Institute features an interesting collection of early farm and industrial machinery imported from Europe, a typical pioneer house and shearing shed (both reconstructed), and a wooden-wheeled trailer that served as shelter for shepherds. Visitors can wander among the outdoor exhibits at will, but ask the caretaker at the library for admission to the buildings.

The library also has a display of historical maps, and a series of historical and scientific publications for sale to the public. A rather overgrown botanical garden, a small zoo, and experimental garden plots and greenhouses are also open to the public.

Admission costs US$1. Hours are weekdays 9 am to 12:30 pm and 2:30 to 6:30 pm. Weekend visits may be possible by prior arrangement. Any taxi colectivo to the Zona Franca (duty-free zone) will drop you across the street.

Organized Tours

Several agencies run trips to tourist sites near Punta Arenas, as well as to more distant destinations like Torres del Paine.

Turismo Pali Aike (☎ 22-3301), Lautaro Navarro 1129, goes to the Seno Otway penguin colony (US$12) daily at 3:30 pm, to Fuerte Bulnes (US$12) daily at 10 am, and to Río Verde (US$15) on Seno Skyring (where there's a hostería); all their tours include sandwiches and soft drinks. Arka Patagonia (☎ 22-6370), Roca 886, Local 7, also runs trips for similar prices, as do Turismo Aonikenk (☎ 22-8332) at Magallanes 619 and Turismo Viento Sur (☎ 22-5167) at Fagnano 565. It's possible to take more than one tour in a day, as these companies usually offer various trips daily.

DAP Antarctica (☎ 22-3340), O'Higgins 891, organizes all-inclusive, four-day kayak trips to Parque Nacional Torres del Paine for US$1600.

Boat Cruises

From November through April, Turismo Comapa (☎ 24-4448, fax 24-7514), Av Independencia 840, runs weeklong luxury cruises on the 100-passenger *Terra Australis* from Punta Arenas through the Cordillera de Darwin, the Beagle Channel and Puerto Williams, Ushuaia (Argentina) and back. While these cruises are expensive, starting at US$1022 per person double occupancy in low season (April) and reaching $3000 for a high season single, all meals are included and they do offer a chance to visit parts of the region that are otherwise very difficult and even more expensive to reach independently. It may be possible to do the leg between Punta Arenas and Ushuaia separately.

Special Events

One LP reader endorses February's Yugoslavian folk festival, with music, dancing and "all four food groups – fat, salt, carbos and alcohol".

Places to Stay – bottom end

Prices for accommodations have risen recently, but there are still good values.

Sernatur maintains a very complete list of accommodations and prices.

Camping *Camping Pudú*, at Km 10.5 north of town, has pleasant woodsy facilities, including barbecue pits and showers, but it's a bit inconvenient for backpackers and expensive for single people at US$10 per site.

Hostels Unquestionably the cheapest accommmodations in town arethe *Ejército de Salvación* (☎ 22-4039), Bellavista 577, for foreigners only (expect a bit of proselytizing). At the recommended *Casa del Deportista*, at O'Higgins 1205 near the port, rates are US$6 per person for a shared room in summer only; they sometimes have private rooms for couples. Open from November through March, the *Albergue Backpacker's Paradise* (☎ 22-2554), Ignacio Carrera Pinto 1022, charges US$6.50 for dormitory accommodations with pleasant common rooms, a kitchen, and cable TV.

Relocated at Bellavista 697 (six blocks south of Plaza Muñoz Gamero) after a fire destroyed its previous site, the *Colegio Pierre Fauré* (☎ 22-6256) is a private school that operates as a hostel in January and February; it may be able to accommodate visitors in other seasons. Singles cost US$7 with breakfast, US$6 without, but campers can also pitch a tent in the side garden for US$4 per person. All bathrooms are shared, but there's plenty of hot water, and it's a good place to hook up with other travellers.

The regular *Albergue Juvenil* (☎ 22-6705), Ovejero 265, is much less central, northeast of the cemetery; rates are US$8 per night. The *Albergue Hostelling International* (☎ 24-8543), part of Residencial Sonia at Pasaje Darwin 175, south of downtown, charges US$10 with hostel card.

Hospedajes There are inexpensive hospedajes in the port zone south of downtown, including the *Casa de Familia* (☎ 24-7687) at Paraguaya 150 for US$8 with breakfast. One reader very much liked *Hospedaje Nena* (☎ 24-2411), at Boliviana 366 four blocks south of the plaza, while others have exuberantly recommended homey *Hospedaje Guisande* (☎ 24-3295) at JM Carrera 1270 between Caupolicán and Quillota near the cemetery, for US$8 with breakfast, US$13 with breakfast and dinner.

Hotels & Residenciales *Residencial Roca* (☎ 24-3903), at Roca 1038 near O'Higgins, welcomes backpackers but is often full. Situated in a well-heated but leaky building, a single bed in a six-bed room costs US$8 without breakfast, while a private single costs US$11 when available. Other modest and modestly priced alternatives include *Residencial Oasis* (☎ 24-2307) at Fagnano 583, and the slightly more expensive *Residencial Sonia* (☎ 24-8543) at Pasaje Darwin 175. Recommended *Hostal Calafate* (☎ 24-8415), Lautaro Navarro 850, charges US$13 per person with a substantial breakfast, while *Hotel El Pionero* (☎ 24-8851), at Chiloé and Errázuriz, costs US$34 double.

Residencial Rubio (☎ 22-6458), Av España 640, is a good value at US$15/21 single/double with shared bath, US$24/29 with private bath; all rates include breakfast. *Residencial París* (☎ 22-3112), 4th floor, Nogueira 1116, half a block from Plaza Muñoz Gamero, costs US$16 per person, while old but spacious *Hotel Montecarlo* (☎ 22-3438), Av Colón 605, charges US$16/26 with shared bath, US$26/39 with private bath. Recommended *Hostal Koiuska* (☎ 22-8520), Waldo Seguel 480, charges US$20 per person.

Places to Stay – middle
Probably the best midrange value is *Hostal Chapital* (☎ 24-2237), Armando Sanhueza 974, which charges US$31/39 with shared bath, US$37/50 with private bath. At reader-endorsed *Hostal de la Patagonia* (☎ 24-1079), O'Higgins 478, rates are US$36/40 with shared bath, US$45/53 with private bath. *Hostal Carpa Manzano* (☎ 24-2296), Lautaro Navarro 336, is also worth a try for US$48/64.

Comfortably modern *Hotel Cóndor de Plata* (☎ 24-7987), Av Colón 556, costs US$46/53 – a better value than others charging considerably more. *Hotel Mercurio* (☎ 22-3430), Fagnano 595, is also modern, clean, and comfortable at US$49/62 with breakfast. Convenient *Hotel Plaza* (☎ 24-1300), at Nogueira 1116 one floor below Residencial París, charges US$54/68.

Places to Stay – top end

Perhaps the best in town, *Hotel Los Navegantes* (☎ 22-4877), José Menéndez 647, has rooms for US$103/131, while the slightly more central and refurbished *Hotel Cabo de Hornos* (☎ 22-2134), on the east side of Plaza Muñoz Gamero, charges US$129/150. The latter has a good but costly bar, and its solarium displays a number of stuffed birds, including rockhopper and macaroni penguins, which visitors to local penguin colonies are unlikely to see.

Part of the Sara Braun mansion has become *Hotel José Nogueira* (☎ 24-8840), half a block from Plaza Muñoz Gamero at Bories 959. It costs US$114/137, but selective backpackers can afford a drink or a meal in its conservatory/restaurant, beneath what may well be the world's most southerly grape arbor. Another new top-end choice is *Hotel Isla Rey Jorge* (☎ 22-2681), 21 de Mayo 1243, for US$102/136.

> **Food from the Sea**
>
> If a constant diet of Argentine beef has become tiresome, visitors to Chilean Patagonia can feast on the superb and varied seafood that typifies Chilean cuisine – both finfish and shellfish. Popular regional dishes include centolla (king crab), cholgas (mussels), cóngrio (conger eel), locos (abalone, the availability of which may be limited because of overexploitation), ostiones (scallops) and erizos (sea urchins), which are definitely an acquired taste. Travelers with a group should consider curanto, a tasty filling stew with shellfish, chicken, mutton, potatoes and vegetables. The traditional Chilean salad, consisting of tomatoes and onions, is simple but tasty. ∎

Places to Eat

Fusión (☎ 22-4704), Mejicana 654, offers a very good fixed price lunch for US$4, if you can tolerate the appalling music. *Quijote*, Lautaro Navarro 1087, also has reasonable lunches. *La Carioca* (☎ 22-4809), José Menéndez 600, offers good sandwiches and lager beer, although its pizzas are small and expensive. A good choice for breakfast and onces ('elevens', Chilean afternoon tea) is *Café Garogha* (☎ 24-1782), Bories 817. A portion of their "selva negra" chocolate cake is large enough for two, as are their sandwiches. *Lomit's*, José Menéndez 722, also serves excellent sandwiches.

A local institution at Mejicana 617 (the ground-level entrance to this upstairs restaurant is inconspicuous), *El Mercado* (☎ 24-7415) prepares a spicy ostiones al pil pil (a spicy scallop dish) and a delicate but filling chupe de locos (an abalone dish); prices are generally moderate. The *Centro Español* (☎ 24-2807), above the Teatro Cervantes on the south side of Plaza Muñoz Gamero, serves delicious cóngrio and ostiones, among other specialties. *Golden Dragon*, a Chinese restaurant at Colón 529, is also very good.

Highly regarded *Sotitos* (☎ 24-5365), O'Higgins 1138, serves outstanding if pricey dishes like centolla, but there are also more reasonably priced items on the menu. The same holds for nearby *El Beagle* (☎ 24-3057), O'Higgins 1077. Prices are moderate at *La Taberna de Silver* (☎ 22-5533), O'Higgins 1037, but its fish dishes are often deep-fried. Another recommendation, specializing in lamb, is *El Mesón del Calvo* (☎ 22-5015) at Jorge Montt 687.

Asturias (☎ 24-3763) at Lautaro Navarro 967 is worth a try at the upper end of the scale, as is *El Infante* (☎ 24-1331) at Magallanes 875. Recent readers' recommendations include *Venus* (☎ 24-1681), Pedro Montt 1046, and *Monaco* on Nogueira near the post office.

Entertainment

Since the end of the military dictatorship, which regularly enforced a curfew, Chilean nightlife has become more exuberant. *Café Garogha* has a lively crowd late into the evening, and sometimes provides live entertainment. As in any port, there are numerous bars: try the *Ñandú Café Grill*, at Waldo Seguel 670, which also serves meals. *Disco Yordi* is on Pedro Montt between O'Higgins and Lautaro Navarro.

Two central cinemas often show North American and European films: *Teatro Cervantes* (☎ 22-3225) is on the south side of Plaza Muñoz Gamero, while the *Cinema* is at Mejicana 777.

On the outskirts of downtown on Av Bulnes are the *Club Hípico* (municipal racetrack) and the *Estadio Fiscal* (stadium), where the local soccer league club plays.

Things to Buy

Punta Arenas' Zona Franca (duty-free zone) is a good place to replace a lost or stolen camera, and to buy film and other luxury items. Fujichrome slide film, 36 exposures, costs about US$5 per roll without developing, but it is increasingly difficult to find; print film is correspondingly cheap. Taxi colectivos run frequently from downtown to the Zona Franca, which is open daily except Sunday.

Chile Típico (☎ 22-5827), Ignacio Carrera Pinto 1015, offers artisanal items in copper, bronze, lapis lazuli, and other materials.

Getting There & Away

The tourist office distributes a useful brochure with complete information on all forms of transportation including those which go to or through Argentina and their schedules to and from Punta Arenas, Puerto Natales, and Tierra del Fuego. Note that discount airfares are available from the major airlines between Punta Arenas and mainland Chile but usually involve some restrictions.

Air LanChile (☎ 24-1232), Lautaro Navarro 999 at Pedro Montt, flies daily to Puerto Montt (US$196) and Santiago (US$317), and Sunday and Monday to Concepción (US$271). Children's fares (ages two to 12) are slightly more than half adult price.

Ladeco (☎ 22-6100), Lautaro Navarro 1155, flies daily to Puerto Montt (US$217) and Santiago (US$311), and on Saturdays and Sundays to Balmaceda/Coyhaique (US$117).

National Airlines (☎ 22-1636), at Bories and Ignacio Carrera Pinto, flies Monday, Tuesday, Friday, and Saturday to Concepción (US$226) and Santiago (US$282), and Wednesday, Friday, and Sunday to Puerto Montt (US$170).

Aerovías DAP (☎ 22-3340, fax 22-1693), O'Higgins 891, flies to Porvenir (US$18) and back at least twice daily, except Sunday, when there is only one flight. Monday, Wednesday, and Friday, it flies to and from Puerto Williams on Isla Navarino (US$69 one-way). It also has Tuesday, Thursday, and Sunday flights to Ushuaia, Argentina (US$60) and to Río Gallegos, Argentina (US$49), and flies daily except Sunday to Río Grande, Argentina (US$50). Children below the age of six travel half-price.

In summer, DAP has Friday flights to the Falkland Islands (US$355 one-way); in winter, these flights leave alternate Fridays. It also has monthly flights to Teniente Marsh air base in Antarctica for US$1000 single. The schedule permits one or two nights in Antarctica before returning to Punta Arenas.

Kaikén Líneas Aéreas (☎ 24-1321), Magallanes 974, flies daily except Sunday to Río Grande (US$60) and nine times weekly to Ushuaia (US$80); there are significant discounts for roundtrip tickets.

Bus Punta Arenas has no central bus terminal; each company has its own office from which its buses depart, although most of these are fairly close together, on or near Lautaro Navarro. There are direct buses to Puerto Natales, Río Grande, and Río Gallegos in Argentina, and to mainland Chilean destinations via Argentina. It makes sense to purchase tickets at least a couple hours in advance.

Buses Fernández (☎ 24-2313), Armando Sanhueza 745, which has a reputation for excellent service, runs five buses daily to Puerto Natales (US$7). Bus Sur (☎ 24-4464), at Magallanes and Colón, has three buses daily to Puerto Natales except Sunday, when it has only two.

Austral Bus (☎ 24-1708), José Menéndez 565, has one bus nightly at 7:30 pm to Puerto Natales, and also goes on Tuesdays to Puerto Montt (US$97). Buses Ghisoni (☎ 22-3205), Lautaro Navarro 971, goes sporadically to Puerto Montt (US$75).

Turibus (☎ 24-1463), José Menéndez 647, goes Tuesday, Thursday, and Saturday to Puerto Montt (US$80) and Santiago (US$100), and Wednesday and Saturday to Concepción (US$97). These trips take as long as two days, but the buses are very comfortable, with regular meal stops.

Several companies have numerous buses to Río Gallegos, Argentina (US$20, five hours). The most frequent is Buses Pingüino (☎ 24-1684), Armando Sanhueza 745. Buses Mansilla (☎ 22-1516) at José Menéndez 556, and Buses Ghisoni and Magallanes Tour (☎ 22-2078), both at Lautaro Navarro 975, also have several departures.

Buses Pacheco (☎ 24-2174), Av Colón 900, goes Tuesday, Thursday, and Saturday at 7 am to Río Grande in Argentine Tierra del Fuego (US$27), with connections to Ushuaia. Tuesday and Saturday at 7 am, Transporte Los Carlos (☎ 24-1321), Magallanes 974, goes to Río Grande and continues directly to Ushuaia (US$49).

Boat Transbordador Austral Broom (☎ 21-8100), Av Bulnes 05075, ferries passengers (US$6) and automobiles (US$35) between Punta Arenas and Porvenir, Tierra del Fuego, in 2½ hours; the *Melinka* sails Tuesday, Wednesday, Friday, Saturday, and Sunday at 9 am from the terminal at Tres Puentes, readily accessible by taxi colectivo from the Braun-Menéndez house. The return from Porvenir is normally at 2 pm, but on Sundays and holidays, when the ferry returns at 5 pm, it is possible to do this as a day trip.

The *Beaulieu*, a small cargo vessel, can take two or three passengers on its monthly trip to Puerto Williams, for US$300 per person return; the trip takes at least several days. Those with patience can sometimes obtain passage to Puerto Williams on board Chilean naval vessels. Inquire at Tercera Zona Naval, a beautiful Victorian building at Lautaro Navarro 1150.

Navimag (☎ 24-4448), which offers ferry service from Puerto Natales to Puerto Montt via the spectacular Chilean fjords, has an office at Av Independencia 830. For details, see the Puerto Natales entry below.

Getting Around
To/From the Airport Aeropuerto Presidente Carlos Ibáñez del Campo is 20 km north of town. Austral Bus runs minibuses to the airport from Hotel Cabo de Hornos, on Plaza Muñoz Gamero. DAP runs its own bus to the airport, while LanChile and Ladeco use local bus companies (US$1.25).

Bus & Colectivo Although most places of interest are within easy walking distance of downtown, public transportation is excellent to outlying sights like the Instituto de la Patagonia and the Zona Franca. Taxi colectivos, with numbered routes, are only slightly more expensive than buses (about US$0.30, a bit more late at night and on Sundays), much more comfortable, and much quicker.

Car Hertz (☎ 24-8742) is at Av Colón 798 and Ignacio Carrera Pinto 700, while Budget (☎ 24-1696) and the Automóvil Club de Chile (☎ 24-3675) are at O'Higgins 964 and 931, respectively. Other agencies include Internacional (☎ 22-8323) at Sarmiento 790-B, Australmag (☎ 24-2174) at Av Colón 900, and Lubag (☎ 24-2023) at Magallanes 970.

To replace a shattered windshield on a private car – not an unusual occurence on Patagonia roads – go to Solovidrios (☎ 22-4835), Mejicana 762. Prices here are a fraction of what they are in Argentina.

AROUND PUNTA ARENAS
Penguin Colonies
Also known as the jackass penguin for its characteristic braying sound, the Magellanic penguin *(Spheniscus magellanicus)* comes ashore in spring to breed and lay its eggs in sandy burrows or under shrubs a short distance inland. There are two substantial colonies near Punta Arenas: the easiest to reach is the mainland pingüinera on **Seno Otway** (Otway Sound), about an hour northwest of the city, while the larger and more interesting **Monumento Natural Los Pingüinos** is accessible only by boat to Isla Magdalena or Isla Marta in the strait. Several species of gulls and cormorants are also common, along with rheas and southern sea lions.

Magellanic penguins are naturally curious and tame, though if approached too quickly they scamper into their burrows or toboggan awkwardly across the sand back into the water. If approached too closely, they will bite, and their bills can open a cut large enough to require stitches – never stick your hand or face into a burrow. The least disruptive way to observe or photograph them is to seat yourself among the burrows and wait for their curiosity to get the better of them.

Since there is no scheduled public transport to either site, it is necessary to rent a car or take a tour to visit them. For details, see the Organized Tours and Getting There & Away entries for Punta Arenas. Admission to the sites costs US$2.50 per person.

Puerto Hambre & Fuerte Bulnes
Founded in 1584 by an overly optimistic Pedro Sarmiento de Gamboa, "Ciudad del Rey don Felipe" was one of Spain's most inauspicious (and short-lived) American outposts. Not until the mid-19th century was there a permanent European presence at suitably named Puerto Hambre ('Port Famine'), where a plaque from 1965 commemorates the 125th anniversary of the arrival of the Pacific Steam Navigation Company's ships *Chile* and *Peru*.

Named for the Chilean president who ordered the occupation of the territory in 1843, the once remote outpost of Fuerte Bulnes is 55 km south of Punta Arenas. Only a few years after its founding, it was abandoned because of its exposed site, lack of potable water, poor, rocky soil, and inferior pasture.

A good gravel road runs from Punta Arenas to the restored wooden fort, where a fence of sharpened stakes surrounds the blockhouse, barracks, and chapel, but there is no interpretive material whatsoever. Nor is there any scheduled public transport, but several travel agencies make half-day excursions to Fuerte Bulnes and Puerto Hambre, now a quiet fishing village where visitors can see the ruins of an early church; for details, see the Organized Tours entry for Punta Arenas. There are good picnic sites and pleasant walks along the coast.

Estancia San Gregorio
Some 125 km northeast of Punta Arenas, straddling Ruta 255 to Río Gallegos (Argentina), this once enormous (90,000 hectares) estancia is now a cooperative. Since the abandonment of most of the main buildings (employee residences, warehouses, chapel, and pulpería), it has the aspect of an enormous ghost town. The casco still belongs to a descendent of the famous and influential Menéndez family, but the cooperative uses the large shearing shed.

The nearest accommodations are *Hostería Tehuelche* (☎ 22-1270), 29 km northeast, where buses to and from Río Gallegos stop for lunch or dinner; this is also the junction for the road to the ferry that crosses the Strait of Magellan from Punta Delgada to Chilean Tierra del Fuego. Until 1968, the hostería was the casco for Estancia Kimiri Aike, pioneered by the Woods, a British immigrant family. It has clean, comfortable rooms for US$25/35 a single/double, and a good restaurant and bar.

PUERTO NATALES
Black-necked swans paddle serenely around the gulls and cormorants that perch on the rotting jetties of scenic Puerto

Natales, on the eastern shore of Seno Última Esperanza (Last Hope Sound). Traditionally dependent on wool, mutton, and fishing, this port of 18,000 people is the southern terminus for the scenic ferry from Puerto Montt and an essential stopover for hikers and other visitors en route to Parque Nacional Torres del Paine. It also offers the best access to Glaciar Serrano in Parque Nacional Bernardo O'Higgins and the famous Cueva del Milodón, and many travelers continue to Argentina's Parque Nacional Los Glaciares via the coal-mining town of Río Turbio.

The visitor season starts in October and runs until April, though the peak is January and February. During the rest of the year, access to attractions like Torres del Paine and the Balmaceda glacier may be much reduced.

History

The first Europeans to visit Última Esperanza were the 16th-century Spaniards Juan Ladrillero and Pedro Sarmiento de Gamboa, in search of a route to the Pacific, but their expeditions left no permanent legacy. In part because of Indian resistance, no Europeans located here until the late 19th century, when German explorer Hermann Eberhard established a sheep estancia near Puerto Prat, the area's initial settlement, later superseded by Puerto Natales.

The dominant economic enterprise was the slaughterhouse and meat packing plant at Bories, operated by the Sociedad Explotadora de Tierra del Fuego, which processed livestock from throughout southwestern Argentina as well. This factory still operates, although it has declined in importance.

Orientation

About 250 km northwest of Punta Arenas via half-paved Ruta 9, Puerto Natales itself is compact enough that walking suffices for most purposes. Although its grid is more irregular than many Chilean cities, most destinations are easily visible from the waterfront, where the Costanera Pedro Montt runs roughly north-south. The other main commercial streets are the east-west Av Bulnes and the north-south Av Baquedano. Bories, and the Cueva del Milodón are north of town on the graveled highway to Torres del Paine.

Information

Tourist Office Sernatur (☎ 41-2125), which has maps and information about hotels, restaurants, and transportation, occupies a chalet on the Costanera Pedro Montt at the intersection with the Philippi diagonal. Its hours are 8:30 am to 1 pm and 2:30 to 6:30 pm weekdays all year, 9 am to 1 pm weekends in summer (December to March) only.

Money Stop Cambios, Baquedano 380, will change US dollars and traveler's checks. There are no ATMs, but Banco O'Higgins at Bulnes 637 will make cash advances on MasterCard.

Post & Telecommunications Correos de Chile is directly on the Plaza de Armas at Eberhard 423, near Tomás Rogers; it also contains the offices of Telex Chile. CTC, Blanco Encalada 298, operates long-distance services 8 am to 10 pm daily. Puerto Natales' area code is 61 (the same as Punta Arenas).

National Parks CONAF (☎ 41-14380 is at Ignacio Carrera Pinto 566.

Travel Agencies Turis-Ann (☎ 41-1141) is at Tomás Rogers 258; see also Organized Tours below.

Laundry Papagayo II, Bulnes 513, offers a 10% discount for loads prior to 10 am.

Medical Services Hospital Puerto Natales (☎ 41-1533) is at the corner of O'Higgins and Ignacio Carrera Pinto.

Museo Histórico Municipal

Puerto Natales' modest municipal museum has natural history items comprised mostly of stuffed animals, archaeological artifacts including arrowheads and spearpoints of

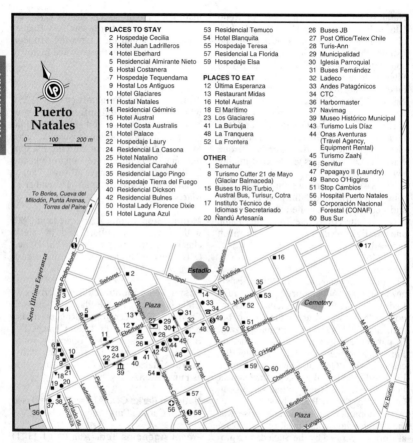

Puerto Natales

0   100   200 m

To Bories, Cueva del
Milodón, Punta Arenas,
Torres del Paine

PLACES TO STAY		
2	Hospedaje Cecilia	
3	Hotel Juan Ladrilleros	
4	Hotel Eberhard	
5	Residencial Almirante Nieto	
6	Hostal Costanera	
7	Hospedaje Tequendama	
9	Hostal Los Antiguos	
10	Hotel Glaciares	
11	Hostal Natales	
14	Residencial Géminis	
16	Hotel Austral	
19	Hotel Costa Australis	
21	Hotel Palace	
22	Hospedaje Laury	
24	Residencial La Casona	
25	Hotel Natalino	
26	Residencial Carahué	
35	Residencial Lago Pingo	
38	Hospedaje Tierra del Fuego	
40	Residencial Dickson	
42	Residencial Bulnes	
50	Hostal Lady Florence Dixie	
51	Hotel Laguna Azul	

53 Residencial Temuco
54 Hotel Blanquita
55 Hospedaje Teresa
57 Residencial La Florida
59 Hospedaje Elsa

PLACES TO EAT
12 Última Esperanza
13 Restaurant Midas
16 Hotel Austral
18 El Marítimo
23 Los Glaciares
41 La Burbuja
48 La Tranquera
52 La Frontera

OTHER
1 Sernatur
8 Turismo Cutter 21 de Mayo
   (Glaciar Balmaceda)
15 Buses to Río Turbio,
   Austral Bus, Turisur, Cotra
17 Instituto Técnico de
   Idiomas y Secretariado
20 Ñandú Artesanía

26 Buses JB
27 Post Office/Telex Chile
28 Turis-Ann
29 Municipalidad
30 Iglesia Parroquial
31 Buses Fernández
32 Ladeco
33 Andes Patagónicos
34 CTC
36 Harbormaster
37 Navimag
39 Museo Histórico Municipal
43 Turismo Luis Díaz
44 Onas Aventuras
   (Travel Agency,
   Equipment Rental)
45 Turismo Zaahj
46 Servitur
47 Papagayo II (Laundry)
49 Banco O'Higgins
51 Stop Cambios
56 Hospital Puerto Natales
58 Corporación Nacional
   Forestal (CONAF)
60 Bus Sur

both stone and whalebone, ethnographic materials like a Yahgan canoe and Tehuelche bolas, and historical photographs of Captain Eberhard and the development of Natales. At Bulnes 285, it's open Tuesday to Sunday, 3 to 6:15 pm.

Language Schools
The Instituto Técnico de Idiomas y Secretariado, Bulnes 1231, offers intensive Spanish courses.

Organized Tours
Puerto Natales' many travel agencies offer visits to the main local attractions like

Bories, the Cueva del Milodón, and Torres del Paine. English-speaking Eduardo Scott at Hotel Austral (see Places to Stay) can take eight to 10 passengers to Torres del Paine and other destinations in his minibus. Andes Patagónicos (☎ 41-1594), Blanco Encalada 226, is a good place to confirm airline reservations, and Stop Cambios (☎ 41-1393), Baquedano 380, has similar services.

Turismo Luis Díaz (☎ 41-1050), Bulnes 433, runs one- and two-day tours to Torres del Paine, and also goes to Cueva del Milodón and to Argentina's Parque Nacional Los Glaciares (see the El Calafate section in the Patagonia chapter). Three-day excursions to Torres del Paine cost about US$120 per person with Buses Fernández.

Onas Aventuras (☎ 41-1321), Bulnes 453, rents camping equipment and also offers sea kayaking and trekking trips. Both Andes Patagónicos and Turismo Díaz rent camping equipment.

Places to Stay – bottom end

Puerto Natales is popular with budget travelers, but competition keep prices reasonable. When your bus arrives, you may be buried in business cards or slips of paper offering bottom-end accommodations, most of which include breakfast. Quality is usually good and often excellent.

Prices start around US$5 per person at recommended *Hospedaje Elsa* (☎ 41-1807), O'Higgins 657, including breakfast and hot showers. *Residencial La Florida* (☎ 41-1361), O'Higgins 431, costs US$5/9 single/double with shared bath, while *Residencial Dickson* (☎ 41-1218), Bulnes 307, charges US$5.50 single. Rates are about US$7 per person at *Residencial Lago Pingo* (☎ 41-1026), Bulnes 808, and *Hospedaje Laury*, Bulnes 222.

Convenient to the ferry, *Hospedaje Tierra del Fuego*, Av Bulnes 29, charges US$8 with shared bath. Comparably priced *Hospedaje Tequendama*, Ladrilleros 141, is very obliging but rooms are basic and some are very dark. For US$8, Swiss-run *Hospedaje Cecilia* (☎ 41-1797), Tomás Rogers 64, has delicious breakfasts with fresh bread and muesli, though some rooms are small. *Hospedaje Teresa*, Esmeralda 463, is very comparable, as is *Residencial Temuco* (☎ 41-1120), Ramírez 310.

Recommended *Residencial Almirante Nieto* (☎ 41-2249), Bories 206, charges US$9 a single. Slightly dearer, around US$10, are *Residencial La Bahía* (☎ 41-1297) at Serrano 434 (three blocks south of Yungay), *Residencial Carahué* (☎ 41-1339) at Bulnes 370, and attractive *Residencial La Casona*, Bulnes 280. Very clean, friendly *Residencial Géminis* (☎ 41-

2081), Philippi 653 at the north end of Blanco Encalada, has doubles for US$15.

Places to Stay – middle

More businesslike than friendly, well-kept *Hostal Los Antiguos* (☎ 41-1885), Ladrilleros 195, charges US$13 single. A traditional midrange favorite is Eduardo Scott's *Hotel Austral* (☎ 41-1593), Valdivia 955; rooms with shared bath cost US$13/21, while those with private bath are US$19/27. For about the same price, *Hostal Costanera* (☎ 41-1273) at Ladrilleros 106 is a lesser value with music in every room – whether or not you want it. *Hostal Natales* (☎ 41-1098), Eberhard 250, charges US$19/27 with private bath.

At *Residencial Bulnes* (☎ 41-1307), Bulnes 407, rates are US$19/27 with shared bath, US$25/37 with private bath. *Hotel Blanquita* (☎ 41-1874), Ignacio Carrera Pinto 409, charges US$29/37 with private bath. At recommended *Hotel Natalino* (☎ 41-1968), Eberhard 371 near Tomás Rogers, rooms with private bath cost US$30/40.

Places to Stay – top end

Top-end rates start around US$47/54 at *Hotel Laguna Azul* (☎ 41-1207), Baquedano 380. The new and attractive *Hostal Lady Florence Dixie* (☎ 41-1158), set back from the street at Bulnes 659, charges US$55/70, while the equally new *Hotel Glaciares* (☎ 41-2189), Eberhard 104, costs US$65/75.

Clearly showing its age, the well-worn *Hotel Palace* (☎ 41-1134) at Ladrilleros 209 costs US$ 68/82, while the comparable *Hotel Juan Ladrilleros* (☎ 41-1652) at Costanero Pedro Montt 161 goes for US$68/79. For US$83/101, the waterfront *Hotel Eberhard* (☎ 41-1208), Costanera Pedro Montt 25 at Señoret, is now badly overpriced but has an excellent dining room with a panoramic view of the sound.

Unfortunately, fast-growing Puerto Natales is presently pouring raw sewage into the sound, directly across from the otherwise sparkling new and attractive *Hotel Costa Australis* (☎ 41-2000), at the corner of the Costanera Pedro Montt and Bulnes. Room rates start at US$100/110 for singles/doubles with a town view, rising to US$120/130 with sea view; suites cost US$240/250. Note that these prices do not include 20% IVA.

Places to Eat

For a small provincial town, Puerto Natales has excellent restaurants, specializing in good and reasonably priced seafood. Highly recommended *La Frontera*, on Bulnes between Baquedano and Ramírez, has superb home-cooked meals for only US$4, but the service can be a bit absent-minded. Popular *El Marítimo*, a moderately priced seafood restaurant at Costanera Pedro Montt 214, corner of Eberhard, is deservedly doing excellent business.

Popular *La Tranquera* (☎ 41-1039), Bulnes 579, has good food, friendly service, reasonable prices and one of the continent's most hilarious English language menus (where else can you get "poor eel" and "chicken in a gas cooker'?). Another good, popular and lively place is *Restaurant Midas* (☎ 41-1606), on the Plaza de Armas at Tomás Rogers 169. Other good choices include *La Burbuja* at Bulnes 371, *Última Esperanza* (☎ 41-1391) at Eberhard 354, and *Los Glaciares* on Eberhard between Barros Arana and Magallanes.

Hotel Austral has a good restaurant (serving a steady diet of salmon), while the huge dining room at unpretentious *La Bahía* (☎ 41-1297), Serrano 434, can accommodate large groups for a superb curanto, with sufficient notice. It's less central than most other restaurants in town, but still reasonable walking distance.

Things to Buy

At Bulnes 44, Ñandú Artesanía has a small but good selection of crafts, and also sells local maps and books.

Getting There & Away

Air Puerto Natales has no regular air services, though they may commence soon; at present, the nearest commercial airport is at Punta Arenas, though the Argentine air force has passenger flights (which must be arranged in Argentina) to nearby Río Turbio, just across the border. Buses to Punta Arenas will drop passengers at the airport.

As of writing, the local Ladeco office (☎ 41-1236) at Bulnes 530 was due to move to Tomás Rogers and Bories. Andes Patagónicos has a computerized airline information service for reservations and information on other airlines, such as Lan-Chile and DAP.

Bus Puerto Natales has no central bus terminal, though several companies stop at the junction of Valdivia and Baquedano. Buses Fernández (☎ 41-1111) at Eberhard 555 and Bus Sur (☎ 41-1325) at Baquedano 534 provide seven buses daily to Punta Arenas (US$7). Austral Bus (☎ 41-1415), at Valdivia and Baquedano, goes daily to Punta Arenas.

In summer, Bus Sur also goes daily to Parque Nacional Torres del Paine (US$7 single, slightly cheaper return), weekdays to Río Turbio (US$3) and twice weekly to Río Gallegos, Argentina (US$19). El Pingüino goes Wednesday and Sunday at noon to Río Gallegos (US$18). Turismo Zaahj (☎ 41-2260), Bulnes 459, runs buses to El Calafate, Argentina, in summer only (US$32) on Monday, Wednesday and Saturday at 7:30 am.

Servitur (☎ 41-1858), Prat 353, goes to Torres del Paine daily, as does Buses JB (☎ 41-1707), Bulnes 370. Turismo Luis Díaz, Bulnes 433, operates buses to Torres del Paine via Laguna Amarga.

Turisur and Cotra have frequent buses from the corner of Philippi and Baquedano to Río Turbio (US$3), where it is possible to make connections to Río Gallegos and to Calafate.

Boat Navimag (☎ 41-1421), Costanera Pedro Montt 380, operates the car/passenger ferry *MV Puerto Edén* to Puerto Montt every seven to 10 days all year, though dates and times vary according to weather and tides. The four-day, three-night voyage is heavily booked in summer, so try to reserve as far ahead as possible.

Accommodations in all categories are very comfortable, and include breakfast, lunch, and dinner, but incidentals like drinks and snacks are extra. There are many activities on board, but no laundry facilities. High season is November through April, while low season is May through October. Fares, which vary according to view and private or shared bath, are as follows:

Cabina Armador	High Season	Low Season
Single	US$800	US$700
Double	US$500	US$400
Triple	US$400	US$300
Cabina AA		
Single	US$650	US$450
Double	US$400	US$300
Triple	US$330	US$250
Quadruple	US$250	US$170
Literas (Bunks)		
AA	US$250	US$170
A	US$220	US$140
B	US$200	US$130
Económica	US$120	US$110

Getting Around

Both Andes Patagónicos and Luis Díaz (above) have rental vehicles, which can be a reasonable alternative to buses if several riders share expenses.

AROUND PUERTO NATALES
Bories

Built in 1913 with British capital, the Sociedad Explotadora's Puerto Bories **Frigorífico** (meat freezer), once processed enormous quantities of beef and mutton, and also shipped tallow, hides and wool from estancias in Chile and Argentina for export to Europe. Its operations, four km north of Puerto Natales, are now much reduced, but there remain several unique metal-clad buildings and houses, classic representatives of hybrid Victorian/Magellanic architecture.

Glaciar Serrano

This otherwise inaccessible glacier in Parque Nacional Bernardo O'Higgins is the final destination of a spectacular four-hour boat ride from Puerto Natales through Seno Última Esperanza to the jetty at Puerto Toro, where a footpath leads to the base of the Serrano Glacier and, on a clear day, the Torres del Paine are visible in the distance to the north. En route, passengers will glimpse the frigorífico at Bories, several small estancias whose only access to Puerto Natales is over water, numerous glaciers and waterfalls, a large cormorant rookery, a smaller sea lion rookery, and occasional Andean condors. The return trip takes the same route.

Daily in summer, weather permitting, Turismo Cutter 21 de Mayo (☎ 41-1176), Ladrilleros 171 in Puerto Natales, runs its namesake cutter or the motor yacht *Alberto de Agostini* to Balmaceda, and will go at other times if demand is sufficient. The cost is US$24 per person. Decent meals are available on board for about US$6, as are hot and cold drinks. For reservations, contact the owners, who can also arrange hiking and rafting excursions to Torres del Paine via Paso de los Toros and Río Serrano.

Cueva del Milodón

In the 1890s, Hermann Eberhard discovered the well-preserved remains of an enormous ground sloth in a cave at this national monument, 24 km northwest of Puerto Natales. Twice the height of a human, the milodón was an herbivorous mammal that pulled down small trees and branches for their succulent leaves; like the mammoth and many other American megafauna, it became extinct near the end of the Pleistocene era.

Bruce Chatwin's literary travelogue *In Patagonia* amusingly recounts the many fanciful stories about the milodón, including legends that Indians kept it penned as a domestic animal and that some specimens remained alive into the last century. Paleo-Indians did occupy the cave as a shelter, long after the animal's extinction. There are smaller caves nearby which can be explored with a torch.

In the cave, which is 30 meters high, 80

meters wide, and 200 meters deep, stands a tacky full-size replica of the animal. LP readers Ru Smith and Cristina Vargas write that the cave itself formed at the base of a Cretaceous conglomeratic submarine channel fill of the Lago Sofia Formation. This formation overlay more easily eroded mudstones and sandstones of the Cerro Toro Formation, which were later uplifted from depths between 1000 and 2000 meters. (Readers interested in more detail should seek out an article by Winn and Dott in the journal *Sedimentology* (Vol. 26, pp 203 – 228, 1979).)

Although the closest hotel accommodations are at Puerto Natales, camping and picnicking are possible near the site. CONAF charges US$4 for admission, less for Chilean nationals and children. Buses to Torres del Paine will drop you at the entrance, which is a several km walk from the cave proper. Alternatively, take a taxi or hitch from Puerto Natales.

The reddish brown guanaco, related to the domesticated llama, chews cud much like a cow.

PARQUE NACIONAL TORRES DEL PAINE

Soaring almost vertically more than 2000 meters above the Patagonian steppe, the Torres del Paine (Towers of Paine) are spectacular granite pillars, which were originally magmatic intrusions that formed resistant granite beneath the surface of the earth; erosion of the weaker surrounding rock exposed them. These pillars dominate the landscape of what may be South America's finest national park, a miniature Alaska of shimmering turquoise lakes, roaring creeks, rivers and waterfalls, sprawling glaciers, dense forests, and abundant wildlife. The issue is not whether to come here, but how much time to spend.

Before its creation in 1959, the park was part of a large sheep estancia; it is now recovering from nearly a century of over-exploitation of its pastures, forests and wildlife. It shelters large and growing herds of guanacos (relatives of the domesticated llama of the central Andes), flocks of the flightless ostrich-like rhea (known locally as the ñandú), Andean condors, flamingos, and many other species. Since 1978, it has been part of the United Nations' World Biosphere Reserve system.

The park's outstanding wildlife conservation success has undoubtedly been the guanaco *(Lama guanicoe)*, which grazes the open steppes where its main natural enemy, the puma, cannot approach undetected. After more than a decade of effective protection from hunters and poachers, the guanaco barely flinches when humans or vehicles approach. The elusive huemul, or Chilean deer, is much more difficult to spot.

For hikers and backpackers, this 240,000-hectare World Biosphere Reserve is an unequalled destination, offering a well-developed trail network as well as opportunities for cross-country travel. The weather is changeable, with the strong westerlies that typify Patagonia, but very long summer days make outdoor activities possible late into the evening. Good foulweather gear is essential, and a warm sleeping bag and good tent are imperative for

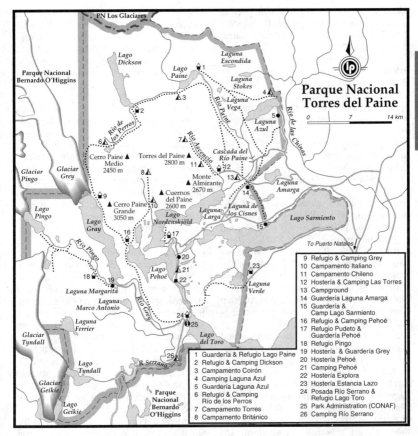

Parque Nacional Torres del Paine

0   7   14 km

1   Guardería & Refugio Lago Paine
2   Refugio & Camping Dickson
3   Campamento Coirón
4   Camping Laguna Azul
5   Guardería Laguna Azul
6   Refugio & Camping Río de los Perros
7   Campamento Torres
8   Campamento Británico
9   Refugio & Camping Grey
10 Campamento Italiano
11 Campamento Chileno
12 Hostería & Camping Las Torres
13 Campground
14 Guardería Laguna Amarga
15 Guardería & Camp Lago Sarmiento
16 Refugio & Camping Pehoé
17 Refugio Pudeto & Guardería Pehoé
18 Refugio Pingo
19 Hostería & Guardería Grey
20 Hostería Pehoé
21 Camping Pehoé
22 Hostería Explora
23 Hostería Estancia Lazo
24 Posada Río Serrano & Refugio Lago Toro
25 Park Administration (CONAF)
26 Camping Río Serrano

To Puerto Natales

those undertaking the extremely popular Paine circuit.

Guided daytrips from Puerto Natales are possible, but permit only a superficial reconnaissance. It is better to explore the several options for staying at the park, including camping at both backcountry and improved sites, or staying at the guest houses and hotels near park headquarters and at Lago Pehoé.

Orientation

Parque Nacional Torres del Paine is 112 km north of Puerto Natales via a decent but sometimes bumpy gravel road that passes Villa Cerro Castillo, where there is a summer border crossing into Argentina at Cancha Carrera. The road continues 38 km north, where there is junction with a 27-km lateral along the south shore of Lago Sarmiento to the little-visited Laguna Verde sector of the park.

Three km north of this junction the highway forks west along the north shore of Lago Sarmiento to the Portería Sarmiento, the park's main entrance; from this intersection it's another 37 km south to the Administración (park headquarters). About 12 km east of Portería Sarmiento, another lateral forks north and, three km farther, forks again; the northern branch goes to Guardería Laguna Azul, while the western branch goes to Guardería Laguna Amarga, the starting point for the Paine Circuit.

Information

Entrances There is an entry charge of US$12 per person (less for Chilean nationals), collected at the Portería Sarmiento, where maps and informational brochures are available, or at Guardería Laguna Amarga (where most buses now stop inbound), Guardería Lago Verde, or Guardería Laguna Azul. There are recent reports of a US$150 fee for climbers.

Books & Maps Both the Sociedad Turística Kaonikén in Puerto Natales and Kiosko Puma in Punta Arenas publish good topographic maps of the park at a scale of 1:100,000 with 100-meter contour intervals, which include detailed routes of the Paine circuit and other park trails. Both are widely available in Punta Arenas, Puerto Natales, and the park itself; the Puma map is more current and detailed, but either is suitable for exploring the park.

For more information on trekking and camping, including detailed contour maps, consult Clem Lindenmayer's LP guide *Trekking in the Patagonian Andes*. Bradt Publications' *Backpacking in Chile & Argentina* and William Leitch's *South America's National Parks* both have useful chapters on Torres del Paine, but are less thorough on practical information. On wildlife, LP readers have recommended *The Fauna of Torres del Paine* (1993) by Gladys Garay N and Oscar Guineo N, available in the Museo Salesiano in Punta Arenas.

Trekking

Paine Circuit Approaching the point of gridlock, this inordinately popular trek usually begins at Guardería Laguna Amarga, where most hikers disembark from the bus and do the route counterclockwise. It's also possible to start at Portería Sarmiento, adding two hours to the

hike, or at the Administración, which means a much longer approach. All hikers destined for the circuit are required to register with the rangers at the guarderías or at the Administración, and to give your passport number. Very determined hikers can probably walk the circuit in five days, but most should schedule seven.

In some ways, the Paine circuit is less challenging than in past years, as simple but sturdy bridges have replaced log crossings and once-hazardous stream fords, and park concessionaires have built comfortable refugios with hot showers and meals at regular intervals along the trail. In theory, this makes it possible to walk from hut to hut without carrying a tent, but the changeable weather still makes a tent desirable because of the possibility of being caught in between. Camping is still possible, but only at designated sites; there is a modest charge for camping the new refugios.

While the trek is tamer than it once was, it is not without difficulty and hikers have suffered serious injuries and even death; for this reason, CONAF no longer permits solo treks, but it is not difficult to link up with others. Allot at least five days, preferably more for bad weather; consider at least one layover day, since the route is strenuous, especially the rough segments and over the 1241-meter pass to or from the Río de los Perros and on the east side of Lago Grey.

Be sure to bring food, since prices at the small grocery at Posada Río Serrano near park headquarters are at least 50% higher than in Punta Arenas or Puerto Natales, and the selection is minimal. In late summer, the abandoned garden at Refugio Dickson still produces an abundant harvest of gooseberries.

Andescape (☎ 41-2592), Prat 353 in Puerto Natales, opened refugios at Lago Pehóe and Lago Grey in the summer of 1994 – 1995, and was scheduled to open others at Río de los Perros and Lago Dickson in the summer of 1995 – 1996. For trekkers from Guardería Laguna Amarga, this would mean roughly an 11-hour hike to the first refugio at Dickson, though there is a rustic shelter at Campamento Coirón, about three hours earlier.

Andescape's refugios have 32 bunks, not including sheets or sleeping bags, for US$12.50 per night, including kitchen privileges. Breakfast is available for US$3, lunch for US$6, and dinner for US$9, or all meals for US$17. Camping costs US$3 per person, with showers an additional US$2. Rental equipment is also available at reasonable prices.

Other Paine Trails Both visitors lacking the time to hike the Paine circuit or those preferring a bit more solitude have alternatives within the park. The next best choice for seeing the high country is the shorter but almost equally popular trail up the **Río Ascencio** to a treeless tarn beneath the eastern face of the Torres del Paine proper. From Guardería Laguna Amarga, there's a narrow but passable road to the trailhead beyond Hostería Las Torres, where a bridge now crosses the river and avoids a sometimes hazardous ford. The trail continues up the canyon to Campamento Chileno and Campamento Torres, which are the only legal campsites.

From Campamento Torres, a steep and sometimes ill-marked trail climbs through patchy beech forests to the barren tarn above, which provides dramatic views of the nearly vertical torres. This is a feasible day hike from Laguna Amarga, and a fairly easy one from Hostería Las Torres, but it's also an exceptional area for camping despite its popularity (try to arrive early to get the best sites).

Comparable to the Río Ascencio trail is the trail up the **Valle Francés**, between 3050-meter Paine Grande to the west and the lower but still spectacular Cuernos del Paine (Horns of Paine) to the east. It's a seven-hour, one-way hike from the Administración, but it is also accessible by going cross-country from Hostería Las Torres along the north shore of Lago Nordenskjöld. Trekkers can pitch their tents at the Campamento Italiano at the foot of the valley, or at the Campamento Británico at its head.

Floods in the early 1980s destroyed several bridges, requiring CONAF to relocate the part of the Paine circuit that formerly crossed the Río Paine at the outlet of **Lago Paine**, the northern shore of which is now accessible only from Laguna Azul. This four-hour, one-way hike, offering considerably greater solitude than the Paine circuit, leads to the rustic Refugio Lago Paine, a former outside house on the former estancia.

From the outlet of Lago Grey, 18 km northwest of the Administación by a passable road, a good trail leads to **Lago Pingo**, on the eastern edge of the Campo de Hielo Sur (southern continental ice field). Much less frequented than other park trails, this route has two very rustic refugios en route.

Horseback Riding
See Brigitte Buhoffer at her house at Río Serrano about riding horses, or contact Baqueano Zamora (☎ 41-1594). Rates are about US$15 for two hours or US$55 a full day, lunch included.

Places to Stay & Eat
Camping The most central organized campsites are *Camping Pehoé*, which charges US$14 for up to six people, and *Camping Río Serrano*, which costs US$11. The fees include firewood and hot showers, available every morning but in evenings by request only.

Camping Las Torres, on the grounds of Estancia Cerro Paine, charges US$4 per person and is popular with hikers acclimatizing by taking the short trek up the Río Ascencio before doing the Paine circuit. The more remote and recently privatized *Camping Laguna Azul* charges US$14 per night.

Hotels & Hosterías Park accommodations are often crowded in summer, despite a construction boom within the park boundaries, and reservations are a good idea. However, low cost and even free accommodations exist – a short distance from the Administración, *Refugio Lago*

Toro has bunks and hot showers for US$5, plus US$2 for hot showers, but your own sleeping bag is essential. Other refugios, such as that at Pudeto on Lago Pehoé are free but *very* rustic (hard wooden bunks, no mattresses, mice).

Posada Río Serrano (☎ 69-1931), a remodeled estancia house near the Administración, has rooms with shared bath for US$47/53, while those with private bath go for US$75/80. It has a reasonably priced restaurant and bar, with occasional informal, live entertainment, but several readers consider it a poor value and suggest that the management is sometimes less than helpful. Arrange bookings in advance in Puerto Natales (☎ /fax 41-1355). *Hostería Estancia Lazo* (☎ 22-3771), with eight cabins and a spacious farmhouse at the Laguna Verde sector of the park, costs US$70/90.

Refugio Grey (☎ 24-1504 in Punta Arenas), at the outlet of its namesake lake, costs US$80/110. *Hostería Pehoé* (☎ 41-1390), on a small island in the lake of the same name and linked to the mainland by a footbridge, charges US$85/111 single/double for views of the Cuernos del Paine and Paine Grande. It has a restaurant and bar, both open to the public. *Hostería Las Torres* (☎ 24-7050), seven km west of Guardería Laguna Amarga, charges US$85/110 and also has a restaurant/bar.

The most extravagant lodging in the park is the new *Hostería Explora* (☎ 41-1247 in Puerto Natales), near the Salto Chico waterfall at the outlet of Lago Pehoé, where rooms start at US$190/260 and rise rapidly.

Getting There & Away

For details of transportation to the park, see the Puerto Natales entry above. Bus services drop you at the Administración at Río Serrano, although you can disembark at Portería Lago Sarmiento or Guardería Laguna Amarga to begin the Paine circuit, or elsewhere upon request. Hitching from Puerto Natales is possible, but competition is heavy.

Sometimes there are summer bus services between Torres del Paine and El Calafate, Argentina, the closest settlement to Parque Nacional Los Glaciares (see the El Calafate section in the Patagonia chapter). Inquire at the Administración.

Getting Around

Hikers can save time and effort by taking the launch *Tzonka* from Refugio Pudeto, at the east end of Lago Pehoé, to Refugio Pehoé at the west end of the lake. The launch runs two to four times daily (US$10), but sometimes erratically – visitors should not rely on connections.

From Hostería Grey, the 38-passenger *Tetramarán Grey I* runs twice daily to Glaciar Grey and back; the three-hour excursion costs US$25.

PORVENIR

Founded less than a century ago to service the new sheep estancias across the Strait of Magellan from Punta Arenas, Porvenir is the largest settlement in Chilean Tierra del Fuego. Many of its 5143 inhabitants claim Yugoslav descent, dating from the brief gold rush of the 1880s and commemorated by several monuments and a pleasant waterfront park.

Porvenir only becomes visible as the ferry approaches its sheltered, nearly hidden harbor. The waterfront road, or costanera, leads from the ferry terminal to a cluster of rusting, metal-clad Victorians that belie the town's optimistic name ('the future'). The beautifully manicured Plaza de Armas has a worthwhile museum, but for most travellers Porvenir is a brief stopover en route to or from Ushuaia, on the Argentine side of Tierra del Fuego.

Motorists will find the gravel road east, along Bahía Inútil to the Argentine border at San Sebastián, in excellent condition though a bit narrow in spots. Northbound motorists from San Sebastián should take the equally good route from Onaisín to Cerro Sombrero and the crossing of the Strait of Magellan at Punta Delgada-Puerto Espora, rather than the heavily traveled and rutted truck route north from San Sebastián.

Information

Tourist Office The Oficina Municipal de Turismo (☎ 58-0100), on the 2nd floor at Valdivieso 402, is open 11:30 am to 1 pm and 2:30 to 4 pm weekdays. Information is also available at the kiosk on the costanera between Mardones and Muñoz Gamero.

Post & Telecommunications Correos de Chile is at the southwest corner of the Plaza de Armas. The Compañía Chilena de Teléfonos is on Damián Riobó between Valdivieso and Briceño. Porvenir's area code is 61.

Medical Services Porvenir's hospital is on Carlos Wood between Señoret and Guerrero.

Museo de Tierra del Fuego Fernando Cordero Rusque

This small but intriguing museum has some unexpected materials, including Selknam mummies and skulls, musical instruments used by mission Indians on Isla Dawson, stuffed creatures from the region, a display on the evolution of police uniforms in Chile, and another on the enigmatic Julio Popper, the onetime "dictator" of Tierra del Fuego. Probably the most unlikely exhibit is one on early Chilean cinematography. The museum is on the Plaza de Armas, in the same building as the tourist office. Hours are weekdays 8:30 am to 12:30 pm and 2:30 to 6 pm.

Places to Stay & Eat

For its size, Porvenir has good accommodations and food, but prices have recently risen. The cheapest rooms are at *Hotel España* (☎ 58-0160), Yugoslavia 698, which has singles for US$10 with shared bath, US$13 with private bath. Basic *Hotel Tierra del Fuego* (☎ 58-0015), Carlos Wood 489, is comparably priced. At *Residencial Colón* (☎ 58-0108), Damián Riobó 198, singles with shared bath cost US$13.

Hotel Central (☎ 58-0077), at Philippi

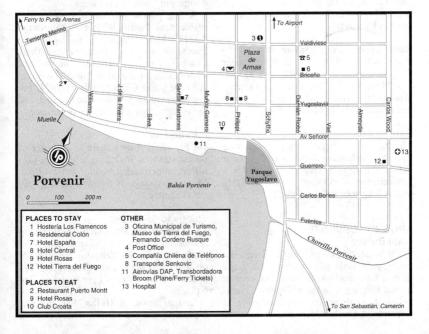

Porvenir

Bahía Porvenir

0   100   200 m

PLACES TO STAY
1 Hostería Los Flamencos
6 Residencial Colón
7 Hotel España
8 Hotel Central
9 Hotel Rosas
12 Hotel Tierra del Fuego

PLACES TO EAT
2 Restaurant Puerto Montt
9 Hotel Rosas
10 Club Croata

OTHER
3 Oficina Municipal de Turismo, Museo de Tierra del Fuego, Fernando Cordero Rusque
4 Post Office
5 Compañía Chilena de Teléfonos
8 Transporte Senkovic
11 Aerovías DAP, Transbordadora Broom (Plane/Ferry Tickets)
13 Hospital

and Yuglosavia, is a good value for US$18/35. Across the street at Philippi 296, *Hotel Rosas* (☎ 58-0088) charges US$26/37 for singles/doubles and has a good seafood restaurant. For upscale comfort, try *Hostería Los Flamencos* (☎ 58-0049), on Teniente Merino overlooking the harbor, where prices are US$55/60.

The *Club Croata*, on the costanera Av Señoret, is worth a try for lunch or dinner, along with the simple *Restaurant Puerto Montt* at Yugoslavia 1199, near Hostería Los Flamencos.

Getting There & Away
Air Aerovías DAP (☎ 58-0089), Av Señoret 542, flies across the Strait of Magellan to Punta Arenas (US$21) at least twice daily except Sunday, when there's only one flight.

Bus Transporte Senkovic (☎ 58-0015), Carlos Wood 489, departs Wednesday and Saturday at 2 pm for Río Grande, in Argentine Tierra del Fuego (US$12.50, seven hours). From Río Grande there are connections to Ushuaia.

Boat Transbordadora Broom (☎ 58-0089) along Av Señoret, operates a car/passenger ferry to Punta Arenas (US$5 per person, US$28 per vehicle, 2½ hours) on Monday, Wednesday, Friday, and Saturday at 2 pm and Sundays and holidays at 5 pm.

Getting Around
The bus to the ferry terminal, departing from the waterfront kiosk about an hour before the ferry's departure, provides a farewell tour of Porvenir for US$1. Taxis cost at least four times as much.

AROUND PORVENIR
Lago Blanco
In the southern part of Chilean Tierra del Fuego, accessible only by private car, Lago Blanco has excellent fishing. The nearest formal lodging is in the village of Timaukel, just south of the large estancia at Camerón (which, despite the Spanish

accent, takes its name from a Scottish pioneer sheep ranching family that first settled in the Falkland Islands).

CERRO SOMBRERO
This semi-ghost town at the north end of Tierra del Fuego, 43 km south of the ferry crossing at Primera Angostura, is a former oil center that has oddball '60s architecture, cheap lodging, a restaurant open until 3 am, and, of all things, an astronomical observatory. It's definitely worth a stop if you have your own car.

PUERTO WILLIAMS
Captain Robert Fitzroy encountered the Yahgan Indians, who accompanied the *Beagle* back to England, near this Chilean naval settlement on Isla Navarino, directly across the Beagle Channel from Argentine Tierra del Fuego. Missionaries in the mid-19th century and fortune-seekers during the local gold rush of the 1890s established a permanent European presence.

A few people of Yahgan descent still reside near Puerto Williams (population 1000), which is named for the founder of Fuerte Bulnes. A dispute over the three small islands of Lennox, Nueva, and Picton, east of Navarino, nearly brought Argentina and Chile to war in 1978, but papal intervention defused the situation and the islands remain in Chilean possession.

Information
On President Ibáñez there is a cluster of public services, including telephone, post office, supermarket, and tourist office. Money exchange is possible at the only travel agency.

Things to See & Do
The **Museo Martín Gusinde**, honoring the German priest and ethnographer who worked among the Yahgans, has exhibits on natural history and ethnography. It's open weekdays 9 am to 1 pm, and daily 3 to 6 pm.

East of town, at **Ukika**, live the few remaining Yahgan people. There is good hiking in the surrounding countryside, but the changeable weather demands warm, water-resistant clothing.

Places to Stay & Eat

Central *Residencial Onashaga* is basic but clean and comfortable for US$14 single. Camping is possible near the upscale, highly recommended *Hostería Patagonia* (☎ 22-6100 in Punta Arenas), which has singles/doubles at US$70/100 (winter prices may be negotiable). Both hotels serve meals.

Getting There & Away

Air Aerovías DAP flies to and from Punta Arenas on Monday, Wednesday, and Friday (US$67 one-way). Seats are limited and advance reservations essential. DAP flights to Antarctica make a brief stopover here.

Boat Chilean naval supply vessels, which sail irregularly between Punta Arenas and Puerto Williams, sometimes take passengers. In summer, there is sporadic service across the Beagle Channel to Ushuaia; inquire at the tourist office in either place.

ARGENTINA

Falkland Islands

Falkland Islands (Islas Malvinas)

Surrounded by the South Atlantic Ocean and centuries of controversy, the Falkland Islands lie some 300 miles (500 km) east of the Patagonian mainland. Consisting of two main islands, East and West Falkland, and several hundred smaller ones, they support a permanent population of about 2000, most of whom live in the capital of Stanley. The remainder live on widely dispersed sheep stations.

FACTS ABOUT THE FALKLANDS
History

Although there is some evidence that Patagonian Indians may have reached the Falklands in rudimentary canoes, the Islands were uninhabited when Europeans began to frequent the area in the late 17th century. Their Spanish name, Islas Malvinas, derives from early French navigators from the Channel port of St Malo.

No European power established a settlement until 1764, when the French built a garrison at Port Louis on East Falkland, disregarding Spanish claims under the papal Treaty of Tordesillas that divided the New World between Spain and Portugal. Unknown to either France or Spain, Britain soon planted a West Falkland outpost at Port Egmont, on Saunders Island. Spain, meanwhile, discovered and then supplanted the French colony after an amicable settlement between the two European states. The Spanish forces then detected and expelled the British in 1767. Under threat of war, Spain restored Port Egmont to the British, who only a few years later abandoned the area without, however, renouncing their territorial claims.

For the rest of the 18th century, Spain maintained the Islands as one of the world's most secure penal colonies. After it abandoned them in the early 1800s, only maverick whalers and sealers visited, until the United Provinces of the River Plate sent a military governor in the early 1820s to assert its claim as successor to Spain. Later, a naturalized Buenos Aires entrepreneur named Louis Vernet initiated a project to monitor uncontrolled sealers and exploit local fur seal populations in a sustainable manner, as well as tame the numerous wild cattle and horses that had multiplied on the abundant pastures since the Spaniards' departure.

Vernet's seizure of three American sealers triggered reprisals from a hotheaded US naval officer, who vandalized the Port Louis settlement beyond restoration in 1831. After Vernet's departure, Buenos Aires kept a token force there until early 1833, when it was expelled by British forces. Vernet pursued his claims for property damages in British courts for nearly 30 years, with little success, but Argentina has since asserted its territorial claim to the Islands by diplomacy and, in 1982, by force.

Under the British, the Falklands languished until the mid-19th century, when sheep began to replace cattle, and wool became an important export commodity. Founded by Samuel Lafone, an Englishman from Montevideo, the Falkland Islands Company became the Islands' largest landholder, but other immigrant entrepreneurs occupied all available pastoral lands in extensive holdings by the 1870s.

The steady arrival of English and Scottish immigrants augmented the early population, which was a mix of stranded mariners and holdover gauchos from the Vernet era. Roughly half resided in the new capital and port of Stanley, founded in 1844, while the remainder became resident laborers on large sheep stations resembling those in Australia. The population has never exceeded its 1931 maximum of 2400.

Most of the original landowners lived and worked in the Falklands, but in time they or their descendants returned to Britain and ran their businesses as absen-

The Warrah, the Yahgans & the Discovery of the Falklands

Who discovered the Falklands? Opinions depend, it seems, on who's speaking and what that person's native language is. Spanish speakers argue forcefully, almost without exception, that a ship from Magellan's 1520 expedition wintered at the Islands, while English speakers strongly assert that privateer John Davis discovered them in 1592. Unfortunately, no Yahgan speakers remain to tell us whether the "Canoe Indians" of Tierra del Fuego might have been the first to set foot on the Islands.

The evidence, admittedly, is slim and the idea seems at first unconventional and unlikely. The Yahgans navigated the waters of the Beagle Channel and the Strait of Magellan in simple beech bark canoes held together with whalebone and shredded saplings. By all accounts, these leaky vessels required constant bailing, but the Yahgans did use sealskin sails in favorable winds. In these canoes they certainly arrived at Staten Island at the eastern tip of Tierra del Fuego and, some speculate, more than 500 miles northeast in the Falklands. Early settlers found canoes washed up on the shores of West Falkland, but the most concrete evidence for at least a temporary Indian presence was the Islands' only native land mammal, the *warrah* or Falklands fox, *Dusicyon australis*.

When Europeans first landed, the Falklands were unpeopled, but the warrah (its name probably derived from the Australian Aboriginal word *warrigal* used to describe the dingo) aroused the interest of visitors like Darwin, who wrote:

> There is no other instance in any part of the world of so small a mass of broken land, distant from a continent, possessing so large an aboriginal quadruped peculiar to itself . . . Within a very few years after these islands shall have become regularly settled, in all probability this fox will be classed with the dodo, as an animal which has perished from the face of the earth.

Darwin and others remarked on the animal's extraordinary tameness, a characteristic which would support British biologist Juliet Clutton-Brock's conclusion that the warrah was a feral dog or a cross of feral dog and South American fox. Analyzing the animal's physical characteristics from specimens in the British Museum, she concluded that, like the Australian dingo, the warrah had been domesticated and likely brought across several hundred miles of open ocean in Yahgan canoes.

Was this possible? No one can be absolutely positive, but indigenous peoples navigated thousands of miles of the open Pacific, although their watercraft were more sophisticated than the Yahgans'. The Yahgans were a hardy people, though, and chances are that a canoe or two might have ridden the prevailing winds and currents from the Strait of Lemaire to the Falklands. If, as usual, they carried a dog or two, perhaps a pregnant bitch, it is reasonable to believe those animals might have bred on the Islands. Whether these presumed discoverers of the Falklands were able to return to Tierra del Fuego is even more speculative, but just considering the idea makes us rethink, once again, the myth of European "discovery." As Darwin predicted, the warrah itself did not survive European settlement – perceived as a threat to sheep, the last individual was shot on West Falkland in the 1870s. ■

tees. For nearly a century the Falkland Islands Company, owner of nearly half the land and livestock, dominated the local economy.

Until the late 1970s, when local government began to encourage the sale and subdivision of large landholdings to slow high rates of emigration, little changed in the

Islands' only industry. Since then, nearly every unit has been sold to local family farmers. Beginning in 1982, change became even more rapid with the Falklands War and the subsequent expansion of long-distance, deep-sea fishing in the surrounding South Atlantic. There is speculation, but still no firm evidence, of offshore petroleum in Falklands waters.

The Falklands War Although Argentina had persistently affirmed its claim to the Falklands since 1833, successive British governments never publicly acknowledged their seriousness until the late 1960s when, apparently, the Foreign & Commonwealth Office had begun to see the Islands as a politically burdensome anachronism to be discarded with all judicious speed. By then, the FCO and the military government of General Juan Carlos Onganía reached a communications agreement giving Argentina a significant voice in matters affecting Falklands transportation, fuel supplies, shipping, and even immigration, beginning in 1971.

Islanders and their supporters in Britain saw the Argentine presence as an ominous development. Only a few years earlier, right-wing guerrillas had hijacked an Aerolíneas Argentinas jet, which crash-landed on the Stanley racecourse (the Islands had no airport at the time); afterward, the guerrillas briefly occupied parts of town. Concerned about Argentina's chronic political instability, Falklanders suspected the FCO of secretly arranging transfer of the Islands to Argentina, and they were probably correct.

This process dragged on for more than a decade, during which Argentina's brutal Dirty War after 1976 gave Falklanders good reason to fear increasing Argentine presence. What was too fast for the Islanders was too slow for the Argentines, especially for the desperate military government of General Leopoldo Galtieri, which invaded the almost undefended Islands on April 2, 1982.

Galtieri's disintegrating government had come under increasing pressure from Argentines fed up with the corruption, economic chaos, and totalitarian ruthlessness of the Proceso, but his seizure of the Malvinas briefly united a divided country and made him an ephemeral hero. Galtieri and his advisers did not anticipate that British Prime Minister Margaret Thatcher, herself in precarious political circumstances, would respond so decisively. In a struggle whose loser would not survive politically, the Argentine sought diplomatic approval of his *fait accompli,* while the Briton organized an enormous naval task force to recover the lost territory.

The military outcome was one-sided, despite substantial British naval losses, as experienced British troops landed at San Carlos Bay and routed ill-trained and poorly supplied Argentine conscripts. The most serious fighting took place at Goose Green, on East Falkland, but the Argentine army's surrender at Stanley averted the destruction of the capital. Near Stanley, and at a few other sites around the Islands, there remain unexploded mines, but mine fields are clearly marked and pose no danger to anyone exercising reasonable caution.

Post-War Politics & Development Since the end of the war, most Islanders have wanted little or nothing to do with Argentina, preferring to emphasize their political, economic, and cultural links with Britain and to renew long-standing commercial ties with the southern Chilean city of Punta Arenas. In early 1995, however, Islanders Graham Bound and Janet Robertson toured Argentina as private citizens, under the auspices of the non-governmental Consejo Argentino de Relaciones Internacionales (Argentine International Relations Council), to establish dialogue and explain recent developments on the Islands to the Argentine public. While many Islanders opposed the visit, Argentine audiences generally treated the visitors cordially and respectfully.

Official Argentina, at the same time, continues to send mixed messages to the Islanders. President Carlos Menem has repeatedly renounced the use of force to support his country's claim to the Malvinas, yet he has also bragged that the Islands will once again be Argentine by the turn of the century. Foreign minister Guido di Tella, meanwhile, has pursued an ineffective policy of buttering up the Islanders by sending Christmas cards, gifts like children's videos, and even Queen's birthday greetings, while simultaneously proposing indemnities of US$100,000 or more per Islander should they vote to accept Argentine sovereignty in a referendum. Nearly all Falklanders angrily dismiss di Tella's efforts to purchase their allegiance as insulting and patronizing, but many have no objection to a strictly economic relationship with their larger neighbor.

Geography & Climate

The Falklands' total land area is 4700 sq miles (13,000 sq km), about the same as that of Northern Ireland or the US state of Connecticut. There are two main islands, East and West Falkland, separated by the Falkland Sound; of the many smaller islands, only a handful are large enough for human habitation. Despite a reputation for dismal weather, the Islands' oceanic climate is temperate, although with frequent high winds. Maximum temperatures rarely reach 75°F (25°C), while even on the coldest winter days the temperature usually rises above freezing at some time during the day. The average annual rainfall at Stanley, one of the Islands' most humid areas, is only about 24 inches (600 mm).

Except for the low-lying southern half of East Falkland, known as Lafonia, the terrain is generally hilly to mountainous, although the highest peaks do not exceed 2300 feet (690 meters). Among the most interesting geological features are the "stone runs" of quartzite boulders that descend from many of the ridges and peaks on East and West Falkland. The numerous bays, inlets, estuaries, and beaches present an often spectacular coastline, with abundant, accessible, and remarkably tame wildlife.

Because the settlements are so far apart, often separated by water, and the Islands'

road network is so limited, light aircraft is the easiest way to visit areas beyond the immediate Stanley area. In some areas, riding is still a common means of travel, but the Land Rover and the motorcycle have for the most part supplanted the horse. For adventurous travelers, walking is feasible, but trekkers must be prepared for changeable and sometimes inclement weather.

Flora & Fauna

Grasslands and prostrate shrubs dominate the Falklands flora; there are no native trees. At the time of European discovery, extensive stands of the native tussock grass *Parodiochloa flabellata* dominated the coastline and provided nutritious fodder for livestock, but it proved highly vulnerable to overgrazing and fire. Today, very little tussock remains on East or West Falkland, although well-managed farms on offshore islands have preserved significant areas of it. Most of the native pasture is rank white grass *(Cortaderia pilosa),* which supports only about one sheep per four or five acres.

Most visitors will find the Falklands' fauna more varied and interesting, and remarkably tame and accessible – only the Galápagos or the Everglades are comparable. The Islands' beaches, headlands, and offshore waters support the largest and finest concentrations of South Atlantic wildlife north of South Georgia Island and Antarctica. The Magellanic penguin, the only species that visits the South American continent, is common, but four other species breed regularly in the Falklands: the rockhopper, the closely related macaroni, the gentoo, and the king. Four other species have been recorded, but do not breed here.

Many other birds, equally interesting and uncommon, breed in the Falklands; for visitors from the Northern Hemisphere, almost all of them will be new. Undoubtedly the most beautiful is the black-browed albatross, but there are also caracaras, cormorants, gulls, hawks, peregrine falcons, oystercatchers, snowy sheathbills,

FALKLANDS

FALKLANDS

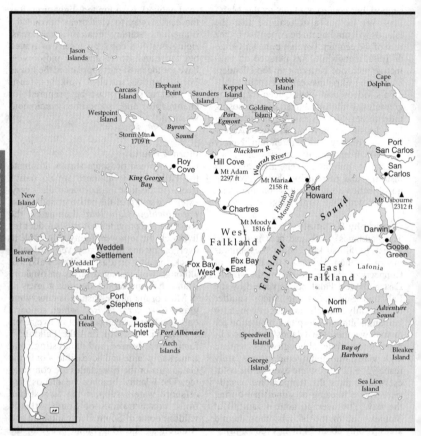

sheldgeese, steamer ducks, and swans – among others. Most are present in very large and impressive breeding colonies and are easy to photograph.

Also present, in locally large numbers, are marine mammals. Elephant seals, southern sea lions, and southern fur seals breed on the beaches, while six species of dolphins have been observed offshore. Killer whales are common, but the larger species of South Atlantic whales are rarely seen.

While the Falklands have no formally designated national parks, there are many outstanding wildlife sites. Over the past decade, local government has encouraged nature-oriented tourism, constructing small lodges near some of the best areas, but there are also less-structured opportunities away from these places. Hiking and trekking possibilities are excellent.

Government
In international politics, the Falklands remain a colonial anachronism, administered by a governor appointed by the Foreign & Commonwealth Office (FCO) in London, but in local affairs the eight-member, elected Legislative Council (Legco)

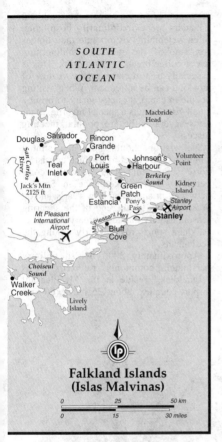

Falkland Islands (Islas Malvinas)

revenue producer under a licensing scheme established by the local government with the approval of the FCO. Asian and European fleets seeking both squid and fin fish have brought as much as £25 million per year into the Islands, most of which has gone to fund overdue improvements in public services, such as roads, telephones, and medical care. Tourist traffic is numerically small, but facilities in Stanley and at some wildlife sites are more than adequate and often excellent. Local government began permitting offshore seismic surveys for oil in 1993, and it is considering issuing licenses for offshore petroleum exploration, a subject that generates great ambivalence among Islanders because of the potential environmental impact. Among the postulants for exploration licenses is the former Argentine state oil company YPF, as a partner of British Petroleum (BP).

Most of the population of Stanley works for the local government (FIG) or for the Falkland Islands Company (FIC), which has been the major landowner and economic power in the Islands for more than a century. FIC has sold all its pastoral property to the government for subdivision and sale to local people, but it continues to provide shipping and other commercial services for ranchers and other residents of the Islands. In the countryside, known colloquially as "camp," nearly everyone is involved in wool-growing on relatively small, widely dispersed family-owned units.

exercises considerable power. Four of the eight members come from Stanley, while the remainder represent the camp, or countryside. Selected Legco members advise the governor as part of his Executive Council (Exco), which also includes the Chief Executive and the Financial Secretary. The present governor is David Tatham.

Economy

From the mid-19th century, the Falklands' economy has depended almost exclusively on the export of wool. Since 1986, however, fishing has eclipsed agriculture as a

Population & People

According to the 1991 census, the population of the Falklands is 2050, of whom about three-quarters live in Stanley and the remainder in camp. About 60% of the population is native-born, some tracing their ancestry back six or more generations, while the great majority of the remainder are immigrants or temporary residents from the United Kingdom. Islanders' surnames indicate that their origins can be traced to a variety of European backgrounds, but English is both the official language and the language of preference, though a few people speak and understand Spanish. There is a handful of immigrants from South America, nearly all of them Chilean.

Because of the Islands' isolation and small population, Falkland Islanders are traditionally versatile and adaptable. Almost every male, for example, is an expert mechanic, while lack of spare parts has encouraged many to become improvisational machinists. This adaptability has also been a virtue for individuals who rely on seasonal labor like sheep shearing and peat cutting, both of which are well paid. Many camp women also perform a variety of tasks, including shearing. Recently, however, these jobs are less sex segregated than they once were.

The Islands' history of colonial rule and the paternalistic social system (see the Stanley section) of the large sheep stations and other workplaces left an unfortunate legacy of public timidity in the face of authority, even when private opinions are very strong. At the same time, Falkland Islanders are extraordinarily hospitable, often welcoming visitors into their homes for "smoko," the traditional midmorning tea or coffee break, or for a drink. This is especially true in camp, where visitors of any kind can be infrequent. When visiting people in camp, it is customary to bring a small gift – rum is a special favorite. Stanley's several pubs are popular meeting places.

No visitor should miss the annual summer sports meetings, which consist of horse racing, bull riding, and similar competitions. These take place in Stanley between Christmas and New Year's, and on West Falkland at the end of the shearing season, usually in late February. The West Falkland sports rotate yearly among the settlements.

Approximately 2000 British military personnel, commonly referred to as "squaddies," reside at the Mt Pleasant airport complex, about 35 miles (60 km)

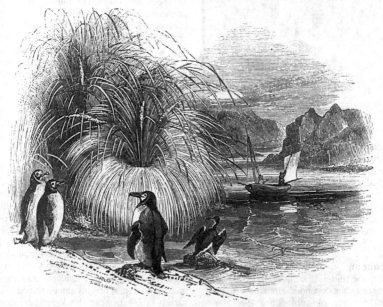

The Falkland Islands are home to a variety of penguins.

southwest of Stanley, and at a few other scattered sites around the Islands. Civilian-military relations are generally cordial but now rather distant.

FACTS FOR THE VISITOR
Although the Falklands are small and Islanders are few, in many ways the Islands are a small country, with their own immigration regulations, customs requirements, currency, and other unique features. Bureaucracy is generally not odious or cumbersome, but government officials sometimes play things "by the book."

Planning
When to Go Since the Islands' primary attraction is wildlife, the best season is October to March, when migratory birds (including penguins) and marine mammals return to the beaches and headlands. December and January are the best months, since very long days permit outdoor activities even if inclement weather spoils part of the day.

What to Bring Since the weather is cool and changeable, visitors should bring good waterproof clothing suitable for spring in the northern British Isles, such as warm sweaters and an anorak. A pair of rubber boots is often useful in wet weather. While summer never gets truly hot, and the wind can lower the ambient temperature considerably, the climate does not justify Antarctic preparations. For trekkers, a *very* sturdy tent with rain fly and a warm sleeping bag are essential.

Maps Excellent topographic maps, prepared by the Directorate of Overseas Surveys, are available from the Secretariat in Stanley for about £2 each. There is a two-sheet, 1:250,000 map of the entire Islands that is suitable for most purposes, but for more detail, obtain the 1:50,000 sheets. For maritime charts, contact the Customs & Immigration Department (☎ 27340) on Ross Rd in Stanley.

Tourist Offices
The local tourist office is the Falklands Islands Tourist Board (☎ 500-25115, fax 22619) in Stanley, but the Islands also have representation in the UK, Europe, and the Americas.

United Kingdom
    Falkland House, 14 Broadway, Westminster, London SW1H 0BH (☎ 171-222-2542, fax 222-2375)
Germany
    HS Travel & Consulting, PO Box 1447, 64529 Moerfelden (☎ /fax 61-05-1304)
USA
    Leo Le Bon & Associates, 190 Montrose Ave, Berkeley, CA 94707 (☎ /fax 510-525-8846)
Chile
    Broom Travel, Roca 924, Punta Arenas (☎ 61-22-8312)

Visas
All nationalities, including British citizens, must carry valid passports. For non-Britons, visa requirements are generally the same as those for foreigners visiting the UK, except that Argentines must obtain a visa in advance (not easily accomplished). For more details, inquire at the Islands' UK representative at Falkland House (☎ 222-2542), 14 Broadway, Westminster, London SW1H 0BH. In Punta Arenas, Chile, contact Aerovías DAP (☎ 22-3340, fax 22-1693) at O'Higgins 891, which operates flights to the Islands, or British consul John Rees (☎ 22-8312) at Roca 924.

Local officials normally allow a four-month visitor's permit on arrival in the Islands, but they may ask to see a return or onward ticket.

Customs
Customs regulations are few except for limits on importation of alcohol and tobacco, which are heavily taxed but readily available locally.

Money & Costs
The legal currency is the Falkland Islands pound (£), on a par with sterling. There are

FALKLANDS

Penguins & Their Feathered Friends

On the Patagonian mainland, the only breeding species of penguin is the burrowing Magellanic. In the cooler waters around the Falklands, large schools of squid are food for many more species of these fascinating birds of the family *Spheniscidae* – rockhoppers, gentoos, kings, and macaronis – plus other seabirds rarely seen on the mainland. In some cases, their numbers are almost incomprehensible, while elsewhere there are just a few, at the limits of their sub-Antarctic range. Rockhoppers and Magellanics spend most of the year at sea, coming ashore to breed in the southern spring, but kings and gentoos remain in the Falklands throughout the year.

Rockhopper penguins *(Eudyptes crestatus)*, affectionately called "rockies," are the most common species in the Falklands. Although resembling the macaroni penguin *(Eudyptes chrysolophus)*, rockies are easily distinguished by their floppy yellow crests, while the macaroni's crest is orange and more erect, resembling the foppish 18th-century male hairstyle that gave the bird its common English name. The rockhopper is also smaller, weighing only 5.5 pounds (2.5 kg), while the macaroni reaches 10 pounds (4.5 kg).

Falklands rockhopper colonies are the largest in the world – in the spring, perhaps as many as five million birds climb rugged, wave-battered headlands to breed in stony amphitheaters like the one on Sea Lion Island. Scaling these nearly vertical cliffs is no easy task – more often than not, as soon as the rocky leaves the water a breaker thrashes it against a rock and it falls back into the sea. Persistence triumphs, as the bird reaches the top after many false starts. Once on the headlands, male and female mate and produce two eggs of unequal size, only the larger of which usually hatches and reaches maturity. The birds must return to the sea daily in search of squid, which they digest and regurgitate for their young.

While rockhoppers can be pugnacious, careful visitors able to tolerate the overpowering odor of ammonia from penguin excreta can walk among them without even disturbing a nesting mother. Rarely do these colonies, which can cover many acres, consist of rockies alone. In their eastern breeding sites, rockies mix with king cormorants *(Phalacrocorax albiventer)*, while in the west they share their space with the strikingly beautiful black-browed albatross *(Diomedea melanophris)*. On rare occasions you will see a solitary pair of macaronis among the breeding rockhoppers, or even a single macaroni who, unable to find a mate of its own species, has nested with a rocky. More common on sub-Antarctic islands like South Georgia, the macaroni is at the limits of its range in the Falklands.

The gentoo *(Pygoscelis papua)* is much more common than the macaroni but not so common as the rocky. Its distinguishing features are its size (although smaller than the king, it weighs up to 13.5 pounds or six kg), its bright orange bill, and the white band that connects the eyes across the crown. For nesting, it favors open, level sites some distance from the ocean. Gentoo routes to and from the sea are like ant trails, often long and indirect. Traditionally, Falkland Islanders have collected gentoo eggs in the spring but, unlike the rockhopper, the gentoo may lay a second egg if the first is removed.

Gentoos are popular with Falklands farmers, since they uproot the common *diddle-dee* shrub

---

bank notes for £5, £10, £20, and £50, and coins for 1p, 2p, 5p, 10p, 20p, 50p, and £1. Sterling notes and coins circulate alongside local currency, but Falklands currency is not legal tender in the UK, nor on Ascension Island, where flights to and from the UK make a brief refueling stop. Ascension/St Helena bank notes and coins are not legal tender in either the Falklands or the UK.

Credit cards are not widely used in the Islands, but traveler's checks are readily accepted with a minimum of bureaucracy. Britons with guarantee cards from Barclays, Lloyds, Midland, and National Westminster Banks can cash personal checks up to £50 at Stanley's Standard Chartered Bank.

Recent tourist development has encouraged short-stay, top-end accommodations and services at prices up to £50 or more per day (with full board), but there are cheaper alternatives, such as B&Bs in Stanley from about £15. In camp, there are low-cost, self-catering cabins for about £10, and opportunities for trekking and camping at virtually no cost. Camp families in some isolated areas still welcome visitors without charge.

Food prices are roughly equivalent to the UK, but fresh meat (chiefly mutton) is extremely cheap. Restaurant meals are

(*Empetrum rubrum*), which has no pasture value, while fine pasture grasses quickly colonize abandoned gentoo nesting sites. The application of the popular name gentoo to the species is obscure, since the word describes a non-Moslem inhabitant of India – one speculation is that the band across the gentoo's head bears resemblance to a turban.

The undisputed monarch of Falklands penguins is, appropriately, the king (*Aptenodytes patagonicus*). This enormous, regal bird is unmistakable, standing more than three feet (nearly a meter) in height and weighing more than 35 pounds (16 kg), with a bright orangeish ear patch connecting to a golden patch on the breast. It resembles the much larger emperor penguin (*Aptenodytes forsteri*) of Antarctica. Once nearly extinct in the Falklands, the king has reappeared at several sites throughout the Islands, most notably Volunteer Point, which has a breeding colony of more than 150 pairs.

King penguins breed on flat, open areas among gentoos, but they do not nest, instead incubating their single egg on their feet and protecting it among loose folds of skin. The most extraordinary thing about the bird is its erratic breeding cycle, which is not synchronized with the seasons or the year – no scientist has successfully explained why 14 to 16 months pass between eggs. Because of the kings' beauty and rarity, Falklands farms that have breeding populations take great pride in their presence.

Many other birds are worth seeing, but one deserves special mention: the black-browed albatross, which nests on precipitous, west-facing headlands on New Island, West Point, Saunders Island, and a few other places. Tiny but inaccessible Beauchene Island, an isolated southern outlier of East Falkland, has an astonishing two million birds. In total, the Falklands have more than three-quarters of the world's population of the species.

With an eight-foot (nearly three-meter) wingspan and flat webbed feet, this enormous bird is ungainly on land, getting airborne only by leaping off cliffs into the prevailing westerlies. It spends most of the winter at sea, and some individuals migrate across the entire South Atlantic in a circular pattern. Like the penguins among which it nests, the black-browed albatross has little fear of humans. By sitting near the colony, you will arouse enough interest that this curious bird will come to you instead of your having to go to it.

Unfortunately, all is not idyllic in this wildlife paradise. Since 1986, revenue from fishing licenses has brought the Islands unprecedented prosperity, but Asian and European fleets may have overexploited the stocks of squid and finfish upon which penguins, black-browed albatrosses, and many other birds feed. Oil exploration in offshore waters poses an additional hazard, though local government has proceeded very deliberately in encouraging petroleum development.

Falklands Conservation, a pro-wildlife organization with branches in both Stanley and the UK, is currently conducting seabird monitoring and research projects to determine the threat that commercial fishing and oil development pose to local wildlife. For more information, see the listing under Useful Organizations in this chapter. ■

fairly expensive, but inexpensive short orders and snacks are available in Stanley.

Post & Telecommunications

Postal services are very dependable. There are two airmail services weekly to and from the UK, but parcels larger than about one lb (0.45 kg) arrive or depart by sea four to five times yearly. The Government Air Service delivers the post to outer settlements and islands. If you're expecting mail in the Islands, instruct correspondents to address their letters to the "Post Office, Stanley, Falkland Islands, via London, England."

Cable and Wireless PLC operates both local and long-distance telephone services; all local numbers have five digits. The Falklands' international country code is 500, valid for numbers in Stanley and in camp.

Local calls cost 5p per minute, calls to the UK 15p for six seconds, and calls to the rest of the world 18p per six seconds. Operator-assisted calls cost the same but have a three-minute minimum. Collect calls are possible only locally and to the UK.

Books

Many books have been written since the 1982 war, but the most readily available general account is the third edition of Ian

Strange's *The Falkland Islands* (David & Charles, 1983), which deals with the geography, history, and natural history of the Islands. More recent are Paul Morrison's *The Falkland Islands* (Aston Publications, 1990), and Tony Chater's *The Falklands* (Penna Press, 1993).

Based on unpublished materials from Cambridge University archives and other sources, Patrick Armstrong's recent *Darwin's Desolate Islands: A Naturalist in the Falklands, 1833 and 1834* (Picton, 1992) is of great historical interest. Michael Mainwaring's *From the Falklands to Patagonia* (Allison & Busby, 1983) is a worthwhile historical work on pioneer sheep farming in the South Atlantic, based on private correspondence.

For a good contemporary account of the Falklands, see Robert Fox's *Antarctica and the South Atlantic: Discovery, Development and Dispute*. Of the numerous books on the war, one of the best is Max Hastings and Simon Jenkins' *Battle for the Falklands*.

Visitors interested in wildlife should acquire Robin Woods' *Falkland Islands Birds*, which is a suitable field guide with excellent photographs. More detailed but unsuitable for field use is his *The Birds of the Falkland Islands*. Strange's *Field Guide to the Wildlife of the Falkland Islands and South Georgia* is also worth a look, along with TH Davies and JH McAdam's *Wild Flowers of the Falkland Islands*. Trekkers might acquire Julian Fisher's *Walks and Climbs in the Falkland Islands*.

Media

Radio is the most important communications medium in the Falklands. The Falkland Islands Broadcasting Service (FIBS) produces local programming and also carries news from the BBC and programs from the British Forces Broadcasting Service (BFBS). Do not miss the nightly public announcements, to which local people listen religiously; they're part of the local news program. The Falklands may be the only place in the world where the purchase of air time is within anybody's reach. Frequencies are 550 kHz on the AM band and 96.5 MHz on the FM band.

Television is available at least ten hours daily from the BFBS station at Mt Pleasant airport; programs are taped and flown in from the UK on a regular basis. The only print media are the weekly newspapers *Penguin News* and *Teaberry Express,* both available from shops in Stanley.

Film & Photography

Color and B&W print film are readily available at reasonable prices, although they're cheaper in the UK and the USA. Color slide film is less dependably available, so you may want to bring all you need. Color print processing is available in the Islands.

Time

The Falklands are four hours behind GMT. In summer, Stanley goes on daylight saving time, but camp remains on standard time.

Electricity

Electric current operates on 220/240 V, 50 cycles. Plugs are identical to those in the UK.

Weights & Measures

The metric system has become official, but in everyday matters people more commonly use English measurements. Since elevations on the Directorate of Overseas Survey maps are in feet and most tourist literature uses English units, this chapter uses the English system, with the metric equivalent in parentheses.

Health

No special health precautions need to be taken in the Falklands, but carry adequate insurance. There are excellent medical and dental facilities at the new King Edward VII Memorial Hospital, a joint civilian-military facility in Stanley.

Despite relatively cool temperatures, unsuspecting visitors may suffer severe sunburn after experiencing the deceptive combination of wind and sun. In the event of inclement weather, the wind can contribute to hypothermia.

Because flights from Brize Norton to Mt Pleasant may be diverted to West Africa or Brazil due to bad weather, the British Ministry of Defence (MOD) recommends that passengers on its flights make sure their yellow fever vaccinations are up-to-date.

Useful Organizations

Based in both the UK and Stanley, Falklands Conservation is a nonprofit organization promoting wildlife conservation research as well as the preservation of wrecks and historic sites in the Islands. Membership, which costs £15 per year and includes its annual newsletter, is available from Falklands Conservation (☎ 181-346-5011), 1 Princes Rd, Finchley, London N3 2DA, England. Its local representative (☎ 22247, fax 22288) is at the Beauchene Complex on John St between Philomel and Dean Sts in Stanley.

The Falkland Islands Association (☎ 171-222-0028), 2 Greycoat Place, Westminster, London SW1P 1SD, is a political lobbying group that publishes a quarterly newsletter on the Falklands with much useful information.

Dangers & Annoyances

Near Stanley and in a few camp locations on both East and West Falkland, there remain unexploded plastic land mines, but mine fields are clearly marked and, in the ten years since the Falklands War, no civilian has been injured. *Never* even consider entering one of these fields – the mines will bear the weight of a penguin or even a sheep, but not of a human. Report any suspicious object to the Explosive Ordinance Disposal (EOD, ☎ 22229) opposite the Stanley police station, which distributes free mine field maps (which, incidentally, are handy for walks in the Stanley area).

Trekking in the camp is safe for anyone with confidence in his or her abilities, but it's better not to trek alone. The camp is so thinly populated that the consequences of an accident, however unlikely, could be very serious. Walkers in camp should be

aware that so-called soft camp, covered by white grass, is boggy despite its firm appearance. There is no quicksand, but step carefully.

Business Hours

Falkland Islands government offices are open weekdays 8 am to noon and 1:15 to 4:30 pm. Most large businesses in Stanley, such as the FIC's West Store (a supermarket with some general interest items), stay open until 7 or 8 pm, but smaller shops are often open only a few hours a day. On weekends, business hours are much reduced. The few stores in camp, such as those at Fox Bay East and Port Howard, have a very limited regular schedule but will often open on request.

Cultural Events & Holidays

On both East and West Falkland, the annual sports meetings have been a tradition since the advent of sheep farming in the 19th century. In a land where most people lived a very isolated existence, they provided a regular opportunity to get together and share news, meet new people, and participate in friendly competitions such as horse racing, bull riding, and sheep-dog trials.

The rotating camp sports meeting on West Falkland carries on this tradition best, hosting "two-nighters," during which Islanders party till they drop, go to sleep for a few hours, and get up and start all over again. Independent visitors should not feel shy about showing up at one of these events, although it is best to arrange for accommodations in advance – this will usually mean floor space for your sleeping bag.

National holidays include the following:

January 1
   New Year's Day
Late February (dates vary)
   Camp Sports
March/April (date varies)
   Good Friday
April 21
   Queen's Birthday
June 14
   Liberation Day

FALKLANDS

August 14
  Falklands Day
December 8
  Battle of the Falklands (1914)
December 25
  Christmas Day
December 26/27
  Boxing Day/Stanley Sports

Activities

Wildlife is the major attraction for most visitors. Penguins, other shorebirds, and marine mammals are tame and easily approached even at developed tourist sites like Sea Lion Island and Pebble Island, but there are other equally interesting, undeveloped sites. Keep a respectful distance from these animals, especially the dangerous southern sea lion (see the Península Valdés sidebar in the Patagonia chapter).

Fishing for sea trout, mullet and smelt is also a popular pastime; the most convenient site is the Murrell River, which is walking distance from Stanley. There are many other suitable places in camp, some easily accessible from the Mt Pleasant Hwy. Early March to late April is best for fishing for sea trout, which requires a license (£10) from the Stanley Post Office; it is obligatory to return the accompanying logbook to the Fisheries Department (☎ 27260) at the Falkland Islands Port and Storage System (FIPASS), anchored in Stanley Harbor east of town. The season runs from September 1 to April 30.

Trekking and camping are possible, but many landowners and the tourist board now discourage camping because of fire danger and disturbance to stock and wildlife. Hikers can visit the 1982 battlefields on both East and West Falkland.

Windsurfing is possible in sheltered waters such as Stanley Harbour (wet suits essential), but probably only the truly adept can avoid sailing to South Africa on the prevailing winds. Experienced divers may find it interesting to explore some of the Falklands' numerous wrecks.

Work

Stanley's labor shortage has eased over the last few years, and work is more difficult to obtain. In the past, it was possible to obtain seasonal work on the large sheep stations belonging to the Falkland Islands Company and other companies, but agrarian reform has nearly eliminated this option. The major employers are FIC and FIG. There is a chronic housing shortage, and rental housing is difficult to come by, except for short-term stays.

Accommodations

Accommodations are limited and improvised in some areas, but are still reasonably good everywhere. Stanley has several B&Bs and two hotels. Several farms have converted surplus buildings into lodges, some very comfortable, to accommodate tourists, but there are also self-catering cottages. A few have caravans or surplus Portakabin shelters obtained from the British military. These shelters are modular shell units similar to cargo containers but with doors and windows. They can be outfitted with beds or more elaborate furnishings, and sometimes plumbing and electricity.

In areas not frequented by tourists, Islanders often welcome houseguests; in addition, many farms have "outside houses" or shanties that visitors may use with permission. Some outside houses, traditionally used by shepherds on distant parts of a farm, are very comfortable if a bit old, while others are very run-down. Camping is possible only with permission.

Food & Drinks

Wool has long been the staple of the Falklands economy and mutton the staple of the Falklander's diet. While it is not true that Islanders eat mutton 365 days a year, it is nearly true – on Christmas Day they eat lamb, or so the story goes. Beef is generally available only in winter. Vegetarians will have a hard time of it, but meat is at least cheap.

Locally grown vegetables and fruits rarely appear on the market, since people grow their own in kitchen gardens, but a hydroponic market garden has begun to produce aubergines (eggplant), tomatoes, lettuce, and other salad greens throughout the year.

Stanley snack bars offer fast food such as fish and chips, mutton burgers (better than they sound), sausage rolls, and pasties. There are respectable restaurants, but nothing of international stature. Stanley has several well-patronized pubs, where beer and hard liquor (whiskey and rum) are the favorites, though wine has gained popularity in recent years. All drinks are imported.

GETTING THERE & AWAY

Since 1986, with the completion of the Mt Pleasant international airport (MPA) 35 miles (60 km) southwest of Stanley, twice-weekly flights have connected the Falklands to RAF Brize Norton, near Burford, Oxfordshire, via the tiny South Atlantic island of Ascension. Southbound, these flights leave Brize Norton Mondays and Thursdays, arriving Tuesdays and Fridays; northbound, they leave Mt Pleasant Wednesdays and Saturdays, arriving Thursdays and Sundays. The flight takes 18 hours, including an hour's stopover for refueling on Ascension.

The economy roundtrip fare is £2180, but there is a reduced Apex roundtrip fare of £1340 with 30-day advance purchase, as well as a £1130 fare for groups of six or more. Travelers continuing to Chile can purchase one-way tickets at half the above fares. For reservations in the UK, contact Carol Stewart, Travel Coordinator at FIG's London offices (☎ 171-222-2542), Falkland House, 14 Broadway, Westminster, London SW1H 0BH. In Stanley, contact the FIC (☎ 27633) on Crozier Place. The baggage limit is normally 40 lbs (18 kg), but enforcement is lax.

Travelers visiting southern South America can reach the Falklands with Aerovías DAP (☎ 22-3340, fax 22-1693), O'Higgins 891 in Punta Arenas (US$355 one-way). These flights, weekly in summer and fortnightly in winter, use Stanley airport near the capital, but sometimes land at MPA depending on the wind. FIC is also the Stanley representative of DAP. There is a possibility that DAP may begin using

larger planes, connecting directly from Santiago via Punta Arenas.

Mount Pleasant has duty-free facilities, as does Wideawake airfield on Ascension Island.

Stanley Services Limited (☎ (500) 22622, fax 22623), on Airport Rd in Stanley, will arrange excursions and itineraries for independent travelers; contact Jacki Draycott, Manager, Travel Division.

GETTING AROUND

Transportation outside the Stanley/Mt Pleasant area is not cheap, since roads are few and the only regular public transportation is the Falkland Islands Government Air Service (FIGAS), an on-demand service that flies ten-passenger Norman-Britten Islander aircraft to grass airstrips throughout the Islands. The approximate charges of £1 per minute would make the fare to Carcass Island, off West Falkland, about £145 roundtrip. The baggage limitation of 30 lbs (14 kg) per passenger is strictly enforced for safety reasons.

Rental vehicles are available in Stanley, while lodges at Pebble Island, Sea Lion Island, Port Howard, and San Carlos have comfortable County Land Rovers available with drivers/guides for guests. Visitors may use their own state or national driver's licenses in the Falklands for up to 12 months.

Stanley

In reality Stanley, the Falklands' capital, is little more than a village which, by historical accident, acquired a political status totally out of proportion to its size. Because many of its houses were built from available materials, often locally quarried stone and timber from shipwrecks, it has a certain ramshackle charm, as the houses' metal cladding and brightly painted corrugated-iron roofs contrast dramatically with the surrounding moorland. Nearly all the houses have large kitchen gardens, where residents grow much of their own food and enough ornamentals to give the townscape a spot of color. The sweetish fragrance of peat fuel still permeates the town on calm evenings, even though many households now use oil, gas, and electricity for cooking and heating.

Stanley was founded in 1844, when the Colonial Office ordered the removal of the seat of government from Port Louis, on Berkeley Sound, to the more sheltered harbor of Port Jackson, since renamed Stanley Harbour. Originally a tiny outpost of colonial officials, vagabond sailors, and British military pensioners, the town grew slowly as a supply and repair port for ships rounding Cape Horn en route to the California gold rush. Some damaged vessels were forced to limp back into port, their cargos legitimately being condemned and sold, but shipping began to avoid the port when others were scuttled under such questionable circumstances that the town acquired an unsavory reputation which undoubtedly discouraged growth. Only as sheep replaced cattle in the late 19th century did Stanley begin to grow more rapidly, as it became the transshipment point for wool between camp and the UK.

As the wool trade grew, so did the influence of the Falkland Islands Company, already the Islands' largest landowner. FIC soon became the town's largest employer, especially after acquiring the property of JM Dean, its only commercial rival, in the late 19th century. Over the next century, FIC's political and economic dominance was uncontested, as it ruled the town no less absolutely than the owners of the large sheep stations ruled the camp. At the same time, the company's relatively high wages and good housing provided a paternalistic security, although these "tied houses" were available only so long as the employee remained with the company.

During the 1982 war, the capital escaped almost unscathed despite its occupation by thousands of Argentine troops. The two major exceptions were both ironic: a British mortar hit a house on the outskirts of Stanley, killing three local women, while Argentine conscripts rioted against their officers after the surrender and burned the historic Globe Store, a business owned by an Anglo-Argentine who had died only a few years earlier.

Stanley remains the service center for the wool industry, but since the declaration of a fisheries protection zone around the Islands, it has become an important port for the deep-water fishing industry, and many Asian and European fishing companies have offices in town.

Orientation

On a steep hillside on the south shore of Stanley Harbour, Port William's sheltered inner harbor on East Falkland, Stanley is surrounded by water and low hills. For protection from the prevailing southwest winds, the town has sprawled east and west along the harbor rather than onto the exposed ridge of Stanley Common, to the south. Ross Rd, running the length of the harbor, is the main street, but most government offices, businesses, and houses are within a few blocks of each other in the compact town center. Most Stanley roads are paved, but outside town they are invariably graveled. The only good roads outside Stanley are those to Mt Pleasant airport, to Darwin/Goose Green, and from Pony's Pass to Port Louis and Volunteer Point.

Information

Tourist Offices The Falkland Islands Tourist Board (☎ 22215, 22281) at the Public Jetty distributes an excellent guide to Stanley, as well as other useful brochures, including a list of accommodations throughout the Islands. Hours are 8 am to noon and 1:15 to 4:30 pm weekdays.

The Mount Pleasant Travel Office (☎ 76691) is at 12 Facility Main Reception, at Mt Pleasant international airport.

Money Standard Chartered Bank, on Ross Rd between Barrack and Villiers Sts, will change foreign currency and traveler's checks, and cash personal checks drawn on several UK banks with the appropriate guarantee card. Hours are weekdays 8:30

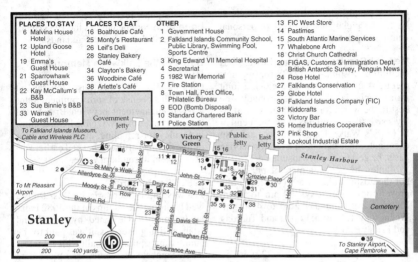

PLACES TO STAY
6 Malvina House Hotel
12 Upland Goose Hotel
19 Emma's Guest House
21 Sparrowhawk Guest House
22 Kay McCallum's B&B
23 Sue Binnie's B&B
33 Warrah Guest House

PLACES TO EAT
16 Boathouse Café
25 Monty's Restaurant
26 Leif's Deli
28 Stanley Bakery Café
34 Clayton's Bakery
36 Woodbine Café
38 Arlette's Café

OTHER
1 Government House
2 Falkland Islands Community School, Public Library, Swimming Pool, Sports Centre
3 King Edward VII Memorial Hospital
4 Secretariat
5 1982 War Memorial
7 Fire Station
8 Town Hall, Post Office, Philatelic Bureau
9 EOD (Bomb Disposal)
10 Standard Chartered Bank
11 Police Station
13 FIC West Store
14 Pastimes
15 South Atlantic Marine Services
17 Whalebone Arch
18 Christ Church Cathedral
20 FIGAS, Customs & Immigration Dept, British Antarctic Survey, Penguin News
24 Rose Hotel
27 Falklands Conservation
29 Globe Hotel
30 Falkland Islands Company (FIC)
31 Kiddcrafts
32 Victory Bar
35 Home Industries Cooperative
37 Pink Shop
39 Lookout Industrial Estate

Stanley

FALKLANDS

am to noon and 1:15 to 3 pm. Most Stanley businesses readily accept traveler's checks.

Remember that Falklands currency is valueless outside the Islands – change your local notes for sterling or US dollars before leaving.

Post & Telecommunications The post office (☎ 27180), in Town Hall on Ross Rd at Barrack St, is open weekdays 8 am to noon and 1:15 pm to 4:30 pm. Stamp collectors should visit the Philatelic Bureau (☎ 27159), in the same building (see Things to Buy for more details). Hours are weekdays 9 am to noon and 1:15 to 4 pm.

Easily identified by its satellite dish, Cable and Wireless PLC (☎ 20804) operates the Falklands' phone, telegram, telex, and fax services from offices on Ross Rd near Government House. To make an overseas call from the booths in the office, purchase a magnetic card over the counter – this is cheaper than an operator-assisted call. Counter hours are 8:30 am to 5 pm weekdays, but public booths are open 24 hours.

Immigration The Customs & Immigration Department (☎ 27340), on Ross Rd next to

Penguin News, also sells maritime charts of the Islands.

Travel Agencies For special itineraries or assistance for groups or individuals within the Islands, contact Jacki Draycott at Stanley Services (☎ 22622, fax 22623), on Airport Rd.

Library Stanley Public Library (☎ 27290), in the Falkland Islands Community School on Reservoir Rd, keeps a large selection of specialist papers and books relating to the Falklands (including my 781-page doctoral dissertation!). Hours are 9 am to noon weekdays, 1:30 to 5:30 pm Monday, Tuesday, and Thursday, 2:30 to 5:30 pm Wednesday, 3 to 6 pm Friday, and 1:45 to 5 pm Saturday.

Film Processing Falkland Printz (☎ 32185), at Mt Pleasant airport, stocks and develops both color print and slide film. In Stanley, leave your film at Pastimes, on Dean St near Ross Rd behind the FIC's West Store, for 36-hour service.

Laundry Stewart's Laundry Service (☎ 22704), in the Lookout Industrial Estate (a very small industrail park) on Davis St East, does pickup and delivery of personal laundry and dry-cleaning. .

Medical Services The King Edward VII Memorial Hospital (☎ 27328 for appointments, ☎ 27410 for emergencies), a joint military-civilian facility, is probably the best in the world for a community of Stanley's size. The hospital is at the west end of St Mary's Walk). Dental services are also excellent. Since care is on a fee-for-service basis, be certain to have insurance.

Stanley has no commercial pharmacy, but the hospital dispensary (☎ 72315) fills prescriptions weekdays 10 am to noon, Monday and Thursday 2:30 to 4:30 pm, Wednesday 1:30 to 5:30 pm, and Tuesday and Friday 3 to 5 pm.

Emergency The police (☎ 27222) are on Ross Rd, and Fire & Rescue (☎ 27333) is on St Mary's Walk.

Government House
Probably Stanley's most photographed landmark, rambling Government House has been home to London-appointed governors since the mid-19th century. It is traditional for all visitors to the Falklands to sign the register of visitors, but this custom has declined with the increased passenger traffic of the postwar period. Once a very minor post within the FCO, the governorship is much more significant now. Government House is just off Ross Rd. There's a register that guests should sign before entering the building.

Christ Church Cathedral
Completed in 1892 and undoubtedly the town's most distinguished landmark, the cathedral, on Ross Rd, is a massive brick-and-stone construction with a brightly painted corrugated-metal roof and attractive stained-glass windows. Several interior plaques honor the memory of local men who served in the British Forces in WWI and WWII. On the small square next to the

cathedral, the recently restored **Whalebone Arch** commemorates the 1933 centenary of British rule in the Falklands.

Battle of the Falklands Memorial (1914)
On Ross Rd West, just past Government House, this obelisk of sorts commemorates a naval engagement between British and German forces in WWI. Nine British ships, in Stanley for refueling, quickly sank four of five German cruisers that had earlier surprised them in southern Chile.

1982 War Memorial
Just west of the Secretariat on Ross Rd is a wall honoring the victims of the 1982 Falklands conflict. Designed by a Falkland Islander living overseas, it was paid for by public subscription and built with volunteer labor. Somber ceremonies take place here every June 14.

Cemetery
At the east end of Ross Rd, Stanley Cemetery is the final resting place for both the Islands' tiny elite and its working class. Note the tombstones of three young Whitingtons, children of an unsuccessful 19th-century pioneer. Other surnames, such as Felton and Biggs, are as common in the Islands as Smith and Jones are in the US and UK.

Falkland Islands Museum
Ironically, the facility that houses the Falklands museum was built for the Argentine Air Force officer who was the local representative of LADE, which until 1982 operated air services between Comodoro Rivadavia and Stanley. For several years after the war, it was the residence of the Commander of British Forces Falkland Islands (BFFI), but after the garrison moved to Mt Pleasant it became the new home of the local museum (☎ 27428), on Holdfast Rd south of Ross Rd West, just beyond the 1914 Battle Memorial.

Curator John Smith is especially conversant with the Islands' maritime history; his booklet *Condemned at Stanley* relates the stories of the numerous shipwrecks that dot the harbor. Hours are Tuesday to Friday 10:30 am to noon and 2 to 4 pm, Sunday 10 am to noon. Admission costs £1.50 for adults, but is free for children.

Activities
Stanley's new public **swimming** pool (☎ 27291), on Reservoir Rd near the Mt Pleasant Hwy, has become a very popular recreational resource. Hours vary – check at the pool or with the tourist office.

Fishing for sea trout, mullet, and smelt is also a popular pastime; the nearest site is the Murrell River, which is walking distance from Stanley. There are many other suitable places in the camp, some easily accessible from the Mt Pleasant Hwy. Fishing for sea trout requires a license, available from the post office for £10. The season runs from September 1 to April 30.

Mel Lloyd's Falcon Tours (☎ 32220) offers **horseback riding**, as does Gardner Fiddes's Tumbledown Trekking (☎ 21494).

Special Events
The capital's most noteworthy public event is the annual Stanley Sports between Christmas and New Year's, which features horse racing (bets are legal), bull riding, and other competitions.

Every March, the Falkland Islands Horticultural Society presents a competitive Horticultural Show, displaying the produce of kitchen gardens in Stanley and camp, plus a wide variety of baked goods. At the end of the day, the produce is sold in a spirited auction.

In August, the annual Crafts Fair in the gymnasium displays the work of local weavers, leather workers, photographers, and artists (there are many talented illustrators and painters). Particularly interesting is the horse gear, the origins of which lie in 19th-century gaucho traditions.

Places to Stay
Accommodations in Stanley are good but limited and not cheap – reservations are a good idea. Several B&Bs also offer the option of full board.

The most economical is *Kay McCallum's B&B* (☎ 21071), 14 Drury St, charging £15 per person. *Sue Binnie's B&B* (☎ 21051), 3 Brandon Rd, charges £25. As of this writing, *Sparrowhawk Guest House* (☎ 21979, fax 21980), 7 Drury St, was undergoing renovation, but it's usually one of the more economical lodgings.

Warrah Guest House (☎ 22649), a renovated 19th-century stone house at 46 John St between Dean and Philomel, charges £25 with breakfast and £44 with full board. Popular *Emma's Guest House* (☎ 21056), 36 Ross Rd near Philomel St, charges £30.50/55 single/double for bed and breakfast, while rates with full board are £48 single, £90 double.

Malvina House Hotel (☎ 21355), 3 Ross Rd, has Stanley's most congenial ambience, with beautiful grounds and a conservatory restaurant. Rates are £37.50 for an economy single with breakfast, £49.95 for a regular single with breakfast, and £47.25 per person for a twin or double with breakfast (£10 supplement for a single). The tourist rate, which includes full board, is £65.50.

The venerable *Upland Goose Hotel* (☎ 21455), a mid-19th century building at 20/22 Ross Rd, charges £39.50 per person for an economy room or £49.50 per person for a twin room with separate facilities (shared bath) and breakfast, and £59.50 per person for a twin/double with breakfast and private bath. There is a single supplement of £20 in all cases. Tourist rates, with full board, are £72.50 per person with a £40 single supplement. The Goose is the only lodging to accept Visa and MasterCard.

Places to Eat
Most of Stanley's eateries are modest and inexpensive snack bars with limited hours. Two bakeries serve bread, snacks, and light meals: *Clayton's Bakery* (☎ 21273) on Dean St (open daily 7:30 am to 1:30 pm), and *Stanley Bakery Café* (☎ 22692), Waverley House, Philomel St (open weekdays 8:30 am to 3:30 pm, Saturday 9 am to 12:30 pm).

The *Boathouse Café* (☎ 21145), on Ross

Rd near the cathedral, is open for lunch 10 am to 4 pm Monday, Wednesday, and Friday, 10 to 2 pm Tuesday and Thursday. *Woodbine Café* (☎ 21002), 29 Fitzroy Rd, serves fish and chips, pizza, sausage rolls, and similar items. It's open Tuesday to Friday 10 am to 2 pm, Wednesday and Friday 7 to 9 pm, and Saturday 10 am to 3 pm. *Arlette's Café* (☎ 22633), Atlantic House, Fitzroy Rd, is open daily except Wednesday, 9 am to 9 pm. *Leif's Deli* (☎ 22721), 23 John St, has specialty foods and snacks; it's open weekdays 9 am to 5 pm, Saturday 9:30 am to noon and 1 to 4 pm. The varied menu at *Monty's Restaurant* on John St includes vegetarian dishes.

Most Stanley hotels also have restaurants, but meals should be booked in advance. Emma's Guest House has more elaborate lunches for £6.50 and dinner for £11, while Warrah Guest House offers lunch for £7 and dinner for £12. The *Conservatory Restaurant* at Malvina House Hotel and the Upland Goose Hotel both serve three-course meals and bar snacks.

Entertainment

Stanley is no mecca for nightlife but has several pubs, open Monday to Saturday 10 am to 2 pm, Monday to Thursday 5:30 to 11 pm, Friday and Saturday 5:30 to 11:30 pm, and Sunday, Good Friday, and Christmas Day noon to 2 pm and 7 to 10 pm. When cruise ships are in port, they are open all day.

The most popular is the *Globe Hotel* (☎ 22703) at Crozier Place and Philomel St, which serves bar meals; try also the *Rose Hotel* (☎ 21067) on Brisbane Rd, the *Victory Bar* (☎ 21199) on Philomel St at Fitzroy Rd, and the *Stanley Arms* (☎ 22258) on John Biscoe Rd at the far west end of town. The Upland Goose Hotel's *Ship Bar* (☎ 21455) is open to the public, as is Monty's bar, *Deano's* (☎ 21292).

In winter Stanley pubs sponsor a popular darts league, and darts tournaments take place in the Town Hall auditorium. For more information, contact the Darts Club (☎ 21199).

Many dances, with live music, and discos also take place throughout the year usually at the town hall. Listen to the nightly FIBS announcements for dates and times. There are no cinemas, but most hotels and guesthouses have video lounges.

Things to Buy

There are a few Falklands souvenirs, but most come from the UK. The exception is locally spun and knitted woolens, some of which are outstanding. Try the Home Industries Cooperative on Fitzroy Rd, open weekdays 9:30 am to noon and 1:30 to 4:30 pm. Kiddcrafts (☎ 21301), 2A Philomel St, makes stuffed penguins and other soft toys appealing to kids.

The Pink Shop (☎ 21399), 33 Fitzroy Rd, sells gifts and souvenirs in general, Falklands and general-interest books (including a selection of Lonely Planet guides), and excellent wildlife prints by owner Tony Chater.

Postage stamps, available from the post office and from the Philatelic Bureau, are popular with collectors. The Bureau also sells stamps from South Georgia and British Antarctic Territory, and accepts Visa credit cards. The Treasury (☎ 27141), in the Secretariat on Thatcher Drive behind the 1982 War Memorial, sells commemorative Falklands coins.

Getting There & Away

Air For information on international flights, see the general Getting There & Away section above.

The Falkland Islands Government Air Service (FIGAS) (☎ 27219), at Stanley airport, sets up itineraries according to demand; as soon as you know when and where you wish to go, contact them, and listen to the FIBS announcements at 6:30 pm the night before your departure to learn your departure time. Flight plans depend on demand; if only one ot two people are headed to a destination, FIGAS may delay a flight until other passengers join the group. On rare occasions, usually around holidays, flights are heavily booked and you may not get on. Because some grass airstrips can only accept a limited payload, luggage is restricted to 30 lbs (13.5 kg) per person.

Passages may also be arranged through the Falkland Islands Tourist Board on the Public Jetty. Sample roundtrip fares from Stanley include Salvador (£50), Darwin (£76), San Carlos (£78), Port Howard (£94), Sea Lion Island (£95), Pebble Island (£106), Fox Bay East or West (£121), and Carcass Island (£145).

Bus There are few places accessible by road in the Falklands, but C&M Travel (☎ 21468) serves Stanley and Mt Pleasant airports, and will also make day trips to Darwin/Goose Green and elsewhere during the summer months. They have two 52-seater coaches, one 28-seater, and a 12-seater minibus.

Getting Around

To/From the Airport The Falklands have two main airports. Mt Pleasant International airport is 35 miles (56 km) southwest of Stanley via a good graveled road, while Stanley airport (☎ 27303), for local flights and flights from Punta Arenas, is about three miles (five km) east of town. C&M Travel (☎ 21468) takes passengers to Mt Pleasant for £13 single; call for reservations the day before. They will also take groups to Stanley airport or meet them there.

Taxi For cabs, contact Ben's Taxi Service (☎ 21191) or Lowe's Taxis (☎ 21381), but be aware that they're expensive.

Car Rental Since roads are so few, it's hard to justify renting a car, but Land Rovers are available from Ian Bury (☎ 21058), 63 Davis St; Ben Claxton (☎ 21437) on Ross Rd East; and the Upland Goose Hotel (☎ 21455) on Ross Rd. Drivers without local experience often get stuck in the boggy soft camp. This problem is so common even for experienced drivers that locals often carry a two-meter radio to call for help if they "get bogged."

AROUND STANLEY

Stanley Harbour Maritime History Trail

See the tourist office on the Public Jetty for Graham Bound's informational brochure on the various wrecks and condemned ships in Stanley Harbour. There are now informational panels near the remains of vessels like the *Jhelum* (a sinking East Indiaman deserted by her crew in 1871), the *Charles Cooper* (an American packet from 1866 still used for storage by the FIC), and the *Lady Elizabeth* (a striking three-masted freighter that limped into Stanley after hitting a reef in 1913).

Penguin Walk & Gypsy Cove

To visit the most convenient penguin colonies, about 1½ hours' walk northeast of Stanley, go to the east end of Ross Rd beyond the cemetery and cross the bridge over the inlet known as The Canache, continuing past the wreck of the *Lady Elizabeth* and Stanley airport. Gentoo penguins crowd the large sand beach at Yorke Bay north of the airport where, unfortunately, the Argentines anticipated a British frontal assault and buried countless plastic mines. While you cannot go onto the beach itself, you can get a good view of the penguins by walking along the mine field fence. Farther on, at Gypsy Cove, are Magellanic penguins, upland geese, kelp geese, and many other shorebirds. There are no known mines in this area, but some may have washed up onshore.

Battlefields

AD (Tony) Smith (☎ 21027) offers tours of 1982 battlefield sites near Stanley, including Wireless Ridge, Mt Tumbledown, and Sapper Hill.

Cape Pembroke Lighthouse

Built in 1855 and rebuilt in 1906, this recently restored lighthouse is a full-day's walk east from Stanley airport. In the late 19th century, the entire Cape Pembroke peninsula constituted one of few small farms on the Islands, leased by the

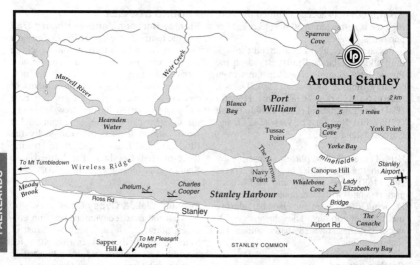

Around Stanley

government to Stanley resident James Smith, a vocal advocate of agrarian reform, which finally came about a century later.

Kidney Island

This small nature reserve north of Port William is covered with tussock grass, forming the habitat for a wide variety of wildlife, including rockhopper penguins, sea lions, and other species. Arrange carefully planned visits through the Agricultural Officer (☎ 27355). Dave and Carol Eynon's South Atlantic Marine Services (☎ 21145) on Ross Rd offers boat transportation.

The Camp

Every part of the Falklands outside Stanley is "camp," including those parts of East Falkland accessible by road from Stanley, all of West Falkland, and the numerous smaller offshore islands, only a few of which are inhabited. Nearly everyone in camp is engaged in sheep ranching, though a few work in tourism and minor cottage industries.

Since the advent of the large sheep stations in the late 19th century, rural settlement in the Falklands has consisted of tiny hamlets, really company towns, near sheltered harbors where coastal shipping could collect the wool clip. In fact, these settlements were the models for the sheep estancias of Patagonia, many of which were founded by Falklands emigrants. On nearly all of them, shepherds lived in "outside houses" that still dot the countryside. Since the agrarian reform of the late 1970s and 1980s, this pattern of residence has not changed greatly despite the creation of many new farms.

Many but not all of the Islands' best wildlife sites are on smaller offshore islands such as Sea Lion Island and Pebble

Island, where there are comfortable but fairly costly tourist lodges. These are described in detail below, but there are also alternatives for budget travelers. Some of the most interesting islands have few or no visitor facilities and very difficult access, but it is worthwhile asking at the Tourist Board about them when you arrive in the Falklands.

EAST FALKLAND

East Falkland has the Islands' most extensive road network, consisting of a good highway to Mt Pleasant international airport and Goose Green. From Pony's Pass on the Mt Pleasant Hwy, there is also a good track north to the Estancia (a farm west of Stanley) and Port Louis, and also one west toward Douglas and Port San Carlos. There's also a Rover track from Darwin north toward San Carlos (which is different from Port San Carlos). Most other tracks are usable for 4WDs only, so FIGAS is still the quickest and most reliable means of transport.

Salvador

Originally founded by Andrés Pitaluga, a Gibraltarian who arrived in the Islands via South America in the 1830s, Salvador is one of East Falkland's oldest owner-occupied sheep farms. On the station's north coast are colonies of five different species of penguins and many other shorebirds and waterfowl, while Centre Island in Port Salvador (also known as Salvador Water) has breeding populations of elephant seals and sea lions. Trekking along the north coast is possible with permission.

Owner Rob Pitaluga of *Salvador Lodge* (☎ 31199) offers self-catering accommodations (they provide the bedding, you provide and cook your own food) for £10 per person per night, £5 for children under 12.

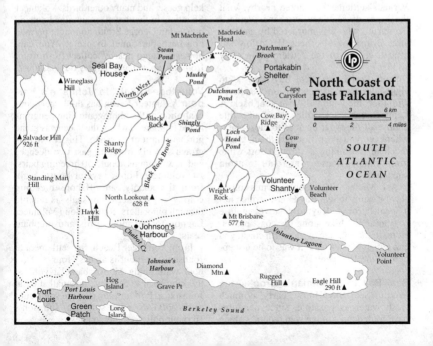

North Coast of East Falkland

Trekking the Northeast Coast

If you can do only one trek in the Islands, this is the one. From Seal Bay to Volunteer Point on the north coast of East Falkland, a mixture of broad, sandy beaches and rugged headlands, a trekker always has penguins in view.

Port Louis to Seal Bay Port Louis is the starting point, reached by car – ask around town for a vehicle – or on foot from Stanley in one very long day. You will need permission from station manager Michael Morrison at Port Louis (☎ 31004) and owner George Smith of Johnson's Harbour (☎ 31399).

Port Louis is the Falklands' oldest settlement, dating from the French foundation of the colony by Louis de Bougainville in 1764. One of the oldest buildings in the colony is the ivy-covered 19th-century farmhouse, still occupied by farm employees, but there are also ruins of the French governor's house and fortress and Louis Vernet's settlement scattered nearby. Visit the grave of Matthew Brisbane, Vernet's lieutenant, who was murdered by gauchos after British naval officer JJ Onslow left him in charge of the settlement in early 1833.

From Port Louis, Seal Bay is a six- to eight-hour walk, depending on weather – with luck, the wind will be at your back. A Land Rover track follows a fence line almost all the way; be sure to close gates whenever you pass through them. Since much of the hiking is through soft white grass camp, choose your route to avoid sinking in.

Ask Michael Morrison's permission to stay or camp at Seal Bay House, which has a peat-burning Rayburn stove, before beginning the hike along the coast proper. Here, in the solitude of the north coast, you can get an idea of what it was to be a shepherd in the 19th century.

Seal Bay to Dutchman's Brook After leaving Seal Bay House, carry as much fresh water as possible, since penguins have fouled most of the watercourses along the way. Follow the arc of the coast eastward, past several colonies of rockhopper penguins and king cormorants, to the sea lion colony at Macbride Head. En route, there are also thousands of burrows of Magellanic penguins and occasional macaronis and gentoos.

Although the 1:250,000 map of East Falkland indicates a large inlet at Swan Pond, there is a broad, sandy beach there that only requires wading one shallow creek. The best campsite is Dutchman's Brook, where there is a Portakabin shelter but no dependable source of fresh water.

Dutchman's Brook to Volunteer Shanty About 1½ hours south of Dutchman's Brook, in a patch of white grass along a fence line near a colony of gentoo penguins, a tiny spring is the only likely source of fresh water until Volunteer Shanty, another four hours south. On the way, you will see many more penguins, elephant seals, nesting turkey vultures, upland and kelp geese, and many other birds. Volunteer Shanty is in fact a well-maintained outside house, but George Smith no longer permits non-farm personnel to use it. You can, however, camp nearby, collect fresh water from the tap, and use its very tidy outhouse.

Volunteer Shanty to Johnson's Harbour Volunteer Beach has the largest concentration of the photogenic king penguins in the Falklands, where the species is at the northern limit of its range. This colony has grown steadily over the past two decades and now contains about 150 breeding pairs. At Volunteer Point, several hours' walk from the shanty, an offshore breeding colony of southern fur seals is visible through binoculars. Return along Volunteer Lagoon to see more birds and elephant seals.

From Volunteer Beach, the settlement at Johnson's Harbour is an easy four- to five-hour walk along Mt Brisbane. If you are trekking back to Stanley, the small store at Johnson's Harbour may provide some supplies. FIGAS now stops at Johnson's Harbour only for emergencies.

AD (Tony) Smith (☎ 21027) runs full-day excursions to Volunteer Beach from Stanley, as does Mel Lloyd's Falcon Tours (☎ 32220). Mike Rendell at Malvina House Hotel (☎ 21084), 8 Ross Rd West in Stanley, arranges overnight excursions for a maximum of five people.

San Carlos

British forces in the 1982 conflict first came ashore at San Carlos settlement, at the south end of San Carlos Water on the Falkland Sound side of East Falkland; there is a small military cemetery nearby. Until 1983, when it was subdivided and sold to half a dozen local families, San Carlos was a traditional large sheep station – the isolated "big house," with its lengthy approach, will give you some idea how farm owners and managers distanced themselves from laborers.

There is fishing on the San Carlos River, north of the settlement, while the comfortable *Blue Beach Lodge,* operated by William and Lynda Anderson, charges £49 for full board, with discounts for children. Self-catering accommodations are available at Robin and Mandy Goodwin's *Waimea Fishing Lodge* (☎ 32220) for £15 per person.

Across San Carlos Water, on Ajax Bay, are the fascinating ruins of the **Ajax Bay Refrigeration Plant,** a Colonial Development Corporation (CDC) boondoggle of the 1950s that failed when farmers did not provide it with sufficient high-quality mutton from flocks raised primarily for wool. After its abandonment, pre-fab houses that were imported for laborers were dismantled and moved to Stanley, where they can be seen on Ross Rd West. Gentoo penguins occasionally wander through the ruins, which served as a military field hospital during the 1982 conflict. Take a flashlight if you plan to explore the ruins, which are about a four-hour walk around the south end of San Carlos Water.

Darwin & Goose Green

Darwin, at the narrow isthmus that separates the southern peninsula of Lafonia from the northern half of East Falkland, was the site of Samuel Lafone's saladero, where the Montevideo merchant's local agents slaughtered feral cattle and processed their hides; later it became the center of the Falkland Islands Company's camp operations and, with nearby Goose Green, the largest settlement in the Falklands outside Stanley.

Built across Bodie Creek in 1926 to improve communications between Goose Green and Darwin, the world's southern-most suspension bridge is an unexpected sight. The heaviest ground fighting of the Falklands war took place at Goose Green, where there are several military landmarks, including an Argentine military cemetery and a memorial to British Colonel H Jones.

Sea Lion Island

The most southerly inhabited island in the Falklands is barely a mile across at its widest point, but still has more wildlife in a smaller area than almost anywhere in the Islands, including all five species of Falklands penguins, enormous colonies of cormorants, giant petrels, and the remarkably tame and charming predator known locally as the "Johnny Rook," more properly the striated caracara *(Phalcoboenus australis).* Hundreds of elephant seals haul up to breed on its sandy beaches every spring, while sea lions line the narrow gravel beaches below the southern bluffs and lurk among the towering tussock grass.

For most of its history, Sea Lion's isolation and difficult access undoubtedly contributed to the continuing abundance of wildlife, but much of the credit has to go to Terry and Doreen Clifton, who farmed Sea Lion Island since the mid-1970s before selling it in the early 1990s – the Cliftons developed their 2300-acre farm with the idea that wildlife, habitat, and livestock were compatible uses. Sea Lion Island is one of few working farms in the Falklands with any substantial cover of native tussock, which once covered the coastal fringe of both East and West Falkland and many offshore islands before careless fires and overgrazing nearly eliminated it.

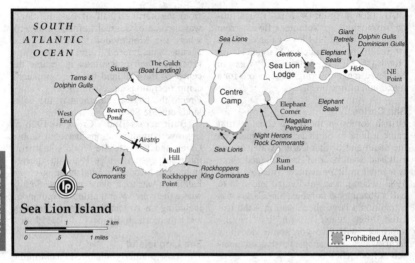

Through improved fencing and other conscientious management decisions, the Cliftons made the island both a successful sheep station and a popular tourist site, mostly for day trips from Stanley and the military base at Mt Pleasant. Since 1986 the modern *Sea Lion Lodge* (☎ 32004), operated by Dave and Pat Grey, has offered twin-bedded rooms with full board for £51 per person, including access to a County Land Rover for visiting wildlife sites, although almost anyone can walk the length of the island in a few hours. To see the island in its entirety, allow at least two full days.

WEST FALKLAND

Nearly as large as East Falkland, West Falkland's only proper road runs from Port Howard on Falkland Sound to Chartres on King George Bay, but a system of rough tracks is also suitable for Land Rovers and motorcycles. Although offshore Saunders Island was the site of the first British garrison in 1765, West Falkland was settled permanently only in the late 1860s, when pioneer sheep farmer JL Waldron founded Port Howard. In short order, British entrepreneurs established stations at Hill Cove,

Fox Bay, Port Stephens, Roy Cove, Chartres, and many smaller offshore islands. One of the most interesting experiments was the founding of a mission for Indians from Tierra del Fuego on Keppel Island.

West Falkland, as well as adjacent offshore islands, has outstanding wildlife sites and good trekking in its interior, which is generally more mountainous than East Falkland. Only a few of these sites have formal tourist infrastructure, but independent travelers should look into visiting all parts of the island. Ask local farmer owners for permission to walk across their properties.

Port Howard

West Falkland's oldest farm is one of very few large sheep stations to survive the major agrarian reform of the past decade. For more than a century it belonged to JL Waldron Ltd, but in 1987 it was sold to local managers Robin and Rodney Lee, who have kept the farm and settlement intact rather than subdividing it. About 40 people live on the 200,000-acre station, which has 42,000 sheep, 800 cattle, and its own dairy, grocery, abattoir, social club, and other amenities. Unusually for the Falklands, employees have been given the opportunity to purchase their houses, and at least one has chosen to retire here rather than move to Stanley. Port Howard will be the West Falkland terminus of the anticipated ferry across Falkland Sound.

Port Howard is a very scenic settlement at the foot of 2158-foot Mt Maria, at the north end of the Hornby range. Although there is wildlife, most of it is distant from the settlement, the immediate surroundings of which offer opportunities for hiking, horseback riding, and fishing. It is also possible to view summer shearing and other camp activities, and there is a small **museum** of artifacts from the 1982 war, when Argentine forces occupied the settlement.

Port Howard Lodge (☎ 42150) is the former manager's house, a classic of its era with a beautiful conservatory that feels like the tropics when the sun comes out – see also the antique West Falkland telephone exchange, which no longer functions. Accommodations cost £48 per person with full board, but make arrangements in advance to lodge at the farm's cookhouse for a fraction of the cost.

From Port Howard it is possible to hike up the valley of the Warrah River, a good trout stream, and past the Turkey Rocks to the Blackburn River and Hill Cove settlement, another pioneer 19th-century farm. Where the track is unclear, look for the remains of the old telephone lines. Ask permission to cross property boundaries, and remember to close gates. There are other, longer hikes south toward Chartres, Fox Bay, and Port Stephens.

Pebble Island

Elongated Pebble, off the north coast of West Falkland, has varied topography, a good sampling of wildlife, and extensive wetlands. *Pebble Island Hotel* (☎ 41093) charges £48 per person for room with full board, but ask about self-catering cottages at the settlement and *Marble Mountain Shanty* at the west end of the island, both of which charge £15 per night.

Keppel Island

In 1853, the South American Missionary Society established an outpost on Keppel Island to catechize Yahgan Indians from Tierra del Fuego and teach them to become potato farmers instead of hunters and gatherers. The mission was controversial because the government suspected that Indians had been brought against their will, but it lasted until 1898, despite the Indians' susceptibility to disease – contrast the unmarked but discernable Yahgan graves with the marked ones of the mission personnel. One Falklands governor attributed numerous Yahgan deaths from tuberculosis to their

> delicacy of constitution . . . developed owing to the warm clothing which they are for the sake of decency required to adopt after having been for 15 or 20 years roaming about in their canoes in a very cold climate without clothing of any kind.

It's likely that hard physical labor, change of diet, European contagion, and harsh living conditions in their small, damp stone houses played a greater role in the Yahgans' demise than any inherent delicacy of constitution. The mission was undoubtedly prosperous, though, bringing in an annual income of nearly £1000 from its herds of cattle, flocks of sheep, and gardens by 1877.

Although Keppel is now exclusively a sheep farm, there remain several interesting ruins. The former chapel is now a wool shed, while the stone walls of the Yahgan dwellings remain in fairly good condition. The mission bailiff's house stands intact, though in poor repair. Keppel is also a good place to see penguins. Visitors interested in exploring the island should contact LR Fell (☎ 41001), the owner of Keppel.

Saunders Island

Only a few miles west of Keppel, Port Egmont on Saunders Island was the site of the first British garrison on the Falklands, built in 1765. In 1767, after France ceded its colony to Spain, Spanish forces dislodged the British from Saunders and nearly precipitated a general war between the two countries. After the British left voluntarily in 1774, the Spaniards razed the settlement, including its impressive blockhouse, leaving the still remaining jetties, extensive foundations, and some of the buildings' walls, plus the garden terraces built by the British marines. One British sailor left a memoir indicating how well developed the settlement was:

The glory of our colony was the gardens, which we cultivated with the greatest care, as being fully convinced how much the comforts of our situation depended on our being supplied with vegetables . . . We were plentifully supplied with potatoes, cabbages, broccoli, carrots, borecole, spinach, parsley, lettuce, English celery, mustard, cresses, and some few, but very fine cauliflowers.

Saunders Island continued to be controversial into the late 1980s because the property passed by inheritance into the hands of Argentine descendants of the Scottish pioneer sheep farmer John Hamilton, who also had extensive properties near Río Gallegos in Santa Cruz province. For years, Islanders agitated for the farm's expropriation, but the owners finally consented to sell the Island to its local managers in 1987.

In addition to historical resources, Saunders Island has an excellent sample of Falklands wildlife and offers good trekking, especially out the north side of Brett Harbour to The Neck. About four hours' walk from the settlement, this sand-pit beach connects Saunders Island to Elephant Point peninsula, once a separate island. The Neck has a Portakabin shelter near a large colony of black-browed albatrosses and rockhopper penguins, as well as a few king penguins. Farther on, toward Elephant Point proper, are thousands of Magellanic penguins, breeding kelp gulls, skuas, and a colony of elephant seals in a very scenic area. From The Neck, Elephant Point is about a four hours' walk one way.

David and Suzan Pole-Evans on Saunders (☎ 41298) rent a comfortable self-catering cottage in the settlement for £10 per person per night, as well as the Porta-

kabin at The Neck, which sleeps six (bedding supplied) and has a gas stove and a chemical toilet outside. Fresh milk and eggs are usually available in the settlement, but otherwise visitors should bring their own food. Depending on the farm workload, transportation to The Neck is available for £10 per person.

Carcass Island
Despite its name, Carcass is a small, scenic island west of Saunders with a good variety of wildlife. It is a popular weekend and holiday vacation spot for Stanleyites. A couple of self-catering cottages in the settlement rent for £15/25 single/double, plus £5 per additional person; for details, contact Rob McGill on Carcass Island (☎ 41106).

Port Stephens
Unquestionably the most scenic part of the Falklands, Port Stephens' rugged headlands are open to the blustery South Atlantic and are battered by storms out of the Antarctic. Thousands upon thousands of rockhopper penguins, cormorants, and other seabirds breed on the exposed coast, only a short distance from the settlement's sheltered harbor, until recently the center of one of the FIC's largest stations. Like many other settlements, Port Stephens has no formal tourist facilities, but it is well worth a visit.

Less than an hour's walk from the settlement, Wood Cove and Stephens Peak are excellent places to see gentoo and rockhopper penguins and other local birds. The peak of Calm Head, about a two hours' walk, has excellent views of the jagged shoreline and the powerful open South Atlantic.

One interesting longer trek goes from the settlement to the abandoned sealing station at Port Albemarle and huge gentoo penguin colonies near the Arch Islands. Hoste Inlet, where there is a habitable outside house, is about a five hours' walk in good weather, while the sealing station, another post-WWII Colonial Development Corporation blunder, is four hours farther. Like the Ajax

Bay freezer, the sealing station is a monument to bureaucratic ineptitude, but photographers and aficionados of industrial archaeology will find its derelict power station, boilers, rail track, water tanks, jetty, and Nissen huts surrealistically intriguing. There is a habitable shanty with a functional Rayburn stove nearby, but unfortunately squaddies from the radar station on Mt Alice have vandalized the larger outside house.

The massive penguin colonies are an hour's walk beyond the sealing station. The Arch Islands, unfortunately inaccessible except by boat, take their name from the opening that the ocean has eroded in the largest of the group – and it is large enough to allow a good-sized vessel to pass through it.

Visitors interested in exploring Port Stephens and trekking in the vicinity should contact Peter or Anne Robertson (☎ 42307) at the settlement, or Leon and Pam Berntsen (☎ 42309) at Albemarle Station.

Weddell Island

Scottish pioneer John Hamilton, also a major landholder in Argentine Patagonia, acquired this western offshore island and others nearby to experiment on various agricultural improvement projects, including the replanting of tussock grass, forest plantations, the importation of Highland cattle and Shetland ponies, and the well-meaning but perhaps misguided introduction of exotic wildlife like guanacos (still present on Staats Island), Patagonian foxes (common on Weddell proper), and otters (apparently extinct). Saunders still hosts abundant local wildlife, including gentoo and Magellanic penguins, great skuas, night herons, giant petrels, and striated caracaras.

Unfortunately, Hamilton's original farmhouse, which had spectacular interior woodwork, burned to the ground a few years ago, but farm owners John and Steph Ferguson (☎ 42398) still welcome guests at *Seaview Cottage* or *Hamilton Cottage* for £15 per person per night (self-catering) or £30 per person per night with full board.

New Island

The Falklands' most westerly inhabited island is almost inaccessible (unless the new grass airstrip has been finished), but it has great historic interest, having been a refuge for whalers from Britain and North America from the late 18th century well into the 19th, despite the objections of Spanish and British authorities. There remain ruins of a shore-based, turn-of-the-century Norwegian whaling factory that failed because there simply were not enough whales.

On the precipitous western coast are gigantic colonies of rockhopper penguins and black-browed albatrosses and a large rookery of southern fur seals. Facilities are few, but potential visitors should contact Tony or Annie Chater (☎ 21399), or Ian or María Strange (☎ 21185) in Stanley.

Uruguay

Facts about Uruguay

About the size of Buenos Aires province, Uruguay is a classic political buffer between the South American megastates of Argentina and Brazil. Increasing numbers of independent travelers are visiting the country – from Buenos Aires, it is only a short hop across the Río de la Plata to the fascinating colonial contraband center of Colonia and a few hours more to Montevideo, one of South America's most interesting capitals. East of Montevideo, sandy Atlantic beaches attract many Uruguayans and Argentines for summer holidays, but the less frequented towns up the Río Uruguay, opposite Argentine Mesopotamia, are also clean and attractive. Uruguay's hilly interior is agreeable but rarely visited gaucho country.

Known officially as the República Oriental del Uruguay (Eastern Republic of Uruguay, often abbreviated as ROU), the area was long called the Banda Oriental or "Eastern Shore" of the River Plate. For most of this century, foreigners considered Uruguay the "Switzerland of South America," but political and economic events of the 1970s and 1980s undermined this favorable image.

HISTORY

Uruguay's aboriginal inhabitants were the Charrúa Indians, a hunting and gathering people who also fished extensively. Hostile to outsiders, they killed Spanish explorer Juan de Solís and most of his party in 1516, which discouraged settlement for more than a century. In any event, there was little to attract the Spanish who, according to William Henry Hudson, "loved gold and adventure above everything, and finding neither in the Banda, they little esteemed it."

In the 17th century, the Charrúas acquired the horse and prospered on wild cattle, eventually trading with the Spanish. Never numerous, they no longer exist as a definable tribal entity, though there remain some mestizo people in the interior along the Brazilian border. Much as the Argentine gauchos of the Pampas, the Uruguayan gauchos subsisted on wild cattle, but in time the establishment of estancias pushed them back into the interior.

European Colonization

The first Europeans on the Banda Oriental were Jesuit missionaries who settled near present-day Soriano, on the Río Uruguay. In 1680 the Portuguese established a beachhead at Nova Colônia do Sacramento, opposite Buenos Aires on the estuary of the Rió de la Plata. As a fortress and contraband center, Colonia posed a direct challenge to Spanish authority, forcing the Spanish to build their own citadel at the sheltered port of Montevideo.

This rivalry between Spain and Portugal led eventually to Uruguayan independence. José Gervasio Artigas, Uruguay's greatest national hero, allied with the United Provinces of the River Plate against Spain, but was unable to prevent Uruguay's takeover

José Gervasio Artigas

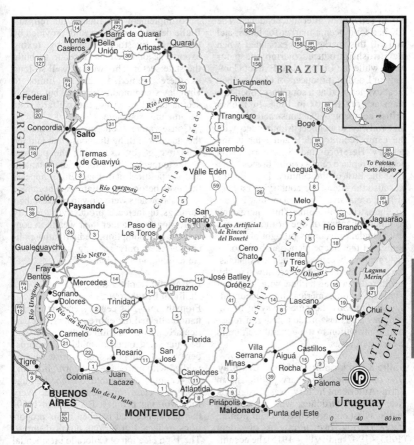

by Brazil. Exiled to Paraguay, he inspired the famous "33 Orientales," Uruguayan patriots under General Juan Lavalleja who, with Argentine support, launched a campaign to liberate the Banda Oriental from Brazilian control. In 1828, after three years' struggle, a British-mediated treaty between Argentina and Brazil established Uruguay as a small independent buffer between the emerging continental powers.

Independence & Development

For most of the 19th century, Uruguay's independence was a fragile one, threatened politically and militarily by Argentina and

Brazil, and economically by Britain. Federalist forces, with the support of the Argentine dictator Rosas, besieged Montevideo from 1838 to 1851. From this period, Uruguay's two major political parties, the Blancos and the Colorados, can trace their origins as armed gaucho sympathizers of the Federalist and Unitarist causes. As Hudson wrote in *The Purple Land* (1922), "Endless struggles for mastery ensued, in which the Argentines and Brazilians, forgetting their solemn compact, were for ever taking sides."

British interest in the Banda Oriental, aroused by that country's occupation of the city in 1807, grew after independence. The UK had long been a market for hides, and in 1840 this market was expanded when the British introduced merino sheep for wool, while the Liebig Meat Extract Company of London (producers of Oxo, a cubed meat extract used as a soup base) opened a plant at Fray Bentos in 1864. In 1868 a British company began construction on the first railway to connect Montevideo with the camp (countryside), and later in the century Hereford and Shorthorn cattle began to replace rangy criollo breeds.

At the turn of the century, Fray Bentos was also the site of the country's first *frigorífico,* a massive Anglo plant that is now an industrial museum. This increasing commercialization of one of the country's few abundant resources brought about the demise of the independent gaucho who, as in Argentina, became attached to estancias, the boundaries of which were now fixed by the introduction of barbed wire. As elsewhere in Latin America, large landholdings *(latifundios)* became a way of life in Uruguay, and these made a major, if reluctant, contribution to the general welfare in the form of taxes.

Batlle & the Modernization of Uruguay
One of the most visionary politicians in Latin American history was Uruguay's José Batlle y Ordóñez, who devised the region's first comprehensive social welfare state. During two terms as president (1903 – 1907 and 1911 – 1915), he accomplished such innovations as modern pensions, farm credits, unemployment compensation, and eight-hour workdays. Despite his own strong presidency and interventionist approach to government, he also sought to overcome the legacy of *caudillismo* (the strong-arm rule of the *caudillo)* by constitutional reform. He created a collegial executive on the Swiss model, but this reform was never completely successful. State intervention in the economy resulted in the nationalization of many industries, the creation of others, and, for a while, an unparalleled general prosperity.

To implement and finance his reforms, Batlle depended on the wealth provided by the rural livestock sector; by taxing exports he obtained the revenue to build the state sector. This worked well so long as there seemed to be no limits to Uruguay's commodity exports, but as this sector failed to grow, the welfare state became unsustainable.

Conservative economists have blamed the state for "killing the goose that laid the golden egg" by exploiting the pastoral sector to the limit for Montevideo's benefit and for political patronage. But it appears that even before the welfare state became a fact, landowners were slow to reinvest their earnings to increase productivity, mainly preferring to squander their wealth in conspicuous consumption. Redistributive policies worked only so long as there was something to redistribute.

Economic Decline & Political Breakdown
From the mid-20th century, economic stagnation affected the entire country, but particularly the city of Montevideo, which had become accustomed to middle-class prosperity. State-supported enterprise became riddled with patronage and corruption, and the economy was unable to support a huge pensioner class (one pensioner for every four working people). By the mid-1960s this unbalance had reached crisis proportions, reflected in serious political unrest. The 1966 election of Colorado presidential candidate Oscar Gestido, a highly regarded retired general, appeared to give some cause for optimism and recovery; however, Gestido died shortly after taking office, and was replaced by Vice President Jorge Pacheco Areco, a virtual unknown who proved to have disturbing authoritarian tendencies.

The country slid into dictatorship as Pacheco outlawed leftist parties, closed newspapers, and invoked state-of-siege measures, citing guerrilla activity. The major guerrilla force was the Movimiento de Liberación Nacional (National Liberation Movement), more commonly known as the Tupamaros, a clandestine socialist faction that had organized as early as 1963 but did not reveal its existence publicly until 1967. Although an urban, middle-class movement in a country populated almost exclusively by descendants of Europeans, the Tupamaros took their name from a Peruvian Indian who led an 18th-century rebellion against the Spanish crown.

At first, public support for the Tupamaros was considerable, but it eroded quickly as Uruguayans began to blame them for the Pacheco government's excesses, which included the dismissal of a police official who openly disapproved of torture. After the Tupamaros kidnapped and executed suspected CIA agent Dan Mitrione (an incident dramatized in Costa-Gavras's film *State of Siege*) (1973), and then engineered the escape of more than one hundred of their comrades from prison, Pacheco put the military rather than the police in charge of counterinsurgency.

Presidential elections occurred as scheduled in November 1971, but Pacheco's handpicked successor, Juan M Bordaberry, invited the military to participate in government, ruling with a National Security Council and eventually dissolving the legislature.

The Military Dictatorship & its Aftermath

While the Uruguayan military takeover exhibited neither the shocking suddenness of the Chilean coup nor the sustained brutality of Argentina's Dirty War, it was perhaps even more insidious in the context of Uruguayan history. Virtually eliminating free expression, the armed forces occupied almost every position of importance in the entire country and increased the military budget dramatically to bolster "national security."

Torture or threat of torture became routine; eventually more than 60,000 citizens were detained. The military established a political classification system that determined eligibility for public employment; subjected all political offenses to military courts; actively censored public libraries;

and even subjected large family gatherings to prior police approval.

Attempting to institutionalize their political role, the armed forces drafted a constitution, but the electorate rejected it in a plebiscite in 1980 despite warnings that rejection would delay any return to civilian rule. Four more years passed before voters could elect Colorado presidential candidate Julio María Sanguinetti under the Constitution of 1967. Sanguinetti, though not a tool of the military, won only because they prohibited the candidacy of Blanco leader Wilson Ferreira Aldunate, a vocal and popular opponent of the dictatorship.

Sanguinetti's presidency, while not a spectacular change, seemed to indicate a return to Uruguay's democratic traditions. He did, however, support a controversial amnesty bill for military human rights violations that was submitted to a referendum of all Uruguayans in April 1989. Despite serious misgivings on the part of many, a majority of voters approved the amnesty. Later that year, Blanco presidential candidate Luis Lacalle succeeded Sanguinetti in a peaceful transition of power. Sanguinetti returned to office as the head of a coalition government in the elections of November 1994.

GEOGRAPHY & CLIMATE

One of South America's smallest countries, Uruguay is still large by European standards. Its area of 187,000 sq km is slightly larger than England and Wales combined, or about the size of the US state of North Dakota. Lacking energy resources (except for a few hydroelectric sites), minerals, and commercial forests, its principal natural asset is agricultural land, which is abundant but less fertile than the Argentine Pampas. For the most part, the country's rolling topography is an extension of southern Brazil, with two main ranges of interior hills, the Cuchilla de Haedo, west of Tacuarembó, and the Cuchilla Grande, south of Melo, neither of which exceeds 500 meters in height. West of Montevideo, the level terrain resembles the Pampas, while the coastal area east of the capital has impressive beaches, dunes, and headlands. There are some large lagoons near the Atlantic border with Brazil, including the huge Laguna Merín.

The climate is mild, even in winter, and frosts are rare. Along the coast, daytime temperatures average 28°C in January and 15°C in June, while nighttime temperatures average 17°C in January and 7°C in June. Annual rainfall, evenly distributed throughout the year, averages about one meter over the whole country. (See Climate Charts on page 755.)

FLORA & FAUNA

Consisting mostly of grasslands and gallery forests (forests along watercourses), Uruguay's native vegetation does not differ greatly from that of the Argentine Pampas or southern Brazil. In the southeast along the Brazilian border some areas of palm savanna remain, but only a very small percentage of the land is forested.

Wild animals of any size are uncommon, although rhea can still be found in areas close to the Río Uruguay. Uruguay's nature reserves are few and offer little out of the ordinary, although the seal colonies near Punta del Este and at Cabo Polonio make worthwhile visits.

GOVERNMENT

The 1967 constitution of the republic of Uruguay establishes three separate branches of government. The president heads the executive branch, while the legislative Asamblea General (General Assembly) consists of a 99-seat Cámara de Diputados (Chamber of Deputies) and a 30-member Senado (Senate). Elections for these seats are held every five years. The Corte Suprema (Supreme Court) is the highest judicial power. Administratively, the country consists of 19 departments organized much like the national government.

The electoral system is very complex. While the legislature is chosen by proportional representation, each party may offer several presidential candidates. The winner is the candidate with the most votes of the party with the most votes. This means that

the winner almost certainly will not win a majority (even within his own party) and may not even be the candidate with the most votes overall. In the eight elections between 1946 and 1984, no winning candidate obtained more than 31% of the vote.

The two major political parties are the Colorados, the inheritors of the legacy of *Batllismo,* and the generally more conservative Blancos. Julio María Sanguinetti of the Colorado party, the first post-military president, ruled between 1984 and 1989, while his successor, Luis Lacalle, who ruled until the 1994, belonged to the Blancos. A third force, which has been growing in power, is the Frente Amplio or Encuentro Progesista, a center-left coalition that controls the mayorship of Montevideo. Ironically, their most prominent figure is a retired general, Liber Seregni. In the presidential election of November 1994, Frente Amplio candidate Tabar Vásquez actually won more votes than any other candidate, but the fact that his party had fewer total votes than the Colorados denied him the presidency.

This closely contested election returned Sanguinetti to the presidency at the head of a Colorado-Blanco coalition that has divided important cabinet posts between the two parties and constitutes, at least in theory, a substantial legislative majority. Whether the coalition of these traditional opponents will hold together for long remains an open question, but Frente Amplio now constitutes the official opposition. Despite continuing links to leftists (when former Tupamaro José Mujica, now an elected deputy, parked his motorcycle at Montevideo's Palacio Legislativo, he responded to staff inquiries as to how long he planned to remain with "Five years, unless the military returns"), it has made surprising inroads into wealthier neighborhoods like Carrasco. As Frente Amplio mayor of Montevideo, Mariano Arana is one of the country's most powerful individuals outside the national government.

The new government faces two major issues: reform of the overburdened social security system, and the country's response to its membership in the recently formed Mercosur common market, which positions Uruguay as a junior partner, for all practical purposes, to economic giants Brazil and Argentina. Uruguay risks being swamped in Mercosur, because the elimination of protective tariffs for state industries is more to the advantage of the larger states with greater productive capacity than it is to Uruguay.

ECONOMY

Uruguay is resource-poor and underpopulated. Historically, the dominant and most productive part of the Uruguayan economy has been the pastoral sector. Cattle and sheep estancias occupy more than three-quarters of the land, grazing over 9 million cattle and 23 million sheep, but as the pastoral economy has stagnated from estancieros' unwillingness to invest in improvements, the country has been unable to sustain the progressive social programs established by José Batlle. The low international price for wool, the country's primary export, has been a major factor in recent years. Only along the southwest littoral does the country support intensive agriculture, although wet-rice cultivation has increased around Laguna Merín near the Brazilian border. Cropland occupies a relatively small area, but makes a disproportionately high contribution to the economy.

Uruguay's manufacturing is restricted mostly to the area around Montevideo. In part because of Batlle's legacy of encouraging self-sufficiency despite a tiny internal market, many inefficient state-supported industries produce inferior products at very high cost, surviving only because of protective tariffs. Among the economic activities traditionally controlled by the government are railroads, banking, insurance, telephone service, electricity, water supply, oil refining, fisheries, and Montevideo's meat supply. This extensive control makes the country's economy the most state-dominated in Latin America. Social security pensions consume 60% of public expenditure.

Tourism plays an increasingly important economic role, as the beaches east of Montevideo attract wealthy Argentines. In many ways, Uruguay is an economic satellite of both Brazil and Argentina as well as a political buffer between the two major South American powers. The new Mercosur common market, which went into effect in 1995, joined these two countries' economies with those of Paraguay and Uruguay; conceivably, by encouraging investment, this opening could reduce the emigration that has deprived Uruguay of many of its most youthful and capable people who have sought employment in neighboring countries. In some ways, Uruguay remains the most maddeningly bureaucratic of South American states, with a bloated and unmotivated state sector.

Hyperinflation has twice required the introduction of new currencies in the past two decades. Inflation has fallen but is still very high by European standards – for the 1994 calendar year, it was roughly 45%, but gradual devaluation of the peso is keeping prices relatively stable in terms of US dollars. Foreign debt is still a major concern, as Uruguay has one of the largest per capita burdens in Latin America. Historically, the country's liberal banking laws have made it a destination for capital from neighboring countries, but usually only as a stop en route to Switzerland or the USA.

Uruguay's minimum wage is approximately US$90 per month, and the unemployment rate about 12%.

POPULATION & PEOPLE

With a population of just over 3.2 million, Uruguay is South America's smallest Spanish-speaking country. Its population is highly urbanized, with more than 85% of Uruguayans residing in cities. Nearly half live in Montevideo, a fact that led one political scientist to call Uruguay a "city-state," even though, historically, the rural sector has produced most of its wealth. The next largest city, Salto, has fewer than 100,000 inhabitants.

By world standards, the welfare of Uruguayans ranks high. Infant mortality rates are low, and the life expectancy of 71 years

URUGUAY

Just as in Argentina, tango is an important part of Uruguayan music and dance. Gardel spent time in Montevideo and clubs in the city feature both tango and candombe (Afro-Uruguayan) dancing.

is the highest in South America and only slightly below that of many Western European countries. Yet limited economic opportunity has forced half a million Uruguayans to live outside the country, mostly in Brazil and Argentina.

Most Uruguayans are predominantly of Spanish and Italian origin. European immigration has overwhelmed the small but still visible Afro-Uruguayan population of perhaps 60,000, descendents of slaves brought to the country in the 19th century who once constituted nearly 20% of the population of Montevideo.

EDUCATION

For more than a century, primary education has been free, secular, and compulsory, with per capita government expenditures among the highest in Latin America. Uruguay's literacy rate is among the foremost in the region, and enrollment in free secondary schools is also very high.

Montevideo's Universidad de la República is the only public university. Since a disproportionate number of university students pursue degrees in law or medicine, professions that are oversupplied, the country lacks trained personnel in more technically oriented professions.

ARTS

For such a small country, Uruguay has an impressive literary and artistic tradition. Uruguay's best known contemporary writers are Juan Carlos Onetti, whose novels *No Man's Land* (Tierra de Nadie), *The Shipyard* (El Astillero), and *A Brief Life* (Una Vida Breve) are available in English, and poet, essayist, and novelist Mario Benedetti. Historian and journalist Eduardo Galeano, whose *Open Veins of Latin America* is mentioned in the section on Argentine history (see Facts for the Visitor), is also Uruguayan.

Uruguay's most famous writer is probably José Enrique Rodó, whose turn-of-the-century essay *Ariel*, contrasting North American and Latin American civilizations, is a classic of the country's literature (it's available in a paperback English translation). While none of 19th-century writer Javier de Viana's work has been translated into English, he and his "gauchesco" novels are the subject of John F Garganigo's biography *Javier de Viana*.

Theater is a popular medium, and playwrights are very prominent. One is Mauricio Rosencof, a Tupamaros founder whose plays have been produced since his release from prison, where he was tortured by the military government in the 1970s.

Uruguayan artists such as Pedro Figari, who paints rural scenes, have earned recognition well beyond the country's borders. Punta Ballena, near Punta del Este, is well known as an artists' colony.

RELIGION

Uruguayans are almost exclusively Roman Catholic, but church and state are officially separate. There is a small Jewish minority, probably numbering only about 25,000, who live almost exclusively in Montevideo. Evangelical Protestantism has made some inroads, and Sun Myung Moon's Unification Church owns the afternoon daily *Últimas Noticias*.

LANGUAGE

Spanish is the official language and is universally understood. Uruguayans fluctuate between use of the *voseo* and *tuteo* (see the Glossary) in their everyday speech, but either are readily understood. In the north, along the Brazilian border, many people are bilingual in Spanish and Portuguese, or speak *fronterizo*, an unusual hybrid of the two. See the Language section in the Facts about Argentina chapter for more information on Latin American Spanish.

Facts for the Visitor

Although Uruguay is a very distinct country, traveling there is very similar to traveling in Argentina. Only those facts that differ significantly from those for travelers in Argentina are mentioned below.

PLANNING
When to Go
Since Uruguay's major tourist attraction is its beaches, most visitors come in summer and dress accordingly, but the year-round temperate climate requires no special preparations. In ritzy resorts like Punta del Este, people often dress their best when going out for the evening.

Visitors to Montevideo can enjoy its urban attractions in any season. Along the Río Uruguay in summer, temperatures can be smotheringly hot, but the interior hill country is slightly cooler, especially at night.

Maps
Uruguayan road maps are only a partial guide to the country's highways, but see the Automóvil Club Uruguayo, and Shell and Ancap service stations for the best ones. For more detailed maps, try the Instituto Geográfico Militar (☎ 81-6868), on the corner of 12 de Octubre and Abreu in Montevideo.

HIGHLIGHTS
For most visitors, Montevideo and the Atlantic beach resorts will be Uruguay's main attractions. The narrow streets and port zone of Montevideo's Ciudad Vieja (Old City), currently being redeveloped, have immense colonial charm, while its hilly topography adds a dimension that even Buenos Aires' more picturesque neighborhoods lack. Besides its sophisticated resorts and broad sandy beaches, the Atlantic coast also has scenic headlands.

Up the estuary of the Río de la Plata, the colonial contraband port of Colonia is one of the continent's least known treasures –

every visitor to Buenos Aires should plan at least a day trip and preferably a weekend here. Further up, on the Río Uruguay, there is first-rate river fishing. Uruguay's undulating interior literally offers relief from the comparative monotony of the Argentine Pampas.

TOURIST OFFICES
As in Argentina, almost every department and municipality has a tourist office, usually on the main plaza or at the bus terminal. Although Uruguayan maps are not quite as good as those in most Argentine tourist offices, many of the brochures have excellent historical information.

A few departments and municipalities maintain offices in Montevideo. The Intendencia Municipal de Maldonado, which includes the key resort of Punta del Este, runs a Centro de Información (☎ 93-0272) in the Pluna building, Colonia 1021. The Intendencia Municipal de Rocha (☎ 92-0133) maintains an information office on the 5th floor of the Galería Kambarrere, 18 de Julio 907 at Convención.

The larger Uruguayan consulates, such as those in New York and Los Angeles, usually have a tourist representative in their delegation, but they are not especially helpful.

Australia
> There is no specific tourist information office in Australia. Tourist inquiries should be directed to the Uruguayan Consulate-General, GPO Box 717, Sydney, NSW, 2001 (☎ 02-232-8029)

Canada
> Suite 1905, 130 Albert St, Ottawa, Ontario (☎ 234-2937)

UK
> Tourist information can be obtained from the Uruguayan Embassy, 140 Brompton Rd, 2nd Floor, London SW31HY (☎ 584-8192)

USA
> 541 Lexington Ave, New York, NY 10022 (☎ 755-1200, ext 346)
> 429 Santa Monica Blvd, Suite 400, Santa

Monica, CA 90401 (☎ 394-5777)
1918 F St NW, Washington, DC 20006
(☎ 331-1313)

VISAS & DOCUMENTS
Uruguay requires visas of all foreigners, except nationals of neighboring countries (who need only national identification cards) and those of Western Europe, Israel, Japan, and the USA. All visitors need a tourist card, which is valid for 90 days and renewable for another 90. To extend your visa or tourist card, visit the Dirección Nacional de Migración (☎ 96-0471) at Misiones 1513 in Montevideo. Summer hours are 7:15 am to 1 pm.

Uruguay has recently imposed visa requirements on Canadians in response to Canada's visa requirements for Uruguayans. The visa requires a return ticket, a photograph, and a payment of US$30 to a Uruguayan consulate, which can make a day trip to Colonia from Buenos Aires a costly and time-consuming process.

Passports are necessary for many everyday transactions, such as cashing traveler's checks and checking into hotels. Theoretically, Uruguay requires the Inter-American Driving Permit rather than the International Driving Permit, but this appeared to make no difference in the one instance in which police asked me for identification.

At border crossings, the Ministerio de Turismo sells a "Tarjeta Turística" (not to be mistaken for the required immigration tourist card), which provides a number of tourist services, such as automobile insurance and medical and legal assistance in case of sickness or accident. It also provides discounts at many tourist sites throughout the country and can be worthwhile if you are spending some time in Uruguay. There are two types: For non-motorists, the "Tarjeta Azul" costs US$20 per month, while the "Tarjeta Roja" for motorists costs US$26 per month.

EMBASSIES
Uruguayan Embassies Abroad
Uruguay has diplomatic representation in neighboring countries and overseas,

although its network is less extensive than Argentina's.

Argentina
    Las Heras 1907, Buenos Aires (☎ 803-6030)
    Uruguay also runs offices in Concordia, Córdoba, Gualeguaychú, Mar del Plata, Mendoza, Rosario, and Salta.
Australia
    1st floor, Suite 107, MLC Tower (GPO Box 318), Woden, ACT, 2606 (☎ 06-282-4800)
Brazil
    SES Av Das Nacoes, Lote 14, Brasilia DF (☎ 224 2415)
    Praja de Botafogo 242, 6 Andar, CEP 22250, Rio de Janeiro (☎ 553-6033)
Canada
    Suite 1905, 130 Albert St, Ottawa, Ontario (☎ 234-2937)
Chile
    Pedro de Valdivia 711, Santiago (☎ 223-8398)
Paraguay
    25 de Mayo 1894, Esquina Gral, Aquinto, Asunción (☎ 203-864)
UK
    140 Brompton Rd, 2nd Floor, London SW31HY (☎ 584-8192)
USA
    1918 F St NW, Washington, DC 20006 (☎ 331-4219)
    429 Santa Monica Blvd, Suite 400, Santa Monica, CA 90401 (☎ 310-394-5777)
    546 Market St, Suite 221, San Francisco, CA 94104 (☎ 415-986-5222)

Foreign Embassies in Uruguay
South American countries, the USA, and most Western European countries have diplomatic representation in Montevideo. Both Argentina and Brazil also have consulates in border towns, which are mentioned in the appropriate chapters of the text.

Argentina
    WF Aldunate 1281 (☎ 39-3953)
Belgium
    Leyenda Patria 2880, 4th floor (☎ 70-1571)
Bolivia
    4th floor, WF Aldunate 1320 (☎ 98-5064)
Brazil
    Convención 1343, 6th floor (☎ 77-2036)
Canada
    Tagle 2828 (☎ 95-8583)

URUGUAY

Chile
1st floor, Andes 1365 (☎ 98-2223)
Denmark
Colonia 981, Oficina 405 (☎ 92-2759)
France
Av Uruguay 853 (☎ 92-0077)
Germany
La Cumparsita 1435 (☎ 91-3970)
Israel
Bulevar Artigas 1585 (☎ 40-4164)
Italy
JB Lamas 2857 (☎ 78-7152)
Japan
Bulevar Artigas 953 (☎ 48-7645)
Netherlands
Leyenda Patria 2880 (☎ 71-2957)
Paraguay
Bulevar Artigas 1256 (☎ 48-5810)
Peru
Soriano 1124 (☎ 92-1113)
Spain
Libertad 2750 (☎ 78-0048)
Sweden
5th floor, Sarandí 693 (☎ 96-1700)
Switzerland
11th floor, Federico Abadie 2936
(☎ 70 4315)
United Kingdom
Marco Bruto 1073 (☎ 62-3630)
USA
Lauro Muller 1776 (☎ 23-6061)

CUSTOMS

Uruguayan customs regulations permit the entry of used personal effects and other articles in "reasonable quantities."

MONEY

The unit of currency is the peso, which replaced the *peso nuevo* (N$) in 1993 (the peso nuevo had replaced an older peso in 1975 after several years' hyperinflation). Older bank notes of N$5000 and N$10,000 are still in circulation, but travelers should deduct three zeros to get current values. There are coins of 5, 10, 20, and 50 *centésimos*, and one, two and five pesos. Older coins of N$100, N$200, and N$500 are still in circulation.

The Uruguayan chapters refer to US dollars for prices because the dollar is far more stable than the Uruguayan peso. While US dollars are not the currency of convenience that they are in Argentina,

they are commonly accepted as payment. Even some budget hotels give travelers their prices in US dollars, and better restaurants always accept dollars (or Argentine pesos at present, though usually at a slightly lower rate than the dollar). Away from major tourist centers along the coast, dollars are less frequently accepted on an everyday basis.

Costs

Inflation, at a current rate of 45%, is running at much higher levels than in Argentina, though steady devaluations keep prices from rising substantially in dollar terms. Travel costs are slightly lower than in Argentina, especially with respect to accommodations and transportation; however, should inflation continue at this rate, prices will soon reach Argentine levels. Prices in this book are given in US dollars.

Currency Exchange

Money is readily exchanged at casas de cambio in Montevideo, Colonia, and the Atlantic beach resorts, but banks are the rule in the interior. Casas de cambio accept traveler's checks at slightly lower rates than cash dollars, and they sometimes charge commissions, although these are not so high as those levied in Argentina; there are some indications that cashing traveler's checks is getting more difficult. There is no black market for dollars or other foreign currency, which can be purchased without difficulty. Most better hotels, restaurants, and shops accept credit cards, but Uruguayan ATMs will not accept North American or European credit cards.

Because the peso is steadily declining against the dollar, exchange rates are likely to work in your favor. At press time exchange rates were the following:

Argentina	Arg$1	=	Ur$6.50
Australia	A$1	=	Ur$4.19
Bolivia	Bol$1	=	Ur$1.36
Brazil	BraR$1	=	Ur$6.90
Canada	Can$1	=	Ur$3.78
Chile	Ch$100	=	Ur$1.67
France	Fr1	=	Ur$1.25

Germany	DM1	=	Ur$4.48
Italy	It£1000	=	Ur$3.98
Japan	Jap¥100	=	Ur$6.65
Netherlands	Nfl	=	Ur$3.67
Paraguay	Par₲100	=	Ur$0.32
Spain	SpPta100	=	Ur$4.91
Switzerland	SwFr1	=	Ur$5.35
United Kingdom	UK£1	=	Ur$10.04
United States	US$1	=	Ur$6.56

POST & TELECOMMUNICATIONS

Rates are reasonable, but postal and telephone services are not any better than in Argentina.

Post

As in Argentina, letters and parcels are likely to be opened and the contents appropriated if they appear to contain anything of value. If something is truly important, send it by registered mail or private courier.

For poste restante, address mail to the main post office in Montevideo. It will hold mail for up to a month, or up to two months with authorization.

Telephone

Antel is the state telephone monopoly, with central long-distance offices resembling those in Argentina. As in Argentina, public telephones take *fichas* (tokens) rather than coins. Each ficha is good for about three minutes. More convenient magnetic cards are also available.

Discount rates for international calls are in effect between 10 pm and 7 am weekdays, midnight to 7 am and 1 pm to midnight Saturdays, and all day Sundays.

Making credit card or collect calls to the US and other overseas destinations is cheaper than paying locally; the list below gives the numbers of foreign direct operators.

Argentina	☎ 000454
Brazil	☎ 000455
Canada	☎ 000419
Chile	☎ 000456
Costa Rica	☎ 0004506
France	☎ 000433
Italy	☎ 000439

Paraguay	☎ 0004595
Spain	☎ 000434
UK	☎ 000444
USA	☎ 000410 AT&T
	☎ 000412 MCI
	☎ 000417 Sprint

BOOKS

For information on Uruguayan literature see the section on Arts found in Facts about Uruguay.

History

Compared to neighboring countries, surprisingly little material is available on Uruguay in English. For a discussion of the rise of Uruguay's unusual social welfare policies, see George Pendle's *Uruguay, South America's First Welfare State,* 3rd ed, and Milton Vanger's *The Model Country: Jose Batlle y Ordóñez of Uruguay, 1907-1915.*

The country's agrarian history is covered in RH Brannon's *The Agricultural Development of Uruguay.* Even those with great patience and a command of Spanish will find José Pedro Barrán and Benjamín Nahum's seven-volume *Historia Rural del Uruguay Moderno* imposing, but the authors summarize their conclusions in "Uruguayan Rural History," an article in the *Hispanic American Historical Review* (November, 1984). William Henry Hudson's novel *The Purple Land* (1916) is a classic portrait of 19th-century Uruguayan life.

For a sympathetic explanation of the rise of the 1960s guerrilla movements, see María Esther Gilio's *The Tupamaro Guerrillas.*

Contemporary Government & Politics

A good starting point for looking at the politics of modern Uruguay is Henry Finch's edited collection *Contemporary Uruguay: Problems and Prospects* (Institute for Latin American Studies, Liverpool, 1980). See also Luis González's *Political Parties and Redemocratization in Uruguay,* and Martin Weinstein's *Uruguay, Democracy at the Crossroads.* For an account of Uruguay's

URUGUAY

own Dirty War, see Lawrence Weschler's *A Miracle, A Universe: Settling Accounts with Torturers.*

FILM

Costa-Gavras's famous and engrossing film *State of Siege,* filmed in 1973 in Allende's Chile, deals with the Tupamaro guerillas' kidnapping and execution of suspected American CIA officer Dan Mitrione.

MEDIA

Newspapers are very important in Uruguay, which ranks second on the continent (after Argentina) in total circulation per 1000 inhabitants. Montevideo has a variety of newspapers, including the morning dailies *El Día* (founded by José Batlle), *La República, La Mañana,* and *El País.*

Gaceta Comercial is the voice of the business community, as is *El Observador Económico.* Afternoon papers are *El Diario, Mundocolor,* and *Ultimas Noticias,* a recent arrival operated by followers of Reverend Sun Myung Moon. For the most part, newspapers are identified with specific political parties, but a relatively new weekly, *Búsqueda,* takes a more independent stance with respect to political and economic matters.

The *Buenos Aires Herald* and other porteño newspapers are readily available in Montevideo, Punta del Este, and Colonia.

Radio and television are popular, with 20 television stations (four in Montevideo) and 100 radio stations (about 40 in the capital) for Uruguay's three million people. While freedom of speech and the press are generally respected, in 1994 the government revoked the license of a radio station operated by the Tupamaros.

HEALTH

Note that Uruguayan hospitals generally demand cash and refuse to accept insurance coverage; travelers needing hospitalization or other medical services may have to pay first and then ask their insurance companies for reimbursement.

SENIOR TRAVELERS

Elderhostel runs several educational programs to Uruguay, all of which begin with a short orientation stay in Montevideo. Course topics include cultural history, the ecosystem of the eastern coast, and a tour of Punta del Este. Participants must be at least 55 years of age. For more information or a catalog, write to Elderhostel, 75 Federal St, Boston, MA 02110-1941, or call ☎ 617-426-8056.

USEFUL ORGANIZATIONS

Uruguay's youth hostel network, while limited, is a good alternative to standard accommodations, and a youth hostel card may prove worthwhile; for US$24, membership is much cheaper than in Argentina. Accommodations cost around US$5 per night. For more information, contact the Asociación de Alberguistas del Uruguay (☎ 40-4245), the local affiliate of Hostelling International, at Calle Pablo de María 1583, Montevideo. It's open weekdays from 11:30 am to 7 pm.

BUSINESS HOURS & PUBLIC HOLIDAYS

Most shops are open weekdays and Saturdays from 8:30 am to 12:30 or 1 pm, and then close until midafternoon and reopen until 7 or 8 pm. Food shops also open on Sunday mornings.

Government office hours vary with the season – in summer, from mid-November to mid-March, offices are open from 7:30 am to 1:30 pm, while the rest of the year their hours are noon to 7 pm. Banks are open weekday afternoons in Montevideo, but outside the capital they are usually open mornings only. Exceptions are noted in the text.

On public holidays, most stores and all public offices are closed. Public transportation does run, but schedules are usually limited. The year's public holidays are as follows:

January 1
    Año Nuevo (New Year's Day)

January 6
Epifanía (Epiphany)
March/April (dates vary)
Viernes Santo/Pascua (Good Friday/Easter)
April 19
Desembarco de los 33 (Return of the 33)
This holiday honors the exiles who returned to Uruguay in 1825 to liberate the country from Brazil with the help of Argentina.
May 1
Día del Trabajador (Labor Day)
May 18
Batalla de Las Piedras (Battle of Las Piedras) This holiday commemorates a major battle of the fight for independence.
June 19
Natalicio de Artigas (Artigas's Birthday)
July 18
Jura de la Constitución (Constitution Day)
August 25
Dia de la Independencia (Independence Day)
October 12
Día de la Raza (Columbus Day)
November 2
Día de los Muertos (All Souls' Day)
December 25
Navidad (Christmas Day)

Uruguay's Carnaval, which takes place the Monday and Tuesday before Ash Wednesday in April, is livelier than its Argentine counterparts but not as lively as in Brazil. Visit Montevideo's Barrio Sur, where the city's black population celebrates with traditional *candombe* (Afro-Uruguayan dance) ceremonies. A good place to check this out is the new Afro cultural center in Montevideo's Mercado Central.

Holy Week (Easter) is also La Semana Criolla, during which traditional gaucho activities like *asados* (barbecues) and folk music take place. Most businesses close for the duration.

FOOD
Per capita, Uruguayans consume even more beef than Argentines, and the *parrillada* (beef platter) is a standard here. Likewise, the kinds of eating places are very similar – *confiterías* (cafés), pizzerias, and restaurants closely resemble their Argentine counterparts. There are good interna-

tional restaurants in Montevideo, Punta del Este and some other beach resorts, but elsewhere the food is fairly uniform. Uruguayan seafood is almost always a good choice.

The standard of Uruguayan short orders is *chivito,* which is not goat but rather a tasty and filling steak sandwich with a variety of additions – cheese, lettuce, tomato, bacon, or other odds and ends. Even more filling is the *chivito al plato,* in which the steak is served topped with a fried egg, with potato salad, green salad, and chips on the side. Other typically Uruguayan short orders include *olímpicos,* which are club sandwiches, and *húngaros,* which are spicy sausages on a hot dog roll (probably too spicy for young children, who will prefer the blander *panchos).*

DRINKS
Uruguayans consume even more *mate* (Paraguayan tea) than Argentines and Paraguayans, many lugging a thermos wherever they go. Uruguayan wines are very decent, especially in the form of *clericó,* a mixture of white wine and fruit juice. Another popular alcoholic drink is the *medio y medio,* a mixture of sparkling wine and white wine. Beers are equally good.

ENTERTAINMENT
Cinema is extremely popular in Montevideo and throughout the country, although the domestic film industry is very limited. Live theater is also very well patronized, especially in Montevideo.

Uruguay has won soccer's World Cup twice in this century. The first time was in the 1930s when it shocked a heavily favored Brazilian team in Brazil, but decades passed before the national team once again upset Brazil in the 1995 Copa de las Américas. Soccer remains the most popular spectator and participant sport; the most notable teams are Nacional and Peñarol both in Montevideo.

Tango is nearly as popular as in Argentina, while Afro-Uruguayan *candombe* music and dance add a unique dimension.

URUGUAY

THINGS TO BUY

Most shoppers will be interested in leather clothing and accessories, woolen clothing and fabrics, agates and gems, ceramics, wood crafts, and decorated gourds.

One of the most popular places for shoppers is the artisans' cooperative Manos del Uruguay, with several locations in Montevideo. For more details, see listings under Montevideo.

Getting There & Away

For getting there and away, Uruguay is almost a satellite of Argentina. Most international flights to and from the country go to Buenos Aires' Ezeiza Airport before continuing to Montevideo, while all river transport and the great majority of land transport also pass through Argentina. There are several direct land crossings from Brazil.

AIR
To/From the USA
From Miami, Lapsa has three flights weekly with a long stopover and change of planes in Asunción, Paraguay. Lloyd Aéreo Boliviano has somewhat better connections from Miami via Santa Cruz de la Sierra on Thursdays and Saturdays. All other flights pass through Ezeiza.

To/From Europe
Pluna, Uruguay's recently privatized national carrier, has Thursday and Sunday flights from Madrid, stopping in Río de Janeiro. KLM flies from Amsterdam via Rio de Janeiro and São Paulo Wednesdays and Sundays, but all other carriers servicing Uruguay stop over in Ezeiza.

To/From Neighboring Countries
There are frequent flights between Montevideo's Aeropuerto Internacional Carrasco and Buenos Aires' Aeroparque Jorge Newbery, as well as between Areoparque and Punta del Este or Colonia. Although it is possible to fly between Carrasco and Ezeiza, it is more expensive and much less convenient unless your ticket is valid for an ongoing flight.

Pluna flies from Montevideo to Brazilian destinations, including Porto Alegre (twice weekly), Florianópolis (twice), Rio de Janeiro (three times), and São Paulo (three times). Varig has similar routes, with some flights continuing to Bahia and Recife.

To/From Other South American Countries
Unless otherwise specified, all flights below originate in Montevideo. Pluna also flies to Asunción, Paraguay (twice weekly, originating in Punta del Este and stopping in Montevideo), and to Santiago, Chile (three times weekly). Líneas Aéreas Paraguayas (Lapsa) flies to Asunción three times weekly, while Lloyd Aéreo Boliviano flies Sundays to Santa Cruz de la Sierra and Sundays and Wednesdays to Asunción and Santa Cruz de la Sierra.

LAND
Uruguay shares borders with the Argentine province of Entre Ríos and the southern Brazilian state of Rio Grande do Sul. Major highways and bus services are generally good, but there are no rail services.

To/From Argentina
There are direct buses from Montevideo to Buenos Aires via Gualeguaychú, but these are slower and less convenient than the land/river combinations across the Rió de la Plata. For more details on the bridge crossings of the Río Uruguay, see the Getting There & Away chapter for Argentina.

To/From Brazil
Chuy to Chui & Pelotas The most frequently used border crossing from Brazil into Uruguay is connected to Montevideo by an excellent paved highway. Chuy and Chui are twin cities whose parallel main streets are separated only by a median strip, but Uruguayan immigration is about one km before the actual border and Brazilian immigration two km beyond it. If you are continuing any distance into Brazil, complete border formalities on both sides.

Río Branco to Jaguarão Less frequently used than the border crossing at Chuy, this is an alternative route to Pelotas and Porto

Alegre via the town of Treinta y Tres, in the department of the same name, or Melo, in the department of Cerro Largo. There are buses from Jaguarão to Pelotas.

Rivera to Livramento The crossing at Rivera and Livramento is frequented by travelers heading from Colón, Argentina, to Brazil, via Paysandú and the interior city of Tacuarembó. There are regular buses from Livramento to Porto Alegre.

Artigas to Quaraí This route crosses the Puente de la Concordia over the Río Quareim, but the principal highway goes southeast to Livramento.

Bella Unión to Barra do Quaraí In the extreme northwest corner of Uruguay, this crossing leads to the Brazilian city of Uruguaiana, where you can cross into the Argentine province of Corrientes and head north to Paraguay or to Iguazú Falls. Overland travel to Iguazú Falls through southern Brazil is slow and difficult.

RIVER & SEA
The most common means of crossing from Montevideo to Argentina involves ferry or hydrofoil, sometimes involving bus combinations to Colonia.

Montevideo to Buenos Aires The so-called Aviones de Buquebus are very comfortable, high-speed ferries that connect the two capitals in about 2½ hours for US$37 one-way. The main passenger salon is tobacco-free.

Colonia to Buenos Aires From Montevideo you can make direct bus connections to Colonia (three hours), from which Ferrytur has morning and evening sailings to Buenos Aires (US$11, 2½ hours). Aliscafos-Belt, the hydrofoil, takes only an hour from Colonia to Buenos Aires (US$21).

Carmelo & Nueva Palmira to Tigre There are launches across the estuary of the Río de la Plata to the Buenos Aires suburb of Tigre. Launches from Carmelo cost US$11 and tale about 2½ hours.

DEPARTURE TAXES
International passengers leaving from Aeropuerto Carrasco pay a departure tax of US$2.50 if headed to Argentina, US$6 to other South American countries, and US$7 for other destinations. For domestic flights, the departure tax is about US$1.

Ferry passengers embarking at Montevideo pay a US$5 port terminal and departure tax, while those at Colonia pay US$3.

Getting Around

AIR

Domestic air services in Uruguay are very limited. The national carrier Pluna has flights to and from Punta del Este, while the military airline Tamu serves the interior cities of Artigas, Salto, Rivera, Paysandú, Melo, and Tacuarembó. Tamu fares are absurdly cheap: Artigas, for example, is 601 km from Montevideo by road, yet the fare is only US$20 one-way, US$36 return. Tamu, however, only flies Fokker F27s.

Both Pluna and Tamu publish timetables, which can easily be obtained at their offices. There are four flights weekly to Salto, two to Artigas and Tacuarembó, four to Paysandú, four to Rivera, and four to Melo.

BUS

Buses in Uruguay are not quite as comfortable as those in Argentina, but the rides are shorter and they are perfectly acceptable; many companies publish accurate timetables. Most Uruguayan cities do not have central bus terminals, but the companies are always within easy walking distance of each other, usually around the central plaza. Montevideo, however, has a new, spacious, and busy terminal.

Buses are very frequent to destinations all around the country, so reservations should only be necessary on or near holidays. Fares are very reasonable – for example, the trip from Montevideo to Fray Bentos, a distance of about 300 km, costs only about US$8.

TRAIN

Passenger services on Uruguayan trains ceased completely in 1988.

CAR

Uruguayans are less ruthless on the road than Argentines, although it has been said that dividing lines are mere decoration.

There are, in any event, plenty of Argentines on the road, so watch out for Argentine license plates. Outside Montevideo and coastal areas, traffic is minimal and poses few problems, although some interior roads are very rough. Visitors lulled to sleep by the endlessly flat Pampas will be forced to pay close attention on Uruguay's winding roads and hilly terrain.

Uruguay ostensibly requires the Inter-American Driving Permit, rather than the International Driving Permit, in addition to a state or national driver's license, but we found that the police paid no attention so long as we had something that looked official. Arbitrary police stops and searches are less common than in Argentina, but the police are not above soliciting a bribe for traffic violations.

Driving can be even more expensive in Uruguay than in Argentina, since Uruguay imports all its oil and cars – there is no domestic automobile industry. Consequently, you will see so many lovingly maintained, truly antique *cachilas* on the streets of Montevideo that you may think you've stumbled onto the set of a gangster movie. If you plan to purchase a car, Argentina is a better bet. Petrol in Uruguay costs about US$0.85 per liter, and car rentals are just as costly as in Argentina.

The Automóvil Club del Uruguay (☎ 91-1251), on the corner of Colonia and Yi in Montevideo, is the equivalent of Argentina's ACA, although it is less widespread. It does have good maps and information.

LOCAL TRANSPORT

Taxi

Taxis have meters, and drivers correlate the meter reading with a photocopied fare chart. Between midnight and 6 am fares are higher. There is a small additional charge for luggage, and passengers generally round off the fare to the next even number.

Montevideo

Montevideo dominates political, economic, and cultural life in Uruguay even more than Buenos Aires does in Argentina. Nearly half of Uruguay's 3.2 million citizens live here (no other city has even 100,000 residents); there is a certain logic to this, as the capital's superb natural port links the country to overseas commerce, and the almost exclusively rural economy hardly requires a competing metropolis for trade and administration. The country's tax burden, though, has fallen unevenly on the rural export sector and has unquestionably contributed to the capital's dominance. The rural sector subsidizes not only inefficient domestic industries, but also the country's progressive social welfare policies.

In many ways, economic stagnation has left modern Montevideo a worn-out city with undistinguished, utilitarian bureaucratic public buildings that would not be out of place in Eastern Europe – according to one graffito, it's "un necrópolis de sueños rotos" (a necropolis of broken dreams). The more affluent residents and their businesses move toward suburbs like Pocitos and Carrasco, leaving the entire central city needing a coat of paint. On the positive side, the municipal administration is at least sprucing up open spaces like Plaza Cagancha (thanks to the relocation of bus companies to the new Tres Cruces bus terminal, just outside the center of town) and creating a few attractive urban spaces like the new peatonal in the Ciudad Vieja, the city's intriguing colonial core.

HISTORY

Spain's 1726 founding of Montevideo was a response to concern over Portugal's growing influence in the River Plate area; since 1680, the fortress and contraband port of Colonia had been a thorn in Spain's side. Montevideo was in turn a fortress against the Portuguese as well as British, French, and Danish privateers who came in search of hides in the Banda Oriental. Even more isolated than Buenos Aires, it was modest and unimpressive despite its official status as port of call for ships en route to the Pacific. In 1797, a British visitor to present-day Plaza Zabala observed:

The fort seems to be the only object on which any attention has been bestowed; it is large, handsomely built, and consists of four bastions, on which are apparently very good brass cannon . . .

The church is the next principal building; it is large and clean, but has nothing remarkable about it: the houses, many of which lie scattered about in a very irregular manner, with very pleasing gardens and little plantations attached to them, are all low and meanly built, very few being higher than the ground floor; but their tiled tops, with the green trees waving over them, have, taken altogether, rather a pretty effect.

Many of Montevideo's early residents were Canary Islanders. The city's port, superior to Buenos Aires' in every respect except its access to the Humid Pampa, soon made it a focal point for overseas shipping. An early-19th-century construction boom resulted in a new Iglesia Matriz, Cabildo, and other neoclassical late colonial monuments, but after independence Uruguayan authorities demolished many of these buildings and planned a new center east of Ciudad Vieja (Old City) and its port. No wonder, since it could be an insalubrious place – one British visitor in 1807 described the hazards of walking in the city at night

through long narrow streets so infested with voracious rats as to make it perilous sometimes to face them . . . Around the offals of carrion, vegetables and stale fruit accumulated there, the rats absolutely mustered in legions. If I attempted to pass near those formidable banditti, or to interrupt their meals or orgies, they gnashed their teeth upon me like so many evening wolves. So far they were from running in affright to their numerous burrows, that they turned round, set up a raven cry, and rushed at my legs in a way to make my blood run chill.

Montevideños had other worries, though. During the mid-19th century, the city endured an almost constant state of siege by the Argentine dictator Rosas, who was determined to create a small client (puppet) state to Buenos Aires. After Rosas' fall in 1851, normal commerce resumed and, between 1860 and 1911, the British-built railroad network assisted Montevideo's growth. Like Buenos Aires, the city absorbed numerous European immigrants in the early 20th century, mostly from Spain and Italy; by 1908, 30% of Montevideo's population was foreign-born.

Around this time, the country became ever more closely linked to the export trade; construction of the city's first locally financed frigorífico was followed by two similar foreign-backed enterprises. Growth has continued to stimulate agricultural expansion near Montevideo in response to the demands of the rapidly increasing urban population. Much of this population, consisting mostly of refugees from rural poverty, lives in *conventillos,* large, older houses converted into multi-family slum dwellings. Many of these are in the Ciudad Vieja, but even this population is being displaced as urban redevelopment usurps the picturesque and valuable central area.

ORIENTATION

Montevideo lies on the east bank of the Río de la Plata, almost directly east of Buenos Aires on the other side of the river. For most visitors, the most intriguing area will be the Ciudad Vieja, where the colonial grid, once surrounded by protective walls, covered a small peninsula near the port and harbor. The center of the Ciudad Vieja is Plaza Matriz, which is also known as Plaza Constitución. Visitors should be aware that many plazas and streets in Monetvideo have two or more official names.

The city's functional center is Plaza Independencia to the east, which has many historic public buildings from the republican era; here begins Av 18 de Julio, a major thoroughfare and traditionally the capital's main commercial and entertainment zone, which runs through Plaza Cagancha. Formerly the main staging area for national and international public transportation, Plaza Cagancha is an open space currently being redeveloped. Theaters, exchange houses, and some restaurants are nearby, especially on the north side of the plaza. Av 18 de Julio divides the tree-shaded barrio known as El Córdon (in earlier times El Cardal, the birthplace of Artigas). Some streets change their name on either side of Av 18 de Julio. Most inexpensive accommodations are on side streets around Plaza Cagancha, though some are in the Ciudad Vieja.

From Plaza del Entrevero, on Av 18 de Julio, the diagonal Av Libertador General Lavalleja leads to the imposing Palacio Legislativo, site of the Asamblea General. The 11th-floor terrace of the Palacio Municipal, at Av 18 de Julio and Ejido, offers spectacular views of the city. At the northeastern end of Av 18 de Julio is Parque José Batlle y Ordóñez, a large public park containing the Estadio Centenario, a 75,000-seat stadium built to commemorate the country's centenary in 1930. Running perpendicular to its terminus is Bulevar Artigas, another major artery, while the nearby Av Italia is the main highway east to Punta del Este and the rest of the Uruguayan Riviera.

Many points of interest are beyond downtown, a result of Montevideo's sprawl both east and west along the river. Across the harbor to the west, the 132-meter Cerro de Montevideo ("a conical mountain of a stupendous height" according to an easily impressed 18th-century English visitor) was a landmark for early navigators and still offers outstanding views of the city. To the east, the Rambla or riverfront road leads past attractive residential suburbs with numerous public parks, including Parque Rodó at the south end of Bulevar Artigas. Further on but well within the city limits are numerous sandy beaches frequented by the capital's residents in summer and on weekends throughout the year.

INFORMATION
Tourist Offices
The Ministerio de Turismo (☎ 90-4148) maintains a cubbyhole information office on the ground floor at Av Lavalleja 1409; it's open 9 am to 6:30 pm weekdays. The main office on the 4th floor is extremely bureaucratic. The Oficina de Informes (☎ 41-8998) at Terminal Tres Cruces, the new bus station at Bulevar Artigas and Av Italia, is open 7 am to 11 pm daily and is better prepared to deal with visitor inquiries. There is also an Oficina de Informes (☎ 50-3812) at Aeropuerto Carrasco in neighboring Canelones, reputed to be next to useless.

The División Turismo de la Intendencia Municipal de Montevideo (☎ 93-0646), on the 3rd floor of the Palacio Municipal at 18 de Julio and Ejido, is also very bureaucratic, but sometimes publishes a useful guide called *Brújula*. Also widely distributed is a small, annually updated booklet entitled *Guía Montevideo*. The very useful, weekly *Guía del Ocio,* which lists cultural events, cinemas, theaters, and restaurants, comes with the Friday edition of the daily *El País.*

If your Spanish is good, dial ☎ 124 for general information on virtually anything in Montevideo. For entertainment information, call Espectáculos (☎ 0900-2323; the call costs US$0.60 per minute).

Visitors bound for Maldonado/Punta del Este should visit the very helpful desk maintained by the Intendencia Municipal de Maldonado (☎ 93-0272) in the Pluna offices at Colonia 1021, open weekdays 9 am to 6 pm. The Intendencia Municipal de Rocha (☎ 92-0133), on the 5th floor of the Galería Kambarrere, 18 de Julio 907, provides information weekday afternoons only.

Foreign Embassies
For diplomatic representatives from overseas and neighboring countries, see the Facts for the Visitor chapter for Uruguay.

Immigration
The Dirección Nacional de Migracion (☎ 96-0471) is at Misiones 1513.

Money
There are many exchange houses around Plaza Cagancha and on Av 18 de Julio. Indamex, at the entrance to the Balmoral Plaza Hotel on Plaza Cagancha, is open 24 hours. Exprinter, Sarandí 700 on Plaza Independencia, is very dependable. American Express (☎ 92-0829), locally represented by Turisport at Mercedes 942, no longer cashes its own traveler's checks, but Cambio Gales at 18 de Julio 1048 will do so.

Post & Telecommunications
The Correo Central (main post office) is at Buenos Aires 451 in the Ciudad Vieja, with

a branch at Ejido 1322. Antel has convenient offices at Rincón 501 in the Ciudad Vieja, San José 1108 (open 24 hours), and Fernández Crespo 1534. Montevideo's area code is 02.

Cultural Centers

Run by the United States Information Service, the Biblioteca Artigas-Washington (☎ 91-5232), Paraguay 1217, is a very substantial library with books and newspapers in English. The center also sponsors special programs and lectures.

The Anglo-Uruguayan Cultural Institute (☎ 90-3708), San José 1426, also operates an English-language library. Montevideo has branches of the Instituto Goethe at Canelones 1524, and the Alianza Francesa (☎ 93-0805) at Soriano 1180.

At the corner of 18 de Julio and Julio Herrera y Obes is the Centro Cultural Uruguayo-Brasileiro.

In the 1820s escaped Brazilian slaves formed Montevideo's Afro-Uruguayan community in the capital's Barrio Sur. Their descendants are now building their own downtown cultural center, called the Centro de Estudios e Informes Afros (☎ /fax95-0247) upstairs in the Mercado Central, Ciudadela 1229. Allied with the Instituto de Arte y Cultura Afro (IDAYCA), it will have a research library, theater, cafe, and other facilities.

Travel Agencies

Among many others, VP Turismo (☎ 90-3730), San José 1073, and Viajes COT (☎ 92-1605), Plaza Cagancha 1124, arrange trips in and out of Montevideo and to neighboring countries.

Bookstores

Montevideo has several excellent bookstores. Linardi y Risso (☎ 95-7129), at Juan Carlos Gómez 1435 in the Ciudad Vieja, is the equivalent of Buenos Aires' Platero, offering outstanding selections in history and literature, including many out-of-print items. The city's largest book dealer is Barreiro y Ramos, at 25 de Mayo and Juan Carlos Gómez in the Ciudad Vieja, with branches at Av 18 de Julio 941 and in the suburbs of Pocitos and Carrasco. The Librería Inglesa-Británica, Sarandí 580 in the Ciudad Vieja, has English-language books, including Penguin paperbacks.

Two worthwhile hybrid bookstore/cafés in Pocitos are Libertad Libros (☎ 71-3460), Libertad 2433, and Casa Gandhi (☎ 77-5870), JB Blanco 975.

Film & Photography

Kilómetro Cero, 18 de Julio 1180 on Plaza Cagancha, and Kodak Uruguaya, Yí 1532, offer dependable developing. Technifilm, 18 de Julio 1202, is the place to go for camera repairs.

Medical Services

The most convenient hospital is the Hospital Maciel (☎ 95-6810) at 25 de Mayo and Maciel, in the Ciudad Vieja. Línea SIDA (☎ 42-1010) is Montevideo's AIDS hotline.

Dangers & Annoyances

While Montevideo is pretty sedate by most standards, visitors will note symptoms of increasing street crime – private security

Street scene along Calle Sarandi and Puerta de la Ciudadela

URUGUAY

guards now lurk at many cafés and restaurants, and all cabs now have a plastic shield between passenger and driver. Take the usual precautions.

WALKING TOUR

To orient yourself in downtown Montevideo, take a walk from **Plaza Independencia** through the Ciudad Vieja to the port. On the plaza, an honor guard keeps 24-hour vigil over the **Mausoleo de Artigas,** which is topped by a 17-meter, 30-ton statue of the country's greatest hero. The 18th-century **Palacio Estévez,** on the south side, was the Presidencia (Government House) until 1985, while the ornate baroque, 26-story **Palacio Salvo,** on the east side, was the continent's tallest building when it opened in 1927 and is still the tallest in the city. Just off the plaza is the **Teatro Solís** (see below).

At the west end of the plaza is **La Puerta de la Ciudadela**, a modified remnant of the colonial citadel that dominated the area before its demolition in 1833. Calle Sarandí, part of which is now a peatonal, leads to **Plaza Constitución,** also known interchangeably as Plaza Matriz, the centerpiece of which is a sculpture by the Italian Juan Ferrari that commemorates the establishment of Montevideo's first waterworks. On the west side of the Plaza Constitución, the **Cabildo** (finished in 1812), a neoclassical stone structure designed by Spanish architect Tomás Toribio, now houses the Museo y Archivo Histórico Municipal. Begun in 1784 and completed in 1799, the **Iglesia Matriz** (cathedral), on the corner of Sarandí and Ituzaingó, is Montevideo's oldest public building, the work of Portuguese architect José de Sáa y Faría.

Detour one block north of the Plaza Constitución to see the outstanding bas-reliefs created by Edmundo Prati in 1941 on the Banco La Caja Obrera, 25 de Mayo at Ituzaingó. Returning to Calle Rincón, continue west to the **Casa Rivera** at Rincón and Misiones, the **Museo Romántico** at 25 de Mayo 428, and the **Casa Lavalleja** at Zabala and 25 de Mayo, all part of the

Museo Histórico Nacional (see below). See also the **Palacio Taranco** (1910), at 25 de Mayo and Primero de Mayo, built in an 18th-century European style by French architects commissioned by a wealthy merchant; it houses the **Museo de Arte Decorativo,** open weekdays 2 to 6 pm. From there, visit **Plaza Zabala,** site of the colonial governor's house until its demolition in 1878; there is a statue dedicated to Bruno Mauricio de Zabala, Montevideo's founder, by Spanish sculptor Lorenzo Coullant Valera. From the plaza, continue west along Washington and north to Colón and 25 de Mayo, where the **Casa Garibaldi** once housed the Italian hero, and then to Piedras and the **Mercado del Puerto** (see below).

Travelers interested in more detail on the Ciudad Vieja's architecture can acquire Julio C Gaeta's *Guía Ciudad Vieja Montevideo* (Guías Elarqa de Arquitectura, Montevideo, 1994) for about US$20.

MUSEUMS & LANDMARKS
Museo Histórico Nacional

The national history museum actually consists of four different houses, most of them former residences of Uruguayan national heroes in the Ciudad Vieja. Built in the late 18th century, the **Casa Lavalleja,** Zabala 1469, was the home of General Lavalleja from 1830 until his death in 1853; in 1940, his heirs donated it to the state. The **Casa Rivera,** a 19th-century building at Rincón 437, belonged to General Fructuoso Rivera, Uruguay's first president and founder of the Colorado party. The **Casa Garibaldi,** at 25 de Mayo 314, belonged to the Italian patriot who commanded the Uruguayan navy from 1843 to 1851, and now contains many of his personal effects. All the houses are open Tuesday through Friday 12:30 to 6:30 pm, Sundays and holidays 2 to 6 pm.

The 18th-century **Museo Romántico,** 25 de Mayo 428, is full of paintings and antique furniture, but its exterior has been modified from the original colonial style. It keeps the same hours as the rest of the museum. The entrance fee is about US$1.

URUGUAY

PLACES TO STAY
2 Alojamiento Piedras
3 Hotel Universal
9 Hotel Capri
23 Hotel City
31 Hotel Arapey
34 Hotel Mediterráneo
35 Residencial Acevedo
38 Hotel Victoria Palace
40 Hotel Internacional
47 Hotel Ideal
59 Hotel Aramaya
62 Hotel Ateneo
63 Residencial Congreso
66 Hospedaje El Aguila,
   Pensión Catalunya
68 Hotel Alvear
70 Hospedaje Nuevo Savoy
71 Hotel Palacio
77 Hotel Reina
78 Hospedaje Solís
86 Hotel Crillón
90 Hotel Español
91 Hotel Cervantes
93 Albergue Juvenil
97 Hotel Casablanca
101 Gran Hotel América
106 Hotel London Palace
108 Hotel Nuevo Ideal
115 Hotel Oxford
116 Hotel Royal,
   Hospedaje del Centro
117 Hotel Lancaster
121 Hotel Lafayette
124 Hotel Balfer
127 Hotel Embajador
129 Hotel Windsor
131 Hotel Libertad
134 Hotel Klee
139 Hotel Libertador
140 Residencial Libertad

PLACES TO EAT
15 Natura
21 Olivier
24 Confitería de la Corte
26 Confitería La Pasiva
27 Club Alemán
28 Club Libanés
33 La Camargue
43 Oro del Rhin
65 Pizza Bros
81 Mercado Central,
   Restaurant Morini
85 Oriente
87 Las Brasas
92 La Suiza
105 El Fogón
107 La Vegetariana
120 Ruffino
122 Vida Natural
123 Taberna Vasca
126 Mesón Viejo Sancho

132 La Vegetariana
133 La Genovesa
136 Mesón del Club Español
143 El Horreo

OTHER
1 Ferry Port
4 Dirección Nacional
   de Migracion
5 Museo Municipal de la
   Construcción Tomás Toribio
6 Casa Mario
7 Hospital Maciel
8 Casa Garibaldi
10 Palacio Taranco,
   Museo de Arte Decorativo
11 Casa Lavalleja
12 Teatro El Picadero
13 Museo Romántico
14 Casa Rivera
16 Cabildo, Museo y Archivo
   Histórico Municipal

17 Antel
18 Banco La Caja Obrera
19 Linardi y Risso (Bookstore)
20 Barreiro y Ramos
22 Correo Central
   (Main Post Office)
25 Librería Inglesa-Británica
29 French Consulate
30 Autocar
32 Budget Rent A Car
36 Kodak Uruguaya
37 National Rent A Car
39 Hertz Rent A Car
41 Chilean Consulate
44 Peletería Holandesa
45 Dollar Rent A Car
46 Intendencia Municipal de Rocha
48 Barreiro y Ramos
49 Turisport (American Express)
50 Tamu, Iberia

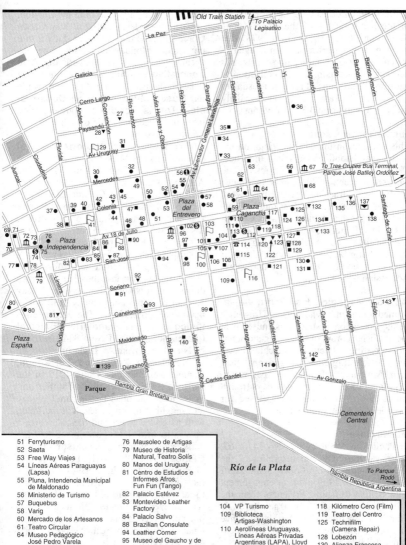

URUGUAY

51 Ferryturismo
52 Saeta
53 Free Way Viajes
54 Líneas Aéreas Paraguayas (Lapsa)
55 Pluna, Intendencia Municipal de Maldonado
56 Ministerio de Turismo
57 Buquebus
58 Varig
60 Mercado de los Artesanos
61 Teatro Circular
64 Museo Pedagógico José Pedro Varela
67 Automóvil Club del Uruguay, Museo del Automóvil
69 Mercado de los Artesanos
72 Museo Torres García
73 American Airlines
74 Exprinter (Cambio, Travel Agency)
75 Puerta de la Ciudadela

76 Mausoleo de Artigas
79 Museo de Historia Natural, Teatro Solís
80 Manos del Uruguay
81 Centro de Estudios e Informes Afros, Fun Fun (Tango)
82 Palacio Estévez
83 Montevideo Leather Factory
84 Palacio Salvo
88 Brazilian Consulate
94 Leather Corner
95 Museo del Gaucho y de la Moneda, Centro Cultural Uruguayo-Brasileiro
98 Peletería Holandesa
99 Centro Artesanal
100 Argentine Consulate
102 Cambio Gales
103 Bolivian Consulate

104 VP Turismo
109 Biblioteca Artigas-Washington
110 Aerolíneas Uruguayas, Líneas Aéreas Privadas Argentinas (LAPA), Lloyd Aéreo Boliviano (LAB)
111 LanChile
112 Indamex, Viajes COT, Balmoral Plaza Hotel
113 Manos del Uruguay
114 Antel
116 Peruvian Consulate

118 Kilómetro Cero (Film)
119 Teatro del Centro
125 Technifilm (Camera Repair)
128 Lobezón
130 Alianza Francesa
135 Multicar
137 Post Office
138 Palacio Municipal
141 La Cumparsita (Nightclub)
142 La Cumparsita (Tango)

Museo Del Gaucho y De La Moneda

In the headquarters of the Banco de la República at Av 18 de Julio 998, this museum displays artifacts from Uruguay's gaucho history, including horse gear, silverwork and weapons, plus a collection of bank notes and coins. It is open Tuesday to Friday from 9:30 am to 12:30 pm, and daily except Monday from 3:30 to 7:30 pm.

Museo Torres García

This museum in the Ciudad Vieja, on the peatonal at Sarandí 683, displays the works of Uruguayan artist Joaquín Torres García, who spent much of his career in France producing abstract and even cubist work like that of Picasso, as well as unusual portraits of historical figures such as Columbus, Mozart, Beethoven, Bach, Rabelais, and the like. Open weekdays from 3 to 7 pm and Saturdays from 11 am to 1 pm, it also has a small gift shop and bookstore. Admission is free.

Museo Pedagógico José Pedro Varela

Named for the man who devised Uruguay's public education system, this museum at the northeast corner of Plaza Cagancha has an interesting collection of teaching materials, suggesting how Uruguayans view their own country. It's usually open weekdays from 10 am to 8 pm, Saturdays from 8 am to noon, but it has been closed for remodeling. Admission is free.

Museo Naval

In Pocitos, reached by bus No 14 or 62, the naval museum contains relics of the German battleship *Graf Spee,* scuttled off Montevideo in 1939 after an engagement with British warships. Prisoners from the ship were later confined at Argentina's Isla Martín García, then shifted to the province of Córdoba, where many of their descendants still live.

Other Museums

Montevideo has many other worthwhile museums, mostly downtown and almost all closed Mondays. The **Museo y Archivo Histórico Municipal** (Municipal Archive and Historical Museum) is in the Cabildo, opposite the Iglesia Matriz at Juan Carlos Gómez and Sarandí; it's open daily 2 to 6 pm except Monday, and offers English-speaking tours. The **Museo de Arte Decorativo** is a fine-arts museum in the Palacio Taranco, 25 de Mayo 376, while the **Museo Municipal de la Construcción Tomás Toribio** (an architectural museum), Piedras 528, is open Tuesday to Friday 2 to 6 pm.

The **Museo de Historia Natural** (Natural History Museum) is in the Teatro Solís building, Buenos Aires 652. The Automóvil Club del Uruguay's **Museo del Automóvil,** 6th floor, Colonia 1251, has a superb collection of antique cars, although you'll see as many or more on city streets. It's open weekends 3 to 9 pm.

Across the harbor, the **Museo del Cerro** in Parque Carlos Vaz Ferreira has an excellent weapons collection and offers good views of the city; take bus No 125 from downtown. It is open Thursday and Friday 1:30 to 5:45 pm and Sunday 9:30 am to noon and 2 to 5:45 pm. The **Jardín Zoológico** (zoo) and **Planetario Municipal** (planetarium) are at Rivera 3245, reached by No 60 tram from Av 18 de Julio.

The **Museo Zoológico Larrañaga,** Rambla República de Chile 4215 in the barrio of Buceo, has exhibits of stuffed animals, birds, and other fauna from Uruguay and neighboring countries. The building, with its gilded tower and tiles, deserves a visit in its own right – it's open 3 to 7 pm daily except Monday. The **Museo Juan M Blanes,** Av Millán 4016 in the suburb of Prado, displays the work of Uruguay's most famous painter, including many historical scenes not just of Uruguay but of the whole River Plate region. Hours are 2 to 7 pm daily except Monday. The Estadio Centenario's **Museo del Fútbol** is open Thursday, weekends, and holidays from noon to 5 pm.

Palacio Legislativo

At the north end of Av Lavalleja, the neoclassical legislature is brilliantly lit at night, and is one of the city's most impressive landmarks. Guided tours (available in English) take place every half hour between 1:30 and 4:30 pm, weekdays only. Admission is free.

Teatro Solís
Named for the first Spaniard to set foot in what is now Uruguayan territory, Montevideo's leading theater opened in 1856 (construction actually began in 1842 but was delayed by Rosas' siege of Montevideo). Artists who have performed here include Caruso, Toscanini, Pavlova, Nijinski, Sarah Bernhardt, Rostropovich, and Twyla Tharpe.

At the southwest corner of Plaza Independencia, at Buenos Aires 678, the Solís (☎ 95-9770) has superb acoustics and offers concerts, ballet, opera, and plays throughout the year. It is also home to the Comedia Nacional, the municipal theater company. You can usually get tickets a few days before events, but the earlier the better.

MARKETS & FAIRS
Mercado Del Puerto
At its opening in 1868, Montevideo's port was the continent's finest, but its market now survives on personality and atmosphere. No visitor should miss the old port market building at the foot of Calle Pérez Castellano. Its impressive wrought-iron superstructure shelters a gaggle of reasonably priced parrillas (choose your cut off the grill) and some more upmarket restaurants with outstanding seafood. About 40 years ago, local entrepreneurs began to add more sophisticated restaurants to the grills that already fed the people who brought their produce to the market, and the market gradually became a local phenomenon.

Especially on Saturdays, it is a lively, colorful place where the city's artists, crafts workers, and street musicians hang out. Cafe Roldos, at the same site since 1886, serves the popular medio y medio, a mixture of white and sparkling wines.

Feria De Tristán Narvaja
A 60-year tradition begun by Italian immigrants, El Cordón's Sunday morning outdoor market sprawls from Av 18 de Julio along Calle Tristán Narvaja to Galicia, spilling over onto side streets. Besides groceries, you can find many interesting trinkets, antiques, and souvenirs in its many dozens of makeshift stalls.

ORGANIZED TOURS
Free Way Viajes (☎ 90-8931), Colonia 994, runs a recommended city tour (US$13) and another by night for US$24 (US$35 with dinner included). It runs additional tours throughout the country, and its tour guides speak several languages.

SPECIAL EVENTS
Much livelier than the one in Buenos Aires, Montevideo's late summer Carnaval is well worth the trip for those who can't make it to Rio de Janeiro. Semana Criolla festivities during Semana Santa (Holy Week) take place at Parque Prado, north of downtown. Because Uruguay is a secular country, official holy week celebrations are more nationalistic than religious. They include displays of gaucho skills, asados, and the like.

PLACES TO STAY
Prices for accommodations have risen faster than inflation in recent years, so that many former bottom-end hotels are now midrange. Bottom-end hotels are often dark and rundown, but there are a few exceptions.

Places To Stay – bottom end
Camping The municipal *Parque Recreativo Punta Espinillo* (☎ 95-9935 for reservations), accessed via Ruta 1 west of town and then the lateral Camino 2° Sanguinetti, is seven km from downtown. It has very basic facilities (no hot water), but is woodsy and sites are free of charge.

Parque Rodó has an authorized campground exclusively for self-contained vehicles, but has a 24-hour limit on stays. There are also sites at *Parque Lecocq*, west of Montevideo on Av Luis Batlle Berres, and at *Parque Nacional Franklin D Roosevelt*, east of the city toward Aeropuerto Carrasco.

Hostel For budget travelers, the most reasonable and central lodging is the *Albergue Juvenil* (☎ 98-1324), the official youth hostel at Canelones 935, which costs about US$8 per night (including breakfast) with hostel card; linens cost an additional US$1.20. It has kitchen facilities, a lounge, and information. Its 11 pm curfew could restrict your nightlife, though it's not impossible to arrange a later arrival with the caretaker. The hostel is closed from noon to 7:30 pm daily.

Hospedajes & Hotels In the Ciudad Vieja, near the Mercado del Puerto, there are two very cheap places on the margins of acceptability: *Alojamiento Piedras* at Piedras 270 and *Hotel Universal* at Piedras 272 both charge about US$5 per person, but they are oriented toward families and workers for longer stays. The former is in slightly better condition. A new and good choice is the simple but friendly *Hospedaje Solís* (☎ 95-0437), Bartolomé Mitre 1314, which charges only US$8 for spacious singles with shared bath; those with private bath cost US$20.

Hotel Nuevo Ideal (☎ 98-2913), Soriano 1073, has mildewy singles/doubles with private bath for US$13/18, but its central location is a strong point. *Hospedaje del Centro* (☎ 90-1419), at Soriano 1126 next to the Peruvian Consulate, charges US$10/13 with shared bath, US$14/17 with private bath; once a luxurious single-family residence, it's clean but declining, and some rooms are very dark. *Hospedaje El Aguila,* an old and ramshackle but friendly place at Colonia 1235, has rooms with shared bath for US$11/16. *Pensión Catalunya,* nearby at Colonia 1223, is very clean and slightly cheaper, but room size varies greatly. The recommended *Hotel Windsor* (☎ 91-5080), Zelmar Michelini 1260, charges US$10/15 for singles/doubles with shared bath, US$13/18 with private bath.

Friendly, appealing *Hotel Libertad,* Carlos Quijano 1223, charges US$14 double with shared bath, US$20 with private bath. No relation to the Hotel Libertad, the musty *Residencial Libertad* (☎ 91-7665), Maldonado 980, charges US$17 double on weekdays, US$20 double on weekends for rooms with private bath. *Hotel Ideal* (☎ 91-6389), Colonia 914, is clean and friendly with good bathrooms; singles/doubles with shared bath are US$15/20, with private bath US$18/25.

One of Montevideo's best budget accommodations has been *Hotel Palacio* (☎ 96-3612) at Bartolomé Mitre 1364, but it seems to be surviving on reputation after unwarranted price increases. Singles with brass beds (some of them sagging), antique furniture, and balconies cost US$17 with shared bath – ask for the 6th-floor rooms, where the balconies are nearly as large as the rooms themselves and provide exceptional views of the Ciudad Vieja. Although still a good place, it's not the value it once was. Across the street at Bartolomé Mitre 1371, *Hospedaje Nuevo Savoy* offers bright, freshly painted doubles with shared bath for as little as US$10, with private bath for US$12. Some rooms are windowless, and there are children, so the place can be noisy at times; still it's very friendly.

Places To Stay – middle
A good choice is *Hotel Arapey* (☎ 90-7032) at Av Uruguay 925, for US$20/25 single/double. At *Hotel Ateneo* (☎ 91-2630), Colonia 1147, rates are US$20/26 for rooms with private bath and television, but some are a bit dark. *Residencial Acevedo,* Av Uruguay 1127, has single or double rooms with shared bath for US$20 or with private bath for US$25.

Hotel Casablanca (☎ 91-0918), conveniently central at San José 1039, charges US$25 per double with private bath. *Residencial Congreso* (☎ 90-6593), Rondeau 1446, has seen better days – it has a classic bird-cage elevator but also sagging beds and peeling paint. Rooms with shared bath are US$20/27 single/double, with private bath US$23/30. Conveniently central and comfortable *Hotel Reina* (☎ 95-9461), Bartolomé Mitre 1343, costs US$24/30.

Rooms at *Hotel Royal* (☎ 98-3115), at Soriano 1120, cost US$23/30 with private bath. *Hotel Capri* (☎ 95-5970), in the Ciudad Vieja's red-light district at Colón 1460, charges US$26 for singles/doubles with private bath and color TV; there's a 20% discount Monday through Thursday. The recommended *Hotel City* (☎ 98-2913), Buenos Aires 462, is comparably priced.

The family-run *Hotel Cervantes* (☎ 90-7991), Soriano 868, charges US$30 double. Probably the best midrange value is *Hotel Mediterráneo* (☎ 90-5090), Paraguay 1486, which charges US$30/40 single/double for well-kept rooms with breakfast and excellent service. Pleasant, comparably priced *Hotel Aramaya* (☎ 98-6192) is at Av 18 de Julio 1103. *Hotel Español* (☎ 90-3816) at Convención 1317 charges US$25/40 single/double for interior rooms, US$35/50 for those facing on the street. *Hotel Hispano-América* (☎ 62-2703), Melitón González 1225 near Pocitos shopping center, is a good value for US$35 double; it also has a downstairs rotisería.

Other typical places in this category include *Hotel Crillón* (☎ 92-0195) at Andes 1318, which has been undergoing remodeling but is usually the US Peace Corps hangout; *Hotel Balfer* (☎ 91-2647) at Zelmar Michelini 1328 for US$35/50; and *Hotel Lancaster* (☎ 92-0029) at Plaza Cagancha 1334 for US$39/58 single/double.

Places To Stay – top end

Montevideo's top-end hotels lack the luxury of those in Buenos Aires, but there are some decent values. Typical amenities include room service, spas, and hairdressers, and all of these hotels include breakfast in their rates. *Gran Hotel América* (☎ 92-0392), WF Aldunate 1330, charges US$48/62 single/double, while the *Hotel London Palace* (☎ 92-0024), WF Aldunate 1278, costs US$47/64. Comparable places, for about US$50/67, include *Hotel Alvear* (☎ 92-0244) at Yí 1372 and *Hotel Internacional* (☎ 90-5794) at Colonia 823. *Hotel Embajador* (☎ 92-0009), San José 1212, is slightly dearer at US$54/73.

At *Hotel Klee* (☎ 91-0671), Yaguarón 1306, rates are US$60/80. The refurbished

Hotel Oxford (☎ 92-0046) at Paraguay 1286 costs US$70/85, including an outstanding breakfast. The upscale *Hotel Libertador* (☎ 92-0079), Florida 1128, also houses US Peace Corps volunteers when they're in town. Near Playa Pocitos at JB Blanco 783, *Hotel Ermitage* (☎ 70-4021) is a good choice for around US$60/80.

The recently built *Hotel Lafayette* (☎ 92-2351), Soriano 1170, is Montevideo's only real luxury hotel specifically catering to international business travelers; it charges US$98/113. The *Hotel Victoria Palace* (☎ 98-9565), Plaza Independencia 759, makes an effort to be one.

PLACES TO EAT

Montevideo falls short of Buenos Aires' sophistication and variety, but its numerous restaurants are unpretentious and offer excellent value for the money. Reasonably priced, worthwhile downtown restaurants include *Morini* (☎ 95-9733), Ciudadela 1229; *Mesón Viejo Sancho* (☎ 90-4063), San José 1229; and *Del Ferrocarril* (☎ 94-0801), in the old train station at Río Negro 1746. *La Genovesa* (☎ 90-8729), San José 1262, has good seafood with abundant portions, but note that IVA is not included in the listed prices, nor is the cubierto or service.

Uruguayans eat even more meat than Argentines, so parrillada is always a popular choice. Central parrillas include *El Fogón* (☎ 90-0900) at San José 1080, *Las Brasas* (☎ 90-2285) at San José 909, and the many stalls at the *Mercado del Puerto*. The *Hotel Victoria Palace* , on Plaza Independencia, has a pricey rooftop parrilla during the summer months. A bit less central but still accessible is *El Entrevero* (☎ 70-0481), in Pocitos at 21 de Setiembre 2774. One of the capital's most highly regarded parrillas is *Forte di Makale* (☎ 71-5934), at Requena García and Rambla Wilson in Parque Rodó. The recommended *Shorthorn Grill* (☎ 42-2955), Av Uruguay 1923, has moderate prices and excellent service.

If you've overdosed on meat, there are several vegetarian restaurants: *La Vegetariana* at Yí 1334 (☎ 90-7661) and San José 1056 (☎ 91-0558); *Natura* (☎ 95-7047) at

Rincón 414; *Sabor Integral* at Fernández Crespo 1531; and *Vida Natural* at San José 1184.

Seafood is another possibility. *La Posada del Puerto* (☎ 95-4279) has two stalls in the Mercado del Puerto, while *La Tasca del Puerto* is outside on the peatonal Pérez Castellano. *La Proa* (☎ 96-2578), a sidewalk café on the peatonal Pérez Castellano, has entrées from about US$7/8; with drinks, dinner for two should cost about US$20. It serves as many as 800 people per day, but the service is still friendly and personal. Another popular place in the Mercado is *El Palenque* (☎ 95-4704).

As in Argentina, Italian immigration has left its mark on the country's cuisine. For pizza, try *Emporio de la Pizza* (☎ 91-4681), Río Negro 1311; less traditional is *Pizza Bros,* Plaza Cagancha 1364, a lively place with good pizza and bright but not overpowering decor. For more elaborate dishes, visit *Ruffino* (☎ 98-3384) at San José 1166, *Gatto Rosso* (☎ 77-1122) at JB Blanco 913 in Pocitos, or the rather pricy *Bellini* (☎ 41-2987) at San Salvador 1644, which also has live entertainment.

Olivier (☎ 95-0617), at Juan Carlos Gómez 1420 just off Plaza Constitución, is a very highly regarded but expensive French restaurant. *La Camargue* at Mercedes 1133 likewise has an outstanding reputation but is not cheap. Ditto for *Dona Flor* (☎ 79-6884), Bulevar Artigas 1034, and *Le Gavroche,* Rivera 1989. Spanish food is available at *Mesón del Club Español* (☎ 91-5145), Av 18 de Julio 1332, and *El Horreo* (☎ 91-7688), Santiago de Chile 1137, which has flamenco shows on Fridays. For Basque food, visit *Taberna Vasca* (☎ 92-3519) at San José 1168.

Other European places include the *Club Alemán* (☎ 92-2832) offering German food at Paysandú 935, as well as *La Suiza,* Soriano 939, and *Bungalow Suizo* (☎ 61-1875), some distance outside the center at Camino Carrasco 150, both offering Swiss specialties including fondue.

For something a bit more exotic, try *Ponte Vecchio,* which, despite its name, is an Armenian restaurant at Rivera 2638.

There's Middle-Eastern food at the *Club Libanés* (☎ 90-1801), Paysandú 898.

Confitería La Pasiva, on Plaza Constitución at Juan Carlos Gómez and Sarandí in the Ciudad Vieja, has excellent, reasonably priced minutas and superb flan casero in a very traditional atmosphere (except for the digital readout menu on one wall); the "pasiva entrecote" has been highly recommended as sufficient for two. There are other branches at Plaza Independencia, and at Av 18 de Julio and Ejido.

Other decent confiterías include *Oro del Rhin* (☎ 92-2833), the oldest in the city at Convención 1403, and *Hamburgo* (☎ 49-2120), offering excellent baked goods, at Rivera 2081. *Confitería de la Corte,* at Ituzaingó 1325 just off Plaza Constitución, has very good, moderately priced lunch specials.

Montevideo's Chinese food outshines that of Buenos Aires, but the tenedor libre aspect is lacking. *Oriente,* Andes 1311, has a good menu, but some dishes are expensive. Try *Canton Chino* (☎ 80-4401) at 8 de Octubre 2611, or *Nan-King* (☎ 40-4619) at Pablo de María 1445. In Pocitos, but easily reached by public transport, is *Taiwan* (☎ 70-7710), 21 de Setiembre 2996, three blocks above Rambla Mahatma Gandhi.

ENTERTAINMENT

Most of the entertainment venues listed below are in the Ciudad Vieja and the central barrio of El Cordón, but the focus of Montevideo's nightlife is shifting eastward toward Pocitos and Carrasco, where there are plenty of clubs and restaurants, and good access to beaches.

Music

Tin-Pan-Alley (☎ 48-4736), Jackson 872, is an informal place for live blues and rock and roll. *Lobezón* (☎ 91-1334), Zelmar Michelini 1264 between San José and Soriano, is a popular pub and hangout that also serves meals.

Tango

Gardel spent time in Montevideo, where the tango is no less popular than in Buenos

Aires. The very informal *Fun Fun* (☎ 95-8005), Ciudadela 1229 in the Mercado Central, has a good mix of young and old in its audience. *La Cumparsita* (☎ 91-6245), appropriately located at Carlos Gardel 1181, gets very crowded, so make reservations. It also features candombe (Afro-Uruguayan) dancing. Prices for show and dinner run about US$20 per person.

Cinema

Montevideo's commercial cinemas offer films from around the world and Latin America, lagging only a little behind Buenos Aires; most of the cinemas are along Av 18 de Julio and Plaza Cagancha. The *Cinemateca Uruguaya* (☎ 48-2460), a film club at Lorenzo Carnelli 1311, has a modest membership fee that allows unlimited viewing at the five cinemas it runs.

Theater

Like Buenos Aires, Montevideo has a lively theater community. Besides the *Teatro Solís,* there is the *Casa del Teatro* (☎ 49-0717) at Mercedes 1788; *Teatro Circular* (☎ 91-5952) at Rondeau 1388; *Teatro del Anglo* (☎ 92-3773) at San José 1426; *Teatro de la Candela* (☎ 70-9298) at 21 de Setiembre 2797 in Pocitos; *Teatro El Picadero* (☎ 95-2337) at 25 de Mayo 390 in the Ciudad Vieja; *Teatro del Centro* (☎ 92-8915) at Plaza Cagancha 1164; and *Teatro El Galpón* (☎ 48-3366) at Av 18 de Julio 1618. Prices are very reasonable, starting at about US$5.

SPECTATOR SPORTS

Soccer, an Uruguayan passion, inspires large and regular crowds. The main stadium, the Estadio Centenario in Parque José Batlle y Ordóñez off Av Italia, opened in 1930 for the first World Cup. Later declared a historic monument, it also contains the Museo del Fútbol.

THINGS TO BUY

Central Montevideo's main shopping area is Av 18 de Julio, although the Ciudad Vieja is becoming more attractive as it is redeveloped. Outlying barrios increasingly offer shopping malls like the unlikely Punta Carretas Shopping, a remodeled former prison that attracts both locals and foreigners. It's near Rambla Mahatma Gandhi at José Ellauri and Solano García; Bus No 121 from downtown is the most convenient public transportation.

For attractive artisanal items at reasonable prices in an informal atmosphere, visit Mercado de los Artesanos, which has branches at Plaza Cagancha and at Bartolomé Mitre 1367 in the Ciudad Vieja. Hours are 10 am to 8 pm weekdays, and 10 am to 2 pm Saturdays. Manos del Uruguay, at San José 1111 (☎ 90-4910) and Reconquista 602 (☎ 95-9522) (diagonally across the street from each other), is famous for its quality goods.

Other crafts centers include Artesanía Rinconada at Bulevar Artigas 2315, Centro Artesanal at WF Aldunate 1183, and Artesanía Candil at Montecaseros 3435. The daily crafts market in Plaza Cagancha is a hangout for many younger Uruguayans.

As in Argentina, leather is a popular item. Shops worth checking out include Casa Mario (☎ 96-2356) at Piedras 641 in the Ciudad Vieja; the Leather Corner (☎ 90-7922), a branch of Casa Mario, at San José 950; and the Montevideo Leather Factory (☎ 91-6226) at Plaza Independencia 832, on the 2nd floor. Sheepskin clothing is good at Peletería Holandesa (☎ 91-5438), Colonia 890 or 18 de Julio 1020. For footwear, try Arbiter-Pasqualini at 18 de Julio 943, or Impel (☎ 79-8176) at Luis B Cavia 2898 in Pocitos, both of which make shoes to order.

Uruguayan woolens are excellent. Besides Manos del Uruguay, try La Calesa, on Río Negro between 18 de Julio and San José, or Uruwool (☎ 41-2868), Tacuarembó 1531.

Uruguay's very limited mining industry produces some worthwhile gemstones, particularly amethysts and agates. Good jewelers include Cabildo Piedras at Sarandí 610, Cuarzos del Uruguay (☎ 95-9210) at Sarandí 604, and Carlos Andersen (☎ 98-2742) at Julio Herrera y Obes 1284.

URUGUAY

GETTING THERE & AWAY
Air
Many more airlines fly via Ezeiza in Buenos Aires than directly to Montevideo's Aeropuerto Internacional Carrasco, although many still have offices in Montevideo. Commuter airlines also provide international services between the two countries. Airlines flying out of Carrasco without stopping in Ezeiza include Pluna (to Buenos Aires's Aeroparque, several Brazilian destinations, Paraguay, Chile, and Spain), Aerolíneas Argentinas (to Aeroparque), Lapsa (to Paraguay), LAB (to Paraguay and Bolivia), and Varig/Cruzeiro (to Brazil). Pluna and Aerolíneas's "Puente Aéreo" ("Air Bridge") offers a US$52 one-way fare between Montevideo and Aeroparque.

Aerolíneas Argentinas
    Colonia 851 (☎ 91-9466)
Aerolíneas Uruguayas
    Plaza Cagancha 1343 (☎ 90-1868)
American
    Sarandí 699 bis (☎ 96-3979)
Saeta
    Colonia 981 (☎ 91-3570)
Iberia
    Colonia 975 (☎ 98-1032)
LanChile
    11th floor, Plaza Cagancha 1335 (☎ 98-2727)
Líneas Aéreas Paraguayas (Lapsa)
    Colonia 1001 (☎ 90-7946)
Líneas Aéreas Privadas Argentinas (LAPA)
    Plaza Cagancha 1339 (☎ 90-8765)
Lloyd Aéreo Boliviano (LAB)
    Oficina 119, Plaza Cagancha 1335
    (☎ 92-2656)
Pluna
    Colonia 1021 (☎ 98-0606, 92-1414)
Varig/Cruzeiro
    Río Negro 1362 (☎ 98-2321)

LAPA (☎ 90-8765), Plaza Cagancha 1339, runs a bus-plane combination to Colonia and Buenos Aires' Aeroparque Jorge Newbery (US$30.50). Aerolíneas Regionales Uruguayas (☎ 93-1608), Yí 1435, flies to Colonia and Aeroparque.

Aviasur (☎ 61-4618), at Carrasco only, flies to the interior destinations of Salto (five times weekly), Paysandú (three times), and Rivera (twice).

The military airline Tamu (☎ 90-0904; 60-8383 at Carrasco), Colonia 959, flies several times weekly to Salto (US$25), Tacuarembó (US$20), Artigas (US$30), Rivera (US$25), and Melo (US$20). You can also make Tamu reservations at Pluna offices.

Bus
International Still reasonably close to downtown, Montevideo's long-overdue Terminal Tres Cruces (☎ 41-8998), at Bulevar Artigas and Av Italia, is a big improvement on the individual bus terminals that once cluttered and congested Plaza Cagancha and nearby side streets. It has decent restaurants, clean toilets, luggage check, public telephones, a casa de cambio, and many other services.

Most companies have kept downtown ticket offices as well; addresses are included below when appropriate. They usually add a small *tasa de embarque* (terminal charge) of around US$0.50 in addition to the ticket price.

COT/Bus de la Carrera (☎ 42-1313; 91-0100 downtown at Plaza Independencia 826) has three direct buses daily to Buenos Aires (US$22 for an eight-hour trip), and one daily to Porto Alegre, Brazil (US$30, taking 12 hours). Cita also goes to Buenos Aires, as does Cacciola.

Several companies go elsewhere in Argentina, including Empresa General Artigas (EGA, ☎ 92-5335) at Río Branco 1409, which travels to Rosario (US$43), Mendoza (US$61, taking 21 hours), and continuing to Santiago de Chile (US$95, taking 28 hours); Expreso Encon (☎ 48-6670; 92-5153 downtown at Av Uruguay 921) traveling to Rosario, Paraná, Santa Fe, and Córdoba; and Cora (☎ 49-8799; 91-7954 at Av Lavalleja 1440), which goes to Córdoba four times weekly. Núñez has one bus daily to Santa Fe (US$40, taking 10 hours), Rosario (US$43, taking 10 hours), Córdoba (US$56, 13 hours), and Villa Carlos Paz (US$62, one hour).

El Rápido Internacional (☎ 41-4764; 92-0474 at Av Uruguay 1252) goes to Rosario and Mendoza, with connections to Chile.

To Chile, also check out Tas Choapa (☎ 49-8598; 98-3539 at Río Negro 1356).

Brújula (☎ 1717; 91-5143 at Av Uruguay 1113) goes to Asunción Tuesday, Friday, and Sunday (US$64), while Coit (☎ 41-5628; 91-6619 at Paraguay 1473) goes Monday, Wednesday, and Saturday via Uruguaiana (Brazil) and Posadas (Argentina). Both have a reputation for excellent service.

Cauvi (☎ 41-9196; 95-4040 at Bacacay 1342) goes to the Brazilian cities of Porto Alegre, Curitiba, and São Paulo. Other companies serving Brazil are Cynsa and TTL (☎ 41-1410; 91-7142 at Plaza Cagancha 1385), which goes nightly to Pelotas (US$30) and Porto Alegre (US$34, taking 11½ hours), and to Florianópolis (US$45, taking 16 hours), Camboriú (US$47, 18 hours), Curitibá (US$55, 23 hours), and São Paulo (US$62, 27 hours). Coche cama sleepers cost US$42 to Pelotas and US$51 to Porto Alegre. EGA also goes daily to Brazilian destinations including Pelotas and Porto Alegre, and leaves three times weekly to Florianópolis, Camboriú, Curitiba, and São Paulo. Planalto (☎ 1717), downtown at Rondeau 1475, also serves Brazilian destinations.

Domestic COT (☎ 49-4949) sends more than 20 buses per day to Punta del Este (US$6, 2½ hours) via Piriápolis (US$4), Pan de Azúcar, San Carlos, and Maldonado; Copsa (☎ 48-1521; 92-1040 at Av Uruguay 1313) also goes to Maldonado. COT also has nine buses daily to Colonia (2½ hours, US$7) and also goes to Rocha (US$8) and La Paloma (US$9). Agencia Central (☎ 1717; 90-1586 downtown at Rondeau 1475) goes to Mercedes, Paysandú (US$17, five hours), Salto (six hours, US$20), and Tacuarembó (US$14, 5½ hours). Turil (☎ 48-3711; 41-1884 at JB Amorín 1384) goes three times daily to Tacuarembó and Rivera (US$18), three times daily to Artigas (US$22), and eight times daily to Colonia (US$7).

Chadre (☎ 1717; 90-1586 at Rondeau 1475), Sabelín (☎ 1717; 91-5143 at Av Uruguay 1113), Copay (☎ 40-9926; 92-

1040 at Av Uruguay 1021), and Intertur (☎ 49-7098; 98-0250 at Av Uruguay 1252) all serve littoral destinations like Colonia, Carmelo, Mercedes, Fray Bentos (five hours), Paysandú, and Salto.

Rutas del Sol (☎ 42-5451; 90-3345 at Paraguay 1375) goes to Rocha and La Paloma eight times daily, and to Barro de Valizas. Cita (☎ 42-5425; 91-0100 at Plaza Independencia 826) goes to Chuy, as do COT and Rutas del Sol. Rutas del Plata (☎ 42-5159) goes to Minas (US$5, two hours), Treinta y Tres (US$10, four hours), and Río Branco (US$15, six hours) four times daily.

Núñez (☎ 48-6670;90-0483 at Av Uruguay 921) serves interior destinations like Minas, Treinta y Tres, Melo (US$15, six hours), Río Branco, Salto, and Rivera, while El Norteño (☎ 42-1042; 91-1898 at Av Uruguay 1291) goes to Salto and Bella Unión. Sharing offices with Núñez, Cynsa (☎ 48-6670; 90-5321) has five buses daily to Chuy (US$12, five hours), and six to La Paloma (US$10, four hours).

Other companies going to Minas (US$5) include Cita, Corporación (☎ 42-1920; 90-8733 at Av Uruguay 1021), Cota (☎ 42-1307; 91-3352 at Av Uruguay 1291), Cromín (☎ 42-5451), Emdal (☎ 49-7098), and Expreso Minuano (☎ 42-5075; 91-5896 at Plaza Independencia 1382).

CUT (☎ 42-50-54; 90-3165 at Av Uruguay 1251) and Corporación go five times daily to Mercedes (US$10) and Fray Bentos (US$11), and twice to Artigas (US$22). Turismar (☎ 49-0999; 90-3712 at Av Lavalleja 1470) goes to Treinta y Tres and Melo three times daily, as does Cota.

Buses Nossar (☎ 1880; 92-5916 at Av Uruguay 1194), has five daily buses to Durazno (US$6), one of which continues to Paso de los Toros (US$9) and Tacuarembó (US$16). CTT (☎ 42-1042) runs similar routes.

River
Most services across the Río de la Plata to Buenos Aires are bus-boat combinations via Colonia, but the so-called Aviones de Buquebus are high-speed ferries that take

URUGUAY

only about 2½ hours for the crossing (US$37) and leave from the port at the foot of Pérez Castellano. Buquebus (☎ 92-0670) is at Río Negro 1400. Cacciola (☎ 91-0755), Plaza Cagancha 1326, runs a bus-launch service to the Buenos Aires suburb of Tigre four times daily.

Aliscafos Belt (☎ 90-4608) at Plaza Cagancha 1325 and Ferryturismo (☎ 90-6617) at Río Branco 1368 both run a bus-hydrofoil combination to Buenos Aires (four hours, US$35 on peak weekends, US$25 weekdays) via Colonia three times daily except Sunday, when it runs only twice. There are slight discounts for round-trips. Deltanave (☎ 91-5143), which runs launches from Nueva Palmira to Tigre, is at Plaza Cagancha 1340.

Most of the boat services across the Río de la Plata have offices at Tres Cruces as well, including Aliscafos Belt (☎ 48-8146), Deltanave (☎ 49-8598), Ferryturismo (☎ 49-8198), and Buquebus (☎ 48-8146), all of which can arrange bus-boat combinations.

GETTING AROUND
To/From the Airport

For US$4, there is a special bus from Pluna's downtown offices to Montevideo's Aeropuerto Internacional Carrasco; see the schedule posted there. Tamu passengers can take advantage of free bus services to Carrasco, but the D-1 Expreso bus from the Ciudad Vieja also goes to Carrasco. COT's buses to Punta del Este also stop at the airport.

Special taxis serve the airport and cost more than regular ones, but any cab can take you there. Since the airport is beyond the city limits, fares will exceed the meter reading (see the Taxi section below).

Bus

Montevideo has an extensive but chaotic public transport system The city's fleet of buses is improving; they less frequently leave you gasping for breath with noxious diesel fumes, and still go everywhere for about US45¢. The *Guia de Montevideo Eureka,* available at bookstores or kiosks, lists routes and schedules, as do the yellow pages of the Montevideo phone book. As in Argentina, the driver or conductor will ask your destination. Retain your ticket, which may be inspected at any time. This is not Buenos Aires – most routes cease service by 10:30 or 11 pm.

Car Rental

Uruguayan car rental costs have risen dramatically and now approach Argentine prices; before signing a contract, ascertain whether insurance and IVA are included. Agencies include Hertz (☎ 92-3920) at Colonia 813, Budget (☎ 91-6363) at Mercedes 935, National (☎ 90-0035) at Ciudadela 1397, and Dollar (☎ 98-4376) at Convención 1432. Local agencies, marginally cheaper, include Multicar (☎ 92-2555) at Yaguarón 1344 bis and Autocar (☎ 98-5153) at Mercedes 863.

Taxi

Taxis have meters, and drivers correlate the meter reading with a photocopied fare chart. Between midnight and 6 am fares are higher. There is a small additional charge for luggage, and riders generally round off the fare to the next higher peso as a tip.

The Uruguayan Littoral

West of Montevideo, the littoral is that portion of Uruguay that fronts the Río de la Plata and the Río Uruguay, opposite Argentine Mesopotamia. Originally Indian and gaucho country, it has become the country's most important agricultural area, the wheat fields and gardens of which feed the growing population of the capital.

The littoral has one can't-miss attraction, the 17th-century Portuguese contraband port and fortress of Colonia opposite Buenos Aires, and several lesser sights that make worthwhile day trips from either Colonia or Montevideo. Overland travelers from Argentine Mesopotamia will find the towns along the Río Uruguay – Salto, Paysandú, Fray Bentos, and Mercedes – pleasant enough to justify a stopover en route to Colonia and Montevideo.

COLONIA

Only an hour or two from Buenos Aires, Colonia (full name Colonia del Sacramento) is one of the Southern Cone's unappreciated gems, attracting many thousands of Argentines but only a handful of the many foreign tourists who visit the Argentine capital.

Founded in 1680 by the Portuguese Manoel Lobo, it occupied a strategic position almost exactly opposite Buenos Aires across the Río de la Plata, but its major importance was as a source of contraband, undercutting Spain's jealously defended mercantile trade monopoly. British goods made their way from Colonia into Buenos Aires and the interior through surreptitious exchange with the Portuguese in the Paraná delta; for this reason, Spanish forces intermittently besieged Portugal's riverside outpost for decades. The Jesuit father Martin Dobrizhoffer vividly described mid-18th-century Colonia:

The houses are few and low, forming a village, rather than city, yet it is far from despicable; opulent merchants, wares of every kind, gold, silver, and diamonds are concealed beneath its miserable roofs. Surrounded with a single and very slender wall . . . the land under Portuguese authority is of such small circumference that the most inactive person might walk round it in half an hour. Portuguese ships, laden with English and Dutch wares, and Negro slaves . . . crowd to this port, and the Spanish sentinels, either bribed or deceived, convey the goods to Paraguay, Peru, or Chili. It is incredible how many millions are lost to the Spaniards in this forbidden traffic.

Although the two powers agreed over the cession of Colonia to Spain around 1750, the agreement failed when Jesuit missionaries on the upper Paraná refused to comply with the proposed exchange of territory in their area. Spain finally captured the city in 1762, but failed to hold it until 1777, when authorities created the Viceroyalty of the River Plate. From this time, the city's commercial importance declined as foreign goods proceeded directly to Buenos Aires.

The capital of its department, Colonia is a pleasant town of about 20,000, the streets of its historic colonial core shaded by sycamores from the summer heat. In the course of the day, the town discloses its many aspects as sunlight strikes whitewashed colonial buildings and the river; the latter, living up to its name, is silvery in the morning but turns brownish by midday. The townspeople are extremely polite, motorists even stopping for pedestrians.

Colonia served as the fictional San José de los Altares in Argentine director María Luisa Bemberg's 1993 film *I Don't Want to Talk About It,* starring Marcelo Mastroianni as an enigmatic Italian immigrant who falls in love and marries a dwarf, the daughter of the widow of the town's mayor, who eventually deserts him to join the circus.

Orientation

Colonia del Sacramento sits on the east bank of the Río de la Plata, 180 km west of

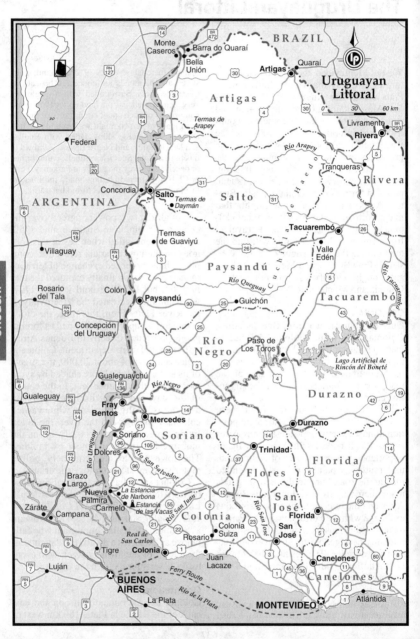

Montevideo via Ruta 1 but only 50 km from Buenos Aires by ferry or hydrofoil. Like Montevideo, it features an irregular colonial nucleus of narrow cobbled streets, now known as the Barrio Histórico, on a small peninsula jutting into the river. The town's commercial center, around Plaza 25 de Agosto, and the river port are a few blocks east, where the Rambla Costanera leads north along the river to the Real de San Carlos, another area of interest to visitors. The diagonal Av Roosevelt is the main highway to Montevideo.

Information

Tourist Offices The municipal Oficina de Información Turística (☎ 2182) is at General Flores 499. While not especially well informed, the staff have numerous brochures that are difficult to obtain elsewhere. Hours are weekdays 7 am to 8 pm, weekends 10 am to 7 pm. The Ministerio de Turismo (☎ 4897) maintains a ferry-port branch that is more efficient and helpful.

Foreign Consulate The Argentine Consulate (☎ 2091) is at General Flores 350 and Virrey Zeballos. It is not especially helpful in renewing visas that have been obtained in other Argentine consulates, so try to renew in Montevideo. It's open weekdays 8 am to 1 pm.

Money Arriving at the port from Buenos Aires, you can change money at Cambio Libertad or Banco República, both of which are alongside the Ministerios de Turismo. Banco República pays slightly lower rates and charges US$1 commission for traveler's checks. In downtown, try Cambio Colonia, at General Flores and Alberto Méndez, or Cambio Viaggio at General Flores 350. The latter is open Sundays 10 am to 6 pm and will change traveler's checks for 2½% commission.

Post & Telecommunications The post office is at Lavalleja 226. Antel, at Rivadavia 420, has direct fiber-optic lines to the USA (AT&T and MCI) and the UK. Colonia's area code is 0522.

Travel Agency Receptivos Colonia (☎ 3388), General Flores 507, arranges air tickets, tours, and car rentals.

Walking Tour

Also known as La Colonia Portuguesa (the Portuguese colony), Colonia's Barrio Histórico begins at the **Puerta de Campo,** the restored Calle Manoel Lobo entrance to the old city, which dates from the governorship of Vasconcellos in 1745. A thick, fortified wall runs south along the Paseo de San Miguel to the river. A short distance west is the **Plaza Mayor 25 de Mayo;** off the plaza leads the narrow, cobbled **Calle de los Suspiros** (Street of Whispers), lined with tile-and-stucco colonial houses. Just beyond, the **Museo Portugués** has good exhibits on the Portuguese period, including Lusitanian and colonial dress. Colonia's museums are generally open 11:30 am to 6 pm.

At the southwest corner of Plaza Mayor are the **Casa de Lavalleja,** once the residence of General Lavalleja, and the ruins of the 17th-century **Convento de San Francisco** and the 19th-century **Faro** (lighthouse, open 10:30 am to noon Thursday for an excellent view of the old town). At its west end, on Calle del Comercio, is the **Museo Municipal;** next door is the so-called **Casa del Virrey,** the Viceroy's House. Strangely enough, there was never a viceroy in Colonia, but the building is an interesting example of colonial architecture. At the northwest corner of the plaza, on Calle de las Misiones de los Tapes, the

Take a stroll down Calle de los Suspiros.

URUGUAY

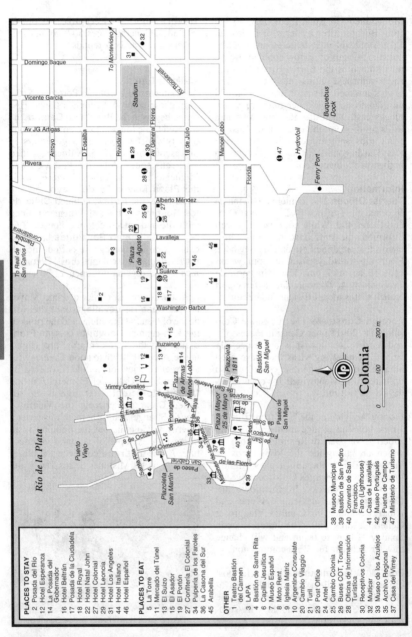

PLACES TO STAY
2   Posada del Río
12 Hotel Esperanza
14 La Posada del Gobernador
16 Hotel Beltrán
17 Posada de la Ciudadela
18 Hotel Royal
22 Hotel Natal John
27 Hotel Colonial
29 Hotel Leoncia
31 Hotel Los Angeles
44 Hotel Italiano
46 Hotel Español

PLACES TO EAT
5   La Torre
11 Mercado del Túnel
13 El Suizo
15 El Asador
19 El Portón
27 Confitería El Colonial
34 Pulpería de los Faroles
36 La Casona del Sur
45 Arabella

OTHER
1   Teatro Bastión del Carmen
3   LAPA
4   Bastión de Santa Rita
6   Capilla Jesuítica
7   Museo Español
8   Moto Rent
9   Iglesia Matriz
10 Argentine Consulate
20 Cambio Viaggio
21 Turil
23 Post Office
24 Antel
25 Cambio Colonia
26 Buses COT, Tourifin
28 Oficina de Información Turística
30 Receptivos Colonia
32 Multicar
33 Museo de los Azulejos
35 Archivo Regional
37 Casa del Virrey
38 Museo Municipal
39 Bastión de San Pedro
40 Convento de San Francisco, Faro (Lighthouse)
41 Casa de Lavalleja
42 Museo Portugués
43 Puerta de Campo
47 Ministerio de Turismo

Colonia

0   100   200 m

Top Left: Communications Tower, Montevideo (RS)
Top Right: Conventillo, Ciudad Vieja, Montevideo
Bottom Left: Colonial Estancia El Talar, Uruguay
Bottom Right: Old car, Colonia, Uruguay (DS)

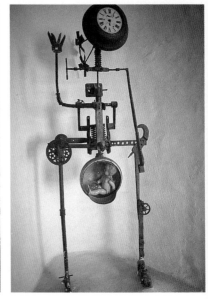

Top: Paysandú, Uruguay
Left: Punta del Este, Uruguay
Right: Sculpture in Casa Pueblo, Punta Ballena, Uruguay

Archivo Regional contains a small museum and bookstore.

At the west end of Misiones de los Tapes is the **Museo de los Azulejos** (Museum of Tiles), a 17th-century house with a sampling of colonial tile work (closed at last report). From there, the riverfront **Paseo de San Gabriel** leads to Calle del Colegio, where a right on Calle del Comercio leads to the **Capilla Jesuítica**, the ruined Jesuit chapel. Going east along Av General Flores and then turning south on Calle Vasconcellos, you reach the landmark **Iglesia Matriz** (see below) on the **Plaza de Armas**, also known as Plaza Manoel Lobo.

Back across General Flores, at España and San José, the **Museo Español** has exhibitions of replica pottery, clothing, and maps of the colonial period. It's closed Tuesday and Wednesday. At the north end of the street is the **Puerto Viejo**, the old port. One block east, at Calle del Virrey Cevallos and Rivadavia, the **Teatro Bastión del Carmen** is a theater building that incorporates part of the city's ancient fortifications.

Iglesia Matriz

Begun in 1680, Uruguay's oldest church has undergone many changes over three centuries. It was expanded between 1722 and 1749 under Portuguese Governor Pedro Vasconcellos, nearly destroyed by fire in 1799, and rebuilt by Spanish architect Tomás Toribio, who also designed the Cabildo of Montevideo.

The church suffered further misfortune when, during the Brazilian occupation of 1823, lightning struck a powder magazine in the sacristy, producing an explosion that destroyed part of the lateral walls, two-thirds of the vault, the altar, and the posterior wall, leaving cracks in many other parts of the building. Between 1836 and 1842, under the direction of Padre Domingo Rama and the sponsorship of General Fructuoso Rivera, it was again rebuilt; changes since then have been primarily cosmetic. It's on Calle Vasconcellos, between General Flores and the Plaza de Armas.

Special Events

In early March, Colonia hosts the Fiesta Nacional de La Leche (National Dairy Festival), which attracts many Uruguayans who come for the excellent local food and music.

Places to Stay

As Colonia has become a more popular destination for Argentine and international travelers, hotel keepers have upgraded their accommodations as well as their prices, but there are still reasonable alternatives. The municipal tourist office on General Flores may help visitors find accommodations in casas de familia. Some hotels charge higher rates on weekends (Friday through Sunday) than weekdays (Monday through Thursday). Except for the very cheapest establishments, most include breakfast in their rates.

Places to Stay – bottom end

Camping The *Camping Municipal de Colonia* (☎ 4444) sits in a eucalyptus grove at the Real de San Carlos, five km from the Barrio Histórico. It has excellent facilities and is close to the Balneario Municipal. Open all year, it's easily accessible by public transport. Fees are about US$3.50 per person.

Hospedajes & Hotels Except for camping, really cheap accommodations have nearly disappeared in Colonia. The cheapest in town is the *Hotel Español* (☎ 2314), Manoel Lobo 377, with large but dark rooms for US$8 single (if available), US$15 double with shared bath. The very central *Hotel Colonial* (☎ 2906), General Flores 440, costs US$13/20 single/double without breakfast.

One of the best values is the very convenient but quiet *Posada del Río* (☎ 3002), on tree-lined Washington Barbot 258 near a pleasant sand beach. Rooms cost US$15 per person with private bath. Another good choice is *Posada de la Ciudadela* (☎ 2683), Washington Barbot 164, where rates are US$20 per person.

URUGUAY

Places to Stay – middle

Hotel Los Angeles (☎ 2335), Av Roosevelt 203, is a modern, rather impersonal building on a busy street some distance from the Barrio Histórico, but service is good for US$25/38 single/double weekdays, US$35/55 weekends, with breakfast. The upgraded *Hotel Italiano* (☎ 2103), Manoel Lobo 341, charges US$35 for doubles with shared bath, US$55 with private bath, breakfast included.

Friendly, usually quiet (noise from a nearby bar occasionally erupts on weekends), and very clean, *Hotel Beltrán* (☎ 2955), General Flores 311, is one of Colonia's oldest hotels; all rooms face onto a central patio. Since remodeling, rates are US$36 double with shared bath, US$45 with private bath, including breakfast, but rise to US$70 double on weekends.

Downtown, *Hotel Natal John* (☎ 2081), General Flores 394, costs US$45/68 single/double. *Hotel Esperanza* (☎ 2922), near the entrance to the Barrio Histórico at General Flores 237, charges US$55 double with breakfast, while double rates at *Hotel Leoncia* (☎ 2369), Rivera 214, are US$60 with breakfast.

Places to Stay – top end

Gran Hotel Casino El Mirador (☎ 2004), distant from the Barrio Histórico on Av Roosevelt, is a high-rise hotel with every modern luxury and nothing of Colonia's unique personality. Rates are US$70 per person with half-board, US$80 with full board. Conveniently central at General Flores 340, *Hotel Royal* (☎ 3139) costs US$60/90 single/double weekdays, US$80/120 weekends. Probably the most distinctive accommodations are at *La Posada del Gobernador* (☎ 3018), 18 de Julio 205 in the Barrio Histórico, but it's arguably overpriced for US$105 double.

Places to Eat

Confitería El Colonial (☎ 2906), General Flores 432, is an excellent and reasonably priced breakfast spot, selling enormous hot croissants. One of Colonia's best values is *El Asador,* Ituzaingó 168, a parrilla jammed with locals. *El Portón,* General Flores 333, is a more upscale but appealing parrilla.

El Suizo, another parrilla at General Flores and Ituzaingó, appears to charge more because of its attractive colonial setting than its food. Down the block at General Flores 229, the extensive menu at *Mercado del Túnel* (☎ 4666) varies in quality – some dishes are very good dishes, but others are unremarkable. Discreetly examine other patrons' dishes to determine what's worth ordering.

Pulpería de los Faroles, at Calle del Comercio and Misiones de los Tapes in the Barrio Histórico, has an upscale ambience but is not outrageously expensive for a good meal. *La Casona del Sur,* two doors away, is a good confitería that doubles as a handicrafts market. At night it has live music.

At the tip of the Barrio Histórico, *La Torre* is a good pizzería in a remodeled tower located on the Bastión de Santa Rita. A recent reader recommendation is *Arabella,* 18 de Julio 360.

Things to Buy

For handicrafts, check out the Sunday market in the Barrio Histórico's Plaza Mayor. La Casona del Sur, a confitería on Misiones de los Tapes, also has a good selection. El Musguito, nearby on Calle de la Playa, is an artisans' cooperative with ceramics, leather work, and wood carvings.

Getting There & Away

Air LAPA (☎ 2006), Rivadavia 383, flies twice daily except Sunday (once only) to Aeroparque in Buenos Aires. The 15-minute crossing costs US$23 one-way. The flights from Aeroparque continue to Montevideo by bus; the trip costs US$7.50, and takes 2½ hours.

Bus Colonia has no central bus terminal. COT (☎ 3121), General Flores 440, has nine buses daily to Montevideo for US$7, taking 2½ hours. It also has nine buses daily to Colonia Suiza, Rosario, and Juan Lacaze, except Sundays when there are only eight.

Turil (☎ 5246), at General Flores and Suárez, one block east of Hotel Beltrán, goes almost hourly to Montevideo. Touriño, General Flores 432, has six daily to Carmelo except Sundays, when there are only two. Klüver (☎ 2934) goes to Mercedes.

Car & Scooter Rental Multicar (☎ 4893) is at Av Roosevelt 220. At Moto Rent (☎ 2266), Virrey Cevallos 223, scooter rentals run about US$6 per hour or $30 - per day.

River Buquebus (☎ 2975), Ferryturismo (☎ 2919), and Aliscafos (☎ 3664), all at the port at the foot of Av Roosevelt, link Colonia with Buenos Aires. All offer discounts on roundtrip fares, especially for same-day returns.

Ferryturismo runs the ferry *Ciudad de Buenos Aires* to the Argentine capital weekdays at noon and 8 pm, weekends at 7:30 pm only; the trip takes 2½ hours and costs US$10, or US$7 for children over three years. The Buquebus ferries *Eladia Isabel* and *Silvia Ana* run two trips daily on weekdays, at 4 am and 8 pm, and one trip per day on weekends. Cars weighing up to 1200 kg cost US$60 exclusive of passenger fares, while those over 1200 kg cost US$70.

Aliscafos has two hydrofoils daily to Buenos Aires, which, although faster than the ferries, are also more crowded, and a luggage limitation is enforced. The trip takes one hour and costs US$21. Ferryturismo (☎ 2919) runs three hydrofoils daily Monday to Saturday, and two on Sunday.

There is a US$3 departure tax from the ferry terminal.

Getting Around

Cotuc, the city bus company, goes to the Camping Municipal and the Real de San Carlos for US$0.50. It runs mostly along Flores. Otherwise, Colonia is extremely compact and excellent for walking.

AROUND COLONIA
Real de San Carlos

At the turn of the century, naturalized Argentine entrepreneur Nicolás Mihanovich invested US$1.5 million to build an enormous tourist complex at the Real de San Carlos, five km west of Colonia, where Spanish troops once camped before attacking the Portuguese outpost. Among the attractions erected by Mihanovich, a Dalmatian immigrant, were a 10,000-seat bullring (Uruguay outlawed bullfights in 1912), a 3000-seat jai alai frontón, a hotel-casino with its own power plant (the casino failed in 1917 when the Argentine government placed a tax on every boat crossing the river), and a racecourse.

Only the racecourse functions today, but the ruins make an interesting excursion. There is also the **Museo Municipal Real de San Carlos,** focusing on paleontology, which is open daily except Monday 2 to 7 pm.

COLONIA SUIZA

In the department of Colonia, Colonia Suiza (also known as Nueva Helvecia) is 120 km east of Montevideo and 60 km east of the city of Colonia del Sacramento along a short lateral off Ruta 1. Settled by Swiss immigrants in 1862, it was the country's first interior agricultural colony, providing wheat for the mills of Montevideo. A quiet, pleasant destination with a demonstrably European ambience, its dairy products are known throughout the country – 60% of Uruguay's cheese comes from here.

Information

Colonia Suiza has no formal tourist office. To change cash, try the Banco de Crédito at Berna 1314, or the Banco La Caja Obrera on 18 de Julio. Antel is at Artigas and Dreyer, across from the OSE water tower. Colonia Suiza's area code is 0552. The hospital (☎ 4057) is at 18 de Julio and C Cunier.

Things to See

The center of the town is the Plaza de los Fundadores, with an impressive sculpture,

URUGUAY

El Surco, commemorating the original Swiss pioneers. Interesting buildings include the ruins of the first flour mill, the **Molino Quemado,** and the historic **Hotel del Prado,** which also functions as a youth hostel.

Places to Stay & Eat

The most reasonable accommodations are at friendly *Hotel Comercio* at 18 de Julio 1209, where singles with private bath cost about US$10 (its entrance near Colón is completely unmarked). Dating from 1884, the 80-room *Hotel del Prado* (☎ 4169), in the Barrio Hoteles on the outskirts of town, is a magnificent if declining building with huge balconies. Rooms are US$25 per person, but it is also the youth hostel, offering beds with shared bath for US$8 with a hostel card.

Dating from 1872, the *Gran Hotel Suizo* (☎ 4002), on Av Federico Fischer, is the country's oldest tourist hotel and has a renowned restaurant. Without a doubt, though, top of the line is luxurious *Hotel Nirvana* (☎ 4081; 90-3823 in Montevideo), on Av Batlle y Ordóñez, where high-season (December 15 to April 1) accommodations cost US$56 per person with breakfast. It offers a swimming pool, tennis courts, horseback riding, facilities for children, and 25 hectares of beautifully landscaped grounds.

Colonia Suiza has several excellent restaurants. Besides Hotel Suizo, try *La Gondola,* Luis Dreyer and 25 de Agosto, *L'Arbalete* on Av Batlle y Ordóñez, and *Don José,* 18 de Julio 1214.

Getting There & Away

COT (☎ 5231), next to Bar Meny at 18 de Julio and Treinta y Tres, has services to Montevideo, Colonia, Fray Bentos (three daily), and Paysandú (one daily).

CARMELO

Where the Río Uruguay broadens and becomes the Río de la Plata, Carmelo sits opposite the Paraná delta, 75 km northwest of Colonia del Sacramento and 235 km from Montevideo. Launches connect it to the Buenos Aires suburb of Tigre. Part of the department of Colonia, it is a center for yachting and boating on the Río Uruguay and the Río de la Plata, and for exploring the delta.

Carmelo dates from 1816, when residents of the village of Las Víboras petitioned Artigas, for whom the town's original central plaza is named, for permission to move to the more hospitable Arroyo de las Vacas. The local economy depends on tourism, livestock, and agriculture – local wines have an excellent reputation.

Orientation

Carmelo straddles the Arroyo de las Vacas, a sheltered harbor on the Río de la Plata. North of the Arroyo, shady Plaza Independencia is now the commercial center. Most of the town's businesses are located along 19 de Abril, which leads to the bridge across the arroyo, where a large park offers open space, camping, swimming, and a huge, tasteless casino.

Information

Tourist Office The municipal Oficina de Turismo (☎ 2001) is at 19 de Abril 250, corner of Barrios, four blocks from the bridge over Arroyo de las Vacas.

Foreign Consulate The Argentine Consulate (☎ 2266) is at Roosevelt 442.

Money Carmelo has two exchange houses: Lerga, at 19 de Abril and Rodríguez, and Viaggio, at 19 de Abril and 12 de Febrero, which is open 10 am to 6 pm weekdays but does not cash traveler's checks.

Post & Telecommunications The post office is at Uruguay 368. Carmelo's area code is 542.

Travel Agency When the tourist office is not open, ask for information at West Tour (☎ 2719), 19 de Abril 267, where the staff is extremely helpful and well informed.

Medical Services The hospital (☎ 2107) is at Uruguay and Av Artigas.

Things to See

The **Santuario del Carmen**, at Lavalleja and El Carmen, dates from 1830. Next door is **Archivo y Museo Parroquial**, featuring documents and objects of local historical importance. Dating from 1860, the **Casa de Ignacio Barrios**, at Barrios and 19 de Abril, once belonged to one of San Martín's lieutenants, also a signer of the Uruguayan declaration of independence.

Special Events

In early February, Carmelo celebrates the Fiesta Nacional de la Uva (National Grape Festival), an established event for more than 20 years.

Places to Stay

Camping *Camping Náutico Las Higueritas* (☎ 2058), on the south side of Arroyo de las Vacas, charges US$3 per person. *Camping Don Mauro* (☎ 2390) is at Ignacio Barros and Arroyo de las Vacas, six blocks from downtown; it's open December to March, and has cold showers only. The fee is also US$3 per person.

Hotels The cheapest town in is the very basic, run-down *Hotel Carmelo*, 19 de Abril 561 at 25 de Mayo, where rooms with shared bath are US$5 per person. *Hotel Oriental*, 19 de Abril 286 near Rodríguez, is also basic, with several beds to a room. Adults pay US$7 per single, and children are an additional US$3.

Hotel Paraná (☎ 2480), 19 de Abril 585, has singles for US$8 with private bath. *Hotel La Unión* (☎ 2028), next to the post office at Uruguay 368, is very nice and clean; singles with shared bath cost US$9, singles/doubles with private bath cost US$12/20. Friendly *Hotel San Fernando* (☎ 2503), 19 de Abril 161 near Barrios, has clean rooms with private bath for US$15/20. At the *Palace Hotel* (☎ 2622), Sarandí 308, doubles are US$30.

The modern and clean but ugly *Hotel Bertoletti* (☎ 2030), Uruguay 171, has singles for US$17 without breakfast. *Hotel Rambla* (☎ 2390), conveniently close to the launch docks at Uruguay 55, doubles

cost US$45 with breakfast. The top of the line is the *Hotel Casino Carmelo* (☎ 2314), on Av Rodó across the Arroyo de las Vacas, where rates are US$37.50 per person with breakfast, US$50 with full half-board.

Places to Eat

El Vesubio, 19 de Abril 451, serves an enormous, tasty chivito al plato, plus a variety of other dishes. Other restaurants include *Perrini* at 19 de Abril 440, and the *Yacht Club, Morales,* and *El Refugio,* all across the bridge in the park.

Getting There & Away

Bus All the bus companies are on or near Plaza Independencia. Sabelín and Chadre (☎ 2987), both at Uruguay and 18 de Julio, go to Montevideo (the trip costs US$9 and takes four hours) and north to Fray Bentos, Paysandú, and Salto. Turil goes to Colonia (costing US$2 and taking one hour), as do Klüver (☎ 3411) and Intertur, both at 18 de Julio and Uruguay.

River Movilán/Deltanave, at Constituyentes 263, has two crossings daily to the Buenos Aires suburb of Tigre, at 4 am and 10:30 am. Cacciola, Constituyentes 219, goes at 4:30 am and 11:30 am except Mondays, when departures are at 11:30 am and 6:30 pm. The fare is US$11 one-way for adults, US$7.50 one-way for children.

AROUND CARMELO
La Estancia de Narbona

Despite the deteriorating condition of its buildings, this 18th-century estancia on the Arroyo Víboras, about 20 km west of Carmelo on the road to Nueva Palmira, is deservedly a national historical monument. Its casco and chapel, with a three-story bell tower, sit on the summit of a small hill about two km from the main road. At the junction and near a hydraulic mill erected to process local wheat, the **Puente Castells,** the first bridge of its kind in the country, has stood for more than 130 years.

Estancia de las Vacas

Just east of Carmelo, Estancia de las Vacas

was an 18th-century Jesuit enterprise, probably the most advanced of its kind in the Banda Oriental, with its chapel, patios, lodging, blacksmiths' and carpenters' workshops, looms, bakery, dairy, and brick and tile factories, as well as Uruguay's first vineyards and 30,000 heads of cattle. More than 200 people, including Indian peons and black slaves, lived here.

After expulsion of the Jesuits in 1767, Juan de San Martín (father of the Argentine hero) was the estancia's administrator until 1774. After his departure, it passed into the hands of another monastic order that proved much less capable, and the estanica fell into disrepair. It is now a national historical monument, also known as the Calera de las Huérfanas.

FRAY BENTOS

Capital of the department of Río Negro, Fray Bentos, about 300 km northwest of Montevideo, is the southernmost overland crossing point from Argentina, reached by the Libertador General San Martín bridge over the Río Uruguay. It lies on the east bank of the river, opposite the Argentine city of Gualeguaychú.

In 1864, Fray Bentos was the site of the country's first meat extract plant; in 1902 British interests located Uruguay's first frigorífico here. The enormous Anglo plant in this former company town has closed, but the Uruguayan government is preserving it as a museum.

Orientation

Fray Bentos has a very regular grid pattern centered on the surprisingly open Plaza Constitución, where scattered palms surround a Victorian band shell, a replica of London's Crystal Palace donated by Liebig Meats in 1902. The main commercial street is 18 de Julio, leading east to Ruta 2 toward Mercedes and Montevideo; northbound 25 de Mayo passes the shadier Plaza Hargain, toward the bridge to Argentina.

Information

Tourist Offices The municipal Oficina de Turismo (☎ 3261) is at 25 de Mayo and 18

de Julio, opposite Plaza Constitución; with a friendly, helpful, and knowledgeable staff, it's open weekdays from 8 am to noon and 5 to 9 pm. There's a satellite office at the bridge over the Río Uruguay.

Foreign Consulate The Argentine Consulate (☎ 2638), Sarandí 3193 near Rincón, is open weekdays, 8 am to 1 pm.

Money Cambio Fagalde, 18 de Julio 1163, is open weekdays and Saturdays 8 am to noon and 3:30 to 7:30 pm.

Post & Telecommunications The post office is at Treinta y Tres 3271, between 18 de Julio and Zorrilla. Antel is at Zorrilla 1127 near Treinta y Tres. Fray Bentos's area code is 535.

Medical Services The Hospital Salúd Pública (☎ 2533) is at Echeverría and Lavalleja.

Things to See

Probably Fray Bentos's most architecturally distinguished landmark, the 400-seat **Teatro Young** bears the name of the wealthy Anglo-Uruguayan estanciero who sponsored its construction between 1909 and 1912. Now municipal property, it hosts cultural events throughout the year, and can be visited upon request. Ask at the theater itself or at the tourist office. It's a block north of Plaza Constitución, at the corner of 25 de Mayo and Zorrilla.

The municipal **Museo Solari** on Treinta y Tres, on the west side of Plaza Constitución, has changing exhibits. In Parque Roosevelt, on the banks of the river at the west end of town, the open-air **Teatro Municipal de Verano** seats 4000 and has excellent acoustics.

In 1865, the Liebig Extract of Meat Company located its pioneer South American plant, which soon became the most important industrial complex in Uruguay, southwest of downtown Fray Bentos. Most installations of the now defunct Frigorífico Anglo del Uruguay make up the dominant landmark in **Barrio Histórico del Anglo**.

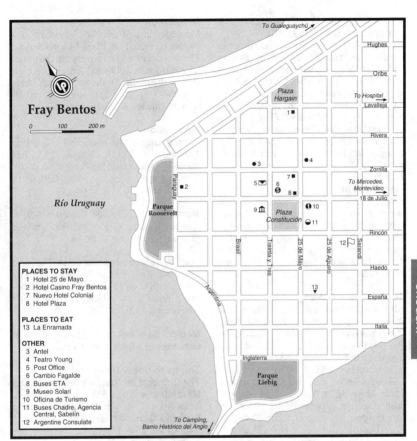

Fray Bentos

0   100   200 m

Río Uruguay

To Gualeguaychú

Hughes

Oribe

Plaza Hargain

To Hospital
Lavalleja

Rivera

Zorrilla

To Mercedes,
Montevideo

18 de Julio

Parque Roosevelt

Plaza Constitución

Rincón

Haedo

España

Italia

Paraguay

Brasil

Treinta y Tres

25 de Mayo

25 de Agusto

Sarandi

Argentina

Inglaterra

Parque Liebig

To Camping,
Barrio Histórico del Anglo

PLACES TO STAY
1   Hotel 25 de Mayo
2   Hotel Casino Fray Bentos
7   Nuevo Hotel Colonial
8   Hotel Plaza

PLACES TO EAT
13   La Enramada

OTHER
3   Antel
4   Teatro Young
5   Post Office
6   Cambio Fagalde
8   Buses ETA
9   Museo Solari
10   Oficina de Turismo
11   Buses Chadre, Agencia
     Central, Sabelin
12   Argentine Consulate

URUGUAY

The landscape and street life of this bustling neighborhood offer great photographic opportunities, and the former plant buildings are undergoing restoration as the **Museo de la Revolución Industrial** (☎ 2918). Note especially the manager's residence and the former British Consulate. Local authorities are also trying to attract light industry to the area.

Places to Stay

Camping The *Club Atlético Anglo* (☎ 2787) maintains a campground, with hot showers and beach access, ten blocks south from Plaza Constitución. Eight km

south of town, the sprawling municipal *Balneario Las Cañas* (☎ 1611), charges US$3 per person and US$2 per tent, plus US$3 per vehicle.

Hotels & Motels For accommodations in private houses, ask at the tourist office.

Nuevo Hotel Colonial (☎ 2260), 25 de Mayo 3293 near Zorrilla, is very clean and friendly, with rooms arranged around an interior patio. Rates are US$18 double with shared bath, US$22 with private bath. *Hotel 25 de Mayo* (☎ 2586), at the corner of 25 de Mayo and Lavalleja, is a modernized 19th-century building offering singles/

doubles with shared bath for US$12/18, with private bath for US$15/20.

Hotel Plaza (☎ 2363), at the corner of 18 de Julio and 25 de Mayo, charges US$22/38 for rooms with private bath. *Balneario Las Cañas* (☎ 1611), eight km south of town, has motel accommodations with private bath and half-board for US$30 per person. *Hotel Casino Fray Bentos* (☎ 2358), on the waterfront at Paraguay 3272 between 18 de Julio and Zorrilla, charges US$34 per person, with breakfast included.

Places to Eat
Food in Fray Bentos is nothing to write home about. *La Enramada*, on España between 25 de Mayo and 25 de Agosto, is basic but cheap and friendly. The best in town may be the *Club de Remeros*, where the yacht crowd hangs out, near Parque Roosevelt.

Getting There & Away
All the bus offices are close to Plaza Constitución. ETA, with offices at the Hotel Plaza, has three buses daily to Gualeguaychú (US$4), as does CUT, which also has four daily to Mercedes (US$1.50) and four to Montevideo (US$11, taking five hours).

Buses Chadre, on Plaza Constitución at 25 de Mayo 3220, has two buses daily in each direction between Bella Unión and Montevideo, stopping at Salto, Paysandú, Fray Bentos, Mercedes, Dolores, Nueva Palmira, Carmelo, and Colonia. Agencia Central (☎ 3470) and Sabelín (in the same offices) and Corporación also have buses going to Montevideo.

MERCEDES
Capital of the department of Soriano, only 30 km from Fray Bentos and 270 km from Montevideo, Mercedes is a livestock center and minor resort on the south bank of the Río Negro, a tributary of the Uruguay. Principal activities are boating, fishing, and swimming along its sandy beaches. It has more frequent connections to Montevideo and other points throughout the country than does Fray Bentos.

Orientation
Mercedes is laid out on a standard grid pattern, centered on Plaza Independencia. The main commercial streets are the parallel north-south Colón and Artigas, on each side of the plaza. To the north, both intersect the very pleasant, shady riverside, which is the town's main attraction.

Information
Tourist Office The municipal Oficina de Turismo (☎ 2733), Artigas 215, has friendly, enthusiastic staff and a good city map. It's open weekdays only, 7:30 am to 1:30 pm and 3:30 to 9:30 pm.

Money Cambio Fagalde, Giménez 709, or Cambio España, Colón 262, will change cash but not traveler's checks.

Post & Telecommunications The post office is at Rodó 650, at the corner of 18 de Julio. Antel is on 18 de Julio between Roosevelt and Castro y Careaga. Mercedes's area code is 532.

Medical Services Hospital Mercedes is at the corner of Sánchez and González.

Things to See & Do
The **Catedral de Nuestra Señora de las Mercedes,** south of Plaza Independencia, dates from 1788. The **Biblioteca Museo Eusebio Giménez,** on Giménez between Sarandí and 25 de Mayo, displays paintings by the local artist. Some distance west of town is the **Museo Paleontológico Alejandro Berro,** displaying a valuable collection of fossils. It's open daily except Mondays 7:30 am to 6:30 pm and is accessible by public transport. On Sunday mornings, east of downtown in Plaza Lavalleja, there is a flea market and crafts fair.

Places to Stay
Camping Only eight blocks from Plaza Independencia, Mercedes' spacious *Camping del Hum* occupies half the Isla del Puerto in the Río Negro, connected to the mainland by a bridge. One of the best campgrounds in the region, it offers excel-

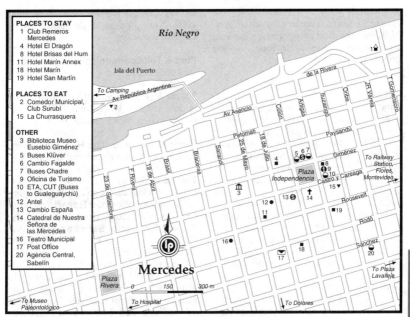

PLACES TO STAY
1 Club Remeros
Mercedes
4 Hotel El Dragón
8 Hotel Brisas del Hum
11 Hotel Marín Annex
18 Hotel Marín
19 Hotel San Martín

PLACES TO EAT
2 Comedor Municipal,
Club Surubí
15 La Churrasquera

OTHER
3 Biblioteca Museo
Eusebio Giménez
5 Buses Klüver
6 Cambio Fagalde
7 Buses Chadre
9 Oficina de Turismo
10 ETA, CUT (Buses
to Gualeguaychú)
12 Antel
13 Cambio España
14 Catedral de Nuestra
Señora de
las Mercedes
16 Teatro Municipal
17 Post Office
20 Agencia Central,
Sabelín

Río Negro

Mercedes

URUGUAY

lent swimming, fishing, and sanitary facilities. Fees are just US$0.75 per person plus US$1 per tent.

Hostel There is a youth hostel at the *Club Remeros Mercedes* (☎ 2534), De la Rivera 949 at Gomensoro.

Hotels The cheapest in town is *Hotel San Martín* (☎ 3212), Artigas 305, with singles for US$6 per person with shared bath, US$8 with private bath. Gloomy *Hotel El Dragón* (☎ 3204), Giménez 659, has singles with shared bath for US$7, with private bath for US$9. The quiet and friendly *Hotel Marín* (☎ 2987), at Rodó 668, has singles for US$9; its annex (☎ 2115) at Roosevelt 627, between 18 de Julio and 25 de Mayo, has more character but is slightly more expensive at US$10, plus US$2 for air-conditioning.

Despite a depressing exterior, *Hotel Brisas del Hum* (☎ 2740), at Artigas 201, is the closest to a luxury hotel in town. Rates are US$34 per person with breakfast.

Places to Eat

La Churrasquera, Castro y Careaga 790, is a moderately priced parrilla with large portions, offering discounts to ACA members. On the Isla del Puerto, near the campground, the *Comedor Municipal* and *Club Surubí* both have good inexpensive food, including river fish selections. The outdoor seating is less than luxurious but very pleasant.

Getting There & Away

Buses Klüver (☎ 22046), on Plaza Independencia at Giménez 701, has three buses daily to Palmar and three weekly to Durazno. For Buses Chadre (at Artigas 176), Mercedes is a stopover en route from Bella Unión to Montevideo (see the Fray Bentos listing for details). Agencia Central and Sabelín, both at Sánchez 782 (☎ 2982), connect Paysandú and Montevideo via Mercedes.

CUT and ETA, with services to Gualeguaychú, Argentina, share offices at Artigas 233. ETA also goes to interior destinations such as Trinidad, Durazno, Paso de los Toros, Tacuarembó, and Rivera. CUT, with the most modern buses, has four services daily to Montevideo, costing US$10 and taking 4½ hours.

PAYSANDÚ

Capital of its department and the second-largest city in Uruguay, Paysandú (population 100,000) traces its origins to the mid-18th century, when it was an outpost of cattle herders from the Jesuit mission at Yapeyú, Corrientes. The first saladero was established in 1840, but construction of its late-19th-century frigorífico was a turning point in its industrial history. Today, it is Uruguay's only significant industrial center outside Montevideo, processing beer, sugar, textiles, leather, and other products. For most independent travelers, it will be a stopover en route to or from Argentina.

Orientation

On the east bank of the Río Uruguay, Paysandú is 370 km from Montevideo via Ruta 3 and 110 km north of Fray Bentos via Ruta 24. The Puente Internacional General Artigas, 15 km north of town, connects it with the Argentine city of Colón, Entre Ríos province. The city is laid out on a slightly irregular grid pattern. The center of activity is Plaza Constitución, while 18 de Julio, the main commercial street, runs east-west along the south side of the plaza. Except for a small area around the port, directly west of downtown, the entire riverfront remains open parkland due to regular flooding, but it provides a welcome refuge from the oppressive summer heat.

Information

Tourist Office The municipal Oficina de Turismo (☎ 6677) is opposite Plaza Constitución at 18 de Julio 1226. It has one of the best city maps in Uruguay and a selection of useful brochures.

Foreign Consulates The Argentine Consulate (☎ 2253) is at Leandro Gómez 1034. Paraguay has a consulate at Cerrito 1295.

Money Cambio Fagalde is at 18 de Julio 1002. Next door at 18 de Julio 1008 is Cambio Bacacay.

Post & Telecommunications Paysandú's area code is 0722.

Travel Agencies Mundi Travel (☎ 4187) is downtown at 18 de Julio 1177. Elvitur (☎ 4449) is at Montecaseros 1024.

Medical Services The Hospital Escuela del Litoral (☎ 4836) is at Montecaseros 520.

Things to See

Downtown landmarks include the **Basílica de Nuestra Señora del Rosario** on Plaza Constitución, dating from 1860, and the **Teatro Florencio Sánchez** (1876) on Herrera between Av España and Leandro Gómez. Paysandú has several worthwhile museums, particularly the gauchesque **Museo de la Tradición** at the Balneario Municipal, north of town. Visit also the **Museo Salesiano** (Salesian Museum) at 18 de Julio and Montecaseros and the **Museo Histórico** at Zorrilla de San Martín and Sarandí.

Places to Stay

Camping Paysandú has two campgrounds: the *Balneario Municipal Parque Guyunusa,* two km north of downtown on the Río Uruguay, and one at the *Parque Sacra,* one km south of Plaza Constitución. Recent reports suggest that the former's basic facilities are ill-maintained; the latter has electricity. Neither has hot water, but both are free.

Hotels The cheapest lodging in town, and also the friendliest, is *Hotel Victoria* (☎ 4320), 18 de Julio 979. Rooms with shared bath cost US$7 per person, with private bath US$10. The talkative owner at *Hotel Concordia* (☎ 2417), which shares the same address, charges US$22 double. *Hotel Artigas* (☎ 4343), Baltasar Brum 943, is slightly dearer at US$10 per person for shared bath, US$12 for private bath.

Hotel Plaza (☎ 2022), Leandro Gómez

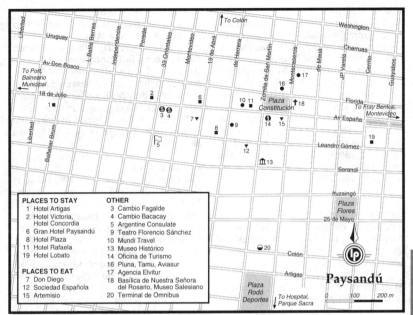

PLACES TO STAY
1 Hotel Artigas
2 Hotel Victoria,
   Hotel Concordia
6 Gran Hotel Paysandú
8 Hotel Plaza
11 Hotel Rafaela
19 Hotel Lobato

PLACES TO EAT
7 Don Diego
12 Sociedad Española
15 Artemisio

OTHER
3 Cambio Fagalde
4 Cambio Bacacay
5 Argentine Consulate
9 Teatro Florencio Sánchez
10 Mundi Travel
13 Museo Histórico
14 Oficina de Turismo
16 Pluna, Tamu, Aviasur
17 Agencia Elvitur
18 Basílica de Nuestra Señora
    del Rosario, Museo Salesiano
20 Terminal de Omnibus

Paysandú

URUGUAY

1121, charges US$34 double with private bath, while *Hotel Rafaela* (☎ 5053), 18 de Julio and Zorrilla de San Martín, costs US$35 double. At *Hotel Lobato* (☎ 2241), Leandro Gómez 1415, singles/doubles with private bath cost US$27/41. Acknowledged as the best in town is *Gran Hotel Paysandú* (☎ 3400), Herrera and 19 de Abril, for US$60 double.

Places to Eat
Don Diego, 19 de Abril 917, has reasonable parrillada, pizza, and minutas. Other good eating spots include the *Sociedad Española,* Leandro Gómez 1192, and the highly recommended *Artemisio,* at 18 de Julio 1248 near the tourist office.

Getting There & Away
Air Pluna (☎ 3071), Florida 1249, sells tickets for occasional Tamu flights to Montevideo (US$20). Aviasur, in the same office, flies twice weekly to Montevideo and three times to Salto.

Bus Paysandú's new Terminal de Omnibus is at Montecaseros and Artigas, directly south of Plaza Constitución. Buses Chadre passes through Paysandú en route from Bella Unión to Montevideo; for details, see the entry for Fray Bentos. Agencia Central goes to interior destinations. Copay, Núñez, and Sabelín also provide service to Montevideo for US$17, taking six hours.

AROUND PAYSANDÚ
Termas de Guaviyú
In a soothing yatay palm savannah 60 km north of Paysandú, this sprawling 109-hectare thermal baths complex (☎ 0722-6677) has eight pools, including four with spas, and a thousand campsites. Motel accommodations cost US$25 triple for category "A," which includes air-conditioning and kitchenettes, or US$15 for the more basic, but still comfortable category "B." Buses between Montevideo and Salto will drop passengers at the Termas, which are directly on Ruta 3 at Km 441.5.

SALTO

Directly across the Río Uruguay from Concordia, Entre Ríos, Salto is the most northerly crossing point into Argentina and site of the enormous Salto Grande hydroelectric project, 520 km from Montevideo via Ruta 3. The reservoir behind the dam is a very conventional recreational resource that attracts some visitors, while the surrounding area is known for its citrus production, mostly consisting of oranges. Horacio Quiroga, who's spent most of his life in Argentine Misiones, and novelist Enrique Amorim are major literary figures associated with Salto.

Orientation & Information

Salto has a very regular grid centered on Plaza Artigas; most points of interest are along Uruguay, the principal street, which runs west toward the port.

Tourist Office The municipal Oficina de Turismo (☎ 34096) is at Uruguay 1052.

Foreign Consulates Argentina's consulate (☎ 32931) is at Artigas 1162. Paraguay keeps a consulate (☎ 32105) at Misiones 77.

Money Cambio Salto Grande is at Joaquín Suárez 20.

Post & Telecommunications The post office is at Artigas and Treinta y Tres. Antel is at Grito de Asencio 55; Salto's area code is 073.

Medical Services The Hospital Regional Salto (☎ 32155) is at 18 de Julio and Varela.

Things to See & Do

Salto has a gaggle of worthwhile museums. Northeast of downtown at Enrique Amorim and Blandengues, the **Museo Histórico Municipal** contains the ashes of cremated writer Horacio Quiroga (see the San Ignacio section in the Mesopotamia chapter for more on Quiroga). The **Museo del Teatro Larrañaga** (☎ 32158), Joaquín Suárez 51, is part of Salto's prime performing arts venue. Other facilities include the **Museo de Bellas Artes y Artes Decorativas** (☎ 35289) at Uruguay 1067, the **Museo del Hombre y la Tecnología** (☎ 33923) at Brasil and Zorrilla (also site of the **Museo Arqueológico**), and the **Museo Escultórico Edmundo Pratti**, a three-dimensional arts museum at Artigas and 25 de Agosto.

To visit the Salto Grande hydroelectric project, make arrangements at the Oficina de Turismo.

Places to Stay

The *Club Remeros de Salto* (☎ 33418), at Rambla César Mayo Gutiérrez (Costanera Norte) and Belén, runs an official hostel. Otherwise, try the very modest *Pensión 33,* Treinta y Tres 269, or inexpensive accommodations like *Hotel Plaza* (☎ 33744) at Uruguay 465, or *Hotel Danaly* (☎ 34350), northeast of downtown at Agraciada 2060, all in the US$10 to US$12 range per person.

Midrange accommodations, including breakfast, cost about US$30/50 single/double at *Hotel Uruguay* (☎ 33051) at Brasil 891, *Hotel Eldorado* (☎ 35450) at Sarandí 20, and *Hotel Los Cedros* (☎ 33984) at Av Uruguay and Joaquín Suárez. Upscale *Gran Hotel Salto* (☎ 33250), 25 de Agosto 5, costs around US$76/88 single/double.

Places to Eat

The *Restaurant Cheff* (☎ 35328), Uruguay 639, is a good downtown choice, while the *Club de Remeros* (☎ 34607) on the Costanera Norte, which has many other restaurants, is also popular. There are many pizzerías, including *Firenze* at Uruguay 945 and *Las Mil y Una* at Uruguay 906.

Getting There & Away

Air Aviasur (☎ 32724), Uruguay 657, flies four or five times weekly to Montevideo, and twice weekly to Rivera. It is also the agent for Pluna and Tamu, though only the latter has flights from here to Montevideo.

Bus The Terminal Municipal de Omnibus

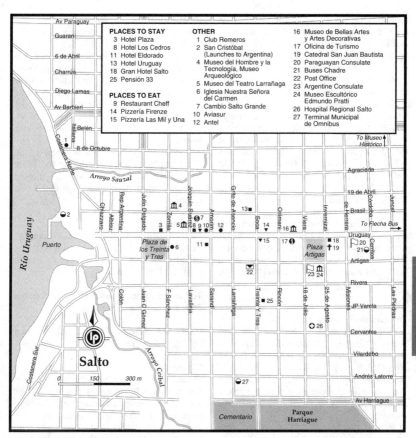

PLACES TO STAY
3 Hotel Plaza
8 Hotel Los Cedros
11 Hotel Eldorado
13 Hotel Uruguay
18 Gran Hotel Salto
25 Pensión 33

PLACES TO EAT
9 Restaurant Cheff
14 Pizzería Firenze
15 Pizzería Las Mil y Una

OTHER
1 Club Remeros
2 San Cristóbal
   (Launches to Argentina)
4 Museo del Hombre y la
   Tecnología, Museo
   Arqueológico
5 Museo del Teatro Larrañaga
6 Iglesia Nuestra Señora
   del Carmen
7 Cambio Salto Grande
10 Aviasur
12 Antel

16 Museo de Bellas Artes
   y Artes Decorativas
17 Oficina de Turismo
19 Catedral San Juan Bautista
20 Paraguayan Consulate
21 Buses Chadre
22 Post Office
23 Argentine Consulate
24 Museo Escultórico
   Edmundo Pratti
26 Hospital Regional Salto
27 Terminal Municipal
   de Omnibus

URUGUAY

is at Larrañaga and Andrés Latorre. Chadre (☎ 32603), Cerrito 66, goes to Concordia daily except Sunday at 8 am and 2 pm, while Flecha Bus (☎ 32150) at Uruguay and Beltrán, six blocks east of Plaza Artigas, goes at 2 and 8:30 pm daily except Sunday. Chadre also has international service to Uruguaiana, Brazil, across the border from Paso de los Libres in Argentina's Corrientes province.

Domestic bus lines to Montevideo include Chadre/Agencia Central, Núñez (☎ 35581) at Brasil and Suárez, and El Norteño (☎ 32150), Beltrán 19, which also goes to Bella Unión.

River From the port at the foot of Brasil, San Cristóbal launches cross the river to Concordia (US$3) five times daily during the week, four times daily weekends and holidays

AROUND SALTO
Termas de Daymán
Only eight km south of Salto, Termas de Daymán is the largest and most developed of several thermal baths complexes in northwestern Uruguay. Surrounded by a cluster of motels and cabañas, it's a popular destination for Uruguayan and Argentine

tourists, offering facilities for a variety of budgets. The Complejo Médico Hidrotermal Daymán (☎ 29090), open daily 9 am to 9:30 pm, provides medically oriented physical therapy, but there are regular facilities available as well. Bus No. 4 from downtown Salto goes directly to the baths.

Hostería Aguasol (☎ 33055) has low-season (December through mid-February) doubles for US$30, but the rest of the year it charges US$40. *La Posta del Daymán* (☎ 29701), at Km 487 on Ruta 3, charges US$24 per person with breakfast, US$32 with half-board, but also offers camping for US$4 per person, with fixed price lunches and dinners for US$9. *Hotel Amazonas* (☎ 35711) is more upscale.

The *Parador Municipal Termas de Daymán* (☎ 33992) has a varied international menu and reasonable prices. *Parrilla San Francisco* (☎ 29690) is also worth a visit, as is *Restaurante Eduardo* (☎ 29675), opposite Hotel Amazonas.

Termas de Arapey

About 45 km north of Salto on the Río Arapey Grande, Termas de Arapey is another popular hot springs resort. The *Hotel Municipal* (☎ 073-34096) charges US$45/50 single/double with breakfast, but there are also cheaper motel and bungalow accommodations, as well as inexpensive camping.

TACUAREMBÓ

Capital of its department, Tacuarembó has sycamore-lined streets and attractive plazas which make it one of the most agreeable towns in Uruguay's interior. Since its founding in 1832, authorities have kept sculptors busy on busts and monuments that pay tribute to the usual military heroes but also to writers, clergy, and educators. The local economy relies on livestock, both cattle and sheep, but local producers also grow rice, sunflowers, peanuts, linseed, tobacco, asparagus, and strawberries. Its late-March gaucho festival merits a detour if you're in the area.

Orientation

Located in rolling hill country along the Cuchilla de Haedo, on the banks of the Río Tacuarembó Chico, Tacuarembó is 230 km east of Paysandú and 390 km north of Montevideo. It's a major highway junction for the Uruguayan interior, as Ruta 26 leads west to Argentina and east to Brazil and the Uruguayan coast, while Ruta 5 from Montevideo continues north to Rivera and Brazil.

The center of the town is Plaza 19 de Abril, but the streets 25 de Mayo and 18 de Julio both lead south past the almost equally important Plaza Colón and Plaza Rivera.

Information

Tourist Office The municipal Oficina de Turismo (☎ 4671) is at 18 de Julio 164. The friendly and helpful staff can offer a simple map and limited brochures.

Telecommunications Antel is at Sarandí 242. Tacuarembó's area code is 0632.

Medical Services The Hospital Regional (☎ 2955) is at Treinta y Tres and Catalogne.

Museums

Tacuarembó's **Museo del Indio y del Gaucho Washington Escobar,** at Flores and Artigas, pays romantic tribute to Uruguay's nearly forgotten Indians and gauchos, and their role in the country's rural history. The **Museo de Geociencias** is an earth sciences facility at Suárez and 18 de Julio.

Special Events

In late March, the three-day **Fiesta de la Patria Gaucha** attracts visitors from around the country to exhibitions of traditional gaucho skills, music, and other activities. It takes place in Parque 25 de Agosto, at the north end of town.

Places to Stay

Camping The densely forested *Balneario Municipal Iporá* (☎ 4761), alongside a reservoir seven km north of town, has both

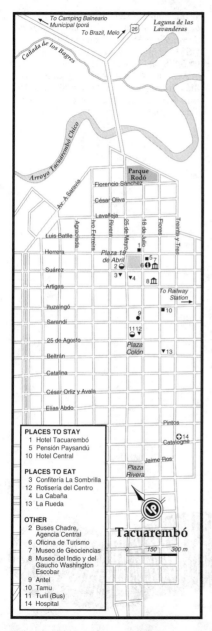

PLACES TO STAY
1 Hotel Tacuarembó
5 Pensión Paysandú
10 Hotel Central

PLACES TO EAT
3 Confitería La Sombrilla
12 Rotisería del Centro
4 La Cabaña
13 La Rueda

OTHER
2 Buses Chadre,
   Agencia Central
6 Oficina de Turismo
7 Museo de Geociencias
8 Museo del Indio y del
   Gaucho Washington
   Escobar
9 Antel
10 Tamu
11 Turil (Bus)
14 Hospital

Tacuarembó

0   150   300 m

free and paying sites. The free sites have clean toilets but lack showers. For US$1.50 per person, campers gain access to showers.

Buses to the campground leave from near Plaza 19 de Abril.

Pensiones & Hotels The friendly *Pensión Paysandú* (☎ 2453), 18 de Julio 154 opposite Plaza 19 de Abril, offers good, clean, but basic accommodations for US$8 single in a shared room, US$10/14 single/double for a private room with shared bath. *Hotel Central* (☎ 2341), Flores 300, charges US$13 per person with private bath. *Hotel Tacuarembó* (☎ 2104/5), 18 de Julio 133, is more comfortable but more impersonal, with singles/doubles for US$27/50 with private bath.

Places to Eat

Hotel Tacuarembó has a good restaurant serving parrillada, the regional standard, and other dishes; two other parrillas are *La Rueda,* Beltrán and Flores, and *La Cabaña,* 25 de Mayo 217. A reasonable confitería is *La Sombrilla,* 25 de Mayo and Suárez. *Rotisería del Centro,* on 18 de Julio near Plaza Colón, sells an enormous, tasty chivito that is a meal in itself.

Getting There & Away

Air Tamu (☎ 2341), Flores 300, flies twice weekly from Montevideo via Artigas to Tacuarembó, then returns directly from Tacuarembó to Montevideo (US$20).

Bus To Montevideo (US$14, taking 5½ hours), try Buses Chadre/Agencia Central (☎ 3455), 25 de Mayo 169, or Turil (☎ 3305), opposite Plaza Colón at 25 de Mayo and 25 de Agosto. Chadre/Agencia Central also serves interior destinations and connects Tacuarembó with the littoral cities of Salto and Paysandú.

AROUND TACUAREMBÓ

Valle Edén

Valle Edén, 30 km west of Tacuarembó on Ruta 26 to Paysandú, is a scenic area featuring a unique hanging bridge over the Arroyo Jabonería and the unusual Cerro

URUGUAY

Cementerio, a granite outcrop on the sides of which locals have entombed their dead.

RIVERA
Across the border from Livramento, Brazil, Rivera is 114 km north of Tacuarembó via Ruta 5. The free *Camping Municipal* (☎ 0622-3803), on Agraciada near Presidente Viera, has hot showers, and there's also a youth hostel, *Albergue Frontera de la Paz* (☎ 6660), at Uruguay 735. *Hotel Sarandí* (☎ 3521), Sarandí 770, charges US$15 single. Brazil has a consulate (☎ 3278) at Ceballos 1159.

Aviasur (☎ 0622-3404), Paysandú 1079, flies Mondays and Fridays to Montevideo. Bus services are an extension of those to Tacuarembó.

The Uruguayan Riviera

East of Montevideo, innumerable beach resorts dot the scenic Uruguayan coast, where sandy river beaches, vast dunes, and dramatic ocean headlands extend all the way to the Brazilian border. The area attracts hordes of tourists during the summer, but relatively few after wealthy Brazilians and Argentines end their holidays in early March. Its showplace is exclusive Punta del Este, where Argentina maintains a summer consulate and the Buenos Aires daily *La Nación* even opens a temporary bureau. Nearby Maldonado offers more reasonably priced accommodations and facilities, but other resorts slightly further out are just as attractive and even more affordable. After summer crowds depart in early March, prices fall, the weather is still ideal, and the pace is much more leisurely.

The modern department of Rocha, between Maldonado and the Brazilian border, was subject to a constant tug-of-war between Portugal and Spain in the colonial era, and between Brazil and Argentina up to the mid-19th century. This conflict left several valuable historical monuments, such as the fortresses of Santa Teresa and San Miguel, while discouraging rural settlement and sparing some of Uruguay's wildest countryside. No one will compare it to trackless Amazonia, but it does have nearly undeveloped areas like Cabo Polonio, with extensive dunes and a large colony of southern sea lions, and Parque Nacional Santa Teresa (more a cultural than a natural park, however). The interior has a varied landscape of palm savannas and marshes, rich in bird life.

Not often visited by foreigners, the interior departments of Treinta y Tres and Cerro Largo offer several alternatives for crossing into Brazil. The route north from the city of Treinta y Tres to Melo is one the most beautiful in Uruguay.

This chapter starts with resorts immediately east of Montevideo, following the Ruta Interbalnearia (coastal highway) east and then north toward the Brazilian border, describing interior destinations where appropriate. Technically, beaches west of Punta del Este are river beaches, but most visitors will note little difference between these and the ocean beaches to the east except for the river's gentle surf.

ATLÁNTIDA

In the department of Canelones, only 50 km from Montevideo, Atlántida is the first major resort along the Interbalnearia. The Oficina de Turismo (☎ 22736) is at the intersection of Calles 14 and 1. Atlántida's area code is 0372.

Camping El Ensueño (☎ 2371) is nine blocks from the Playa Brava, Atlántida's most popular beach. Fees are about US$6 for two persons and include 24-hour hot water and sanitary facilities. COT (☎ 3888), Calle 18 and Av Artigas, has regular buses to Montevideo and on down the coast.

Accommodations start at around US$20 per person, breakfast included, at *Hotel Playa Mansa* (☎ 4370), Calles 11 and 26, but most hotels are in the US$30 range. One of these is the *Hotel Rex* (☎ 2009), on the waterfront Rambla at the corner of Calle 1. Just west of town is the highly regarded *Hostería del Fortín de Santa Rosa*, a popular hideaway for well-heeled folks from Montevideo, where per-person rates start around US$50, US$75 with half-board, US$100 with full board.

PIRIÁPOLIS

The westernmost beach resort in the department of Maldonado, Piriápolis is less pretentious and more affordable than Punta del Este. It was founded about 100 km from Montevideo in 1893 but was developed as a tourist resort in the 1930s by Argentine entrepreneur Francisco Piria, who built the imposing landmark Hotel Argentino and an

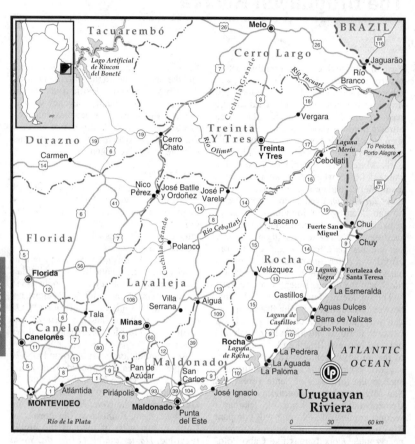

Tacuarembó

BRAZIL

Melo

Cerro Largo

Jaguarão

Lago Artificial
de Rincon
del Boneté

Río Tacuari

Río
Branco

Cuchilla Grande

Vergara

Durazno

Cerro
Chato

Treinta
Y Tres

Río Olimar

Treinta
Y Tres

Laguna
Merín

To Pelotas,
Porto Alegre

Carmen

Cebollati

Nico
Pérez

José Batlle
y Ordoñez

José P
Varela

Lascano

Fuerte San
Miguel

Chui

Florida

Río Cebollati

Polanco

Cuchilla Grande

Chuy

Rocha

Velázquez

Laguna
Negra

Fortaleza de
Santa Teresa

Lavalleja

Aiguá

Castillos

La Esmeralda

Villa
Serrana

Aguas Dulces

Barra de Valizas

Laguna de
Castillos

Cabo Polonio

Tala

Minas

Canelones

Canelones

Rocha

Laguna
de Rocha

La Pedrera

ATLANTIC
OCEAN

Pan de
Azúcar

San
Carlos

La Aguada

La Paloma

José Ignacio

Uruguayan
Riviera

Atlántida

Piriápolis

MONTEVIDEO

Maldonado

Punta
del Este

Río de la Plata

0   30   60 km

Florida

Maldonado

eccentric residence known as "Piria's Castle" (the latter now part of a city park). At one time Piria's ferries brought tourists directly from Argentina.

In the surrounding countryside are many interesting features, including Cerro Pan de Azúcar, one of Uruguay's highest points, and the hill resort of Minas.

Orientation

With a permanent population of only about 6000, Piriápolis is very compact. Almost everything is within reasonable walking distance in an area bounded by the water-front Rambla de los Argentinos to the south, Bulevar Artigas in the west, Calle Misiones in the north, and Av Piria on the east. Most residents give directions by noting a site's proximity to the Hotel Argentino.

Information

Tourist Office The private Asociación de Fomento y Turismo (☎ 22560) is at Rambla de los Argentinos 1348, near Hotel Argentino. It's open daily 9:30 am to 1 pm and 3:30 to 9 pm, and has maps, a few brochures, and a listing of current hotel prices.

Money Banco del Uruguay is at Tucumán and Sanabria. You can change cash, but not traveler's checks, at Hotel Argentino.

Post & Telecommunications The post office is on Rambla de los Argentinos, between Armenia and Manuel Freire. Antel is on Tucumán, behind the enormous skyscraper near the corner of Manuel Freire. Piriápolis's area code is 43.

Things to See & Do
The landmark **Hotel Argentino** is an attraction in itself. For a good view of Piriápolis, climb the **Cerro del Inglés** (also known as Cerro San Antonio) at the east end of town. For real lazybones, there is a chair lift to the top.

Swimming and sunbathing are the most popular activities, but there is good fishing off the rocks at the west end of the Playa de Piriápolis, where Rambla de los Argentinos becomes Rambla de los Ingleses.

Places to Stay
In Piriápolis and most of the Uruguayan Riviera, there are abundant accommodations, but prices and availability are highly seasonal. Many places open only between December and April, and nearly all raise prices dramatically between December 15 and March 1, after which prices drop, the weather is delightful, and crowds are gone. From April 1 to December 1, prices are extremely reasonable.

Places to Stay – bottom end
Camping Open from mid-December to late April, *Camping Piriápolis FC* (☎ 23275) is at Misiones and Niza, 350 meters behind Hotel Argentino. It has every necessary facility, including electricity and hot showers, for US$7 for two persons, while there are a few rooms with shared bath available for US$7 per person. Ten km west of town on Ruta 10, *Camping Las Flores* (☎ 3546) charges US$6 for two people, US$8 for three.

Hostels Piriápolis has two spacious hostels close behind Hotel Argentino: *Albergue Piriápolis 1* (☎ 20394) at Simón del Pino 1106, and *Albergue Antón Grassi* (☎ 22157) at Simón del Pino 1136. Both charge around US$7 per person with hostel card and are open all year, but reservations are essential in January and February.

Pensiones & Hotels Nearly all accommodations include breakfast. The cheapest in town are *Residencial Uruguay* (☎ 22424) at Uruguay 1026, and *Hotel El Paso* (☎ 22632) at Piria and Chacabuco, where singles off-season cost US$15, rising to US$22 in summer. The highly recommended *Petite Pensión* (☎ 22471) is a tiny (seven-room) but clean and friendly family-run hotel at Sanabria 1084 near Ayacucho, two blocks from the beach. Rates are US$18 off-season, US$22 per person in summer.

Places to Stay – middle
There is an abundance of midrange accommodations, such as *Hotel Danae* (☎ 22594) at the Rambla de los Argentinos and Freire, for US$18 off-season or US$25 in summer; *Hotel San Sebastián* (☎ 22546), Sanabria 942, for US$18 off-season, US$27 in summer; and *Hotel Sierra Mar* (☎ 22613), Sanabria 1051, which charges US$18 per person off-season, US$28 in summer. Off-season rates are comparable at *Hotel Centro* (☎ 22516), Sanabria 931, but summer rates are US$38 per person. Try also *Hotel Alcázar* (☎ 22507), Piria and Tucumán, where singles are US$18 off-season, US$36 in summer.

Places to Stay – top end
Quieter but less central than most midrange hotels, the highly recommended *Hotel Colonial* (☎ 23366), at Piria 790 near the verdant Cerro del Inglés, costs US$50 with half-board.

Even if you don't stay at *Hotel Argentino* (☎ 22791), you should visit this elegant, 350-room European-style spa on the Rambla de los Argentinos, with thermal baths, a casino, a classic dining room, and other luxuries. Rates are US$86 per person with half-board, US$107 with full board.

Places to Eat

La Langosta (☎ 23382), Rambla de los Argentinos 1212, has fine seafood and parrillada at moderate prices. Other appealing restaurants along the rambla include *Viejo Martín* (☎ 22501), at the corner of Trápani, and *Delta* (☎ 22364), at the corner of Atanasio Sierra.

Things to Buy

For artisanal items, visit the Paseo de la Pasiva, an attractive colonnaded gallery along the Rambla de los Argentinos.

Getting There & Away

All the bus companies have offices along the Rambla de los Argentinos. In high season, COT (☎ 22259) runs up to 27 buses daily to and from Punta del Este. Díaz has 14 buses daily to Pan de Azúcar and Minas. The fare to Montevideo is about US$2.50.

AROUND PIRIÁPOLIS
Pan de Azúcar

West of the highway between Piriápolis and the town of Pan de Azúcar, ten km to the north, an obvious hiking trail reaches the 493-meter summit of **Cerro Pan de Azúcar,** the third-highest point in the country. At the nearby Parque Municipal is a small but well-kept **Reserva de Fauna Autóctona** of native species like the capybara, grey fox, and ñandú. On the opposite side of the highway is the **Castillo de Piria,** Francisco Piria's opulent, outlandish residence.

MINAS

In the Cuchilla Grande of the department of Lavalleja, 120 km northeast of Montevideo and 60 km north of Piriápolis, Minas is an agreeable hill town offering a change of pace from the unrelentingly flat Pampas. It draws its name from the nearby quarries of building materials, but its most popular attraction is **Parque Salus** ten km west of town, source of Uruguay's best known mineral water and site of a brewery. Every April 19, up to 70,000 pilgrims visit the **Cerro y Virgen del Verdún,** 6 km west of town.

The municipal Oficina de Turismo (☎ 4118) is at Lavalleja 572, but visit also the **Casa de la Cultura** at Lavalleja and Rodó. Minas's area code is 0442.

Places to Stay

Camping is possible at woodsy *Parque Arequita,* nine km north of Minas on the road to Polanco (public transport is available from Minas). Sector "A" is more basic, with cold showers only, but is ridiculously cheap at US$.75 per person per day. Sector "B," which has swimming pools and hot showers, costs US$1.50 per person per day. A limited number of two-bed cabañas, with shared bath, are available for US$5 per night; others with private bath cost US$17.

Minas's *Hotel Verdún* (☎ 2110), 25 de Mayo 444, charges US$23 per person, but also has hostel accommodations for US$8; for inexpensive lodging, try also *Residencial Minas,* 25 de Mayo 502. At Parque Salus, accommodations are available at *El Parador Salus.*

Getting There & Away

Most bus companies are near the plaza. Olivera Hermanos (☎ 4111) goes twice daily to Maldonado (US$3), a trip that Coom does eight times daily. Cota (☎ 2256) links Montevideo with Minas, Treinta y Tres, and Melo. Emdal (☎ 2405), Núñez, and Corporación also go to Montevideo (US$5, two hours).

AROUND MINAS

In **Villa Serrana,** 23 km northeast of Minas, there are hostel accommodations at *Chalet Las Chafas,* with kitchen facilities, a swimming pool, and a lake. Buses from Minas pass no closer than three km from the hostel, so you'll need to walk or hitch; make reservations, which are essential, through the Asociación de Albergistas in Montevideo. Weekends and holidays can be uncomfortably crowded.

More upscale is *Mesón de las Cañas* (☎ 1611), which charges US$24 per person with full board.

MALDONADO
Capital of its namesake department, Maldonado is a popular beach resort that has retained a certain colonial atmosphere despite having sprawled because of its proximity to fashionable Punta del Este. It remains a more economical alternative to Punta del Este, which is easily accessible by public transport.

Maldonado dates from 1755, when Governor JJ de Viana of Montevideo sent the first settlers to establish an outpost to provision ships at the mouth of the Río de la Plata. British forces occupied the town during the siege of Buenos Aires in 1806, and in 1832 Darwin used it as a base during ten weeks spent collecting natural history specimens.

Because Maldonado and Punta del Este have grown together, only convenience separates them in this book, and readers will find themselves referring back and forth between the two entries.

Orientation
Maldonado is 130 km east of Montevideo and only 30 km from Piriápolis. Its center is Plaza San Fernando, and most points of interest (except the beaches) are within a few blocks of it. The original city plan is a standard rectangular grid, but between Maldonado and Punta del Este it becomes highly irregular. To the west, along the Río de la Plata, the Rambla Claudio Williman is the main thoroughfare, while to the east Rambla Lorenzo Batlle Pacheco follows the Atlantic coast. Locations along these routes are usually identified by numbered *paradas* (bus stops). There are many attractive beaches along both routes, but the ocean beaches have rougher surf. For more beach information, see the entry for Punta del Este below.

Information
Tourist Office Open weekdays 12:30 to 6:30 pm, the Dirección de Turismo (☎ 21920) is in the Intendencia Municipal, on Sarandí between Juan A Ledesma and Enrique Burnett; the branch at the bus terminal no longer exists. Papelería Sienra,

Sarandí 812, sells an excellent, up-to-date street map of Maldonado and Punta del Este for US$6. If you plan to stay more than a few days, it's a very worthwhile purchase.

Money Maldonado has several exchanges houses, including Cambio Maldonado at Dodero and Florida, Cambio Bacacay on Florida near 18 de Julio, Cambio Dominus at 25 de Mayo and 18 de Julio, and Cambio Porto at Florida 764, in the same building as Hotel Le Petit.

Post & Telecommunications The post office is at Ituzaingó and San Carlos. Antel is at the corner of Av Artigas and Florida; Maldonado's area code is 042.

Laundry Espumas del Virrey (☎ 20582) is at Sarandí 679. Lavadero Bahía is across the street, slightly to the south.

Medical Services Hospital Maldonado (☎ 25889) is on Calle Ventura Alegre, about eight blocks west of Plaza San Fernando.

Things to See & Do
On Plaza San Fernando is the **Catedral de Maldonado,** completed in 1895 after nearly a century of construction. At Gorriti and Pérez del Puerto, the **Plaza de la Torre del Vigía** features a colonial watchtower built with peepholes for viewing the approach of hostile forces or other suspicious movements.

Another colonial relic is the **Cuartel de Dragones y de Blandengues,** a block of military fortifications with stone walls and iron gates, built between 1771 and 1797, located along 18 de Julio and Pérez del Puerto. Its **Museo Didáctico Artiguista** (☎ 25378), in honor of Uruguay's hero of independence, is open daily 8 to 11 pm.

The **Museo San Fernando de Maldonado** (☎ 25929) is a fine arts museum at the corner of Sarandí and Pérez del Puerto, open Monday to Saturday 12:30 to 8 pm, Sunday 4:30 to 8 pm. Although currently undergoing restoration as a cultural center, it is still open to the public.

URUGUAY

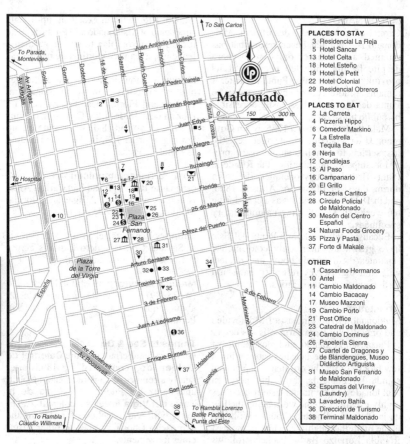

To San Carlos

Maldonado

0   150   300 m

PLACES TO STAY
3 Residencial La Reja
5 Hotel Sancar
13 Hotel Celta
18 Hotel Esteño
19 Hotel Le Petit
22 Hotel Colonial
29 Residencial Obreros

PLACES TO EAT
2 La Carreta
4 Pizzería Hippo
6 Comedor Markino
7 La Estrella
8 Tequila Bar
9 Nerja
12 Candilejas
15 Al Paso
16 Campanario
20 El Grillo
25 Pizzería Carlitos
28 Círculo Policial
de Maldonado
30 Mesón del Centro
Español
34 Natural Foods Grocery
35 Pizza y Pasta
37 Forte di Makale

OTHER
1 Cassarino Hermanos
10 Antel
11 Cambio Maldonado
14 Cambio Bacacay
17 Museo Mazzoni
19 Cambio Porto
21 Post Office
23 Catedral de Maldonado
24 Cambio Dominus
26 Papelería Sienra
27 Cuartel de Dragones y
de Blandengues, Museo
Didáctico Artiguista
31 Museo San Fernando
de Maldonado
32 Espumas del Virrey
(Laundry)
33 Lavadero Bahía
36 Dirección de Turismo
38 Terminal Maldonado

Maldonado's most unusual sight is the eclectic, eccentric Mazzoni house, dating from 1782. With all the family's furniture and belongings, and a particularly weird natural history room, the **Museo Mazzoni** defies description – see the sculpted rockhopper penguin on the patio fountain. At Ituzaingó 789, the Museo (☎ 21107) is open Tuesday to Friday, 4 to 10 pm. Admission is free.

Activities

Sport fishing for corvina, conger eel, bonito, shark, and other species is a popular pastime along the coast, at sea, and on Isla

Gorriti and Isla de Lobos. The tourist office publishes a brochure with a map of recommended fishing spots. Cassarino Hermanos (☎ 23735), Sarandí 1253, will arrange boat trips.

Other water sports include surfing, windsurfing, and diving. Another tourist office brochure recommends sites for each of these activities.

Places to Stay

Accommodations in the Maldonado/Punta del Este area are abundant but generally costly. Prices decline considerably after the summer high season, but can vary even within it – the first three weeks of January tend to be very expensive, but prices begin dropping after mid-February. Much depends on economic conditions in Argentina – if Argentina's economy and currency are weak, prices will drop in Uruguay. Unless otherwise indicated, prices below are high-season and can be volatile. For Punta del Este proper, see the separate entry below.

Camping *Camping San Rafael* (☎ 86715), on the outskirts of Maldonado beyond Aeropuerto El Jagüel, has well-kept facilities on woodsy grounds, complete with store, restaurant, automatic laundry, 24-hour hot water, and other amenities. It's organized almost to the point of regimentation, but at least you can expect quiet after midnight. Sites cost US$11 for two in January and February, US$10 the rest of the year. It accepts Uruguayan pesos, US dollars, and almost all credit cards. Bus No 5 from downtown Maldonado drops you at the entrance.

Hostel The best bargain is the recently opened *Albergue Puebla Nueva* (☎ 71427), across from the Club de Pesca in Manantiales east of Maldonado, which charges US$8. Accessed by Codesa bus, it's open November through March.

Residenciales & Hotels At *Residencial La Reja* (☎ 23712), 18 de Julio 1092 at José Pedro Varela, singles/doubles with shared bath cost US$18/20, and with private bath US$25/28. Try also *Residencial Obreros* at 19 de Abril and Pérez del Puerto.

Irish-owned *Hotel Celta* (☎ 30139), Ituzaingó 839, is a popular choice for foreign travelers. Standard rates are US$20 per person, but cheaper budget rooms are available, especially outside peak season. Rates are similar or a little higher at *Hotel Sancar* (☎ 23563), Juan Edye 597.

Hotel Esteño (☎ 25222), Sarandí 881, charges US$26 per person in peak season. *Hotel Colonial* (☎ 23346), on 18 de Julio near the cathedral, charges US$56 double,

but is no longer the value it once was. *Hotel Le Petit* (☎ 23044), at Florida and Sarandí opposite Plaza San Fernando, charges US$40 per person in peak season, less than half that off-season.

Places to Eat
Maldonado restaurants are often a better value than their pricier and more prestigious counterparts in Punta del Este. The modest *Tequila Bar,* Ituzaingó and Román Guerra, offers good value for the money. Other inexpensive choices include *Comedor Markino* at Dodera and Ituzaingó, and the *Círculo Policial de Maldonado* at Pérez del Puerto 780. *Pizzería Carlitos,* Sarandí 834, is an inexpensive but ordinary pizzería on Plaza San Fernando; alternatives include *Campanario,* at the corner of Florida and 18 de Julio, and *Pizzería Hippo,* at the corner of Sarandí and Juan Edye. For more elaborate Italian meals with better atmosphere, try *Pizza y Pasta* on the grounds of the Circolo Italiano at Sarandí 642.

Economical *La Estrella,* on 18 de Julio between Ventura Alegre and Ituzaingó, has a standard Uruguayan menu specializing in chicken and is a good choice for takeout meals. *El Grillo,* at the corner of Ituzaingó and Sarandí, prepares typical Uruguayan fare like chivitos. *Al Paso* (☎ 22881), a favorite parrilla at 18 de Julio 888, is more expensive but a good value. *La Carreta,* at the corner of 18 de Julio and José Pedro Varela, and *Candilejas,* on Dodera between Ituzaingó and Florida, are comparable.

More upmarket is *Mesón del Centro Español* at 18 de Julio 708, with excellent but costly Spanish seafood. Locals also recommend the seafood at *Nerja,* in the 800 block of Ituzaingó. Another highly regarded place is the Maldonado branch of Montevideo's *Forte di Makale,* on Sarandí near Enrique Burnett.

There's a natural foods grocery at San Carlos and Treinta y Tres.

Getting There & Away
Air Most air traffic to Maldonado/Punta del Este takes place in summer, when there are flights from Argentina, Brazil, and

Paraguay. For details, see the entry for Punta del Este.

Aeropuerto Carlos Carbelo (☎ 78782), at Laguna del Sauce west of Maldonado, cannot handle aircraft larger than 737s at present, but there are plans to expand it to international standards. (Aeropuerto Carlos Carbelo is also known as Aeropuerto Laguna del Sauce.) Aeropuerto El Jagüel (☎ 84378) is mainly used by small private craft, but some commercial flights land there.

Bus The Terminal Maldonado (☎ 25701) is at Av Roosevelt and Sarandí, eight blocks south of Plaza San Fernando. COT (☎ 25026) goes to Piriápolis, Montevideo, and Colonia, while Copsa (☎ 34733) goes 20 times daily to Montevideo. TTL (☎ 69224) serves Montevideo, Porto Alegre, and São Paulo from San Carlos. Expreso del Este (☎ 20040) goes to Rocha and Treinta y Tres, along with Tur-Este (☎ 37323).

Transporte Núñez (☎ 30170) has two buses daily to Montevideo. Olivera Hermanos (☎ 28330) goes twice daily to Minas (US$3).

Getting Around

Codesa (☎ 23481), on Av Velásquez, runs local buses to Punta del Este, La Barra, Manantiales, and San Carlos. Olivera (☎ 24039) connects Maldonado and Punta del Este (US$0.50) with San Rafael, Punta Ballena, Portezuelo, and Aeropuerto Carlos Carbelo in Laguna del Sauce.

AROUND MALDONADO
Casa Pueblo

At Punta Ballena, a scenic headland 10 km west of Maldonado, Uruguayan artist Carlos Páez Vilaró built this unconventional, sprawling, multilevel Mediterranean hillside villa and art gallery using no right angles. For an admission charge of US$3, visitors can tour the gallery, view a slide presentation on the building's creation, and dine or drink at the bar-cafeteria. Parts of Casa Pueblo (☎ 78041) are open to member-patrons only, but you can sneak a

view from the outside. Regular hours are 10 am to 6 pm daily.

José Ignacio

This once tranquil fishing village, 30 km east of Maldonado, has become the latest "in" spot among upscale beach towns on the Uruguayan Riviera. There are two to three buses daily from Maldonado.

PUNTA DEL ESTE

Where an early Jesuit visitor once remarked that "you see nothing here but a few cabins, the abodes of misery," one of South America's most glamorous summer resorts typically swarms with upper-class Argentines who disdain Mar del Plata since the latter lost its exclusivity. Strictly speaking, Punta del Este is part of Maldonado, but economically and socially, its elegant seaside homes, yacht harbor, and expensive hotels and restaurants make it a world apart.

Punta's main street, Av Gorlero, is a clutter of neon and plastic signs so dense it's hard to make sense of them – Uruguay's counterpart of the Las Vegas strip. After a bad summer in 1995, much of the property bought on speculation in previous years went up for grabs at bargain prices. Rates were negotiable, but even then some Argentines who stayed at comfortable hotels in previous years stayed at campgrounds instead. Budget travelers are still likelier to visit than to lodge here, but there is a small selection of reasonable accommodations.

Orientation

Geographically, the tiny peninsula of Punta del Este is south of Maldonado proper, but is easily accessible by public transport. The Rambla General Artigas circles the peninsula, passing the protected beach of the Playa Mansa and the yacht harbor on the west side, the exclusive residential zone at its southern tip, and the rugged Playa Brava, open to the South Atlantic, in the east.

Punta del Este has two separate grid systems, dictated by a constricted neck just

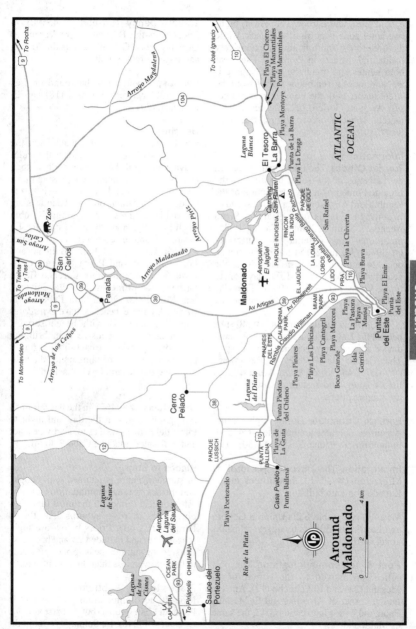

Around Maldonado

0   2   4 km

URUGUAY

east of the yacht harbor. The newer, high-rise hotel zone is north of this neck, while the area to the south is almost exclusively residential. Streets in Punta del Este bear both names and numbers; when appropriate, addresses given below refer first to the street name, with the number in parentheses. Av Juan Gorlero (22), the main commercial street, is universally referred to as just "Gorlero."

Information

Tourist Offices The municipal Dirección de Turismo, in the same building as the Liga de Fomento, at the intersection of the Rambla and Angostura near the west end of Inzaurraga (31), is open 9 am to 9 pm weekdays, 9 am to 3 pm weekends. It also maintains an Oficina de Informes (☎ 89467/73, Int 24) at the bus terminal, open 24 hours in summer. The rest of the year it's open Monday and Tuesday 8 am to 6 pm, Wednesday 8 am to 9 pm, Thursday and Friday 8 am to 8 pm, and weekends 9 am to 9 pm.

The Ministerio de Turismo (☎ 40514), behind the Liga de Fomento, is open weekdays 8 am to 6 pm, weekends 8 am to 3 pm. The Centro de Hoteles y Restoranes (☎ 40512, 44093) on Plaza Artigas, has a list of hotels and restaurants, with up-to-the-minute prices.

Foreign Consulate During high season, Argentina operates a consulate (☎ 43530) in the Edificio Padua, Las Focas (30) 619.

Immigration The Dirección Nacional de Migración (☎ 40513) has offices in the Liga de Fomento building.

Money Try Cambio Bella Unión at Gorlero and Las Focas (30) or any of several banks along Gorlero.

Post & Telecommunications The post office has moved to the corner of El Mesana (24) and El Estrecho (17). Antel is on the corner of Arrecifes and El Mesana. Punta del Este's area code is 042, the same as Maldonado's.

Travel Agency Turisport (☎ 45500), at Local 9 in the Edificio Torre Verona at Gorlero and La Galerna (21), is the American Express representative.

Laundry Laverap can be found on Las Focas (30) between Baupres (18) and El Remanso (20).

Beaches

On the west side of Punta del Este, the Rambla Artigas snakes along the calm Playa Mansa on the Río de la Plata, then circles around the peninsula, passing Playa de Los Ingleses and Playa El Emir to the wilder Playa Brava on the Atlantic side. From Playa Mansa, west along Rambla Williman, the main beach areas are La Pastora, Marconi, Cantegril, Las Delicias, Pinares, La Gruta at Punta Ballena, and Portezuelo, beyond Punta Ballena. Eastward, along the Rambla Lorenzo Batlle Pacheco, the prime sites are La Chiverta, San Rafael, La Draga, and Punta de la Barra. All these beaches have *paradores* (small restaurants) with beach service, which is more expensive than bringing your own goodies. Beach-hopping is a popular activity, depending on local conditions and the general level of action.

Organized Tours

Green Tours (☎ 89467), in the bus terminal, runs guided tours in the day and night to Punta del Este, as well as to nearby beaches and outlying sights like Cabo Polonio.

Places to Stay

In summer, Punta is jammed with people, and prices for accommodations can be astronomical (although the most luxurious places are in ritzy suburbs like Barrio Parque del Golf). Prices below are high-season rates and include IVA and breakfast. Outside the summer peak, prices may drop to half or even less than those indicated.

Places to Stay – bottom end

Modest accommodations are scarce in Punta del Este proper, but do exist at *Hotel Ocean* (☎ 43248), La Salina (9) 636, in the

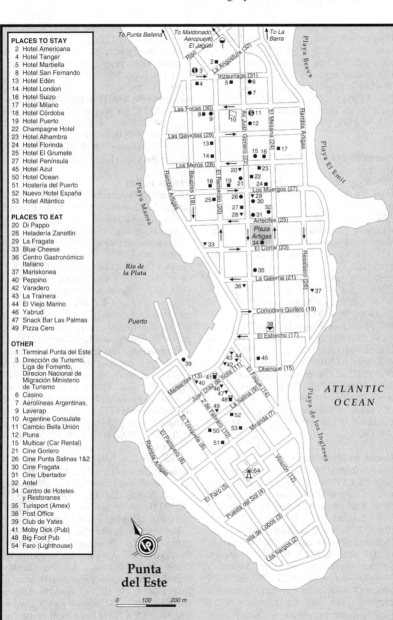

PLACES TO STAY
2 Hotel Americana
4 Hotel Tanger
5 Hotel Marbella
8 Hotel San Fernando
13 Hotel Edén
14 Hotel London
16 Hotel Suizo
17 Hotel Milano
18 Hotel Córdoba
19 Hotel Puerto
22 Champagne Hotel
23 Hotel Alhambra
24 Hotel Florida
25 Hotel El Grumete
27 Hotel Península
45 Hotel Azul
50 Hotel Ocean
51 Hostería del Puerto
52 Nuevo Hotel España
53 Hotel Atlántico

PLACES TO EAT
20 Di Pappo
28 Heladería Zanettin
29 La Fragata
33 Blue Cheese
36 Centro Gastronómico Italiano
37 Mariskonea
40 Peppino
42 Varadero
43 La Trainera
44 El Viejo Marino
46 Yabrud
47 Snack Bar Las Palmas
49 Pizza Cero

OTHER
1 Terminal Punta del Este
3 Dirección de Turismo, Liga de Fomento, Direcion Nacional de Migración Ministerio de Turismo
6 Casino
7 Aerolíneas Argentinas,
9 Laverap
10 Argentine Consulate
11 Cambio Bella Unión
12 Pluna
15 Multicar (Car Rental)
21 Cine Gorlero
26 Cine Punta Salinas 1&2
30 Cine Fragata
31 Cine Libertador
32 Antel
34 Centro de Hoteles y Restoranes
35 Turisport (Amex)
38 Post Office
39 Club de Yates
41 Moby Dick (Pub)
48 Big Foot Pub
54 Faro (Lighthouse)

URUGUAY

Punta del Este

0   100   200 m

quiet, residential part of town (it occasionally gets noisy at night, however). Doubles with shared bath cost US$30 without breakfast, but ring ahead for reservations. The next cheapest is *Hostería del Puerto* (☎ 45345), Capitán Miranda (7) and Calle 2 de Febrero (10), a pleasant, older-style hotel, with singles/doubles with private bath for US$25/35.

Places to Stay – middle

Midrange accommodations start around US$40 per person with breakfast at *Hotel Marbella* (☎ 41814), a good value on Inzaurraga between Gorlero and El Remanso (20); *Hotel Córdoba* (☎ 40008), at Los Muergos (27) 660; and recommended *Hotel Americana* (☎ 80794), at Angostura (32) 638, around the corner from the bus terminal.

Slightly more expensive at around US$45 per person are *Hotel Puerto* (☎ 40332) at Los Muergos 622; *Hotel El Grumete* (☎ 41009) at El Remanso (20) 797; *Hotel San Fernando* (☎ 40720) at Las Focas (30) 691 between Baupres (18) and El Remanso (20); *Hotel Edén* (☎ 40504) at El Remanso (20) 887; and *Hotel Península* (☎ 41533) at Gorlero 761. Several places charge about US$50 per person, including *Hotel Florinda* (☎ 40022) on Los Muergos (27) between Gorlero and El Mesana (24), and *Hotel Milano* (☎ 40039) at El Mesana (24) 880.

Places to Stay – top end

Hotel Atlántico (☎ 40229), across from the Hostería del Puerto in the residential part of town, charges US$60 per person, as do *Hotel Azul* (☎ 40106) at Gorlero 540 and *Hotel London* (☎ 41911) at El Remanso (20) 877. *Nuevo Hotel España* (☎ 40228), La Salina (9) 660, costs US$63 per person in high season, but half that off season. Comparably priced are *Hotel Alhambra* (☎ 40094) at Los Meros (28) 573 and *Hotel Tanger* (☎ 40601), Inzaurraga (31) between Baupres (18) and El Remanso (20). Slightly more expensive are *Hotel Suizo* (☎ 41517) at Los Meros (28) 590 for

US$70 and *Champagne Hotel* (☎ 45276), Gorlero 828, for US$75.

Real luxury accommodations are not in Punta del Este proper, but out on the Ramblas and into the suburbs. If you have money to burn, check out *La Posta del Cangrejo* (☎ 70021) in Barra del Maldonado (US$112 per person); *Hotel Solana del Mar* (☎ 78888), at Km 126.5 in Punta Ballena (US$84); or the truly extravagant *Hotel L'Auberge* (☎ 82601) in Barrio Parque del Golf (US$135).

Places to Eat

The narrow peninsula of Punta del Este is jammed with probably half the restaurants in Uruguay. Most tend to the expensive, but there are several reasonably priced pizzerías and cafés along Gorlero, such as *Di Pappo* (☎ 42869), Gorlero 841. Other choices for Italian food include *Pizza Cero* (☎ 45954) at La Salina (9) and 2 de Febrero (10), and *Peppino* at the corner of 2 de Febrero (10) and Rambla Artigas. There are several moderately priced restaurants at the *Centro Gastronómico Italiano* at the corner of Gorlero and La Galerna (21).

International restaurants are too numerous for an exhaustive list. Good seafood is available at *Mariskonea* (☎ 40408), Resalsero (26) 650. Other seafood options include *La Fragata* (☎ 40001), Gorlero 800 at Los Muergos (27); *Varadero,* on Rambla Artigas between El Foque (14) and Virazón (12); and *El Viejo Marino* (☎ 43565), at the corner of Solís (11) and El Foque (14). *Snack Bar Las Palmas,* on Virazón (12) between Solís (11) and La Salina (9), is a more economical alternative. Farther east, at La Barra, *La Posta del Cangrejo* (☎ 70021), in the hotel of the same name, has outstanding but costly seafood.

Between Punta and Maldonado, the very expensive *La Bourgogne* (☎ 82007), Pedragosa and Av Córdoba, imports its chefs from France. Another highly regarded but expensive French restaurant is *Blue Cheese* (☎ 40354), Rambla Artigas and El Corral (23). Montevideo's *Bungalow Suizo* (☎ 82358) has a local branch on the Rambla Batlle at Parada 8, near Av

Roosevelt. For variety, try the Basque *La Trainera* (☎ 45960) at Rambla Artigas and El Foque (14), or the Arab/Armenian *Yabrud* at the corner of Solís (11) and Virazón (12).

Heladería Zanettin, Gorlero and Arrecifes (25), has first-rate ice cream.

Entertainment

Punta del Este is lively at night. Many cinemas line Av Gorlero, and pubs are concentrated near the port. Cinemas include *Cine Fragata* (☎ 40002) at Gorlero 798, *Cine Gorlero* (☎ 44437) on Gorlero between Los Meros (28) and Los Muergos (27), *Cine Libertador* (☎ 44437) on Gorlero near Arrecifes (25), and the *Cine Punta Salinas 1&2* (☎ 46406/7) at the corner of Gorlero and Los Muergos (27).

Near the yacht harbor are two entertaining pubs: *Moby Dick* on Rambla Artigas between Virazón (12) and 2 de Febrero (10), and the colorful *Big Foot* at the corner of Virazón (12) and La Salina (9). There is a *casino* at Gorlero and Inzaurraga (31). Most discos are along the Rambla Batlle, east of Playa Brava.

Things to Buy

For souvenirs and handicrafts, visit the Feria de los Artesanos (once known as the "Feria de los Hippies") on Plaza Artigas. In high season, December to March, hours are from 6 pm to 1 am daily, while the rest of the year it's open from 11 pm to 5 weekends only – later if business is good. Much of the material is tacky, but there are a few worthwhile items.

Manos del Uruguay has a leather outlet at Gorlero and Las Gaviotas (29).

Getting There & Away

Air Pluna (☎ 40004), Gorlero 940, has numerous flights to Buenos Aires' Aeroparque. In summer, it has daily flights to Montevideo which, depending on the day, continue to Porto Alegre, São Paulo, and Rio de Janeiro in Brazil, Asunción (Paraguay), and Santiago (Chile).

Aerolíneas Argentinas (☎ 43801) is in the Edificio Santos Dumont on Gorlero between Inzaurraga (31) and Las Focas (30). It flies to Aeroparque Thursday, Friday, and twice Sunday.

Bus The Terminal Punta del Este (☎ 89467) is at Riso and Av Artigas. Bus services to Punta del Este are an extension of those to Maldonado; for details on bus services, see Getting There & Away under Maldonado. Transporte Núñez, Coom, and TTL have offices at the terminal; COT (☎ 86810) is the only one to have a separate phone line.

Buquebus (☎ 84995) is also in the terminal; see the chapter on Montevideo for more detailed information on their services.

Getting Around

To/From the Airport Maldonado and Punta del Este share two airports. Aerolíneas Argentinas and Pluna use Aeropuerto Laguna de Sauce (aka Aeropuerto Carlos Carbelo), west of Portezuelo, reached by Buses Olivera (☎ 24039) from Maldonado. Aeropuerto El Jagüel (☎ 84378), which has sporadic commercial flights, is at the west end of Av Aparicio Saravia, five km from downtown Maldonado, also served by Olivera.

Bus Maldonado Turismo (☎ 81725), Gorlero and Las Focas (30), connects Punta del Este with La Barra and Manantiales. Its buses leave from La Angostura behind the bus terminal.

Car Rental Budget (☎ 46363) has offices at Los Muergos (27) and Gorlero. Multicar (☎ 43143) is at Gorlero 860, while Uruguay Car (☎ 41036) is in the Galería Sagasti alongside the Casino on Gorlero.

AROUND PUNTA DEL ESTE
Isla Gorriti

Boats leave every half-hour or so from the yacht harbor for this nearby island, which has excellent sandy beaches and ruins of the **Baterías de Santa Ana,** an 18th-century fortress. It also has two restaurants, *Parador Puerto Jardín* and *Playa Onda*.

Isla de Lobos

About six miles offshore, the nature reserve of Isla de Lobos hosts a population of some 300,000 southern fur seals. During the invasion of 1806, British forces stranded numerous prisoners here without food or water, and many perished while swimming to Maldonado. To arrange trips to the reserve, contact the Unión de Lanchas (☎ 42594) in Punta del Este.

ROCHA

Founded in 1793 by Rafael Pérez del Puerto, picturesque Rocha is capital of the department and merits at least an afternoon for visitors staying on the beach at La Paloma. In the narrow alleyways off Plaza Independencia are a number of interesting houses from the late colonial and early independence eras.

Virtually everything of interest, including hotels and transport, is on or near Plaza Independencia. The municipal Oficina de Turismo (☎ 2995) is at General Artigas 176. Money exchange is available at Banco de la República or Banco Comercial. Rocha's area code is 472.

Places to Stay & Eat

Accommodations are very reasonable, perhaps enough so to justify staying here rather than in La Paloma. Try the tidy *Hotel Municipal Rocha* (☎ 2404), a block off the plaza on 19 de Abril between Ramírez and Presbítero Aquiles, which charges US$17/24 single/double. The modest *Hotel Centro* (☎ 2349), Ramírez 152, is slightly dearer. *Hotel Trocadero* (☎ 2267), at 25 de Agosto and 18 de Julio, charges US$25/36. *Confitería La Candela,* on the plaza, has tasty and visually appealing sweets and pastries.

Getting There & Away

Rocha is a hub for bus travel between Montevideo and the Brazilian border. Rutas del Sol runs eight buses daily to Montevideo and five daily to Chuy via La Paloma, La Pedrera, and Castillos, plus six daily to Barra de Valizas (US$3.50). Cynsa has ten daily to La Paloma and nine from La

Paloma back to Rocha, where you can catch the service to Chuy. COT also serves Rocha.

LA PALOMA

Some 28 km south of Rocha and 250 km from Montevideo, placid La Paloma (population 5000) is less developed, less expensive, and much less crowded than Punta del Este, but still has almost every important comfort and amenity except Punta's hyperactive nightlife. As elsewhere on the coast, there are attractive sandy beaches in town and beyond – those to the east are less protected from ocean swells.

Orientation

La Paloma occupies a small peninsula at the south end of Ruta 15. The center, on both sides of the Av Nicolás Solari, is small and compact. Although the streets are named, the buildings, including hotels and restaurants, lack numbers and are more easily located by their relationship to prominent intersections and other landmarks. At the eastern entrance to town, on the highway to Rocha, is the woodsy and spacious Parque Andresito, an appealing camping area with excellent facilities.

Information

Tourist Office The Oficina de Turismo (☎ 6107) is on the traffic circle at the east end of Av Nicolás Solari. In summer, it's open 8 am to 11 pm, but the rest of the year only 9 am to 9 pm.

Money You can change US dollars at Banco de la República, at Av Nicolás Solari and Titania.

Post & Telecommunications The post office is on Av Nicolás Solari, just east of the former Onda bus terminal. Antel is on Av Nicolás Solari between Av El Navío and De La Virgen. La Paloma's area code is 473.

El Faro del Cabo Santa María

In 1874, construction of the local lighthouse marked the beginning of La Palo-

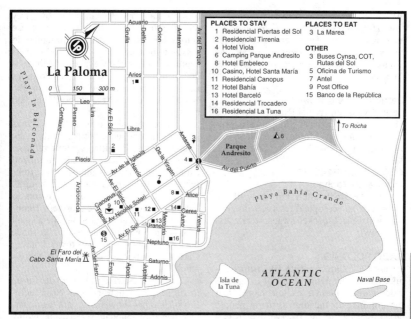

La Paloma

0   150   300 m

PLACES TO STAY	PLACES TO EAT
1 Residencial Puertas del Sol	3 La Marea
2 Residencial Tirrenia	
4 Hotel Viola	**OTHER**
6 Camping Parque Andresito	3 Buses Cynsa, COT,
8 Hotel Embeleco	Rutas del Sol
10 Casino, Hotel Santa María	5 Oficina de Turismo
11 Residencial Canopus	7 Antel
12 Hotel Bahía	9 Post Office
13 Hotel Barceló	15 Banco de la República
14 Residencial Trocadero	
16 Residencial La Tuna	

ma's growth as a summer beach resort. It's open to the public 7 to 8 pm in summer, 6 to 7 pm the rest of the year.

Places to Stay

Camping *Camping Parque Andresito* (☎ 6107), at the northern entrance to town, has such amenities as hot showers, a supermarket, a restaurant, and electricity for US$10 for two persons; there is excellent beach access. Inexpensive cabañas are also available.

Hostels For budget travelers, the most reasonable accommodations are at the *Albergue Altena 5000* (☎ 6396), in Parque Andresito. It's open November through March; make reservations in Montevideo through the Asociación de Alberguistas in Montevideo.

Residenciales & Hotels La Paloma used to have a wider selection of economical alternatives than either Punta del Este or Maldonado, but its growing popularity has caused prices to rise. For US$45 double, *Residencial Canopus* (☎ 6068) on Av Nicolás Solari near Sirio, is now one of the best values in town.

Most others are in the US$60 double range, including *Residencial Trocadero* (☎ 6007) on Juno near Ceres, *Residencial Puertas del Sol* (☎ 6066) on Delfín near Aries, *Residencial Tirrenia* (☎ 6230) on Av El Navío, *Residencial La Tuna* (☎ 6083) on Neptuno between Juno and Av El Navío, and *Hotel Viola* (☎ 6020) on Av Nicolás Solari near Antares.

Hotel Bahía (☎ 6029), at Av El Navío and Av El Sol, charges US$75 double. Somewhat more upscale accommodations are available at *Hotel Barceló* (☎ 6052), on Av El Sol at its intersection with Urano and Jupiter. *Hotel Embeleco* (☎ 6108), at Av El Sol and De La Virgen, has rooms for US$100 double with half-board.

Places to Eat

La Marea, on Av del Parque, has good, fresh, and reasonably priced seafood, but

URUGUAY

the waiters are overworked and service is slow. *Hotel Bahía* and *Hotel Embeleco* also have restaurants. There are several pizzerías, including *La Currica* on Av Nicolás Solari and *Ponte Vecchio* on Playa La Aguada.

Getting There & Away
Buses Cynsa, on Av del Parque next to La Marea, goes to Rocha (US$1) and also provides service to Montevideo (US$10), along with COT and Rutas del Sol.

AROUND LA PALOMA
Laguna de Rocha
Laguna de Rocha, ten km west of La Paloma, is an ecological reserve with populations of black-necked swans, storks, and waterfowl.

CABO POLONIO
East of La Paloma on Ruta 10, visitors can hike 10 km over dunes in one of Uruguay's wildest areas to visit a sea lion colony. Near the entrance to the dunes, many people advertise rides to the reserve, which is a hefty but feasible full day's walk. Dune walking is very tiring – be sure to take water.

AGUAS DULCES
This quaint fishing village, 11 km directly southeast of the town of Castillos, is the place for a *really* quiet seaside holiday. Its only accommodations are the modest *Hotel Gainfor* and an equally modest municipal campground. Sample the seafood at any of several restaurants, but do not leave without tasting the messy but flavorful fruit of the *butía* palm, for sale in almost every tiny shop.

At nearby Barra de Valizas, the youth hostel *Albergue Artigas* (no phone), for which you must make reservations with the Asociación de Alberguistas in Montevideo, has kitchen facilities and hot showers. Rutas del Sol buses from Montevideo stop nearby.

PARQUE NACIONAL SANTA TERESA
More a historical than a natural attraction, this coastal park 35 km south of Chuy incorporates the hilltop **Fortaleza de Santa Teresa,** begun by the Portuguese in 1762 but finished by the Spaniards after its capture by Governor Cevallos of Montevideo in 1793. Across Ruta 9, the enormous Laguna Negra and the marshes of the Bañado de Santa Teresa support abundant bird life.

By international standards, Santa Teresa is a very humble unit, but it attracts many Uruguayan and Brazilian visitors, offering uncrowded beaches and decentralized camping in forest plantations of trees spaced so randomly that they seem natural. But look closely: Eucalyptus is native to Australia and pine to the Northern Hemisphere only. Other features include a small zoo, an indoor plant nursery, and a shade nursery. The park gets very crowded during Carnaval, but most of the time there's ample space.

Camping fees are US$10 per site, for up to six people, which includes basic facilities such as hot showers. At park headquarters, there are abundant services, including phone and post offices, a supermarket, a bakery, a butchery, and a restaurant.

CHUY
Chuy is the grubby but energetic Uruguayan-Brazilian border town at the terminus of Ruta 9, 340 km from Montevideo. Pedestrians and vehicles cross freely between the Uruguayan and Brazilian sides, which are separated only by a median strip along the main avenue (on the Uruguayan side, it's Av Brasil; on the Brazilian side, it's Av Uruguay). There are several exchange houses along Av Brasil, although changing traveler's checks is problematic. Chuy's area code is 474.

Hotel Plaza (☎ 2309), at Av Artigas and Arachanes, has singles for US$22, but accommodations are usually cheaper at *Hotel Rivero* or *Hotel San Francisco* on the Brazilian side. Ten km south of Chuy, a side road on the coast leads to well-equipped *Camping Chuy* (☎ 2425), which charges US$10 per site, and *Camping de la*

Top Left: Ñandutí lace, Itauguá, Paraguay
Top Right: Canecutter, Piribebuy, Paraguay
Bottom Left: Jesuit ruins of Trinidad, Paraguay
Bottom Right: Parque Nacional Ybycuí, Paraguay

Top: Trinidad mission, Paraguay
Bottom: Steam train, Asunción to Areguá, Paraguay

Barra (☎ 1611), which costs US$4 per person, with all facilities. Local buses from Chuy go directly to both.

If proceeding beyond Chuy into Brazil, complete Uruguayan emigration formalities at the border post on Ruta 9, 1 km south of town. If you need a visa, Brazil has a consulate at Fernández 147. Change your Uruguayan money before entering Brazil, as Uruguayan currency is worthless any distance into Brazil.

Entering Uruguay, you will find an extremely helpful and well-informed tourist office which, with a little polite cajoling, will give you a computer printout of up-to-date hotel and restaurant information for the whole department. Several bus companies connect Chuy with Montevideo (costing US$12 and taking five hours) including Rutas del Sol, Cynsa, Cita, and COT, all on or very near Av Brasil. There is also bus service to Treinta y Tres. Brazilian buses have a central terminal three blocks north of the border.

Seven km west of Chuy, the restored **Fuerte San Miguel,** a pink-granite fortress built in 1734 during hostilities between Spain and Portugal, merits a visit. Its entrance, protected by a moat, overlooks the border from an isolated high point. It's closed Mondays, but you can still glimpse the interior and visit the nearby gaucho museum.

TREINTA Y TRES

Little-visited Treinta y Tres (population 30,000) is a gaucho town in the very scenic rolling hill country of the Cuchilla Grande on the Río Olimar, inland 150 km west from Chuy via Ruta 14, and 290 km northeast of Montevideo via Ruta 8. Founded in 1853 on the interior route to Brazil via

Melo or Río Branco, it is also the departmental capital. The route north to Melo is one of the most beautiful in Uruguay.

On the plaza at Lavalleja 564, simple but clean and friendly *Hotel Olimar* (☎ 0452-2115) has singles for US$12.50 with shared bath, US$16 with private bath; about the same price is *Hotel Treinta y Tres* (☎ 2325), Lavalleja 698. *Restaurant London,* also on the plaza at Lavalleja and Zufriátegui, has good, filling, and inexpensive meals.

Núñez, Expreso Minuano (☎ 5364) at Araujo 242, Cota (☎ 3617) at Manuel Freire 3617, and Rutas del Plata have eight buses daily to Melo and to Montevideo via Minas. Tur-Este (☎ 3516), Zufriátegui 209, goes daily to Maldonado and takes four hours.

MELO

Capital of the department of Cerro Largo, 110 km north of Treinta y Tres via Ruta 8, Melo is a transport hub for Uruguay's interior, with bus connections to Río Branco, Aceguá, and Rivera, all of which have border crossings to Brazil. There is a Brazilian consulate (☎ 2084) at Saravia 711. Founded in 1795, the town has a few late colonial buildings and a stone post building now housing the **Museo del Gaucho.**

Parque Rivera has a public *campground,* while the *Crown Hotel* (☎ 0462-2261), Ituzaingó 609, has rooms for US$20/26 single/double. For meals, try *La Rueda,* a parrilla at Saravia 541, or *Cerro Largo* (☎ 2197) at Saravia 636.

Tamu has inexpensive flights to and from Montevideo several times weekly. Cota (☎ 2253) at Colón 627, Núñez, and Turismar have buses to Montevideo and also provide local services.

Paraguay

Facts about Paraguay

Paraguay is South America's "empty quarter," little known even to its neighbors. For much of its history, sustained by geographical isolation, it has distanced itself from the Latin American mainstream, but economic developments since the 1970s and political developments since the late 1980s appear to have brought about irrevocable changes. Once South America's most notorious and durable police state, the country now welcomes foreign visitors and offers many worthwhile sights, including the riverside capital of Asunción and its scenic surroundings, the Jesuit missions of the upper Río Paraná, the massive Argentine/Paraguayan and Brazilian/Paraguayan hydroelectric projects at Itaipú and Yacyretá, and several national parks, although access is difficult to most of them. The Gran Chaco, west of the Río Paraguay, is a paradise for bird-watchers and other nature-oriented travelers.

HISTORY

Paraguay's pre-Columbian cultural patterns were more complex than either Argentina's or Uruguay's. At the time of first European contact, Guaraní-speaking people inhabited most of what is now eastern Paraguay, while west of the Río Paraguay a multitude of Indian groups, known collectively as "Guaycurú" to the Guaraní, inhabited overlapping territories in the Chaco. Among these groups were the Tobas, Matacos, Mbayás, Abipones, and many others, some of whom are now extinct.

The Guaraní were semisedentary cultivators, while groups of hunter-gatherers such as the Aché (Guayakí) lived in enclaves of dense tropical and subtropical forests near the borders of present-day Brazil. The Chaco Indians were mostly hunter-gatherers who also fished along the Río Pilcomayo and other permanent watercourses.

Although predominantly a peaceful people, the Guaraní did not always refrain from venturing into Guaycurú territory and battling with them. They even raided the foothills of the Andes, where they obtained gold and silver objects that later aroused the interest of the Spaniards. The Guaycurú, for their part, did not hesitate to fight back, and later Spanish-Guaraní expeditions into the Chaco were frequently violent. Well into this century, Indian hostility deterred settlement of many parts of the region.

European Exploration & Settlement

Europeans first entered the upper Paraná in 1524 when Alejo García, a survivor of Juan de Solís' ill-fated expedition to the Banda Oriental, walked across southern Brazil, Paraguay, and the Chaco to the foothills of Bolivia with Guaraní guides. Although he found silver in the Andes, García died on the return journey. His discoveries resulted in the renaming of the Río de Solís as the Río de la Plata (River of Silver).

Sebastián Cabot sailed up the Río Paraguay in 1527, but Pedro de Mendoza's expedition made the major advance; after failing to establish a permanent settlement at Buenos Aires, his men founded a fortress called Nuestra Señora de la Asunción on the east bank of the Río Paraguay. At Asunción, the Guaraní were far more tolerant of the Spanish presence and made a military alliance with them against the hostile Chaco peoples.

The Guaraní were more sedentary than the nomadic Chaco tribes, though not so settled as the civilizations of the Andean, so relations between the Indians and the Spaniards took an unusual course: the Guaraní absorbed the 350 Spaniards (and a few other Europeans) into their social system by providing them with women and, therefore, with food, since women bore the major responsibility for Guaraní agriculture. The Spaniards, in effect, became the heads of the household, and the *encomienda,* when it was introduced, merely ratified this informal arrangement. The Spaniards adopted Guaraní food, customs, and even language, but cultural assimilation was a two-way process. Gradually there emerged a hybrid, Spanish-Guaraní society in which the Spaniards were politically dominant. The mestizo children of the Spaniards adopted Spanish cultural values, despite their acquisition of the Guaraní language and other local customs.

The Jesuit Missions

In the colonial period, Paraguay comprised a much larger area than it does now and included large sections of present-day Brazil and Argentina. In part of this area, on both sides of the upper Río Paraná, Jesuit missionaries conducted a remarkable experiment, creating a series of highly organized settlements in which the Guaraní learned many aspects of European high culture as well as new crafts, crops, and methods of cultivation. For more than a century and a half, until the expulsion of the Jesuits in 1767 because of local jealousies and Madrid's concern that their power had become too great, Jesuit organization deterred Portuguese intervention in

PARAGUAY

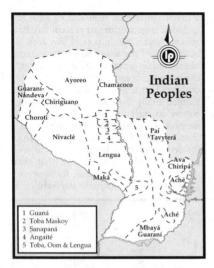

Indian Peoples

Ayoreo
Chamacoco
Guaraní-Ñandeva
Chiriguano
Choroti
Nivaclé
1
2
3
4
Lengua
Paí Tavyterá
Maká
Ava Chiripá
Aché
5
Aché
Mbayá Guaraní

1 Guaná
2 Toba Maskoy
3 Sanapaná
4 Angaité
5 Toba, Oom & Lengua

The savage Guaycurus, Lenguas, Mocobios, Tobas, Abipones, and Mbayas, wretchedly wasted the province with massacres and pillage, without leaving the miserable inhabitants a place to breathe in, or the means of resistance. To elude their designs, little fortlets are every where erected on the banks of the Paraguay, fitted up with a single cannon, which, being discharged whenever the savages come in sight, admonishes the neighbours to fight or fly.

For these Indians, admitted Dobrizhoffer, the Chaco was a refuge "which the Spanish soldiers look upon as a theatre of misery, and the savages as their Palestine and Elysium." There, he wrote, they had "mountains for observatories, trackless woods for fortifications, rivers and marshes for ditches, and plantations of fruit trees for storehouses." Having acquired the horse, groups like the Abipones and Tobas were mobile and flexible in their opposition, while the riverine Payaguá could prey upon riverboats:

the region and protected the interests of the Spanish crown. For more information on the missions themselves, see the chapter on Argentine Mesopotamia.

Jesuit influence was less effective among the non-Guaraní peoples of the Chaco, whose resistance to the Spaniards discouraged any proselytizing. Martin Dobrizhoffer, an Austrian Jesuit who spent nearly 20 years in the region, wrote about these people:

These atrocious pirates, infesting the rivers Paraguay and Parana, had for many years been in the habit of intercepting Spanish vessels freighted with wares for the port of Buenos-Ayres . . . and of massacring the crews . . . .

They have two sorts of canoes; the lesser for fishing and daily voyages, the larger for the uses of war. If their designs are against the Spaniards, many of them join together in one fleet, and are the more dangerous from their drawing so little

Because they resisted the Spaniards, the Lengua Indians were depicted as savage and unruly.

water, which enables them to lurk within the shelter of the lesser rivers, or islands, till a favourable opportunity presents itself of pillaging loaded vessels, or of disembarking and attacking the colonies . . . . For many years they continued to pillage the Spanish colonies, and all the ships that came in their way, from the city of Asumpcion, forty leagues southwards.

Several Jesuit missionaries, some like Dobrizhoffer being excellent amateur ethnographers and naturalists, managed to live among the Chaco tribes from the mid-17th century, but the area remained an Indian refuge from Europeans even into this century. After secular Spaniards realized that the Chaco route promised neither gold nor silver, they abandoned the area entirely, and the most important political and economic developments occurred east of the Río Paraguay.

Independence &
the Reign of El Supremo

When Paraguayans deposed their Spanish governor and declared independence in 1811, the Spanish crown declined to contest the action, since the colony was so isolated and economically insignificant. Within a few years, José Gaspar Rodríguez de Francia emerged as the strongest member of the governing junta. From 1814 to 1840, the autocratic Francia ruled the country as El Supremo.

In the late 16th century, Spanish official López de Velasco wrote that Paraguay had "all which is necessary for sustenance, but no wealth in money, for . . . all their wealth is in the agriculture of the country." Even in 18th-century Asunción, wrote Dobrizhoffer, money was so scarce that the "want or ignorance of metals may be reckoned among the divine blessings and advantages of Paraguay." Francia, recognizing 19th-century Paraguay's inability to compete with its neighbors, made a virtue of necessity by virtually sealing off the country's borders to commerce and promoting self-sufficiency – subsistence on a country-wide scale.

To accomplish his goals, Francia expropriated the properties of landholders, mer-

chants, and even the Church (converting monasteries into army barracks), establishing the state as the dominant economic as well as political power. The small agricultural surplus – mostly *yerba mate* and tobacco – was state controlled. Like his successors almost to the present day, Francia ruled by fear, confining his opponents in what JP Robertson, who claimed to be the first Englishman to visit Paraguay during the Francia dictatorship, described as "state dungeons":

They are small, damp vaulted dungeons, of such contracted dimensions that to maintain an upright posture in them is impossible, except under the centre of the arch.

Here it is, that loaded with irons, with a sentinel continually in view, bereft of every comfort, left without the means of ablution, and under a positive prohibition to shave, pare their nails, or cut their hair – here, in silence, solitude and despair, the victims of the Dictator's vengeance . . . pass a life to which death would be preferable . . . . The wretched, and in most cases innocent victim is left to pine away his hours in darkness and solitude.

In a precocious example of newspeak that anticipated Orwell by more than a century, Francia called his most notorious dungeon the "Chamber of Truth."

Francia himself was not immune to the climate of terror. After escaping an assassination attempt in 1820, El Supremo so feared assassination that his food and drink were consistently checked for poison, no one could approach him closer than six paces, the streets were cleared for his carriage, and he slept in a different place every night. In 1840 he died a natural death and was replaced by Carlos Antonio López. In 1870, political opponents who knew how to hold a grudge disinterred Francia's remains and threw them into the Río Paraguay.

The López "Dynasty" &
the War of the Triple Alliance

With the income from state enterprises, Carlos Antonio López ended Paraguay's extreme isolation, building railways, a tele-

PARAGUAY

graph, an iron foundry, a shipyard, and – most importantly – an army. Ruling just as autocratically as Francia, he amassed a standing army of 28,000 men and another 40,000 reserves by the early 1860s (Argentina, at the time, had only 6000 men in uniform). His megalomaniacal son Francisco Solano López succeeded him and led the country into the catastrophic War of the Triple Alliance against Argentina, Uruguay, and Brazil.

Supporting a federalist Blanco faction in Uruguay, Solano López marched his forces across the Argentine territory of Misiones and even captured Corrientes, but Triple Alliance forces destroyed his navy and, after four years, captured Asunción. Solano López retreated into the bush but died in 1870 at the hands of Brazilian forces at Cerro Corá, near present-day Pedro Juan Caballero.

Paraguay lost 150,000 sq km of territory, but even worse, it also lost much of its population through combat, famine, and disease – it was often said that only women, children, and burros remained. By some contemporary accounts, women outnumbered men three to one at the end of the war; others said that the country lost more than half its population. However, recent research indicates that the total loss may not have exceeded 20%. Still, this was a blow from which the country has never completely recovered.

Reconstruction & the Chaco War

After 1870, despite a new constitution, Paraguay underwent a sustained period of political instability that lasted for decades. As borders opened, a trickle of European and Argentine immigrants arrived and slowly resuscitated the agricultural economy. The Colorado Party, formed in 1887, helped reestablish the country as a sovereign state, encouraged agricultural development, and brought about reforms in public education. The other major party, the Liberals, took power after the turn of the century.

About this time, tension began to arise between Paraguay and Bolivia over the ill-defined borders of the Chaco, which neither country effectively occupied. As early as 1907, both began to build fortifications in anticipation of war, but full-scale hostilities did not erupt until 1932. After a 1935 cease-fire that left no clear victor, a peace treaty awarded Paraguay three-quarters of the territory in dispute. The country paid dearly, however, both financially and in the loss of another sizable portion of its population.

The reasons underlying the war remain unclear. The Paraguayans, by encouraging Mennonite immigrants to settle in the Chaco, certainly provoked the Bolivian government. However, Bolivia's war effort was rumored to have been underwritten by oil companies – one Paraguayan tourist brochure even makes the extraordinary claim that maverick United States Senator Huey Long, for whom a settlement on the Trans-Chaco highway is named, was assassinated for openly criticizing Standard's involvement on behalf of Bolivia. In any event, no oil was ever discovered, and the region is still a thinly populated backwater.

Modern Developments

After the end of the Chaco War, Paraguay endured more than a decade of disorder until the end of a brief civil war, which returned the Colorados to power in 1949. A military coup in 1954 removed the constitutional president and brought to power General Alfredo Stroessner, who despite completely bogus elections ("guided democracy"), ruled the country for 35 years in a manner that, in the former Soviet Union, might have been denounced as a "cult of personality."

Since Stroessner's overthrow by General Andrés Rodríguez in 1989, the government has made a concerted effort to eradicate the thousands of monuments to General Stroessner and his relatives, even renaming the city of Puerto Presidente Stroessner to Ciudad del Este, but reminders of his brutal regime linger. Some Paraguayans even express a certain nostalgia for Stroessner (now suffering poor health and in Brazilian exile), who has publicly sought permission to return to Asunción. Most, though, appreciate the demise of the Stroessner police state even if they are skeptical that it will bring any benefits beyond the freedom to say publicly what they have always thought.

For more information on the Stroessner regime and its successors, see the Government section below.

GEOGRAPHY & CLIMATE

Landlocked and isolated in the heart of South America, surrounded by gigantic Brazil, Argentina, and Bolivia, Paraguay appears much smaller than it really is. Its area of 407,000 sq km makes the country slightly larger than Germany and almost exactly the size of California. More than half of it is forested, but most of its timber has little commercial value.

The Río Paraguay, which connects the capital of Asunción with the Río Paraná, the rest of the River Plate drainage, and the Atlantic Ocean, divides the country into two unequal halves. In the smaller eastern sector, comprising about 40% of the country's territory and containing the great majority of the population, a well-watered, elevated plateau of rolling grasslands and patches of subtropical forest separates the valley of the Río Paraguay from the upper Paraná. These rivers and the Río Pilcomayo form much of Paraguay's borders with Brazil and Argentina. The Paraná constitutes an outstanding hydroelectric resource whose development may turn Paraguay into an energy colony of its larger neighbors. Mineral resources, including petroleum, are almost nonexistent.

Eastern Paraguay's climate is humid, with rainfall distributed fairly evenly throughout the year. In the east, near the Brazilian border, it averages an abundant 2000 mm per annum, declining to about 1500 mm near Asunción. Since elevations do not exceed 600 meters, temperatures are almost uniformly hot in summer – the average high in December, January, and February is 35°C. Winter temperatures are milder, with an average high of 22°C in July, the coldest month, although frosts are not unknown. Paraguay is vulnerable to cold fronts known as *pamperos,* which work their way north from temperate Argentina in the spring and fall, causing temperatures to drop dramatically – as much as 20°C in only a few hours.

Paraguay's western sector is an extensive plain, known as the Gran Chaco, rising gradually toward the Bolivian border. Only about 4% of all Paraguayans live in the Chaco, whose principal economic activity is cattle ranching on very large estancias. Temperatures are even higher than in eastern Paraguay, often exceeding 40°C, and rainfall is erratic; precipitation does not exceed 1000 mm. This, combined with high evaporation rates, makes rain-fed agriculture undependable. German Mennonite settlers have nevertheless successfully raised cotton, sorghum, and other commercial crops, as well as dairy cattle, in the region.

FLORA & FAUNA

Paraguay's vegetation correlates strongly with rainfall and diminishes from east to west. Its humid subtropical forest is densest in the moist valleys of eastern Paraguay, near the Brazilian frontier, and sparser on the thinner upland soils. The most important tree species are lapacho *(Tabebula* spp), quebracho colorado *(Schinopsis balansae),* trébol *(Amburana cearensis),* peroba *(Aspidosperma polyneuron),* and guatambú *(Balfourodendron riedelanium).*

Between this forest and the Río Paraguay, the dominant vegetation is savanna, with occasional gallery forests along watercourses, while west of the Río Paraguay, caranday palm savanna gradually gives way to scrub and thorn forest, including the valuable quebracho, a source of natural tannin. Throughout the country, there is a particular abundance of aroid plants (such as philodendrons) and orchids.

Paraguayan wildlife is equally diverse, but the dense human population of rural eastern Paraguay has put great pressure on the local fauna. Paraguayan mammals in danger of extinction include the giant anteater, giant armadillo, maned wolf, river

PARAGUAY

otter, Brazilian tapir, jaguar, pampas deer, and marsh deer. One modest but notable wildlife success has been the rediscovery in the mid-1970s of the Chacoan peccary, which was thought to be extinct for at least half a century, and its nurture by a joint effort of Paraguayan and international conservationists.

Bird life is abundant, especially in the Chaco, and Paraguay has 365 bird species, including 21 species of parrots and parakeets, jabirú and wood storks, plumed ibis, and waterfowl, among many others. In the riverine lowlands, there are numerous reptiles, including two species of caiman, anacondas, and boa constrictors. Short-term visitors are unlikely to see the truly rare species, but they have a good chance of seeing many reptiles they have never seen before.

NATIONAL PARKS

Paraguay has several national parks and lesser reserves protecting an impressive diversity of habitats throughout the country, but only a few are easily accessible to travelers. The three largest are in the Chaco, while the smaller and more biologically diverse units are in eastern Paraguay. For detailed information on Paraguayan parks and reserves, contact the Dirección de Parques Nacionales y Vida Silvestre (☎ 445-214), on the 12th floor of the Edificio Garantía, 25 de Mayo 640, Asunción. The Fundación Moisés Bertoni (☎ 440-238), Rodríguez de Francia 770 in Asunción, is a private organization that works with landowners and the government in the interest of environmental conservation, and is also a good source of information on biological conservation in Paraguay.

Unfortunately, because of corruption, economic pressure, and a traditionally weak political commitment, some of Paraguay's parks have experienced serious disruption. Despite these difficulties, organizations like the Fundación Bertoni have accomplished a great deal by publicizing environmental issues both locally and abroad.

Parque Nacional Defensores del Chaco

In semi-arid northwest Chaco, 830 km from Asunción, this 780,000-hectare (6084-sq-mile) park is by far the country's largest, although direct protective activities are minimal over most of the area. Its dominant vegetation is thorn forest of *quebracho, algarrobo,* and *palo santo,* and large mammals include jaguar, puma, tapir, peccary, and monkeys. Access is difficult but not impossible.

Parque Nacional Tinfunqué

On the Río Pilcomayo, 300 km from Asunción, this 280,000-hectare (2184-sq-mile) unit of savanna and marshlands is the country's second-largest park. Consisting entirely of private estancias, it is effectively a paper park, with neither a management plan nor direct protective activities, but landowners do not object to visitors. Wildlife includes capybara, swamp deer, caiman, and a great variety of bird life.

Parque Nacional Teniente Enciso

In semi-arid upper Chaco, 665 km from Asunción on the Ruta Trans-Chaco, 40,000-hectare (312-sq-mile) Teniente Enciso features low, dense thorn forest and wildlife similar to that of the larger and less accessible Defensores del Chaco, and it also preserves battle sites from the Chaco War. Managed jointly by the Ministerio de Defensa and Ministerio de Agricultura y Ganadería, it has resident rangers and some visitor facilities.

Parque Nacional Caaguazú

Tripled in size by recent acquisitions, 16,000-hectare (125-sq-mile) Caaguazú is an area of mixed secondary Brazilian rainforest with considerable historical and anthropological interest, situated 250 km southeast of Asunción in the department of Caazapá. The most common wildlife species are the coatimundi, deer, and reptiles, and there are several cave sites with aboriginal inscriptions. Because of pressure from agricultural colonists, its size has been reduced from an original 200,000 hectares, and direct protective activities are few.

Parque Nacional Cerro Corá
In the department of Amambay, 500 km from Asunción, 22,000-hectare (174-sq-mile) Cerro Corá is probably the most scenic of Paraguay's parks, with transitional humid subtropical forest among isolated peaks up to 450 meters high. It also features numerous cave sites and was the scene of the famous battle at which Francisco Solano López died during the War of the Triple Alliance. The park has a visitor center, camping area, and several *cabañas* (cabins) where visitors can lodge.

Parque Nacional Ybycuí
In the department of Paraguarí, only 150 km from Asunción, 5000-hectare (39-sq-mile) Ybycuí, with its humid subtropical forest, is the most accessible and probably best managed of Paraguay's parks, despite the presence of agricultural colonists and problems with timber poachers. There are several self-guided nature trails, a longer backpack trail, a visitors center, and a campground, plus the ruins of Paraguay's first iron foundry. A small restaurant serves meals on weekends.

Parque Nacional Serranía San Luis
In the department of Concepción, 6870 km north of Asunción, 10,000-hectare (78-sq-mile) San Luis is an area of rugged subtropical forest near the Brazilian border. It has limited visitor infrastructure.

GOVERNMENT
On paper, Paraguay is a republic with a 1992 constitution that establishes a strong president, popularly elected for a five-year term, who in turn appoints a seven-member cabinet to assist in governing. Congress consists of a lower Cámara de Diputados (Chamber of Deputies) and an upper Senado (Senate), elected concurrently with the president. The Corte Suprema (Supreme Court) is the highest judicial authority. Administratively, the country comprises 17 departments, the counterparts of states or provinces in other countries.

For most of the post-WWII era, however, Paraguay has been one of the Western Hemisphere's most odious and long-lasting dictatorships, whose extremely corrupt electoral politics has been controlled by a government that has allowed only token opposition. Lack of any limitation to presidential or congressional terms helped solidify the Stroessner dictatorship for 35 years until his overthrow in early 1989.

Historically, the electoral system has been simple and unrepresentative. The party with the most votes automatically gained two-thirds of the seats in Congress, effectively marginalizing the opposition. Controlling the machinery of government, the Colorado Party has been the dominant formal organization in Paraguayan political life since winning the civil war of 1947. For most of this period, the Colorados relied on Stroessner and the Paraguayan military for their privileged status. Political torture and assassination were common in those years.

Shortly after deposing Stroessner in 1989, General Andrés Rodríguez won the presidency, unopposed, in an election in which the entire spectrum of opposition parties obtained a larger percentage of congressional seats than ever before. In December 1991, in what was probably the fairest election ever held in Paraguay (undoubtedly faint praise), General Rodríguez's Colorado Party won a legislative majority. Even before the 1991 election, however, political activity and dialogue had flourished on a scale unprecedented in recent Paraguayan history.

Both the Liberals and the Febreristas, a moderate labor-oriented party, operated within the stringent bounds of acceptable public dialogue under the Stroessner regime, but others, including Liberal and Colorado factions, boycotted bogus elections. With the Liberals and Febreristas, the Christian Democrats and Mopoco (a dissident Colorado faction) now constitute the Acuerdo Nacional (national accord) of political opposition.

Paraguay's 46 senators are now chosen

by proportional representation in nation-wide elections, while the 80 deputies are chosen geographically, by department. Mayoral elections are due in early to mid-1996, while the next presidential election will take place in 1998. Thanks to political decentralization, the various departments now choose their own civilian governors.

Whether these promising developments will result in an enduring democracy is still uncertain because of Paraguay's authoritarian tradition and continuity among the entrenched Colorado elite. One of the great ironies of Stroessner's overthrow was Rodríguez's triumphant appearance on Paraguayan television with his daughter and grandchildren who are also Stroessner's grandchildren, since Rodríguez's daughter is married to Stroessner's son, Gustavo – so far, Paraguayans have managed to keep it in the family. The Colorado Party, now a congressional minority, has lobbied for an amnesty to permit Stroessner's return from Brazilian exile.

Juan Carlos Wasmosy, Paraguay's first elected civilian president in eons, was nominated by the then ruling Colorados as a figurehead, but he has since come into conflict with the still-powerful military, most notably coup-monger General Lino Oviedo. Nicknamed the "bonsai horseman" for his diminutive stature and cavalry background, Oviedo once dressed as Julius Caesar at a costume party, but one senator remarked that the general more closely resembled Caligula. At the same time, military prestige and authority continue to come under scrutiny as groups like the Movimiento de Objeción de la Conciencia publicize problems like the abuse of conscripts. Wasmosy, at the same time, has come under scrutiny for shady business dealings associated with Paraguay's massive hydroelectric projects.

ECONOMY

Historically, Paraguay's economy has depended on agriculture and livestock. Its principal exports have been beef, maize, sugar cane, soybeans, lumber, and cotton, but a large proportion of the rural populace cultivates subsistence crops on small landholdings, selling any surplus at local markets and laboring on large estancias and plantations to supplement the household income. High transport costs, due primarily to Paraguay's landlocked isolation, have driven up the cost of its exports in comparison with other Latin American countries.

While Paraguay lacks mineral energy resources, it has begun to develop its abundant hydroelectric potential over the past 15 years through participation with Brazil and Argentina in enormous dam projects. Brazil takes most of the electricity from Itaipú, located on the upper Paraná above Ciudad del Este, while corruption-plagued Yacyretá, on the border with the Argentine province of Corrientes, may never be finished (see the chapter on Argentine Mesopotamia). So far Paraguay has benefited by playing South America's two major economic and military powers off each other, but it risks becoming an energy colony, especially if the price of competing sources of energy drops and Paraguay cannot repay its share of capital costs, which Brazil and Argentina have already paid, and maintenance.

Paraguayan industry, which consists for the most part of the processing of agricultural products, benefits little from this enormous hydroelectric capacity. The slowdown in construction with the completion of Itaipú and Yacyretá's continuing problems have nearly eliminated the economic growth of the 1970s. The economic growth rate for 1994 was a modest 3.6%, while inflation has been running at roughly 45%. The official minimum wage is approximately US$200 per month, but the Ministerio de Justicia y Trabajo (Ministry of Justice and Labor) is unable to enforce regulations, and probably 70% of Paraguayan workers fall below this level.

Paraguay's major industry remains contraband, including electronics and agricultural produce, most of which passes through Ciudad del Este to or from Brazil. Stolen cars and illegal drugs, including cocaine, are other unfortunate goods that pass into or through Paraguay.

The gradual reduction of tariffs in Mercosur (see Economy in the Facts about Argentina chapter), to which Paraguay is a charter member, may reduce the prevalence of smuggling by making imported goods cheaper in the neighboring member countries of Argentina, Brazil, and Uruguay. Some Paraguayans envision the country's becoming a financial center, but the *Wall Street Journal* has noted that financial irregularities are widespread, quoting the president of the Asunción stock exchange to the effect that "Paraguayan corporate accounting statements typically contain certain anomalies. Assets are misrepresented, sales are misrepresented, and profits are misrepresented."

POPULATION & PEOPLE

Paraguay has a population of 4.1 million, approximately one-seventh that of the state of California, which has about the same area. With 500,000 residents, Asunción is by far the largest city, but only 43% of Paraguayans live in urban areas, compared with more than 80% in Argentina and Uruguay. Many Paraguayans are peasant cultivators who produce a small surplus for sale.

By world and even South American standards of welfare, Paraguayans rank relatively low. Infant mortality rates are higher than any other South American country except Colombia, Bolivia, and Peru, and the life expectancy of 65 years is lower than any other country in South America except Bolivia and Peru. For both political and economic reasons, many Paraguayans live outside the country, mostly in Brazil and Argentina – between 1950 and 1970, more than 350,000 Paraguayans sought work in Argentina. Many political exiles have returned since the overthrow of the Stroessner dictatorship.

More than 75% of Paraguayans are mestizos, of mixed Spanish-Guaraní heritage. Almost all of these are bilingual, speaking Guaraní by preference, although Spanish is the official language of government and commerce. Even upper-class Paraguayans speak Guaraní, however.

Approximately 20% of Paraguayans are descendants of European immigrants, including about 100,000 Germans. Since the 1930s, agricultural settlement by German Mennonites, who have prospered in the difficult environment of the central Chaco, has caused ethnic friction and continuing problems with some Indian groups. Japanese immigrants have settled in parts of eastern Paraguay, along with Brazilian agricultural colonists, many of German origin, who have moved across the border in recent years. Asunción has seen a substantial influx of Koreans, mostly involved in commerce. Since the end of apartheid, a number of South Africans have moved to the department of Caaguazú.

In the Chaco and in scattered areas of eastern Paraguay, there are small but significant populations of indigenous people, some of whom, until very recently, still relied on hunting and gathering for their livelihood. According to many credible accounts, the Stroessner dictatorship conducted an active campaign of genocide against the Aché (Guayakí) Indians of eastern Paraguay in the 1970s.

Most of Paraguay's Indians are in the Chaco, where isolated groups such as the Ayoreo lived almost untouched by European civilization until very recently. The largest groups are the Nivaclé and Lengua, both of whom number around 10,000. Many of them have become dependent labor for the region's agricultural colonists. In total, Indians comprise about 3% of the population.

EDUCATION

Education is compulsory only to the age of 12. In the country as a whole, literacy is only 81%, the lowest of the River Plate republics but higher than all the Andean countries except Ecuador. Higher education is largely the responsibility of the Universidad Nacional and the Universidad Católica in Asunción, but both have branches throughout the country.

ARTS

In general, very little Paraguayan literature

is available to English-speaking readers, but novelist and poet Augusto Roa Bastos put Paraguay on the international literary map by winning the Spanish government's Cervantes Prize in 1990. Despite having spent much of his adult life in exile from the Stroessner dictatorship, Roa Bastos focuses on Paraguayan themes and history in the larger context of politics and repressive government.

Some of his best work is available in English. *Son of Man,* originally published in 1961, is a novel tying together several episodes in Paraguayan history, including the Francia dictatorship and the Chaco War. *I the Supreme* is a historical novel about the paranoid dictator Francia.

Works by other important Paraguayan writers, such as novelist Gabriel Casaccia and poet Elvio Romero, are not readily available in English. Josefina Pla's historical and critical works on Guaraní-Baroque art and the British in Paraguay have been translated, but her poetry has not. For books on history and other aspects of Para-

guay, see the Books section in the Paraguay Facts for the Visitor chapter.

As in Buenos Aires and Montevideo, theater is a popular medium, with occasional offerings in Guaraní as well as Spanish. In 1933, during the Chaco War, Asunción theatergoers swarmed to see the Guaraní dramatist Julie Correa's *Guerra Ayaa.* The visual arts are very important and popular; Asunción has numerous galleries, most notably the Museo del Barro, which emphasizes modern, sometimes very unconventional, works. Both classical and folk music are performed at venues in Asunción.

Paraguay's most famous traditional craft is the production of multicolored *ñandutí* (spider-web lace) in the Asunción suburb of Itauguá. Paraguayan harps and guitars, as well as filigree gold and silver jewelry and leather goods, are made in the village of Luque, while other high-caliber artisanal goods come from the Indian communities of the Chaco. While production for sale rather than for use may have debased the

Paraguayan crafts range from ñandutí (spider-web lace) to filigree gold jewelry.

quality of certain items, such as spears and knives, wood carvings are truly appealing (the eastern Paraguayan village of Tobatí is well known for this).

CULTURE

English-speaking visitors will find Paraguay, in some ways, more "exotic" than either Argentina or Uruguay because of the country's unique racial and cultural mix; however, Paraguayans in general are eager to meet and speak with foreign visitors. Take advantage of any invitation to drink *mate,* often in the form of ice-cold *tereré,* which can be a good introduction to Paraguay and its people.

In the Mennonite colonies of the Chaco, an ability to speak German will quickly dissolve barriers in this culturally insular community. It is much more difficult, however, to make contact with the region's indigenous people, and it is undiplomatic to probe too quickly into the relations between the two, which are a controversial subject. From regular contact with the Mennonites, many Chaco Indians speak German rather than Spanish as a second language.

Paraguayans in general are very sports-minded; the most popular soccer team, Olímpia, has beaten the best Argentine sides. Tennis and basketball have also become popular spectator sports, but golf and squash are exclusively the province of the elite.

RELIGION

Roman Catholicism is Paraguay's official religion, but folk variants are important, and the Church is weaker and less influential than in most other Latin American countries. One 19th-century visitor, undoubtedly a Protestant, wrote that

Paraguayans were steeped in religious ignorance and floundering in idolatry . . . . The priests were ignorant and immoral, great cockfighters and gamblers, possessing vast influence over the women, a power which they turn to the basest of purposes.

Traditionally, Paraguay's isolation and the state's indifference to religion have resulted in a wide variety of irregular religious prac-

---

Common Guaraní Words & Phrases

The following is a small sample of Guaraní words and phrases that many travelers may find useful, if only to break the ice. Those given are not so consistently phonetic as Spanish but are still fairly easy to pronounce. A few have obviously been adapted from Spanish.

I	*she*	woman	*kuñá*
you	*nde*	man	*kuimbaé*
we	*ñande*	person	*hente*
this	*péva*	road	*tapé*
that	*amóa*	rain	*amá*
no	*naháníri*	cloud	*araí*
all	*entéro*	mountain	*sero*
many	*hetá*	new	*piahú*
big	*guazú*	good	*porá*
small	*mishí*	name	*héra*
one	*peteí*	How are you?	*Mba'eichapa?*
two	*mokoi*	Fine, and you?	*Iporãiterei, ha nde?*
eat	*okarú*	I'm fine, too.	*Iporãiterei avei.*
drink	*hoiú*	Where are you from?	*Moõguápa nde?*
water	*y*	I'm from Australia.	*Che Australia gua.*
meat	*soó*	Where do you live?	*Moõpa reiko?*
hot	*hakú*	I live in California.	*Che aiko California.*
cold	*roí*		

tices – according to one anthropologist, rural Paraguayans view priests more as healers or magicians than spiritual advisers. Women express greater religious devotion than men.

Protestant sects have made fewer inroads in Catholic Paraguay than in some other Latin American countries, although fundamentalist Mennonites have proselytized among Chaco Indians since the 1930s. Other evangelical groups, including the highly controversial New Tribes Mission, used to operate with the collusion and, some say, active support of the Stroessner dictatorship. This regime was no friend to the country's indigenous people, who, of course, have their own religious beliefs, many of which they have retained or only slightly modified, despite nominal allegiance to Catholicism or evangelical Protestantism.

LANGUAGE

Paraguay is officially bilingual in Spanish and Guaraní, a legacy of colonial times when vastly outnumbered Spaniards had no alternative but to interact with the indigenous population. Though undoubtedly influenced by Spanish, Guaraní has also modified the European language in its vocabulary and pattern of speech. During the Chaco War of the 1930s, Guaraní enjoyed resurgent popularity for both practical and nationalist reasons when, for security purposes, field commanders prohibited the use of Spanish on the battlefield. Listeners tuned to Paraguayan radio will hear otherwise familiar soft-drink jingles in Guaraní rather than Spanish.

Several other Indian languages are spoken in the Chaco and isolated parts of eastern Paraguay, including Lengua, Nivaclé, and Aché.

Facts for the Visitor

Travelers will find Paraguay similar to Argentina and Uruguay in some respects but very different in others. Only facts for the visitor that differ significantly from the other River Plate republics are mentioned in this chapter.

PLANNING
When to Go & What to Bring

Because of Paraguay's intense summer heat, visitors from midlatitudes may prefer the winter months from, say, May to August or September, when the country will seem positively springlike. Days will normally be warm, but nights can be very cool, and frosts are not unusual.

During the summer heat, Paraguayans dress very informally. Light cotton clothing will suffice for almost all conditions except in winter, but a sweater or light jacket is advisable for changeable spring weather. If you're spending any time outdoors in the brutal subtropical sun, do not neglect a wide-brimmed hat or baseball cap, a light-weight long-sleeved shirt, and sunblock. Mosquito repellent is imperative in the Chaco and many other places. (See Climate Charts on page 755.)

Maps

The best maps come from the Instituto Geográfico Militar on Av Artigas in Asunción, but the new *Guía Shell* (see Travel Guides below) contains the most useful road map of the country (despite the prominent Shell logos indicating their service station locations). The guide also includes a good general country map at a scale of 1:2,000,000, and a very fine map of Asunción, with a street index, at a scale of 1:25,000.

The Dirección de Turismo in Asunción distributes a very good city map, which includes an even more detailed *microcentro* (downtown) section, free of charge. In Filadelfia, it is possible to purchase an excellent, detailed map of the Mennonite colonies, but other maps of the country's interior towns and cities are hard to find.

HIGHLIGHTS

For independent travelers with an open mind, little-visited Paraguay has much to offer. As one of Latin America's oldest cities, Asunción's historical significance is considerable, even though it has relatively few colonial remains. Southeastern Paraguay, between Asunción and Encarnación, has important colonial remains, including those of Jesuit missions like Jesús and Trinidad, which in some ways surpasses that of Argentina's San Ignacio Miní. Fishing along the Río Paraná and the Río Paraguay is, obviously, similar to that in Argentina.

On the Brazilian frontier, the massive binational hydroelectric complex at Itaipú deserves a visit, if only to mourn Sete Quedas, a series of falls that surpassed even Iguazú before their disappearance under a massive reservoir. Iguazú itself is easily visited from Ciudad del Este (ex-Puerto Presidente Stroessner), but Paraguay has important natural assets of its own in several widely dispersed national parks. The most accessible of these is Ybycuí, which preserves a representative sample of subtropical rainforest. Other reserves can be found both in eastern Paraguay and the nearly vacant Chaco region, one of South America's great wildernesses. Paraguay's bird life is exceptionally rich both in eastern Paraguay and the Chaco, although mammals and reptiles have suffered by comparison.

TOURIST OFFICES
Local Tourist Offices

Paraguayan tourist offices are fewer than in Argentina or Uruguay and less well organized. They can be found in Asunción, Encarnación, Ciudad del Este, and a handful of other places.

Foreign Representatives

The larger Paraguayan consulates, such as in New York and Los Angeles (see the list below), usually have a tourist representative in their delegation. North American offices of Líneas Aéreas Paraguayas (Lapsa, ☎ 800-795-2772) also serve as de facto tourist representatives. Lapsa offices in the USA are:

Suite 375, 6033 W Century Blvd, Los Angeles, CA 90045 (☎ 310-670-0807)
Suite 402, 7200 NW 19th St, Miami, FL 33126 (☎ 305-477-2104)
Suite 2050, 500 5th Ave, New York, NY 10110 (☎ 212-302-0004)

VISAS & DOCUMENTS

Paraguay requires visas of all foreigners, except those from neighboring countries and Chileans (who need only national identification cards) and nationals of most Western European countries and the USA. According to the Paraguayan Consulate in Washington, DC, Canadians, Australians, and New Zealanders need a clean police record and a bank statement and must pay a fee of US$10 for a visa. Canadians should do this through the Paraguayan Consulate in New York. French visitors also require visas.

Paraguay has dispensed with the tourist card it formerly required, and there are no longer any border charges except for airport departure taxes.

Passports are necessary for many everyday transactions, such as cashing traveler's checks, checking into hotels, and passing the various military and police checkpoints in the Chaco. Paraguay requires that foreign drivers possess the International Driving Permit, although document checks are usually perfunctory.

EMBASSIES
Paraguayan Embassies & Consulates

Paraguay has diplomatic representation in neighboring countries and overseas, but its network is less extensive than Argentina's.

Argentina
    Viamonte 1851, Buenos Aires (☎ 01-812-0075)
Australia
    Paraguay does not have diplomatic representation in Australia.
Bolivia
    Av Arce, Edificio Venus, La Paz (☎ 322-018)
Brazil
    No 1208, Rua do Carmo 20, Centro, Río de Janeiro (☎ 242-9671)
    10th floor, Av São Luis 112, São Paulo (☎ 255-7818)
Chile
    Huérfanos 886, Santiago (☎ 639-4640)
UK
    Braemar Lodge, Cornwall Gardens, London SW7 4AQ (☎ 0171-937-1253)
Uruguay
    Bulevar Artigas 1256, Montevideo (☎ 40-3801)
USA
    2400 Massachusetts Ave NW, Washington, DC (☎ 202-483-6960)
    2800 Viscayne Blvd, Miami, FL (☎ 305-573-5588)
    675 3rd Ave, Suite 1604 New York, NY (☎ 212-682-9441)
    8322 Seaport Drive, Huntington Beach, CA (☎ 714-536-2259)

Foreign Embassies in Paraguay

South American countries, the USA, and most Western European countries have diplomatic representation in Asunción, but Australians and New Zealanders must depend on their consulates in Buenos Aires or upon the British Consulate.

Argentina and Brazilian consulates in border towns appear in the appropriate chapters of the text.

Argentina
    corner of Avs España & Perú (☎ 212-320)
Belgium
    5th floor, Juan O'Leary 409 (☎ 610-603)
Bolivia
    Eligio Ayala 2002 (☎ 210-676)
Brazil
    3rd floor, General Díaz 521 (☎ 448-084)
Canada
    Edificio Colón, El Paraguayo Independiente & Colón, Entrepiso (☎ 449-505)
Chile
    Guido Spano 1687 (☎ 600-671)

France
Av España 676 (☎ 212-439)
Germany
Av Venezuela 241 (☎ 214-009)
Israel
8th floor, Edificio San Rafael, Yegros 437
(☎ 495-097)
Italy
Av Mariscal López 1104 (☎ 25918)
Japan
Av Mariscal López 2364 (☎ 604-616)
Netherlands
Chile 668 (☎ 492-137)
Peru
Av Mariscal López 648 (☎ 200-949)
Spain
6th floor, Yegros 437 (☎ 490-686)
Switzerland
4th floor, Estrella & O'Leary (☎ 490-848)
UK
4th floor, Presidente Franco 706 (☎ 496-067)
Uruguay
25 de Mayo 1894 (☎ 203-864)
USA
Av Mariscal López 1776 (☎ 213-715)

CUSTOMS

Paraguayan customs officially admit into the country "reasonable quantities" of personal effects, alcohol, and tobacco; since contraband is the national sport, however, officials at overland crossings wink at anything that is not flagrantly illegal. At Ciudad del Este, customs officials declined even to look at our car, let alone process its papers (our Argentine license plates may have been a factor in our being treated so routinely).

Nevertheless, foreign motorists may run into corrupt customs officials who claim that their vehicles may not enter the country without posting a bond of half the vehicle's local value – which is much higher than what it is overseas. Anyone encountering such a problem should politely but firmly remind them that Mercosur regulations, which establish a common external tariff among Brazil, Argentina, Uruguay, and Paraguay, do not require this. Keep photocopies of vehicle documentation from neighboring countries for proof and reference when crossing borders.

MONEY

The unit of currency is the *guaraní* (plural *guaraníes*), indicated by a capital letter G with a forward slash (/). Banknote values are 100, 500, 1000, 5000, 10,000, and 50,000 guaraníes, and there are coins for 1, 5, 10, 20, 50, and 100 guaraníes.

Inflation in Paraguay is much less serious than in Argentina, and prices in general are slightly lower than in Uruguay. Money is readily exchanged at casas de cambio in Asunción, Ciudad del Este, Encarnación, and Pedro Juan Caballero, but banks are the rule in the interior. Street changers give slightly lower rates than cambios, but they can be helpful on weekends or in the evening, when cambios are closed.

Most better hotels, restaurants, and shops in Asunción accept credit cards, but their use is less common outside the capital. Paraguayan ATMs generally do not recognize foreign credit cards, but the Banco Unión in Asunción at the corner of Alberdi and Estrella, which is linked to the Cirrus system, is a welcome exception.

Exchange Rates

Exchange houses accept traveler's checks at slightly lower rates than cash dollars, and sometimes charge commissions, although these are not as high as those levied in Argentina. German marks are more welcome in Asunción than in other South American capitals, although prices are given in US dollars, still the most popular foreign currency. There is no black market. Some travelers have reported that exchange houses will not cash traveler's checks without the bill of sale.

At press time exchange rates were as follows:

Argentina	Arg$1	=	G 1945
Australia	A$1	=	G 2000
Bolivia	Bol$1	=	G 400
Brazil	BraR$1	=	G 2280
Canada	Can$1	=	G 1360
Chile	Ch$1	=	G 2.5
France	FFr1	=	G 370
Germany	DM1	=	G 1293

Italy	It£1	=	₲ 20
Netherlands	NLf1	=	₲ 1153
Spain	SpPta1	=	₲ 14.8
Switzerland	SwFr1	=	₲ 1528
UK	UK£1	=	₲ 3018
Uruguay	Urg$1	=	₲ 300
USA	US$1	=	₲ 1950

POST & TELECOMMUNICATIONS

Postal rates are cheaper in Paraguay than in Argentina or Uruguay, but as elsewhere in Latin America, truly essential mail should be registered. Paraguayan post offices charge about US25¢ per item for poste restante services.

Antelco, the state telephone monopoly, has central long-distance offices resembling those of Uruguay's Antel; it may soon undergo privatization. Central offices in Asunción have fiber-optic lines with direct connections to operators in the USA (ATT, MCI, Sprint), Britain, Australia, Germany, Argentina, Uruguay, Brazil, and Japan. Credit card or collect calls to the US and other overseas destinations are cheaper than paying locally. For local calls, public phone boxes (which take fichas rather than coins) are few and far between.

For an international operator, dial 0010; for Discado Directo Internacional (DDI), dial 002.

BOOKS
History

Despite a slightly misleading title, J Richard Gorham's edited collection *Paraguay: Ecological Essays* (Academy of the Arts and Sciences of the Americas, 1973) contains excellent material on pre-Columbian and colonial Paraguayan history and geography. For a standard historical account of rural Paraguay, see Elman and Helen Service's *Tobatí: Paraguayan Town.* Harris Gaylord Warren's *Rebirth of the Paraguayan Republic* tells the story of Paraguay's incomplete recovery, under the direction of the Colorado Party, from the disaster of the War of the Triple Alliance.

For a general account of human rights abuses under Stroessner, see *Rule by Fear: Paraguay After Thirty Years Under Stroess-*
ner (Americas Watch, 1985). Richard Arens's edited collection *Genocide in Paraguay* is an account of the Paraguayan government's role in the attempted extermination of the Aché Indians. Carlos Miranda's *The Stroessner Era* is a thoughtful, nonpolemical analysis of Stroessner's rise and consolidation of power, plus a short political obituary.

Travel Guides

While its tourist information is limited and conventional, the new *Guía Shell* contains the most useful road map of the country. It also includes a good general country map and a very fine map of Asunción. A worthwhile acquisition for anyone spending more than a few days in the country, the guide and maps cost about US$7.50, but the Touring y Automóvil Club Paraguayo sells it for a slight discount to its members and to members of its international affiliates.

MEDIA

The Stroessner dictatorship severely punished press criticism, closed opposition papers, jailed and tortured editors and reporters, and monitored foreign press agencies. Nevertheless, Asunción's daily *ABC Color* made its reputation as nearly the sole opposition to Stroessner, despite being subject to severe restrictions. An independent radio station, Radio Ñandutí, also criticized the Stroessner regime. The editorially bold newspaper *Ultima Hora* is very independent, breaking stories such as the deaths of army conscripts – usually termed "suicides" – under suspicious circumstances; it also has an excellent cultural section.

El Pueblo, a small circulation organ of the Febrerista party, is independent of the government but has had little impact. *Hoy* and *Patria* (the official Colorado Party newspaper) are controlled by Stroessner relatives.

Asunción's German-speaking community publishes a twice-monthly newspaper, *Neues für Alle,* which is widely distributed throughout the country. The *Buenos Aires Herald* and other Argentine newspapers are available in Asunción, at a kiosk on the corner of Chile and Palma, but they are hard to find elsewhere.

FILM & PHOTOGRAPHY

Asunción is one of the best places in South America to buy film, with Fujichrome 100 slide film readily available for about US$5 per roll without developing. This is suitable for Paraguay's tropical light conditions and verdant greens, although in the dense subtropical rainforests of eastern Paraguay it would be useful to have high-speed film, which is much more expensive and best brought from overseas.

TIME

Paraguay is three hours behind GMT except in winter (April 1 to September 30), when daylight savings time adds an hour.

HEALTH

According to US Peace Corps volunteers, who have close contact with both rural and urban health conditions, Paraguay presents few health problems for travelers. Peace Corps officials recommend that volunteers follow the "20-meter rule" with respect to drinking water in rural areas – if the water source is within 20 meters of a latrine, do not drink it. I drank tap water from Ciudad del Este all the way to Filadelfia with no ill effects, but if you have any doubts, stick to mineral water, which is readily available.

Malaria is not a major health hazard in Paraguay, but the monstrous Itaipú hydroelectric project on the Brazilian border appears to have created a new habitat for mosquito vectors. The US Centers for Disease Control in Atlanta recommend chloroquine for malaria prophylaxis.

Other causes for concern, but not hysteria, are Chagas' disease, tuberculosis, typhoid, hepatitis, and hookworm *(susto)* – avoid going barefoot. Cutaneous leishmaniasis *(ura)*, a malady transmitted by sandflies that bite and resulting in open sores, is very unpleasant and can be dangerous if untreated. Yellow fever is uncommon, and there is a low risk of mosquito-transmitted dengue fever.

WOMEN TRAVELERS

Paraguay is generally safe for women travelers, but modesty is important, and women should, in general, avoid eye contact with unfamiliar males, especially in the countryside. Single women should avoid even "friendly" conversation with men on buses. There have been reports of kidnap and rape attempts of single women in the country.

USEFUL ORGANIZATIONS

For visitors interested in natural history and conservation, the Fundación Moisés Bertoni (☎ 440-238), Rodríguez de Francia 770, Asunción, is an indispensable organization that welcomes foreign visitors. Named after a 19th-century Swiss-Paraguayan naturalist, it sponsors projects that encourage biological diversity and restoration of degraded ecosystems, cooperates with the state in strengthening national parks and other reserves, promotes environmental education and research, and tries to involve Paraguayan citizens and private enterprise in conservation. Many if not most of the staff speak English. Now building a new center in the suburb of Lambaré, it also administers the Fundación Mbaracayú.

The government organization in charge of Paraguay's national parks, working in concert with the Fundación Bertoni and the US Peace Corps, is the Ministerio de Agricultura's Dirección de Parques Nacionales y Vida Silvestre (☎ 495-568, 494-914), 12th floor, 25 de Mayo 640, Asunción.

For motorists, the Touring y Automóvil Club Paraguayo is less widespread than its Argentine equivalent, but it's still a useful resource, providing information, road services, and excellent maps and guidebooks for its own members and those of overseas affiliates. Its Asunción office (☎ 210-550, 210-553) is on Calle Brasil between Cerro Corá and 25 de Mayo.

DANGERS & ANNOYANCES

In the Chaco, especially, watch for poisonous snakes. As elsewhere in the world, you're not likely to find them unless you go looking, but the consequences of snakebite

PARAGUAY

are so serious that you won't care to chance it. Differing from its northern counterparts, the Brazilian rattlesnake *(Crotalus durissus)* transmits a highly potent neurotoxin that can cause paralysis so severe that neck muscles cannot hold up the head, and the neck appears broken. However, you are more likely to be troubled by mosquitos, so bring repellent, lightweight long-sleeved shirts, and a hat to protect yourself from both them and the sun.

Since the end of the Stroessner dictatorship, the police operate with less impunity than formerly, but it is not wise to aggravate either them or the military. Surprisingly, highway police appear less arbitrary than in Argentina; however, at Chaco highway checkpoints you will encounter teenage conscripts with automatic rifles as big as they are – although the rumor is that officers don't dare issue them ammunition for fear of being turned upon. Be polite, show your papers, and you are unlikely to be seriously inconvenienced. There is tension between the pacifist Mennonites and the Paraguayan military and police in the Chaco.

BUSINESS HOURS & PUBLIC HOLIDAYS

Most shops are open weekdays and Saturdays from 7 am to noon, then close until midafternoon and stay open until 7 or 8 pm. Banking hours are usually 7:30 to 11 am weekdays, but exchange houses keep longer hours.

Because of the summer heat, Paraguayans go to work very early – in summer, from mid-November to mid-March, government offices open as early as 6:30 am and usually close before noon. The following is a list of national holidays on which government offices and businesses are closed.

1 January
  Año Nuevo (New Year's Day)
3 February
  Día de San Blas (Patron Saint of Paraguay)
February (date varies)
  Carnaval – Paraguay's celebration of this popular Latin American festival is liveliest in

Asunción, Encarnación, Ciudad del Este, Caacupé, and Villarrica
1 March
  Cerro Corá (Death of Mariscal Francisco Solano López) – commemorates the War of the Triple Alliance in the 1860s
March/April (dates vary)
  Viernes Santo/Pascua (Good Friday/Easter)
1 May
  Día de los Trabajadores (Labor Day)
15 May
  Independencia Patria (Independence Day)
12 June
  Paz del Chaco (End of Chaco War)
15 August
  Fundación de Asunción (Founding of Asunción)
29 September
  Victoria de Boquerón (Battle of Boquerón) – commemorating the Chaco War of the 1930s
8 December
  Día de la Virgen (Immaculate Conception) – the religious center of Caacupé is the most important site for this widespread Roman Catholic holiday
25 December
  Navidad (Christmas Day)

FOOD

Paraguayan food resembles in some aspects that of Argentina and Uruguay, but differs in others. Meat consumption is much lower than in either of the other River Plate republics, although *parrillada* (grilled meat) is still a restaurant standard. Tropical and subtropical foodstuffs, with their origins in the country's Guaraní heritage, play a much greater role in the Paraguayan diet.

Grain, particularly maize, and tubers such as *mandioca* (manioc or cassava) are part of almost every meal. *Locro* is a maize stew resembling its Argentine namesake, while *mazamorra* is a corn mush. *Sopa paraguaya,* the national dish and a dietary staple, is not soup but rather a cornbread with cheese and onion. *Chipa guazú,* a recommended choice, is a variant of sopa paraguaya – it's a sort of cheese soufflé. *Mbaipy so-ó* is a hot maize pudding with chunks of meat, while *bori-bori* is a chicken soup with cornmeal balls. *Sooyo sopy* is a thick soup of ground meat, accompanied by rice or noodles. *Mbaipy he-é* is a dessert of corn, milk, and molasses.

Manioc dishes are the province of the rural poor, since the crop yields abundantly on poor to mediocre soils. *Chipa de almidón* resembles chipa guazú, but manioc flour dominates instead of cornmeal. *Mbeyú,* also known as *torta de almidón,* is a plain grilled manioc pancake that in some ways resembles the Mexican tortilla. During Holy Week, the addition of eggs, cheese, and spices transforms ordinary food into a holiday treat.

Paraguay may be the best place in South America, other than the Guianas, to sample a variety of Asian food – Chinese, Korean, and Japanese – after a wave of immigration over the past decade. It certainly has the widest selection of any Spanish-speaking country on the continent.

DRINKS
Like Argentines and Uruguayans, Paraguayans consume enormous amounts of *mate,* but do it more commonly in the form of *tereré,* served refreshingly ice cold in the withering summer heat. A common story says that tereré became popular among soldiers during the Chaco War, when it was used to filter the region's muddy water, but as early as the 18th century, a Jesuit father noted that mate "assuages both hunger and thirst, especially if … drunk with cold water without sugar."

Throughout eastern Paraguay, roadside stands offer *mosto* – sugar-cane juice. *Caña,* cane alcohol, is a popular alcoholic beverage.

ENTERTAINMENT
Cinema and live theater are popular in Asunción, and the capital's cultural life is much livelier since the overthrow of Stroessner.

SPECTATOR SPORTS
As elsewhere, soccer is the most popular spectator and participant sport: Asunción's most popular team, Olímpico, is competitive with the best Argentine and Uruguayan sides.

THINGS TO BUY
Paraguay's most well-known handicraft is its ñandutí lace, which ranges in size from doilies to bedspreads. The women of Itauguá, a village east of Asunción, are the best-known weavers. In the town of Luque, artisans produce stunningly beautiful handmade musical instruments, particularly guitars and harps, for surprisingly reasonable prices.

Paraguayan leather goods are excellent, and bargains are more readily available than in either Argentina or Uruguay. Chaco Indians produce carvings of animals from the aromatic wood of the palo santo, replicas of spears and other weapons, and traditional string bags *(yiscas).*

Asunción and Ciudad del Este are good places to look for electronics, particularly to replace a lost or stolen camera. The selection is not so great as the *zona franca* (free zone) of Iquique, Chile, but prices are very reasonable.

Getting There & Away

Paraguay is a hub of sorts for Southern Cone air traffic, but overland travelers to destinations other than Iguazú Falls and Posadas will find it a bit out of the way. There is a difficult but intriguing and increasingly popular land crossing from Bolivia.

AIR
To/From the USA
Now owned by the Ecuadorena airline Saeta, Líneas Aéreas Paraguayas (Lapsa or Air Paraguay) is the successor to the former state-owned enterprise of the same name; it has traditionally been a discount carrier, but fares no longer differ from those of other IATA (International Air Transport Association) airlines. It has flights from Miami to Asunción Wednesday and Friday, with connections to Río de Janeiro, São Paulo, Buenos Aires, Montevideo, and Santiago de Chile.

American Airlines flies daily from New York and Miami via São Paulo, while Lloyd Aéreo Boliviano (LAB) has Sunday, Thursday, and Saturday flights from Miami via Santa Cruz (Bolivia).

To/From Canada
Canadian Airlines International flies Wednesday, Friday, and Sunday from Toronto to São Paulo, making a convenient Asunción connection with Varig.

To/From UK & Europe
Lapsa has at least temporarily discontinued flights to Europe, but several European airlines have services to and from the continent. Lufthansa has the highest number of flights, which are from Frankfurt via Rio de Janeiro, São Paulo, or Buenos Aires. Air France flies three times weekly to Asunción via São Paulo, while Alitalia has services from Milan and Rome via São Paulo or Buenos Aires.

Iberia flies daily from Madrid via Buenos Aires, but most of its flights require a change to Aerolíneas Argentinas at Ezeiza. British Airways flights from Heathrow also connect with Aerolíneas Argentinas at Ezeiza.

To/From Neighboring Countries
Lapsa flies to Buenos Aires daily; to São Paulo Monday, Wednesday, Thursday, Friday, and Saturday; and to Santa Cruz (Bolivia) Saturday, continuing to Quito. Lloyd Aéreo Boliviano also flies to Santa Cruz Tuesday, Friday, and Sunday, with onward connections in Bolivia and elsewhere. Aeroperú also flies to Santa Cruz and onward to Lima.

Aerolíneas Argentinas flies at least daily to Asunción from Ezeiza, while Lufthansa, Varig, Alitalia, Canadian Airlines International, and American Airlines fly to and from São Paulo.

To/From Other South American Countries
Lapsa and Pluna (Uruguay's national carrier) fly between Asunción and Montevideo, with some Pluna flights going directly to Punta del Este. Lapsa flies to Santiago, Chile, five times weekly, while Ladeco does so seven times weekly, sometimes via Iquique in northern Chile. The new Chilean discount carrier National Airlines now flies between Asunción and Santiago and also to Iquique. Lapsa connects Asunción with Lima, Quito, and Guayaquil.

LAND
Paraguay's relatively few overland crossings underscore the country's geographical isolation. There are only three legal border crossings from Argentina, two from Brazil, and one from Bolivia.

To/From Argentina

There are two direct border crossings between Paraguay and Argentina, plus one requiring a brief detour through Brazil. If the corruption-plagued Yacyretá hydroelectric project on the Río Paraná is ever completed, another will open from Ayolas to Ituzaingó via a bridge over the top of the dam.

Asunción to Clorinda There is frequent bus service via the Puente Internacional Ignacio de Loyola between Asunción and Clorinda, in the Argentine province of Formosa, which is renowned for ferocious customs checks.

Encarnación to Posadas Frequent bus service across the Paraná has facilitated this crossing on the new Puente Internacional Beato Roque González to Posadas, in the Argentine province of Misiones. It is still possible to take a launch between the river docks, at least until the Yacyretá Dam floods the low-lying parts of both cities.

Ciudad del Este to Puerto Iguazú Frequent buses connect Ciudad del Este (ex-Puerto Presidente Stroessner) to the Brazilian city of Foz do Iguaçu, with easy connections to Puerto Iguazú in the Argentine province of Misiones. Alternatively, you can cross by launch from Puerto Presidente Franco, a few kilometers south of Ciudad del Este, directly to Puerto Iguazú across the Paraná without passing through Brazil.

To/From Brazil

Ciudad del Este to Foz do Iguaçu This is the most frequently used overland border crossing between the two countries. Vehicles and pedestrian traffic move freely across the Puente de la Amistad (Friendship Bridge) that connects the two cities across the Paraná. If you plan to spend more than a day in either country, be sure to complete the immigration procedures.

Pedro Juan Caballero to Ponta Porã Pedro Juan Caballero is a small town on the Paraguayan/Brazilian border, while Ponta Porã is its Brazilian counterpart. Each town has a consulate of the neighboring country. There is a regular bus service from Asunción to Pedro Juan Caballero, to which Ruta 5 is being paved. From the Brazilian city of Campo Grande, there are several buses and two trains daily.

To/From Bolivia

This has been one of the most difficult overland border crossings in South America, lacking regular public transport between Estancia La Patria, on the Ruta Trans-Chaco, 85 km from the border, and the Bolivian town of Boyuibe, a further 135 km west. Recently, however, Stel Turismo and Yacyretá have begun an experimental bus service to the Bolivian city of Santa Cruz de la Sierra. Beyond Filadelfia, the dirt road is subject to long delays in the event of heavy, if infrequent, rains.

In the absence of a bus, there are countless military checkpoints where you can wait for days in the hope of catching a truck across the border. One alternative is the Nasa bus from Asunción to Estancia La Patria, although Mariscal Estigarribia, where there is lodging, food, and a petrol station, would be a more comfortable place to wait.

RIVER

This is not a conventional means of travel to Paraguay, but it is possible. In winter, there are occasional tour boats from Buenos Aires to Asunción, although there is no ordinary passenger service. From Asunción, the Flota Mercante del Estado (State Merchant Fleet) no longer carries passengers on its irregular sailings to and from the Brazilian city of Corumbá, but Cruceros SRL (☎ /fax 445-098), 14 de Mayo 150, Asunción, has taken up some of the slack with improved upriver services. For details, see the chapter on Asunción.

DEPARTURE TAX

Paraguay collects a departure tax of US$15 for international flights from Asunción's Aeropuerto Silvio Pettirossi.

PARAGUAY

TOURS

Intertours (☎ 211-747), Perú 436, Asunción, is Paraguay's largest and most experienced tour operator, offering brief or extended excursions to Asunción and its surroundings, the Jesuit mission area around Encarnación, and the Iguazú Falls of Brazil and Argentina.

Outside Asunción, organized tourism is in its infancy and logistics are difficult, but Intertour's Natur (☎ 27804, fax 211-870), at the same address, arranges trips of greater or lesser duration to the Chaco, Parque Nacional Ybycuí, Lago Ypacaraí, and other destinations. Per person rates range from US$35 for day trips to easily accessible destinations like Ypacaraí and the more accessible parts of the Chaco to US$230 for four-day, three-night excursions. All trips include an English-speaking guide, and there are also specialized 10- to 20-day trips emphasizing birds, vegetation, insect life, butterflies, and environmental education.

Getting Around

Public transport in Paraguay is generally cheap and efficient, if not always quite so comfortable as in Argentina or Uruguay.

AIR

Domestic air services are limited. Lapsa has only international flights, but the new private carriers Ladesa and Arpa serve Pedro Juan Caballero, Ciudad del Este, and Encarnación. Líneas Aéreas de Transporte Nacional (LATN) and Transporte Aéreo Militar (TAM), the air force's passenger service, fly to a very few isolated parts of the Chaco. Domestic fares are now expensive; a roundtrip from Asunción to Pedro Juan Caballero costs around US$180, for example. For further details, see the appropriate geographical sections.

BUS

The quality of Paraguayan bus services varies considerably, depending on whether you take *servicio removido,* which makes flag stops, or *servicio directo,* which stops only at fixed locations in each city or town. Other common terms are *regular* (buses that stop at every shady spot along the highway), *común* (a basic bus that stops in only a limited number of places), and *ejecutivo* (a faster deluxe bus with toilets, tea and coffee service, and other facilities).

Larger Paraguayan cities have central bus terminals, but in those cities that do not, bus companies are within easy walking distance of one another, usually around the central plaza.

Buses run very frequently to destinations all around the country, and only on or near holidays should reservations be necessary. Fares are very reasonable – for example, Asunción to Filadelfia, a distance of about 450 km, costs only about US$10 removido or US$13 directo.

TRAIN

Paraguay's antique, wood-burning trains are more interesting than practical. Visitors to Asunción should not miss the short ride to Areguá, on the shores of Lago Ypacaraí, but it's basically a day excursion.

CAR

Unfortunately, Paraguayans appear to be taking driving lessons from their Argentine neighbors, with all the highway hazards that implies – like high-speed tailgating and passing on blind curves. Driving in Paraguay also presents some problems that are less common to Argentina and Uruguay, most notably the presence of high-wheeled wooden oxcarts and livestock on the road. For the most part, carts stick to tracks that parallel the highway, but on occasion they must cross. Everywhere in the country, but especially in the Chaco, watch for cattle on the road. Such hazards make driving at night inadvisable.

Paraguay formally requires the International Driving Permit, in addition to a state or national driver's license, but cars with foreign number plates are rarely stopped except at military checkpoints in the Chaco. Car theft is very common in Paraguay, and many so-called *mau* vehicles are "imported" illegally from Argentina and Brazil, with authorities turning a blind eye. If your vehicle is conspicuous, be especially certain it is secure.

Operating a car in Paraguay is more economical than in either Argentina or Uruguay because the price of super petrol, at about US45¢ per liter, is about half that in Argentina. There has also been a flood of cheap spares – if you need to purchase tires, for example, Asunción is the place to do so. If you need repairs, Paraguayan mechanics are very competent, and labor is much cheaper than in Argentina.

The Touring y Automóvil Club Paraguayo (☎ 210-550, 210-253), on Calle Brasil between Cerro Corá and 25 de Mayo, Asunción, is the equivalent of

Argentina's ACA. Though less widespread than ACA, they are nonetheless friendly and helpful.

BOAT

Cruceros SRL (☎ 445-098), 14 de Mayo 150, Asunción, operates passenger services up the Río Paraguay to Concepción and other river ports, as far as Corumbá, Brazil. For more details, see the Asunción chapter.

LOCAL TRANSPORTATION
To/From the Airport

Except in Asunción, air travel is infrequent in Paraguay, but Asunción city buses go to Aeropuerto Silvio Pettirossi. For details, see the chapter on Asunción. Lapsa and TAM run airport buses for their own passengers, while the taxi fare is about US$10.

Bus & Tram

Asunción has an extensive public transport system, but late-night buses are less frequent than in Buenos Aires. As in Argentina, the driver or conductor will ask your destination. Retain your ticket, since an inspector may check it. The standard fare is about US30¢.

Buses to Asunción suburbs like San Lorenzo, Villa Hayes, and Areguá leave from downtown as well as from the bus terminal.

Taxi

Cabs in Paraguay operate on the basis of direct meter readings. Fares are slightly cheaper than Argentina and Uruguay, but after midnight drivers are likely to levy a surcharge. There is often a small surcharge for luggage as well.

Asunción

From its central location on the Río Paraguay, Asunción has always been the landlocked country's link to the outside world and the pivot of its political, economic, and cultural life. Even though only about 20% of the country's population lives in the capital and its suburbs, most of the remainder lives within about 150 km. Unlike Buenos Aires and other Latin American metropolises, Asunción has sprouted relatively few skyscrapers, so the sun still reaches the sidewalks of narrow downtown streets – a mixed blessing in summer's overpowering heat, which is relieved only by shady plazas and streets. Although Asunción has some industry on its outskirts, mostly the processing of agricultural materials, its economy is really administrative and commercial.

HISTORY

Asunción was founded in 1537 by Juan de Salazar, an officer from Mendoza's failed colony at Buenos Aires. Early Spaniards were attracted to its abundant food supplies and the hospitable Guaraní. By 1541, its European population was about 600, and for more than 40 years, until the refounding of Buenos Aires in 1580, it was the most important settlement in the River Plate region. Spaniards initially expected Asunción to be the gateway to Perú, but the hot, dry Chaco, with its many hostile Indians, proved to be an insuperable barrier to travel, and it was superseded by the route down the eastern side of the Andes to Salta, Tucumán, Córdoba, and Buenos Aires.

By European standards, colonial Asunción was a stagnant backwater. The Austrian Jesuit missionary Martin Dobrizhoffer, visiting in the mid-18th century, was not impressed with either the city or its society:

Neither splendid edifices nor city fortifications are here to be found. Many of the houses are of stone or brick, and roofed with tiles, but none of them are above one story high. The monasteries are nearly of the same description, possessing nothing by which you could recognise the church. The streets are crooked, and impeded with ditches and stones thrown out of their places, to the imminent peril of both men and horses. It has but one market-place, and that covered with grass. The governor and bishop have resided here since the time of Charles V, though neither has any proper seat . . . . Even matrons of the higher rank, boys, girls, and all the lower orders speak Guarany, though the generality have some acquaintance with Spanish. To say the truth, they mingle both, and speak neither correctly . . . . The Spanish miserably corrupted the Indian, and the Indian the Spanish language.

After independence in 1811, little changed during the isolationist dictatorship of Francia. Englishman JP Robertson, during a visit near the end of Francia's rule, also saw the capital through European eyes, but thought more highly of its residents:

In extent, architecture, convenience, or population, it does not rank with a fifth-rate town in England . . . . Its government-house, with the title of palace, is a mean, low, whitewashed, though extensive structure. Its largest buildings – though anything but sumptuous – are the convents . . . while the great bulk of the dwellings were simple huts, constituting narrow lanes, or standing apart, surrounded by a few orange-trees. There could not be said to be more than one street in the town, and that was unpaved . . . .

The inhabitants of Assumption and its suburbs amounted . . . to ten thousand . . . . The great bulk of the population was of a breed between Spaniards and Indians, so attenuated . . . as to give the natives the air and appearance of descendants from Europeans. The men were generally well made and athletic; the women almost invariably pretty.

Only with Francia's death in 1840 did Asunción's isolation end, as Carlos Antonio López opened the country to foreign influence and nearly obliterated all colonial remains in the process. López and his son, Francisco Solano López, built Asunción's major public buildings, including the Palacio de Gobierno (once intended as Francisco Solano López's residence, now housing the Congress), the Panteón de los Héroes, the train station, and an opera house modeled on La Scala (now the internal revenue building). But Francisco Solano López effectively ended this brief era of material progress by foolishly plunging Paraguay into the War of the Triple Alliance.

Ten years after the war, in 1880, a British journalist commented that these López family legacies were nothing more than "extravagant luxuries" that stuck out like sore thumbs among their surroundings:

These ruins of past greatness, glaring at the wretched buildings all around, looking down on the poverty-stricken people that wander under their rumbling pillars, tottering arcades, and dangling rafters, are unique. They are not grand, rather the reverse, but they must have appeared colossal to a people living in primitive dwellings.

Public improvements were indeed slow to come in the capital. Well into the 20th century, much of central Asunción went unpaved, although from 1873 a horse-drawn tramway, later upgraded to a steam locomotive, operated into Villa Morra and the northeast of the city. As European immigrants trickled in, the city gradually improved its appearance and developed exclusive residential suburbs to the east.

The Chaco War of the 1930s further retarded progress, but the city has since sprawled to encompass ever more distant areas, such as the university center of San Lorenzo. In recent decades, there has been a minor boom in high-rise downtown office and hotel construction, but the city still retains much of its 19th-century structure, with low buildings lining narrow streets. At the same time, the influx of people from the impoverished countryside has resulted in enormous shantytowns along the riverfront, the railway, or anywhere else there happens to be a vacant lot.

ORIENTATION

Asunción sits on a bluff above the east bank of the Río Paraguay. Like most colonial cities, it features a conventional grid pattern, refashioned by the irregularities of a riverside location, a slightly hilly topography, and some modern developments. Like Buenos Aires and Montevideo, the city consists of numerous barrios, but most key sights, as well as inexpensive hotels and restaurants, are located within an area bounded by the riverfront, Av Colón in the west, Haedo and Luis A Herrera in the south, and Estados Unidos to the east. There are few colonial remains.

The city center is Plaza de los Héroes, bounded by Independencia Nacional to the east, Palma to the north side, Chile to the west, and Oliva to the south. Street names change on either side of Independencia Nacional. The city's commercial and financial institutions are concentrated along Palma and its eastward extension, Mariscal Estigarribia; from Plaza de los Héroes to Plaza Uruguaya, Palma and Mariscal Estigarribia are being redeveloped as a pedestrian walk.

Plaza Uruguaya is bounded by Eligio Ayala to the north, México to the west, 25 de Mayo to the south, and Antequera to the east (do not confuse Eligio Ayala with Eusebio Ayala, a major arterial leading east out of town). Although Plaza Uruguaya is an attractive, shady refuge from the midday heat, prostitutes frequent the area at night and single women will probably prefer to avoid it.

To the north, along the riverfront, irregular Plaza Constitución is bounded by Independencia Nacional to the east, El Paraguayo Independiente to the south, and 14 de Mayo to the west. It contains the Palacio Legislativo, but below the bluff, subject to flooding, lie the so-called *viviendas temporarias,* Paraguay's shantytown counterpart of Argentina's *villas miserias.* El Paraguayo Independiente, a diagonal, leads west to the Palacio de Gobierno, the presidential palace.

Asunción's most prestigious residential areas are east of downtown, out Avs España and Mariscal López toward Aeropuerto Silvio Pettirossi (ex-Aeropuerto Presidente Stroessner). Most of the capital's embassies and its best restaurants are here, in barrios like Recoleta and Villa Morra. Northeast of downtown, at the end of Av Artigas, the Jardín Botánico was once the López family estate and is now the city's largest open space, a popular site for weekend outings.

INFORMATION
Tourist Offices

The Dirección de Turismo (☎ 441-530, 441-620), Palma 468 between Alberdi and 14 de Mayo, is friendly but not especially knowledgeable or helpful. It has a good city center map/brochure and several looseleaf notebooks full of tourist information you can consult. It's open weekdays from 7 am to 7 pm and Saturday from 8 am to noon. There's a satellite office at the bus terminal.

The Touring y Automóvil Club Paraguayo (☎ 210-550, 210-553), on Brasil between Cerro Corá and 25 de Mayo, sells the *Guía Shell* and its accompanying maps at a discount to its own members and those of affiliated overseas clubs. It's happy to provide other member services as well.

For more detailed maps, visit the Dirección del Servicio Geográfico Militar (☎ 206-344), Av Artigas 920 at Perú.

Foreign Consulates

For information on foreign diplomatic missions, see the Paraguay Facts for the Visitor chapter.

Immigration

The Dirección de Migraciones (☎ 493-646) is at the corner of O'Leary and General Díaz, 1st floor.

Money

Cambios Guaraní is at Palma 449, but there are several other exchange houses on Palma and nearby side streets: Internacional Cambios (which does not insist on bill of sale for cashing traveler's checks) is at Palma 364, Yguazú Cambios at Palma

547, and Banco Amambay at the corner of Estrella and 14 de Mayo. The only ATM that seems to function with a foreign credit card is at Banco Unión, at the corner of Alberdi and Estrella, which is linked to the Cirrus system. Banco Unión will also give advances on Visa and MasterCard.

The information desk at the bus terminal will change US dollars and Argentine or Uruguayan pesos into guaraníes, but there are reports of poor rates. There are also moneychangers with name tags near ticket offices on the 2nd floor of the terminal.

Post & Telecommunications

The Correo Central (main post office), at the corner of Alberdi and El Paraguayo Independiente, is open weekdays from 7:30 am to noon and 2:30 to 7:30 pm, Saturday from 8 am to 1 pm. It also has an attractive patio garden, a museum (worthwhile if you're already in the building or nearby), and good views of downtown Asunción from the roof.

Antelco, at the corner of 14 de Mayo and General Díaz, has direct fiber-optic lines to connect with operators in the USA (ATT, MCI, Sprint), Britain, Australia, Germany, Argentina, Uruguay, Brazil, and Japan for collect or credit card calls. There is another office, much less state-of-the-art, at the bus terminal. Asunción's area code is 021.

Cultural Centers

Asunción's several international cultural centers offer artistic and photographic exhibitions, as well as films, at little or no cost. These include the Casa de la Cultura Paraguaya (ex-Colegio Militar) at the corner of 14 de Mayo and El Paraguayo Independiente; the Centro Juan de Salazar (☎ 449-221) at Luis A Herrera 834; the Centro Anglo-Paraguayo (☎ 25525) at Av España 457; the Alianza Francesa (☎ 210-382) at Mariscal Estigarribia 1039; the Instituto Cultural Paraguayo Alemán (☎ 26242) at Juan de Salazar 310, off Av España; and the Centro Cultural Paraguayo-Japonés (☎ 661-914) at the corner of Julio Correa and Portillo in Barrio San Miguel, near Av Santísima

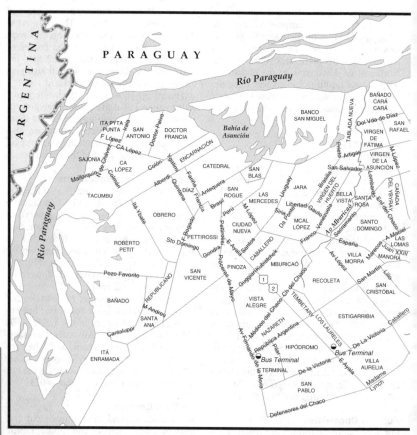

Trinidad. The Centro Cultural Paraguayo-Americano, Av España 352, has American books, magazines, videos, and a small café.

Travel Agencies

Asunción has a multitude of downtown travel agencies, such as Exprinter (☎ 444-639) at 25 de Mayo 135, Guaraní Turismo (☎ 448-379) at Palma 449, and the Mennonite-operated Menno Travel (☎ 441-210) at Azara 532, an especially good source for information on the Chaco. Paula Braun at Paula's Tours (☎ 446-021), Cerro Corá 795, is an English-speaking Mennonite travel agent. Americana Tours (☎ 490-

672), Alberdi 517, also has English-speaking staff.

American Express (☎ 490-111), in the Edificio Inter-Express at Yegros 690, gives poor rates for traveler's checks.

Bookstores

Librería Comuneros, Cerro Corá 289, offers a good selection of historical and contemporary books on Paraguay. Another good shop is Librería Internacional, Caballero 270, next to the Chaco Hotel. There are interesting open-air bookstalls on Plaza Uruguay.

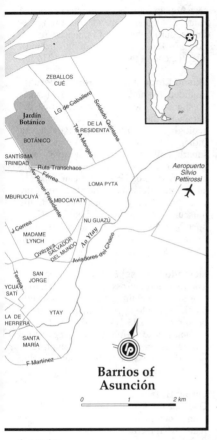

**Barrios of
Asunción**

0   1   2 km

and a number of respectable museums, most of which keep erratic opening hours – it's better to phone before visiting, unless you're already in the area.

Begun in 1860 but not completed until 1892, the **Palacio de Gobierno** (presidential palace) on El Paraguayo Independiente between Ayolas and Juan O'Leary was intended as a residence for Francisco Solano López, who died in the War of the Triple Alliance. It is safe to approach it for photographs, at least since the ousting of Stroessner, who apparently followed the precedent of his 19th-century counterpart Francia – according to JR Robertson, El Supremo once ordered that "every person observed gazing at the front of his palace should be shot in the act." A flag ceremony takes place daily at sunset.

One of the few colonial buildings to survive the Francia years, the restored **Casa Viola** (1750), across the street at Ayolas and El Paraguayo Independiente, is now a cultural center, open weekdays from 8 am to 9 pm, and weekends from 10 am to 8 pm. It presents art exhibitions, distributes a free calendar of events, and houses a cafe and the **Museo Memoria de la Ciudad**, chronicling Asunción's urban development. Two blocks east, at 14 de Mayo, the **Casa de Cultura Paraguaya** is a remnant of late Jesuit times that most recently served as the Colegio Militar. Overlooking the river, on Plaza Constitución at the foot of Alberdi, the **Palacio Legislativo,** begun in 1844 and completed in 1857, is home to both houses of the legislature.

At the east end of Plaza Constitución is the neoclassical **Catedral Metropolitana** (1845), whose **Museo del Tesoro de la Catedral** is open daily from 8 to 11 am except Sundays. South of Plaza Constitución, on Alberdi between El Paraguayo Independiente and Benjamín Constant, the turn-of-the-century **Edificio de Correos** is the central post office and also the site of the **Museo Postal Telegráfico.** At the corner of Alberdi and Presidente Franco, the **Teatro Municipal** (1893) sits on the foundations of an earlier theater that faced the river. One block west, at the corner of

Laundry

Laverap is downtown at Hernandarias 636 and at Presidente Franco 661. There's also a convenient laundry at the rear of Hotel Stella d'Italia, Cerro Corá 933.

Medical Services

Asunción's Hospital de Clínicas (☎ 80982) is at the corner of Av Dr J Montero and Lagerenza, about one km west of downtown.

WALKING TOUR

Asunción's compact downtown has a handful of remaining colonial buildings

Presidente Franco and 14 de Mayo, Paraguayans declared independence in 1811 at the **Casa de la Independencia** (1772), which also has a museum (☎ 493-918).

On the Plaza de los Héroes, at the corner of Chile and Calle Palma, the **Panteón de los Héroes** is a public mausoleum for the country's greatest military figures (see separate entry below), several of whom led the country into disastrous wars. Four blocks east, the small and disappointing **Museo de Bellas Artes** (☎ 447-716), on the corner of Iturbe and Mariscal Estigarribia, is open weekdays from 8 am to noon. Next door, the **Archivo Nacional** has fabulous woodwork and an interesting spiral staircase. At the foot of Iturbe are the remains of the **Cárcel Pública**, one of the dungeons in which Doctor Francia kept political enemies such as Pedro Juan Caballero, who committed suicide here. Two blocks east, on the north side of Plaza Uruguaya, the British-built **Estación Ferrocarril Central** dates from 1856 and displays antique steam locomotives, some of which still function on the short line to Areguá. The building served as a hospital during the Chaco War with Bolivia.

Political activists with a macabre sense of history may want to visit the site of the assassination of former Nicaraguan dictator Anastasio Somoza, on Av España between América and Venezuela. Interestingly and perhaps fittingly, this segment of Av España is officially "Generalísimo Franco," perhaps the only street in Latin America named for the late Spanish dictator. The name itself may fall victim to the de-Stroessnerization process, since most people prefer and continue to use "Avenida España."

THINGS TO SEE
Panteón de Los Héroes
On the Plaza de los Héroes, at the corner of Chile and Calle Palma, a somber honor guard protects the remains of Carlos Antonio López, his son Francisco Solano López, Bernardino Caballero, José Félix Estigarribia, and other key figures (it's difficult to call most of them heroes) of Paraguay's

catastrophic wars. Work commenced on the Panteón, originally intended as a religious shrine, during the rule of Francisco Solano López in 1863, but it was not finished until after the end of the Chaco War in 1936.

Museo Etnográfico Andrés Barbero
Founded by and named for the former president of the Sociedad Científica del Paraguay, this anthropological and archaeological museum displays Paraguayan Indian tools, ceramics, weavings, and a superb collection of photographs, with good maps to indicate where everything comes from. For US$2, you can purchase an excellent illustrated guide to accompany your tour. One of Asunción's best, the museum (☎ 41696), Av España 217, is open Monday through Thursday from 8 am to 11 am and 3 to 5:30 pm. The museum library keeps slightly different hours.

Mercado Petrossi & Mercado Cuatro
The Mercado Petrossi is a lively Saturday morning market lining both sides of several blocks east along Av Pettirossi from its beginning at Calle Brasil. It deserves a visit, but don't make the mistake of trying to drive through it or, even worse, attempting to park. Farther east, at Pettirossi and Eusebio Ayala, is the similar Mercado Cuatro.

Jardín Botánico
Once the estate of the López family, Asunción's botanical gardens are no longer really what the name implies, but they are the city's largest open space and a popular area for weekend outings. The park contains a rather pathetic zoo (home to exotic rather than Paraguayan species), is the site of the municipal campground, and is also home to the displaced Maká Indians of the Chaco, for whose plight no one seems to take responsibility. Attendants collect a modest admission charge at the entrance to the gardens, at the corner of Av Artigas and Av Primer Presidente, near the house where Uruguayan independence hero José Artigas spent his later years in exile.

Within the park, the **Museo de Historia Natural** (☎ 290-172) is a vintage building housing an impressive collection of specimens, but the exhibits are poorly labeled and displayed, with no attempt to place them in any ecological context. The collection is worth seeing for the spectacular display of insects – one butterfly has a wingspan of 274 mm – but some visitors may find the variety of bugs outdoors nearly as impressive. The museum is open Monday to Saturday from 7:30 to 11:30 am and 1 to 5 pm, Sunday and holidays from 8 am to 1 pm.

From downtown, the most direct bus to the gardens is the No 44 ("Artigas") from the corner of Oliva and 15 de Agosto, which goes directly to the gates. Or take Nos 23 or 35.

Museo del Barro

Asunción's foremost modern art museum, in the newly developed area of Isla de Francia, displays some very unconventional work, but there are also other interesting exhibits from the 18th century to the present, including political caricatures of prominent Paraguayans. The Museo del Barro (☎ 607-996) is open daily from 4 to 8:30 pm except Sunday.

To get there, take any No 30 bus beyond the end of Av San Martín out Av Aviadores del Chaco and look for the prominent sign – otherwise it's difficult to locate. It occupies a new facility at Callejón Cañada and Calle 1, just off Av Aviadores del Chaco; ask the driver to drop you at Av Molas López.

Museo Boggiani

From 1887 to the turn of the century, Italian ethnographer Guido Boggiani conducted fieldwork among the Chamacoco Indians of the upper Río Paraguay. After he declined to marry a Chamacoco woman, the group, fearing that he would live with another faction of their tribe or with their traditional enemies, the Caduveo, killed him.

Before his death, Boggiani sent some of his impressive collection of feather art to the Museum für Volkerkunde in Berlin; part of it remains on exhibit in this new and well-organized museum (☎ 584-717),

Coronel Bogado 888 in the suburb of San Lorenzo. The museum, which is in the process of expansion, is open Tuesday to Saturday from 10 am to noon and from 3 to 6 pm, and it's well worth the 45-minute bus ride from downtown out Av Mariscal López on Línea 27. Artisanal items are available.

San Lorenzo also has a noteworthy Gothic-style cathedral.

Art Galleries

In addition to the cultural centers and museums listed above, Asunción's arts community displays its work in numerous private galleries, among them Artesanos (☎ 27853) at Cerro Corá and 22 de Setiembre; Fábrica (☎ 204-081) at Mariscal Estigarribia 1384; Belmarco (☎ 23361) at Brasil 265; the Sala Agustín Barrios (☎ 24831) at Av España 532; Forum Galería (☎ 204-491) at Eligio Ayala 1184; Pequeña Galería (☎ 603-177), Local 39 in the Shopping Center de Villa Morra at Mariscal López and De Gaulle; Liliana Boccia (☎ 23518) at 25 de Mayo 1316; and Cristina Osnaghi-Atelier (☎ 491-348) at Manduvirá 120. La Dirección de Turismo distributes a complete list.

ORGANIZED TOURS

For city tours during the day or night, as well as excursions to outlying areas such as San Bernardino, the Cataratas del Iguazú (Iguazú Falls), and the Jesuit missions, contact Lions Tur (☎ 490-591), Alberdi 454. Some travelers consider its seven-hour circuito central tour overpriced at $45, but it includes a good buffet at San Bernardino.

For environmentally oriented tours, contact English-speaking Carlos (Charlie) Sandoval at Intertours' Natur (☎ 27804, 211-747; fax 211-870), Perú 436 near Av España; for more information, see the Tours entry in the Getting There & Away chapter for Paraguay.

PLACES TO STAY

Asunción has an abundance of inexpensive accommodations, much of it Korean-owned after heavy immigration over the past decade or so. Most of these hotels are

PLACES TO STAY
2 Residencial Ambassador
3 Hotel América
22 Residencial Jacarandá
33 Hotel Embajador
34 Ñandutí Hotel
46 Chaco Hotel
47 Plaza Hotel
56 Hotel Cecilia
65 Hotel de la Paz
67 Hotel Asunción Palace
68 Hotel Sahara
69 Hotel Zaphir
71 Hotel Palma
72 Hotel Continental
76 Gran Hotel Renacimiento
82 Hotel Nueva Aurora
83 Gran Hotel Paraná
84 Hotel Miami
88 Hotel Stella d'Italia
91 Hotel Internacional
94 Hotel España
105 Hotel Guaraní
107 Hotel Hispania
110 Hotel Amigo
112 Hotel Lord
115 Residencial La Española
116 Residencial Siria
119 Residencial Antequera
120 Hospedaje Oasis
121 Hotel Azara
124 Hotel Itapúa
127 Hotel Amalfi
131 Hotel Excelsior
132 Hotel Manduvirá Plaza
135 Residencial Notre Dame
138 Hotel Tayí

PLACES TO EAT
14 Confitería El Molino
19 Il Capo
20 La Pérgola Jardín
26 Anahi
31 Periplö
37 Confitería El Molino
41 Lido Bar
42 Munich
43 4-D
53 Talleyrand
54 Rincón Chileno
57 La Preferida
58 Café San Francisco
62 Buon Appetito
66 Don Vito, Copetín Immanuel
86 Gasthaus Arche Noah
87 Vieja Bavaria
92 Taberna El Antojo
117 Nick's
123 Celestial
125 Sukiyaki
128 La Flor de Canela
133 Sugar's

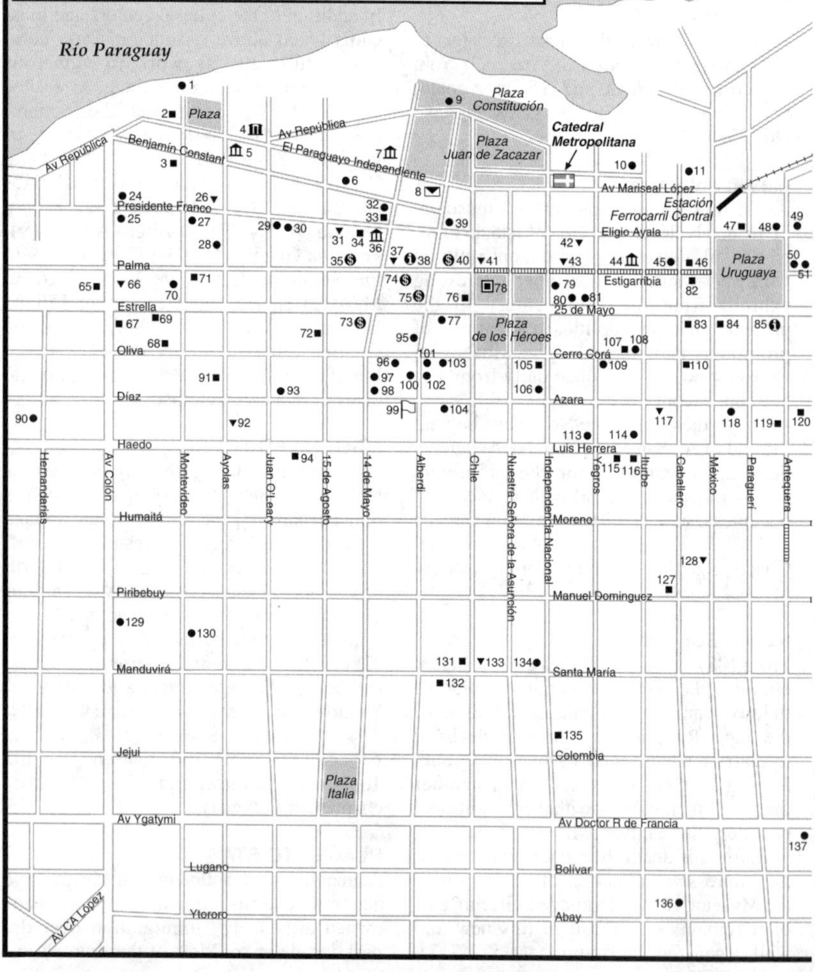

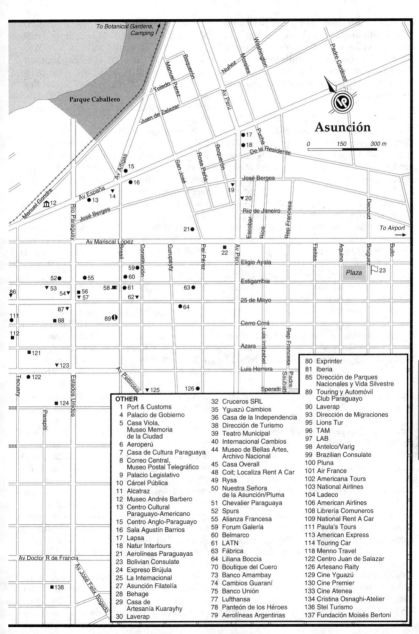

Asunción

0   150   300 m

Parque Caballero

To Botanical Gardens, Camping

To Airport

Plaza

PARAGUAY

OTHER

1 Port & Customs
4 Palacio de Gobierno
5 Casa Viola,
  Museo Memoria
  de la Ciudad
6 Aeroperú
7 Casa de Cultura Paraguaya
8 Correo Central,
  Museo Postal Telegráfico
9 Palacio Legislativo
10 Cárcel Pública
11 Alcatraz
12 Museo Andrés Barbero
13 Centro Cultural
   Paraguayo-Americano
15 Centro Anglo-Paraguayo
16 Sala Agustín Barrios
17 Lapsa
18 Natur Intertours
21 Aerolíneas Paraguayas
23 Bolivian Consulate
24 Expreso Brújula
25 La Internacional
27 Asunción Filatelía
28 Behage
29 Casa de
   Artesanía Kuarayhy
30 Laverap

32 Cruceros SRL
35 Yguazú Cambios
36 Casa de la Independencia
38 Dirección de Turismo
39 Teatro Municipal
40 Internacional Cambios
44 Museo de Bellas Artes,
   Archivo Nacional
45 Casa Overall
48 Coit; Localiza Rent A Car
49 Rysa
50 Nuestra Señora
   de la Asunción/Pluma
51 Chevalier Paraguaya
52 Spurs
55 Alianza Francesa
59 Forum Galería
60 Belmarco
61 LATN
63 Fábrica
64 Liliana Boccia
70 Boutique del Cuero
73 Banco Amambay
74 Cambios Guaraní
75 Banco Unión
77 Lufthansa
78 Panteón de los Héroes
79 Aerolíneas Argentinas

80 Exprinter
81 Iberia
85 Dirección de Parques
   Nacionales y Vida Silvestre
89 Touring y Automóvil
   Club Paraguayo
90 Laverap
93 Dirección de Migraciones
95 Lions Tur
96 TAM
97 LAB
98 Antelco/Varig
99 Brazilian Consulate
100 Pluna
101 Air France
102 Americana Tours
103 National Airlines
104 Ladeco
106 American Airlines
108 Librería Comuneros
109 National Rent A Car
111 Paula's Tours
113 American Express
114 Touring Car
118 Menno Travel
122 Centro Juan de Salazar
126 Artesano Raity
129 Cine Yguazú
130 Cine Premier
133 Cine Atenea
134 Cristina Osnaghi-Atelier
136 Stel Turismo
137 Fundación Moisés Bertoni

clean and basic, and quite a few have with air-conditioning, a welcome feature in steamy Asunción. Midrange hotels are often a very good value, while the best top-end places are superior to those in Montevideo but not quite the equal of those in Buenos Aires.

Places to Stay – bottom end

Camping Asunción's campground is in the shady Jardín Botánico, the city's botanical gardens, about five km from downtown. It is generally quiet and secure, and the staff are friendly, but the animals in the nearby zoo may keep you awake. There are luke-warm showers and adequate toilet facili-ties, but take care not to pitch your tent over an ant colony – their bites are painful. Bring mosquito repellent.

Fees are negligible at US25¢ per person plus US$1 per vehicle or tent, plus US25¢ per person for admission to the gardens. When returning to your site at night, tell the guard at the entrance on Av Artigas that you are staying in the campground.

From downtown, the most direct bus is the No 44 ("Artigas") from the corner of Oliva and 15 de Agosto. Or take Nos 23 or 35.

Hostel Affiliated with Hostelling Interna-tional, the new *Albergue Juvenil* is at 15 de Agosto 155, between Av República and El Paraguayo Independiente. Rates are US$6 per person. Another hostel is due to open on Presidente Franco between 14 de Mayo and 15 de Agosto.

Hospedajes, Residenciales & Hotels

Probably the cheapest acceptable lodging is *Residencial Ambassador* (☎ 445-901), Montevideo 110 at El Paraguayo Indepen-diente, just a stone's throw from the Palacio de Gobierno. For US$5 it's very basic and a bit musty, but it's friendly and has ceiling fans in most rooms. Up the block, at Mon-tevideo 160, *Hotel América* (☎ 493-251) has singles/doubles with shared bath for US$6/10, or singles with private bath for US$9.

Hotel Nueva Aurora (☎ 445-625), Mariscal Estigarribia 442, charges US$6 per person with shared bath, as does *Resi-dencial Notre Dame* (☎ 449-723), Indepen-dencia Nacional 1076. In the same range are *Hospedaje Oasis* at Azara 736 and *Res-idencial Antequera* at Antequera 630, both of which have received some negative reports.

Hotel Hispania (☎ 444-018), Cerro Corá 265, has been a popular budget alternative for years, with clean but rather gloomy downstairs rooms for US$5/7 with shared bath, US$7/10 with private bath; there are recent complaints of declining cleanliness, and noise from a nearby pub has disturbed some travelers. At *Hotel Lord* (☎ 446-087), Tacuary 576, rates are US$6 per person with shared bath, while *Hotel Palma* (☎ 490150), Palma 873, charges US$6/10 with shared bath. *Hotel Itapúa* (☎ 445-121), Moreno 943, costs about US$7/12, as does *Residencial Siria* (☎ 447-258), Luis A Herrera 166.

Korean-run *Hotel Amigo* (☎ 491-987), Caballero 521, charges US$10/14 for rooms with air-con, and it has a downstairs restaurant. Clean, friendly *Hotel Stella d'Italia* (☎ 448-731), a US Peace Corps hangout at Cerro Corá 933, charges US$11/15 with shared bath, a bit more with private bath. *Hotel Azara* (☎ 449-754), Azara 850, has singles/doubles with private bath, fridge, and air-con for US$13/17.

Clean and spacious, with high ceilings, *Hotel Embajador* (☎ 493-393) at Presi-dente Franco 514 has doubles with shared bath for US$13, with private bath for US$21. At recommended *Hotel Miami* (☎ 444-950), México 449, rates are US$13/20 with private bath, breakfast and air-con; take a room away from the busy front door. *Hotel Tayí* (☎ 490-147), Simón Bolívar 930, is a bit less central but away from the busy downtown area, and it costs US$10 per person.

If catching an early bus, you may prefer a place across from the terminal – try friendly and quiet *Hotel Familiar Yasy* (☎ 551-623), Fernando de la Mora 2390, which charges US$7 per person with private bath; next door is an anonymous restaurant with outstanding chicken empanadas.

Places to Stay – middle
The congenial *Ñandutí Hotel* (☎ 446-780), Presidente Franco 551, offers excellent value for US$13/20 with shared bath, US$17/25 with private bath. Opposite Plaza Uruguaya and next to the train station, the *Plaza Hotel* (☎ 444-772), Eligio Ayala 609, is clean, quiet, secure, and also friendly, with singles/doubles for US$15/22 with shared bath, US$23/30 with private bath.

Near the bus terminal, *Hotel 2000* (☎ 551-628), Fernando de la Mora 2332, charges US$15/26. *Residencial Jacarandá* (☎ 23861), Mariscal López 1458 at Perú, has spacious rooms for US$16/30 with private bath.

Hotel España (☎ 443-192), Haedo 667, is slightly more expensive at US$20/26, as is *Residencial La Española* (☎ 447-312), Luis A Herrera 142, for US$23/28. At downtown *Hotel Sahara* (☎ 494-935), Oliva 920, singles/doubles cost US$20/28 with bath and breakfast; the street is noisy but interior rooms are quiet.

Hotel Asunción Palace (☎ 600-966), Av Colón 415, is more modest than its name suggests, charging US$28/45 with air-con and private bath; rooms facing the street have pleasant balconies. *Hotel de la Paz* (☎ 490-786), Av Colón 350, costs US$30/37, while *Hotel Amalfi* (☎ 494-154), Caballero 877, costs US$33/44. Try also *Hotel Zaphir* (☎ 490-025), Estrella 955, which charges about US$36/43. *Gran Hotel Paraná* (☎ 444-545), at the corner of 25 de Mayo and Caballero, has singles/doubles for US$39/44, as does *Hotel Continental* (☎ 493-760), 15 de Agosto 420.

Places to Stay – top end
One of downtown's older hotels, *Gran Hotel Renacimiento* (☎ 445-165), Chile 388 opposite Plaza de los Héroes, has more personality than most others. Rates are US$45/56 with breakfast, television, telephone, and other amenities. *Hotel Mandu-*

virá Plaza (☎ 447-533), Manduvirá 345, is a bit more expensive for US$46/54.

Hotel Internacional (☎ 496-587), Ayolas 520, costs US$59/74, while the modern *Chaco Hotel* (☎ 492-066), Caballero 285, has rooms for US$74/94 with breakfast, plus a rooftop swimming pool; another step up is *Hotel Cecilia* (☎ 210-365), Estados Unidos 341, for US$86/109. Rates at the extravagant *Hotel Excelsior* (☎ 495-632), Chile 980, start at US$87/96.

High-rise *Hotel Guaraní* (☎ 491-131), opposite Plaza de los Héroes at Oliva and Independencia Nacional, has standard rooms for US$98/118. Asunción's very best is the *Yacht y Golf Club Paraguayo* (☎ 36117), whose very name suggests its price: US$157/187. It's at Av del Yacht 11 in the ritzy western suburb of Lambaré.

PLACES TO EAT
From its modest snack bars to formal international restaurants, Asunción has a surprising variety of quality food. The best dining areas are downtown and barrios to the east, around Avs Mariscal López and España.

One of Asunción's best breakfast and lunch choices is the *Lido Bar,* opposite the Panteón de los Héroes at the corner of Chile and Palma, which offers a variety of tasty, reasonably priced Paraguayan specialties. Packed with locals, it's good for snacks at any hour. Readers swear by the empanadas at *Don Vito/Copetín Immanuel,* Av Colón 346.

Anahi, at the corner of Presidente Franco and Ayolas, is an outstanding confitería with good food and ice cream at moderate prices; it's open Sunday, when most downtown restaurants close. A few doors west, toward Montevideo, is an outstanding German bakery. *Nick's,* Azara 348, is a good and inexpensive lunch or dinner choice.

Another worthwhile stop is *Confitería El Molino,* with branches at Palma 488 and at Av España 382 (☎ 210-671). For Asunción's best coffee, visit hole-in-the-wall *Café San Francisco* at the corner of Brasil and Estigarribia. *Periplô,* Presidente Franco 583, has an inexpensive fixed-price lunch that is good enough to overlook the atrocious service, but you would expect better service for the more expensive dinner. It is known for a delicious Spanish paella, however.

Rincón Chileno, with good, moderately priced Chilean food at Estados Unidos 314, is popular with US Peace Corps volunteers (a good source of information on the country), but the owner can be hostile if you question his mathematics. One block south, at Estados Unidos 422, *Vieja Bavaria* has good beer and short orders. It's a hangout for German visitors, but everyone is welcome. *Munich* (☎ 447-604), Eligio Ayala 163, also comes recommended.

As elsewhere in the River Plate republics, parrillas (grills) are the standard. There are several along the Av Brasilia, north of Av España, in the barrio of Mariscal López: *La Paraguaya* at Av Brasilia 624, *Maracaná* at the corner of Av Brasilia and Salazar, and *Anrejó* (also a pizzería) at Av Brasilia 572. *La Paraguayita,* at the corner of Av Brasilia and República Siria, belongs to the owners of La Paraguaya, across the street.

For Italian food, try the traditionally excellent and congenial *Buon Appetito,* in a pleasant outdoor setting at 25 de Mayo 1199, corner of Constitución. Also try *Il Capo* at Perú 291, *La Stampa* (☎ 606-085) at Austria and Viena in Villa Morra, or the *Spaghettoteca* Av San Martín 893 at Austria in Villa Morra. *Pizzometro,* Bruselas 1789 in Barrio Luis Herrera, has good all-you-can-eat pizza. Another attractive dinner choice is *La Pérgola Jardín* (☎ 210-219), Perú 240.

Highly regarded *Talleyrand* (☎ 441-163), a French/international restaurant at Mariscal Estigarribia 932, is expensive but worthwhile for a special occasion. *La Maison des Alpes,* at the corner of Bruselas and Viena in Villa Morra, and *La Preferida* (☎ 441-637), a German restaurant at 25 de Mayo 1005, also deserve a visit. *Taberna El Antojo* (☎ 441-743), Ayolas 631 between General Díaz and Haedo, has good fixed-price meals for US$7 as well as live music and dance.

Open for lunch only, on México near Moreno, *La Flor de Canela* serves excellent Peruvian food – try the surubí al ajo. *Gasthaus Arche Noah* (☎ 490-717), 25 de Mayo at Tacuary, has an extensive German menu, reasonable prices, and outstanding service.

Asunción probably has better Asian food and greater variety than either Buenos Aires or Montevideo because of the influx of Koreans – in the area around Mercado Cuatro, at Pettirossi and Rodríguez de Francia, try *Copetín Koreano* on Eusebio Ayala, one block from Rodríguez de Francia and Perú. For Japanese food, check out *Sukiyaki* (☎ 22038), Constitución 763 at Av Pettirossi. Chinese food is still the most common; try *Formosa* (☎ 211-075) at Av España 780 near Perú, or *Celestial* at Luis A Herrera 919.

Asunción's popular ice creamery *4-D* now has a downtown branch on Mariscal Estigarribia near Independencia Nacional, but the original at Av San Martín and Olegario Andrade (reached by bus Nos 12, 16, or 28) carries a wider selection of flavors. Some visitors prefer *Sugar's,* on Chile near Manduvirá, opposite Hotel Excelsior.

ENTERTAINMENT

The useful Spanish-English monthly *Amerindia* and the weekly *Fin de Semana,* a calendar of entertainment and cultural events, are both widely distributed throughout the city.

Cinemas

Most of Asunción's downtown cinemas rarely offer anything more challenging than cheap porno or the latest Arnold Schwarzenegger flick, but a few are worth checking out. First-run films cost about US$5 at *Cine Premier* (☎ 491-106) at Montevideo and Piribebuy, *Cine Yguazú* (☎ 494-427) at Colón and Piribebuy, *Cine Cosmos* (☎ 490-306) at Independencia Nacional and Manduvirá, and *Cine Atenea* (☎ 443-015) in the Mall Excelsior at Chile and Manduvirá.

The capital's many cultural centers (see Information) offer the best of foreign cinema; check *Fin de Semana* for current listings. In summer, the *Patio del Aguacate del Teatro Municipal,* at Alberdi and Presidente Franco, offers good films outdoors (rain or not) for US$3.

Nightclubs
Several readers have praised the shows, often including traditional harp music, at *Jardín de la Cerveza* (☎ 600-752), at República Argentina and Castillo in the Barrio of Recoleta (opposite the elite cemetery of the same name). Most were unimpressed with the food, however.

Bars
The informal *Spurs,* on Mariscal Estigarribia near Estados Unidos, is popular with both foreigners and Paraguayans.

Dance Clubs
Downtown, try *Piano Bar* at the Hotel Internacional, Ayolas 520; *La City* at the corner of Presidente Franco and 15 de Agosto¡ and *Alcatraz* at Caballero 1. Most others are in residential neighborhoods east of downtown, such as the *Muzak Mall* (☎ 662-792) at the corner of Ocampos and Bertoni in Villa Morra.

Theater
Asunción has numerous venues for live theater and music; the season generally runs March to October. Possibilities include the Casa de la Cultura Paraguaya (see Cultural Centers under Information); the *Teatro Arlequín* (☎ 605-107) at the corner of De Gaulle and Quesada in Villa Morra; *Escuela de Teatro Arlequín* at the corner of Zalazar and Av Artigas; *Teatro de las Américas* (☎ 24772) at José Berges 297; and *Placita Ayolas,* at the corner of Ayolas and Humaitá.

THINGS TO BUY
Most shops are open weekdays from 8 am to noon and 3 to 7 pm, mornings only on Saturday. Some keep slightly longer hours. All other shops listed are on the map.

Artesanía Viva, José Berges 993 at Perú, features Chaco Indian crafts, including ponchos, hammocks, and bags, plus books and information on Chaco Indian groups. Artesanía Hilda (☎ 447-620), at the corner of Presidente Franco and O'Leary, sells ñandutí and other Paraguayan handicrafts. Nearby Casa de Artesanía Kuarayhy (☎ 497-930), Presidente Franco 663, specializes in musical instruments, pottery, and tapestries.

Casa Overall (☎ 448-694), Mariscal Estigarribia 397 near Caballero, has a good selection of ñandutí and leather goods. Galería Artesanos (☎ 27853), at Cerro Corá and 22 de Setiembre, offers local paintings. For wood crafts, try Behage (☎ 493-279), Ayolas 222, or carver Zenón Páez (☎ 490-717), Lillo 1360 in Villa Morra. Artesano Raity (☎ 25285), Paí Pérez 778, has Paraguayan handicrafts and leatherwork as well as artwork by Korean immigrants.

The open-air market on Plaza de los Héroes is a good place for crafts, but remember that items made with feathers are probably subject to endangered species regulations overseas. For leather goods, try Boutique del Cuero (☎ 495-239) at Montevideo 329. Stamp collectors should visit Asunción Filatelía, Presidente Franco 845.

GETTING THERE & AWAY
Air
Because of its central location on the continent, Asunción is a good place to catch flights to neighboring countries, Europe, and the USA. Aeropuerto Internacional Silvio Pettirossi (☎ 22012) is in the suburb of Luque, east of Asunción, but is easily reached by buses on Av Aviadores del Chaco.

Airlines with representatives in Asunción include the following:

Aerolíneas Argentinas
    Independencia Nacional 365 (☎ 491-012)
Aeroperú
    Benjamín Constant 536 (☎ 493-122)
Air France
    Oliva 393 (☎ 498-768)
American Airlines
    Independencia Nacional 557 (☎ 443-331)
Iberia
    25 de Mayo 161 (☎ 493-351)

Líneas Aéreas del Cobre (Ladeco)
    General Díaz 347 (☎ 447-028)
Lapsa (Líneas Aéreas Paraguayas)
    Perú 456 (☎ 491-040, fax 496-484)
Lloyd Aéreo Boliviano (LAB)
    14 de Mayo 563 (☎ 441-586)
Lufthansa
    3rd floor, Estrella 345 (☎ 447-964)
National Airlines
    Oliva 381 (☎ 440-831)
Pluna
    Alberdi 513 (☎ 490-128)
Varig
    General Díaz & 14 de Mayo (☎ 497-351)

Aerolíneas Paraguayas (Arpa, ☎ 206-634), San José 136 at Mariscal López, links Asunción with Ciudad del Este five to seven times daily, with Pedro Juan Caballero twice daily on weekdays and daily on weekends, and with Encarnación daily except Sunday. Líneas Aéreas del Este (Ladesa, ☎ 600-948), Mariscal López 4531 in Barrio San Cristóbal, also flies to Ciudad del Este.

The Paraguayan air force's Transporte Aéreo Militar (TAM, ☎ 445-843), at Oliva 471, serves off-the-beaten-track destinations in the Chaco and along the northern Río Paraguay, including Concepción, Valle Mí, La Victoria, Fuerte Olimpo, San Carlos, and Bahía Negra.

Líneas Aéreas de Transporte Nacional (LATN, ☎ 212-277), at Brasil and Mariscal Estigarribia, flies to Concepción and Juan Pedro Caballero, the upper Río Paraguay destinations of Puerto Pinasco, Puerto Casado and Valle Mí, and to the Río Pilcomayo outposts of Fortín Caballero, Fortín Teniente Martínez, and Fortín Rojas Silva, which is the best access to Parque Nacional Tinfunqué.

Bus

Asunción's Terminal de Omnibus (☎ 551-728, 551-740) is at Av Fernando de la Mora and República Argentina in the Barrio Terminal, from downtown take buses Nos 8, 10, 25, 31, or 38 from Oliva. Asunción-bound passengers should note that the toilets at the terminal charge US75¢; it's best to use the ones on the bus before you arrive.

Asunción has excellent and frequent international as well as national connections; fares vary depending on the quality of the service. Some companies, most notably Pluma, Chevallier, and Nuestra Señora de la Asunción, continue to operate ticket offices on Plaza Uruguaya, enabling you to avoid an unnecessary trip to the terminal.

Traveling into Argentina or Brazil, it may be slightly cheaper to take a local bus across the border (for example, Asunción to Clorinda or Encarnación to Posadas) and then to purchase a long-distance bus ticket. The inconvenience of changing buses usually offsets the minor financial advantage.

Domestic There are countless buses to Ciudad del Este (US$8.50, 4½ hours): try Rápido Yguazú (Rysa, ☎ 551-601, 442-244 downtown at Eligio Ayala and Antequera); Rápido Caaguazú (☎ 553-908); and Nuestra Señora de la Asunción (☎ 551-667, 492-274 at Mariscal Estigarribia 727). To Encarnación (US$10, five hours), try Rysa, Nuestra Señora, Flecha de Oro (☎ 553-800), and La Encarnaceña (☎ 551-745).

For Pedro Juan Caballero, try San Jorge (☎ 554-782), Cometa del Amambay (☎ 554-923), La Santaniana (☎ 551-580), or La Ovetense (☎ 551-737). Connections between Asunción and Concepción are offered by Nueva Asunción (Nasa, ☎ 551 731), La Ovetense, San Jorge, La Santaniana, and Ciudad de Concepción (☎ 551-912).

La Chaqueña serves nearby Chaco destinations like Presidente Hayes and Benjamín Aceval. Long-distance Chaco carriers are Nasa (☎ 551-731), Stel Turismo (☎ 450-043) at Caballero 1340, and Ecmetur (☎ 555-852), with services to Pozo Colorado and Concepción (weather permitting on the dirt road from Pozo), Filadelfia (US$11, eight hours), Neuland, Mariscal Estigarribia (US$13), and Estancia La Patria, the last stop on the Ruta Trans-Chaco. Nasa is the only company to do this route in partial daylight.

Popular destinations near Asunción, such as San Bernardino and Caacupé, have such frequent services that it would be inconvenient to list them all here; instead, refer to the destination itself for such information.

International Nuestra Señora de la Asunción (☎ 551-667) and Expreso Brújula (☎ 551-662, downtown 491-720) at Presidente Franco 976, run buses to Falcón, on the Argentine border, from downtown Asunción (US$2). These leave hourly from the corner of Presidente Franco and Av Colón from 5 to 11 am and 12:30 to 5:30 pm. Nuestra Señora, Brújula, and Empresa Godoy also run eight to ten buses daily from the terminal directly to Clorinda.

Nuestra Señora also has frequent service to Posadas (US$11, five hours), Buenos Aires (US$42, 20 hours; US$73 in *coche cama* sleeper), and to Foz do Iguaçu, Brazil (five hours), and one service weekly to Rosario, Argentina. Chevalier Paraguaya (☎ 551-660, downtown 493-375) at Mariscal Estigarrribia 767, serves Buenos Aires via Formosa and Santa Fe. Expreso Brújula also serves Resistencia and Buenos Aires frequently, Montevideo (Uruguay) and São Paulo (Brazil) less often. La Internacional (☎ 551-662, downtown 491-720) at Presidente Franco 995, goes to Buenos Aires via Formosa; in the same offices, Empresa Godoy serves Resistencia via Formosa and Buenos Aires via both Formosa and Encarnación.

La Encarnaceña (☎ 551-745) also has regular service to Buenos Aires, while Cacorba (☎ 551-662) has twice-weekly buses to Córdoba (18 hours). Expreso Pullman Sur operates the only buses to Santiago, Chile (30 hours), Monday and Thursday.

Coit (☎ 551-738, downtown 496-197) at Eligio Ayala 693, goes to Río de Janeiro Monday, Wednesday, and Saturday evenings, and to Montevideo Monday, Wednesday, and Saturday mornings (US$64). Pluma (☎ 551-758, downtown 445-024) at Mariscal Estigarribia and Antequera, frequently connects Asunción with Foz (US$10, five hours), São Paulo (18 hours), Río de Janeiro (US$42, 22 hours), Curitiba

(14 hours), and Paranaguá (16 hours). Rysa also goes to Foz and São Paulo. Unesul goes to Porto Alegre, and Catarinense (☎ 551-738) provides a service to Florianópolis (US$31) via Blumenau.

Stel Turismo and Yacyretá (☎ 551-617) now operate two to three services weekly to the Bolivian destinations of Boyuibe (US$56, 24 hours) and Santa Cruz (US$67, 30 hours). Meals are included, but carry extra water on this hot, dusty trip. If wishing to explore the Paraguayan Chaco before continuing to Bolivia, it's still a good idea to purchase your ticket in Asunción, even if you wish to board in Filadelfia or Mariscal Estigarribia.

Train
Built in 1856, the Ferrocarril Central del Paraguay (☎ 447-316) is on Plaza Uruguay, at the corner of Eligio Ayala and México. Departing Sundays only at 8:30 am, the steam train to Lago Ypacaraí tours the backyards of Asunción's shantytowns en route to the Jardín Botánico, Luque, Isla Valle, and Areguá; it returns at 5 pm. The fare to Areguá, a US Peace Corps training center, is US75¢ return.

Boat
An alternative way of crossing to Argentina is the launch from Puerto Itá Enramada, west of downtown, to Puerto Pilcomayo, Formosa. These leave every half hour weekdays from 7 am to 5 pm, and Saturday irregularly from 7 to 10 am. It's possible to return by bus from Clorinda.

For scheduled long-distance boat services up the Río Paraguay, visit Cruceros SRL (☎ /fax 445-098), 14 de Mayo 150, which has recently acquired the former Flota Mercante state concession for the riverboat *Presidente Carlos Antonio López* and offers monthly excursions as well as straightforward transportation upriver to Concepción (310 km, 26 hours), continuing to Corumbá, Brazil (another 830 km, 72 hours more) if river conditions permit. Fares for the 10-day roundtrip to the Brazilian Pantanal and back, including meals and excursions, start at US$372 per person in quadruple rooms, rising to US$1263 for a luxury single, but fares are correspondingly lower for those who disembark in Corumbá.

Classes of tickets include 3rd (Tercera), 2nd (Turista), 1st (Primera), Ejecutivo, and Matrimonio. Third-class accommodations include only deck space for hammocks; all other fares include cabins with bunks or beds of increasing size and comfort. First class and above include private bath. Fares according to destination are:

Concepción	US$11 to US$76
Punto Pinasco	US$16 to US$113
Fuerte Olimpo	US$24 to US$178
Bahía Negra	US$53 to US$209
Corumbá	US$41 to US$290

As many as a dozen naval supply boats per week also carry passengers up the Río Paraguay as far as Concepción; inquire at the port at the river end of Calle Montevideo. These go to Isla Margarita on the Brazilian border, then cross to Porto Murtinho, Brazil, with buses to Corumbá.

GETTING AROUND
To/From the Airport
From downtown, bus No 30A takes 50 to 60 minutes to Aeropuerto Silvio Pettirossi and costs US30¢. Taxis cost about US$10.

To/From the Bus Terminal
Bus No 8 runs from Cerro Corá to the bus terminal, as does Bus No 25 from Plaza Uruguaya.

Buses
Asunción city buses go almost everywhere for around US30¢, but Paraguayans are less night people than Argentines or Uruguayans, and buses are few after about 10 or 11 pm. Plan your late night trip well or else take a cab. On the other hand, buses start running very early in the morning, since Paraguayans start work around 6:30 or 7 am. Around noon, buses are jammed with people going home for an extended lunch, so avoid travel into outlying barrios or suburbs at this hour.

Car Rental
Asunción has several car rental agencies: Hertz (☎ 605-708) at Eusebio Ayala, Km 4.5, or at Aeropuerto Silvio Pettirossi (☎ 206-195); National (☎ 491-379) at Yegros 501; Localiza (☎ 446-233) at Eligio Ayala 695; and Touring Car (☎ 447-945) at Iturbe 682.

Taxi
Cabs are metered and reasonable, but they may tack on a surcharge late at night. A cab to the bus terminal costs about US$5, to the airport about US$10.

Eastern Paraguay

East of the Río Paraguay and beyond Asunción is the nucleus of historical Paraguay, the homeland of the Guaraní people among whom the Spaniards began to settle in the 16th century. More than 90% of the country's population now lives here, mostly within 100 km of Asunción, but the border towns of Encarnación, across the Río Paraná from the Argentine city of Posadas, and Ciudad del Este (ex-Puerto Presidente Stroessner), across the Paraná from the Brazilian city of Foz do Iguaçu, have grown dramatically because of the enormous binational hydroelectric projects at Itaipú and Yacyretá.

Many of Paraguay's finest cultural, historical, and natural attractions are within a short distance of Asunción, on a convenient and popular circuit from the capital. These include the weaving center of Itauguá, the lakeside resorts of San Bernardino and Areguá, the celebrated shrine of Caacupé, colonial villages like Piribebuy and Yaguarón, and, a bit farther, Parque Nacional Ybycuí. On and near the highway between Asunción and Encarnación, numerous Jesuit ruins are in equal or better repair than those in Argentine Misiones. The fast-growing contraband center of Ciudad del Este is Paraguay's gateway to the Cataratas del Iguazú, and the gigantic Itaipú hydroelectric project is itself a tourist attraction of sorts.

The Circuito Central

With great hyperbole, tourist brochures label this itinerary, roughly a 200 km roundtrip from Asunción, the Circuito de Oro (Golden Circuit), but its lack of truly glittering attractions should not deter you from making day trips, weekend excursions, or even longer outings from the capital.

In most of these towns and villages, people pay little attention to street names, if indeed there are any.

AREGUÁ
On the south shore of Paraguay's largest lake, Lago Ypacaraí, the resort town of Areguá is slightly higher and cooler than Asunción. Just 28 km from the capital, it is also a US Peace Corps training center, but volunteers warn that pollution from a nearby fertilizer plant has made the lake unsuitable for swimming. On the main avenue from the train station to the lake, *Hospedaje Ozli* has rooms with fans for US$6 per person, pleasant gardens, and good food at reasonable prices.

Sunday visitors arrive by the antique steam train, which leaves downtown Asunción around 8:30 am and returns around 5 pm, but there are also frequent buses on Línea 11 from Av Perú in Asunción. For a longer excursion, there is a launch across the lake to San Bernardino from the pier at the Balneario Municipal, departing every half hour from 10:15 am to 2:15 pm, but there have been complaints of overcharging and poor service.

ITAUGUÁ
Founded in 1728 and only 30 km from Asunción, Itauguá is the home of Paraguay's famous ñandutí lace, a cottage industry practiced by skilled women from childhood to old age. On both sides of Ruta 2, the main highway to Ciudad del Este, weavers display their multicolored merchandise, ranging in size from doilies to bedspreads. It's possible to visit the artisans' houses, where you can see the women working on their latest project.

There are two cooperatives, the Mutual Tejedoras at Km 28 and the Taller Artesanal at Km 29, both open daily from 9 am to 5 pm except Sunday. Lessons and demonstrations are free. Across from the

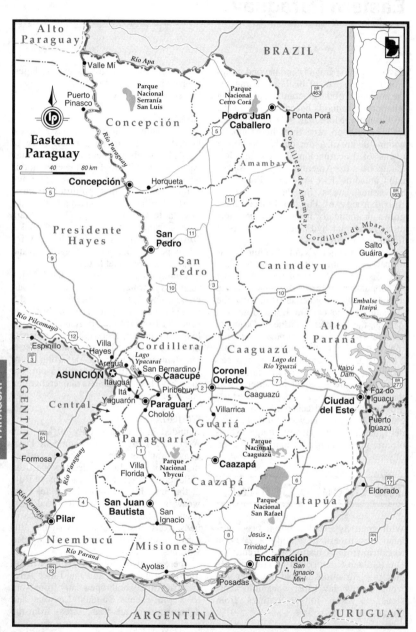

Taller, Casa Myriam is a good choice for anyone in search of a US$1500 wedding dress, hand sewn for nine months by four women. Smaller pieces cost only a few dollars, larger ones range from US$50 upward, but you can bargain with shopkeepers. Casa Servín also has quality ñandutí.

Two blocks south of the highway, opposite the plaza, the **Museo Parroquial San Rafael** displays religious and secular relics from the colonial era to the present, including Jesuit- and Franciscan-influenced indigenous artwork as well as very early samples of ñandutí. Although it's dark and conditions are less than ideal for preservation, the quality of the artifacts definitely justifies a visit. It's open daily from 8 to 11:30 am and 3 to 6 pm. In July the town celebrates the annual **Festival del Ñandutí.**

Meals are available in the local market for less than US$1, mostly for spaghetti with meat and manioc or rice. From the Asunción bus terminal, Itauguá, Caacupé, Tobatí, and Atyrá buses leave for Itauguá (US50¢, one hour) about every 15 minutes all day and night.

SAN BERNARDINO

In 1881, German colonists settled San Bernardino, which is on the eastern shore of Lago Ypacaraí, 48 km from Asunción on a northern spur off Ruta 2. It soon became a recreational refuge from the capital, and it's still a weekend resort for Asunción's elite, with a wide selection of restaurants, cafés, and hotels along its shady streets and the lakeshore. There are some reasonable budget alternatives, and the lake is cleaner here than at Areguá. Artisans in the nearby village of Altos create exceptional wood carvings, particularly animal masks.

Hotel Santa Rita (☎ 0512-2258) is probably the best bargain for accommodations, with singles around US$9. The traditionally distinguished *Hotel del Lago* (☎ 2201), at Caballero and Teniente Weiler, has singles/doubles for US$21/26; more upscale lodging, for around US$27/33, is available at *Hotel Acuario* (☎ 2375), at Km

45 on Ruta 2. The extravagant new *San Bernardino Pueblo Hotel* (☎ 2195), at Paseo del Pueblo and Mbocayá, charges US$59/74. *Restaurant Las Palmeras* and the German bakery on Colonos Alemanes are good places to eat in town. At Km 44 on Ruta 2, *Cuckaroochoo*, run by an American, serves burgers and apple, pecan, and lemon pies.

From the Asunción terminal, Transporte Villa del Lago (Línea 210) runs buses to San Bernardino every 20 to 30 minutes for most of the day. Transporte Cordillera de los Andes (Línea 103) has slightly less frequent service.

CAACUPÉ

Every December 8 since the mid-18th century, hordes of pilgrims have descended upon Caacupé, Paraguay's most important religious center, for the **Día de la Virgen** (Immaculate Conception), but the faithful continue to arrive throughout the year. After ending their tour of duty in the Chaco, military conscripts from eastern Paraguay often walk the length of the Ruta Trans-Chaco and the last 54 km across Asunción and its suburbs to the imposing **Basílica de Nuestra Señora de Los Milagros.** The Basílica dominates the townscape over the huge cobblestone plaza, which easily accommodates the 300,000 pilgrims who often gather here.

Hospedaje Uruguayo, midway between Ruta 2 and the Basílica, has comfortable rooms in a subtropical garden setting for US$10 single with private bath and fan, US$15 with air-conditioning. *Hotel La Giralda,* at the corner of Alberdi and 14 de Mayo, has singles for US$10. *Hospedaje San Blas I,* north of the highway but still only 1½ blocks from the Basílica, has singles/doubles for US$5/9 with shared bath.

Opposite the plaza is a block of cheap restaurants and tacky souvenir stands; try also *Restaurant Edelweiss* for meals. At Km 69 on Ruta 2, American-owned *Casa de Maní* has good food.

Transporte La Caacupeña (Línea 119)

PARAGUAY

Each year thousands of pilgrims visit the Basílica de Nuestra Señora de los Milagros in Caacupé.

and Transporte Villa Serrana (Línea 110) run buses from Asunción almost every 10 minutes between 5 am and 10 pm.

AROUND CAACUPÉ
Tobatí

About 20 km north of Caacupé, this village's skilled artisans produce outstanding wood carvings – a comparatively recent development, since the craft is not even mentioned in Elman and Helen Service's classic, 1954 ethnography *Tobatí: Paraguayan Town*.

For carvings, contact Zenón Páez (☎ 0516-229), who also has a studio in Asunción .

PIRIBEBUY

During the War of the Triple Alliance, the village of Piribebuy briefly served as the national capital and also saw serious combat. Founded in 1640, it features a mid-18th century church in excellent repair, which retains some of the original wood-

work and sculpture. The **Museo Histórico Comandante Pedro Juan Caballero**, opposite the church on the plaza, has interesting but deteriorating artifacts on local history and the Chaco War; it's open daily from 7:30 am to noon and 1 to 6 pm except Sunday.

Only 74 km from Asunción, on a southern branch off Ruta 2, Piribebuy is a good place for a glimpse of rural Paraguay. At its northern entrance is the government's experimental sugar cane plantation, with a nearby mill, while across the highway peasants grow maize, beans, and manioc. At the south end of town, a skilled carpenter produces up to five traditional wooden-wheeled oxcarts of hard lapacho wood per year.

Hotel Rincón Viejo (☎ 0515-251), a block east of the plaza at Maestro Fermín López 1051, has doubles with private bath for US$20 including breakfast, but try bargaining. *Hotel Los Carlos* (☎ 0515-223), Mariscal Estigarribia 668, charges US$18/21 for singles/doubles.

Transporte Piribebuy (Línea 197) has buses from Asunción every half hour between 5 am and 9 pm.

AROUND PIRIBEBUY
Chololó
South of Piribebuy, the narrow, scenic paved road leads to Chololó, less a village than a series of riverside campgrounds in a verdant, relatively undeveloped area; there is a branch road to the modest **Saltos de Piraretá,** a waterfall with nearby camping areas.

Paraguarí
The landscape around Paraguarí, where the road connects with Ruta 1 back to Asunción, consists of attractive hill country, but the town itself is notable only for having expunged "Presidente Stroessner" as a street name – though the children's playground still bears a plaque honoring Stroessner's wife, Eligia. *Hotel Chololó* (☎ 0531-242) offers reasonable rooms for US$26/36 single/double. Transporte Ciudad Paraguarí (Línea 193) has buses to Asunción every 15 minutes between 5 am and 8 pm.

About 21 km south of Paraguarí on Ruta 1, the village of **Carapeguá** is known for its cotton hammocks, known by the Guaraní term *poyvi*. The **Festival del Poyvi** takes place in November.

YAGUARÓN
Yaguarón's pride is its landmark 18th-century Franciscan church, a wooden structure 70 meters long and 30 meters wide with a baroque altar (the free-standing bell tower is a 20th-century reconstruction, however). It's open daily from 7:30 am to noon and 2 to 5 pm except Sunday, when it's open for mass only.

Yaguarón is also home to the **Museo del Doctor Francia,** 2½ blocks from the church in a well-preserved colonial house in which Francia was appointed colonial administrator. Its collection of colonial and early independence portraiture includes likenesses of El Supremo at different ages.

It's open daily from 7 to 11 am and 2 to 5 pm except Sunday.

Across Ruta 1 from the church is an inexpensive, unnamed restaurant that has mediocre food but excellent homemade ice cream; it also provides basic accommodation for US$4 per person. From Asunción, 48 km north, Transporte Ciudad Paraguarí (Línea 193) has buses every 15 minutes between 5 am and 8:15 pm.

ITÁ
Founded in 1539 by Domingo Martínez de Irala, Itá is known for its *gallinita* pottery of local black clay. There are very frequent buses to and from Asunción, 37 km away, with Transporte 3 de Febrero (Línea 159).

Southeastern Paraguay

PARQUE NACIONAL YBYCUÍ
In the department of Paraguarí, 5000-hectare Parque Nacional Ybycuí preserves one of eastern Paraguay's last remaining stands of Brazilian rainforest. Its rugged topography consists of steep hills, reaching up to 400 meters, dissected by creeks that form a number of attractive waterfalls and pools. In structure and species composition, the forests resemble those of Argentina's Parque Nacional Iguazú. Created in 1973, Ybycuí is the most accessible unit in the Paraguayan system.

Wildlife, though abundant, is rarely seen because the mostly secondary forest is so dense; animals are so difficult to spot that they usually hide rather than run. The exception is a remarkable number of stunningly colorful butterflies. Annual rainfall is about 1500 mm, while temperatures average around 22° C to 24° C.

Things to See & Do
Ybycuí is remarkably tranquil and undeveloped, although the influx of weekenders from Asunción can disrupt its peacefulness. When this happens, you can take

refuge on any of several hiking trails, which are more extensive and accessible than those at Iguazú. There is now a visitor center, with rangers on duty, and a brochure for a self-guided nature hike. For more detailed information, contact the Dirección de Parques Nacionals (☎ 445-214) in Asunción.

Sendero Mirador West of the campground, on the opposite side of the road from the ranger's house, this short but steep trail to an overlook doesn't quite repay the climb, since the forest is so dense it's hard to see out. There is wildlife, but you are likelier to hear it than see it.

Salto Guaraní Below this waterfall near the campground, a bridge leads to a pleasant creekside trail that continues to the old iron foundry at La Rosada. You will see a wealth of butterflies, including the large metallic blue morpho. Watch for poisonous snakes, but bear in mind that the rattler and coral snake are not normally aggressive, and the very aggressive yarará is nocturnal.

La Rosada The first of its kind in South America, this iron foundry was built during the government of Carlos Antonio López, but Brazilian forces destroyed it during the War of the Triple Alliance. The old waterwheel is of special interest. Located at the park entrance, two km west of the campground, it has an adjacent museum that keeps irregular hours.

Much of Ybycuí's forest is secondary, having recovered from overexploitation during the years when the foundry operated on wood charcoal, two tons of which were required to produce a single ton of iron. Engineers dammed Arroyo Mina to provide water and power for the bellows, while oxcarts hauled ore from several different sites more than 25 km away.

Places to Stay
The park has no hotels, so your only alternative is to camp at Arroyo Mina, which has adequate sanitary facilities, cold showers, and a confitería serving meals on weekends. Level sites are scarce. Fortunately, mosquitos are also few, but swarming moths and flealike insects are a nighttime nuisance, even though they do not bite.

At the cotton-mill village of Ybycuí, *Hotel Pytu'u Renda* (☎ 05328-264) charges US$13 per double.

Getting There & Away
Parque Nacional Ybycuí is 151 km southeast of Asunción. Ruta 1, the paved highway to Encarnación, leads 84 km south to Carapeguá, where there is a turnoff to the park, which is a further 67 km via the villages of Acahay and Ybycuí. From Asunción, Transporte Emilio Cabrera has eight buses daily to Acahay, where it is necessary to make local connections to the village of Ybycuí – a bus leaves daily at noon for the park entrance, returning to the village every morning at 7 am and 2 pm. Covered trucks also continue through the park to the village of Sargento Barrientos.

If driving, do not mistake Parque Nacional Bernardino Caballero, a historical monument with a semi-abandoned museum, for Parque Nacional Ybycuí, which is several km farther down the road.

VILLA FLORIDA
On the banks of the Río Tebicuary, 161 km southeast of Asunción, Villa Florida is a popular but relatively expensive *balneario* (bathing resort) and fishing and camping spot. *Hotel La Misionera,* while spotlessly clean, is very basic for US$18 per person, but it does have a good, reasonably priced restaurant with fish dishes.

ENCARNACIÓN
Once the site of the early Jesuit *reducción* (mission) of Itapúa, of which nothing remains, Encarnación is the southern gateway to Paraguay. This lively city of 50,000 is a town in limbo. As the rising waters behind the massive Yacyretá dam inundate the city's oldest barrios, most established businesses are moving onto high ground, and the public buildings and housing are left to decay. The old town center has become nothing more than a tawdry but

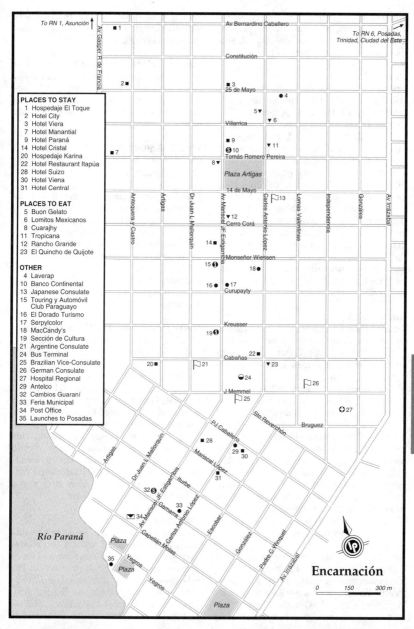

To RN 1, Asunción

Av Gasper R de Francia

Av Bernardino Caballero

To RN 6, Posadas,
Trinidad, Ciudad del Este

Constitución

25 de Mayo

Villarrica

Tomás Romero Pereira

Plaza Artigas

14 de Mayo

Cerro Corá

Monseñor Wiessen

Curupayty

Kreusser

Cabañas

J Memmel

Sto Reverchón

Bruguez

Antequera y Castro

Artigas

Dr. Juan L Mallorquín

Av Mariscal JF Estigarribia

Carlos Antonio López

Lomas Valentinas

Independencia

Gonzáles

Av Irrazabal

PJ Caballero

Mariscal López

Dr. Juan L Mallorquín

Av Mariscal JF Estigarribia

Gamarra

Iturbe

Carlos Antonio López

Escobar

Gonzáles

Padre G Winquel

Capellán Molas

Yegros

Yegros

Artigas

Río Paraná

Plaza

Plaza

Plaza

PLACES TO STAY
1 Hospedaje El Toque
2 Hotel City
3 Hotel Viera
7 Hotel Manantial
9 Hotel Paraná
14 Hotel Cristal
20 Hospedaje Karina
22 Hotel Restaurant Itapúa
28 Hotel Suizo
30 Hotel Viena
31 Hotel Central

PLACES TO EAT
5 Buon Gelato
6 Lomitos Mexicanos
8 Cuarajhy
11 Tropicana
12 Rancho Grande
23 El Quincho de Quijote

OTHER
4 Laverap
10 Banco Continental
13 Japanese Consulate
15 Touring y Automóvil
   Club Paraguayo
16 El Dorado Turismo
17 Serpylcolor
18 MacCandy's
19 Sección de Cultura
21 Argentine Consulate
24 Bus Terminal
25 Brazilian Vice-Consulate
26 German Consulate
27 Hospital Regional
29 Antelco
32 Cambios Guaraní
33 Feria Municipal
34 Post Office
35 Launches to Posadas

PARAGUAY

Encarnación

0   150   300 m

vibrant bazaar of cheap imported trinkets – digital watches, personal cassette players, and other electronic goodies that Argentines swarm to buy at bargain prices.

Orientation

Encarnación sits on the north bank of the Río Paraná, directly opposite the much larger city of Posadas, Argentina. The Puente Internacional Beato Roque González, built by Argentina at Paraguay's insistence as part of the Yacyretá agreement, links the two cities.

Encarnación now comprises two very different parts: an older, colonial-style quarter along the flood-prone riverfront and a newer section on the bluff overlooking the river. From the riverside, Av Mariscal JF Estigarribia leads from the old commercial center to the new one around Plaza Artigas, site of the original Jesuit mission. Most government offices and businesses have relocated to higher ground, but a few hang on.

Information

Tourist Offices The Sección de Cultura at the Municipalidad, on the corner of Av Estigarribia and Kreusser, is helpful but lacks printed matter. It's open weekdays from 7 am to 12:30 pm.

The Touring y Automóvil Club Paraguayo (☎ 2203) is at the corner of Av Estigarribia and Monseñor Wiessen.

Foreign Consulates The Argentine Consulate (☎ 3446), Mallorquín 788, is open weekdays from 7:30 am to 1:30 pm. The Brazilian Vice-Consulate (☎ 3950), directly across from the bus terminal at Memmel 452, is open weekdays from 8 am to noon. Japan has a consulate (☎ 2288) at Carlos Antonio López 1290; Germany (☎ 4041) at Memmel 631.

Money In the old city, change money at Cambios Guaraní at Av Estigarribia 307. In the newer part of town, try Banco Continental, Av Estigarribia 1418, or the nearby branch of Citibank. Outside regular hours and on weekends, the bus terminal is loaded with money changers. Travelers with ATM or credit cards will have to cross the river to Posadas.

Post & Telecommunications The post office is at Capellán Molas 337, in the old city. Antelco is at the corner of PJ Caballero and Carlos Antonio López, next to Hotel Viena. Encarnación's area code is 071.

Travel Agencies El Dorado Turismo (☎ 2558) is in the Galería San Jorge at Curupayty and Av Estigarribia.

Film Serpylcolor, on the corner of Av Estigarribia and Curupayty, has cheap Fuji film, but slide film is harder to come by. Still, travelers in Posadas may want to cross the border to load up before continuing to Iguazú or Buenos Aires.

Laundry Laverap is on 25 de Mayo between Carlos Antonio López and Lomas Valentinas.

Medical Services The Hospital Regional (☎ 2272) is at the corner of Independencia and General Bruguez.

Feria Municipal

At the corner of Carlos Antonio López and General Gamarra, the municipal market is a warren of stalls staffed by petty merchants intent on milking every last peso out of visiting Argentines before the flood. This description may sound pejorative, but in truth the place has a vitality that transcends the dubious quality of the baubles and gadgets that change hands here. It is also a good, inexpensive place to eat.

Places to Stay

Encarnación does not lack reasonable accommodations, and visitors to Posadas may find it almost as convenient and much cheaper to stay on the Paraguayan side. The windowless singles at *Hospedaje Karina*, at the corner of Cabañas and General Artigas, are the cheapest alternative at US$4, and the shared toilets are clean. *Hospedaje*

El Toque, on Av B Caballero between Francia and Antequera, has clean but small and basic singles for US$5 with shared bath, US$7.50 with private bath, but the hot water supply is erratic and the rooster next door starts early.

Homey *Hotel Manantial* (☎ 3546), at Tomás Romero Pereira 44 near the train station, has rooms with shared bath for US$7.50. Convenience is the major attraction of *Hotel Itapúa* (☎ 3346), directly across from the bus terminal on the corner of Cabañas and Carlos Antonio López, which costs US$6/9 with shared bath, US$8/13 with private bath. *Hotel Suizo* (☎ 3692), Av Estigarribia 562 between PJ Caballero and Mariscal López, is slightly dearer at US$9/15.

At *Hotel Central* (☎ 3454), Carlos Antonio López 542, and *Hotel City* (☎ 2432), Antequera y Castro 1659, rates are around US$10/18. Rooms at clean, quiet *Hotel Viena* (☎ 3486), PJ Caballero 568, are an excellent value for US$10/17 with private bath – German speakers may get a small discount and special attention. Do not confuse it with *Hotel Viera* (☎ 2038), 25 de Mayo 413, which is pricier at about US$13/18.

Hotel Paraná (☎ 4440), at Av Estigarribia 1414, has singles/doubles with private bath for US$34/48, while *Hotel Cristal* (☎ 2371), Av Estigarribia 1157, is the best in town at US$36/51. Just outside town, in Villa Quitería at Ruta 1, Km 361, the *Novotel* (☎ 071-5120) has first-class accommodations for US$60/76.

Places to Eat

Packed with both locals and Argentines, *Cuarajhy,* on Plaza Artigas at the corner of Av Estigarribia and Tomás Romero Pereira, is a good, moderately priced parrilla. *Rancho Grande,* at the corner of Av Estigarribia and Cerro Corá, is a large pleasant parrilla under a thatched roof, also popular with locals; at night, Paraguayan folk musicians perform, including harpists.

El Quincho de Quijote, opposite the bus terminal at Carlos A López and General Cabañas, is good value for decent food and excellent service at very moderate prices. *Tropicana,* on Carlos Antonio López between Villarrica and Tomás Romero Pereira, is a reasonably priced parrilla with US$3 lunch specials. *Lomitos Mexicanos,* at the corner of Villarrica and Carlos Antonio López, is the only place in Paraguay to get a taco.

Buon Gelato, on Carlos Antonio López between 25 de Mayo and Villarrica, is a dependable ice creamery.

Things to Buy

MacCandy's, on Carlos Antonio López between Monseñor Wiessen and Curupayty, has a varied selection of craft items.

Getting There & Away

Air ARPA now flies daily except Sunday to Asunción; consult travel agencies for details. The Argentine side has air connections with Buenos Aires and Puerto Iguazú – see the entry for Posadas in the Argentine Mesopotamia chapter.

Bus Between 6 am and 11 pm, frequent buses cross the Puente Internacional Beato Roque González to Posadas for US$1 regular, US$2 servicio diferencial (the latter are air-conditioned and pass more quickly through customs at busy morning hours). These begin at Av Bernardino Caballero and travel down Av Estigarribia, passing the bus terminal and the port. The trip takes about 50 minutes, including the stop for customs and immigration, on the Argentine side of the bridge for both countries.

La Encarnaceña (☎ 3448) has daily bus service to Buenos Aires (US$38, 18 hours) at 2:30 pm. Río Paraná has an identical service at 3 pm. There is a much greater selection of departures from Posadas, where prices are slightly lower. Rysa (☎ 3311) also goes to Buenos Aires.

Within Paraguay, there are numerous buses to Asunción (US$10, five hours), with Flecha de Oro, La Encarnaceña, Nuestra Señora (☎ 3527), and Rysa. Ten companies, including La Encarnaceña, Rysa, Transparanaense (☎ 4121), and Yacyretá, run some 30 buses daily to Ciudad del Este

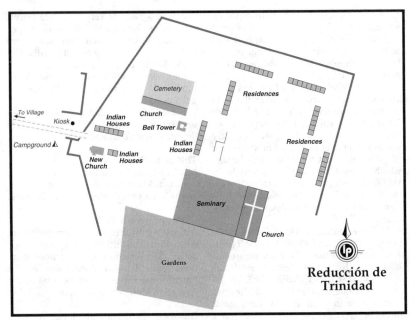

To Village
Kiosk
Campground

Cemetery
Church
Indian Houses
Bell Tower
Indian Houses
New Church
Indian Houses
Residences
Residences
Seminary
Church
Gardens

Reducción de Trinidad

(US$8, four to five hours). There are also connections to Ayolas, San Cosme y Damián, Villarrica, and many lesser destinations.

Train Passenger services have ceased on the Ferrocarril Central between Encarnación and Asunción.

Boat For the time being, launches still cross the Paraná to Posadas every half hour on weekdays from 6:30 am to 5 pm, Saturday and "semi-holidays" from 7 am to 10:15 am and 1 to 4:30 pm, and Sunday and holidays from 8:15 to 9:15 am and 3:30 to 4:30 pm. The trip takes 30 minutes and costs US$1. The former dock is now submerged by the rising waters, so passengers board from the temporary floating dock at the foot of Av Estigarribia.

Getting Around
Encarnación has a good local bus system, but for all practical purposes, your feet should get you around town. Most buses to

the old town use Carlos Antonio López and return by General Artigas. There are both horse-drawn and petrol-powered cabs.

AROUND ENCARNACIÓN
Trinidad & Jesús
Paraguay's best preserved Jesuit reducción, Trinidad occupies an imposing hilltop site 28 km from Encarnación. Though its church is smaller and its grounds are less extensive than those at San Ignacio Miní, Trinidad is in many ways its equal. From its bell tower, the Jesuit mission at Jesús de Tavarangue, 10 km north as the crow flies, is easily visible – Jesús is, strictly speaking, not ruins but rather an incomplete construction project, interrupted by the Jesuits' expulsion in 1767.

Founded only in 1706, Trinidad was one of the later Jesuit establishments, but by 1728 it boasted a Guaraní population of more than 4000. Designed by Italian Jesuit architect Juan Bautista Prímoli, who spent 12 years on the project, it was not finished until 1760, only a few years before the

Jesuit expulsion in 1767. Its church, whose truly elaborate pulpit, frescos, statues, and other adornments remain in excellent repair, was the centerpiece of the reducción.

As elsewhere, the Jesuits introduced European crafts and industry, so that Trinidad became famous for the manufacture of bells, organs, harps, and statuary. It also operated three cattle estancias, two large *yerba mate* plantations, and a sugar plantation and mill.

The fenced grounds at Trinidad, along with the museum, are open Monday through Saturday from 7:30 to 11:30 am and 1:30 to 5:30 pm; Sunday and holiday hours are 8 am to 5 pm. The fences are not especially secure, however, and many people climb through and wander about after closing time, with no apparent complaint from the staff. Admission costs US$1 for adults, US$0¢ for children under age 12. Parking costs US$1. Camping is possible outside the ruins.

Jesús, 11 km north of Trinidad by a generally good dirt road off Ruta 6, keeps nearly identical hours and collects the same fees.

At Capitán Miranda, 21 km from Encarnación on Ruta 6, *Hotel Tirol* (☎ 075-555) has outstanding accommodations from US$39/53. From the bus terminal at Encarnación, Empresa Ciudad de Encarnación goes to Trinidad nine times daily between 6 am and 7 pm, and it has two buses daily to Jesús at 8 and 11:30 am.

Coronel Pirapó

One of rural Paraguay's most incongruous sights is in this small village along Ruta 6 east of Trinidad, Jesús, and Hohenau: a substantial stadium, seating well over a thousand people, with an electronic scoreboard. Here you will hear not Spanish, not Guaraní, but Japanese, thanks to immigrants who designed the park not for soccer but for baseball. Paraguayan participants are not unusual, however.

SAN IGNACIO GUAZÚ

About 140 km northwest of Encarnación on Ruta 1, San Ignacio was also an 18th-century Jesuit reducción. It preserves only

a modest sample of ruins, but it has two commendable museums. The **Museo Jesuítico,** open daily from 8 to 11:30 am and 2 to 5 pm, holds a valuable collection of Guaraní Indian carvings; admission costs US$1. The **Museo Histórico Semblanza de Héroes** is open Monday to Saturday from 7:45 to 11:45 am and 2 to 5 pm, Sunday and holidays from 8 to 11 am.

Budget accommodations are available at the *Hotel del Puerto,* on Ruta 1 across from the plaza, which is most convenient for bus connections since the bus drivers stay at this hotel. Singles/doubles cost US$4/6 with shared bath. Only a little better, but a lot less convenient, is the pretentiously named *Gran Hotel Parador Arapizandú* (☎ 082-203), at the turnoff to Ayolas at the north end of town, which charges US$5 per person with private bath.

There are more than 30 buses per day to Asunción (3½ hours), 20 to Encarnación, 20 to the departmental capital of San Juan Bautista, and 15 to the Río Paraná port of Ayolas. There are also five buses daily to the Jesuit village of Santa María.

SANTA MARÍA

Twelve km from San Ignacio off Ruta 1, Santa María is a one-time Jesuit reducción with dirt roads and a shady plaza. Its **Museo Jesuítico,** with a superb collection of Jesuit statuary, is open daily from 8:30 to 11:30 am and 1:30 to 5 pm. Admission is US$1.

Basic *Pensión San José,* on the plaza, charges US$3 per person. There are five buses daily from San Ignacio Guazú, the most convenient of which leave at 11:30 am and 4:30 pm.

Northeastern Paraguay

Easternmost Paraguay, along the Brazilian frontier, is Paraguay's economic boom zone. The world's largest hydroelectric project, found at Itaipú, has spurred this development, and while it's a marvelous object lesson in Third World debt and environmental catastrophe, it has propelled the town of Ciudad del Este into unprecedented, if ephemeral, prosperity (based also on contraband). Brazilian agricultural colonists are moving across the border, deforesting the countryside for coffee and cotton while squeezing out Paraguayan peasants and the region's few remaining Aché Indians.

CIUDAD DEL ESTE

Formerly Puerto Presidente Stroessner, Ciudad del Este is a key border crossing, a transportation hub, and one of the gateways to the world-famous Cataratas del Iguazú. It is perhaps more significant, in the words of the *Wall Street Journal,* as the site of "15,000 shops jammed into 20 blocks," a "chaos of mass consumption" that turned over US$13 billion of dubious, sometimes shady merchandise in 1994.

While it's hard to ignore its ragged and undisciplined squalor, Ciudad del Este has an infectious boomtown vitality. Hidden behind handtrucks piled high with cardboard boxes containing imported VCRs and stereos, young boys wheel their merchandise up and down the sloping streets, while frenzied Brazilians stagger like overloaded porters beneath the weight of enormous satchels holding everything acquired on shopping sprees financed with overvalued reals. You can buy or sell just about anything in Ciudad del Este, so long as it's not made in Paraguay.

Asian immigrants play a major role in legitimate commerce, but some locals worry that Mercosur tariff reductions may undercut the undisciplined contraband sector of the city's economy. One "businessman," quoted in the *Wall Street Journal,* expressed it this way: "As I understand it, we will no longer be able to live by smuggling products but will have to begin producing things."

Ciudad del Este

PLACES TO STAY
1 Hotel Munich
2 Hotel Austria
3 City Hotel
4 Hotel Paraná
8 Hotel Puerta del Sol
9 Convair Hotel
15 Hotel Mi Abuela
18 Executive Hotel
22 Hotel San Rafael
26 Gran Hotel Acaray

PLACES TO EAT
7 Restaurant Cavi
12 Mi Ranchito
16 New Tokio
19 Restaurant Oriental
20 Osaka

OTHER
5 Immigration & Customs, Dirección de Turismo
6 Guaraní Cambios
10 Lavandería La Veloz
11 International Travel Service
13 TAM
14 Aerolíneas Paraguayas (Arpa)
17 Laveya
21 Lapsa
23 Municipalidad
24 Antelco
25 Brazilian Consulate

Orientation

Ciudad del Este sits on the west bank of the Río Paraná, linked to the Brazilian city of Foz do Iguaçu by the Puente de la Amistad (Bridge of Friendship). Created only in 1957 (Paraguayans joke that it has no cemetery because there are virtually no locals), the town has a somewhat irregular plan. The main street is Av San Blas, the westward extension of the Puente de la Amistad, which becomes Ruta 7 to Caaguazú, Coronel Oviedo, and Asunción (via Ruta 2). While a bit complex, irregular, and very disorderly, the center is compact and easily manageable on foot.

Information

Tourist Offices The Dirección de Turismo (☎ 62417, 66051) at the immigration border post is friendly but not particularly well informed or well supplied with printed matter. Try instead the Municipalidad on Av Alejo García, which opens very early but closes before noon. Many places around town distribute a small brochure with a basic map.

The Touring y Automóvil Club Paraguayo (☎ 62340) is on Av San Blas, at the Shell station about one km west of Plaza Madame Lynch, on Ruta 7 to Asunción. It sells the new *Guía Shell,* which includes the best available road maps of Paraguay, for US$8.

Foreign Consulates The Brazilian Consulate (☎ 62308), Tte Coronel Pampliega 337 at Paí Pérez, is open weekdays from 7 am to noon.

Money Money changers are everywhere, especially at the border, but they give poorer rates than banks or cambios. Guaraní Cambios is at the corner of Av Monseñor Rodríguez and Tte Coronel Pampliega.

Post & Telecommunications The post office is at Alejo García and Oscar Rivas Ortellado, across from the bus station.

Antelco is on the corner of Av Alejo García and Paí Pérez, across from the

Municipalidad. Ciudad del Este's telephone code is 061.

Travel Agencies International Travel Service (☎ 500812), Av Adrián Jara 202 at Pampliega, serves as agent for Arpa and other airlines.

Laundry Lavandería La Veloz (☎ 64294) is on Tte Coronel Pampliega, between Av Monseñor Rodríguez and Adrián Jara. Laveya is on Pampliega between Adrián Jara and Paí Pérez.

Places to Stay

Accommodations are abundant in Ciudad del Este, but demand is high and rooms are costlier than in other Paraguayan cities; still, given present price levels in Brazil, they're a fairly good value. The most reasonably priced place is *Hotel Paraná* (☎ 62568), Camilo Recalde 128, where singles/doubles cost US$12/16. Cozy, friendly *Hotel Mi Abuela* (☎ 62373), with an attractive garden courtyard at Alejo García and Adrián Jara, has singles/doubles with private bath, ceiling fans, and breakfast for US$12/18; for air-con, add US$3 per person.

Also a good value is the German-run *Hotel Munich* (☎ 62371), at the corner of Emiliano Fernández and Capitán Miranda, where singles/doubles with private bath, good breakfast, and air-con cost US$12/17. Down the block, at Emiliano Fernández 165, is the comparably priced, enthusiastically recommended *Hotel Austria* (☎ 68614). *City Hotel* (☎ 62730), Regimiento Sauce 301 at Capitán Miranda, charges US$16/22.

At the modern *Hotel Puerta del Sol* (☎ 68081), Av Boquerón 111, rates are US$18/24 with private bath and air-con. *Hotel San Rafael* (☎ 68105), at the corner of Av Adrián Jara and Abay, charges US$24/35 for rooms with breakfast and air-con, while the modernistic *Executive Hotel* (☎ 68981), at Av Adrián Jara and Curupayty, is slightly dearer at US$27/37. Recently upgraded, *Convair Hotel* (☎ 62349), across the street from Hotel Mi

Abuela, has rooms with air-conditioning, television, telephone, and other amenities for US$37/45. The *Gran Hotel Acaray* (☎ 61471), on Av 11 de Septiembre near the river, is also Ciudad del Este's casino; singles/doubles cost US$37/42. It's quieter because it's away from the rowdy downtown.

Places to Eat

The pleasant surprise in Ciudad del Este is the outstanding Asian food – Japanese, Chinese, and Korean – at reasonable prices. *Restaurant Oriental,* on Adrián Jara near Av Boquerón, has very good Japanese/Chinese food, especially agropicante (hot-and-sour) soup. Alongside side it is *Osaka,* which has an equally appealing menu but keeps shorter hours. *New Tokio,* on Pampliega between Adrián Jara and Paí Pérez, comes highly recommended.

Mi Ranchito, a sidewalk parrilla at the corner of Curupayty and Av Adrián Jara, offers a good, complete meal for around US$4. *Restaurant Cavi,* at the corner of Monseñor Rodríguez and Nanawa, is a popular Paraguayan restaurant.

Getting There & Away

Air Ciudad del Este's new Aeropuerto Internacional Guaraní is 30 km west of town on Ruta 7, but flights are as yet very limited. Lapsa (☎ 68830) is on Av Adrián Jara near Abay, but has no flights to or from Ciudad del Este. The military airline TAM (☎ 68352), in the Edificio SABA just off Monseñor Rodríguez, offers occasional flights to Asunción, as does Aerolíneas Paraguayas (Arpa, ☎ 62995), on Nanawa near Adrián Jara.

There are also major airports at Foz do Iguaçu in Brazil and Puerto Iguazú in Argentina. From Foz, Varig and other Brazilian airlines have flights to São Paulo, Curitiba, Rio de Janeiro, and Asunción; from Puerto Iguazú, Aerolíneas, Austral, and LAPA have regular services to Aeroparque in Buenos Aires.

Bus Catch buses for Foz do Iguaçu, which leave every 10 minutes weekdays and Sat-

urday, and every half hour Sunday and holidays, at the entrance to the bridge over the Paraná after going through Paraguayan immigration. On the other side, unless just crossing for the day, disembark to go through Brazilian immigration; if you hold on to your ticket, any following bus will take you to Foz.

There are half a dozen international services daily to São Paulo (18 hours), Rio de Janeiro (25 hours), Florianópolis (15 hours), and Curitiba (13 hours) with Pluma (☎ 60343), Rysa (☎ 63057), Catarinense, and La Paraguaya. There is, of course, a wider selection of Brazilian bus services in Foz proper.

From Ciudad del Este to Asunción (US$8.50, five hours), there are 34 buses daily with Rysa, Rápido Caaguazú (☎ 68124), and Nuestra Señora (☎ 60095). There are nearly as many to Encarnación, with CarepeguEña (☎ 60178), Nuestra Señora, Transporte Paraná, Rysa, Empresa Ciudad del Este, and others. Salto Cristal has two per day via Villarrica to Ybycuí, convenient for Parque Nacional Ybycuí, while Piribebuy and La Guaireña also go to Villarrica several times daily.

Boat If you prefer to bypass Brazil for lack of a visa or some other reason, try to locate one of the (infrequent) launches from Puerto Presidente Franco, south of Ciudad del Este, to Puerto Iguazú, Argentina.

Getting Around

Ciudad del Este's public transport system has managed to keep pace with the city's rapid development, but for most travelers the central area is compact enough that it will not be necessary to use it. The exception is the bus terminal on Av Bernardino Caballero, two km south of downtown; take the "Mburucuyá" bus from Av Alejo García or a cab for about US$3.

AROUND CIUDAD DEL ESTE
Itaipú Dam

With an installed capacity of 12.6 million kilowatts, the binational Itaipú Dam is the world's largest hydroelectric project and an extraordinary illustration of the ways in which massive development projects have put countries like Brazil many billions of dollars into debt without hope of repayment. Paraguay, though, has benefited economically from Itaipú because of the construction boom, its own low domestic demand, and Brazil's need to purchase the Paraguayan surplus. It risks, however, becoming an energy colony of its mammoth neighbor. At the same time, should the price of competing sources of energy drop, reduced Brazilian demand could saddle Paraguay with the repayment of an unexpected share of the project's enormous capital and maintenance costs.

Project propaganda omits any reference to the costs of the US$25 billion project, and environmental concerns figured not at all in the Itaipú equation. The dam created a reservoir covering 1350 sq km, 220 meters deep, which drowned the falls at Sete Quedas, a larger and even more impressive natural feature than Iguazú. Recent research indicates that the reservoir's stagnant waters have provided new habitat for anopheline mosquitos, posing an increased malaria risk in an area where the disease had nearly been eradicated.

On both sides of the border, well-rehearsed guides lead tours that stop long enough for visitors to take photographs. On the Paraguayan side, these leave from the Centro de Recepción de Visitas, north of Ciudad del Este near the town of Hernandarias. Hours are Monday to Saturday at 8:30, 9:30, and 10:30 am; passports are required. There is a documentary film, also available in English-language video format, half an hour before the tour departs.

From Ciudad del Este, take any Hernandarias Transtur or Tacurú Pucú bus from the roundabout at the intersection of Av San Blas and Av Alejo García. These leave every 10 to 15 minutes throughout the day – ask to be dropped at the entrance to the unmistakably conspicuous project.

Salto Monday

They're not Sete Quedas, but these falls on the Río Monday, near Puerto Presidente Franco, are the best Paraguay now has to offer. They're only 10 km from Ciudad del Este, but there is no scheduled public transport, so taxi is the best alternative. Otherwise it should be possible to catch one of the frequent buses from Ciudad del Este to Puerto Presidente Franco and to walk to the falls from there.

Colonia Iguazú

Forty km west of Ciudad del Este on the highway to Asunción, Colonia Iguazú is a Japanese agricultural colony, established in 1960 with the assistance of the Japanese government, which specializes in cotton. Buses from Ciudad del Este stop at the Esso Servicentro, where the restaurant serves excellent Japanese food along with Paraguayan dishes.

CORONEL OVIEDO

Just off Ruta 2 midway between Asunción and Ciudad del Este, Coronel Oviedo is a major crossroads in eastern Paraguay – long-distance buses pass through town at least every 15 minutes all day. Ruta 3 goes north toward Pedro Juan Caballero (with branches to Salto del Guáira and Concepción), while Ruta 8 heads south to Villarrica, center of an area of German colonization on the Asunción-Encarnación railway.

At the crossroads, *Hotel Alemán* is a reasonable place to stay, while nearby *Parador La Tranquera* has good food. In the town proper, three km north of the crossroads, highly recommended *Hotel Colonial* (☎ (0521) 2393) has singles for US$13. *Hotel del Rey* (☎ 2117), Av Mariscal JF Estigarribia 261, charges US$16/20.

Between Coronel Oviedo and San José, a branch road off Ruta 2 leads to the frequently renamed town of **Nueva Australia,** a short-lived socialist experiment populated by the descendants of late-19th-century Australian immigrants. Named Hugo Stroessner, for Alfredo's immigrant father, on some maps, the dissension-ridden agricultural colony attracted its earliest participants with exaggerated propaganda on the area's economic potential until it finally broke apart in 1896. Colonia Cosme, an offshoot south of Villarrica, struggled on a few years more.

VILLARRICA

Settled by German agricultural immigrants, Villarrica is a quiet provincial town known as one of Paraguay's cultural capitals, due in part to the impressive Franciscan church that dates from colonial times. It is about 40 km south of Coronel Oviedo via paved Ruta 8, which becomes Av Thompson past the plaza and then Av Carlos Antonio López at Bulevar Ayolas.

The nearby village of Yataity is renowned for artisans who produce *ao po'i* or *lienzo* (loose-weave cotton) garments. The **Fiesta del Ao po'i** takes place in November.

Friendly, family-run *Hospedaje Porvenir,* Av Thompson 144, is basic but good value, offering singles/doubles with shared bath for US$5/9. *Hotel Ybyturutzú* (☎ (0541) 2390), at Carlos Antonio López and Dr Bottrell, has clean, spacious rooms with breakfast, private bath, and air-con for US$13/18, but some downstairs rooms are slightly musty. Good meals are available, and it has pleasant gardens and common spaces. For breakfast, try *Tirol* down the block.

Villarrica's only night spot is Petroleo's Pub, also on Carlos Antonio López.

PEDRO JUAN CABALLERO

Capital of the department of Amambay, 532 km northeast of Asunción by Ruta 3 and Ruta 5 from Coronel Oviedo, Pedro Juan Caballero is the Paraguayan counterpart of the Brazilian town of Ponta Porã. There is no clearly marked border, and locals cross from one side to the other at will. You can do the same, but before continuing any distance into either country, visit immigration at Naciones Unidas 144, open daily from 8 am to noon except Sunday. There are reports of contraband drug traffic in the area, so beware of unsavory characters.

Exchange houses are numerous, including Guaraní Cambios on Rodríguez de Francia. The Brazilian Consulate (open weekdays from 8 am to noon and 2 to 6 pm) is in the *Hotel La Siesta* (☎ (036) 3021), at the corner of Alberdi and Dr Francia, which has singles/doubles for US$7/10. Other economical accommodations are available at several hotels along Mariscal López: the recommended *Hotel Guavirá* (☎ 2743), Mariscal López 1325, charges US$5.50 for a single with shared bath, US$9 with private bath; *Hotel Peralta* (☎ 2346), Mariscal López 1257, has rooms for US$5/8; and *Hotel La Negra* (☎ 2262), Mariscal López 1342, for US$8/12. *Hotel Eiruzú* (☎ 2259), Av Mariscal JF Estigarribia 48, charges US$22/31, while the *Hotel Casino Amambay* (☎ 2718), Rodríguez de Francia 1, is the town's best for US$26/32.

Getting There & Away

Air Agrotur (☎ 2710), at Mariscal López and Curupayty, is the agent for Arpa, which flies twice daily weekdays and daily on weekends to Asunción. State-owned LATN has reduced services, but its fares are cheaper.

Bus Ten buses daily connect Pedro Juan Caballero with Asunción via Coronel Oviedo, with San Jorge, Cometa del Amambay, La Santaniana or La Ovetense; the trip traditionally takes 8 to 12 hours, depending on weather and road conditions, but the highway is now almost entirely paved.

There are also 10 buses daily to Concepción, where it is possible to travel downriver to Asunción, and one per day to Ciudad del Este. Nasa goes daily to Campo Grande, Brazil, but there are more bus services, plus two trains per day, across the border in Ponta Porã.

PARQUE NACIONAL CERRO CORÁ

Visitors passing through northeastern Paraguay should not bypass 22,000-hectare Parque Nacional Cerro Corá, only 40 km southwest of Pedro Juan Caballero, which protects an area of dry tropical forest and savanna grasslands in a landscape of steep, isolated hills rising above the central plateau. Besides a representative sample of Paraguayan flora and fauna, the park also has cultural and historical landmarks, including pre-Columbian caves and petroglyphs, and was the site of the battle in which a Brazilian soldier killed Francisco Solano López at the end of the War of the Triple Alliance.

The park has nature trails, a camping area, and a few basic cabañas where travelers can lodge. There are rangers, but no formal visitor center.

CONCEPCIÓN

On the east bank of the Río Paraguay, 310 km upstream from Asunción, the small provincial town of Concepción conducts considerable river trade with Brazil and has an interesting market. There are two inexpensive hotels: the so-so *Hotel Victoria* (☎ 031-2826), at Presidente Franco and Juan Pedro Caballero, costs around US$8/13 for singles/doubles with shared bath, while the recommended *Hotel Francés* (☎ 2750), at Presidente Franco and Carlos Antonio López, charges US$10/16 with a good breakfast. A recent reader's

suggestion is *Hospedaje Imperial*, at General Garay and Villarrica, for US$7 single.

Getting There & Away

Air TAM, the Paraguayan air force passenger service, flies to Asunción, Valle Mí, La Victoria, Fuerte Olimpo, San Carlos, and Bahía Negra. LATN flies to Asunción, Juan Pedro Caballero, and the upper Río Paraguay destinations of Puerto Pinasco, Puerto Casado, and Valle Mí.

Boat For details of boat traffic from Asunción to Corumbá, Brazil, see the Getting There & Away entry under Asunción.

Bus Bus services to Asunción, subject to suspension due to road conditions, can go either via Pozo Colorado in the Chaco or via Coronel Oviedo, the latter a 9- to 11-hour trip. The main carriers are Nasa, La Ovetense, San Jorge, La Santaniana, and Ciudad de Concepción. There are daily Nasa buses to Pedro Juan Caballero (US$8.50, 5½ hours, continuing to Campo Grande, Brazil), and others to Ciudad del Este.

PARAGUAY

The Paraguayan Chaco

With more than 60% of the country's territory and only 4% of its population, the Gran Chaco is the Paraguayan frontier, where great distances separate tiny settlements. Paved Ruta 9, popularly known as the Ruta Trans-Chaco, leads 450 km to the town of Filadelfia, center of an area colonized by European Mennonite immigrants since the late 1920s. Beyond Filadelfia, the pavement ends but the highway continues to the Bolivian border at Eugenio Garay, another 300 km northwest.

Geographically, the Paraguayan Chaco is the northernmost segment of an almost featureless plain rising slowly from southeast to northwest, its surface consisting of sediments eroded from the Andes. It comprises three rather distinct zones that emerge gradually as one travels east to west. Immediately west of the Río Paraguay, the Low Chaco landscape becomes a soothing, verdant savanna of caranday palms with scattered islands of thorny scrub, commonly known as *monte*. In this poorly drained area, ponds and marshes shelter large numbers of colorful birds, including the ungainly South American storks. Peasant farmers build picturesque houses of palm logs, but the primary industry is cattle ranching, as Paraguayan gauchos herd scrawny cattle on estancias even larger than many in Argentina or Uruguay.

As the Ruta Trans-Chaco continues northwest, rainfall declines and the drought-tolerant monte expands, with substantial groves of quebracho, palo santo, and the unique *palo borracho,* which conserves water in its bulbous trunk. Despite erratic environmental conditions, Mennonite colonists have built successful agricultural communities in the Middle Chaco, but no one has yet established anything but army bases and cattle estancias in the High Chaco beyond Mariscal Estigarribia, where the thorn forest is denser and rainfall even more undependable.

Historically, the Chaco has been the last refuge of indigenous peoples like the Ayoreo and Nivaclé, who managed an independent subsistence until very recently by hunting, gathering, and fishing. Later industries included cattle ranching and extraction of the tannin-rich quebracho. It was the Mennonite colonists, first arriving in 1927, who proved that parts of the Chaco were suitable for more intensive agriculture and permanent settlement. The first Mennonite settlers arrived in the heart of the Chaco not by the Ruta Trans-Chaco (not completed until 1964 and not paved until very recently), but rather by a railway from Puerto Casado, on the upper Río Paraguay.

A glance at the map reveals an inordinate number of Chaco place names that begin with the word *Fortín*; these were the numerous fortifications and trenches, many of which remain nearly unaltered, from the Chaco War (1932-35) with Bolivia. Most of these sites are abandoned, but small settlements have grown up near a few. The Paraguayan military still retains a visible presence throughout the Chaco.

The Chaco War gave Paraguay the incentive to build a network of dirt roads, most of which have deteriorated since hostilities ended. This generality does not apply in the Mennonite communities, which have done an outstanding job of maintaining those roads within their autonomous jurisdiction. Most others are impassable except to 4WD vehicles.

Travel in the Chaco can be rough, and accommodations are scarce outside the few main towns; it is possible to camp almost anywhere, but beware of snakes. In a pinch, the estancias or the *campesinos* (peasants) along the Trans-Chaco will put you up in a bed with a mosquito net if they have one. Otherwise, you're on your own.

VILLA HAYES

Only a short distance from Asunción across

the Puente Remanso, Villa Hayes takes its name from one of the USA's most obscure and undistinguished presidents who, strangely, is a hero in the hearts and minds of all Paraguayans. Many consider him an honorary Paraguayan.

Rutherford Birchard Hayes (pronounced "eye-zhess" in Paraguay's River Plate accent) occupied the White House from 1877-81, leaving office without even seeking a second term. Even in his hometown of Delaware, Ohio, the only monument to his memory is a modest plaque on the site of his birthplace – now a gasoline station. In Paraguay, by contrast, he is commemo-

rated by the Club Presidente Hayes, which sponsors the local soccer team, an Escuela Rutherford B Hayes, and a separate monument outside the school. In 1928 and 1978, the town held major festivities to honor Hayes.

Why this homage to a man almost forgotten in his own country, who never even set foot in Paraguay, 7400 km to the south? At the end of the War of the Triple Alliance, Argentina claimed the entire Chaco, but after delicate negotiations, both countries agreed to submit claims over a smaller area, between the Río Verde and the Río Pilcomayo, to arbitration. In 1878,

Argentine and Paraguayan diplomats traveled to Washington to present their cases to Hayes, who decided in Paraguay's favor; in gratitude, the Congreso in Asunción immortalized the American president by renaming the territory's largest town, Villa Occidental, in his honor.

To attend the Hayes sesquicentennial in 2028, take bus No 46 from Estados Unidos or Av España in downtown Asunción. It leaves every half hour between 5:30 am and noon, and every 45 minutes from noon to 9 pm.

POZO COLORADO

Pozo Colorado, 274 km northwest of Asunción, has little of interest, but it's the only major crossroads in the entire Chaco. From here, Ruta 5 is a dry-weather route east to Concepción, where it's possible to catch a bus back to Asunción or on to the Brazilian border at Pedro Juan Caballero. There is a military checkpoint just before arriving at Pozo.

The unnamed restaurant on the north side of the highway has decent food and very cold beer; it may be able to offer a bed for the night, but if not, try the Shell station across the highway. From Concepción, Nasa runs two buses daily to Asunción via Pozo Colorado, at 7:30 am and 11 pm. These should arrive 2½ to 3 hours later in Pozo. Several other buses continue from Pozo on to the Mennonite settlements at Filadelfia, Loma Plata, and Neu-Halbstadt.

FILADELFIA

Filadelfia is the administrative and service center for Mennonite farmers of Fernheim colony. It is the most visited of the three colonies, with the most reasonable accommodations and outgoing people. In some ways, it resembles the cattle towns of the Australian outback or the American West, but dairy products and cotton are the primary products rather than beef. Just as aboriginal people work the cattle stations of Australia, so Nivaclé, Lengua, Ayoreo, and other indigenous people work the Mennonite farms. The very controversial New

Tribes Mission, an evangelical group not related to the Mennonites, maintains an office in town.

Filadelfia is still a religious community and shuts down almost completely on Sundays. On weekday mornings, you will see Mennonite farmers drive to town in their pickup trucks in search of Indians for day labor, returning with them in the afternoon. At noon, when the heat can be overpowering, the town is exceptionally quiet, as Mennonites have adopted the custom of the tropical siesta.

Orientation

Filadelfia is about 450 km northwest of Asunción via the Trans-Chaco. The town itself lies about 20 km north of the highway, on a spur whose paved ends about one km south of town.

Filadelfia's dusty, unpaved streets form a very orderly grid. The *Hauptstrasse* (main street) is north-south Hindenburg, named after the German general and president

PLACES TO STAY
6 Hotel Florida
13 Hotel Safari

PLACES TO EAT
7 La Estrella
11 Girasol

OTHER
1 New Tribes Mission
2 Monument
3 Hospital
4 Museo Unger
5 Reisebüro
8 Cooperativa Mennonita
9 Post Office
10 Antelco
12 Librería El Mensajero
14 Stel Turismo
15 Ecmetur
16 Nasa Bus Terminal

whose government helped the Fernheim refugees escape the Soviet Union. The other main thoroughfare is Trébol, which leads east to Loma Plata, the center of Menno colony, and west to the Trans-Chaco and Fortín Toledo. Nearly every important public service is on or near Hindenburg.

Information
Tourist Office Filadelfia's de facto tourist office is the Reisebüro, the travel agency on Hindenburg between Calle Trébol and Unruh. Hotel Florida shows a video on the Mennonite colonies.

Money To change cash, try the Reisebüro or the Cooperativa Mennonita supermarket, near the corner of Unruh and Hindenburg.

Post & Telecommunications The post office and Antelco are both at the corner of Hindenburg and Unruh. Filadelfia's area code is 091.

Medical Services Filadelfia's modern hospital is at the corner of Hindenburg and Trébol.

Museo Unger
This well-arranged museum, opposite Hotel Florida on Hindenburg, tells the story of Fernheim colony from its foundation in 1930 to the present, and it also contains ethnographic materials on the Chaco Indians. It keeps no regular schedule, but Hartmut Wohlgemuth, manager of the Florida, provides guided tours in Spanish or German when his schedule permits. There is an admission charge of about US$1.

Places to Stay
Camping Camping is possible free of charge in shady Parque Trébol, five km east of Filadelfia, but there is no water and only a single pit toilet. While camping there one evening, we saw a highly poisonous (but timid) coral snake.

Hotels Filadelfia's most established accommodation is *Hotel Florida* (☎ 258),

at the corner of Hindenburg and Unruh. It has motel-style double rooms with private bath and air-con for US$25, but its budget annex is an excellent bargain at US$7 per person with comfortable beds, shared bath with cold showers (not a bad idea here), and fans.

The new *Hotel Safari* (☎ 218), on Industrie between Hindenburg and Miller, charges US$20 single and also has a pool. Spartan *Hotel Edelweiss,* on Hindenburg 1½ blocks south of Boquerón, is a last ditch choice for US$5 double, using an outhouse and outdoor tap.

Places to Eat
Hotel Florida has a very decent restaurant, while several shops along Hindenburg offer snacks and homemade ice cream. Try also the parrillada at *La Estrella,* around the corner from the Hotel Florida on Unruh, which has a shady outdoor dining area. *Girasol,* across the street, also serves a good asado. The modern Cooperativa Mennonita supermarket has excellent dairy products and other groceries.

Things to Buy
Librería El Mensajero, behind Antelco and across from the Mennonite cooperative, is an evangelical bookshop that also offers a good selection of Chaco Indian crafts. There is a better crafts selection at Neu-Halbstadt.

Getting There & Away
Several bus companies serve Filadelfia. Nasa, on Chaco Boreal near the corner of Miller, goes daily at 2:30 pm to Asunción (seven hours) and at 2 am to Mariscal Estigarribia (two hours) and Estancia La Patria (five hours), the last stop for public transport on the Trans-Chaco before the Bolivian border. It also has a 1 pm Saturday minibus service (US$3) to Mariscal Estigarribia for those who care to see the landscape.

Stel Turismo, on the east side of Hindenburg between Industrie and Chaco Boreal, connects Filadelfia with Asunción daily at 7 pm except Saturday; Tuesday at 7:45 pm,

PARAGUAY

The Mennonite Colonies

Mennonites are Anabaptists, believing in adult rather than infant baptism. This might sound innocuous enough today, but in 16th-century Holland and Switzerland it got them into serious trouble with both Catholics and other Protestants. As pacifists, the Mennonites also believed in separation of church and state and rejected compulsory military service, making their situation even worse and causing them to flee to Germany, Russia, and Canada. By the early 20th century, political upheaval once again caused them to seek new homes, this time in Latin America. Their primary destinations were Mexico and Paraguay.

For Mennonites, Paraguay's attractions were large extents of nearly uninhabited land, on which they could follow their traditional agricultural way of life, and the government's willingness to grant them political autonomy under a Privilegium: They were responsible for their own schools, with German-language instruction, and community law enforcement, and they had separate economic organization, freedom from taxation, religious liberty, and exemption from military service. The first group to arrive in Paraguay, in 1927, were the *Sommerfelder* (Summerfield) Mennonites from the Canadian prairies, who left after Canadian authorities failed to live up to their promise of exemption from military service. These Sommerfelder formed Menno colony, the first of three distinct but territorially overlapping Mennonite groups. Centered around the town of Loma Plata, it is still the most conservative and traditional of the colonies.

Only a few years after the founding of Menno colony, refugees from the Soviet Union established Fernheim (Distant Home), with its "capital" at Filadelfia. Neuland (New Land) was founded in 1947 by Ukrainian-German Mennonites, many of whom had served unwillingly in the German army in WWII and had managed to stay in the west after being released from prisoner-of-war camps. Its largest settlement is Neu-Halbstadt.

Mennonite immigrants obtained major concessions under the Privilegium, but they soon found that the Paraguayans had exploited their desire to live in peaceful isolation by granting them land in the midst of a zone of conflict. Since the early part of the century, Paraguay and Bolivia had been building fortifications in anticipation of armed conflict over an area that had been a cause of antagonism since colonial days. In 1932, this erupted into open warfare, with Mennonite settlements the scene of ground fighting and even Bolivian air attacks.

Because of their isolation, the Mennonites saw Paraguayans only infrequently, but regularly came into contact, and sometimes conflict, with Chaco Indians. During the war, nomadic Indians,

a bus leaves Filadelfia for Cruce de los Pioneros, connecting with their westbound service across the Chaco to Boyuibe and Santa Cruz, Bolivia. Ecmetur, at the corner of Hindenburg and Chaco Boreal, has buses to the capital daily at 7 or 8 pm.

The local bus line Expreso CV connects Filadelfia with Loma Plata (25 km) daily at 8 am, returning at 9 am. Nasa minibuses go Monday, Wednesday, and Friday at 11:30 am to Neu-Halbstadt, returning at 1 pm.

Buses from Asunción also stop at Loma Plata and most continue to Neu-Halbstadt. Hitching or asking for lifts is worth a try if you plan to go anywhere else, like Fortín Toledo, Neu-Halbstadt, or Loma Plata at odd hours.

AROUND FILADELFIA
Cruce de los Pioneros
A traditional stopping place on the Trans-Chaco, *Hotel Cruce de los Pioneros*

(☎ 094-820, 605-740 in Asunción) has good accommodations and a restaurant; the owner will organize trips into the Chaco interior. Singles/doubles are US$35/46.

Fortín Toledo
About 40 km west of Filadelfia, Fortín Toledo was the site of trench warfare during the Chaco conflict, and it's also home to the **Proyecto Taguá**, a small reserve that is nurturing a population of the Chaco or Wagner's peccary *(Catagonus wagneri)*, thought extinct for nearly half a century until its rediscovery in a remote area in 1975. The current project manager, Christopher Jahncke, is a Chicago doctoral student doing research on three-banded armadillos, and he welcomes visits if his schedule permits.

The peccaries are confined within a large fenced and forested area with a large pond, which attracts many Chaco birds. Directors

who felt allegiance to neither country, were targets for both the Bolivians and Paraguayans. Some found refuge with the Mennonites, but others so strongly resented the Mennonite intrusion that they resisted violently. As late as the 1940s, Ayoreo hunter-gatherers attacked and killed members of a Mennonite family in the northwestern Chaco, although it is not clear who was at fault.

Such extreme cases were unusual, but more than a few Indians thought the Mennonites invaders and did not hesitate to let their cattle graze on Mennonite crops. From motives that were both religious and expedient, Mennonites encouraged the Indians to become settled cultivators, following their own example. But the Mennonites also distanced themselves from the Indians – those who adopted the Mennonite religion were encouraged to form their own church, and to integrate more closely into Paraguayan rather than Mennonite society. Over time, many Lengua and Nivaclé (Chulupí) Indians became seasonal laborers on Mennonite farms. This opportunistic exploitation and some Mennonites' patronizing attitudes alienated many Indians whose cultural system was more egalitarian and reciprocal. There is no doubting the sincerity of the Mennonites' Christian convictions and their pacifism, but as one member of the community said, "Not all of us live up to our ideals."

As more Paraguayans settle in the Chaco, the Mennonite communities have come under pressure from authorities, and there is concern that the government may abrogate the Privilegium. Few Mennonites are reinvesting their earnings in Paraguay, and some are openly looking for alternatives elsewhere. On the other hand, the election of a Mennonite governor of the department of Boquerón, whose capital is Filadelfia, perhaps indicates a desire to participate more directly in a wider Paraguayan context.

Some Mennonites are disgruntled, however, with developments in Filadelfia, whose material prosperity has contributed to a generation more interested in motorbikes and videos than traditional Mennonite values. Beer and tobacco, once absolutely *verboten* in Mennonite settlements, are now sold openly, although only non-Mennonites would normally consume them in public.

There are perhaps 15,000 Mennonites and a roughly larger number of Indians in the region. Among themselves, Mennonites prefer to speak *Plattdeutsch* (Low German) dialect, but they readily speak and understand *Hochdeutsch* (High German), which is the language of instruction in the schools. Most adults now speak Spanish and a number speak passable English. Local Indians are as likely to speak German as Spanish, although most prefer their native languages. ∎

of the project, sponsored in part by the San Diego Zoo, hope to be able to expand the reserve, but there are legal problems with acquisition of adjacent property, which is part of an inheritance dispute. Nearby you can visit the fortifications of Fortín Toledo, some of which are still in excellent repair, and a Paraguayan military cemetery. Try to imagine yourself in the dusty or muddy trenches, awaiting the charge of the Bolivians.

To get to Fortín Toledo from Filadelfia, hitch or take a bus (such as the Nasa bus to Estancia La Patria) out Calle Trébol to the intersection with the Ruta Trans-Chaco. From there, cross the highway and continue about three km to an enormous tire on which are painted the words "pasar prohibido." Continue on the main road another seven km, passing several buildings occupied by squatters on an old estancia, before taking a sharp right that leads to a sign

reading "Proyecto Taguá" (if walking, avoid the midday heat). You may be able to hitch this segment as well.

LOMA PLATA

Loma Plata, 25 km east of Filadelfia, is the administrative and service center of Menno colony, the oldest and most traditional of the Mennonite settlements. It has an excellent museum with an outdoor exhibit of early farming equipment and a typical pioneer house, plus an outstanding photographic exhibit on the colony's history. Ask for the key at the Secretariat, the large building next door to the museum.

Accommodations are available at *Hotel Loma Plata* for about US$7 with shared bath, but it's also possible to make a day trip from Filadelfia, where there are daily bus connections. Buses from Filadelfia to Asunción stop half an hour later in Loma

Plata. Likewise, buses from Asunción to Filadelfia stop first in Loma Plata.

NEU-HALBSTADT

Founded in 1947 by Ukrainian-German Mennonites, 33 km south of Filadelfia, Neu-Halbstadt is the service center of Neuland colony. *Hotel Boquerón* has singles/doubles for US$15/22, with a good restaurant as well, and there is also a campground north of town. Nearby Fortín Boquerón preserves a sample of the trenches of the Chaco War.

South of Neuland are the largest Indian reserves, where many Lengua and Nivaclé have settled with the assistance of the Asociación del Servicio de Cooperación Indígena Menonita (ASCIM) to become farmers. Neu-Halbstadt is a good place to obtain Indian handicrafts, including bags and hammocks and woven goods, including belts and blankets colored with natural dyes. For excellent information on local Indians and access to a great selection of crafts, contact Walter and Verena Regehr in Neu-Halbstadt, who distribute Indian crafts on a nonprofit basis and also own Artesanía Viva in Asunción.

Several buses from Asunción to Filadelfia continue to Neu-Halbstadt, while others come directly from Asunción. Nasa has Tuesday and Thursday buses to Asunción at 6:30 pm, while Stel Turismo leaves for the capital daily except Monday at the same hour.

PARQUE NACIONAL DEFENSORES DEL CHACO

Created in 1980, the High Chaco park of Defensores del Chaco is Paraguay's largest (780,000 hectares) and most remote unit. Once the exclusive province of nomadic Ayoreo hunter-gatherers, it is mostly a forested alluvial plain about 100 meters in elevation, but the isolated 500-meter peak of Cerro León is the park's greatest landmark.

Quebracho, algarroba, palo santo, and cactus are the dominant species in the dense thorn forest, which harbors populations of important animal species despite the pressures of illicit hunting, which has proved difficult to control over such a large, thinly populated area. This is the most likely place in Paraguay to view large cats such as jaguar, puma, ocelot, and Geoffroy's cat, plus other unique species, although, as everywhere, such species are only rarely seen.

Defensores del Chaco is 830 km from Asunción over roads that are impassable to most ordinary vehicles, especially after rain. Park headquarters are reached by a road north from Filadelfia to Fortín Teniente Martínez and then to Fortín Madrejón, another 213 km north. Further facilities are at Aguas Dulces, 84 km beyond Madrejón.

As there is no regular public transportation to Defensores del Chaco, access is difficult, but not impossible. Inquire at the Dirección de Parques Nacionales (☎ 445-214) in Asunción, which may be able to put you in contact with rangers who must occasionally travel to Asunción. They will sometimes, if space is available, take passengers on the return trip. Getting away may present some difficulty, but have patience – you are unlikely to be stranded forever.

MARISCAL ESTIGARRIBIA

According to LP reader Jerry Azevedo, the last sizeable settlement on the Trans-Chaco before the Bolivian border has "300 soldiers, half that many civilians, and an equal number of roosters." Mariscal Estigarribia is 540 km from Asunción; motorists should bear in mind that there is no dependable source of gasoline beyond here, so be sure to fill up and carry extra gas, food, and water.

Lodging is available at *Hotel Alemán* for US$16 double, and food can be had at *Restaurant Achucarro* (which also has simple accommodations); there is also a police checkpoint and a gas station, which is a good place to try to catch a lift onward to Bolivia. It's conceivable to board buses to Santa Cruz (Bolivia) here, but it's advisable to purchase your ticket in Asunción.

Every Friday at 8 am, a Nasa bus goes to

Estancia La Patria (three hours), the last Trans-Chaco outpost accessible by public transport. Buses to Asunción (US$12.50, 10 hours) leave daily, twice on Sunday.

ESTANCIA LA PATRIA

Only 85 km from the Bolivian border, Estancia La Patria is being developed as a rural service center for the estancias of the High Chaco, with running water, a power station, school, hospital, phone system, motel, and petrol station. Every Friday at 2 pm, eastbound buses go to Mariscal Estigarribia (three hours), Filadelfia (five hours), and Asunción (14 hours). Gasoline may be available here.

Glossary

Unless otherwise indicated, the terms below apply to all three River Plate countries of Argentina, Uruguay, and Paraguay. Terms specific to the Falkland Islands are also noted. The list includes common geographical and biological terms as well as slang terms from everyday speech. The latter includes *lunfardo*, the street slang of Buenos Aires.

AAA – Argentine Anti-communist Alliance, a right-wing death squad probably organized by Peron's mysterious advisor José López Rega.

ACA – Automóvil Club Argentino, which provides maps, road service, insurance and other services, and operates hotels, motels, and campgrounds throughout the country. A valuable resource even for travelers without motor vehicles.

acequia – irrigation canal, primarily in the Cuyo region.

Acuerdo Nacional – in Paraguay, a broad coalition of opponents of the Stroessner dictatorship.

aerosilla – chairlift.

alameda – street lined with poplar trees.

albergue transitorio – not to be mistaken for an *albergue juvenil* (youth hostel), this is very short-term accommodations normally utilized by young couples in search of privacy. Some places cater exclusively to this trade, while some lower end hotels rely on it in part for financial viability. An alternative euphemism, used in Uruguay, is *hotel de alta rotatividad*.

alerce – large coniferous tree, resembling California redwood, for which Argentina's Parque Nacional Los Alerces is named.

alfajores – biscuit sandwiches with chocolate, dulce de leche, or fruit.

alíscafo – hydrofoil, from Buenos Aires across the Río de la Plata to Colonia, Uruguay.

altiplano – high Andean plain, often above 4000 meters, in the northwestern Argentine provinces of Jujuy, Salta, La Rioja, and Catamarca.

apunamiento – altitude sickness.

argentinidad – rather nebulous concept of Argentine national identity, often associated with extreme nationalistic feelings.

arrayan – tree of the myrtle family, for which Argentina's Parque Nacional Los Arrayanes is named.

arroyo – creek, stream.

asado – barbecue, usually a family outing in summer.

autopista – freeway or motorway.

bache – pothole (in a road or highway).

balneario – bathing resort or beach.

balsa – a launch or raft.

bañado – marsh or seasonally flooded zone on the rivers of northern Argentina. Bañados are good habitat for migratory birds, but are also often used for temporary cultivation.

banda negativa – low-cost air tickets in Argentina, where limited seats on particular flights are available for up to 40% less than the usual price.

baqueano – back-country tracker.

barrio – neighborhood.

bencina – white gas, used for camp stoves. Also known as *nafta blanca*.

BFFI – British Forces Falkland Islands.

bicho – any small creature, from insect to mammal.

biota – the fauna and flora of a region.

boleadoras – heavily weighted thongs, used by Pampas and Patagonian Indians for hunting guanaco and rhea. Also called *bolas*.

boga – tasty river fish from the rivers of Argentine Mesopotamia.

bonos – bonds used as legal currency in the provinces of Jujuy, Salta, and Tucumán, but worthless outside the province of issue. Bonos usually have a date of expiration beyond which they have no value.

cabildo – colonial town council.
cachila – in Uruguay, an antique automobile, often beautifully maintained.
cacique – Indian chief.
cajero automático – automatic teller machine (ATM).
caldén – *Prosopis caldenia*, a characteristic tree of the Dry Pampa.
calle – street.
Camp, The – in the Falkland Islands, the area beyond Stanley, ie the countryside. Anglo-Argentines use the same term to refer to the countryside, but it can also mean a given field or paddock, in both Falklands or Anglo-Argentine usage.
campo – the countryside. Alternately, a field or paddock.
caracoles – a winding road, usually in a mountainous area.
característica – telephone area code.
carapintada – in the Argentine military, extreme right-wing, ultranationalist movement of disaffected junior officers, responsible for several attempted coups during the Alfonsín and Menem administrations.
carpincho – capybara, a large aquatic rodent which inhabits the Paraná and other subtropical river areas.
casa de familia – modest family accommodations, usually in tourist centers.
casa de gobierno – literally "government house", a building now often converted to a museum, offices, etc.
casco – "big house" of a cattle or sheep estancia.
cataratas – waterfalls.
caudillo – in 19th-century Argentine politics, a provincial strongman whose power rested more on personal loyalty than political ideals or party organization.
cerro – mount, mountain.
chachacoma – Andean shrub whose leaves produce a herbal tea which relieves symptoms of altitude sickness.
chacra – small, independent farm.
chivito – Uruguayan steak sandwich.
chusquea – solid bamboo of the Valdivian rain forest in Patagonia.
ciervo – deer.
coima – a bribe. One who solicits a bribe is a *coimero*.

comedor – basic cafeteria or dining room in a hotel.
CONAF – Corporación Nacional Forestal, Chilean state agency in charge of forestry and conservation, including management of national parks like Torres del Paine.
confitería – café which serves coffee, tea, desserts and simple food orders. Many confiterías are important social centers in Argentina.
congregación – in colonial Latin America, the concentration of dispersed native populations in central settlements, usually for purposes of political control or religious instruction (see also *reducción*).
congrio – conger eel, a popular and delicious Chilean seafood.
Conquista del Desierto – "Conquest of the Desert", a euphemism for General Julio Argentino Roca's late 19th-century war of extermination against the Mapuche of northern Patagonia.
conventillo – tenements which housed immigrants in older neighborhoods of Buenos Aires and Montevideo. On a reduced scale, these still exist in the San Telmo area of Buenos Aires and the Ciudad Vieja of Montevideo.
cordobazo – 1969 uprising against the Argentine military government in the city of Córdoba, which eventually paved way for the return of Juan Perón from exile.
cospel – token used in Argentine public telephones in lieu of coins. Cospeles are also common in Uruguay and Paraguay.
costanera – seaside, riverside, or lakeside road.
criollo – in colonial period, an American-born Spaniard, but the term now commonly describes any Argentine of European descent. The term also describes the feral cattle of the Pampas.
cuatrerismo – cattle rustling.
curanto – Chilean seafood stew.

démedos – literally "give me two", a pejorative nickname for Argentines who travel to Miami, where everything is so cheap that they buy things they don't need.
DDI – Discado Directo Internacional (International Direct Dialing), which provides

direct access to home-country operators for long distance collect and credit card calls. This is cheaper than the Argentine companies Telecom and Telefónica, but is not yet available in all areas.

dique – a dam. The reservoir created by a dique is often used for recreational purposes. In some cases, a dique refers to a dry dock.

Dirty War – see *Guerra Sucia*.

dulce de leche – caramelized milk, an Argentine invention and obsession, often spread on bread or crackers and stuffed in pastries.

dorado – large river fish in the Paraná drainage, known among fishing enthusiasts as the "Tiger of the Paraná" for its fighting spirit. The flesh is tasty but rather bony.

encomienda – colonial labor system, under which Indian communities were required to provide workers for Spaniards *(encomenderos)*, in exchange for which the Spaniards were to provide religious and language instruction. In practice, the system benefited Spaniards far more than native peoples.

EOD – Explosive Ordnance Disposal, British army unit in charge of dealing with unexploded land mines and other weapons from the Falklands War of 1982.

ERP – Ejército Revolucionario del Pueblo, revolutionary leftist group which mimicked Cuban-style revolution in the sugar-growing areas of Tucumán province in 1970s. Wiped out by the Argentine army during the Dirty War.

esquí alpino – downhill skiing.

esquí de fondo – Nordic or cross-country skiing.

estancia – extensive grazing establishment, either for cattle or sheep, with a dominating owner or manager and dependent resident labor force.

estanciero – owner of an estancia.

facturas – pastries.

ficha – token used in the Buenos Aires subway system (Subte) in lieu of coins.

FIBS – Falkland Islands Broadcasting Service.

FIC – Falkland Islands Company.

FIDC – Falkland Islands Development Corporation.

FIG – Falkland Islands Government.

FIGAS – Falkland Islands Government Air Service.

forro – slang term for condom or, when used to describe a person, a "scumbag"; to be avoided in polite conversation.

frigorífico – meat freezing factory.

fronterizo – hybrid Spanish-Portuguese dialect spoken along the border between Uruguay and Brazil.

Gardeliano – fan of the late tango singer Carlos Gardel.

gas-oil – diesel fuel.

gasolero – motor vehicle which uses diesel fuel, which is much cheaper than ordinary petrol in Argentina.

guapoy – strangler fig of subtropical forests.

guardaganado – cattle guard (on a road or highway).

Guerra Sucia – in the 1970s, the Dirty War of the Argentine military against left-wing revolutionaries and anyone suspected of sympathizing with them.

guita – in lunfardo, money.

gurí – Guaraní word meaning "child" which has been adopted into regional speech in Argentine Mesopotamia and Paraguay.

hacienda – in the Andean Northwest, a large but often underproductive rural landholding, with a dependent resident labor force, under a dominant owner. In Argentina, a less common form of *latifundio* than in other Latin American countries.

ichu – bunch grass of the Andean steppe (altiplano).

ida – one-way.

ida y vuelta – roundtrip.

iglesia – church.

indigenismo – movement in Latin American art and literature which extolls aboriginal traditions, usually in a romantic or patronizing manner.

ingenio – industrial sugar mill.

interno – extension off a central telephone number or switchboard.

IVA – *impuesto de valor agregado*, value added tax (VAT), often added to restaurant or hotel bills in Argentina and Uruguay. If there is any question, ask whether IVA is included in the bill.

jabalí – wild European boar, a popular game dish in Argentine Patagonia.

jineteada – any horseback riding competition, as in a rodeo.

lapacho – important timber tree in subtropical northern Argentina.

latifundio – large landholding, such as a cattle or sheep estancia.

legua – vernacular "league" of about five km, commonly used to measure distance in rural areas of Argentina.

literatura gauchesca – literature *about* idealized gauchos and their values, usually written *by* urban and rural elites, as opposed to literature *by* gauchos, whose traditions were oral rather than written.

lunfardo – street slang of Buenos Aires, with origins in immigrant neighborhoods at the turn of the century.

manta – a shawl or bedspread.

mara – Patagonian hare.

maragato – native or resident of the city of Carmen de Patagones, in southern Buenos Aires province.

mazamorra – thickish maize soup, typical of the Northwest Andean region.

mate – see *yerba mate.*

mazorca – political police of 19th-century Argentine dictator Juan Manuel de Rosas.

mediero – sharecropper, a tenant who farms another's land in exchange for a percentage of the crop.

meseta – interior steppe of eastern Patagonia.

mestizo – a person of mixed Indian and Spanish descent.

minifundio – small landholding, such as a peasant farm.

minuta – in restaurant or confitería, a short order such as spaghetti or milanesa.

mirador – viewpoint, usually on a hill but often in a building.

Montoneros – left-wing faction of the Peronist party, which became an underground urban guerrilla movement in 1970s.

monte – scrub forest. The term is often applied to any densely vegetated area.

municipalidad – city hall.

museo – museum.

nafta – gasoline or petrol.

novela – television soap opera.

ñandú – large, flightless bird, resembling the ostrich. There are two Argentine species.

ñandutí – delicate "spider-web" lace woven by the women of Itauguá, a small town near Asunción, Paraguay.

ñoqui – a public employee whose primary interest is collecting a monthly paycheck. So-called because potato pasta, or ñoquis (from the Italian *gnocchi*), are traditionally served in financially strapped Argentine households on the 29th of each month, the implication being that the employee shows up at work around that time.

oligarquía terrateniente – derogatory term for the Argentine landed elite.

onces – "elevens", Chilean afternoon tea.

pampero – South Atlantic cold front which brings dramatic temperature changes to Uruguay, Paraguay, and the interior of northern Argentina.

parada – bus stop.

parrillada, parrilla – respectively, a mixed grill of steak and other beef cuts, and a restaurant specializing in such dishes.

pasaperros – professional dog walker in Buenos Aires.

pasarela – catwalk across a stream or bog.

paseo – an outing, such as a walk in the park or downtown.

peatonal – pedestrian mall, usually in the downtown area of major Argentine cities.

pehuén – Araucaria, or "monkey puzzle" tree of southern Patagonia.

peña – club which hosts informal folk music gatherings.

peones golondrinas – "swallows", term frequently applied to seasonal laborers from Bolivia in the Tucumán sugar harvest, but also used in similar contexts elsewhere in Argentina.

picada – in rural areas, a trail, especially through dense woods or mountains; in the context of food, hors d'oeuvres.

pingüinera – penguin colony.

piropo – sexist remark, ranging from complimentary and relatively innocuous to rude and offensive.

Porteño – inhabitant of Buenos Aires, a "resident of the port"

precordillera – foothills of the Andes.

primera – 1st-class on a train.

Privilegium – agreement between the government of Paraguay and Mennonite agricultural colonists, granting the latter land and political autonomy, including the right to German-language schools, freedom of religion, exemption from military service, cooperative economic organization, and independent law enforcement.

Proceso – in full, "El Proceso de Reorganización Nacional", a military euphemism for its brutal attempt to remake Argentina's political and economic culture between 1976 and 1983.

propina – a tip, eg in a restaurant or cinema.

pucará – in the Andean Northwest, an indigenous fortification, generally on high ground commanding an unobstructed view in several directions.

puchero – soup combining vegetables and meats, served with rice.

puesto – "outside house" on cattle or sheep estancia.

pucho – in lunfardo, a cigarette or cigarette butt.

pulpería – rural shop or "company store" on cattle or sheep estancia.

puna – Andean highlands, usually above 3000 meters.

puntano – a native or resident of Argentina's San Luis province.

quebracho – literally, the "axe-breaker" tree (*Quebrachua lorentzii*) of the Chaco, a natural source of tannin for the leather industries of the River Plate.

quilombo – in lunfardo, a mess. Originally a Brazilian term describing a settlement of runaway slaves, it came to mean a house of prostitution in Argentina.

quinoa – a native Andean grain, the dietary equivalent of rice in pre-Columbian times.

rambla – avenue or shopping mall.

rancho – a rural house, generally of adobe, with a thatched roof.

recargo – additional charge, usually 10%, which many Argentine businesses add to credit card transactions because of high inflation and delays in payment.

reducción – like congregación, the concentration of native populations in towns modeled on the Spanish grid pattern, for purposes of political control or religious instruction. The term also refers to the settlement itself.

remise – a taxi with a radio connection to a dispatcher.

refugio – a usually rustic shelter in a national park or remote area.

río – river.

RN – Ruta Nacional, in Argentina, a national highway.

RP – Ruta Provincial, in Argentina, a provincial highway.

ruta – highway.

sábalo – popular river fish in the Paraná drainage.

saladero – establishment for salting meat and hides.

salar – salt lake or salt pan, usually in the high Andes or Argentine Patagonia.

SIDA – AIDS.

siesta – lengthy afternoon break for lunch and, occasionally, a nap.

s/n – "sin número", indicating a street address without a number.

smoko – in the Falkland Islands, mid-morning tea or coffee break, usually served with cakes and other homemade sweets.

sobremesa – after-dinner conversation.

soroche – altitude sickness.

Southern Cone – in political geography,

the area comprising Argentina, Chile, Uruguay and parts of Brazil and Paraguay. So-called after the area's shape on the map.

squaddies – British enlisted men on four-month tours-of-duty in the Falkland Islands.

Subte – the Buenos Aires underground.

surubí – popular river fish in Argentine Mesopotamia and in the River Plate drainage. It is frequently served in restaurants.

taguá – Wagner's peccary, a species of wild pig thought extinct but recently rediscovered in the Paraguayan Chaco.

tapir – large hoofed mammal of subtropical forests in northern Argentina and Paraguay, a distant relative of the horse.

teleférico – gondola cable-car.

tenedor libre – "all-you-can-eat" restaurant. Also known as *diente libre*.

tereré – cold mate, as consumed by Paraguayans.

todo terreno – mountain bike.

tola – high-altitude shrubs in the altiplano of northwestern Argentina.

trapiche – antique sugar mill.

trasnochador – one who stays up very late or all night, as do many Argentines.

trucho – bogus, a term widely used by Argentines to describe things which are not what they appear to be.

turco – "Turk", an often derogatory term for any Argentine of Middle Eastern descent.

turismo aventura – term used to describe non-traditional forms of tourism, such as trekking and river rafting.

turista – 2nd-class on a train, usually not very comfortable.

tuteo – use of the pronoun *tú* in Spanish and its corresponding verb forms.

two-nighter – in the Falkland Islands, a traditional party for visitors from distant sheep stations, who would invariably stay the weekend.

vado – dip (in a road highway).

vicuña – wild relative of domestic llama and alpaca, found only at high altitudes in Argentina's Andean Northwest.

villas miserias – shantytowns on the outskirts of Buenos Aires and other Argentine cities.

vinchuca – biting insect, living in thatched dwellings with dirt floors, which is a vector for Chagas' disease.

viviendas temporarias – riverfront shantytowns of Asunción, Paraguay.

vizcacha – wild relative of the domestic chinchilla. There are two common species in Argentina, the mountain vizcacha (*Lagidium vizcacha*) of the Andean highlands and the plains vizcacha (*Lagostomus maximus*) of the subtropical lowlands. Some regard the latter as a pest.

voseo – the use of the pronoun *vos* and its corresponding verb forms in the River Plate republics of Argentina, Uruguay, and Paraguay.

warrah – the now extinct but possibly domesticated Falklands fox or wolf, *Dusicyon australis*, presumptive evidence of Yahgan Indian presence on the Falklands.

yacaré – South American alligator, found in humid, subtropical parts of Argentina, Uruguay, and Paraguay.

YCF – Yacimientos Fiscales Carboníferos, Argentina's state coal company.

yerba mate – "Paraguayan tea" (*Ilex paraguariensis*), which Argentines consume in very large amounts, but many Paraguayans, Uruguayans and Brazilians also use regularly. Taking *mate* is an important everyday social ritual.

yisca – bag made of vegetable fiber, traditional among the Toba Indians of the Chaco.

YPF – Yacimientos Fiscales Petrolíferos, Argentina's former state oil company.

yungas – in northwestern Argentina, transitional subtropical lowland forest.

yuyos – "herbs", mixed with *yerba mate* in northern Argentina.

zafra – sugar harvest.

Zonda – in the central Andean provinces, a powerful, dry north wind like the European *Föhn* or North American *Chinook*.

Index

748

TEXT

map references are in **bold** type

Thanks

Thanks to all the following travelers and others (apologies if we have misspelled your name) who took time to writie to us about their experiences in Argentina, Uruguay, the Falkland Islands, and Paraguay.

Jeremy Paul and Mark Adams (UK), Kim Adams (UK), Bill Aherne (UK), Stephen Aichele (USA), Didier and Sandrine Aique (Sw), Adrian Allan (UK), David Allan (Aus), Robert and Lynn Anderson (USA), Bryony Angell and Samantha Everett, Sandra Arkin (USA), Mats Areskoug (Swe), Rosa Arko (Arg), Jason Ashworth (UK), Pamela Attree (O), Jerry Azevedo (USA), Dr Irmgard Bauer (Aus), Thorsten Becker (D), Howard M Behr (USA), Alberto Bennici (I), Armando de Berardinis (I), Caroline Blick (SA), Jean-Roch Bouchard (C), Ronald Boyle (USA), Paul Brach (O), Wim Brack (B), Ingrid Bremer (D), Hendrik J van Broekhuizen (NL), Richard Browne (UK), Nils Brüchert-Pastor (D), Ulrich Bünstorf (D), Wolfgang Bußmann (D), R and A Beyne-Pille (B), Hazel Cant (UK), Glynn Carré (UK), Sean Casey (USA), Uttom Chowdhury (UK), Gavin Crichton (Aus), JK Clark (NZ), Eric Clauwaert (Sw), Alan Cohen (USA), Rachel Cohen (USA), Greg Contaoi (Uru), Ann Corder (Arg), C Brian Cramm (USA), Gavin Chricton (Aus), Rosemary Cummings (USA), Ken Darcovich (C), Bill Davis (USA/Arg), Robin and Keith Daus (USA), Lilian Deenen (NL), Didier and Sandrine (CH), Jeri and Hugh Dingle (USA), Carsten Dittmann (D), Michael Dixon (UK), Monique Dodinet (F), Patrick and Elisabeth Duffy (C), Dolan Eargle and Nadine Gray (USA), Eva Echenberg (C), Sue Edelstein (USA), Christian Elling and Kåre Lundquist (Swe), Louis and Curtis Fazen (USA), Vincent Fernández (C), Stefano Ferrari (I), Maurice Frank (UK), Olivier and Dominique Frering (F), Dirk Frewing (USA), Miguel Fuertes and Helena Centeno (Sp), Christian Gaebler (Sw), Asunción Gallego (Sp), Horacio García (Arg), Christophe Gautier (F), Ruud van Ginkel (NL), Kate Goodwin (UK), Daniel Guerrero C (Ch), Kenneth Hake (USA), Liz Hall (USA), Paul Hatfield and Gareth Sellors, Kimberly Y Heath (USA), John Heinzel (USA), N G Hetterley (UK), Pat Hickey and Carol Paulsen (USA), Jana Hinken (USA), Eric and Ingrid Holzman (USA), Debra Iles, Arjen and Marianne Jaarsma (NL), Georg Jaggi, Douglas Jasch (Aus), Ruben Jazquez (Arg), Marie Jenneteg (Swe), Sabine Joyce (USA), Stephen Kay (USA), Paul Kempf (Sw), Rob Kent (USA), Andy King and Helen Moody (UK), Daniel King (Aus), Christoph Kohler (Sw), Daniel Alberto Kormann (Arg), Paul Kretkowski (USA), Wolfgang Krones (D), Lucy Kunkel (USA), Bob Langford (C), Kai Larsen (Den), J M Layman (UK), Ben Lemlich (USA), Keith Liker (USA), Andrea Löbbecke (D), Dawn Lock (UK), William Löfberg (UK), Julie Lomax and Nina Grinnell (USA), Sarah Love (UK), Julio César Lovece (Arg), Mabel Macdonald (USA), Carlo Mattio (I), Bernhard Matz (D), Mike McDonald (UK), Peter McFadden (UK), Bruce and Cheryl McLaren (NZ), R N McLean (NZ), Sheila Mee (UK), Martin Meier and Catarina Pfister (Sw), Edith Meijer-Swart (N), Daniel de Rezende Melo and Renata Soto (Bra), Zan Mendonça (USA), Manfred Meyer (D), Patrick Miller (Aus), Nicoletta and Lionello Morganti (I), Marilyn Moyer (USA), Kerry Mullan and Graham Neilson (UK), Erik Muller (USA), Gustavo Damián Muriel (Arg), Robert S Neus (USA), Susanne Nickel (D), John F Nixon (UK), Professor and Mrs Nixon (UK), Miguel Nogales (USA), Michele Novosad (C), Rick O'Connell (USA), Francis X O'Donoghue (Ire), Reiner Oesterreicher and Natalie Funk (D), Eugene and Mayuki Orwell (Aus), Martin Pagel and Susi Schuegraf (USA), Gennaro Pastore (UK), Bill Pelke (USA), Bridget Percy (NZ), Hans-Joachim Philipp (D), Marianne Pirker (Arg), Mark Plotkin (USA), Dr Benjamin Poensgen (D), Nigel Poole (UK), E Pounds (UK), Philip Preston (USA), Guner Quaisser (D), Eric Raff (USA), P G Raheen (UK), Joe Rathbun (USA), Tammo Rieg (NL), Eduardo Riestra (Arg), Cornelia Risch (Sw), Alison Robins (NL), Richard Robson-Smith (UK), A M Roddick (Arg), Deborah Rowland (UK), Stig Sandberg (N), Richard Sanford (USA), Roger and Kitana, Ruud (C) Julia Schaay (NL), Christian Schindler (D), Philipp Schlagenhauf (Sw), Tim Schmith (Den), K Shayes (USA), Ola Sköld (Swe), Arie Sluijter (NL), Ru Smith (UK) , Jorge Antolin Solache (Arg), Jorge Staude (Arg), Patrick Sterckx (B), Rafaela Suárez Buela de Bertolini (Uru), Yvette Szepesi (NL), Silvia Taussik (Arg), C and A Terashita (C), Robert Thomas (Aus), Liz Tremlett and Charlotte Spencer (UK) for a particularly amusing contribution, Arnoud Troost and Fenna den Hartog (NL), Daniel Turkewitz (USA), Marie Vallat (F), John van der Rest and Marian de Vries (NL), Cristina Vargas (Ch), Rubén Vásquez (Arg), François Vincent (Arg), Marianne Vincken (NL), John Vinks (Arg), Joeren Vrakking (NL), Guido Vuarambón (Arg), Ken Walker (C), Lina and Jens Weibull (Swe), Peter J Wheelan (USA), Helen Whitford (Aus), R R Willis (Aus), Diarmuid Wilson (UK/Aus) Gareth Wilson (UK), Ronald S Winters (USA), Felice Wyndham, and Julian Yates (Aus).

Arg - Argentina, Aus - Australia, B - Belgium, C - Canada, Ch - Chile, D - Germany, Den - Denmark, F - France, I - Italy, Ire - Ireland, N - Norway, NL - Netherlands, O - Austria, S - Sweden, SA - South Africa, Sp - Spain, Sw - Switzerland, Swe - Sweden, UK - United Kingdom, Uru - Uruguay, USA - United States.

Climate Charts

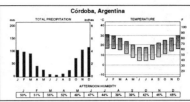

Córdoba, Argentina

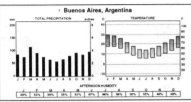

Buenos Aires, Argentina

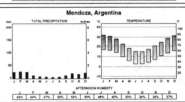

Mendoza, Argentina

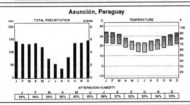

Montevideo, Uruguay

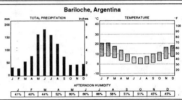

Bariloche, Argentina

Asunción, Paraguay

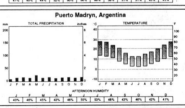

Puerto Madryn, Argentina

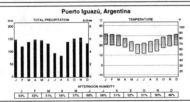

Puerto Iguazú, Argentina

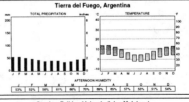

Tierra del Fuego, Argentina

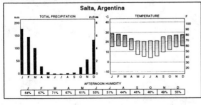

Salta, Argentina

Stanley, Falkland Islands (Islas Malvinas)

LONELY PLANET PHRASEBOOKS

Nepali phrasebook

Ethiopian Amharic phrasebook

Latin American Spanish phrasebook

Ukrainian phrasebook

Greek phrasebook

Vietnamese phrasebook

Building bridges,
Breaking barriers,
Beyond babble-on

Listen for the gems

Speak your own words

Ask your own questions

Master of your own image

- handy pocket-sized books
- easy to understand Pronunciation chapter
- clear and comprehensive Grammar chapter
- romanisation alongside script to allow ease of pronunciation
- script throughout so users can point to phrases
- extensive vocabulary sections, words and phrases for every situation
- full of cultural information and tips for the traveller

'...vital for a real DIY spirit and attitude in language learning' – Backpacker

'the phrasebooks have good cultural backgrounders and offer solid advice for challenging situations in remote locations' – San Francisco Examiner

'...they are unbeatable for their coverage of the world's more obscure languages' – The Geographical Magazine

---

Arabic (Egyptian)
Arabic (Moroccan)
Australia
 Australian English, Aboriginal and Torres Strait languages
Baltic States
 Estonian, Latvian, Lithuanian
Bengali
Brazilian
Burmese
Cantonese
Central Asia
Central Europe
 Czech, French, German, Hungarian, Italian and Slovak
Eastern Europe
 Bulgarian, Czech, Hungarian, Polish, Romanian and Slovak
Ethiopian (Amharic)
Fijian
French
German
Greek

Hindi/Urdu
Indonesian
Italian
Japanese
Korean
Lao
Latin American Spanish
Malay
Mandarin
Mediterranean Europe
 Albanian, Croatian, Greek, Italian, Macedonian, Maltese, Serbian and Slovene
Mongolian
Nepali
Papua New Guinea
Pilipino (Tagalog)
Quechua
Russian
Scandinavian Europe
 Danish, Finnish, Icelandic, Norwegian and Swedish

South-East Asia
 Burmese, Indonesian, Khmer, Lao, Malay, Tagalog (Pilipino), Thai and Vietnamese
Spanish (Castilian)
 Basque, Catalan and Galician
Sri Lanka
Swahili
Thai
Thai Hill Tribes
Tibetan
Turkish
Ukrainian
USA
 US English, Vernacular, Native American languages and Hawaiian
Vietnamese
Western Europe
 Basque, Catalan, Dutch, French, German, Irish, Italian, Portuguese, Scottish Gaelic, Spanish (Castilian) and Welsh

---

LONELY PLANET JOURNEYS

JOURNEYS is a unique collection of travel writing – published by the company that understands travel better than anyone else. It is a series for anyone who has ever experienced – or dreamed of – the magical moment when they encountered a strange culture or saw a place for the first time. They are tales to read while you're planning a trip, while you're on the road or while you're in an armchair, in front of a fire.

JOURNEYS books catch the spirit of a place, illuminate a culture, recount a crazy adventure, or introduce a fascinating way of life. They always entertain, and always enrich the experience of travel.

'Idiosyncratic, entertainingly diverse and unexpected . . . from an international writership'
– The Australian

'Books which offer a closer look at the people and culture of a destination, and enrich travel experiences'
– American Bookseller

FULL CIRCLE
A South American Journey
Luis Sepúlveda
Translated by Chris Andrews

Full Circle invites us to accompany Chilean writer Luis Sepúlveda on 'a journey without a fixed itinerary'. Whatever his subject – brutalities suffered under Pinochet's dictatorship, sleepy tropical towns visited in exile, or the landscapes of legendary Patagonia – Sepúlveda is an unflinchingly honest yet lyrical storyteller. Extravagant characters and extraordinary situations are memorably evoked: gauchos organising a tournament of lies, a scheming heiress on the lookout for a husband, a pilot with a corpse on board his plane . . . Part autobiography, part travel memoir, *Full Circle* brings us the distinctive voice of one of South America's most compelling writers.

Luis Sepúlveda was born in Chile in 1949. Imprisoned by the Pinochet dictatorship for his socialist beliefs, he was for many years a political exile. He has written novels, short stories, plays and essays. His work has attracted many awards and has been translated into numerous languages.

'Detachment, humour and vibrant prose' – El País

'an absolute cracker' – The Bookseller

 This project has been assisted by the Commonwealth Government through the Australia Council, its arts funding and advisory body.

LONELY PLANET TRAVEL ATLASES

Lonely Planet has long been famous for the number and quality of its guidebook maps. Now we've gone one step further and in conjunction with Steinhart Katzir Publishers produced a handy companion series: Lonely Planet travel atlases – maps of a country produced in book form.

Unlike other maps, which look good but lead travellers astray, our travel atlases have been researched on the road by Lonely Planet's experienced team of writers. All details are carefully checked to ensure the atlas corresponds with the equivalent Lonely Planet guidebook.

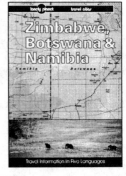

The handy atlas format means no holes, wrinkles, torn sections or constant folding and unfolding. These atlases can survive long periods on the road, unlike cumbersome fold-out maps. The comprehensive index ensures easy reference.

- full-colour throughout
- maps researched and checked by Lonely Planet authors
- place names correspond with Lonely Planet guidebooks
  – no confusing spelling differences
- legend and travelling information in English, French, German, Japanese and Spanish
- size: 230 x 160 mm

Available now:
Chile & Easter Island • Egypt • India & Bangladesh • Israel & the Palestinian Territories •Jordan, Syria & Lebanon • Kenya • Laos • Portugal • South Africa, Lesotho & Swaziland • Thailand • Turkey • Vietnam • Zimbabwe, Botswana & Namibia

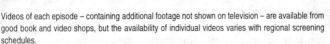

LONELY PLANET TV SERIES & VIDEOS

Lonely Planet travel guides have been brought to life on television screens around the world. Like our guides, the programmes are based on the joy of independent travel, and look honestly at some of the most exciting, picturesque and frustrating places in the world. Each show is presented by one of three travellers from Australia, England or the USA and combines an innovative mixture of video, Super-8 film, atmospheric soundscapes and original music.

Videos of each episode – containing additional footage not shown on television – are available from good book and video shops, but the availability of individual videos varies with regional screening schedules.

Video destinations include: Alaska • American Rockies • Australia – The South-East • Baja California & the Copper Canyon • Brazil • Central Asia • Chile & Easter Island • Corsica, Sicily & Sardinia – The Mediterranean Islands • East Africa (Tanzania & Zanzibar) • Ecuador & the Galapagos Islands • Greenland & Iceland • Indonesia • Israel & the Sinai Desert • Jamaica • Japan • La Ruta Maya • Morocco • New York • North India • Pacific Islands (Fiji, Solomon Islands & Vanuatu) • South India • South West China • Turkey • Vietnam • West Africa • Zimbabwe, Botswana & Namibia

The Lonely Planet TV series is produced by:
Pilot Productions
The Old Studio
18 Middle Row
London W10 5AT UK

For video availability and ordering information contact your nearest Lonely Planet office.

Music from the TV series is available on CD & cassette.

PLANET TALK

Lonely Planet's FREE quarterly newsletter

We love hearing from you and think you'd like to hear from us.

When...is the right time to see reindeer in Finland?
Where...can you hear the best palm-wine music in Ghana?
How...do you get from Asunción to Areguá by steam train?
What...is the best way to see India?

For the answer to these and many other questions read PLANET TALK.

Every issue is packed with up-to-date travel news and advice including:

* a letter from Lonely Planet co-founders Tony and Maureen Wheeler
* go behind the scenes on the road with a Lonely Planet author
* feature article on an important and topical travel issue
* a selection of recent letters from travellers
* details on forthcoming Lonely Planet promotions
* complete list of Lonely Planet products

To join our mailing list contact any Lonely Planet office.

Also available: Lonely Planet T-shirts. 100% heavyweight cotton.

LONELY PLANET ONLINE

Get the latest travel information before you leave or while you're on the road

Whether you've just begun planning your next trip, or you're chasing down specific info on currency regulations or visa requirements, check out Lonely Planet Online for up-to-the minute travel information.

As well as travel profiles of your favourite destinations (including maps and photos), you'll find current reports from our researchers and other travellers, updates on health and visas, travel advisories, and discussion of the ecological and political issues you need to be aware of as you travel.

There's also an online travellers' forum where you can share your experience of life on the road, meet travel companions and ask other travellers for their recommendations and advice. We also have plenty of links to other online sites useful to independent travellers.

And of course we have a complete and up-to-date list of all Lonely Planet travel products including guides, phrasebooks, atlases, Journeys and videos and a simple online ordering facility if you can't find the book you want elsewhere.

www.lonelyplanet.com
or
AOL keyword: lp

LONELY PLANET PRODUCTS

Lonely Planet is known worldwide for publishing practical, reliable and no-nonsense travel information in our guides and on our web site. The Lonely Planet list covers just about every accessible part of the world. Currently there are nine series: *travel guides, shoestring guides, walking guides, city guides, phrasebooks, audio packs, travel atlases, Journeys – a unique collection of travel writing and Pisces Books - diving and snorkeling guides.*

EUROPE

Amsterdam • Austria • Baltic States phrasebook • Britain • Central Europe on a shoestring • Central Europe phrasebook • Czech & Slovak Republics • Denmark • Dublin • Eastern Europe on a shoestring • Eastern Europe phrasebook • Estonia, Latvia & Lithuania • Finland • France • French phrasebook • Germany • German phrasebook • Greece • Greek phrasebook • Hungary • Iceland, Greenland & the Faroe Islands • Ireland • Italian phrasebook • Italy • Lisbon • London • Mediterranean Europe on a shoestring • Mediterranean Europe phrasebook • Paris • Poland • Portugal • Portugal travel atlas • Prague • Romania & Moldova • Russia, Ukraine & Belarus • Russian phrasebook • Scandinavian & Baltic Europe on a shoestring • Scandinavian Europe phrasebook • Slovenia • Spain • Spanish phrasebook • St Petersburg • Switzerland • Trekking in Spain • Ukrainian phrasebook • Vienna • Walking in Britain • Walking in Italy • Walking in Switzerland • Western Europe on a shoestring • Western Europe phrasebook

Travel Literature: The Olive Grove: Travels in Greece

NORTH AMERICA

Alaska • Backpacking in Alaska • Baja California • California & Nevada • Canada • Chicago • Deep South • Florida • Hawaii • Honolulu • Los Angeles • Mexico • Mexico City • Miami • New England • New Orleans • New York City • New York, New Jersey & Pennsylvania • Pacific Northwest USA • Rocky Mountain States • San Francisco • Southwest USA • USA phrasebook • Washington, DC & the Capital Region

Travel Literature: Drive thru America

CENTRAL AMERICA & THE CARIBBEAN

•Bahamas and Turks & Caicos •Bermuda •Central America on a shoestring • Costa Rica • Cuba •Eastern Caribbean •Guatemala, Belize & Yucatán: La Ruta Maya • Jamaica

SOUTH AMERICA

Argentina, Uruguay & Paraguay • Bolivia • Brazil • Brazilian phrasebook • Buenos Aires • Chile & Easter Island • Chile & Easter Island travel atlas • Colombia Ecuador & the Galápagos Islands • Latin American Spanish phrasebook • Peru • Quechua phrasebook • Rio de Janeiro • South America on a shoestring • Trekking in the Patagonian Andes • Venezuela

Travel Literature: Full Circle: A South American Journey

ISLANDS OF THE INDIAN OCEAN

Madagascar & Comoros • Maldives • Mauritius, Réunion & Seychelles

AFRICA

Africa - the South • Africa on a shoestring • Arabic (Moroccan) phrasebook • Cairo • Cape Town • Central Africa • East Africa • Egypt • Egypt travel atlas • Ethiopian (Amharic) phrasebook • Kenya • Kenya travel atlas • Malawi, Mozambique & Zambia • Morocco • North Africa • South Africa, Lesotho & Swaziland • South Africa, Lesotho & Swaziland travel atlas • Swahili phrasebook • Tunisia Trekking in East Africa • West Africa • Zimbabwe, Botswana & Namibia • Zimbabwe, Botswana & Namibia travel atlas

Travel Literature: The Rainbird: A Central African Journey • Songs to an African Sunset: A Zimbabwean Story

MAIL ORDER

Lonely Planet products are distributed worldwide. They are also available by mail order from Lonely Planet, so if you have difficulty finding a title please write to us. North American and South American residents should write to 150 Linden St, Oakland CA 94607, USA; European and African residents should write to 10a Spring Place, London NW5 3BH; and residents of other countries to PO Box 617, Hawthorn, Victoria 3122, Australia.

NORTH-EAST ASIA

Beijing • Cantonese phrasebook • China • Hong Kong • Hong Kong, Macau & Guangzhou • Japan • Japanese phrasebook • Japanese audio pack • Korea • Korean phrasebook • Mandarin phrasebook • Mongolia • Mongolian phrasebook • North-East Asia on a shoestring • Seoul • Taiwan • Tibet • Tibet phrasebook • Tokyo

Travel Literature: Lost Japan

MIDDLE EAST & CENTRAL ASIA

Arab Gulf States • Arabic (Egyptian) phrasebook • Central Asia • Central Asia phrasebook • Iran • Israel & the Palestinian Territories • Israel & the Palestinian Territories travel atlas • Istanbul • Jerusalem • Jordan & Syria • Jordan, Syria & Lebanon travel atlas • Lebanon • Middle East • Turkey • Turkish phrasebook • Turkey travel atlas • Yemen

Travel Literature: The Gates of Damascus • Kingdom of the Film Stars: Journey into Jordan

ALSO AVAILABLE:

Brief Encounters • Travel with Children • Traveller's Tales

INDIAN SUBCONTINENT

Bangladesh • Bengali phrasebook • Delhi • Goa • Hindi/Urdu phrasebook • India • India & Bangladesh travel atlas • Indian Himalaya • Karakoram Highway • Nepal • Nepali phrasebook • Pakistan • Rajasthan • Sri Lanka • Sri Lanka phrasebook • Trekking in the Indian Himalaya • Trekking in the Karakoram & Hindukush • Trekking in the Nepal Himalaya

Travel Literature: In Rajasthan • Shopping for Buddhas

SOUTH-EAST ASIA

Bali & Lombok • Bangkok • Burmese phrasebook • Cambodia • Ho Chi Minh City • Indonesia • Indonesian phrasebook • Indonesian audio pack • Jakarta • Java • Laos • Lao phrasebook • Laos travel atlas • Malay phrasebook • Malaysia, Singapore & Brunei • Myanmar (Burma) • Philippines • Pilipino phrasebook • Singapore • South-East Asia on a shoestring • South-East Asia phrasebook • Thailand • Thailand's Islands & Beaches • Thailand travel atlas • Thai phrasebook • Thai audio pack • Thai Hill Tribes phrasebook • Vietnam • Vietnamese phrasebook • Vietnam travel atlas

AUSTRALIA & THE PACIFIC

Australia • Australian phrasebook • Bushwalking in Australia • Bushwalking in Papua New Guinea • Fiji • Fijian phrasebook • Islands of Australia's Great Barrier Reef • Melbourne • Micronesia • New Caledonia • New South Wales • New Zealand • Northern Territory • Outback Australia • Papua New Guinea • Papua New Guinea phrasebook • Queensland • Rarotonga & the Cook Islands • Samoa • Solomon Islands • South Australia • Sydney • Tahiti & French Polynesia • Tasmania • Tonga • Tramping in New Zealand • Vanuatu • Victoria • Western Australia

Travel Literature: Islands in the Clouds • Sean & David's Long Drive

ANTARCTICA

Antarctica

THE LONELY PLANET STORY

Lonely Planet published its first book in 1973 in response to the numerous 'How did you do it?' questions Maureen and Tony Wheeler were asked after driving, bussing, hitching, sailing and railing their way from England to Australia.

Written at a kitchen table and hand collated, trimmed and stapled, *Across Asia on the Cheap* became an instant local bestseller, inspiring thoughts of another book.

Eighteen months in South-East Asia resulted in their second guide, *South-East Asia on a shoestring*, which they put together in a backstreet Chinese hotel in Singapore in 1975. The 'yellow bible', as it quickly became known to backpackers around the world, soon became *the* guide to the region. It has sold well over half a million copies and is now in its 9th edition, still retaining its familiar yellow cover.

Today there are over 240 titles, including travel guides, walking guides, language kits & phrasebooks, travel atlases and travel literature. The company is the largest independent travel publisher in the world. Although Lonely Planet initially specialised in guides to Asia, today there are few corners of the globe that have not been covered.

The emphasis continues to be on travel for independent travellers. Tony and Maureen still travel for several months of each year and play an active part in the writing, updating and quality control of Lonely Planet's guides.

They have been joined by over 70 authors and 170 staff at our offices in Melbourne (Australia), Oakland (USA), London (UK) and Paris (France). Travellers themselves also make a valuable contribution to the guides through the feedback we receive in thousands of letters each year and on our web site.

The people at Lonely Planet strongly believe that travellers can make a positive contribution to the countries they visit, both through their appreciation of the countries' culture, wildlife and natural features, and through the money they spend. In addition, the company makes a direct contribution to the countries and regions it covers. Since 1986 a percentage of the income from each book has been donated to ventures such as famine relief in Africa; aid projects in India; agricultural projects in Central America; Greenpeace's efforts to halt French nuclear testing in the Pacific; and Amnesty International.

'I hope we send people out with the right attitude about travel. You realise when you travel that there are so many different perspectives about the world, so we hope these books will make people more interested in what they see. Guidebooks can't really guide people. All you can do is point them in the right direction.'

– Tony Wheeler

LONELY PLANET PUBLICATIONS

Australia
PO Box 617, Hawthorn 3122, Victoria
tel: (03) 9819 1877 fax: (03) 9819 6459
e-mail: talk2us@lonelyplanet.com.au

USA
150 Linden St
Oakland, CA 94607
tel: (510) 893 8555 TOLL FREE: 800 275-8555
fax: (510) 893 8563
e-mail: info@lonelyplanet.com

UK
10a Spring Place,
London NW5 3BH
tel: (0171) 428 4800 fax: (0171) 428 4828
e-mail: go@lonelyplanet.co.uk

France:
71 bis rue du Cardinal Lemoine, 75005 Paris
tel: 01 44 32 06 20 fax: 01 46 34 72 55
e-mail: bip@lonelyplanet.fr

World Wide Web: http://www.lonelyplanet.com
or *AOL keyword: lp*